# Archivi Reali di Ebla

## Testi

## XXI

On behalf of the Università degli Studi di Roma
„La Sapienza“ edited by
Paolo Matthiae, Frances Pinnock,
and Alfonso Archi

M
A
I
S



2023
Harrassowitz Verlag · Wiesbaden

Alfonso Archi, Gabriella Spada

# Annual Documents of the Metal Expenditures (è) from Minister Ibrium's Period

(Archive L. 2769)

Part 1

2023
Harrassowitz Verlag · Wiesbaden

Publication of this book was supported by a grant of the Fondazione OrMe.

The images of the plates can be downloaded at:
https://www.harrassowitz-verlag.de/isbn_9783447120937.ahtml
© Missione Archeologica Italiana in Siria - Sapienza Università di Roma

Inventory code: So for example 04o-10077.jpg refers to the text 4 obverse

Bibliografische Information der Deutschen Nationalbibliothek
Die Deutsche Nationalbibliothek verzeichnet diese Publikation in der Deutschen Nationalbibliografie; detaillierte bibliografische Daten sind im Internet über https://dnb.de abrufbar.

Bibliographic information published by the Deutsche Nationalbibliothek
The Deutsche Nationalbibliothek lists this publication in the Deutsche Nationalbibliografie; detailed bibliographic data are available in the Internet at https://dnb.de

For further information about our publishing program consult our website http://www.harrassowitz-verlag.de


Printed on permanent/durable paper.
Printing and binding: Memminger MedienCentrum AG
Printed in Germany
ISSN 1828-3039
ISBN 978-3-447-12093-7
eISBN 978-3-447-39475-8

# Contents

# Foreword

This volume includes the annual documents (nos. 1–21) concerning the "expenditures", è, of metals (silver as well as gold, tin, and copper, which were usually valued in silver) from the eighteen years that Ibrium served as minister, which coincide with the first half of Išᶜar-damu's reign. Texts nos. 22–25 complete the documentation for this period.

The tablets were restored (as far as possible) and transcribed by Alfonso Archi over several periods of time working at the Museum of Idlib during the years 1990–2010. Tragically, in later years the Museum was severely damaged and plundered during the Syrian War.

The translation of the documents, the chapters on the list of offerings to the gods, and on the ki-$lam_7$ markets, and the Indices are by Gabriella Spada.

The work at the Museum of Idlib was made possible by the authorities of the General Directorate of Antiquities and Museums of the Syrian Arab Republic. Alfonso Archi is particularly indebted to Mr. Abdo Asfari and Mr Fajjar aj Mohammed, who succeeded each other as Director of the Idlib Museum for their cooperative friendship.

The photographs are by Maurizio Necci. Special thanks to Enrico Guida for the layout and graphic design.

The publication of this volume was made possible through the generosity of the Fondazione OrMe.

Alfonso Archi Gabriella Spada

Rome, July 2023

# Abbreviations

Abbreviations are according to *RlA* (= E. Ebeling et al., *Reallexikon der Assyriologie*. Berlin–Leipzig–New York 1928–) except for the following:

| | |
|---|---|
| *ARES* I | A. Archi (ed.), *Eblaite Personal Names and Semitic Name-Giving. Papers of a Symposium held in Rome, July 15–17, 1985*, (Archivi Reali di Ebla – Studi I), Roma 1988. |
| *ARES* II | A. Archi – P. Piacentini – F. Pomponio, *I nomi di luogo dei testi di Ebla* (*ARET I–IV, VII–X, e altri testi editi e inediti*), (Archivi Reali di Ebla – Studi II), Roma 1993. |
| *ARES* IV | M. Civil, *The Early Dynastic Practical Vocabulary* (*Archaic HAR-ra A*), (Archivi Reali di Ebla – Studi IV), Roma 2008. |
| *ARET* I | A. Archi, *Testi amministrativi*: *assegnazioni di tessuti* (*Archivio L. 2769*), (Archivi Reali di Ebla – Testi I), Roma 1985. |
| *ARET* II | D. O. Edzard, *Verwaltungstexte verschiedenen Inhalts aus dem Archiv L. 2769* (Archivi Reali di Ebla – Testi II), Roma 1981. |
| *ARET* III | A. Archi – M. G. Biga, *Testi amministrativi di vario contenuto* (*Archivio L. 2769*: *TM.75.G:3000–4101*), (Archivi Reali di Ebla – Testi III), Roma 1982. |
| *ARET* VII | A. Archi, *Testi amministrativi*: *registrazioni di metalli e di tessuti* (*Archivio L. 2769*), (Archivi Reali di Ebla – Testi VII), Roma 1988. |
| *ARET* IX | L. Milano, *Testi amministrativi*: *assegnazioni di prodotti alimentari* (*Archivio L. 2712-I*), (Archivi Reali di Ebla – Testi IX), Roma 1985. |
| *ARET* X | A. Archi – M. G. Biga, *Testi amministrativi*: *assegnazioni di prodotti alimentari* (*Archivio L. 2712-II*), (Archivi Reali di Ebla – Testi X), (*forthcoming*). |
| *ARET* XI | P. Fronzaroli, *Testi rituali della regalità* (*Archivio L. 2769*), (Archivi Reali di Ebla – Testi XI), Roma 1993. |
| *ARET* XII | M. Lahlouh – A. Catagnoti, *Testi amministrativi di vario contenuto* (*Archivio L. 2769*: *TM.75.G.4102-6050*), (Archivi Reali di Ebla – Testi XII), Roma 2006. |
| *ARET* XIII | P. Fronzaroli, *Testi di cancelleria*: *i rapporti con le città* (*Archivio L. 2769*), (Archivi Reali di Ebla – Testi XIII), Roma 2003. |
| *ARET* XV | F. Pomponio, *Testi amministrativi*: *assegnazioni mensili di tessuti* (*Archivio L. 2769*), (Archivi Reali di Ebla – Testi XV, 1, 2), Roma 2008 / 2013. |
| *ARET* XIX | I. Samir, *Wirtschaftstexte. Monatliche Buchführung über Textilien aus Ibriums Amtszeit* (*Archiv L: 2769*), (Archivi Reali di Ebla – Testi XIX), Wiesbaden 2020. |
| *ARET* XX | A. Archi, *Administrative Documents. Allotments of Clothing for the Palace Personnel* (*Archive L. 2769*), (Archivi Reali di Ebla – Testi XX), Wiesbaden 2019. |
| *ARET* XXII | A. Archi – G. Spada, *The Annual Documents of Expenditures of Metals from Minister Ibbi-zikir's Period* (*Archive L. 2769*), (Archivi Reali di Ebla – Testi XXII), (in preparation). |
| *LLE*,I | Archi, A. – Krebernik, M., *The Bilingual Lexical Lists from Ebla* (forthcoming) |
| *MEE* 2 | G. Pettinato, *Testi amministrativi della biblioteca L. 2769* (Materiali Epigrafici di Ebla – 2), Napoli 1980. |
| *MEE* 4 | G. Pettinato, *Testi lessicali bilingui della biblioteca L. 2769* (Materiali Epigrafici di Ebla – 4), Napoli 1982. |
| *MEE* 7 | F. D'Agostino *Testi amministrativi di Ebla. Archivio L. 2769* (Materiali Epigrafici di Ebla – 7), Roma 1996. |
| *MEE* 10 | P. Mander, *Administrative Texts of the Archive L. 2769* (Materiali Epigrafici di Ebla – 10), Roma 1990. |
| *MEE* 12 | H. Waetzoldt, *Wirtschafts- und Verwaltungstexte aus Ebla. Archiv L. 2769* (Materiali Epigrafici di Ebla – 12), Roma 2001. |
| *Sign List* | Archi, A., 1987, "The 'Sign-list' from Ebla", *Eblaitica* I, Winona Lake, Indiana, |

| | |
|---|---|
| Ibr. | Ibrium |
| I.Z. | Ibbi-zikir |
| kb | kù-babbar "silver" |
| kbg | kù:babbar-gi "silver and gold" |
| kg | kù-gi "gold" |
| o. | obverse |
| r. | reverse |

# References


Archi, A. 1986, "Bemerkungen von Zuwendungen an Personengruppen in Ebla", *AoF* 13, pp. 191–205.

Archi, A. 1988, "Studies in Eblaite Prosopography", pp. 205–284 in: A. Archi (ed.) *Eblaite Personal Names and Semitic Name-Giving* (ARES I), Roma.

Archi, A. 1992, "Transmission of the Mesopotamian Lexical and Literary Texts from Ebla", pp. 1–39 in: P. Fronzaroli (ed.), *Literature and Literary Language at Ebla* (Quaderni di Semitistica18), Firenze.

Archi, A. 1995, "Šalaš Consort of Dagan and Kumarbi", pp. 1–6 in: Th. Van den Hout – Johan de Roos. (eds.), *Studies Presented to Philo H.I. Houwink ten Cate on the Occasion of his 65th Birthday,* Leiden.

Archi, A. 1998a, "The High Priestess, dam-dingir, at Ebla", pp. 43–53 in: M. Dietrich – I. Kottsieper (eds.), 'Und Moses schrieb dieses Lied auf'. *Studien zum Alten Testament und zum Alten Orient. Festschrift für Oswald Loretz zur Vollendung seines 70. Lebensjahres mit Beiträgen von Freunden, Schülern und Kollegen* (AOAT 250), Münster.

Archi, A. 1998b, "The Stele (na-rú) in the Ebla documents", pp. 15–24 in: J. Braun – Kr. Łyczkowsa – M. Popko – P. Stenkeller (eds.), *Written on Clay and Stones. Studies Presented to Krystyna Szarzyńska on the Occasion of her 80th Birthday*, Warsawa.

Archi, A. 1998c, "The Regional State of Nagar According to the State of Ebla", pp. 1–15 in: M. Lebeau (ed.), *About Subartu / À propos de Subartu, Studies Devoted to Upper Mesopotamia* (Subartu IV,2), Turnhout.

Archi, A. 2002a, "Prepositions at Ebla", pp. 1–21 in: C.H. Gordon – G.A, Rendsburg (eds.), *Eblaitica* 4, Winona Lake, Indiana.

Archi, A. 2002b, "šeš-ii-ib: A Religious Confraternity at Ebla", pp. 23–55 in: C.H. Gordon – G.A, Rendsburg (eds.), *Eblaitica* 4, Winona Lake, Indiana

Archi, A. 2003, "In margine", pp. 27–41 in: (P. Marrassini ed.), *Semitic and Assyriological Studies Presented to Pelio Fronzaroli by Pupils and Colleagues*, Wiesbaden.

Archi, A. 2010a, "The God Hay(y)a (Ea/Enki) at Ebla", pp. 15–36 in: C. Melville – A.L. Slotsky (eds.), *Opening the Tablet Box. Near Eastern Studies in Honor of Benjamin, R. Foster*, Leiden/Boston.

Archi, A. 2010b, "Hamath. Niya and Tunip in the 3rd Millennium B.C. According to the Ebla Documents, *SMEA* 52, pp. 33–39.

Archi, A. 2010c, "Divination at Ebla", pp. 45–56 in: J.C. Fincke (ed.), *Festschrift für Gernot Wilhelm anläßlich seines 65. Geburtstages an 28. Januar 2010*, Dresden.

Archi, A. 2013a, "Ritualization at Ebla", *JANER* 13, pp. 212–237.

Archi, A. 2013b, "History of Syria in the Third Millennium: the Written Sources", pp. 75–88 in: W. Orthmann – M. al-Maqdissi – P. Matthiae, *Archéologie et Histoire de la Syrie* I: *La Syrie de l'époque* néolithique à l'âge du fer, Wisbaden.

Archi, A. 2015, *Ebla and its Archives. Texts, History, and Society* (SANER 7), Boston/Berlin.

Archi, A. 2016a, "Egypt or Iran in the Ebla Texts?", *Orientalia* 85, pp. 1–49.

Archi, A. 2016b, "Iritum(/Irrite) at the Time of the Archives of Ebla". Pp. 35–43 in: S. Erkut – O. Sir Gavaz (eds.), *Studies in Honour of Ahmet Ünal Armağani*, Istanbul.

Archi, A. 2018a, "IGI-ḪI-DU$_8$ 'To Pass in Review; Review'", pp. 19–26 in: A. Vacca – S. Pizzimenti – M. G. Micale (eds.), *A Oriente del Delta. Scritti sull'Egitto ed il Vicino Oriente antico in onore di Gabriella Matthiae Scandone,* (*CMAO* 18), Roma.

Archi, A. 2018b, "Guests at the Court of Ebla", pp. 17–42 in: Kr. Kleber – G. Neumann – S. Paulus (eds.), *Grenzüberschreitungen. Studien zur Kulturgeschichte des Alten Orients. Festschrift für Hans Neumann zum 65. Geburtstag am 9. Mai 2018* (dubsar 5), Münster.

Archi, A. 2018c, Eblaite $^{d}$*Gú-šar* and $^{d}$*Gú-ša-ra-tum* – Ugaritic *kṯr* and *kṯrt*, *N.A.B.U.* 2018/2, pp. 1–3.

Archi, A. 2019a, "The Defeat of Mari and the Fall of Ebla (EB IVA). Focusing on the Philological Data", *Orientalia* 88, pp. 141–190.

Archi, A. 2019b, "Wars at the Time of Irkab-damu, King of Ebla", *Studia Eblaitica* 5, pp. 1–13.

Archi, A. 2020a, "Personal Names of Proto-Anatolian Indo-European-Speaking Populations East of the Euphrates (24th Cent. BC)", pp. 27–36 in: M. Cammarosano – E. Devecchi – M. Viano (eds.), "*talugaeš witteš*. Ancient Near Eastern Studies Presented to Stefano de Martino on the Occasion of his 65th Birthday" (Kasion 2), Münster.

Archi, A. 2020b, "The Overseers of the Teams of Mules and Asses, ugula sur$_x$-BAR.AN/IGI.NITA", *Asia Anteriore Antica* 2 (2020), pp. 45–51.

Archi, A. 2021a, "The Wars of Ebla at the Time of Minister Ibrium"; *AoF* 48, pp. 189–220.

Archi, A. 2021b, "The Royal Wedding at Ebla", *Studia Eblaitica* 7, pp. 1–32.

Archi, A. 2022a, "Minima Eblaitica 26bis. A Point of History: The Death of King Irkab-damu and the Synchronism between the Death of two Kings of Mari and two Kings of Kakmiun", *N.A.B.U.* 2022/46, pp. 103–104.

Archi, A. 2022b, "Minima Eblaitica 27. Sumerian KA-ma, Eblaite *bù-gú-*⌜*ú*⌝*-um* 'monkey'", *N.A.B.U.* 2022/80, pp. 176–177.

Archi, A. 2024, "Metals in the Third Millennium BC: the Case of Ebla", (forthcoming).

Archi, A., "Tiša-lim of Ebla, queen of Emar" (forthcoming)-

Astour, M.C. 1992, "History of Ebla", *Eblaitica* 3, pp. 3–82.

Biga, M.G. 2000, "Wet-nurses at Ebla: a Prosopograhic Study", *VO* 12, pp. 59–88.

Biga, M.G. 2002, "Les foires d'après les archives d'Ébla", pp. 277–288 in: *Florilegium marianum* VI, Paris.

Biga, M.G. 2003, "Feste e fiere a Ebla", pp. 55–68 in: C. Zaccagnini (ed.), *Mercato e politica nel mondo antico*, Roma.

Catagnoti, A. 1997, "Les listes des ḪÚB(.KI) dans les textes administratifs d'Ébla et l'onomastique de Nagar", *Amurru* 8, pp. 563–597.

Catagnoti, A. 2016, "Il legno di bosso", pp. 29–53 in: P. Corò – E. Devecchi – N. De Zorzi – M. Maiocchi (eds.), Libiamo ne' lieti calici. Ancient Near Eastern Studies Presented to Lucio Milano on the Occasion of his 65th Birthday by Pupils, Colleagues and Friends (AOAT 436), Münster.

Civil, M. 2008, *The Early Dynastic Practical Vocabulary A* (*Archaic HAR-ra A*) (ARES IV) Roma.

Conti, G. 1997, "Carri ed equipaggi nei testi di Ebla", pp. 23–71 in: P. Fronzaroli (ed.), *Miscellanea Eblaitica* 4 (Quaderni di Semitistica 19), Firenze.

Conti, G. 2003, "Il Pennsylvania Sumerian Dictionary e il Sumerico di Ebla", pp. 116–135 in: (P. Marrassini ed.), *Semitic and Assyriological Studies Presented to Pelio Fronzaroli by Pupils and Colleagues*, Wiesbaden.

Conti, G. – Bonechi, M. 1992, "*tišānum* éblaite = akkadien de Mari *tišānum*", *N.A.B.U.* 1992/11, pp. 9–10.

Fronzaroli, P. 1988, "Il culto dei re defunti in ARET 3. 178", pp. 1–33 in: P. Fronzaroli (ed.), *Miscellanea Eblaitica* 1 (Quaderni di Semitistica 15), Firenze.

Fronzaroli, P. 1992, "The Ritual Texts of Ebla", pp. 163–183 in: P. Fronzaroli (ed.), *Literature and Literary Language at Ebla* (Quaderni di Semitistica 18), Firenze.

Fronzaroli, P. 1997, "Divinazione a Ebla (TM.76.G.86", pp. 1–22 in: P. Fronzaroli (ed.), *Miscellanea Eblaitica* 4 (Quaderni di Semitistica 19), Firenze.

Fronzaroli, P. 2022, "Betyls in the Ebla Texts", *Studia Eblaitica* 8, pp. 75–86.

Krecher, J. 1981, "Sumerogramme und syllabische Orthographie in den Texten von Ebla", pp. 135–154 in: L. Cagni (ed.), *La lingua di Ebla. Atti del Convegno Internazionale* (*Napoli 21–23 aprile 1980*), Napoli.

Pasquali, 2004, "Le figure dei tori androcefali ("lu$_x$") come «apotropaion» su un ariete d'assedio ad Ebla", *N.A.B.U.* 2004/67.

Pettinato, G. 1981, "Gasur nella documentazione epigrafica di Ebla", pp. 297–307 in: M.A. Morrison – D.I. Owen (eds.), *Studies on the Civilization and Culture of Nuzi and the Hurrians. In Honor of Ernest .R. Lacheman*, Winona Lake, Indiana.

Pomponio, F. – Xella, P. 1997, *Les dieux d'Ebla* (AOAT 245), Münster.

Sallaberger, W. – Shrakamp, I. 2015, "Philological Data for a Historical Chronology of Mesopotamia in the 3rd Millennium", pp. 1–136 in: Sallaberger, W., and Shrakamp (eds.), History & Philology (ARCANE III). Turnhout.

Steinkeller, P. 1987, "Battering Ram and Siege Engines at Ebla", *N.A.B.U.* 1987/27.

Steinkeller, P. 2021, "International Trade in Greater Mesopotamia during Late Pre-Sargonic Times", pp. 173–193, in L. Rahmstorf – G. Barjamovic – N. Ialongo (eds.), *Merchants, Measures and Money* (Understanding Technologies of Early Trade in a Comparative Perspective 2), Kiel/Hamburg.

# List of the documents and the find spots[1]

| Text | Inv. no. TM.75/76.G | mm. | Locus | Datation |
|---|---|---|---|---|
| 1 | 76.672+674+677(+)675(+)676(+)678(+)679(+)681 | | Locus 2769 Wall, sector | 00 |
| 2 | 75.2333 | | Est, B, d | 01a |
| 3 | 75.1705+3822+5114+12173 | (191×183×20) | Est, C | 01b |
| 4 | 75.10077 | | Est | 02a |
| 5 | 75.2362+4188 | | Est, B, d | 02b |
| 6 | 75.2464 | (207×193×38) | Est, B, d | 03 |
| 7 | 75.1771 | (240×223×41) | Est, B, c | 04 |
| 8 | 75.3052(ARET III 41)+3316(ARET III 247)+4391+11988 (obv.) 75.3106(ARET III 91)+3706(ARET III 635)+ 11631+11632+12036 (rev.) | | | 05 |
| 9 | 75.3481(ARET III 417)+4589+4633+5487+5515+ 5518+5521+5529+5531+5532+5533+5534+ 5547+5552+5556+5559+5562+5568+5578+5584+5613 | | | 06 |
| 10 | 75.1904+12094+12109 | (211×196×51) | Est, B, c | 07 |
| 11 | 75.10148+4196+10149+11548 | | | 08 |
| 12 | 75.2359 | | Est, B, a | 09 |
| 13 | 75.10143+3861(ARET III 772)+5021+5022+5128 5129+11694+11695 | | | 10 |
| 14 | 75.10144 | | | 11 |
| 15 | 75.1464+12628 | (258×243×43) | Est, A | 12 |
| 16 | 75.2365+11439 | | Est, B, d | 13 |
| 17 | 75.1730+3233+3242(ARET III 200)+ 3372(ARET III 326)+12631+13693+XL(1, 2) | (269×246×46) | | 14 |
| 18 | 75.2502 | (273×253×47) | Est, C | 15 |
| 19 | 75.2465 | | Nord, C | 16 |
| 20 | 75.10210+11381+11382(+)16852+XIV+XVIII | | | 17 |
| 21 | 75.1923+3497(ARET III 433)+3500(ARET III 436) | | Nord, C | 18 |
| 22 | 75.2596 | | Est, C | |
| 23 | 75.1696 | | Est, B | |
| 24 | 75.2261 | (113×123×22) | Est, A | |
| 25 | 75.2630 | | Est, C | |

1 The Museum of Idlib was not accessible after the year 2010. The registered measures of some tablets can suggest the standard dimension of this typology of documents.

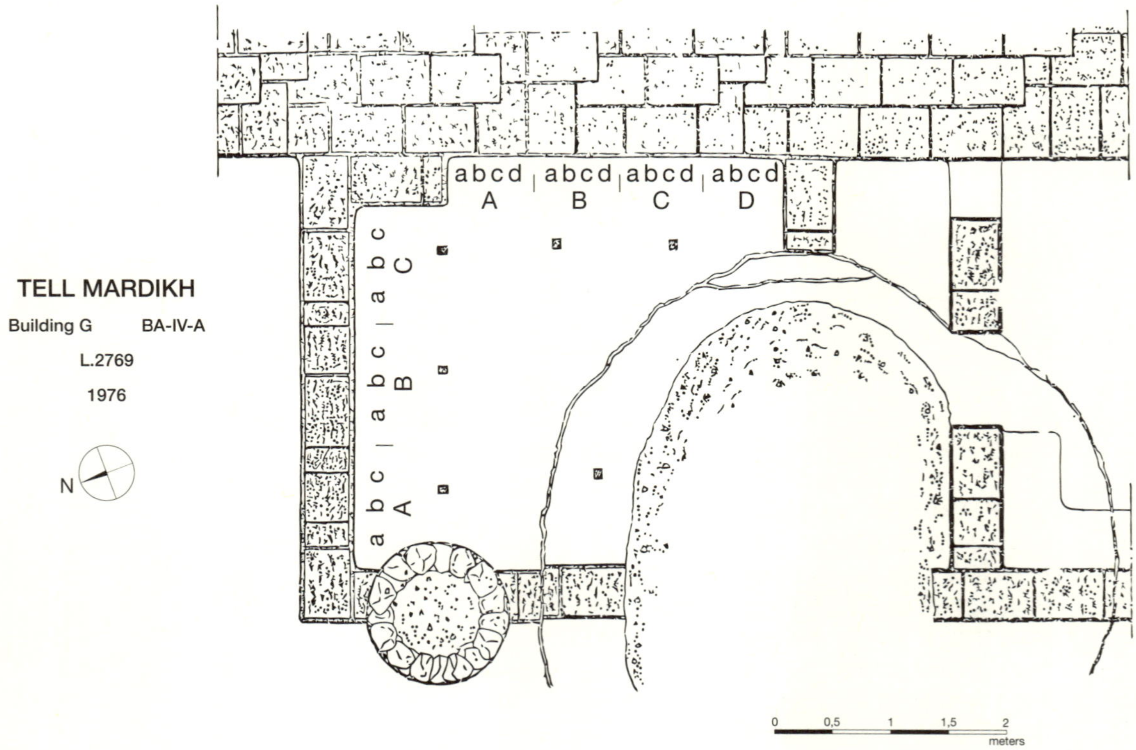


Ebla: Archive, L. 2769

# List of the inventory numbers of the tablets

| Inv. no. TM.75.G | |
|---|---|
| 1464+ | 15 |
| 1696 | 23 |
| 1705+ | 3 |
| 1730+ | 17 |
| 1771 | 7 |
| 1904+ | 10 |
| 1923+ | 21 |
| 2261 | 24 |
| 2333 | 2 |
| 2359 | 12 |
| 2362+ | 5 |
| 2365+ | 16 |
| 2464 | 6 |
| 2465 | 19 |
| 2502 | 18 |
| 2596 | 22 |
| 2630 | 25 |
| 3052+ | 8 |
| 3106+ | 8 |
| 3233+ | 17 |
| 3242+ | 17 |
| 3316+ | 8 |
| 3372+ | 17 |
| 3481+ | 9 |
| 3497+ | 21 |
| 3500+ | 21 |
| 3706+ | 8 |
| 3822+ | 3 |
| 3861+ | 13 |
| 4188+ | 5 |
| 4196+ | 11 |
| 4391+ | 8 |
| 4589+ | 9 |
| 4633+ | 9 |
| 5021+5022+ | 13 |
| 5114+ | 3 |
| 5128+5129+ | 13 |
| 5487+ | 9 |
| 5515+5518+5521+ | 9 |
| 5529+5531+5532+5533+5534+ | 9 |
| 5547+5552+5556+5559+ | 9 |
| 5562+5568+5578+5584+ | 9 |
| 5613+ | 9 |
| 10077 | 4 |
| 10143+ | 13 |
| 10144 | 14 |
| 10148+10149 | 11 |
| 10210+ | 20 |
| 11381+11382+ | 20 |
| 11439+ | 16 |
| 11548 | 11 |
| 11631+11632+ | 8 |
| 11694+11695+ | 13 |
| 11988+ | 8 |
| 12036+ | 8 |
| 12094+ | 10 |
| 12109+ | 10 |
| 12173+ | 3 |
| 12631+ | 17 |
| 12628 | 15 |
| 13693+ | 17 |
| 16852+ | 20 |
| Tiny fragments from bags XIV, XVIII, XL | |

| Inv. no. TM.76.G | |
|---|---|
| 672+674+675+676+677+678+679+681 | 1 |

# Introduction

Minister Arrukum died after having served in this role for about five or six years, (the last of the eleven years of king Irkab-damu's reign) and was succeeded by Ibrium shortly before Irkab-damu's death. The king had been ill for several months, probably suffering from a wound received in battle against Enna-Dagan of Mari (Archi 2022a). Peace was sealed in the year Ibr. 03.

Ibrium had previously served as a "lord", lugal, in the corps of the twelve / fifteen officials at the head of the central administration already from the first six years of Irkab-damu's reign (see *ARET* XIV 33, 34, 35). According to *ARET* XIV 36 o. I 5–II 1, he was at the head of 600 "men", ĝuruš. Several documents of Arrukum's period mention him (they are listed in *ARET* XV,2, p. 329). When Ebla decided to be involved in the conflict between the cities of Abarsal and Armi (see Archi 2019b, pp. 3–7) Ibrium assisted Arrukum in his diplomatic action (*ARET* XV,1 8 § 9; 26 §§ 63–64).

Four documents concern the year in which Ibrium succeeded Arrukum.

*a*) *ARET* XIV 54 registers the gifts in silver, gold, and garments delivered by more than forty city-states or small centres in connection to Irkab-damu's death. The gifts of nine officials follow, with Ibrium listed first. It is specified that he gave 1 mina (470 g) of gold and a mantel for the "purification rite", ì-ĝiš-saĝ, of Dusigu, Irkab-damu's spouse of second rank, and mother of Išᶜar-damu, the new king. Only the seven minas (3.29 kg) of gold sent by Kablul, the city that usually supplied Ebla with gold, surpassed (and by far) Ibrium's gift. Dusigu also received fourteen toggle-pins of 3 minas (1.41 kg) of silver for her "purification rite" (§ 53). Išᶜar-damu was still a child, so it was Dusigu who in some way assured dynastic continuity. In total more than 30 minas (14.10 kg) of silver and 9 minas (4.23 kg) of gold were received as "competence of Irkab-damu when he went to his destiny", níĝ-ki-za *Ìr-kab-da-mu si-mi* úš-*sù*.

*b*) Text XXI 22 first registers the very last expenditures of gold and silver during Arrukum's mandate, and then the expenditure of 4;33 minas of gold "delivered", mu-DU, by Ibrium for a funerary rite for the "royal ancestors, É×PAP en-en (§ 27).

*c*) An annual document concerning the expenditures of gold for that year, *MEE* 10, 4, has a total of "7;30 minas (3.525 kg) of gold (expended) at Irkab-damu's death", è *in* ud *Ìr-kab-da-mu si-mi* úš-*sù* (o. VIII 7–12). A final total of 52;40 minas (24.753 kg) of gold (r. XII 1') may concern an earlier period.

*d*) Text XXI 1 presents the same dating formula: è in ud *Ìr-kab-da-mu si-mi* úš-*sù* (§ 25). It concerns the silver and gold "expenditures", è, from the last year of Irkab-damu's reign, up until his death.

The Administration included in this last document not only the accounts of metal expenditures until the end of Arrukum's mandate, but also the following ones up until the end of the accounting year, which must have occurred sometime around Irkab-damu's death. In this way Ibrium would appear to have been in office at the beginning of the new administrative year.

The registration of the expenditure accounts for Ibrium's first two years required two large tablets for each year (differently from all the other documents of this typology). Text 2 (the first part of the first year) closes with the total of the expended silver (§ 76). Text 3 has: "x silver expended; second tablet", ... kù:babbar è 2 dub: this total only considers the silver from the second tablet, which is followed by the total of the silver "present", $al_6$-ĝál, (in the Treasury) at the end of that year. Text 4 similarly has: "x silver expended in (the first part of) Ibrium's second year", kù:babbar è in ud *Ib-rí-um* 2 mu (§ 126), while text 5 specifies: "x silver expended in (the second part of Ibrium's) second year, second tablet", kù:babbar è 2 mu 2 dub; the total amount of the silver in the Treasury is omitted.

No annual document of expenditures receives a dating, with the exception of *ARET* XXI 1 and two texts from the period of Ibbi-zikir, Ibrium's son and successor, which are also dated by an event: *ARET* XXII 3 (I.Z. 4): DIŠ mu úš ama-gal en iti *ga-sum* úš-*sù* "year of the death of (Dusigu) the king's mother; month VII" (one felt to precise the month of this important woman's death!); XXII 10 (I.Z. 11): DIŠ mu šu-ba$_4$-ti *Ì-li-ga-ù*$^{ki}$ "year of the taking of the city of Iliga'u".

The sequence of the large annual tablets of "expenditures", è, could be deduced by their order on the shelves of the central archive, differently from the much smaller annual documents concerning the "deliveries", mu-DU, to the Administration. The scribes, therefore, must have felt the need to fix the sequence of these last documents at a certain point, by carving a numeral on the already dry tablets (simple lines, not cuneiform signs) after having moistened that part of the surface. This was done, unfortunately, in different periods and sometimes not carefully. They considered *ARET* XIV 54 as the first document in the series of Ibrium's annual mu-DU documents. It was written at Irkab-damu's death, when Ibrium was just recently installed as minister, so that *ARET* XIV 55 – the first document which lists the annual deliveries to the Administration from Ibrium's period – is dated to the "second year (from) the king's death", 2 mu úš en (§ 32), (see *ARET* XIV, pp. 171–172, 179, 185).

Starting with the second year (text 4, § 1), these annual documents open with the registration of the expenditure of 1 mina (470 g) of silver for the "head" (saĝ) of Kura, the city-god, (§ 1), a renewal rite celebrated at the beginning of the new year. This rite is already attested in minister Arrukum's annual documents, but not in the opening lines. Three more shekels (23 g) of silver were needed for a subsequent rite which again involved the head of the god's statue (see the commentary to text no. 4).

Already text no. 2 (Ibr. 01) registers in § 2 the delivery of a considerable amount of silver for Tinib-dulum, a "king's sister", nin-ni en, priestess of the god 'Adabal. This expenditure would always follow (in § 2) that for Kura, beginning in the year Ibr. 05 (text no. 8), which shows how Kura and 'Adabal were the most important deities for the Ebla dynasty. Some documents associate her younger sister Tirin-damu with this priestess (see Archi 1998a).

Text no. 17 (Ibr. 14) registers the marriage of king Iš'ar-damu with Tabur-damu, daughter of his father's brother, and therefore his cousin, who received the title of "queen", *ma-lik-tum*.

Ibrium died after being minister for eighteen years; the end of text no. 21 registers his funerary gifts.

The expenditures of objects in silver and gold especially concerned the gods (see the List of offerings, below), the king, his mother, and daughters (including those of the previous king Irkab-damu). Some of these princesses had married kings of city-states that recognized Ebla's hegemony. Some officials received plaques of gold as a reward for special missions. Weapons decorated with silver and gold were distributed to members of the Administration.

Silver was given to some members of the Administration, particularly to Wabarum (qualified as a "collector", ur$_4$), who had to buy goods at several markets (see below).

The period of minister Ibrium, like the preceding one of Arrukum (and the following one of minister Ibbi-zikir) was characterized by a series of wars both to maintain and extend Ebla's hegemony over minor centers, or for contrasting the expansionist policy of Mari, whose more direct opponent was Nagar. This common enemy made Nagar, which controlled the Ḫabur triangle, a trustworthy ally of Ebla. The wars of Ibrium's period have already been object of a detailed analysis (Archi 2021a).

Even events in Babylonia were considered of interest; for example, messengers from Mari brought the news of the defeat of Kiš (years 10–12).

The list here below, in the left column, first registers the total of silver, gold, copper, bronze, and tin (in kg) delivered by the minister over a year, followed by the deliveries by the lords, the towns and the city-states (when totals are given). The "(final) total" is given at the end. Objects in gold and silver are not considered when their weight is not given. A distinction is made (although not in a consequent way) between unworked silver and gold, and the metals employed for objects. The totals of the delivered clothes are not given here.

The totals of silver in the right column concern the expenditures in that same year according to the annual documents of the "expenditures" (è). Some documents register the total not only of the expended (è) silver, but also the amount of silver that remained ("present", $al_6$-ĝál), in the Treasury.

The weights of the metals are given in kg (silver = **s.**; gold = **g.**; copper = **co.**; bronze = **br.**; refined copper = **r.co.**; tin: **t.**).

| | *Incomes* (*mu*-DU *documents*) | *Expenditures* (*è documents*) |
|---|---|---|
| 1st year | *ARET* XIV 55<br>Ibrium: **s.** 38[+x] kg.<br>Total: **s.** 105.20 kg; **g.** 14.18 kg | *a*) *ARET* XXI 2:<br>**s.** 92.98 kg expended<br>*b*) *ARET* XXI 3:<br>**s.** 73.12 kg expended; 227.01 kg present |
| 2nd year | *ARET* XIV 56<br>Ibrium: **s.** 111.39 kg; **g.** 20.41 kg<br>Lords: **s.** 36.66 kg<br>Total: **s.** 148.05 kg; **g.** 14.18 kg | *a*) *ARET* XXI 4:<br>**s.** [ ] expended<br>*b*) ARET XXI 5:<br>**s.** 62.43 kg expended |
| 3rd year | *ARET* XIV 57<br>Ibrium: **s.** 178.60 kg<br>Lords: **s.** 39.60 kg<br>Total: **s.** 229.67 kg | a) *ARET* XXI 6:<br>**s.** 82.16 kg; **t.** kg 10.90 expended |
| 4th year | *ARET* XIV 58<br>Ibrium: **s.** 329 kg; **g.** 4.70 kg; **co.** 211.50kg; **br.** 39.24 kg<br>Lords: **s.** 35.34 kg<br>Cities: **s.** 5.36 kg<br>Total: **s.** 371.62 kg; **g.** 4.77 kg | *ARET* XXI 7:<br>**s.** 70.03 kg expended |
| 5th year | *ARET* XIV 59<br>Ibrium: **s.** 190.35 kg; **g.** 1.54 kg<br>Lords: **s.** 20.21 kg<br>Cities: **s.** 3.79 kg<br>Total: **s.** 209.93 kg | *ARET* XXI 8<br>[ ] |
| 6th year | *ARET* II 13<br>Ibrium: **s.** 32.90 kg; **g.** 1.52 kg<br>Lords: **s.** 18.17 kg<br>Cities: **s.** 2.51 kg<br>Total: **s.** 53.58 kg; **g.** 2.14 kg | *ARET* XXI 9<br>[ ] |
| 7th year | *ARET* XIV 60<br>Ibrium: **s.** 70.50 kg<br>Lords: **s.** 32.19 kg<br>Cities: **s.** 52.11 kg<br>Total: **s.** 108.29 kg; **g.** 0.62 kg | *ARET* XXI 10<br>**s.** 42.50 kg expended; [ ] present |
| 8th year | *ARET* XIV 61<br>Ibrium: **s.** 87.89 kg; **g.** 0.47 kg; **br.** 70.03 kg<br>Lords: **s.** 29.84 kg<br>Cities: **s.** 5.67 kg; **g.** 0.08 kg<br>Total: **s.**137.33 kg; **g.** 0.55 kg | *ARET* XXI 11<br>[ ] |

| | | |
|---|---|---|
| 9th year | *ARET* XIV 62<br>Ibrium: **s.** 150.40 kg; **co.** 35.25 kg<br>Lords: **s.** 31.96 kg<br>Cities: **s.** 5.46 kg; **g.** 0.94 kg<br>Total: **s.** 188 kg; **g.** 1.17 kg | *ARET* XXI 12<br>**s.** [ ] expended; 141.47 kg present |
| 10th year | *ARET* XIV 63<br>Ibrium: [...]<br>Lords: **s.** 31.96(?) kg<br>Cities: [...]<br>Total: [...] | *ARET* XXI 13<br>**s.** 80.22 expended; [ ] |
| 11th year | *ARET* XIV 64<br>Ibrium: **s.** 136.30 kg; **g.** 7.98 kg<br>Lords: **s.** 30.08 kg<br>Cities: **s.** 4.78 kg<br>Total: **s.** 175.09 kg; **g.** 8.01 kg | *ARET* XXI 14<br>[ ] |
| 12th year | *ARET* XIV 65<br>Ibrium: **s.** 188 kg; **g.** 2.76 kg; **r.co.** 188 kg<br>Lords: **s.** 30;31 kg<br>Cities: **s.** 4.08 kg<br>Total: **s.** 226.54 kg; **g.** 4.68 kg | *ARET* XXI 15<br>**s.** 109.04 expended; 164.50 kg present |
| 13th year | *ARET* XIV 66<br>Ibrium: **s.** 161.68 kg; **g.** 19.50 kg; **r.co.** 329 kg<br>Lords: **s.** 30.39 kg<br>Cities: **s.** 9.59 kg<br>Total: **s.** 201.19 kg; **g.** [...] | *ARET* XXI 16<br>**s.** 139,67/92.67 expended; 94[+x] kg present |
| 14th year | *ARET* XIV 67<br>Ibrium: **s.** 141 kg; **g.** 1.98 kg; **r.co.** 138.65 kg<br>Lords.: **s.** 28.70 kg<br>Cities: **s.** 5.92 kg; **g.** 1.24 kg<br>Total: **s.** 176.62 kg; **g.** 3.22 kg; **r.co.** 145.70 kg | *ARET* XXI 17<br>**s.** 124.58 kg expended; 51.07(?) kg present |
| 15th year | *ARET* XIV 68<br>Ibrium: **s.** 183.06[a] + 152.04[b] kg; **g.** 9.76 kg;<br>**r.co.** 322.42 kg<br>Lords: **s.** 28.67 kg<br>Cities: **s.** 7.54 kg; **g.** 2.85 kg<br>Total: **s.** 365.19 kg; **g.** 12.30 kg | *ARET* XXI 18<br>**s.** 128.63 kg expended; 205.39 kg present |
| 16th year | *ARET* XIV 69<br>Ibrium: **s.** 211.5[a] + 141[b] kg; **g.** 0.76 kg; **r.co.** 329 kg<br>Lords: **s.** 28.51 kg<br>Cities: **s.** 10.92 kg<br>Total: **s.** 250.93[a] + 141[b] kg; **g.** 4.90[a] + 2.58[b] kg<br>a: wrought; b: unwrought | *ARET* XXI 19<br>**s.** 175.98 kg expended; 75.20 kg present |
| 17th year | *ARET* XIV 70<br>Ibrium: **s.** 298.92 kg; **g.** 4.79 kg; **r.co.** 385.40 kg<br>Lords: **s.** 29.53 kg<br>Cities: **s.** 7.46 kg; g. 3.19 kg<br>Total: **s.** 335.92 kg; g. 7.99 kg | *ARET* XXI 20<br>**s.** 112.80[+x] kg expended; [ ] |

| | | |
|---|---|---|
| 18th year | *ARET* XIV 71<br>Ibrium: **s.** 329 kg; **g.** 5.40 kg; **co.** 512.30 kg<br>Lords: **s.** 30.16 kg<br>Cities: **s.** 7.52 kg; **g.** 3.29 kg<br>Total: **s.** 366.60 kg | *ARET* XXI 21<br>[ ] |

Final totals (in kg) of the delivered (mu-DU) metals: silver 3,890.75[+x] kg;[2] gold 81.29 kg[+x];[3] refined copper 2,458.57[+x] kg; bronze 109.27[+x] kg.

2 The amount of the 10th year is not preserved.
3 Several documents do not give the totals of gold.

TEXTS AND COMMENTARIES

# 1
(Plates I–II)

o. I–IV. (in lacuna)

(1’)
V. 1. ˹50˺ gín DILMUN kù:babbar
[š]u-bal-ak
3. 10 gín DILMUN kù-gi
níĝ-sa$_{10}$ 1 BAR.AN
5. *Ba-˹ḫa˺-ni-um*$^{ki}$

(2’)
10 ma-na kù:babbar
7. kin$_{5}$-ak
17 íb-lá 17 *si-ti-tum* 17 ĝír-kun
9. ˹ME˺-sig
é

(3’)
11. 2 ma-na 10 gín DILMUN kù:babbar
níĝ-sa$_{10}$ 11 dam
13. [*A*-]*šum*
[šu-b]a$_{4}$-[ti]

(4’)
[x gín DILMUN kù:babbar]
15. níĝ[-kaskal]
*Ìr-kab-ar*
17. DU.DU
*si-in*
19. *Ar-mi*$^{ki}$

(5’)
VI. 1 50 gín DILMUN
níĝ-sa$_{10}$ ˹ĝeštin˺
3. *Bu$_{x}$-ma-ì*
šu-ba$_{4}$-ti

(6’)
5. 1 ma-na ŠÚ+ŠA gín DILMUN
[kù:]bab[bar]
*ni-zi-mu*
7. 2 níĝ-anše-ak 4 kù-sal
*Ìr-am$_{6}$-da-mu*
9. lú *I-rí-gú-nu*

(7’)
7 gín DILMUN kù:babbar
11. níĝ-sa$_{10}$ 1 ĝír mar-tu *ba-du-u$_{4}$*
kù:babbar-gi
*Ba-šu-rúm*
13. lú *A-zú-gú-ra*

(8’)
ŠÚ+ŠA g[ín DILMUN] kù:babbar
15. níĝ-kaskal
*Na*-N[E]
17. *Na-gà*[*r*$^{ki}$]
VII. 1. DU.DU
*si-in*
3. *Ar-mi*$^{ki}$

(9’)
6 gín DILMUN kù:babbar
5. níĝ-kaskal
*Ne-zi-ma-ì*
7. ˹*Puzur$_{4}$*˺-*ra-a-gú*
DU.DU
9. *si-in*
*Na-gàr*$^{ki}$

(10’)
11. ˹15˺ gín DILMUN [k]ù:[babbar]
*ni-zi-mu*
13. 1 íb-lá
*Du-bí-šum*
15. lú *Ba-zi-da*
tuš-LÚ×TIL
17. *Kak-mi-um*$^{ki}$

(11’)
TAR kù:babbar
19. [*ni*]-*zi-mu*
1 íb-lá [1] *si-ti*[-*tum* 1 ĝír-kun]

(1’) 50 shekels of silver in exchange for 10 shekels of gold, for the purchase of 1 mule (from) the city of Baḫaniʾum.
(2’) 10 minas of silver for making 17 belts, 17 sheaths, 17 dagger pendants for the watchmen of the (king’s) house.
(3’) 2 minas (and) 10 shekels of silver for the purchase of 11 women, [A]šum [has rece]iv[ed].
(4’) [x shekels of silver]: [travel] provision for Irkab-ar (who) went to the city of Armi.
(5’) 50 shekels of silver for the purchase of wine: Buma-i(l) has received.
(6’) 1;20 minas of silver for decorating 2 bridles (and) 4 buckles for Iram-damu, (son) of Iri-gunu.
(7’) 7 shekels of silver for the purchase of 1 *b.* mar-tu dagger (decorated with) silver (and) gold for Bašurum (son) of Azu-gura.
(8’) 20 shekels of silver: travel provision for NANE of the city of Nagar (who) went to the city of Armi.
(9’) 6 shekels of silver: travel provision for Nezima-i(l) (and) Puzurra-agu (who) went to the city of Nagar.
(10’) 15 shekels of silver for decorating 1 belt for Dubišum, (son) of Bazida who resided in the city of Kakmium.
(11’) 30 (shekels) of silver for decorating 1 belt, [1] she[ath, 1 dagger pendant …] for Agab, (son) of Ḫazu[…].

21. [ ]
[ ]
23. [ ]
VIII. 1. *A-ga-ab*
lú
3. *Ḫ*[*a-*]*zu-*[ ]

(12’)
[15] gín DILMUN kù:babbar
5. šu-bal-ak
3 gín DILMUN ⸢kù-gi⸣
7. *ni-*[*zi-*]*m*[*u*]
2 ⸢ĜIŠ⸣ [ ] 2 ĜIŠ-⸢x⸣
9. dumu-nita
*In-da-mu*

(13’)
11. 5 gín DILMUN kù:[bab]bar
šu-bal-ak
13. 1 gín DILMUN kù-gi
2 ĝeštu$_x$-lá
15. *Ù-ra-rí*
lú *I-gi*

(14’)
17. 5 gín DILMUN kù:babbar
šu-bal-ak
19. 1 gín DILMUN kù-gi
[ ]
21. [ ]
[ ]
23. [ ]

(15’)
IX. 1. 5 gín DILMUN kù:babbar
šu-bal-ak
3. [1 gín] ⸢kù-gi⸣
nu$_{11}$-za
5. *sa-ga-ti*
1 ĝír ⸢mar⸣[-tu]
7. [ ]
1 ma-na ŠA.PI gín DILMUN
kù:babbar
9. šu-bal-ak
ŠÚ+ŠA gín DILMUN kù-gi
11. 1 íb-lá 1 *si-ti-tum* 1 ĝír-kun
en
13. *Ì-ra-ar*$^{ki}$
*Wa-ba-rúm*
15. šu-mu-tak$_4$
É×PAP

(16’)
17. 14 gín DILMUN kù:babbar
*Za-zú*
19. *Ga-ga-*⸢*ba*⸣*-an*$^{ki}$

(17’)
[ -]⸢x⸣
21. [ ]
X. 1. 10 gín DILMUN kù:babbar
šu-bal-ak
3. 2 gín DILMUN kù-gi
nu$_{11}$-za-*sù*
5. dumu-nita
⸢*Ri*⸣*-ì*[*-ma-lik*]
7. [ ]

(18’)
[x] gín DILMUN kù:babbar
9. 1 *gú-li-lum*
15 gín DILMUN kù:babbar
11. šu-⸢bal-[ak]⸣
3 gín DILMUN kù-gi
13. nu$_{11}$-za-*sù*
*wa*
15. [1] kù-sal
NI-*gu*
17. dumu-munus
*A-ba-la*
19. *I-da-ni-ki-mu*

(19’)
6 gín DILMUN kù:babbar
21. *Ḫi-la-zu*$^{ki}$

(20’)
[x] gín [DILMUN kù:babbar]
XI. 1. *Maš-da-ru*$_{12}$
dumu-nita
3. *En-na-*$^{d}$Utu

(12’) [15] shekels of silver in exchange for 3 shekels of gold for decorating 2 … (and) 2 … for the son of Indamu.
(13’) 5 shekels of silver in exchange for 1 shekel of gold for 2 earrings for Urari, (son) of Igi.
(14’) 5 shekels of silver in exchange for 1 shekel of gold […].
(15’) 5 shekels of silver in exchange for [1 shekel] of gold for plating the *s.* of 1 mar[-tu] dagger; […] 1;40 minas of silver in exchange for 20 shekels of gold for 1 belt, 1 sheath, 1 dagger pendant for the king of the city of Irar, Wabarum has handed over for (his) funerary rite.
(16’) 14 shekels of silver for Zazu of the city of Gagaban.
(17’) [x silver for …], 10 shekels of silver in exchange for 2 shekels of gold for its plating for the son of Reʾi-[malik] […].
(18’) [x] shekels of silver for 1 bracelet, 15 shekels of silver in exchange for 3 shekels of gold for its plating, and for [1] buckle for NIgu, daughter of Abala of Ida-nikimu.
(19’) 6 shekels of silver for (someone of) the city of Ḫilazu.
(20’) [x] shekels [of silver] for Mašdaru, son of Enna-Utu.

(21')
ŠÚ+ŠA 5 gín DILMUN kù:babbar
5. [ ]
1 ma-na kù:babbar
7. šu-bal-ak
12 gín DILMUN kù-gi
9. nu$_{11}$-[za] 2 ⌜x⌝
[

(22')
XII. 1. [x gín DILMUN] kù:babbar
*I-ti-ne*
3. [l]ú [ ]
*Ib*[- ]
5. ⌜x⌝[

(23')
XIII. x+1. [x gín DIL]MUN [k]ù:[babbar]
[níĝ-s]a$_{10}$ [2 ĝí]r [mar-]tu [kù-g]i
3'. [*D*]*u-si*
*wa*
5'. *A-ku-*$^{d}$Utu
[

**(a) 681**

o. x+I. x+1. *I-šar*
lú
3'. [

II'. x+1. *Du-*⌜*rí*⌝*-um*
[

III'. x+1. ⌜x⌝

r. x+I. x+1. [ ] íb+III-TÚG babbar
ki:lam$_{7}$
3'. [

II'. 1. kù-gi
*Ḫa-ra-ì*
3. *Iš-da-má*
[

**(b) 679**

r. x+I. x+1. [ ] k[ù-gi]
50 gín DILMUN kù:babbar
3'. níĝ-sa$_{10}$ 20 ⌜ĝír⌝ [
[

II'. x+1. [*Ì*]*r-ku*$^{ki}$
*A-bù-*Kur$^{ki}$
3'. 10 lá-1 ma-na ŠÚ+ŠA 2 kù:babbar
níĝ-sa$_{10}$ ⌜x-x⌝
5'. [

**(c) 675**

r. x+I. x+1. [ ]⌜x⌝
[ĜIŠ-]⌜banšur⌝
3'. $^{d}$*Ku-r*[*a*]
[

II'. x+1. 15 gín DILMUN kù:babbar
[

III'. x+1. [ kù-]gi
[

**(d) 676**

r. x+I. x+1. *Si-*NE[*-su*]$^{ki}$
1 ma-na ŠÚ+ŠA gín [DILMUN kù:babbar]
3'. [

II'. x+1. 40[(+x)] *gú-li-lum*-II ŠÚ+ŠA-ŠÚ+ŠA
[

**(e) 678**

(24'')
r. x+I. x+1. [x ĝír] ma[r-tu] ⌜kù⌝[-gi]
1 ĝír mar-⌜tu⌝ ti kù-gi
3'. 46 íb+III-TÚG sa$_{6}$ gùn
2 *mi-at* 80 lá[-x] íb[+III]-TÚG gùn
5'. [

(25'')
II'. x+1. *Da-d*[*ub*]
*Ìr-m*[*u-*]*da-mu*
3'. lú *Íl-zi*
*Ìr-ga-bù*
5'. è
*in* ud
7'. *Ìr-kab-da-mu*
*si-mi*
9'. úš-*sù*

(21') 20 shekels of silver […], 1 mina of silver in exchange for 12 shekels of silver for plating 2 […].
(22') [x shekels] of silver for Itine, (son) of [PN] (and) Ib[…].
(23') [x shekels of silver for the purcha]se of [2 mar]-tu daggers [(decorated with) gold] for Dusi and Aku-Utu […].
(*fragmentary section*)
(24'') [x] ma[r-tu dagger(s)] (decorated with) gold, 1 pointed mar-tu dagger (decorated with) gold, 46 kilts, 280-[x] kilts […].
(25'') […] Dad[ub], Irm[u-]damu, (son) of Ilzi, Irgabu. Expended (silver) when (for) Irkab-damu his death was established.

(26")
6 ma-na 10 kù:babbar
11'. [

(27")
III'. 1. ⌜x⌝
šu-[ba$_4$-ti]

(28")
3. 10 g[ín] D[ILMUN kù:]babbar
maškim
5. *Ḫal-ba$_x$*(PÉŠ)
*Na-a*[*m$_6$*]$^{ki}$

(29")
7. 3 gín DILMUN kù:babbar
níĝ-kaskal
9. *I-ga-iš-lu*
DU.DU
11. *si-in*
*Ma-rí*$^{ki}$

(30")
13. 10 gín DILMUN kù:babbar
*Tar$_5$-ḫa-um*$^{ki}$

(31")
15. 1 ma-na 10 gín kù:babbar
NE-*a-du*
17. 2 BAR.AN
[ ]⌜x⌝[ ]
19. [

(32")
IV'. 1. [*i*]*n* ud
⌜ḫi⌝-úš
3. *I-ti-ì*
simug

(33")
5. 2 ma-na kù:babbar
níĝ-sa$_{10}$ 5 IGI.NITA u$_5$
7. *In-ti*
šu-ba$_4$-ti

(34")
9. 3 gín DILMUN kù:babbar
lú nu-kiri$_6$
11. [*Du-*]*bí-šum*
*ʾÀ-šu*$^{ki}$

(35")
13. 20 lá-2 ma-na kù:babbar
*si-*[*in*]
15. [x+]10 [ ]
[

(26") 6;10 minas of silver [...].
(27") [...] has re[ceived].
(28") 10 shekels of silver for the representative of Ḫalba of the city of Naʾam.
(29") 3 shekels of silver: travel provision for Iga-išlu (who) went to the city of Mari.
(30") 10 shekels of silver for (someone of) the city of Tarḫaum.
(31") 1;10 minas of silver for NEadu, 2 mules [...].
(32") [...] on the occasion of the death of Iti-i(l), the smith.
(33") 2 minas of silver for the purchase of 5 donkeys to ride, Inti has received.
(34") 3 shekels of silver for the gardeners of [Du]bišum of the city of Ašu.
(35") 18 minas of silver for [...].

## Commentary

This document is dated by the event mentioned in § 25": *in* ud *Ìr-kab-da-mu si-mi* úš-*sù* "when (for) Irkab-damu his death was established"; *si-mi* should be a stative form /šīm/, from **śym*, cf. *šīmtu*, OAkk. *śīmtum* "destiny", see Fronzaroli, 1992, p. 182, note 69; Pettinato, *apud MEE* 10, p. 35. Another text, *MEE* 10, 4 (TM.75.G.1796), concerns this same year and presents the same dating formula, obv. VIII 7–11: AN.ŠÈ.GÚ 7 ma-na TAR kù-gi è *in* ud *Ìr-kab-da-mu si-mi* úš-*sù*. *ARET* XIV 54 (§ 54), a mu-DU document which registers the deliveries of silver, gold, and garments by more than forty cities, as well as by Dusigu (mother of Išʿar-damu, Irkab-damu's son and successor), along with Ibrium and other officials on the occasion of king Irkab-damu's death, has a similar colophon: níĝ-ki-za ("competence of") *Ìr-kab-da-mu si-mi* úš-*sù*. A number concerning its dating is a cryptic notation: 10+1, which can be interpreted as "eleventh year of Irkab-damu", or "tenth year of Irkab-damu, first year of the minister Ibrium". In any case, it concerns the year that Ibrium succeeded Arrukum.

Ibrium was chosen as minister at Arrukum's death, just a few months before Irkab-damu's death. Both the redaction of the present document and that of *ARET* XIV 54, therefore, fall in months preceding the end of what one has to consider the final year of Arrukum's mandate.

The last two lines of the annual mu-DU document *ARET* XIV 55, which chronologically follows text XIV 54, attribute it to the "second" year of Ibrium. The Administration therefore considered the year that Ibrium succeeded Arrukum (completing Arrukum's last year) to be the first year of his mandate, and his second year was the first full year of his mandate (see *ARET* XIV, pp. 172, and 185). This filing is not followed here.

§ 1'. *Ba-ḫa-ni-um*$^{ki}$ (cf. *Ba-ḫa-ne-um*$^{ki}$ in *ARET* XV 40 § 55), the town where a mule was acquired, probably belonged to the region of Nagar, from where Ebla was usually provided with such animals.

§ 4'. Irkab-ar (who went to Armi) was an important official of the time of Arrukum, see *ARET* XV,2, p. 336.

§ 8' *Na*-NE, a messenger from Nagar, received a particularly high "travel provision" (20 shekels instead the usual 5 shekels), having to go to Armi.

§ 15' The king of *Ì-ra-ar*$^{ki}$, for whose death Wabarum handed over a belt decorated with 20 shekels of gold, should have been *I-ku-li-im*, mentioned in 75.1915+ r. I 6–7, a text of the period of Arrukum.

§ 29'' Iga-išlu, who went to Mari, is mentioned also in *ARET* XV 22 § 3 (*I-ga-iš-ru*$_{12}$).

# 2
## (Plates III–IV)

(1)

o. I. 1. [5 gín DILMUN kù:babbar]
[šu-bal-a]k
3. [1] gín DILMUN kù-gi
*ni-zi-mu*
5. 1 dib
*Ar-si-a-ḫa*
7. lú NI-*na-ad*

(2)

5 gín DILMUN kù:babbar
9. šu-bal-ak
1 gín DILMUN kù-gi
11. kin$_5$-ak
5 *zi-ba-tum*
13. *Di-ne-íb-du-lum*
nin-ni
15. en

(3)

5 gín DILMUN kù:babbar
17. šu-bal-ak
1 gín DILMUN kù-gi
19. *ni-zi-mu*
1 dib
21. *Ìr-am$_6$-ma-lik*
*Zi-ig*$^{ki}$

(4)

23. 5 gín DILMUN kù:babbar
II. 1. šu-bal-ak
1 gín DILMUN kù-gi
3. kin$_5$-ak
1 kù-sal
5. níĝ-ba
en
7. $^{d}$*Ba-ra-ma*
*in* ud
9. ne:saĝ-*sù*

(5)

50 gín DILMUN kù:babbar
11. níĝ-sa$_{10}$
1 ĝír mar-tu kù-gi
13. *Íl-ru$_{12}$-ga-lu*
*Ì-ra-ar*$^{ki}$

(6)

15. TAR kù:babbar
šu-bal-ak
17. 6 gín DILMUN kù-gi
nu$_{11}$-za
19. 1 bur-KAK ĜIŠ-taškarin
15 gín DILMUN kù:babbar
21. šu-bal-ak
3 gín DILMUN kù-gi
III. 1. nu$_{11}$-za 2 saĝ 2 *bu*-DI
ŠÚ+ŠA gín DILMUN kù:babbar
3. 2 *bu*-DI
10 gín DILMUN kù:babbar
5. 1 an-zam$_x$
3 gín DILMUN kù:babbar
7. 1 zi-bar
16 gín DILMUN kù:babbar
9. 2 ĜIŠ-du
2 ma-na kù:babbar
11. 1 ĜIŠ-šú 1 níĝ-bànda
*Da-ti-*$^{d}$TU
13. *ma-lik-tum*
*Lum-na-an*$^{ki}$

(7)

15. 5 gín DILMUN kù:babbar
šu-bal-ak
17. 1 gín DILMUN kù-gi
*ni-zi-mu*
19. 1 dib
*I-bí-zi-kir*
IV. 1. dumu-nita
*Ib-ri-um*

(1) [5 shekels of silver in exchange for 1] shekel of gold for decorating 1 plaque for Arsi-aḫa, (son) of NInad.

(2) 5 shekels of silver in exchange for 1 shekel of gold for making 5 handles for Tinib-dulum, sister of the king.

(3) 5 shekels of silver in exchange for 1 shekel of gold for decorating 1 plaque for Iram-malik of the city of Zig.

(4) 5 shekels of silver in exchange for 1 shekel of gold for making 1 buckle: gift of the king for the goddess Barama, on the occasion of her first-fruit offering.

(5) 50 shekels of silver for the purchase of 1 mar-tu dagger (decorated with) gold for Ilru-galu of the city of Irar.

(6) 30 shekels of silver in exchange for 6 shekels of gold for plating 1 bur-KAK vessel of boxwood; 15 shekels of silver in exchange for 3 shekels of gold for plating 2 heads of 2 toggle-pins; 20 shekels of silver for 2 toggle-pins; 10 shekels of silver for 1 an-zam$_x$ goblet; 3 shekels of silver for 1 zi-bar goblet; 16 shekels of silver for 2 foot rings; 2 minas of silver for 1 jug (and) 1 goblet: for Dati-TU, the queen of the city of Lumnan.

(7) 5 shekels of silver in exchange for 1 shekel of gold for decorating 1 plaque for Ibbi-zikir, son of Ibrium.

(8)
3. 55 gín DILMUN kù:babbar
šu-bal-ak
5. 11 gín DILMUN kù-gi
*ni-zi-mu*
7. 1 dib
*Iš*$_{11}$*-gi-wa-aš*
9. *Áb-su*$^{ki}$

(9)
TAR kù:babbar
11. šu-bal-ak
6 gín DILMUN kù-gi
13. nu$_{11}$-za
1 *ḫa-bù*
15. 15 gín DILMUN kù:babbar
nu$_{11}$-za-*sù*
17. níĝ-ba
*Ib-rí-um*
19. $^{d}$*ʾA*$_{5}$*-da-"bal"*
*ʾÀ-ma-ad*$^{ki}$

(10)
21. 10 gín DILMUN kù:babbar
V. 1. 1 an-zam$_{x}$
3 gín DILMUN kù:babbar
3. 1 zi-bar
ŠÚ+ŠA gín DILMUN kù:babbar
5. 2 *bu*-DI
15 gín DILMUN kù:babbar
7. šu-bal-ak
3 gín DILMUN kù-gi
9. nu$_{11}$-za 2 saĝ-*sù*
*Dar-maš-da-mu*
11. dumu-munus en
*gal-tum*
13. BAD-*da-mu*

(11)
50 gín DILMUN kù:babbar
15. níĝ-sa$_{10}$ 1 ĝír mar-tu kù-gi
*En-na-il*
17. ugula *Lum-na-an*$^{ki}$

(12)
1 ma-na ŠA.PI gín DILMUN
kù:babbar
VI. 1. šu-bal-ak
ŠÚ+ŠA gín DILMUN kù-gi
3. kin$_{5}$-ak
2 *ti-ki-na*
5. en

(13)
10 gín DILMUN kù:babbar
7. šu-bal-ak
2 gín DILMUN kù-gi
9. maš-maš
1 ĜIŠ-banšur
11. *wa*
1 kù-sal
13. níĝ-ba
*Ib-rí-um*
15. $^{d}$*Ku-ra*
*in* ud
17. ne:saĝ-*sù*

(14)
7 ½ gín DILMUN kù:babbar
19. šu-bal-ak
1 ½ gín DILMUN kù-gi
21. 1 kù-sal
níĝ-ba
23. *Du-si-gú*
$^{d}$*Iš:šára*
VII. 1. *Zi-da-ra*$^{ki}$

(15)
1 ma-na 8 gín DILMUN kù:babbar
3. níĝ-sa$_{10}$ 6 *ʾà-da-um*-TÚG 6 aktum-TÚG 3 gada-TÚG 1 íb+III-TÚG sa$_{6}$ gùn
ki:lam$_{7}$
5. *gi-ba-lu*
*ʾÀ-da-ni*$^{ki}$

(8) 55 shekels of silver in exchange for 11 shekels of gold for decorating 1 plaque for Išgi-waš of the city of Absu.

(9) 30 shekels of silver in exchange for 6 shekels of gold for plating 1 mace; 15 shekels of silver for its plating: gift of Ibrium for the god ʾAdabal of the city of ʾAmadu.

(10) 10 shekels of silver for 1 an-zam$_{x}$ goblet; 3 shekels of silver for 1 zi-bar goblet; 20 shekels of silver for 2 toggle-pins; 15 shekels of silver in exchange for 3 shekels of gold for plating their 2 heads: for Tarmaš-damu, daughter of the king (and) daughter-in-law of BAD-damu.

(11) 50 shekels of silver for the purchase of 1 mar-tu dagger (decorated with) gold for Enna-il, the overseer of the city of Lumnan.

(12) 1;40 minas of silver in exchange for 20 shekels of gold for making 2 torques for the king.

(13) 10 shekels of silver in exchange for 2 shekels of a striped (decoration) of gold for 1 table and 1 buckle: gift of Ibrium for the god Kura, on the occasion of his first-fruit offering.

(14) 7 ½ shekels of silver in exchange for 1 ½ shekel of gold for 1 buckle: gift of Dusigu for the goddess Išḫara of the city of Zidara.

(15) 1;08 minas of silver for the purchase of 15 garments (and) 1 kilt at the market of the *gibalu* of the city of ʾAdani.

(16)
7. šú+ša 7 gín DILMUN kù:babbar
níĝ-sa$_{10}$ *gàr-su*
9. NI-*a-ba-mu*
šu-ba$_{4}$-ti

(17)
11. 4 ma-na kù:babbar
šu-bal-ak
13. 10 lá-2 ma-na gìn-gìn
4 ma-na 11 gín DILMUN kù:babbar
15. níĝ-sa$_{10}$
VIII. 1. 6 zara$_{6}$-TÚG
11 aktum-TÚG
3. 1 íb+III-TÚG babbar gíd
5 *ʾà-da-um*-TÚG-I
5. 31 siki na$_{4}$ *Ma-rí*$^{ki}$
*áš-da*
7. *Du-tum*
*Ma-rí*$^{ki}$

(18)
9. 1 ma-na kù:babbar
níĝ-sa$_{10}$ 1 BAR.AN
11. *Sag-gar*$^{ki}$

(19)
4 ma-na šú+ša 6 gín DILMUN
kù:babbar
13. níĝ-sa$_{10}$ 42 aktum-TÚG
15 sal-TÚG
15. 5 *ʾà-da-um*-TÚG-I
10 íb+III-TÚG sa$_{6}$ gùn
17. 11 íb+III-TÚG gùn
ki:lam$_{7}$
IX. 1. *zi-ba-tum*
*ʾÀ-da-ni*$^{ki}$

(20)
3. 1 ma-na kù:babbar
níĝ-sa$_{10}$ 1 ĝír mar-tu kù-gi
5. *Ib-rí-um*

(21)
5 gín DILMUN kù:babbar
7. šu-bal-ak
1 gín DILMUN kù-gi
9. nu$_{11}$-za
*ba-na-a*
11. *wa*
íb+III-TÚG
13. $^{d}$*Ša-ma-gan*
en
15. 3 gín DILMUN kù:babbar
kin$_{5}$-ak
17. saĝ-*sù*

(22)
5 gín DILMUN kù:babbar
19. šu-bal-ak
1 gín DILMUN kù-gi
21. *ni-zi-mu*
X. 1. 2 ĝeštu$_{x}$-lá
*Di-ni-íb-du-lum*
3. nin-ni
en

(23)
5. 11 ma-na TAR 8 gín DILMUN
kù:babbar
níĝ-sa$_{10}$ 4 *mi-at* 10 siki na$_{4}$ *Ma-rí*$^{ki}$
7. 10 lá-2 aktum-TÚG
24 *ʾà-da-um*-TÚG-I
9. 32 íb+III-TÚG babbar
ki:lam$_{7}$
11. SA.ZA$_{x}$$^{ki}$

(24)
ŠA.PI 5 gín DILMUN kù:babbar
13. níĝ-sa$_{10}$ 13 íb+III-TÚG sa$_{6}$ gùn
TAR kù:babbar
15. níĝ-sa$_{10}$ ĜIŠ-sal
[*Wa-ba-*]*rúm*
17. šu-ba$_{4}$-ti
XI. 1. ki:lam$_{7}$
$^{d}$*A-da-ma*

(16) 20 shekels of silver for the purchase of bags, NI(l)abamu has received.
(17) 4 minas of silver in exchange for 8 minas of lapis lazuli, 4;11 minas of silver for the purchase of 22 garments, 1 kilt (and) 31 stone weights of wool from the city of Mari, by Dutum of the city of Mari.
(18) 1 mina of silver for the purchase of 1 mule (from) the city of Saggar.
(19) 4;26 shekels of silver for the purchase of 62 garments (and) 21 kilts at the market of the *zibatum* of the city of ʾAdani.
(20) 1 mina of silver for the purchase of 1 mar-tu dagger (decorated with) gold for Ibrium.
(21) 5 shekels of silver in exchange for 1 shekel of gold for plating the face and the kilt of (the statue of) the god Šamagan by the king; 3 shekels of silver for making its head.
(22) 5 shekels of silver in exchange for 1 shekel of gold for decorating 2 earrings for Tinib-dulum, sister of the king.
(23) 11;38 minas of silver for the purchase of 410 stone weights of wool from the city of Mari, 32 garments (and) 32 kilts at the market of the Palace.
(24) 45 shekels of silver for the purchase of 13 kilts; 30 shekels of silver for the purchase of GIŠ-sal: [Waba]rum has received at the market of Adamma.

(25)
3. TAR 3 3 NI gín DILMUN kù:babbar
šu-bal-ak
5. 6 gín DILMUN 2 NI kù-gi
2 *gú-li-lum*
7. níĝ-ba
$^{d}$*Ku-ra*

(26)
9. 15 gín DILMUN kù:babbar
šu-bal-ak
11. 3 gín DILMUN kù-gi
nu$_{11}$-za
13. 1 ĝír mar-tu *ra-ʾà-tum* tur
en
15. *Ì-mar*$^{ki}$

(27)
10 gín DILMUN kù:babbar
17. šu-bal-ak
2 gín DILMUN kù-gi
19. nu$_{11}$-za
1 *ma-ḫa-ni-gúm*
21. *Ib-rí-um*

(28)
[50 gín D]IL[MUN kù:babbar]
XII. 1. šu-bal-ak
10 gín DILMUN kù-gi
3. kin$_{5}$-ak
saĝ
5. $^{d}$*ʾA$_{5}$-da-ra*

(29)
5 gín DILMUN kù:babbar
7. šu-bal-ak
1 gín DILMUN kù-gi
9. *ni-zi-mu*
1 dib
11. *En-na-ma-lik*
*Ma-nu-wa-ad*$^{ki}$

(30)
13. 10 gín DILMUN kù:babbar
šu-bal-ak
15. 2 gín DILMUN kù-gi
*ni-zi-mu*
17. maš-maš
íb-lá
19. *I-ti-aš-dar*
lú
21. nídba ì-ĝiš

(31)
ŠÚ+ŠA gín DILMUN k[ù]:⌜babbar⌝
23. [šu-bal-a]k
XIII. 1. 4 gín DILMUN kù-gi
*ni-zi-mu*
3. 1 pad
1 an-zam$_{x}$
5. *Ib-rí-um*

(32)
15 gín DILMUN kù:babbar
7. šu-bal-ak
3 gín DILMUN kù-gi
9. *ni-zi-mu*
nu$_{11}$-za ĜIŠ-sur$_{x}$
11. ĜIŠ-gígir-II$^{!}$(III)
en

(33)
13. 11 gín DILMUN 3 NI kù:babbar
šu-bal-ak
15. 2 gín DILMUN 2 NI kù-gi
*ni-zi-mu*
17. 4 ĝeštu$_{x}$-lá
*Du-si-gú*

(34)
19. 10 gín DILMUN kù:babbar
šu-bal-ak
21. 2 gín DILMUN kù-gi
*ni-zi-mu*

(25) 33 shekels (and) 3 NI of silver in exchange for 6 shekels (and) 2 NI of gold for 2 bracelets: gift for the god Kura.
(26) 15 shekels of silver in exchange for 3 shekels of gold for plating 1 small mar-tu dagger (decorated with) shells for the king of the city of Imar.
(27) 10 shekels of silver in exchange for 2 shekels of gold for plating 1 necklace for Ibrium.
(28) [50 shekels of silver] in exchange for 10 shekels of gold for making the head of the goddess ʾAdara.
(29) 5 shekels of silver in exchange for 1 shekel of gold for decorating 1 plaque for Enna-malik of the city of Manuwat.
(30) 10 shekels of silver in exchange for 2 shekels of gold for a striped (decoration) of (1) belt for Iti-ašdar (on the occasion) of the offering of the oil.
(31) 20 shekels of silver [in exchange] for 4 shekels of gold for decorating 1 lid of 1 an-zam$_{x}$ goblet for Ibrium.
(32) 15 shekels of silver in exchange for 3 shekels of gold for decorating with lamination the double yoke of the chariot of the king.
(33) 11 shekels (and) 3 NI of silver in exchange for 2 shekels (and) 2 NI of gold for decorating 4 earrings for Dusigu.
(34) 10 shekels of silver in exchange for 2 shekels of gold for decorating 1 plaque for Ridam-malik, the overseer of the city of Šutigu.

XIV. 1. 1 dib
*Rí-dam-ma-lik*
3. ugula *Šu-ti-gú*$^{ki}$

(35)
10 gín DILMUN kù:babbar
5 šu-bal-ak
2 gín DILMUN kù-gi
7. *ni-zi-mu*
1 dib
9. *Iš-má-ga-lu*

(36)
ŠA.PI 5 gín DILMUN kù:babbar
11. šu-bal-ak
9 gín DILMUN kù-gi
13. *ni-zi-mu*
nu$_{11}$-za
15. ḫaš-ḫaš
4 *gú-li-lum* kù:babbar
17. *wa*
ḫaš-ḫaš
19. 5 *gú-li-lum* a-gar$_5$-gar$_5$
lú ĝuruš-ĝuruš
21. SA.ZA$_x$$^{ki}$

(37)
10 gín DILMUN kù:babbar
XV. 1. šu-bal-ak
2 gín DILMUN kù-gi
3. *ni-zi-mu*
6 ĝeštu$_x$-lá
5. *Da-mur-da-mu*
dam
7. *Ib-rí-um*

(38)
50 gín DILMUN kù:babbar
9. šu-bal-ak
10 gín DILMUN kù-gi
11. nu$_{11}$-za
*sa-ga-tum*
13. *wa*
*kam$_4$-ma-a-tum*
15. 10 lá-1 ĝír mar-tu zú
*Gi-a-da-mu*
17. *Gú-zi*
lú *Iš$_{11}$-gi-ba-ir*
19. *I-šar*
lú *Ba-ti*
21. *En-na-gú-nu*
lú *A-da-mu*
r. I. 1. ⸢*Ḫa*⸣*-ra-du*
lú
3. *Ba-lu-zú*
*Íl-ba-ma-lik*
5. lú *Da-*NE*-ga*
*I-rí-ig*
7. lú-kar
*Ḫa-zu-wa-an*$^{ki}$
9. *Mi-ga-il*
lú *I-ti-ki-šum*
11. *Ma-gal-lu*
lú
13. (blank)

(39)
10 gín DILMUN kù:babbar
15. šu-bal-ak
2 gín DILMUN kù-gi
17. *ni-zi-mu*
1 dib
19. *Ig-rí-iš*
lú *I-rí-gú-nu*

(40)
21. 10 gín DILMUN kù:babbar
šu-bal-ak
23. 2 gín DILMUN kù-gi
kin$_5$-ak
25. 1 *gú-li-lum*
II. 1. 1 kù-sal
níĝ-ba
3. *Ib-rí-um*
$^{d}$*Ku-ra*
5. *in* ud
lú nídba

(41)
7. ŠÚ+ŠA gín DILMUN kù:babbar
2 *ʾà-ra-ma-tum*
9. 15 gín DILMUN kù:babbar

(35) 10 shekels of silver in exchange for 2 shekels of gold for decorating 1 plaque for Išma-galu.
(36) 45 shekels of silver in exchange for 9 shekels of gold for decorating with lamination and granulation 4 bracelets of silver and 5 bracelets of copper for the men of the Palace.
(37) 10 shekels of silver in exchange for 2 shekels of gold for decorating 6 earrings for Tamur-damu, spouse of Ibrium.
(38) 50 shekels of silver in exchange for 10 shekels of gold for plating the ... (*sa-ga-tum*) and the knobs of 9 serrated mar-tu daggers for Giadamu, Guzi (son) of Išgi-bair, Išar (son) of Bati, Enna-gunu (son) of Adamu, Ḫaradu (son) of Baluzu, Ilba-malik (son) of DaNEga, Irig, trader of the city of Ḫasuwan, Miga-il (son) of Itikišum, Magallu son of (…).
(39) 10 shekels of silver in exchange for 2 shekels of gold for decorating 1 plaque for Igriš, (son) of Iri-gunu.
(40) 10 shekels of silver in exchange for 2 shekels of gold for making 1 bracelet (and) 1 buckle: gift of Ibrium for the god Kura, on the occasion of (his) offering.
(41) 20 shekels of silver for 2 pectorals; 15 shekels of silver in exchange for 3 shekels of gold for plating its 2 ... (*zé*): gift of Ibrium for the god Utu of the Palace.

šu-bal-ak
11. 3 gín DILMUN kù-gi
nu$_{11}$-za
13. 2 zé-*sù*
níĝ-ba
15. *Ib-rí-um*
$^{d}$Utu
17. SA.ZA$_{x}^{ki}$

(42)
4 ma-na ŠA.PI gín DILMUN
kù:babbar
19. šu-bal-ak
55 gín DILMUN kù-gi
21. nu$_{11}$-za
III. 1. [x *gú-li-lum*] 10 ⌜gín⌝ kù:babbar
3 *gú-li-lum* a-gar$_{5}$-gar$_{5}$ TAR-II esi
3. 2 *gú-li-lum* a-gar$_{5}$-gar$_{5}$ ŠÚ+ŠA-II esi
20 *gú-li-lum* a-gar$_{5}$-gar$_{5}$ 10-I esi
5. gaba-ru
é
7. en

(43)
12 ½ gín DILMUN kù:babbar
9. šu-bal-ak
2 ½ gín DILMUN kù-gi
11. 1 *gú-li-lum* 1 kù-sal
níĝ-ba
13. *Du-si-gú*
$^{d}$*Ra-sa-ap*
15. *ʾÀ-da-ni*$^{ki}$

(44)
TAR kù:babbar
17. nu$_{11}$-za 2 *ḫa-bù*
1 ma-na kù:babbar
IV. 1. [šu-bal-ak]
[ŠÚ+ŠA] g[ín DIL]MUN kù-gi
3. nu$_{11}$-za-*sù*
níĝ-ba
5. $^{d}$*Ra-sa-ap*
⌜*ʾÀ-da*⌝-*ni*$^{ki}$
7. *wa*
$^{d}$*ʾÀ-da*
9. $^{d}$AMA-*ra*

(45)
10 gín DILMUN kù:babbar
11. šu-bal-ak
2 gín DILMUN kù-gi
13. 2 ĝeštu$_{x}$-lá
*I-bí-zi-kir*
15. dumu-nita
*Ib-rí-um*

(46)
17. 1 ½ kù:babbar
maš-maš
19. 1 banšur
2 ½ gín DILMUN kù:babbar
21. šu-bal-ak
½ kù-gi
23. maš-maš-*sù*
níĝ-ba
25. en
$^{d}$*Ì-lam*

(47)
V. 1. [x ma-na] 5 gín DILMUN kù:babbar
níĝ-sa$_{10}$ 35 gud-gud
3. 10 ma-na 7 gín DILMUN kù:babbar
níĝ-sa$_{10}$ 10 lá-2 zara$_{6}$-TÚG
5. 44 aktum-TÚG
2 íb+III-TÚG babbar gíd
7. 20 *ʾà-da-um*-TÚG-I
1 túg-NI.NI ḫul
9. 2 níĝ-<lá->gaba
75 íb+III-TÚG sa$_{6}$ gùn
11. 7 íb+III-TÚG babbar
55 gín DILMUN kù:babbar
13. níĝ-sa$_{10}$ raš-SAR Kur$^{ki}$
2 ma-na 7 gín DILMUN kù:babbar
15. níĝ-sa$_{10}$
VI. 1. [ ]
[x gín DILMUN] kù:babbar
3. níĝ-sa$_{10}$ ĜIŠ-ád
ki:lam$_{7}$
5. *ʾÀ-da-ni*$^{ki}$

(42) 4;40 shekels of silver in exchange for 55 shekels of gold for plating [x bracelets] of silver of 10 shekels; 3 double bracelets of 30 shekels of copper each (and) diorite; 2 double bracelets of 20 shekels of copper each (and) diorite; 20 single bracelets of 10 shekels of copper each (and) diorite: supply for the king's house.
(43) 12 ½ shekels of silver in exchange for 2 ½ shekels of gold for 1 bracelet (and) 1 buckle: gift of Dusigu for the god Rašap of the city of ʾAdani.
(44) 30 shekels of silver for plating 2 maces; 1 mina of silver [in exchange for 20 sheke]ls of gold for its plating: gift for the god Rašap of the city of ʾAdani and for the god Hadda, at the AMA-ra (festival).
(45) 10 shekels of silver in exchange for 2 shekels of gold for 2 earrings for Ibbi-zikir, son of Ibrium.
(46) 1 ½ (shekel of) silver for a striped (decoration) of 1 table; 2 ½ shekels of silver in exchange for ½ (shekel of) gold for its striped (decoration): gift of the king for the god Ilam.
(47) [x];05 [minas] of silver for the purchase of 35 oxen; 10;07 minas of silver for the purchase of 75 garments (and) 84 kilts; 55 shekels of silver for the purchase of leek from the mountain region; 2;07 minas of silver for the purchase of […]; [x shekels] of silver for the purchase of myrtle: at the market of the city of ʾAdani.

(48)
⸢2⸣ [ma-]na TAR kù:babbar
7. šu-bal-ak
TAR kù-gi 1 íb-lá ĝír-kun
9. en
*Ma-nu-wa-ad*$^{ki}$
11. *in* ᵓ*À-da-ni*$^{ki}$
šu-ba$_4$-ti

(49)
13. 6 ma-na 55 gín DILMUN kù:babbar
šu-bal-ak
15. ŠA.PI 3 gín DILMUN kù-gi
kin$_5$-ak
17. 1 dib lú ĜIŠ-ĝeštin
*wa*
19. 1 dib-II ŠA.PI gín DILMUN kù-gi
VII. 1. [ ]

(50)
1 ma[-na] TAR kù:babbar
3. níĝ-sa$_{10}$ 2 gud
1 ma-na kù:babbar
5. nu$_{11}$-⸢za⸣ 4 si-*sù*
nídba
7. en
$^{d}$*Ra-sa-ap*
9. ᵓ*À-da-ni*$^{ki}$
$^{d}$AMA-*ra*

(51)
11. 3 ma-na ŠÚ+ŠA 7 gín DILMUN kù:babbar
níĝ-sa$_{10}$ 6 gud-gud
13. ⸢ki⸣:lam$_7$
$^{d}$*Ì-lam*

(52)
15. 15 gín DILMUN kù:babbar
nu$_{11}$-za 1 an-dùl
17. ŠÚ+ŠA 5 gín DILMUN kù:babbar
šu-bal-ak
19. 5 gín DILMUN kù-gi
nu$_{11}$-za
VIII. 1. [*ba-na-a*]
*wa*
3. íb+III-TÚG
níĝ-ba
5. *Ib-rí-um*
$^{d⌜}$BAD *Du*⸣-*du*-⸢*la*$^{ki}$⸣

(53)
7. TAR 3 3 NI gín DILMUN kù:babbar
šu-bal-ak
9. 6 2 NI gín DILMUN kù-gi
2 *gú-li-lum*
11. níĝ-ba
$^{d}$*Ku-ra*

(54)
13. 5 gín DILMUN kù:babbar
šu-bal-ak
15. 1 gín DILMUN kù-gi
maš-maš 1 banšur
17. *wa*
1 kù-sal
19. 1 gín DILMUN kù:babbar
maš-maš-*sù*
21. níĝ-ba
*Ib-rí-um*
23. $^{d}$ᵓ*A*$_5$-*da*-"*bal*"
IX. 1. *La-ru*$_{12}$-*ga-du*$^{ki}$

(55)
11 ma-na TAR 3 gín DILMUN kù:babbar
3. níĝ-sa$_{10}$ 95 aktum-TÚG
20 lá-2 túg-NI.NI ḫul
5. 4 zara$_6$-TÚG
10 lá-2 ᵓ*à-da-um*-TÚG-I
7. 11 sal-TÚG
2 íb+III-TÚG babbar gíd
9. 16 íb+III-TÚG sa$_6$ gùn
5 íb+III-TÚG babbar
11. 8 gín DILMUN kù:babbar
níĝ-sa$_{10}$ ú-ḫáb

(48) 2;30 [mi]nas of silver in exchange for 30 (shekels) of gold for 1 belt (and) dagger pendant: the king of the city of Manuwat has received in the city of ᵓAdani.
(49) 6;55 minas of silver in exchange for 43 shekels of gold for making 1 plaque (decorated with) a grapevine and 1 plaque, double, of 40 shekels of gold [...].
(50) 1;30 mi[na] of silver for the purchase of 2 oxen; 1 mina of silver for plating their 4 horns: offering of the king for the god Rašap of the city of ᵓAdani, at the AMA-ra (festival).
(51) 3;27 minas of silver for the purchase of 6 oxen at the market of the god Ilam.
(52) 15 shekels of silver for plating 1 statue; 25 shekels of silver in exchange for 5 shekels of gold for plating [(its) face] and (its) kilt: gift of Ibrium for the god Dagan of the city of Tuttul.
(53) 33 shekels (and) 3 NI of silver in exchange for 6 shekels (and) 2 NI of gold for 2 bracelets: gift for the god Kura.
(54) 5 shekels of silver in exchange for 1 shekel of gold for the striped (decoration) of 1 table, and 1 buckle; 1 shekel of silver for its striped (decoration): gift of Ibrium for the god ᵓAdabal of the city of Larugadu.
(55) 11;33 minas of silver for the purchase of 136 garments (and) 23 kilts; 8 shekels of silver for the purchase of dull red dye; 4 minas of silver for the purchase of GIŠ-ti-ḪAR-wood; 6;06 minas of silver for the purchase of 11 oxen; 55 shekels of silver for the purchase of 1 onagre; 2;02 minas of silver for the purchase of 4 donkeys to ride: at the market of the city of NIab.

13. 4 ma-na kù:babbar
níĝ-sa$_{10}$ ĜIŠ-ti-ḪAR
15. 6 ma-na 6 gín DILMUN kù:babbar
X. 1. níĝ-sa$_{10}$ 11 gud
55 gín DILMUN kù:babbar
3. níĝ-sa$_{10}$ 1 BAR.NITA
2 ma-na 2 kù:babbar
5. níĝ-sa$_{10}$ 4 IGI.NITA u$_5$
ki:lam$_7$
7. NI-*ab*$^{ki}$

(56)
ŠA.PI gín DILMUN kù:babbar
9. níĝ-sa$_{10}$
1 ĝír mar-tu kù-gi
11. *Íl-da-ar*
*Kak-mi-um*$^{ki}$

(57)
13. TAR 5 gín DILMUN kù:babbar
níĝ-sa$_{10}$ 1 ĝír mar-tu kù-gi
15. *Du-bí-šum*
lú-kar
17. ŠA.PI kù:babbar
níĝ-sa$_{10}$
19. 1 ĝír mar-tu kù-gi
*Ì-lum-na-im*
21. lú-kar
*Ma-nu-wa-ad*$^{ki}$

(58)
XI. 1. 1 ma-na ŠÚ+ŠA 5 gín DILMUN
kù:babbar
níĝ-sa$_{10}$ 2 ĝír mar-tu ti kù-gi 1 ĝír
mar-tu *ba-du-u$_9$* kù-gi
3. 3 *gú-li-lum* a-gar$_5$-gar$_5$ kù-gi
*Bù-da-ma-lik*
5. BÍL-*ma-lik*
*A-da-mu*
7. lú-kar
*Ḫa-zu-wa-an*$^{ki}$

(59)
9. 10 gín DILMUN kù:babbar
níĝ-sa$_{10}$ 1 ĝír mar-tu *ba-du-u$_9$* kù-gi
11. *Bu-da-na-im*
dumu-nita
13. ga-du$_8$

(60)
50 gín DILMUN kù:babbar
15. šu-bal-ak
10 gín DILMUN kù-gi
17. 1 íb-lá
níĝ-ba
19. $^{d\text{ʾ}}$*A$_5$-da-ra*

(61)
15 gín DILMUN kù:babbar
XII. 1. šu-bal-ak
3 gín DILMUN kù-gi
3. *n[i-z]i-⸢mu⸣*
1 dib
5. *Zé-da-mu*
lú *Dab-da-ar*

(62)
7. 11 ma-na 11 gín DILMUN kù:babbar
níĝ-sa$_{10}$ 76 aktum-TÚG
9. 3 *gu-zi-tum*-TÚG
20 lá-1 *ʾà-da-um*-TÚG-I
11. 7 túg-NI.NI ḫul
31 gada-TÚG
13. íb+III-TÚG gíd
4 níĝ-lá-saĝ
15. 30 íb+III-TÚG sa$_6$ gùn
30 íb+III-TÚG gùn
17. 20 siki na$_4$ sa$_6$
18 gín DILMUN kù:babbar
19. níĝ-sa$_{10}$
6 udu-nita sa$_6$
21. ki:lam$_7$
XIII. 1. ⸢SA⸣.ZA$_x$$^{⸢ki⸣}$

(56) 40 shekels of silver for the purchase of 1 mar-tu dagger (decorated with) gold for Il-dar of the city of Kakmium.

(57) 35 shekels of silver for the purchase of 1 mar-tu dagger (decorated with) gold for Dubišum, the trader; 40 shekels of silver for the purchase of 1 mar-tu dagger (decorated with) gold for Ilum-naʾim, trader of the city of Manuwat.

(58) 1;25 minas of silver for the purchase of 2 pointed mar-tu daggers (decorated with) gold, 1 *b.* mar-tu dagger (decorated with) gold, 3 bracelets of copper and gold for Buda-malik, BIL-malik (and) Adamu, traders of the city of Ḫasuwan.

(59) 10 shekels of silver for the purchase of 1 *b.* mar-tu dagger (decorated with) gold for Buda-naʾim, son of the wet-nurse.

(60) 50 shekels of silver in exchange for 10 shekels of gold for 1 belt: gift for the goddess ʾAdara.

(61) 15 shekels of silver in exchange for 3 shekels of gold for decorating 1 plaque for Ze-damu, (son) of Dab-dar.

(62) 11;11 minas of silver for the purchase of 140 garments, 60 kilts (and) 20 stone weights of wool of good quality; 18 shekels of silver of silver for the purchase of 6 rams of good quality: at the market of the Palace.

(63)
15 ma-na 5 gín DILMUN kù:babbar
3. níĝ-sa$_{10}$ 10 lá-1 zara$_6$-TÚG
90 aktum-TÚG
5. 52 aktum-TÚG-II
14 túg-NI.NI ḫul
7. 7 sal-TÚG
10 lá-2 níĝ-<lá->gaba
9. 1 *mi-at* 50 siki na$_4$ sa$_6$
ki:lam$_7$
11. *Ìr-ku*$^{ki}$
*A-bù*-Kur$^{ki}$

(64)
13. TAR 3 3 NI gín DILMUN kù:babbar
šu-bal-ak
15. 6 gín DILMUN 2 NI kù-gi
2 *gú-li-lum*
17. níĝ-ba
$^{d}$*Aš-da-bíl*

(65)
19. 15 gín DILMUN kù:babbar
nu$_{11}$-za
21. 1 *ḫa-bù*
TAR kù:babbar
XIV. 1. šu-bal-ak
6 gín DILMUN kù-gi
3. nu$_{11}$-za-*sù*
6 2 NI gín DILMUN kù:babbar
5. 2 *gú-li-lum*
níĝ-ba
7. en
$^{d}$*Am-ma-rí-ig*

(66)
9. 1 ma-na kù:babbar
nu$_{11}$-za
11. 10 *gú-li-lum* a-gar$_5$-gar$_5$ ŠÚ+ŠA-II esi
*wa*
13. 20 *gú-li-lum* a-gar$_5$-gar$_5$ 10-I esi
4 ma-na 10 gín DILMUN kù:babbar
15. kin$_5$-ak
5 *gú-li-lum* TAR-II esi
17. *wa*
5 *gú-li-lum* ŠÚ+ŠA-II esi
19. 4 ma-na 10 gín DILMUN kù:babbar
šu-bal-ak
21. [52] gín DILMUN [k]ù-gi
XV. 1. nu$_{11}$-za-*sù*
50 gín DILMUN kù:babbar
3. kin$_5$-ak
5 *gú-li-lum* 10-I esi
5. 50 gín DILMUN kù:babbar
šu-bal-ak
7. 10 gín DILMUN kù-gi
nu$_{11}$-za-*sù*
9. gaba-ru
é en

(67)
11. 7 gín DILMUN kù:babbar
nu$_{11}$-za 1 an-dùl
13. 2 ½ gín DILMUN kù:babbar
šu-bal-ak
15. ½ gín DILMUN kù-gi
nu$_{11}$-za
17. *ba-na-a-ša*
níĝ-ba
19. [(ca. 8 lines)]

(68)
XVI. 1. nu$_{11}$-za-*sù*
en
3. $^{d}$*Á-la*
*Zi-ig*$^{ki}$

(69)
5. 1 ma-na kù:babbar
níĝ-sa$_{10}$
7. 1 ĝír mar-tu *ra-ʾà-tum* kù-gi
*Ib-rí-um*

(63) 15;05 minas of silver for the purchase of 180 garments (and) 150 stone weights of wool of good quality, at the market of the city of Irku, Abu-Kur (has received).
(64) 33 shekels (and) 3 NI of silver in exchange for 6 shekels (and) 2 NI of gold for 2 bracelets: gift for the god Ašdabil.
(65) 15 shekels of silver for plating 1 mace; 30 (shekels) of silver in exchange for 6 shekels of gold for its plating; 6 shekels (and) 2 NI of silver for 2 bracelets: gift of the king for the god Ammarik.
(66) 1 mina of silver for plating 10 double bracelets of 20 (shekels) of copper each (and) diorite and 20 single bracelets of 10 (shekels) of copper each (and) diorite; 4;10 minas of silver for making 5 double bracelets of 30 (shekels) each (and) diorite and 5 double bracelets of 20 (shekels) each (and) diorite; 4;10 shekels of silver in exchange for [52] shekels of gold for their plating; 50 shekels of silver for making 5 single bracelets of 10 (shekels) each (and) diorite; 50 shekels of silver in exchange for 10 shekels of gold for their plating: supply for the king's house.
(67) 7 shekels of silver for plating 1 statue; 2 ½ shekels of silver in exchange for ½ shekels of gold for plating its face: gift for [the god(dess) …].
(68) […] for its plating: (gift) of the king for the god Ala of the city of Zig.
(69) 1 mina of silver for the purchase of 1 mar-tu dagger (decorated with) shells (and) gold for Ibrium.

(70)
9. 3 ma-na TAR 8 gín DILMUN
kù:babbar
níĝ-sa$_{10}$ 20 lá-2 *ᵓa-da-um*-TÚG-I
11. 34 aktum-TÚG
ki:lam$_7$
13. *Du-du-la*$^{ki}$

(71)
3 ma-na TAR[(+x) kù:babbar]
15. [(ca. 6 lines)]
XVII. 1. níĝ-sa$_{10}$
1 ĝír mar-tu kù-gi
3. 1 ma-na ŠA.PI ½ gín DILMUN
kù:babbar
níĝ-sa$_{10}$ ĜIŠ-ti-ḪAR
5. *Wa-ba-rúm*
ki:lam$_7$
7. $^{d}$*Áš-da-bíl*

(72)
3 ma-na TAR 3 gín DILMUN
kù:babbar
9. 55 ˹aktum˺-TÚG
1 túg-NI.NI ḫul
11. ˹2˺$^{?}$ kù:[b]abbar
níĝ-sa$_{10}$ 1 *gàr-su*
13. NI-*a-ba-mu*
ki:lam$_7$
15. *Šè-ᵓà-am*$^{ki}$

(73)
1 ma-na 10 gín DILMUN kù:babbar
17. šu-bal-ak
14 gín [DILMUN] k[ù-gi]
19. [(ca. 7 lines)]

(74)
l.ed. 1. 2 ma-na TAR kù:babbar
šu-bal-ak
3. TAR kù-gi 1 íb-lá
*I-bí-zi-kir*
5. lú *I-rí-gú-nu*

(75)
5 ma-na kù:babbar
7. šu-bal-ak
1 ma-na kù-gi 2 íb-lá
9. ME-sig
(blank)

(76)
11. AN.ŠÈ.GÚ 1 *mi-at* 97 ma-na 50 gín
DILMUN kù:babbar
è
13. (blank)

(70) 3;38 minas of silver for the purchase of 52 garments at the market of the city of Tuttul.
(71) 3;3[x] minas [of silver] […] for the purchase of 1 mar-tu dagger (decorated with) gold; 1;40 ½ minas of silver for the purchase of GIŠ-ti-ḪAR-wood: Wabarum (has received), at the market of the god Ašdabil.
(72) 3;33 minas of silver for 56 garments; 2$^{?}$ (shekels of) silver for the purchase of 1 bag: NI(l)abamu (has received), at the market of the city of Šeᵓam.
(73) 1;10 minas of silver in exchange for 14 shekels of g[old …].
(74) 2;30 minas of silver in exchange for 30 (shekels of) gold for 1 belt for Ibbi-zikir, (son) of Iri-gunu.
(75) 5 minas of silver in exchange for 1 mina of gold for 2 belts for the watchmen (of the king's house).
(76) Total: 197;50 minas of silver: expenditure.

## Commentary

This document registers the expended silver, and the expended gold (valued in silver in a ratio of 5 : 1) during the first part of the first year in which Ibrium served as minister, for a total of 197;50 minas (92.981 kg) of silver.

The name of the minister is mentioned in §§ 7, 9, 13, 20, 27, 31, 37 (his spouse Tamur-damu), 40, 41, 45, 52, 54, and 69, in several cases on the occasion of offerings to several gods. Ibbi-zikir, his son and successor, is mentioned in §§ 7 and 45.

Dusigu, king Išᶜar-damu's mother, received four gold earrings (§ 33). She offered a buckle (kù-sal) to the goddess Išḫara of Zidara, as well as a bracelet and a buckle to Rašap of ᵓAdani (§§ 14, 43).

The text presents the writing *La-ru*$_{12}$*-ga-du*$^{ki}$ (§ 54), as well as the documents nos. 03–07 to be dated to the years 1–4. This is the predominant writing in documents from the time of Arrukum (see *ARET* XV,2, p. 388), later superseded by *A-ru*$_{12}$*-ga-du*$^{ki}$.

The "men", ĝuruš-ĝuruš, of the Palace received four "bracelets", *gú-li-lum*, of silver and five "bracelets" of unrefined copper (§ 36). The "watchmen", ME-sig, of the "house" (of the king) received two belts (§ 75).

§§ 2, 22. Tinib-dulum, a "sister of the king", received some jewels. She became one of the two high priestesses (dam-diĝir "spouse of the god") at the service of ᵓAdabal of Luban at least from this year until the fifth year of minister Ibbi-zikir (the date of her death). This priestess (to whom later her sister Tirin-damu will be associated) would receive a substantial amount of silver for all the following years of Ibrium's period. The registration of these expenses following that for the head of Kura, is one of the data which demonstrate that Kura and ᵓAdabal were the most important deities of north-west Syria, perhaps going back to the pre-Semitic period (Archi 1998a = 2015a, pp. 699–710), (§§ 1, 2).

§ 6. Gifts given to princess Dati-TU on the occasion of her marriage with the king of Lumnan: 9 shekels (70 g) of gold and 2;59 minas (1.401 kg) of silver were required. 6 shekels of gold decorated the bur-KAK vase of boxwood which had to be used for the celebration of the rite; and 2 minas of silver were used for another two vessels.

Dati-TU is mentioned together with other princesses (daughters of king Irkab-damu) in documents of minister Arrukum: *ARET* XV,1 26 § 40 (together with eleven sons and seven daughters of the king, §§ 37–39); 34 § 142; 59 § 87. Her name occurs in several texts of some later years: *ARET* XXI 3 (Ibr. 1b) § 5, a supplementary gift of ten earrings; XXI 6 (Ibr. 3) § 67; XXI 10 (Ibr. 07) § 30; XXI 11 (Ibr. 8) §§ 27, 29; XXI 12 (Ibr. 09) § 31. On her death, see the commentary to text XXI 11.

Dati-TU's death is registered in the monthly document TM.75.G.2632 o. IV 10–V 1 (dated to Ibrium): (gifts) *Da-ti-*ᵈTU *ma-lik-tum Lum-na-an*ᵏⁱ É×PAP.

§ 10. Tarmaš-damu, "a daughter of the king, (and) daughter-in-law (*gal-tum*) of BAD-*da-mu*", received goblets and jewels. *LLE*,I no. 318 has the equivalence: É.GI.A = *gal-la-tum/du* / *gal-tum* (Akk. *kallatum* "daughter-in-law"). She had to be (for a chronological reason) a daughter of king Irkab-damu. This same lady, qualified as é-gi of BAD-*da-mu*, delivered a kilt "on the occasion of the festival (ḫúl) of the king in Luban", according to *ARET* XIV 65 § 28 (the mu-DU document of the year Ibrium 12). She is also mentioned (always with this qualification) in the annual documents XXI 17 § 16, and *ARET* XXII 2 r. X 28–32 (Ibbi-zikir 02), as well as in the monthly documents TM.75.G.2499 o. IX 19–X 2 and TM.75.G.10159 o. II 1–5 (both of the time of Ibbi-zikir).

Tamur-dašeli, daughter of Riti, was a "daughter-in-law" of the king, *ARET* VIII 529 § 8 VIII 25–IX 2: *Da-mur-da-šè-li* dumu-munus *Rí-ti* é-gi-a en. The term *gal-tum* occurs again in a fragmentary passage, *ARET* III 144 III 3–9: 4 ga-du$_8$ 4 dumu-nita en *gal-tum wa* ga-du$_8$ *Za-a-šè* "four wet-nurses of four sons of the king, (and) the daughter-in-law, and the wet-nurse of Zaᵓaše".

§ 17. Dutum of Mari brought 3.700 kg of lapis lazuli at the value 2 : 1 in a ratio with silver, and several garments. Dutum reached Ebla also in the following years, see texts nos. 3, 6, 8 and 10 (the latter dated to the year Ibrium 07).

§ 18. Saggar, the town where a mule was bought, belonged to the region under the hegemony of Nagar: the Ḫabur triangle.

§ 37 Tamur-damu, "spouse", dam, of Ibrium, is still mentioned in the document of the year Ibbi-zikir 01 (*ARET* XXII 1 o. II 5).

§ 66 Receipt concerning 45 "bracelets", *gú-li-lum*, decorated with silver or gold for the king's house.

# 3
(Plates V–VI)

(1)

o. I. 1. ⌜5⌝ ma-na kù:babbar
níĝ-sa$_{10}$ še
3. *Rí-ì-ma-lik*
ugula *A-da-⌜áš⌝*$^{ki}$
5. 5 ma-na kù:babbar
níĝ-sa$_{10}$ še
7. *Rí-ì-ma-lik*
ugula *Ig-du-ra*$^{ki}$
9. 5 ma-na kù:babbar
níĝ-sa$_{10}$ še
11. *Ru*$_{12}$*-zu-mu*
5 ma-na kù:babbar
13. níĝ-sa$_{10}$ še
[*Sa*]*g-da-mu*
15. 7 ma-na kù:babbar
níĝ-sa$_{10}$ še
17. *Puzur*$_4$*-ra-ḫa-al*$_6$
II. 1. 5 ma-na kù:babbar
níĝ-sa$_{10}$ še
3. *Ḫa-ra-il*
5 ma-na kù:babbar
5. níĝ-sa$_{10}$ še
*En-a-mar*
7. 5 ma-na kù:babbar
níĝ-sa$_{10}$ še
9. *En-na*-BAD ⌜"ur$_4$"⌝
BAD é
11. *Ib-rí-um*

(2)

TAR kù:babbar
13. *I-ti*
*Ma-rí*$^{ki}$
15. *Ìr-am*$_6$*-ma-lik*
šu-mu-tak$_4$

(3)

17. 10 gín DILMUN kù:babbar
níĝ-ba
19. *Daš-na*
*wa*
21. *Wa-ru*$_{12}$*-tum*
*Ma-rí*$^{ki}$

(4)

III. 1. 1 ½ gín DILMUN kù:babbar
nu$_{11}$-za
3. 1 zag
ĜIŠ-gígir-II
5. *Ib-rí-um*

(5)

ŠÚ+ŠA gín DILMUN kù:babbar
7. šu-bal-ak
4 gín DILMUN kù-gi
9. *ni-zi-mu*
10 ĝeštu$_x$-lá
11. *Da-ti*-⌜$^{d}$TU⌝
*ma-lik-tum*
13. *Lum-na-an*$^{ki}$

(6)

15 gín DILMUN kù:babbar
15. kin$_5$-ak
6 ĜIŠ-kak-ĜIŠ-kak
17. lú ĜIŠ-asari
kaskal
19. en

(7)

10 gín DILMUN kù:babbar
21. šu-bal-ak
2 gín DILMUN kù-gi
IV. 1. *ni-zi-mu*
1 dib
3. *I-bí-um*
lú
5. *I*[*š*]*-má-ga-lu*

(1) 5 minas of silver for the purchase of barley for Reʾi-malik, the overseer of the city of Adaš; 5 minas of silver for the purchase of barley for Reʾi-malik, the overseer of the city of Igdura; 5 minas of silver for the purchase of barley for Ruzumu; 5 minas of silver for the purchase of barley for [Sa]g-damu; 7 minas of silver for the purchase of barley for Puzurra-ḫal; 5 minas of silver for the purchase of barley for Ḫara-il; 5 minas of silver for the purchase of barley for En-amar; 5 minas of silver for the purchase of barley for Enna-BAD, the collector (of goods) (and) the majordomo of the house of Ibrium.

(2) 30 (shekels of) silver for Iti of the city of Mari: Iram-malik has handed over.

(3) 10 shekels of silver: gift for Dašna and Warutum of the city of Mari.

(4) 1 ½ shekel of silver for plating 1 side of the chariot of Ibrium.

(5) 20 shekels of silver in exchange for 4 shekels of gold for decorating 10 earrings for Dati-TU, the queen of the city of Lumnan.

(6) 15 shekels of silver for making 6 pegs of a travel tray for the king.

(7) 10 shekels of silver in exchange for 2 shekels of gold for decorating 1 plaque for Ibbium, (son) of Išma-galu.

(8)
TAR gín 3 DI[LMUN] 3 NI kù:babbar
7. šu-bal-ak
6 gín DILMUN 2 NI kù-gi
9. 2 *gú-li-lum*
níĝ-ba
11. $^{d}$*Ku-ra*

(9)
13 gín DILMUN kù:babbar
13. nu$_{11}$-za 1 *ḫa-bù*
ŠÚ+ŠA 5 gín DILMUN kù:babbar
15. šu-bal-ak
5 gín DILMUN kù-gi
17. nu$_{11}$-za *ar-ra-si-su*
níĝ-ba
19. $^{d}$ʾ*A*$_5$*-da-*⸢*bal*⸣
*La-ru*$_{12}$*-ga-du*$^{ki}$
21. *Ib-rí-um*
ì-na-sum

(10)
V. 1. ŠÚ+ŠA gín DILMUN kù:babbar
níĝ[-sa$_{10}$]
3. 40[+x] diri ĝír mar-tu
ĝuruš-ĝuruš

(11)
5. 2 ma-na kù:babbar
*zi-du*
7. 60 ĝír mar-tu
SA.ZA$_x$$^{ki}$

(12)
9. 7 ma-na ŠA.PI gín DILMUN kù:babbar
níĝ-sa$_{10}$ 2 ʾ*à-da-um*-TÚG-II
11. 1 ʾ*à-da-um*-TÚG-I
14 aktum-TÚG
13. 8 gada-TÚG
1 íb+III-TÚG gíd babbar
15. 1 *mi-at* 20 íb+III-TÚG sa$_6$ gùn
5 íb+III-TÚG gùn
17. ki:lam$_7$
SA.ZA$_x$$^{ki}$

(13)
19. 10 ma-na 6 gín DILMUN kù:babbar
VI. 1. níĝ-sa$_{10}$ 10 lá-1 *gu-zi-tum*-TÚG
1$^?$ ʾ*à-da-um*-TÚG-I
3. 4 gada-TÚG
1 *mi-at* íb+III-TÚG sa$_6$ gùn 40 íb+III-TÚG gùn
5. 13 gín DILMUN kù:babbar
níĝ-sa$_{10}$ 1 *mi-at* 34 níĝ-saĝšu
7. 13 gín DILMUN kù:babbar
níĝ-sa$_{10}$ raš-SAR Kur$^{ki}$
9. 1 ma-na TAR kù:babbar
níĝ-sa$_{10}$ 1 BAR.AN
11. *Rí-ì-Ḫa-lab*$_x$
šu-ba$_4$-ti

(14)
13. TAR kù:babbar
níĝ-sa$_{10}$
VII. 1. 1 IGI.NITA u$_5$
*Bù-da-ma-lik*
3. šu-ba$_4$-ti

(15)
2 ma-na kù:babbar
5. níĝ-sa$_{10}$ ĜIŠ-ti-ḪAR
*Wa-ba-rúm*
7. šu-ba$_4$-ti
ki:⸢lam$_7$⸣
9. $^{d}$*Ga-mi-iš*

(16)
4 gín DILMUN kù:babbar
11. lú nu-kiri$_6$
DU.DU
13. *al*$_6$
dumu-nita
15. *Ru*$_{12}$*-zi-da-mu*
*Ma-nu-wa-ad*$^{ki}$

(8) 33 shekels (and) 3 NI of silver in exchange for 6 shekels (and) 2 NI of gold for 2 bracelets: gift for the god Kura.
(9) 13 shekels of silver for plating 1 mace; 25 shekels of silver in exchange for 5 shekels of gold for plating its handle: gift for the god ʾAdabal of the city of Larugadu, Ibrium has given.
(10) 20 shekels of silver for the pur[chase] of 40[+x] mar-tu daggers in addition for the men.
(11) 2 minas of silver as alloy for 60 mar-tu daggers for the Palace.
(12) 7;40 minas of silver for the purchase of 25 garments (and) 126 kilts at the market of the Palace.
(13) 10;06 minas of silver for the purchase of 14 garments (and) 140 kilts; 13 shekels of silver for the purchase of 134 helmets; 13 shekels of silver for the purchase of leek from the mountain region; 1;30 shekels of silver for the purchase of 1 mule: Reʾi-Ḫalab has received.
(14) 30 (shekels) of silver for the purchase of 1 donkey to ride, Buda-malik has received.
(15) 2 minas of silver for the purchase of GIŠ-ti-ḪAR-wood, Wabarum has received at the market of the god Kamiš.
(16) 4 shekels of silver for the gardener (who) went on behalf of the son of Ruzi-damu of the city of Manuwat.

(17)

17. 10 gín DILMUN kù:babbar
šu-bal-ak
19. 2 gín DILMUN kù-gi
*Zú-zu*
VIII. 1. [ ]
[ ]
3. [ ]
níĝ-kas$_4$
5. nu-du$_{11}$-nu-du$_{11}$
šu-ba$_4$-ti
7. *si-in*
*Ib-al*$_6^{ki}$
9. *in* ud
dumu-nita
11. en
*Ḫa-zu-wa-an*$^{ki}$
13. ḫi-úš
*in*
15. *Ga-ra-ma-an*$^{ki}$
lú
17. *Ḫar-sum*$^{ki}$

(18)

ŠA.PI 6 gín DILMUN kù:babbar
19. níĝ-sa$_{10}$ 30 ĝír mar-tu zú-ak
ì-na-sum
21. ĝuruš-ĝuruš
*Ar-si-a-ḫa*
23. *wa*
IX. 1. [ ]
[ ]
3. [ ]
[ ]
5. [ ]
[ ]

(19)

7. ŠÚ+ŠA [+x] gín DILM[UN] kù:babbar
níĝ-sa$_{10}$ 1 ĝír mar-tu ti kù-gi
9. NI-*gi*
saĝ-du$_8$
11. lú-kar
*A-da-bí-ig*$^{ki}$
13. 8 gín DILMUN kù:babbar
níĝ-sa$_{10}$ 1 ĝír mar-tu *ba-du-u*$_4$
kù:babbar kù-gi
15. *Ù-ra*-AN
maškim-*sù*

(20)

17. 4 ma-na TAR kù:babbar
X. (ca. 12 lines)

(21)

x+1. ŠA.P[I] 1 gín DILMUN kù:babbar
níĝ-sa$_{10}$ ĜIŠ-ti-ḪAR
3'. *Wa-ba-rúm*
šu-ba$_4$-ti
5'. ki:lam$_7$
$^{d}$*Áš-da-bíl*

(22)

XI. 1. [ ]
[ ]
3. [ ]
2 gín DILMUN kù:babbar
5. maš-maš 1 ĜIŠ-banšur
2 ½ gín DILMUN kù:babbar
7. šu-bal-ak
½ gín DILMUN kù-gi
9. [ ]⌜x⌝
[níĝ-ba]
11. $^{[d]}$ↄ*À-da*
lú *Du-ub*$^{ki}$

(23)

13. 10 gín DILMUN kù:babbar
⌜2⌝ *bu*-DI
15. ì-ĝiš-saĝ
*Tíš-*⌜*má*⌝*-da-mu*
17. dam
en

(24)

19. ŠA.PI gín DILMUN kù:babbar
XII. 1. [šu-bal-ak]
⌜8⌝ gín DILMUN kù-gi
3. *ni-zi-mu*
1 dib
5. *Zi-ba-da*

(17) 10 shekels of silver in exchange for 2 shekels of gold for Zuzu [… to] the military expedition against the city of Ibˤal—received without authorization—when the son of the king of the city of Ḫasuwan was killed in the city of Garaman of the city of Ḫaršum.
(18) 46 shekels of silver for the purchase of 30 serrated mar-tu daggers given to the men of Arsi-aḫa and […].
(19) 20[+x] shekels of silver for the purchase of 1 pointed mar-tu dagger (decorated with) gold for NIgi, at the disposal of a trader of the city of Adabik; 8 shekels of silver for the purchase of 1 *b.* mar-tu dagger. (decorated with) silver and gold for Ura-AN, his representative.
(20) 4;30 minas of silver […]
(21) 41 shekels of silver for the purchase of GIŠ-ti-ḪAR-wood, Wabarum has received at the market of the god Ašdabil.
(22) […] 2 shekels of silver for a striped (decoration) of 1 table; 2 ½ shekels of silver in exchange for ½ shekel of gold for […: gift] for the god Hadda of the city of Dub.
(23) 10 shekels of silver for 2 toggle-pins for the purification rite of Tišma-damu, woman of the king.
(24) 40 shekels of silver [in exchange for] 8 shekels of gold for decorating 1 plaque for Zibada.

(25)
TAR 5 gín DILMUN kù:babbar
7. nu$_{11}$-za 1 an-dùl
TAR kù:babbar
9. šu-bal-ak
6 gín DILMUN kù-gi
11. nu$_{11}$-za
*ba-na-*⌜*ʾà*⌝
13. *wa*
2 šu 2 DU-*sù*
15. níĝ-ba
$^{d}$*Am-ma-rí-ig*

(26)
17. 6 gín DILMUN 2 NI kù:babbar
⌜2⌝ [*gú-*]*l*[*i-lum*]
19. níĝ-b[a]
$^{d}$*Am-ma-rí-ig*

(27)
21. 1 gín DILMUN kù:babbar
XIII. 1. [1 za]g$^{?}$
ĜIŠ-gígir-II
3. en
*Ì-ra-ar*$^{ki}$

(28)
5. 5 gín DILMUN kù:babbar
EN-*mar*
7. *Kak-mi-um*$^{ki}$
lú ĜIŠ-kiri$_{6}$

(29)
9. 1 gín DILMUN kù:babbar
*ni-zi-mu*
11. nu$_{11}$-za 1 *za-ḫa-da*
*I*[*b-rí-um*]

(30)
13. 13 gín ⌜DILMUN⌝ kù:babbar
níĝ-ba
15. *Daš-na*
*wa*
17. *Wa-ru*$_{12}$*-tum*
*Ma-rí*$^{ki}$

(31)
19. 15 gín DILMUN kù:babbar
[nu$_{11}$-za 1 *ḫa-*]*b*[*ù*]
21. TAR [gín DILMUN] kù:babbar
XIV. 1. šu[-bal]-ak
6 gín DILMUN kù-gi
3. nu$_{11}$-za 1 *ar-ra-si-su*
níĝ-ba
5. $^{d}$*ʾÀ-da*

(32)
[(ca. 7 lines)]
13. *ni-zi-mu*
2 *ba-ga-ni-sa*
15. en

(33)
1 ma-na ŠA.PI gín DILMUN
kù:babbar
17. šu-bal-ak
ŠÚ+ŠA gín [DILMUN kù-gi]
19. 1 dib
XV. 1. [ ]
[ ]

(34)
3. 1 ma-na 50 gín DILMUN kù:babbar
šu-bal-ak
5. [ŠÚ+ŠA 5 gín DILMUN kù-gi]
[1 dib]
7. [(ca. 8 lines)]

(35)
15. *n*[*i-zi-*]*m*[*u*]
1 dib
17. *I-bí-zi-kir*
l[ú *Ib-rí-um*]
19. [1 ma-na ŠA.PI gín DILMUN]
⌜kù:babbar⌝
r. I. 1. šu-bal-ak
ŠÚ+ŠA gín DILMUN kù-gi 1 dib
3. *Šum*-bàd$^{ki}$
šeš-*sù*

(25) 35 shekels of silver for plating 1 statue, 30 shekels of silver in exchange for 6 shekels of gold for plating its face and their 2 hands and feet: gift for the god Ammarik.
(26) 6 shekels (and) 2 NI of silver for 2 [bracelets]: gift for the god Ammarik.
(27) 1 shekel of silver [for 1 sid]e of the chariot of the king of the city of Irar.
(28) 5 shekels of silver for ENmar of the city of Kakmium, of the garden.
(29) 1 shekel of silver for decorating with lamination 1 battle-axe for I[brium].
(30) 13 shekels of silver: gift for Dašna and Warutum of the city of Mari.
(31) 15 shekels of silver [for plating 1 mace], 30 [shekels] of silver in exchange for 6 shekels of gold for plating its handle: gift for the god Hadda.
(32) […] for decorating 2 *clasps* for the king.
(33) 1;40 minas of silver in exchange for 20 shekels [of gold] for 1 plaque […].
(34) 1;50 minas of silver in exchange for [25 shekels of gold for 1 plaque …].
(35) […] for deco[rating] 1 plaque for Ibbi-zikir, (son) o[f Ibrium; 1;40 shekels] of silver in exchange for 20 shekels of gold for 1 plaque for Šum-bad, his brother.

(36)

5. 1 ma-na ŠA.PI gín DILMUN
kù:babbar
šu-bal-ak
7. ŠÚ+ŠA gín DILMUN kù-gi
*ni-zi-mu*
9. ḫaš-ḫaš
*gú-li-lum*
11. ⸢x⸣ [ ]
[(ca. 8 lines)]

(37)

II. 1. 1 ma-na ŠA.PI gín DILMUN
kù:babbar
níĝ-sa$_{10}$
3. ĜIŠ-ti-ḪAR
*Wa-ba-rúm*
5. šu-ba$_4$-ti

(38)

5 ma-na kù:babbar
7. níĝ-sa$_{10}$ 10 gud
*Ib-bí-um*
9. ugula é
šu-ba$_4$-ti
11. ki:lam$_7$
[(ca. 7 lines)]

(39)

III. 1. é
en

(40)

3. 56 gín DILMUN kù:babbar
*ni-zi-mu*
5. 2 níĝ-anše-ak 4 kù-sal
*I-bí-zi-kir*
7. dumu-nita
*Ib-rí-um*

(41)

9. 17 gín DILMUN kù:babbar
níĝ-sa$_{10}$ 1 ĝír mar-tu zú
A.LAGAB×ḪAL
11. [ ]
diri
13. ĝír mar-tu
ĝuruš-ĝuruš
15. *in* ud
igi-ḫi-du$_8$
17. SA.ZA$_x$$^{ki}$

(42)

TAR 3 gín DILMUN 3 NI kù:babbar
19. šu-bal-ak
6 gín DILMUN [2 NI] kù-gi
IV. 1. 2 *gú-li-lum*
níĝ-ba
3. $^d$*Aš-da-bíl*

(43)

4 gín DILMUN kù:babbar
5. kin$_5$-ak
1 šu-dub
7. *Ib-rí-um*
*in* ud
9. ḫúl
na-rú-*sù*

(44)

11. ŠÚ+ŠA 2 gín DILMUN 2 *bu*-DI
ama-gal
13. ⸢*Ib-rí*⸣-[*um*]
*Du-si-gú*
15. šu-mu-tak$_4$

(45)

3 ma-na ŠÚ+ŠA gín DILMUN
kù:babbar
17. šu-bal-ak
ŠA.PI gín DILMUN kù-gi 1 ⸢dib⸣
V. 1. *Ḫáb-ra-ar*
ugula *ʾA$_5$-da-tum*$^{ki}$
3. 2 ma-na TAR kù:babbar
šu-bal-ak
5. TAR kù-gi 1 dib
*La-da-da-áš*
7. šeš-*sù*

(36) 1;40 shekels of silver in exchange for 20 shekels of gold for decorating with granulation bracelets […].
(37) 1;40 shekels of silver for the purchase of GIŠ-ti-ḪAR-wood, Wabarum has received.
(38) 5 minas of silver for the purchase of 10 oxen, Ibbium, overseer of the house (of the king?) has received at the market [of .. ].
(39) […] of the king's house.
(40) 56 shekels of silver for decorating 2 bridles (and) 4 buckles for Ibbi-zikir, son of Ibrium.
(41) 17 shekels of silver for the purchase of 1 mar-tu dagger (decorated with) hippopotamus ivory […] for the men on the occasion of the review of the Palace.
(42) 33 shekels (and) 3 NI of silver in exchange for 6 shekels (and) [2 NI] of gold for 2 bracelets: gift for the god Ašdabil.
(43) 4 shekels of silver for making 1 ring for Ibrium, on the occasion of the feast of his stele.
(44) 22 shekels of silver for 2 toggle-pins for Ibrium's mother, Dusigu has handed over.
(45) 3;20 minas of silver in exchange for 40 shekels of gold for 1 plaque for Ḫabrar, overseer of the city of ʾAdatum; 2;30 minas of silver in exchange for 30 (shekels of) gold for 1 plaque for Ladadaš, his brother.

(46)
TAR kù:babbar
9. šu-bal-ak
6$^{1}$ gín DILMUN kù-gi
11. nu$_{11}$-za 1 bur-KAK
*na-⸢kar?-ra⸣-tim*
13. *Ib-rí-um*

(47)
ŠÚ+ŠA gín DILMUN kù:babbar
15. níĝ-ba
*Iš-má-il*
17. *wa*
*Ba-ga-ar*
VI. 1. *Ma-rí*$^{ki}$

(48)
2 ma-na TAR kù:babbar
3. šu-bal-ak
TAR kù-gi <1 dib>
5. *I-ku-i-šar*
en
7. *Ma-rí*$^{ki}$
*Du-tum*
9. *Ma-rí*$^{ki}$
šu-mu-tak$_4$

(49)
11. ŠA.PI gín DILMUN kù:babbar
níĝ[-ba]
13. BAD-*sù*-BAD
*wa*
15. *Maḫ-mu*
*M*[*a-rí*$^{ki}$]

(50)
17. 3 ma-na ŠA.PI 2 gín DILMUN kù:babbar
níĝ-sa$_{10}$ 16 *ʾà-da-um*-TÚG-I
19. 6 aktum-TÚG
VII. 1. 1 níĝ-lá-gaba
70 íb+III-TÚG gùn
3. ki:lam$_7$
*gi-ba-lu*
5. *ʾÀ-da-ni*$^{ki}$

(51)
12 gín DILMUN kù:babbar
7. níĝ-du$_8$
1 lú
9. šitim
*Ab-ru*$_{12}$*-ti-um*$^{ki}$
11. *áš-ti*
*Ir-i-tum*$^{ki}$

(52)
13. 8 gín DILMUN kù:babbar
*zi-ba-tum*
15. 4 ĜIŠ-šú 1 níĝ-bànda
l[ú 2 šu]
17. 1 ma-na TAR 1 gín DILMUN kù:babbar
níĝ-sa$_{10}$ 20 *gàr-su*
VIII. 1. NI-*la-ba-mu*
šu-ba$_4$-ti

(53)
3. 1 ma-na 2 gín DILMUN kù:babbar
níĝ-ba
5. *Ib-gi-tum*
*wa*
7. maškim-*sù*
*Ma-rí*$^{ki}$
9. *in*
*Ša-dab*$_6$$^{ki}$
11. šu-ba$_4$-ti

(54)
5 ma-na kù:babbar
13. níĝ-sa$_{10}$ (blank) a-gar$_5$-gar$_5$
*A-bù*-Kur$^{ki}$

(46) 30 (shekels of) silver in exchange for 6$^{1}$ shekels of gold for plating 1 bur-KAK vessel ... (*na-kar-ra-tim*) for Ibrium.
(47) 20 shekels of silver: gift for Išma-il and Bagar of the city of Mari.
(48) 2;30 minas of silver in exchange for 30 (shekels of) gold (for) <1 plaque> for Iku-išar, king of the city of Mari, Dutum of the city of Mari has handed over.
(49) 40 shekels of silver, gi[ft] (to) BADSUBAD and Maḫmu of the city of M[ari].
(50) 3;42 minas of silver for the purchase of 23 garments (and) 70 kilts at the market of the *gibalu* of the city of ʾAdani.
(51) 12 shekels of silver for the ransom of 1 man, a house builder of the city of Abrutium, from the city of Iritum.
(52) 8 shekels of silver for the handles of 4 GIŠ-šú vessels (and) 1 níg-bànda vessel o[f the hands]; 1;31 minas of silver for the purchase of 20 bags: NIlabamu has received.
(53) 1;02 minas of silver: gift for Ibgitum and his representative, of the city of Mari, received in the city of Šadab.
(54) 5 minas of silver for the purchase of copper, Abu-Kur (has received).

(55)
15. 16 gín DILMUN kù:babbar
níĝ-sa$_{10}$ 2 na$_4$
17. *Ša-ma*
simug

(56)
19 3 gín DILMUN kù:babbar
IX. 1. nu$_{11}$-za 2 zag
2 ĜIŠ-gígir-II
3. *Ib-rí-um*
*wa*
5. en
*Bur-ma-an*$^{ki}$

(57)
7. 2 ma-na ŠA.PI 4 gín DILMUN kù:babbar
níĝ-sa$_{10}$ 15 *ʾà-da-um*-TÚG-I
9. 1 *mi-at* 4 íb+III-TÚG gùn
1 m[a-]na 10 [gín DILMUN kù:babbar]
11. níĝ-sa$_{10}$ 1 BAR.AN
ŠÚ+ŠA gín DILMUN k[ù:bab]bar
13. níĝ-sa$_{10}$ ĜIŠ-ti-ḪAR
*Wa-ba-rúm*
15. šu-ba$_4$-ti
ki:lam$_7$
17. šeš-II-ib
X. 1. *ʾÀ-da-ni*$^{ki}$

(58)
4 ma-na kù:babbar
3. níĝ-sa$_{10}$ 1 BAR.AN
*áš-ti*
5. en
*Ra-ʾà-ak*$^{ki}$
7. *Íl-ba-ma-lik*
šu-mu-tak$_4$

(59)
9. 4 gín DILMUN kù:babbar
*Ḫa-ra-an*$^{ki}$

(60)
11. 4 gín DILMUN kù:babbar
[n]íĝ-ba
13. *Ib-gi-tum*
lú *I-ti*
15. *Ma-rí*$^{ki}$

(61)
51 gín DILMUN kù:babbar
17. níĝ-ba
diĝir-diĝir-diĝir

(62)
19. 4 gín DILMUN k[ù]:babbar
[ ]
XI. 1. níĝ-ba
$^{d}$*ʾA*$_5$*-da-"bal"*
3. *La-ru*$_{12}$*-ga-du*$^{ki}$
*Ib-rí-um*
5. ì-na-sum

(63)
10 gín DILMUN kù:babbar
7. níĝ-ba
*ʾÀ-du*$^{ki}$

(64)
9. ŠÚ+ŠA gín DILMUN kù:babbar
níĝ-ba
11. *Kùn-*$^{d}$*Aš-dar*
lú ˹*I*˺*-ti*
13 [*Ma-rí*$^{ki}$]

(65)
53 gín DILMUN kù:babbar
15. 6 *bu*-DI
níĝ-ba
17. 3 dam
*Zi-ba-da*
19. *in* ud
níĝ-mu-sá
21. dumu-munus
*Ib-rí-um*

(55) 16 shekels of silver for the purchase of 2 stones, Šama the metalworker (has received).
(56) 3 shekels of silver for plating 2 sides of 2 chariots of Ibrium and the king of the city of Burman.
(57) 2;44 minas of silver for the purchase of 15 garments (and) 104 kilts; 1;10 minas [of silver] for the purchase of 1 mule; 20 shekels of s[ilv]er for the purchase of GIŠ-ti-ḪAR-wood: Wabarum has received, at the market of the šeš-II-ib confraternity of the city of ʾAdani.
(58) 4 minas of silver for the purchase of 1 mule from the king of the city of Raʾak, Ilba-malik has handed over.
(59) 4 shekels of silver (for someone) of the city of Ḫarran.
(60) 4 shekels of silver: gift for Ibgitum, (son) of Iti of the city of Mari.
(61) 51 shekels of silver: gift for the gods.
(62) 4 shekels of silver […]: gift for the god ʾAdabal of the city of Larugadu, Ibrium has given.
(63) 10 shekels of silver: gift for (someone of) the city of ʾAddu.
(64) 20 shekels of silver: gift for Kun-Ašdar, (son) of Iti [of the city of Mari].
(65) 53 shekels of silver for 6 toggle-pins: gift for 3 women of Zibada, on the occasion of the marriage of a daughter of Ibrium.

(66)
23. ŠA.PI gín DILMUN kù:babbar
XII. 1. níĝ-sa$_{10}$ 40 siki na$_{4}$
*áš-da*
3. *Ma-rí*$^{ki}$

(67)
1 ma-na kù:babbar
5. níĝ-ba
*Ù-da-aḫ*
7. *Ma-rí*$^{ki}$
kuš$_{7}$

(68)
9. 5 ma-na kù:babbar
šu-bal-ak
11. [1 ma-na] kù-gi
kin$_{5}$-ak
13. 2 íb-lá kù-gi
ì-ĝiš-saĝ
15. 2 en
*Ma-nu-wa-ad*$^{ki}$
17. *Ba-ga-ma*
šu-mu-tak$_{4}$
19. *in* ud
úš
21. *ma-lik-tum*

(69)
ŠÚ+ŠA gín kù:babbar
XIII. 1. níĝ-ba
*A-ku-da*
3. *wa*
*Daš-na*
5. *Ma-rí*$^{ki}$

(70)
3 ma-na 55 gín DILMUN kù:babbar
7. níĝ-sa$_{10}$ 27 íb+III-TÚG sa$_{6}$ gùn
1 *mi-at* 67 íb+III-TÚG gùn
9. 4 ma-na ŠÚ+ŠA gín kù:babbar
[níĝ-]⌜sa$_{10}$⌝ ĜIŠ-ti-ḪAR
11. *Wa-ba-rúm*
ki:lam$_{7}$
13. $^{d}$*A-da-ma*
*wa*
15. ki:lam$_{7}$
bàd-diĝir$^{ki}$

(71)
17. ŠÚ+ŠA gín DILMUN kù:babbar
níĝ-ba
19. *Daš-na*
*A-ba-du*
21. *Ma-rí*$^{ki}$

(72)
50 gín DILMUN kù:babbar
XIV. 1. níĝ-[s]a$_{10}$ 2 ĝír mar-tu ti kù-gi
*Du-bí-zi-kir*
3. *wa*
*Íl-ba-šum*
5. lú-kar

(73)
4 ma-na kù:babbar
7. níĝ-sa$_{10}$ 71 *ʾà-da-um*-TÚG-I
1 íb+III-TÚG gíd babbar
9. 3 gada-TÚG
⌜ki:lam$_{7}$⌝
11. *Ma-rí*$^{ki}$
*Na-zi*
13. (blank)
XV. 1. (blank)

(74)
AN.ŠÈ.GÚ 1 *mi-at* 56! ma-na TAR 4 gín DILMUN!(NI.<TUK>) kù:babbar
3. è
2 dub[a)]
l.ed.[a)] 1. *ap*
4 *mi-at* 83 ma-na kù:babbar
3. al$_{6}$-ĝál (blank)

*a*) added in a second time

(66) 40 shekels of silver for the purchase of 40 stone weights of wool from the city of Mari.
(67) 1 mina of silver: gift for Udaḫ, a (horse) groom of the city of Mari.
(68) 5 minas of silver in exchange for [1 mina] of gold for making 2 belts (decorated with) gold for the purification ceremony for the 2 kings of the city of Manuwat: Bagama has handed over on the occasion of the queen's death.
(69) 20 shekels of silver: gift for Akuda and Dašna of the city of Mari.
(70) 3;55 minas of silver for the purchase of 194 kilts; 4;20 minas of silver for [the pur]chase of GIŠ-ti-ḪAR-wood, Wabarum (has received), at the market of the god Adamma and the market of the Fortress of the god.
(71) 20 shekels of silver: gift for Dašna (and) Abadu of the city of Mari.
(72) 50 shekels of silver for the purchase of 2 pointed mar-tu daggers (decorated) with gold for Dubi-zikir and Ilbašum, the traders.
(73) 4 minas of silver for the purchase of 74 garments (and) 1 kilt at the market of the city of Mari, Nazi (has received).
(74) Total: 156;34 minas of silver: expenditure; second document; and further 483 minas of silver are present.

## Commentary

The colophon (§ 74) states that this is the "2nd document", 2 dub, which means that this is the annual document concerning the expenditures of silver and gold for the second part of Ibrium's first full year: the year in which he had already been minister from its first month.

The expended silver and the gold valued in silver (in a gold to silver ratio of 5 : 1) amounted to 156;34 minas (73.583 kg), which summed to the silver expended in the first part of the year (text no. 2, above) gives a total of 354;24 minas (168.564 kg) for this year. The silver "present", al$_{6}$-ĝál, (that is which remained in the Treasury) amounted to 483 minas (227.010 kg).

The god Kura received two "bracelets" that required 6 ⅔ shekels (52 g) of gold (§ 8); this would become an annual rite.

Ibrium celebrated his stele (*in* ud ḫúl na-rú-*sù*) this year (§ 43), and again in his year 05, (text no. 8 § 4). One of these two celebrations is also mentioned in the monthly document *ARET* XIX 4 § 32'. On this festival, see Archi 1998b.

The minister received a drinking vessel (§ 46), and accessories for his chariot (§§ 4, 56). He dedicated some objects to various gods (§§ 9, 62). His mother received a gift from Dusigu, the king's mother (§ 44). Gifts were given to three women on the occasion of the marriage of one of his daughters (§ 65). His son Ibbi-zikir received a plate (§ 35), and a pair of reins decorated with silver (§ 40).

Relations with Mari intensified, as demonstrated by the numerous messengers from this city who reached Ebla (some of them even more than once this year): *I-ti* (§ 2); his sons *Ib-gi-tum* (§ 60), and *Kùn-*$^{d}$*Aš-dar* (§ 64); *Daš-na* and *Wa-ru*$_{12}$*-tum* (§§ 3, 30); *Daš-na* and *A-ku-da* (§ 69); *Daš-na* and *A-ba-du* (§ 71); *Iš-má-il* and *Ba-ga-ar* (§ 47); BAD-*sù*-BAD and *Máḫ-mu* (§ 49); *Ib-gi-tum* again together with one of his representatives (§ 53); and *Ù-da-aḫ*, a groom (kuš$_{7}$), (§ 67). Wool and clothing were purchased from Mari (§§ 66, 73).

Enna-Dagan, the king of Mari, had died the previous year, the same year as king Irkab-damu's death, and a certain *Du-tum* announced that *I-ku-i-šar* was the new king of Mari (§ 48). Ebla decided to send the modest gift of 235 g of gold to re-establish diplomatic relations after Enna-Dagan's military expedition. On these events, see Archi, 2019a, pp. 146–150; Id., 2022a.

§ 1. The document opens with an expenditure of barley evaluated at 42 minas (19.740 kg) of silver in favour of eight officials: the first two, both named Reʾi-malik, were "overseers", ugula, of a village; the last person, Enna-BAD, was the majordomo of Ibrium's house. This registration could mean that the Administration had cancelled their obligation of an annual delivery of barley for that year.

§ 5. On *Da-ti-*$^{d}$TU, see the commentary of text no. 2 § 6.

§ 13. *Rí-ì-Ḫa-lab*$_{x}$ should have been a trader, who received silver from the Administration for providing several goods, including a mule. He is probably the same Reʾi-Ḫalab mentioned in the fragment *ARET* III 81 II, who received silver for acquiring 3 mules, and also in *ARET* I 12 § 32 (dated to Ibrium), according to which he received wool for six teams of mules of the king.

§ 17. Zuzu (and at least another man associated to him) received – without authorization – 2 shekels of gold in a military expedition against Ibᶜal, when "a son of the king of Ḫasuwan was killed in Garaman of the city of Ḫarsum". A parallel passage in the monthly document *ARET* XIX 6 § 56, mentions seven men who had received a garment each for having killed this "son": *A-na-lum Ib-dur-ì A-ba-ru* $_{2}^{ki}$ *Ḫa-lam* NE-NE-*ni*$^{ki}$ *I-ti-a-gú Mu-rí-ig*$^{ki}$ *Ša-da-ar*$^{ki}$ *Ba-u*$_{9}$*-ra-du*$^{ki}$ *Du-rí Ar-ra-ì A-ra-mi-iš*$^{ki}$ *Nu-zú* ḫi-úš dumu-nita en *Ḫa-zu-wa-an*$^{ki}$ *in Ib-al*$_{6}^{ki}$. One of these men, Nuzu from Aramiš, further received five simple garments for having reached Ibᶜal, § 49: *Nu-zú A-ra-mi-iš*$^{ki}$ DU.DU *si-in Ib-al*$_{6}^{ki}$.

These events related to the war against Ibᶜal, in particular to the expedition against Garaman (one of its cities), have been already discussed in Archi 2021a, 199–201.

§ 68. A monthly document, to be dated to Ibrium, registers the same expenditure. *ARET* XIX 9 (TM.75.G.1324) § 46: "two sets of garments and two belts decorated with 1 mina of gold Bagama handed over for the two kings of Manuwat on the occasion of the death of the queen of Manuwat (*Ba-ga-ma* šu-mu-tak$_4$ *in* ud ḫi-úš *ma-lik-tum Ma-nu-wa-ad*$^{ki}$)". *MEE* 2, 25 o. VII 9–VIII 6 (also a monthly document) registers a similar expenditure, probably on the same occasion: "two sets of garments and two belts Bagama has handed over for the purification rite of the two kings of Manuwat" (ì-ĝiš-saĝ 2 en *Ma-nu-wa-at*$^{ki}$ *Ba-ga-ma* šu-mu-tak$_4$). The two kings of Manuwat coexisted already in the preceding years because they are also mentioned in some documents dated to the minister Arrukum: *ARET* XV 10 § 53; 59 § 76'; *MEE* 10, 4 o. VII 3–10; r. IV 8; TM.75.G.1872+3385 (an annual document) o. 13–VI 4: "1 mina of gold for the decoration of two belts for the two kings of Manuwat, Ilba-IGI-DU$_8$ has handed over", and o. VIII 18–IX 2: "<1 mina> of gold for the decoration of two belts for the two kings of Manuwat, [*Í*]*l*-[*g*]*ú*-⌜*uš*⌝-<*li*>-*im* has handed over". The two kings are also mentioned in *ARET* III 192 r. IV 7–8, and 271 III 2'–3', too fragmentary to be dated.

# 4
## (Plates VII–VIII)

**(10077+4195)**

(1)
o. I. 1. 1 ma-na kù:babbar
sag̑ kù:babbar
3. $^{d}$*Ku-ra*

(2)
3 ma-na 7 gín DILMUN kù:babbar
5. *ni-zi-mu*
20 íb-lá *si-ti-tum* g̑ír-kun
7. lú g̑uruš-g̑uruš
SA.ZA$_{x}^{ki}$

(3)
9. 3 m[a-]na [ ]
[ ]
11. [ ]
12$^{?}$. [x *g*]*ú*-[*l*]*i*-[*lum* x gí]n [DILM]UN
13. [ì]-na-sum
SA.ZA$_{x}^{ki}$
15. *in*
zar$^{ki}$
17. en

(4)
II. 1. 4 gín DILMUN kù:babbar
Šubur
3. *Na-gàr*$^{ki}$
ḫi-mu-DU
5. 2 *na-se*$_{11}$
*Ma-rí*$^{ki}$

(5)
7. TAR kù:babbar
níg̑-sa$_{10}$
9. 1 *mi-at* 20 ḪU.UD-ḪU.UD
*áš-ti*
11. *Áš-da-ti-u*[*m*]⸢$^{ki}$⸣

(6)
5 gín DILMUN kù:babbar
13. 1 níg̑-bànda
[níg̑-ba]
15. [$^{d}$]⸢*ʾA*$_{5}$⸣-*da*-[“*ba*]*l*”
*L*[*a-r*]*u*$_{12}$-*ga*[-*du*]$^{ki}$

(7)
17. 3 gín DILMUN kù:babbar
níg̑-kaskal
19. *Ni-zi-ma-il*
DU.DU
21. *Na-gàr*$^{ki}$

(8)
6 gín DILMUN kù:babbar
23. 2 *bu*-DI
III. 1. *Du-si-gú*
ama-gal
3. en

(9)
10 ½ gín DILMUN kù:babbar
5. ZU.PIRIG̑
kin$_{5}$-ak
7. *gú-li-lum*
*wa*
9. níg̑-anše-ak kù-sal
SA.ZA$_{x}^{ki}$

(10)
11. TAR kù:babbar
*Na-gàr*$^{ki}$
13. šu-ba$_{4}$-ti
*in*
15. ⸢*Za*$^{?}$-*ù*$^{?}$⸣$^{ki}$

(11)
4 gín DILMUN kù:babbar
17. *Ù-ḫa*

(1) 1 mina of silver for the silver head of the god Kura.
(2) 3;07 minas of silver for decorating 20 belts, sheaths (and) dagger pendants for the men of the Palace.
(3) 3;[xx] minas […] [x b]racel[ets (weighing) x shek]els, the Palace has given in the wharehouse of the king.
(4) 4 shekels of silver for Šubur of the city of Nagar, (who) delivered 2 people of the city of Mari.
(5) 30 (shekels of) silver for the purchase of 120 ḪU.UD-ḪU.UD from the city of Ašdatium.
(6) 5 shekels of silver for 1 níg-bànda vessel: [gift] for the god ʾAdabal of the city of Larugadu.
(7) 3 shekels of silver: travel provision for Nizima-il (who) went to the city of Nagar.
(8) 6 shekels of silver for 2 toggle-pins for Dusigu, the king’s mother.
(9) 10 ½ shekels of silver for hangers for making bracelets and bridles (and) buckles for the Palace.
(10) 30 (shekels of) silver (for someone) of the city of Nagar, received in the city of Zau.
(11) 4 shekels of silver for Uḫa of the city of ʾAma, [re]ceived in […].

⸢ʾ*À*?⸣-*ma*$^{ki}$
19. [šu-]ba$_4$-ti
*in*
21. [ ]

(12)
[ ]
23. [1+]1 *zú-zú-ba-tum*
*Ib-rí-um*

(13)
IV. 1. 2 ma-na kù:babbar
níĝ-sa$_{10}$ ĝeštin-ĝeštin
3. *Ib-bí-um* "ur$_4$"
šu-ba$_4$-ti

(14)
5. 2 ma-na kù:babbar
*Wa-ra-núm*
7. *Ma-rí*$^{ki}$

(15)
TAR kù:babbar
9. 2 *bu*-DI
ama-gal
11. [ ]
[ ]

(16)
13. 12 gín DILMUN kù:babbar
nu$_{11}$-za$^{!}$(KUR)
15. 3 ĜIŠ-banšur 3 ĝír mar-tu
níĝ-ba
17. ŠA.PI gín DILMUN k[ù]:b[abbar]
[níĝ-b]a
19. [DN]

(17)
6 gín DILMUN kù:babbar
21. ì-na-sum
V. 1. *Zi-rí-gú*
níĝ-du$_8$
3. dumu-nita
*Lá-da-il*
5. *Ma-rí*$^{ki}$

(18)
ŠA.PI gín DILMUN kù:babbar
7. 2 *gú-li-lum*
*Gú-gi*
9. šu-i

(19)
TAR kù:babbar
11. níĝ-sa$_{10}$
[1 *mi-a*]*t* 30 ḪU.UD-ḪU.UD
13. *áš-ti*
*Áš-da-ti-um*$^{ki}$

(20)
15. 1 ½ gín DILMUN kù:babbar
nu$_{11}$-za$^{!}$(KUR)
17. 1 zag
ĜIŠ-gígir-II
19. *Sá-gú-šum*

(21)
1 ma-na 10 gín kù:babbar
21. 6 *bu*-D[I]
3 dam
VI. 1. *Ib-rí-um*
*Ḫa-zu-wa-an*$^{ki}$

(22)
3. TAR kù:babbar
*Mi-su-wa-du*
5. *Ma-rí*$^{ki}$

(23)
ŠÚ+ŠA gín DILMUN kù:babbar
7. *Na-gàr*$^{ki}$

(24)
ŠÚ+ŠA gín DILMUN kù:babbar
9. *Ga-ga-ba-an*$^{ki}$
10 gín DILMUN kù:babbar
11. maškim-*sù*

(25)
10 gín DILMUN kù:babbar
13. *A-bù-li-um*$^{ki}$

(12) […] for 2 ... (*zú-zú-ba-tum*) for Ibrium.
(13) 2 minas of silver for the purchase of wine: Ibbium, the collector (of goods), has received.
(14) 2 minas of silver for Waranum of the city of Mari.
(15) 30 (shekels of) silver for 2 toggle-pins for the mother of […].
(16) 12 shekels of silver for plating 3 tables (and) 3 mar-tu daggers: gift; 40 shekels of si[lver: gif]t for [the god(dess) …].
(17) 6 shekels of silver given by Zirigu for the ransom of the son of Lada-il of the city of Mari.
(18) 40 shekels of silver for 2 bracelets for Gugi, the barber.
(19) 30 (shekels of) silver for the purchase of [1]30 ḪU.UD-ḪU.UD (from) the city of Ašdatium.
(20) 1 ½ shekel of silver for plating 1 side of the chariot of Sagušum.
(21) 1;10 minas of silver for 6 toggle-pins for 3 women of Ibrium (from) the city of Ḫasuwan.
(22) 30 (shekels of) silver for Misuwadu of the city of Mari.
(23) 20 shekels of silver for (someone of) the city of Nagar.
(24) 20 shekels of silver for (someone of) the city of Gagaban; 10 shekels of silver for his representative.
(25) 10 shekels of silver for (someone of) the city of Abulium.

(26)
10 gín DILMUN kù:babbar
15. *Na-ba-ti-um*$^{ki}$

(27)
6 gín DILMUN kù:babbar
17. *maš-da-ù*
1 dumu-nita 1 dumu-munus
19. [x-]*da*[- ]

(28)
VII. 1. 50 gín DILMUN kù:babbar
níĝ-sa$_{10}$ ĝeštin-ĝeštin
3. *Dim-ma-il*
3 šu-ba$_{4}$-ti

(29)
5. TAR 7 gín DILMUN kù:babbar
2 *bu*-DI 10 lá-2 ĝeštu$_{x}$-lá 30 *du-ru*$_{12}$-*gú*
7. 1 *gu*-⌜*za*$_{x}$⌝-*gú*
1 šu-dub 1 *ma-ḫa-na-gúm*
9. *Ma-za-a-du*
*ma-lik-tum*
11. *Ib-al*$_{6}^{ki}$

(30)
ŠÚ+ŠA 7 gín DILMUN kù:babbar
13. níĝ-sa$_{10}$ 1 ĝír mar-tu ti kù-gi
*Du-bù-uš-da-mu*
15. *Ib-al*$_{6}^{ki}$

(31)
VIII. 1. 8 gín DILMUN kù:babbar
*zi-tum*
3. 4 ĝír-ĝír šu-du$_{8}$-máš
1 ma-na kù:babbar
5. níĝ-sa$_{10}$ 1 ĝír mar-tu kù-gi
*Sá-gu-šum*

(32)
7. 1 ma-na kù:babbar
níĝ-sa$_{10}$ 1 ĝír mar-tu kù-gi
9. *Ìr-am*$_{6}$*-da-mu*
lú
11. *Íl-zi*

(33)
10 gín DILMUN kù:babbar
13. *Na-gàr*$^{ki}$

(34)
TAR kù:babbar
15. *ᵓÀ-du*$^{ki}$

(35)
3 gín DILMUN kù:babbar
17. níĝ-kaskal
*Ìr-a*[*m*$_{6}$-]*ma-lik*
19. DU.DU
IX. 1. *Na-gàr*$^{ki}$

(36)
10 gín DILMUN kù:babbar
3. *Na-gàr*$^{ki}$
ĜIŠ.DUG.DU
5. *Ib-rí-um*

(37)
17 gín DILMUN kù:babbar
7. níĝ-sa$_{10}$ 1 na$_{4}$ maḫ
*in*
9. mè
*Kab-lu*$_{5}$*-ul*$^{ki}$

(38)
11. 1 ma-na ŠÚ+ŠA gín DILMUN kù:babbar
10 lá-2 *bu*-DI
13. níĝ-ba
4 dam
15. *Ì-ra-ar*$^{ki}$

(26) 10 shekels of silver for (someone of) the city of Nabatium.
(27) 6 shekels of silver for a *pallium* for 1 son (and) 1 daughter of […].
(28) 50 shekels of silver for the purchase of wine: Dimma-il has received in three (issues).
(29) 37 shekels of silver for 2 toggle-pins, 8 earrings, 30 pearls, 1 ... (*gu-za*$_{x}$*-gú*), 1 ring (and) 1 necklace for Maza-ᵓadu, the queen of the city of Ibᶜal.
(30) 27 shekels of silver for the purchase of 1 pointed mar-tu dagger (decorated with) gold for Dubuš-damu of the city of Ibᶜal.
(31) 8 shekels of silver in alloy for 4 knives to perform *extispicia*; 1 mina of silver for the purchase of 1 mar-tu dagger (decorated with) gold for Sagušum.
(32) 1 mina of silver for the purchase of 1 mar-tu dagger (decorated with) gold for Iram-damu, (son) of Ilzi.
(33) 10 shekels of silver for (someone of) the city of Nagar.
(34) 30 (shekels of) silver for (someone of) the city of ᵓAddu.
(35) 3 shekels of silver: travel provision for Iram-malik, (who) went to the city of Nagar.
(36) 10 shekels of silver for (someone of) the city of Nagar (who) came by Ibrium.
(37) 17 shekels of silver for the purchase of a big stone (in coincidence with) the battle (against) the city of Kablul.
(38) 1;20 minas of silver for 8 toggle-pins: gift for 4 women of the city of Irar.

(39)
5 ma-na TAR kù:babbar
17. kin$_5$-ak
3 íb<-lá> ĜÁ×LÁ ŠA.PI
19. 7 íb-lá *si-ti-tum* ĝír-kun
níĝ-ba ĝuruš-ĝuruš
X. 1. *Ì-ra-ar*$^{ki}$
*in* ud
3. *ma-lik-tum*
*Ì-ra-ar*$^{ki}$
5. DU.DU

(40)
ŠÚ+ŠA gín DILMUN kù:babbar
7. nu$_{11}$-za$^!$(KUR)
20 *gú-a-tum*
9. 4 ma-na TAR kù:babbar
1 ĜIŠ-šú 1 níĝ-bànda
11. 5 gín DILMUN kù:babbar
1 *mar-wa-ga-tum*
13. 3 gín DILMUN kù:babbar
*ḫa-za-nu*
15. 2 *da-ni-da*
8 gín DILMUN kù:babbar
17. níĝ-ba
diĝir-diĝir-diĝir
19. lú
dumu-munus
21. *Ib-rí-um*
šu-mu-tak$_4$
23. *si-in*
*Ì-ra-ar*$^{ki}$

(41)
XI. 1. 2 ma-na TAR kù:babbar
šu-bal-ak
3. TAR kù-gi
nu$_{11}$-za$^!$(KUR)
5. 4 bur-KAK-bur-KAK ĜIŠ-taškarin
TAR kù:babbar
7. 2 ĜIŠ-du
*Du-si-gú*
9. ama-gal
en

(42)
11. 3 ma-na TAR kù:babbar
šu-bal-ak
13. ŠA.PI 2 gín DILMUN kù-gi
2 ĜIŠ-du
15. *Du-si-gú*
ama-gal
17. en

(43)
1 ma-na kù:babbar
19. kin$_5$-ak
12 zi-bar tur
21. lú
sagi
23. kas$_4$-kas$_4$
XII. 1. é en

(44)
8 gín DILMUN kù:babbar
3. *ni-zi-mu*
10 lá-2 *gú-li-lum*
5. ĝuruš-ĝuruš
*Da-rí-ib*$^{ki}$

(45)
7. 10 gín DILMUN kù:babbar
*Si-zú*$^{ki}$

(46)
9. TAR kù-gi
níĝ-sa$_{10}$ 30 lá-2 ĜIŠ-ma-dul$_{10}$
11. 6 2 NI gín DILMUN kù:babbar
2 *gú-li-lum*
13. $^{d.?}$*À-ma-rí-ig*

(47)
1 ½ gín DILMUN kù:babbar
15. níĝ-sa$_{10}$ 1 na na$_4$
12 ma-na kù:babbar
17. en
*Na-gàr*$^{ki}$
19. Šubur
XIII. 1. [šu-mu-tak$_4$]

(39) 5;30 minas of silver for making 3 belts weighing 40 (shekels), 7 belts (with) sheaths (and) dagger pendants: gift for the men of the city of Irar, on the occasion of the coming of the queen of the city of Irar.

(40) 20 shekels of silver for plating 20 *gú-a-tum* vessels; 4;30 minas of silver for 1 GIŠ-šú vessel (and) 1 níg-bànda vessel; 5 shekels of silver for 1 *mar-wa-ga-tum* vessel; 3 shekels of silver for beads for 2 *da-ni-da*; 8 shekels of silver: gift for the gods, a daughter of Ibrium has handed over in the city of Irar.

(41) 2;30 minas of silver in exchange for 30 (shekels of) gold for plating 4 bur-KAK vessels of boxwood; 30 (shekels of) silver for 2 foot rings for Dusigu, the king's mother.

(42) 3;30 minas of silver in exchange for 42 shekels of gold for 2 foot rings for Dusigu, the king's mother.

(43) 1 mina of silver for making 12 small zi-bar goblets of the steward for the couriers of the king's house.

(44) 8 shekels of silver for decorating 8 bracelets for the men of the city of Darib.

(45) 10 shekels of silver for (someone of) the city of Sizu.

(46) 30 (shekels of) silver for the purchase of 28 chariot shafts; 6 shekels (and) 2 NI of silver for 2 bracelets for the god Ammarik.

(47) 1 ½ shekel of silver for the purchase of 1 palette of stone; 12 minas of silver for the king of the city of Nagar: Šubur [has handed over].

(48)
3 g[ín DILMUN kù:babbar]
3. saĝ kù:babbar
$^{d}$*Ku-ra*

(49)
5. 10 gín DILMUN kù:babbar
EN-NE$^{ki}$

(50)
7. 1 ½ gín DILMUN kù:babbar
nu$_{11}$-za$^{!}$(KUR) 1 zag
9. ĜIŠ-gígir-II
*Ib-rí-um*

(51)
11. ŠÚ+ŠA gín DILMUN kù:babbar
níĝ-kaskal
13. *ʾÀ-daš*
*ma-za-lum*
15. DU.DU
*Ar-mi*$^{ki}$

(52)
17. 2 gín DILMUN kù:babbar
nam-kud
19. *Ì-ra-ar*$^{ki}$
é
21. $^{d}$*Ku-ra*

(53)
2 ma-na kù:babbar
XIV. 1. [ ]⌜x⌝[ ]
*Ma*[- ]

(54)
3. 10 gín DILMUN kù:babbar
*Na-gàr*$^{ki}$

(55)
5. 5 gín DILMUN kù:babbar
níĝ-kaskal
7. *Du-nu*$^{ki}$

(56)
15 gín DILMUN kù:babbar
9. níĝ-kaskal
*Ga-zú-wa-ti-um*$^{ki}$

(57)
11. 4 gín DILMUN kù:babbar
níĝ-kaskal
13. maškim
*Ḫa-ra-il*

(58)
15. 4 gín DILMUN kù:babbar
níĝ-kaskal
17. *A-zú*$^{ki}$

(59)
3 gín DILMUN kù:babbar
19. níĝ-kaskal
*Ni-zi-ma-il*
21. DU.DU
*Na-gàr*$^{ki}$

(60)
23. 2 gín DILMUN kù:babbar
XV. 1. ZU.PIRIĜ
2 *ḫu-bù*
3. [ ]
3 gí[n] DI[LMUN] kù:babbar
5. ZU.PIRIĜ
1 útul urudu
7. lú gùn-gùn
íb+III-TÚG

(61)
9. 6 gín DILMUN kù:babbar
níĝ-kaskal
11. *Za-ba-ra*
maškim
13. *Ḫa-ra-il*

(62)
ŠÚ+ŠA gín DILMUN kù:babbar
15. níĝ-ba
diĝir-diĝir-diĝir

(48) 3 sh[ekels of silver] for the silver head of the god Kura.
(49) 10 shekels of silver for (someone of) the city of ENNE.
(50) 1 ½ shekel of silver for plating 1 side of the chariot of Ibrium.
(51) 20 shekels of silver: travel provision for ʾAdaš, a courier (who) went to the city of Armi.
(52) 2 shekels of silver for the oath (of someone) of the city of Irar, at the temple of the god Kura.
(53) 2 minas of silver […].
(54) 10 shekels of silver for (someone of) the city of Nagar.
(55) 5 shekels of silver: travel provision for (someone of) the city of Dunu.
(56) 15 shekels of silver: travel provision for (someone of) the city of Gazuwatium.
(57) 4 shekels of silver: travel provision for the representative of Ḫara-il.
(58) 4 shekels of silver: travel provision for (someone of) the city of Azu.
(59) 3 shekels of silver: travel provision for Nizima-il (who) went to the city of Nagar.
(60) 2 shekels of silver for the hangers of 2 ... (*ḫu-bù*) […]; 3 shek[els] of silver for the hangers of 1 kettle of copper for dyeing kilts.
(61) 6 shekels of silver: travel provision for Zabara, the representative of Ḫara-il.
(62) 20 shekels of silver: gift for the gods.

(63)
17. 3 ma-na ŠÚ+ŠA gín DILMUN
kù:babbar
kin$_5$-ak 20 *gú-li-lum*
19. gaba-ru
é en
21. tak$_4$
igi-igi

(64)
23. 7 gín DILMUN kù:babbar
r. I. 1. kin$_5$-ak
3 *zú-zú-ba-tum*
3. ĜIŠ-gígir-II
*Ib-rí-um*

(65)
5. 3 gín DILMUN kù:babbar
ugula ĝiš
7. E[N-]⌜X-X⌝-*tum*
3 íb-lá *si-ti-tum* ĝír-kun
9. lú ĝuruš-ĝuruš

(66)
10 gín DILMUN kù:babbar
11. *Ba-sa-ḫu*
*Na-gàr*$^{ki}$

(67)
13. 10 gín DILMUN kù:babbar
Ku-tu
15. *A-bù-li-um*$^{ki}$

(68)
10 gín DILMUN kù:babbar
17. *La-⌜a⌝-[na-ma]*
*[G]a-ga-[b]a-an*$^{ki}$

(69)
19. 5 gín DILMUN kù:babbar
*A*-NI-*ʾà*
21. *Ša-ga-bal*$^{ki}$

(70)
II. 1. 5 gín DILMUN kù:babbar
*A-tar*$_x$(BAN)-*il*
3. SA.ZA$_x$$^{ki}$

(71)
5 gín DILMUN kù:babbar
5. *Zú-zu*
*Ir-i-tum*$^{ki}$

(72)
7. 4 ma-na ⌜kù:babbar⌝
níĝ-sa$_{10}$ ĝeštin-ĝeštin
9. *Ib-bi-um* "ur$_4$"
šu-ba$_4$-ti

(73)
11. 2 gín DILMUN kù:babbar
*Ki-ti-ir*
13. *La-ru*$_{12}$*-ga-du*$^{ki}$

(74)
8 gín DILMUN kù:babbar
15. níĝ-sa$_{10}$ 1 na$_4$
*A-ʾà-lu*

(75)
17. 4 gín DILMUN kù:babbar
⌜níĝ⌝[-sa$_{10}$ 1 n]a$_4$
19. *U*$_9$*-da-ar*

(76)
III. 1. 3 gín DILMUN kù:babbar
níĝ-sa$_{10}$ 1 na$_4$(UD.NI)
3. *Puzur*$_4$*-ra-ma-lik*

(77)
3 gín DILMUN kù:babbar
5. níĝ-sa$_{10}$ 1 na$_4$(UD.NI)
*Ìr*-NI-*ba*

(78)
7. 4 g[ín DILMUN kù:babbar]
*[n]i-zi-mu*

(63) 3;20 minas of silver for making 20 bracelets as supply for the king's house, deposited as a provision.
(64) 7 shekels of silver making 3 ... (*zú-zú-ba-tum*) of the chariot of Ibrium.
(65) 3 shekels of silver for the grove's overseer …, 3 belts (with) sheath (and) dagger pendants for (his) men.
(66) 10 shekels of silver for Basaḫu of the city of Nagar.
(67) 10 shekels of silver for Kutu of the city of Abulium.
(68) 10 shekels of silver for La[nama] of the city of Gagaban.
(69) 5 shekels of silver for ANIʾa of the city of Šagabal.
(70) 5 shekels of silver for Atar-il of the Palace.
(71) 5 shekels of silver for Zuzu of the city of Iritum.
(72) 4 minas of silver for the purchase of wine: Ibbium, the collector (of goods), has received.
(73) 2 shekels of silver for Kitir of the city of Larugadu.
(74) 8 shekels of silver for the purchase of 1 stone for Aʾalu.
(75) 4 shekels of silver for the pur[chase of 1 sto]ne for Udar.
(76) 3 shekels of silver for the purchase of 1 stone for Puzurra-malik.
(77) 3 shekels of silver for the purchase of 1 stone for IrNIba.
(78) 4 sh[ekels of silver for de]corating with lamination 2 knives to perform *extispicia* for Ibrium.

9. nu$_{11}$-za$^!$(KUR)
2 ĝír šu-du$_8$-máš
11. lú
*Ib-rí-um*

(79)
13. 1 ma-na 53 gín DILMUN kù:babbar
šu-bal-ak
15. 1 ma-na 53 an-na
kin$_5$-ak
17. níĝ-anše-ak kù-sal
10 u$_5$
19 SA.ZA$_x$$^{ki}$

(80)
IV. 1. 1 gín DILMUN kù:babbar
nu$_{11}$-za$^!$(KUR)
3. 2 šu-i
*Ib-rí-um*

(81)
5. 5 2 NI g[ín DILMUN kù:babbar]
nu$_{11}$-za
7. 1 *ma-ḫa-ni-gúm*
*Ib-rí-um*

(82)
9. 2 NI g[ín DILMUN kù:babbar]
1 *bu*-DI sal
11. *Du-si-gú*
ama-gal
13. en

(83)
TAR kù:babbar
15. nu$_{11}$-za$^!$(KUR)
2 *ḫa-bù*
17. níĝ-ba
$^d$*Ra-sa-ap*
19. lú
*ʾÀ-da-ni*$^{ki}$
21. *wa*
$^{d}$*ʾÀ-da*

(84)
23. 2 ma-na kù:babbar
*Bù-šu-sum*
V. 1. *Ma-rí*$^{ki}$

(85)
1 ma-na kù:babbar
3. níĝ-sa$_{10}$ ĝeštin-ĝeštin
*Ib-bí-um* "ur$_4$"
5. šu-ba$_4$-ti

(86)
1 ma-na TAR kù:babbar
7. níĝ-sa$_{10}$ 1 BAR.AN
lú
9. [ ]
*áš-ti*
11. *Ra-ʾà-ak*$^{ki}$

(87)
1 ma-na kù:babbar
13. níĝ-sa$_{10}$ 2 ĜIŠ-banšur kù-gi
1 ½ gín DILMUN kù:babbar
15. 1 šu-dub
sikil
17. lú en
$^d$*Ra-sa-ap*
19. *ʾÀ-da-ni*$^{ki}$

(88)
1 ma-na ŠÚ+ŠA 5 gín DILMUN
kù:babbar
VI. 1. níĝ-sa$_{10}$ 1 BAR.AN
*Mi-na-i-um*$^{ki}$

(89)
3. TAR kù:babbar
níĝ-sa$_{10}$ 1 ĝír mar-tu ti kù-gi
5. *Iš$_{11}$-gi-wa-aš*
*Áb-su*$^{ki}$

(90)
7. TAR kù:babbar
[níĝ-]s[a$_{10}$ 1 ĝír mar-tu] ⌜ti⌝ kù-gi

(79) 1;53 minas of silver in exchange for 1;53 minas of tin for making bridles (and) buckles for 10 couriers of the Palace.
(80) 1 shekel of silver for plating 2 šu-i vessels for Ibrium.
(81) 5 she[kels] (and) 2 NI [of silver] for plating 1 necklace for Ibrium.
(82) 2 NI sh[ekels of silver] for 1 thin toggle-pin for Dusigu, the king's mother.
(83) 30 (shekels of) silver for plating 2 maces: gift for the god Rašap of the city of ʾAdani and for the god Hadda.
(84) 2 minas of silver for Bušusum of the city of Mari.
(85) 1 mina of silver for the purchase of wine: Ibbium, the collector (of goods), has received.
(86) 1;30 minas of silver for the purchase of 1 mule of [...] from the city of Raʾak.
(87) 1 mina of silver for the purchase of 2 tables (decorated with) gold; 1 ½ shekel of silver for 1 ring for the purification of the king by the god Rašap of the city of ʾAdani.
(88) 1;25 minas of silver for the purchase of 1 mule (from) the city of Minaʾium.
(89) 30 (shekels of) silver for the purchase of 1 pointed mar-tu dagger (decorated with) gold for Išgi-waš of the city of Absu.
(90) 30 (shekels of) silver for [the purchase of 1] pointed [mar-tu dagger] (decorated with) gold for NImati, trader of the city of Kakmium.

9. NI-*má-ti*
lú-kar
11. *Kak-mi-um*$^{ki}$

(91)
ŠÚ+ŠA gín DILMUN kù:babbar
13. níĝ-sa$_{10}$ 1 ĝír [m]ar-tu zú kù-gi
*I-ga-li-im*
15. en
*Ib-al*$_6^{ki}$

(92)
VII. 1. TAR kù:babbar
níĝ-sa$_{10}$ 1 ĝír mar-tu ti kù-gi
3. *Sa-ḫa-a*
ugula *Ù-si-gú*$^{ki}$

(93)
5. TAR kù:babbar
níĝ-sa$_{10}$ 1 ĝír mar-tu ti kù-gi
7. ⸢*I*⸣*-i-*⸢*bù*⸣
[ ]
9. [ ]-⸢*ig*⸣
maškim
11. *A-ag*

(94)
2 ma-na [x g]ín [DIL]MUN
[kù:babbar]
13. níĝ[-sa$_{10}$] 2 ĜI[š-x]
*Ib-bí-um* "ur$_4$"
15. šu-ba$_4$-ti
ki:lam$_7$
17. *ᵓÀ-da-ni*$^{ki}$

(95)
20 ma-na kù:babbar
VIII. 1. en
*Na-gàr*$^{ki}$
3. *Ni-zi-ma-il*
šu-mu-tak$_4$

(96)
5. 3 gín DILMUN kù:babbar
níĝ-kaskal
7. *Ni-zi-ma-il*
DU.DU
9. *Na-gàr*$^{ki}$

(97)
5 gín DILMUN kù:babbar
11. [ ]
*wa*
13. *ma-z*[*a-*]*lum*[*-sù*]
DU.DU
15. *Ar-mi*$^{ki}$

(98)
2 gín DILMUN kù:babbar
17. *ni-zi-mu*
2 *gú-li-lum*
19. *ša-ti*
lú *Di-bí-zi-kir*

(99)
21. TAR kù:babbar
IX. 1. *I-du-bù*
tuš-LÚ×TIL
3. *Ḫa-z*[*u-*]*wa-an*$^{ki}$

(100)
TAR kù:babbar
5. 2 *gú-li-lum*-I esi
*En-na-ma-lik*
7. lú-kar
*Ma-nu-wa-ad*$^{ki}$

(101)
9. 5 gín DILMUN kù:babbar
[kin$_5$-ak]
11. [1 *gú-*]*li-lum*
dumu-nita
13. *Mu-gàr*
NE-di

(102)
15. 1 ma-na kù:babbar
Šubur
17. *Na-gàr*$^{ki}$
šu-mu-tak$_4$

(91) 20 shekels of silver for the purchase of 1 serrated mar-tu dagger (decorated with) gold for Iga-lim, the king of the city of Ibᶜal.
(92) 30 (shekels of) silver for the purchase of 1 pointed mar-tu dagger (decorated with) gold for Saḫaᵓa, the overseer of the city of Usigu.
(93) 30 (shekels of) silver for the purchase of 1 pointed mar-tu dagger (decorated with) gold for Iᵓibu […] for […], the representative of Aᵓag.
(94) 2;[xx] minas [of silver] for the pur[chase] of 2 […]: Ibbium, the collector (of goods), has received at the market of the city of ᵓAdani.
(95) 20 minas of silver for the king of the city of Nagar, Nizima-il has handed over.
(96) 3 shekels of silver: travel provision for Nizima-il (who) went to the city of Nagar.
(97) 5 shekels of silver for [PN] and [his] courier (who) went to the city of Armi.
(98) 2 shekels of silver for decorating 2 bracelets, those of Dibi-zikir.
(99) 30 (shekels of) silver for Idubu (who) resided in the city of Ḫasuwan.
(100) 30 (shekels of) silver for 2 single bracelets of diorite for Enna-malik, trader of the city of Manuwat.
(101) 5 shekels of silver for [making 1 bra]celet for the son of Mugar, the dancer.
(102) 1 mina of silver for Šubur of the city of Nagar (who) has handed over kilt(s) (in the) Mari (fashion) (and reported) its (i.e. Mari's) defeat.

19. íb+III-TÚG babbar
*Ma-rí*$^{ki}$
21. *wa*
til-*sù*

(103)
X. 1. 12 gín DILMUN kù:babbar
kin$_5$-ak
3. 6 *zú-zú-ba-tum*
2 ĜIŠ-gígir-II
5. en

(104)
2 ma-na kù:babbar
7. kin$_5$-ak
2 níĝ-anše-ak 4 kù-sal
9. *Sá-gú-šum*

(105)
15 gín DILMUN [kù]:b[abbar]
11. [ ]
níĝ-"mul"
13. àga-"kár"(ŠÈ)
*Ma-rí*$^{ki}$
15. *wa*
til
17. *Wa-ru*$_{12}$*-tum*

(106)
8 gín DILMUN kù:babbar
19. *ᵓÀ-du*$^{ki}$

(107)
8 gín DILMUN kù:babbar
21. nu$_{11}$-za$^!$(KUR)
1 an-dùl
23. níĝ-ba
XI. 1. $^d$*A*$^!$(DA)*-la*
*Ib-rí-um*
3. ì-na-sum

(108)
1 ma-na ŠA.PI gín DILMUN
kù:babbar
5. šu-bal-ak
1 dib ĜÁ×LÁ ŠÚ+ŠA gín DILMUN kù-gi
7. ì-na-sum
*Ìr-am*$_6$*-ma-lik*
9. maškim
*Du-si*
11. [ ]
šeš[-mu]
13. en
*Du-lu*$^{ki}$
15. *I-bí-ga-lu*
šu-mu-tak$_4$

(109)
17. 14 gín DILMUN kù:babbar
níĝ-sa$_{10}$ raš-SAR Kur$^{ki}$

(110)
19. 15 gín DILMUN kù:babbar
nu$_{11}$-za$^!$(KUR)
XII. 1. 1 *ḫa-bu*
níĝ-ba
3. $^{dᵓ}$*À-da*

(111)
2 gín DILMUN kù:babbar
5. *ni-zi-mu*
2 *gú-li-lum*
7. *Bar-za-ma-li*
lú
9. *Iš-da-má*

(112)
2 gín DILMUN kù:babbar
11. *ni-zi-mu*
nu$_{11}$-za$^!$(KUR)
13. 1 *ma-ḫa-ni-gúm*
*Ib-rí-um*

(113)
15. ŠÚ+ŠA gín DILMUN k[ù]:babbar
[níĝ-kaskal]
17. *A-ᵓà-⸢lu⸣*
*wa*
19. *Ù-da-a*$^{ᵓ)}$*-ḫa*
*Ma-rí*$^{ki}$
21. heš$_5$
DU.DU

(103) 12 shekels of silver for making 6 ... (*zú-zú-ba-tum*) of 2 chariots of Ibrium.
(104) 2 minas of silver for making 2 bridles (and) 4 buckles for Sagušum.
(105) 15 shekels of [silver] for [PN] (who) brought the news that the city of Mari had been vanquished and defeated, (confirmed by) Warutum.
(106) 8 shekels of silver for (someone of) the city of ᵓAddu.
(107) 8 shekels of silver for plating 1 statue: gift for the god Ala, Ibrium has given.
(108) 1;40 minas of silver in exchange for 1 plaque weighing 20 shekels of gold, given by Iram-malik, the representative of Dusi, […], the brother of the king of the city of Dulu: Ibbi-galu has handed over.
(109) 14 shekels of silver for the purchase of leek from the mountain region.
(110) 15 shekels of silver for plating 1 mace: gift for the god Hadda.
(111) 2 shekels of silver for decorating 2 bracelets for Barza-mali, (son) of Išdama.
(112) 2 shekels of silver for decorating with lamination 1 necklace for Ibrium.
(113) 20 shekels of silver: [travel provision] for Aᵓalu and Udaᵓ-aḫa of the city of Mari (who escorted) some prisoners back (to their own city).

(114)
23. 4 gín DILMUN kù:babbar
ZU.PIRIĜ
25. 2 dib
*Lu-a-tum*$^{ki}$

(115)
XIII. 1. 1 ma-na 12 gín DILMUN kù:babbar
kin$_5$-ak
3. 4 íb-lá *si-ti-tum* ĝír-kun
*Du-bù-uš-da-mu*
5. *I-ga-li-im*
*Zú-ga-du*
7. *Ì-lum-a-rí-ḫu*
4 en
9. *Ib-al*$_6^{ki}$
*in* ud
11. [nídba ì-ĝiš]

(116)
[x gín DILMUN k]ù:[babbar]
13. kin$_5$-ak
4 íb-lá
15. gaba-ru
é en

(117)
17. 10 gín DILMUN kù:babbar
*Na-gàr*$^{ki}$

(118)
19. 1 ma-na ŠA.PI gín DILMUN
kù:babbar
šu-bal-ak an-na
XIV. 1. PA níĝ-*sù*-níĝ-*sù*
50 ma-na zabar
3. kin$_5$-ak
5 *mi-at* ĜIŠ-gu-kak-gíd
5. 5 ma-na TAR 3 NI gín DILMUN
kù:babbar
šu-bal-ak
7. 5 ma-na TAR 3 NI an-na
kin$_5$-ak
9. [ ] ĜIŠ-g[u-]kak-gíd
1 ma-na ŠÚ+ŠA gín DILMUN
kù:babbar
11. 2 níĝ-anše-ak 4 kù-sal
*Du-bí-zi-kir*
13. lú
*Ti-ša-rum*$^?$

(119)
15. 1 ma-na ŠÚ+ŠA gín DILMUN
kù:babbar
2 níĝ-anše-ak 4 kù-sal
XV. 1. *A-bu*

(120)
5 ma-na kù:babbar
3. šu-bal-ak
1 ⌜ma-na⌝ [kù-g]i
5. en
*Kak-mi-um*$^{ki}$
7. ⌜*I*⌝*-ti-*[$^d$]*Aš-dar*
[šu-]mu-[ta]k$_4$

(121)
9. [x m]a-na kù:[bab]bar
[níĝ-]sa$_{10}$ [1$^?$] BAR.AN
11. *A-šu*$^{ki}$
*ᵓÀ-bí*
13. lú
$^d$*Ra-sa-ap*
15. ŠE.SAĜ×ḪA-mul

(122)
[x k]ù[:babbar]
17. ZU.PIRIĜ
1 útul urudu
19. lú
sada(ĜIŠGAL)-titab(MUNU$_4$.GÚG)

(123)
21. 5 kù:babbar
1 bur-KAK
23. aš-ḫal
ì-ĝiš

(114) 4 shekels of silver for the hangers of 2 plaques for (2 men of) the city of Luatum.
(115) 1;12 minas of silver for making 4 belts (with) sheaths (and) dagger pendants for Dubuš-damu, Iga-lim, Zugadu, Ilum-ariḫu, 4 kings of the city of Ibᶜal, on the occasion of [the offering of the oil].
(116) [x shekels of silver] for making 4 belts as supply for the king's house.
(117) 10 shekels of silver for (someone of) the city of Nagar.
(118) 1;40 minas of silver in exchange for tin for …; 50 minas of bronze for making 500 spearheads; 5;30 minas (and) 3 NI of silver in exchange for 5;30 minas (and) 3 NI of tin for making [x] spearheads; 1;20 minas of silver for 2 bridles (and) 4 buckles for Dubi-zikir, (son) of Tišarum.
(119) 1;20 minas for 2 bridles (and) 4 buckles for Abu.
(120) 5 minas of silver in exchange for 1 mina [of gold] for the king of the city of Kakmium, Iti-Ašdar has handed over.
(121) [x m]ina(s) of sil[ver] for [the pur]chase of [1] mule (from) the city of Ašu, ᵓAbi the man of the god Rašap (took) on debt.
(122) [x shekels of silver] for the hangers for 1 kettle of copper for beer mash.
(123) 5 (shekels of) silver for 1 bur-KAK vessel, with a filter, for the oil.

(124)
25. ŠA.PI gín DILMUN kù:babbar
XVI. 1. 1 á-MUŠEN níĝ-saĝšu
[ ]k[ù:bab]bar
3. [ca. 8 lines]

(125)
11?. 1 ma-na ŠA.PI kù:babbar
šu-bal-ak
13. ŠÚ+ŠA gín DILMUN kù-gi 1 an-zam$_x$
(blank)
15?. (blank and then lacuna)

(126)
[AN.ŠE.GÚ x ma-na (x)] kù:[bab]bar
17. è
*in* ud
19. *Ib-rí-um*
2 mu
21. (blank)

*a*) it follows a vertical wedge

(124) 40 shekels of silver for 1 helmet; [...] of si[lver ...].
(125) 1;40 minas of silver in exchange for 20 shekels of silver for 1 an-zam$_x$ goblet.
(126) [Total: x minas] of sil[ver]: expenditure during the second year of Ibrium.

## Commentary

The colophon (§ 126) states that this document concerns the silver (the total is in lacuna) "expended (by the Administration in the first part of the) second year of Ibrium", è *in* ud *Ib-rí-um* 2 mu.

This is the first annual document concerning the "expenditures", è, of metals which starts with the registration of the expenditure of 1 mina (470 g) of silver for the "head" (saĝ) of Kura, the city-god, (§ 1), a renewal rite probably celebrated at the beginning of the new year. A similar registration opens all the following documents of this series. This registration is not preserved in the two preceding texts. Although the rite is already attested in minister Arrukum's annual documents, it is not mentioned in the opening lines: TM.75.G.1406 o. X 1–3 (2! ma-na kù-babbar); TM.75.G.1871 r. III 11–13; TM.75.G.1872 r. VI 18–VII 2.

The head of Kura was of bronze (urudu, see text 10 o. I 2), on which the silver mask was applied. Three more shekels (23 g) were needed for a subsequent rite which again involved the head of the statue (§ 48). The rite probably fell on the third month (Archi 2005, p. 81 = 2015a, pp. 736–737; Id. 2013a, pp. 214–216 = 2015a, pp. 501–503).

The mu-DU document from the year Ibrium 02, *ARET* XIV 56 o. I 1–3, registers "43;26 minas (20.414 kg) of gold and 117 minas (54.990 kg) of silver of Kablul". The extraordinary tribute paid by this city was the consequence of a military defeat mentioned in the present document in § 37: "(a silver expenditure on the occasion of) the battle (mè) of Kablul". Kablul was already a city under the hegemony of Ebla: it delivered 7 minas (3.290 kg) of gold and 2 minas (940 g) of tin on the occasion of Irkab-damu's death, *ARET* XIV 54 § 28. This city was a major source of gold for Ebla (see the *ARET* XIV, pp. 513–514), and therefore must have been located in an area where this metal was easily accessible, in the Taurus range.

Two passages allude to a diplomatic activity by Ibrium, § 36: "10 shekels of silver (to someone of) Nagar (who) came (by) Ibrium", *Na-gàr*$^{ki}$ ĜIŠ.DUG.DU *Ib-rí-um*; § 21 "6 toggle-pins (to) 3 women of Ibrium (from) Ḫasuwan", 3 dam *Ib-rí-um Ḫa-zu-wa-an*$^{ki}$. The city of Ḫasuwan was probably conquered by Ebla the previous year (Archi 2019b, pp. 10–11).

Dusigu, "the king's mother", ama-gal en, received several gifts in silver and also in gold (1;12 minas = 464 g), §§ 8, 41, 42, 82.

Iga-lim of Ibᶜal received a dagger decorated with gold (§ 91); he later came to Ebla to swear an oath of alliance together with another three kings of the confederation of Ibᶜal: Dubuš-damu, Zugadu and Ilum-ariḫu, each receiving a belt each (§ 115). A dagger decorated with gold was given to Dubuš-damu, while Maza-ʾadu, "the queen of Ibᶜal" (probably his spouse) received several pieces of jewelry (§§ 29, 30). Dubuš-damu of Ibᶜal is also mentioned in *ARET* XII 302 r. II 8.

Iga-lim had become one of the kings of the confederation of Ibᶜal the same year of Irkab-damu's death, according to *ARET* XIII 13 §§ 2, 4–5: "the year of king Irkab-damu's death (DIŠ mu úš en *I.*), Iga-lim, the son of Inkar was king [more precisely: one of the kings!] of (the confederation of) Ibᶜal ... He performed the offering of the oil (of the alliance), and the son of Iga-lim and his brothers joined together for the military expedition (of Ebla against) Mari (níĝ-kas$_4$ *Ma-rí*$^{ki}$)" (Archi 2019a, pp. 148–149).

According to §§ 38–39, four women and seven men from Irar received gifts "when the queen of Irar went (DU.DU)", i.e.: [this lady] left Ebla to become queen of Irar. Because the text also states that one of Ibrium's daughters had to hand over gifts for the gods in Irar, § 40, it seems probable that one of the minister's daughters married the king of Irar, who may have come to Ebla in person to swear an oath in the temple of Kura (§ 52). The four women and the seven men had come to Ebla to accompany the young lady to Irar. This queen received a gift from Dusigu, the king's mother, according to text no.15 § 60.

Ibrium received several gifts: §§ 12, 50, 64, 78, 81, 112, and even two knives to perform *extispicia*, šu-du$_8$-máš (§ 78).

Šubur of Nagar consigned two men from Mari (§ 4). He brought a stone (?), and 12 minas (5.640 kg) of silver (§ 47) to his king. The passage in § 102 could be interpreted as Šubur receiving another mina (470 g) of silver for having presented a garment from Mari, announcing that Mari "had been defeated".

The news came that Mari had been vanquished and defeated, níĝ-"mul" àga-"kár" *Ma-rí*$^{ki}$ *wa* til, was confirmed by Warutum (§ 105). The syntax is awkward because it could also be understood to mean that Mari's emissary to Ebla brought the news that Warutum had died in the course of that war. Other documents however show that Warutum was active in subsequent years. On the relation with Mari during this period, see Archi 2019a. pp. 146–153

Some other unnamed envoys from Nagar received 30 shekels (235 g) of silver (§ 10), and 20, 10, and again 10 shekels (157 / 78 g) respectively (§§ 23, 33, 54). Basaḫu and another man from Nagar received 10 shekels (78 g) each (§§ 66, 117), and a messenger from Nagar came to meet Ibrium personally, receiving 10 shekels (78 g) of silver (§ 36).

From Ebla's side, Nizima-il went to Nagar twice (§§ 7, 59), and on his third journey, he delivered 20 minas (9.400 kg) of silver to the king of Nagar (§§ 95, 96). For each of these journeys, he received 3 shekels (23 g) of silver as travel expenses, as did Iram-malik, who was also sent to Nagar (§ 35).

This document gives clear evidence of an alliance between Ebla and Nagar, and Ebla's interest in supporting this city.

The messengers from Mari were *Wa-ra-núm*, *Mi-su-wa-du*, and *Bù-šu-sum* (§§ 14, 22, 84). The ransom for a man from Mari was paid (§ 17). Two men from Mari, Aʾalu and Udaʾ-aḫ(u) (a "trader", lú-kar, *ARET* IV 2 o. 6 1–2) escorted some prisoners back to their own city (§ 113). These two officials performed the same function a year later, according to text XXI 6 § 41.

§ 3. On zar$^{ki}$ (LAGAB×SUM), see Archi 2010a, p. 28 = Id. 2015a, p. 672 nt. 45.

§§ 5, 19. The good ḪU.UD-ḪU.UD was received in both these cases from *Áš-da-ti-um*$^{ki}$, a city apparently not mentioned elsewhere. This good is always mentioned in high numbers, respectively in 120 and 130 units in these two registrations; their value was in both cases of 30 shekels in total. According to *ARET* VII 77 § 1, an indeterminate number of this item was acquired in *Ga-sur*$_x^{ki}$ for 47 shekels of silver. It was therefore probably an exotic good. A certain Ibbium acquired 120 items of it for 30 shekels of silver, together with "wheat", gig, for four minas (text XXI 6 § 2). Two documents of Arrukum register the purchase of ḪU.UD-ḪU.UD: *a*) TM.75.G.1352 r. IV 6–8 = VI 5: 80 items for 35 shekels of silver; *b*) TM.75.G.10050+ o. XI 1'–3': 177 items for 1;26 minas of silver. The *LLE*,I 758 have: UD.ḪU = *ḫa-ḫa-tum*.

§ 34. The city of *ʾÀ-du*$^{ki}$ was located south of Nagar, near the border of the areas under Ebla and Mari's hegemony (Archi 2019a, pp. 180–181).

# 5
## (Plates IX–X)

(1)
o. I. 1. 14 ma-na ŠÚ+ŠA 7 gín DILMUN
kù:babbar níĝ-sa$_{10}$
27 ᵓ*à-da-um*-TÚG-I
3. 34 gada-TÚG
1 aktum-TÚG 1 túg-NI.NI 1 íb-lá saĝ
5. 1 gu-dùl-TÚG
[x íb+III-TÚG] sa$_6$ gùn
7. 2 *mi-at* 10 íb+III-TÚG gùn
4 ĝír mar-tu zú-ak
9. 4 ĝír zú-ak
3 *mi-at* 54 na$_4$ siki sa$_6$
II. 1. 3 ma-na ŠÚ+ŠA 1 gín DILMUN
kù:babbar níĝ-sa$_{10}$
ĜIŠ-ti-ḪAR ĜIŠ-ád
3. *Wa-ba-rúm* "ur$_4$"
šu-ba$_4$-ti
5. ki:lam$_7$
<d>*A-da-ma*
7. ᵓ*À-da-ni*$^{ki}$

(2)
8 gín DILMUN kù:babbar níĝ-sa$_{10}$
9. 1 ĝír mar-⸢tu⸣ [kù:babbar]
[n⸢í⸣ĝ-ba]
11. *Ib-ḫur-ma-lik*
lú-kar
13. *Kak-mi-um*$^{ki}$

(3)
TAR kù:babbar
15. níĝ-ba
*Daš-na*
17. *wa*
*Wa-ru*$_{12}$*-tum*
19. *Ma-rí*$^{ki}$
*in*
III. 1. *Má*-NE$^{ki}$
lú *Ì-mar*$^{ki}$
3. šu-ba$_4$-ti

(4)
1 ma-na kù:babbar
5. níĝ-sa$_{10}$ 1 ĝír mar-tu kù-gi
*Ba-ga-ma* ugula

(5)
7. ŠA.PI gín DILMUN kù:babbar
šu-bal-ak
9. 8 gín DILMUN kù-gi
nu$_{11}$-za 2 *gú-li-lum*
11. *A-bù-sa*

(6)
[1 ma-na 50 gí]n DILMUN kù:babbar
13. šu-bal-ak
ŠÚ+ŠA 2 gín DILMUN kù-gi
15. nu$_{11}$-za 3 *gú-li-lum*-II esi 10 *gú-li-lum*-I esi
ME-sig é

(7)
17. 10 gín DILMUN kù:babbar níĝ-sa$_{10}$
ĜIŠ-ma-dul$_{10}$
19. 14 gín DILMUN kù:babbar níĝ-sa$_{10}$
IV. 1. ĜIŠ-ti-ḪAR
*Wa-ba-rúm*
3. šu-ba$_4$-ti
ki:lam$_7$
5. SA.ZA$_x^{ki}$

(8)
2 ½ gín DILMUN kù:babbar
7. šu-bal-ak
½ gín DILMUN kù-gi
9. *ni-zi-mu* 1 dib

(1) 14;27 minas of silver for the purchase of 65 garments, [x]+210 kilts, 4 serrated mar-tu daggers, 4 serrated daggers, 354 stone weights of wool of good quality; 3;21 minas of silver for the purchase of GIŠ-ti-ḪAR-wood (and) myrtle: Wabarum, the collector (of goods), has received at the market of the god Adamma of the city of ᵓAdani.
(2) 8 shekels of silver for the purchase of 1 mar-tu dagger (decorated with) [silver]: [gift for] Ibḫur-malik, trader of the city of Kakmium.
(3) 30 shekels of silver: gift for Dašna and Warutum of the city of Mari, in the city of MaNE (someone) of the city of Imar has received.
(4) 1 mina of silver for the purchase of 1 mar-tu dagger (decorated with) gold for Bagama, the overseer.
(5) 40 shekels of silver in exchange for 8 shekels of gold for plating 2 bracelets for Abusa.
(6) [1;50] minas of silver in exchange for 22 shekels of gold for plating 3 double bracelets of diorite (and) 10 single bracelets of diorite for the watchmen of the (king's) house.
(7) 10 shekels of silver for the purchase of chariot shafts; 14 shekels of silver for the purchase of GIŠ-ti-ḪAR-wood: Wabarum has received at the market of the Palace.
(8) 2 ½ shekels of silver in exchange for ½ shekel of gold for decorating 1 plaque for Arsi-aḫa, (son) of Bulugu.

*Ar-si-a-ḫa*
11. lú *Bù-lu-gú*

(9)
5 gín DILMUN kù:babbar
13. šu-bal-ak
1 gín DILMUN kù-gi
15. *ni-zi-mu* 1 dib
*Íl-ba-ma-lik*
17. lú *I-gi*

(10)
ŠA.PI 6 gín DILMUN kù:babbar
19. nu$_{11}$-za 3 *gú-li-lum*-II a-gar$_5$-gar$_5$ 10 *gú-li-lum*-I
V. 1. esi a-gar$_5$-gar$_5$
ME-sig
3. é en
3 gín DILMUN kù:babbar
5. dàra-*sù*

(11)
10 gín DILMUN kù:babbar
7. níĝ-sa$_{10}$ ĝeštin
*Bu*$_x$-*ma-ì*
9. šu-ba$_4$-ti

(12)
1 ma-na 20 gín DILMUN kù:babbar
11. lul-gu-ak 2 níĝ-anše-ak 4 NE-*na-tum*
*Du-si-gú*
13. ama-gal en

(13)
10 gín DILMUN kù:babbar
15. *ni-zi-mu*
24 íb[?]-lá ĝír-kun
17. *ìr-a-núm*
*I-rí-ig-ma-lik*
19. 12 ½ gín DILMUN kù:babbar
VI. 1. šu-bal-ak
2 ½ gín DILMUN kù-gi
3. *ni-zi-mu*
nu$_{11}$-za *gú-li-lum*
5. *ìr-a-núm-sù*

(14)
ŠÚ+ŠA gín DILMUN kù:babbar 2 *bu*-DI
7. ama-gal *I-bí-zi-kir*
*in* ud
9. níĝ-mu-sá
dumu-munus
11. *Ib-rí-um*
*Gi-ti*-NE$^{ki}$

(15)
13. 5 gín DILMUN kù:babbar
nu$_{11}$-za 1 bur-KAK ĜIŠ-taškarin
15. *Ib-rí-um*

(16)
1 ma-na kù:babbar
17. níĝ-sa$_{10}$ 1 ĝír mar-tu kù-gi
*Ib-rí-um*
19. *in* ud
nídba
VII. 1. $^{d}$[*Iš*:]*šára* ĜIŠ-kiri$_6$

(17)
1 ma-na ŠA.PI gín DILMUN kù:babbar
3. níĝ-sa$_{10}$ 2 *gú-li-lum* a-gar$_5$-gar$_5$ kù-gi
*Bu-ra*
5. maškim
*A-šum*

(18)
7. TAR kù:babbar
níĝ-sa$_{10}$ 1 gud
9. *Ib-gi-da-mu*
ugula kad$_4$-kad$_4$

(9) 5 shekels of silver in exchange for 1 shekel of gold for decorating 1 plaque for Ilba-malik, (son) of Igi.
(10) 46 shekels of silver for plating 3 double bracelets of copper (and) 10 single bracelets of diorite (and) copper for the watchmen of the king's house; 3 shekels of silver for its (toggle-pin in the shape of a) mountain goat.
(11) 10 shekels of silver for the purchase of wine: Buma-i(l) has received.
(12) 1;20 minas of silver as replacement of 2 bridles, 4 ... (NE-*na-tum*) for Dusigu, the king's mother.
(13) 10 shekels of silver for decorating 24 belts (and) dagger pendants for the gang of Irig-malik; 12 ½ shekels of silver in exchange for 2 ½ shekels of gold for decorating with lamination the bracelets for his gang.
(14) 20 shekels of silver for 2 toggle-pins for Ibbi-zikir's mother on the occasion of the marriage of a daughter of Ibrium (who resided in) the city of GitiNE.
(15) 5 shekels of silver for plating 1 bur-KAK vessel of boxwood for Ibrium.
(16) 1 mina of silver for the purchase of 1 mar-tu dagger (decorated with) gold for Ibrium, on the occasion of the offering to [Iš]ḫara of the garden.
(17) 1;40 minas of silver for the purchase of 2 bracelets of copper (and) gold for Bura, the representative of Ašum.
(18) 30 shekels of silver for the purchase of 1 ox (received) by Ibgi-damu, the overseer of the kad$_4$-workers, and received by Buma-i(l) for the purchase of wine; 25 shekels of silver for the purchase of 1 ox by his representative: offering of the king for the god Hadda; 1 mina of silver for plating their 4 horns at the AMA-ra (festival).

11. *wa*
šu-ba$_4$-ti
13. *Bu$_x$-ma-ì*
níĝ-sa$_{10}$ ĝeštin
15. ŠÚ+ŠA 5 gín DILMUN kù:babbar
níĝ-sa$_{10}$ 1 gud
17. maškim-*sù*
nídba
19. en
$^{d}$*ʾÀ-da*
21. 1 ma-na kù:babbar
VIII. 1. nu$_{11}$-za 4 si-*sù*
*in*
3. AMA-*ra*

(19)
1 ma-na 13 gín DILMUN kù:babbar
5. níĝ-sa$_{10}$ 2 gud
nídba
7. en
$^{d}$*ʾÀ-da*
9. *ʾÀ-da-ni*$^{ki}$
1 ma-na kù:babbar
11. nu$_{11}$-za 4 si-*sù*
*in*
13. AMA-*ra*

(20)
14 ma-na 13 gín DILMUN kù:babbar
níĝ-sa$_{10}$
15. 7 *ʾà-da-um*
1 *mi-at* 33 íb+III-TÚG sa$_6$ gùn
IX. 1. 4 *mi-at* 74 íb+III-TÚG gùn
17 ĝír mar-tu zú-ak
3. 1 ĝír zú-ak
4 ma-na kù:babbar
5. níĝ-sa$_{10}$ ĜIŠ-ti-ḪAR
*Wa-ba-rúm*
7. šu-ba$_4$-ti
ki:lam$_7$
9. AMA-*ra*

(21)
ŠÚ+ŠA gín DILMUN kù:babbar <2>
*bu*-DI
11. *ma-lik-tum*
*Ì-la-ar*$^{ki}$

13. *in*
*ʾÀ-da-ni*$^{ki}$
15. šu-ba$_4$-ti

(22)
6 gín DILMUN kù:babbar
17. níĝ-sa$_{10}$ ĝeštin
*En-na-ma-lik*
19. šu-ba$_4$-ti
X. 1. *in*
[ ]

(23)
3. 10 gín DILMUN kù:babbar
*Na*-NE
5. *wa*
⌜Šubur⌝
7. *Na-gàr*$^{ki}$
*in*
9. níĝ-kas$_4$
*A-da-[bí-]⌜ig⌝*$^{ki}$
11. šu-ba$_4$-ti

(24)
TAR kù:babbar
13. šu-bal-ak
5 gín DILMUN kù-gi
15. *ni-zi-mu*
1 dib *Ki-ti-ir*
17. lú *I-rí-ig-gú-nu*

(25)
10 gín DILMUN kù:babbar
19. šu-bal-ak
2 gín DILMUN kù-gi
21. *ni-zi-mu*
1 dib
XI. 1. [ ]
[ ]

(26)
3. [ ]
[ ]
5. [ ]
[ ]
7$^{?}$. lú *A-ma-ʾà*

(19) 1;13 minas of silver for the purchase of 2 oxen: offering of the king for the god Hadda of the city of ʾAdani; 1 mina of silver for plating their 4 horns at the AMA-ra (festival).
(20) 14;13 minas of silver for the purchase of 7 garments, 607 kilts (and) 18 serrated mar-tu daggers; 4 minas of silver for the purchase of GIŠ-ti-ḪAR-wood: Wabarum has received at the market of the AMA-ra (festival).
(21) 20 shekels of silver for <2> toggle-pins for the queen of the city of Irar, received in the city of ʾAdani.
(22) 6 shekels of silver for the purchase of wine: Enna-malik has received in […].
(23) 10 shekels of silver for NANE and Šubur of the city of Nagar (who) have received on (the occasion of) the military expedition (against) the city of Ada[bi]k.
(24) 30 shekels of silver in exchange for 5 shekels of gold for decorating 1 plaque for Kitir, (son) of Iri-gunu.
(25) 10 shekels of silver in exchange for 2 shekels of gold for decorating 1 plaque […].
(26) […] of Amaʾa.

(27)
TAR kù:babbar íb-lá
9. ŠÚ+ŠA gín DILMUN kù:babbar níĝ-
sa$_{10}$
1 ĝír mar-tu ti kù-gi
11. *I-bí-šum*
lú *I-gi*
13. É×PAP

(28)
10 gín DILMUN kù:babbar
15. šu-bal-ak
2 gín DILMUN kù-gi
17. *ni-zi-mu*
1 dib *A-ti*
XII. 1. [ ]

(29)
[ ]
3. [ ]
[ ]
5. [ ]
[ ]

(30)
7. 13 gín DILMUN kù:babbar
nu$_{11}$-za 1 *ḫa-bù*
9. TAR kù:babbar
šu-bal-ak
11. 6 gín DILMUN kù-gi
nu$_{11}$-za *ar-ra-si-sù*
13. $^{d}$*Ra-sa-ap*
*ᵓÀ-da-ni*$^{ki}$
15. AMA-*ra*

(31)
3 ma-na kù:babbar
17. nu$_{11}$-za 1 ĜIŠ-banšur
15 gín DILMUN an-na šub
XIII. 1. [ ]
[ ]
3. [ ]

(32)
[ ]
5. [ ]
[ ]
7. *Du-⸢bí⸣-zi-kir*
lú *Ab-a-nu*

(33)
9. TAR kù:babbar
níĝ-sa$_{10}$ ĝeštin
11. *Bu*$_{x}$*-ma-i*
šu-ba$_{4}$-ti

(34)
13. 10 gín DILMUN kù:babbar
šu-bal-ak
15. 2 gín DILMUN kù-gi
*ni-zi-mu*
17. 1 dib *Du-bí-zi-kir*
lú *I-rí-ig-ma-lik*

(35)
19. TAR 3 2 NI gín DILMUN kù:babbar
XIV. 1. [ ]
[ ]
3. [ ]
[ ]
5. [ ]

(36)
[x kù:babbar níĝ-sa$_{10}$]
7. [x *ᵓà-da-um*-TÚG-I]
2 gada-TÚG 4 aktum-TÚG
9. 40 lá-2 íb+III-TÚG sa$_{6}$ gùn 3 *mi-at*
70 íb+III-TÚG gùn
10 gín DILMUN kù:babbar
11. níĝ-sa$_{10}$ ú-ḫáb
13 gín DILMUN kù:babbar níĝ-sa$_{10}$
13. 4 ĝír mar-tu kù:babbar
XV. 1. [ ]
[ ]
3. [ ]
[ ]
5. [ ]
[ ]
7. [ ]

(37)
[x kù:babbar]
9. níĝ-sa$_{10}$
1 BAR.AN

(27) 30 shekels of silver for (1) belt; 20 shekels of silver for the purchase of 1 pointed mar-tu dagger (decorated with) gold for the funerary rite of Ibišum, (son) of Igi.
(28) 10 shekels of silver in exchange for 2 shekels of gold for decorating 1 plaque for Ati […].
(29) […]
(30) 13 shekels of silver for plating 1 mace; 30 shekels of silver in exchange for 6 shekels of gold for plating its handle: (gift for) the god Rašap of the city of ᵓAdani, at the AMA-ra (festival).
(31) 3 minas of silver for plating 1 table; 15 shekels of tin to be melted [with …].
(32) […] Dubi-zikir, (son) of Abanu.
(33) 30 shekels of silver for the purchase of wine: Buma-i(l) has received.
(34) 10 shekels of silver in exchange for 2 shekels of gold for decorating 1 plaque for Dubi-zikir, (son) of Irig-malik.
(35) 33 shekels (and) 2 NI of silver […].
(36) [x silver for the purchase of x]+6 garments (and) 408 kilts; 10 shekels of silver for the purchase of dull red dye; 13 shekels of silver for the purchase of 4 mar-tu daggers (decorated with) silver […].
(37) [x silver] for the purchase of 1 mule: Reᵓi-malik has received.

11. *Rí-ì-ma-lik*
šu-ba$_4$-ti

(38)
13. 3 ma-na kù:babbar níĝ-sa$_{10}$ ĜIŠ-ti-ḪAR
*Wa-ba-rúm*
15. šu-ba$_4$-ti
ki:lam$_7$
17. $^{d}$*Ga-mi-iš*

(39)
3 ma-na ŠÚ+ŠA gín DILMUN kù:babbar
XVI. 1. [ ]
[ ]
3. [ ]
[ ]
5. [ ]
[ ]
7. [ ]

(40)
[ ]
9. [níĝ-sa$_{10}$] 2 [*gú-*]*li-lum*
*Bù-da-il*
11. *Ù-la-bù*$^{ki}$
*wa*
13. *I-si-rúm*
lú *Ib-gú-nu*
15. 10 gín DILMUN kù:babbar
šu-bal-ak
17. 2 gín DILMUN kù-gi
*ni-zi-mu*
19. nu$_{11}$-za-*sù*

(41)
r. I. 1. ˹x˺ g[ín] DILMUN kù:babbar
lul-gu-ak
3. 1 *zú-zú-ba-tum*
zàḫ
5. *Ib-rí-um*

(42)
5 gín DILMUN kù:babbar
7. šu-bal-ak
1 gín DILMUN kù-gi
9. *ni-zi-mu*
1 dib *Ḫal-za-um*

(43)
11. 8 gín DILMUN kù:babbar
*ni-zi-mu*
13. 2 <níĝ->anše-ak 4 kù-sal
[10 gín DILMUN kù:babbar]
15. šu-b[al-ak]
2 gín DILMUN kù-gi
17. *ni-z*[*i-*]*m*[*u*]
nu$_{11}$-z[a-]*sù*
19. [x gín DILMUN kù:babbar]
[kin$_5$-ak]
II. 1. 3 *zú-zú-ba-tum*
*I-bí-zi-kir*
3. dumu-nita
*Ib-rí-um*

(44)
5. 15 gín DILMUN kù:babbar
níĝ-ba
7. *Wa-ru*$_{12}$*-tum*
*Ma-rí*$^{ki}$

(45)
9. ŠÚ+ŠA gín DILMUN kù:babbar
níĝ-sa$_{10}$ raš-SAR Kur$^{ki}$
11. 1 ma-na TAR 6 gín DILMUN kù:babbar
níĝ-sa$_{10}$ 3 gud
13. ki:lam$_7$
SA.ZA$_x^{ki}$

(46)
15. 5 gín DILMUN kù:babbar
níĝ-ba
17. *I-ku-il*
*Ma-rí*$^{ki}$

(47)
19. ŠÚ+ŠA gín DILMUN kù:babbar
níĝ-sa$_{10}$ 85[+1]
III. 1. íb+II-TÚG babbar
ir$_{11}$-ir$_{11}$
3. en

(38) 3 minas of silver for the purchase of GIŠ-ti-ḪAR-wood: Wabarum has received at the market of the god Kamiš.
(39) 3;20 minas of silver […].
(40) [x silver for the purchase] of 2 [bra]celets for Buda-il of the city of Ulabu and Isirum, (son) of Ibgunu; 10 shekels of silver in exchange for 2 shekels of gold for decorating their lamination.
(41) [x] shekels of silver as replacement of 1 lost ... (*zú-zú-ba-tum*) for Ibrium.
(42) 5 shekels of silver in exchange for 1 shekel of gold for decorating 1 plaque for Ḫalzaum.
(43) 8 shekels of silver for decorating 2 bridles (and) 4 buckles; [10 shekels of silver] in exchange for 2 shekels of gold for decorating their lamination; [x shekels of silver for making] 3 ... (*zú-zú-ba-tum*) for Ibbi-zikir, son of Ibrium.
(44) 15 shekels of silver: gift for Warutum of the city of Mari.
(45) 20 shekels of silver for the purchase of leek from the mountain region; 1;36 minas of silver for the purchase of 3 oxen at the market of the Palace.
(46) 5 shekels of silver: gift for Iku-il of the city of Mari.
(47) 20 shekels of silver for the purchase of 86 kilts for the servants of the king.

(48)
17 gín DILMUN kù:babbar
5. níĝ-sa$_{10}$ 1 ĝír mar-tu kù-gi zú
LAGAB×A
*Ḫáb-ra-ar*
7. lú *Ib-ga-iš-lu*

(49)
ŠÚ+ŠA gín DILMUN kù:babbar
9. níĝ-sa$_{10}$ 7 íb+II-TÚG sa$_6$ gùn
7 íb+II-TÚG gùn
11. ki:lam$_7$
SA.ZA$_x^{ki}$

(50)
13. 3 gín DILMUN kù:babbar
nu$_{11}$-za 1 ĝír mar-tu
15. 5 gín DILMUN kù:babbar
šu-bal-ak
17. 1 gín DILMUN kù-gi 1 kù-sal
IV. 1. níĝ-ba
$^{d}$*ᵓA$_5$-da-"bal"*
3. *Lu-ba-an*$^{ki}$
*Ib-rí-um*
5. ì-na-sum
*in* ud
7. ne:saĝ-*sù*

(51)
2 ma-na TAR kù:babbar
9. šu-bal-ak
TAR kù-gi 1 íb-lá
11. BÍL-*ma-lik*
lú *Ba-ḫa-ga*
13. *in* ud
*Gú-rá-ma-an*$^{ki}$
15. tuš-LÚ×TIL

(52)
10 gín DILMUN kù:babbar
17. níĝ-ba
*Wa-ru$_{12}$-tum*
19. *wa*
maškim
21. *Ma-rí*$^{ki}$

(53)
5 gín DILMUN
V. 1. kù:babbar
níĝ-ba
3. *Daš-na*
*Ma-rí*$^{ki}$
5. *in*
níĝ-kas$_4$
7. *Gú-rá-ma-an*$^{ki}$
šu-ba$_4$-ti

(54)
9. 1 ma-na ŠÚ+ŠA 5 gín DILMUN
kù:babbar
nu$_{11}$-za 1 ĜIŠ-banšur
11. 1 ma-na ŠÚ+ŠA gín DILMUN
kù:babbar
šu-bal-ak
13. ŠÚ+ŠA gín DILMUN kù-gi
nu$_{11}$-za 3 saĝ lu$_5$
15. 10 gín DILMUN an-na
šub
17. *si-in*
urudu-*sù*
19. níĝ-b[a]
$^{d}$*ᵓA$_5$-da-"bal"*
VI. 1. *La-ru$_{12}$-ga-du*$^{ki}$
en
3. ì-na-sum

(55)
1 ma-na 50 gín DILMUN kù:babbar
5. šu-bal-ak
ŠÚ+ŠA 2 gín DILMUN kù-gi
7. 1 dib *I-ti-gi-ma-lik*
ugula *Mug-rí-ì*$^{ki}$

(56)
9. 8 gín DILMUN kù-gi
2 zi-bar

(48) 17 shekels of silver for the purchase of 1 serrated mar-tu dagger (decorated with) gold (and) horn for Ḫabrar, (son) of Ibga-išlu.
(49) 20 shekels of silver for the purchase of 14 kilts at the market of the Palace.
(50) 3 shekels of silver for plating 1 mar-tu dagger; 5 shekels of silver in exchange for 1 shekel of gold for 1 buckle: gift for the god ᵓAdabal of the city of Luban, Ibrium has given on the occasion of his first-fruit offering.
(51) 2;30 minas of silver in exchange for 30 (shekels of) gold for 1 belt for BIL-malik, (son) of Baḫaga when he occupied the city of Guraman.
(52) 10 shekels of silver: gift for Warutum and (his) representative of the city of Mari.
(53) 5 shekels of silver: gift for Dašna of the city of Mari (who) has received on (the occasion of) the military expedition (against) the city of Guraman.
(54) 1;25 minas of silver for plating 1 table; 1;20 minas of silver in exchange for 20 shekels of gold for plating 3 heads of androcephalus bulls; 10 shekels of tin to be melted with its copper: gift for the god ᵓAdabal of the city of Larugadu, the king has given.
(55) 1;50 minas of silver in exchange for 22 shekels of gold for 1 plaque for Itigi-malik, the overseer of the city of Mugri-il.
(56) 8 shekels of gold for 2 zi-bar goblets: gift for the Lord of the city of MANE, Dusigu has given.

11. níĝ-ba
$^{d}$BAD *Má*-NE$^{ki}$
13. *Du-si-gú*
ì-na-sum

(57)
15. 4 ma-na kù:babbar
níĝ-sa$_{10}$ še
17. ĝuruš-ĝuruš-*sù*
*wa*
VII. 1. da[m]-*sù*
*Za-ba-rúm*
3. še-<SAĜ×>ḪA-mul

(58)
10 gín DILMUN kù:babbar
5. šu-bal-ak
2 gín DILMUN kù-gi
7. *ni-zi-mu*
1 dib *Ig-rí-iš*
9. lú *I-rí-ig-gú-nu*

(59)
1 ½ gín DILMUN kù:babbar
11. šu-bal-ak
½ gín DILMUN kù-gi
13. *ni-zi-mu*
1 dib *Zé-da-ar*
15. lú-kar

(60)
TAR 3 3 NI gín DILMUN kù:babbar
17. šu-bal-ak
VIII. 1. 6 2 NI gín DILMUN kù-gi
2 *gú-li-lum*
3. $^{d}$*Áš-da-bíl*

(61)
4 gín DILMUN an-na
5. šub
ĜIŠ-zú
7. 1 gín DILMUN kù:babbar
nu$_{11}$-za 1 zag
9. ĜIŠ-gígir-II
*I-nu-ud-da-mu*
11. *Kak-mi-um*$^{ki}$

(62)
6 2 NI gín DILMUN kù:babbar
13. 2 *gú-li-lum*
$^{d}$*Am-ma-rí-ig*

(63)
15. 3 gín DILMUN kù:babbar
níĝ-sa$_{10}$ 1 ĜIŠ-banšur
17. níĝ-ba
*I-bí-zi-kir*
19. dumu-nita
*Ib-rí-um*
IX. 1. $^{d\text{ʾ}}$*A*$_{5}$*-da-"bal"*
*La-ru*$_{12}$*-ga-du*$^{ki}$

(64)
3. 4 ma-na 52 gín DILMUN kù:babbar
níĝ-sa$_{10}$
5. 3 *ʾà-da-um*-TÚG-I
22 íb+II-TÚG sa$_{6}$ gùn
7. 2 *mi-at* 31 íb+III-TÚG gùn
1 ma-na kù:babbar
9. níĝ-sa$_{10}$ ĜIŠ-ti-ḪAR
*Wa-ba-rúm*
11. šu-ba$_{4}$-ti
ki:lam$_{7}$
13. $^{d}$*Áš-da-bíl*

(65)
4 gín DILMUN kù:babbar
15. lú ĜIŠ-kiri$_{6}$
*Ba-ga-ma*
17. šu-ba$_{4}$-ti

(66)
X. 1. 2 ma-na kù:babbar
šu-bal-ak
3. ŠÚ+ŠA 4 gín DILMUN kù-gi <1 dib>
en
5. *Ša-bir*$_{5}$*-ti-um*$^{ki}$

(57) 4 minas of silver for the purchase of barley for his workers and his spouse, debited to Zabarum.
(58) 10 shekels of silver in exchange for 2 shekels of gold for decorating 1 plaque for Igriš, (son) of Iri-gunu.
(59) 1 ½ shekel of silver in exchange for ½ shekel of gold for decorating 1 plaque for Zedar, the trader.
(60) 33 shekels (and) 3 NI of silver in exchange for 6 shekels (and) 2 NI of gold for 2 bracelets for the god Ašdabil.
(61) 4 shekels of tin to be melted for hooks; 1 shekel of silver for plating 1 side of a chariot of Inud-damu of the city of Kakmium.
(62) 6 shekels (and) 2 NI of silver for 2 bracelets for the god Ammarik.
(63) 3 shekels of silver for the purchase of 1 table: gift of Ibbi-zikir, son of Ibrium, for the god ʾAdabal of the city of Larugadu.
(64) 4;52 minas of silver for the purchase of 3 garments (and) 253 kilts; 1 mina of silver for the purchase of GIŠ-ti-ḪAR-wood: Wabarum has received at the market of the god Ašdabil.
(65) 4 shekels of silver for the garden, Bagama has received.
(66) 2 minas of silver in exchange for 24 shekels of gold <for 1 plaque> for the king of the city of Šabirtium.

(67)
15 gín DILMUN kù:babbar
7. nu$_{11}$-za 1 *ḫa-bù*
TAR kù:babbar
9. šu-bal-ak
6 gín DILMUN kù-gi
11. nu$_{11}$-za *ar-ra-su-sù*
níĝ-ba
13. $^{d}$*ʾÀ-da*
ŠÚ+ŠA 5 gín DILMUN kù:babbar
15. *ʾà-na-gu*
si 2 gud
17. lú en
nídba
19. $^{d}$*ʾÀ-da*

(68)
ŠÚ+ŠA 5 gín DILMUN kù:babbar
XI. 1. *ʾa$_5$-na-gu*
si 2 gud
3. lú *Ib-rí-um*
nídba
5. $^{d}$*ʾÀ-da*
*in*
7. iti *ʾa$_5$-nun*

(69)
4 gín DILMUN kù:babbar
9. lú ĜIŠ-kiri$_6$
*in*
11. *Am$_6$-ma-šu*$^{ki}$
[šu]-ba$_4$-ti

(70)
13. 14 gín DILMUN kù:babbar
níĝ-sa$_{10}$ 1 *gu-zi-tum*-TÚG
15. ⌜4⌝ gada-TÚG
14 ma-na kù:babbar
17. níĝ-sa$_{10}$ 61 gud
ki:lam$_7$
19. $^{d}$*ʾÀ-da*
*in*
21. iti *ʾa$_5$-nun*

(71)
1 ma-na ŠA.PI 8 gín DILMUN
kù:babbar
XII. 1. níĝ-sa$_{10}$ 43 *ʾà-da-um*-TÚG-I
*in*
3. *Ša-bir$_5$-ti-um*$^{ki}$
*Puzur$_4$-ra-il*
5. *Na-gàr*$^{ki}$

(72)
ŠÚ+ŠA gín DILMUN kù:babbar
7. šu-bal-ak
5 gín DILMUN kù-gi
9. nu$_{11}$-za
*ba-na-a*
11. $^{d}$*Gú-šar*
ŠÚ+ŠA 3 gín DILMUN kù:babbar
13. nu$_{11}$-za 2 šu-*sù*

(73)
15 gín DILMUN kù:babbar
15. šu-bal-ak
3 gín DILMUN kù-gi
17. *ni-zi-mu*
nu$_{11}$-za 2 *gú-li-lum*
19. *I-du-bù*

(74)
7 gín DILMUN kù:babbar
21. šu-bal-ak
XIII. 1. 1 ½ gín DILMUN kù-gi
*ni-zi-mu*
3. nu$_{11}$-za
2 *gú-li-lum*
5. *En-gi-iš-ar*
a:zu$_5$

(75)
7. ŠA.PI gín DILMUN kù:babbar
nu$_{11}$-za 20 *gú-li-lum*
9. ME-sig$^{!}$
é en

(67) 15 shekels of silver for plating 1 mace; 30 shekels of silver in exchange for 6 shekels of gold for plating its handle: gift for the god Hadda; 25 shekels of silver for the circular stand of the 4 horns of 2 bulls: offering of the king for the god Hadda.
(68) 25 shekels of silver for the circular stand of the horns of 2 bulls: offering of Ibrium for the god Hadda, in month VIII.
(69) 4 shekels of silver for the garden, received in the city of Ammašu.
(70) 14 shekels of silver for the purchase of 5 garments; 14 minas of silver for the purchase of 61 oxen, at the market of the god Hadda, in month VIII.
(71) 1;48 minas of silver for the purchase of 43 garments in the city of Šabirtium, Puzurra-il of the city of Nagar (has received).
(72) 20 shekels of silver in exchange for 5 shekels of gold for plating the face of the god Gušar; 23 shekels of silver for plating its hands.
(73) 15 shekels of silver in exchange for 3 shekels of gold for decorating with lamination 2 bracelets for Idubu.
(74) 7 shekels of silver in exchange for 1 ½ shekel of gold for decorating with lamination 2 bracelets for Engi-išar, the physician.
(75) 40 shekels of silver for plating 20 bracelets for the watchmen of the king's house.

(76)
11. 10 gín DILMUN kù:babbar
2 *ḃu*-DI
13. 2 *ti-ša-na*
níĝ-ba
15. $^{d}$*Ga-na-na*
ĜIŠ.DUG.DU maḫ

(77)
17. 15 gín DILMUN kù:babbar
šu-bal-ak
19. 3 gín DILMUN kù-gi
nu$_{11}$-za 1 ĝír mar-tu
21. níĝ-ba
$^{d}$ʾ*A*$_{5}$-*da*-“*bal*”
23. ʾ*À-ma-du*$^{ki}$
*Ib-rí-um*
XIV. 1. in-na-sum

(78)
2 gín DILMUN kù:babbar
3. nu$_{11}$-za 1 ĝír mar-tu
2 ½ gín DILMUN kù:babbar
5. šu-bal-ak
½ kù-gi 1 kù-sal
7. níĝ-ba
$^{d}$*Ra-sa-ap*
9. ʾ*À-da-ni*$^{ki}$
*in*
11. SA.ZA$_{x}^{ki}$
*Ib-rí-um*

(79)
13. 2 gín DILMUN kù:babbar
nu$_{11}$-za 1 ĝír mar-tu
15. 2 ½ gín DILMUN kù:babbar
šu-bal-ak
17. ½ kù-gi 1 kù-sal
níĝ-ba
19. $^{d}$*Ra-sa-ap*
*gú-núm*$^{ki}$
21. en
in-na-sum
23. ne:saĝ-*sù*

(80)
15 gín DILMUN kù:babbar
25. šu-bal-ak
XV. 1. 3 gín DILMUN kù-gi
*ni-zi-mu*
3. 1 dib
*Íl-mi*

(81)
5. 10 gín DILMUN kù:babbar
šu-bal-ak
7. 2 kù-gi
*ni-zi-mu*
9. 1 dib
*Ib-lu*$_{5}$-*zú*

(82)
11. 1 ½ gín DILMUN kù:babbar
níĝ-sa$_{10}$ *a-gú*
13. TAR 5 gín DILMUN kù:babbar
*ni-zi-mu*
15. 3 ĜIŠ-šú 3 níĝ-bànda
10 gín DILMUN kù:babbar
17. níĝ-sa$_{10}$
*in*
19. é
$^{d}$*Ra-sa-ap*
21. ʾ*À-da-ni*$^{ki}$
SA.ZA$_{x}^{ki}$

(83)
23. 1 ma-na kù:babbar
níĝ-ba
25. *Gú-šu*$^{?}$

(84)
10 gín DILMUN kù:babbar
27. níĝ-ba
*Wa-ru*$_{12}$-*tum*
XVI. 1. *Ma-rí*$^{ki}$
šu-mu-tak$_{4}$
3. íb+III-TÚG
*Ga-ga-ba-an*$^{ki}$

(76) 10 shekels of silver for 2 toggle-pins (decorated with) 2 (couples) of ... (*ti-ša-na*): gift for the goddess Ganana (on the occasion of) the great presentation.
(77) 15 shekels of silver in exchange for 3 shekels of gold for plating 1 mar-tu dagger: gift for the god ʾAdabal of the city of Amadu, Ibrium has given.
(78) 2 shekels of silver for plating 1 mar-tu dagger; 2 ½ shekels of silver in exchange for ½ (shekel of) gold for 1 buckle: gift for the god Rašap of the city of ʾAdani at the Palace, Ibrium (has given).
(79) 2 shekels of silver for plating 1 mar-tu dagger; 2 ½ shekels of silver in exchange for ½ (shekel of) gold for 1 buckle: gift for the god Rašap *gunum*, the king has given (on the occasion of) his first-fruit offering.
(80) 15 shekels of silver in exchange for 3 shekels of gold for decorating 1 plaque for Ilmi.
(81) 10 shekels of silver in exchange for 2 (shekels of) gold for decorating 1 plaque for Ibluzu.
(82) 1 ½ shekel of silver for the purchase of antimony paste; 35 shekels of silver for decorating 3 jugs (and) 3 goblets; 10 shekels of silver for purchases in the temple of the god Rašap of the city of ʾAdani of the Palace.
(83) 1 mina of silver: gift for Gušu.
(84) 10 shekels of silver: gift for Warutum of the city of Mari (who) has handed over kilt(s) (at) the city of Gagaban.

(85)
5. 1 ma-na TAR kù:babbar
níĝ-ba
7. diĝir-diĝir-diĝir

(86)
4 ma-na ŠÚ+ŠA gín DILMUN
kù:babbar
9. šu-bal-ak
52 gín DILMUN kù-gi
11. *ni-zi-mu*
1 *zi-ru*$_{12}$
13. *wa*
2 *gi-zu*
15. *wa*
LAGAB-LAGAB

(87)
17. 1 ma-na kù:babbar[a)]
níĝ-sa$_{10}$ siki
19. *I-bu*$_{16}$*-bù*$^{ki}$
ugula é
21. en
šu-ba$_{4}$-ti[a)]

(88)
XVII. 1. (blank) AN.ŠÈ.GÚ 1 *mi-at* 32 ma-na
50 gín DILMUN kù:babbar
è
3. 2 mu
2 dub[a)]

*a*) written in a second time

(85) 1;30 minas of silver: gift for the gods.
(86) 4;20 minas of silver in exchange for 52 shekels of gold for decorating 1 *zi-ru*$_{12}$ vessel and 2 *gi-zu* vessels and blocks.
(87) 1 mina of silver for the purchase of wool from the city of Ibubu, the overseer of the king's house has received.
(88) Total: 132;50 minas of silver: expenditure during the second year (of Ibrium), second document.

## Commentary

The colophon (§ 88) states that this is the "2nd document" of the second year of minister Ibrium: 2 mu 2 dub. The expended (è) silver and the silver with which the expended gold was valued (in a ratio of 5 : 1) amounted to 132;50 minas (62.431 kg). The total amount of silver expended in the first part of the year (text XXI 4) is in lacuna.

This document preserves the writing *La-ru*$_{12}$*-ga-du*$^{ki}$ instead of the later *A-ru*$_{12}$*-ga-du*$^{ki}$.

Ibrium performed offerings to several deities, and received some gifts (a vessel, § 15; and a *zú-zú-ba-tum* in substitution of a lost one, § 41). Section 14 should be interpreted as follows: "Two toggle-pins of silver (for) the mother of Ibbi-zikir (i.e. Ibrium's wife, mother of the son who will succeed Ibrium as minister) on the occasion of the marriage of a daughter of Ibrium who resided in GitiNE". This small centre was bound to Ibrium, see TM.75.G.1759+ r. I 6–9: "1 garment to the son of Ibrium in G(itiNE)."; TM.75.G.1795+ obv. II 1–3: "[garments to the spouse] of Ibrium who gave birth in G."; TM.75.G.10078 r. III 1–9): "a garment (to) ENdaza of G. who brought the news of the omen (for) Ibrium (concerning his) departure against Adaradu (máš *Ib-rí-um* è *al*$_{6}$ *A-da-ra-du*$^{ki}$)". According to TM.75.G.2159 obv. VII 1–IX 2, several "men", ĝuruš-ĝuruš, resided in GitiNE on behalf of the Central Administration.

Dusigu, "the king's mother", received a new harness for her chariot (§ 12); she offered a gift to the "Lord", $^{d}$BAD, of MaNE (§ 56).

Ibbi-zikir, the son of Ibrium, received some gifts (§ 43), and performed an offering to ᵓAdabal of Larugadu (§ 63).

The messengers of Mari who came to Ebla were *Daš-na* and *Wa-ru*$_{12}$*-tum* (§ 3); *Daš-na* (§ 53); *Wa-ru*$_{12}$*-tum* (§§ 44, 52, 84); *I-ku-il* (§ 46). Those of Nagar were *Na*-NE and Šubur (§ 23); *Puzur*$_{4}$*-ra-il* (§ 71).

§ 13. Irik-malik and his gang of workers (*ìr-a-núm*) are also mentioned in *ARET* XX 5 (dated to Ibrium) r. VIII 11–13 (the number of the workers is not preserved).

§§ 18, 19. The value of the two oxen which the king offered to the god Hadda of Ebla was respectively of 30 shekels (235 g) and 25 shekels (196 g.) of silver, while that for the two oxen sacrificed to Hadda of ᵓAdani (§ 19) was of 1;13 minas (571 g). The decoration for each of the two pairs of horns needed 1 mina (470 g) of silver.

§ 21 The lady who married the crown prince of Irar (probably a daughter of Ibrium, see above text 4 §§ 38–40) came to (the temple of Hadda in) ᵓAdani and received two toggle-pins of silver.

§ 23. Adabik, a town belonging to Ebla, rebelled (see Archi 2021a, p. 201), and two messengers of the city of Nagar took part in the military expedition. This city had been already defeated (til) at the time of minister Arrukum, see *ARET* XV,2 46 § 6.

§ 27. Death of Ibišum (son) of Igi, an official mentioned also in *ARET* XV,1 29 § 36.

§§ 51, 53. Ga/uraman, a town administrated by an "overseer", ugula, (see *ARES* II, pp. 232, 253) was occupied, and an Eblaite official, BÍL-*ma-lik*, received a belt decorated with 235 g of gold. The town had been defeated the previous year, see text no. 3 § 17 (see also Archi 2021a, pp. 199–200).

§ 53. Dašna, a messenger of Mari, who joined the military expedition against the city of Ga/uraman, received 5 shekels (39 g.) of silver.

§ 54. A "table", ĜIŠ-banšur, devoted by the king to the god ᵓAdabal of Larugadu, needed 1;25 minas (666 g) of silver for its decoration, and 20 shekels (157 g) of gold for three heads of androcephalus bull applied to it. This table needed 10 shekels (78 g) of tin to be alloyed with the copper. A similar passage occurs in text no. 14 § 64.

§ 56. *Má*-NE$^{ki}$, the Ebla's harbour on the Euphrates by Imar, was the seat of a sanctuary dedicated to Išḫara, and of the cult of a "Lord", $^{d}$BAD (see *ARES* II, pp. 379–380).

§ 57. *Za-ba-rúm* received 4 minas (1.880 kg) of silver for acquiring barley for his workers and spouse. He received other 3 minas (1.410 kg) of silver in the year Ibrium 06 for having again to provide barley, according to text no. 9 § 70. According to TM.75.G.1959 o. IV 2–5, this official was at the head of a "gate", ká.

§ 66. A king (en) of Šabirtium is also mentioned in *ARET* XXII 11 (Ibbi-zikir 11) r. VI 6–7: en *Ša-bir*$_5$*-tum*$^{ki}$. This city has to be placed in the region of Nagar (cf. § 71).

§ 72. The god *Gú-šar* is the Ugaritic *kṯr*. The Ebla documents mention usually the pl. feminine $^{d}$*Gú-ša-ra-tum*, Ugaritic *kṯrt*, see Archi 2018c.

# 6
## (Plates XI–XII)

(1)
o. I. 1. 1 ma-na kù:babbar
saĝ kù:babbar
3. $^{\text{d}}$*Ku-ra*

(2)
TAR kù:babbar
5. níĝ-sa$_{10}$ 1 *mi-at* 20 ḪU.UD-ḪU.UD
4 ma-na kù:babbar
7. níĝ-sa$_{10}$ gig
*Ib-bí-um*
9. šu-ba$_{4}$-ti

(3)
3 ma-na kù:babbar
11. šu-bal-ak
3 ma-na an-na
13. en
*Ma-nu-wa-ad*$^{\text{ki}}$

(4)
15. 1 ma-na kù:babbar
šu-bal-ak
17. 1 ma-na an-na
II. 1. en
*Kak-mi-um*$^{\text{ki}}$

(5)
3. 1 ma-na kù:babbar
níĝ-ba
5. ḫúb-ki
*in* ud
7. *a-<lu->nu*
ĝiš
9. ba:tuš

(6)
ŠÚ+ŠA gín DILMUN kù:babbar
11. níĝ-sa$_{10}$ 2 dam túg-nu-tag *Ma-rí*$^{\text{ki}}$

(7)
3 gín DILMUN kù:babbar
13. saĝ kù:babbar
$^{\text{d}}$*Ku-ra*
15. 2 mu-ti

(8)
5 ma-na kù:babbar
17. níĝ-ba
*A-ḫa-ar-si*

(9)
19. 3 ma-na kù:babbar
níĝ-ba
21. *ʾÀ-sa*

(10)
2 ma-na kù:babbar
23. níĝ-ba
III. 1. *Íl-a*

(11)
1 ma-na kù:babbar
3. níĝ-ba
ĝuruš-ĝuruš maškim-*sù*
5. *Ma-rí*$^{\text{ki}}$
*in* ud
7. nídba ì-ĝiš
*Ma-rí*$^{\text{ki}}$

(12)
9. 10 gín DILMUN kù:babbar
níĝ-ba
11. *Du-tum*
*Ma-rí*$^{\text{ki}}$

(13)
13. 50 gín DILMUN kù:babbar
nu$_{11}$-za

(1) 1 mina of silver for the silver head of the god Kura.
(2) 30 (shekels of) silver for the purchase of 120 ḪU.UD-ḪU.UD; 4 minas of silver for the purchase of wheat: Ibbium has received.
(3) 3 minas of silver in exchange for 3 minas of tin for the king of the city of Manuwat.
(4) 1 mina of silver in exchange for 1 mina of tin for the king of the city of Kakmium.
(5) 1 mina of silver: gift for the acrobat who stays on the pole.
(6) 20 shekels of silver for the purchase of 2 female weavers from the city of Mari.
(7) 3 shekels of silver for the silver head of the god Kura: second delivery.
(8) 5 minas of silver: gift for Aḫarsi.
(9) 3 minas of silver: gift for ʾAsa.
(10) 2 minas of silver: gift for Ila.
(11) 1 mina of silver: gift for men (and) their representatives of the city of Mari on the occasion of the offering of the oil of the city of Mari.
(12) 10 shekels of silver: gift for Dutum of the city of Mari.
(13) 50 shekels of silver for plating the tablet of the oath between the cities of Ebla and Mari for the temple of the god Kura.

15. 1 dub
lú
17. nam-kud
*Ib-la*$^{ki}$
19. *wa*
*Ma-rí*$^{ki}$
21. é
$^{d}$*Ku-ra*

(14)
23. 5 ma-na kù:babbar níĝ-ba
IV. 1. *Zú-gú-uš*
*Na-gàr*$^{ki}$

(15)
3. TAR kù:babbar
*Ga-ga-ba-an*$^{ki}$
5. TAR kù:babbar
*A-bù-li-um*$^{ki}$
7. TAR kù:babbar
*Na-ba-ti-um*$^{ki}$
9. TAR kù:babbar
*La-dab*$_6$*-bí-um*$^{ki}$
11. TAR kù:babbar
*Ba-sa-ḫi-um*$^{ki}$
13. TAR kù:babbar
*Zàr-ʾà-*NI*-um*$^{ki}$
15. TAR kù:babbar
*Ḫi-la-zi-um*$^{ki}$
17. 2 gín DILMUN kù:babbar
níĝ-kaskal
19. *Ìr-am*$_6$*-ma-lik*
DU.DU
21. *Na-gàr*$^{ki}$

(16)
V. 1. TAR kù:babbar
ZU.PIRIĜ
3. kin$_5$-ak
23 dib a-gar$_5$-gar$_5$ kù-gi
5. ME-sig
é
7. en

(17)
15 gín DILMUN kù:babbar
9. níĝ-kaskal
*ʾÀ-daš*
11. DU.DU
*si-in*
13. *Ar-mi*$^{ki}$

(18)
17 gín DILMUN kù:babbar
15. 1 an-zam$_x$
*Di-ni-íb-du-lum*
17. nin-ni
en

(19)
19. 10 ma-na kù:babbar
níĝ-sa$_{10}$ 20 ĝír mar-tu kù-gi
21. 1 ma-na kù:babbar
VI. 1. *zi-tum*
20 ĝír mar-tu *ba-du-u*$_9$ kù:babbar
kù-gi
3 13 ma-na ŠÚ+ŠA gín DILMUN
kù:babbar
kin$_5$-ak
5. 20 íb-lá 20 ĝír-kun ĜÁ×LÁ ŠA.PI
11 ma-na ŠA.PI kù:babbar
7. kin$_5$-ak
10 *gú-li-lum*-II esi TAR
9. *wa*
10 *gú-li-lum*-II esi ŠÚ+ŠA
11. *wa*
20 *gú-li-lum* 10-I esi
13. [ ]

(20)
VII. 1. 2 ma-na kù:babbar
níĝ-sa$_{10}$ 1 *za-ḫa-da ra-ʾà-tum* kù-gi
3. níĝ-ba
$^{d}$*ʾÀ-da*
5. ì-na-sum

(14) 5 minas of silver: gift for Zuguš of the city of Nagar.
(15) 30 (shekels of) silver for (someone of) the city of Gagaban, 30 (shekels of) silver for (someone of) the city of Abulium, 30 (shekels of) silver for (someone of) the city of Nabatium, 30 (shekels of) silver for (someone of) the city of Ladabium, 30 (shekels of) silver for (someone of) the city of Basaḫium, 30 (shekels of) silver for (someone of) the city of ZarʾaNIum, 30 (shekels of) silver for (someone of) the city of Ḫilazium; 2 shekels of silver: travel provision for Iram-malik (who) went to the city of Nagar.
(16) 30 (shekels of) silver for the hangers of 23 plaques (decorated with) copper (and) gold for the watchmen of the king's house.
(17) 15 shekels of silver: travel provision for ʾAdaš (who) went to the city of Armi.
(18) 17 shekels of silver for 1 an-zam$_x$ goblet for Tinib-dulum, sister of the king.
(19) 10 minas of silver for the purchase of 20 mar-tu daggers (decorated with) gold; 1 mina of silver in alloy for 20 *b.* mar-tu daggers (decorated with) silver and gold; 13;20 minas of silver for making 20 belts (and) 20 dagger pendants weighing 40 (shekels); 11;40 minas of silver for making 10 double bracelets of 30 (shekels) each (and) diorite and 10 single bracelets of 20 (shekels) each (and) diorite and 20 single bracelets of 10 (shekels) each (and) diorite […].
(20) 2 minas of silver for the purchase of 1 battle-axe (decorated with) shells (and) gold: gift given to the god Hadda.

(21)
ŠU+ŠA 5 gín DILMUN kù:babbar
7. níĝ-sa$_{10}$ 1 ĝír mar-tu ti kù-gi
*Ru$_{12}$-zi-ma-lik*
9. dumu-nita
*I-gi*

(22)
11. TAR kù:babbar
níĝ-sa$_{10}$ 1 ĝír mar-tu ti kù-gi
13. *Ib-gi-da-mu*
lú *Si-gi*

(23)
15. 5 gín DILMUN kù:babbar
VIII. 1. nu$_{11}$-za 1 ĜIŠ-banšur
níĝ-ba
3. $^{d}$ʾ*À-da*
lú *Lu-ub*$^{ki}$
5. *wa*
nu$_{11}$-za 1 ĝír mar-tu
7. níĝ-ba
$^{d}$*Wa-da-ʾà-an*
9. lú
*Ga-ra-mu*$^{ki}$

(24)
11. 1 ma-na 50 kù:babbar
níĝ-ba
13. diĝir-diĝir-diĝir-diĝir

(25)
2 ½ gín DILMUN kù:babbar
15. níĝ-sa$_{10}$ 1 kir$_{11}$ sa$_6$ siki

(26)
5 gín DILMUN kù:babbar
17. níĝ-kaskal
*A-ir-ra*
19. *wa*
*A-zú-bù-lu*
21. [*Ù-t*]*i-*[*g*]*ú*$^{ki}$
[*w*]*a*
23. *A-zú*

IX. 1. DU.DU
*Ar-mi*$^{ki}$

(27)
3. ŠU+ŠA gín DILMUN kù:babbar
šu-bal-ak
5. 1 ma-na an<-na>
5 gín DILMUN kù:babbar
7. níĝ-ba
*A-mu-ra*
9. *Du-ub*$^{ki}$

(28)
2 gín DILMUN kù:babbar
11. nu$_{11}$-za
1 zag
13. ĜIŠ-gígir-II
*Ib-rí-um*

(29)
15. 1 ½ gín DILMUN kù:babbar
nu$_{11}$-za
17. 1 zag
ĜIŠ-gígir-II
19. en
*Kab-lu$_5$-ul*$^{ki}$

(30)
21. 10 ma-na kù:babbar
níĝ-sa$_{10}$
X. 1. 5 *mi-at* ma-na a-gar$_5$-gar$_5$

(31)
10 ma-na kù:babbar
3. zi-du$_8$
en
5. $^{d}$ʾ*À-da*

(32)
10 gín DILMUN kù:babbar
7. *ru$_{12}$-du-ga-tum*
ĝír mar-tu kù-gi
9. 3 ma-na kù:babbar
níĝ-ba

(21) 25 shekels of silver for the purchase of 1 pointed mar-tu dagger (decorated with) gold for Ruzi-malik, son of Igi.
(22) 30 (shekels of) silver for the purchase of 1 pointed mar-tu dagger (decorated with) gold for Ibgi-damu, (son) of Sigi.
(23) 5 shekels of silver for plating 1 table: gift for the god Hadda of the city of Lub, and for plating 1 mar-tu dagger: gift for the god Wadaʾan of the city of Garamu.
(24) 1;50 minas of silver: gift for the gods.
(25) 2 ½ shekels of silver for the purchase of 1 female lamb (with) wool of good quality.
(26) 5 shekels of silver: travel provision for Airra and Azu-bulu of the city of Utig and Azu (who) went to the city of Armi.
(27) 20 shekels of silver in exchange for 1 mina of tin; 5 shekels of silver: gift for Amura of the city of Dub.
(28) 2 shekels of silver for plating 1 side of a chariot of Ibrium.
(29) 1 ½ shekel of silver for plating 1 side of a chariot of the king of the city of Kablul.
(30) 10 minas of silver for the purchase of 500 minas of copper.
(31) 10 minas of silver for the entitlement by the king to the god Hadda.
(32) 10 shekels of silver for a ... (*ru$_{12}$-da-ga-tum*) of a mar-tu dagger (decorated with) gold; 3 minas of silver: gift for Wabarum of the city of Mari; 1 mina of silver: gift for ʾAsa, his representative.

11. *Wa-ba-rúm*
*Ma-rí*$^{ki}$
13. 1 ma-na kù:babbar
níĝ-ba
15. *ˀÀ-sa*
maškim-*sù*

(33)
17. 2 ma-na kù:babbar
níĝ-ba
19. *I-ti*
ga:eš$_{8}$
21. *Ma-rí*$^{ki}$

(34)
XI. 1. 1 ma-na kù:babbar
níĝ-sa$_{10}$ ĜIŠ-ti-ḪAR
3. ki:lam$_{7}$
$^{d}$*A-da-ma*
5. *ˀÀ-da-ni*$^{ki}$
*Wa-ba-rúm*
7. šu-ba$_{4}$-ti

(35)
ŠA.PI gín DILMUN kù:babbar
9. 2 *bu*-DI
10 gín DILMUN kù:babbar
11. 1 an-zam$_{x}$
50 gín DILMUN kù:babbar
13. nu$_{11}$-za 1 ĜIŠ-banšur
*wa*
15. 1 *ḫa-bù*
$^{d}$*Iš:šára*
17. [*Má-*]NE$^{ki}$

(36)
5 gín DILMUN kù:babbar
19. níĝ-kaskal
*Ni-zi-ma-il*
21. DU.DU
XII. 1. *Ma-rí*$^{ki}$

(37)
1 ma-na ŠA.PI gín DILMUN
kù:babbar
3. níĝ-sa$_{10}$ 1 *mi-at* si-si ĝír mar-tu kù-gi

(38)
50 gín DILMUN kù:babbar
5. 1 íb-lá *si-ti-tum* ĝír-⌜kun⌝
*Sá-gú-šum*
7. É×PAP

(39)
2 ma-na kù:babbar
9. níĝ-ba
*Ab-ba*
11. *Ma-rí*$^{ki}$

(40)
1 ma-na kù:babbar
13. níĝ-ba
*Ib-ḫur-úr*
15. 5 gín DILMUN kù:babbar
níĝ-ba
17. *Sa*-NI-*gú*
maškim-*sù*
19. níĝ-"mul"
XIII. 1. *ˀÀ-du*$^{ki}$
àga-"kár"(ŠÈ)

(41)
3. 10 gín DILMUN kù:babbar
níĝ-kaskal
5. *A-ˀà-lu*
*wa*
7. *Ù-da-aḫ*
heš$_{5}$(LÚ×KÁR)
9. DU.DU
*Ma-rí*$^{ki}$

(42)
11. 5 gín DILMUN kù:babbar
nu$_{11}$-za 1 saĝ lu$_{5}$
13. ĜIŠ-ĝidru
$^{d}$*Ra-sa-ap*
15. *ˀÀ-da-ni*$^{ki}$

(33) 2 minas of silver: gift for Iti, travelling merchant of the city of Mari.
(34) 1 mina of silver for the purchase of GIŠ-ti-ḪAR-wood: at the market of the god Adamma of the city of ˀAdani, Wabarum has received.
(35) 40 shekels of silver for 2 toggle-pins; 10 shekels of silver for 1 an-zam$_{x}$ goblet; 50 shekels of silver for plating 1 table and 1 mace for the goddess Išḫara of the city of [Ma]NE.
(36) 5 shekels of silver: travel provision for Nizima-il (who) went to the city of Mari.
(37) 1;40 minas of silver for the purchase of 100 mar-tu daggers (decorated with) ivory (and) gold.
(38) 50 shekels of silver for 1 belt (with) sheath (and) dagger pendant for the funerary rite of Sagušum.
(39) 2 minas of silver: gift for Abba of the city of Mari.
(40) 1 mina of silver: gift for Ibḫurur; 5 shekels of silver: gift for SaNIgu, his representative (who brought) the news that the city of ˀAddu had been vanquished.
(41) 10 shekels of silver: travel provision for Aˀalu and Udaˀ-aḫ(u) (who) escorted some prisoners to the city of Mari.
(42) 5 shekels of silver for plating 1 head of androcephalus bull (on) a stick for the god Rašap of the city of ˀAdani.

(43)
6 gín DILMUN kù:babbar
17. *Na*-NE
*Na-gàr*$^{ki}$

(44)
19. 5 gín DILMUN kù:babbar
*La-a-na-ma*
21. *Ga-ga-ba-an*$^{ki}$

(45)
15 gín DILMUN kù:babbar
23. nu$_{11}$-za 1 *ḫa-bù*
XIV. 1. níĝ-ba
$^{d}$BAD *Ga-na-na-im*

(46)
3. 10 gín DILMUN kù:babbar
2 ĜIŠ-du
5. en
*in* ud
7. SIG$_{7}$
è
9. *si-in*
ki
11. $^{d}$*Ra-sa-ap*

(47)
15 gín DILMUN kù:babbar
13. nu$_{11}$-za 1 *ḫa-bù*
níĝ-ba
15. $^{d\text{ʾ}}$*A*$_{5}$*-da-"bal"*
*La-ru*$_{12}$*-ga*$_{x}$(ZÀR)*-du*$^{ki}$

(48)
17. 2 ma-na kù:babbar
níĝ-sa$_{10}$ 1 BAR.AN
19. EN-NE$^{ki}$

(49)
ŠÚ+ŠA gín DILMUN kù:babbar
21. níĝ-sa$_{10}$ raš-SAR

(50)
5 gín DILMUN kù:babbar
XV. 1. níĝ-kaskal
*A-ir-ra*
3. *wa*
*A-zú-bù-lu*
5. DU.DU
*Ar-mi*$^{ki}$
7. maškim
*Ḫa-ra-il*

(51)
9. 10 gín DILMUN kù:babbar
níĝ-ba
11. *Puzur*$_{4}$*-ra-*$^{d}$Utu
*Ma-rí*$^{ki}$
13. šu-mu-tak$_{4}$
túg-túg
15. *áš-da*
*Na-zi*

(52)
17. 15 gín DILMUN kù:babbar
níĝ-ba
19. *Ù*-NE-NE
*Ma-rí*$^{ki}$

(53)
21. 8 gín DILMUN kù:babbar
nu$_{11}$-za 4 ĝír šu-du$_{8}$-máš
23. 4 gín DILMUN kù:babbar
3 *zú-zú-ba-tum*
XVI. 1. en
*Gú-da-da-núm*$^{ki}$
3. *Za-a-ti*
šu-mu-tak$_{4}$

(54)
5. 4 gín DILMUN kù:babbar
níĝ-kaskal
7. *Ni-zi-ma-il*
*wa*
9. *I-ib-ma-lik*

(43) 6 shekels of silver for NANE of the city of Nagar.
(44) 5 shekels of silver for Lanama of the city of Gagaban.
(45) 15 shekels of silver for plating 1 mace: gift for the Lord of Ganana.
(46) 10 shekels of silver for 2 foot rings for the king on the occasion of … (SIG$_{7}$) for the departure to the place of the god Rašap.
(47) 15 shekels of silver for plating 1 mace: gift for the god ʾAdabal of the city of Larugadu.
(48) 2 minas of silver for the purchase of 1 mule (from) the city of ENNE.
(49) 20 shekels of silver for the purchase of leek.
(50) 5 shekels of silver: travel provision for Airra and Azu-bulu, representatives of Ḫara-il, (who) went to the city of Armi.
(51) 10 shekels of silver: gift for Puzurra-Utu of the city of Mari, (who) handed over textiles to Nazi.
(52) 15 shekels of silver: gift for UNENE of the city of Mari.
(53) 8 shekels of silver for plating 4 daggers for taking omens; 4 shekels of silver for 3 ... (*zú-zú-ba-tum*) for the king of the city of Gudadanum, Zati has handed over.
(54) 4 shekels of silver: travel provision for Nizima-il and Ib-malik (who) went to the city of Mari.

DU.DU
11. *Ma-rí*$^{ki}$

(55)
10 gín DILMUN kù:babbar
13. níĝ-ba
*Ìr*-NI-*ba*
15. *wa*
*Sá-ba*
17. *Ma-rí*$^{ki}$

(56)
3 gín DILMUN kù:babbar
19. níĝ-du$_8$
dumu-nita
21. *Ù-du-bù*$^{ki}$
*áš-ti*
23. *Kak-mi-um*$^{ki}$

(57)
TAR kù:babbar
25. nu$_{11}$-za 2 *ḫa-bù*
níĝ-ba
27. $^{d}$*Ra-sa-ap*
r. I. 1. *ʾÀ-da-ni*$^{ki}$
*wa*
3. $^{dʾ}$*À-da*
$^{d}$AMA-*ra*

(58)
5. 10 gín DILMUN kù:babbar
níĝ-ba
7. *Daš-na*
*wa*
9. *I-da-il*
*Ma-rí*$^{ki}$

(59)
11. 5 gín DILMUN kù:babbar
níĝ-kaskal
13. *Ìr-am*$_6$*-ma-lik*
*wa*
15. *I-ib-ma-lik*
DU.DU
17. *Ma-rí*$^{ki}$

(60)
ŠÚ+ŠA gín DILMUN kù:babbar
19. ZU.PIRIĜ
3 útul-útul$^{!}$ urudu maḫ
21. 4 gín DILMUN kù:babbar
kin$_5$-ak
23. 10 lá-2 ĝeštu$_x$-lá
*Ki-sa-du*
25. ga-du$_8$
en

(61)
II. 1. 5 gín DILMUN kù:babbar
níĝ-kaskal
3. *Za-gàr*
*A-dar-ki-zú*$^{ki}$
5. DU.DU
*Ar-mi*$^{ki}$

(62)
7. 1 ma-na kù:babbar
níĝ-sa$_{10}$ 1 ĝír mar-tu kù-gi
9. *Ib-ri-um*

(63)
ŠA.PI gín DILMUN kù:babbar
11. níĝ-sa$_{10}$ 1 ĝír mar-tu kù-gi
*I-bí-gàr-du*
13. ugula *ʾÀ-ma-du*$^{ki}$

(64)
10 gín DILMUN kù:babbar
15. nu$_{11}$-za 1 ĝír mar-tu
níĝ-ba
17. $^{d}$*Da-i-in*
*wa*
19. maš-maš 1 ĜIŠ-banšur
III. 1. níĝ-ba
$^{d}$*Ga-mi-iš*
3. *in* ud
en
5. e$_{11}$
é
7. $^{d}$*Ga-mi-iš*

(55) 10 shekels of silver: gift for IrNIba and Saba of the city of Mari.
(56) 3 shekels of silver for the ransom of a young man of the city of Udubu, from the city of Kakmium.
(57) 30 (shekels of) silver for plating 2 maces: gift for the god Rašap of the city of ʾAdani and for the god Hadda, at the AMA-ra (festival).
(58) 10 shekels of silver: gift for Dašna and Ida-il of the city of Mari.
(59) 5 shekels of silver: travel provision for Iram-malik and Ib-malik (who) went to the city of Mari.
(60) 20 shekels of silver for the hangers of 3 large kettles of not refined copper; 4 shekels of silver for making 8 earrings for Kisadu, the wet-nurse of the king.
(61) 5 shekels of silver: travel provision for Zagar of the city of Adarkizu (who) went to the city of Armi.
(62) 1 mina of silver for the purchase of 1 mar-tu dagger (decorated with) gold for Ibrium.
(63) 40 shekels of silver for the purchase of 1 mar-tu dagger (decorated with) gold for Ibbi-gardu, the overseer of the city of ʾAmadu.
(64) 10 shekels of silver for plating 1 mar-tu dagger: gift for the god Dayin, and for the striped (decoration) of 1 table: gift for the god Kamiš, when the king ascended to the temple of Kamiš.

(65)
11 gín DILMUN kù:babbar
9. 6 ĜIŠ-kak-ĜIŠ-kak
2 ĜIŠ-banšur
11. kaskal
en

(66)
13. 5 gín DILMUN kù:babbar
níĝ-ba
15. *Na*-NE
*Na-gàr*$^{ki}$

(67)
17. 4 gín DILMUN kù:babbar
níĝ-sa$_{10}$ 4 *ba-rí-zú* im-ĝi$_6$
19. ŠÚ+ŠA gín DILMUN kù:babbar
2 *bu*-DI
21. *Da-ti*-$^{d}$TU
*ma-lik-tum*
23. *Lum-na-an*$^{ki}$

(68)
IV. 1. ŠÚ+ŠA gín DILMUN kù:babbar
níĝ-ba
3. *Daš-na*
*wa*
5. *I-da-il*
*Ma-rí*$^{ki}$

(69)
7. 10 gín DILMUN kù:babbar
níĝ-kaskal
9. *Ḫar-zàr-du*$^{ki}$
DU.DU
11. *Ar-mi*$^{ki}$

(70)
10 gín DILMUN kù:babbar
13. níĝ-ba
*A-gàr*
15. *wa*
*Gú-zú-gú-zú*
17. *Ma-rí*$^{ki}$

(71)
TAR 2 gín DILMUN kù:babbar
19. nu$_{11}$-za
$^{d}$*Ba-li-ḫa*-II
21. lú 8 bàd$^{ki}$

(72)
2 gín DILMUN kù:babbar
23. níĝ-kaskal
*En-na-ì*
V. 1. lú kas$_4$-kas$_4$
DU.DU
3. *Ma-rí*$^{ki}$

(73)
TAR kù:babbar
5. nu$_{11}$-za
$^{d}$*Wa-da-ʾà-an*
7. *wa*
$^{d}$*Ša-la-ša*
9. lú
*Ga-ra-mu*$^{ki}$

(74)
11. 1 ma-na ŠÚ+ŠA gín kù:babbar
⸢2⸣ níĝ-anše-ak 4 kù-sal
13. *Du-si-gú*
níĝ-ba
15. en

(75)
2 gín DILMUN kù:babbar
17. nu$_{11}$-za
1 zag
19. ĜIŠ-gígir-{II-}II
*Ib-rí-um*

(76)
21. 1 ma-na kù:babbar
níĝ-ba
23. *ʾÀ-sa*
*wa*
25. *Gú-gi*
VI. 1. *I-ku-il*
*wa*

(65) 11 shekels of silver for 6 pegs of 2 travel tables for the king.
(66) 5 shekels of silver: gift for NANE of the city of Nagar.
(67) 4 shekels of silver for the purchase of 4 *ba-rí-zú* containers for black dye; 20 shekels of silver for 2 toggle-pins for Dati-TU, the queen of the city of Lumnan.
(68) 20 shekels of silver: gift for Dašna and Ida-il of the city of Mari.
(69) 10 shekels of silver: travel provision for (someone of) the city of Ḫarzadu (who) went to the city of Armi.
(70) 10 shekels of silver: gift for Agar and Guzuguzu of the city of Mari.
(71) 32 shekels of silver for plating (the statues of) the two Baliḫ of the eight fortresses.
(72) 2 shekels of silver: travel provision to Enna-i(l) for the couriers (who) went to the city of Mari.
(73) 30 (shekels of) silver for plating (the statues of) the god Wadaʾanu and the goddess Šalaša of the city of Garamu.
(74) 1;20 minas of silver for 2 bridles (and) 4 buckles for Dusigu: gift of the king.
(75) 2 shekels of silver for plating 1 side of a chariot of Ibrium.
(76) 1 mina of silver: gift for ʾAsa and Gugi, to Iku-il and Badulum of the city of Mari (who brought) the news that the city of Nagar had been vanquished.

3. *Ba-du-lum*
*Ma-rí*$^{ki}$
5. níĝ-"mul"
*Na-gàr*$^{ki}$
7. àga-"kár"(ŠE)

(77)
5 gín DILMUN kù:babbar
9. níĝ-ba
*I-i-bù*
11. *Ir-i-tum*$^{ki}$

(78)
ŠÚ+ŠA gín DILMUN kù:babbar
13. 2 *bu*-DI
*ma-lik-tum*
15. *Ra-ʾà-ak*$^{ki}$
É×PAP
17. EN-*mar*
šu-mu-tak$_4$

(79)
19. 6 2 NI gín DILMUN kù:babbar
2 *gú-li-lum*
21. níĝ-ba
$^{d}$*ʾÀ-ma-rí-ig*

(80)
VII. 1. ŠÚ+ŠA gín DILMUN kù:babbar
kin$_5$-ak
3. 2 bur-KAK
aš-ḫal ì-ĝiš
5. kaskal
en

(81)
7. 1 ma-na kù:babbar
1 íb-lá 1 *si-ti-tum* 1 ĝír-kun
9. *Ba-lu-zú* "ur$_4$"
*Ì-mar*$^{ki}$
11. *in* ud
ḫúl
13. na-rú-*sù*
*Zú-ba-núm*
15. šu-mu-tak$_4$

(82)
13 gín DILMUN kù:babbar
17. níĝ-sa$_{10}$
1 *gú-li-lum* a-gar$_5$-gar$_5$ kù-gi
19. (blank)

(83)
ŠA.PI kù:babbar
21. 1 íb-lá *si-ti-tum* ĝír-kun kù:babbar
VIII. 1. maš-maš kù-gi
*Na-bù-mu*
3. ŠA.PI gín DILMUN kù:babbar
1 íb-lá *si-ti-tum* ĝír-kun maš-maš kù-gi
5. *Ma-gal-lu*
2 lú-kar

(84)
7. ŠA.PI gín DILMUN kù:babbar
1 íb-lá 1 ĝír-kun
9. *I-bí-šum*
lú *Ti-ir*
11. *in* ud
tuš-LÚ×TIL
13. *Zú-ti*$^{ki}$

(85)
12 ma-na kù:babbar
15. níĝ-sa$_{10}$ 1 *mi-at* 62 aktum-TÚG
15 zara$_6$-TÚG
17. 1 gada-TÚG
IX. 1. 11 dùl-TÚG
5 níĝ-lá-saĝ
3. ki:lam$_7$
*Ma-rí*$^{ki}$
5. *Na-zi*

(86)
5 ma-na 16 gín DILMUN kù:babbar
7. níĝ-sa$_{10}$ 10 *à-da-um*-TÚG-II
⌜10⌝?+1 aktum-TÚG
9. 10 túg-NI.NI
4 gada-TÚG
11. 40 íb+III-TÚG sa$_6$ gùn
1 *mi-at* 45 íb+III-TÚG gùn

(77) 5 shekels of silver: gift for Ibu of the city of Iritum.
(78) 20 shekels of silver for 2 toggle-pins for the funerary rite of the queen of the city of Raʾak, ENmar has haded over.
(79) 6 shekels (and) 2 NI of silver for 2 bracelets: gift for the god Ammarik.
(80) 20 shekels of silver for making 2 bur-KAK vessels, with a filter, for the oil for the king's journey.
(81) 1 mina of silver for 1 belt, 1 sheath, 1 dagger pendant for Baluzu, the collector (of goods) of the city of Imar on the occasion of the feast of his stele, Zubanum has handed over.
(82) 13 shekels of silver for the purchase of 1 bracelet (decorated with) copper (and) gold.
(83) 40 (shekels of) silver for 1 belt (with) sheath (and) dagger pendant of silver with a striped (decoration) of gold for Nabumu; 40 shekels of silver for 1 belt (with) sheath (and) dagger pendant with a striped (decoration) of gold for Magallu, (who are) 2 traders.
(84) 40 shekels of silver for 1 belt (with) dagger pendant for Ibišum, (son) of Tir when he resided in the city of Zuti.
(85) 12 minas of silver for the purchase of 194 garments at the market of the city of Mari, Nazi (has received).
(86) 5;16 minas of silver for the purchase of 35 garments, 185 kilts (and) 12 mar-tu daggers of poor quality; 1 mina of silver for the purchase of GIŠ-ti-ḪAR-wood: Wabarum has received at the market of the cities of ʾAdani and NIab and Larugadu.

13. 12 ĝír mar-tu ḫul
1 ma-na kù:babbar
15. níĝ-sa$_{10}$ ĜIŠ-ti-ḪAR
*Wa-ba-rúm*
X. 1. šu-ba$_{4}$-ti
ki:lam$_{7}$
3. *ʾÀ-da-ni*$^{ki}$
*wa*
5. NI-*ab*$^{ki}$
*wa*
7. *La-ru*$_{12}$*-ga-du*$^{ki}$

(87)
ŠA.PI gín DILMUN kù:babbar
9. níĝ-sa$_{10}$ 1 ĝír mar-tu kù-gi
*Ru*$_{12}$*-zu-il*
11. ugula sur$_{x}$-BAR.AN

(88)
TAR kù:babbar
13. níĝ-sa$_{10}$ 1 ĝír mar-tu ti kù-gi
*Ba-ga-ma*
15. ugula sur$_{x}$-BAR.AN
*Ib-rí-um*

(89)
17. 17 gín DILMUN kù:babbar
níĝ-sa$_{10}$ 1 ĝír mar-tu *ba-du-u*$_{9}$
kù:babbar kù-gi
19. *Šu*-NE
ugula sur$_{x}$-BAR.AN
21. en

(90)
XI. 1. [
[níĝ-s]a$_{10}$ 1 ĝír mar-tu ti kù-gi
3. *Ig-rí-iš-li-im*
dumu-nita
5. *Ib-gi-da-mu*

(91)
8 ma-na 50 gín DILMUN kù:babbar
7. níĝ-sa$_{10}$ 31 aktum-TÚG
2 sal-TÚG
9. 2 túg-NI.NI
10 *ʾà-da-um*-TÚG-I
11. 47 gada-TÚG
50 lá-1 íb+III-TÚG sa$_{6}$ gùn
13. 1 ĜIŠ-banšur kù-gi
ki:lam$_{7}$
15. SA.ZA$_{x}$$^{ki}$

(92)
1 ma-na ŠÚ+ŠA gín DILMUN
kù:babbar
XII. 1. [šu-bal-ak]
[ ] kù-g[i]
3. *Du-bù-uš-da-mu*
*wa*
5. *Il-il*
*Ib-al*$_{6}$$^{ki}$

(93)
7. 1 ma-na 8 gín DILMUN kù:babbar
níĝ-sa$_{10}$ 3 aktum-TÚG
9. 7 gada-TÚG
10 íb+III-TÚG sa$_{6}$ gùn
11. ki:lam$_{7}$
$^{d}$*Áš-da-bíl*

(94)
13. 7 ma-na TAR 3 gín DILMUN
kù:babbar
níĝ-sa$_{10}$ 50 lá-3 aktum-TÚG
15. 25 *ʾà-da-um*-TÚG-I
15 gada-TÚG
17. 12 sal-TÚG
3 níĝ-lá-saĝ
XIII. 1. ŠA.PI 7 gín DILMUN kù:babbar
níĝ-sa$_{10}$ 5 ma-na ŠA.PI zabar
3. 2 ma-na TAR urudu
1 útul tur
5. 6 gín DILMUN kù:babbar
níĝ-sa$_{10}$ 1 ĝír kù-gi
7. 2 ma-na kù:babbar
níĝ-sa$_{10}$ 4 gud
9. TAR 6 gín DILMUN kù:babbar
níĝ-sa$_{10}$ *gàr-su*
11. NI-*a-ba-mu*
šu-ba$_{4}$-ti

(87) 40 shekels of silver for the purchase of 1 mar-tu dagger (decorated with) gold for Ruzu-il, the overseer of the team of mules.
(88) 30 (shekels of) silver for the purchase of 1 pointed mar-tu dagger (decorated with) gold for Bagama, the overseer of the team of mules of Ibrium.
(89) 17 shekels of silver for the purchase of 1 *b.* mar-tu dagger (decorated with) gold for ŠuNE, the overseer of the team of mules of the king.
(90) [x silver for the purcha]se of 1 pointed mar-tu dagger (decorated with) gold for Igriš-lim, son of Ibgi-damu.
(91) 8;50 minas of silver for the purchase of 92 garments, 49 kilts (and) 1 table (decorated with) gold, at the market of the Palace.
(92) 1;20 minas of silver [in exchange for x] gold for Tubuš-damu and Ilil of the city of Ibʿal.
(93) 1;08 minas of silver for the purchase of 10 garments (and) 10 kilts at the market of the god Ašdabil.
(94) 7;33 minas of silver for the purchase of 102 garments; 47 shekels of silver for the purchase of 5;40 minas of bronze (and) 2;30 minas of copper for 1 small kettle; 6 shekels of silver for the purchase of 1 dagger (decorated with) gold; 2 minas of silver for the purchase of 4 oxen; 36 shekels of silver for the purchase of bags: NI(l)abamu has received at the market of the god Hadda.

13. ki:lam$_7$
$^{d?}$*À-da*

(95)
15. 3 ma-na ŠÚ+ŠA kù:babbar
1 ĜIŠ-šú 1 níĝ-bànda
17. lú šu-šu
en

(96)
19. 10 gín DILMUN kù:babbar
XIV. 1. 2 *bu*-DI 2 *ti-ša-na*
níĝ-ba
3. $^{d}$*Ga-na-na*
ĜIŠ.DUG.DU maḫ

(97)
5. 8 gín DILMUN kù:babbar
saĝ
7. $^{d}$*À-la*
*wa*
9. $^{d}$*Da-bí-na-ad*
lú *A-ra-ab*$^{ki}$

(98)
11. 1 ma-na ŠÚ+ŠA kù:babbar
2 níĝ-anše-ak
13. 4 kù-sal
*Ba-ga-ma*
15. ugula SA.ZA$_{x}^{ki}$

(99)
50 kù:babbar[a)]
17. 1 íb-lá kù:babbar maš-maš kù-gi
(blank)

(100)
19. ŠA.PI kù:babbar
1 íb-lá maš-maš kù-gi
21. (blank)

(101)
XV. 1. 3 ma-na ŠA.PI gín DILMUN an-na
kin$_5$-ak
3. 40 ĝír mar-tu kù-gi
20 ĝír mar-tu zú
5. 20 ĝír mar-tu *ba-du-u*$_9$ kù:babbar kù-gi
11 ma-na 6 gín DILMUN an-na
7. kin$_5$-ak
1 *li-im* ĜIŠ-gu-kak-gíd zabar

(102)
9. 1 ma-na an-na
en
11. *Kak-mi-um*$^{ki}$

(103)
1 ma-na an-na
13. *Na-zú-ù*
*Ki-ma-lik*
15. *wa*
*I-bí-iš-lu*
17. šu-mu-tak$_4$

(104)
13 gín DILMUN an-na
XVI. 1. šub-šub
2 ĜIŠ-zú
3. 2 ĜIŠ-gígir-II
*Ib-rí-um*

(105)
5. 13 an-na šub
2 ĜIŠ-zú
7. ĜIŠ-gígir-II
en

(106)
9. 5 an-na
1 sig$_7$-igi[!](ME)
11. *Du-si-gú*

(107)
TAR an-na
13. šub
4 *ma-ḫa-ni-gi*
15. *Ib-rí-um*

(95) 3;20 minas of silver for 1 GIŠ-šú vessel (and) 1 níg-bànda vessel for the hands of the king.
(96) 10 shekels of silver for 2 toggle-pins (decorated with) 2 (couples of) ... (*ti-ša-na*): gift for the goddess Ganana (on the occasion of) the great presentation.
(97) 8 shekels of silver for the head of the god Ala and the goddess Dabinad of the city of Arab.
(98) 1;20 minas of silver for 2 bridles (and) 4 buckles for Bagama, the overseer of the Palace.
(99) 50 (shekels of) silver for 1 belt of silver with a striped (decoration) of gold.
(100) 40 (shekels of) silver for 1 belt with a striped (decoration) of gold.
(101) 3;40 minas of tin for making 40 mar-tu daggers (decorated with) gold, 20 serrated mar-tu daggers, 20 *b.* mar-tu daggers (decorated with) silver (and) gold; 11;06 minas of tin for making 1000 bronze spearheads.
(102) 1 mina of tin for the king of the city of Kakmium.
(103) 1 mina of tin Nazu, Kimalik and Ibišlu have handed over.
(104) 13 shekels of tin to be melted in 2 hooks for 2 chariots of Ibrium.
(105) 13 (shekels of) of tin to be melted in 2 hooks for a chariot of the king.
(106) 5 (shekels of) tin for 1 eyebrow (decoration) for Dusigu.
(107) 30 (shekels of) tin to be melted in 4 necklaces for Ibrium.

(108)
4 an-na
17. kin$_{5}$-ak
4 ĝír šu-du$_{8}$-máš

(109)
19. ŠÚ+ŠA an-na
kin$_{5}$-ak
21. $^{d}$*A-lum*
*wa*
23. $^{d}$*Si-gar*
*A-ḫa-da-mu*$^{ki}$

(110)
25. TAR an-na
*ni-zi-mu*
27. ZA$_{x}$
naĝar

(111)
29. TAR an-na
en
31. *Du-lu*$^{ki}$
*Iš-má-da-mu*
XVII. 1. šu-mu-tak$_{4}$

(112)
3 an-na
3. 1 ĜIŠ-banšur
$^{d}$*Iš:šára*
5. *Má*-NE$^{ki}$

(113)
TAR an-na
7. *Zú-gú-uš*
*Na-gàr*$^{ki}$

(114)
9. 3 an-na
2 ĜIŠ-zú
11. 1 ĜIŠ-gígir-II
en
13. *Kab-lu*$_{5}$*-ul*$^{ki}$

(115)
1 ma-na an-na
15. en
*Ma-rí*$^{ki}$

(116)
17. TAR an-na
en
19. *Ša-bir*$_{5}$*-ti-tum*$^{ki}$

(117)
15 an-na
21. šub-šub
nu$_{11}$-za
23. 1 *ḫa-bù*
níĝ-ba
25. $^{d}$*Ga-mi-iš*
en
27. ì-na-sum

(118)
1 ma-na an-na
29. kin$_{5}$-ak
$^{d}$*Á-la*
31. *wa*
dam-*sù*
33. lú
*A-ra-ab*$^{ki}$

(119)
35. 2 an-na
šub 1 šu-i
37. *Ib-rí-um*

(120)
l.ed. 1. ŠA.PI an-na
kin$_{5}$-ak
3. $^{d}$*Ì-lam*
lú *Za-za-u*$_{9}$
5. (blank)

(108) 4 (shekels of) tin for making 4 daggers for taking omens.
(109) 20 (shekels of) tin for making (statues) of the god Alum and the goddess Sigar of the city of Aḫadamu.
(110) 30 (shekels of) tin for decorating objects of the carpenters.
(111) 30 (shekels of) tin for the king of the city of Dulu, Išma-damu has handed over.
(112) 3 (shekels of) tin for 1 table for the goddess Išḫara of the city of MaNE.
(113) 30 (shekels of) tin for Zuguš of the city of Nagar.
(114) 3 (shekels of) tin for 2 hooks for a chariot of the king of the city of Kablul.
(115) 1 mina of tin for the king of the city of Mari.
(116) 30 (shekels of) tin for the king of the city of Sabirtitum.
(117) 15 (shekels of) tin to be melted for plating 1 mace: gift for the god Kamiš, the king has given.
(118) 1 mina of tin for making (statues) of the god Ala of the city of Arab and his spouse.
(119) 2 (shekels of) tin to be melted in 1 šu-i vessel for Ibrium.
(120) 1;20 (minas of) tin for making (1 statue) of the god Ilam of the city of Zazaʾu.

(121)
AN.ŠÈ.GÚ 1 *mi-at* 74 ma-na ŠA.PI 8
gín DILMUN kù:babbar
7. è
23 ma-na 12 gín DILMUN an-na
9. è

(122)
šu-níĝin 1 *mi-at* 98 ma-na
kù:babbar an-na
11. (blank)

*a*) lines 16-17 and 19-20 added in a second time

(121) Total: 174;48 minas of silver: expenditure; 23;12 minas of tin: expenditure.
(122) Grand total: 198 minas of silver (and) tin.

## Commentary

This document registers the expenditure (è) of silver and the amount of silver with which the expended gold was valued (in a ratio of 5 : 1), for a total of 174;48 minas (82.156 kg). The colophon (§ 121) also oddly includes the total of the expended tin (an-na) of 23;12 minas (10.904 kg). The Grand total, šu-nígin (§ 122), of 198 minas, adds this tin to the silver, which is anomalous. This sum is justified by the fact that silver and tin had the same value, as §§ 3 and 4 show. The mina of tin in § 27 was instead valued at only 20 shekels of silver.

The sum of tin, of 23;14 minas, is 1 shekels higher than the total of 23;13 minas (§ 121): 3;40 + 11;06 (§ 101), 1;00 (§ 102), 1;00 (§ 103), 0;13 (§ 104), 0;13 (§ 105), 0;05 (§ 106), 0;30 (§ 107), 0;04 (§ 108), 0:20 (§ 109), 0;30 (§ 110), 0;30 (§ 111), 0;03 (§ 112), 0;30 (§ 113), 0;03 (§ 114), 1;00 (§ 115). 0;30 (§ 116), 0;15 (§ 117), 1;00 (§ 118), 0;02 (§ 119), 0;40 (§ 120).

The four minas of tin in §§ 3 and 4 are not included in the final sum of the tin, because the grand total already contains its equivalent value in silver.

The document opens with the registration of 1 mina (470 g) of silver for the renewal rite of the head of the city-god Kura (§ 1), (see the commentary to text no. 4). This would become the rule for all of Ibrium's subsequent annual documents concerning the expenditures of metals, as well as those of his son and successor Ibbi-zikir.

Ibrium received a dagger (§ 62) (as did Bagama, his overseer of teams of mules, § 88), some decorations and accessories for his chariot (§§ 28, 75, 104), and some jewels (§§ 107, 119).

Dusigu, "the king's mother", is mentioned in §§ 74 and 106.

Tinib-dulum, a sister of the king, and priestess, dam-diĝir, of the god ᵓAdabal of Luban, received a silver drinking vessel (§ 18).

It was only sometime this year that peace was sealed with Mari (§§ 8–13). The war had broken out during the last year of king Irkab-damu's reign; it is quite probably that he died as a consequence of having been wounded in battle. Enna-Dagan of Mari had likely suffered the same fate, because he died the same year (Archi 2022). It was Dutum who brought the news that Mari had a new king: Ikun-išar, according to text no. XXI 3 § 48 (Ibr. 01b). According to text no. XXI 4, from the following year (Ibr. 02a; see the commentary above), the city of Ibᶜal supported Ebla in this war. The present document (from the year Ibr. 03) mentions a delegation of several people, led by *A-ḫa-ar-si*, *ᵓÀ-sa* and *Íl-a*, which reached Ebla for the "offering of the oil (of peace)", nídba ì-ĝiš (§§ 8–11). Of these people, *Íl-a*/*e*, is attested as a man from Mari in *ARET* VIII 532 XIV 13–14, a document from the final years of the archive, where he is qualified as a "trader", lú-kar. These envoys received respectively 5, 3 and 2 minas (2.35 and 1.410 kg; 940 g) of silver. The "men", ĝuruš-ĝuruš, who accompanied them received 1 mina (470 g) of silver all together, and *Du-tum* (who had returned to Ebla) received 10 shekels (78 g) of silver. A "tablet", dub, decorated with 50 shekels (391 g) of silver was deposited in the temple of Kura, where an "oath", nam-kud, was sworn (§ 13). A similar ceremony had to be performed in Mari. One mina (470 g) of tin was sent to the king of Mari (§ 115).

Other officials from Mari who reached Ebla were *Wa-ba-rúm* and his maškim *ʾÀ-sa* (§ 32); *I-ti* "the travelling merchant", ga:eš$_8$ (§ 33); *Ab-ba* (§ 39); *Puzur$_4$-ra*-$^{d}$Utu (§ 51); *Ù*-NE-NE (§ 52); *Ìr*-NI-*ba* and *Sá-ba* (§ 55); *Daš-na* and *I-da-il* (§§ 58 and 68); *A-gàr* and *Gú-zú-gú-zú* (§ 70); *ʾÀ-sa*, *Gú-gi*, *I-ku-il* and *Ba-du-lum* (§ 76), who brought the news that Nagar had suffered a defeat: níg-"mul" *Na-gàr*$^{ki}$ àga-"kár".

The officials from Ebla who went to Mari were: *Ni-zi-ma-il* (§ 36); again *Ni-zi-ma-il* and *I-ib-ma-lik* (§ 54); *Ìr-am$_6$-ma-lik* and *I-ib-ma-lik* (§ 59); *En-na-ì* lú kas$_4$-kas$_4$ (§ 72). *A-ʾà-lu* and *Ù-da-aḫ* of Mari accompanied some prisoners back to their city receiving 10 shekels (78 g) of silver as a travel provision (§ 41); the preceding year they had received 20 shekels (157 g) for the same task, see text XXI 4 § 113. Two "female weavers", túg-nu-tag, were "acquired", níĝ-sa$_{10}$, from Mari (§ 6)

*Zú-gú-uš* of Nagar received the gift of 5 minas (2.350 kg) of silver plus 30 shekels (235 g) of tin (§§ 14, 113). A list of seven towns belonging to Nagar follows in § 15: *A-bù-li-um*$^{ki}$, *Ba-sa-ḫi-um*$^{ki}$, *Ga-ga-ba-an*$^{ki}$, *Ḫi-la-zi-um*$^{ki}$, *La-dab$_6$-bí-um*$^{ki}$, *Na-ba-ti-um*$^{ki}$, and *Zàr-ʾà*-NI-*um*$^{ki}$; they received 30 shekels (235 g) of silver each. The messengers from Nagar were *Na*-NE (§§ 43, 66); and *La-a-na-ma* (from the city of Gagaban) (§ 44). It was Iram-malik who travelled to Nagar, receiving 2 shekels (16 g) of silver as travel provision (§ 15), and 5 shekels (39 g) in addition to travelling to Mari (§ 59).

§§ 3, 4. The kings of Manuwat and Kakmium received respectively 3 and 1 minas (1.410 kg and 470 g) of tin evaluated in silver in a ratio of 1 : 1.

§ 5. ḫub-ki "dancer, acrobat". A parallel passages is text no. 16 § 70; cf. also *ARET* III 865 II 1–4: *A-da-mi* ba:tuš *a-lu-nu* sig$_4$$^{ki}$.

§ 29. The king of Kablul received a silver decoration for his chariot.

§ 30. The ratio between silver and copper was 1 : 50.

§ 31. 10 minas of silver are "entitled", zi-du$_8$, to the god Hadda by the king. This term occurs also in *ARET* XVI 21 o. V 8, and VI 5. "silver / sheep from GN allotted to PN". The *LLE*,1 1028 has: ZI.DU$_8$ = *ʾà*/*a-ma-zu-um*.

§ 40. The defeat (àga-"kár") of the city of ʾAddu was probably inflicted by Mari, whose last target seems to have been Nagar, more to the north (see § 76). The city of ʾAddu is perhaps to be identified with Tell Malhat ed-Dēru, 75 km north of the place where the Ḫabur flows in the Euphrates (Archi 2019a, pp. 179–181).

§ 50. Expenditure for a travel provision concerning a second journey by Airra and Azu-bulu to Armi. For a first journey to Armi, see § 26.

§ 60. *Ki-sa-du*, the wet-nurse (ga-du$_8$) of the king, is mentioned, together with her colleague *Iš$_{11}$-lu-ì-la*, in *ARET* IV 11 r. XI 6, and XII 1250 o.$^{?}$ 2'–4'; in a list in text XXI 17 § 90, she follows a sister of Dusigu. In TM.75.G.2417 r. XIII 5–8 Kisadu is mentioned as the wet-nurse of king Išʿar-damu (Archi 2021b, p. 9). The wet nurses of the Ebla documents are listed in Biga 2000.

§ 70. For the name of the second messenger of Mari: *Gú-zú-gú-zú*, cf. *Gú-zú* in *ARET* IX 36 § 8.

§ 76. The defeat of the city of Nagar followed that of ʾAddu (§ 40) in an expansionist campaign of Mari towards the north, which took its revenge from the defeat suffered the year before (see XXI 4 §§ 102, 105).

# 7
## (Plates XIII–XIV)

(1)
o. I. 1. [1 m]a-[n]a kù[:babbar]
[s]aĝ kù:babbar
3. [$^{d}$*K*]*u-ra*

(2)
10 gín DILMUN kù:babbar
5. níĝ-ba
NE-*a-da-nu*
7. *ˀÀ-du*$^{ki}$

(3)
2 gín DILMUN kù:babbar
9. nu$_{11}$-za 1 ĝír mar-tu
níĝ-ba
11. $^{d}$*Wa-da-ˀà-nu*
[l]ú [*Ša-*]*dab*$_{6}^{ki}$
13. *Ib-rí-um*
in-na-sum

(4)
15. 5 gín DILMUN kù:babbar
níĝ-sa$_{10}$ 1 *gàr-su*
17. *Ḫáb-ra-ar*
lú ⸢*Ib*⸣-*ga-*[*i*]*š-lu*

(5)
19. [x gí]n [DILM]UN [kù:babbar]
[(ca. 5 lines)]
II. 1. *Du-bí*
ugula *A-ru*$_{12}$-*lu*$^{ki}$
3. šu-ba$_{4}$-ti

(6)
5 gín DILMUN kù:babbar
5. níĝ-sa$_{10}$ 1 *gàr-su*
*Ù-zi*
7. šeš
*A-zú-ma*

(7)
9. 4 gín DILMUN kù:babbar
níĝ-sa$_{10}$ 1 *gàr-su*
11. *Ib-lu*$_{5}$-*zú*
lú-kar
13. *Ma-nu-wa-ad*$^{ki}$

(8)
10 gín DILMUN kù:babbar
15. ⸢2⸣ *ti-gi-na* 2 ĜIŠ-du
*Ir*-NE
17. dumu-nita
*I-ib-ma-lik*

(9)
19. [x] kù:[bab]bar
[(ca. 4 lines)]

(10)
24$^{?}$. [5 gín DILMUN]
III. 1. kù:babbar
šu-bal-ak
3. 1 gín DILMUN kù-gi
1 kù-sal
5. níĝ-ba
ama-gal en
7. $^{d}$Nin-kar

(11)
12 gín DILMUN kù:babbar
9. níĝ-sa$_{10}$ 1 megida$^{?}$ níĝ-sikil
*I-ba*$_{x}$-*zi-mi-nu*

(12)
11. 3 gín DILMUN kù:babbar
nu$_{11}$-za 1 ĝír mar-tu
13. *wa*
1 kù-sal
15. níĝ-ba
*Ib-rí-um*

(1) [1 m]i[n]a of sil[ver] for the silver head of the god Kura.
(2) 10 shekels of silver: gift for NEadanu of the city of ˀAddu.
(3) 2 shekels of silver for plating 1 mar-tu dagger: gift for the god Wadaˀanu of the city of [Ša]dab, Ibrium has given.
(4) 5 shekels of silver for the purchase of 1 bag for Ḫabrar, (son) of Ibga-išlu.
(5) [x she]kels of [silver] […] Dubi, the overseer of the city of Arulu, has received.
(6) 5 shekels of silver for the purchase of 1 bag for Uzi, brother of Azuma.
(7) 4 shekels of silver for the purchase of 1 bag for Ibluzu, trader of the city of Manuwat.
(8) 10 shekels of silver for 2 torques (and) 2 foot rings for IrNE, son of Ib-malik.
(9) [x] silver […].
(10) [5 shekels of] silver in exchange for 1 shekel of gold for 1 buckle: gift of the king's mother to the goddess Ninkar.
(11) 12 shekels of silver for the purchase of 1 sow (megida$^{?}$) for the purification (níg-sikil) of Ibaziminu.
(12) 3 shekels of silver for plating 1 mar-tu dagger and 1 buckle: gift of Ibrium to the god Rašap of the city of Tunip.

17. $^{d}$*Ra-sa-ap*
*Du-ne-ib*$^{ki}$

(13)
19. 5 ma-na kù:babbar
[n]íĝ-sa$_{10}$ [x ĝír mar-t]u [(x) kù-gi]
21. [(ca. 4 lines)]

(14)
IV. 1. nu$_{11}$-za AN.Á.DAḪ
diĝir-diĝir

(15)
3. 3 ma-na ŠA.PI gín DILMUN
kù:babbar
níĝ-sa$_{10}$ 10 lá-2 ĝír mar-tu ti kù-gi
5. 2 ma-na TAR kù:babbar
šu-bal-ak
7. TAR kù-gi
*zi-du*
9. 10 ĝír mar-tu ti kù-gi
ŠA.PI gín DILMUN kù:babbar
11. nu$_{11}$-za 20 ĝír mar-tu ti kù:babbar
TAR kù:babbar
13. šu-bal-ak
6 gín DILMUN kù-gi
15. *ga-ma-a-tum-sù*
1 ma-na ŠÚ+ŠA gín DILMUN
kù:babbar
17. [(ca. 4 lines)]
V. 1. šub *si-in*
kin$_5$-ak-*sù*
3. lú ì-na-sum
SA.ZA$_x$$^{ki}$
5. *in*
*Du-du-lu*$^{ki}$
7. *in*
níĝ-kas$_4$
9. *Ma-ri*$^{ki}$

(16)
2 gín DILMUN kù:babbar
11. nu$_{11}$-za 1 ĝír mar-tu ti
*Da-zi-ma-ad*
13. šu-i
*Ib-rí-um*

(17)
15. ŠA.PI gín DILMUN kù:babbar
níĝ-sa$_{10}$ 1 ĝír mar-tu kù-gi
17. *Lá-da*
lú-kar
19. *A-da-bí-ig*$^{ki}$

(18)
ŠA.PI gín DILMUN kù:babbar
21. níĝ-sa$_{10}$ 1 ĝír mar-tu kù-gi
*Ḫáb-ra-ar*
23. [l]ú [*Ib-ga-iš-lu*]
[(ca. 3 lines)]

(19)
VI. 1. 3 ma-na ŠÚ+ŠA gín DILMUN
kù:babbar
šu-bal-ak
3. ŠA.PI gín DILMUN kù-gi
1 dib
5. *Wa-na*
ugula BAR.AN-BAR.AN

(20)
7. ŠÚ+ŠA 5 gín DILMUN kù:babbar
níĝ-sa$_{10}$ 1 ĝír mar-tu ti kù-gi
9. *Ti-ra-ì*
maškim
11. EN-*mar*
šu-du$_8$
13. *in*
*Ma-ri*$^{ki}$

(21)
15. 5 gín DILMUN kù:babbar
níĝ-sa$_{10}$ 1 ĝír mar-tu *ba-du-u*$_4$
kù:babbar-gi
17. *Bu-ma-ì*
*Gú-ra-"bal"*$^{ki}$

(13) 5 minas of silver for the purchase of [x mar-tu daggers (decorated with) gold ...].
(14) [...] for plating ... (AN.Á.DAḪ) for the gods.
(15) 3;40 minas of silver for the purchase of 8 pointed mar-tu daggers (decorated with) gold; 2;30 minas of silver in exchange for 30 (shekels of) gold in alloy for 10 pointed mar-tu daggers (decorated with) gold; 40 shekels of silver for plating 20 pointed mar-tu daggers (decorated with) gold; 30 (shekels of) silver in exchange for 6 shekels of gold for their knobs; 1;20 minas of silver [...] melted for its making: the Palace has given to the city of Tuttul for the military expedition of the city of Mari.
(16) 2 shekels of silver for plating 1 pointed mar-tu dagger for Dazimad, the barber of Ibrium.
(17) 40 shekels of silver for the purchase of 1 mar-tu dagger (decorated with) gold for Lada, trader of the city of Adabik.
(18) 40 shekels of silver for the purchase of 1 mar-tu dagger (decorated with) gold for Ḫabrar, (son of) [Ibga-išlu].
(19) 3;20 minas of silver in exchange for 40 shekels of gold for 1 plaque for Wana, the overseer of the mules.
(20) 25 shekels of silver for the purchase of 1 pointed mar-tu dagger (decorated with) gold: Tira-il, the representative of ENmar took possession for the city of Mari.
(21) 5 shekels of silver for the purchase of 1 *b.* mar-tu dagger (decorated with) silver (and) gold for Buma-i(l) of the city of Gurabal.

(22)
19. 50 gín DILMUN an-na
š[ub] *s*[*i-in*]
21. [(ca. 3 lines)]
VII. 1. 2 lu$_5$
lú *I-dam-na*
3. gud-si-dili gibil

(23)
1 gín DILMUN kù:babbar
5. *ni-zi-mu*
nu$_{11}$-za 1 *za-ḫa-da*
7. *Ib-rí-um*

(24)
ŠA.PI gín DILMUN an-na
9. šub *si-in*
*ni-zi-mu*
11. ZA$_x$
naĝar

(25)
13. TAR 3 gín DILMUN 3 NI kù:babbar
šu-bal-ak
15. 6 gín DILMUN 2 NI kù-gi
2 *gú-li-lum*
17. níĝ-ba
$^d$*Ku-ra*

(26)
19. 5 ma-na kù:babbar
šu-bal-ak
21. 1 m[a-]⌜na⌝ [kù-gi]
[(ca. 3 lines)]
VIII. 1. tuš-LÚ<×TIL>
*Ma-rí*$^{ki}$
3. *áš-ti*
*Du-du-lu*$^{ki}$

(27)
5. TAR kù:babbar 1 íb-lá 1 *si-ti-tum* 1
ĝír-kun
níĝ-ba
7. *Ib-ḫur-ma-lik*
*Kak-mi-um*$^{ki}$
9. tuš-LÚ<×TIL>
*in*
11. *Ar-ḫa-du*$^{ki}$

(28)
10 lá-1 ma-na ŠÚ+ŠA gín DILMUN
kù:babbar
13. níĝ-sa$_{10}$ 12 aktum-TÚG ti-TÚG
12 túg-NI.NI
15. 1 dùl-TÚG *Ma-rí*$^{ki}$
26 *ʾà-da-um*-TÚG-I
17. 33 [ -TÚG]
[ca. 3 lines]
IX. 1. 10 lá-2 na$_4$ siki *Ma-rí*$^{ki}$
2 ma-na kù:babbar
3. 96 ĜIŠ-ti-ḪAR
*Wa-ba-rúm*
5. šu-ba$_4$-ti

(29)
6 gín DILMUN kù:babbar
7. n[íĝ-sa$_{10}$] ĜIŠ-ád
ki:lam$_7$
9. $^d$*A-da-ma*
*wa*
11. SA.ZA$_x$$^{ki}$

(30)
2 ma-na kù:babbar
13. níĝ-sa$_{10}$ 1 BAR.AN
*Ba-na-i-um*$^{ki}$
15. *in*
níĝ-kas$_4$
17. *Ma-rí*$^{ki}$

(31)
TAR kù:babbar
19. níĝ-sa$_{10}$ raš-SAR Kur$^{ki}$

(32)
[1 ma-na kù:]b[abbar]
21. [ní]ĝ-s[a$_{10}$] 10 ĝ[ír$^?$ ]

(22) 50 shekels of tin to be melted in […] 2 androcephalus bulls for Idamna (for a) new battering ram.
(23) 1 shekel of silver for decorating with lamination 1 battle-axe for Ibrium.
(24) 40 shekels of tin to be melted for decorating objects of the carpenters.
(25) 33 shekels (and) 3 NI of silver in exchange for 6 shekels (and) 2 NI of gold for 2 bracelets: gift for the god Kura.
(26) 5 minas of silver in exchange for 1 mina of [gold for … for PN (who)] resided in the city of Mari, (coming) from the city of Tuttul.
(27) 30 (shekels of) silver for 1 belt, 1 sheath, 1 dagger pendant: gift for Ibḫur-malik of the city of Kakmium, (who) resided in the city of Arḫadu.
(28) 9;20 minas of silver for the purchase of 84 garments […] (and) 8 stone weights of wool from the city of Mari; 2 minas of silver (for the purchase of) 96 GIŠ-ti-ḪAR-wood, Wabarum has received.
(29) 6 shekels of silver for the pur[chase] of myrtle at the markets of the god Adamma and of the Palace.
(30) 2 minas of silver for the purchase of 1 mule from the city of Banaʾium for the military expedition of the city of Mari.
(31) 30 (shekels of) silver for the purchase of leek from the mountain region.
(32) [1 mina of silver] for the pur[chase of] 10 da[ggers …].

(33)

[ ]
23. [ ]
X. 1. *Ib-rí-um*
níĝ-ba
3. $^{d}$BAD *Du-du-lu*$^{ki}$

(34)

ŠA.PI gín DILMUN kù:babbar
5. nu$_{11}$-za 1 an-dùl munus
1 ma-na ŠÚ+Š[A 5] gín DILMUN kù:babbar
7. [šu]-bal-ak
17 gín DILMUN kù-gi
9. nu$_{11}$-za saĝ-*sù* 2 šu-*sù* DU-*sù*
níĝ-ba
11. $^{d}$*Sa-a-ša*
*si-in*
13. *Du-du-lu*$^{ki}$
*Ib-rí-um*
15. šu-mu-tak$_{4}$

(35)

3 gín DILMUN kù:babbar
17. nu$_{11}$-za 1 ĝír mar-tu
[ ]
19. [ ]
[ ]

(36)

XI. 1. 2 ½ gín DILMUN kù:babbar
šu-bal-ak
3. ½ gín DILMUN kù-gi
*ni-zi-mu*
5. 1 dib
*Du-ur-ì*
7. *Bù-ur-tin*$^{ki}$

(37)

15 gín DILMUN kù:babbar
9. nu$_{11}$-za 1 ešda
TAR kù:babbar
11. šu-bal-ak
6 gín DILMUN kù-gi
13. nu$_{11}$-za 1 *ar-ra-sù*
níĝ-ba
15. $^{d}$*Ra-sa-ap*

(38)

ŠÚ+ŠA gín DILMUN kù:babbar
17. *ʾa$_{5}$-na-gu*
4 si 2 gud
19. nídba
en
21. [$^{d}$*Ra-sa-ap*]
[*ʾÀ-da-ni*$^{ki}$]
23. [*in*]
XII. 1. $^{d}$AMA-*ra*

(39)

15 gín DILMUN kù:babbar
3. nu$_{11}$-za 1 ešda
TAR kù:babbar
5. šu-bal-ak
6 gín DILMUN kù-gi
7. nu$_{11}$-za 1 *ar-ra-sù*
ŠÚ+ŠA gín DILMUN kù:[bab]bar
9. *ʾa$_{5}$-na-gu*
4 si 2 gud
11. nídba
en
13. $^{dʾ}$*À-da*
*in*
15. $^{d}$AMA-*ra*

(40)

10 gín DILMUN kù:babbar
17. šu-bal-ak
2 gín DILMUN kù-gi
19. *ni-zi-mu*
nu$_{11}$-za 1 ĝír mar-tu
21. *Ig-na-*[*d*]*a-*[*a*]*r*

(41)

[ ]
XIII. 1. kù:babbar

(33) […] gift of Ibrium to the Lord of the city of Tuttul.
(34) 40 shekels of silver for plating 1 female statue; 1;2[5] shekels of silver in exchange for 17 shekels of gold for plating its head, its 2 hands (and) its feet: gift for the goddess Salaša to the city of Tuttul, Ibrium has handed over.
(35) 3 shekels of silver for plating 1 mar-tu dagger […].
(36) 2 ½ shekels of silver in exchange for ½ shekel of gold for decorating 1 plaque for Dur-il of the city of Burtin.
(37) 15 shekels of silver for plating 1 mace; 30 (shekels of) silver in exchange for 6 shekels of gold for plating its handle: gift for the god Rašap.
(38) 20 shekels of silver for the circular stand of the 4 horns of 2 bulls: offering of the king [for the god Rašap of the city of ʾAdani, at] the AMA-ra (festival).
(39) 15 shekels of silver for plating 1 mace; 30 (shekels of) silver in exchange for 6 shekels of gold for plating its handle; 20 shekels of silver for the circular stand of the 4 horns of 2 bulls: offering of the king for the god Hadda, at the AMA-ra (festival).
(40) 10 shekels of silver in exchange for 2 shekels of gold for decorating with lamination 1 mar-tu dagger for Ignadar.
(41) [x] silver for decorating 2 bridles (and) 1 buckle; 10 shekels of silver in exchange for 2 shekels of gold for a striped decoration of 4 buckles for Ibrium.

*ni-zi-mu*
3. 2 níĝ-anše-ak 1 kù-sal
10 gín DILMUN kù:babbar
5. šu-bal-ak
2 gín DILMUN kù-gi
7. *ni-zi-mu*
maš-maš 4 kù-sal
9. *Ib-rí-um*

(42)
2 ½ gín DILMUN kù:babbar
11. šu-bal-ak
½ gín DILMUN kù-gi
13. *ni-zi-mu*
nu$_{11}$-za 1 ĝír
15. en

(43)
10 gín DILMUN kù:babbar
17. šu-bal-ak
2 gín DILMUN kù-gi
19. *ni-zi-mu*
nu$_{11}$-za 2 *za-ḫa-da*
21. en

(44)
[x] g[ín DILMUN kù:babbar]
XIV. 1. *ni-zi-mu*
maš-maš ĜIŠ-bar-ús
3. 15 gín DILMUN kù:babbar
šu-bal-ak
5. 3 gín DILMUN kù-gi
maš-maš-*sù*
7. lú 2 ĜIŠ-gígir-II
en

(45)
9. ŠA.PI gín DILMUN kù:babbar
šu-bal-ak
11. 8 gín DILMUN kù-gi
nu$_{11}$-za 1 *za-ḫa-da*
13. *Ib-rí-um*

(46)
8 gín DILMUN an-na
15. šub *si-in*
1 tùn tur 1 dub-naĝar sal
17. 1 *ma-za-ḫa-rúm*
1 UŠ×KÍD
19. *si-in*
ZA$_x$
21. ˹*Ib*˺-[*r*]*í-um*

(47)
[x ma-na x]
XV. 1. gín DILMUN kù:babbar
kin$_5$-ak
3. 6 *zú-zú-ba-tum*
ĜIŠ-bar-ús
5. zú-ak
2 ĜIŠ-gígir-II
7. en

(48)
ŠÚ+ŠA gín DILMUN kù:babbar
9. níĝ-ba
*Da-ti*

(49)
11. 5 gín DILMUN kù:babbar
níĝ-ba
13. *A*-LUM-*mu-d*[*a*]
*Ma-r*[*í*$^{ki}$]

(50)
15. 2[+x$^?$ gín] ˹DILMUN˺ kù:babbar
nu$_{11}$-za 1 gud-<si->dili
17. lú sig$_{17}$
lú ZA$_x$
19. *Ib-rí-um*

(51)
10 gín DILMUN kù:babbar
21. níĝ-ba
˹*Wa*˺-[*r*]*u*$_{12}$[-*tum*]
23. [*Ma-rí*$^{ki}$]

(52)
XVI. 1. 12 ½ gín DILMUN kù:babbar
šu-bal-ak
3. 2 ½ gín DILMUN kù-gi
*ni-zi-mu*

(42) 2 ½ shekels of silver in exchage for ½ shekel of gold for decorating with lamination 1 dagger for the king.
(43) 10 shekels of silver in exchange for 2 shekels of gold for decorating with lamination 2 battle-axes for the king.
(44) [x] sh[ekels of silver] for a striped decoration of goads; 15 shekels of silver in exchange for 3 shekels of gold for the striped decoration of 2 chariots of the king.
(45) 40 shekels of silver in exchange for 8 shekels of gold for plating 1 battle-axe for Ibrium.
(46) 8 shekels of tin to be melted in 1 small axe, 1 thin hammer, 1 pliers, 1 blade, for the property of Ibrium.
(47) [x;xx minas] of silver for making 6 ... (*zú-zú-ba-tum*), goads (and) hooks of 2 chariots of the king.
(48) 20 shekels of silver: gift for Dati.
(49) 5 shekels of silver: gift for ALUM-muda of the city of Mari.
(50) 2[+x shekels] of silver for plating 1 battering ram of yellow stone for the property of Ibrium.
(51) 10 shekels of silver: gift for Waru[tum of the city of Mari].
(52) 12 ½ shekels of silver in exchange for 2 ½ shekels of gold for decorating 1 plaque for Bagama.

5. 1 dib
*Ba-ga-ma*

(53)
7. TAR 3 gín DILMUN 3 NI kù:babbar
šu-bal-ak
9. 6 gín DILMUN 2 NI kù-gi
[2 *gú-l*]*i*-[*lu*]*m*
11. [níĝ-]ba
[$^{d}$*K*]*u-ra*

(54)
13. ŠA.PI gín DILMUN kù:babbar
1 ĝír mar-tu kù-gi
15. *Puzur$_{4}$-ra-ma-lik*
lú *Iš$_{11}$-da-mu*

(55)
17. 15 gín DILMUN kù:babbar
níĝ-ba
19. *D*[*a-* ]
XVII. 1. *in*
NI-*rúm*$^{ki}$
3. šu-ba$_{4}$-ti

(56)
6 ma-na ŠA.PI gín DILMUN
kù:babbar
5. níĝ-sa$_{10}$ 33 túg-NI.NI
1 *ʾà-da-um*-TÚG-II
7. 24[+2$^{?}$] íb[+III]-TÚG sa$_{6}$ [gùn]
2 *m*[*i-at*] íb[+III-TÚG] gùn
9. 2 ĝír zabar
12 ma-na 11 gín DILMUN kù:babbar
11. níĝ-sa$_{10}$ 33 gud-gud
ki:lam$_{7}$
13. $^{d}$*ʾÀ-da*

(57)
10 gín DILMUN kù:babbar
15. níĝ-kaskal
⸢*Nap*⸣-*ḫ*[*a-il*]
XVIII. 1. DU.DU
*si-in*
3. *Ma-rí*$^{ki}$

(58)
ŠA.PI gín DILMUN kù:babbar
5. níĝ-sa$_{10}$ 1 ĝ[ír] mar[-tu] kù-g[i]
$^{d}$[*ʾÀ*]-*d*[*a*](?)
7. [ ]
[ ]
9. [ ]

(59)
[x] g[ín DILMUN kù:]babba[r]
11. [ ]
T[AR gín DILMUN kù:babbar]
13. šu-b[al-ak]
6 g[ín DILMUN] kù-g[i]
15. *N*[*a*$^{?}$- ]
[ ]
17. [ ]
⸢x⸣[ ]
19. [ ] K[A$^{?}$ ]
[ ]
XIX. 1. [ ]

(60)
[ kù:]b[abbar$^{?}$]
3. [ ]

(61)
r. I. [(ca. 6 lines)]
7$^{?}$. ⸢x⸣[
*i*[*n*]
9. *g*[*i*-NI] (?)

(62)
10[+x] gí[n] DI[LMUN kù:]b[abbar]
11. nu$_{11}$-[za] 1 e[šda]
[6$^{?}$ gín DILMUN kù-gi]
13. 1 *a*[*r-*]*ra-sù*
2 ½ gín DILMUN kù:babbar
15. šu-bal-ak
½ gín D[ILMUN] kù-g[i]
17. 1 [
⸢x⸣[
19. ⸢x⸣[
[ ]
21. [ ]

(53) 33 shekels (and) 3 NI of silver in exchange for 6 shekels (and) 2 NI of gold [for 2 bracele]ts: [gi]ft for [the god K]ura.
(54) 40 shekels of silver for 1 mar-tu dagger (decorated with) gold for Puzurra-malik, (son) of Išdamu.
(55) 15 shekels of silver: gift for D[a…] (that) he has received in the city of NIrum.
(56) 6;40 minas of silver for the purchase of 34 garments, 226 kilts (and) 2 daggers (decorated with) bronze; 12;11 minas of silver for the purchase of 33 oxen, at the market of the god Hadda.
(57) 10 shekels of silver: travel provision for Napḫ[a-il] (who) went to the city of Mari.
(58) 40 shekels of silver for the purchase of 1 mar[-tu]da[gger] (decorated with) gold for [the god Hadda …].
(59) [x] sh[ekels of sil]ver […]; 3[0 shekels of silver] in ex[change for] 6 sh[ekels] of gold for N[a…] […].
(60) [… silver] […].
(61) […] i[n (month) I]V.
(62) 10[+x] she[kels of silver] for pla[ting] 1 m[ace; 6 shekels of gold] for ist handle; 2 ½ shekels of silver in exchange for ½ shekel of gold for 1 […].

(63)

II. 1. [ ]
[ ]
3. [ ]
[ ]
5. [ ]

(64)

2 g[ín DILMUN] kù:babbar
7. nu$_{11}$-z[a] 1 ĝír mar-tu
2 ½ gín DILMUN kù:babbar
9. šu-bal-ak
½ gín DILMUN [k]ù-gi
11. [1 k]ù-sal
níĝ-ba
13. $^{d}$*Ra-sa-ap*
*Du-ne-íb*$^{ki}$

(65)

15. 2 gín DILMUN kù:babbar
nu$_{11}$-za 1 ĝír mar-tu
17. 2 ½ gín DILMUN kù:babbar
šu-bal-ak
19. ½ g[ín DILMUN] kù-g[i]
1 kù-s[al]
21. níĝ-ba
III. 1. [$^{d}$ ]

(66)

[ ]
3. [ ]
[ ]⸢x⸣
5. [x] ⸢*ʾà-ra*⸣*-ma-tum*
10 gín DILMUN kù:babbar
7. šu-bal-ak
2 gín DILMUN kù-gi
9. n[u$_{11}$]-za [ ]
[níĝ-ba]
11. $^{d}$Utu
SA.ZA$_{x}$$^{ki}$

(67)

13. 2 gín DILMUN kù:babbar
nu$_{11}$-za 1 ĝír mar-tu
15. 3 gín DILMUN 3 NI kù:babbar
šu-bal-ak
17. 2 NI gín DILMUN kù-gi
1 kù-sal
19. níĝ-ba
$^{d}$*Ku-ra*

(68)

21. ½ gín DILMUN
IV. 1. [kù:babbar]
[*ʾa$_{5}$-na-gu*]
3. [1 ĜIŠ-banšur]
[3 gín DILMUN 3 NI kù:babbar]
5. [šu-bal-ak]
2 N[I gín] DI[LMUN] kù-gi
7. 1 kù-sal
níĝ-ba
9. $^{dʾ}$*A$_{5}$-da-"bal"*
[*Lu-b*]*a-an*$^{[ki]}$

(69)

11. ½ g[ín] DILMUN kù:babbar
*ʾa$_{5}$-na-gu*
13. 1 ĜIŠ-banšur
3 gín DILMUN 3 NI kù:babbar
15. šu-bal-ak
2 NI gín DILMUN kù-gi
17. 1 kù-sal
níĝ-ba
19. $^{d}$*Am-ma-rí-ig*

(70)

½ gín DILMUN kù:babbar
21. *ʾa$_{5}$-na-gu*
1 ĜIŠ-banšur
23. 2 ½ gín DILMUN kù:babbar
šu-bal-ak
V. 1. [½ gín DILMUN kù-gi]
[1 kù-sal]
3. [níĝ-ba]
⸢$^{d}$⸣[ ]
5. ⸢x⸣[
šu-mu-t[ak$_{4}$]
7. diri
diĝir-diĝir-diĝir

(63) […].
(64) 2 sh[ekels] of silver for plati[ng] 1 mar-tu dagger; 2 ½ shekels of silver in exchange for ½ shekel of gold [for 1 b]uckle: gift for the god Rašap of the city of Tunip.
(65) 2 shekels of silver for plating 1 mar-tu dagger; 2 ½ shekels of silver in exchange for ½ sh[ekel] of gold for 1 buckle: gift for [the god(dess) …].
(66) […] [x] pectoral(s); 10 shekels of silver in exchange for 2 shekels of gold for plating […:gift] for the god Utu of the Palace.
(67) 2 shekels of silver for plating 1 mar-tu dagger; 3 shekels (and) 3 NI of silver in exchange for 2 NI of gold for 1 buckle: gift for the god Kura.
(68) ½ shekel [of silver for the circular stand of a table; 3 shekels (and) 3 NI of silver in exchange for] 2 NI of gold for 1 buckle: gift for the god ʾAdabal of [the city of Lub]an.
(69) ½ sh[ekel] of silver for the circular stand of a table; 3 shekels (and) 3 NI of silver in exchange for 2 NI of gold for 1 buckle: gift for the god Ammarik.
(70) ½ shekel of silver for the circular stand of a table; 2 ½ shekels of silver in exchange for [½ shekel of gold for 1 buckle: gift for the god(dess) …], […] has handed over, as surplus for the gods.

(71)
9. [x] gín [DI]LMUN [kù:babbar]
[ ]
11. *Ib*$^{?}$[-*du*$^{?}$-$^{d}$]En-ki

(72)
TAR 3 gín DILMUN 3 NI kù:babbar
13. šu-bal-ak
˹6˺ gín DILMUN [1+]1 NI k[ù-gi]
15. 2 *gú-li-lum*
[ní]ĝ-ba
17. $^{d}$*Áš-da-bíl*

(73)
10 gín DILMUN kù:babbar
19. šu-bal-ak
2 gín DILMUN kù-gi
21. nu$_{11}$-za 1 ĝír mar-tu
níĝ-ba
23. $^{d}$*Áš-da-bíl*
*Ib-rí-um*
25. in-na-sum

(74)
VI. 1. ˹5˺ gín DILMUN ˹kù:babbar˺
šu-bal-ak
3. 1 gín DILMUN kù-gi
1 kù-sal 1 buru$_{4}$-MUŠEN
5. [níĝ-ba]
[ ]
7. [$^{d}$*Ra-sa-*]*a*[*p*]
*ˀÀ-da-ni*$^{ki}$
9. šu-mu-tak$_{4}$
$^{d}$AMA-*ra*

(75)
11. 10 lá-3 ma-na TAR kù:babbar
níĝ-s[a$_{10}$] 3 zara$_{6}$-TÚG 2 aktum-TÚG
13. 40 lá-3 túg-NI.NI
1 níĝ-lá-saĝ
15. 20 lá-2 íb+III-TÚG sa$_{6}$ gùn
2 *mi-at* 50 lá-3 íb+IV-TÚG gùn
17. ki:lam$_{7}$
$^{d}$*Áš-da-bíl*
19. *wa*
[*Ši-*]˹*ˀà*˺-*mu*$^{ki}$

(76)
VII. 1. 10 lá-2 ma-na ŠÚ+ŠA 5 gín DILMUN
kù:babbar
[níĝ-]sa$_{10}$ [10$^{?}$ l]á-1 ˹*ra*˺[-*ˀà*]-*tum*
3. 3 *ˀà-da-um*-TÚG-I
46 aktum-TÚG
5. 4 *mi-at* na$_{4}$ siki *Ma-rí*$^{ki}$
ba-ba
7. 1 ma-na ŠA.PI gín ˹DILMUN˺
[kù:babbar]
níĝ-sa$_{10}$ 1 *li-im* ĜIŠ-gu-kak-gíd
9. 1 ma-na 6 gín DILMUN kù:babbar
níĝ-sa$_{10}$ 24 *gàr-su*
11. NI-*la-ba-mu*
šu-ba$_{4}$-ti
13. ki:lam$_{7}$
$^{d}$*ˀÀ-da*

(77)
15. 15 gín DILMUN kù:babbar
nu$_{11}$-za 1 ešda
17. TAR [kù:]babba[r]
VIII. 1. šu-bal-ak
6 gín DILMUN [kù-]gi
3. [nu$_{11}$-]za *ar-r*[*a-*]*sù*
níĝ-ba
5. $^{d}$*ˀÀ-da*
*in*
7. iti *ˀa*$_{5}$-*nun*

(78)
6 ma-na 10 gín DILMUN kù:babbar
9. níĝ-sa$_{10}$ 40 lá-2 gud
*in*
11. *Ša-dab*$_{6}$$^{ki}$
˹lú *Ì*˺-[*m*]*ar*$^{ki}$
13. ˹*wa*˺
[ ]˹$^{ki}$˺

(71) [x] shekels of [silver …] for Ib[du]-Enki.

(72) 33 shekels (and) 3 NI of silver in exchange for 6 shekels (and) 2 NI of g[old] for 2 bracelets: gift for the god Ašdabil.

(73) 10 shekels of silver in exchange for 2 shekels of gold for plating 1 mar-tu dagger: gift for the god Ašdabil, Ibrium has given.

(74) 5 shekels of silver in exchange for 1 shekel of gold for 1 buckle (and) 1 shield: [gift of … for the god Raš]a[p] of the city of ˀAdani, handed over at the AMA-ra (festival).

(75) 7;30 minas of silver for the purchase of 43 garments (and) 265 kilts at the market of the god Ašdabil and of the city of [Ši]ˀamu.

(76) 8;25 minas of silver [for the pur]chase of 9 shells, 49 garments, 400 stone weights of wool from the city of Mari (and) carapaces; 1;40 minas of [silver] for the purchase of 1000 spearheads; 1;06 minas of silver for the purchase of 24 bags: NIlabamu has received, at the market of the god Hadda.

(77) 15 shekels of silver for plating 1 mace; 30 (shekels of) [si]lver in exchange for 6 shekels of [go]ld [for pla]ting its handle: gift for the god Hadda, in month VIII.

(78) 6;10 minas of silver for the purchase of 38 oxen in the city of Šadab of the city of I[m]ar and [the city of …].

(79)
15. ŠA.PI gín DILMUN kù:babbar
níĝ-ba
17. *I-ti-ì*

(80)
10 gín DILMUN kù:babbar
19. níĝ-ba
*Iš-dub-ì*
21. *Ma-rí*$^{ki}$
níĝ-"mul"
23. *Ar-ti-na-an*$^{ki}$
til

(81)
25. 1 ma-na kù:babbar
níĝ-sa$_{10}$
IX. 1. 1 [ĝír] mar-[tu kù-g]i
*Ib-r[í-um]*

(82)
3. 5 ma-na ŠÚ+ŠA 5 gín DILMUN kù:babbar
šu-bal-ak
5. 1 ma-[n]a 5 gín DILMUN kù-gi
nu$_{11}$-za 10 *gú-li-lum* a-gar$_5$-gar$_5$ TAR-II
7. 5 *gú-li-lum* a-gar$_5$ ŠÚ+ŠA-II
10 *gú-li-lum* ⸢a⸣-gar$_5$-gar$_5$ ⸢15$^?$⸣-I
9. 10 *gú-l[i]-lum* a-gar$_5$-gar$_5$ 10-I 10-I
2 gín DILMUN kù:babbar
11. ZU.PIRIĜ-[*s*]*ù*
ME-sig
13. é
en

(83)
15. 1 ma-na ŠA.PI gín DILMUN kù:babbar
šu-bal-ak
17. ŠÚ+ŠA gín DILMUN kù-gi
*ni-zi-mu*
19. 1 dib
en

(84)
X. 1. 5 gín DILMUN kù:babbar
šu-bal-ak
3. 1 gín DILMUN kù-gi
*ni-zi-mu*
5. 1 dib
*I-bí-um*
7. lú *Iš-má-ga-l*[*u*]

(85)
⸢5⸣ [gín DILM]UN [k]ù[:babbar]
9. [šu-bal-a]k
[1] gín DILMUN kù-gi
11. *ni-zi-mu*
1 ⸢dib⸣
13. *En-n*[*a-*]⸢*ì*⸣
lú *Rí-ì-ma-lik*

(86)
15. 14 gín DILMUN kù:babbar
níĝ-ba
17. *Wa-ru*$_{12}$*-tum*
*Ma-rí*$^{ki}$

(87)
19. 2 gín DILMUN kù:babbar
*ni-zi-mu*
21. 2 *zú-zú-ba-tum*
en

(88)
23. ŠÚ+ŠA gín DILMUN kù:babbar
*A-a-lu*
XI. 1. *Kab-lu*$_5$*-ul*$^{ki}$
al$_6$-tuš
3. *Mi-da-ḫi*$^{ki}$

(89)
TAR kù:babbar
5. šu-bal-ak
6 gín DILMUN kù-gi
7. *ni-zi-mu*
2 *gú-li-lum*
9. *Ib-rí-um*

(79) 40 shekels of silver: gift for Iti-i(l).
(80) 10 shekels of silver: gift for Išdub-i(l) of the city of Mari (who brought) the news that the city of Artinan had been defeated.
(81) 1 mina of silver for the purchase of 1 mar-[tu dagger (decorated with) gol]d for Ibr[ium].
(82) 5;25 minas of silver in exchange for 1;05 minas of gold for plating 10 double bracelets of 30 shekels of copper each, 5 double bracelets of 20 shekels of copper each, 10 single bracelets of 15 shekels of copper each, 10 single bracelets of 10 shekels copper each; 2 shekels of silver for their hangers, for the watchmen of the king's house.
(83) 1;40 minas of silver in exchange for 20 shekels of gold for decorating 1 plaque for the king.
(84) 5 shekels of silver in exchange for 1 shekel of gold for decorating 1 plaque for Ibbium, (son) of Išma-galu.
(85) 5 [shekels of silver in exchange for 1] shekel of gold for decorating 1 plaque for Enna-i(l), (son) of Reʾi-malik.
(86) 14 shekels of silver: gift for Warutum of the city of Mari.
(87) 2 shekels of silver for decorating 2 ... (*zú-zú-ba-tum*) for the king.
(88) 20 shekels of silver for Aʾalu of the city of Kablul (who) resided in the city of Midaḫi.
(89) 30 (shekels of) silver in exchange for 6 shekels of gold for decorating 2 bracelets for Ibrium.

(90)
50 gín DILMUN k[ù]:babbar
11. n[íĝ-b]a
*Gul-la*
13. ⌜x-x-x⌝
*Sa-ma-na-nu*
15. [*S*]*i-mi*[- ]
[ ]
17. *Iš-ba-ì*
*A-ša*$^{\text{ki}}$
19. *in* ud
DU.DU
21. nam-kud
é
23. $^{\text{d}}$*Ku-ra*

(91)
5 gín DILMUN kù:babbar
25. níĝ-kaskal
*Ur-sá-um*$^{\text{ki}}$

(92)
27. TAR kù:babbar
níĝ-sa$_{10}$
XII. 1. [1 ĝír mar]-tu kù-gi
*Ig-rí-iš*
3. lú *I-rí-ig-gú-nu*
É×PAP

(93)
5. 10 ma-na kù:babbar
níĝ-sa$_{10}$ 26 zara$_6$-TÚG aktum-TÚG
7. 6 níĝ-lá-DU
*I-na-ni-gi*
9. *Kab-lu*$_5$*-ul*$^{\text{[ki]}}$
[
11. [
*wa*
13. maškim:<e>-gi$_4$
DU.DU

(94)
15. TAR 5 gín DILMUN kù:babbar
šu-bal-ak
17. 7 gín DILMUN kù-gi
*zi-du*
19. 1 ĝír mar-tu
en

(95)
21. 1 ma-na kù:babbar
XIII. 1. [níĝ-ba]
*Daš-na*
3. *Ma-rí*$^{\text{ki}}$
níĝ-"mul"
5. Kiš$^{\text{ki}}$
til

(96)
7. 10 gín DILMUN kù:babbar
níĝ-sa$_{10}$ 1 ĝír mar-tu *ba-du-u*$_4$
kù:babbar-gi
9. *En-na-ì*
lú BÍL-*za-ì*
11. DU.DU
*si-in*
13. Ki[š$^{\text{ki}}$]
[x ma-na] an-na
15. sagi
*Ma-rí*$^{\text{ki}}$
17. *En-na-ì*
šu-mu-tak$_4$

(97)
19. 10 gín DILMUN kù:babbar
níĝ-ba
21. *Iš-dub-ì*
maškim
23. ga:eš$_8$
*Du-du-lu*$^{\text{ki}}$
25. ḫi-mu-DU
ḪU.UD

(98)
27. 10 gín DILMUN
XIV. 1. [kù:babbar]
4 *ti-ša-nu* 2 *bu*-DI
3. níĝ-ba

(90) 50 shekels of silver as g[if]t for Gulla, …, Samananu, Simi[…], […], Išba-i(l) of the city of Aša, when they went to swear an oath in the temple of the god Kura.
(91) 5 shekels of silver: travel provision for (someone of) the city of Ursaʾum.
(92) 30 (shekels of) silver for the puchase of [1 mar]-tu [dagger] (decorated with) gold for the funerary rite of Igriš, (son) of Iri-gunu.
(93) 10 minas of silver for the purchase of 32 garments for Inanigi of the city of Kablul […] and (his) representative(s) to travel.
(94) 35 shekels of silver in exchange for 7 shekels of gold as alloy for 1 mar-tu dagger for the king.
(95) 1 mina of silver: [gift] for Dašna of the city of Mari (who brought) the news that the city of Kiš had been defeated.
(96) 10 shekels of silver for the purchase of 1 *b.* mar-tu dagger (decorated with) silver and gold for Enna-i(l), (son) of BILza-i(l), (who) went to the city of Ki[š]; [x mina(s)] of tin for the steward of the city of Mari, Enna-i(l) has handed over.
(97) 10 shekels of silver: gift for Išdub-i(l), representative of the travelling merchant of the city of Tuttul, (who) delivered ḪU.UD.
(98) 10 shekels [of silver] for 4 ... (*ti-ša-nu*) (decorating) 2 toggle-pins, as gift for the goddess Ganana (on the occasion of) the great presentation.

$^{d}$*Ga-na-na*
5. *in* ud
GIŠ DUG.DU
7. maḫ

(99)
6 gín 2 NI kù:babbar
9. 2 *gú-li-lum*
níĝ-ba
11. $^{d}$*Am-ma-rí-ig*

(100)
2 ma-na kù:babbar
13. níĝ-ba
diĝir-diĝir-diĝir

(101)
15. 2 [ma-n]a [k]ù[:babbar]
níĝ-ba
17. *Wa-ru*$_{2}$*-tum*
*Da-ti*
19. *Bù-sum*
*Ma-rí*$^{ki}$

(102)
21. 5 gín DILMUN kù:babbar
šu-bal-ak
23. 1 gín DILMUN kù-gi
*ni-zi-mu*
25. 1 dib
*I-ti-um*
XV. 1. [*Ma-nu*]-⸢*wa*⸣-[*a*]*d*$^{ki}$

(103)
[1+]1 ma-na TAR kù:babbar
3. šu-bal-ak
TAR kù-gi
5. 1 dib
*Ne-zi-ma-lik*
7. lú-kar
*Kak-mi-um*$^{ki}$

(104)
9. 10 ma-na kù:babbar
ŠÚ+ŠA 7 gín DILMUN kù-gi sikil
11. lú *Maš-ga-du*$^{ki}$
*wa*
13. ì-na-sum
nu$_{11}$-za $^{d}$*Ra-sa-ap*
15. *Du-ne-íb*$^{ki}$

(105)
2 ma-na kù:babbar
17. šu-bal-ak
ŠÚ+ŠA 4 gín DILMUN kù-gi
19. daḫ(MU.MU)
kù-gi
21. lú en
*wa*
23. [l]ugal-[lu]gal
[ì-n]a-sum
25. [nu$_{11}$-z]a(?) [$^{d}$*Ra-s*]*a-ap*

(106)
XVI. 1. [x ma-na x gí]n DILMUN kù:babbar
[níĝ-s]a$_{10}$
3. [1 ĝí]r mar-[t]u kù-gi
[1 ĜIŠ]-gu-kak-gíd
5. $^{d}$*Ra-sa-ap*
*Du-ne-íb*$^{ki}$
7. en
in-na-sum
9. (blank)

(107)
AN.ŠÈ.GÚ 1 *mi-at* 50 lá-1 ma-na
kù:babbar
11. è
(blank)

(99) 6 shekels (and) 2 NI of silver for 2 bracelets: gift for the god Ammarik.
(100) 2 minas of silver: gift for the gods.
(101) 2 [min]as of [silver]: gift for Warutum, Dati, (and) Busum of the city of Mari.
(102) 5 shekels of silver in exchange for 1 shekel of gold for decorating 1 plaque for Itium of [the city of Manu]w[a]t.
(103) 2;30 minas of silver in exchange for 30 (shekels of) gold for 1 plaque for Nezi-malik, trader of the city of Kakmium.
(104) 10 minas of silver (and) 27 shekels of gold (for) the purification of the city of Mašgadu and given for plating (the statue of) the god Rašap of the city of Tunip.
(105) 2 minas of silver in exchange for 24 shekels of gold to add to the gold that the king and the lords have given [for the lamination of (the statue) of the god Raš]ap.
(106) [x;xx mina(s)] of silver [for the purchase of 1] mar-tu [dagger] (decorated with) gold (and) [1 sp]earhead for the god Rašap of the city of Tunip, given by the king.
(107) Total: 149 minas of silver: expenditure.

## Commentary

This document concerns the expenditure (è) of silver and the amounts of silver with which the expended gold was valued: a total of 149 minas (70.030 kg) of silver (§ 107) for the year Ibr. 04. The first registration concerns 1 mina (470 g) of silver for the renewal rite of the head of the city-god Kura (§ 1); the god further received a pair of gold bracelets of 6 ⅔ shekels (52 g) as annual offering (§ 25).

The king received two daggers (§§ 42, 94), two "battle-axes", *za-ḫa-da* (§ 43); decorations and accessories for his chariot (§§ 44, 47, 87); and a plaque of 20 shekels (157 g) of gold (§ 83).

Ibrium received accessories for the harness of his chariot (§ 41), two battle-axes (§§ 23, 45), several objects (*si-in* ZA$_x$ *Ib-rí-um*, §§ 46, 50), one dagger (§ 81), and two bracelets (§ 89). He performed offerings to several gods.

Dusigu, the king's mother, presented a buckle to the goddess $^d$Nin-kar (10).

Dašna of Mari brought the news that Kiš was "defeated", til (§ 95). Even so, this event must have been a minor battle, a prelude to the war ascribed to Enšakušana of Uruk which ended with the defeat of Kiš (see Sallaberger, Schrakamp 2015, pp. 89, 97). The final campaign would not start until the year Ibr. 10, and it ended in the year Ibr. 12 (texts nos. 13, 14, 15, see below). As a consequence of this first defeat, *En-na-ì*, son of BÍL-*za-ì*, was sent to Kiš, to take personal note of the situation, receiving a dagger decorated with gold and silver; and a certain amount of tin to be handed over to the "steward", sagi, of Mari (a high-ranking official entrusted with diplomatic relations), when passing through that city (§ 96). This remarkable datum shows how the capitals of regional states were concerned with events that could change the political balance of power, even within a range as far away as 1000 km. This Enna-i(l), son of BÍLza-i(l) was the same person who was sent to Kiš many years later according to *ARET* XXII 3 obv. XII 17–23 (I.Z. 04) and *ARET* XXII 8 obv. XXVII 31–37 (I.Z. 9).

The other messengers from the side of Mari who came to Ebla were: *Da-ti* (§ 48); *A*-LUM-*mu-da* (§ 49); *Wa-ru*$_{12}$*-tum* (§ 51, 86); *Iš-dub-ì* (§ 80, who brought the news of the defeat of the city of Artinan); *Wa-ru*$_{12}$*-tum*, *Da-ti*, *Bù-sum* (§ 101). Clothing, wool, and shells were bought from Mari (§ 76).

The city of Artinan (§ 80) had to be in the region of Mari. According to text no. 12 § 13, Ibrium devoted a dagger to the "Lord", $^d$BAD, of Artinan.

*Ti-ra-ì* maškim EN-*mar* (§ 20) and *Nap-ḫa-il* (§ 57) went to Mari.

§. 15. The Palace delivered in Tuttul thirty-eight daggers decorated with gold and silver "for the military expedition (níg-kas$_4$) of Mari (against Kiš?)". It is possible that Mari contributed to the defeat of Kiš attacked from the south by a Sumerian city (probably Uruk). Weapons decorated with gold are also registered in § 26, probably for someone from Tuttul who had resided in Mari.

§ 30. A mule was bought in *Ba-na-i-um*$^{ki}$ (the ending of this name places this town in the region of Nagar, see Archi, 1998c, pp. 7–8), in order to provide a messenger to join the "military expedition of Mari", *in* níĝ-kas$_4$ *Ma-rí*$^{ki}$, perhaps against Kiš.

§ 82. Expenditure of gold for the decoration of thirty-five bracelets for the "watchmen", ME-sig, of "the house of the king".

§ 90. Five people from *A-ša*$^{ki}$ came to swear an oath in the temple of Kura. This city, ruled by a "king", en (*ARET* III 231 r. III' 2'–3'), lay presumably in the region of Ḫarran (*ARET* XII 332 r. IV' 2'–4').

# 8
## (Plates XV)

(1)
o. I. 1. 1 ma-na kù:babbar
saĝ
3. $^{d}$*Ku-ra*

(2)
4 ma-na kù:babbar
5. *Di-rín-da-mu*
*Di-ne-íb-du-lum*
7. nin-ni
[en]

(3)
9. [(ca. 5 lines)]
14$^{?}$. [1 ĝír mar-tu *ra-ʾà-t*]*um* [kù-g]i
15. [1] ĝír mar-tu kù-gi
*Ib-rí-um*
17. è

(4)
⌜1⌝ ĝír mar-[t]u
II. 1. ⌜1⌝ *r*[*a*]-⌜*ʾà*⌝-*tum* kù-gi
*Ib-rí-um*
3. en
šu-mu-tak$_4$
5. *in* ud
ḫúl
7. na-rú
[ ]

(5)
[(ca. 4 lines)]
12$^{?}$. ⌜*Za*⌝-*gi*-[*t*]*i*-[*m*]*a*

(6)
13. 1 ĝír mar-tu kù-gi
*Iš-má-ga-lu*
15. lú EN-*sa-rí*

(7)
TAR kù:babbar
17. *Du-bí*
III. 1. *wa*
maškim-*sù*
3. *Ma-rí*$^{ki}$

(8)
12 gín DILMUN kù:babbar
5. níĝ-sa$_{10}$ 2 *gàr-su* ĝi$_6$
*I-nu-ud-da-mu*
7. ugula *Kak-mi-um*⌜$^{ki}$⌝
[ ]
9. [ ]
[ ]

(9)
11. [3 gín DILMUN kù:babbar]
saĝ
13. $^{d}$*Ku-ra*

(10)
ŠA.PI gín DILMUN kù:babbar
15. *Ib-bu-tum*

(11)
ŠÚ+ŠA gín DILMUN kù:babbar
17. *Daš-na*
IV. 1. *Ma-rí*$^{ki}$

(12)
ŠÚ+ŠA gín DILMUN kù:babbar
3. [ ]⌜x⌝[ ]⌜x⌝
[ ]
5. [ ]

(13)
[1+]1 ma-na [kù:babbar]
7. [ ]

(1) 1 mina of silver for the head of the god Kura.
(2) 4 minas of silver for Tirin-damu (and) Tinib-dulum, sisters [of the king].
(3) […] [1 mar-tu dagger (decorated with) shel]ls (and) [gold, 1] mar-tu dagger (decorated with) gold for Ibrium: expenditure.
(4) 1 mar-tu dagger (decorated with) shells (and) gold for Ibrium, the king has handed over on the occasion of the feast of (his) stele.
(5) […] Zagitima.
(6) 1 mar-tu dagger (decorated with) gold for Išma-galu, (son) of ENsari.
(7) 30 (shekels of) silver for Dubi and his representative, of the city of Mari.
(8) 12 shekels of silver for the purchase of 2 black bags for Inud-damu, the overseer of the city of Kakmium […].
(9) [3 shekels of silver] for the head of the god Kura.
(10) 40 shekels of silver for Ibbutum.
(11) 20 shekels of silver for Dašna of the city of Mari.
(12) 20 shekels of silver […].
(13) 2 minas [of silver …].

[ ]
9. [ ]
[ ]

(14)
11?. 1 ma-na kù:babbar
*I-ti*
13. ga:eš$_8$
*I-ga-iš-ru*$_{12}$
15. šu-mu-tak$_4$

(15)
4 ma-na ŠÚ+ŠA 3 gín DI[LMUN kù:babbar]
V. 1. níĝ-sa$_{10}$ 33 aktum-TÚG 14 *ᵓà-da-um*-TÚG-I
1 *gu-zi-tum* 10 íb+III-TÚG sa$_6$ gùn
3. 40 lá-2 íb+III-TÚG gùn
[ ]
5. [ -g]*i*
*Ib-lu*$_5$*-zú*
7. *wa*
*I-za-iš-ru*$_{12}$
9. lú-kar *Ma-nu-wa-ad*$^{ki}$
ki:lam$_7$
11. šeš-˹ib˺[-II]
VI. 1. *ᵓÀ-da-ni*$^{ki}$

(16)
2 ma-na TAR kù:babbar
3. šu-bal-ak
TAR kù-gi
5. daḫ
nu$_{11}$-za 1 an-dùl
7. níĝ-ba
$^{d}$BAD *Ga-na-na-um*

(17)
9. 6 gín [DILMUN kù:babbar]
[ ]
11. *in*
*Ša-dab*$_6^{ki}$
13. šu-ba$_4$-ti

(18)
10 gín DILMUN kù:babbar
15. *Na*-NE
*Na-gàr*$^{ki}$

(19)
17. 10 gín DILMUN k[ù]:babbar
[ ]
VII. 1. *ᵓÀ-du*$^{ki}$

(20)
4 gín DILMUN kù:babbar
3. nu$_{11}$-za 1 ĝír mar-tu
níĝ-ba
5. $^{d}$*ᵓA*$_5$*-da-“bal”*
*ᵓÀ-ma-du*$^{ki}$

(21)
7. 1 ma-na 15 gín DILMUN kù:babbar
níĝ-ba
9. diĝir-diĝir-diĝir

(22)
3 ma-na 50 gín DILMUN [kù:babbar]
11. 1 aš-ḫal 1 LAGAB al$_6$-ĝál
é siki

(23)
13. 8 ma-na 10 gín [DILMUN kù]:babbar
[ ]
VIII. 1. [x-]˹x˺-*na*-˹x˺
[5+]3 ma-na ŠÚ+ŠA gín DILMUN kù:babbar
3. [šu-]bal-ak
1 ma-na ˹ša˺-pi [g]ín DI[LMUN] kù-gi
5. 20 ĝír mar-tu ti kù-gi 3 gín DILMUN k[ù]-˹gi˺
*wa*
7. 10 ĝír [ ]
IX. 1. [ ]
*ga-ma-[a-]tum*
3. 13 ma-na ŠÚ+ŠA gín DILMUN kù:babbar

(14) 1 mina of silver for Iti, the travelling merchant, Igaišru has handed over.
(15) 4;23 minas [of silver] for the purchase of 48 garments (and) 48 kilts [...]: Ibluzu and Izaišru, traders of the city of Manuwat, (have received), at the market of the šeš-II-ib confraternity of the city of ᵓAdani.
(16) 2;30 minas of silver in exchange for 30 (shekels of) gold, to add (to that) for plating 1 statue: gift for the Lord of Ganana.
(17) 6 shekels [of silver ...] received in the city of Šadab.
(18) 10 shekels of silver for NaNe of the city of Nagar.
(19) 10 shekels of silver [for ...] of the city of ᵓAddu.
(20) 4 shekels of silver for plating 1 mar-tu dagger: gift for the god ᵓAdabal of the city of ᵓAmadu.
(21) 1;15 minas of silver: gift for the gods.
(22) 3;50 minas [of silver] for 1 filter of 1 ... (LAGAB) stored in the Treasury.
(23) 8;10 minas [of sil]ver [...]; 8;20 minas of silver in exchange for 1;40 minas of gold for 20 pointed mar-tu daggers (decorated with) gold (weighing) 3 shekels of gold each and 10 [...] daggers [...] for (their) knobs; 13;20 minas of silver for making 20 belts (and) 20 dagger pendants of 40 (shekels) each, given by the Palace for the review on the occasion of the offering [...].

kin$_5$-ak 20 íb-lá 20 kun ŠA.PI
5. ì-na-sum
SA.ZA$_x$$^{ki}$
7. *in*
igi-ḫi-du$_8$
9. *in* ud
⸢nídba⸣
X. 1. [ ]

(24)
⸢x⸣ gín DILMUN kù:babbar
3. *Ib-bu-tum*
7 gín DILMUN kù:babbar
5. maškim-*sù*
*Ma-rí*$^{ki}$

(25)
7. 4 gín DILMUN kù:babbar
nu$_{11}$-za 1 ⸢ĝír mar⸣-[tu]
9. [$^d$*Ra-sa-ap*]
[*ʾÀ-d*]*a*-[*n*]*i*$^{ki}$
11. *in*
[SA.]ZA$_x$$^{ki}$

(26)
13. [(ca. 3 lines)]
XI. 1. [ ]
en
3. *Kab-lu$_5$-ul*$^{ki}$
šu-ba$_4$-ti

(27)
5. 3 ma-na 57 gín DILMUN kù:babbar
níĝ-sa$_{10}$ 2 íb+III-TÚG babbar gíd 65 íb+III-TÚG sa$_6$ gùn 60 lá-1 [íb+III-TÚG gùn]
7. 3 ma-na 10 gín DILMUN kù:babbar
<níĝ-sa$_{10}$ ĜIŠ-ti-ḪAR>
*Wa-ba-rúm* "ur$_4$"
9. [šu]-⸢ba$_4$⸣-[ti]
[ki:lam$_7$]
XII. 1. [ ]$^{ki}$

(28)
10 gín DILMUN kù:babbar
3. lú ĜIŠ-kiri$_6$
*Kak-mi-um*$^{ki}$

(29)
5. 10 gín DILMUN kù:babbar
šu-bal-ak
7. 2 gín DILMUN kù-gi
*ni-zi-mu*
9. 2 *gú-li-lum*
*Wa-na*
11. ugula sur$_x$-BAR.AN

(30)
ŠÚ+ŠA gín ⸢DILMUN⸣ kù:babbar
13. šu-bal$^!$(KUL)-ak
4 gín ⸢DILMUN⸣ kù-g[i]
15. *ni-zi-mu*
1 dib
17. *Aḫ-ra-ma-lik*
[ ]

(31)
XIII. 1. TAR 4 gín DILMUN kù:babbar
šu-bal-ak
3. 6 2 NI gín DILMUN kù-gi
2 *gú-li-lum*
5. $^d$*Ku-ra*

(32)
ŠA.PI gín DILMUN kù:babbar
7. URI
1 íb-lá 1 kun
9. *Zi-ba-da*

(33)
1 ma-na 8 ½ gín DILMUN kù:babbar
11. šu-bal-ak
13 2 NI gín DILMUN ⸢kù-gi⸣
13. [...]
XIV. 1. *sa-ga-tum*
10 ĝír mar-tu zú LAGAB×AN.A
3. ì-na-sum

(24) [x] shekels of silver for Ibbutum; 7 shekels of silver for his representative of the city of Mari.
(25) 4 shekels of silver for plating 1 mar-[tu] dagger [for the god Rašap of the city of ʾAdani] in [the Pal]ace.
(26) [...] the king of the city of Kablul has received.
(27) 3;57 minas of silver for the purchase of 126 kilts; 3;10 minas of silver <for the purchase of GIŠ-ti-ḪAR-wood>, Wabarum, the collector (of goods), has received [at the market of the city of ...].
(28) 10 shekels of silver for the garden of the city of Kakmium.
(29) 10 shekels of silver in exchange for 2 shekels of gold for decorating 2 bracelets for Wana, the overseer of the team of mules.
(30) 20 shekels of silver in exchange for 4 shekels of gold for decorating 1 plaque for Aḫra-malik [...].
(31) 34 shekels of silver in exchange for 6 shekels (and) 2 NI of gold for 2 bracelets for the god Kura.
(32) 40 shekels of silver for the URI-decoration of 1 belt (and) 1 dagger pendant for Zibada.
(33) 1;08 ½ minas of silver in exchange for 13 shekels (and) 2 NI of gold [...] *sa-ga-tum* 10 serrated mar-tu daggers (decorated with) ivory, given for the review.

*in*
5. igi-ḫi-du$_8$

(34)
12 ma-na ŠA.PI gín DILMUN
kù:babbar
7. šu-bal-ak
2 ma-na TAR 2 gín DIL[MUN] kù-g[i]
9. ki[n$_5$-ak]
4 s[aĝ ] 4 *zi-[kir-]ra-tu[m]*
11. en

(35)
TAR kù:babbar
13. šu-˹bal˺[-ak]
XV. 1. 6 gín DILMUN kù:babbar
*ni-zi-mu*
3. 10 lá-2 kù-sal 2 níĝ-anše-ak
lú en

(36)
5. 10 g[ín DILMUN kù:babbar]
6–11. [ ]
12?. 2 ˹x˺[
13. [ ]
r. II?. x+1. [š]u-bal-ak
4 gín DILMUN kù-gi
3'. nu$_{11}$-za *ba-na-i-sa*
níĝ-ba
5'. *Ib-rí-um*
$^{d}$*Ra-sa-ap*
7'. [ ]

(37)
III?. x+1. *I-t[i]-a-gú*
DU.D[U]
3'. ˹*Za*˺*-bù-rúm*$^{ki}$

(38)
5 gín DILMUN kù:babbar
5'. *Du-tum*
*Ma-rí*$^{ki}$

(39)
7'. 1 ma-na kù:babbar
šu-bal-ak
9'. 1 ma-na ŠÚ+ŠA za:gìn
*áš-tum*
11'. *I-ti*
ga:eš$_8$
13'. *Ma-rí*$^{ki}$

(40)
10 gín DILMUN kù:babbar
15'. níĝ-ba
*Daš-na*
17'. *Ma-rí*$^{ki}$
[ ]
19'. [ ]

(41)
IV?. x+1. [z]áḫ

(42)
2 gín DILMUN ˹kù:babbar˺
3'. *ni-˹zi˺-mu*
1 níĝ-[anše-]a[k]
5'. *A-bu*

(43)
6 gín DILMUN kù:˹babbar˺
7'. lú ĜIŠ-kiri$_6$
*I-lum-na-im*
9'. šu-ba$_4$-ti

(44)
2 ma-na ŠÚ+ŠA gín DILMUN
kù:babbar
11'. níĝ-sa$_{10}$ ĜIŠ-ti-ḪAR
*Wa-ba-rúm* "ur$_4$"
13'. šu-ba$_4$-ti

(45)
3 ma-na ŠA.PI 5 gín DI[LMUN
kù:babbar]
V?. x+1. *[Ib-lu$_5$]-˹zú˺*
*wa*

(34) 12;40 minas of silver in exchange for 2;32 minas of gold for ma[king] 4 h[eads …] 4 fasteners for the king.
(35) 30 (shekels of) silver in exchange for 6 shekels of gold for decorating 8 buckles (and) 2 bridles for the king.
(36) 10 she[kels of silver … 20 shekels of silver] in exchange for 4 shekels of gold for plating its face: gift of Ibrium for the god Rašap […].
(37) […] for Itiagu (who) went to the city of Zabarum.
(38) 5 shekels of silver for Dutum of the city of Mari.
(39) 1 mina of silver in exchange for 1;20 minas of lapis lazuli from Iti, travelling merchant of the city of Mari.
(40) 10 shekels of silver: gift for Dašna of the city of Mari […].
(41) [… lo]st.
(42) 2 shekels of silver for decorating 1 bridle for Abu.
(43) 6 shekels of silver for the garden, Ilum-naim has received.
(44) 2;20 minas of silver for the purchase of GIŠ-ti-ḪAR-wood, Wabarum, the collector (of goods), has received.
(45) 3;45 minas [of silver for Iblu]zu and Iza-išru, [trade]rs of the city of Manuwat; 6 shekels of silver for the purchase of 1 black cloak for his spouse.

3'. *I-za-iš-ru*$_{12}$
[lú-k]ar
5'. *Ma-nu-wa-ad*$^{ki}$
6 gín DILMUN kù:babbar
7'. níĝ-sa$_{10}$ 1 gu-dùl-TÚG gi$_{6}$
dam-*sù*

(46)
9'. 1 ma-na kù:babbar
nu$_{11}$-za 8 si
11'. 4 gud
nídba
13'. en
*wa*
15'. *Ib-rí-um*
nídba
17'. $^{d}$*Ra-sa-ap*
[*ʾÀ-da-ni*$^{ki}$]

(47)
VI$^{?}$. x+1. [x ma-na x gín] ⌜DILMUN⌝
kù:babbar
níĝ-sa$_{10}$ ⌜18⌝ gud
3'. en

(48)
53 gín DILMUN kù:babbar
5'. níĝ-sa$_{10}$ 7 *mi-at* 80 <ĜIŠ->gu-kak-gíd
1 gín DILMUN kù:babbar
7'. níĝ-sa$_{10}$ 2 si dàra
15 gín DILMUN kù:babbar
9'. níĝ-sa$_{10}$ 1 ĝír mar-tu zú LAGAB×AN.A
NI-*gi*
11'. *A-da-bí-ig*$^{ki}$

(49)
VII$^{?}$. x+1. 1 ĝ[ír] mar-t[u] *ba-du-*[*u*$_{4}$] kù-g[i]
⌜kù⌝:[babbar]
*Ma-zú-ru*$_{12}$
3'. [ -]*du*[- ]

(50)
9 gín DILMUN kù:babbar
5'. níĝ-sa$_{10}$ 1 ĝír mar-tu *ba-du-u*$_{4}$ kù-gi
kù:babbar
*Ib-dur-ti-lu*
7'. dumu-nita
*A-mur-li-im*

(51)
9'. ŠA.PI gín DILMUN kù:babbar
níĝ-sa$_{10}$ 1 ĝír mar-tu kù-gi
11'. *Gú-ra*-BÀD$^{[ki]}$

(52)
VIII$^{?}$. x+1. 10 gín DILMUN kù:babbar
níĝ-sa$_{10}$ 1 ĝír mar-tu *ba-du-u*$_{4}$ kù-gi
3'. [X-N]E[- ]
lú *Ḫáb-la-ar*

(53)
5'. 8 gín DILMUN kù:babbar
níĝ-sa$_{10}$ 1 ĝír mar-tu *ba-du-u*$_{4}$ kù-gi
kù:babbar
7'. *Ù-da-sa*
di-kud

(54)
9'. 55 gín DILMUN kù:babbar
šu-bal-ak
11'. 11 gín DILMUN kù-gi
[ ]

**TM.75.G.3706 (ARET III 635)**

(55)
r. IX$^{?}$. x+1. ⌜X-*na*⌝-*ra-tum*
*Da-ḫi-ir-ma-lik*
3'. *maš-ar-tum*

(56)
10$^{?}$ gín DILMUN kù:babbar
5'. [nu$_{11}$-za 1 *ḫa-bù*]

(46) 1 mina of silver for plating 8 horns of 4 oxen: offering of the king and Ibrium for the god Rašap [of the city of ʾAdani].
(47) [x;xx mina(s)] of silver for the purchase of 18 oxen for the king.
(48) 53 shekels of silver for the purchase of 780 spearheads; 1 shekel of silver for the purchase of 2 horns of a mountain goat; 15 shekels of silver for the purchase of 1 serrated mar-tu dagger (decorated with) ivory for NIgi of the city of Adabik.
(49) 1 *b.* mar-tu dagger (decorated with) silver (and) gold for Mazuru […].
(50) 9 shekels of silver for the purchase of 1 *b.* mar-tu dagger (decorated with) silver (and) gold for Ibdur-tilu, son of Amur-lim.
(51) 40 shekels of silver for the purchase of 1 mar-tu dagger (decorated with) gold for Gura-BAD.
(52) 10 shekels of silver for the purchase of 1 *b.* mar-tu dagger (decorated with) gold for […], (son) of Ḫablar.
(53) 8 shekels of silver for the purchase of 1 *b.* mar-tu dagger (decorated with) silver (and) gold for Udasa, the judge.
(54) 55 shekels of silver in exchange for 11 shekels of gold […].
(55) […] ... (for) Daḫir-malik (for$^{?}$ her$^{?}$) stele.
(56) 10 shekels of silver [for plating 1 mace]; 30 [shekels of silver] in exchange for 6 shekels of gold for plating its handle for the Lord of Ganana.

⸢TAR⸣ [gín DILMUN k]ù:b[abbar]
7'. šu-bal-ak
6 gín DILMUN kù-gi
9'. nu$_{11}$-za *ar-ra-si-su*
$^{\mathrm{d}}$BAD *Ga-na-na-um*

(57)
11'. 5 gín DILMUN kù:babbar
⸢šu⸣-bal-ak
13'. 1 gín DILMUN kù-gi
*ni-zi-mu*
15'. [ ]
X$^{?}$. x+1. [*Kak*]-⸢*mi*⸣-*um*$^{\mathrm{ki}}$

(58)
1 ma-na 10 gín DILMUN kù:babbar
3'. 12 gada-TÚG
[ ]

(59)
5'. [TAR 3 gín DILMUN 3 NI] kù[:babba]
r
šu-bal-ak
7'. 6 2 NI gín DILMUN kù-gi
2 *gú-li-lum*
9'. $^{\mathrm{d}}$*Ku-ra*

(60)
2 ½ gín DILMUN kù:babbar
11'. šu-bal-ak
½ gín DILMUN kù-gi
13'. *ni-zi-mu*
1 dib
15'. *Du-bí-ab*
[ ]

(61)
XI$^{?}$. x+1. [x] g[ín] ⸢DILMUN⸣ kù:babbar
nu$_{11}$-za 1 dub
3'. ki
*Ib-rí-um*
5'. [ ]

(62)
[ ]
7'. [ ]
[ ]
9'. lú an-zam$_{\mathrm{x}}$
*wa*
11'. šu-du$_{8}$
*Šè-na-um*$^{\mathrm{ki}}$

(63)
13'. 3 ma-na ŠÚ+ŠA gín DILMUN
kù:babbar
[*z*]*i-du*
15'. 1 *mi-at* ĝír mar-tu *ba-du-u*$_{4}$
kù:[babba]r
[ ]

(57) 5 shekels of silver in exchange for 1 shekel of gold for decorating [… of the city of Kak]mium.
(58) 1;10 minas of silver for 12 linen clothes […].
(59) [33 shekels (and) 3 NI] of sil[ver] in exchange for 6 shekels (and) 2 NI of gold for 2 bracelets for the god Kura.
(60) 2 ½ shekels of silver in exchange for ½ shekel of gold for decorating 1 plaque for Dubiab […].
(61) [x] she[kels] of silver for plating 1 tablet … Ibrium […].
(62) […] of the an-zam$_{\mathrm{x}}$ goblet and taken in possession in the city of Šenaʾum.
(63) 3;20 minas of silver as alloy for 100 *b.* mar-tu daggers (decorated with) sil[ver …].

## Commentary

The following text, no. 9, has to be dated to the year Ibrium 06, what compels to date this document to the year Ibrium 05.

The total silver expended is not preserved. The first registration concerns the mina (470 g) of silver for the renewal rite of the city-god Kura (§ 1): an additional 3 shekels for an unspecified ceremony in the course of the year (but again concerning his head) is then mentioned in § 9 (see the commentary to text no. 4). The documents XXI 9 and 10 from the following years instead register the additional 3 shekels in the first section, together with the mina expended at the beginning of the year. Kura also twice received a pair of gold bracelets of 6 ⅔ shekels (52 g) as annual offering (§§ 31, 59). The "gods", diĝir-diĝir-diĝir, received 1;15 minas (587 g) of silver (§ 21).

Four minas of silver were given to Tirin-damu and Tinib-dulum, two sisters (nin-ni) of the king, in relation to their function as priestesses, dam-diĝir, of the god ʾAdabal of Luban (Archi 1998a = 2015a, pp. 699–710), (§§ 1, 2). A silver delivery for these priestesses is often registered in the documents of the later years.

The king received decorations for his chariot (§§ 34, 35), and he was provided with eighteen oxen (§ 47).

The minister Ibrium celebrated the "festival of his stele", ḫúl na-rú<-*sù*> (§ 4), as he already had done in his first year (text no. XXI 3 § 43). He received two daggers (§ 3), and one plaque of silver (§ 61).

The envoys of Mari who came to Ebla were *Du-bí* with his representative (§ 7), *Daš-na* (§§ 11, 40), *Ib-bu-tum* with his representative (§ 24); *Du-tum* (§ 38); *I-ti* ga:eš$_8$ (§ 39)

A distribution of weapons to the personnel of the Palace in relation to a "review", igi-ḫi-du$_8$, of the personnel is registered in §§ 23, 33.

§ 48. Adabik was provided with 780 spearheads, and NIgi received a dagger. This city had been defeated in the year Ibr. 02 (see Archi 2021a, pp. 201–202).

§ 50. Ibdur-tilu, the son of Amur-lim, received a similar dagger according to *ARET* I 17 § 10, and *ARET* III 635 r. V 5.

§ 55. Daḫir-malik should be a daughter of Ibrium.

# 9
(Plates XVI–XVII)

(1)
o. I. 1. 1 ma-na 3 gín kù:babbar
saĝ [kù:]babba[r]
3. $^{d}$*Ku-ra*
[

(2)
II. 1. 1 ma-na kù:babbar
níĝ-ba
3. diĝir-diĝir-diĝir

(3)
8 gín DILMUN kù:babbar
5. níĝ-kaskal
*Gi-li-ti-um*$^{ki}$
7. DU.DU
[*A*]*r-mi*$^{ki}$

(4)
9. [x gí]n [DILMUN kù:babbar]
[níĝ-kaskal]
11. [*A-ir-ra*$^{?}$]
[*wa*]
13. [*A-zú-bù-lu*$^{?}$]
14$^{?}$. DU.DU
15. *Ar-mi*$^{ki}$
maškim
17. *Ḫa-ra-ì*

(5)
[x] ˹gín DILMUN˺ kù:babbar
19. [(ca. 4 lines)]
III. 1. níĝ-sa$_{10}$ 7 sila$_{4}$ ḪI.DIM[1]
lú
3. níĝ-lá-gaba
en
5. sikil

(6)
TAR kù:babbar
7. nu$_{11}$-za 2 *ḫa-bù*
1 ma-na kù:babbar
9. šu-bal-ak
[12 gín DILMUN kù-gi]
11. [ ]
[ ]
13. [ ]
[*a*]*r-ra-sa-sù*
15. níĝ-ba
$^{d}$*Ra-sa-ap*
17. *ʾÀ-da-ni*$^{ki}$
*wa*
19. $^{d}$*ʾÀ-da*
*Ḫa-lab*$_{x}^{ki}$
21. AMA-*ra*

(7)
[1 ma-na kù-babbar]
23. [nu$_{11}$-za si-si]
IV. 1. 2 gud
nídba
3. en
$^{d}$*Ra-sa-ap*
5. *ʾÀ-da-ni*$^{ki}$

(8)
1 ma-na kù:babbar
7. nu$_{11}$-za si-si
2 gud
9. nídba
en
11. $^{d}$*ʾÀ-da*
[*Ḫ*]*a-lab*$_{x}^{ki}$
13. [*i*]*n*
AMA-*ra*

[1] The transcription of this fragment (TM.75.G.3481) in *ARET* III 417 has wrongly: 7 sila$_{4}$ gíd ša$_{6}$.

(1) 1;03 minas of silver for the [sil]ver head of the god Kura.
(2) 1 mina of silver: gift for the gods.
(3) 8 shekels of silver: travel provision (for someone of) the city of Gilitium (who) went to the city of Armi.
(4) [x shekels of silver: travel provision for Airra and Azubulu] representatives of Ḫara-il, (who) went to the city of Armi.
(5) [x] shekels of silver […] for the purchase of 7 lamb's *fleeces* for the breast-band of the king for the purification rite.
(6) 30 (shekels of) silver for plating 2 maces; 1 mina of silver in exchange for [12 shekels of gold] […] for their handles: gift for the god Rašap of the city of ʾAdani and for the god Hadda of the city of Ḫalab, at the AMA-ra (festival).
(7) [1 mina of silver for plating the horns] of 2 oxen: offering of the king for the god Rašap of the city of ʾAdani.
(8) 1 mina of silver for plating the horns of 2 oxen: offering of the king for the god Hadda of [the city of Ḫ]alab, at the AMA-ra (festival).

(9)

15\. 10 gín DILMUN kù:babbar
šu-bal-ak
17\. 2 gín DILMUN kù-gi
*ni-zi-mu*
19\. 1 dib
*Ma-gal-lu*
21\. lú-kar
[*M*]*a-nu-*[*wa-ad*$^{ki}$]

(10)

23\. [x kù:babbar]
V. 1. níĝ-sa$_{10}$ 2 ĝír mar-tu *ba-du-u*$_4$ kù:babbar
*Šè-na*$^{ki}$
3\. šu-du$_8$
*wa*
5\. *En-na-il*
lú an:zam$_x$
7\. ugula IGI.NITA

(11)

3 gín DILMUN kù:babbar
9\. nu$_{11}$-za 3 ĝír šu-du$_8$-m[áš]
*Ib-rí-um*

(12)

11\. ŠA.PI 2 gín DILMUN kù:babbar
níĝ-sa$_{10}$ 7 gada-TÚG
13\. ki:lam$_7$
SA.ZA$_x$$^{ki}$

(13)

15\. 1 ma-na ŠA.PI gín DILMUN kù:babbar
[ ]
17\. [ ]

(14)

VI. 1. 20 gín DILMUN kù-gi
[(ca. 7 lines)]

(15)

9?. š[Ú+ŠA] g[ín] D[ILMUN ]
e[n]
11\. *Ì-ra-ar*$^{ki}$

(16)

ŠÚ+ŠA gín DILMUN kù:babbar 2 *bu*-DI
13\. 10 gín DILMUN kù:babbar
šu-bal-ak
15\. 2 gín DILMUN kù-gi
[ ]
VII. 1–11. [ ]

(17)

[ ]
13?. níĝ-s[a$_{10}$] 10 *ʾà-da-um*-TÚG-I
7 gada-TÚG
15\. 40 lá-2 íb+III-TÚG sa$_6$ gùn
1 *mi-at* [ ]
17\. [ ]
VIII. 1. [ ]
2–6. [ ]
7?. [ki:lam$_7$]
*ʾÀ-da-ni*$^{ki}$
9\. AMA-*ra*

(18)

TAR 3 gín DILMUN 3 NI kù:babbar
11\. šu-bal-ak
[6 g]ín DILMUN [3 N]I [kù-gi]
13\. 2 *gú-li-lum*
níĝ-ba
15\. $^{d}$*Ku-*[*ra*]

(19)

ŠÚ+ŠA gín DILMUN kù:babbar
17\. níĝ-ba
*Na-gàr*$^{ki}$
19\. *wa*
[ ]
21\. [ ]
IX. 1–6. [ ]

(9) 10 shekels of silver in exchange for 2 shekels of gold for decorating 1 plaque for Magallu of [the city of Ma]nu[wat].
(10) [x silver] for the purchase of 2 *b.* mar-tu daggers (decorated with) silver, taken in possession in the city of Šena, and (for) the an:zam$_x$ goblet for Enna-il, the overseer of the donkeys.
(11) 3 shekels of silver for plating 3 daggers for taking omens for Ibrium.
(12) 42 shekels of silver for the purchase of 7 linen clothes at the market of the Palace.
(13) 1;40 minas of silver […].
(14) 20 shekels of gold […].
(15) 20 sh[ekels of silver] for the ki[ng] of the city of Irar.
(16) 20 shekels of silver for 2 toggle-pins; 10 shekels of silver in exchange for 2 shekels of gold […].
(17) […] for the purchase of 17 garments (and) 138[+x] kilts […], [at the market] of the city of ʾAdani, at the AMA-ra (festival).
(18) 33 shekels (and) 3 NI of silver in exchange for [6 sh]ekels (and) [3 N]I [of gold] for 2 bracelets: gift for the god Ku[ra].
(19) 20 shekels of silver: gift for (someone of) the city of Nagar and […].

(20)
7$^{?}$. 5 gín DILMUN kù:babbar
*Sal-bí-um*$^{ki}$
9. *I-ga-iš-lu*
šu-mu-tak$_4$
11. *si-in*
NI-*rúm*$^{ki}$

(21)
13. 10 gín DILMUN kù:babbar
[níĝ-]⌜sa$_{10}$⌝
15. ⌜raš⌝-SAR
Kur⌜$^{ki}$⌝
17. ki:lam$_7$
$^{d}$*Ì-lam*

(22)
19. [ ]
[ ]
21. [ ]
X. 1–6. [ ]

(23)
7$^{?}$. ŠÚ+ŠA gín DILMUN kù:babbar
níĝ-sa$_{10}$ 40 si-si ĝír mar-tu
9. 1 ma-na ŠÚ+ŠA gín DILMUN kù:babbar
*zi-du*
11. [20$^{?}$+]10$^{?}$ g[ír] mar-tu
lú
13. simug
*Ga-sa*$^{ki}$

(24)
15. [ ]
[ ]
17. [ ]
[ ]
19. [ ]

(25)
XI. 1–6. [ ]
7$^{?}$. *Ma-rí*$^{ki}$
*in*
9. *Zi-ma-du*$^{ki}$
šu-ba$_4$-ti

(26)
11. 10 gín DILMUN kù:babbar
*Šu-ga-du*
13. *in*
*An-ga-li-lu*$^{ki}$
15. šu-ba$_4$-ti

(27)
TAR kù:babbar
17. *Na-gàr*$^{ki}$
*wa*
19. *Ga-ga-ba-an*$^{ki}$
*in*
21. [ $^{ki}$]
šu-ba$_4$-ti

(28)
23. ŠÚ+ŠA gín DILMUN kù:babbar
XII. 1–5. [ ]

(29)
6$^{?}$. 5 gín DILMUN kù:babbar
7. níĝ-kaskal
*Ìr-am$_6$-ma-lik*
9. *wa*
*En-na*-BAD
11. DU.DU
[*M*]*a-rí*$^{ki}$

(30)
13. ŠÚ+ŠA gín DILMUN kù:babbar
níĝ-ba
15. *Daš-na*
*wa*
17. *Šu-ga-du*
*Ma-r*[*í*]$^{ki}$
19. *in*
*Gi-da*-NE$^{ki}$
21. šu-ba$_4$-ti

(31)
[x] gín DILMUN kù:babbar
23. *Wa-ru$_{12}$-tum*
*Ma-rí*$^{ki}$
XIII. 1–4. [ ]

(20) 5 shekels of silver (for someone of) the city of Salbium, Iga-išlu has handed over for the city of NIrum.
(21) 10 shekels of silver [for the pur]chase of leek from the mountain region, at the market of the god Ilam.
(22) [...].
(23) 20 shekels of silver for the purchase of 40 mar-tu daggers (decorated with) horn; 1;20 minas of silver as alloy for 30 mar-tu da[ggers] for the metalworkers of the city of Gasa.
(24) [...].
(25) [...] of the city of Mari has received in the city of Zimadu.
(26) 10 shekels of silver Šugadu has received in the city of Angalilu.
(27) 30 (shekels of) silver for (someone of) the cities of Nagar and Gagaban, received in [...].
(28) 20 shekels of silver [...].
(29) 5 shekels of silver: travel provision for Iram-malik and Enna-BAD (who) went to [the city of M]ari.
(30) 20 shekels of silver: gift for Dašna and Šugadu of the city of Mari (who) have received it in the city of GidaNE.
(31) [x] shekels of silver for Warutum of the city of Mari [...].

(32)
5?. 2 ma-na 5 gín DILMUN kù:babbar
šu-bal-ak
7. ŠÚ+ŠA 5 gín DILMUN kù-gi
1 dib
9. *Zé-ba-da-ar*
l[ú]-ka[r]

(33)
11. TAR 3 gín DILMUN 3 NI kù:babbar
šu-bal-ak
13. 6 gín DILMUN 2 NI kù-gi
2 *gú-li-lum*
15. níĝ-⸢ba⸣
$^{d}$*Áš-da-bíl*

(34)
17. 4 ma-na ŠA.PI gín DILMUN
kù:babbar
níĝ-sa$_{10}$ 1 *mi-at* sal-TÚG
XIV. 1–4. [ ]
5?. 14 íb+III-TÚG gùn
ki:lam$_{7}$
7. $^{d}$*Áš-da-bíl*

(35)
10 ma-na TAR 2 gín DILMUN
kù:babbar
9. níĝ-sa$_{10}$ 3 [ ] ⸢x⸣
1 túg-NI.NI sa$_{6}$ 40 *ʾà-da-um*-TÚG-I
11. 10 túg-NI.NI
40 *ʾà-da-um*-TÚG-I
13. 1 *mi-at* 15 sal-TÚG
1 *mi-at* 12 gu-mug-TÚG
15. 12 íb+III-TÚG babbar
ki:lam$_{7}$
17. *Ìr-ku*$^{ki}$

(36)
XV. 1–4. [ ]

(37)
5?. TAR kù:babbar
níĝ-sa$_{10}$ ĝeštin
7. *Ib-gi-da-mu*
šu-ba$_{4}$-ti

(38)
9. 5 kù:babbar
níĝ-sa$_{10}$ 2 ĝír mar-tu ti kù-gi
11. *Ib-rí-um*
uru-bar
13. *in* níĝ-kas$_{4}$
lú sikil

(39)
15. ŠÚ+ŠA 5 gín [DILMUN] kù:babbar
níĝ-sa$_{10}$ 1 ĝír mar-tu ti kù-gi
17. *A-šu-úr-il*
ugula

(40)
XVI. x+1. šu-⸢du$_{8}$⸣

(41)
ŠA.PI gín DILMUN kù:babbar
3'. níĝ-sa$_{10}$ 1 ĝír mar-tu kù-gi
*Ìr-da-ma-lik*
5'. lú
[

(42)
XVII. x+1. ⸢x⸣[ ]⸢x⸣[ ]
maš[kim]
3'. *Ib-rí-um*

(43)
1 ma-na kù:babbar
5'. níĝ-sa$_{10}$ 1 ĝír mar-tu kù-gi
[

(44)
XVIII. x+1. [ -]*il*
šu-ba$_{4}$-ti

(45)
3'. TAR 5 gín DILMUN kù:babbar
níĝ-sa$_{10}$

(32) 2;05 minas of silver in exchange for 25 shekels of gold for 1 plaque for Zebadar, the trader.
(33) 33 shekels (and) 3 NI of silver in exchange for 6 shekels (and) 2 NI of gold for 2 bracelets: gift for the god Ašdabil.
(34) 4;40 minas of silver for the purchase of 100[+x] garments (and) 14 kilts, at the market of the god Ašdabil.
(35) 10;32 minas of silver for the purchase of 321 garments (and) 12 kilts, at the market of the city of Irku.
(36) […].
(37) 30 (shekels of) silver for the purchase of wine, Ibgi-damu has received.
(38) 5 (shekels of) silver for the purchase of 2 pointed mar-tu daggers (decorated with) gold for Ibrium, (received in) the suburbs, for the purification (on the occasion) of the military expedition.
(39) 25 shekels of silver for the purchase of 1 pointed mar-tu dagger (decorated with) gold for Ašur-il, the overseer.
(40) […] taken in possession.
(41) 40 shekels of silver for the purchase of 1 mar-tu dagger (decorated with) gold for Irda-malik, (son) of […].
(42) […] the repre[sentative] of Ibrium.
(43) 1 mina of silver for the purchase of 1 mar-tu dagger (decorated with) gold […].
(44) […] has received.
(45) 35 shekels of silver for the purchase of 1 mar-tu dagger (decorated with) gold, Ilum-aḫa has received (for) a young man of the suburbs.

r. I. 1. 1 ĝír mar-tu kù-gi
*Ì-lum-a-ḫa*
3. dumu-nita
uru-bar
5. šu-ba$_4$-ti

(46)
ŠÚ+ŠA 5 [g]ín DILMUN kù:babbar
7. [(ca. 7 lines)]

(47)
13?. 1 ma-na TAR 7 gín DILMUN
kù:babbar
níĝ-sa$_{10}$ 8 gada-TÚG
15. 68 íb+III-TÚG gùn
ki:lam$_7$
17. *gi-*[*ba-lu*]
II. 1. *ʾÀ-da-ni*$^{ki}$

(48)
2 ma-na TAR kù:babbar
3. šu-bal-ak
TAR kù-gi
5. [(ca. 7 lines)]

(49)
13?. *Du-bí*
lú *Iš-da-má*
15. tuš-LÚ×TIL
*Ar-mi*$^{ki}$
17. *áš-ti*
*Gul-da-ad*$^{ki}$

(50)
19. 2 ma-na TAR kù:babbar
*šu-ti*
III. 1. TAR kù-gi 1 dib
*En-àr-li-im*
3. [dumu-ni]ta
*Du-*[*bí*]*-šum*
5. *A-ba-ad*$^{ki}$
tuš-LÚ×TIL
7. *Ar-mi*$^{ki}$
*áš-ti*
9. *Zú-mu-šar*$^{ki}$

(51)
10 ma-na TAR kù:babbar
11. šu-bal-ak
[2 ma-na 6 gín DILMUN] kù-[gi] 1
[dib]
13. [ŠÚ+]ŠA 5 [gí]n [DILM]UN
[kù:babbar]
⸢*wa*⸣(?)
15. [x] gín DILMUN kù-gi
nu$_{11}$-za 1 ĝír mar-tu
17. *Du-ur-il*
IV. 1. *Bù-ra-tin*$^{ki}$
tuš-LÚ×TIL
3. *Ar-mi*$^{[ki]}$
[*áš-ti*]
5. [ $^{ki}$]

(52)
2 ⸢ma⸣-na TAR [kù:babbar]
7. šu-ba[l]-ak
TAR kù-gi 1 dib
9. TAR kù:babbar
níĝ-sa$_{10}$ 1 ĝír mar-tu kù-gi
11. *Šu-ma-lik*
lú
13. *Iš$_{11}$-da-mu*

(53)
TAR kù:babbar
15. 2 *bu*-DI
*Za-ne-ḫi-Ma-rí*$^{ki}$
17. é-gi
*Ib-ʾà-ra*
19. *ʾÀ-šu*$^{⸢ki⸣}$

(54)
V. 1. 6 gín DILMUN kù:babbar
⸢ZU.PIRIĜ⸣
3. 2[+x] ⸢x⸣[- ] 3 [ ]
⸢x⸣[- ]
5. *Ir*[- ]

(55)
4 gín DILMUN kù:babbar
7. nam-kud

(46) 25 shekels of silver [...].
(47) 1;37 minas of silver for the purchase of 8 garments (and) 68 kilts, at the market of the *gi*[*balu*] of the city of ʾAdani.
(48) 2;30 minas of silver in exchange for 30 (shekels of) gold [...].
(49) [...] for Dubi, (son) of Išdama (who) resided in the city of Armi from the city of Guldad.
(50) 2;30 minas of silver, those (for) 30 (shekels of) gold for 1 plaque for Enar-lim, [so]n of Du[bi]šum of the city of Abad, (who) resided in the city of Armi from the city of Zumušar.
(51) 10;30 minas of silver in exchange for [2;06 minas of] go[ld] for 1 [plaque]; 25 [shek]els of [silver] and [x] shekels of gold for plating 1 mar-tu dagger for Dur-il of the city of Buratin, (who) resided in the city of Armi [from the city of ...].
(52) 2;30 minas [of silver] in exchange for 30 (shekels of) gold for 1 plaque; 30 (shekels of) silver for the purchase of 1 mar-tu dagger (decorated with) gold for Šu-malik, (son) of Iš-damu.
(53) 30 (shekels of) silver for 2 toggle-pins for Zaneḫi-Mari, daughter-in-law of Ibʾara of the city of ʾAšu.
(54) 6 shekels of silver for the hangers of 2+[x ...].
(55) 4 shekels of silver for the king of the city of Burman (who) swore an oath in the temple of the god Kura.

en
9. *Bur-ma-an*$^{ki}$
é
11. $^{d}$*Ku-ra*

(56)
12 gín DILMUN kù:babbar
13. nu$_{11}$-za
1 *ḫa-bù*
15. níĝ-ba
$^{d}$*Ga-mi-iš*
17. *ḫu-ru*$_{12}$-˹*mu*˺

(57)
ŠÚ+ŠA gín DILMUN kù:babbar
19. [níĝ-]˹sa$_{10}$˺
VI. 1. ĜIŠ-ti-ḪAR
*Wa-ba-*˹*rúm*˺
3. šu-ba$_{4}$-ti
*in* ud
5. šu-mu-níĝin
SA.ZA$_{x}^{ki}$

(58)
7. TAR kù:babbar 1 *bu*-DI
10 gín DILMUN kù:babbar
9. šu-bal-ak
2 gín DILMUN kù-gi
11. nu$_{11}$-za 2 saĝ-*sù*
níĝ-ba
13. *Kir-su-ud*

(59)
ŠÚ+ŠA gín DILMUN kù:babbar
15. 4 *bu*-DI
níĝ-ba
17. *Ib-ʾà-ra*
*wa*
19. nin-ni-˹*sù*˺
VII. 1. *in* ud
níĝ-mu-sá
3. ˹*Za*˺*-ne-ḫi-Ma-*[*r*]*í*$^{ki}$
é-gi
5. *Ib-ʾà-ra*
*ʾÀ-šu*$^{ki}$

(60)
7. 2 ma-na TAR kù:babbar
šu-bal-ak
9. TAR kù-gi 1 dib
*En-na-il*
11. ugula *Lum-na-an*$^{ki}$

(61)
13 gín DILMUN kù:babbar
13. nu$_{11}$-za 1 *ḫa-bù*
TAR kù:babbar
15. šu-bal-ak
6 gín DILMUN ˹kù-gi˺
17. nu$_{11}$-za 1 *ar-ra-sù*
VIII. 1. [níĝ-b]a$^{?}$
$^{d}$BAD *Ga-*[*na-*]*na-im*

(62)
3. ŠÚ+ŠA 6 gín DILMUN
nu$_{11}$-za 1 an-dùl
5. TAR kù:babbar
šu-bal-ak
7. 6 gín DILMUN kù-gi
nu$_{11}$-za
9. *ba-na-ʾà-sa*
*wa*
11. íb+III-TÚG
[*w*]*a*
13. an-zam$_{x}$
*wa*
15. 2 *gú-li-lum-sù*
níĝ-ba
17. $^{dʾ}$*A*$_{5}$*-da-ra*

(63)
5 ma-na 5 gín ˹DILMUN˺
[kù:babbar]
IX. 1. nu$_{11}$-za 1 an-dùl
lú
3. *Ib-rí-um*
šu-mu-tak$_{4}$
5. $^{d}$BAD *Du-du-la*$^{ki}$

(56) 12 shekels of silver for plating 1 mace: gift for the god Kamiš, in month VI.
(57) 20 shekels of silver [for the pur]chase of GIŠ-ti-ḪAR-wood, Wabarum has received on the occasion of the cultic journey of the Palace.
(58) 30 (shekels of) silver for 1 toggle-pin; 10 shekels of silver in exchange for 2 shekels of gold for plating their heads: gift for Kirsud.
(59) 20 shekels of silver for 4 toggle-pins: gift of Ibʾara and his sister, on the occasion of the marriage of Zaneḫi-Mari, daughter-in-law of Ibʾara of the city of ʾAšu.
(60) 2;30 minas of silver in exchange for 30 (shekels of) gold for 1 plaque for Enna-il, the overseer of the city of Lumnan.
(61) 13 shekels of silver for plating 1 mace; 30 (shekels of) silver in exchange for 6 shekels of gold for plating its handle: [gif]t to the Lord of Ga[na]na.
(62) 36 shekels (of silver) for plating 1 statue; 30 (shekels of) silver in exchange for 6 shekels of gold for plating its face and kilt and (its) an-zam$_{x}$ goblet (and) 2 bracelets: gift for the goddess ʾAdara.
(63) 5;05 minas [of silver] for plating 1 statue, Ibrium has handed over to the Lord of the city of Tuttul.

(64)

ŠÚ+ŠA ⌜gín⌝ [DILMUN] kù:babbar 2 *bu*-DI
7. *ma-lik-tum*
*Lum-na-an*$^{ki}$
9. *I-lu*$_5$-*za*$_x$-*ma-lik*
šu-mu-tak$_4$

(65)

11. 7 ma-na TAR kù:babbar
šu-bal-ak 1 ma-na TAR kù-gi
13. *ni-zi-mu*
nu$_{11}$-za ḫaš-ḫaš
15. 7 *gú-li-lum*
X. 1. ⌜kù:babbar⌝-II esi ĜÁ×LÁ TAR-*sù*
*wa*
3. 10 *gú-li-lum* kù:babbar-II esi ĜÁ×LÁ ŠÚ+ŠA gín DILMUN
1 *gú-li-lum* kù:babbar-I esi 1 gín DILMUN ĜÁ×LÁ-*sù*
5. 7 ma-na 1 gín DILMUN kù:babbar
šu-bal-ak
7. 1 ma-na ŠÚ+ŠA 6 gín DILMUN kù-gi
*ni-zi-mu*
9. nu$_{11}$-za ḫaš-ḫaš
1 dib a-gar$_5$-gar$_5$ lú 4 *gú-li-lum*
11. [ ]
1 dib a-gar$_5$-gar$_5$
XI. 1. [ ]
15 *gú-li-lum* a-gar$_5$-gar$_5$-II esi
3. *wa*
2 *gú-li-lum* a-gar$_5$-gar$_5$ *sa-ḫ*[*a*-]*wa*-II esi ĜÁ×LÁ TAR
5. *wa*
1? *gú-li-lum* a-gar$_5$-gar$_5$ *sa-ḫa-wa* 20 esi
7. 12 *gú-li-lum* a-gar$_5$-gar$_5$ *sa-ḫa-wa* 12 esi
5 gín DILMUN kù:babbar
9. *ni-zi-mu*
nu$_{11}$-za ḫaš-ḫaš
11. 1 *gú-li-lum* a-gar$_5$-gar$_5$-II esi
*wa*
13. 4 *gú-li-lum* [a-]gar$_5$-gar$_5$[-I] esi
XII. 1. [1 ma-na ŠA.PI gín DILMUN kù:babbar]
[šu-]bal-ak
3. ŠÚ+ŠA gín DILMUN kù-gi
*ni-zi-mu*
5. nu$_{11}$-za
10 ĝír mar-tu kù-gi
7. 2 ĝír mar-tu ti [kù]-⌜gi⌝
[x] ĝír mar-tu zú LAGAB×AN
9. 6 ĝír mar-tu *ba-du-u*$_4$ kù-gi
3 gín DILMUN kù:babbar
11. *ni-zi-mu*
*zi-tum*
13. 4 ĝír mar-tu *ba-du-u*$_4$ kù:babbar
lú
15. [ĝuruš-ĝuruš]
XIII. 1. [SA.]ZA$_x^{ki}$

(66)

[ ]
3. [ ]
[ ]
5. [*D*]*u-du-la*$^{ki}$

(67)

1 gín DILMUN kù:babbar
7. nu$_{11}$-za
[ ]x
9. [ ]
*Ib-r*[*í*-]*um*

(68)

11. 1 ma-na kù:babbar
[ ]
13. [ ]
šu-ba$_4$-ti

(64) 20 shekels of silver for 2 toggle-pins for the queen of the city of Lumnan, Iluza-malik has handed over.
(65) 7;30 minas of silver in exchange for 1;30 minas of gold for decorating with lamination and granulation 7 double bracelets of 30 (shekels of) silver each (and) diorite and 10 double bracelets of 20 shekels of silver each (and) diorite, 1 single bracelet of 1 shekel of silver (and) diorite; 7;01 minas of silver in exchange for 1;26 minas of gold for decorating with lamination and granulation 1 plaque of copper of 4 bracelets […] 1 plaque of copper […] 15 double bracelets of copper (and) diorite and 2 double bracelets (and) pendants of 30 (shekels) of copper each (and) diorite and 1 bracelet (and) pendant of 20 (shekels) of copper (and) diorite, 12 bracelets (and) pendants of 12 (shekels) of copper each (and) diorite; 5 shekels of silver for decorating with lamination and granulation 1 double bracelet of copper (and) diorite and 4 single bracelets of copper (and) diorite; [1;40 minas of silver in] exchange for 20 shekels of gold for decorating with lamination and granulation 10 mar-tu daggers (decorated with) gold, 2 pointed mar-tu daggers (decorated with) gold, [x] serrated mar-tu daggers (decorated with) ivory, 6 *b.* mar-tu daggers (decorated with) gold; 3 shekels of silver for decorating in alloy 4 *b.* mar-tu daggers (decorated with) silver, for [the men of the Pa]lace.
(66) [… of the city of T]uttul.
(67) 1 shekel of silver for plating […] for Ibrium.
(68) 1 mina of silver […] has received.

(69)
15. 5 gín DILMUN
*gú-la-⸢zi⸣-na-tum*
17. 3 *gú-li-lum* a-gar$_5$-gar$_5$
lú *Wa-su*-LUM
19. lú *Ib-ni-ḫar*
*wa*
21. *En-nu-lum*
XIV. 1. BÍL-*da-mu*
*I-ti-a-gú*
3. lú *En-na-il*
[ ]
5. [ ]
[ ]
7. ki[n$_5$-ak]
*gú-li-lum*
9. ĝuruš-ĝuruš
SA.ZA$_x^{ki}$

(70)
11. 3 ma-na kù:babbar
*Za-ba-rúm*
13. šu-ba$_4$-ti
níĝ-sa$_{10}$ še-še

(71)
15. ŠA.PI gín DILMUN kù:babbar
níĝ-sa$_{10}$ 1 ĝír mar-tu kù-gi
17. *Íl-zi*
lú *Iš*$_{11}$*-gú-nu*
19. *⸢Ba⸣*?*-sa-⸢rí-im*$^{ki}$⸣

(72)
XV. 1. ⸢15⸣ gín DILMUN kù:babbar
níĝ-sa$_{10}$ 1 ĝír mar-tu zú LAGAB×AN
k[ù-]g[i]
3. [*Gi-ra*]-*m*[*a-lik*]
lú *I-b*[*í*]-*šum*

(73)
5. ŠA.PI gín DILMUN kù:babbar
níĝ-sa$_{10}$ 1 ĝír mar-tu kù-gi
7. 4 ma-na 10 gín DILMUN kù:babbar
šu-bal-ak
9. 50 gín DILMUN kù-gi 1 dib
TAR kù:babbar
11. URI
1 íb-lá 1 ĝír-kun
13. 2 ma-na TAR kù:babbar
šu-bal-ak
XVI. 1. [TAR] kù-g[i]
nu$_{11}$-za-*sù*
3. *En-na-⸢il⸣*
[ ]
5. *Rí-ì-ma-lik*
lú-kar
7. *Kak-mi-um*$^{ki}$

(74)
50 gín DILMUN kù:babbar
9. níĝ-sa$_{10}$ 50 íb+III-TÚG gùn
TAR 2 gín DILMUN kù:babbar
11. níĝ-sa$_{10}$ ĜIŠ-gu-kak-gíd
*Wa-ba-rúm*
13. ⸢šu⸣-ba$_4$-ti
ki:⸢lam$_7$⸣
15. *zi-ba-tum*
*ʾÀ-da-ni*$^{ki}$

(75)
17. ⸢TAR⸣ [k]ù:b[abbar]
[ ]
XVII. 1–3. [ ]
[5 gín DILMUN kù:babbar]
5?. šu-bal-ak
1 gín DILMUN kù-gi
7. *ni-zi-mu*
1 dib
9. *Maḫ-ra-da-mu*
dumu-nita en

(69) 5 shekels (of silver) … (*gú-la-zi-na-tum*) for 3 bracelets of copper for WasuLUM, (son) of Ibniḫar and Ennulum, BIL-damu, Itiagu, (son) of Enna-il […] for m[aking] bracelets for the men of the Palace.
(70) 3 minas of silver, Zabarum has received for the purchase of barley.
(71) 40 shekels of silver for the purchase of 1 mar-tu dagger (decorated with) gold for Ilzi, (son) of Iš-gunu of the city of Basarim.
(72) 15 shekels of silver for the purchase of 1 serrated mar-tu dagger (decorated with) ivory and go[ld for Gira]-m[alik], (son) of Ibišum.
(73) 40 shekels of silver for the purchase of 1 mar-tu dagger (decorated with) gold; 4;10 minas of silver in exchange for 50 shekels of gold for 1 plaque; 30 (shekels of) silver for the URI-decoration of 1 belt (and) 1 dagger pendant; 2;30 minas of silver in exchange for [30] (shekels of) gol[d] for its lamination for Enna-il, […], Reʾi-malik, trader of the city of Kakmium.
(74) 50 shekels of silver for the purchase of 50 kilts; 32 shekels of silver for the purchase of spearheads, Wabarum has received, at the market of the *zibatum* of the city of ʾAdani.
(75) 30 (shekels of) [sil]ver […] [5 shekels of silver] in exchange for 1 shekel of gold for decorating 1 plaque for Maḫra-damu, son of the king.

(76)
11. ŠA.PI 7 gín DILMUN an-na
[šu]b [*si-i*]*n*
13. [ ] x [ ]
[ ]
15. [ ]
1 ĜIŠ-gígir-II
17. *Ib-rí-um*

(77)
ŠÚ+ŠA kù:babbar
19. níĝ-sa$_{10}$ 1 ĝír mar-tu ti kù-gi
*Ma-li-gú*
21. *Ga-rí-*⌜*u*$_9$⌝$^{[ki]}$

(78)
XVIII. 1–4. [ ] ⌜x⌝
5?. è
[DI]š mu

(79)
7. [x+]2 kù:babbar[a)]
níĝ-sa$_{10}$
9. [
(blank)

*a*) lines 7–8 written in graffito

(76) 47 shekels of tin to be melted in […] for a chariot of Ibrium.
(77) 20 (shekels of) silver for the purchase of 1 pointed mar-tu dagger (decorated with) gold for Maligu of the city of Gariu.
(78) […]: expenditure, (for) one year.
(79) [x+]2 (shekels of) silver for the purchase of […].

## Commentary

The synchronism established by the registration of the oath of Enar-Ḫalab king of Burman in § 55 and in *ARET* XIV 59a § 17, the mu-DU document to be dated to the year Ibr. 06 (see *ARET* XIV, p. 212), fixes this document in the chronological order of the series of the annual documents concerning the "expenditures", è, of metals.

The first registration concerns (as usual) 1 mina (470 g) of silver for the renewal rite of the head of the city-god Kura (§ 1), and another 3 shekels (23 g) for a later ceremony; the following one (§ 2) concerns 1 mina for "the gods", diĝir-diĝir-diĝir. Kura then received a pair of gold bracelets of 6 ⅔ shekels (52 g), as an annual offering (§ 18).

The wool of seven "... lambs (for) the breast-band of the king (for) a purification rite (sikil)" is registered in § 5; cf. *ARET* XII 510 I' 1': 1 zara$_6$-T[ÚG] en sikil; *MEE* 10, 3 o. V 5–10: 1 zara$_6$- TÚG sikil en in ud nídba $^{d}$En-ki.

The minister Ibrium received several daggers (§§ 11, 38, 67?), and some decorations for his chariots (§ 76).

Several messengers of Mari came to Ebla: [X] (§ 25); *Šu-ga-du* (§ 26); *Daš-na* and *Šu-ga-du* (§ 30); *Wa-ru*$_{12}$*-tum* (§ 31). *Ìr-am*$_6$*-ma-lik* and *En-na-*BAD were sent to Mari (§ 29).

§ 23. Silver was given to the "metalworkers", simug, of the city of Gasa for the decoration of some daggers. The metalworkers of this city are mentioned also in *ARET* III 964 r. IV 2': in number of 41.

§ 30. The city of *Gi-da-*NE$^{ki}$ (other writing *Gi-ti-*NE$^{ki}$) was related to Ibrium and his family, see also *ARET* III 628 I 2'–4': *Ib-rí-um in Gi-da-*NE$^{ki}$ šu-ba$_4$-ti.

§§ 49–50. Plaques in gold were given to several officials who "resided", tuš-LÚ×TIL, in the city of Armi.

§§ 53, 59. Princess *Za-ne-ḫi-Ma-rí*$^{ki}$, probably a daughter of king Irkab-damu, is mentioned in two documents of minister Arrukum as *Za-ne-Ma-rí* (*ARET* XV,1 26 §§ 39–40, 34 § 142) together with *Da-ti-*$^{d}$TU, (who became queen of the city of Lumnan. § 64), and *Dab-za-da-mu*. She is always qualified as "daughter-in-law", é-gi (see LL é-gi-a = *gal-la-tum/du* / *gal-tum*; Akk. *kallatum*) of *Ib-*ʾ*à-ra* (a chief) of the city of ʾ*À-šu*$^{ki}$ (see the *Indices*).

§ 55. The king of Burman came to swear an oath in the temple of Kura (see above).

§ 58. Kirsud was “a woman of the king”, dam en.

§ 64. The queen of Lumnan was the Eblaite princess Dati-TU (see the commentary to the text XXI 2 § 6).

§ 65. Gold was employed for the decoration of many bracelets of silver and copper, and of daggers for the men of the Palace. See also § 69.

§ 70. 3 minas (1.41 kg) were given to Zabarum for the purchase of barley. He had already received barley for his “men” and spouse in the year Ibrium 02 (see XXI 5 § 57).

# 10
## (Plates XVIII–XIX)

(1)
o. I. 1. 1 ma-na 3 gín DILMUN kù:babbar
saĝ urudu
3. $^{d}$*Ku-ra*

(2)
1 ma-na ŠÚ+ŠA gín DILMUN
kù:babbar
5. *Di-ne-íb-du-lum*
nin-ni
7. en
šu-ba$_4$-ti

(3)
9. TAR kù:babbar
níĝ-ba
11. *Du-tum*
*Ma-rí*$^{ki}$
13. lú ga:eš$_8$

(4)
10 gín DILMUN kù:babbar
15. lú ĜIŠ-kiri$_6$
*Kak-mi-um*$^{ki}$

(5)
17. 10 gín DILMUN kù:babbar
[(níĝ-)]kaskal
II. 1. *A-dar-*KA*-mu*$^{ki}$

(6)
2 ma-na kù:babbar
3. nu$_{11}$-za 1 ĜIŠ-banšur
1 ma-na ŠA.PI gín DILMUN
kù:babbar
5. šu-bal-ak
ŠÚ+ŠA gín DILMUN kù-gi
7. nu$_{11}$-za 1 saĝ ⸢lu$_5$⸣
1 ĜIŠ-banšur
9. níĝ-ba
$^{d}$*Am-ma-rí-ig*

(7)
11. 1 ma-na ŠÚ+ŠA gín DILMUN
kù:babbar
níĝ-ba
13. *Wa-ru*$_{12}$*-tum*
III. 1. *Daš-na*
*Iš*$_{11}$*-ga-um*
3. *ᵓÀ-bí-su*
*Ma-rí*$^{ki}$

(8)
5. ŠA.PI gín DILMUN kù:babbar
2 *šu-ba*$^{?}$*-la*
7. *Ib-rí-um*

(9)
⸢5⸣ gín DILMUN kù:babbar
9. níĝ-ba
*A-mu-ra*
11. *Du-ub*$^{ki}$

(10)
5 gín DILMUN kù:babbar
13. níĝ-ba
*Ša-nap-zu-gúm*$^{ki}$

(11)
15. 10 gín DILMUN kù:babbar
níĝ-ba
17. *Ba-na-*⸢*i*⸣*-um*$^{ki}$

(12)
10 gín DILMUN kù:babbar
IV. 1. níĝ-ba
*Daš-na*
3. *Ma-rí*$^{ki}$

(1) 1;03 minas of silver for the bronze head of the god Kura.
(2) 1;20 minas of silver, Tinib-dulum, sister of the king, has received.
(3) 30 (shekels of) silver: gift for Dutum of the city of Mari, the travelling merchant.
(4) 10 shekels of silver for the garden of the city of Kakmium.
(5) 10 shekels of silver: travel [provision] for (someone of) the city of AdarKAmu.
(6) 2 minas of silver for plating 1 table; 1;40 minas of silver in exchange for 20 shekels of gold for plating 1 head of androcephalus bull of 1 table: gift for the god Ammarik.
(7) 1;20 minas of silver: gift for Warutum, Dašna, Išgaum (and) ᵓAbišu of the city of Mari.
(8) 40 shekels of silver for 2 … (*šu-ba-la*) for Ibrium.
(9) 5 shekels of silver: gift for Amura of the city of Dub.
(10) 5 shekels of silver: gift for (someone of) the city of Šanapzugum.
(11) 10 shekels of silver: gift for (someone of) the city of Banaᵓium.
(12) 10 shekels of silver: gift for Dašna of the city of Mari.

(13)
10 gín DILMUN kù:babbar
5. *ni-zi-mu*
*iš-ki-lum*
7. en

(14)
10 gín DILMUN kù:babbar
9. nu$_{11}$-za 1 ĜIŠ-sal
lú DU.DU
11. lu$_{5}$
tuš
13. $^{d}$*Á-la*
lú *Zi-ig*$^{ki}$

(15)
15. 2 gín DILMUN kù:babbar
*ni-zi-mu*
17. nu$_{11}$-za 1 *za-ḫa-da*
*Ib-rí-um*

(16)
19. 15 gín DILMUN [kù:babbar]
V. 1. nu$_{11}$-za 1 *ḫa-bù*
TAR kù:babbar
3. šu-bal-ak
6 gín DILMUN kù-gi
5. nu$_{11}$-za 1 *ar-ra-sù*
níĝ-ba
7. $^{d}$*ʾÀ-da*

(17)
10 gín DILMUN kù:babbar
9. nu$_{11}$-za 1 ĜIŠ-banšur
níĝ-ba
11. $^{d}$*Ku-ra*
*Ib-rí-um*
13. in-na-sum
*in* ud
15. ne:s[aĝ]-*sù*

(18)
10 gín DILMUN kù:babbar
17. [ ]
[ ]
19. [ ]
[ ]
21. [ ]
[ ]
VI. 1. DU.DU
*Du-gú-ra-su*$^{ki}$

(19)
3. 10 gín DILMUN kù:babbar
níĝ-ba
5. *Zú-zú*
*Ir-i-tum*$^{ki}$
7. *in*
*A-bí-na-du*$^{ki}$
9. šu-ba$_{4}$-ti

(20)
ŠA.PI gín DILMUN kù:babbar
11. 4 *bu*-DI
dumu-munus
13. e[n]
[*Ra-ʾà-ak*$^{ki}$]
15. [*m*]*a*-[*li*]*k*-[*t*]*um*
⌈*A*⌉*-bar-sal*$_{4}^{ki}$
17. *wa*
*ma-lik-tum*
19. *Ir-i-tum*$^{ki}$
EN-*mar*
21. šu-mu-tak$_{4}$

(21)
[ ]
23. [ ]
[ ]
VII. 1. ME-sig
é en

(22)
3. 10 gín DILMUN kù:babbar
lú ĜIŠ-kiri$_{6}$
5. *Kak-mi-um*$^{ki}$

(23)
50 gín DILMUN kù:babbar
7. nu$_{11}$-za 1 dub
nam-kud
9. *Ib-rí-um*

(13) 10 shekels of silver for decorating the … (*iš-ki-lum*) for the king.
(14) 10 shekels of silver for plating 1 ... (GIŠ-sal) for the hoofs of the androcephalus bull (that) lies by the god Ala of the city of Zig.
(15) 2 shekels of silver for decorating with lamination 1 battle-axe for Ibrium.
(16) 15 shekels [of silver] for plating 1 mace; 30 (shekels of) silver in exchange for 6 shekels of gold for plating its handle: gift for the god Hadda.
(17) 10 shekels of silver for plating 1 table: gift for the god Kura, Ibrium has given on the occasion of his first-fruit offering.
(18) 10 shekels of silver […] (who) went to the city of Dugurasu.
(19) 10 shekels of silver: gift for Zuzu of the city of Iritum, (that) he has received in the city of Abinadu.
(20) 40 shekels of silver for 4 toggle-pins for the daughter of the ki[ng of the city of Raʾak], (who is) the queen of the city of Abarsal, and for the queen of the city of Iritum; ENmar has handed over.
(21) […] for the watchmen of the king's house.
(22) 10 shekels of silver for the garden of the city of Kakmium.
(23) 50 shekels of silver for plating the tablet of the oath of Ibrium […] Ibbi-zikir, son of Ibrium.

[ ]
11. [ ]
*I-bí-zi-kir*
13. dumu-nita
*Ib-rí-um*

(24)
15. TAR kù:babbar
níĝ-ba
17. *Bù-sum*
*Ma-rí*$^{ki}$
19. ĜIŠ.DUG.DU
izi-ĝar

(25)
21. 10 gín DILMUN kù:babbar
níĝ-ba
23. *I-ti-il*
VIII. 1. *Ma-rí*$^{ki}$
šu-mu-tak$_4$
3. 1 aktum-TÚG
*Ib-rí-um*

(26)
5. 10 gín DILMUN kù:babbar
níĝ-ba
7. *Daš-na*
*Ma-rí*$^{ki}$

(27)
9. 10 gín DILMUN kù:babbar
[ ]
11. [ ]

(28)
ŠÚ+ŠA gín DILMUN kù:babbar
13. 2 *bu*-DI
dam
15. BAD-*da-mu*
*in* ud
17. níĝ-mu-sá

(29)
8 gín DILMUN kù:babbar
19. nu$_{11}$-za
balaĝ
21. lú *gú-za-rí-tum*
lú *Ib-rí-um*

(30)
IX. 1. 10 gín DILMUN kù:babbar
2 *bu*-DI
3. ama-gal
en
5. *Lum-na-an*$^{ki}$
*Da-ti-*$^{d}$TU
7. šu-mu-tak$_4$

(31)
13 m[a-]n[a] ŠÚ[+ŠA gí]n [DILM]UN kù:[bab]bar
9. kin$_5$-ak
20 íb-lá 20 ĝír-kun
11. in-na-sum
1 é-duru$_5$$^{ki}$
13. dumu-nita-dumu-nita

(32)
10 gín DILMUN kù:babbar
15. níĝ-ba
"ur$_4$"
17. *Mar-da-ma*-LUM$^{ki}$

(33)
4 ma-na kù:babbar
19. níĝ-ba
*Wa-ba-rúm*
21. *Ma-rí*$^{ki}$
X. 1. *in* ud
di-kud
3. DU.DU

(34)
10 gín DILMUN kù:babbar
5. en
*Du-lu*$^{ki}$

(35)
7. 10 gín [DILMUN kù:babbar]
n[íĝ-]ba

(24) 30 (shekels of) silver: gift for Busum of the city of Mari (who) attended the izi-ĝar ceremony.
(25) 10 shekels of silver: gift for Iti-il of the city of Mari (who) handed over 1 garment for Ibrium.
(26) 10 shekels of silver: gift for Dašna of the city of Mari.
(27) 10 shekels of silver [...].
(28) 20 shekels of silver for 2 toggle-pins for the spouse of BAD-damu, on the occasion of her marriage.
(29) 8 shekels of silver for plating a harp, (that is its) clasp for Ibrium.
(30) 10 shekels of silver for 2 toggle-pins for the mother of the king of the city of Lumnan, Dati-TU has handed over.
(31) 13;20 minas of silver for making 20 belts (and) 20 dagger pendants given to a work-gang of young men.
(32) 10 shekels of silver: gift for the collector (of goods) of the city of MardamaLUM.
(33) 4 minas of silver: gift for Wabarum of the city of Mari, when he came (with) a judge.
(34) 10 shekels of silver for the king of the city of Dulu.
(35) 10 shekels [of silver]: gift for Šugadu (and) Ruzilum of the city of Mari.

9. *Šu-ga-du*
*Ru*$_{12}$*-zi-lum*
11. *Ma-rí*$^{ki}$

(36)
3 gín DILMUN kù:babbar
13. nu$_{11}$-za 1 ĝír mar-tu
níĝ-ba
15. *Ìr-ba*$_{x}$*-zé*
*ᵓÀ-da-ni*$^{ki}$
17. en
in-na-sum

(37)
19. 1 ma-na TAR 3 gín DILMUN
kù:babbar
níĝ-ba
21. diĝir-diĝir-diĝir

(38)
5 gín DILMUN kù:babbar
XI. 1. ĝeštu-ĝeštu
1 ĜIŠ-šú
3. lú šu-šu
en

(39)
5. 15 gín DILMUN kù:babbar
níĝ-ba
7. *Ba-zú-zi*
*Ma-[r]í*$^{ki}$

(40)
9. 1 ma-na kù:babbar
nu$_{11}$-za 4 si-si
11. 2 gud
lú en
13. nídba
$^{d}$*ᵓÀ-da*
15. *in*
AMA-*ra*

(41)
17. 5 gín DILMUN kù:babbar
níĝ-ba
19. *Ir-i-tum*$^{ki}$

(42)
1 ma-na kù:babbar
21. níĝ-ba
*Daš-na*
23. *Wa-ru*$_{12}$*-tum*
*Puzur*$_{4}$*-ra*-BAD
XII. 1. *I-ti-il*
*Ma-rí*$^{ki}$

(43)
3. 1 gín DILMUN kù:babbar
nu$_{11}$-za 1 zag
5. 1 ĜIŠ-gígir-II
*Ba-ga-ma*

(44)
7. 3 gín DILMUN kù:babbar
[ZU.]PIRIĜ
9. ĜIŠ-šú níĝ-bànda
šu-šu

(45)
11. 1 ma-na kù:babbar
*I*[*š*- ]
13. *A*[- ]

(46)
[x+]1 [gí]n DILMUN kù[:babbar]
15. ⌜níĝ⌝-ba
[*L*]*a*$^{?}$*-la*-LUM
17. [ ]
[ ]
19. [ ]
[ ]

(47)
XIII. 1. [x gí]n [DIL]MUN kù:babbar
níĝ-ba
3. NE-*da*-ḪI
*Na-gàr*$^{ki}$

(48)
5. 1 ½ gín DILMUN kù:babbar
nu$_{11}$-za 1 zag
7. 1 ĜIŠ-gígir-II
*Ib-rí-um*

(36) 3 shekels of silver for plating 1 mar-tu dagger as gift for Irbaze of the city of ᵓAdani, the king has given.
(37) 1;33 minas of silver: gift for the gods.
(38) 5 shekels of silver for the handles of 1 jug for the king's hands.
(39) 15 shekels of silver: gift for Bazuzi of the city of Mari.
(40) 1 mina of silver for plating 4 horns of 2 oxen: offering of the king for the god Hadda, at the AMA-ra (festival).
(41) 5 shekels of silver: gift for (someone of) the city of Iritum.
(42) 1 mina of silver: gift for Dašna, Warutum, Puzurra-BAD (and) Iti-il of the city of Mari.
(43) 1 shekel of silver for plating 1 side of a chariot of Bagama.
(44) 3 shekels of silver for the hangers of 1 jug (and) 1 goblet for the hands.
(45) 1 mina of silver for I[š…] A[…].
(46) [x+]1 [shek]els of sil[ver]: gift for [L]alaLUM […].
(47) [x shek]els of silver: gift for NEdaḪI of the city of Nagar.
(48) 1 ½ shekel of silver for plating 1 side of a chariot of Ibrium.

(49)
9. 5 gín DILMUN kù:babbar
maš-maš
11. 1 [ĜIŠ]-⌜banšur⌝
*wa*
13. nu$_{11}$-za 1 ĝír mar-tu
níĝ-ba
15. $^{d}$*Ku-ra*
lú
17. *ᵓÀ-ti-ni*$^{ki}$

(50)
3 gín DILMUN kù:babbar
19. 2 ĝeštu$_{x}$-lá
2[+2] ⌜*ba*⌝-*ga-ne-su*
21. dumu-nita-dumu-nita
NE-di

(51)
XIV. 1 10 gín DILMUN kù:babbar
níĝ-ba
3. *Gul-la*
ḫi-mu-DU
5. 1 BAR.AN

(52)
10 gín DILMUN kù:babbar
7. níĝ-ba
*Ù-da-aḫ*
9. *Na-gàr*$^{ki}$

(53)
ŠÚ+ŠA gín DILMUN kù:babbar
11. níĝ-ba
*Daš-na*
13. *Wa-ru*$_{12}$*-tum*
*Ma-rí*$^{ki}$

(54)
15. 14 gín DILMUN kù:babbar
níĝ-kaskal
17. *En-na*-BAD
*Zú-ti*$^{ki}$
19. maškim
*Du-bí*
21. DU.DU
*Ar-mi*$^{ki}$

(55)
23. 8 gín DILMUN kù:babbar
XV. 1. *Na-gàr*$^{ki}$

(56)
5 gín DILMUN kù:babbar
3. níĝ-ba
*Ga-ga-ba-an*$^{ki}$

(57)
5. 2 ma-na ŠA.PI gín DILMUN
kù:babbar
nu$_{11}$-za 2 si
7. am
lú $^{d}$*Ra-sa-ap*
9. *gú-núm*

(58)
2 gín DILMUN kù:babbar
11. níĝ-du$_{8}$
*Ù-ba-nu*
13. KAR
kù-gi
15. en
*Ma-nu-wa-ad*$^{ki}$

(59)
17. 5 gín DILMUN kù:babbar
níĝ-kaskal
19. *Íl-ra*-BAD
maškim
21. NI-*ba-rúm*
XVI. 1. DU.DU
*si-in*
3. *Ar-mi*$^{ki}$

(60)
1 [ma-]na kù:babbar
5. níĝ-ba
*Ib-gi-tum*
7. *Ma-rí*$^{ki}$
níĝ-"mul"

(49) 5 shekels of silver for a striped (decoration) of 1 [ta]ble and for plating 1 mar-tu dagger: gift for the god Kura of the city of ᵓAtini.
(50) 3 shekels of silver for 2 earrings (and) 4 *clasps* for the young dancers.
(51) 10 shekels of silver: gift for Gulla (who) delivered 1 mule.
(52) 10 shekels of silver: gift for Udaḫ of the city of Nagar.
(53) 20 shekels of silver: gift for Dašna (and) Warutum of the city of Mari.
(54) 14 shekels of silver: travel provision for Enna-BAD of the city of Zuti, the representative of Dubi (who) went to the city of Armi.
(55) 8 shekels of silver for (someone of) the city of Nagar.
(56) 5 shekels of silver: gift for (someone of) the city of Gagaban.
(57) 2;40 minas of silver for plating 2 tusks of elephant for the god Rašap *gunum.*
(58) 2 shekels of silver for the ransom of Ubanu, for the … (KAR) of gold for the king of the city of Manuwat.
(59) 5 shekels of silver: travel provision for Ilra-BAD, the representative of NIbarum (who) went to the city of Armi.
(60) 1 [mi]na of silver: gift for Ibgitum of the city of Mari (who brought) the news that the city of Nagar had been defeated.

9. *Na-gàr*$^{ki}$
[t]il

(61)
11. 5 gín DILMUN kù:babbar
*A-da-bí-ig*$^{ki}$
13. ì-ti
*mi-nu*
15. *Ar-mi*$^{ki}$

(62)
ŠÚ+ŠA gín DILMUN kù:babbar
17. níĝ-ba
*Iš*$_{11}$*-ga-um*
19. *Ma-rí*$^{ki}$

(63)
ŠÚ+ŠA gín DILMUN kù:babbar
r. I. 1. níĝ-ba
*Daš-na*
3. *wa*
*Wa-ru*$_{12}$*-tum*
5. *Ma-rí*$^{ki}$

(64)
1 ½ gín DILMUN kù:babbar
7. 1 *zú-zú-ba-tum*
*Ib-rí-um*

(65)
9. TAR kù:babbar
2 *bu*-DI
11. *ma-lik-tum*
*Ì-mar*$^{ki}$
13. *Du-si-*⌜*gú*⌝
[šu]-mu-tak$_4$

(66)
15. ŠÚ+ŠA gín DILMUN kù:babbar
*Na-gàr*$^{ki}$
17. *in*
⌜kaskal⌝
19. šu-ba$_4$-ti

(67)
TAR kù:babbar
21. níĝ-ba
*Daš-na*
II. 1. *wa*
*Wa-ru*$_{12}$*-tum*
3. *Ma-rí*$^{ki}$

(68)
5 gín DILMUN kù:babbar
5. 1 *mar-wa-ga*$_x$(ZÀR)*-tum*
šu-šu
7. en

(69)
5 gín DILMUN kù:babbar
9. *ni-zi-mu*
nu$_{11}$-za
11. 4 *gú-li-lum*
esi[-esi-II]
13. ⌜4⌝ gín DILMUN kù:babbar
ZU.PIRIĜ
15. ⌜5⌝ *gú-li-lum* a-gar$_5$-gar$_5$ II:esi
[ŠA].PI gín DILMUN kù:babbar
17. kin$_5$-ak
4 *gú-li-lum*
III. 1. I:esi
gaba-ru
3. é
en

(70)
5. 6 gín DILMUN kù:babbar
nu$_{11}$-za
7. 1 *ma-ḫa-ni-gúm*
*Ib-rí-um*

(71)
9. 10 gín DILMUN kù:babbar
níĝ-ba
11. *Na*-NE
*Na-gàr*$^{ki}$

(72)
13. [x] gín DILMUN [k]ù[:babbar]
níĝ-ba
15. *La-sa-nu*
*Ḫa-ra-an*$^{ki}$

(61) 5 shekels of silver for (someone of) the city of Adabik (who) came back from the city of Armi.
(62) 20 shekels of silver: gift for Išgaum of the city of Mari.
(63) 20 shekels of silver: gift for Dašna and Warutum of the city of Mari.
(64) 1 ½ shekel of silver for 1 ... (*zú-zú-ba-tum*) for Ibrium.
(65) 30 (shekels of) silver for 2 toggle-pins for the queen of the city of Imar, Dusigu has handed over.
(66) 20 shekels of silver for (someone of) the city of Nagar, received for the journey.
(67) 30 (shekels of) silver: gift for Dašna and Warutum of the city of Mari.
(68) 5 shekels of silver for 1 *mar-wa-ga-tum* vessel for the king's hands.
(69) 5 shekels of silver for decorating with lamination 4 double bracelets of diorite; 4 shekels of silver for the hangers of 5 double bracelets of copper and diorite: 40 shekels of silver for making 4 single bracelets of diorite: supply for the king's house.
(70) 6 shekels of silver for plating 1 necklace for Ibrium.
(71) 10 shekels of silver: gift for NANE of the city of Nagar.
(72) [x] shekels of [silver]: gift for Lasanu of the city of Ḫarran.

(73)
17. ŠA.PI gín DILMUN kù:babbar
níĝ-ba
19. *Ib-gi-tum*

(74)
ŠÚ+ŠA gín DILMUN kù:babbar
IV. 1. níĝ-ba
*Wa-ru$_{12}$-tum*
3. *wa*
*Daš-na*
5. *Ma-rí$^{ki}$*

(75)
1 ma-na 15 gín DILMUN kù:babbar
7. níĝ-sa$_{10}$
3 *mi-at* ma-na níĝ-saĝ
9. [x gí]n [DILMUN] kù:babbar
ZU.PIRIĜ
11. ⌜10⌝ útul! urudu!
lú dam
13. lú sada(ĜIŠGAL)-titab(MUNU$_4$.A)
*wa*
15. ZU.PIRIĜ
10 útul urudu
17. lú *Du-si-gú*

(76)
10 gín DILMUN kù:babbar
19. *ma-za-um*
V. 1. ĝír mar-tu
3 ma-na 5 gín DILMUN kù:babbar
3. šu-bal-ak
TAR 7 gín DILMUN kù-gi
5. *ma-za-um*
3 ĝír mar-tu
7. en

(77)
ŠÚ+ŠA gín DILMUN kù:babbar
9. 2 *bu*-DI
*Sa-mu-sá-sal*
11. *Da-bí*
šu-mu-tak$_4$

(78)
13. 3 gín DILMUN kù:babbar
nu$_{11}$-za
15. *gú-za-ru$_{12}$-tum*
lú
17. [x]-⌜x-x⌝

(79)
1 ma-na kù:babbar
19. níĝ-ba
VI. 1. *Iš$_{11}$-ga*
*wa*
3. *Daš-na*
*Ma-rí$^{ki}$*

(80)
5. 5 ma-na kù:babbar
níĝ-sa$_{10}$
7. 66 *ʾà-da-um*-TÚG-I
10 aktum-túg
9. ⌜1⌝? ma-na ŠA.⌜PI⌝ gín DILMUN
kù:babbar
níĝ-sa$_{10}$ ĜIŠ-ti-ḪAR
11. *Wa-ba-rúm*
šu-ba$_4$-ti

(81)
13. 1 ma-na kù:babbar
níĝ-sa$_{10}$ *gàr-sù*
15. NI-*la*-[*ba-m*]*u*
[šu-ba$_4$-ti]

(82)
17. [10 gín DILMUN kù:babbar]
šu-bal-ak
19. 2 gín DILMUN kù-gi
VII. 1. en
*A-la-u$_9$*$^{[ki]}$
3. *in*
⌜ki⌝:lam$_7$
5. $^{d}$*ʾÀ-da*

(83)
8 ⌜ma⌝-na ŠÚ+Š[A] gín DI[LMUN]
kù:babbar

(73) 40 shekels of silver: gift for Ibgitum.
(74) 20 shekels of silver: gift for Warutum and Dašna of the city of Mari.
(75) 1;15 minas of silver for the purchase of 300 minas of … (níĝ-saĝ); [x sheke]ls of silver for the hangers of 10 copper kettles for the women processing the malt and for the hangers of 10 copper kettles for Dusigu.
(76) 10 shekels of silver for the … (*ma-za-um*) of mar-tu daggers; 3;05 minas of silver in exchange for 37 shekels of gold for the … (*ma-za-um*) of 3 mar-tu daggers for the king.
(77) 20 shekels of silver for 2 toggle-pins for Samusasal, Dabi has handed over.
(78) 3 shekels of silver for plating the clasp of […].
(79) 1 mina of silver: gift for Išga(um) and Dašna of the city of Mari.
(80) 5 minas of silver for the purchase of 76 garments; 1;40 minas of silver for the purchase of GIŠ-ti-ḪAR-wood, Wabarum has received.
(81) 1 mina of silver for the purchase of bags, NIla[bam]u [has received].
(82) [10 shekels of silver] in exchange for 2 shekels of gold for the king of the city of Alau, at the market of the god Hadda.
(83) 8:20 minas of silver for the purchase of 100 garments (and) 16 kilts, at the market of the *gibalu* of the city of ʾAda[ni].

7. níĝ-sa$_{10}$
80 aktum-TÚG
9. 20 *ʾà-da-um*-TÚG-I
16 íb+III-TÚG sa$_6$ gùn
11. ki:lam$_7$
*gi-ba-lu*
13. ˹*ʾÀ*˺-*da*-[*ni*]$^{ki}$

(84)
[(ca. 3 lines)]
17$^?$. ˹*ni-zi*˺-*mu*
[1] an-zam$_x$
19. en

(85)
VIII. 1. 50 gín DILMUN kù:babbar
šu-bal-ak
3. 10 gín DILMUN kù-gi
1 pad
5. an-zam$_x$
en

(86)
7. T[AR] ˹kù:babbar˺
˹šu-bal˺-ak
9. 6 gín DILMUN
1 zi-bar
11. en

(87)
50 gín DILMUN kù:babbar
13. šu-bal-ak
10 gín DILMUN kù-gi
[(ca. 5 lines)]
20$^?$. *Du*-˹*si*˺$^?$-*gú*

(88)
ŠÚ+ŠA gín DILMUN
IX. 1. kù:babbar
níĝ-ba
3. *Na*-NE
*wa*
5. maškim-*sù*
*Na-gàr*$^{ki}$

(89)
7. ŠÚ+ŠA gín DILMUN kù:babbar
níĝ-ba
9. *ʾÀ-du*$^{ki}$

(90)
5 gín DILMUN kù:babbar
11. níĝ-ba
*Zi-ti-ru*$_{12}^{ki}$

(91)
13. 50 gín DILMUN kù:babbar
[níĝ-s]a$_{10}$
15. [(ca. 6 lines)]

(92)
21$^?$. 3 gín DILMUN kù:babbar
X. 1. nu$_{11}$-za 1 ĝír mar-tu
1 kù-sal
3. níĝ-ba
$^{d}$*Ku-ra*
5. *Ib-rí-um*
ì-na-sum
7. *in*
ne-saĝ-*sù*

(93)
9. 10 gín DILMUN kù:babbar
šu-bal-ak
11. 2 gín DILMUN kù-gi
maš-maš 1 ĜIŠ-banšur
13. *wa*
[x] kù-sal
15. [(ca. 6 lines)]
21$^?$. 20 t[ùn] gal zabar
XI. 1. 10 tùn tur zabar
1 ma-na an-na
3. šub
30 tùn ˹gal˺ urudu
5. 5 gín DILMUN an-na
šub
7. 1 *ma-ga-um* zabar
[ ]˹x˺
[(ca. 7 lines)]
16$^?$. *Du*-[*ub*]$^{ki}$

(84) […] for decorating [1] an-zam$_x$ goblet for the king.
(85) 50 shekels of silver in exchange for 10 shekels of gold for a lid of 1 an-zam$_x$ goblet for the king.
(86) 30 (shekels of) silver in exchange for 6 shekels (of gold) for 1 zi-bar goblet for the king.
(87) 50 shekels of silver in exchange for 10 shekels of gold […] for Dusigu.
(88) 20 shekels of silver: gift for NANE and his representative, of the city of Nagar.
(89) 20 shekels of silver: gift for (someone of) the city of ʾAddu.
(90) 5 shekels of silver: gift for (someone of) the city of Zitiru.
(91) 50 shekels of silver [for the purcha]se of […].
(92) 3 shekels of silver for plating 1 mar-tu dagger (and) 1 buckle: gift for the god Kura, Ibrium has given on (the occasion) of his first-fruit offering.
(93) 10 shekels of silver in exchange for 2 shekels of gold for a striped (decoration) of 1 table and [x] buckle(s) […] 20 big axes of bronze (and) 10 small axes of bronze; 1 mina of tin to be melted in 30 big axes of copper; 5 shekels of tin to be melted in 1 … (*ma-ga-um*) of bronze […] of the city of Du[b].

(94)

XII. 1. [x m]a-na [x gín DILM]UN
[k]ù[:babbar]
[x-(x-)n]a
3. [ ]-⌜x⌝$^{ki}$
ḫi-mu-DU
5. ⌜ĜIŠ⌝-ti-ḪAR

(95)

1 ma-na ⌜an⌝-na
7. en
[*M*]*a-rí*$^{ki}$

(96)

9. [ ]⌜x⌝
[(ca. 9 lines)]
19?. [šu-ba$_4$-]ti (?)

(97)

XIII. x+1. [x ma-na ] a[n-na]
E[N ]
3'. DU [ ]

(98)

7 gín DILMUN an-na
5'. [šu]b
[
XIV. 1. 8 ĝír mar-tu
ĝuruš-ĝuruš
3. SA.ZA$_x$$^{ki}$

(99)

3 ma-na [ ]
5. [
XV. (blank)

(100)

XVI. 1. AN.ŠÈ.GÚ 90 ma-na
ŠÚ+ŠA 6 gín DILMUN kù:babbar
3. ⌜è⌝
*w*[*a*]
5. [

(94) [x;xx m]ina(s) of s[ilver] [...] for the delivery of GIŠ-ti-ḪAR-wood.
(95) 1 mina of tin for the king of [the city of M]ari.
(96) [...] [has receiv]ed.
(97) [x mina(s)] of t[in] [...].
(98) 7 shekels of tin [to be melt]ed [...] 8 mar-tu daggers for the men of the Palace.
(99) 3 minas [...].
(100) Total: 90;26 minas of silver: expenditure, an[d ...].

## Commentary

Only the total of the expended silver is preserved: it amounted to 90;26 minas (42.503 kg), (§ 100).

The document first registers the mina (470 g) of silver for the usual renewal rite of the city-god Kura, then another 3 shekels (23 g) for a later ceremony, and 1;33 minas (730 g) of silver were given to "the gods", diĝir-diĝir-diĝir (§ 37).

Following this is the expenditure of 1;20 minas (627 g) of silver for Tinib-dulum, sister (nin-ni) of the king, who was priestess, dam-diĝir, of the god ʾAdabal of Luban (§ 2).

The king received amounts of silver for the decoration of several objects (§§ 13, 38, 68, 76); other silver was exchanged for gold for other objects (§§ 84, 85, 86).

Ibrium received a battle-axe (§ 15) and a plaque of 50 shekels (391 g) of silver when he swore an oath (probably together with his son Ibbi-zikir, § 23); as well as some objects either in silver or decorated with silver (§§ 8, 29, 70), and decorations for his chariot (§ 48, 64). He also received a garment brought by a messenger from Mari (§ 25).

The relations with Mari were particular intense. The envoys of this city were *Du-tum* (§ 3), *Daš-na* (§§ 12, 26), *I-ti-il* (§ 25), *Wa-ba-rúm*, who came to Ebla in conjunction with a judge (§ 33), *Šu-ga-du* and *Ru*$_{12}$*-zi-lum* (35), *Ba-zú-zi* (§ 39), *Daš-na*, *Wa-ru*$_{12}$*-tum*, *Puzur*$_4$*-ra*-BAD, *I-ti-il* (§ 42), *Daš-na* with *Wa-ru*$_{12}$*-tum* (§§ 53, 63, 67, 74), *Ib-gi-tum*, who brought the news that Nagar had again been "defeated", til (§§ 60, 73), *Iš*$_{11}$*-ga-um* (§ 62), *Iš*$_{11}$*-ga(-um)* and *Daš-na* (§ 79), again *Wa-ba-rúm* (80). The king of Mari sent 1 mina (470 g) of tin (§ 95).

Mari "defeated", til, Nagar (§ 60), the city that controlled the Ḫabur triangle and was Ebla's ally. Before this event three messengers from Nagar: NE-*da*-ḪI (§ 47), *Ù-da-aḫ* (52), and an unnamed envoy (§ 55) had reached Ebla together with an envoy from Gagaban, a city placed in the territory controlled by Nagar (§ 56). After the defeat, another of its messengers, *Na*-NE, also came (§§ 71, and 88; this time with one of his representatives).

The relations between Ebla and Nagar can be summarized in the following way. According to text XXI 4 (Ibrium 02) Nagar was an ally of Ebla in function of its rivalry against Mari. Nagar was "defeated", àga-"kár" a first time, as several messengers of Mari informed Ebla (text XXI 6 § 76, Ibrium 03). A messenger from Mari, Ibgitum, brought the news that Nagar "had been defeated", til, again in the year Ibrium 07 (text XXI 10 § 60).

§ 18. This section registers the expenditure of 10 shekels (78 g) of silver as travel provision for a messenger sent to Dugurasu (Tukriš), in the Zagros region. This is one of the first contacts on which the basis of a regular exchange of caravans between Ebla and Dugurasu was established (Archi 2016a, pp. 5–6).

§ 20. ENmar brought two toggle-pins, of 10 shekels (78 g) each, to the queen of Abarsal (a daughter of the king of Raᵓak), and to the queen of Iritum: cities which have been respectively identified with Tell Khuēra and with a tell in the plain of Suruç (see Archi 2019b, p. 1, and 2016b, respectively). See also the monthly document of garments deliveries TM.75.G.1867 r. III 8–17: ... 4 *bu*-DI ... 2 dumu-munus en *Ra-ᵓà-ak*$^{ki}$ *ma-lik-tum A-bar-sal*$_4^{ki}$ *wa ma-lik-tum Ir-i-tum*$^{ki}$ EN-*mar* šu-mu-tak$_4$.

§ 30. Dati-TU, the Eblaite princess who had married the king of Lumnan, gave to her mother-in-law two toggle-pins of 10 shekels (78 g) of silver.

# 11

(Plates XX–XXI)

(1)

o. I. 1. 1 ma-na 3 gín DILMUN kù:babbar
saĝ [kù:]babbar
3. $^{d}$*K*[*u-ra*]

(2)

3 ma-na ⌜kù:babbar⌝
5. [*Di-rín-da-mu*]
[*Di-ne-íb-du-lum*]
[nin-ni]
[en]

(3)

II. 1. ⌜x⌝-[x]-⌜x⌝
kù:[babb]ar X
3. Ur-é

(4)

15 gín DILMUN kù:babbar
5. šu-bal-ak
3 gín DILMUN kù-gi
7. *Da-zi-ma-ad*
maškim
9. *Ìr-am*$_6$*-da-mu*
[l]ú [*I*]*l-zi*

(5)

11. [x g]ín DILMUN kù:[babbar]
[níĝ]-sa$_{10}$ [x] sila$_4$
13. lú šu-du$_8$-máš

(6)

[x kù:babbar]
15. níĝ-sa$_{10}$ 10 lá-2 *ʾà-da-um*-TÚG-II 31
*ʾà-da-um*-TÚG-I
3 zara$_6$-TÚG
III. 1. 14 aktum-TÚG
44 gada-TÚG
3. 50 íb+IV-TÚG sa$_6$ gùn
93 "KIN" siki sa$_6$
5. 10 lá-3 ĝír mar-tu zú[-ak]
10 lá-2 ma-na TAR kù:babbar
7. níĝ-sa$_{10}$ 22 gud-gud
50 gín DILMUN kù[:babbar]
9. [ ]
[ -]N[E]
11. šu-ba$_4$-ti
ki:lam$_7$
13. *gi-ba-ù*
IV. 1. [*wa*]
$^{d}$*A-d*[*am-*]*ma*
3. *ʾÀ-da-ni*$^{ki}$

(7)

15 gín DILMUN kù:babbar
5. šu-bal-ak
3 gín DILMUN kù-gi
7. nu$_{11}$-za *maš-ar-tum*
níĝ-ba
9. dumu-munus
[*I*]*b-rí-*[*u*]*m*
11. é-gi<-a>
*Zi-ba-da*
13. é
$^{dʾ}$*À-da*

(8)

15. 2 ½ gín DILMUN kù:babbar
[š]u-bal-ak
17. [½ gí]n [DILMUN k]ù-[g]i
1 kù-sal
19. 2 gín DILMUN kù:babbar
nu$_{11}$-za [1 g]ír mar-⌜tu⌝
21. níĝ-⌜ba⌝
V. 1. [$^{d}$*Ku-ra*]
[*Ib-rí-um*$^{?}$]
3. [ì-na-sum]
[*i*]*n* ⌜ud⌝
5. ne:saĝ

(1) 1;03 minas of silver for the [sil]ver head of the god K[ura].

(2) 3 minas of silver [for Tirin-damu (and) Tinib-dulum, 2 sisters of the king].

(3) […] of sil[ver] for Ur-e(gal).

(4) 15 shekels of silver in exchange for 3 shekels of gold for Dazimad, the representative of Iram-damu, (son) [o]f [I]lzi.

(5) [x sh]ekels of sil[ver for the pur]chase of [x] lambs for taking omens.

(6) [x silver] for the purchase of 100 garments, 50 kilts, 93 KIN measures of wool of good quality (and) 7 serrated mar-tu daggers; 8;30 minas of silver for the purchase of 22 oxen; 50 shekels of sil[ver …]: […N]E has received at the markets of the *gibalu* [and] of the god Ad[am]ma of the city of ʾAdani.

(7) 15 shekels of silver in exchange for 3 shekels of gold for plating a stele: gift of a daughter of Ibrium, (who is) the daughter-in-law of Zibada, to the temple of the god Hadda.

(8) 2 ½ shekels of silver in exchange for [½ shek]el of [g]old for 1 buckle; 2 shekels of silver for plating [1] mar-tu [da]gger: gift for [the god Kura, Ibrium has given o]n the occasion of the first-fruit offering.

(9)

2 ½ gín DILMUN kù:babbar
7. šu-bal-ak
½ gín DILMUN kù-gi
9. 1 kù-sal
2 gín DILMUN kù:babbar
11. nu$_{11}$-za 1 ĝír mar-tu
níĝ-ba
13. *Ib-rí-um*
$^{d}$*Ra-s[a-ap]*
15. *g[ú-n]úm*
*in* ud
17. ne:saĝ

(10)

1 ma-na an-na
19. šub *si-in*
*ni-zi-mu*
21. ZA$_x$
VI. 1. naĝar-naĝar

(11)

[10] gín DILMUN kù:babbar
3. šu-bal-ak
2 gín DILMUN kù-gi
5. *ni-zi-mu*
1 *mar-wa-ga-tum*
7. lú 2 šu
en

(12)

9. TAR 3 gín DILMUN 3 NI kù:babbar
šu-bal-ak
11. 6 gín DILMUN 2 NI kù-gi
2 *gú-li-lum*
13. níĝ-[b]a
⸢d⸣[*Ku-ra/Áš-da-bíl*]

(13)

15. ŠÚ+ŠA gín DILMUN kù:babbar
šu-bal-ak
17. 4 gín DILMUN kù-gi
*ni-zi-mu*
19. 2 níĝ-anše-ak 2 kù-sal
lú 2 IGI.NITA
21. ⸢en⸣

(14)

VII. 1. 2 ma-na kù:babbar
níĝ-sa$_{10}$ 2 ĝír mar-tu kù-gi
3. *ra-ʾà-tum*
*Ib-rí-um*

(15)

5. ŠÚ+ŠA gín DILMUN kù:babbar
níĝ-ba
7. *Ma-rí*$^{ki}$
níĝ-"mul"
9. *Na-gàr*$^{ki}$
til

(16)

11. 2 ma-na TAR
šu-bal-ak
13. TAR kù-gi
1 dib
15. *Íl-gú-uš-ti*
lú *I-gi*
17. tuš-LÚ×TIL
Kiš$^{ki}$
19. lú *A-bar-sal*$_4^{ki}$

(17)

2 ma-na TAR kù:babbar
21. šu-bal-ak
[TAR kù-g]i
23. [1 íb-lá]
VIII. 1. 1 *si-ti-tum* 1 ĝír-kun
*I-rí-ig-da-mu*
3. lú *Gi-gi*
šu-du$_8$
5. *ba-da-lum*
*A-bar-sal*$_4^{ki}$

(9) 2 ½ shekels of silver in exchange for ½ shekel of gold for 1 buckle; 2 shekels of silver for plating 1 mar-tu dagger: gift of Ibrium for the god Raš[ap] *gunum*, on the occasion of the first-fruit offering.
(10) 1 mina of tin to be melted for decorating objects of the carpenters.
(11) [10] shekels of silver in exchange for 2 shekels of gold for decorating 1 *mar-wa-ga-tum* vessel for the hands of the king.
(12) 33 shekels (and) 3 NI of silver in exchange for 6 shekels (and) 2 NI of gold for 2 bracelets: gift for [the god …].
(13) 20 shekels of silver in exchange for 4 shekels of gold for decorating 2 bridles (and) 2 buckles for 2 mules of the king.
(14) 2 minas of silver for the purchase of 2 mar-tu daggers (decorated with) gold (and) shells for Ibrium.
(15) 20 shekels of silver: gift for (someone of) the city of Mari (who brought) the news that the city of Nagar had been defeated.
(16) 2;30 minas (of silver) in exchange for 30 (shekels of) gold for 1 plaque for Ilgušti, (son) of Igi, (who) resided in the city of Kiš, (and was a man) of the city of Abarsal.
(17) 2;30 minas of silver in exchange for [30 (shekels of) gol]d [for 1 belt], 1 sheath (and) 1 dagger pendant for Irik-damu, (son) of Gigi, (who) has taken in possession for? the minister of the city of Abarsal.

(18)
7. 15 gín DILMUN kù:babbar
níĝ-du$_8$
9. šeš
*Ti-la-rí-im*$^{ki}$
11. *ʾÀ-bí-gú*$^{ki}$
*áš-da*
13. *Tar$_5$-ḫa-um*$^{ki}$

(19)
TAR kù:babbar
15. níĝ-ba
*Wa-ru$_{12}$-tum*
17. *Daš-na*
*I-ku*[!](DÚR)-*ku*[!](DÚR)-*tu*
19. *Ma-rí*$^{ki}$

(20)
2 gín DILMUN kù:babbar
21. níĝ-sa$_{10}$ 1 ĜIŠ-⸢x-x⸣
[ ]
IX. 1. lú *Gur-ad*$^{ki}$

(21)
5 gín DILMUN kù:babbar
3. níĝ-sa$_{10}$ 1 ĝír mar-tu *ba-du-u$_4$*
kù:babbar
*Ba*-NE
5. lú-kar
*A-da-bí-ig*$^{ki}$

(22)
7. 14 ma-na ŠA.PI 4 gín DILMUN
kù:babbar
níĝ-sa$_{10}$ 35 *ʾà-da-um*-TÚG-II
9. 25 *ʾà-da-um*-TÚG-I
52 aktum-TÚG ti-TÚG
11. 3 níĝ-lá-saĝ 20 íb+IV-TÚG sa$_6$ gùn
2 *mi-at* [(x) íb+IV-TÚG gùn]
X. 1. [ŠA.]PI 6 kù[:babbar]
níĝ-sa$_{10}$ raš-SAR Kur$^{ki}$
3. ki:lam$_7$
$^{d}$AMA-*ra*

(23)
5. 13 gín DILMUN kù:babbar
nu$_{11}$-za 1 ešda
7. TAR kù:babbar
šu-bal-ak
9. 6 gín DILMUN kù-gi
nu$_{11}$-za 1 *ar-ra-sù*
11. ŠÚ+ŠA gín DILMUN kù:babbar
*ʾa$_5$-na-gu*
13. 4 si 2 gud
nídba
15. en
$^{d}$*Ra-sa-ap*
17. *ʾÀ-da-ni*$^{ki}$

(24)
13 gín DILMUN kù:babbar
19. nu$_{11}$-za 1 ešda
TAR kù:babbar
21. šu-bal-ak
6 gín DILMUN kù-gi
23. nu$_{11}$-za [1 *ar-r*]*a*-[*sù*]
XI. 1. ŠÚ+ŠA gín DILMUN kù:babbar
*ʾa$_5$-na-gu*
3. 4 si 2 gud
nídba
5. en
$^{d}$*ʾÀ-da*
7. *in*
$^{d}$AMA-*ra*

(25)
9. 1 ma-na ŠA.PI gín DILMUN
kù:babbar
níĝ-ba
11. diĝir-diĝir-diĝir

(26)
1 ma-na kù:babbar
13. níĝ-sa$_{10}$ 4 gud
*Wa-ba-rúm*
15. *En-na-ì*
lú-kar
17. *Kak-mi-um*$^{ki}$

(18) 15 shekels of silver for the ransom of (his?) brother of the city of Tilarim (belonging to) the city of Abigu, from the city of Tarḫaum.
(19) 30 (shekels of) silver: gift for Warutum, Dašna (and) Ikukutu of the city of Mari.
(20) 2 shekels of silver for the purchase of 1 […] of the city of Gurad.
(21) 5 shekels of silver for the purchase of 1 *b.* mar-tu dagger (decorated with) silver for BaNE, trader of the city of Adabik.
(22) 14;44 minas of silver for the purchase of 115 garments (and) 220+[x] kilts; 46 (shekels of) sil[ver] for the purchase of leek from the mountain region, at the market of the AMA-ra (festival).
(23) 13 shekels of silver for plating 1 mace; 30 (shekels of) silver in exchange for 6 shekels of gold for plating its handle; 20 shekels of silver for the circular stand of the 4 horns of 2 bulls: offering of the king for the god Rašap of the city of ʾAdani.
(24) 13 shekels of silver for plating 1 mace; 30 (shekels of) silver in exchange for 6 shekels of gold for plating [its hand]le; 20 shekels of silver for the circular stand of the 4 horns of 2 bulls: offering of the king for the god Hadda, at the AMA-ra (festival).
(25) 1;40 minas of silver: gift for the gods.
(26) 1 mina of silver for the purchase of 4 oxen: Wabarum (and) Enna-i(l), traders of the city of Kakmium (have received).

(27)

2 gín DILMUN kù:babbar
19. *ni-zi-mu*
1 an-zam$_x$
21. *Da-ti-*$^d$TU
XII. 1. *ma-lik-tum*
*Lum-na-an*$^{ki}$

(28)

3. 1 ma-na TAR kù:babbar
níĝ-sa$_{10}$ geštin
5. *Bu*$_x$*-ma-ì*
šu-ba$_4$-ti

(29)

7. ŠÚ+ŠA gín DILMUN kù:babbar
2 *bu*-DI
9. 10 gín DILMUN kù:babbar
šu-bal-ak
11. 2 gín DILMUN kù-gi
nu$_{11}$-za 2 saĝ-*sù*
13. 7 ½ gín DILMUN kù:babbar
šu-bal-ak
15. 1 ½ gín DILMUN kù-gi
1 kù-sal
17. *Da-ti-*$^d$TU
*ma-lik-tum*
19. *Lum-na-an*$^{ki}$
É×PAP
21. *I-šar*
šu-mu-tak$_4$

(30)

23. 13 ma-na
XIII. 1. [x] gín DILMUN kù:babbar
níĝ-sa$_{10}$ 53 zara$_6$-TÚG[a)]
3. 13 *ʾà-da-um-*TÚG-II
16 *ʾà-da-um-*TÚG-I
5. 35 íb+IV-TÚG sa$_6$ gùn
3 *mi-at* 6 íb+IV-TÚG gùn
7. 10 ĝír mar-tu ḫul
ŠA.PI 2 gín DILMUN kù:babbar
9. níĝ-sa$_{10}$ 2 gud
*Ib-lu*$_5$*-zú*
11. ki:lam$_7$
$^d$*Ga-mi-iš*

r. I. [(in lacuna)]

(31)

II. 1. [ ]
[ ]
3. 80 í[b-lá] 80 ĝír m[ar-tu]
21 á-MUŠEN zabar
5. SUD.SI.PA.SAL-*sù*
*in* ud
7. è
níĝ-kas$_4$
9. *Gú-da-da-núm*$^{ki}$

(32)

5 gín DILMUN kù:babbar
11. ZU.PIRIĜ
*gú-li-lum-gú-li-lum*
13. ĝuruš-ĝuruš

(33)

14 ma-na kù:babbar
15. níĝ-sa$_{10}$ 26 túg-NI.NI
52 *ʾà-da-um-*TÚG-I
17. [x í]b[+III]-TÚG-sa$_6$-gùn
III. 1. [ ]
[ ]
3. [ ]
ki:lam$_7$
5. SA.ZA$_x$$^{ki}$
$^d$*Áš-da-bíl*
7. *Ši-ʾà-mu*$^{ki}$

(34)

2 ma-na kù:babbar
9. níĝ-ba
en
11. *Ša-bir*$_5$*-ti-du*$^{ki}$
16 gín DILMUN kù:babbar
13. *Na-mi-ir*
maškim-*sù*

(27) 2 shekels of silver for decorating 1 an-zam$_x$ goblet for Dati-TU, the queen of the city of Lumnan.

(28) 1;30 minas of silver for the purchase of wine, Buma-i(l) has received.

(29) 20 shekels of silver for 2 toggle-pins; 10 shekels of silver in exchange for 2 shekels of gold for plating their 2 heads; 7 ½ shekels of silver in exchange for 1 ½ shekel of gold for 1 buckle for the funerary rite of Dati-TU, the queen of the city of Lumnan, Išar has handed over.

(30) 13;[xx] minas of silver for the purchase of 82 garments, 341 kilts (and) 10 mar-tu daggers of poor quality; 42 shekels of silver for the purchase of 2 oxen: Ibluzu (has received), at the market of Kamiš.

(31) […] for 80 b[elts], 80 m[ar-tu] daggers, 21 helmets of bronze, their … (SUD.SI.PA.SAL), on the occasion of the departure to the military expedition (against) the city of Gudadanum.

(32) 5 shekels of silver for the hangers of bracelets for the men.

(33) 14 minas of silver for the purchase of 78 garments, [x ki]lts […] at the markets of the Palace, of the god Ašdabil (and) of the city of Šiʾamu.

(34) 2 minas of silver: gift for the king of the city of Šabirtidu; 16 shekels of silver for Namir, his representative.

(35)

15. TAR kù:babbar
níĝ-kaskal
17. *Kab-lu$_5$-ul$^{ki}$*
5 gín DILMUN kù:babbar
19. níĝ-du$_8$
2 dumu-nita
21. *Bur-ḫa-áš*

(36)

[ ]
23. [ ]
IV. 1. níĝ-ba
*Bù-za-lum*
3. *Am$_6$-mu-tum*
*Ma-rí$^{ki}$*
5. ĜIŠ.DUG.D[U]
izi-ĝar

(37)

7. 13 gín DILMUN kù:babbar
nu$_{11}$-za 1 ešda
9. níĝ-ba
*$^{d\text{ʾ}}$À-da*
11. lú *Lu-ub$^{ki}$*
*in*
13. *gi*-NI

(38)

4 gín DILMUN kù:babbar
15. lú ĜIŠ-kiri$_6$
*Zi-la-da-mu*
17. šu-ba$_4$-ti

(39)

6 2 NI gín DILMUN kù:babbar
19. 2 *gú-li-lum*
níĝ-ba
21. *$^d$Am-rí-ig*

(40)

1 gín DILMUN kù:babbar
23. *ʾa$_5$-na-gu*
1 ĜIŠ-banšur
25. [$^d$BAD]
V. 1. *Ga-na-na-im*
lú *Lu-wa-šum$^{ki}$*

(41)

3. 2 gín DILMUN kù:babbar
nu$_{11}$-za 1 ĝír mar-tu
5. níĝ-ba
*$^d$Am-rí-ig*

(42)

7. 1 ⌜ma-na kù⌝:babbar
[ní]ĝ-sa$_{10}$ 1 na$_4$ maḫ
9. *áš-ti*
*Uš-ga* "ur$_4$"
11. *A-da-bí-ig$^{ki}$*

(43)

ŠA.PI gín DILMUN kù:babbar
13. níĝ-sa$_{10}$ 1 ĝír mar-tu kù-gi
en
15. *Ša-bir$_5$-ti-du$^{ki}$*

(44)

13 gín DILMUN kù:babbar
17. nu$_{11}$-za 1 ešda
níĝ-ba
19. [*$^{d\text{ʾ}}$A$_5$-d*]*a*-"*bal*"
[ ]
VI. 1. *in* ud
NI.DU

(45)

3. 1 gín DILMUN kù:babbar
*ʾa$_5$-na-gu*
5. 1 ĜIŠ-banšur
níĝ-ba
7. *$^d$Ra-sa-ap*
*Du-bí-tum$^{ki}$*
9. [ ]⌜x⌝
[*in*] ud
11. ḫúl
*é-sù*

(35) 30 (shekels of) silver: travel provision for (someone of) the city of Kablul; 5 shekels of silver for the ransom of 2 sons of Burḫaš.
(36) […]: gift of Buzalum (and) Ammutum of the city of Mari (who) attended the izi-ĝar ceremony.
(37) 13 shekels of silver for plating 1 mace: gift for the god Hadda of the city of Lub, in month IV.
(38) 4 shekels of silver for the garden, Zila-damu has received.
(39) 6 shekels (and) 2 NI of silver for 2 bracelets: gift for the god Ammarik.
(40) 1 shekel of silver for the circular stand of a table for [the Lord] of Ganana of the city of Luwašum.
(41) 2 shekels of silver for plating 1 mar-tu dagger: gift for the god Ammarik.
(42) 1 mina of silver for the purchase of 1 big stone by Ušga, the collector (of goods) of the city of Adabik.
(43) 40 shekels of silver for the purchase of 1 mar-tu dagger (decorated with) gold for the king of the city of Šabirtidu.
(44) 13 shekels of silver for plating 1 mace: gift for [the god ʾAd]abal [of the city …], in month VII.
(45) 1 shekel of silver for the circular stand of a table: gift for the god Rašap of the city of Dubitum […], on the occasion of the feast of his temple.

(46)
13. 15 gín DILMUN kù:babbar
*ni-zi-mu*
15. 2 níĝ-anše-ak 4 kù-sal
*Ìr-am$_{6}$-da-mu*
17. lú *Íl-zi*

(47)
ŠÚ+ŠA gín DILMUN kù:babbar
19. 2 *ʾà-ra-ma-tum*
1 ma-na ŠA.PI gín DILMUN kù:babbar
21. šu-bal-ak
ŠÚ+ŠA kù-gi
VII. 1. nu$_{11}$-za-*sù*
níĝ-ba
3. *Ib-rí-um*
$^{d}$Utu
5. lú SA.ZA$_{x}^{ki}$

(48)
ŠA.PI gín DILMUN kù:babbar
7. 1 íb-lá 1 ĝír-kun
ŠA.PI gín DILMUN kù:babbar
9. šu-bal-ak
8 gín DILMUN kù-g[i]
11. maš-[maš-*sù*]
[2 ma-na TAR gín DILMUN kù:babbar]
13. [šu-]bal-ak
TAR kù-gi
15. 1 dib
TAR kù:babbar
17. níĝ-sa$_{10}$ 1 ĝír mar-tu kù-gi
*Zi-ir-a-ḫu*
19. ugula *A-bar-sal$_{4}$*$^{ki}$
*in* ud
21. šu-du$_{8}$

(49)
10 gín DILMUN kù:babbar
23. *zi-du*
$^{d}$En-ki

(50)
VIII. 1. [x] gín DILMUN kù:babbar
níĝ-kaskal
3. *Ḫa-ra-ì*

(51)
5 gín DILMUN kù:babbar
5. níĝ-kaskal
*Kab-lu$_{5}$-ul*$^{ki}$
7. DU.DU
*Ar-mi*$^{ki}$

(52)
9. 15 gín DILMUN kù:babbar
nu$_{11}$-za 1 ešda
11. ŠÚ+ŠA gín DILMUN kù:babbar
*ʾa$_{5}$-n*[*a-gu*]
13. 1[+3 si 2 gud]
⌜nídba⌝
15. en
$^{d}$*ʾÀ-da*
17. lú *Ḫa-lab$_{x}$*$^{ki}$
*in*
19. iti *ʾa$_{5}$-nun*
(blank)
IX. (blank)
X. (in lacuna)

(53)
XI. 1. [AN.ŠÈ.G]Ú [x *m*]*i-at* [x+]4 m[a-]n[a ]
[ ]

*a*) on erasure

(46) 15 shekels of silver for decorating 2 bridles (and) 4 buckles for Iram-damu, (son) of Ilzi.
(47) 20 shekels of silver for 2 pectorals; 1;40 minas of silver in exchange for 20 (shekels of) gold for their lamination: gift of Ibrium to the god Utu of the Palace.
(48) 40 shekels of silver for 1 belt (and) 1 buckle; 40 shekels of silver in exchange for 8 shekels of gold for their striped (decoration); [2;30 minas of silver in ex]change for 30 (shekels of) gold for 1 plaque; 30 (shekels of) silver for the purchase of 1 mar-tu dagger (decorated with) gold for Ziʾir-aḫu, the overseer of the city of Abarsal when he took possession.
(49) 10 shekels of silver as alloy for the god Enki.
(50) [x] shekels of silver: travel provision for Ḫara-i(l).
(51) 5 shekels of silver: travel provision for (someone) of the city of Kablul (who) went to the city of Armi.
(52) 15 shekels of silver for plating 1 mace; 20 shekels of silver for the circular [stand of the 4 horns of 2 bulls]: offering of the king for the god Hadda of the city of Ḫalab, in month VIII.
(53) [Tota]l: [xx]4 min[as of silver …].

**Commentary**

This document is dated to the year Ibr. 08 because it mentions the military expedition led by Ibrium against Gudadanum, a city to be located north of Karkamiš (§ 31; see Archi 2021a, pp. 197, 203). The total of the expended silver and gold is not preserved.

The text opens with the usual registration of 1 mina (470 g) of silver for the head of Kura, and the 3 shekels (23 g) for a supplementary rite which fell later in the year. Kura perhaps also received a pair of gold bracelets of 6 ⅔ shekels (52 g) as an annual offering (§ 12: $^{d}$*Ku-ra* / $^{d}$*Áš-da-bíl*). The "gods", diĝir-diĝir-diĝir, received 1;40 minas (783 g) of silver, (§ 25).

The expenditure of 3 minas (1.410 kg) of silver follows: for Tirin-damu and Tinib-dulum, sisters (nin-ni) of the king, and priestesses, dam-diĝir, of the god ᵓAdabal of Luban (§ 2).

A messenger from Mari brought the news that Nagar "had been defeated", til (§ 15). This was the continuation of a military action that had begun the previous year, when Ibgitum of Mari had already reported that Nagar "had been defeated", til, text no. 10 § 60. A first confrontation between the two cities had occurred in year Ibr. 03, when Mari was already victorious (*Na-gàr*$^{ki}$ àga-"kár"; text no. 6 § 76), (see the commentary of the preceding document).

The king received a "drinking-cane (?) (*mar-wa-ga-tum*) for (his) hands", for which 2 shekels (16 g) of gold were employed (§ 11), and also reins decorated with 4 shekels (32 g) of gold (§ 13).

Ibrium received two daggers decorated with gold, of the value of 2 minas (940 g) of silver (§ 14).

Three envoys of Mari: *Wa-ru*$_{12}$*-tum*, *Daš-na*, and *I-ku-ku-tu* received all together 30 shekels (235 g) of silver (§ 19). *Bù-za-lum* (mentioned together with *Daš-na* in *ARET* XXII 1 o. III 2–5 (I.Z. 01), and *Am*$_{6}$*-mu-tum* (both also from Mari) received a gift when they came to Ebla for the izi-ĝar ceremony (§ 36).

§ 5. Silver was expended for acquiring lambs for a divination inquiry, perhaps concerning the military expedition against Gudadanum (mentioned in § 31).

§ 7. Offering of an object to the temple of Hadda by the daughter of Ibrium, who became Zibada's daughter-in-law (see text no. 3 § 65).

§ 16. Ilgušti, son of Igi, "resided", tuš-LÚ×TIL, in Kiš. The awkward syntax could suggest that Kiš belonged to Abarsal! According to text no. 17 (Ibr. 14) § 3, this same official "resided" in Kakmium by [GN$^{?}$].

§ 27. A gift for Dati-TU, queen of Lumnan (a vessel decorated with 2 shekels, 16 g, of silver) is followed by the gifts sent to Lumnan for her funerary rite (É×PAP, § 29): 2 toggle-pins of 20 shekels (157 g) of silver whose heads were decorated with 2 shekels (16 g) of gold, and 1 buckle of 1 ½ shekels (12 g) of gold (§ 29). Dati-TU had married the king of Lumnan in the year Ibr. 01: her dowry is listed in text no. 2 § 6; she died, therefore, eight years later. The year after her death, Dusigu, mother of king Išᶜar-damu, sent two buckles to her daughter, text no. 12 § 31. Dati-TU is already mentioned in two documents dated to the minister Arrukum, *ARET* XV,1 26 §§ 39–40, which lists eight princesses, first *Ti-ne-ib-da-mu*, *Dag-mu-mu*(*mul*$^{!}$)*-da-mu* (cf. *Dag*$^{(!)}$*-mul-da-mu* in 30 § 39), *Dar-maš-da-mu*, *Ma-ù-ud*, *I-ti-mu-ud* (§ 39), and then *Da-ti-*$^{d}$TU, *Za-ne-*<*ḫi-*>*-Ma-rí*, and *Dab-za-da-mu* (§ 40). Four of the first princesses are also listed in XV 27 § 107, while the last three appear in XV 34 § 142. It seems quite probable that all the eight ladies were daughters of king Igriš-Ḫalab.

§ 31. Ebla went to war with Gudadanum, a city to be placed in the north, because it precedes Karkamiš in the list of the cities under the control of Ebla as a consequence of the Treaty of Abarsal (*ARET* XIII 5 § 4), (Archi 2021a, pp. 196–197).

§ 43. The city of *Ša-bir*$_{5}$*-ti-du*$^{ki}$, *Ša-bir*$_{5}$*-ti-*(*t*)*um*$^{ki}$, ruled by a "king", en, lay in the Ḫabur triangle, the area dominated by Nagar, see no. 5 §§ 66, 71. This city delivered in the course of the years just two and one garments: years Ibr. 11 and 12, see *ARET* XIV 64 § 36; 65 § 36.

§ 48. A remarkable gift: a belt decorated with 40 shekels (313 g) of silver and 8 shekels (63 g) of gold, a dagger decorated with silver and gold, and a plaque of 20 shekels (235 g) of gold, was given to Ziᵓir-aḫu, the "overseer", ugula, of Abarsal, "when he took possession", *in* ud šu-du$_{8}$.

This anodyne expression is explained in *ARET* IV 13 § 1, a monthly document of expenditure of garments, which registers the same goods for this official of Abarsal "on the occasion of the conquest of the cities of Zurigi and Abala". This monthly document has therefore to be dated to the year Ibr. 08. Another major official of this city was a *badalum* (above, § 17), and text XXI 10 § 20 mentions a "queen", *maliktum*, of Abarsal together with that of Iritum and a daughter of the king of Raʾak. Abarsal had been defeated first by Igriš-Ḫalab of Ebla, and later by the city of Armi (Archi 2019b, pp. 3–7; Id. 2021a, p. 202).

## 12
## (Plates XXII–XXIII)

(1)
o. I. 1. 1 ma-na 3 gín DILMUN kù:babbar
saĝ kù:babbar
3. $^{d}$*Ku-ra*

(2)
6 ma-na TAR 4 gín DILMUN
kù:babbar
5. níĝ-sa$_{10}$ 1 zara$_{6}$-TÚG 14 túg-NI.NI 2
níĝ-lá-gaba
53 íb+III-TÚG sa$_{6}$ gùn
7. 2 *mi-at* 10 íb+III-TÚG gùn
2 ma-na [x+]3 [g]ín DILMUN
[kù]:babbar
9. níĝ-[sa$_{10}$] 10 [ ]
[š]A.PI [g]ín [DI]LMUN [kù:babbar]
11. [ ]
[ ]
13. [ ]
II. 1. níĝ-sa$_{10}$ 2 IGI.NITA
*Bù-da-ma-lik*
3. šu-ba$_{4}$-ti

(3)
11 gín DILMUN kù:babbar
5. níĝ-sa$_{10}$ raš-SAR Kur$^{ki}$
ki:lam$_{7}$
7. $^{d}$*Ga-mi-iš*
*wa*
9. ki:lam$_{7}$
$^{d}$ʾ*A*$_{5}$*-da-“bal”*
11. *A-ru*$_{12}$*-ga-du*$^{ki}$

(4)
ŠÚ+ŠA 5 gín DILMUN kù:babbar
13. níĝ-ba
*Ib-gi-tum*
15. *wa*
Ku-tu-ʾ*à-bù*
17. *wa*
*Ib-du-nu*
19. [ -]⌈x⌉
[ ]
21. [ ]
III. 1. *Du-du-lu*$^{ki}$
níĝ-“mul”
3. *Ag-sa-gú*$^{ki}$
šu-ba$_{4}$-ti

(5)
5. 1 ma-na kù:babbar
nu$_{11}$-za 2 an-dùl
7. *ap* kù-gi
lú dib
9. *Puzur*$_{4}$*-ra-ḫa-al*$_{6}$
ŠÚ+ŠA 2 gín DILMUN kù-gi
11. nu$_{11}$-za
*ba-na-i-su-ma*
13. *wa*
2 šu-šu-*sù*
15. 2 DU.DU-*sù*
níĝ-ba
17. ⌈d⌉ʾ*A*$_{5}$*-da-*[“*b*]*al*”
[*A-*]*ru*$_{12}$*-*[*ga-d*]*u*$^{ki}$
19. [e]n
[*i*]*n*
21. [ ]

(6)
IV. 1. 4 ma-na 10 gín DILMUN kù:babbar
šu-bal-ak
3. 50 gín DILMUN kù-gi
1 dib
5. *I-bí-zi-kir*
dumu-nita
7. *Ib-ri-um*
10 gín DILMUN kù:babbar
9. šu-bal-ak
2 gín DILMUN kù-gi 2 ĝeštu$_{x}$-lá
11. *Gi-rí*
šeš-*sù*

(1) 1;03 shekels of silver for the silver head of the god Kura.

(2) 6;34 minas of silver for the purchase of 17 garments (and) 263 kilts; 2;[x+]3 minas of [sil]ver for the pur[chase] of 10 […]; 40 [she]kels of [silver] […] for the purchase of 2 donkeys, Buda-malik has received.

(3) 11 shekels of silver for the purchase of leek from the mountain region at the market of the god Kamiš and the market of the god ʾAdabal of the city of Arugadu.

(4) 25 shekels of silver: gift for Ibgitum and Kutu-ʾabu and Ibdunu […] of the city of Tuttul (who brought) the news that the city of Akšak had been conquered.

(5) 1 mina of silver for plating 2 statues and also gold for a plaque for Puzurra-ḫal; 22 shekels of gold for plating their faces and their hands and feet: gift of the king for the god ʾAdabal of [the city of A]ru[gad]u, in […].

(6) 4;10 minas of silver in exchange for 50 shekels of gold for 1 plaque for Ibbi-zikir, son of Ibrium; 10 shekels of silver in exchange for 2 shekels of gold for 2 earrings for Giri, his brother.

(7)
13. 2 gín DILMUN kù:babbar
nam-kud
15. en
*Ì-ra-ar*$^{ki}$
17. é
$^{⌜d⌝}$*Ku-ra*

(8)
19. 1 ma-na 10[+30 gín DILMUN]
kù:[babba]r
V. 1. šu-bal-ak
ŠÚ+ŠA gín DILMUN kù-gi
3. en
*Sa-ḫa-ru*$_{12}$$^{ki}$

(9)
5. 5 gín DILMUN kù:babbar
lú ĜIŠ-nu-kiri$_6$
7. *Zi-la-da-mu*
ugula
9. kas$_4$
šu-ba$_4$-ti

(10)
11. 4 gín DILMUN kù:babbar
nu$_{11}$-za 2 ĝír mar-tu
13. 7 ½ gín DILMUN kù:babbar
šu-bal-ak
15. 1 ½ gín DILMUN kù-gi
2 kù-sal
17. [ní]ĝ-ba
$^{d}$BAD *Ga-na-na-im*
19. [*w*]*a*
[$^{d?}$*A*$_5$*-d*]*a*[*-ra*]
VI. 1. *Gi-rí*
*wa*
3. *Ni-ir-da-mu*
2 dumu-nita
5. *Ib-rí-um*
in-na-sum
7. *in* ud
gi$_4$
9. *mi-nu*
*Du-du-lu*$^{ki}$

(11)
11. 4 ma-na kù:babbar
níĝ-ba
13. *Wa-ba-rúm*
ga:eš$_8$
15. *Du-du-lu*$^{ki}$
2 ma-na kù:babbar
17. níĝ-ba
*Na-na-tum*
19. dam-*sù*
1 ma-na kù:babbar
21. níĝ-ba
dumu-nita-*sù*
23. šu-mu-tak$_4$
ŠE+TIN
25. 1 ma-na kù:babbar
VII. 1. níĝ-ba
2 maškim-*sù*
3. *in*
*Sa-gàr-du*$^{ki}$
5. šu-ba$_4$-ti

(12)
2 ma-na kù:babbar
7. níĝ-ba
*Ab-bu*$_{16}$
9. *Ma-rí*$^{ki}$
níĝ-"mul"
11. *Ag-sa-gú*$^{ki}$
šu-ba$_4$-ti

(13)
13. 2 gín DILMUN kù:babbar
nu$_{11}$-za 1 ĝír mar-tu
15. níĝ-ba
$^{d}$BAD *Ar-ti-na-an*$^{ki}$
17. *Ib-rí-um*
in-na-sum

(14)
19. ŠÚ+ŠA gín DILMUN kù:babbar 2 *bu*-DI
*Za-ne-ḫi-Ma-rí*$^{ki}$
21. dumu-munus
en

(7) 2 shekels of silver for the oath of the king of the city of Irar in the temple of the god Kura.
(8) 1;40 minas of sil[ver] in exchange for 20 shekels of gold for the king of the city of Saḫaru.
(9) 5 shekels of silver for the gardeners, Zila-damu, the overseer of the messengers has received.
(10) 4 shekels of silver for plating 2 mar-tu daggers; 7 ½ shekels of silver in exchange for 1 ½ shekel of gold for 2 buckles: [gi]ft for the Lord of Ganana [an]d for [the goddess ᵓAd]a[ra], Giri and Niᵓir-damu, 2 sons of Ibrium, have given when came back from the city of Tuttul.
(11) 4 minas of silver: gift for Wabarum, travelling merchant of the city of Tuttul; 2 minas of silver: gift for Nanatum, his spouse; 1 mina of silver: gift for his son, (since) they have handed over beer; 1 mina of silver: gift for 2 of his representatives; they have received it in the city of Sagardu.
(12) 2 minas of silver: gift for Abbu of the city of Mari (who brought) the news that the city of Akšak had been conquered.
(13) 2 shekels of silver for plating 1 mar-tu dagger: gift for the Lord of the city of Artinan, Ibrium has given.
(14) 20 shekels of silver for 2 toggle-pins for Zaneḫi-Mari, daughter of the king (and) daughter-in-law of Ibᵓara.

23. é-gi

VIII. 1. *Ib-ˀà-ra*

(15)

TAR 3 gín DILMUN 3 NI kù:babbar

3. šu-bal-ak

6 gín DILMUN 2 NI kù-gi

5. 2 *gú-li-lum*

níĝ-ba

7. $^{d}$*Áš-da-bíl*

(16)

7 ma-na TAR 3 gín DILMUN

kù:babbar

9. níĝ-sa$_{10}$ 31 túg-NI.NI

1 gada-TÚG

11. 10 lá-2 íb+III-TÚG sa$_6$ gùn

3 *mi-at* 53 íb+III-TÚG gùn

13. ki:lam$_7$

$^{d}$*Áš-da-bíl*

(17)

15. 6 gín DILMUN 2 NI kù:babbar

2 *gú-li-lum*

IX. 1. níĝ-ba

$^{d}$*Am-ma-rí-ig*

(18)

3. 11 ma-na 10 gín DILMUN an-na

kin$_5$-ak

5. 1 *li-im* ĜIŠ-gu-kak-gíd zabar

1 ma-na kù:babbar

7. níĝ-sa$_{10}$ 1 ĝír mar-tu kù-gi

*Ib-rí-um*

9. *in* ud

è

11. *si-in*

níĝ-kas$_4$

13. *Ma-nu-wa-ad*$^{ki}$

(19)

1 ma-na kù:babbar

15. níĝ-ba

*Wa-ru*$_{12}$*-tum*

17. *Ma-rí*$^{ki}$

níĝ-"mul"

X. 1. *Ag-sa-gú*$^{ki}$

šu-ba$_4$-ti

(20)

3. ŠA.PI 4 gín DILMUN an-na

šub

5. *si-in*

6 ma-na 10 gín DILMUN a-gar$_5$-gar$_5$

7. *ni-zi-mu*

ZA$_x$

9. naĝar-naĝar

(21)

7 gín DILMUN an-na

11. šub

*si-in*

13. 2 *ma-ga-za-ˀà* zabar

gibil

15. 2 zú

bulug$_4$

17. *Wa-ba-rúm*

šu-ba$_4$-ti

(22)

19. 3 ½ gín DILMUN an-na

šub

21. *si-in*

XI. 1. 1 ĜIŠ-gu-kak-šub

sur$_x$-BAR.AN

3. *Ib-rí-um*

(23)

5 gín DILMUN an-na

5. šub

*si-in*

7. 1 ĜIŠ-zú

ĜIŠ-gígir-II

9. *Ib-rí-um*

(24)

7 gín DILMUN an-na

11. šub

*si-in*

13. *ba-na-a*

1 níĝ-saĝšu

15. lú *Ma-za-um*

(15) 33 shekels (and) 3 NI of silver in exchange for 6 shekels (and) 2 NI of gold for 2 bracelets: gift for the god Ašdabil.

(16) 7;33 minas of silver for the purchase of 32 garments (and) 361 kilts, at the market of the god Ašdabil.

(17) 6 shekels (and) 2 NI of silver for 2 bracelets: gift for the god Ammarik.

(18) 11;10 minas of tin for making 1000 spearheads of bronze; 1 mina of silver for the purchase of 1 mar-tu dagger (decorated with) gold for Ibrium, on the occasion of (his) departure to the military expedition (against) the city of Manuwat.

(19) 1 mina of silver: gift for Warutum of the city of Mari (who brought) the news that the city of Akšak had been conquered.

(20) 24 shekels of tin to be melted with 6;10 minas of copper for decorating objects of the carpenters.

(21) 7 shekels of tin to be melted in 2 new rasps of bronze (and) 2 blades for chisel, Wabarum has received.

(22) 3 ½ shekels of tin to be melted in 1 goad for the team of mules of Ibrium.

(23) 5 shekels of tin to be melted in 1 hook for the chariot of Ibrium.

(24) 7 shekels of tin to be melted in the visor of a helmet for Mazaum.

(25)
TAR 5 gín DILMUN kù:babbar
17. níĝ-sa$_{10}$ 1 ĝír mar-tu ti kù-gi
*wa ʾà-lum*
19. *A-bur-li-im*
lú
XII. 1. *Ig-rí-iš*

(26)
10 gín DILMUN kù:babbar
3. šu-bal-ak
2 gín DILMUN kù-gi 2 ĝeštu$_x$-lá
5. *I-bí-zi-kir*
dumu-nita
7. *Ib-rí-um*
*in* ud
9. šu-du$_8$
*in*
11. *Ma-nu-wa-ad*$^{ki}$

(27)
10 gín DILMUN kù:babbar
13. šu-bal-ak
2 gín DILMUN kù-gi
15. 2 ĝeštu$_x$-lá
*I-bí-zi-kir*
17. lú *I-rí-gú-nu*
*in* ud
19. tuš-LÚ×TIL
XIII. 1. *in*
*Ma-nu-wa-ad*$^{ki}$

(28)
3. 8 gín DILMUN kù:babbar
šu-bal-ak
5. 1 ½ gín DILMUN kù-gi
*ni-zi-mu*
7. nu$_{11}$-za 1 *gú-li-lum* 15 gín DILMUN
a-gar$_5$-gar$_5$
1 gín DILMUN kù:babbar
9. 2 *gú-a-zi-da-su*
*Iš-má-ga-lu*
11. lú *Mu-gàr*
NE-di

(29)
13. 10 gín DILMUN kù:babbar
šu-bal-ak
15. 2 gín DILMUN kù-gi
*ni-zi-mu*
17. nu$_{11}$-za
XIV. 1. 2 *gú-li-lum* kù:babbar
lú *Sa-mu-um*
3. lú *En-ti*
*wa*
5. lú dumu-nita
*I-da-ad-mu*
7. *in*
*ìr-a-núm*
9. *I-rí-ig-ma-lik*

(30)
6 gín DILMUN kù:babbar
11. 2 zi-bar
níĝ-ba
13. $^{d}$BAD *Má*-NE$^{ki}$
*wa*
15. $^{d}$BAD *Zu-ra-mu*$^{ki}$
*Du-si-gú*
17. šu-mu-tak$_4$

(31)
7 ½ gín DILMUN kù:babbar
19. šu-bal-ak
XV. 1. 1 ½ gín DILMUN kù-gi 2 kù-sal
dumu-munus
3. *Da-ti-*$^{d}$TU
*ma-lik-tum*
5. *Lum-na-an*$^{ki}$
*Du-si-gú*
7. šu-mu-tak$_4$

(32)
1 ma-na ŠA.PI gín DILMUN
kù:babbar
9. šu-bal-ak
ŠÚ+ŠA gín DILMUN kù-gi
11. 10 ĝeštu$_x$-lá
ama-gal
13. *Ib-rí-um*

(25) 35 shekels of silver for the purchase of 1 pointed mar-tu dagger (decorated with) gold and … (*ʾà-lum*) for Abur-lim, (son) of Igriš.

(26) 10 shekels of silver in exchange for 2 shekels of gold for 2 earrings for Ibbi-zikir, son of Ibrium, when he took possession in the city of Manuwat.

(27) 10 shekels of silver in exchange for 2 shekels of gold for 2 earrings for Ibbi-zikir, (son) of Iri-gunu when he occupied the city of Manuwat.

(28) 8 shekels of silver in exchange for 1 ½ shekel of gold for decorating with lamination 1 bracelet of 15 shekels of copper; 1 shekel of silver for 2 … (*gú-a-zi-da-su*) for Išma-galu, (son) of Mugar, the dancer.

(29) 10 shekels of silver in exchange for 2 shekels of gold for decorating with lamination 2 bracelets of silver for Samum, (son) of Enti and for the son of Idadmu, (belonging) to the gang of Irig-malik.

(30) 6 shekels of silver for 2 zi-bar goblets: gift for the Lord of the city of MANE and for the Lord of the city of Zuramu, Dusigu has handed over.

(31) 7 ½ shekels of silver in exchange for 1 ½ shekel of gold for 2 buckles for the daughter of Dati-TU, the queen of the city of Lumnan, Dusigu has handed over.

(32) 1;40 minas of silver in exchange for 20 shekels of gold for 10 earrings for Ibrium's mother.

(33)
3 ma-na ŠÚ+ŠA gín DILMUN
kù:babbar
15. šu-bal-ak
ŠA.PI gín DILMUN kù-gi
r. I. 1. 1 íb-lá 1 *si-ti-tum* 1 ĝír-kun
*I-bí-du-lum*
3. en
*Ma-nu-wa-ad*$^{ki}$
5. *in* ud
DU.DU
7. nam-kud
é
9. $^{d}$*Ku-ra*

(34)
15 gín DILMUN kù:babbar
11. nu$_{11}$-za 1 *ḫa-*⸢*bù*⸣
TAR kù:babbar
13. šu-ba[l-]ak
6 gín DIL[MUN] kù-gi nu$_{11}$-za 1 *ar-ra-sù*
15. níĝ-ba
$^{d}$*ʾÀ-da*

(35)
17. ŠÚ+ŠA gín DILMUN kù:babbar
*ʾa*$_{5}$*-na-gu*
II. 1. 4 si-si
2 gud
3. nídba
en
5. $^{d}$*ʾÀ-da*
*in*
7. iti *ʾa*$_{5}$*-nun*

(36)
ŠÚ+ŠA gín DILMUN kù:babbar
9. šu-bal-ak
5 gín DILMUN kù-gi
11. níĝ-ba
*Ša-ḫa-ru*$_{12}$$^{ki}$

(37)
13. 6 gín DILMUN kù:babbar
*Bù-sum*
15. *Ma-rí*$^{ki}$
*a-dè*
17. túg-*sù*
ugula ki:lam$_{7}$
19. ga:eš$_{8}$
*in*
21. *Maš-a*$^{ki}$

(38)
2 ma-na 50 gín DILMUN kù:babbar
23. níĝ-sa$_{10}$
III. 1. 2 *ʾà-da-um*-TÚG-I
23 gada-TÚG mu$_{4}$$^{mu}$
3. 10 gada-TÚG ḫul
4 gada-TÚG *kir-na-nu*
5. 18 íb+III-TÚG sa$_{6}$ gùn
18 siki na$_{4}$ *Ma-rí*$^{ki}$
7. 10 ma-na 52 gín DILMUN kù:babbar
níĝ-sa$_{10}$ 80 gud-gud
9. ki:lam$_{7}$
$^{d}$*ʾÀ-da*

(39)
11. TAR kù:babbar
níĝ-ba
13. diĝir-diĝir-diĝir

(40)
5 gín DILMUN kù:babbar
15. šu-bal-ak
1 gín DILMUN kù-gi
IV. 1. *ni-zi-mu*
1 níĝ-anše-ak
3. IGI.NITA
*Ib-rí-um*

(41)
5. 1 ma-na kù:babbar
níĝ-sa$_{10}$ 1 ĝír mar-tu kù-gi
7. *Ib-rí-um*
*in* ud
9. è
*si-in*
11. á-daḫ
lú *A-te-na-ad*$^{ki}$

(33) 3;20 minas of silver in exchange for 40 shekels of gold for 1 belt, 1 sheath (and) 1 dagger pendant for Ibbi-dulum, the king of the city of Manuwat, when he went to swear an oath in the temple of the god Kura.
(34) 15 shekels of silver for plating 1 mace; 30 (shekels of) silver in exchange for 6 shekels of gold for plating its handle: gift for the god Hadda.
(35) 20 shekels of silver for the circular stand of the 4 horns of 2 bulls: offering of the king for the god Hadda, in month VIII.
(36) 20 shekels of silver in exchange for 5 shekels of gold: gift for (someone of) the city of Šaḫaru.
(37) 6 shekels of silver for Busum of the city of Mari as a replacement for his clothing, the overseer of the market (who is) a travelling merchant, in the city of Maša.
(38) 2;50 minas of silver for the purchase of 39 garments, 18 kilts (and) 18 stone weights of wool from the city of Mari; 10;52 mina of silver for the purchase of 80 oxen, at the market of the god Hadda.
(39) 30 (shekels of) silver: gift for the gods.
(40) 5 shekels of silver in exchange for 1 shekel of gold for decorating 1 bridle of the donkey of Ibrium.
(41) 1 mina of silver for the purchase of 1 mar-tu dagger (decorated with) gold for Ibrium, on the occasion of the departure to help the city of Atenat.

(42)

13. 4 gín DILMUN kù:babbar
níĝ-sa$_{10}$ 1 *gàr-su* ĝi$_{6}$
15. *Ib-rí-um*

(43)

ŠÚ+ŠA 4 gín DILMUN kù:babbar
17. níĝ-sa$_{10}$ 8 *gàr-su* ĝi$_{6}$ si$_{4}$-si$_{4}$
V. 1. lú gaba-ru

(44)

3 ma-na TAR kù:babbar
3. šu-bal-ak
ŠA.PI 2 gín DILMUN kù-gi
5. *ni-zi-mu*
2 *gú-li-lum*
7. en

(45)

10 gín DILMUN kù:babbar
9. níĝ-sa$_{10}$ še-in
*Wa-na*
11. ugula BAR.AN
šu-ba$_{4}$-ti

(46)

13. 1 ma-na kù:babbar
níĝ-ba
15. *Ib-gi-tum*
*Ma-rí*$^{ki}$
17. ĜIŠ.DUG.DU
izi-ĝar

(47)

19. 5 gín DILMUN kù:babbar
VI. 1. daḫ
níĝ-du$_{8}$
3. 1 ĝuruš
*Lu-wa-šum*$^{ki}$
5. *áš-ti*
*Ba-na-i-um*$^{ki}$

(48)

7. 3 gín DILMUN kù:babbar
níĝ-du$_{8}$
9. 1 dumu-nita
*Ti-in*$^{ki}$
11. lú *A-da-su*$^{ki}$
*I-šar*
13. *Da-ti-um*$^{ki}$
šu-ba$_{4}$-ti

(49)

15. TAR kù:babbar
níĝ-sa$_{10}$ 2 zara$_{6}$-TÚG
17. ŠA.PI gín DILMUN kù:babbar
níĝ-sa$_{10}$ 1 níĝ-lá-gaba 3 níĝ-lá-saĝ
19. *I-in-zé*
*in*
21. Kiš$^{ki}$

(50)

VII. 1. ŠÚ+ŠA gín DILMUN kù:babbar
níĝ-du$_{8}$
3. *Dam-da-il*
*Ib-su*$^{ki}$
5. *in*
Kiš$^{ki}$
7. lú
*Na-zu-mu*
9. níĝ-du$_{8}$

(51)

2 gín DILMUN kù:babbar
11. nu$_{11}$-za 1 ĝír mar-tu
½ gín DILMUN kù:babbar
13. 1 kù-sal
níĝ-ba
15. *Ib-rí-um*
$^{d}$ʾ*A*$_{5}$*-da-“bal”*
17. *Ne-a-ù*$^{ki}$

(52)

1 ma-na kù:babbar
19. níĝ-ba
*Daš-na*
21. *Ma-rí*$^{ki}$
DU.DU
23. *áš-da*
VIII. 1. [ ]
[ ]

(42) 4 shekels of silver for the purchase of 1 black bag for Ibrium.
(43) 24 shekels of silver for the purchase of 8 black and red bags: receipt.
(44) 3;30 minas of silver in exchange for 42 shekels of gold for decorating 2 bracelets for the king.
(45) 10 shekels of silver for the purchase of straw, Wana, the overseer of the mules, has received.
(46) 1 mina of silver: gift for Ibgitum of the city of Mari, (who) attended the izi-ĝar ceremony.
(47) 5 shekels of silver, in addition, for the ransom of 1 man of the city of Luwašum from the city of Banaʾium.
(48) 3 shekels of silver for the ransom of a young man of the city of Tin (from) the city of Adasu, Išar of the city of Datium has received.
(49) 30 (shekels of) silver for the purchase of 2 mantels; 40 shekels of silver for the purchase of 1 breast-band and 3 headbands for Iʾin-ze in the city of Kiš.
(50) 20 shekels of silver for the ransom of Damda-il of the city of Ibsu in the city of Kiš, (who) Nazumu has ransomed.
(51) 2 shekels of silver for plating 1 mar-tu dagger; ½ shekel of silver for 1 buckle: gift of Ibrium for the god ʾAdabal of the city of Neau.
(52) 1 mina of silver: gift for Dašna of the city of Mari (who) went from [the city of …].

(53)
3. 50 gín DILMUN kù:babbar
níĝ-sa$_{10}$ 1 ĝír mar-tu kù-gi
5. *Ib-rí-um*
*in* ud
7. ká gibil
lú *I-bí-zi-kir*
9. igi-ḫi-du$_{8}$

(54)
2 ma-na 10 gín DILMUN kù:babbar
11. šu-bal-ak
ŠÚ+ŠA 6 gín DILMUN kù-gi
13. kin$_{5}$-ak
saĝ
15. $^{d}$*Ra-sa-ap*
*Du-ne-íb*$^{ki}$
17. *wa*
nu$_{11}$-za
IX. 1. íb+III-TÚG-*sù*
lú
3. *al*$_{6}$
[iti]
5. NI.DU

(55)
TAR 3 gín DILMUN kù:babbar
7. nu$_{11}$-za 2 an-dùl
ŠA.PI gín DILMUN kù:babbar
9. šu-bal-ak
8 gín DILMUN kù-gi
11. nu$_{11}$-za *ba-na-a-sa*
*wa*
13. 2 šu-*sù*
*wa*
15. 2 DU-*sù*
níĝ-ba
17. *Du-si-gú*
$^{d}$*Ku-ra*
19. *in* ud
ne:saĝ

(56)
21. 1 gín DILMUN kù:babbar
nam-kud
X. 1. *Ar-ru*$_{12}$*-šum*
*Na-gàr*$^{ki}$

(57)
3. [x] gín DILMUN kù:babbar
níĝ-sa$_{10}$ ĜIŠ-*šè-bir*$_{5}$*-gi-nu*
5. *Wa-ba-rúm*
šu-ba$_{4}$-ti

(58)
7. 3 ma-na 5 gín DILMUN kù:babbar
šu-bal-ak
9. TAR 7 gín DILMUN kù-gi 1 dib
*I-da-ne-gi-mu*
11. dumu-nita en

(59)
3 ma-na ŠÚ+ŠA gín DILMUN
kù:babbar
13. šu-bal-ak
XI. 1. ŠA.PI gín DILMUN kù-gi
kin$_{5}$-ak
3. 2 níĝ-anše-ak
sur$_{x}$-BAR.AN
5. [am]a-gal
en

(60)
7. 1 ma-na ŠÚ+ŠA 3 gín DILMUN an-na
šub
9. *si-in*
9 ma-na TAR gín DILMUN a-gar$_{5}$-gar$_{5}$
11. kin$_{5}$-ak
6 tùn tur lú TAR.TAR
13. 6 dub-naĝar šu-mu-LAGAB ŠÚ+ŠA-ŠÚ+ŠA
6 dub-naĝar sal
15. lú 15 gín DILMUN

(53) 50 shekels of silver for the purchase of 1 mar-tu dagger (decorated with) gold for Ibrium when he passed in review the new "gate" of Ibbi-zikir.

(54) 2;10 minas of silver in exchange for 26 shekels of gold for making the head of the god Rašap of the city of Tunip and for plating its kilt, on [month] VII.

(55) 33 shekels of silver for plating 2 statues; 40 shekels of silver in exchange for 8 shekels of gold for plating their faces and their hands and feet: gift of Dusigu for the god Kura, on the occasion of (his) first-fruit offering.

(56) 1 shekel of silver for the oath of Arrušum of the city of Nagar.

(57) [x] shekels of silver for the purchase of … (ĜIŠ-*šè-bir*$_{5}$*-gi-nu*), Wabarum has received.

(58) 3;05 minas of silver in exchange for 37 shekels of gold for 1 plaque for Ida-nikimu, son of the king.

(59) 3;20 minas of silver in exchange for 40 shekels of gold for making 2 bridles for the team of mules of the king's [mo]ther.

(60) 1;23 shekels of tin to be melted with 9;30 shekels of copper for making 6 small axes of 30 (shekels), 6 hammers with a square head of 20 (shekels), 6 thin hammers of 15 shekels, 6 thin hammers of 10 (shekels), 6 pliers of 10 (shekels), 6 saws of 10 (shekels), 6 saws of 5 (shekels), 6 small hammers of 5 (shekels), 12 blades, 6 new seal pins of of a chariot; 57 shekels of tin to be melted with 6;46 minas of copper for making 5 small axes of 30 (shekels), 5 thin hammers of 15 (shekels), 5 thin hammers of 10 (shekels), 5 rasps of 10 (shekels), 5 pliers of 30 (shekels) […] 5 new seal pins of boxwood: Wabarum [has] received.

6 dub-naĝar sal 10
XII. 1. 6 *ma-za-ḫa-*$ru_{12}$ 10
6 *ḫa-ra-nu* 10
3. 6 *ḫa-ra-nu* 5
6 dub-naĝar tur 5
5. 12 ˹UŠ×KÍD˺
6 $bulug_4$-$bulug_4$ gibil lú ĜIŠ-gígir-II
7. 57 gín DILMUN an-na
šub
9. *si-in*
6 ma-na ŠA.PI 6 gín DILMUN a-$gar_5$-$gar_5$
11. $kin_5$-ak
5 tùn tur TAR.TAR
13. 5 dub-naĝar sal 15
5 dub-naĝar sal 10
15. 5 *ma-ga-za-*$u_9$ 10
5 *ma-za-ḫa-*$ru_{12}$ TAR
XIII. 1. [ ]
[ ]
3. [ ]˹x˺
5 $bulug_4$-$bulug_4$ gibil lú ĜIŠ-taškarin
5. *Wa-ba-rúm*
[šu-]$ba_4$-ti

(61)
7. 3 ma-na 50 gín DILMUN kù:babbar
*Di-ni-ib-du-lum*
9. dam-diĝir
nin-ni
11. en
šu-$ba_4$-ti
(blank)
XIV. (blank)

(62)
XV. 1. [AN.ŠÈ.GÚ x kù:babbar]
[è]
3. *ap*
3 *mi-at* 1 ma-na kù:babbar
5. [$al_6$-ĝá]l
é en
7. diri
(blank)

(61) 3;50 minas of silver: Tinib-dulum, the priestess, sister of the king, has received.
(62) [Total: x silver: expenditure], and 301 minas of silver [are present] in the king's house, as remainder.

## Commentary

This document is to be dated to the year Ibr. 09 because it mentions the military expedition against the city-state of Manuwat led by Ibrium (§§ 18, 26, 27, 33; see Archi 2021a, pp. 198, 203). The total of the expended silver is not preserved; the silver which remained in the "house of the king", é en, amounted to 301 minas (141.47 kg), (§ 62).

The document opens with the usual registration of the expenditures of 1 mina (470 g) of silver for the renewal rite at the beginning of the new year, and 3 more shekels (23 g) for a subsequent rite which perhaps fell in the third month (see the commentary of text no. 4). Thirty shekels (23 g) were expended for "the gods", diĝir-diĝir-diĝir (§ 39).

The 3;50 minas (1.801 kg) of silver received by Tinib-dulum in her function as priestess of the god ʾAdabal, is registered at the end of the document (§ 61).

Minister Ibrium received a dagger decorated with gold valued at 1 mina of silver for the "military expedition", níg-$kas_4$, against the city of Manuwat, and 11;10 minas (5.25 kg) of tin were employed to forge 1,000 spearheads for his army (§ 18). Ibbi-dulum, the defeated king of Manuwat, later came to Ebla to swear an "oath", nam-kud, in the temple of Kura. This event is also registered in *ARET* XIV 62 § 32, the annual mu-DU document from the year Ibr. 09, where it is said that on that occasion Ibbi-dulum delivered eight garments, four kilts, a belt decorated with 1 mina (470 g) of gold, a plaque of 58 shekels (454 g) of gold, and a dagger decorated with a statuette of gold. Ebla reciprocated this gift with a belt decorated with 40 shekels (313 g) of gold (§ 33). Relations between the two cities had been good for years, and the quality of the gift and the counter gift shows the will to resume previous relations.

Three or more messengers from Tuttul, who had brought the news that Akšak (a city to the north of Kiš) had been "conquered", šu-$ba_4$-ti, received all together 25 shekels (20 g) of silver (§ 4). This news was confirmed by two envoys from Mari: *Ab-bu*$_{16}$ (*Ab-ba* is the more frequent writing, see the Index), and Warutum (§§ 12, 19). This event was so highly appreciated that Abbu received 2 minas of silver and Warutun 1 mina (940 and 470 g respectively). The reason for the dramatically different amounts given as rewards to the envoys from Tuttul as opposed to those from Mari was probably related to the status of the two cities.

Other envoys from Mari who reached Ebla were *Bù-sum* (§ 37), *Ib-gi-tum* (§ 46), and *Daš-na* (52).

Ibrium received two expenditures of tin for his chariot and gold decorations for the harness (§§ 22, 23, 40); a bag of the value of 4 shekels (31 g) of silver (§ 42). He also received a dagger decorated with gold when he "went to help", á-daḫ, Atenat, a city bound to his family (§ 41). His mother received 5 pairs of earrings of 20 shekels (157 g) of gold (§ 32)

Ibbi-zikir, Ibrium's son, received a pair of earrings decorated with 2 shekels (16 g) of gold, having taken part in the expedition against Manuwat (§ 26).

Ibbi-zikir, the son of Iri-gunu, who served as "lord", lugal, for most of the period of Ibrium (see *ARET* XIV, p. 499), "occupied", tuš-LÚ×TIL, Manuwat (§ 27). Ibrium received another dagger decorated with gold when he "passed in review" the "new gate of Ibbi-zikir", probably this Ibbi-zikir (§ 53).

§ 2. Buda-malik received 6;34 minas (3.09 kg) of silver for purchasing a large amount of clothing; other silver was employed in acquiring other goods, including two donkeys (these passages are only in part preserved). The markets where he provided these goods are not mentioned.

§ 6. Ibbi-zikir, the son of Ibrium, and his brother Giri, received respectively 1 plaque of 50 shekels (391 g) of gold, and a pair of earrings of 2 shekels (16 g) of gold.

§ 7. The king of Irar came to Ebla to swear an oath in the temple of Kura. He had already come to swear a first oath in the year Ibrium 02 (text 4 § 52).

§ 10. Giri and Niʾir-damu, two sons of Ibrium, offered a buckle decorated with gold both to the Lord of Ganana, and his *paredra* ʾAdara.

The relation between these two deities is confirmed by several passages, such as *ARET* XXII 6 r. V 29–31 $^{d}$BAD *Ga-na-na-um* $^{d}$ʾ*$A_{5}$-da-la*; XXII 9 (*MEE* 12, 37) o. XXI 16–18: $^{d}$ʾ*$A_{5}$-da-la wa* $^{d}$BAD *Ga-na-na*$^{!}$(GA)-*um*; TM.75.G.2398 rev. I 7–9: $^{d}$ʾ*$A_{5}$-da-ra wa Ga-na-na.* This last passage belongs to a monthly document of sheep offerings, which the goddess always received outside Ebla, with the exception of a couple of cases, when she was offered "by the wood of the god Ašdabil" (at Ebla), cf. TM.75.G.2398 obv. I 11–17: 3 udu $^{d}$ʾ*$A_{5}$-da-ra* en nídba *áš-da* ĝiš $^{d}$*Áš-da-bíl.* The writing ʾ*$A_{5}$-da-ra* is preserved in *ARET* XII 597 o. II' 2', 699 r. II 10; XV 41 r. VI 12; *MEE* 10, 27 o. XI' 3; ʾ*$A_{5}$-da-la* in *ARET* XII 32 o.$^{?}$ 4' 1. For the Lord of Ganana, see Archi 2021b, p. 3.

§ 11. Wabarum, the most important "travelling merchant", ga:eš, of Tuttul, apparently presented his whole family to the Eblaite administration: he received 4 minas of silver, his spouse 2 minas, and one of his sons 1 mina (for a total of 3.29 kg), because they had handed over ŠE+TIN beer. Another mina of silver (470 g) was given to two of his representatives.

§ 14. On the princess Zaneḫi-Mari see the commentary to text no. 9.

§ 20. The alloy had 10.62% of tin.

§ 29. The *ìr-a-núm* of Irig-malik is also mentioned in *ARET* XX 5 r. VII 12–13.

§ 31. Dusigu, the king's mother, sent a pair of earrings to the daughter of Dati-TU, the Eblaite princess who had married the king of Lumnan, and died the previous year (Ibr. 08), (see the commentary of XXI 11).

§ 46. Ibgitum of Mari received 1 mina (470 g) of silver when he came back for the izi-ĝar ceremony.

§ 49. A certain Iʾin-ze received 30 shekels (235 g) of silver in order to purchase some garments in Kiš.

§ 50. Nazumu received 20 shekels (146 g) of silver in order to ransom a certain Damda-il in Kiš.

§ 51. *Ne-a-ù*[ki], one of the cult seat of the god ᵓAdabal, has been identified with the Egyptian Niya, and [uru]*Ni-ḫi* /*Ni-ya*/*Ni-i*, of the cuneiform sources, placed in the Orontes valley, see Astour 1992, p. 9 and nt. 31; Archi 2010b, pp.37–38.

§ 56. Arrušum, a representative of the city of Nagar came to swear an oath.

§ 57. Wabarum (of Tuttul) received a (not preserved amount of silver) in order to provide an object.

§ 58. Ida-nikimu received a plaque of 37 shekels (290 g) of gold.

§ 59. The new harness of the mules of the queen mother required 40 shekels (313 g) of gold.

§ 60. Wabarum received amounts of tin and copper in order to provide work tools.

# 13
## (Plates XXIV–XXV)

(1)

o. I. 1. 1 ma-na kù:babbar
saĝ kù:babbar
3. ${}^{d}$*Ku-ra*

(2)

[2+]1 ma-na ⸢ŠÚ+ŠA⸣ 5 gín DILMUN kù:babbar
5. [*Di-n*]*e*-[*í*]*b*-[*du*-]*lum*
[ni]n-ni
7. [e]n
[šu-b]a$_4$-[t]i

(3)

9. [x m]a-na [kù:bab]bar [x í]b-lá [x *si*-]*ti-tum* [x ĝí]r-kun
[e]n
11. [*Du*-]*lu*${}^{ki}$
[ŠA.]PI [gí]n [DI]LMUN k[ù:babbar]
13. [ ]⸢x-x⸣
[ -*w*]*a*
15. [2 *b*]*u*-DI
[*m*]*a-lik*-[*t*]*um*
17. [*D*]*u-lu*${}^{ki}$

(4)

[š]A.PI gín DILMUN [kù]:babbar [1 íb-lá 1] *si-ti-tum* 1 ĝír-kun
19. 1 ma-na an-na
II. 1. *Ar-ra-du-lum*
ŠÚ+ŠA gín DILMUN kù:babbar 2 *bu*-DI
3. dam-*sù*
*Iš-má-ga-lu*
5. šu-mu-tak$_4$

(5)

2 ma-na kù:babbar
7. 2 íb-lá 2 *si-ti-tum* 2 ĝ[í]r-kun
*Mu-zi*
9. šeš
en
11. *wa*
*Lu-wa-sa-ra-du*
13. *Du-lu*${}^{ki}$

(6)

1 ma-na kù:babbar
15. 1 íb-lá 1 *si-ti-tum* 1 ĝír-kun
*Mu*-NE-*a-du*
17. ugula *Ar-ḫa-du*${}^{ki}$
*in* ud
19. DU.DU
nam-kud
21. é
${}^{d}$*Ku-ra*

(7)

23. 2 ma-na
III. 1. ŠA.PI gín DILMUN kù:babbar
šu-bal-ak
3. TAR 2 gín DILMUN kù-gi
nu$_{11}$-za 2 ĜIŠ.GAM.GAM
5. 10 gín DILMUN kù:babbar
šu-bal-ak
7. [2 gín DILMUN kù-g]i
nu$_{11}$-za 1 zag
9. 5 gín DILMUN an-na
šub *si-in*
11. 1 ĜIŠ-zú
ĜIŠ-gígir-II
13. en

(8)

4 gín DILMUN kù:babbar
15. lú ĜIŠ-nu-kiri$_6$
*Du-bí*
17. šu-ba$_4$-ti

(1) 1 mina of silver for the silver head of the god Kura.

(2) 3;25 minas of silver, [Tin]ib-[du]lum, [si]ster [of the ki]ng [has receiv]ed.

(3) [x m]ina(s) of [silv]er for [x b]elt(s), [x sh]eath(s) (and) [x dagger pen]dant(s) for the [ki]ng of the city of [Du]lu; 40 [she]kels of s[ilver …] […] [2 tog]gle-pins for the [qu]een of the city of [D]ulu.

(4) 40 shekels of silver [for 1 belt, 1] sheath (and) 1 dagger pendant; 1 mina of tin for Arra-dulum; 20 shekels of silver for 2 toggle-pins for his spouse, Išma-galu has handed over.

(5) 2 minas of silver for 2 belts, 2 sheaths (and) 2 dagger pendants for Muzi, the king's brother and for Luwa-saradu of the city of Dulu.

(6) 1 mina of silver for 1 belt, 1 sheath (and) 1 dagger pendant for MuNEadu, the overseer of the city of Arḫadu, when he went to swear an oath in the temple of the god Kura.

(7) 2;40 minas of silver in exchange for 32 shekels of gold for plating 2 wheels; 10 shekels of silver in exchange for [2 shekels of gold] for plating 1 side; 5 shekels of tin to be melted in 1 hook of a chariot of the king.

(8) 4 shekels of silver for a gardener, Dubi has received.

(9)
3 gín DILMUN an-na
19. šub *si-in*
1 ĜIŠ-gu-kak-šub
21. en
*Ì-ra-ar*$^{ki}$

(10)
23. ½ gín DILMUN kù:babbar
IV. 1. nam-kud
*Na-ḫal*$^{ki}$
3. *Ki-li-im*
šu-mu-tak$_4$

(11)
5. 4 gín DILMUN kù:babbar
níĝ-sa$_{10}$ 1 ĝír mar-tu *ba-du-u*$_4$
kù:babbar
7. [*Rí-*]*dam-ma-lik*
ugula *Su-ti-gú*$^{ki}$

(12)
9. 14 gín DILMUN kù:babbar
lú ĜIŠ-nu-kiri$_6$
11. *Ti-ti-nu*
*wa*
13. *Gú-zi*
šu-ba$_4$-ti
15. *in*
*A-te-na-ad*$^{ki}$

(13)
17. 1 ma-na an-na
sagi(SÌLA.ŠU.DU$_8$)
19. *Ma-rí*$^{k}$
ŠÚ+ŠA gín DILMUN kù:babbar
21. níĝ-ba
*Wa-ru*$_{12}$*-tum*
23. *wa*
V. 1. *Šu-ga-du*
*Ma-rí*$^{ki}$

(14)
3. 2 gín DILMUN kù:babbar
nu$_{11}$-za 1 ĝír mar-tu
5. níĝ-ba
*Ib-rí-um*
7. $^{d}$*Ra-sa-ap*
$^{d}$En-ki

(15)
9. 7 ma-na TAR 4 gín DILMUN
kù:babbar
níĝ-sa$_{10}$ 60 lá-2 íb+III-TÚG sa$_6$ gùn
11. 30 íb+III-TÚG gùn
2 *mi-at* 45 "KIN" siki *Ma-rí*$^{ki}$
13. 5 ma-na TAR 3 gín DILMUN
kù:babbar
níĝ-sa$_{10}$ 20 gud
15. 1 ma-na kù:babbar
níĝ-sa$_{10}$ ĜIŠ-ti-ḪAR
17. *Wa-ba-rúm*
šu-ba$_4$-ti
VI. 1. ki:lam$_7$
šeš-II-ib
3. *wa*
$^{d}$*A-da-ma*
5. *ʾÀ-da-ni*$^{ki}$

(16)
4 gín DILMUN an-na
7. šub *si-in*
1 ĜIŠ-zú
9. 1 gín DILMUN kù:babbar
nu$_{11}$-za 1 zag
11. ĜIŠ-gígir-II
*I-bí-zi-kir*
13. dumu-nita
*Ib-rí-um*

(17)
15. TAR kù:babbar
níĝ-ba
17. *Ib-gi-tum*

(9) 3 shekels of tin to be melted in 1 spearhead for the king of the city of Irar.
(10) ½ shekel of silver for the oath of the city of Naḫal, Kilim has handed over.
(11) 4 shekels of silver for the purchase of 1 *b.* mar-tu dagger (decorated with) silver for [Ri]dam-malik, the overseer of the city of Sutigu.
(12) 14 shekels of silver for the gardeners: Titinu and Guzi have received in the city of Atenat.
(13) 1 mina of tin for the steward of the city of Mari; 20 shekels of silver: gift for Warutum and Šugadu of the city of Mari.
(14) 2 shekels of silver for plating 1 mar-tu dagger: gift of Ibrium for the gods Rašap (and) Enki.
(15) 7;34 minas of silver for the purchase of 88 kilts (and) 245 KIN measures of wool from the city of Mari; 5;33 minas of silver for the purchase of 20 oxen; 1 mina of silver for the purchase of GIŠ-ti-ḪAR-wood: Wabarum has received, at the markets of the šeš-II-ib confraternity and of the god Adamma of the city of ʾAdani.
(16) 4 shekels of tin to be melted in 1 hook; 1 shekel of silver for plating 1 side of the chariot of Ibbi-zikir, son of Ibrium.
(17) 30 (shekels of) silver: gift for Ibgitum, Badulum, Lali (and) Ikukutu of the city of Mari.

*Ba-du-lum*
19. *La-li*
*I-ku*$^!$(DÚR)-*ku*$^!$(DÚR)-*tu*
21. *Ma-ri*$^{ki}$

(18)
TAR [x] gí[n] DIL[MUN] kù:babbar
23. *ni-zi-mu*
nu$_{11}$-za 1 bur-KAK
25. $^{d}$*Á-la*
*Zi-gú*$^{ki}$

(19)
VII. 1. 1 ma-na kù:babbar
níĝ-sa$_{10}$ ĝeštin
3. *si-in*
*In-gàr*
5. *Gú-zi*
šu-mu-tak$_{4}$

(20)
7. 15 gín DILMUN kù:babbar
šu-bal-ak
9. 3 gín DILMUN kù-gi
kin$_{5}$-ak
11. 1 *du-rúm*
níĝ-ba
13. *Ib-rí-um*
$^{d}$*Ḫa-a-ba-du*
15. lú *Ḫa-lab*$_{x}^{ki}$

(21)
ŠA.PI 3 gín DILMUN kù:babbar
17. nu$_{11}$-za 2 an-dùl
50 gín DILMUN kù:babbar
19. šu-bal-ak
10 gín DILMUN kù-gi
21. nu$_{11}$-za [I]GI.DUB-*sù*
*wa*
23. 4 šu-*sù*
VIII. 1. 4 DU-*sù*
níĝ-ba
3. *Du-si-gú*
$^{d}$*Ra-sa-ap*
5. $^{d}$*A-da-ma*
*ʾÀ-da-ni*$^{ki}$

(22)
7. 3 gín DILMUN kù:babbar
saĝ kù:babbar
9. $^{d}$*Ku-ra*
mu-ti-II

(23)
11. 12 gín DILMUN kù:babbar
nu$_{11}$-za 1 an-dùl
13. 15 gín DILMUN kù:babbar
šu-bal-ak
15. 3 gín DILMUN kù-gi
nu$_{11}$-za
17. IGI.DUB-*sù*
2 šu-*sù* 2 DU-*sù*
19. níĝ-ba
*Du-si-gú*
21. $^{d}$*Iš:šára*
*Wa*-NE-*du*$^{ki}$

(24)
23. ŠÚ+ŠA gín DILMUN kù:babbar
šu-bal-ak
IX. 1. 4 gín DILMUN kù-gi
*ni-zi-mu*
3. 4 *ʾà-ra-ma-tum*
*Zi-mi-ni*-kù:babbar
5. *ma-lik-tum*
*Bur-ma-an*$^{ki}$

(25)
7. 2 ½ gín DILMUN kù:babbar
nu$_{11}$-za 1 ĝír mar-tu 1 kù-sal
9. níĝ-ba
*Ib-rí-um*
11. $^{d}$*Ga-ra-ru*$_{12}$

(26)
2 ½ gín DILMUN kù:babbar
13. šu-bal-ak
½ gín DILMUN kù-gi 1 kù-sal

(18) 30[+x] shek[els] of silver for decorating with lamination 1 bur-KAK vessel for the god Ala of the city of Zigu.
(19) 1 mina of silver for the purchase of wine for Ingar, Guzi has handed over.
(20) 15 shekels of silver in exchange for 3 shekels of gold for making 1 … (*du-rúm*): gift of Ibrium for the goddess Ḫaʾabadu of the city of Ḫalab.
(21) 43 shekels of silver for plating 2 statues; 50 shekels of silver in exchange for 10 shekels of gold for plating their faces and their 4 hands and 4 feet: gift of Dusigu for the god Rašap (and) the god Adamma of the city of ʾAdani.
(22) 3 shekels of silver for the silver head of the god Kura: second delivery.
(23) 12 shekels of silver for plating 1 statue; 15 shekels of silver in exchange for 3 shekels of gold for plating its head, its 2 hands (and) feet: gift of Dusigu for the goddess Išḫara of the city of WaNEdu.
(24) 20 shekels of silver in exchange for 4 shekels of gold for decorating 4 pectorals for Zimini-kubabbar, the queen of the city of Burman.
(25) 2 ½ shekels of silver for plating 1 mar-tu dagger (and) 1 buckle: gift of Ibrium for the god Gararu.
(26) 2 ½ shekels of silver in exchange for ½ shekel of gold for 1 buckle; 1 shekel of silver for 1 buckle: gift for NEtiadu, the god of the city of Dulu, Išma-galu has handed over.

15. 1 gín DILMUN kù:babbar
1 kù-sal
17. níĝ-ba
$^{d}$NE-*ti-a-du*
19. diĝir *Du-lu*$^{ki}$
*Iš-má-ga-lu*
21. šu-mu-tak$_4$

(27)
6 gín DILMUN kù:babbar
X. 1. [x k]ù:babbar
*Ti-ra-ì*
3. *A-da-bí-ig*$^{ki}$

(28)
3 ma-na an-na
5. šub *si-in*
24 ma-na a-gar$_5$-gar$_5$
7. kin$_5$-ak
IGI.DUB
9. 40 níĝ-saĝšu

(29)
10 lá-2 ma-na kù:babbar
11 níĝ-sa$_{10}$ 1 *mi-at* 50 aktum-TÚG 1 zara$_6$-TÚG 20 dùl-TÚG *Ma-rí*$^{ki}$
ki:lam$_7$
13 *Ma-rí*$^{ki}$
dam-gàr

(30)
15 ŠA.PI gín DILMUN kù:babbar
níĝ-sa$_{10}$ 1 ĝír mar-tu kù-gi
17. *ba-da-lum*
XI. 1. ⌜*Ḫa*⌝*-ra-a*[*n*$^{ki}$]

(31)
15 gín DILMUN kù:babbar
3. nu$_{11}$-za 1 *ḫa-bù*
TAR kù:babbar
5. šu-bal-ak
6 gín DILMUN kù-gi
7. nu$_{11}$-za 1 *ar-ra-sù*
ŠÚ+ŠA gín DILMUN kù:babbar
9. *ʾa$_5$-na-gu*
4 si 2 gud
11 nídba
en
13 $^{d}$*Ra-sa-ap*
*ʾÀ-da-ni*$^{ki}$

(32)
15 1 íb-lá TAR kù:babbar
maš-maš kù-gi
17. lú mu-DU
*Ib-rí-um*
19. *ap*
10 gín DILMUN kù:babbar
21. 1 ĝír-kun
5 gín DILMUN kù:babbar
23. šu-bal-ak
1 gín DILMUN kù-gi maš-maš-*sù*

(33)
XII. 1. [x kù:babbar]
[níĝ]-sa$_{10}$ [1 g]ír m[ar-t]u kù-g[i]
3. *Ù-zu* “ur$_4$”
*Ì-mar*$^{ki}$
5. É×PAP
*Ba-ga-ma*
7. šu-mu-tak$_4$

(34)
4 gín DILMUN an-na
9. šub *si-in*
2 ĝír mar-tu
11. 4 gín DILMUN kù:babbar
nu$_{11}$-za-*sù*
13. 3 gín DILMUN 3 NI kù:babbar
šu-bal-ak
15. 3 NI gín DILMUN kù-gi
*kam$_4$-ma-a-tum-sù*
17. *In-gàr*
*wa*
19. *Ne-zi-ma-lik*
lú-kar
21. *Kak-mi-um*$^{ki}$

(35)
ŠÚ+ŠA gín DILMUN kù:babbar
23. šu-bal-ak
XIII. 1. ⌜4⌝ gín DILMUN kù-gi

(27) 6 shekels of silver [for … of s]ilver for Tira-i(l) of the city of Adabik.
(28) 3 minas of tin to be melted with 24 minas of copper for making the visors of 40 helmets.
(29) 8 minas of silver for the purchase of 171 garments at the market of the city of Mari, the merchant(s) (have handed over).
(30) 40 shekels of silver for the purchase of 1 mar-tu dagger (decorated with) gold for the minister of the city of Ḫarran.
(31) 15 shekels of silver for plating 1 mace; 30 (shekels of) silver in exchange for 6 shekels of gold for plating its handle; 20 shekels of silver for the circular stand of the 4 horns of 2 bulls: offering of the king for the god Rašap of the city of ʾAdani.
(32) 1 belt of 30 (shekels of) silver for a striped (decoration) of gold: delivery for Ibrium, and also 10 shekels of silver for 1 dagger pendant; 5 shekels of silver in exchange for 1 shekel of gold for its striped (decoration).
(33) [x silver for the pur]chase of [1] m[ar-t]u [dag]ger (decorated with) gol[d] for the funerary rite of Uzu, the collector (of goods) of the city of Imar, Bagama has handed over.
(34) 4 shekels of tin to be melted in 2 mar-tu daggers; 4 shekels of silver for their lamination; 3 shekels (and) 3 NI of silver in exchange for 3 NI of gold for their knobs: for Ingar and Nezi-malik, traders of the city of Kakmium.
(35) 20 shekels of silver in exchange for 4 shekels of gold for 4 buckles on the account of buckles of Zibada.

4 kù-sal
3. *al*$_{6}$
kù-sal
5. ⌜*Zi*⌝-*ba*-⌜*da*⌝

(36)
7 g[ín] DILMUN kù:babbar
7. šu-bal-ak
1 ½ gín DILMUN kù-gi
9. *ni-zi-mu*
maš-maš 4 kù-sal
11. *Ib-rí-um*

(37)
2 ma-na TAR kù:babbar
13. šu-bal-ak
TAR kù-gi 1 dib
15. ì-ĝiš-saĝ
en
17. *Ì-mar*$^{ki}$

(38)
1 ma-na kù:babbar
19. 2 *bu*-DI
15 gí[n] DILMUN kù:babbar
21. šu-bal-ak
3 gín DILMUN kù-gi
23. nu$_{11}$-za 2 saĝ-*sù*
ì-ĝiš-saĝ
XIV. 1. *Ti-šè-li-im*
ama-gal-*sù*

(39)
3. 2 ma-na 50 gín DILMUN kù:babbar
[níĝ-sa$_{10}$]
5. [x *mi-at*] 30+[3(?)+]2 íb+III-TÚG sa$_{6}$ gùn
1 *mi-at* íb+III-TÚG gùn
7. 2 níĝ-saĝšu
3 ma-na ŠÚ+ŠA 4 gín DILMUN kù:babbar
9. níĝ-sa$_{10}$ 12 gud
13 gín DILMUN kù:babbar
11. níĝ-sa$_{10}$ ĜIŠ-ti-ḪAR
12 ma-na ŠÚ+ŠA gín DILMUN kù:babbar
13. šu-bal-ak
40 lá-3 ma-na gìn-gìn
15. ki:lam$_{7}$
*ᵓÀ-da-ni*$^{ki}$
XV. 1. AMA-*ra*

(40)
16 gín DILMUN an-na
3. šub *si-in*
3 ĜIŠ-zú
5. 3 ĜIŠ-gígir-II
en
7. *wa*
ama-gal-*sù*
9. *wa*
*Ib-rí-*[*u*]*m*

(41)
11. 3 gín DILMUN kù:babbar
nu$_{11}$-za 2 zag
13. 2 ĜIŠ-gígir-II
ama-gal
15. en
*wa*
17. *Ib-rí-um*

(42)
TAR kù:babbar
19. 2 *bu*-DI
15 gín DILMUN kù:babbar
21. šu-bal-ak
3 gín DILMUN kù-gi
23. nu$_{11}$-za 2 saĝ-*sù*
níĝ-ba
25. *Ti-šè-li-im*
*ma-lik-tum*
XVI. 1. *Ì-mar*$^{ki}$
*in* ud
3. DU.DU
*si-in*
5. SA.ZA$_{x}^{ki}$
tak$_{4}$
7. AMA-*ra*

(43)
1 gín DILMUN kù:babbar
9. nu$_{11}$-za 2 si
[gud]-I

(36) 7 she[kels] of silver in exchange for 1 ½ shekel of gold for a striped (decoration) of 4 buckles for Ibrium.
(37) 2;30 minas of silver in exchange for 30 (shekels of) gold for 1 plaque for the purification rite of the king of the city of Imar.
(38) 1 mina of silver for 2 toggle-pins; 15 shek[els] of silver in exchange for 3 shekels of gold for plating their 2 heads for the purification rite of Tiša-lim, his mother.
(39) 2;50 minas of silver [for the purchase of x+]135 kilts (and) 2 helmets; 3;24 minas of silver for the purchase of 12 oxen; 13 shekels of silver for the purchase of GIŠ-ti-ḪAR-wood; 12;20 minas of silver in exchange for 37 minas of lapis lazuli, at the market of the city of ᵓAdani, at the AMA-ra (festival).
(40) 16 shekels of tin to be melted in 3 hooks for the 3 chariots of the king and his mother and Ibrium.
(41) 3 shekels of silver for plating 2 sides of the 2 chariots of the king's mother and of Ibrium.
(42) 30 (shekels of) silver for 2 toggle-pins; 15 shekels of silver in exchange for 3 shekels of gold for plating their 2 heads: gift for Tiša-lim, the queen of the city of Imar, when she went to the Palace, handed over at the AMA-ra (festival).
(43) 1 shekel of silver for plating 2 horns [of a bull] […] for Ibrium.

11. ˹x˺ 1 ˹x˺
*Ib-rí-um*

(44)
13. 50 gín DILMUN kù:babbar
níĝ-ba
15. *Daš-na*
*wa*
17. *Šu-ga-du*
*Ma-rí*$^{ki}$

(45)
19. 3 gín DILMUN kù:babbar
níĝ-ba
21. *A-za-ba*
*Ir-i-tum*$^{ki}$
23. á-áĝ
*a-dè*
25. šir

(46)
7 ma-na ŠA.PI
XVII. 1. 2 gín DILMUN kù:babbar
níĝ-sa$_{10}$ 10 túg-NI.NI
3. 40 íb+III-TÚG sa$_{6}$ gùn
4 *mi-at* 40 íb+III-TÚG gùn
5. ŠÚ+ŠA gín DILMUN [k]ù:babbar
níĝ-s[a$_{10}$] raš-SAR Kur$^{ki}$
7. 1 ma-na 1 gín DILMUN kù:babbar
níĝ-sa$_{10}$ 3 IGI.NITA u$_{5}$
9. en
18 gín DILMUN kù:babbar
11. níĝ-sa$_{10}$ ĜIŠ-ma-dul$_{10}$
ki:lam$_{7}$
13. $^{d}$*Ga-mi-iš*

(47)
ŠÚ+ŠA gín DILMUN kù:babbar
15. níĝ-ba
*Bù-sum*
17. *Ma-rí*$^{ki}$

(48)
r. I. 1. 2 ma-na kù:babbar
níĝ-ba
3. *Ìr-am*$_{6}$-kur$^{ki}$
sagi
5. *Ma-rí*$^{ki}$
*in* ud
7. kin$_{5}$-ak
kú
9. en

(49)
ŠA.PI gín DILMUN kù:babbar
11. níĝ-ba
*Da-ti*
13. *Iš-da-maḫ*
*Ù-lu-li*
15. [ ]
[ ]
17. [ ]
ḫi-mu-DU
19. 1 BAR.AN
*Na-zu-mu*
21. zàḫ

(50)
10 m[a-]na kù:babbar
23. níĝ-s[a$_{10}$] 60 [ ]
[ ]
II. 1. 24 dùl-TÚG *Ma-rí*$^{ki}$
ki:lam$_{7}$
3. SA.ZA$_{x}$$^{ki}$

(51)
1 ma-na 2 gín DILMUN kù:babbar
5. lul-gu-ak
gur$_{8}$
7. ˹*Sa-mu-ù*˺
dam-gàr
9. *Ga-ra-ma-an*$^{ki}$

(52)
10 gín DILMUN kù:babbar
11. lul-gu-ak
gur$_{8}$
13. *Puzur*$_{4}$*-ra-m[a-]lik*
lú-kar
15. *Kak-mi-um*$^{ki}$
KAK*-bar-zú*
17. *wa*

(44) 50 shekels of silver: gift for Dašna and Šugadu of the city of Mari.
(45) 3 shekels of silver: gift for Azaba of the city of Iritum, (who) gave instructions for a song.
(46) 7;42 minas of silver for the purchase of 10 garments (and) 480 kilts; 20 shekels of [si]lver for the purcha[se] of leek from the mountain region; 1;01 minas of silver for the purchase of 3 donkeys to ride for the king; 18 shekels of silver for the purchase of chariot shafts: at the market of the god Kamiš.
(47) 20 shekels of silver: gift for Busum of the city of Mari.
(48) 2 minas of silver: gift for Iram-kur, the steward of the city of Mari, when (he came to) prepare meals for the king.
(49) 40 shekels of silver: gift for Dati, Išda-mah, Ululi, […], (who) delivered 1 mule (that) Nazumu had lost.
(50) 10 minas of silver for the purcha[se] of 84[+x] garments at the market of the Palace.
(51) 1;02 minas of silver for the replacement of a raft for Samuʾu, the merchant of the city of Garaman.
(52) 10 shekels of silver for the replacement of a raft for Puzurra-malik, trader of the city of Kakmium: KAKbarzu and Dubi-zikir have handed over for the king of the city of Kakm[i]u[m].

*Du-bí-zi-kir*
19. šu-mu-tak$_4$
*si-in*
21. en
*Kak-m*[*i-*]*u*[*m*$^{ki}$]

(53)
23. [x kù:babbar]
[ ]
III. 1. 1 ĝír mar-tu ti kù-gi
*wa*
3. 1 *gú-li-lum* a-gar$_5$-gar$_5$ kù-gi
[ ]
5. ugula sur$_x$-BAR.AN
*Ib-rí-um*

(54)
7. TAR 3 gín DILMUN 3 NI kù:babbar
šu-bal-ak
9. 6 gín DILMUN 2 NI kù-gi 2 *gú-li-lum*
níĝ-ba
11. $^{d}$*Ku-ra*

(55)
2 ma-na kù:babbar
13. níĝ-ba
*Kùn*-NE
15. *wa*
*Ab-ba*
17. muḫaldim
*Ma-rí*$^{ki}$
19. ḫi-mu-DU
mè
21. *si-in*
*Ma-nu-wa-ad*$^{ki}$

(56)
23. 2 gín DILMUN an-na
[ ]
25. [ ]
[ ]
IV. 1. nu$_{11}$-za-*sù*
*Ib-rí-um*

(57)
3. [13 g]ín [DILM]UN [kù:babbar]
[nu$_{11}$-za 1 *ḫa-bù*]
5. níĝ[-ba]
$^{d}$*ʾÀ-da*
7. lú *Lu-ub*$^{ki}$

(58)
13 gín DILMUN kù:babbar
9. nu$_{11}$-za 1 *ḫa-bù*
níĝ-ba
11. $^{d}$*ʾA$_5$-da-"bal"*
*A-ru$_{12}$-ga-du*$^{ki}$

(59)
13. TAR 4 gín DILMUN kù:babbar
nu$_{11}$-za 2 an-dùl
15. níĝ-ba
*Ib-rí-um*
17. $^{d}$*Ra-sa-ap*
*wa*
19. $^{d}$*A-da-ma*
*ʾÀ-da-ni*$^{ki}$

(60)
21. 5 gín DILMUN kù:babbar
nu$_{11}$-za ⌜1⌝ an-dùl
23. [níĝ-ba]
[ ]
25. [$^{d}$X]

(61)
V. 1. 14 gín DILMUN kù:[babba]r
[ ]
3. [ ]
[ ]
5. kin$_5$-ak
$^{d}$*A-gi*
7. *Su-ti-ig*$^{ki}$

(62)
12 ma-na TAR kù:babbar
9. níĝ-sa$_{10}$ 42 túg-NI.NI
35 aktum-TÚG
11. 16 *ʾà-da-um*-TÚG
40 íb+III-TÚG sa$_6$ gùn
13. 4 *mi-at* 72 íb+III-TÚG gùn
ki:lam$_7$
15. $^{d}$*Áš-da-bíl*

(53) [x silver ...] for 1 pointed mar-tu dagger (decorated with) gold and 1 bracelet of copper (and) gold [for ...] the overseer of the team of mules of Ibrium.
(54) 33 shekels (and) 3 NI of silver in exchange for 6 shekels (and) 2 NI of gold for 2 bracelets: gift for the god Kura.
(55) 2 minas of silver: gift for KunNE and Abba, (2) cooks from the city of Mari, (when) they joined the battle (against) the city of Manuwat.
(56) 2 shekels of tin [...] for its lamination for Ibrium.
(58) [13 sh]ekels [of silver for plating 1 mace]: gi[ft] for the god Hadda of the city of Lub.
(58) 13 shekels of silver for plating 1 mace: gift for the god ʾAdabal of the city of Arugadu.
(59) 34 shekels of silver for plating 2 statues: gift of Ibrium for the gods Rašap and Adamma of the city of ʾAdani.
(60) 5 shekels of silver for plating 1 statue: [gift of ... for ...].
(61) 14 shekels of sil[ver ...] for making (a statue of) the god Agi of the city of Šutik.
(62) 12;30 minas of silver for the purchase of 93 garments (and) 512 kilts, at the market of the god Ašdabil.

(63)
6 gín DILMUN 2 NI kù:babbar 2 *gú-li-lum*
17. níĝ-ba
$^{d}$*Am-ma-*⸢*rí*⸣[*-ig*]

(64)
VI. 1. ŠA.PI gín D[ILMUN kù:babbar]
[ ]
3. [ ]
*Iš*$_{11}$*-la-ab*
5. lú *Ru*$_{12}$*-zi-da-mu*
*wa*
7. *I-ša-ni-ki-mu*
šeš
9. *Ar-si-a-ḫa*
2 lú-kar
11. *Ma-nu-wa-ad*$^{ki}$

(65)
ŠA.PI gín DILMUN kù:babbar
13. níĝ-sa$_{10}$ 1 ĝír mar-tu kù-gi
*Na-zu-mu*
15. *in* ud
níĝ-kas$_{4}$
17. *si-in*
Kiš$^{ki}$

(66)
19. 1 ma-na kù:babbar
[ ]
21. [ ]
[ ]
VII. 1. Kiš$^{ki}$

(67)
TAR 3 gín [DILMUN 2 NI kù:babbar]
3. [šu-bal-ak]
[6 gín DILMUN 2 NI kù-gi]
5. 2 *gú-li-lum*
níĝ-ba
7. $^{d}$*Ku-ra*

(68)
16 gín DILMUN kù:babbar
9. níĝ-sa$_{10}$ 7 *gàr-su* ĝi$_{6}$
*Ar-wa*
11. BÍL*-za-ì*
*wa*
13. *En-na-ì*
2 dumu-nita
15. šeš
*Ib-rí-um*
17. *wa*
Lugal*-na-*⸢*i*⸣*-iš*
19. *Íl-ba-šum*
*Íl-ba-zi-kir*
21. *A-ma-*NI
lú-kar
23. [ ]

(69)
[15 gín DILMUN kù:babbar]
25. [šu-bal-ak]
VIII. 1. 3 gín DILMUN kù-gi
*ni-zi-m*[*u*]
3. [ ]
[*Ì-lum-a-ḫi*]
5. *wa*
*I-in-*$^{d}$ʾ*À-da*
7. 2 dumu-nita
en

(70)
9. ŠÚ+ŠA gín DILMUN kù:babbar
šu-bal-ak
11. 4 gín DILMUN kù-gi
nu$_{11}$-za saĝ 4 *bu-*DI
13. ama-gal
en

(71)
15. 3 ma-na ŠÚ+ŠA gín DILMUN
kù:babbar
[ ]
17. [ ]

(63) 6 shekels (and) 2 NI of silver for 2 bracelets: gift for the god Ammar[ik].
(64) 40 shekels [of silver …] for Išlab, (son) of Ruzi-damu and Iša-nikimu, brother of Arsi-aḫa, 2 traders of the city of Manuwat.
(65) 40 shekels of silver for the purchase of 1 mar-tu dagger (decorated with) gold for Nazumu, on the occasion of the military expedition against the city of Kiš.
(66) 1 mina of silver […] the city of Kiš.
(67) 33 shekels [(and) 3 NI of silver in exchange for 6 shekels (and) 2 NI of gold] for 2 bracelets: gift for the god Kura.
(68) 16 shekels of silver for the purchase of 7 black bags for Arwa, BILza-i(l) and Enna-i(l), 2 sons of a brother of Ibrium, and Lugal-naiš, Ilbašum, Ilba-zikir, AMANI, traders of [the city of …].
(69) [15 shekels of silver in exchange for] 3 shekels of gold for decorating [… for Ilum-aḫi] and Iʾin-Hadda, 2 sons of the king.
(70) 20 shekels of silver in exchange for 4 shekels of gold for plating the heads of 4 toggle-pins for the king's mother.
(71) 3;20 minas of silver […] Pu[zur]ra[-malik], (son) of Iš-damu.

[ ]
19. *Pu*[*zur*$_4$-]*ra*[-*ma-lik*]
lú *Iš*$_{11}$-*da-mu*

(72)
21. [3 ma-na ŠÚ+ŠA gín DILMUN kù:babbar]
IX. 1. šu-bal-ak
[š]A.PI g[ín DILMUN kù-gi]
3. 1 dib
2 ma-na TAR kù:babbar
5. šu-bal-ak
TAR kù-gi 1 íb-lá 1 *si-ti-tum* 1 ĝ[ír-kun]
7. [ ]
[ ]
9. [ ]
[…-]⸢x⸣$^{ki}$

(73)
11. [2] ma-na TAR kù:babbar
[šu-b]al-[a]k
13. [TAR gín DILMUN kù-gi]
[ ]
15. *B*[*ù*-]*du-d*[*u*]
ugula *Ar-ʾà-mu*$^{ki}$
17. *in* ud
*Si-da-rí-in*$^{ki}$
19. til

(74)
[x kù:babbar]
21. [níg-sa$_{10}$]
X. 1. ⸢10⸣[+x *ʾà-da-um*-TÚG-II]
[x *ʾà*]-*da*-[*u*]*m*-TÚG-I
3. 80 aktum-TÚG
30 íb+III-TÚG sa$_6$ gùn
5. 4 *mi-at* 96 íb+III-TÚG gùn
ŠÚ+ŠA g[ín] D[ILMUN] kù:babbar
7. níĝ-sa$_{10}$ 10 gud
1 ma-na kù:babbar
9. níĝ-sa$_{10}$ 22 [ ]
[ki:]⸢lam$_7$⸣
11. *Si*-⸢*ʾà*⸣-*mu*$^{ki}$
*wa*
13. ki:lam$_7$
$^{d}$*ʾÀ-da*

(75)
15. 2 ma-na kù:babbar
1 ĜIŠ-šú 1 níĝ-bànda
17. lú 2 šu
TAR [kù]:babbar 2 *t*[*i-gi-na*]
XI. 1. 2 ĜIŠ-du
⸢13⸣[+(x) g]ín DILMUN [kù:babbar]
3. [ ]
[x] kù:[bab]bar
5. 1 zi-bar
2 gín DILMUN kù-babbar
7. 1 *bu*-DI tur
[ ]
9. [x gín DILMUN a]n-na
šub *si-in*
11. 1 igi-igi
15 gín DILMUN kù:babbar
13. *Dag*-⸢*mul*⸣-*da-mu*
*ma-lik-tum*
15. *Lum-na-an*$^{ki}$
šu-mu-tak$_4$
17. 2 gín DILMUN kù:babbar
géme-*sù*

(76)
19. 10 gín DILMUN kù:babbar
[ ]
XII. 1. *Ú-mu*-⸢*ti*⸣
[(ca. 10 lines)]

(77)
12.? [ -N]E?-[N]E
13. *Ma-rí*$^{ki}$
*in*
15. ⸢x⸣-[x-]*ma*-⸢x⸣
šu-ba$_4$-ti

(78)
17. 2 ma-na TAR kù:babbar
šu-bal-ak

(72) [3;20 minas of silver] in exchange for 40 sh[ekels of gold] for 1 plaque; 2;30 minas of silver in exchange for 30 (shekels of) gold for 1 belt, 1 sheath (and) 1 dagger pen[dant for … of the city of …].
(73) [2];30 minas of silver [in excha]nge for [30 shekels of gold for …] for B[u]dud[u], the overseer of the city of Arʾamu, when the city of Sidarin had been defeated.
(74) [x silver for the purchase of] 90[+x] garments (and) 526 kilts; 20 she[kels] of silver for the purchase of 10 oxen; 1 mina of silver for the purchase of 22 […]: at the [mar]ket of the city of Siʾamu and the market of the god Hadda.
(75) 2 minas of silver for 1 GIŠ-šú vessel (and) 1 níg-bànda vessel for the hands; 30 (shekels of) [sil]ver for 2 t[orques] (and) 2 foot rings; 13[+x she]kels of [silver] [for …]; [x] silver for 1 zi-bar goblet; 2 shekels of silver for 1 small toggle-pin […] [x shekels of t]in to be melted in 1 (jewel in shape of) a pair of eyes; 15 shekels of silver: Dagmul-damu, the queen of the city of Lumnan has handed over; 2 shekels of silver for her maidservant.
(76) 10 shekels of silver […] Umuti […].
(77) […] […N]E[N]E of the city of Mari has received in […].
(78) 2;30 minas of silver in exchange for 30 (shekels of) gold (that) the minister of the city of Abarsal received in […].

19. TAR kù-gi
*ba-da-lum*
21. *A-bar-sal*$_4$$^{ki}$
šu-du$_8$
23. *in*
[ ]

(79)
25. [x gín DILMUN kù:babbar]
XIII. 1. 4 ĝeštu$_x$-lá
[(ca. 11 lines)]

(80)
13.? [ -]⌜x⌝
[ -]⌜x⌝
15. DU.DU
*Ma-ri*$^{ki}$

(81)
17. 2 ma-na kù:babbar
kin$_5$-ak
19. 2 *gú-li-lum*-II ŠÚ+ŠA
2 *gú-li-lum*-I 10
21. [ ]
XIV. 1. ŠÚ+ŠA 4 g[ín DILMUN ]
[(ca. 14 lines)]

(82)
16.? ŠA.PI gín DILMUN kù:babbar
17. nu$_{11}$-za
5 *gú-li-lum*-II a-gar$_5$-gar$_5$ TAR
19. *wa*
5 *gú-li-lum*-II a-gar$_5$-gar$_5$ ŠÚ+ŠA
21. [ ]
XV. 1. ME-sig
é
3. [en]
[(ca. 15 lines; then blank)]
XVI. (blank)

(83)
XVII. 1. AN.ŠÈ.GÚ 1 *mi-at* 70 m[a-]n[a]
40[+x] g[ín DILMUN kù:babbar]
[ ] (then blank)

(79) [x shekels of silver] for 4 earrings […].
(80) […] (who) went to the city of Mari.
(81) 2 minas of silver for making 2 double bracelets of 20 (shekels), 2 single bracelets of 10 (shekels) […]; 24 she[kels of …] […].
(82) 40 shekels of silver for plating 5 double bracelets of 30 (shekels) of copper each and 5 double bracelets of 20 (shekels) of copper each […] for the watchmen of the [king's] house.
(83) Total: 170;40[+x] minas [of silver …].

## Commentary

This document is to be dated to the year Ibr. 10. The expended silver amounts to 170;40 + x minas (80.213 + x kg), § 83. It opens with the registration of the expenditure of 1 mina (470 g) of silver for the renewal rite concerning the city-god Kura which fell at the beginning of the new year. Kura also received a pair of gold bracelets of 6 ⅔ shekels (52 g) twice (§§ 54, 67).

Tinib-dulum, a sister of the king, received 3;25 minas (1.606 kg) in her function as priestess of the god ʾAdabal (§ 2).

Lavish gifts were sent to some members of the elite of Dulu, a city which lay between Armi(um), identified as Samsat (on the Upper Euphrates) and Ebla. Its king received a belt decorated with silver (whose amount is not preserved), and its queen jewelry for which 40 shekels (313 g) of silver were employed. Arra-dulum received a belt decorated with 40 shekels (313 g) of silver, and 1 mina (470 g) of tin; his spouse two toggle-pins of 20 shekels (157 g) of silver. Muzi, the king's brother, and Luwa-saradu (in text no 14 § 18 this name is written *Ḫu-wa-sa-ra-du*) each received a belt decorated with 1 mina (470 g) of silver each (§§ 3–5). Dulu reciprocated these gifts with clothing, in particular *kir-na-nu*, probably lengths of linen (see *ARET* XIV 63 §§ 30–32, and 39, the annual mu-DU document from the same year): the cities of Dulu and Dugurasu were both renowned producers of this cloth. The occasion of this exchange of gifts between Ebla and Dulu was the alliance which the two cities entered, as can be deduced from the fact that Ebla sent two buckles (one in gold, the other in silver) as a gift to $^{d}$NE-*ti-a-du*, the god of Dulu (§ 26). The gift for the god as well as those for the members of the royal court were brought to Dulu by a certain Išma-galu. An exchange of goods between the two cities continued the following year (XXI 14 §§ 5, 18, 52, 67). It has been suggested that the city of Dulu, to be localized north of Ebla, could perhaps be identified as Titriş Höyük (see Archi 2016a, pp. 17, 27–29, 42; Id. 2020a, pp. 29–31).

The king received a new chariot, for which 34 shekels (266 g) of gold and 5 shekels (39 g) of tin (§ 7) were employed. His mother, ama-gal en, also received some decorations for her chariot (§§ 40, 41), in addition to four toggle-pins decorated with gold (§ 70). Two of the king's sons, Ilum-aḫi and Iʾin-Hadda, received an object decorated with a small amount of gold each (§ 69).

Minister Ibrium received a belt of 30 shekels (235 g) of silver to be fused with gold, a pendant decorated with 10 shekels (78 g) of silver to be fused with 1 shekel (8 g) of gold (§ 32), and a decoration for his chariot (§ 41). He also received four earrings whose alloy required 12 g (94 g) of gold (§ 36). Ibbi-zikir, his son, received a decoration for his chariot (§ 16).

Among the several messengers from Mari who came to Ebla, its "steward", sagi, received 1 mina (470 g) of tin. He was accompanied by *Wa-ru*$_{12}$*-tum* and *Šu-ga-du* (who knew well the way to Ebla), who received together 20 shekels (157 g) of silver (§ 13). A delegation of four messengers, *Ib-gi-tum*, *Ba-du-lum*, *La-li*, and *I-ku-ku-tu*, received 30 shekels (235 g) of silver (§ 17). Šugadu, together with *Daš-na*, came a second time to Ebla; they received 50 shekels (391 g) of silver (§ 44). *Bù-sum* received 20 shekels (157 g) of silver, (§ 47). The steward *Ìr-am*$_6$-kur$^{ki}$ (probably the steward mentioned previously) had come "to prepare dinners for the king", *in* ud kin$_5$-ak kú en; he was rewarded with 2 minas (940 g) of silver (§ 48). The two "cooks", muḫaldim, *Kùn*-NE and *Ab-ba*, who accompanied him, together received 2 minas (940 g) of silver. The king of Ebla therefore appreciated Mari's cuisine, which these cooks had introduced to him when they joined the Ebla expedition against Manuwat the previous year, ḫi-mu-DU mè *si-in Ma-nu-wa-at*$^{ki}$ (§ 55).

After this war, two "traders", lú-kar, of Manuwat reached Ebla (§ 64)

§ 6 The "overseer", ugula, of the city of Arḫadu came to Ebla to swear an oath in the temple of Kura.

§ 9. The king of Irar received a spearhead for which were employed 3 shekels (23 g) of tin.

§10. 4 g of silver were given to a representative of the city of Naḫal (a city very rarely mentioned, who belonged to Gasur, see *ARET* XIII 4 r. I 13–II 5: *Na-al*$^{ki}$ ... kalam$^{tim}$-kalam$^{tim}$ *Ga-sur*$_x$$^{ki}$), because it swore an oath.

§ 24. Zimini-kubabbar, the queen of Burman, received a jewel (in four strips) of 4 shekels (31 g) of gold. She was a princess of Ebla, probably a daughter of Irkab-damu (see the sequence of princesses in *ARET* XII 723 II'; XIX 2 §§ 9'–11', 5 § 35, etc.). She married the king of Burman in the year Ibr. 10 (see *ARET* XIV 63 § 33, and the monthly document TM.75.G.1793 o. III 15–IV 6). Two monthly documents register that she gave birth to a girl, TM.75.G.1704 o. VIII 10–15, and a boy, TM.75.G. r. III 1'–5'). She was still alive in the year I.Z. 05, see *ARET* XIV 81 § 63. Text no. 15 § 63 registers a gift for the funerary rite of Natum, queen of Burman, *Na-tum ma-lik-tum Bur-ma-an*$^{ki}$ É×PAP, who was probably the spouse of the father of the king who married Zimini-kubabbar.

§ 30. The *badalum* of Ḫarran received a dagger decorated with 40 shekels (313 g) of silver.

§ 34. Two "traders", lú-kar, from Kakmium received a dagger each, which were decorated with small amounts of tin, silver, and gold.

§§ 37, 38 The king of Imar received a plaque of 30 shekels (235 g) of gold, and (his spouse) Tiša-lim received two toggle-pins of 1 mina (470 g) of silver, whose heads were decorated with 3 shekels (23 g) of gold. The occasion was the purification rite (ì-ĝiš-saĝ) in relation with the death of the king's mother: ama-gal-*sù* (o. XIV 2), i.e. of "the king of Imar (o. XIII 16–17)". Tiša-lim visited very often Ebla from the beginning of the Ibrium's period and had therefore to be an Eblaite princess. She is, however, never mentioned in the list of king Irkab-damu's women (see Archi, *forthcoming*).

§§ 40, 41. Expenditure of 16 shekels (125 g) of tin for three "hooks", ĜIŠ-zú, of the chariots of the king, his mother, and Ibrium. The side of the chariots of the king's mother and Ibrium required further 3 shekels (23 g) of silver.

§ 42. Tiša-lim, the queen of Imar, went to Ebla after this death. She received two toggle-pins of 30 shekels (235 g) of silver, whose heads were decorated with 3 shekels (23 g) of gold.

§ 45. Azaba of the city of Iritum (later: Irrite) is mentioned in some fragmentary passages: *ARET* III 261 o.? III' 8', 615 o.? II' 3'; XII 243 o.? II' 8'.

§ 49. 40 shekels (313 g) of silver were given to some messengers from Mari who had to supply Nazumu with a mule to replace his own which had been lost. He had to join the army of Mari in the war against Kiš (see § 65).

§ 65. Nazumu received a dagger decorated with 8 shekels (39 g) of gold because he was sent to Mari to join the military expedition of this city against Kiš. Another gift of the value of 1 mina (470 g) of silver, was given to someone else for a similar task (§ 66, is in part in lacuna).

§ 68. Allotment of black bags: one to each of seven men, probably all "traders", lú-kar. Two of them, BÍLza-i(l) and Enna-i(l), were sons of a Ibrium's brother.

§ 73. It is reported that the city of Sidarin "was defeated", til. The mu-DU documents mention a "conquest", TUM×SAL, of Sidarin only for the year Ibr. 15, *ARET* XIV 69 § 28.

§ 75. The former queen of Lumnan, the Eblaite princess Dati-TU, had died two years earlier (Ibr. 08; text XXI 11 § 29); she was succeeded by Dagmul-damu. The list of vessels and jewels in this section can only be interpreted as part of her dowry. Another list of jewelry, which also includes a bur-KAK vessel to be used in the marriage ceremony, is included in text XXI 24 § 14, which therefore has to be dated to this same year. At this time, king Išʿar-damu must have been about fourteen or fifteen years old. Dagmul-damu was therefore one of his sisters, a daughter of king Irkab-damu. Dati-TU, whose marriage has to be dated to the year Ibr. 01 (see the commentary in text XXI 2 § 6), should have been a daughter of king Igriš-Ḫalab (see above the commentary to text 11 § 27, above). A princess Dagmul-damu is mentioned in some documents from the time of minister Arrukum (see Archi 1996, p. 121; *MEE* 10, 4 I 3–5: *Dag-mul-da-mu* [dumu-mu]nus [e]n (i.e, of Irkab-damu).

§ 78. The *badalum* of the city of Abarsal received 30 shekels (235 g) of gold.

§ 82. Distribution of ten bracelets of copper decorated with silver for the "watchmen" ME-sig, of "the house of the king", é en.

## 14
(Plates XXVI–XXVII)

(1)
o. I. 1. 1 ma-na kù:babbar
sa$\hat{g}$ kù:babbar
3. $^{d}$*Ku-ra*

(2)
5 ma-na TAR 5 gín DILMUN
k[ù:babbar]
5. [*Di-ni-íb-du-lum*]
[nin-ni]
7. [en]
[šu-ba$_4$-ti]

(3)
9. [x kù:babbar]
[šu-ba]l-[a]k
11. [x] gín DILMUN [kù-]gi
kin$_5$-ak
13. 1 *mu-ḫar-tim*
TAR 5 gín DILMUN kù:babbar
15. šu-bal-ak
7 gín DILMUN kù-gi
17. *zi-tum*
1 $\hat{g}$ír mar-tu
19. en

(4)
II. 1. 5 gín DILMUN kù:babbar
šu-bal-ak
3. 1 gín DILMUN kù-gi
1 kù-sal
5. ní$\hat{g}$-ba
ama-gal
7. en
$^{d}$*Ba-ra-ma*
9. [ ]
[ ]

(5)
11. 7 gín DILMUN kù:babbar
*zi-tum*
13. 1 ⸢$\hat{g}$ír⸣ mar-tu
*Ar-ra-du-lum*
15. *Du-lu*$^{ki}$
*Ib-gi-da-mu*
17. šu-mu-tak$_4$

(6)
5 gín DILMUN kù:babbar
19. ní$\hat{g}$-ba
*Šu-a-ḫa*
21. maškim
ga:eš$_8$
23. *Du-du-lu*$^{ki}$

(7)
1 gín DILMUN kù:babbar
III. 1. lú $\hat{G}$IŠ-nu-kiri$_6$
*Zi-la-da-mu*
3. šu-ba$_4$-ti

(8)
5 gín DILMUN kù:babbar
5. ní$\hat{g}$-ba
*A-ku-a-ḫa*
7. *Ma-rí*$^{ki}$

(9)
4 gín DILMUN k[ù:babba]r
9. ní$\hat{g}$-sa$_{10}$ 1 *gàr-su*
en
11. *Sa-nap-zu-gúm*$^{ki}$

(10)
10 gín DILMUN kù:babbar
13. n[í$\hat{g}$-ba]

(1) 1 mina of silver for the silver head of the god Kura.
(2) 5;35 minas of si[lver: Tinib-dulum, sister of the king, has received].
(3) [x silver in exchange for x] shekels of [go]ld for making 1 … (*mu-ḫar-tim*); 35 shekels of silver in exchange for 7 shekels of gold in alloy for 1 mar-tu dagger for the king.
(4) 5 shekels of silver in exchange for 1 shekel of gold for 1 buckle: gift of the king's mother for the goddess Barama […].
(5) 7 shekels of silver in alloy for 1 mar-tu dagger for Arra-dulum of the city of Dulu, Ibgi-damu has handed over.
(6) 5 shekels of silver: gift for Šu-aḫa, representative of the travelling merchant of the city of Tuttul.
(7) 1 shekel of silver for a gardener, Zila-damu has received.
(8) 5 shekels of silver: gift for Aku-aḫa of the city of Mari.
(9) 4 shekels of s[ilver] for the purchase of 1 bag for the king of the city of Sanapzugum.
(10) 10 shekels of silver: g[ift] for Išdub-i(l) and Ibgitum, representatives of the travelling merchant of the city of Tuttul (who) had handed over food provisions.

*Iš-⌜dub⌝-ì*
15. *wa*
*Ib-gi-tum*
17. maškim
ga:eš$_8$
19. *Du-du-lu*$^{ki}$
šu-mu-tak$_4$
21. *ʾà:bíl*

(11)
6 ma-na ŠA.PI gín DILMUN an-na
23. šub-šub
IV. 1. *si-in*
kin$_5$-ak
3. 2 *mi-at* ĝír mar-tu
4 ma-na ŠÚ+ŠA 7 gín DILMUN kù:babbar
5. kin$_5$-ak
*kam$_4$-ma-a-tum-⌜sù⌝*
7. ì-na-sum
ĝuruš-ĝuruš
9. SA.ZA$_x$$^{ki}$
*in*
11. níĝ-kas$_4$
*Kak-mi-um*$^{ki}$

(12)
13. 4 ma-na TAR an-na
šub *si-in*
15. kin$_5$-ak
IGI.DUB
17. 60 níĝ-saĝšu
1 ma-na kù:babbar
19. níĝ-sa$_{10}$ 2 *gú-li-lum* a-gar$_5$-gar$_5$ kù-gi esi-I ⌜x⌝

(13)
V. 1. 1 ma-na gín DILMUN
*Mu*-NE-*a-du*
3. ugula *Ar-ḫa-du*$^{ki}$
*Puzur$_4$-ra-ma-lik*
5. lú kas$_4$-kas$_4$
šu-mu-tak$_4$

(14)
7. ŠÚ+ŠA gín DILMUN kù:babbar
2 *bu*-DI
9. dumu-munus
en
11. *Ì-ra-ar*$^{ki}$
É×PAP
13. *Zú-ba-núm*
šu-mu-tak$_4$

(15)
15. 11 gín DILMUN kù:babbar
níĝ-sa$_{10}$ 11 *ra-ʾà-tum*
17. 10 gín DILMUN kù:babbar
níĝ-sa$_{10}$ LAGAB×UD-LAGAB×UD
19. kin$_5$-ak
ĜIŠ-asari
21. sagi

(16)
11 [ma-na]
VI. 1. ŠÚ+ŠA gín DILMUN kù:babbar
níĝ-sa$_{10}$ 8 zara$_6$-TÚG
3. 7 gíd-TÚG
30 lá-2 *ʾà-da-um*-TÚG-I dùl-TÚG-I
5. 1 *mi-at* 90 lá-2 aktum-TÚG
ki:lam$_7$
7. *Ma-rí*$^{ki}$
dam-gàr

(17)
9. 3 gín DILMUN kù:babbar
saĝ kù:babbar
11. $^{d}$*Ku-ra*
*in*
13. mu-ti-II

(18)
2 ma-na kù:b[abbar]
15. 2 ma-⌜na⌝ an-na
*Ḫu-wa-sa-ra-du*$^{\{ki\}}$
17. *Du-lu*$^{ki}$
ḫi-mu-DU

(11) 6;40 minas of tin to be melted for making 200 mar-tu daggers; 4;27 minas of silver for making their knobs, given to the men of the Palace for the military expedition (against) the city of Kakmium.
(12) 4;30 minas of tin to be melted for making the visors of 60 helmets; 1 mina of silver for the purchase of 2 single bracelets of copper, gold (and) diorite.
(13) 1 mina <of silver> for MuNEadu, the overseer of the city of Arḫadu, Puzurra-malik, (the overseer) of the messengers has handed over.
(14) 20 shekels of silver for 2 toggle-pins for the funerary rite of a daughter of the king of the city of Irar, Zubanum has handed over.
(15) 11 shekels of silver for the purchase of 11 shells; 10 shekels of silver for the purchase of ostrich shells for making a tray for the steward <of the city of Mari>.
(16) 11;20 [minas] of silver for the purchase of 231 garments at the market of the city of Mari, the merchant(s) (have handed over).
(17) 3 shekels of silver for the silver head of the god Kura: second delivery.
(18) 2 minas of sil[ver] (and) 2 minas of tin for Ḫuwa-saradu of the city of Dulu, (who) presented a monkey and 8 linen cloths.

19. 1 kir$_4$-ma
*wa*
21. 10 lá-2 gada-TÚG

(19)
TAR kù:babbar
VII. 1. URI
1 íb-lá 1 ĝír-kun
3. kù-gi
*En-na-il*
5. lú *Zi-ba-da*

(20)
ŠA.PI gín DILMUN kù:babbar
7. šu-bal-ak
8 gín DILMUN kù-gi
9. *ni-zi-mu*
1 dib
11. *Šum*-bàd$^{ki}$
dumu-nita
13. *Ib-rí-um*

(21)
ŠA.PI gín DILMUN kù:babbar
15. 1 íb-lá 1 ĝír-kun
TAR [5] g[ín DILMUN] k[ù:babbar]
17. šu-bal-ak
7 gín DILMUN kù-gi
19. maš-maš-*sù*
*Zú-za-bir*$_5$
VIII. 1. lú *A-da-ad*
tuš-LÚ×TIL
3. *in*
*Am*$_6$-*ʾà-rúm*$^{ki}$

(22)
5. [x] gín DILMUN kù[:babbar]
*Áš-da-ma-ì*
7. maškim
ga:eš$_8$
9. *Du-du-lu*$^{ki}$

(23)
ŠA.PI 5 gín DILMUN kù:babbar
11. šu-bal-ak
9 gín DILMUN kù-gi
13. *ni-zi-mu*
4 ĜIŠ-ban
15. 2 ĜIŠ-gígir-II
en
17. 2 ½ gín DILMUN kù[:babbar]
šu-bal-ak
19. ½ gín DILMUN kù-gi
*ni-zi-mu*
21. nu$_{11}$-za 2 zag
2 ĜIŠ-gígir-II
23. 3 ½ gín DILMUN kù:babbar
IX. 1. šu-bal-ak
2 NI gín DILMUN kù-gi
3. *ni-zi-mu*
*ma-wa-ù*
5. 2 ĜIŠ-bar-ús
ĜIŠ-gígir-II
7. e[n]

(24)
[10 gín] D[ILMUN] kù:babbar
9. šu-bal-ak
2 gín DILMUN kù-gi
11. *ni-zi-mu*
1 dib
13. *Daš-na*

(25)
18 gín DILMUN kù:babbar
15. níĝ-s[a$_{10}$] 1 [ ]
[ ]
17. [ ]

(26)
ŠÚ+ŠA gín DILMUN kù:babbar
19. *ʾa*$_5$-*na-gu*
4 si 2 gud
21. 15 gín DILMUN kù:babbar
nu$_{11}$-za
23. 1 *ḫa-bù*
X. 1. TAR [gín DILMUN] kù:babbar
šu-bal-ak
3. 6 gín DILMUN kù-gi
nu$_{11}$-za 1 ⸢*ar*⸣-*ra*[-*sù*]

(19) 30 (shekels of) silver for the URI-decoration of 1 belt (and) 1 dagger pendant (decorated with) gold for Enna-il, (son) of Zibada.
(20) 40 shekels of silver in exchange for 8 shekels of gold for decorating 1 plaque for Šum-bad, son of Ibrium.
(21) 40 shekels of silver for 1 belt (and) 1 dagger pendant; 3[5] sh[ekels] of s[ilver] in exchange for 7 shekels of gold for their striped (decoration) for Zuzabir, (son) of Adad, (who) occupied the city of Amʾarum.
(22) [x] shekels of sil[ver] for Ašdama-i(l), representative of the travelling merchant of the city of Tuttul.
(23) 45 shekels of silver in exchange for 9 shekels of gold for decorating 4 bows of 2 chariots of the king; 2 ½ shekels of silver in exchange for ½ shekel of gold for decorating with lamination 2 sides of 2 chariots; 3 ½ shekels of silver in exchange for 2 NI of gold for decorating the … (*ma-wa-ù*) of 2 goads of the chariot of the ki[ng].
(24) [10 shekels] of silver in exchange for 2 shekels of gold for decorating 1 plaque for Dašna.
(25) 18 shekels of silver for the purcha[se] of 1 […].
(26) 20 shekels of silver for the circular stand of the 4 horns of 2 bulls; 15 shekels of silver for plating 1 mace; 30 [shekels] of silver in exchange for 6 shekels of gold for plating [its] handle: [offering] of the king for the god Rašap of [the city of ʾAdani], at the AMA-ra (festival), and also 1 mace of silver and gold for the god Hadda for the purification rite of Bagama, received in the city of Manuwat.

5. [nídba]
en
7. $^{d}$*Ra-sa-ap*
[*ʾÀ-da-ni*$^{ki}$]
9. *in*
$^{d}$AMA-*ra*
11. *ap*
1 *ḫa-bù*
13. $^{dʾ}$*À-da*
kù:babbar kù-gi
15. sikil
lú *Ba-ga-ma*
17. šu-ba$_{4}$-ti
*in*
19. *Ma-nu-wa-ad*$^{ki}$

(27)
1 ½ gín DILMUN kù:babbar
21. 2 ½ gín DILMUN kù:babbar
šu-bal-ak
23. ½ gín DILMUN kù-gi
*ni-zi-mu*
25. nu$_{11}$-za
XI. 1. [ ]
[ ]
3. [ ]

(28)
[1] ma-na ŠÚ+ŠA gín DILMUN kù:babbar
5. *n*[*i-zi-*]*m*[*u*]
2 níĝ-anše-ak 2[+2] kù-sal
7. *En-na-ì*
lú *Ša-ù-um*

(29)
9. 10 gín DILMUN kù:babbar
*ni-zi-mu*
11. 2 *gú-li-lum*
*Bu*$_{x}$*-ma-il*
13. šeš
*Ib-rí-um*
15. ŠÚ+ŠA 2 ½ gín DILMUN kù:babbar
šu-bal-ak
17. 4 ½ gín DILMUN kù-gi
*ni-zi-mu*
19. nu$_{11}$-za-*sù*

(30)
10 gín DILMUN kù:babbar
XII. 1. [šu-bal-ak]
2 gín DILMUN kù-gi
3. *ni-zi-mu*
nu$_{11}$-za
5. 2 *gú-li-lum* a-gar$_{5}$-gar$_{5}$ esi-I
*A-zú-gú-ra*
7. šeš
*Ra-ù-tum*

(31)
9. 10 gín DILMUN kù:babbar
lú *I-šar*
11. *in*
*Am*$_{6}$*-ma-šu*$^{ki}$
13. šu-ba$_{4}$-ti

(32)
2 ½ gín DILMUN kù:babbar
15. šu-bal-ak
[½ gín DILMUN k]ù[-gi]
17. *ni-zi-mu*
maš-maš
19. 4 kù-sal
*Ib-rí-um*

(33)
21. 3 gín DILMUN kù:babbar
*mu-sa-du*
XIII. 1. ⌜LUM⌝?-[ ]
ĜIŠ-taškarin
3. lú en
*wa*
5. ama-gal-*sù*

(34)
4 gín DILMUN kù:babbar
7. níĝ-sa$_{10}$ 1 ĝír mar-tu *ba-du-u*$_{4}$ kù:babbar
*Iš-ra-il*
9. lú-kar
*Kak-mi-um*$^{ki}$

(27) 1 ½ shekel of silver; 2 ½ shekels of silver in exchange for ½ shekel of gold for decorating with lamination […].
(28) [1];20 minas of silver for d[ecora]ti[ng] 2 bridles (and) 4 buckles for Enna-i(l), (son) of Šaum.
(29) 10 shekels of silver for decorating 2 bracelets for Buma-il, brother of Ibrium; 22 ½ shekels of silver in exchange for 4 ½ shekels of gold for decorating their lamination.
(30) 10 shekels of silver [in exchange for] 2 shekels of gold for decorating with lamination 2 single bracelets of copper (and) diorite for Azu-gura, brother of Raʾutum.
(31) 10 shekels of silver Išar has received in the city of Ammašu.
(32) 2 ½ shekels of silver in exchange for [½ shekel of gold] for a striped (decoration) of 4 buckles for Ibrium.
(33) 3 shekels of silver … (*mu-sa-du*) […] of boxwood for the king and his mother.
(34) 4 shekels of silver for the purchase of 1 *b.* mar-tu dagger (decorated with) silver for Išra-il, trader of the city of Kakmium.

(35)
11. ŠÚ+ŠA gín DILMUN kù:babbar
níĝ-ba
13. *Daš-na*
*Ma-rí*$^{ki}$

(36)
15. ⌜2⌝ gín [DI]LMUN [an-n]a
[šub *si-in*]
17. [x] gí[n] DIL[MUN] a-gar$_5$-gar$_5$
lul-gu-ak
19. 4 ĜIŠ-gu-kak-šub
lú *Daš-na*
21. *M*[*a-*]*rí*$^{⌜ki⌝}$
XIV. 1. *i*[*n*]
*Bar-ga-u*$_9^{ki}$
3. zàḫ
*in* kaskal
5. $^{d}$AMA-*ra*

(37)
5 gín DILMUN kù:babbar
7. [šu-bal-ak]
⌜1⌝ gín DILMUN kù-gi
9. [*ni-*]*zi-mu*
1 dib
11. *ʾÀ-bí*
lú NI-BAD
13. *wa*
in-na-sum
15. *Ig-na-da-ar*
lú *Mi-ga-il*

(38)
17. 10 gín DILMUN kù:babbar
šu-bal-ak
19. 2 gín DILMUN kù-gi
*ni-zi-mu*
21. nu$_{11}$-za 2 *gú-li-lum* kù-gi
lú
23. *I*[*g-n*]*a-*[*da-ar*]
XV. 1. *Mi-ga-il*
ì-na-sum
3. (blank)

(39)
10 gín DILMUN kù:babbar
5. [šu-bal-ak]
[2 gín DILMUN k]ù-g[i]
7. *zi-ba-tum*
1 balag zabar
9. lú en

(40)
5 gín DILMUN kù:babbar
11. šu-bal-ak
1 gín DILMUN kù-gi
13. *ni-zi-mu*
nu$_{11}$-za
15. 1 *gú-li-lum* a-gar$_5$-gar$_5$
*Ig-bù-ul-ma-lik*
17. NE-di

(41)
3 gín DILMUN an-na
19. šub *s*[*i-*]*in*
2 ĜIŠ-gu-kak-gíd
XVI. 1. en

(42)
[
3. [
[
5. é
*Ib-rí-um*
7. šu-ba$_4$-ti

(43)
13 ma-na [x] gín[a)] DILMUN kù:babbar
9. níĝ-sa$_{10}$
96 aktum-TÚG
11. 3 zara$_6$-TÚG
2 íb+III-TÚG *Sa-ma-rí*$^{ki}$
13. 22 túg-NI.NI
[ ]
15. 54[b)] íb+III-TÚG sa$_6$ gùn
2 *mi-at* 50 íb+III-TÚG gùn
17. 5 ĝír mar-tu zú-ak

(35) 20 shekels of silver: gift for Dašna of the city of Mari.
(36) 2 shekels of [ti]n, [to be melted with x] she[kels] of copper for the replacement of 4 spearheads that Dašna of the city of Mari had lost in the city of Bargaʾu, during (his) journey, at the AMA-ra (festival).
(37) 5 shekels of silver [in exchange for] 1 shekel of gold [for de]corating 1 plaque for ʾAbi, (son) of NIBAD and given by Ignadar, (son) of Miga-il.
(38) 10 shekels of silver in exchange for 2 shekels of gold for decorating with lamination 2 bracelets of gold that I[gn]a[dar] has given to Miga-il.
(39) 10 shekels of silver [in exchange for 2 shekels of g]old for the handle of a bronze harp for the king.
(40) 5 shekels of silver in exchange for 1 shekel of gold for decorating with lamination 1 bracelet of copper for Igbul-malik, the dancer.
(41) 3 shekels of tin to be melted in 2 spearheads for the king.
(42) […] the house of Ibrium has received.
(43) 13[;xx] minas of silver for the purchase of 121[+x] garments, 306 kilts (and) 5 serrated mar-tu daggers; 40 [shekels] of silver for the purchase of leek from the mountain region; 3;34 minas of silver for the purchase of 11 oxen for the king; 30 (shekels of) silver for the purchase of GIŠ-ti-ḪAR-wood: W[ab]aru[m] has received, at the market of the city of ʾAdani, at the AMA-ra (festival).

XVII. 1. ŠA.PI [gín DILMUN] kù:babbar
níĝ-sa$_{10}$ raš-SAR Kur$^{ki}$
3. 3 ma-na TAR 4 gín DILMUN kù:babbar
níĝ-sa$_{10}$ 11 gud
5. en
TAR kù:babbar
7. níĝ-sa$_{10}$ ĜIŠ-ti-ḪAR
*W*[*a-b*]*a-rú*[*m*]
9. šu-ba$_4$-ti
ki:lam$_7$
11. *ʾÀ-da-ni*$^{ki}$
*in*
13. $^{d}$AMA-*ra*

(44)
5 m[a-]na ⸢TAR⸣ [kù:babbar]
15. 1 *gú-li-lum*-II lú TAR
5 *gú-li-lum*-II lú ŠÚ+ŠA-ŠÚ+ŠA
17. 20 *gú-li-lum*-I lú 10 10
5 ma-na TAR kù:babbar
XVIII. 1. šu-bal-⸢ak⸣
1 ma-na 6 gín DILMUN kù-gi
3. nu$_{11}$-za-*sù*
7 ma-na 18 gín DILMUN kù:babbar
5. šu-bal-ak
1 ma-na ŠÚ+ŠA 7 ½ gín DILMUN kù-gi
7. [nu$_{11}$-za]
10 *gú-li-lum*-II lú TAR.TAR a-gar$_5$-gar$_5$
9. *wa*
10 *gú-li-lum* a-gar$_5$-gar$_5$-II ⸢lú⸣[ŠÚ+ŠA-ŠÚ+ŠA]
11. [*wa*]
10 *gú-li-lum* a-gar$_5$-gar$_5$-I lú 15 10
13. 10 ma-na ŠÚ+ŠA 7 gín DILMUN kù:babbar
nu$_{11}$-za
15. 10 *gú-li-lum*
XIX. 1. a-gar$_5$-g[ar$_5$]-II ⸢lú⸣ TAR.TAR
*wa*
3. 4 *gú-li-lum* a-gar$_5$-gar$_5$-II lú ŠÚ+ŠA-ŠÚ+ŠA
*wa*
5. 20 *gú-li-lum* a-gar$_5$-gar$_5$-I lú 15 10
5 gín DILMUN kù:babbar
7. Z[U].PI[RIG]
[(ca. 12 lines)]

(45)
20.$^{?}$ *Du-du-lu*$^{ki}$

(46)
XX. 1. [ k]ù:[b]abbar
*Iš-dub-il*
3. maškim
ga:eš$_8$
5. *Du-du-lu*$^{ki}$
šu-mu-tak$_4$
7. *ʾà:bíl*

(47)
2 gín DILMUN kù:babbar
9. *ma-za-lum*
[
11. [
ugula *Kul-ba-an*$^{ki}$
13. ga:eš$_8$
šu-ba$_4$-ti

(48)
15. 10 gín DILMUN [an-]na
[(ca. 8 lines)]
24$^{?}$. lú
XXI. 1. *I-bí-zi-kir*

(49)
6 ma-na ŠÚ+ŠA 2 ½ gín DILMUN kù:babbar
3. níĝ-sa$_{10}$ 34 túg-NI.NI
*wa*
5. 6 zara$_6$-TÚG
1 gu-dù[l-TÚG]
7. [x í]b+III-TÚG [s]a$_6$ gùn
*wa*
9. 2 *mi-at* 60 íb+III-TÚG gùn
6 gín D[ILMUN kù:b]abbar
[(ca. 8 lines)]

(44) 5;30 minas [of silver] for 1 double bracelet of 30 (shekels) each, 5 double bracelets of 20 (shekels) each, 20 single bracelets of 10 (shekels) each; 5;30 minas of silver in exchange for 1;06 minas of gold for their lamination; 7;18 minas of silver in exchange for 1;27 ½ minas of gold [for plating] 10 double bracelets of 30 (shekels) of copper each and 10 double bracelets of [20 (shekels)] of copper each [and] 10 single bracelets of 15 (and) 10 (shekels) of copper each; 10;27 minas of silver for plating 10 double bracelets of 30 (shekels) of copper each and 4 double bracelets of 20 (shekels) of copper each and 20 single bracelets of 15 (and) 10 (shekels) of copper each; 5 shekels of silver for the han[gers] of [...].
(45) [...] of the city of Tuttul.
(46) [... sil]ver for Išdub-il, representative of the travelling merchant of the city of Tuttul (who) had handed over food provisions.
(47) 2 shekels of silver for the courier [...] the overseer of the city of Kulban, the travelling merchant has received.
(48) 10 shekels of [ti]n [...] of Ibbi-zikir.
(49) 6;22 ½ minas of silver for the purchase of 41 garments and 260[+x] kilts; 6 shekels of [sil]ver [...].

(50)

19.$^?$ [$^{d?}$*A*$_5$-]*d*[*a*-]"*bal*" (?)

(51)

r. I. 1. TAR kù:babbar
níĝ-sa$_{10}$ ĜIŠ-ti-ḪAR
3. [ ]
[ ]
5. 9 gín DILMUN kù:babbar
níĝ-sa$_{10}$ [siki$^?$] ⸢si$_4$$^?$ x⸣ [siki *ba-r*]*a-i*
7. [x] ⸢KI/DI⸣
[x *i*]*n*$^?$-K[A]$^?$-[*i*]*š*$^?$

(52)

9. [1+]1 ma-na kù:b[abbar]
2 ma-na an-na
11. *Ar-ra-du-lum*
[*Du-lu*$^{ki}$]
13. *S*[*a-m*]*u*-⸢*ù*⸣
dam-⸢gàr⸣
15. šu-mu-tak$_4$

(53)

TAR 3 gín DILMUN 3 NI kù:babbar
17. šu-bal-ak
6 gín DILMUN ⸢2⸣ NI kù-gi
II. 1. 2 *gú-li-lum*
níĝ-ba
3. [$^{d}$*Ku-ra*/$^{d}$*Áš-da-bíl*]

(54)

[5 gín DILMUN kù:babbar]
5. [šu-bal-ak]
1 gín DILMUN kù-gi
7. *ni-zi-mu*
[nu$_{11}$-za]
9. 1 ĝír mar-tu
*Íl-gú-uš-ti*
11. lú *I-gi*

(55)

13 gín DILMUN kù:babbar
13. nu$_{11}$-za
1 *ḫa-bù*
15. TAR kù:babbar
šu-bal-ak
17. 6 gín DILMUN kù-gi
nu$_{11}$-za 1 *ar-ra-su-sù*
19. níĝ-ba
$^{d?}$*A-da*
21. lú *Lu-ub*$^{ki}$
[*i*]*n*
23. [*gi*-NI]

(56)

III. 1. ⸢10⸣+2 gín DILMUN kù:babbar
[(ca 6 lines)]
8$^?$. maš-maš-*sù*
9. 5 gín DILMUN kù:babbar
šu-bal-ak
11. 1 gín DILMUN kù-gi
nu$_{11}$-za [1 g]ír [mar-t]u [t]i
13 *Ir-da-mu*
dumu-nita
15. *Ib-rí-um*

(57)

[x g]ín DILMUN an-na
17. šub *si-in*
3 ĝír
19. lú
*Sa-d*[*a-* ]
21. [ ]
[ ]

(58)

IV. 1. 50 gín DILMUN [ ]
[(ca. 9 lines)]

(59)

11.$^?$ [ k]ù:b[abbar]
níĝ-ba
13. *Iš-dub-il*
maškim
15. ga:eš$_8$
*Du-du-lu*$^{ki}$

(50) [… the god ᵓA]d[a]bal.

(51) 30 (shekels of) silver for the purchase of GIŠ-ti-ḪAR-wood […]; 9 shekels of silver for the purchase of [wool$^?$] […].

(52) 2 minas of sil[ver] (and) 2 minas of tin for Arra-dulum [of the city of Dulu], S[am]uᵓu, the merchant, has handed over.

(53) 33 shekels (and) 3 NI of silver in exchange for 6 shekels (and) 2 NI of gold for 2 bracelets: gift [for the god …].

(54) [5 shekels of silver in exchange for] 1 shekel of gold for decorating [with lamination] 1 mar-tu dagger for Ilgušti, (son) of Igi.

(55) 13 shekels of silver for plating 1 mace; 30 (shekels of) silver in exchange for 6 shekels of gold for plating its handle: gift for the god Hadda of the city of Lub, [i]n [month IV].

(56) 12 shekels of silver […] for its striped (decoration); 5 shekels of silver in exchange for 1 shekel of gold for plating [1 poin]ted [mar-t]u [dag]ger for Ir-damu, son of Ibrium.

(57) [x she]kels of tin to be melted in 3 daggers for Sad[a…] […].

(58) 50 shekels [of …] […].

(59) […s]il[ver]: gift for Išdub-il, representative of the travelling merchant of the city of Tuttul.

(60)

17. TAR 3 gín DILMUN 3 NI kù:babbar
šu-bal-⸢ak⸣
19. [6 gín DILMUN 2 NI kù-gi]
[2 *gú-li-lum*]
21. [níĝ-ba]
V. 1. [$^{d}$*Áš-da*]-*bí*[*l*]

(61)

6 gín DILMUN 2 NI kù-gi [2]
*gú*-[*l*]*i-lum*
3. [níĝ-ba]
$^{d}$*Am-ma-rí-ig*

(62)

5. 2 ma-na 16 gín DILMUN kù:babbar
níĝ-sa$_{10}$ 40 lá-1 íb+III-TÚG sa$_{6}$ gùn
7. [ ]
[ki:lam$_{7}$]
9. $^{d}$*Áš-da-bíl*

(63)

1 ma-na k[ù:babba]r
11. [níĝ-ba]
*Wa-ru*$_{12}$*-tum*
13. *Ma-rí*$^{ki}$
níĝ-"mul"
15. Kiš$^{ki}$
til-til
17. *wa*
[ ]
19. šu-mu-tak$_{4}$

(64)

50 gín DILMUN kù:babbar nu$_{11}$-za
VI. 1. 1 ĜIŠ-banšur maḫ
10 gín DILMUN an-na
3. [šub *si-in*]
[x gín DILMUN a-ga]r$_{5}$-gar$_{5}$
5. urudu-*sù*
ŠA.PI 5 gín DILMUN kù:babbar
7. šu-bal-ak
9 gín DILMUN kù-gi
9. *ᵓa*$_{5}$*-na-gu-sù*
[níĝ-ba]
11. $^{dᵓ}$*A*$_{5}$*-da-"bal"*
*ᵓÀ-ma-du*$^{ki}$
13. en
šu-mu-tak$_{4}$

(65)

15. 16 gín DILMUN an-na
šub
17. *si-in*
1 ma-na 54 gín DILMUN a-gar$_{5}$-g[ar$_{5}$]
19. nu$_{11}$-za 1 ĜIŠ-asari
6 gín DILMUN kù:babbar
21. nu$_{11}$-za 4 saĝ
VII. 1. lu$_{5}$
*al*$_{6}$*-sù*
3. níĝ-ba
$^{dᵓ}$*A*$_{5}$*-da-"bal"*
5. *Ne-a-ù*$^{<ki>}$
*Ib-rí-um*
7. šu-mu-tak$_{4}$

(66)

10 gín DILMUN kù:babbar
9. [2 *b*]*u*-DI
*wa*
11. 4 *ti-ša-nu*
níĝ-ba
13. $^{d}$*Ga-na-na*
ĜIŠ.DUG.DU maḫ

(67)

15. 9 gín DILMUN kù:babbar
níĝ-ba
17. Šubur
*Du*<*-lu*>$^{ki}$
19. kin$_{5}$-ak
*šè-li*

(68)

21. 2 gín DILMUN an-na
šub
23. *si-in*
16 gín DILMUN a-⸢gar$_{5}$⸣-gar$_{5}$
25. kin$_{5}$-ak

(60) 33 shekels (and) 3 NI of silver in exchange for [6 shekels (and) 2 NI of gold for 2 bracelets: gift for the god Ašda]bi[l].
(61) 6 shekels (and) 2 NI of gold for [2] bracelets: [gift] for the god Ammarik.
(62) 2;16 minas of silver for the purchase of 39 kilts […, at the market] of the god Ašdabil.
(63) 1 mina of s[ilver: gift] for Warutum of the city of Mari (who brought) the news that the city of Kiš had been defeated and […] has handed over.
(64) 50 shekels of silver for plating 1 big table; 10 shekels of tin [to be melted with x shekels of refined cop]per: its copper; 45 shekels of silver in exchange for 9 shekels of gold for its circular stand: [gift] for the god ᵓAdabal of the city of ᵓAmadu, the king has handed over.
(65) 16 shekels of tin to be melted with 1;54 minas of copp[er] for plating 1 tray; 6 shekels of silver for plating 4 heads of androcephalus bulls on it: gift for the god ᵓAdabal of the city of Neau, Ibrium has handed over.
(66) 10 shekels of silver [for 2 tog]gle-pins and 4 … (*ti-ša-nu*): gift for the goddess Ganana (on the occasion of) the great presentation.
(67) 9 shekels of silver: gift for Šubur of the city of Du<lu>, for making (an object in) malachite.
(68) 2 shekels of tin to be melted with 16 shekels of copper for making goads for the king.

ĜIŠ-bar-ús
27. en

(69)
ŠÚ+ŠA gín DILMUN kù:babbar
29. šu-bal-ak
VIII. 1. [4 gín DILMUN kù-gi]
[kin$_5$-ak]
3. [1 ĜIŠ-ba]nšur
[*wa*]
5. 1 kù-sal
$^{d}$*Ra-sa-ap*
7. *Du-ne-íb*$^{ki}$
en
9. šu-mu-tak$_4$

(70)
4 ma-na ŠÚ+ŠA gín DILMUN
kù:babbar
11. šu-bal-ak
ŠA.PI gín DILMUN kù:babbar 1 dib
13. *A-mur-da-mu*
tuš-LÚ×TIL
15. *Dur-zi-lum*$^{ki}$

(71)
ŠA.PI gín DILMUN kù:babbar
17. 1 íb-lá 1 ĝír-kun
TAR 5 gín DILMUN
19. [šu-bal-ak]
[7 gín DILMUN kù-gi]
21. [maš-maš-*sù*]
IX. 1. [ ]
[ ]
3. [ ]
[ ]
5. [dum]u-nita
*I-bí-zi-kir*
7. [tuš-LÚ×TIL]
[*in*]
9. *Ib-al*$_6^{ki}$

(72)
2 ma-na TA[R] kù:babbar
11. [šu-b]al[-ak]
[TAR kù-gi]
13. [1 íb-lá 1 ĝír-kun]
e[n]
15. *Ì-ra-ar*$^{ki}$
TAR kù:babbar 2 *bu*-DI
17. 15 gín DILMUN kù:babbar
šu-bal-ak
19. 3 gín DILMUN kù-gi
nu$_{11}$-za 2 saĝ-*sù*
21. *ma-lik-tum*
*Ì-ra-ar*$^{ki}$
23. *En-na-ì*
X. 1. [šu-mu-tak$_4$]

(73)
[(ca. 5 lines)]

(74)
7.? [x kù:babbar]
[šu-bal-ak]
9. [x kù-gi]
nu$_{11}$-za
11. 1 ĝír mar-tu
AN-NI-NE

(75)
13. 4 gín DILMUN kù:babbar
níĝ-ba
15. *Ù-li-li*
maškim
17. [ga:eš$_8$]
[*Du-du-lu*]$^{ki}$

(76)
19. 5 gín DILMUN kù:babbar
níĝ-kaskal
21. [*Ì*]*r-am*$_6$-[*m*]*a-lik*
[ ]⌜x⌝
23. [DU.DU]
*si-in*
25. Kiš$^{ki}$

(77)
1 ma-na kù:babbar níĝ-kaskal
XI. 1. ĝuruš-ĝuruš
šu-mu-tak$_4$

(69) 20 shekels of silver in exchange for [4 shekels of gold, for making 1 tab]le [and] 1 buckle for the god Rašap of the city of Tunip, the king has handed over.
(70) 4;20 minas of silver in exchange for 40 shekels of gold for 1 plaque for Amur-damu, (who) resided in the city of Durzilum.
(71) 40 shekels of silver for 1 belt (and) 1 dagger pendant; 35 shekels <of silver> [in exchange for 7 shekels of gold for their striped (decoration) …], [s]on of Ibbi-zikir, (who) [resided in] the city of Ib$^{c}$al.
(72) 2;30 minas of silver [in exchange for 30 (shekels of gold for 1 belt (and) 1 dagger pendant] for the ki[ng] of the city of Irar; 30 (shekels of) silver for 2 toggle-pins; 15 shekels of silver in exchange for 3 shekels of gold for plating their 2 heads for the queen of the city of Irar; Enna-i(l) [has handed over].
(73) […].
(74) [x silver in exchange for x gold] for plating 1 mar-tu dagger for ANNINE.
(75) 4 shekels of silver: gift for Ulili, representative of the [travelling merchant of the city of Tuttul].
(76) 5 shekels of silver: travel provision for [I]ram-[m]alik [… (who) went] to the city of Kiš.
(77) 1 mina of silver: travel provision for the men; handed over.

(78)
3. 2 gín DILMUN kù:babbar
kin$_5$-ak
[(ca. 6 lines)]

(79)
11.? *Ab-ra-ḫu*
*wa*
13. *Iš$_{11}$-a-ma-lik*
ba-za

(80)
15. 6 m[a-]na TAR [kù:]babbar
níĝ-sa$_{10}$ 43 gada-TÚG-gada-TÚG
[(ca. 6 lines)]
23. [x gín DILMU]N kù:b[abbar]
níĝ-sa$_{10}$ zú AN.LAGAB×AN
25. 1 ma-na
XII. 1. [
[
3. [
*Wa-ba-rúm*
5. [šu-ba$_4$-ti]

(81)
[x ma-na kù:babbar]
7. níĝ-sa$_{10}$ 10 gud
*Rí-ì-ma-lik*
9. lú *I-bí-zi-im*
ki:lam$_7$
11. [$^d$*A-*]*da-ma*

(82)
5 gín DILMUN kù:[babb]ar
13. [šu-ba]l-⌜ak⌝
1 kù-gi
15. *ni-zi-mu*
1 pad
17. an-zam$_x$
*Ib-r*[*í-*]⌜*um*⌝

(83)
19. 1 ma-na ŠA.PI gín DILMUN
kù:babbar
šu-ba[l-ak]
21. [ŠÚ+ŠA gín DILMUN kù-gi]
[ ]
23. 1 kù:babbar 1 ĜIŠ-[ ]
[ ]
25. dumu-nita
*Ib-rí-um*

(84)
XIII. 1. 6 2 NI [k]ù:babbar
[šu-bal-ak]
3. 1 ½ kù-g[i]
*ni-zi-mu*
5. 1 níĝ-anše-ak 1 kù-sal
1 IGI.NITA
7. en

(85)
1 ma-na ŠÚ+ŠA kù:babbar
9. šu-bal-ak
16 kù-gi
11. 3 kù:babbar
*zi-ba-tum*
13. *wa*
*kam$_4$-ma-tum*
15. 16 ĝír mar-tu kù-gi
⌜10⌝ ĝír ⌜mar⌝-tu ti kù-gi
17. 15 ĝ[ír] mar-tu zú AN.LAGAB×AN
2 ĝír mar-tu *ba-du-u$_4$* kù-gi
19. 6 ĝír mar-tu kù:babbar
1 ma-na 16 kù:babbar
21. *ni-zi-mu*
URI
23. 10 lá-2 íb-lá 5 g[ír-kun] kù:b[abbar]
maš-maš
XIV. x+1. [x g]*ú-li-lum* kù:b[abbar]
[T]AR.TAR-II

(78) 2 shekels of silver for making […].
(79) […] for Abraḫu and Iš-malik, the dwarfs.
(80) 6;30 minas of [sil]ver for the purchase of 43[+x] garments […]; [x shekels] of sil[ver] for the purchase of teeth of hippopotamus; 1 mina […] Wabarum [has received].
(81) [x mina(s) of silver] for the purchase of 10 oxen: Reʾi-malik, (son) of Ibbi-zim (has received), at the market of [the god A]damma.
(82) 5 shekels of sil[ve]r [in exchan]ge for 1 (shekel of) gold for decorating the lid of 1 an-zam$_x$ goblet for Ibr[i]um.
(83) 1;40 minas of silver in exchan[ge for 20 shekels of gold for …]; 1 (shekel of) silver for 1 […, for …], son of Ibrium.
(84) 6 (shekels and) 2 NI of [si]lver [in exchange for] 1 ½ (shekel of) gold for decorating 1 bridle (and) 1 buckle of a donkey for the king.
(85) 1;20 minas of silver in exchange for 16 (shekels of) gold; 3 (shekels of) silver for handles and knobs of 16 mar-tu daggers (decorated with) gold, 15 mar-tu daggers (decorated with) ivory, 2 *b.* mar-tu daggers (decorated with) gold, 6 mar-tu daggers (decorated with) silver; 1;16 minas of silver for a URI-decoration of 8 belts (and) 5 bu[ckles] of sil[ver], [x] double bracelets of 30 (shekels) of sil[ver] each, 9 double bracelets of 20 (shekels) of silver each, […]; 50 shekels of silver in exchange for 10 shekels of gold to add for decorating with lamination 2 double bracelets of 40 (shekels) of copper each and 1 single bracelet of 20 (shekels) of copper (and their) pendants and 1 bracelet of […] of copper […]; 3 shekels of silver for the purchase of 13 fat-tailed sheep; 20 shekels of silver for the purchase of 10 big stones: Iram-malik […].

10 lá-1 *gú-li-lum* kù:babbar šú+ša-šú+ša-ii
3'. [ ]˹x˺[ ]
˹50˺ gín dilmun kù:babbar
5'. ˹šu-bal˺-ak
10 gín dilmun kù-gi
7'. daḫ$_{x}$(mu.mu.mu)
*ni-zi-mu*
9'. nu$_{11}$-za-*sù*
2 *gú-li-lum* a-gar$_{5}$-gar$_{5}$ lú ša.pi-ša.pi-ii
11'. *wa*
1 *gú-li-lum* a-gar$_{5}$-gar$_{5}$ lú šú+ša-i
13'. *sa-ḫa-wa*
*wa*
15'. 1 *gú-li-lum* a-gar$_{5}$-gar$_{5}$ [ ]
XV. [(ca. 9 lines)]
10.? 3 gín dilmun kù:babbar
11. níĝ-sa$_{10}$ 13 gukkal?
šú+ša gín dilmun kù:babbar
13. níĝ-sa$_{10}$ 10 na$_{4}$ maḫ
*Ìr-am$_{6}$-ma-lik*
15. ˹x-x-x-x˺

(86)
3 gín dilmun [kù:]bab[bar]
17. [ ]

XVI.
XVII. (only few signs: last line:)
x+1. 1 gín dilmun kù-g[i]
XVIII. 1. [ ]
[ ]
3. 2 ma-na ˹5˺ gín dilmun kù:babbar
šu-bal-ak
5. šú+ša ˹5˺ gín dilmun [kù-gi]
[
x+1. níĝ-sa$_{10}$
XIX. 1. 2 [ ]
diĝir-diĝir-diĝir
3. 5 gín dilmun kù:babbar
šu-bal-ak
5. [1 g]ín [dil]mun [kù-gi]
[

x+1. ˹*Sa*˺-[*ḫa-a*]
ugula *Ù-si-gú*$^{ki}$
XX. x+1. ˹è˺
*ni-zi-mu*
3'. za$_{x}$
ĝuruš-ĝuruš

*a*) on erasure; *b*) 4 unities added in a second time

(86) 3 shekels of [sil]ver [...].
(87) [...] 1 shekel of gold [...]; 2;05 minas of silver in exchange for 25 shekels of [gold ...] for the purchase of 2 [...] for the gods; 5 shekels of silver in exchange for [1 she]kel of [gold ...] [...], the overseer of the city of Usigu: expenditure for decorating objects of the men.

## Commentary

This document has to be dated to the year Ibr. 11. The last sections of the text, with the sum of the expended silver and the amount of the silver "present", al$_{6}$-ĝál, in the Treasury are not preserved.

It opens with the registration of the expenditure of 1 mina (470 g) of silver for the renewal rite concerning the city-god Kura which fell at the beginning of the new year. The 3 shekels (23 g) of silver to be given to the god in a later period of the year are registered in § 17. The "gods", diĝir-diĝir-diĝir, received a gift (r. XIX 1–2). Tinib-dulum, a sister of the king, received 5.35 minas (2.624 kg) of silver in her function as priestess of the god ᵓAdabal (§ 2).

Warutum of Mari, who had brought the news that Kiš had been defeated by the alliance of Mari with a Sumerian city, received 1 mina (470 g) of silver (§ 63). This war, which had started the previous year (see text XXI 13 § 65), ended the following year (see the commentary to text no. 15). Iram-malik was sent to Kiš to take note of the situation (§ 76). On this synchronism between Ebla and Babylonia, see Archi 2013b, p. 85; Sallaberger, Shrakamp 2015, p. 97), where the campaigns against Akšak and Kiš are attributed to Enšakušana.

Members of Dulu's elite received some presents again this year: Arradulum a dagger decorated with 7 shekels (55 g) of silver (§ 5); Ḫuwa-saradu, who had presented a "monkey", kir$_{4}$-ma, and eight pieces of linen clothing, received 2 minas of silver and 2 minas of tin (940 g of each), (§ 18). The latter envoy must be Luwa-saradu, mentioned in text no. 13 § 5. In a second mission, Arrudulum again received 2 minas of silver and 2 minas of tin (940 g of each); it was Samuᵓu, the merchant, who brought this gift to him (§ 52).

A "mace", *ḫa-bù*, of silver and gold which Bagama had brought back from the military expedition against Manuwat (year Ibr. 09) was dedicated to the god Hadda for a "purification rite", sikil (§ 26).

The king received a dagger and some objects decorated with gold (whose amount is partially in lacuna), (§ 3); decorations for his chariot required ten shekels (78 g) of gold (§ 23); a vessel (?) of boxwood decorated with 3 shekels (23 g) was provided for him and his mother (§ 33); he received a decoration of 2 shekels (16 g) of gold for a harp of bronze, and two spearheads of bronze, (§§ 39, 41). Eleven oxen were bought for the king at the market in the city of ᵓAdani (§ 43); a new goad of bronze, as well as a new harness with 1 ½ shekels (12 g) of gold were given to him (§§ 68, 84).

Ibrium received four buckles decorated with half a shekel (4 g) of gold (§ 32), and a cup with a lid decorated with 1 shekel (8 g) of gold (§ 82). A delivery for his "house", é, is in lacuna (§ 42).

Ibbi-zikir, Ibrium's son, received a gift (in lacuna), (§ 48). Among Ibrium's other sons, *Šum*-bàd$^{ki}$ received a plaque decorated with 8 shekels (63 g) of gold (§ 20), and Ir-damu a dagger decorated with silver and gold (§ 56). His brother Buma-il received two bracelets decorated with 10 shekels (78 g) of silver and 4.5 shekels (34 g) of gold (§ 29). A delivery for another of his sons is badly preserved (§ 83).

The messengers from Mari who came to Ebla were *A-ku-a-ḫa* (§ 8); *Daš-na* (§§ 24, 35, 36); and *Wa-ru*$_{12}$*-tum* (§ 63).

§ 11. The production of 200 daggers for "the men of the Palace" who had to go in a "military expedition", níĝ-kas$_4$, against Kakmium, needed the expenditure of 6;40 minas (3,133 kg) of tin; their *kam*$_4$*-ma-a-tum* required 4;27 minas (2.091 kg) of silver. A second expedition against this city is dated to the year Ibr. 14 (see Archi 2021a, p. 206).

§§ 14, 72. Two toggle-pins of 20 shekels (157 g) of silver were handed over for the funerary rite of a daughter of the king of Irar. This expenditure, together with that of a "mantel", zara$_6$-TÚG, for the funerary rite of a daughter of the king of Irar is registered also in the monthly document TM.75.G.10155 o. IV 2–10, where it is also specified that the messengers who brought these goods to Irar were not only Zibalum, but also Zibada. This delivery is explained by the fact that the queen, mother of the dead girl, was a Ibrium's daughter (see text 4 § 40). A more substantial gift was later sent to Irar: 1 belt with pendant decorated with 30 shekels (235 g) of gold for its king, and two toggle-pins of 30 shekels (235 g) of silver, whose heads were decorated with 3 shekels (23 g) of gold for its queen (§ 72).

§ 15. The encrusting of a tray for the "steward", sagi, <of Mari> required eleven "shells", *ra-ᵓà-tum*, of the value of 11 shekels (86 g) of silver, and of some ostrich shells (?), LAGAB×UD-LAGAB×UD, of the value of 10 shekels (78 g) of silver.

§ 21. Zuzabir, the son of Adad, received a belt of 40 shekels (313 g) of silver, in which 7 shekels (54 g) of gold were melted, because he had "occupied", tuš-LÚ×TIL, the city of Amᵓarum. The "military expedition", níĝ-kas$_4$, against this city is mentioned in *ARET* XIV 63 § 38, the annual mu-DU document of this year.

§ 23. The decorations of five chariots (three of belonging to the king) required 12 shekels (94 g) of gold.

§ 29. Buma-il, a brother of Ibrium, received two bracelets decorated with 10 shekels (78 g) of silver and plated with 4 ½ shekels (35 g) of gold.

§ 30. Raᵓutum, whose brother Azu-gura received two bracelets, was a "woman", dam, of the king, see text XXI 17 § 90.

§ 44. Expenditure of silver (in part to be changed for gold) for decorations of bracelets (several of which were in copper). The end of the section is in lacuna.

§ 56. Ir-damu, Ibrium's son, received a dagger decorated with silver and gold.

§ 70. Amur-damu "resided", tuš-LÚ×TIL, in Darzilum.

§ 71 A son of Ibbi-zikir (whose name is in lacuna) "resided" in Ibᶜal.

§ 85. Expenditures of silver and gold for daggers and bracelets (in part in lacuna).

# 15
## (Plates XXVIII–XXIX)

(1)

o. I. 1. 1 ma-na kù:babbar
saĝ kù:babbar
3. $^{d}$*Ku-ra*

(2)

12 ma-na kù:babbar
5 *Di-ni-ib-du-lum*
nin-ni
7. en
šu-ba$_4$-ti

(3)

9. 5 gín DILMUN kù:babbar
šu-bal-ak
11. 1 gín DILMUN kù-gi 1 kù-sal
níĝ-ba
13. *Da-bur-da-mu*
$^{d}$*Iš:šára*
15. *Zi-da-ra*$^{ki}$

(4)

10 gín DILMUN kù:babbar
17. šu-bal-ak
2 gín DILMUN kù-gi
19. en
*Uš-ḫu-lum*$^{ki}$

(5)

21. 16 gín DILMUN kù:babbar
šu-bal-ak
II. 1. 3 2$^{?}$ NI$^{?}$ gín DILMUN kù-gi
*ʾa$_5$-na-gu*
3. 1 ĜIŠ-banšur
*wa*
5. 1 kù-sal
níĝ-ba
7. *Ib-rí-um*
$^{d}$BAD *Du-du-lu*$^{ki}$

(6)

9. 15 gín DILMUN kù:babbar
níĝ-du$_8$
11. 1 dumu-nita
*A-ba-ti-lum*$^{ki}$
13. maškim
*Za-ba-rúm*
15. *áš-ti*
*Ìr-ku*$^{ki}$

(7)

17. 15 gín DILMUN kù:babbar
šu-bal-ak
19. 3 gín DILMUN kù-gi
1 *gú-li-lum*
21. *a-li-iš*
ĜIŠ-gu-kak-gíd
23. $^{dʾ}$*A$_5$-da-"bal*"
[ ]$^{ki}$
25. en
ì-na-sum
27. *in* ud
šeš-II-ib

(8)

29. TAR kù:babbar
níĝ-⌜ba⌝
III. 1. *Daš-na*
*Ma-rí*$^{ki}$
3. níĝ-"mul"
Kiš$^{ki}$
5. til

(1) 1 mina of silver for the silver head of the god Kura.
(2) 12 minas of silver: Tinib-dulum, sister of the king, has received.
(3) 5 shekels of silver in exchange for 1 shekel of gold for 1 buckle: gift of Tabur-damu for the goddess Išḫara of the city of Zidara.
(4) 10 shekels of silver in exchange for 2 shekel of gold for the king of the city of Ušḫulum.
(5) 16 shekels of silver in exchange for 3 shekels (and) 2 NI of gold for the circular stand of a table and 1 buckle: gift of Ibrium for the Lord of the city of Tuttul.
(6) 15 shekels of silver for the ransom of a young man of the city of Abatilum, through a representative of Zabarum, from the city of Irku.
(7) 15 shekels of silver in exchange for 3 shekels of gold for 1 bracelet above a spearhead for the god ʾAdabal of [the city of …], the king has given on the occasion (of the presence of) the confraternity of the šeš-II-ib.
(8) 30 (shekels of) silver: gift for Dašna of the city of Mari (who brought) the news that the city of Kiš had been defeated and handed over a kilt.

*wa*
7. íb-III-TÚG
šu-mu-tak$_4$

(9)
9. ŠA.PI gín DILMUN kù:babbar
1 íb-lá 1 ĝír-kun
11. TAR 5 gín DILMUN kù:babbar
šu-bal-ak
13. 7 gín DILMUN kù-gi
maš-maš-*sù*
15. 2 ma-na TAR kù:babbar
šu-bal-ak
17. TAR kù-gi 1 dib
TAR kù:babbar
19. níĝ-sa$_{10}$ 1 ĝír-mar-tu kù-gi
*Si-ti*-BAR.AN
21. lú-kar
*Kak-mi-um*$^{ki}$
23. [ ]
*Ḫa-ra-il*
25. *áš-du*
1 dib-*sù*
27. til
IV. 1. *in*
*Ša-nu-gú*$^{ki}$

(10)
3. 1 ma-na ŠA.PI gín DILMUN
kù:babbar
šu-bal-ak
5. ŠÚ+ŠA gín DILMUN kù-gi 1 dib
*Bar-za-ma-ù*
7. ugula *ˀÀ-šu*$^{ki}$
*in* ud
9. tuš-LÚ×TIL
*A-a-lu*$^{ki}$
11. 4 gín DILMUN kù:babbar
níĝ-sa$_{10}$ 1 ĝír mar-tu *ba-du-u*$_4$
kù:babbar
13. *La-gi*
maškim-*sù*

(11)
15. 10 gín DILMUN kù:babbar
šu-bal-ak
17. 2 gín DILMUN kù-gi
*ni-zi-mu*
19. nu$_{11}$-za 4 kù-sal
5 gín DILMUN kù:babbar
21. *ni-zi-mu*
2 níĝ-anše-ak
23. *Ib-rí-um*

(12)
15 gín DILMUN
V. 1. kù:babbar
šu-bal-ak
3. 3 gín DILMUN kù-gi
*ni-zi-mu*
5. 1 dib
GABA-*da-mu*
7. lú *I-rí-ig*

(13)
15 gín DILMUN kù:babbar
9. šu-bal-ak
3 gín DILMUN kù-gi 2 ĜIŠ-ĝidru
11. 2 šu-dub
ama-gal
13. en

(14)
50 gín DILMUN kù:babbar
15. šu-bal-ak
10 gín DILMUN kù-gi 1 dib
17. *Du-bù-ḫu-*$^{d.}$*ˀÀ-da*
dumu-nita
19. *I-bí-zi-kir*

(15)
50 gín DILMUN kù:babbar
21. šu-bal-ak
10 gín DILMUN kù-gi 1 dib
23. *Dar-ib-da-mu*
dumu-munus
25. en

(16)
VI. 1. 6 gín DILMUN kù:babbar
níĝ-sa$_{10}$ 2 *gàr-su*
3. *Ì-lum-a-ḫi*

(9) 40 shekels of silver for 1 belt (and) 1 dagger pendant; 35 shekels of silver in exchange for 7 shekels of gold for their striped (decoration); 2;30 minas of silver in exchange for 30 (shekels of) gold for 1 plaque; 30 (shekels of) silver for the purchase of 1 mar-tu dagger (decorated with) gold for Siti-BARAN, trader of the city of Kakmium […] Ḫara-il as a replacement of his plaque, completed in the city of Šanugu.

(10) 1;40 minas of silver in exchange for 20 shekels of gold for 1 plaque for Barzamaˀu, the overseer of the city of ˀAšu, when he resided in the city of Aˀalu; 4 shekels of silver for the purchase of 1 *b.* mar-tu dagger (decorated with) silver for Lagi, his representative.

(11) 10 shekels of silver in exchange for 2 shekels of gold for decorating with lamination 4 buckles; 5 shekels of silver for decorating 2 bridles for Ibrium.

(12) 15 shekels of silver in exchange for 3 shekels of gold for decorating 1 plaque for GABA-damu, (son) of Irig.

(13) 15 shekels of silver in exchange for 3 shekels of gold for 2 sticks (and) 2 rings for the king's mother.

(14) 50 shekels of silver in exchange for 10 shekels of gold for 1 plaque for Dubuḫu-Hadda, son of Ibbi-zikir.

(15) 50 shekels of silver in exchange for 10 shekels of gold for 1 plaque for Tarib-damu, daughter of the king.

(16) 6 shekels of silver for the purchase of 2 bags for Ilum-aḫi and Iˀin-Hadda, 2 sons of the king.

*wa*
5. *I-in-*$^{d}$*ʾÀ-da*
2 dumu-nita
7. en

(17)
1 gín DILMUN kù:babbar
9. níĝ-sa$_{10}$ ĜIŠ-ád
*Sa-nap-zu-gúm*$^{ki}$

(18)
11. TAR 3 gín DILMUN 3 NI kù:babbar
šu-bal-ak
13. 6 gín DILMUN 2 NI kù-gi 2 *gú-li-lum*
níĝ-ba
15. $^{d}$*Ku-ra*

(19)
10 ma-na ŠA.PI 2 gín DILMUN
kù:babbar
17. níĝ-sa$_{10}$ 1 *ʾà-da-um*-TÚG-II
2 zara$_{6}$-TÚG
19. 30 gada-TÚG
16 sal-TÚG
21. 5 gíd-TÚG
20 íb+III-TÚG sa$_{6}$ ⌜gùn⌝
23. 1 *mi-at*
VII. 1. 46 íb+III-TÚG gùn
3 *mi-at* 85 "KIN" siki *Ma-rí*$^{ki}$
3. 2 ma-na kù:babbar
níĝ-sa$_{10}$ ĜIŠ-ti-ḪAR
5. *Wa-ba-rúm*
šu-ba$_{4}$-ti
7. ki:lam$_{7}$
šeš-II-ib
9. *wa*
$^{d}$*A-da-ma*
11. *ʾÀ-da-ni*$^{ki}$

(20)
TAR kù:babbar
13. níĝ-ba
*Wa-ru*$_{12}$*-tum*
15. *Ma-rí*$^{ki}$
níĝ-"mul"
17. *in*
uru$^{ki}$-uru$^{ki}$
19. Kiš$^{ki}$
šu-ba$_{4}$-ti

(21)
21. 6 gín DILMUN kù:babbar
níĝ-ba
23. *Iš-dub-il*
*wa*
25. *Dab*$_{6}$*-ti*
VIII. 1. *Ma-rí*$^{ki}$
maškim
3. ga:eš$_{8}$
*Du-du-lu*$^{ki}$

(22)
5. 1 ma-na 55 gín DILMUN kù:babbar
níĝ-sa$_{10}$ 10 lá-1 túg-NI.NI
7. 1 túg-NI.NI sa$_{6}$
64 sal-TÚG
9. ki:lam$_{7}$
*Ìr-ku*$^{ki}$

(23)
11. 1 gín DILMUN kù:babbar
nu$_{11}$-za 1 zag
13. ĜIŠ-gígir-II
*I-bi-zi-kir*
15. dumu-nita
*Ib-rí-um*

(24)
17. 2 gín DILMUN kù:babbar
lul-gu-ak
19. 1 *zú-zú-ba-tum*
en
21. zàḫ

(25)
15 gín DILMUN kù:babbar
23. šu-bal-ak
3 gín DILMUN kù-gi 1 zi-bar
IX. 1. en
*Uš-ḫu-lum*$^{ki}$
3. *Ib-dur-i-šar*
šu-mu-tak$_{4}$

(17) 1 shekel of silver for the purchase of myrtle from the city of Sanapzugum.
(18) 33 shekels (and) 3 NI of silver in exchange for 6 shekels (and) 2 NI of gold for 2 bracelets: gift for the god Kura.
(19) 10;42 minas of silver for the purchase of 54 garments, 166 kilts (and) 385 KIN measures of wool from the city of Mari; 2 minas of silver for the purchase of GIŠ-ti-ḪAR-wood: Wabarum has received, at the markets of the šeš-II-ib confraternity and of the god Adamma of the city of ʾAdani.
(20) 30 (shekels of) silver: gift for Warutum of the city of Mari (who brought) the news in the cities that the city of Kiš had been conquered.
(21) 6 shekels of silver: gift for Išdub-il and Dabti of the city of Mari, representatives of the travelling merchant of the city of Tuttul.
(22) 1;55 minas of silver for the purchase of 74 garments at the market of the city of Irku.
(23) 1 shekel of silver for plating 1 side of the chariot of Ibbi-zikir, son of Ibrium.
(24) 2 shekels of silver as replacement of 1 ... (*zú-zú-ba-tum*) for the king, which got lost.
(25) 15 shekels of silver in exchange for 3 shekels of gold for 1 zi-bar goblet for the king of the city of Ušḫulum, Ibdur-išar has handed over.

(26)
5. 10 ma-na kù:babbar
šu-bal-ak
7. 2 ma-na kù-gi
*ni-zi-mu*
9. 4 *su-da-ni*
4 ma-na kù:babbar
11. šu-bal-ak
ŠA.PI 8 gín DILMUN kù-gi
13. *ni-zi-mu*
4 kù-sal-*sù*
15. 50 gín DILMUN kù:babbar
šu-bal-ak
17. 10 gín DILMUN kù-gi
*ni-zi-mu*
19. nu$_{11}$-za 2 ĜIŠ-ban
ĜIŠ-gígir-II lú *ra-ʾà-tum*
21. *ša-ti*
en

(27)
23. 15 gín DILMUN kù:babbar
X. 1. nu$_{11}$-za 1 *ḫa-bù*
TAR kù:babbar
3. šu-bal-ak
6 gín DILMUN kù-gi
5. nu$_{11}$-za 1 *ar-ra-si-su*
ŠÚ+ŠA gín DILMUN kù:babbar
7. *ʾa$_5$-na-gu*
4 si 2 gud
9. nídba
en
11. $^{d}$*Ra-sa-ap*
*ʾÀ-da-ni*$^{ki}$
13. *in*
$^{d}$AMA-*ra*

(28)
15. 1 ma-na 10 kù:babbar
šu-bal-ak
17. 14 gín DILMUN kù-gi
2 *ti-gi-na* 2 ĜIŠ-du
19. 1 KA-*ḫu-a-tum*
*Dar-ib-da-mu*
21. dumu-munus
en

(29)
23. 10 gín DILMUN kù:babbar
šu-bal-ak
25. 2 gín DILMUN kù-gi
*ni-zi-mu*
XI. 1. 1 *gú-li-lum* a-gar$_5$-gar$_5$
*Ib-ga-il*
3. ugula sur$_x$-BAR.AN

(30)
6 ma-na 10 gín DILMUN kù:babbar
5. šu-bal-ak
1 ma-na 14 gín DILMUN kù-gi
7. kin$_5$-ak
10 ĝeštu$_x$-lá
9. 2 *ti-gi-na*
62 *du-ru$_{12}$-gú*
11. 1 *mi-at kur-gú-ru$_{12}$*
2 kù-sal
13. 1 *ma-ḫa-na-gúm*
*ḫa-za-nu*
15. 1 šu-dub
1 *ša-mu*
17. 2 *ti-ba-ra-núm*
*wa*
19. nu$_{11}$-za 2 saĝ 2 *bu*-DI
TAR kù:babbar 2 *bu*-DI
21. *Ar-za-du*
dumu-munus
23. *En-na*-$^{d}$Utu

(31)
5 gín DILMUN kù:babbar
XII. 1. šu-bal-ak
1 gín DILMUN kù-gi 1 kù-sal
3. níĝ-ba
*Du-si-gú*
5. $^{d}$*Ra-sa-ap*
*ʾÀ-da-ni*$^{ki}$

(26) 10 minas of silver in exchange for 2 minas of gold for decorating 4 … (*su-da-ni*); 4 minas of silver in exchange for 48 shekels of gold for decorating their 4 buckles; 50 shekels of silver in exchange for 10 shekels of gold for decorating with lamination 2 bows of the chariot (decorated with) shells for the king.

(27) 15 shekels of silver for plating 1 mace; 30 (shekels of) silver in exchange for 6 shekels of gold for plating ist handle; 20 shekels of silver for the circular stand of the 4 horns of 2 bulls: offering of the king for the god Rašap of the city of ʾAdani, at the AMA-ra (festival).

(28) 1;10 minas of silver in exchange for 14 shekels of gold for 2 torques, 2 foot rings (and) 1 … (KA-*ḫu-a-tum*) for Tarib-damu, daughter of the king.

(29) 10 shekels of silver in exchange for 2 shekels of gold for decorating 1 bracelet of copper for Ibga-il, the overseer of the team of mules.

(30) 6;10 minas of silver in exchange for 1;14 minas of gold for making 10 earrings, 2 torques, 62 pearls, 100 beads, 2 buckles, 1 necklace (with) beads, 1 ring, 1 frontlet, 2 headdresses, and for plating 2 heads of 2 toggle-pins; 30 (shekels of) silver for 2 toggle-pins for Arzadu, daughter of Enna-Utu.

(31) 5 shekels of silver in exchange for 1 shekel of gold for 1 buckle: gift of Dusigu for the god Rašap of the city of ʾAdani.

(32)
7. 4 gín DILMUN kù:babbar
níĝ-sa$_{10}$ 1 gín mar-tu *ba-du-u*$_4$
kù:babbar
9. *I-lu*$_5$*-za*$_x$*-ma-lik*
NE-*na-áš*$^{ki}$

(33)
11. 10 lá-1 ma-na 5 gín DILMUN
kù:babbar
níĝ-sa$_{10}$ 5 túg-NI.NI
13. 3 níĝ-lá-saĝ
10 *ʾà-da-um*-TÚG
15. 1 *mi-at* 53 sal-TÚG
50 lá-3 íb+III-TÚG sa$_6$ gùn
17. 1 *mi-at* 20 íb+III-TÚG gùn
3 íb+III-TÚG *Ma-rí*$^{ki}$
19. 10 gín DILMUN kù:babbar
níĝ-sa$_{10}$ 10 sila$_4$ sa$_6$
XIII. 1. 1 ma-na TAR kù:babbar
níĝ-sa$_{10}$ ĜIŠ-ti-ḪAR
3. *Wa-ba-rúm*
ki:lam$_7$
5. $^{d}$AMA-*ra*
*ʾÀ-da-ni*$^{ki}$

(34)
7. 12 gín DILMUN kù:babbar
níĝ-sa$_{10}$ 3 ĝír mar-tu *ba-du-u*$_4$
9. kù:babbar
*Dab-da-ar*
11. *wa*
*A-a-gú-nu*
13. *ʾÀ-su*$^{ki}$
*wa*
15. *Ib-te-ar*
*Su-ti-ig*$^{⌜ki⌝}$

(35)
17. TAR [kù]:babbar
1 íb[-lá] 1 ĝír-kun
19. 2 ma-na TAR kù:babbar
šu-bal-ak
21. TAR kù-gi
nu$_{11}$-za-*sù*
23. *I-in-il*
ugula *Ù-ša-li-ik*$^{ki}$
25. *in* ud
tuš-LÚ×TIL
27. *Kak-mi-um*$^{ki}$

(36)
XIV. 1. [3 g]ín DILMUN k[ù:babbar]
saĝ kù:babbar
3. $^{d}$*Ku-ra*
mu-ti

(37)
5. 1 ma-na kù:babbar
níĝ-sa$_{10}$ 1 ĝír mar-tu kù-gi
7. en
*áš-du*
9. 1 ĝír mar-tu-*sù*
sikil
11. $^{dʾ}$*A*$_5$*-da-"bal"*
*Lu-ba-an*$^{ki}$

(38)
13. 50 ma-na kù:babbar
šu-bal-ak
15. 10 ma-na kù-gi
kin$_5$-ak
17. é
$^{d}$*Ku-ra*

(39)
19. 3 gín DILMUN kù:babbar
lú ĜIŠ-nu-kiri$_6$
21. *A-ru*$_{12}$*-ga-du*$^{ki}$

(40)
1 ma-na 10 gín DILMUN an-na
23. šub *si-in*
*ni-zi-mu*
25. ZA$_x$
nagar-nagar

(32) 4 shekels of silver for the purchase of 1 *b.* mar-tu dagger (decorated with) silver for Iluza-malik of the city of NEnaš.
(33) 9;05 minas of silver for the purchase of 171 garments (and) 170 kilts; 10 shekels of silver for the purchase of 10 lambs of good quality; 1;30 minas of silver for the purchase of GIŠ-ti-ḪAR-wood: Wabarum (has received), at the market of the AMA-ra (festival) of the city of ʾAdani.
(34) 12 shekels of silver for the purchase of 3 *b.* mar-tu daggers (decorated with) silver for Dab-dar and Aʾagunu of the city of ʾAšu and for Ibtear of the city of Sutig.
(35) 30 (shekels of) [sil]ver for 1 be[lt] (and) 1 dagger pendant; 2;30 minas of silver in exchange for 30 (shekels of) gold for its lamination for Iʾin-il, the overseer of the city of Ušalik, when resided in the city of Kakmium.
(36) [3 sh]ekels of s[ilver] for the silver head of the god Kura: (second) delivery.
(37) 1 mina of silver for the purchase of 1 mar-tu dagger (decorated with) gold for the king as a replacement of his mar-tu dagger (given for) the purification rite to the god ʾAdabal of the city of Luban.
(38) 50 minas of silver in exchange for 10 minas of gold for making the temple of the god Kura.
(39) 3 shekels of silver for the gardener of the city of Arugadu.
(40) 1;10 minas of tin to be melted for decorating objects of the carpenters.

(41)
XV. 1. 27 gín DILMUN kù:babbar
*kam$_4$-ma-a-tum*
3. 20 ĝír mar-tu
ME-sig

(42)
5. TAR 3 gín DILMUN 3 NI kù:babbar
šu-bal-ak
7. 6 gín DILMUN 2 NI kù-gi 2 *gú-li-lum*
níĝ-ba
9. $^d$*Ku-ra*

(43)
12 gín DILMUN an-na
11. šub *si-in*
1 ma-na 10 a-gar$_5$-gar$_5$
13. kin$_5$-ak
2 ⸢ĜIŠ⸣-zú
15. 3 gín DILMUN kù:babbar
nu$_{11}$-za
17. 2 ĜIŠ-gígir-II gibil
*Ib-rí-um*

(44)
19. 2 gín DILMUN kù:babbar
*ni-zi-mu*
21. 1 íb-lá
*Ir-da-mu*
23. 2 ½ gín DILMUN kù:babbar
šu-bal-ak
25. ½ kù-gi
*ni-zi-mu*
XVI. 1. maš-maš-*sù*
2 ½ gín DILMUN kù:babbar
3. šu-bal-ak
½ gín DILMUN kù-gi
5. *ni-zi-mu*
1 *si-ti-tum*
7. *Gi-ir-da-mu*
2 dumu-nita
9. *Ib-rí-um*

(45)
2 gín kù:babbar
11. *zi-ba-du*
1 ĜIŠ-šú 1 níĝ-bànda kù:babbar
13. lú kaskal
*Ib-rí-um*

(46)
15. ŠÚ+ŠA gín DILMUN kù:babbar 2 *bu*-DI
15 gín DILMUN kù:babbar
17. šu-bal-ak
3 gín DILMUN kù-gi
19. nu$_{11}$-za 2 saĝ-*sù*
*Zi-mi-ni*-kù:babbar
21. *ma-lik-tum*
*Bur-ma-an*$^{ki}$
23. *in* ud
dumu-munus
25. tu-da
*I-lu$_5$-za$_x$-ma-lik*
XVII. 1. [šu-mu-ta]k$_4$

(47)
ŠÚ+ŠA gín DILMUN kù:babbar
3. níĝ-ba
*Wa-ru$_{12}$-tum*
5. *Ma-rí*$^{ki}$
e$_{11}$ (dul$_6$-DU)
7. *áš-ti*
*Na-zu-mu*
9. *mi-nu*
Kiš$^{ki}$

(48)
11. 10 lá-1 ma-na 12 gín DILMUN kù:babbar
níĝ-sa$_{10}$ 10 lá-2 túg-NI.NI
13. 15 *ʾà-d*[*a-*]*um*-TÚG[-II$^?$]
1 *mi*[*-at*] 10 sal-TÚG
15. 30 íb+III-TÚG sa$_6$ gùn
4 *mi-at* íb+III-TÚG gùn
17. TAR 3 gín DILMUN kù:babbar

(41) 27 shekels of silver for the knobs of 20 mar-tu daggers for the watchmen.
(42) 33 shekels (and) 3 NI of silver in exchange for 6 shekels (and) 2 NI of gold for 2 bracelets: gift for the god Kura.
(43) 12 shekels of tin to be melted with 1;10 minas of copper for making 2 hooks; 3 shekels of silver for plating 2 new chariots for Ibrium.
(44) 2 shekels of silver for decorating 1 belt for Ir-damu; 2 ½ shekels of silver in exchange for ½ (shekel of) gold for decorating 1 sheath for Giʾir-damu, 2 sons of Ibrium.
(45) 2 shekels of silver for the handle of 1 GIŠ-šú vessel (and) 1 níg-bànda vessel of silver for Ibrium's journey.
(46) 20 shekels of silver for 2 toggle-pins; 15 shekels of silver in exchange for 3 shekels of gold for plating their 2 heads for Zimini-kubabbar, the queen of the city of Burman, when she gave birth to a daughter; Iluza-malik [has handed ove]r.
(47) 20 shekels of silver: gift for Warutum of the city of Mari (who) came back together with Nazumu from the city of Kiš.
(48) 9;12 minas of silver for the purchase of 133 garments (and) 430 kilts; 33 shekels of silver for the purchase of leek; 1;25 mina of silver for the purchase of 4 donk[eys]: Puz[urra]-mal[ik] (has received), at the market of the god Kamiš.

níĝ-sa$_{10}$ raš-SAR
19. 1 ma-na ŠÚ+ŠA 5 gín DILMUN kù:babbar
níĝ-sa$_{10}$ 4 IGI.N[ITA]
21. *Puz*[*ur*$_4$-*ra*]-*ma*-*l*[*ik*]
r. I. 1. ki:lam$_7$
$^{d}$*Ga-mi-iš*

(49)
3. 10 gín DILMUN kù:babbar
níĝ-sa$_{10}$ 1 ma-na 7 gín DILMUN *nap-ḫu*
5. 13 gín DILMUN kù:babbar
nu$_{11}$-za 1 *ḫa-bù*
7. [ŠÚ+ŠA gín DILMUN kù:babbar]
[šu-bal-ak]
9. 4 gín DILMUN kù-g[i]
nu$_{11}$[-za] 1 ˹*ar*˺-*ra-su*[-*sù*]
11. níĝ-ba
$^{d}$ʾ*À-d*[*a*]
13. *Lu-u*[*b*$^{ki}$]
*i*[*n*]
15. *g*[*i*-NI]

(50)
3 m[a-na] ŠÚ+ŠA [gín] DILMUN kù:babbar
17. šu-bal-ak
ŠA.PI gín DILMUN kù-gi
19. kin$_5$-ak 1 an-zam$_x$
II. 1. *wa*
1 pad-*sù*
3. *Ib-rí-um*

(51)
50 gín DILMUN kù:babbar
5. šu-bal-ak
10 gín DILMUN kù-gi
7. nu$_{11}$-za 2 *gú-li-lum* 50 gín DILMUN a-gar$_5$-gar$_5$
*An-na-aḫ*
9. lú-kar
*Kak-mi-um*$^{ki}$

(52)
11. 1 gín DILMUN kù:babbar
ZU.PIRIĜ-*sù*
13. 10 gín DILMUN an-na
šub *si-in*
15. 1 ma-na a-gar$_5$-gar$_5$
kin$_5$-ak
17. 1 *ma-ḫa-ni-gúm*
*wa*
19. 1 tùn gal
en

(53)
21. {1} ŠA.PI gín DILMUN kù:babbar
níĝ-sa$_{10}$ 1 ĝír mar-tu kù-gi
III. 1. *Gi-a-da-mu*

(54)
2 gín DILMUN [kù:babbar]
3. nu$_{11}$-za 1 ĝír mar-tu
níĝ-ba
5. *Ib-rí-um*
$^{d}$ʾ*À-da*
7. *gi*-NI

(55)
15 ma-na 52 gín DILMUN kù:babbar
9. níĝ-sa$_{10}$ 6 dùl-TÚG *Ma-rí*$^{ki}$
4 ʾ*à-da-um*-TÚG-II
11. 11 túg-NI.NI
46 sal-TÚG
13. 40 gada-TÚG-gada-TÚG
2 níĝ-lá-gaba
15. 80 lá-2 íb+III-TÚG sa$_6$ gùn
5 *mi-at* 80 íb+III-TÚG gùn
17. 2 kuš babbar ùz-nita
lú 2 níĝ-anše-ak kù-gi maḫ$^?$
19. en
ki:lam$_7$
21. SA.ZA$_x^{ki}$

(56)
IV. 1. ŠA.PI 8 gín DILMUN kù:babbar
níĝ-sa$_{10}$ 10 *gàr-su*

(49) 10 shekels of silver for the purchase of 1;07 minas of rock crystal; 13 shekels of silver for plating 1 mace; [20 shekels of silver in exchange for] 4 shekels of gol[d] for plat[ing its] handle: gift for the god Had[da] of the city of Lu[b], i[n] mon[th IV].

(50) 3;20 m[inas] of silver in exchange for 40 shekels of gold for making 1 an-zam$_x$ goblet and its lid for Ibrium.

(51) 50 shekels of silver in exchange for 10 shekels of gold for plating 2 bracelets of 50 shekels of copper each for Anaḫ, trader of the city of Kakmium.

(52) 1 shekel of silver for its hangers; 10 shekels of tin to be melted with 1 mina of copper for making 1 necklace and 1 big axe for the king.

(53) 40 shekels of silver for the purchase of 1 mar-tu dagger (decorated with) gold for Giʾa-damu.

(54) 2 shekels of [silver] for plating 1 mar-tu dagger: gift of Ibrium for the god Hadda, (in) month IV.

(55) 15;52 minas of silver for the purchase of 109 garments, 658 kilts (and) 2 hides of white goats for 2 large bridles (decorated with) gold for the king, at the market of the Palace.

(56) 48 shekels of silver for the purchase of 10 bags at the market of the god Hadda and 8 bags at the market of the Palace.

3. ki:lam$_7$
$^{dʾ}$*À-da*
5. *wa*
10 lá-2 *gàr-su*
7. ki:lam$_7$
SA.ZA$_x^{ki}$

(57)
9. TAR 3 gín DILMUN 3 NI kù:babbar
šu-bal-ak
11. 6 gín DILMUN 2 NI kù-gi
2 *gú-li-lum*
13. níĝ-ba
$^{d}$*Aš-da-bíl*

(58)
15. 6 gín DILMUN 2 NI kù:babbar
2 *gú-li-lum*
17. níĝ-ba
$^{d}$*Am-ma-rí-ig*

(59)
19. 5 gín DILMUN kù:babbar
šu-bal-ak
21. 1 gín DILMUN kù-gi 1 kù-sal
níĝ-ba
23. *Da-bur-da-mu*
V. 1. $^{d}$Utu
SA.ZA$_x^{ki}$

(60)
3. ŠÚ+ŠA gín DILMUN kù:babbar 2 *bu*-DI
15 gín DILMUN kù:babbar
5. šu-bal-ak
3 gín DILMUN kù-gi
7. nu$_{11}$-za 2 saĝ-*sù*
*ma-lik-tum*
9. *Ì-ra-ar*$^{ki}$
ama-gal
11. en
šu-mu-tak$_4$
13. *in* ud
DU.DU
15. *Ga-wa-na*$^{ki}$

(61)
1 ma-na kù:babbar
17. níĝ-sa$_{10}$ 1 ĝír mar-tu kù-gi
*Ib-rí-um*
19. *áš-du*
ĝír mar-tu-*sù*
21. sikil
$^{dʾ}$*À-da*

(62)
23. TAR kù:babbar
VI. 1. 1 ⌜íb⌝-lá 1 *si-ti-tum* 1 ĝír-kun
sikil
3. $^{dʾ}$*A$_5$-da-*⌜*bal*⌝
*Lu-ba-an*$^{ki}$
5. *Ib-rí-um*
šu-mu-tak$_4$
7. *al$_6$*
tu-ra-*sù*

(63)
9. ŠÚ+ŠA gín DILMUN kù:babbar 2 *bu*-DI
15 gín DILMUN kù:babbar
11. šu-bal-ak
3 gín DILMUN kù-gi
13. nu$_{11}$-za 2 saĝ-*sù*
níĝ-ba
15. *Na-tum*
*ma-lik-tum*
17. *Bur-ma-an*$^{ki}$
É×PAP
19. *Gi-ba-da*
*Ib-dur-i-šar*
21. šu-mu-tak$_4$

(64)
TAR kù:babbar
23. šu-bal-ak
6 gín DILMUN kù-gi

(57) 33 shekels (and) 3 NI of silver in exchange for 6 shekels (and) 2 NI of gold for 2 bracelets: gift for the god Ašdabil.
(58) 6 shekels (and) 2 NI of silver for 2 bracelets: gift for the god Ammarik.
(59) 5 shekels of silver in exchange for 1 shekel of gold for 1 buckle: gift of Tabur-damu for the god Utu of the Palace.
(60) 20 shekels of silver for 2 toggle-pins; 15 shekels of silver in exchange for 3 shekels of gold for plating their 2 heads for the queen of the city of Irar: the king's mother has handed over, when she went to the city of Gawana.
(61) 1 mina of silver for the purchase of 1 mar-tu dagger (decorated with) gold for Ibrium, as replacement of his mar-tu dagger (given for) the purification rite to the god Hadda.
(62) 30 (shekels of) silver for 1 belt, 1 sheath (and) 1 dagger pendant for the purification rite to the god ʾAdabal of the city of Luban, Ibrium has handed over on the occasion of his illness.
(63) 20 shekels of silver for 2 toggle-pins; 15 shekels of silver in exchange for 3 shekels of gold for plating their 2 heads: gift for the funerary rite of Natum, the queen of the city of Burman; Gibada (and) Ibdur-išar have handed over.
(64) 30 (shekels of) silver in exchange for 6 shekels of gold for decorating 10 […] for Giri; 10 shekels of silver in exchange for 2 shekels of gold for decorating 6 earrings for Giri and Ir-damu (and) Napḫa-il, sons of Ibrium.

25. *ni-zi-mu*
10 ⸢x⸣-[x]
27. *Gi-rí*
VII. 1. ⸢10⸣ gín DILMUN kù:babbar
šu-bal-ak
3. 2 gín DILMUN kù-gi
*ni-zi-mu*
5. 6 ĝeštu$_x$-lá
*Gi-rí*
7. *wa*
*Ir-da-mu*
9. *Nap-ḫa-il*
dumu-nita
11. *Ib-rí-um*

(65)
15 gín DILMUN kù:babbar
13. šu-bal-ak
3 gín DILMUN kù-gi
15. *ʾa$_5$-na-gu*
1 ĜIŠ-banšur
17. *wa*
1 kù-sal
19. níĝ-ba
en

(66)
21. 13 gín DILMUN 3 NI kù:babbar
šu-bal-ak
23. 2 gín DILMUN 2 NI kù-gi
nu$_{11}$-za 1 ĝír mar-tu
25. *wa*
1 kù-sal
27. níĝ-ba
⸢ama⸣-gal
VIII. 1. [e]n

(67)
15 gín DILMUN kù:babbar
3. šu-bal-ak
3 gín DILMUN kù-gi
5. nu$_{11}$-za 1 ĝír mar-tu
*wa*
7. 1 kù-sal
níĝ-ba
9. *Ib-rí-um*
$^{d}$*Ra-sa-ap*
11. *Du-ne-íb*$^{ki}$

(68)
4 ma-na 10 gín DILMUN kù:babbar
13. šu-bal-ak
50 gín DILMUN kù-gi
15. kin$_5$-ak
1 an-zam$_x$
17. *wa*
1 pad-*sù*
19. en

(69)
TAR 5 gín DILMUN kù:babbar
21. šu-bal-ak
7 gín DILMUN kù-gi
23. *ni-zi-mu*
1 an-zam$_x$ an-dùl
25. libir
lú *Ib-rí-um*

(70)
IX. 1. 3 ma-na ŠÚ+ŠA gín DILMUN kù:babbar
šu-bal-ak
3. ŠA.PI gín DILMUN kù-gi
1 dib
5. *A-ḫu-šu-da-mu*
dumu-nita
7. *Zé-ma-lik*
šeš
9. *I-nu-ud-da-mu*

(71)
12 gín DILMUN kù:babbar
11. nu$_{11}$-za 1 *ḫa-bù*
*ap*
13. nu$_{11}$-za
1 *ar-ra-sù*
15. kù-gi sikil
ŠÚ+ŠA gín DILMUN kù:babbar
17. *ʾa$_5$-na-gu*
4 si 2 gud

(65) 15 shekels of silver in exchange for 3 shekels of gold for the circular stand of a table and 1 buckle: gift of the king.

(66) 13 shekels (and) 3 NI of silver in exchange for 2 shekels (and) 2 NI of gold for plating 1 mar-tu dagger and 1 buckle: gift of the [ki]ng's mother.

(67) 15 shekels of silver in exchange for 3 shekels of gold for plating 1 mar-tu dagger and 1 buckle: gift of Ibrium for the god Rašap of the city of Tunip.

(68) 4;10 minas of silver in exchange for 50 shekels of gold for making 1 an-zam$_x$ goblet and its lid for the king.

(69) 35 shekels of silver in exchange for 7 shekels of gold for decorating an old an-zam$_x$ goblet (with the image of) a statue for Ibrium.

(70) 3;40 minas of silver in exchange for 40 shekel of gold for 1 plaque for Aḫušu-damu, son of Ze-malik, brother of Inud-damu.

(71) 12 shekels of silver for plating 1 mace and also for plating its handle (with) pure gold; 20 shekels of silver for the circular stand of the 4 horns of 2 bulls: offering of the king for the god Hadda, in month VIII.

19. nídba
en
21. $^{d}$ʾÀ-*da*
*in*
23. iti ʾ*a*$_{5}$-*nun*

(72)
5 gín DILMUN kù:babbar
25. šu-bal-ak
1 kù-gi 1 kù-sal
X. 1. [níĝ-b]a
en
3. $^{d}$*Ḫa-a-ba-du*
*al*$_{6}$
5. tu-ra
ama-gal-*sù*

(73)
7. 10 gín DILMUN kù:babbar
šu-bal-ak
9. 2 gín DILMUN kù-gi 2 kù-sal
níĝ-ba
11. *Da-bur-da-mu*
$^{d}$*Iš*:*šára*
13. *Zu-ra-mu*$^{ki}$
*wa*
15. $^{d}$*Iš*:*šára*
*Má*-NE$^{ki}$
17. *I-lu*$_{5}$-*za*$_{x}$-*ma-lik*
šu-mu-tak$_{4}$

(74)
19. 1 ma-na kù:babbar
níĝ-ba
21. *Daš-na*
*Ma-rí*$^{ki}$
23. níĝ-"mul"
Kiš$^{ki}$
25. til-til

(75)
5 gín DILMUN kù:babbar
27. níĝ-kaskal
*En-na-ì*
29. DU.DU
Kiš$^{ki}$

(76)
31. 2 ½ gín DILMUN kù:babbar
nu$_{11}$-za
XI. 1. [1 ĝír mar-tu]
[*w*]*a*
3. 1 kù-sal
níĝ-ba
5. *Ib-rí-um*
$^{d}$*A-dar-a-an*
7. *Da-na-áš*$^{ki}$

(77)
10 gín DILMUN kù:babbar
9. šu-bal-ak
2 gín DILMUN kù-gi
11. *ni-zi-mu*
2 ĜIŠ-du
13. *Da-bur-da-mu*

(78)
1 gín DILMUN 2 NI kù:babbar
15. šu-bal-ak
3 NI kù-gi
17. 1 *gú-li-lum*
$^{d}$*Da-bí-ir*
19. diĝir *Ib-la*$^{ki}$

(79)
10 ma-na kù:babbar
21. šu-bal-ak
2 ma-na kù-gi
23. kin$_{5}$-ak
2 *gú-li-lum*
25. 10 lá-2 ma-na ŠÚ+ŠA gín DILMUN kù:babbar
šu-bal-ak
27. 1 ma-na
XII. 1. ŠA[.PI gín DILMUN kù-gi]
1 dib
3. en
*áš-du*
5. dib-*sù*
sikil
7. $^{d}$ʾÀ-*da*
*al*$_{6}$
9. tu-ra

(72) 5 shekels of silver in exchange for 1 (shekel of) gold for 1 buckle: [gif]t of the king for the goddess Ḫaʾabadu, in relation to the illness of his mother.
(73) 10 shekels of silver in exchange for 2 shekels of gold for 2 buckles: gift of Tabur-damu for the goddess Išḫara of the city of Zuramu and the goddess Išḫara of the city of MaNE; Iluza-malik has handed over.
(74) 1 mina of silver: gift for Dašna of the city of Mari (who brought) the news that the city of Kiš had been completely defeated.
(75) 5 shekels of silver: travel provision for Enna-i(l) (who) went to the city of Kiš.
(76) 1 ½ shekels of silver for plating [1 mar-tu dagger an]d 1 buckle: gift of Ibrium for the god Adaranu of the city of Današ.
(77) 10 shekels of silver in exchange for 2 shekels of gold for decorating 2 foot rings for Tabur-damu.
(78) 1 shekel (and) 2 NI of silver in exchange for 3 NI of gold for 1 bracelet for Dabiru, the god of Ebla.
(79) 10 minas of silver in exchange for 2 minas of gold for making 2 bracelets; 8;20 minas of silver in exchange for 1;40 minas [of gold] for 1 plaque for the king, as replacement of his plaque (given for) the purification rite to the god Hadda, in relation to the illness of his mother, and 2 bracelets (given for) the purification rite to the god ʾAdabal of the city of Luban, in relation to his illness.

ama-gal-
11. *sù*
*wa*
13. 2 *gú-li-lum-sù*
sikil
15. $^{dʾ}$*A*$_5$*-da-"bal"*
*Lu-ba-an*$^{ki}$
17. *al*$_6$
tu-ra-*sù*

(80)
19. 10 ma-na kù:babbar
šu-bal-ak
21. 2 ma-na kù-gi
kin$_5$-ak
23. 2 *gu-lí-lum*
*Ib-rí-um*
25. *áš-du*
2 *gu-lí-lum-sù*
27. sikil
$^{dʾ}$*À-da*
29. *al*$_6$
tu-ra
31. en

(81)
10 ma-na kù:babbar
XIII. 1. šu-bal-ak
2 ma-na k[ù-gi]
3. 1 dib
*Ib-rí-um*
5. *áš-du*
1 dib-*sù*
7. sikil
$^{dʾ}$*À-da*
9. *al*$_6$
tu-ra
11. en

(82)
5 gín DILMUN kù:babbar
13. šu-bal-ak
1 gín DILMUN kù-gi
15. *ni-zi-mu*
1 dib
17. *Ù-ti*

(83)
ŠÚ+ŠA 5 gín DILMUN kù:babbar
19. šu-bal-ak
5 gín DILMUN kù-gi
21. ʾ*a*$_5$*-na-gu*
1 ĜIŠ-banšur
23. *wa*
1 kù-sal
25. sikil
*al*$_6$
27. ama-gal
en
29. $^{d}$*Ra-sa-ap*
ʾ*À-da-ni*$^{ki}$

(84)
XIV. 1. 2 gín DILMUN kù:babbar
1 buru$_4$-MU[ŠEN]
3. [ ]
[níĝ-]ba
5. $^{d}$*Áš-da-bíl*
*Ba-šè*$^{ki}$
7. *Ib-rí-um*
šu-mu-tak$_4$

(85)
9. 5 gín DILMUN kù:babbar
šu-bal-ak
11. 1 gín DILMUN kù-gi
*ni-zi-mu*
13. 1 dib
*Iš*$_{11}$*-gi-bar-zú*
15. lú
*Sá-gú-šum*

(86)
17. 10 gín DILMUN kù:babbar
ZU.PIRIĜ
19. kin$_5$-ak
3 útul urudu maḫ
21. 1 ma-na TAR kù:babbar
šu-bal-ak
23. 18 gín DILMUN kù-gi
nu$_{11}$-za
25. 4 sur$_x$-lu$_x$
lú *al*$_6$
27. ĜIŠ-ĝidru-ĜIŠ-ĝidru

(80) 10 minas of silver in exchange for 2 minas of gold for making 2 bracelets for Ibrium, as replacement of his 2 bracelets (given for) the purification rite to the god Hadda, in relation to the illness of the king.
(81) 10 minas of silver in exchange for 2 minas of g[old] for 1 plaque for Ibrium, as replacement of his plaque (given for) the purification rite to the god Hadda, in relation to the illness of the king.
(82) 5 shekels of silver in exchange for 1 shekel of gold for decorating 1 plaque for Uti.
(83) 25 shekels of silver in exchange for 5 shekels of gold for the circular stand of a table and 1 buckle (given for) the purification rite, on the account of king's mother to the god Rašap of the city of ʾAdani.
(84) 2 shekels of silver for 1 shie[ld …: gi]ft for the god Ašdabil of the city of Baše, Ibrium has handed over.
(85) 5 shekels of silver in exchange for 1 shekel of gold for decorating 1 plaque for Išgibarzu, (son) of Sagušum.
(86) 10 shekels of silver for the hangers for making 3 big kettles of copper; 1;30 minas of silver in exchange for 18 shekels of gold for plating 4 androcephalus bulls on the sticks of the throne of the king.

XV. 1. ĜIŠ-uštil
en

(87)
3. 4 ma-na [10 gín DILMUN kù:babbar]
šu-bal-ak
5. 50 gín DILMUN kù-gi
1 dib
7. *Ḫáb-ra-ar*
lú *Ib-ga-iš-lu*

(88)
9. 50 gín DILMUN kù:babbar
šu-bal-ak
11. 10 gín DILMUN kù-gi
*zi-ba-du*
13. 1 *gú-bù* kù-gi libir
1 ma-na kù:babbar
15. níĝ-sa$_{10}$ 1 ĝír mar-tu kù-gi
en
17. *áš-du*
ĝír mar-tu-*sù*
19. sikil
XVI. 1. $^{dʾ}$*A*$_5$*-da-"bal"*
*Lu-ba-an*$^{ki}$

(89)
3. 1 [ma-]n[a] kù:babbar
[níĝ-sa$_{10}$ 1 ĝír mar-t]u kù-gi
5. *Ib-rí-um*
*áš-du*
7. ĝír mar-tu-*sù*
sikil
9. $^{d}$*Áš-da-bíl*
*al*$_6$
11. tu-ra
en

(90)
13. 2 ma-na kù:babbar
in-na-sum
15. *si-in*
šu-bal-ak
17. kù-gi
lú $^{d}$*Ra-sa-ap*
19. *Du-ne-íb*$^{ki}$
lú *Da*-NE-*du*
21. *Kab-lu*$_5$*-ul*$^{ki}$

(91)
1 ma-na ŠÚ+ŠA 3 gín DILMUN
kù:babbar
XVII. 1. níĝ-ba-níĝ-ba
diĝir-diĝir-diĝir
(blank)

(92)
XVIII. 1. AN.ŠÈ.GÚ 2 ⌜*mi-at*⌝ 32 ma-na
kù:babbar
è
3. 1 mu
⌜*ap*⌝
5. ⌜3⌝ *mi-at* 50 ma-na kù:babbar
al$_6$-ĝál
(blank)

(87) 4[;10] minas [of silver] in exchange for 50 shekels of gold for 1 plaque for Ḫabrar, (son) of Ibga-išlu.
(88) 50 shekels of silver in exchange for 10 shekels of gold for the handle of 1 old *gú-bú* vessel (decorated with) gold; 1 mina of silver for the purchase of 1 mar-tu dagger (decorated with) gold for the king, as replacement of his mar-tu dagger (given for) the purification rite to the god ʾAdabal of the city of Luban.
(89) 1 [mi]n[a] of silver [for the purchase of 1 mar-t]u [dagger] (decorated with) gold for Ibrium, as replacement of his mar-tu dagger (given for) the purification rite to the god Ašdabil, in relation to the illness of the king.
(90) 2 minas of silver given to be changed into gold for the god Rašap of the city of Tunip, DaNEdu of the city of Kablul.
(91) 1;23 minas of silver: gift for the gods.
(92) Total: 232 minas of silver: expenditure for 1 year, and 350 minas of silver are present.

## Commentary

This document registers the end of the war against Kiš, which was ended with its defeat; it must therefore be dated to the year Ibr. 12. The expended silver this year (è 1 mu) amounted to 232 minas (109.040 kg), and that "present", al$_6$-ĝál, in the Treasury was 350 minas (164.500), (§ 92).

The registration of the expenditure of 1 mina (470 g) of silver for the renewal rite concerning the city-god Kura, which fell at the beginning of the new year, opens this text as in the other annual documents. The 3 shekels (23 g) of silver to be given to the god for a ceremony which fell in a later period of the year are registered in § 36. Kura also received a pair of gold bracelets of 6 ⅔ shekels (52 g) twice as annual offering (§§ 18, 42), and the "gods", diĝir-diĝir-diĝir, 1;23 minas (650 g) of silver (§ 91). Tinib-dulum, a sister of the king, received 12 minas (5.640 kg) of silver in her function as priestess of the god ᵓAdabal (§ 2).

It was Dašna, a messenger of Mari, who announced that Kiš had been "defeated", til (§ 8). This war had started two years earlier (see the commentary to text no. 14). Warutum (also a messenger from Mari who often travelled to Ebla) confirmed that "Kiš had been conquered" (§ 20). He received a supplementary gift of 20 shekels (157 g) of silver, when "he came back (a second time) from Kiš together with Nazumu" (§ 47). This Nazumu – an envoy from Ebla – who had already been sent to Kiš two years earlier (Ibr. 10), was provided with a mule (text no. 13 §§ 49, 65). In Kiš the preceding year, he had ransomed Damda-il of the city of Ibsu, paying 20 shekels of silver: *Dam-da-il Ib-su*$^{ki}$ *in* Kiš$^{ki}$ lú *Na-zu-mu* níĝ-du$_8$ (text no. 12 § 50; Ibr. 09). Dašna also returned to Ebla this year a second time with more information: Kiš had been completely defeated, níĝ-"mul" Kiš$^{ki}$ til-til, and he received 1 mina (470 g) of silver (§ 74). At this point Ebla decided to send one of his agents, Enna-i(l), to become directly aware of the situation; he received the usual travel provision of 5 shekels (39 g) of silver (§ 75).

An element of the king's chariot had to be replaced with the expenditure of 2 shekels (16 g), of silver (§ 24), and also other parts of his chariots needed decorations (§ 26). The king received a big axe with a necklace, for which one needed 1 mina (470 g) of copper and 10 shekels (78 g) of tin, besides 1 shekel (8 g) of silver for its decoration (§ 52). Two white goat skins were bought at the market of the Palace for the harness of the king (§ 55). He also received a table and a buckle decorated with 3 shekels (23 g) of gold (§ 65), and a vessel, with its lid, in gold, whose weight was 50 shekels (391 g), (§ 68). Ten shekels (78 g) of silver were used for the decoration of three big vessels, while a quadriga that decorated the king's throne was plated with 18 shekels (141 g) of gold (§ 86). The king fell ill: for this reason, he dedicated several objects to the gods Hadda (§§ 80, 81), and Ašdabil (§ 89). Two king's sons, Ilum-aḫi and Iᵓin-Hadda, (already mentioned together in text no. 13 § 69, from the year Ibr. 10) each received two bags decorated with a small amount of silver (§ 16).

Ibrium received a new harness, for which 2 shekels (16 g) of gold and 5 shekels (39 g) of silver were employed (§ 11); other elements of this chariot needed 1.394 kg of gold (§ 26). The minister further received two "travel (kaskal) cups, for which 2 shekels (16 g) of silver were utilized (§ 45). Another vessel and its lid required 40 shekels (313 g) of gold (§ 50). An old vessel for the minister, with the image of a statue, was decorated with 7 shekels (55 g) of gold (§ 69).

Ibbi-zikir, Ibrium's son, received a decoration for his chariot of 1 shekel (8 g) of gold (§ 23). Small amounts of silver and gold were needed for the decoration of a belt and a sheath respectively for Ir-damu, and Giᵓir-damu, another two of Ibrium's sons (§ 44). They, together with Napḫa-il, their brother, received some jewels decorated with 8 shekels (63 kg) of gold (§ 64).

The messengers from Mari who came to Ebla where: *Daš-na* (§§ 8, 74), *Wa-ru*$_{12}$*-tum* (§§ 20, 47), *Iš-dub-il* with *Dab*$_6$*-ti*, (§ 21) who acted as a representative of (Wabarum), the "travelling merchant", ga-eš$_8$, of Tuttul.

§§ 4, 25. The king of Ušḫulum received 2 shekels (16 g) of gold, and a "goblet", zi-bar, of 3 shekels (24 g) of gold.

§§ 13, 66. Dusigu, the king's mother, received a stick and two necklaces, for which 3 shekels (23 g) of gold were needed, and further a dagger and a buckle decorated with 2 ⅔ shekels (19 g) of gold.

§ 14. Dubuḫu-Hadda, the young son of Ibbi-zikir, whom his father will later appoint as his successor as minister, received a plaque of 10 shekels (78 g) of gold.

§§ 15, 28. Tarib-damu, a daughter of the king, received a plaque of 10 shekels (78 g) of gold, and some jewels for which 14 shekels (109 g) of gold were employed.

§ 30. Arzadu, a daughter of the princess (dam en) Enna-$^{d}$Utu, received a substantial number of jewels for which 1;14 minas (580 g) of gold were employed, together with two toggle-pins whose heads were plated with gold. She has probably to be identified with the "sister of the king", nin-ni en, mentioned in texts nos. 16 and 18. A "daughter of the king" also bore this name (see Archi 1988, pp. 238-239).

§ 35. Iˀin-il, the "overseer", ugula, of the city of Ušalik, "resided", tuš-LÚ×TIL, in Kakmium.

§ 41. A "watchman", ME-sig, received twenty daggers decorated with silver.

§ 46. Zimini-kubabbar, queen of Burman (an Eblaite princess) received two toggle-pins of 20 shekels (157 g) of silver, whose heads were decorated with 3 shekels (23 g) of gold, because she gave birth to a daughter.

§§ 59, 77. Tabur-damu, who will marry king Išʿar-damu in the year Ibr. 14, presented to the god Utu of the Palace a buckle of 1 shekel (8 g), and received two foot rings of 2 shekels (16 g) of gold. She was the daughter of Irib-damu, a brother of Irkab-damu, who was still alive at the time of minister Ibbi-zikir, see TM.75.G.2504 r. VII 10–15: 2 *bu*-DI NE-*ti-bù-du* 1 dam *Ìr-ib-da-mu* a-mu *ma-lik-tum*. On this queen, see Archi 2021b, p. 15.

§ 60. The queen of Irar received from the king's mother two toggle-pins of 20 shekels (157 g) of silver, whose heads were decorated with 3 shekels (23 g) of gold, when she went to Gawana, perhaps a cult-place of the goddess Išḫara (cf. *ARET* IX 17 § 11: $^{d}$BARA$_{10}$-*iš ga-wa-nu*).

§ 63. Ebla sent two toggle-pins of 20 shekels (157 g) of silver, whose heads were decorated with 3 shekels (23 g) of gold, for the funerary rites., É×PAP, of Natum, the queen of Burman.

§ 78. The theonym *Da-bí-ir* is also a personal name, see *ARET* XV 4 o. V 1; 43 o. VI 2: *Da-bí-ra* (this a FPN).

§ 82. Uti, the son of Ibrium, received a plaque decorated with 1 shekel (8 g) of gold.

# 16
## (Plates XXX–XXXI)

(1)

o. I. 1. [1] ma-na kù:babbar
saĝ kù:babbar
3. $^{d}$*Ku-ra*

(2)

14 ma-na kù:babbar
5. [*Di-ni-í*]*b*-[*d*]*u-lum*
nin-ni
7. en
⸢šu⸣-ba$_4$-ti
9. 1 ma-na kù:babbar
*Dar-ib-da-mu*
11. nin-ni-*sù*
⸢šu⸣-ba$_4$-ti

(3)

13. 6 ma-na kù:babbar
šu-bal-ak
15. 1 ma-na 12 gín DILMUN kù-gi 1 dib
*Ru*$_{12}$*-zi-da-mu*
17. en
*Ì-mar*$^{ki}$

(4)

19. 10 ma-na TAR kù:babbar
1 ĜIŠ-šú 1 níĝ-bànda 10 kù:babbar
kù-gi
II. 1. ama-gal
en

(5)

3. 20 ma-na kù:babbar
níĝ-sa$_{10}$
5. ⸢1⸣ *li-im* 2 *mi-at* ma-na a-gar$_5$-gar$_5$
2 gín DILMUN kù:babbar
7. 1 á-MUŠEN
1 gín DILMUN kù:babbar
9. šu-bal-ak
5 NI kù-gi
11. saĝ-*sù*
níĝ-ba
13. ama-gal
en
15. $^{d}$TU
é
17. $^{d}$*Ku-ra*

(6)

7 ½ gín DILMUN kù:babbar
19. šu-bal-ak
1 ½ gín DILMUN kù-gi
21. kin$_5$-ak
6 *da-ne-a-tum*
23. *si-ti-tum*
ama-gal
25. en

(7)

III. 1. ⸢15⸣ gín [DILMUN] kù:babbar
šu-[bal-]ak
3. 3 gín DILMUN kù-gi
4 ĝeštu$_x$-lá
5. *Dar-ib-da-mu*
*wa*
7. *Tíš-te-da-mu*
10 gín DILMUN kù:babbar
9. šu-bal-ak
2 gín DILMUN kù-gi
11. 2 kù-sal
*Tíš-te-da-mu*
13. 2 dumu-munus
en

(1) [1] mina of silver for the silver head of the god Kura.
(2) 14 minas of silver: [Tini]b-[d]ulum, sister of the king, has received; 1 mina of silver: Tarib-damu, her sister, has received.
(3) 6 minas of silver in exchange for 1;12 minas of gold for 1 plaque for Ruzi-damu, the king of the city of Imar.
(4) 10;30 minas of silver for 1 GIŠ-šú vessel (and) 1 níg-bànda vessel: (the remaining) 10 (shekels of) silver (are to be exchanged for 2 shekels of) gold (for their decoration) for the king's mother.
(5) 20 minas of silver for the purchase of 1200 minas of copper; 2 shekels of silver for 1 helmet; 1 shekel of silver in exchange for 5 NI of gold for its head: gift of the king's mother for the goddess TU, (in) the temple of the god Kura.
(6) 7 ½ shekels of silver in exchange for 1 ½ shekel of gold for making 6 … (*da-ne-a-tum*) of the sheath for the king's mother.
(7) 15 shekels of silver in ex[chan]ge for 3 shekels of gold for 4 earrings for Tarib-damu and Tište-damu; 10 shekels of silver in exchange for 2 shekels of gold for 2 buckles for Tište-damu, 2 daughters of the king.

(8)

15. 11 gín DILMUN an-na
šub *si-in*
17. *zi-ba-ti*
1 útul urudu maḫ
19. 5 gín DILMUN kù:babbar
ZU.PIRIĜ-*sù*
21. 1 ma-na ŠÚ+ŠA 5 gín DILMUN
kù:babbar
níĝ-sa$_{10}$
IV. 1. 1 *mi-at* 70 siki na$_4$ *Ma-rí*$^{ki}$
TAR kù:babbar
3. níĝ-sa$_{10}$ ĜIŠ-ti-ḪAR
BAD.MUŠ.LU$_5$
5. šu-ba$_4$-ti
ki:lam$_7$
7. šeš-II-ib
*ᵓÀ-da-ni*$^{ki}$

(9)

9. 3 ma-na TAR 2 gín DILMUN
kù:babbar
níĝ-sa$_{10}$ 12 aktum<-TÚG> 1 zara$_6$-
TÚG 1 túg-NI.NI *Ma-rí*$^{ki}$
11. 2 *ᵓà-da-um*-TÚG-I
2 níĝ-lá-gaba
13. 3 *mi-at* 20 siki na$_4$ *Ma-rí*$^{ki}$
15 gín DILMUN kù:babbar
15. níĝ-sa$_{10}$ 65 *ra-ᵓà-tum*
*in*
17. Kiš$^{ki}$
dam-gàr

(10)

V. 1. ŠÚ+ŠA gín DILMUN kù:babbar
2 *bu*-DI
3. *Da-dub*
dam
5. en
lú *A-ru*$_{12}$*-ga-du*$^{ki}$

(11)

7. 7 ma-na TAR kù:babbar
nu$_{11}$-za 1 an-dùl
9. 10 ma-na ŠÚ+ŠA 5 gín DILMUN
kù:babbar
šu-bal-ak
11. 2 ma-na 5 gín DILMUN kù-gi
nu$_{11}$-za IGI.DUB-*sù*
13. *wa*
2 DU-*sù*
15. *wa*
2 šu-*sù*
17. níĝ-ba
$^{d}$BAD *Ga-na-na-im*

(12)

19. 3 gín DILMUN kù:babbar
saĝ kù:babbar
21. $^{d}$*Ku-ra*
mu-ti-II

(13)

23. 2 ma-na 5 gín DILMUN babbar:kù
VI. 1. šu-bal-ak
ŠÚ+ŠA 5 gín DILMUN kù-gi
3. *ni-zi-mu*
2 níĝ-anše-ak 4 kù-sal libir
5. *Ib-rí-um*

(14)

2 ma-na 15 gín DILMUN kù:babbar
7. šu-bal-ak
ŠÚ+ŠA 7 gín DILMUN kù-gi
9. nu$_{11}$-za 2 ĜIŠ.GAM.GAM
7 gín DILMUN kù:babbar
11. šu-bal-ak
1 ½ gín DILMUN kù-gi
13. nu$_{11}$-za 1 zag
5 gín DILMUN an-na
15. šub *si-in*
1 ĜIŠ-zú
17. 1 ĜIŠ-gígir-II
12 ma-na TAR kù:babbar
19. šu-bal-ak
2 ma-na TAR kù-gi
21. kin$_5$-ak
VII. 1. 2 níĝ-anše-ak 4 kù-sal

(8) 11 shekels of tin to be melted in a handle of 1 big kettle of copper; 5 shekels of silver for its hangers; 1;25 minas of silver for the purchase of 170 stone weights of wool from the city of Mari; 30 (shekels of) silver for the purchase of GIŠ-ti-ḪAR-wood: BAD.MUŠ.LU has received, at the market of the šeš-II-ib confraternity of the city of ᵓAdani.

(9) 3;32 minas of silver for the purchase of 18 garments (and) 320 stone weights of wool from the city of Mari; 15 shekels of silver for the purchase of 65 shells, at <the market of> the city of Kiš, the merchant(s) (have handed over).

(10) 20 shekels of silver for 2 toggle-pins for Dadub, the spouse of the king of the city of Arugadu.

(11) 7;30 minas of silver for plating 1 statue; 10;25 minas of silver in exchange for 2;05 minas of gold for plating its face and its 2 hands and feet: gift for the Lord of Ganana.

(12) 3 shekels of silver for the silver head of the god Kura: second delivery.

(13) 2;05 minas of silver in exchange for 25 shekels of gold for decorating 2 old bridles (and) 4 buckles of Ibrium.

(14) 2;15 minas of silver in exchange for 27 shekels of gold for plating 2 wheels; 7 shekels of silver in exchange for 1 ½ shekel of gold for plating 1 side; 5 shekels of tin to be melted in 1 hook of a chariot; 12;30 minas of silver in exchange for 2;30 minas of gold for making 2 new bridles (and) 4 buckles for Ibrium.

gibil
3. *Ib-rí-um*

(15)
10 gín DILMUN kù:babbar
5. šu-bal-ak
2 gín DILMUN kù-gi
7. *ni-zi-mu*
2 níĝ-anše-ak 4 kù-sal
9. 2 IGI.NITA
*Ib-rí-um*

(16)
11. 2 ma-na TAR 5 gín DILMUN
kù:babbar
šu-bal-ak
13. TAR 1 gín DILMUN kù-gi
*ni-zi-mu*
15. 2 dib lú <1> ma-na
3 dib lú 50 gín DILMUN
17. 8 dib lú ŠA.PI gín DILMUN
3 dib lú TAR.TAR
19. 3 dib lú ŠÚ+ŠA gín DILMUN
6 gín DILMUN kù:babbar
VIII. 1. *ni-zi-mu*
7 íb-lá 5 ĝír-kun
3. lú URI
lú kù-gi
5. TAR kù:babbar
šu-bal-ak
7. 6 gín DILMUN kù-gi
*ni-zi-mu*
9. nu$_{11}$-za-*sù*
10 gín DILMUN kù:babbar
11. *ni-zi-mu*
8 á-MUŠEN kù:babbar
13. 12 gín DILMUN kù:babbar
*ni-zi-mu*
15. 17 íb-lá maš-maš kù-gi
10 gín DILMUN kù:babbar
17. šu-bal-ak
2 gín DILMUN kù-gi
19. *ni-zi-mu*
maš-maš-*sù*
21. 52 gín DILMUN kù:babbar
*ni-zi-mu*
23. 32 ĝír
IX. 1. 55 íb-lá kù:babbar
10 gín DILMUN kù:babbar
3. *ni-zi-mu*
3 *gú-li-lum* kù:babbar ŠA.PI-II
5. 2 *gú-li-lum* kù:babbar TAR-II
15 *gú-li-lum* kù:babbar ŠÚ+ŠA-II
7. 7 *gú-li-lum* 11 kù:babbar
3 ma-na 5 gín kù:babbar
9. šu-bal-ak
TAR 7 gín DILMUN kù-gi
11. *ni-zi-mu*
nu$_{11}$-za-*sù*
13. 2 ma-na ŠA.PI gín DILMUN
kù:babbar
šu-bal-a[k]
X. 1. TAR 2 gín DILMUN kù-gi
*ni-zi-mu*
3. nu$_{11}$-za
6 *gú-li-lum* a-gar$_5$-gar$_5$ TAR-II
5. 14 *gú-li-lum* a-gar$_5$-gar$_5$ ŠÚ+ŠA-II
5 *gú-li-lum* a-gar$_5$-gar$_5$ 10-I
7. 2 gín DILMUN kù:babbar
*ni-zi-mu*
9. nu$_{11}$-za
3 *gú-li-lum* a-gar$_5$-gar$_5$ 10-I
11. 15 gín DILMUN kù:babbar
ZU.PIRIĜ
13. 13 á-MUŠEN zabar
TAR an-na
15. SUD.PA.SIKIL
5 íb-lá 20 ĝír-kun zabar
17. 35 á-MUŠEN zabar
XI. 1. 1 ma-na TAR an-na
šub *si-in*
3. [x ma-na (x gín DILMUN) a-gar$_5$-
gar$_5$]
[x ma-na (x gín DILMUN)
kù:babbar]
5. [šu-bal-ak]

(15) 10 shekels of silver in exchange for 2 shekels of gold for decorating 2 bridles (and) 4 buckles for 2 donkeys of Ibrium.

(16) 2;35 minas of silver in exchange for 31 shekels of gold for decorating 2 plaques of <1> mina each; 3 plaques of 50 shekels each, 8 plaques of 40 shekels each, 3 plaques of 30 (shekels) each, 3 plaques of 20 shekels each; 6 shekels of silver for decorating 7 belts (and) 5 dagger pendants with a URI-decoration of gold; 30 (shekels of) silver in exchange for 6 shekels of gold for decorating their lamination; 10 shekels of silver for decorating 8 shields of silver; 12 shekels of silver for decorating 17 belts with a striped (decoration) of gold; 10 shekels of silver in exchange for 2 shekels of gold for its striped decoration; 52 shekels of silver for decorating 32 daggers (and) 55 belts (decorated with) silver; 10 shekels of silver for decorating 3 double bracelets of 40 (shekels of) silver each, 2 double bracelets of 30 (shekels of) silver each, 15 double bracelets of 20 (shekels of) silver each, 7 bracelets of 11 (shekels of) silver each; 3;05 minas of silver in exchange for 37 shekels of gold for decorating their lamination; 2;40 minas of silver in exchange for 32 shekels of gold for decorating with lamination 6 double bracelets of 30 (shekels of) copper each, 14 double bracelets of 20 (shekels of) copper each, 5 single bracelets of 10 (shekels of) copper each; 2 shekels of silver for decorating with lamination 3 single bracelets of 10 (shekels of) copper each; 15 shekels of silver for the hangers of 13 bronze helmets; 30 (shekels of) tin for the … (SUD.PA.SIKIL)

TAR[(+x)] kù-g[i]
7. *zi-ba-d[u]*
14 ĝír mar-tu kù-gi
9. 7 ĝír mar-tu ti kù-gi
17 ĝír mar-tu zú LAGAB×A kù-gi
11. 6 gín DILMUN kù:babbar
*ni-zi-mu*
13. nu$_{11}$-za
12 ĝír mar-tu kù:babbar
15. lú ĝuruš-ĝuruš
*A-zi-mu-tum*

(17)
17. 1 ma-na 50 gín DILMUN <an-na>
XII. 1. šub *si-in*
3[+3[?] ma-n]a [T]AR gín DILMUN ⌜a⌝-gar$_5$-gar$_5$
3. *ni-zi-mu*
ZA$_x$-ZA$_x$
5. naĝar-naĝar

(18)
[(ca. 5 lines)]
11[?]. [d]*Ku-ra*

(19)
5 gín DILMUN kù:babbar
13. šu-bal-ak
1 gín DILMUN kù-gi
15. *ni-zi-mu*
nu$_{11}$-za 2 ĝír
17. lú ZA$_x$
*Ib-rí-um*

(20)
19. 7 ma-na 10 gín DILMUN kù:babbar
níĝ-sa$_{10}$
XIII. 1. [ ]
[ -]*ma*-[x]
3. ugula sur$_x$-B[AR.AN]
*Zú-ba[-núm]*

5. *in*
*Na-gàr*[ki]

(21)
7. 6 ma-na kù:babbar
[ní]g-sa$_{10}$ [x[?]+]2 BAR.AN
9. *Na-gàr*[ki]
[TA]R [3] gín DILMUN kù:b[abbar]
11. [šu-bal-]ak
6 gín DILMUN 2 NI kù-gi 2
*gú-li[-lum]*
13. <x gín DILMUN kù:babbar> níĝ-sa$_{10}$
24 túg-NI.NI
30 gada-TÚG
15. 3 níĝ-lá-gaba
TAR 4 gín DILMUN kù:babbar
17. níĝ-sa$_{10}$ raš-SAR Kur[ki]
ki:lam$_7$
19. *ᵓÀ-da-ni*[ki]
[d]AMA-*ra*

(22)
21. TAR kù:babbar 1 íb-lá 1 *si-ti-tum* 1 ĝír-kun
XIV. 1. [(ca. 6 lines)]
8.[?] *ᵓa$_5$-⌜na⌝[-gu]-sù*

(23)
9. 2 ½ gín DILMUN kù:babbar
šu-bal-ak
11. ½ gín kù-gi 1 kù-sal
[[d]*A-dar-a-an*]
13. *Da-na-áš*[ki]
en
15. šu-mu-tak$_4$

(24)
TAR kù:babbar
17. níĝ-ba
*Wa-ru$_{12}$-tum*
19. *Ma-rí*[ki]

of 5 belts (and) 20 dagger pendants of bronze, 35 helmets of bronze; 1;30 minas of tin to be melted with [x minas of copper; x;xx mina of silver in exchange for] 30[+x] (shekels of) gol[d] for the handles of 14 mar-tu daggers (decorated with) gold, 7 pointed mar-tu daggers (decorated with) gold, 17 mar-tu daggers (decorated with) ivory (and) gold; 6 shekels of silver for decorating with lamination 12 mar-tu daggers (decorated with) silver: for the men of Azimutum.

(17) 1;50 minas <of tin> to be melted with 6;[30 min]as of copper for decorating objects of the carpenters.

(18) […] the god Kura.

(19) 5 shekels of silver in exchange for 1 shekel of gold for decorating with lamination 2 daggers, property of Ibrium.

(20) 7;10 minas of silver for the purchase of […] […], the overseer of the m[ule] teams of Zuba[num] in the city of Nagar.

(21) 6 minas of silver for the purchase of [x+]2 mules (from) the city of Nagar; [33] shekels of sil[ver in exchan]ge for 6 shekels (and) 2 NI of gold for 2 bracel[ets]; <x silver> for the purchase of 57 garments; 34 shekels of silver for the purchase of leek from the mountain region: at the market of the city of ᵓAdani, at the AMA-ra (festival).

(22) 30 (shekels of) silver for 1 belt, 1 sheath (and) 1 dagger pendant […] for its circular stand.

(23) 2 ½ shekels of silver in exchange for ½ shekel of gold for 1 buckle [for the god Adaranu] of the city of Današ, the king has handed over.

(24) 30 (shekels of) silver: gift for Warutum of the city of Mari (who) had handed over a present.

šu-mu-tak$_4$
21. igi-du$_8$

(25)
13 gín DILMUN kù:babbar
23. nu$_{11}$-za
1 *ḫa-bù*
25. TAR kù:babbar
šu-bal-ak
r. I. 1. 6 gín DILMUN kù-gi
nu$_{11}$-za
3. 1 *ar-ra-sù*
ŠÚ+ŠA gín DILMUN kù:babbar
5. *ʾa$_5$-na-gu*
si 2 gud
7. nídba
en
9. $^{d}$*Ra-sa-ap*
*ʾÀ-da-ni*$^{ki}$

(26)
11. 13 gín DILMUN kù:babbar
nu$_{11}$-za 1 *ḫa-bù*
13. *ap*
kù-gi ˹sikil˺
15. ŠÚ+ŠA 5 gín DILMUN kù:babbar
*ʾa$_5$-na-gu*
17. si 2 gud
[níd]ba
19. en
$^{d}$*ʾÀ-da*
21. *in*
$^{d}$AMA-*ra*

(27)
23. ŠÚ+ŠA 5 gín DILMUN kù:babbar
nu$_{11}$-[za] 6 níĝ-[ ]
25. [ ]
[ ]
II. 1. 10 gín DILMUN kù:babbar
*ni-zi-mu*
3. 10 ĝeštu$_x$-lá
5 gín DILMUN kù:babbar
5. šu-bal-ak
1 gín DILMUN kù-gi
7. *ni-zi-mu*
1 kù-sal
9. *Di-ni-íb-du-lum*
nin-ni
11. en

(28)
ŠÚ+ŠA gín DILMUN kù:babbar
13. níĝ-du$_8$
3 *na-se*$_{11}$
15. *Ib-la*$^{ki}$
*áš-ti*
17. *Ir-i-tum*$^{ki}$
*Mi-ga-ì*
19. lú gud-gud
[šu]-ba$_4$-ti

(29)
21. 10 gín DIL[MUN] kù:babbar
níĝ-sa$_{10}$ še-in
23. *I-ba-zi-mi-nu*
ugula ir$_{11}$

(30)
25. 1 ma-na ŠA.PI gín DILMUN kù:babbar
šu-ba[l-ak]
III. 1. [ŠÚ+ŠA k]ù-gi
*ni-zi-mu*
3. *su-da-*˹*nu*˺$^?$
*wa*
5. 4 kù-sal-*sù*
en

(31)
7. 5 gín DILMUN kù:babbar
šu-bal-ak
9. 1 gín DILMUN kù-gi
*ni-zi-mu*
11. maš-maš kù-sal
ama-gal
13. en

(25) 13 shekels of silver for plating 1 mace; 30 (shekels of) silver in exchange for 6 shekels of gold for plating its handle; 20 shekels of silver for the circular stand of the (4) horns of 2 bulls: offering of the king for the god Rašap of the city of ʾAdani.

(26) 13 shekels of silver for plating 1 mace, and also pure gold; 25 shekels of silver for the circular stand of the (4) horns of 2 bulls: [offe]ring of the king for the god Hadda, at the AMA-ra (festival).

(27) 25 shekels of silver for pla[ting] 6 [...]; 10 shekels of silver for decorating 10 earrings; 5 shekels of silver in exchange for 1 shekel of gold for decorating 1 buckle for Tinib-dulum, sister of the king.

(28) 20 shekels of silver for the ransom of 3 people of the city of Ebla from the city of Iritum: Miga-i(l), (the overseer) of the oxen, [has] received.

(29) 10 shekels of silver for the purchase of straw: Ibazi-minu, the overseer of the servants (has received).

(30) 1;40 minas of silver in excha[nge for 20 (shekels of) g]old for decorating the ... (*su-da-nu*) and its 4 buckles for the king.

(31) 5 shekels of silver in exchange for 1 shekel of gold for a striped (decoration) of a buckle for the king's mother.

(32)
2 gín DILMUN kù:babbar
15. *ni-zi-mu*
*ma-wa-lu*
17. 10 gín DILMUN kù:babbar
šu-bal-ak
19. 2 gín DILMUN kù-gi
*ni-zi-mu*
21. *ma-wa-lu*
ĜIŠ-bar-ús
23. ĜIŠ-gígir-II
en

(33)
25. 17 gín DILMUN kù:babbar
níĝ-sa$_{10}$ 1 ĝír mar-tu ti kù-gi
27. *Bu$_x$-ma-ì*
NE-di

(34)
29. 1 ma-na ŠA.PI gín DILMUN
IV. 1. kù:babbar
šu-bal-ak
3. ŠÚ+ŠA gín DILMUN kù-gi
1 dib
5. *Ḫa-bù-zú*
*ʾÀ-bar-du$^{ki}$*
7. maškim
*Za-ba-rúm*
9 tuš-LÚ×TIL
*Ḫal-sum$^{ki}$*

(35)
11. 1 ma-na 50 gín DILMUN kù:babbar
šu-bal-ak
13. ŠÚ+ŠA 2 gín DILMUN kù-gi
*ni-zi-mu*
15. 1 dib
*Íl-a-i-šar*
17. di-kud

(36)
1 ma-na ŠA.PI 1 gín DILMUN
kù:babbar
19. níĝ-sa$_{10}$ 6 IGI.NITA u$_5$
[x+]2 gín DILMUN kù:babbar
21. [ ]
[ ]
23. [š]u-ba$_4$-t[i]
ki:lam$_7$
25. ⸢é⸣?
*mi-i*[*š*-x]

(37)
V. 1. 3 gín DILMUN an-na
šub *si-in*
3. 17 gín DILMUN a-gar$_5$-gar$_5$
kin$_5$-ak
5. 6 ĜIŠ-kak-ĜIŠ-kak
lú 2 asari
7. kaskal
en

(38)
9. 10 gín DILMUN kù:babbar
šu-bal-ak
11. 2 gín DILMUN kù-gi
*ni-zi-mu*
13. 1 dib
*En-na-ì*
15. lú *Rí-ì-ma-lik*

(39)
5 gín DILMUN kù:babbar
17. šu-bal-ak
1 gín DILMUN kù-gi
19. *ni-zi-mu*
1 dib
21. *Bar-za-ma-ù*
ugula *A-ru$_{12}$-ga-du$^{ki}$*

(40)
23. 10 gín DILMUN kù:babbar
šu-bal-ak
25. 2 gín DILMUN kù-gi
*ni-zi-mu*
27. 1 dib
*Ir-ti*

(32) 2 shekels of silver for decorating the … (*ma-wa-lu*); 10 shekels of silver in exchange for 2 shekels of gold for decorating the … (*ma-wa-lu*) of the goads of the chariot of the king.
(33) 17 shekels of silver for the purchase of 1 pointed mar-tu dagger (decorated with) gold for Buma-i(l), the dancer.
(34) 1;40 minas of silver in exchange for 20 shekels of gold for 1 plaque for Ḫabuzu of the city of ʾAbardu, representative of Zabarum, (who) occupied the city of Ḫalsum.
(35) 1;50 minas of silver in exchange for 22 shekels of gold for decorating 1 plaque for Ila-išar, the judge.
(36) 1;41 minas of silver for the purchase of 6 donkeys to ride; [x+]2 shekels of silver […] [… h]as receiv[ed], at the market of the temple of […].
(37) 3 shekels of tin to be melted with 17 shekels of copper for making 6 pegs of 2 travel trays for the king.
(38) 10 shekels of silver in exchange for 2 shekels of gold for decorating 1 plaque for Enna-i(l), (son) of Reʾi-malik.
(39) 5 shekels of silver in exchange for 1 shekel of gold for decorating 1 plaque for Barzamau, the overseer of the city of Arugadu.
(40) 10 shekels of silver in exchange for 2 shekels of gold for decorating 1 plaque for Irti; 10 shekels of silver in exchange for 2 shekels of gold as a replacement for 2 earrings of Giri, 2 sons of Ibrium.

29. 10 gín DILMUN
VI. 1. kù:babbar
šu-bal-ak
3. 2 gín DILMUN kù-gi
lul-gu-ak
5. 2 ĝeštu$_x$-lá
*Gi-rí*
7. 2 dumu-nita
*Ib-rí-um*

(41)
9. 5 gín DILMUN kù:babbar
šu-bal-ak
11. 1 gín DILMUN kù-gi
*ni-zi-mu*
13. nu$_{11}$-za 1 *za-ḫa-da*
*Ib-rí-um*

(42)
15. 3 gín DILMUN kù:babbar
lú ĜIŠ-nu-kiri$_6$
17. *Za-a-ti*
šu-ba$_4$-ti
19. *in*
*Ša-dab$_6$*$^{ki}$

(43)
21. TAR 3 gín DILMUN 3 NI kù:babbar
šu-bal-ak
23. 6 gín DILMUN 2 NI kù-gi 2 *gú-li-lum*
níĝ-ba
25. $^{d}$*Aš-da-bíl*
6 gín DILMUN 2 NI kù:babbar 2 *gú-li-lum*
VII. 1. níĝ-ba
$^{d}$*Am-rí-ig*

(44)
3. 10 gín DILMUN kù:babbar
*ni-zi-mu*
5. 2 níĝ-anše-ak ⸢4⸣ kù-sal
*Ìr-am$_6$-da-mu*
7. lú *Íl-zi*

(45)
2 gín DILMUN kù:babbar
9. 1 *ma-da-ḫu*
*Ar-za-du*
11. nin-ni
en

(46)
13. 12 gín DILMUN kù:babbar
nu$_{11}$-za
15. 1 *ḫa-bù*
TAR kù:babbar
17. šu-bal-ak
6 gín DILMUN kù-gi
19. nu$_{11}$-za
1 *ar-ra-sù*
21. níĝ-ba
$^{d?}$*À-da*
23. lú *Lu-ub*$^{ki}$
*in*
25. *gi*-NI

(47)
10 gín DILMUN kù:babbar
27. *ni-zi-mu*
nu$_{11}$-za
29. 2 ĝír mar-tu kù:babbar *wa*
VIII. 1. 3 ĝír mar-tu ti kù:babbar
*wa*
3. *ga-ma-tum*
17 ĝír mar-tu
5. 1 ma-na kù:babbar
šu-bal-ak
7. 12 gín DILMUN kù-gi
*ni-zi-mu*
9. nu$_{11}$-za
4 ĝír mar-tu kù-gi
11. *wa*
4 ĝír mar-tu ti kù-gi
13. *wa*
5 ĝír mar-tu *ba-du-u$_4$* kù-gi
15. *wa*
*ga-ma-tum*
17. 5 ĝír mar-tu kù:babbar

(41) 5 shekels of silver in exchange for 1 shekel of gold for decorating with lamination 1 battle-axe for Ibrium.
(42) 3 shekels of silver for the gardener(s): Zaᵓati has received in the city of Šadab.
(43) 33 shekels (and) 3 NI of silver in exchange for 6 shekels (and) 2 NI of gold for 2 bracelets: gift for the god Ašdabil; 6 shekels (and) 2 NI of silver for 2 bracelets: gift for the god Ammarik.
(44) 10 shekels of silver for decorating 2 bridles (and) 4 buckles for Iram-damu, (son) of Ilzi.
(45) 2 shekels of silver for 1 clip for Arzadu, sister of the king.
(46) 12 shekels of silver for plating 1 mace; 30 (shekels of) silver in exchange for 6 shekels of gold for plating its handle: gift for the god Hadda of the city of Lub, in month IV.
(47) 10 shekels of silver for decorating with lamination 2 mar-tu daggers (decorated with) silver and 3 pointed mar-tu daggers (decorated with) silver and the knobs of 17 mar-tu daggers; 1 mina of silver in exchange for 12 shekels of gold for decorating with lamination 4 mar-tu daggers (decorated with) gold and 4 pointed mar-tu daggers (decorated with) gold and 5 *b.* mar-tu daggers (decorated with) gold and the knobs of 5 mar-tu daggers (decorated with) silver: to be distributed to the men (sent) to the city of Ḫalsum as representatives.

lú ĝuruš-ĝuruš
19. tar-tar
*in*
21. maškim
*Ḫal-sum*$^{ki}$

(48)
23. 5 ma-na kù:babbar
šu-bal-ak
25. 1 ma-na kù-gi kin$_{5}$-ak
IX. 1. 2 níĝ-anše-ak 4 kù-sal
*I-bí-zi-kir*
3. dumu-nita
*Ib-rí-um*
5. *in* ud
tuš-LÚ×TIL
7. *Ḫal-sum*$^{ki}$

(49)
5 gín DILMUN kù:babbar
9. šu-bal-ak
1 gín DILMUN kù-gi
11. *ni-zi-mu*
1 šu-dub
13. ama-gal
en

(50)
15. 5 gín DILMUN kù:babbar
šu-bal-ak
17. 1 gín DILMUN kù-gi
1 íb-lá 1 *si-ti-tum* 1 ĝír-kun
19. níĝ-ba
*Ib-rí-um*
21. $^{d}$*Ra-sa-ap*
*Da-ra-um*$^{ki}$

(51)
23. 3 gín DILMUN kù:babbar
níĝ-sa$_{10}$ 1 *gàr-su*
25. dumu-nita
*Ig-rí-iš*
27. šu-du$_{8}$
*in*
29. *Ḫal-sum*$^{ki}$

(52)
11 gín DILMUN kù:babbar
X. 1. níĝ-sa$_{10}$ 2 na$_{4}$ 3
4 ma-na 10 gín DILMUN kù:babbar
3. šu-bal-ak
50 gín DILMUN kù-gi 1 dib
5. níĝ-ba
*ba-da-lum*
7. *Ḫa-ra-an*$^{ki}$

(53)
5 ma-na kù:babbar
9. níĝ-ba
*Ar-rúm*
11. *Ma-rí*$^{ki}$
1 ma-na kù:babbar
13. níĝ-ba
maškim-*sù*

(54)
15. ŠÚ+ŠA gín DILMUN kù:babbar
šu-bal-ak
17. 4 gín DILMUN kù-gi
nu$_{11}$-za 1 ĝír mar-tu
19. *wa*
1 kù-sal
21. níĝ-ba
*Ib-rí-um*
23. $^{d}$ʾ*A*$_{5}$*-da-bal*
*A-ru*$_{12}$*-ga-du*$^{ki}$

(55)
25. 12 gín DILMUN kù:babbar
XI. 1. nu$_{11}$-za 1 *ḫa-bù*
*ap*
3. kù-gi sikil
ŠÚ+ŠA gín DILMUN kù:babbar
5. ʾ*a*$_{5}$*-na-gu*
si 2 gud
7. nídba
en
9. $^{d}$ʾ*À-da*

(48) 5 minas of silver in exchange for 1 mina of gold for making 2 bridles (and) 4 buckles for Ibbi-zikir, son of Ibrium, when he occupied the city of Ḫalsum.
(49) 5 shekels of silver in exchange for 1 shekel of gold for decorating 1 ring for the king's mother.
(50) 5 shekels of silver in exchange for 1 shekel of gold for 1 belt, 1 sheath (and) 1 dagger pendant: gift of Ibrium for the god Rašap of the city of Daraum.
(51) 3 shekels of silver for the purchase of 1 bag for the son of Igriš, taken in possession in the city of Ḫalsum.
(52) 11 shekels of silver for the purchase of 2 stones ...; 4;10 minas of silver in exchange for 50 shekels of gold for 1 plaque: gift for the minister of the city of Ḫarran.
(53) 5 minas of silver: gift for Arrum of the city of Mari; 1 mina of silver: gift for his representative.
(54) 20 shekels of silver in exchange for 4 shekels of gold for plating 1 mar-tu dagger and 1 buckle: gift of Ibrium for the god ʾAdabal of the city of Arugadu.
(55) 12 shekels of silver for plating 1 mace, and also pure gold; 20 shekels of silver for the circular stand of the (4) horns of 2 bulls: offering of the king for the god Hadda of the city of Ḫalab, in month VIII.

*Ḫa-lab*$_{x}^{ki}$
11. *in*
iti *ᵓa*$_{5}$*-nun*

(56)
13. 2 ma-na ŠA.PI 6 gín DILMUN
kù:babbar
níĝ-sa$_{10}$ 30 lá-2 túg-NI.NI
15. 4 dùl-TÚG *Ma-rí*$^{ki}$
20 "KIN" siki *Ma-rí*$^{ki}$
17. 1 ma-na ŠÚ+ŠA 3 gín DILMUN
kù:babbar
níĝ-sa$_{10}$ 15 si$_{4}$ *gàr-su*
19. 14 ĝi$_{6}$ *gàr-su*
ki:lam$_{7}$
21. $^{d}$*ᵓÀ-da*

(57)
5 gín DILMUN kù:babbar
23. šu-bal-ak
1 gín kù-gi
25. *ni-zi-mu*
nu$_{11}$-za
XII. 1. šum
ZA$_{x}$
3. *Ib-rí-um*

(58)
5 gín DILMUN kù:babbar
5. *ni-zi-mu*
2 níĝ-anše-ak 4 kù-sal
7. *Ù-ti*
10 gín DILMUN kù:babbar
9. šu-bal-ak
2 gín DILMUN kù-gi
11. *ni-zi-mu*
maš-maš-*sù*

(59)
13. 4 gín DILMUN kù:babbar
*wa*
15. ŠÚ+ŠA gín DILMUN kù:babbar
šu-bal-ak
17. 4 gín DILMUN kù-gi
*ni-zi-mu*
19. nu$_{11}$-za
1 balaĝ nar
21. 5 gín DILMUN kù:babbar
šu-bal-ak
23. 1 gín DILMUN kù-gi
*ni-zi-mu*
25. nu$_{11}$-za 1 bur-KAK ga:eš$_{8}$
4 ma-na 10 gín DILMUN kù:babbar
27. [šu]-bal-ak
[50 g]ín [DIL]MUN [kù-]gi
XIII. 1. nu$_{11}$-za 15 *gú-li-lum* a-gar$_{5}$-gar$_{5}$ 15-I
*wa*
3. 14 *gú-li-lum* a-gar$_{5}$-gar$_{5}$ 12-I
ME-sig
5. é
en

(60)
7. 2 ma-na 10 gín DILMUN kù:babbar
šu-bal-ak
9. ŠÚ+ŠA 6 gín DILMUN kù-gi
kin$_{5}$-ak
11. lul-gu-ak
2 ĝeštu$_{x}$-lá 15
13. sikil
$^{d}$*Iš:šára*
15. *Zu-ra-mu*$^{ki}$
*wa*
17. 1 *ù*-NAM-*mi-lu* 8 gín DILMUN
sikil
19. $^{d}$BAD-munus
*Lu-ba-an*$^{ki}$
21. *wa*
1 kù-sal 4 gín DILMUN
23. sikil
[ ]ʳxˀ
25. [ ]
s[ikil]
27. *in* ud
tu-da

(56) 2;46 minas of silver for the purchase of 32 garments (and) 20 KIN measures of wool from the city of Mari; 1;23 minas of silver for the purchase of 15 red bags (and) 14 black bags: at the market of the god Hadda.

(57) 5 shekels of silver in exchange for 1 shekel of gold for decorating with lamination a saw, property of Ibrium.

(58) 5 shekels of silver for decorating 2 bridles (and) 4 buckles for Uti; 10 shekels of silver in exchange for 2 shekels of gold for their striped decoration.

(59) 4 shekels of silver and 20 shekels of silver in exchange for 4 shekels of gold for decorating with lamination 1 harp of a singer; 5 shekels of silver in exchange for 1 shekel of gold for decorating with lamination 1 bur-KAK vessel for a travelling merchant; 4;10 minas of silver [in ex]change for [50 sh]ekels of [go]ld for plating 15 single bracelets of 15 (shekels of) copper each and 14 single bracelets of 12 (shekels of) copper each: for the watchmen of the king's house.

(60) 2;10 minas of silver in exchange for 26 shekels of gold for making a replacement of 2 earrings of 15 (shekels each), (given) for the purification rite to the goddess Išḫara of the city of Zuramu and 1 … (*ù*-NAM-*mi-lu*) of 8 shekels, (given) for the purification rite to the Lady of the city of Luban, and 1 buckle of 4 shekels, (given) for the purification rite to […] for the pu[rification rite] for giving birth.

(61)

XIV. 1. 5 g[ín] DILMUN kù:babbar
šu-bal-ak
3. 1 gín kù-gi
*zi-ba-du*
5. 1 zag-*sù* kù-gi
en

(62)

7. 4 gín DILMUN kù:babbar
gur$_8$
9. má-gal-má-gal
mu-DU
11. *na-se$_{11}$-na-se$_{11}$*
*in* ud
13. [ ]
[ ]

(63)

15. 6 gín DILMUN an-na
šub *si-in*
17. *zi-ba-du*
1 útul urudu maḫ
19. 15 gín DILMUN kù:babbar
ZU.PIRIG
21. 3 útul urudu maḫ
10 gín DILMUN kù:babbar
23. [šu-]bal-ak
[2 g]ín DILMUN kù-gi
25. [ ]
níĝ[-ba]
27. *Ib-rí-um*
$^{d}$BAD-munus
29. *Lu-ba-an*$^{ki}$

(64)

5 gín DILMUN kù:babbar
XV. 1. 3 *zú-zú-ba-tum*
ĜIŠ-gígir-II
3. *Wa-na*
TAR an-na
5. šub *si-in*
4 ma-na ŠÚ+ŠA a-gar$_5$-gar$_5$
7. kin$_5$-ak
5 tùn gal TAR.TAR
9. 5 dub-naĝar šu-mu-LAGAB 15
5 dub-naĝar 10 sal
11. *Wa-na*
ugula *A-la-ga*$^{ki}$

(65)

13. 2 ½ gín DILMUN kù:babbar
šu-bal-ak
15. ½ kù-gi
*ni-zi-mu*
17. 4 ĝeštu$_x$-lá
*Ir-ti*
19. *Nap-ḫa-ì*
2 dumu-nita
21. *Ib-rí-um*

(66)

3 ma-na TAR kù:babbar
23. [šu-b]al-[a]k
ŠA.[PI 1+]˹1˺ gín DILMUN kù-gi
25. nu$_{11}$-za 2 bur-KAK ĜIŠ-˹taškarin˺
kaskal
27. en
*wa*
29. 2 bur-KAK ĜIŠ-taškarin
kaskal
XVI. 1. ˹*Ib*˺*-rí-um*

(67)

13 ma-na ŠÚ+ŠA an-na
3. šub *si-in*
4 *mi-at* ma-na a-gar$_5$-gar$_5$
5. kin$_5$-ak
2 útul urudu maḫ gibil
7. 50 kù:babbar
šu-bal-ak
9. 10 kù-gi
*ni-zi-mu*
11. 1 dib
*En-na-il*
13. lú *A-ma-za*

(61) 5 she[kels] of silver in exchange for 1 shekel of gold for the handle (and) its side of gold for the king.

(62) 4 shekels of silver for platforms of ships: delivery for the people on the occasion of […].

(63) 6 shekels of tin to be melted in the handle of a big kettle of copper; 15 shekels of silver for the hangers of 3 big kettles of copper; 10 shekels of silver [in ex]change for [2 she]kels of gold [for …]: gi[ft] of Ibrium for the Lady of the city of Luban.

(64) 5 shekels of silver for 3 … (*zú-zú-ba-tum*) of a chariot for Wana; 30 (shekels of) tin to be melted with 4;20 minas of copper for making 5 big axes of 30 (shekels) each, 5 hammers with a square head of 15 (shekels) each, 5 thin hammers of 10 (shekels) each for Wana, the overseer of the city of Alaga.

(65) 2 ½ shekels of silver in exchange for ½ (shekel of) gold for decorating 4 earrings for Irti (and) Napḫa-i(l), 2 sons of Ibrium.

(66) 3;30 minas of silver [in exchan]ge for 42 shekels of gold for plating 2 travel bur-KAK vessels of boxwood for the king and 2 travel bur-KAK vessels of boxwood for Ibrium.

(67) 13;20 minas of tin to be melted with 400 minas of copper for making 2 new big kettles of copper; 50 (shekels of) silver in exchange for 10 (shekels of) gold for decorating 1 plaque for Enna-il, (son) of Amaza.

(68)
50 kù:babbar
15. šu-bal-ak
10 kù-gi
17. *ni-zi-mu*
1 dib
19. *Wa-na*
ugula *A-la-ga*$^{ki}$

(69)
21. 10 kù:babbar
*Na-gàr*$^{ki}$
23. 10 [kù]:babbar
*ᵓÀ-du*$^{ki}$
25. 10 kù:babbar
*A-bù-li-um*$^{ki}$
27. 10 kù:babbar *Gú-ra-du*$^{ki}$
[ ]
29. [ ]
[ ]

(70)
XVII. 1. [1 m]a-[n]a kù:babbar
níĝ-ba
3. ḫúb-ki
ba:tuš
5. *a-lu-nu*
ĝiš

(71)
7. 1 kù:babbar
1 kù-sal
9. níĝ-ba
˹d˺[*Aš-d*]*ar*$^{?}$
11. en
[x-*g*]*a*-[x]$^{ki}$

(72)
13. 1[+x] ma-na [ ]
[níĝ-]ba
15. [diĝir-diĝir]-diĝir

(73)
[TAR 3 3 NI gín kù:babbar šu-ba]
l-ak
17. [6] gín DILMUN 2 NI kù-gi 2 *gú-li-lum*
[níĝ-]ba
19. $^{d}$*Ku-ra*

(74)
AN[.ŠÈ].GÚ ˹1˺[+1$^{?}$] *mi-at* 97 ma-na
10 kù:babbar
21. è
*ap*
23. ˹2˺ *m*[*i-at* x ma-na x kù:babbar]
[al$_6$-ĝál]
25. [é siki] (?)

(68) 50 (shekels of) silver in exchange for 10 (shekels of) gold for decorating 1 plaque for Wana, the overseer of the city of Alaga.
(69) 10 (shekels of) silver for (someone of) the city of Nagar, 10 (shekels of) [sil]ver for (someone of) the city of ᵓAddu, 10 (shekels of) silver for (someone of) the city of Abulium, 10 (shekels of) silver for (someone of) the city of Guradu [...].
(70) [1 m]i[n]a of silver: gift for the acrobat who stayed on the pole.
(71) 1 (shekel of) silver for 1 buckle: gift for the god [Ašd]ar by the king of the city of [...].
(72) 1[+x] minas [of silver: gi]ft [for the god]s.
(73) [33 shekels (and) 3 NI of silver in exchan]ge for [6] shekels (and) 2 NI of gold for 2 bracelets: [gi]ft for the god Kura.
(74) To[ta]l: 297;10 minas of silver: expenditure and also 200+[ minas of silver are present in the Treasury].

## Commentary

This document has to be dated to the year Ibr. 13. The "expended", è, silver amounted to 297;10 minas (139.668 kg), and that "present", al$_6$-ĝál, in the Treasury was more than 200 minas (ca 90 kg), (§ 74): the number is only preserved in part. The text opens with the registration of the expenditure of 1 mina (470 g) of silver for the renewal rite concerning the city-god Kura, which fell at the beginning of the year. A second delivery of 3 shekels (23 g) of silver for a further ceremony for the god in a later period is registered in § 12. Kura then received a pair of gold bracelets of 6 ½ shekels (52 g) as an offering (§ 73). Tinib-dulum, a sister of the king, received 14 minas (6.58 kg) of silver in her function as priestess of the god ᵓAdabal. Tarib-damu, her sister, was associated with her in service of the god from this year onward; she received 1 mina (470 g) of silver (§ 2). On these "priestesses", dam-diĝir, see Archi 1998a.

The war against the city of Ḫalsum started this year. Ḫabuzu, from the city of ᵓAbardu, a representative of Zabarum (this official is also mentioned in text 15 § 6) received a plaque of 20 shekels (157 g) of gold because he had "occupied", tuš-LÚ×TIL, Ḫalsum (§ 34). The decoration of twenty-two daggers for the "men", ĝuruš-ĝuruš, to be distributed to the "representatives", maškim, in Ḫalsum needed 10 shekels (78 g) of silver, and 12 shekels (94 g) of gold for another eighteen daggers (§ 47). Ibbi-zikir, Ibrium's son, also "occupied", tuš-LÚ×TIL, Ḫalsum, receiving 1 mina (470 g) of gold "in order to make bridles" for him, (§ 48). Another Eblaite official: the son of Igriš, received a bag in Ḫalsum (§ 51). For the wars against Ḫalsum, see Archi 2021a, pp. 205, 207–210.

Ruzi-damu, king of Imar, received the substantial gift of 1;12 minas (564 g) of gold, probably because he had succeeded his father Išgi-damu (§ 3). This king is mentioned also in *ARET* IV 7 § 17, and 24 § 1, both to be dated to the minister Ibbi-zikir's period. His spouse was Tiša-lim (see above no 13 §§ 37, 38, 42).

The king received some jewelry, including four buckles, for which 20 shekels (156 g) of gold were needed (§ 30). Two shekels (16 g) of silver and 2 shekels (16 g) of gold were used for the decorations of his chariot (§ 32). Three shekels (23 g) of tin, fused with 17 shekels (133 g) of copper, were used to make six "pegs", ĜIŠ-kak-ĜIŠ-kak, as pedestal for two "travel trays", asari kaskal (§ 37), and 1 shekel (8 g) of gold for the decoration of the rear part of the chariot case (§ 61). The plating of two "travel bowls", kaskal bur-KAK, of boxwood, one for the king and the other for Ibrium, needed 21 shekels (164 g) of gold each (§ 66).

The king's mother received decorations for a case for which 1 ½ shekels (12 g) of gold were employed (§ 6). The decoration for a buckle needed 1 shekel (8 g) of gold (§ 31), and another shekel of gold for the decoration of a ring (§ 49).

Ibrium received decorations for his "former harness", which needed 25 shekels (196 g) of gold (§ 13). The decorations of his chariot needed 2;58 ½ minas (1.394 kg) of gold and 5 shekels (39 g) of tin (§ 14); those for his new harness for a team of donkeys needed 2 shekels (16 g) of gold (§ 15). One shekel (8 g) of gold was employed for two daggers "property ($ZA_x$) of Ibrium" (§ 19). His "battle-axe, *za-ḫa-da*, was decorated with 1 shekel (8 g) of gold (§ 41), as was his saw (§ 57).

*Wa-ru*$_{12}$*-tum* of Mari received 30 shekels (235 g) of silver because he had delivered a gift (§ 24). *Ar-rúm* received the substantial amount of 5 minas (2.35 kg) of silver, and his "representative", maškim, another mina (470 g), without any further explanation (§ 53). This official is mentioned also in *ARET* XIV 77 § 42, of the year I.Z. 1, and in *ARET* XIII 15 §§ 8–9, a document concerning Mari.

§ 4. The ĜIŠ-šú and the níg-bànda could be rather heavy vessels. One has to understand from this in part anomalous registration that 10;30 minas (4.857 kg) of silver were employed for the two vessels, while the remaining "10 shekels (78 g) of silver (exchanged) for (2 shekels) of gold" for their decoration.

§ 5. The ratio 1 : 60 between silver and copper is anomalous because the usual one was 1 : 30, and exceptionally 1 : 40 (see Archi 2024, 000).

§ 7. Tarib-damu and Tište-damu, two "daughters of the king", received two earrings each, for which 3 shekels (23 g) of gold were employed; the second princess further received two buckles of 2 shekels (16 g) of gold. They were daughters of Išᶜar-damu, who at this time should have been about eighteen years old. Tište-damu married in the year I.Z. 9, according to *ARET* I 3 § 55, a document which has to be dated to that year on the basis of some data registered also in *ARET* XXII 8: the annual "è" document of that year.

§ 10. Dadub, "a spouse, dam, of the king", who resided in Arugadu, received two toggle-pins of 20 shekels (157 g) of silver. She is mentioned also in late documents, as *ARET* VIII 525 obv. IV 12; XX 17 rev. IV 20; XX 24 obv. X 26.

§ 16. Expenditures of silver and gold for decorations for plaques, belts, bracelets, helmets, and daggers given to "men", ĝuruš-ĝuruš, under the command of a certain Azimutum.

§ 17. Expenditure of 1;50 minas of tin and 6;30 minas of copper given to the carpenters.

§ 27. Tinib-dulum, the priestess of ᵓAdabal, received some gifts, among which ten earrings and a buckle. They needed 35 shekels (274 g) of silver and 1 shekel (8 g) of gold.

§ 28. Miga-i(l) received 20 shekels (157 g) of silver in order to ransom 3 men from Ebla in the city of Iritum.

§ 35. The judge Ila-išar was in service in the years 12–18 of Ibrium (see *ARET* XIV, p. 170).

§ 40. Irti, son of Ibrium, received a plaque of 2 shekels (16 g) of gold; his brother Giri two earrings of gold of the same weight.

§ 58. Uti (son of Ibrium) received bridles decorated with 5 shekels (39 g) of silver and 2 shekels (16 g) of gold.

§ 59. Expenditure of 4 shekels of silver and 4 shekels of gold (32 + 32 g) for plating a harp of the singers; 1 shekel (8 g) of gold for plating a vessel; and 50 shekels (391 g) of gold for plating 29 bracelets for the "watchmen of the king's house", ME-sig é en.

§ 65. ½ shekel (4 g) of gold for decorating four earrings of Irti and Napḫa-il, two sons of Ibrium.

§ 66. 42 shekels (329 g) of gold for decorating four travel vessels of boxwood: two for the king, and two for Ibrium.

## 17
## (Plates XXXII–XXXIII)

(1)
o. I. 1. 1 ma-na kù:babbar
saĝ kù:babbar
3. $^{d}$*Ku-ra*

(2)
10 lá-2 ma-na kù:babbar
5. *Di-ne-íb-du-lum*
[nin-ni]
7. [en]
šu-ba$_4$-ti

(3)
9. 3 ma-na ŠÚ+ŠA gín DILMUN
kù:babbar
šu-bal-ak
11. ŠA.PI gín DILMUN kù-gi 1 dib
*Íl-gú-uš-ti*
13. lú *I-gi*
tuš-LÚ×TIL
15. *Kak-mi-um*$^{ki}$
⌜*áš-ti*⌝
17. [GN]

(4)
[x kù:babbar]
19. [šu-ba]l-[a]k
[x kù-g]i
21. [ ]
[ ]
23?. [ ]

(5)
II. 1. TAR kù:babbar
níĝ-sa$_{10}$ 2 *gú-li-lum* a-gar$_5$-gar$_5$ TAR
5 gín DILMUN *sa-ḫa-wa*
3. *Ì-na-ar*
[*Za-*ʾ*à-ar*]$^{ki}$

(6)
5. ŠÚ+ŠA gín DILMUN kù:babbar
2 *bu*-[DI]
7. ⌜x⌝[ ]
[ ]
9. [ ]
[ ]
11. [ ]
dumu[-munus]
13. *I-l*[*u*$_5$-]-*z*[*a*$_x$]-⌜*ma*⌝-*lik*
šu-mu-tak$_4$

(7)
15. 6 ma-na kù:babbar
níĝ-sa$_{10}$ 2 BAR.AN
17. ḪI-*ra-ù*
*Na-gàr*$^{ki}$
19. šu-mu-tak$_4$

(8)
ŠÚ+ŠA gín DILMUN k[ù:babbar]
21. [2 *bu*-DI]
[dumu-munus]
III. 1. en
*Bur-ma-an*$^{ki}$
3. É×PAP
é-gi
5. en
*Ra-*ʾ*à-ak*$^{ki}$
7. *Iš*$_{11}$*-da-mu*
[ ]
9. [ -]a[- ]
[(ca. 7 lines)]

(9)
17.? [ŠÚ+ŠA 5 gín DILMUN kù:babbar]
[šu-bal-ak]
19. 5 gín DILMUN kù-gi
*ni-zi-mu*

(1) 1 mina of silver for the silver head of the god Kura.
(2) 8 minas of silver: Tinib-dulum, [sister of the king], has received.
(3) 3;20 minas of silver in exchange for 40 shekels of gold for 1 plaque for Ilgušti, (son) of Igi, (who) occupied the city of Kakmium from [the city of …].
(4) [x silver in exchange for x gol]d […]
(5) 30 (shekels of) silver for the purchase of 2 bracelets of 35 shekels of copper (with) pendants for Inaʾar [of the city of Zaʾar].
(6) 20 shekels of silver for 2 toggle-[pins] […] , the daugh[ter] of Il[u]z[a]-malik has handed over.
(7) 6 minas of silver for the purchase of 2 mules, ḪIrau of the city of Nagar has handed over.
(8) 20 shekels of si[lver for 2 toggle-pins] for the funerary rite [of the daughter] of the king of the city of Burman, the daughter-in-law of the king of the city of Raʾak; Iš-damu […].
(9) [25 shekels of silver in exchange for] 5 shekel of gold for decorating with lamination 1 bracelet of 50 (shekels of) copper: ʾAgar, the overseer of the mules of Ibbi-zikir, son of [Ibrium, has received].

21. nu$_{11}$-za
1 *gú-li-lum* a-gar$_5$-gar$_5$ 50
23. *ʾÀ-gàr*
ugula BAR.AN
25. *I-bí-zi-kir*
dumu-nita
27. [*Ib-rí-um*]
[šu-ba$_4$-ti]

(10)
29. [x ma-na x]
IV. 1. gín DILMUN kù:babbar
níĝ-sa$_{10}$ 2 IGI.NITA u$_5$
3. lú *Du-ur-i*[*l*]

(11)
[(ca. 11 lines)]
15.? lul-gu-ak
1 íb-lá 1 ĝír-kun
17. *Du-ur-il*

(12)
5 gín DILMUN kù:babbar
19. šu-bal-ak
1 gín DILMUN kù-gi 1 kù-sal 1 buru$_4$-MUŠEN
21. [níĝ-ba]
[...]
V. 1. dumu-munus
en
3. $^{d}$*Ku-ra*
ì-na-sum
5. *in*
ne:saĝ-*sù*

(13)
7. [ ]
[ ]
9. [ ]
⌜x⌝[ ]
11?. 2 šu-i
10 gín DILMUN kù:babbar
13. šu-bal-ak
2 gín DILMUN kù-gi
15. nu$_{11}$-za-*sù*
en

(14)
17. 1 gín DILMUN an-na
šub *si-in*
19. 5 gín DILMUN a-gar$_5$-gar$_5$
[ ]
21. 7 gín DILMUN kù:babbar
šu-bal-ak
23. 1 ½ gín DILMUN kù-gi
nu$_{11}$-za-*sù*
25. en

(15)
[ ]
27. [ ]
[ ]
VI. 1. 5 gín DILMUN kù:babbar
níĝ-kaskal
3. *En-na-il*
[DU.DU]
5. *si-in*
Kiš$^{ki}$

(16)
7. [ ]
[ ]
9. [ ]
[*Dar-maš-da-mu*]
11?. dumu-munus
en
13. é-gi
BAD-*da-mu*
15. *in* ud
DU.DU
17. nídba
é
19. diĝir
en

(17)
21. 1 ma-na ŠA.PI gín DILMUN kù:babbar
[šu-bal-ak]
23. ⌜20⌝ gín DILMUN kù-gi 1 dib
*I-ib-ma-lik*
25. dumu-nita
*Aḫ-ra-ma-lik*

(10) [x;xx mina(s)] of silver for the purchase of 2 donkeys to ride for Dur-i[l].
(11) [...] as replacement of 1 belt (and) 1 dagger pendant for Dur-il.
(12) 5 shekels of silver in exchange for 1 shekel of gold for 1 buckle (and) 1 helmet: [gift of ...], daughter of the king, for the god Kura, given on the occasion of his first-fruit offering.
(13) [...] 2 šu-i vessels; 10 shekels of silver in exchange for 2 shekels of gold for their lamination, for the king.
(14) 1 shekel of tin to be melted with 5 shekels of copper [...]; 7 shekels of silver in exchange for 1 ½ shekel of gold for its lamination, for the king.
(15) [...] 5 shekels of silver: travel provision for Enna-il, (who) [went] to the city of Kiš.
(16) [...] [Tarmaš-damu], daughter of the king (and) daughter-in-law of BAD-damu, when she went to (perform) an offering in the temple of the god of the king.
(17) 1;40 minas of silver [in exchange for] 20 shekels of gold for 1 plaque for Iʾib-malik, son of Aḫra-malik.

(18)

27. [ ]
[ ]
29. [ ]
VII. 1. ⸢níĝ-ba⸣
*Ù-rí-rí*
3. maškim
ga:eš$_8$
5. *in* kaskal
é
7. $^{d}$BAD *Ga-na-na*

(19)

[4] ma-na [10 gí]n [DILMUN]
k[ù:babbar]
9. [šu-bal-ak]
50 gín DILMUN kù-gi
11. kin$_5$-ak
2 níĝ-anše-ak 4(2) kù-sal
13. 2 IGI.NITA
ama-gal
15. en

(20)

1 ma-na ŠA.PI gín DILMUN
kù:babbar
17. šu-bal-ak
[ŠÚ+Š]A gín DILMUN kù-gi 2 *bu*-DI
19. níĝ-ba
*Ti-ša-li-im*
21. *ma-lik-tum*
*Ì-mar*⸢$^{ki}$⸣
23. *i*[*n* ud]
[ ]
25. [*I-bí-zi-kir*]
VIII. 1. [dumu-]nita
*Ib-rí-um*

(21)

3. 5 ma-na kù:babbar
níĝ-sa$_{10}$ BAR.AN
5. *áš-ti*
*A-ša*$^{ki}$
7. *Wa-na*
šu-ba$_4$-ti

(22)

9. [x ma-n]a [kù:babbar]
níĝ[-ba]
11. EZEN-*il*
*Ma-rí*$^{ki}$
13. ḫi-mu-DU
LAGAB×UD.LAGAB×UD

(23)

15. 4 ma-na kù:babbar
níĝ-sa$_{10}$ 34 aktum-TÚG
17. 2 zara$_6$-TÚG
5 *ʾà-da-um*-TÚG-I
19. [(ca. 8 lines)]

(24)

IX. 1. *Za-rí-ba*
2 gín DILMUN kù:babbar
3. níĝ-kaskal-*sù*

(25)

5 ma-na kù:babbar
5. níĝ-sa$_{10}$ 1 *mi-at* 10 lá-2 aktum-TÚG
1 zara$_6$-TÚG
ki:lam$_7$
7. *Ma-rí*$^{ki}$
dam-gàr
9. [šu-]mu-[t]ak$_4$

(26)

5 gín DILMUN kù:babbar
11. šu-bal-ak
1 gín DILMUN kù-gi
13. *zi-du*
*ša-ga-tum*
15. 1 ĝír mar-tu kù-gi
*I-šar*
17. lú *I-du-a*

(18) […]: gift for Uriri, representative of the travelling merchant, for (his) travel to the temple of the Lord of Ganana.
(19) [4;10] minas of s[ilver in exchange for] 50 shekels of gold for making 2 bridles (and) 4 buckles for 2 donkeys of the king's mother.
(20) 1;40 minas of silver in exchange for [20] shekels of silver for 2 toggle-pins: gift for Tiša-lim, the queen of the city of Imar, on [the occasion of … Ibbi-zikir, so]n of Ibrium.
(21) 5 minas of silver for the purchase of mules from the city of Aša: Wana has received.
(22) [x min]a(s) [of silver]: gi[ft] for EZEN-il of the city of Mari, (who) delivered ostrich shells.
(23) 4 minas of silver for the purchase of 41[+x] garments […].
(24) […] for Zariba; 2 shekels of silver for his travel provision.
(25) 5 minas of silver for the purchase of 109 garments, at the market of the city of Mari, the merchant(s) [have] handed over.
(26) 5 shekels of silver in exchange for 1 shekel of gold as alloy for the … (*ša-ga-tum*) of 1 mar-tu dagger (decorated with) gold for Išar, (son) of Idua.

(27)

[(ca. 8 lines)]

X. 1. 43 sal-TÚG
43 íb+III-TÚG $sa_6$ gùn
3. 1 *mi-at* 10 íb+III-TÚG gùn
3 *mi-at* 80 siki $na_4$ *Ma-rí*$^{ki}$
5. 1 ma-na kù:babbar
níĝ-$sa_{10}$ 26 gu-dù[l]-TÚG m[aḫ]
7. lú é-$duru_5$$^{⌜ki⌝}$
6 gín DILMUN kù:babbar
9. níĝ-$sa_{10}$ 25[(+x) *ra-*]*ˀà-t*[*um*]
1 m[a-]n[a] TAR kù:babbar
11. [(ca. 9 lines)]

(28)

XI. 1. 1 *gàr-sù*
*I-ib-ma-lik*

(29)

3. TAR 3 gín DILMUN 3 NI kù:babbar
šu-bal-ak
5. 6 gín DILMUN 2 NI kù-gi
2 *gú-li-lum*
7. níĝ-ba
$^{d}$*Ku-ra*

(30)

9. 10 gín DILMUN kù:babbar
šu-bal-ak
11. 2 gín DILMUN kù-gi
*ni-zi-mu*
13. 1 íb-lá 1 *si-ti-tum* 1 ĝír-kun
*Gi-ir-da-mu*

(31)

15. 12 gín DILMUN kù:babbar
1 íb-lá 1 ĝír-kun
17. [x gí]n [DIL]MUN k[ù:babbar]
šu-bal-ak
19. [x] gín DILMUN kù-gi
[*ba-d*]*u-*$u_4$
21. [1] ĝír [mar-]tu
[*Nap*]*-ḫa-⌜i⌝*
23. [dumu-n]ita
[*Ib-rí-u*]*m*

(32)

25. [ ]
[2 *b*]*u*-DI
27. *ma-lik-tum*
XII. 1. *Lum-na-an*$^{ki}$
ama-gal
3. en
šu-mu-$tak_4$
5. *in* ud
DU.DU
7. *si-in*
$U_9$*-gú-a-aš*$^{ki}$

(33)

9. 1 ma-na kù:babbar
níĝ-$sa_{10}$ 50 ma-na a-$gar_5$-$gar_5$
11. ŠA.PI gín DILMUN kù:babbar
1 íb-lá 1 ĝír-kun
13. *Ḫa-zu-um*
maškim
15. *Ib-rí-um*
tuš-LÚ×TIL
17. *Ti-ma-tim*$^{ki}$
lú *Kak-mi-um*$^{ki}$

(34)

19. ŠA.PI gín DILMUN kù:babbar
1 íb-lá 1 ĝír-kun
21. *Du-bí-šum*
lú *Gú-ma-ni-du*
23. maškim
*I-bí-zi-kir*
25. tuš-LÚ×TIL
*Kak-mi-um*$^{ki}$
27. *áš-ti*
*Šu-ra-an*$^{ki}$

(27) [x silver for the purchase of x+]43 garments, 153 kilts (and) 380 stone weights of wool from the city of Mari; 1 mina of silver for the purchase of 26 la[rge] garments for a work gang; 6 shekels of silver for the purchase of 25[+x sh]el[ls]; 1;30 min[a] of silver [...].

(28) [...] 1 bag for Iˀib-malik.

(29) 33 shekels (and) 3 NI of silver in exchange for 6 shekels (and) 2 NI of gold for 2 bracelets: gift for the god Kura.

(30) 10 shekels of silver in exchange for 2 shekels of gold for decorating 1 belt, 1 sheath (and) 1 dagger pendant for Giˀir-damu.

(31) 12 shekels of silver for 1 belt (and) 1 dagger pendant; [x shek]els of s[ilver] in exchange for [x] shekels of gold for [1 *b.* mar]-tu dagger for [Nap]ḫa-i(l), [a so]n of [Ibriu]m.

(32) [x silver for 2 to]ggle-pins for the queen of the city of Lumnan, the king's mother has handed over when she went to the city of Uguaˀaš.

(33) 1 mina of silver for the purchase of 50 minas of copper; 40 shekels of silver for 1 belt (and) 1 dagger pendant for Ḫazum, representative of Ibrium, (who) occupied the city of Timatim, (belonging) to the city of Kakmium.

(34) 40 shekels of silver for 1 belt (and) 1 dagger pendant for Dubišum, (son) of Gumanidu, representative of Ibbi-zikir, (who) occupied the city of Kakmium, from the city of Šuran.

(35)
XIII. 1. 12 gín DILMUN kù:babbar
níĝ-sa$_{10}$ 1 ĝír mar-tu zú kù-gi
3. *Ru*$_{12}$*-zi-ma-lik*
lú *I-rí-ig*
5. al$_{6}$-tuš
*Ab-ra-ti-ig*$^{ki}$

(36)
7. ŠA.PI gín DILMUN kù:babbar
níĝ-sa$_{10}$ 2 gud
9. *in*
SA.ZA$_{x}$$^{ki}$
11. *Rí-ì-ma-lik*
*I-bí-zi-im*

(37)
13. 3 gín DILMUN kù:babbar
saĝ kù:babbar
15. $^{d}$*Ku-ra*
mu-ti

(38)
17. 15 gín DILMUN kù:babbar
šu-bal-ak
19. 3 gín DILMUN kù-gi
*ni-zi-mu*
21. *zi-du*
3 *ša-ga-tum*
23. 3 ĝír mar-tu
*Šu-ma-lik*
25. lú
XIV. 1. *Iš*$_{11}$*-da-mu*
*Iš*$_{11}$*-gi-da-mu*
3. *A-ba-ù*
NI-*ti-ba*$^{ki}$

(39)
5. 8 gín DILMUN kù:babbar
níĝ-sa$_{10}$ 1 ĝír mar-tu zú kù-gi
7. *I-lu*$_{5}$*-za*$_{x}$*-ma-lik*
*Su-ti-ig*$^{ki}$
9. šu-du$_{8}$
*in*
11. *Ù-nu-bu*$^{ki}$

(40)
10 ma-na kù:babbar
13. šu-bal-ak
2 ma-na kù-gi 1 íb-lá 1 *si-ti-tum* 1 ĝír-kun
15. 1 dib
50 gín DILMUN kù:babbar
17. níĝ-sa$_{10}$ 1 ĝír mar-tu kù-gi
4 gín DILMUN an-na
19. šub *si-in*
ŠÚ+ŠA 6 a-gar$_{5}$-gar$_{5}$ 1 ĜIŠ-zú
21. 1 gín DILMUN kù:babbar
nu$_{11}$-za
XV. 1. 1 zag
ĜIŠ-gígir-II
3. 4 gín DILMUN kù:babbar
2 *zú-zú-ba-tum*
5. *Íl-ba-da-mu*
en
7. *Kak-mi-um*$^{ki}$
*in*
9. SA.ZA$_{x}$$^{ki}$
šu-ba$_{4}$-ti

(41)
11. 5 ma-na 15 gín DILMUN kù:babbar
šu-bal-ak
13. 1 ma-na 15 gín DILMUN kù-gi
nu$_{11}$-za 5 *gú-li-lum* a-gar$_{5}$-gar$_{5}$ TAR-II
15. 10 *gú-li-lum* a-gar$_{5}$-gar$_{5}$ ŠÚ+ŠA ŠÚ+ŠA-II
5 *gú-li-lum* a-gar$_{5}$-gar$_{5}$ 15-I
17. 10 *gú-li-lum* a-gar$_{5}$-gar$_{5}$ 10-I
2 gín DILMUN kù:babbar
19. ZU.PIRIĜ-*sù*
ME-sig
21. é
en

(35) 12 shekels of silver for the purchase of 1 serrated mar-tu dagger (decorated with) gold for Ruzi-malik, (son) of Irig, (who) occupied the city of Abratik.
(36) 40 shekels of silver for the purchase of 2 oxen for the Palace: Reʾi-malik (son of) Ibbi-zim (has received).
(37) 3 shekels of silver for the silver head of the god Kura: (second) delivery.
(38) 15 shekels of silver in exchange for 3 shekels of gold for decorating as alloy 3 … (*ša-ga-tum*) of 3 mar-tu daggers for Šu-malik, (son) of Iš-damu, Išgi-damu (and) Abau of the city of NItiba.
(39) 8 shekels of silver for the purchase of 1 serrated mar-tu dagger (decorated with) gold: Iluza-malik of the city of Sutig has taken possession of it in the city of Unubu.
(40) 10 minas of silver in exchange for 2 minas of gold for 1 belt, 1 sheath (and) 1 dagger pendant, 1 plaque; 50 shekels of silver for the purchase of 1 mar-tu dagger (decorated with) gold; 4 shekels of tin to be melted with 26 (shekels of) copper for 1 hook; 1 shekel of silver for plating 1 side of a chariot; 4 shekels of silver for 2 ... (*zú-zú-ba-tum*): Ilba-damu, the king of the city of Kakmium has received in the Palace.
(41) 5;15 minas of silver in exchange for 1;15 minas of gold for plating 5 double bracelets of 30 (shekels of) copper each, 10 double bracelets of 20 (shekels of) copper each, 5 single bracelets of 15 (shekels of) copper each, 10 single bracelets of 10 (shekels of) copper each; 2 shekels of silver for their hangers: for the watchmen of the king's house.

(42)

XVI. 1. 1 ma-na kù:babbar
níĝ-sa$_{10}$ 1 ĝír mar-tu kù-gi
3. *Ib-rí-um*
*in* ud
5. è
níĝ-kas$_{4}$
7. al-kur$_{6}$
še
9. *Kak-mi-um*$^{ki}$

(43)

ŠA.PI 5 gín DILMUN kù:babbar
11. níĝ-sa$_{10}$ 2 ĝír mar-tu *ba-du-u*$_{4}$ kù-gi
1 ĝír mar-tu zú kù-gi
13. 1 ĝír mar-tu *ba-du-u*$_{4}$ kù:babbar-gi
Lugal-*na-i-iš*
15. *Íl-ba-šum*
*Du-bí-ga-lu*
17. *Ša-gú-bù*
dumu-nita
19. en
*Ma-nu-wa-ad*$^{ki}$

(44)

21. ŠÚ+ŠA 2 gín DILMUN kù:babbar
*ni-zi-mu*
XVII. 1. 2 níĝ-anše-ak 4 kù-sal
*Ìr-am*$_{6}$*-da-mu*
3. lú *Íl-zi*

(45)

TAR kù:babbar
5. níĝ-ba
*Wa-ru*$_{12}$*-tum*
7. *wa*
*I-ku-uḫ*
9. *Ma-rí*$^{ki}$
ḫi-mu-DU
11. 1 az$^{!}$ maḫ

(46)

10 ma-na kù:babbar
13. níĝ-sa$_{10}$ 1 *mi-at* 46 aktum-TÚG
10 lá-2 zara$_{6}$-TÚG
15. 7 gíd-TÚG
33 *ˀà-da-um*-TÚG-I
17. ki:lam$_{7}$
*Ma-rí*$^{ki}$
19. dam-gàr

(47)

10 gín DILMUN kù:babbar
21. gur$_{8}$
ĜIŠ-gígir-sum
23. šu-mu-tak$_{4}$
túg-túg

(48)

25. 2 ma-na TAR kù:babbar
šu-bal-ak
27. TAR kù-gi
XVIII. 1. 1 dib
TAR kù:babbar
3. níĝ-sa$_{10}$ 1 ĝír mar-tu kù-gi
*ˀÀ:daš*
5. tuš-LÚ×TIL
*Ša-ra-bi-ig*$^{ki}$

(49)

7. 10 ma-na an-na
kin$_{5}$-ak
9. 3 *mi-at* ĝír mar-tu zabar
1 ma-na 10 gín DILMUN kù:babbar
11. níĝ-sa$_{10}$ si-si-*sù*
6 ma-na TAR kù:babbar
13. kin$_{5}$-ak
*kam*$_{4}$*-ma-a-tum-sù*
15. 1 ma-na ŠA.PI gín an-na
šub *si-in*
17. kin$_{5}$-ak
1 *mi-at* ĝír mar-tu zú-ak

(42) 1 mina of silver for the purchase of 1 mar-tu dagger (decorated with) gold for Ibrium on the occasion of the departure to the military expedition in order to uproot the barley of the city of Kakmium.

(43) 45 shekels of silver for the purchase of 2 *b.* mar-tu daggers (decorated with) gold, 1 serrated mar-tu dagger (decorated with) gold, 1 *b.* mar-tu dagger (decorated with) silver and gold for Lugal-naiš, Ilbašum, Dubigalu (and) Šagubu, the sons of the king of the city of Manuwat.

(44) 22 shekels of silver for decorating 2 bridles (and) 4 buckles for Iram-damu, (son) of Ilzi.

(45) 30 (shekels of) silver: gift for Warutum and Ikuḫ of the city of Mari, (who) delivered an adult bear.

(46) 10 minas of silver for the purchase of 194 garments at the market of the city of Mari; the merchant(s) (have handed over).

(47) 10 shekels of silver for the platform of a wagon, (used) to hand over textiles.

(48) 2;30 minas of silver in exchange for 30 (shekels of) gold for 1 plaque; 30 (shekels of) silver for the purchase of 1 mar-tu dagger (decorated with) gold for ˀAdaš, (who) occupied the city of Šarabig.

(49) 10 minas of tin for making 300 bronze mar-tu daggers; 1;10 minas of silver for the purchase of the horns (for) its (decoration); 6;30 minas of silver for making their knobs; 1;40 minas of tin to be melted for making 100 serrated mar-tu daggers; 56 shekels of tin to be melted with 5;40 minas of copper for making 17 serrated mar-tu daggers and 3 *b.* mar-tu daggers (decorated with) silver and gold; 2;30 minas of silver in exchange for 30 (shekels of) gold for plating their … (*ša-ga-tum*) and their knobs; 7 shekels of silver for the *ba-du-u*$_{4}$ of 3 mar-tu daggers; 1;40 minas of tin to be melted with 26;40 minas of copper for making 100 pointed mar-tu daggers; 2;10 minas of silver for making their knobs: the Palace has given on the occasion of the military expedition (against) the city of Aḫ[aza]nig.

19. 56 gín DILMUN an-na
šub *si-in*
21. 5 ma-na ŠA.PI gín DILMUN
XIX. 1. a-gar$_5$-gar$_5$
kin$_5$-ak 17 ĝír mar-tu zú
3. *wa*
3 ĝír mar-tu *ba-du-u$_4$* kù:babbar-gi
5. 2 ma-na TAR kù:babbar
šu-bal-ak
7. TAR kù-gi
nu$_{11}$-za
9. *ša-ga-tum-sù*
*wa*
11. *kam$_4$-ma-a-tum-sù*
7 gín DILMUN kù:babbar
13. *ba-du-u$_4$*
3 ĝír mar-tu-*sù*
15. 1 ma-na ŠA.PI gín DILMUN an-na
šub *si-in*
17. 26 ma-na ŠA.PI a-gar$_5$-gar$_5$
kin$_5$-ak
19. 1 *mi-at* ĝír mar-tu ti{-la}
2 ma-na 10 gín DILMUN kù:babbar
21. kin$_5$-ak
XX. 1. *kam$_4$-ma-a-tum-sù*
in-na-sum
3. SA.ZA$_x$$^{ki}$
*in* ud
5. níĝ-kas$_4$
*A-ḫ*[*a-za-*]*ni-ig*⸢$^{ki}$⸣

(50)
7. 3 ma-na kù:babbar
lul-gu-ak
9. kù:babbar
lú mu-DU
11. *Áb-zu*$^{ki}$
*I-bí-zi-kir*
13. šu-mu-tak$_4$

(51)
1 ma-na ŠÚ+ŠA 4 gín DILMUN an-na
15. šub *si-in*
11 ma-na a-gar$_5$-gar$_5$
17. kin$_5$-ak 6 *ḫar-ʾà-ru$_{12}$* maḫ
lú gud-si-dili
19. 10 gín DILMUN an-na
šub *si-in*
21. 10 lá-2 ma-na a-gar$_5$-gar$_5$
kin$_5$-ak
23. 6 ĜIŠ-kak-ĜIŠ-kak
r. I. 1. eme
gud-si-dili
3. 3 ma-na ŠÚ+ŠA gín DILMUN
kù:babbar
šu-bal-ak
5. ŠA.PI gín DILMUN kù-gi
1 dib
7. NI.GI
*ma-lik-tum*

(52)
9. 10 gín DILMUN an-na
šub *si-in*
11. 2 ĜIŠ-zú
3 gín DILMUN kù:babbar
13. nu$_{11}$-za 2 zag
2 ĜIŠ-gígir-II
15. 5 gín DILMUN kù:babbar
kin$_5$-ak
17. 3 *zú-zú-ba-tum*
*Ib-rí-um*

(53)
19. 2 ma-na TAR kù:babbar
šu-bal-ak
21. TAR kù-gi
*ni-zi-mu*
23. 1 dib
en

(54)
25. 2 gín DILMUN kù:babbar
*ni-zi-mu*
27. nu$_{11}$-⸢za⸣
1 *za-*⸢*ḫa*⸣*-d*[*a*]
29. *wa*
1 ĜIŠ-MUNŠUB
31. 3 gín DILMUN 3 NI kù:babbar
II. 1. šu-bal-ak
2 NI gín DILMUN kù-gi
3. *ni-zi-mu*
*ma-wa-lu*
5. ĜIŠ-bar-ús
*wa*
7. nu$_{11}$-za
1 *za-ḫa-da*
9. en

(50) 3 minas of silver, as a replacement of the silver that had been delivered from the city of Abzu; Ibbi-zikir has handed over.

(51) 1;44 minas of tin to be melted with 11 minas of copper for making 6 big … (*ḫar-ʾà-ru$_{12}$*) of the battering ram; 10 shekels of tin to be melted with 8 minas of copper for making 6 pegs for the blade of the battering ram; 3;20 minas of silver in exchange for 40 shekels of gold for 1 plaque for the … (NI.GI) of the queen.

(52) 10 shekels of tin to be melted in 2 hooks; 3 shekels of silver for plating 2 sides of 2 chariots; 5 shekels of silver for plating 3 ... (*zú-zú-ba-tum*) for Ibrium.

(53) 2;30 minas of silver in exchange for 30 (shekels of) gold for decorating 1 plaque for the king.

(54) 2 shekels of silver for decorating with lamination 1 battle-axe and 1 … (ĜIŠ-MUNŠUB); 3 shekels (and) 3 NI of silver in exchange for 2 NI of gold for decorating the …(*ma-wa-lu*) of a goad and for plating 1 battle-axe for the king.

(55)
15 gín DILMUN kù:babbar
11. šu-bal-ak
3 gín DILMUN kù-gi
13. *ni-zi-mu*
2 níĝ-anše-ak 4 kù-sal
15. sur$_x$-BAR.AN
10 gín DILMUN kù:babbar
17. šu-bal-ak
2 gín DILMUN kù-gi
19. *ni-zi-mu*
1 níĝ-anše-ak 1 kù-sal
21. 2 IGI.NITA
en

(56)
23. ŠÚ+ŠA 5 gín DILMUN kù:babbar
šu-bal-ak
25. 5 gín DILMUN kù-gi
*ni-zi-mu*
27. nu$_{11}$-za
*si-gi*
29. 1 ĜIŠ-gu-kak-šub
en

(57)
III. 1. 2 gín DILMUN kù:babbar
kin$_5$-ak
3. *kam$_4$-ma-a-tum*
zàḫ
5. *ša-ti*
kù-sal
7. ama-gal
en

(58)
9. 5 gín DILMUN kù:babbar
šu-bal-ak
11. 1 gín DILMUN kù-gi
*ni-zi-mu*
13. nu$_{11}$-za
2 *gú-li-lum* kù:babbar-gi
15. *Ki-li-im*
lú *Íl-gú-uš-ma-lik*

(59)
17. 15 gín DILMUN kù:babbar
šu-bal-ak
19. 3 gín DILMUN kù-gi
*ni-zi-mu*
21. maš-maš kù-sal
*Ib-rí-um*

(60)
23. 7 gín DILMUN kù:babbar
šu-bal-ak
25. 1 gín DILMUN 3 NI kù-gi
*ni-zi-mu*
27. 1 dib
*En-na-ni-il*
29. lú
IV. 1. *Rí-ì-ma-lik*

(61)
4 gín DILMUN kù:babbar
3. níĝ-sa$_{10}$ 1 ĝír mar-tu *ba-du-u$_4$*
kù:babbar
NI-*na-du*
5. ugula sur$_x$-BAR.AN
*Gi-ir-da-mu*
7. dumu-nita
*Ib-rí-um*

(62)
9. 5 gín DILMUN kù:babbar
kin$_5$-ak
11. 1 *zi-zi-ḫi-tum*
*Dar-ib-da-mu*
13. dumu-munus
en

(63)
15. 15 gín DILMUN kù:babbar
nu$_{11}$-za 1 *ḫa-bù*
17. TAR kù:babbar
šu-bal-ak
19. 6 gín DILMUN kù-gi
nu$_{11}$-za 1 *ar-ra-si-sù*
21. ŠÚ+ŠA gín DILMUN kù:babbar

(55) 15 shekels of silver in exchange for 3 shekels of gold for decorating 2 bridles (and) 4 buckles for the team of mules; 10 shekels of silver in exchange for 2 shekels of gold for decorating 1 bridle (and) 1 buckle of 2 donkeys of the king.

(56) 25 shekels of silver in exchange for 5 shekels of gold for decorating with lamination a spearhead for the king.

(57) 2 shekels of silver for making the lost knob of the buckle of the king's mother.

(58) 5 shekels of silver in exchange for 1 shekel of gold for decorating with lamination 2 bracelets of silver and gold for Kilim, (son) of Ilguš-malik.

(59) 15 shekels of silver in exchange for 3 shekels of gold for a striped decoration of a buckle for Ibrium.

(60) 7 shekels of silver in exchange for 1 shekel (and) 3 NI of gold for decorating 1 plaque for Ennani-il, (son) of Reʾi-malik.

(61) 4 shekels of silver for the purchase of 1 *b.* mar-tu dagger (decorated with) silver for NInadu, the overseer of the team of mules of Giʾir-damu, son of Ibrium.

(62) 5 shekels of silver for making 1 … (*zi-zi-ḫi-tum*) for Tarib-damu, daughter of the king.

(63) 15 shekels of silver for plating 1 mace; 30 (shekels of) silver in exchange for 6 shekels of gold for plating its handle; 20 shekels of silver for the circular stand of the 4 horns of 2 bulls: offering of the king for the god Rašap of the city of ʾAdani, at the AMA-ra (festival).

ʾ*a*$_5$-*na-gu*
23. 4 si 2 gud
nídba
25. en
$^{d}$*Ra-sa-ap*
27. ʾ*À-da-ni*$^{ki}$
*in*
29. $^{d}$AMA-*ra*

(64)
16 ma-na
V. 1. TAR kù:babbar
níĝ-sa$_{10}$ 1 *mi-at* aktum-TÚG
3. 5 zara$_6$-TÚG
30 lá-1 túg-NI.NI
5. 80 ʾ*à-da-um*-TÚG-I
1 dùl-TÚG *Ma-rí*$^{ki}$
7. 4 gada-TÚG
46 sal-TÚG
9. 62 íb+III-TÚG sa$_6$ gùn
1 *mi-at* 80 íb+III-TÚG gùn
11. 1 *mi-at* 50 kuš-kuš sa$_6$ ĝi$_6$
ŠA.PI gín DILMUN kù:babbar
13. níĝ-sa$_{10}$ ĜIŠ-bar-ús
*Wa-ba-rúm*
15. <ki:lam$_7$> ʾ*À-da-ni*$^{ki}$

(65)
5 gín DILMUN kù:babbar
17. šu-bal-ak
1 gín DILMUN kù-gi
19. 1 kù-sal 1 buru$_4$-MUŠEN
níĝ-ba
21. ama-gal
en
23. $^{d}$*Ra-sa-ap*
ʾ*À-da-ni*$^{ki}$

(66)
25. TAR kù:babbar 2 *bu*-DI
*Ti-ša-li-im*
VI. 1. *ma-lik-tum*
*Ì-mar*$^{ki}$
3. *in* ud
DU.DU
5. *mi-nu*
ʾ*À-da-ni*$^{ki}$

(67)
7. TAR 3 gín DILMUN 3 NI kù:babbar
šu-bal-ak
9. 6 gín DILMUN 2 NI kù-gi
2 *gú-li-lum*
11. níĝ-ba
$^{d}$*Ku-ra*

(68)
13. 10 gín DILMUN kù:babbar
nu$_{11}$-za 1 an-dùl $^{d}$*Iš*:*šára*
15. en
7 gín DILMUN kù:babbar
17. šu-bal-ak
1 gín 3 NI kù-gi
19. nu$_{11}$-za *ba-na-i-sù*
*wa*
21. íb-lá-*sù*
*wa*
23. šu-kešda gùn-*sù*

(69)
ŠA.PI lá-1 gín DILMUN kù:babbar
25. *a-dè*
1 an-dùl
27. *sa-du*
en
29. *wa*
*ma-lik-tum*
31. *si-in*
NE-*na-áš*$^{ki}$

(70)
33. 2 gín DILMUN kù:babbar *ḫa-za-nu*
VII. 1. *a-ḫa-šum*
gaba
3. $^{d}$*Ku-ra*
*wa*
5. en

(71)
1 gín DILMUN kù:babbar
7. 1 *gú-li-lum*
ùz-munus

(64) 16;30 minas of silver for the purchase of 265 garments, 242 kilts (and) 150 black hides of good quality; 40 shekels of silver for the purchase of goads: Wabarum (has received) <at the market of> the city of ʾAdani.

(65) 5 shekels of silver in exchange for 1 shekel of gold for 1 buckle (and) 1 shield: gift of the king's mother for the god Rašap of the city of ʾAdani.

(66) 30 (shekels of) silver for 2 toggle-pins for Tiša-lim, the queen of the city of Imar, when she went from the city of ʾAdani.

(67) 33 shekels (and) 3 NI of silver in exchange for 6 shekels (and) 2 NI of gold for 2 bracelets: gift for the god Kura.

(68) 10 shekels of silver for plating 1 statue of the goddess Išḫara of the king; 7 shekels of silver in exchange for 1 shekel (and) 3 NI of gold for plating its face and its belt and its multicoloured *pair of gloves*.

(69) 39 shekels of silver for 1 statue of the protective spirits of the king and the queen (to take) to the city of NEnaš.

(70) 2 shekels of silver for beads (and) … (*a-ḫa-šum*) for the pectoral of (the statues of) the god Kura and the king.

(71) 1 shekel of silver for 1 *collar* for a female goat for the lustration of the mausoleum of the city of NEnaš, for the enthroning of the king.

9. a:tu$_{22}$
é *ma-tim*
11. NE-*na-áš*$^{ki}$
*ma-lu-gi-iš*
13. en

(72)
3 gín DILMUN 3 NI kù:babbar
15. šu-bal-ak
2 NI gín DILMUN kù-gi
17. *ni-zi-mu*
nu$_{11}$-za
19. *ša-ga-ti*
1 ĝír mar-tu zú
21. *I-ti-ne*
*A-da-bí-gú*$^{ki}$
23. maškim
*Ba-ga-ma*

(73)
25. 5 gín DILMUN kù:babbar
šu-bal-ak
27. 1 gín DILMUN kù-gi
*ni-zi-mu*
29. 1 dib
*Ti-ti-nu*
31. maškim
*Ib-rí-um*

(74)
VIII. 1. 2 ma-na TAR kù:babbar
šu-bal-ak
3. TAR kù-gi 1 dib
*A-a-zi-kir*
5. lú NI-*wa-lum*

(75)
2 ½ gín DILMUN kù:babbar
7. šu-bal-ak
½ gín DILMUN kù-gi
9. *ni-zi-mu*
1 dib
11. *En-na-il*
*Ga-sa*$^{ki}$

(76)
13. 5 gín DILMUN kù:babbar
*ni-zi-mu*
15. 2 níĝ-anše-ak 4 kù-sal
*Šum*-bàd$^{ki}$
17. dumu-nita
*Ib-rí-um*

(77)
19. 10 gín DILMUN an-na
šub *si-in*
21. 1 ma-na 10 gín DILMUN a-gar$_5$-gar$_5$
kin$_5$-ak
23. 3 ĝír mar-tu
ugula *Ib-al*$_6$$^{ki}$
25. DU.DU
*Du-gú-ra-su*$^{ki}$
27. šu-mu-tak$_4$
ŠÚ+ŠA 5
IX. 1. gín DILMUN kù:babbar
níĝ-kaskal-*sù*

(78)
3. ŠÚ+ŠA gín DILMUN an-na
šub *si-in*
5. 20 lá-2 ma-na a-gar$_5$-gar$_5$
kin$_5$-ak
7. 1 šum maḫ

(79)
5 gín DILMUN kù:babbar
9. kin$_5$-ak
1 ĝír
11. 5 gín DILMUN kù:babbar
šu-bal-ak
13. 1 gín DILMUN kù-gi
nu$_{11}$-za-*sù*
15. lú TAR
*sa*
17. šu-dub
en
19. *wa*
*ma-lik-tum*

(72) 3 shekels (and) 3 NI of silver in exchange for 2 NI of gold for decorating with lamination the … (*ša-ga-ti*) of 1 serrated mar-tu dagger for Itine of the city of Adabik, representative of Bagama.
(73) 5 shekels of silver in exchange for 1 shekel of gold for decorating 1 plaque for Titinu, representative of Ibrium.
(74) 2;30 minas of silver in exchange for 30 (shekels of) gold for 1 plaque for Aya-zikir, (son) of NIwalum.
(75) 2 ½ shekels of silver in exchange for ½ shekel of gold for decorating 1 plaque for Enna-il of the city of Gasa.
(76) 5 shekels of silver for decorating 2 bridles (and) 4 buckles for Šumbad, son of Ibrium.
(77) 10 shekels of tin to be melted with 1;10 minas of copper for making 3 mar-tu daggers, handed over to the overseer of the city of Ibᶜal, (who) has to go to the city of Dugurasu; 25 shekels of silver for his travel provision.
(78) 20 shekels of tin to be melted with 18 minas of copper for making 1 big saw.
(79) 5 shekels of silver for making 1 dagger; 5 shekels of silver in exchange for 1 shekel of gold for its lamination (and its) half for a ring: for the king and the queen.

(80)

21. 3 NI kù:babbar
1 bar:ús
23. lú
dur
25. 2 si-dù
en
27. *wa*
*ma-lik-tum*

(81)

29. ŠÚ+ŠA gín DILMUN kù:babbar
2 *bu*-DI
31. *Ti-ša-li-im*
*ma-lik-tum*
33. *Ì-mar*$^{ki}$
*in* ud
35. DU.DU
*mi-nu*

X. 1. NI-*ab*$^{ki}$
*si-in*
3. SA.ZA$_x$$^{ki}$

(82)

12 ma-na kù:babbar
5. níĝ-sa$_{10}$ 30 lá-1 túg-NI.NI
60 *ˀà-da-um*-TÚG-I
7. 82 sal-TÚG
6 dùl-TÚG *Ma-rí*$^{ki}$
9. 17 gada-TÚG
52 íb+III-TÚG sa$_6$ gùn
11. 2 *mi-at* 40 íb+III-TÚG gùn
1 ma-na kù:babbar
13. níĝ-sa$_{10}$ raš-SAR Kur$^{ki}$
ŠÚ+ŠA 5 gín DILMUN kù:babbar
15. níĝ-sa$_{10}$ 1 gud
ki:lam$_7$
17. $^{d}$*Ga-mi-iš*

(83)

55 gín DILMUN kù:babbar
19. níĝ-sa$_{10}$ 2 gud
ki:lam$_7$
21. *Kab-lu*$_5$*-ul*$^{ki}$
šu-mu-tak$_4$

XI. 1. ⌜$^{d}$*Ku-ra*⌝
[ ]
3. [ -U]D

(84)

[ ] k[ù:babbar]
5. níĝ-[b]a
⌜*Ne-zi*⌝
7. *wa*
*Ìr-*[*b*]*a-il*
9. *Ma-rí*$^{ki}$
maškim
11. ga:eš$_8$
Saḫar$^{ki}$
13. [šu-m]u-[ta]k$_4$

(85)

1 níĝ-lá-gaba 1 níĝ-lá-saĝ
15. [1 šu-d]ub
[x g]ín DILMUN kù[:babbar]
17. kin$_5$-ak
[*ḫ*]*a-za-nu*
19. 2 šu-dub
en
21. *wa*
*ma-lik-tum*
23. 5 gín DILMUN an-na
šub *si-in*
25. 1 sig$_7$-igi
*ma-lik-tum*
27. 1 ma-na ŠA.PI gín DILMUN
kù:babbar
šu-bal-ak
29. ŠÚ+ŠA gín DILMUN kù-gi
kin$_5$-ak
31. 2 šu-dub
en
33. *wa*
*ma-lik-tum*
35. sikil

XII. 1. [1 ma-na kù:babbar(?)]
[šu-bal-ak]
3. 12[(+x)] gín DILMUN kù-gi
kin$_5$-ak
5. 1 šu-dub

(80) 3 NI of silver for 1 staff of the chain of 2 betyls of the king and the queen.

(81) 20 shekels of silver for 2 toggle-pins for Tiša-lim, the queen of the city of Imar, when she came from the city of NIab to the Palace.

(82) 12 minas of silver for the purchase of 194 garments (and) 292 kilts; 1 mina of silver for the purchase of leek from the mountain region; 25 shekels of silver for the purchase of 1 OX: at the market of the god Kamiš.

(83) 55 shekels of silver for the purchase of 2 oxen, at the market of the city of Kablul, handed over for the god Kura […].

(84) [x] s[ilver]: gi[f]t for Nezi and Ir[b]a-il of the city of Mari, representatives of the travelling merchant of the city of Saḫar: [hande]d [ove]r.

(85) 1 breast-band, 1 headband (and) [1 rin]g; [x she]kels of sil[ver] for making beads of 2 rings for the king and the queen; 5 shekels of tin to be melted in 1 eyebrow (decoration) for the queen; 1;40 minas of silver in exchange for 20 shekels of gold for making 2 rings for the king and the queen (for their) purification rite; [1 mina of silver in exchange for] 12 shekels of gold for making 1 ring … (*ˀà-lum*) for the queen.

*ma-lik-tum*
7. *ʾà-lum*

(86)
50 gín DILMUN kù:babbar
9. níĝ-sa$_{10}$ 1 ĝír mar-tu kù-gi
*I-bí-zi-kir*
11. dumu-nita
*Ib-rí-u*[*m*]

(87)
13. [x ma-na x gín DILMUN kù:babbar]
[šu-ba]l-[a]k
15. [x kù-g]i
[1 í]b-lá [1 *si-t*]*i*-[*tu*]*m* [1 gí]r-[ku]n
17. ⌜56⌝ gín DILMUN kù:babbar
níĝ-sa$_{10}$ 1 ĝír mar-tu kù-gi
19. níĝ-ba
*Ib-rí-um*
21. *in* ud
níĝ-mu-sá
23. *ma-lik-tum*

(88)
15 ma-na kù:babbar
25. [šu]-bal-ak
XIII. 1. 3 ma-na kù-gi
kin$_5$-ak
3. 6 íb-lá 6 *si-ti-tum* 6 ĝír-kun
níĝ-ba
5. *Maḫ-ra-da-mu*
*Ì-lum-a-ḫi*
7. *I-da-ni-ki-mu*
*I-in-*$^{d}$*ʾÀ-da*
9. *Ku-ra-da-mu*
dumu-nita
11. en
*wa*
13. *I-ib-ma-lik*
šeš
15. ama-gal
en

(89)
17. TAR kù:babbar
kin$_5$-ak 1 íb-lá 1 *si-ti-tum* 1 ĝír-kun
19. níĝ-ba
*ʾÀ-daš*
21. dumu-nita
*A-du-ba*
23. *ʾÀ-ru*$_{12}$*-gú*$^{ki}$

(90)
5 ma-na ŠA.PI kù:babbar
25. [10+]7 [*b*]*u*$^{?}$-DI [ŠÚ+Š]A-ŠÚ+ŠA
[níĝ-b]a
27. *Ra-ù-tum*
*Kir-*[*s*]*u-*[*u*]*d*
29. [*En-na-*$^{d}$Utu]
XIV. 1. *Ra-ba*$_x$*-tum*
*Maš-ga-sa-du*
3. *Ma-ga-ra-du*
*Tíš-má-da-mu*
5. *Ra-ba*$_x$*-tum*-II
dam
7. en
*wa*
9. *Ma-ù-ud*
*Za-ni-ḫi-Ma-rí*$^{ki}$
11. 2 dumu-munus
en
13. *wa*
ama-gal
15. *Ib-rí-um*
*wa*
17. *A-zi-mu*
*Ti-lu-du*
19. *Ti-a-da-mu*
*Kir-su-ud*
21. dam-*sù*
*wa*
23. *Iš-ru*$_{12}$*-ud*
nin-ni
25. *Du-si-gú*
*Ki-sa-du*

(91)
27. 50 gín DILMUN kù:babbar
kin$_5$-ak
29. 2 *bu*-DI
[ ]
31. [ ]

(86) 50 shekels of silver for the purchase of 1 mar-tu dagger (decorated with) gold for Ibbi-zikir, son of Ibriu[m].

(87) [x silver in exchange for x gold for 1 be]lt, [1 sh]ea[t]h (and) [1 pen]d[an]t; 56 shekels of silver for the purchase of 1 mar-tu dagger (decorated with) gold: gift for Ibrium on the occasion of the marriage of the queen.

(88) 15 minas of silver [in ex]change for 3 minas of gold for making 6 belts, 6 sheaths (and) 6 dagger pendants: gift for Maḫra-damu, Ilum-aḫi, Ida-nikimu, Iʾin-Hadda, Kura-damu, sons of the king, and for Iʾib-malik, brother of the king's mother.

(89) 30 (shekels of) silver for making 1 belt, 1 sheath (and) 1 dagger pendant: gift for ʾAdaš, son of Aduba of the city of ʾArugu.

(90) 5;40 minas of silver for [1]7 [tog]gle-pins of 20 (shekels) each: [gif]t for Raʾutum, Kir[s]ut, [Enna-Utu], Rabatum, Mašgasadu, Magaradu, Tišma-damu, Rabatum, (who are) women of the king, and for Mauʾut, Zaniḫi-Mari, (who are) 2 daughters of the king, and for the mother of Ibrium, and for Azimu, Tiludu, Tia-damu, Kirsut, (who are) his (= Ibrium's) women and for Išrut, sister of Dusigu, and for Kisadu.

(91) 50 shekels of silver for making 2 toggle-pins […].

(92)
[ ]
33. [x *bu-*]DI
[ ]-⌜x⌝
XV. 1. šu-ba$_4$-ti

(93)
50 gín DILMUN kù:babbar
3. šu-bal-ak
10 gín DILMUN kù-gi
5. *ni-zi-mu*
1 dib
7. *Bù-sum*
*Ù-ti-ig*$^{ki}$

(94)
9. 15 gín DILMUN kù:babbar
nu$_{11}$-za 1 *ḫa-bu*
11. TAR kù:babbar
šu-bal-ak
13. 6 gín DILMUN kù-gi
nu$_{11}$-za *ar-ra-si-sù*
15. níĝ-ba
$^{d?}$*À-da*
17. lú *Lu-ub*$^{ki}$
*in*
19. *gi*-NI

(95)
10 gín DILMUN kù:babbar
21. níĝ-ba
*Daš-na*
23. *M[a-]rí*$^{ki}$

(96)
[(ca. 7 lines)]
XVI. 1. ⌜nu$_{11}$-za⌝ 1 ĝír mar-tu
níĝ-ba
3. $^{d}$*Ra-sa-ap*
10 gín DILMUN kù:babbar
5. 2 *bu*-DI
níĝ-ba
7. $^{d}$*A-da-ma*
*gú-núm*
9. *ma-lik-tum*
ì-na-sum
11. *in* ud
šu-mu-níĝin
13. é
diĝir-diĝir-diĝir

(97)
15. TAR 3 gín DILMUN 3 NI kù:babbar
šu-bal-ak
17. 6 gín DILMUN 2 NI kù-gi
2 *gú-li-lum*
19. níĝ-ba
$^{d}$*Aš-da-bíl*
21. 6 gín DILMUN 2 NI kù:babbar
2 *gú-li-lum*
23. níĝ-ba
$^{d}$*Am-ma-rí-ig*
25. [x g]ín [DILMUN x NI kù:babbar]
[(ca. 7 lines)]

(98)
XVII. 1. [ ]
kin$_5$-ak
3. 1 *mu-rúm*
*wa*
5. 1 *gúm-a-nu*
⌜*wa*⌝
7. 2 ĜIŠ.ALAM
*su-da$_5$-lik*
9. en

(99)
16 gín DILMUN 3 NI kù:babbar
11. šu-bal-ak
3 gín DILMUN 2 NI kù-gi
13. kin$_5$-ak
4 ĝeštu$_x$-lá
15. *I-bí-zi-kir*
dumu-nita
17. *Ib-rí-um*
*wa*
19. *En-na-ni-il*
lú *Ša-ù-um*
21. *wa*
*En-na-ì*

(92) [x silver for x toggle]-pins, […] has received.

(93) 50 shekels of silver in exchange for 10 shekels of gold for decorating 1 plaque for Busum of the city of Utig.

(94) 15 shekels of silver for plating 1 mace; 30 (shekels of) silver in exchange for 6 shekels of gold for plating its handle: gift for the god Hadda of the city of Lub, in month IV.

(95) 10 shekels of silver: gift for Dašna of the city of M[a]ri.

(96) […] for plating 1 mar-tu dagger: gift for the god Rašap; 10 shekels of silver for 2 toggle-pins: gift for the god Adamma *gunum*: the queen has given on the occasion of the procession to the gods' temple.

(97) 33 shekels (and) 3 NI of silver in exchange for 6 shekels (and) 2 NI of gold for 2 bracelets: gift for the god Ašdabil; 6 shekels (and) 2 NI of silver for 2 bracelets: gift for the god Ammarik; [x shek]els [(and) x NI of silver …].

(98) […] for making 1 *mu-rúm*-container and 1 *gúm-a-nu*-container and the 2 statues (on the occasion of) the king's accession to the throne.

(99) 16 shekels (and) 3 NI of silver in exchange for 3 shekels (and) 2 NI of gold for making 4 earrings for Ibbi-zikir, son of Ibrium, and for Ennani-il, (son) of Šaum and Enna-i(l), (son) of Zibada (and) […].

23. lú *Zi-ba-da*
[ ]-⸢x⸣-*aš*
25. [ -*t*]*i*

(100)
[(ca. 7 lines)]
XVIII. 1. [
73 íb+III-TÚG sa$_6$ gùn
3. 1 *mi-at* 60 íb+III-TÚG gùn
ki:lam$_7$
5. $^{d}$*Áš-da-bíl*
*Du-ub*$^{ki}$
7. *Ìr-ku*$^{ki}$

(101)
5 kù:babbar
9. šu-bal-ak
1 kù-gi 1 kù-sal
11. níĝ-ba
*Da-bur-da-mu*
13. *al*$_6$
*gú-a-ti*
15. $^{d}$*Ba-ra-ma*

(102)
2 ma-na TAR kù:babbar
17. šu-bal-ak
TAR kù-gi 2 *bu*-DI
19. ama-gal
*Ib-rí-um*

(103)
21. ŠÚ+ŠA kù:babbar
daḫ$_x$(MU.MU.MU)
23. ⸢níĝ⸣-sa$_{10}$
[(ca. 9 lines)]
XIX. 1. [ ]
[ ]

(104)
3. 10 kù:babbar
lul-gu-ak
5. 1 *zú-zú-ba-tum*
*Ib-rí-um*
7. zàḫ

(105)
2 ½ kù:babbar
9. šu-bal-ak
½ kù-gi
11. *ni-zi-mu*
1 dib
13. *A-mi-du*
lú *I-bí-um*

(106)
15. 50 kù:babbar
šu-bal-ak
17. 10 kù-gi
*ni-zi-mu*
19. 1 dib
*Ib-du-*<d>*Aš-dar*
21. dumu-nita
*A-šum*

(107)
23. 5 kù:babbar
šu-bal-ak
25. 1 kù-gi
*ni-zi-mu*
27. 1 dib
*Ir*-NE
29. lú
*Iš*$_{11}$*-gú-ma*

(108)
31. 7 ½ kù:babbar
šu-bal-ak
33. 1 ½ kù-gi
*ni-zi-m*[*u*]
35. 1 di[b]
[(ca. 8 lines)]

(109)
XX. 1. [ ]
[ ]
3. 2 gíd:TÚG
4 *ʾà-da-*<*um*-TÚG>-I
5. 12 aktum-TÚG
7 gada-TÚG
7. 3 gu-dùl-TÚG

(100) [x silver for the purchase of] 233 kilts, at the market of the god Ašdabil of the city of Dub which (took place in) the city of Irku.
(101) 5 (shekels of) silver in exchange for 1 (shekel of) gold for 1 buckle: gift of Tabur-damu above a vessel (*gú-a-ti*) for the goddess Barama.
(102) 2;30 minas of silver in exchange for 30 (shekels of) gold for 2 toggle-pins for the mother of Ibrium.
(103) 20 (shekels of) silver, in addition, for the purchase of […].
(104) 10 (shekels of) silver, as replacement of a lost … (*zú-zú-ba-tum*) for Ibrium.
(105) 2 ½ (shekels of) silver in exchange for ½ (shekel of) gold for decorating 1 plaque for Amidu, (son) of Ibbium.
(106) 50 (shekels of) silver in exchange for 10 (shekels of) gold for decorating 1 plaque for Ibdu-Ašdar, son of Ašum.
(107) 5 (shekels of) silver in exchange for 1 (shekel of) gold for decorating 1 plaque for IrNE, (son) of Išguma.
(108) 7 ½ (shekels of) silver in exchange for 1 ½ (shekel of) gold for decorati[ng] 1 plaq[ue for …].
(109) [x silver for the purchase of x+]28 garments for the work gang (and) 49 kilts; 1;20 minas of silver for the purchase of 9 black bags (and) 24 red bags; 8 (shekels of) silver for the purchase of goads: at the market of the god Hadda.

é-duru$_5^{ki}$
9. 10 lá-1 íb+III-TÚG sa$_6$ gùn
40 íb+III-TÚG gùn
11. 1 ma-na ŠÚ+ŠA kù:babbar
níĝ-sa$_{10}$ 10 lá-1 *gàr-su* ĝi$_6$
13. 24 *gàr-su* si$_4$-si$_4$
8 kù:babbar
15. níĝ-sa$_{10}$ ĜIŠ-bar-ús
ki:lam$_7$
17. $^{d.?}$*À-da*

(110)
5 kù:babbar
19. 15 *ḫa-za-nu*
2 gìn-gìn 2 si$_4$
21. 1 šu-dub
*Ib-rí-um*

(111)
23. 4 kù:babbar
15 *ḫa-za-nu*
25. 2 gìn-gìn 2 si$_4$
1 šu-dub
27. *I-bí-zi-kir*

(112)
ŠÚ+ŠA 2 ½ ⸢kù:babbar⸣
29. šu-bal-ak
4 ½ kù-gi
31. *ʾa$_5$-na-gu*
2 banšur
33. *maš-ar-da*
*Ib-rí-um*
35. *<I->bí-zi-kir*

(113)
2 kù:babbar
37. [*m*]*u-ḫar-t*[*um*]
[ ]
39. [ ]
XXI. 1. [ ]
[ ]
3. dumu-munus tur
en

(114)
5. 2 ma-na TAR kù:babbar
šu-bal-ak
7. TAR kù-gi 2 *bu-*DI
*Di-rin$_x$-da-mu*
9. ŠÚ+ŠA kù:babbar 2 *bu-*DI
15 kù:babbar
11. šu-bal-ak
3 kù-gi nu$_{11}$-za 2 saĝ-*sù*
13. ŠÚ+ŠA kù:babbar
šu-bal-ak
15. 4 kù-gi 2 kù-sal
*Tir$_5$-bù-da-mu*
17. nin-ni-*sù*

(115)
3 ma-na ŠÚ+ŠA an-na
19. šub *si-in*
26 ma-na ŠÚ+ŠA a-gar$_5$-gar$_5$
21. kin$_5$-ak
1 *mi-at* 10 ĝír gibil
23. 10 ma-na kù:babbar
šu-b[al-]a[k]
25. 2 ma-na kù-gi
kin$_5$-ak 2 íb-lá 2 *si-ti-tum* 2 ĝír-kun
27. 1 ma-na TAR kù:babbar
níĝ-sa$_{10}$ 2 ⸢ĝír⸣ [ ]
29. [ ]
XXII. 1. [ ]
[ ]

(116)
3. [ ]
[ ]
5?. [ ] ⸢15⸣
9. 2 ĜIŠ-gu-kak-šub
2 gu-x šub 8
11. en

(117)
1 ma-na 10 kù:babbar
13. ⸢níĝ-ba⸣
diĝir-diĝir-diĝir

(110) 5 (shekels of) silver for 15 beads. 2 (beads) in lapis lazuli, 2 (beads) in carnelian, of a ring for Ibrium.
(111) 4 (shekels of) silver for 15 beads. 2 (beads) in lapis lazuli, 2 (beads) in carnelian, of a ring for Ibbi-zikir.
(112) 22 ½ (shekels of) silver in exchange for 4 ½ (shekels of) gold for the circular stand of 2 tables for the steles of Ibrium (and) Ibbi-zikir.
(113) 2 (shekels of) silver for a … (*mu-ḫar-tum*) […] for the king's little daughter.
(114) 2;30 minas of silver in exchange for 30 (shekels of) gold for 2 toggle-pins for Tirin-damu; 20 (shekels of) silver for 2 toggle-pins; 15 (shekels of) silver in exchange for 3 (shekels of) gold for their 2 heads; 20 (shekels of) silver in exchange for 4 (shekels of) gold for 2 buckles for Terbu-damu, her sister.
(115) 3;20 minas of tin to be melted with 26;20 minas of copper for making 110 new daggers; 10 minas of silver in exchan[ge] for 2 minas of gold for making 2 belts, 2 sheaths (and) 2 dagger pendants; 1;30 minas of silver for the purchase of 2 daggers […].
(116) […] 2 spearheads, 2 … (gu-x šub 8) for the king.
(117) 1;10 minas of silver: gift for the gods.

(118)
15. 1 ma-na kù:babbar
níĝ-sa$_{10}$ 1 ĝír mar-tu kù-gi
17. en
*Ì-mar*$^{ki}$
19. *Ib-rí-um*
šu-mu-tak$_4$

(119)
21. 1 ma-na TAR kù:babbar
níĝ-sa$_{10}$ 2 gu-dùl-TÚG é-duru$_5$$^{ki}$
23. *áš-ti*
*Ša-bir*$_5$*-ti-um*$^{ki}$

(120)
25. 1 ma-na 20[+x
[níĝ-]sa$_{10}$ [20+]10 íb+III-TÚG sa$_6$
gùn
27. ki:[la]m$_7$
[*g*]*i-*⌜*ba*⌝*-lu*
29. [*ʾA-da-ni*$^{ki}$]
[ ]
31. ŠU/D[A]-⌜X⌝[ ]
12 [ ]
l. ed. 1. [ ]
(blank)

(121)
x+1. AN.ŠÈ.GÚ 2 *mi-at* 65 ma-na 4 gín
DILMUN kù:babbar
è
x+3. [(1+$^?$)]1 *mi-at* 10 lá-2 ma-na š[A.PI]
gí[n] DI[LMUN] kù:babbar
al$_6$-ĝál
x+5. lú diri

(118) 1 mina of silver for the purchase of 1 mar-tu dagger (decorated with) gold for the king of the city of Imar, Ibrium has handed over.
(119) 1;30 minas of silver for the purchase of 2 garments for the work gang from the city of Šabirtium.
(120) 1;20[+x] minas [of silver for the pur]chase of 30 kilts, at the mar[ke]t of the [*g*]*ibalu* [of the city of ʾAdani …].
(121) Total: 265;04 minas of silver: expenditure; 208;40 minas of silver are present, as remainder.

## Commentary

This document (already published as *MEE* 7, 34) has to be dated to the year Ibr. 14. It opens with the registration of the expenditures of 1 mina (470 g) of silver for the renewal rite related to the city-god Kura, which fell at the beginning of the new year. The 3 shekels (23 g) of silver to be given to the god for a further ceremony concerning his head in a later period of the year are registered in § 37. Kura also received a pair of gold bracelets of 6 ½ shekels (52 g) as an annual offering (§ 67). The "gods" received a gift of 1;10 minas (548 g) of silver (§ 117). Tinib-dulum, a sister of the king, received 8 minas (3.76 kg) of silver in her function as a priestess of the god ʾAdabal (§ 2).

The "expended", è, silver this year amounted to 265;04 minas (124.863 kg). The total (partially preserved) of the silver "present", al$_6$-ĝal, in the Treasury was quite probably 208;40 minas (98.073 kg), (§ 121).

This was the year that king Išʿar-damu married Tabur-damu, his "queen", *maliktum*. She was a daughter of Irib-damu, a brother of his father Irkab-damu, and therefore Išʿar-damu's cousin. This lady had already been mentioned in the annual document from two years earlier, XXI 15 § 77, according to which she had received two pieces of gold jewelry.

Irkab-damu had married his "queen", *maliktum* (whose name is unknown) around the sixth year of his reign, when he was probably still rather young, and he died about six years later as a consequence of a wound he received in the battle against Enna-Dagan of Mari near ʾAtidu (see Archi 2022a). Išʿar-damu, the son of Dusigu (a spouse of second rank of Irkab-damu), was borne sometime during those years. He was chosen by Irkab-damu as his heir after the death of the queen. Išʿar-damu must have therefore wed when he was eighteen or nineteen years old. He already had a "small daughter", dumu-munus tur en (§ 113), and perhaps two sons (Archi 2021b, p. 8). On this occasion Tabur-damu offered a buckle of 1 shekel (8 g) of gold to Barama, the *paredra* of Kura

(§ 101). The "women of the king", dam en, his two daughters, minister Ibrium's mother and his four spouses, and the sister of Dusigu (the king's mother) received toggle-pins (§ 90).

The gifts delivered on the occasion of Išʿar-damu's marriage are also listed in the ritual document *ARET* XI 2, and in the monthly document of delivery of garments TM.75.G.2417 (see Archi 2021b, pp. 7–15). This marriage is also mentioned in the annual mu-DU document *ARET* XIV 67 § 30 (from the year Ibr. 14): *in* NE-*na-aš in mu-lu-gi* en "in NEnaš, on (the occasion) of the king's attaining to sovereignty". Some of these gifts are also listed here: § 87 (a belt with a dagger for Ibrium); § 88 (five brothers of the king: Maḫra-damu, Ilum-aḫi, Ida-nikimu, Iʾin-Hadda, Kura-damu, and Iʾib-malik – a brother of Dusigu, the king's mother – received a dagger each, whose decorations had needed 3 minas [1.41 kg] of gold); § 89 (a belt of 30 shekels [235 g] of silver for ʾAdaš, son of Aduba, from ʾArugu).

This is the year in which fell the war against the city of Kakmium. Ilgušti, the son of Igi, "occupied", tuš-LÚ×TIL, Kakmium (§ 3). Ḫazum, a representative of Ibrium, occupied Timatim, a city belonging to Kakmium (§ 33), while Dubišum, son of Gumanidu, occupied Kakmium, from the city of Šuran (§ 34), and Ruzi-malik, the son of Irig, occupied Abratig (§ 35). Ibrium instead went "to uproot the barley of Kakmium" (§ 42). Šarabig, another city which belonged to Kakmium, was occupied by ʾAdaš (§ 48), (cf. also *ARET* III 802 rev. I: en *Kak-mi-um*$^{ki}$ šu-du$_8$ *in Ša-ra-bí-ig*$^{ki}$). For this war, see Archi 2021a, p. 206.

After these events, Ilba-damu, the king of Kakmium, came to Ebla to seal the peace. He received a notable gift: a belt with a dagger and a plaque which needed 2 minas (940 g) of gold, another dagger decorated with gold valued at 50 shekels (391 g) of silver, and two tools for his chariot, for which were employed 4 shekels (31 g) of tin and 26 shekels (203 g) of copper, together with 4 shekels (31 g) of silver (§ 40). The alloy contained 13.34% of tin.

The king received some objects (listed in a lacuna) plated with 2 shekels (16 g) and 1 ½ shekels (12 g) of gold respectively (§§ 13, 14); a plaque decorated with 30 shekels (235 g) of gold (§ 53); a battle-axe plated with 2 shekels (16 g) of silver, while ⅔ of a shekel (5 g) of gold were used to plate a goad (§ 54). Three shekels (23 g) of gold were employed for the decoration of the bridle of a team of mules, and 2 shekels (16 g) of gold for the bridle of a team of donkeys (§ 55); another 5 shekels (39 g) of gold were needed for the decoration of a spear (§ 56).

Ten shekels (78 g) of tin and 8 shekels (63 g) of silver were expended for an Ibrium's chariot (§ 52), and 3 shekels (23 g) of gold were fused for making a buckle for him (§ 59). On the occasion of the marriage of the queen, Ibrium received a belt decorated with gold (whose weight is not preserved), and a dagger valued at 56 shekels (438 g) of silver (§ 87). A *zú-zú-ba-tum* of 10 shekels (78 g) of silver, which had been lost, had to be substituted for him (§ 104). His mother received two toggle-pins of 30 shekels (235 g) of gold (§ 102). Both Ibrium and his son Ibbi-zikir, received jewelry of the value of 5 and 4 shekels (39 and 31 g) of gold respectively (§§ 110, 111), and also two plaques decorated with 4 ½ shekels (35 g) of gold (§ 112).

Ibbi-zikir further received a dagger decorated with gold of the value of 50 shekels (291 g) of silver (§ 86).

An envoy from Mari, EZEN-*il*, brought ostrich eggs (§ 22), and *Wa-ru*$_{12}$*-tum* with *I-ku-uḫ* an adult bear (§ 45). *Ne-zi* and *Ìr-ba-il* received an amount (in lacuna) of silver (§ 84). *Daš-na* received 10 shekels (78 g) of silver (§ 95).

§ 7. The price of the two mules brought to Ebla from Nagar was of 3 minas (1.41 kg) of silver each.

§ 8. Two toggle-pins of the weight of 20 shekels (16 g) of silver were sent for the "funerary rite", É×PAP, of a daughter of the king of Burman who had married the son of the king of Raʾak. A funerary rite for a queen of Raʾak fell on the year I.Z. 11 according to *ARET* XXII 10 (= *MEE* 12, 36) o. XIII 9–11, see also *ARET* III 537 IV 4–6; XII 302 r. III 4–6.

§ 9. ʾAgar, the overseer of the mules of Ibbi-zikir, the son of Ibrium, received a bracelet of 50 shekels (391 g) of copper, decorated with 5 shekels (39 g) of gold.

§ 15. Enna-il was sent to Kiš, where he had been already two years earlier (text no. 15 § 73); he received 5 shekels (39 g) of silver as "travel provision".

§ 16. Tarmaš-damu, a "daughter of the king", is mentioned already in text no. 2 § 10. She had performed an offering in "the temple of the god of the king" (either a sacellum at Ebla, or in the "House of Death", the Mausoleum, at NEnaš): a place where rites for the king's ancestors were performed; in this particular case for Irkab-damu, Tarmaš-damu's father.

§ 19. The new bridles of the mules of the king's mother required 50 shekels (391 g) of gold.

§ 20. Tiša-lim, queen of Imar, met Ibbi-zikir, the son of Ibrium, and received two toggle-pins of 20 shekels (157 g) of gold.

§ 21. Wana (an overseer of mules, see Archi 2020b, p. 50) expended 5 minas (3.91 kg) of silver for some mules. According to XXI 20 § 78 (Ibr.17), he acquired one mule for the price of 1 mina (470 g) of silver.

§§ 30, 31. Giᵓir-damu, son of Ibrium, received a dagger decorated with 2 shekels (8 g) of gold, and Napḫa-i(l), his brother, a belt and a dagger decorated with gold, whose amount is not preserved.

§ 32. The queen of Lumnan received two toggle-pins (whose value is not preserved) from the mother of the king, when she went to Uguaᵓaš, the cult place of the Lord, ${}^{d}$BAD, of that city, and his *paredra*, ${}^{d}$BAD-munus, see the indices of *ARET* III, IV XII, XV. She took the place of the previous queen: Dati-TU, a princess of Ebla, who had died in the year Ibr. 08 (see XXI 11 § 29). She, presumably an Eblaite princess, died in the year Ibr. 15 (see XXI 18 § 67).

§ 41. The "watchmen of the house of the king", ME-sig é en, received thirty bracelets of copper decorated with 1;15 minas (587 g) of gold.

§ 43. Four sons of the king of Manuwat, the city which had been defeated by Ebla in the years Ibr. 09, and 10) (see XXI 12, and 13), received a dagger decorated with gold each.

§ 49. It is uncertain if the "military expedition", níĝ-kas$_4$, against Ahazanigu belonged to the war against Kakmium. The Palace provided 523 daggers of different types. The alloy of the 56 shekels (438 g) of tin with the 5;40 minas (2.663 kg) of copper for making 20 daggers had 16.45% of tin (XVIII 19–XIX 4). Each dagger weighed 155 g. The first 300 daggers of "bronze", zabar, needed 10 minas (4.70 kg) of tin, but it is not said the amount of copper used for them (XVIII 9–10). These last were decorated with 7;40 minas (3.603 kg) of silver. All the daggers listed in this section had ornaments in silver.

§ 57. The substitution of a lost element of the buckle of the king's mother needed 2 shekels (16 g) of silver.

§ 61. NInadu, the overseer of the team of mules of Giᵓir-damu, a son of Ibrium, received a dagger decorated with 4 shekels (31 g) of silver.

§ 62. Tarib-damu, a "king's daughter" (that is: daughter of Irkab-damu), received a jewel, for which 5 shekels (9 g) of silver were expended.

§ 66. Tiša-lim, the queen of Imar, received two toggle-pins when she came from ᵓAdani, the major cult place of the god Rašap.

§§ 69, 70, 71. See the parallel passages in the wedding ritual, *ARET* XI 1 §§ 98, 54; 2 §§ 57, 108.

§ 76. *Šum*-bàd${}^{ki}$, a son of Ibrium, received bridles decorated with 5 shekels (39 g) of silver.

§ 77. A "chief", ugula, of the confederation of Ibᶜal, received three daggers for which were employed 10 shekels (78 g) of tin and 1;10 minas (548 g) of copper (that is 12.46% of tin), so that each dagger weighed 160 g. He planned to go on mission to Dugurasu (Tukriš), south of the Caspian Sea. Ebla assigned him 25 shekels (196 g) of silver as "travel provision", níĝ-kaskal: a rather larger amount, what means that he received the task to establish political relations with that state also from the side of Ebla.

§ 78. A "big saw", šum maḫ, needed 20 shekels (157 g) of tin and 18 minas (8,46 kg) of copper: that is with a minimal percentage of tin.

§§ 79. 5 shekels (39 g) of silver and 1 shekel (8 g) of gold used for the decoration of a dagger, and also for a ring, for the king and the queen.

§ 81. Tiša-lim. the queen of Imar, who had already visited the temple of Rašap at ᵓAdani (see § 66), went to the temple of Kamiš at NIab, and then took the occasion to pass by the Palace, at Ebla. She received two toggle-pins of 20 shekels (157 g) of silver.

§ 85. Expenditures of metals for jewels of the king and the queen

§ 98. The amount of metals needed to make a *mu-rúm*, a container: *gúm-a-nu*, and the statues of Kura and Barama, which had to be carried to the mausoleum in NEnaš (see *ARET* XI 2 § 25), is not preserved.

§ 99. Ibbi-zikir received an earring of gold of about 1 shekel (8 g) of gold, as also other three people.

§ 102. The mother of Ibrium received two toggle-pins of 30 shekels (235 g) of gold.

§ 114. Tirin-damu should be the first known priestess of ᵓAdabal (see Archi 1998a, pp. 44–46 = Id. 2015a, pp. 699–702). She received two toggle-pins of gold of 30 shekels (235 g), whose heads were decorated with 3 shekels (23 g) of gold. Her younger sister Terbu-damu received two buckles of 4 shekels (31 g) of gold.

# 18
## (Plates XXXIV–XXXV)

(1)

o. I. 1. 1 ma-na kù:babbar
saĝ kù:babbar
3. $^{d}$*Ku-ra*

(2)

10 lá-1 ma-na ŠA.PI gín DILMUN
kù:babbar
5. *Di-ni-ib-du-lum*
nin-ni
7. en
šu-ba$_4$-ti
9. 1 ma-na kù:babbar
*Dar-ib-da-mu*
11. nin-ni-*sù*
šu-ba$_4$-ti

(3)

13. ŠÚ+ŠA gín DILMUN kù:babbar
ZU.PIRIĜ
15. 3 útul maḫ urudu
*in* ud
17. *ir-me*

(4)

3 ma-na ŠÚ+ŠA gín DILMUN
kù:babbar
19. šu-bal-ak
ŠA.PI gín DILMUN kù-gi
21. 1 *a-ba-lum*
*wa*
23. pad-[*s*]*ù*
II. 1. *Ib-rí-um*

(5)

1 ma-na 10 gín DILMUN kù:babbar
3. šu-bal-ak
14 gín DILMUN kù-gi
5. 2 *gú-li-lum*
*wa*
7. 2 *ti-gi-na*
*wa*
9. 2 ĜIŠ-du
*A-ḫu-su-ub-da-mu*
11. 1 ma-na 10 gín DILMUN kù:babbar
šu-bal-ak
13. 14 gín DILMUN kù-gi
2 *gú-li-lum*
15. *wa*
2 *ti-gi-na*
17. *wa*
2 ĜIŠ-du
19. *A-a-du*-LUM
2 dumu-nita
21. en

(6)

1 ma-na ŠA.PI gín DILMUN
kù:b[abbar]
III. 1. šu-bal-ak
ŠÚ+ŠA gín DILMUN kù-gi 1 dib
3. *Ba-d*[*u-lum*]
[dumu-nita]
5. *Ib-rí-um*

(7)

1 ma-na 55 gín DILMUN kù:babbar
7. šu-bal-ak
ŠÚ+ŠA 3 gín DILMUN kù-gi
9. 1 an-zam$_x$ ĜIŠ-ĝidru
*ma-lik-tum*

(8)

11. 50 gín DILMUN kù:babbar
šu-bal-ak
13. 10 gín DILMUN kù-gi
1 zi-bar
15. ama-gal
en

(9)

17. ŠÚ+ŠA gín DILMUN kù:babbar
2 *bu*-DI
19. *Ar-za-du*

(1) 1 mina of silver for the silver head of the god Kura.
(2) 9;40 minas of silver: Tinib-dulum, sister of the king, has received; 1 mina of silver: Tarib-damu, her sister, has received.
(3) 20 shekels of silver for the hangers of 3 big kettles of bronze, on the occasion of the *ir-me* (festival).
(4) 3;20 minas of silver in exchange for 40 shekels of gold for 1 *a-ba-lum*-vessel and its lid for Ibrium.
(5) 1;10 minas of silver in exchange for 14 shekels of gold for 2 bracelets and 2 torques and 2 foot rings for Aḫsub-damu; 1;10 minas of silver in exchange for 14 shekels of gold for 2 bracelets and 2 torques and 2 foot rings for Aʾadulum, 2 sons of the king.
(6) 1;40 minas of sil[ver] in exchange for 20 shekels of gold for 1 plaque for Bad[ulum, son of] Ibrium.
(7) 1;55 minas of silver in exchange for 23 shekels of gold for 1 an-zam$_x$ goblet (with) handle for the queen.
(8) 50 shekels of silver in exchange for 10 shekels of gold for 1 zi-bar goblet for the king's mother.
(9) 20 shekels of silver for 2 toggle-pins for Arzadu, sister of the king.

nin-ni
21. en

(10)

IV. 1. 3 ma-na ŠÚ+ŠA gín DILMUN an-na
šub
3. *si-in*
56 ma-na ŠA.PI gín DILMUN a-gar$_5$-gar$_5$
5. kin$_5$-ak
2 *mi-at* ĝír mar-tu zú-ak
7. 17 gín DILMUN a-gar$_5$-gar$_5$
*wa*
9. 1 gín DILMUN an-na
kin$_5$-ak
11. 1 ĝír mar-tu
*mu-lu-iš*
13. 1 *li-im* ĝír mar-tu
*A-la-ga*$^{ki}$

(11)

15. 1 ma-na kù:babbar
níĝ-ba
17. lú NI-*dim* "ur$_4$"
*Na-gàr*$^{ki}$

(12)

19. 2 gín DILMUN kù:babbar 2 *bu*-DI
V. 1. níĝ-ba
ama-gal
3. en
$^{d}$*Iš:šára*
5. *Zi-da-ra*$^{ki}$

(13)

2 gín DILMUN kù:babbar
7. *ma-sa-da-ù*
*A-a-du*-LUM
9. dumu-nita
en

(14)

11. 10 gín DILMUN kù:babbar
níĝ-ba
13. *Ḫu-ra*-NE
*Na-gàr*$^{ki}$

(15)

15. 10 gín DILMUN kù:babbar
níĝ-ba
17. *Da-a-nu*
*Bu-si*
19. *ʾÀ-wa-ra*
Mar-tu$^{ki}$

(16)

21. 1 ma-na kù:babbar
níĝ-sa$_{10}$ la-ḫa
23. ĝeštin
en
25. *Gú-da-da-núm*$^{ki}$
*Za-ba-rúm*
27. šu-ba$_4$-ti

(17)

VI. 1. 1 ma-na 10 gín DILMUN kù:babbar
šu-bal-ak
3. [10+]4 [gín DILMUN kù-gi]
*ni-zi-mu*
5. 4 kù-sal
*I-bí-zi-kir*
7. dumu-nita
*Ib-rí-um*

(18)

9. 5 gín DILMUN kù:babbar
níĝ-ba
11. *Sal-bí-um*$^{ki}$

(19)

5 gín DILMUN kù:babbar
13. šu-bal-ak
1 gín DILMUN kù-gi
15. *ni-zi-mu*
nu$_{11}$-za
17. 1 *gú-li-lum* a-gar$_5$-gar$_5$
*Ib-ga-ì*
19. ugula sur$_x$-BAR.AN
en

(10) 3;20 minas of tin to be melted with 56;40 minas of copper for making 200 serrated mar-tu daggers, (that is) 17 shekels of copper and 1 shekel of tin for making 1 mar-tu dagger, in order to reach (the number of) 1000 mar-tu daggers (to be deposited in) the city of Alaga.

(11) 1 mina of silver: gift for NIdim, the collector (of goods) of the city of Nagar.

(12) 2 shekels of silver for 2 toggle-pins: gift of the king's mother for the goddess Išḫara of the city of Zidara.

(13) 2 shekels of silver for a *pallium* for AʾaduLUM, son of the king.

(14) 10 shekels of silver: gift for ḪuraNE of the city of Nagar.

(15) 10 shekels of silver: gift for Daʾanu, Busi (and) ʾAwara of the Martu (confederation).

(16) 1 mina of silver for the purchase of jars of wine for the king of the city of Gudadanum, Zabarum has received.

(17) 1;10 minas of silver in exchange for [1]4 [shekels of gold] for decorating 4 buckles for Ibbi-zikir, son of Ibrium.

(18) 5 shekels of silver: gift for (someone of) the city of Salbium.

(19) 5 shekels of silver in exchange for 1 shekel of gold for decorating with lamination 1 bracelet of copper for Ibga-i(l), the overseer of the team of mules of the king.

(20)

21. TAR 6 gín DILMUN kù:babbar
kin$_5$-ak

VII. 1. 15 ĜIŠ-kak-ĜIŠ-kak
*ša-ti*
3. 5 ĜIŠ-asari
kaskal
5. ⌜en⌝

(21)

7 ma-na kù:babbar
7. šu-bal-ak
1 ma-na ŠÚ+ŠA 4 gín DILMUN kù-gi
nu$_{11}$-za
9. 12 *gú-li-lum* a-gar$_5$-gar$_5$
*wa*
11. 12 *gú-li-lum* a-gar$_5$-gar$_5$ ŠÚ+ŠA-ŠÚ+ŠA-II
5 ma-na ŠÚ+ŠA gín DILMUN kù:babbar
13. kin$_5$-ak
10 *gú-li-lum* lú ŠÚ+ŠA-ŠÚ+ŠA-II
15. *wa*
12 *gú-li-lum* lú 20-I
17. 4 ma-na

VIII. 1. ŠÚ+ŠA gín DILMUN kù:babbar
šu-bal-ak
3. 1 ma-na 4 gín DILMUN kù-gi
[*wa*]
5. 3 ma-na kù:babbar
nu$_{11}$-za
7. 20 *gú-li-lum* a-gar$_5$-gar$_5$ lú TAR-II
*wa*
9. 40 *gú-li-lum* lú 15-I
20 *gú-li-lum* a-gar$_5$-gar$_5$ lú 12-I
11. 4 gín DILMUN kù:babbar
ZU.PIRIĜ-*sù*
13. ME-sig
é
15. en

(22)

11 ma-na an-na
17. šub *si-in*
$3^{!}$ *mi-at*

IX. 1. ma-na a-gar$_5$-gar$_5$
daḫ$_x$(MU.MU.MU)
3. kin$_5$-ak
2 útul gibil
5. 5 m[a-]na [kù:babbar]
ZU.PIRIĜ-*sù*
7. 2 ma-na 12 gín DILMUN an-na
šub *si-in*
9. 13 ma-na TAR a-gar$_5$-gar$_5$
kin$_5$-ak
11. 10 lá-1 *ma-ba-ra-zú*
kin$_5$-ak-*sù*

(23)

13. 4 ma-na ŠA.PI gín DILMUN kù:babbar
níĝ-sa$_{10}$ 23 túg-NI.NI
15. 4 dùl-TÚG *Ma-rí*$^{ki}$
26 gada-TÚG
17. 1 *mi-at* siki na$_4$ *Ma-rí*$^{ki}$
ki:lam$_7$

X. 1. $^{d}$*A-da-ma*
*ʾÀ-da-ni*$^{ki}$

(24)

3. 1 ma-na 15 gín DILMUN kù:babbar
šu-bal-ak
5. 15 gín DILMUN kù-gi
*ni-zi-mu*
7. 2 *ti-gi-na*
10 gín DILMUN kù:babbar
9. šu-bal-ak
2 gín DILMUN kù-gi
11. *ni-zi-mu*
2 ĜIŠ-du
13. *Da-bur-da-mu*
*ma-lik-tum*

(25)

15. 50 gín DILMUN kù:babbar
šu-bal-ak
17. [10 gín DILMUN kù-gi]
1 íb-lá 1 *si-ti-tum* 1 ĝír-kun

(20) 36 shekels of silver for making 15 pegs of 5 travel trays for the king.

(21) 7 minas of silver in exchange for 1;24 minas of gold for plating 12 bracelets of copper and 12 double bracelets of 20 (shekels of) copper each; 5;20 minas of silver for making 10 double bracelets of 20 (shekels of) copper each and 12 single bracelets of 20 (shekels) each; 4;20 minas of silver in exchange for 1;04 minas of gold [and] 3 minas of silver for plating 20 double bracelets of 30 (shekels of) copper each and 40 single bracelets of 15 (shekels) each, 20 single bracelets of 12 (shekels of) copper each; 4 shekels of silver for their hangers: for the watchmen of the king's house.

(22) 11 minas of tin to be melted with 300 minas of copper, in addition, for making 2 new kettles; 5 m[i]nas [of silver] for their hangers; 2;12 minas of tin to be melted with 13;30 minas of copper for making 9 … (*ma-ba-ra-zú*): for their manufacture.

(23) 4;40 minas of silver for the purchase of 53 garments (and) 100 stone weights of wool from the city of Mari, at the market of the god Adamma of the city of ʾAdani.

(24) 1;15 minas of silver in exchange for 15 shekels of gold for decorating 2 torques; 10 shekels of silver in exchange for 2 shekels of gold for decorating 2 foot rings for Tabur-damu, the queen.

(25) 50 shekels of silver in exchange for [10 shekels of gold] for 1 belt, 1 sheath (and) 1 dagger pendant for Giri, and also 7 shekels of silver for decorating 1 belt, 1 sheath (and) 1 dagger pendant; 5 shekels of silver in exchange for 1 shekel of gold for their striped decoration for Irti; 8 shekels of silver for decorating 1 belt (and) 1 dagger pendant for Napḫa-i(l), 3 sons of Ibrium.

XI. 1. *Gi-rí*
*ap*
3. 7 gín DILMUN kù:babbar
*ni-zi-mu*
5. 1 íb-lá 1 ĝír-kun kù:babbar
5 gín DILMUN kù:babbar
7. šu-bal-ak
1 gín DILMUN kù-gi
9. *ni-zi-mu*
maš-maš-*sù*
11. *Ir-ti*
8 gín DILMUN kù:babbar
13. *ni-zi-mu*
1 íb-lá 1 ĝír-kun
15. *Nap-ḫa-ì*
3 dumu-nita
17. *Ib-rí-um*

(26)
5 gín DILMUN kù:babbar <šu-bal-ak>
19. 1 gín DILMUN kù-gi
*ni-zi-mu*
21. 1 dib
*Du-bí-zi-kir*
23. lú *A-ba-an*

(27)
XII. 1. 10 gín DILMUN kù:babbar
níĝ-ba
3. *Ag-ga*
*Na-gàr*$^{ki}$

(28)
5. TAR 3 g[ín DILMUN 3 NI k]ù:[babbar]
šu-bal-ak
7. 6 2 NI gín DILMUN kù-gi
2 *gú-li-lum*
9. níĝ-ba
$^{d}$*Ku-ra*

(29)
11. 2 ma-na TAR kù:babbar
šu-bal-ak
13. TAR kù-gi
*zi-ba-tum*
15. 2 KA-si
en

(30)
17. 1 ma-na kù:babbar
šu-bal-ak
19. 12 gín DILMUN kù-gi
1 *a-ba-lum*
21. níĝ-ba
$^{d}$ʾ*A*$_5$*-da-"bal"*
23. ʾ*À-ma-du*$^{ki}$
*Ib-rí-um*

(31)
XIII. 1. 1 ma-na ŠA.PI gín DILMUN kù:babbar
šu-bal-ak
3. ŠÚ+ŠA gín DILMUN kù-gi
*ba-da-lum*
5. *Ḫa-ra-an*$^{ki}$

(32)
5 gín DILMUN kù:babbar
7. níĝ-ba
*En-na-ì*
9. *Ḫa-la-bi-du*$^{ki}$
*in*
11. ʾ*À-da-ni*$^{ki}$
šu-ba$_4$-ti

(33)
13. ŠÚ+ŠA 4 gín DILMUN kù:babbar
níĝ-sa$_{10}$ 10 na$_4$
15. *Šu-mi-nu*
kin$_5$-ak
17. 2 útul urudu
10 gín DILMUN kù:babbar
19. níĝ-sa$_{10}$ 1 na$_4$
*Ìr*-[NI-*ba*]

(34)
21. 12 gín DILMUN kù:babbar
níĝ-sa$_{10}$ 1 na$_4$
23. EN-*mar*

(26) 5 shekels of silver <in exchange for> 1 shekel of gold for decorating 1 plaque for Dubi-zikir, (son) of Aban.
(27) 10 shekels of silver: gift for Agga of the city of Nagar.
(28) 33 sh[ekels (and) 3 NI of s]il[ver] in exchange for 6 shekels (and) 2 NI of gold for 2 bracelets: gift for the god Kura.
(29) 2;30 minas of silver in exchange for 30 (shekels of) gold for the handle of 2 … (KA-si) for the king.
(30) 1 mina of silver in exchange for 12 shekels of gold for 1 *a-ba-lum*-vessel: gift for the god ʾAdabal of the city of ʾAmadu (by) Ibrium.
(31) 1;40 minas of silver in exchange for 20 shekels of gold for the minister of the city of Ḫarran.
(32) 5 shekel of silver: gift for Enna-i(l) of the city of Ḫalabidu, he has received in the city of ʾAdani.
(33) 24 shekels of silver for the purchase of 10 stones for Šuminu for making 2 kettles of copper; 10 shekels of silver for the purchase of 1 stone for Ir[NIba].
(34) 12 shekels of silver for the purchase of 1 stone for ENmar.

(35)
13 gín DILMUN kù:babbar níĝ-sa$_{10}$
XIV. 1. [1 na$_4$]
*Ib-u$_9$-mu-ud*

(36)
3. 5 gín DILMUN kù:babbar
níĝ-sa$_{10}$ 1 na$_4$
5. *Ni-zi-ma-ì*

(37)
5 gín DILMUN kù:babbar
7. níĝ-sa$_{10}$ 1 na$_4$
*ᵓÀ-la-ga*-NE
9. kin$_5$-ak
2 útul
11. *Ša-ma*

(38)
10 gín DILMUN kù:babbar
13. níĝ-ba
*Du-tum*
15. *wa*
*Ìr-íb-sá-mu*
17. *ᵓÀ-du*$^{ki}$

(39)
10 gín DILMUN kù:babbar
19. níĝ-kaskal
*A*-LUM$^{ki}$
21. maškim
*Ḫa-ra-ì*
23. lú ĜIŠ-nu-kiri$_6$

(40)
ŠA.PI gín DILMUN kù:babbar
25. níĝ-sa$_{10}$ 2 ĝír mar-tu ti kù-gi
*Iš$_{11}$-gi-bar-zú*
27. *wa*
*Du-bí-ab*
XV. 1. ugula *Ti*-[*sum*]$^{ki}$

(41)
2 ma-na 10 gín DILMUN kù:babbar
3. níĝ-sa$_{10}$ 1 *mi-at* sal-TÚG
*si-in*
5. *A-la-ga*$^{ki}$

(42)
10 gín DILMUN kù:babbar
7. níĝ-ba
*Du-tum*
9. *wa*
*Da-mi-gu*
11. *ᵓÀ-du*$^{ki}$

(43)
5 gín DILMUN kù:babbar
13. *Šu*-NE-ḪAR
maškim
15. *A-mur-da-mu*
lú ĜIŠ-nu-kiri$_6$

(44)
17. ŠÚ+ŠA gín DILMUN kù:babbar
níĝ-ba
19. *I-ba$_x$-ì*
*Zi-rí-gu*
21. *ᵓÀ-du*$^{ki}$
*wa*
23. *Ib-rí*
*Na-gàr*$^{ki}$
25. *wa*
*I-ku-a-ḫu*
27. *Sag-gar*$^{ki}$

(45)
15 gín DILMUN kù:babbar
29. šu-bal-ak
3 kù-gi
31. *ni-zi-mu*
nu$_{11}$-za
33. 1 *za-ḫa-da*
1 [ĜI]Š$^?$-PA-⌜x⌝-ga
XVI. 1. *Ib-rí-um*

(46)
14 ma-na kù:babbar
3. níĝ-sa$_{10}$ 9 *mi-at* 80 ma-na a-gar$_5$-gar$_5$

(35) 13 shekels of silver for the purchase of [1 stone] for Ibumut.
(36) 5 shekels of silver for the purchase of 1 stone for Nizima-i(l).
(37) 5 shekels of silver for the purchase of 1 stone for ᵓAlagaNE, for making 2 kettles for Šama.
(38) 10 shekels of silver: gift for Dutum and Irib-samu of the city of ᵓAddu.
(39) 10 shekels of silver: travel provision for ALUM, the representative of Ḫara-i(l), the gardener.
(40) 40 shekels of silver for the purchase of 2 pointed mar-tu daggers (decorated with) gold for Išgi-barzu and Dubi-ab, (2) overseers of the city of Ti[sum].
(41) 2;10 minas of silver for the purchase of 100 garments for the city of Alaga.
(42) 10 shekels of silver: gift for Dutum and Damigu of the city of ᵓAddu.
(43) 5 shekels of silver for ŠUNEḪAR, representative of Amur-damu, the gardener.
(44) 20 shekels of silver: gift for Iba-i(l) (and) Zirigu of the city of ᵓAddu and Ibri of the city of Nagar and Ikuaḫu of the city of Saggar.
(45) 15 shekels of silver in exchange for 3 (shekels of) gold for decorating with lamination 1 battle-axe (and) 1 … for Ibrium.
(46) 14 minas of silver for the purchase of 980 minas of copper.

(47)
1 ma-na kù:babbar
5. níĝ-sa$_{10}$ 1 ĝír mar-tu kù-gi
en

(48)
7. 2 ma-na TAR kù:babbar
šu-bal-ak
9. TAR kù-gi 1 dib
GABA-*da-mu*
11. lú *Ìr-am$_6$-da-mu*

(49)
7 ma-na TAR kù:babbar
13. šu-bal-ak
1 ma-na TAR kù-gi
15. kin$_5$-ak
2 *ti-gi-na*
17. 10 lá-2 ĝeštu$_x$-lá
92 *gur-gú-ru$_{12}$*
19. 3 *mi-at* 60 *ḫa-za-nu*
1 šu-dub
21. 1 *ma-ḫa-na-gúm*
XVII. 1. 2 kù-sal
1 *a-a-nu*
3. 2 ĜIŠ-du
TAR kù:babbar
5. 2 ĜIŠ-du
*Tal-du-du*
7. dam
en

(50)
9. 3 gín DILMUN kù:babbar
saĝ kù:babbar
11. $^{d}$*Ku-ra*
mu-ti-II

(51)
13. 10 gín DILMUN kù:babbar
*Na-gàr*$^{ki}$
15. *in*
*Sal-ba-ù*$^{ki}$
17. šu-ba$_4$-ti

(52)
7 gín DILMUN kù:babbar
19. *zi-ba-du*
1 ĜIŠ-šú 2 níĝ-bànda
21. kaskal-kaskal
*Ib-rí-um*

(53)
23. TAR kù:babbar
šu-bal-ak
25. 6 gín DILMUN kù-gi
*ni-zi-mu*
27. 10 lá-2 ĝeštu$_x$-lá
*Di-ni-ib-du-lum*
29. nin-ni
en

(54)
31. ŠA.PI gín DILMUN kù:babbar
XVIII. 1. šu-bal-ak
8 gín DILMUN kù-gi
3. *ni-zi-mu*
4 *ti-gi-na*
5. 4 ĜIŠ-du
4 ĝeštu$_x$-lá
7. 2 kù-sal
*Dar-ib-da-mu*
9. *wa*
*Tiš-te-da-mu*
11. 2 dumu-munus
en

(55)
13. 15 gín DILMUN kù:babbar
nu$_{11}$-za 1 *ḫa-bù*
15. TAR kù:babbar
šu-bal-ak
17. 6 gín DILMUN kù-gi
nu$_{11}$-za 1 *ar-ra-sù*
19. ŠÚ+ŠA gín DILMUN kù:babbar
*ʾa$_5$-na-gu*
21. si 2 gud
nídba
23. en
$^{d}$*Ra-sa-ap*
25. *ʾÀ-da-ni*$^{ki}$

(47) 1 mina of silver for the purchase of 1 mar-tu dagger (decorated with) gold for the king.
(48) 2;30 minas of silver in exchange for 30 (shekels of) gold for 1 plaque for GABA-damu, (son) of Iram-damu.
(49) 7;30 minas of silver in exchange for 1;30 minas of gold for making 2 torques, 8 earrings, 92 spherical beads, 360 beads in the shape of cloves, 1 ring, 1 necklace, 2 buckles, 1 …, 2 foot rings; 30 (shekels of) silver for 2 foot rings: for Taldud, a spouse of the king.
(50) 3 shekels of silver for the silver head of the god Kura: second delivery.
(51) 10 shekels of silver for (someone of) the city of Nagar, received in the city of Salbaʾu.
(52) 7 shekels of silver for the handle of 1 GIŠ-šú vessel 2 níg-bànda vessels for travelling, for Ibrium.
(53) 30 (shekels of) silver in exchange for 6 shekels of gold for decorating 8 earrings for Tinib-dulum, sister of the king.
(54) 40 shekels of silver in exchange for 8 shekels of gold for decorating 4 torques, 4 foot rings, 4 earrings, 2 buckles for Tarib-damu and Tiste-damu, 2 daughters of the king.
(55) 15 shekels of silver for plating 1 mace; 30 (shekels of) silver in exchange for 6 shekels of gold for plating its handle; 20 shekels of silver for the circular stand for the (4) horns of 2 bulls: offering of the king for the god Rašap of the city of ʾAdani.

(56)
5 gín DILMUN kù:babbar
XIX. 1. šu-bal-ak
1 kù-gi 1 kù-sal
3. buru$_4$-MUŠEN
níĝ-ba
5. ama-gal
en
7. $^{d}$*Ra-sa-ap*
*ᵓÀ-da-ni*$^{ki}$

(57)
9. 15 gín DILMUN kù:babbar
nu$_{11}$-za
11. 1 *ḫa-bù*
*ap*
13. kù-gi
sikil
15. nu$_{11}$-za
*ar-ra-sù*
17. ŠÚ+ŠA gín DILMUN kù:babbar
*ᵓa$_5$-na-gu*
19. si 2 gud
nídba
21. en
$^{d}$*ᵓÀ-da*
23. *Ḫa-lab$_x$*$^{ki}$
*in*
25. $^{d}$AMA-*ra*

(58)
10 gín DILMUN kù:babbar
27. šu-bal-ak
2 gín DILMUN kù-gi
29. *ni-zi-mu*
nu$_{11}$-za
r. I. 1. 2 ĜIŠ.GAM.GAM ĜIŠ-gígir-II
*Ib-rí-um*
3. 15 gín DILMUN kù:babbar
šu-bal-⸢ak⸣
5. 3 gín DIL[MUN] kù-g[i]
*ni-zi-⸢mu⸣*
7. 2 níĝ-anše-ak 2 kù-sal
2 IGI.NITA
9. *wa*$^{a)}$
*su-da-nu*
11. kù-sal
en

(59)
13. 5 gín DILMUN kù:babbar
šu-bal-ak
15. 1 gín DILMUN kù-gi
*wa*
17. 1 gín DILMUN kù:babbar
*ni-zi-mu*
19. *ma-wa-⸢lu⸣*
ĜIŠ-bar-ús
21. ĜIŠ-gígir-II
en

(60)
23. TAR kù:babbar
šu-bal-ak
25. 6 g[ín] D[ILMUN] kù-gi
*ni-zi-mu*
27. nu$_{11}$-za 1 *za-ḫa-da*
⸢en⸣$^{b)}$

(61)
II. 1. 5 gín DILMUN kù:babbar
níĝ-ba
3. *A-daš*$^{ki}$

(62)
2 ma-na an-na
5. šub
*si-in*
7. 12 ma-na a-gar$_5$-gar$_5$
*ni-zi-mu*
9. ZA$_x$-ZA$_x$
naĝar-naĝar

(63)
11. 10 gín DILMUN kù:babbar
níĝ-ba
13. *Kùn-i-šar*
*ᵓÀ-du*$^{ki}$

(56) 5 shekels of silver in in exchange for 1 shekel of gold for 1 buckle (and) 1 shield: gift of the king's mother for the god Rašap of the city of ᵓAdani.
(57) 15 shekels of silver for plating 1 mace and also pure gold for the plating of its handle; 20 shekels of silver for the circular stand for the (4) horns of 2 bulls: offering of the king for the god Hadda of the city of Ḫalab, at the AMA-ra (festival).
(58) 10 shekels of silver in in exchange for 2 shekels of gold for decorating with lamination 2 wheels of a chariot for Ibrium; 15 shekels of silver in in exchange for 3 shekels of gold for decorating 2 bridles (and) 2 buckles of 2 donkeys and … (*su-da-nu*) of a buckle for the king.
(59) 5 shekels of silver in in exchange for 1 shekel of gold and 1 shekel of silver for decorating the … (*ma-wa-lu*) of the goads of a chariot for the king.
(60) 30 (shekels of) silver in exchange for 6 sh[ekels] of gold for decorating with lamination 1 battle-axe for the king.
(61) 5 shekels of silver: gift for (someone of) the city of Adaš.
(62) 2 minas of tin to be melted with 12 minas of copper for decorating objects of the carpenters.
(63) 10 shekels of silver: gift for Kun-išar of the city of ᵓAddu, received in the city of Šadab.

15. *in*
*Ša-dab*$_6$$^{ki}$
17. šu-ba$_4$-ti

(64)
5 gín DILMUN kù:babbar
19. níĝ-ba
*A-ag*
21. *Na-gàr*$^{ki}$

(65)
ŠÚ+ŠA gín DILMUN kù:babbar
23. 2 *bu*-DI
ì-ĝiš-saĝ
25. *Gi-ù-du*
dam
III. 1. *Za-ba-rúm*

(66)
11 ma-na 10 gín DILMUN kù:babbar
3. níĝ-sa$_{10}$ 50 túg-NI.NI
2 zara$_6$-TÚG
5. 22 *ʾà-da-um*-TÚG-I
4 dùl-TÚG *Ma-rí*$^{ki}$
7. 70 gada-TÚG
2 *mi-at* 10 siki na$_4$ *Ma-rí*$^{ki}$
9. ŠÚ+ŠA gín DILMUN kù:babbar
níĝ-sa$_{10}$ raš-SAR Kur$^{ki}$
11. 55 gín DILMUN kù:babbar
níĝ-sa$_{10}$ 3 IGI.NITA u$_5$
13. en
ki:lam$_7$
15. *ʾÀ-da-ni*$^{ki}$
$^{d}$AMA-*ra*

(67)
17. ŠÚ+ŠA gín DILMUN kù:babbar
2 *bu*-DI
19. *ma-lik-tum*
IV. 1. *Lum-na-an*$^{ki}$
É×PAP
3. *Ìr-ba*$_x$*-zé*
šu-mu-tak$_4$

(68)
5. 15 gín DILMUN kù:babbar
šu-bal-ak
7. 3 gín DILMUN kù-gi
*ni-zi-mu*
9. nu$_{11}$-za 1 níĝ-PA
en

(69)
11. 10 gín DILMUN kù:babbar
[n]íĝ-du$_8$
13. 1 dumu-nita
*Ku-a*-NE
15. lú NE-*da-mu*
SA.ZA$_x$$^{ki}$
17. *áš-ti*
*Ìr-ku*$^{ki}$

(70)
19. ŠÚ+ŠA gín DILMUN kù:babbar
2 *bu*-DI
21. ì-ĝiš-saĝ
*Di-rín-da-mu*
23. dam-diĝir
*áš-du*
25. úš
*ma-lik-tum*
27. *Lum-na-an*$^{ki}$

(71)
V. 1. TAR 3 gín DILMUN an-na
šub *si-in*
3. 24 ma-na a-gar$_5$-gar$_5$
kin$_5$-ak
5. 1 šum maḫ
6 gín DILMUN an-na
7. šub *si-in*
5 ma-na a-gar$_5$-gar$_5$
9. kin$_5$-ak
2 šum maḫ
11. 5 gín DILMUN kù:babbar
kin$_5$-ak
13. 3 *zú-zú-ba-tum*

(64) 5 shekels of silver: gift for Aʾag of the city of Nagar.
(65) 20 shekels of silver for 2 toggle-pins for the purification ceremony of Giʾudu, the spouse of Zabarum.
(66) 11;10 minas of silver for the purchase of 148 garments (and) 210 stone weights of wool from the city of Mari; 20 shekels of silver for the purchase of leek from the mountain region; 55 shekels of silver for the purchase of 3 donkeys to ride for the king: at the market of the city of ʾAdani, at the AMA-ra (festival).
(67) 20 shekels of silver for 2 toggle-pins for the funerary rite of the queen of the city of Lumnan, Irbaze has handed over.
(68) 15 shekels of silver in exchange for 3 shekels of gold for decorating with lamination 1 … (níg-PA) for the king.
(69) 10 shekels of silver for the [ra]nsom of 1 son of KuaNE, (son) of NE-damu of the Palace from the city of Irku.
(70) 20 shekels of silver for 2 toggle-pins for the purification ceremony of Tirin-damu, the priestess, (in relation) of the death of the queen of the city of Lumnan.
(71) 33 shekels of tin to be melted with 24 minas of copper for making 1 big saw; 6 shekels of tin to be melted with 5 minas of copper for making 2 big saws; 5 shekels of silver for making 3 … (*zú-zú-ba-tum*) for the chariot of Ibrium.

ĜIŠ-gígir-II
15. *Ib-rí-um*

(72)
2 gín DILMUN an-na
17. šub *si-in*
10 gín DILMUN a-gar$_5$-gar$_5$
19. kin$_5$-ak
2 šu-i
21. *Na-am*$_6$*-ḫa-lu*

(73)
4 gín DILMUN an-na
23. šub *si-in*
ŠÚ+ŠA 6
VI. 1. a-gar$_5$-gar$_5$
kin$_5$-ak
3. bar-ús
en

(74)
5. 2 gín DILMUN kù:babbar
níĝ-ba
7. *I-ti-*$^{d}$*Aš-dar*
*Ir-i-tum*$^{ki}$

(75)
9. TAR 3 gín 3 NI gín DILMUN kù:babbar
šu-bal-ak
11. 6 gín DILMUN 2 NI kù-gi
2 *gú-li-lum*
13. níĝ-ba
$^{d}$*Ku-ra*

(76)
15. TAR kù:babbar
níĝ-sa$_{10}$ 1 ĝír mar-tu kù-gi
17. *Iš*$_{11}$*-ru-ud*
ugula *Sal-ba-ù*$^{ki}$

(77)
19. 1 ma-na ŠA.PI 6 gín DILMUN 2 NI an-na
šub
21. *si-in*
12 ma-na ŠÚ+ŠA[c)]
VII. 1. gín DILMUN a-gar$_5$-gar$_5$
kin$_5$-ak
3. 40 ĝír mar-tu kù-gi
20 ma-na kù:babbar
5. šu-bal-ak
4 ma-na kù-gi
7. *zi-du-sù*
*ap*
9. ŠÚ+ŠA gín DILMUN a-gar$_5$-gar$_5$
*wa*
11. 2 gín DILMUN 2 NI an-na
kin$_5$-ak
13. 1 ĝír mar-tu
6 gín DILMUN kù-gi
15. *zi-du-sù*
50 gín DILMUN an-na
17. šub
*si-in*
19. 6 ma-na ŠÚ+ŠA gín DILMUN a-gar$_5$-gar$_5$
kin$_5$-ak
VIII. 1. 20 ĝír mar-tu ti kù-gi *ʾà-lum*
5 ma-na kù:babbar
3. šu-bal-ak
1 ma-na kù-gi
5. *zi-du-sù*
*ap*
7. 18 gín DILMUN a-gar$_5$-gar$_5$
*wa*
9. 2 ½ gín DILMUN an-na
kin$_5$-ak
11. 1 ĝír mar-tu
3 gín DILMUN kù-gi
13. *zi-du-sù*
1 ma-na 52 ½ gín DILMUN an-na

(72) 2 shekels of tin to be melted with 10 shekels of copper for making 2 šu-i vessels for Naʾam-ḫalu.
(73) 4 shekels of tin to be melted with 26 (shekels of) copper for making a goad for the king.
(74) 2 shekels of silver: gift for Iti-Ašdar of the city of Iritum.
(75) 33 shekels (and) 3 NI of silver in exchange for 6 shekels (and) 2 NI of gold for 2 bracelets: gift for the god Kura.
(76) 30 (shekels of) silver for the purchase of 1 mar-tu dagger (decorated with) gold for Išrut, the overseer of the city of Salbau.
(77) 1;46 minas (and) 2 NI of tin to be melted with 12;20 minas of copper for making 40 mar-tu daggers (decorated with) gold; 20 minas of silver in exchange for 4 minas of gold (to make) their alloy; that is: 20 shekels of copper and 2 shekels (and) 2 NI of tin for making each mar-tu dagger; 6 shekels of gold (to make) its alloy. 50 shekels of tin to be melted with 6;20 minas of copper for making 20 pointed mar-tu daggers (decorated with) gold … (*ʾà-lum*); 5 minas of silver in exchange for 1 mina of gold (to make) their alloy; that is: 18 shekels of copper and 2 ½ shekels of tin for making each mar-tu dagger; 3 shekels of gold (to make) its alloy. 1;52 ½ minas of tin to be melted with 15 minas of copper for making 50 pointed mar-tu daggers (decorated with) gold; 12;30 minas of silver in exchange for 2;30 minas of gold (to make) their alloy; that is: 17 (shekels of) copper, 2 shekels (and) 3 NI of tin for making each mar-tu dagger; 3 shekels of gold (to make) its alloy. 9;26 minas of tin to be melted with 75;36 minas of copper for making 252 ma[r-tu] daggers (decorated with) 4[0 (shekels of)] silver; 5;22 minas (and) 2 NI of silver for their knobs; that is: 38 (shekels of) copper and 2 (shekels and) 4 NI of tin for making each mar-tu dagger; 1 shekel (and) 3 NI of silver for the knob. 1;30 minas of silver for the purchase of 88 serrated mar-tu daggers in order to reach (the number of) the mar-tu daggers to be given to the men.

15. šub
*si-in*
17. 15 ma-na a-gar$_5$-gar$_5$
kin$_5$-ak
IX. 1. 50 ĝír mar-tu ti kù-gi
12 ma-na TAR kù:babbar
3. šu-bal-ak
2 ma-na TAR kù-gi
5. *zi-du-sù*
*ap*
7. 17 a-gar$_5$-gar$_5$
2 gín DILMUN 3 NI an-na
9. kin$_5$-ak
1 ĝír mar-tu
11. 3 gín DILMUN kù-gi
*zi-du-sù*
13. 10 lá-1 ma-na ŠÚ+ŠA 6 gín DILMUN an-na
šub *si-in*
15. 75 ma-na TAR 6 a-gar$_5$-gar$_5$
kin$_5$-ak
17. 2 *mi-at* 52 ĝír ma[r-tu] š[A.PI]
X. 1. kù:babbar
5 ma-na ŠÚ+ŠA 2 gín DILMUN 2 NI kù:babbar
3. *ga-ma-a-tum-sù*
*ap*
5. [TA]R 8 ⌜a⌝-gar$_5$-gar$_5$
*wa*
7. 2 4 NI an-na
kin$_5$-ak
9. 1 ĝír mar-tu
1 gín DILMUN 3 NI kù:babbar
11. *kam$_4$-ma-a-tum*
1 ma-na TAR kù:babbar
13. níĝ-sa$_{10}$ 90 lá-2 ĝír mar-tu zú-ak
lú *mu-lu-iš*
15. ĝír mar-tu
ĝuruš-ĝuruš
17. in-na-sum

(78)
TAR kù:babbar
19. níĝ-kaskal
*Gi-ba-rí-a*
21. *Kab-lu$_5$-ul*$^{ki}$
DU.DU
23. *si-in*
*Ir-bí-ì-lum*$^{ki}$

(79)
XI. 1. 15 gín DILMUN kù:babbar
nu$_{11}$-za 1 *ḫa-bù*
3. TAR kù:babbar
šu-bal-ak
5. 6 gín DILMUN kù-gi
nu$_{11}$-za *ar-ra-sù*
7. níĝ-ba
$^{d.}$*À-da*
9. lú *Lu-ub*$^{ki}$
*in*
11. *gi*-NI

(80)
ŠÚ+ŠA gín DILMUN kù:babbar
13. 1 *a-ba-lum*
5 gín DILMUN kù:babbar
15. 1 zi-bar
níĝ-ba
17. *Gú-sa*
dumu-nita
19. en
*Na-gàr*$^{ki}$

(81)
21. 2 ma-na an-na
níĝ-ba
23. en
*A-daš*$^{ki}$

(82)
25. 10 gín DILMUN kù:babbar
3 zi-bar
27. níĝ-ba
ama-gal
29. en
$^{d}$*Iš:šára*
31. *Má*-NE$^{ki}$
XII. 1. *U$_9$-gú-a-áš*$^{ki}$
*wa*
3. *Zu-ra-mu*$^{ki}$

(83)
16 gín DILMUN kù:babbar
5. 4 níĝ-bànda
2 dumu-nita
7. 2 dumu-munus
en

(78) 30 (shekels of) silver: travel provision for Gibaria of the city of Kablul, (who) went to the city of Irbilum.
(79) 15 shekels of silver for plating 1 mace; 30 (shekels of) silver in exchange for 6 shekels of gold for plating its handle: gift for the god Hadda of the city of Lub, in month IV.
(80) 20 shekels of silver for 1 *a-ba-lum*-vessel; 5 shekels of silver for 1 zi-bar goblet: gift for Gusa, son of the king of the city of Nagar.
(81) 2 minas of tin: gift for the king of the city of Adaš.
(82) 10 shekels of silver for 3 zi-bar goblets: gift of the king's mother to the goddess Išḫara of the city of MaNE, of the city of Uguaš and of the city of Zuramu.
(83) 16 shekels of silver for 4 níg-bànda vessels for 2 sons and 2 daughters of the king.

(84)

9. šú+ša gín DILMUN kù:babbar
2 *bu*-DI
11. 15 gín DILMUN kù:babbar
šu-bal-ak
13. 3 gín DILMUN kù-gi
nu$_{11}$-za 2 saĝ-*sù*
15. ama-gal
*Ib-rí-um*
17. É×PAP

(85)

2 gín DILMUN kù:babbar
19. níĝ-sa$_{10}$ ĜIŠ-šim ĜÁ×LÁ
ki:lam$_{7}$
21. $^{d}$*Ga-mi-iš*
*Du-bí-ga-lu*

(86)

23. 5 ma-na kù:babbar
šu-bal-ak
25. 1 ma-na kù-gi
1 íb-lá 1 *si-ti-tum* 1 ĝír-kun
XIII. 1. ì-ĝiš-saĝ
*Ib-rí-um*

(87)

3. 13 ma-na šú+ša kù:babbar
níĝ-sa$_{10}$ 72 dùl-TÚG *Ma-rí*$^{ki}$
5. 60 lá-3 *ʾà-da-um*-TÚG-I
40 lá-3 túg-NI.NI
7. 2 aktum-TÚG ti-TÚG
4 ma-na ŠA.PI 4 kù:babbar
9. níĝ-sa$_{10}$ 3 *mi-at* 40 siki na$_{4}$ *Ma-rí*$^{ki}$
ki:lam$_{7}$
11. $^{d}$*Ga-mi-iš*
*wa*
13. $^{d}$*Áš-da-bíl*
*wa*
15. $^{d}$BAD
*Du-du-lu*$^{ki}$

(88)

17. [ ] kù:babbar
níĝ-sa$_{10}$ 1 ĝír mar-tu *ba-du-u*$_{4}$
kù:babbar-gi
19. *Min-na-ì*
ugula sur$_{x}$-BAR.AN
21. *Ib-rí-um*

(89)

2 ma-na TAR kù:babbar
23. šu-bal-ak
TAR kù-gi
XIV. 1. nu$_{11}$-za 2 ĜIŠ.GAM-ĜIŠ.GAM ĜIŠ-gígir-II
10 ma-na kù:babbar
3. šu-bal-ak
2 ma-na kù-gi
5. 2 níĝ-anše-ak 4 kù-sal
5 an-na
7. šub *si-in*
TAR 5 a-gar$_{5}$
9. 1 ĜIŠ-zú
5 kù:babbar
11. šu-bal-ak
1 kù-gi
13. nu$_{11}$-za 1 zag ĜIŠ-gígir-II
en
15. *Ì-mar*$^{ki}$

(90)

11 ½ kù:babbar
17. níĝ-sa$_{10}$ 75 ma-na níĝ-NE
4 ma-na TAR kù:babbar
19. nu$_{11}$-za 1 an-dùl munus
6 ma-na 10 kù:babbar
21. šu-bal-ak
⌜1⌝ ma-na 14 gín kù-gi
23. nu$_{11}$-za IGI.DUB-*sa*
2 šu 2 DU-*sù*
25. 4 ma-na šú+ša kù:babbar
nu$_{11}$-za 1 an-dùl nita

(84) 20 shekels of silver for 2 toggle-pins; 15 shekels of silver in exchange for 3 shekels of gold for plating their 2 heads for the funerary rite of the mother of Ibrium.

(85) 2 shekels of silver for the purchase of weighed aromatic essence at the market of the god Kamiš, Dubigalu (has received).

(86) 5 minas of silver in exchange for 1 mina of gold for 1 belt, 1 sheath (and) 1 dagger pendant for the purification ceremony of Ibrium.

(87) 13;20 minas of silver for the purchase of 168 garments; 4;44 minas of silver for the purchase of 340 stone weights of wool from the city of Mari, at the markets of the gods Kamiš and Ašdabil and of the Lord of the city of Tuttul.

(88) [x] silver for the purchase of 1 *b.* mar-tu dagger (decorated with) silver and gold for Minna-i(l), the overseer of the team of mules of Ibrium.

(89) 2;30 minas of silver in exchange for 30 (shekels of) gold for plating 2 wheels of a chariot; 10 minas of silver in exchange for 2 minas of gold for 2 bridles (and) 4 buckles; 5 (shekels of) tin to be melted with 35 (shekels of) copper for 1 hook; 5 (shekels of) silver in exchange for 1 (shekel of) gold for plating 1 side of a chariot for the king of the city of Imar.

(90) 11 ½ (shekels of) silver for the purchase of 75 minas of … (níg-NE); 4;30 minas of silver for plating 1 female statue; 6;10 minas of silver in exchange for 1;14 minas of gold for plating its face, its 2 hands and feet; 4;20 minas of silver for plating 1 male statue; 11 minas of silver in exchange for 2;12 minas of gold for plating its face and belt, sheath, kilt; 6 (shekels of) tin to be melted with 40 (shekels of) copper for 1 table (and) its mar-tu dagger: gift for the Lord of the city of Tuttul.

27. 11 ma-na kù:babbar
šu-bal-ak
XV. 1. 2 ma-na 12 kù-gi
nu$_{11}$-za IGI.DUB-*sù*
3. *na*
íb-lá *si-ti-tum*
5. íb+III-TÚG
6 an-na
7. šub *si-in*
ŠA.PI a-gar$_5$-gar$_5$
9. 1 banšur
1 ĝír mar-tu-*sù*
11. níĝ-ba
$^{d}$BAD
13. *Du-du-lu*$^{ki}$

(91)
TAR 3 3 NI kù:babbar
15. šu-bal-ak
6 2 NI kù-gi 2 *gú-li-lum*
17. $^{d}$*Áš-da-bíl*

(92)
6 2 NI kù:babbar 2 *gú-li-lum*
19. $^{d}$*Am-rí-ig*

(93)
5 kù:babbar
21. šu-bal-ak
1 kù-gi
23. *ni-zi-mu*
nu$_{11}$-za 1 ĝír mar-tu
25. *Gú-zi*

(94)
1 ma-na kù:babbar
27. *Na-gàr*$^{ki}$

(95)
1 ma-na kù:babbar
29. *A-bù-li-um*$^{ki}$
1 ma-na kù:babbar
31. *Na-ba-ti-um*$^{ki}$

XVI. 1. 1 ma-na kù:babbar
*ʾÀ-du*$^{ki}$
3. ŠA.PI kù:babbar
*Sag-gar*$^{ki}$
5. ŠÚ+ŠA kù:babbar
EN-NE$^{ki}$

(96)
7. 4 kù:babbar
lú ĜIŠ-nu-kiri$_6$
9. DU$^{ki}$

(97)
2 ½ kù:babbar
11. 1 ĝír
10 kù:babbar
13. šu-bal-ak
2 kù-gi
15. nu$_{11}$-za-*sù*
ama-gal
17. en

(98)
1 ma-na 10 kù:babbar
19. níĝ-ba
diĝir-diĝir-diĝir

(99)
21. 15 kù:babbar
níĝ-sa$_{10}$ 1 ĝír mar-tu zú LAGAB×AN
kù-gi
23. *Ga-nu-bù*
*Sal-ba-um*$^{ki}$
25. tuš-LÚ×TIL
*Ḫal-sum*$^{ki}$

(100)
27. 2 an-na
šub *si-in*
29. 10 a-gar$_5$-gar$_5$
2 šu-i
31. 2 kù:babbar nu$_{11}$-za-*sù*
*Ib-rí-um*

(91) 33 (shekels and) 3 NI of silver in exchange for 6 (shekels and) 2 NI of gold for 2 bracelets for the god Ašdabil.
(92) 6 (shekels and) 2 NI of silver for 2 bracelets for the god Ammarik.
(93) 5 (shekels of) silver in exchange for 1 (shekel of) gold for decorating with lamination 1 mar-tu dagger for Guzi.
(94) 1 mina of silver for (someone of) the city of Nagar.
(95) 1 mina of silver for (someone of) the city of Abulium; 1 mina of silver for (someone of) the city of Nabatiʾum; 1 mina of silver for (someone of) the city of ʾAddu; 40 (shekels of) silver for (someone of) the city of Saggar; 20 (shekels of) silver for (someone of) the city of ENNE.
(96) 4 (shekels of) silver for the gardener of the city of DU.
(97) 2 ½ (shekels of) silver for 1 dagger; 10 (shekels of) silver in exchange for 2 (shekels of) gold for its lamination for the king's mother.
(98) 1;10 minas of silver: gift for the gods.
(99) 15 (shekels of) silver for the purchase of 1 serrated mar-tu dagger (decorated with) ivory and gold for Ganubu of the city of Salbaʾum, (who) occupied the city of Ḫalšum.
(100) 2 (shekels of) tin to be melted with 10 (shekels of) copper for 2 šu-i vessels; 2 (shekels of) silver for their lamination, for Ibrium.

(101)
33. 6 gín kù:babbar
nu$_{11}$-za 2 ĝír mar-tu
35. 10 kù:babbar
šu-bal-ak
37. 2 kù-gi 2 kù-sal
níĝ-ba
39. ama-gal
XVII. 1. en
$^{d}$*Ra-sa-ap*
3. *Du-ne-íb*$^{ki}$
*wa*
5. $^{d}$*ʾA$_5$-da-"bal"*
*ʾÀ-ma-du*$^{ki}$
7. NI.DU

(102)
50 kù:babbar
9. šu-bal-ak
10 kù-gi
11. *ni-zi-mu*
nu$_{11}$-za
13. 2 ĜIŠ.GAM.GAM
ĜIŠ-gígir-II
15. *ra-ʾà-tum*
en

(103)
17. 10 kù:babbar
*Ag-ga*
19. 10 kù:babbar
*Gul-la*
21. *Ḫu-ra*-NE
*Na-gàr*$^{ki}$
23. *in* kaskal
*Su-da-ma-an*$^{ki}$

(104)
25. 1 ma-na 10 kù:babbar
níĝ-sa$_{10}$ 2 ĝír mar-tu kù-gi
27. *Ìr-am$_6$-ma-lik*
lú *Ib-ga-iš-lu*
29. *wa*
*Íl-ba-ma-lik*
31. lú *Ìr-am$_6$-ma-lik*

(105)
15 kù:babbar
33. nu$_{11}$-za 1 *ḫa-bù*
*ap*
35. kù-gi sikil
ŠÚ+ŠA kù:babbar
37. *ʾa$_5$-na-gu*
si 2 gud
39. nídba
XVIII. 1. en
$^{[d]}$*ʾÀ-da*
3. *Ḫa-lab$_x$*$^{ki}$
*ʾa$_5$-nun*

(106)
5. 1 ma-na kù:babbar
níĝ-sa$_{10}$ 1 ĝír mar-tu kù-gi
7. *Ib-rí-um*
*áš-du*
9. ĝír mar-tu-*sù*
sikil

(107)
11. 10 kù:babbar
*I-ba$_x$-ì*
13. *Zi-rí-gú*
*ʾÀ-du*$^{ki}$

(108)
15. 2 an-na
šub *si-in*
17. 10 a-gar$_5$-gar$_5$
kin$_5$-ak
19. 2 ĝír
15 kù:babbar
21. šu-bal-ak
3 kù-gi
23. nu$_{11}$-za-*sù*
en

(101) 6 (shekels of) silver for plating 2 mar-tu daggers; 10 (shekels of) silver in exchange for 2 (shekels of) gold for 2 buckles: gift of the king's mother for the god Rašap of the city of Tunip and for the god ʾAdabal of the city of ʾAmadu, in month VII.

(102) 50 (shekels of) silver in exchange for 10 (shekels of) gold for decorating with lamination 2 wheels of a chariot (decorated with) shells for the king.

(103) 10 (shekels of) silver for Agga; 10 (shekels of) silver for Gulla (and) ḪuraNE of the city of Nagar, for a journey to the city of Sudaman.

(104) 1;10 minas of silver for the purchase of 2 mar-tu daggers (decorated with) gold for Iram-malik, (son) of Ibga-išlu and Ilba-malik, (son) of Iram-malik.

(105) 15 (shekels of) silver for plating 1 mace and also pure gold; 20 (shekels of) silver for the circular stand of the (4) horns of 2 bulls: offering of the king for the god Hadda of the city of Ḫalab, in month VIII.

(106) 1 mina of silver for the purchase of 1 mar-tu dagger (decorated with) gold for Ibrium, as a replacement for his mar-tu dagger (given for) the purification rite.

(107) 10 (shekels of) silver for Iba-i(l) (and) Zirigu of the city of ʾAddu.

(108) 2 (shekels of) tin to be melted with 10 (shekels of) copper for making 2 daggers; 15 (shekels of) silver in exchange for 3 (shekels of) gold for their lamination, for the king.

(109)
25. 1 ma-na TAR 3 kù:babbar
níĝ-sa$_{10}$ 10 lá-1 *gàr-su* ĝi$_6$
27. 16 *gàr-su* si$_4$
2 ma-na 6 kù:babbar
29. níĝ-sa$_{10}$ 36 *ʾà-da-um*-TÚG-I
1 ma-na 4 kù:babbar
31. níĝ-sa$_{10}$ 85 siki na$_4$ *Ma-rí*$^{<ki>}$
XIX. 1. [ ]
[ ]
3. [ ]
[ ] ⌜x⌝ urudu
5. 7 kù:babbar
níĝ-sa$_{10}$ ĜIŠ-ti-ḪAR
7. <ki:lam$_7$> SA.ZA$_x^{ki}$
*Wa-ba-rúm*
9. šu-ba$_4$-ti

(110)
ŠÚ+ŠA kù:babbar
11. níĝ-ba
*Gú-ra-du*$^{ki}$
13. 10 kù:babbar
níĝ-ba
15. *ʾÀ-lu*$^{ki}$
*in*
17. *Ša-dab*$_6^{ki}$
šu-ba$_4$-ti
19. (blank)
l.ed. (blank)

(111)
1. AN.ŠÈ.GÚ 2 *mi-at* 80 lá-3 ma-na
ŠA.PI 6 gín DILMUN kù:babbar
è
3. *ap*
4 *mi-at* 40 lá-3 ma-na kù:babbar
5. al$_6$-ĝál
(blank)

*a*) it follows a vertical sign; *b*) perhaps unintentionally erased; *c*) followed by erasure

(109) 1;33 minas of silver for the purchase of 9 black bags (and) 16 red bags; 2;06 minas of silver for the purchase of 36 garments; 1;04 minas of silver for the purchase of 85 stone weights of wool from the city of Mari; […] copper; 7 (shekels of) silver for the purchase of GIŠ-ti-ḪAR-wood: <at the market> of the Palace, Wabarum has received.
(110) 20 (shekels of) silver: gift for (someone of) the city of Guradu; 10 (shekels of) silver: gift for (someone of) the city of ʾAlu, received in the city of Šadab.
(111) Total: 277;46 minas of silver: expenditure; and also 437 minas of silver are present.

## Commentary

This document has to be dated to the year Ibr. 15. It opens with the registration of the expenditures of 1 mina (470 g) of silver for the renewal rite concerning the city-god Kura, which fell at the beginning of the new year. The 3 shekels (23 g) of silver to be given in a later period of the year to the god for a further ceremony concerning his head are registered in § 50. Kura also received a pair of gold bracelets of 6 ½ shekels (52 g) as an annual offering (§ 75). Tinib-dulum, a sister of the king, received in her function as a priestess of the god ʾAdabal, 9;40 minas (4.23 kg) of silver, and her sister Tarib-damu, also a priestess of this god, 1 mina (470 g) of silver (§ 2).

The "expended", è, silver that year amounted to 277;46 minas (130.55 kg). The total silver "present", al$_6$-ĝál, in the Treasury was 437 minas (205.39 kg) (§ 111).

A substantial amount of "refined copper", a-gar$_5$-gar$_5$, weighing 980 minas (460.60 kg), was "acquired", níg-sa$_{10}$, with the expenditure of 14 minas (6.58 kg) of silver, that is, in a ratio of 70 : 1 copper – silver of (§ 46). Annual mu-DU documents from this period onward register large quantities of "refined copper" (a-gar$_5$-gar$_5$), and "copper" (urudu) stocked in the Treasury; the one from the year Ibr. 16, *ARET* XIV 69 obv. II 9, registers 700 minas (329 kg) of refined copper in the Treasury.

At the end of this year, the war against Ḫalsum broke out, and Ganubu (from the city of Salbaʾum) occupied the city (§ 99). This war ended the following year (Archi 2021a, pp. 197–198)

The king received fifteen "pegs", ĜIŠ-kak-ĜIŠ-kak, for a pedestal for five "travel trays", ĜIŠ-asari kaskal (§ 20). He received an element of a harness for which 30 shekels (235 g) of gold (§ 29) were employed, and also a dagger decorated with gold, valued at 1 mina (470 g) of silver (§ 47). Five shekels (39 g) of gold were needed for decorations on the wheels of his chariot and its harness (§ 58), as well as 1 shekel (8 g) of gold and 1 shekel of silver for other parts of the chariot (§ 59). A goad required 4 shekels of tin (31 g) together with 26 shekels (203 g) of copper (in a ratio of 1 : 15; § 73). Another 10 shekels (78 g) of gold were employed for the shell decoration on the wheels (§ 102). The king further received a battle-axe decorated with 6 shekels (47 g) of gold (§ 60), and another object (níĝ-PA) for which 3 shekels (23 g) of gold (§ 68) were employed. Two of his sons and two of his daughters all received a gold níg-bànda vessel weighing 4 shekels (313 g) (§ 83).

Tabur-damu, the queen, received a drinking cup with a handle of 23 shekels (180 g) of gold (§ 7), and two sets of jewelry: two *ti-gi-na* and two ĜIŠ-du, which required 17 shekels (133 g) of gold (§ 24).

The king's mother received a goblet of 10 shekels (78 g) of gold (§ 8), and a knife decorated with 2 ½ shekels (20 g) of silver, and 2 shekels (16 g) of gold (§ 97).

Minister Ibrium received a vessel, with its lid, of 40 shekels (313 g) of gold (§ 4); a battle-axe decorated with 3 shekels (23 g) of gold (§ 45); and three vessels for "travelling", kaskal-kaskal (§ 52). Two shekels (16 g) of gold were employed for a decoration on the wheels of his chariots (§ 58). He further received a big saw for which 33 shekels (258 g) of tin and 24 minas (11;28 kg) of copper were needed, and another two big saws which together required 6 shekels (47) of tin and 5 minas (2.35 kg) of copper (therefore an alloy with a very small amount of tin); in addition to a part of the chariot which needed 5 shekels (39 g) of silver (§ 71). The death of Ibrium's mother required items for her "funerary rite", É×PAP, two toggle-pins of 20 shekels (157 g) of silver, whose heads were decorated with 3 shekels (23 g) of gold (§ 84), while Ibrium received a belt decorated with 1 mina (470 g) of gold for his purification rite (ì-ĝiš-saĝ), (§ 86). Lastly the minister received two vessels of bronze for which 2 shekels of tin and 10 shekels (78 g) of copper were employed, in a ratio of 1 : 2, decorated with 2 shekels (16 g) of silver (§ 100). The minister received a dagger for the value of 1 mina (470 g) of silver in replacement of a dagger he gave for a purification rite (§ 106).

No messenger from Mari is mentioned for this year.

1 mina of silver was given to NIdim, a collector of the city of Nagar (§ 11), and 10 shekels (78 g) to Ḫura NE, of the same city (§ 14). A messenger from Nagar, Agga, received as a "gift", níg-ba, 10 shekels (78 g) of silver (§ 27). Ibri from Nagar is mentioned in § 44 together with envoys from ᵓAddu and Saggar; each of them received 5 shekels (39 g) of silver. Another envoy from Nagar received 10 shekels (78 g) of silver in Salbaᵓu (§ 51). Aᵓag of Nagar (presumably the Agga mentioned above) received 5 shekels (39 g) of silver (§ 64). Gusa, a son of the king of Nagar, received 25 shekels (196 g) of silver for an *a-ba-lum* and a goblet of silver (§ 80). 1 mina (470 g) of silver was sent to Nagar (§ 94). Enna-i(l), an envoy of Ḫalabidu, a city belonging to Nagar, received 5 shekels (39 g) of silver (§ 32). Three other cities belonging to Nagar, Abulium, Nabatiᵓum, and Saggar received 1 mina (470 g) of silver each (the first two), and 40 shekels (313 g) of silver (the third one); ᵓAddu (which is again associated to Nagar and its cities) received also 1 mina (70 g) of silver (§ 95). Three men from Nagar received 20 shekels (157 g) of silver for a journey to Sudaman (§ 103). These intense relations with Nagar were in function of the alliance with Ebla which was sworn in the temple of Dagan of Tuttul the following year (see the commentary to text 19).

Two men of ᵓAddu, a city located south of the kingdom of Nagar, received 10 shekels (78 g) of silver (§ 38). See further § 44.

§ 5. Each of two sons of the king received a bracelet, a torque, and a foot ring decorated with 14 shekels (110 g) of gold.

§ 6. Badulum, a son of Ibrium, received a plaque of 20 shekels (157 g) of gold.

§ 8. Dusigu, the king's mother, received a goblet of 10 shekels (78 g) of gold.

§ 9. Arzadu, a king's sister , received two toggle-pins decorated with 20 shekels (16 g) of silver.

§§ 10, 41. An expenditure of 3;20 minas (1.565 kg) of tin to be melted with 56;40 minas (26.633 kg) of copper (at a ratio 1 : 17, as it is stated there) concerned 200 daggers (§ 10). This was the first delivery of the thousand daggers expected to be deposited in Alaga, the place where military forces used to gather before launching an expedition (Archi 2021a, p. 212). A hundred of garments, evaluated 2;10 minas (1.018 g) of silver, were also sent to Alaga (§ 41).

§ 13. Aʾadu-LUM, a son of the king, received an object for which 2 shekels (16 g) of silver were employed.

§ 15. Three people of the Martu confederation, Daʾanu, Busi, and ʾAwara, received together 10 shekels (78 g) of silver,

§ 16. Wine in jars, valued 1 mina (470 g) of silver, was consigned to the king of Gudadanum by a certain Zabarum.

§ 17. Ibbi-zikir, the son of Ibrium, received four buckles decorated with 14 shekels (110 g) of gold.

§ 19. A bracelet of copper decorated with 1 shekel (8 g) of gold was given to Ibga-i(l), an overseer of the mules of the king.

§ 21. The "watchmen of the house of the king", ME-sig é en, received 126 bracelets of copper whose decorations required 8;24 minas (3.948 kg) of silver and 2;28 (1.159 kg) of gold.

§ 22. Two new containers required 11 minas (5.17 kg) of tin and 300 minas (141 kg) of copper in addition, $dah_x$, (tin: 3.54%). Its five clasps required 5 minas (2.35 kg) of silver, and its nine *ma-ba-ra-zú* 13;30 minas (6.11 kg) of copper and 2;12 minas (1.34 kg) of tin (14.02%).

§ 25. Three sons of Ibrium, Giri, Irti, and Napḫa-il, received respectively: *a*) a belt decorated with 10 shekels (78 g) of gold, *b*) a belt decorated with 7 shekels (55 g) of silver, melted with 1 shekel (8 g) of gold, and *c*) a belt decorated with 8 shekels (63 g) of silver.

§ 31. The minister of the city of Ḫarran received 20 shekels (18 g) of gold.

§ 39. *A*-LUM$^{ki}$, the representative of Ḫara-i(l), the gardener, received 10 shekels (78 g) of silver as "travel provision". According to *ARET* XX 7 § 8, *A*-LUM$^{ki}$ had delivered to the central administration 60 garments and sixty kilts.

§ 40. Both Išgi-barzu and Dubi-ab, overseers of Tisum, received a dagger decorated with 40 shekels (313 g) of gold. The expenditure of these "two daggers (decorated with) gold" is registered also in *ARET* XX 2 § 20.

§ 44. 20 shekels (157) of silver were given as a "gift" níg-ba, to two men from ʾAddu, one from Nagar, and one from Saggar, which confirms that the three cities were located in the same region, as also the cities of Abulium, Nabutium and Saggar (§ 95).

§ 49. Taldud, one of the two "spouses", dam, of the king who resided in Lub, received several kinds of jewels decorated with 1;30 minas (705 g) of gold, and 30 shekels (235 g) of silver, perhaps for the birth of a child.

§ 53. Tinib-dulum, the sister of the king, received eight earrings decorated with 6 shekels (47 g) of gold.

§ 54. Tarib-damu and Tište-damu, two "daughters of the king", received several jewels for which were employed 8 shekels (63 g) of gold in total. The two princesses had received jewels already two years earlier (XXI 16 § 7).

§ 62. Two minas (940 g) of tin and 12 minas (5.64 kg) of copper were delivered to the carpenters for decorations.

§§ 63, 64. Two envoys: Kun-išar from the city of ʾAddu (in the city of Šadab), and Aʾag from the city of Nagar, received a "gift", níĝ-ba, respectively of 10 and 5 shekels (78 and 39 g).

§ 65. Giʾudu, the spouse of Zabarum (an official mentioned in several documents of Ibrium, see the Index of the Personal Names) received 2 toggle-pins of 20 shekels (157 g) of silver for the purification rite on the occasion of her husband's death.

§§ 67, 70. Death of the queen of Lumnan, on which occasion two toggle-pins of 20 shekels (157 g) of silver were handed over in that city for her "funerary rite", É×PAP. She was an Eblaite princess who had married the king of Lumnan after the death of Dati-TU, the previous queen: she also an Eblaite princess (see the commentary to XXI 17 § 32). Tirin-damu, the priestess (her sister) received two toggle-pins of 20 shekels (157 g) of silver for her "purification rite", ì-ĝiš-saĝ, on the same occasion.

§ 77. Tin and copper expended for 450 daggers, and silver with gold for their decorations. These daggers "had to be added", *mu-lu-iš*, to those already stored in Alaga; see § 10.

§ 78. Travel provision of 30 shekels (235 g) of silver for Gibaria, a man of the city of Kablul, who had to go to Irbilum (Erbil, see ARET IV, pp. 34–35). The high amount of this provision was in relation of this unusual mission.

§ 81. The king of Adaš received 2 minas (940 g) of tin. The writing *A-daš*$^{ki}$ (see also § 61) is unusual; see *A-da-áš*$^{ki}$ in ARES IV, pp. 92–93. The authority usually referred to this city was an "overseer", ugula.

§ 88. Minna-i(l), an overseer of the mules of Ibrium, required a dagger decorated with gold and silver, whose amount is not preserved.

§ 89. The king of Imar received a chariot with decorations which needed the following expenses: 30 shekels (235 g) of gold for the wheels, 2 minas (940 g) of gold for the bridle; 5 shekels (39 g) of tin and 35 shekels (274 g) of copper (12.5% of tin) for a hook; and 1 shekel (8 g) of gold for the edge the chariot case.

# 19
## (Plates XXXVI–XXXVII)

(1)

o. I. 1. 1 ma-na kù:babbar
saĝ kù:babbar
3. $^{d}$*Ku-ra*

(2)

6 ma-na ŠÚ+ŠA gín DILMUN
kù:babbar
5. *Di-ne-íb-du-lum*
nin-ni
7. en
1 ma-na kù:babbar
9. *Dar-ib-da-mu*
[n]in-ni-*sù*
11. šu-ba$_4$-ti

(3)

2 ma-na kù:babbar
13. níĝ-sa$_{10}$ 2 ĝír mar-tu kù-gi
*Ib-rí-um*
15. *wa*
sikil-*sù*
17. *al*$_6$
tu-ra
19. *I-bí-zi-kir*
*wa*
21. *al*$_6$
tu-ra
23. en

(4)

1 ma-na kù:babbar
25. níĝ-sa$_{10}$ 1 ĝír mar-tu kù-gi
*Ib-rí-um*
27. [*áš*-]*du*
[1 ĝ]ír [mar-t]u
II. 1. [-*s*]*ù*
sikil

(5)

3. 5 gín DILMUN kù:babbar
šu-bal-ak
5. 1 gín DILMUN kù-gi 1 kù-sal
níĝ-ba
7. en
$^{d}$*Ba-tum-ma-du*
9. *áš-t*[*i*]
ĝír mar-tu-*sù*
11. šu-mu-tak$_4$
*al*$_6$
13. tu-ra
*Ib-rí-um*

(6)

15. TAR kù:babbar 2 *bu*-DI
ŠÚ+ŠA gín DILMUN kù:babbar
17. šu-bal-ak
4 gín DILMUN kù-gi
19. nu$_{11}$-za
2 saĝ-*sù*
21. níĝ-ba
*Ti-šè-li-im*
23. *ma-lik-tum*
*Ì-mar*$^{ki}$

(7)

25. 5 gín DILMUN kù:babbar
3 *bu*-DI 2 saĝ
27. 6 gín DILMUN an-na
šub *si-in*
29. TAR 4 a-gar$_5$-gar$_5$
III. 1. 1 SIG$_7$.IGI
*Di-ne-íb-du-lum*
3. nin-ni
en

(8)

5. ŠÚ+ŠA 2 gín DILMUN an-na
šub *si-in*

(1) 1 mina of silver for the silver head of the god Kura.

(2) 6;20 minas of silver for Tinib-dulum, sister of the king; 1 mina of silver for Tarib-damu, her [s]ister: they have received it.

(3) 2 minas of silver for the purchase of 2 mar-tu daggers (decorated with) gold for Ibrium and for his purification rite in relation to the illness of Ibbi-zikir and the illness of the king.

(4) 1 mina of silver for the purchase of 1 mar-tu dagger (decorated with) gold for Ibrium, [as a repla]cement for [his mar-t]u [dag]ger, (given for) the purification rite.

(5) 5 shekels of silver in exchange for 1 shekel of gold for 1 buckle: gift of the king for the god Batum-madu, as a replacement of his mar-tu dagger, (that) had been handed over in relation to the illness of Ibrium.

(6) 30 (shekels of) silver for 2 toggle-pins; 20 shekels of silver in exchange for 4 shekels of gold for plating their 2 heads: gift for Tiše-lim, the queen of the city of Imar.

(7) 5 shekels of silver for 2 toggle-pins (and their) 2 heads; 6 shekels of tin to be melted with 34 (shekels of) copper for 1 eyebrow (decoration) for Tinib-dulum, sister of the king.

(8) 22 shekels of tin to be melted with 1;08 m[i]na of copper for making 3 small axes of 40 (shekels) each to be handed over to the city of Alaga, on the occasion of the *review*[!] in the city of Alaga.

7. 1 m[a-]na TAR [4+]4 gín DILMUN
a-gar$_5$-gar$_5$
kin$_5$-ak
9. 3 tùn tur
ŠA.PI-ŠA.PI
11. lú
šu-mu-tak$_4$
13. *si-in*
*A-la-ga*$^{ki}$
15. *in* ud[a)]
igi-ḫi-du$_8$$^!$(šu-du$_8$[a)])
17. *A-la-ga*$^{ki}$

(9)
ŠÚ+ŠA gín DILMUN kù:babbar
19. *Daš-na*
*wa*
21. *Ì-lum-a-ḫi*
*Ma-rí*$^{ki}$

(10)
23. 15 gín DILMUN kù:babbar
níĝ-ba
25. ḪI-*la-um*
*Na-gàr*$^{ki}$

(11)
27. 15 gín DILMUN kù:babbar
šu-bal-ak
29. 3 gín [DILM]UN
IV. 1. kù-gi
lul-gu-ak
3. 1 iti
lú
5. é
$^{d\text{ʾ}}$*À-da*
7. lú-máš

(12)
1 ma-na ŠA.PI gín DILMUN
kù:babbar
9. níĝ-sa$_{10}$ 1 *mi-at* ma-na a-gar$_5$-gar$_5$

(13)
7 ½ gín DILMUN kù:babbar
11. šu-bal-ak
1 ½ gín DILMUN kù-gi
13. *ni-zi-mu*
nu$_{11}$-za
15. 2 *gú-li-lum* kù:babbar
*Ib-dur-i-šar*
17. lú *Da-si*-KA

(14)
20 lá-1 ma-na ŠÚ+ŠA 7 gín DILMUN
an-na
19. šub *si-in*
1 *mi-at* 50 ma-na a-gar$_5$-gar$_5$
21. kin$_5$-ak
1 *li-im* ĜIŠ-gu-kak-g[íd]
V. 1. zabar
1 gín DILMUN 6 NI an-na
3. šub *si-in*
9 gín DILMUN a-gar$_5$-gar$_5$
5. 1 ĜIŠ-gu-kak-gíd

(15)
10 lá-2 ma-na ŠÚ+ŠA kù:babbar
7. šu-bal-ak
1 ma-na ŠA.PI gín DILMUN kù-gi
9. 1 dib
*I-bí-zi-kir*
11. dumu-nita
*Ib-rí-um*
13. *áš-du*
dib-*sù*
15. sikil
$^{d\text{ʾ}}$*À-da*

(16)
17. 20 ma-na kù:babbar
níĝ-ba
19. en
*Na-gàr*$^{ki}$
21. 7 ma-na kù:babbar
níĝ-ba
23. dumu-nita-dumu-nita-*sù*

(17)
5 ma-na kù:babbar
25. níĝ-ba
en-en
VI. 1. lú *áš-ti*
en

(9) 20 shekels of silver for Dašna and Ilum-aḫi of the city of Mari.
(10) 15 shekels of silver: gift for ḪIlaʾum of the city of Nagar.
(11) 15 shekels of silver in exchange for 3 shekels of gold, as a replacement for (the image of) a month in the temple of the god Hadda for taking an omen.
(12) 1:40 minas of silver for the purchase of 100 minas of copper.
(13) 7 ½ shekels of silver in exchange for 1 ½ shekel of gold for decorating with lamination 2 bracelets of silver for Ibdur-išar, (son) of DasiKA.
(14) 19;27 minas of tin to be melted with 150 minas of copper for making 1000 bronze spearheads; that is: 1 shekel (and) 6 NI of tin to be melted with 9 shekels of copper for each spearhead.
(15) 8;20 minas of silver in exchange for 1;40 minas of gold for 1 plaque for Ibbi-zikir, son of Ibrium, as a replacement of his plaque, (given for) for the purification rite to the god Hadda.
(16) 20 minas of silver: gift for the king of the city of Nagar; 7 minas of silver: gift for his sons.
(17) 5 minas of silver: gift for the kings (who were) with the king of the city of Nagar, (who) went to swear an oath in the temple of the Lord of the city of Tuttul.

3. *Na-gàr*$^{ki}$
DU.DU
5. nam-kud
é
7. $^{d}$BAD
*Du-du-lu*$^{ki}$

(18)
9. 10 gín DILMUN kù:babbar
níĝ-ba
11. *Ḫu-ra*-NE
*Na-gàr*$^{ki}$
13. *in*
*Du-du-lu*$^{ki}$
15. šu-ba$_4$-ti

(19)
ŠÚ+ŠA gín DILMUN kù:babbar
17. níĝ-ba
*ʾÀ-du*$^{ki}$
19. é
$^{d}$BAD *Ga-na-na-im*
21. šu-ba$_4$-ti

(20)
11 ma-na ŠA.PI gín DILMUN kù:babbar
23. níĝ-sa$_{10}$ 30 lá-2 túg-NI.NI
1 *mi-at* 46 sal-TÚG
25. 80 gada-TÚG
60 siki na$_4$ *Ma-rí*$^{ki}$
27. 2 ma-na kù:babbar
níĝ-sa$_{10}$ ĜIŠ-ti-ḪAR
29. ki:lam$_7$
VII. 1. $^{d}$*A-da-ma*
*ʾÀ-da-ni*$^{ki}$

(21)
3. TAR kù:babbar
1 íb-lá 1 *si-ti-tum* 1 ĝír-kun
5. *I-in-*$^{d}$*ʾÀ-da*
dumu-nita
7. en
É×PAP

(22)
9. 3 gín DILMUN kù:babbar
nu$_{11}$-za
11. 2 zag ĜIŠ-gígir-II
10 gín DILMUN an-na
13. šub *si-in*
1 ma-na a-gar$_5$-gar$_5$
15. 2 ĜIŠ-zú ĜIŠ-gígir-II
zú-ak
17. *Ib-rí-um*
*wa*
19. *I-bí-zi-kir*
dumu-nita-*sù*

(23)
21. 2 ma-na TAR kù:babbar
šu-bal-ak
23. TAR kù-gi
1 íb-lá 1 *si-ti-tum* 1 ĝír-kun
25. *Mu-gàr*
dumu-nita
27. *A-ba-rúm*
*in* ud
29. ḫúl-*sù*
VIII. 1. *A-šum*
šu-mu-tak$_4$

(24)
3. 15 gín DILMUN kù:babbar
šu-bal-ak
5. [3 gín DILMUN kù-g]i
*wa*
7. 2 gín DILMUN kù:babbar
ì-na-sum
9. 1 banšur
*wa*
11. 1 kù-sal
níĝ-ba
13. *Ib-rí-um*
$^{d}$*Aš-dar*

(25)
15. ŠÚ+ŠA gín DILMUN kù:babbar
níĝ-kaskal
17. NE-*iš-da-ar*

(18) 10 shekels of silver: gift for ḪuraNE of the city of Nagar, received in the city of Tuttul.
(19) 20 shekels of silver: gift for (someone of) the city of ʾAddu, received in the temple of the Lord of Ganana.
(20) 11;40 minas of silver for the purchase of 254 garments (and) 60 stone weights of wool from the city of Mari; 2 minas of silver for the purchase of GIŠ-ti-ḪAR-wood: at the market of the god Adamma of the city of ʾAdani.
(21) 30 (shekels of) silver for 1 belt, 1 sheath (and) 1 dagger pendant for the funerary rite of Iʾin-Hadda, son of the king.
(22) 3 shekels of silver for plating 2 sides of a chariot; 10 shekels of tin melted with 1 mina of copper for 2 pointed hooks of the chariots for Ibrium and Ibbi-zikir, his son.
(23) 2;30 minas of silver in exchange for 30 (shekels of) gold for 1 belt, 1 sheath (and) 1 dagger pendant for Mugar, son of Abarum, on the occasion of his feast, Ašum has handed over.
(24) 15 shekels of silver in exchange for [3 shekels of gold] and 2 shekels of silver, given for 1 table and 1 buckle: gift of Ibrium for the god Ašdar.
(25) 20 shekels of silver: travel provision for NEišdar of the city of Kablul (who) went to the city of Armi.

*Kab-lu$_5$-ul*[ki]
19. DU.DU
*si-in*
21. *Ar-mi*[ki]

(26)
5 gín DILMUN kù:babbar
23. šu-bal-ak
1 gín DILMUN kù-gi
25. *ni-zi-mu*
4 kù-sal
27. *a-li-iš*
kù-sal-kù-sal
29. *Zi-ba-da*

(27)
10 lá-1 ma-na 20 gín DILMUN an-na
IX. 1. šub *si-in*
2 *mi-at* 17 ma-na a-gar$_5$-g[ar$_5$]
3. [k]in$_5$-ak
sig$_4$-KI
5. 2 útul urudu gibil maḫ

(28)
TAR 3 gín DILMUN kù:babbar 3 NI
7. šu-bal-ak
6 gín DILMUN 2 NI kù-gi
9. 2 *gú-li-lum*
níĝ-ba
11. [d]*Ku-ra*

(29)
10 gín DILMUN kù:babbar
13. šu-bal-ak
2 gín DILMUN kù-gi
15. 2 kù-sal
níĝ-ba
17. [d]*Ba-tum-ma-du*
*wa*
19. [d]*Da-bí-na-du*
*áš-ti*
21. 2 ĝír mar-tu kù-gi
*al$_6$*
23. tu-ra
en

(30)
25. TAR kù:babbar
lú ĜIŠ-nu-kiri$_6$
27. *En-na-il*
ugula engar
29. *Zú-ba-núm*
X. 1. 2 šu-ba$_4$-ti

(31)
1 ma-na 15 ⸢gín⸣ DILMUN kù:babbar
3. šu-bal-ak
15 gín DILMUN kù-gi
5. 1 dib
*Dar-ib-da-mu*
7. dumu-munus
en

(32)
9. ŠÚ+ŠA gín DILMUN kù:babbar 2 *bu*-DI
ì-ĝiš-saĝ
11. *Di-rín-da-mu*
dam-diĝir
13. *Ìr-ba$_x$-zé* "ur$_4$"
šu-mu-tak$_4$

(33)
15. 1 gín DILMUN kù:babbar
nu$_{11}$-za 1 zag ĜIŠ-gígir-II
17. *Ba-ga-ma*

(34)
13 gín DILMUN kù:babbar
19 nu$_{11}$-za 1 *ḫa-bù*
TAR kù:babbar
21. šu-bal-ak
6 gín DILMUN kù-gi
23. nu$_{11}$-za
1 *ar-ra-sù*
25. ŠÚ+ŠA gín DILMUN kù:babbar

(26) 5 shekels of silver in exchange for 1 shekel of gold for decorating 4 buckles in addition to the buckles of Zibada.
(27) 9;20 minas of tin melted with 217 minas of coppe[r for m]aking the … (sig$_4$-KI) of 2 new big kettles of copper.
(28) 33 shekels and 3 NI of silver in exchange for 6 shekels and 2 NI of gold for 2 bracelets: gift for the god Kura.
(29) 10 shekels of silver in exchange for 2 shekels of gold for 2 buckles: gift for the god Batum-madu and the goddess Dabinadu, as a replacement of 2 mar-tu daggers (decorated with) gold (that had been handed over) in relation to the illness of the king.
(30) 30 (shekels of) silver for the gardeners: Enna-il, the overseer of the farmers (and) Zubanum have received.
(31) 1;15 minas of silver in exchange for 15 shekels of gold for 1 plaque for Tarib-damu, daughter of the king.
(32) 20 shekels of silver for 2 toggle-pins for the purification ceremony of Tirin-damu, the priestess; Irbaze, the collector (of goods) has handed over.
(33) 1 shekel of silver for plating 1 side of a chariot for Bagama.
(34) 13 shekels of silver for plating 1 mace; 30 (shekels of) silver in exchange for 6 shekels of gold for plating its handle; 20 shekels of silver for the circular stand of the (4) horns of 2 bulls: offering of the king for the god Rašap of the city of ʾAdani.

*ʾa*$_{5}$*-na-gu*
27. si 2 gud
XI. 1. nídba
en
3. $^{d}$*Ra-sa-ap*
*ʾÀ-da-ni*$^{ki}$

(35)
5. 15 gín DILMUN kù:babbar
nu$_{11}$-za 1 *ḫa-bù*
7. *ap*
nu$_{11}$-za
9. *ar-ra-sù*
kù-gi sikil
11. ŠÚ+ŠA gín DILMUN kù:babbar
*ʾa*$_{5}$*-na-gu*
13. si 2 gud
nídba
15. en
$^{dʾ}$*À-da*
17. *Ḫa-lab*$_{x}^{ki}$
*in*
19. $^{d}$AMA-*ra*

(36)
ŠA.PI gín DILMUN kù:babbar
21. šu-bal-ak
8 gín DILMUN kù-gi
23. nu$_{11}$-za 2 gí[r] mar-tu
*wa*
25. 2 kù-sal
f níĝ-ba
27. $^{dʾ}$*A*$_{5}$*-da-"bal"*
*A-ru*$_{12}$*-ga-du*$^{ki}$
29. *wa*
$^{dʾ}$*A*$_{5}$*-da-"bal"*
31. *ʾÀ-ma-du*$^{ki}$
XII. 1. [ ]-⸢x⸣
[šu-m]u-tak$_{4}$
3. *al*$_{6}$
tu-ra-*sù*

(37)
5. ŠÚ+ŠA gín DILMUN kù:babbar
šu-bal-ak
7. 4 gín DILMUN kù-gi
*ni-zi-mu*
9. 1 an-zam$_{x}$
en

(38)
11. 4 ma-na gín DILMUN kù:babbar
šu-bal-ak
13. 50 gín DILMUN kù-gi
*ni-zi-mu*
15. *su-da-nu*
*wa*
17. kù-sal
sur$_{x}$-BAR.AN
19. en

(39)
15 gín DILMUN kù:babbar
21. šu-bal-ak
3 gín DILMUN kù-gi
23. *ni-zi-mu*
2 [n]íĝ-anše-ak 4 kù-sal
25. *I-bí-zi-kir*

(40)
TAR kù:babbar
27. šu-bal-ak
6 gín DILMUN kù-gi
29. *ni-zi-mu*
nu$_{11}$-za
XIII. 1. 2 ĜIŠ-ban
ĜIŠ-gígir-II
3. *Ib-rí-um*

(41)
3 ma-na ŠÚ+ŠA gín DILMUN kù:babbar
5. šu-bal-ak
ŠA.PI gín DILMUN kù-gi

(35) 15 shekels of silver for plating 1 mace and also for plating its handle (with) pure gold; 20 shekels of silver for the circular stand of the (4) horns of 2 bulls: offering of the king for the god Hadda of the city of Ḫalab, at the AMA-ra (festival).

(36) 40 shekels of silver in exchange for 8 shekels of gold for plating 2 mar-tu daggers and 2 buckles: gift for the god ʾAdabal of the city of Arugadu and for the god ʾAdabal of the city of ʾAmadu; [... has han]ded over in relation to his illness.

(37) 20 shekels of silver in exchange for 4 shekels of gold for decorating 1 an-zam$_{x}$ goblet for the king.

(38) 4 minas of silver in exchange for 50 shekels of gold for decorating the ... (*su-da-nu*) and the buckles for the team of mules of the king.

(39) 15 shekels of silver in exchange for 3 shekels of gold for decorating 2 bridles (and) 4 buckles for Ibbi-zikir.

(40) 30 (shekels of) silver in exchange for 6 shekels of gold for decorating with lamination 2 bows of a chariot for Ibrium.

(41) 3;20 minas of silver in exchange for 40 shekels of gold for 1 an-zam$_{x}$ goblet and its lid for Ibrium.

7. 1 an-zam$_x$
*wa*
9. 1 pad-*sù*
*Ib-rí-um*

(42)
11. 15 gín DILMUN kù:babbar
šu-bal-ak
13. 3 gín DILMUN kù-gi
kin$_5$-ak
15. ZA$_x$
*a-si-ga-tim*
17. ama-gal
en

(43)
19. 5 gín DILMUN kù:babbar
šu-bal-ak
21. 1 gín DILMUN kù-gi 1 kù-sal
níĝ-ba
23. ama-gal
en
25. $^{d}$*Ra-sa-ap*
*ʾÀ-da-ni*$^{ki}$
27. AMA-*ra*

(44)
53 gín DILMUN 3 NI an-na
29. šub *si-in*
6 ma-na ŠA.PI a-gar$_5$
31. kin$_5$-ak
20 ĝír mar-tu kù-gi
33. *ap* 2 ma-na kù-gi
XIV. 1. lú mu-DU
*Kab-lu$_5$-ul*$^{ki}$
3. *zi-du-sù*
*ap*
5. ŠÚ+ŠA a-gar$_5$-gar$_5$
2 an-na 2 NI
7. [kin$_5$]-ak
1 ĝír mar-tu
9. 6 kù-gi
*zi-du-sù*
11. 50 gín DILMUN an-na
šub *si-in*
13. 6 ma-na ŠÚ+ŠA a-gar$_5$
kin$_5$-ak
15. 20 ĝír mar-tu ti kù-gi *ʾà-lum*
5 ma-na kù:babbar
17. šu[-bal-ak]
1 ma-na kù-gi
19. nu$_{11}$-za-*sù*
*ap*
21. 19 a-gar$_5$
2 ½ an-na
23. kin$_5$-ak
1 ĝír mar-tu
25. 3 kù-gi nu$_{11}$-za-*sù*
1 [m]a-na TAR an-na
27. šub *si-in*
12 ma-na a-gar$_5$-gar$_5$
29. kin$_5$-ak
40 ĝír mar-tu ti kù-gi
31. 10 ma-na kù:babbar
XV. 1. šu-bal-ak
2 ma-na kù-gi
3. *zi-du-sù*
*ap*
5. 18 a-gar$_5$
2 4 NI
7. kin$_5$-ak
1 ĝír mar-tu
9. 3 kù-gi
*zi-du-sù*
11. TAR an-na
šub *si-in*
13. 3 ma-na TAR 5 a-gar$_5$
kin$_5$-ak
15. 12 ĝír mar-tu zú AN.LAGAB×A
1 ma-na ŠÚ+ŠA 7 ½ gín DILMUN
kù:babbar
17. šu-bal-ak
17 gín DILMUN ½ kù-gi
19. nu$_{11}$-za *ša-ga-tum-sù*

(42) 15 shekels of silver in exchange for 3 shekels of gold for making objects of a … (*a-si-ga-tum*) for the king's mother.

(43) 5 shekels of silver in exchange for 1 shekel of gold for 1 buckle: gift of the king's mother for the god Rašap of the city of ʾAdani, at the AMA-ra (festival).

(44) 53 shekels (and) 3 NI of tin to be melted with 6;40 minas of copper for making 20 mar-tu daggers (decorated with) gold, and also 2 minas of gold delivered by the city of Kablul, for their alloy; that is: 20 (shekels of) copper (and) 2 (shekels and) 2 NI of tin [for ma]king each mar-tu dagger (and) 6 (shekels of) gold for its alloy. 50 shekels of tin to be melted with 6;20 minas of copper for making 20 pointed mar-tu daggers (decorated with) gold … (*ʾà-lum*); 5 minas of silver in ex[change for] 1 mina of gold for their lamination; that is: 19 (shekels of) copper (and) 2 ½ (shekels of) tin for making each mar-tu dagger (and) 3 (shekels of) gold for its lamination. 1;30 [m]inas of tin to be melted with 12 minas of copper for making 40 pointed mar-tu daggers (decorated with) gold (and) 10 minas of silver in exchange for 2 minas of gold for their alloy; that is: 18 (shekels of) copper (and) 2 (shekels and) 4 NI (of tin) for making each mar-tu dagger (and) 3 (shekels of) gold for its alloy. 30 (shekels of) tin to be melted with 3;35 minas of copper for making 12 serrated mar-tu daggers (decorated with) ivory (and) 1;27 ½ minas of silver in exchange for 17 ½ shekels of gold for plating their … (*ša-ga-tum*) and knobs; that is: 18 (shekels of) copper (and) 2 ½ (shekels of) tin for making each mar-tu dagger (and) 1 ½ (shekel of) gold for its plating. And also 8 serrated mar-tu daggers (decorated with) ivory (and) gold: to be handed over for the military review by the city of Zarudu.

*wa*
21. *ga-ma-a-tum*
*ap*
23. 18 a-gar$_5$
2 ½ an-na
25. kin$_5$-ak
1 ĝír mar-tu
27. 1 ½ kù-gi
nu$_{11}$-za-*sù*
29. *ap*
10 lá-2 ĝír mar-tu zú AN.LAGAB×A
kù-gi
31. lú tak$_4$
igi-ḫi-du$_8$
33. *Za-ru$_{12}$-du*<ki>

(45)

XVI. 1. 1 ma-na TAR an-na
šub *si-in*
3. 12 ma-na a-gar$_5$-gar$_5$
kin$_5$-ak
5. 40 ĝír mar-tu *ba-du-u$_9$* kù-gi
10 lá-2 ma-na ŠÚ+ŠA DILMUN
kù:babbar
7. šu-bal-ak
1 ma-na ŠA.PI gín DILMUN kù-gi
9. *zi-du-sù*
*ap*
11. 18 a[-gar$_5$]
[x an-na]
13. kin$_5$-ak
1 ĝír mar-tu
15. 2 ½ kù-gi
*zi-du-sù*
17. 2 ma-na 15 gín an-na
šub *si-in*
19. 20 lá-2 ma-na a-gar$_5$-gar$_5$
kin$_5$-ak
21. 60 ĝír mar-tu *ba-du-u$_9$* kù:babbar-gi
2 ma-na TAR kù:babbar
23. šu-bal-ak
TAR kù-gi
25. 3 ma-na kù:babbar

XVII. 1. *zi-du-sù*
*ap*
3. 18 a-gar$_5$
2 4 NI an-na
5. kin$_5$-ak
1 ĝír mar-tu
7. 3 kù:babbar
*wa*
9. ½ kù-gi
*zi-du-sù*
11. 11 ma-na 15 gín DILMUN an-na
šub *si-in*
13. 90 ma-na a-gar$_5$-gar$_5$
kin$_5$-ak
15. 3 *mi-at* ĝír [ma]r-tu
*ga-me-ù* kù:babbar
17. 6 ma-na ŠA.PI gín DILMUN
kù:babbar
*ga-ma-a-tum-sù*
19. *ap*
18 a-gar$_5$
21. 2 an-na 4 NI
kin$_5$-ak
23. 1 ĝír mar-tu
1 3 NI kù:babbar
25. *ga-ma-a-tum-sù*
5 ma-na kù:babbar níĝ-sa$_{10}$

XVIII. 1. 3 *mi-at* ĝír mar-tu zú-ak
10 ma-na kù:babbar
3. šu-bal-ak
2 ma-na kù-gi
5. nu$_{11}$-za
16 *gú-li-lum* TAR-II a-gar$_5$
7. *wa*
50 *gú-li-lum* 10-I a-gar$_5$-gar$_5$
9. 3 ma-na kù:babbar
nu$_{11}$-za
11. 10 *gú-li-lum*-II TAR a-gar$_5$-gar$_5$
*wa*
13. 1 *mi-at gú-li-lum*-I 10 a-gar$_5$
3 gín DILMUN kù:babbar
15. ZU.PIRIĜ-*sù*
lú
17. šu-mu-tak$_4$
*si-in*
19. *A-la-ga*[ki]

(45) 1;30 minas of tin to be melted with 12 minas of copper for making 40 *b.* mar-tu daggers (decorated with) gold (and) 8;20 minas of silver in exchange for 1;40 minas of gold for their alloy; that is: 18 (shekels of) co[pper (and) x tin] for making each mar-tu dagger (and) 2 ½ (shekels of) gold for its alloy. 2;15 minas of tin to be melted with 18 minas of copper for making 60 *b.* mar-tu daggers (decorated with) silver (and) gold (and) 2;30 minas of silver in exchange for 30 (shekels of) gold (and) 3 minas of silver for their alloy; that is: 18 (shekels of) copper (and) 2 (shekels and) 4 NI of tin for making each mar-tu dagger (and) 3 (shekels of) silver and ½ (shekel of) gold for its alloy. 11;15 minas of tin to be melted with 90 minas of copper for making 300 *g.* [ma]r-tu daggers (decorated with) silver (and) 6;40 minas of silver for their knobs; that is: 18 (shekels of) copper (and) 2 (shekels and) 4 NI of tin for making each mar-tu dagger (and) 1 (shekel and) 3 NI of silver for its knob. 5 minas of silver for the purchase of 300 serrated mar-tu daggers; 10 minas of silver in exchange for 2 minas of gold for plating 16 double bracelets of 30 (shekels of) copper each and 50 single bracelets of 10 (shekels of) copper each; 3 minas of silver for plating 10 double bracelets of 30 (shekels of) copper each and 10 single bracelets of 10 (shekels of) copper each; 3 shekels of silver for their hangers: they were handed over to the city of Alaga.

(46)
3 ma-na TAR 3 gín DILMUN 2 NI an-
na
21. šub *si-in*
26 ma-na
r. I. 1. ŠA.PI gín DILMUN a-gar$_5$-gar$_5$
kin$_5$-ak
3. 80 ĝír mar-tu kù-gi
*ap*
5. 10 lá-2 ma-na kù-gi
*zi-du-sù*
7. lú mu-DU
*Kab-lu$_5$-ul*$^{ki}$
9. *ap*
ŠÚ+ŠA a-gar$_5$-gar$_5$
11. 2 gín DILMUN 2 NI an-na
kin$_5$-ak
13. 1 ĝír mar-tu
6 gín DILMUN kù-gi
15. *zi-du-sù*
50 gín DILMUN an-na
17. šub *si-in*
6 ma-na ŠÚ+ŠA gín DILMUN a-gar$_5$-
gar$_5$
19. kin$_5$-ak
20 ĝír mar-tu ti kù-gi *ʾà-lum*
21. 6 ma-na ŠA.PI gín DILMUN
kù:babbar
š[u-]bal-ak
23. 1 [ma-na] ŠÚ+ŠA g[ín DILMUN] kù-
gi
*zi-du-sù*
25. *ap*
19 gín DILMUN a-gar$_5$-gar$_5$
II. 1. 3$^{?}$ an-na
kin$_5$-ak
3. 1 ĝír mar-tu
4 gín kù-gi
5. *zi-du-sù*
3 ma-na ŠÚ+ŠA gín DILMUN an-na
7. šub *si-in*
34 ma-na a-gar$_5$-gar$_5$
9. kin$_5$-ak
90 ĝír mar-tu ti kù-gi
11. 22 ma-na TAR kù:babbar
šu-bal-ak
13. 4 ma-na TAR kù-gi
*zi-du-sù*
15. *ap*
18 a-gar$_5$
17. *wa*
2 gín DILMUN 4 NI an-na
19. kin$_5$-ak
1 ĝír mar-tu
21. 3 kù-gi
*zi-du-sù*
23. 1 ma-na 52 [g]ín DILMUN an-na
šub *si-in*
25. 15 ma-na a-gar$_5$-gar$_5$
kin$_5$-ak
27. 50 ĝír mar-tu *ba-du-u$_9$*
III. 1. kù-gi
⌜10⌝ma-na 25 gín DILMUN
kù:babbar
3. šu-bal-ak
2 ma-na 5 gín DILMUN kù-gi
5. *zi-du-sù*
*ap*
7. 18 a-gar$_5$
2 gín DILMUN 4 NI an-na
9. kin$_5$-ak
1 ĝír mar-tu
11. 2 ½ kù-gi
*zi-du-sù*
13. 2 ma-na 15 gín DILMUN an-na
šub *si-in*
15. 20 lá-2 ma-na a-gar$_5$-gar$_5$
kin$_5$-ak
17. 60 ĝír mar-tu *ba-du-u$_9$* kù:babbar-gi
2 ma-na TAR kù:babbar
19. šu-bal-ak
[30 k]ù-gi

(46) 3;33 minas (and) 2 NI of tin to be melted with 26;40 minas of copper for making 80 mar-tu daggers (decorated with) gold, and also 8 minas of gold for their alloy delivered by the city of Kablul; that is: 20 (shekels of) copper (and) 2 shekels (and) 2 NI of tin for making each mar-tu dagger (and) 6 shekels of gold for its alloy. 50 shekels of tin to be melted with 6;20 minas of copper for making 20 pointed mar-tu daggers (decorated with) gold … (*ʾà-lum*); 6;40 minas of silver in exchange for 1;20 [minas] of gold for their alloy; that is: 19 shekels of copper and 3 (shekels of) tin for making each mar-tu dagger (and) 4 shekels of gold for its alloy. 3;20 minas of tin to be melted with 34 minas of copper for making 90 pointed mar-tu daggers (decorated with) gold (and) 22;30 minas of silver in exchange for 4;30 minas of gold for their alloy; that is: 18 (shekels of) copper and 2 shekels (and) 4 NI of tin for making each mar-tu dagger (and) 3 (shekels of) gold for its alloy. 1;52 minas of tin to be melted with 15 minas of copper for making 50 *b.* mar-tu daggers (decorated with) gold (and) 10;25 minas of silver in exchange for 2;05 minas of gold for their alloy; that is: 18 (shekels of) copper (and) 2 (shekels and) 4 NI of tin for making each mar-tu dagger (and) 2 ½ (shekels of) gold for its alloy. 2;15 minas of tin to be melted with 18 minas of copper for making 60 *b.* mar-tu daggers (decorated with) silver (and) gold; 2;30 minas of silver in exchange for [30 (shekels of g]old [an]d 3 minas of silver for their alloy; that is: 18 (shekels of) copper (and) 2 shekels (and) 4 NI of tin for making each mar-tu dagger (and) 3 shekels of silver (and) ½ (shekel of) gold for its alloy. 13;30 minas of tin to be melted with 108 minas of copper for making 360 *g.* mar-tu daggers (decorated with) silver (and) 8 minas of silver for (their) knobs; that is: 18 (shekels of) copper (and) 2 shekels (and) 4 NI of tin for making each mar-tu dagger (and) 1 shekel (and) 3 NI of silver for (its) knob […]. 1[+x minas of s]ilver for the purchase of 40 serrated mar-tu daggers. They were given to the men of the Palace.

21. [*w*]*a*
3 ma-na kù:babbar
23. *zi-du-sù*
*ap*
25. 18 a-gar$_{5}$
2 gín DILMUN 4 NI an-na
27. kin$_{5}$-ak
1 ĝír mar-tu
29. 3 gín DILMUN kù:babbar
IV. 1. ½ kù-gi
*zi-du-sù*
3. 13 ma-na TAR an-na
šub *si-in*
5. 1 *mi-at* 10 lá-2 ma-na a-gar$_{5}$-gar$_{5}$
kin$_{5}$-ak
7. 3 *mi-at* 60 ĝír mar-tu
*ga-mi-ù* kù:babbar
9. 10 lá-2 ma-na kù:babbar
*ga-ma-a-tum*
11. *ap*
18 a-gar$_{5}$
13. 2 gín DILMUN 4 NI an-na
kin$_{5}$-ak
15. 1 ĝír mar-tu
1 gín DILMUN 3 NI kù:babbar
17. ⌜*ga*⌝*-ma-*[*a-t*]*um*
[ ] x
19. 1[+x$^{?}$ ma-na k]ù:babbar
níĝ-sa$_{10}$ 40 ĝír mar-tu zú-ak
21. lú ĝuruš-ĝuruš
SA.ZA$_{x}^{ki}$
23. in-na-sum

(47)
3 gín DILMUN kù:babbar
25. saĝ kù:babbar
$^{d}$*Ku-ra*
27. mu-ti-II

(48)
12 gín DILMUN kù:babbar
V. 1. níĝ-sa$_{10}$ ĜIŠ-ti-ḪAR
ki:lam$_{7}$
3. SA.ZA$_{x}^{ki}$
*Wa-ba-rúm*
5. šu-ba$_{4}$-ti

(49)
1 ma-na ŠA.PI 4 gín DILMUN
kù:babbar
7. níĝ-sa$_{10}$ 70 lá-3 túg-NI.NI
2 *mi-at* 80 sal-TÚG
9. 46 siki na$_{4}$ *Ma-rí*$^{ki}$
1 ma-na ŠA.PI gín DILMUN
kù:⌜babbar⌝
11. [ ]
[ ]
13. [ ]
[ ]
15. ĜIŠ-ma-dul$_{10}$
*Wa-ba-rúm*
17. šu-ba$_{4}$-ti
ki:lam$_{7}$
19. *ʾÀ-da-ni*$^{ki}$
*wa*
21. $^{d}$*Ga-mi-iš*

(50)
10 gín DILMUN kù:babbar
23. *si-in*
al$_{6}$-tuš
25. $^{d}$*Ga-mi-iš*
en
VI. 1. ì-na-sum

(51)
10 gín DILMUN kù:babbar
3. nu$_{11}$-za
1 dub
5. lú nam-kud
en
7. *wa*
*Ib-rí-um*
9. é
$^{d}$*ʾÀ-da*

(52)
11. 10 gín DILMUN kù:babbar
nu$_{11}$-za 1 dub
13. *ma-lik-*[*t*]*um*
[ ]
15. ⌜é⌝ (?)
$^{d}$⌜*ʾÀ*⌝[*-da*] (?)

(47) 3 shekels of silver for the silver head of the god Kura: second delivery.
(48) 12 shekels of silver for the purchase of GIŠ-ti-ḪAR-wood, at the market of the Palace, Wabarum has received.
(49) 1;44 minas of silver for the purchase of 347 garments (and) 46 stone weights of wool from the city of Mari; 1;40 minas of silver […] (for the puchase of) chariot shafts; Wabarum has received at the markets of the city of ʾAdani and of the god Kamiš.
(50) 10 shekels of silver for […] (that) lies by the god Kamiš, the king has given.
(51) 10 shekels of silver for plating a tablet of the oath (taken) by the king and Ibrium in the temple of the god Hadda.
(52) 10 shekels of silver for plating a tablet of the oath (taken) by the queen […] in the temple of the god Ha[dda].

(53)
17. 12 gín DILMUN kù:babbar
níĝ-sa$_{10}$
19. ĜIŠ-sal
é
21. *A-ru*$_{12}$*-ga-du*$^{ki}$
*Ib-bí-um* "ur$_4$"
23. šu-ba$_4$-ti

(54)
TAR 3 gín DILMUN 3 NI kù:babbar
25. šu-bal-ak
6 gín DILMUN 2 NI kù-gi
27. 2 *gú-li-lum*
níĝ-ba
29. $^{d}$*Ku-ra*

(55)
17 gín DILMUN kù:babbar
VII. 1. níĝ-ba
3 ĝuruš
3. *ʾÀ-du*$^{ki}$
*in*
5. *Ḫa-lab*$_x^{ki}$
šu-ba$_4$-ti

(56)
7. 5 gín DILMUN kù:babbar
ḪI-*la-um*
9. *Na-gàr*$^{ki}$
é
11. $^{d}$*Ì-lam*
šu-ba$_4$-ti

(57)
13. 7 gín DILMUN k[ù-gi]
*Š[u-/D[a-* ]
15. *A-b[ù-]li-um*$^{ki}$

(58)
10 gín DILMUN kù:babbar
17. *Ḫu-ra*-NE
*Na-gàr*$^{ki}$
19. *in*
*A-ru*$_{12}$*-ga-du*$^{ki}$
21. šu-ba$_4$-ti

(59)
10 gín DILMUN kù:babbar
23. šu-bal-ak
2 gín DILMUN kù-gi
25. *ni-zi-mu*
1 dib
27. *Ḫa-zu-um*

(60)
10 gín DILMUN kù:babbar
29. šu-bal-ak
2 gín DILMUN kù-gi
31. *ni-zi-mu*
2 dib
33. *Ib-du-*$^{d}$*Aš-dar*
VIII. 1. dumu-nita
*A-šum*
3. *wa*
*Íl-gú-uš-ti*

(61)
5. TAR 2 ½ gín DILMUN kù:babbar
šu-bal-ak
7. 6 gín DILMUN ½ kù-gi
kin$_5$-ak
9. 6 še-šu-še-tag
*wa*
11. 1 buru$_4$-MUŠEN
níĝ-ba
13. $^{dʾ}$*A*$_5$*-da-"bal"*
*wa*
15. $^{d}$BAD-munus
*A-ru*$_{12}$*-ga-du*$^{ki}$
17. ama-gal
en
19. šu-mu-tak$_4$

(62)
12 gín DILMUN kù:babbar
21. nu$_{11}$-za 1 *ḫa-bù*
TAR kù:babbar
23. šu-bal-ak
6 gín DILMUN kù-gi
25. nu$_{11}$-za 1 *ar-ra-sù*
níĝ-ba
27. $^{dʾ}$*À-da*

(53) 12 shekels of silver for the purchase of a … (GIŠ-sal) for the (king's) house in the city of Arugadu, Ibbium, the collector (of goods) has received.
(54) 33 shekels and 3 NI of silver in exchange for 6 shekels and 2 NI of gold for 2 bracelets: gift for the god Kura.
(55) 17 shekels of silver: gift for 3 men of the city of ʾAddu, received in the city of Ḫalab.
(56) 5 shekels of silver for ḪIlaʾum of the city of Nagar, received in the temple of the god Ilam.
(57) 7 shekels of g[old] for […] of the city of Ab[u]lium.
(58) 10 shekels of silver for ḪuraNE of the city of Nagar, received in the city of Arugadu.
(59) 10 shekels of silver in exchange for 2 shekels of gold for decorating 1 plaque for Ḫazum.
(60) 10 shekels of silver in exchange for 2 shekels of gold for decorating 2 plaques for Ibdu-Ašdar, son of Ašum, and Ilgusti.
(61) 32 ½ shekels of silver in exchange for 6 ½ shekels of gold for making 6 … (še-šu-še-tag) and 1 shield: gift for the god ʾAdabal and the Lady of the city of Arugadu, the king's mother has handed over.
(62) 12 shekels of silver for plating 1 mace; 30 (shekels of) silver in exchange for 6 shekels of gold for plating its handle: gift for the god Hadda of the city of Lub, in month IV.

lú *Lu-ub*$^{ki}$
29. *in*
*gi*-NI

(63)
31. TAR 3 gín 3 NI kù:babbar
IX. 1. šu-bal-ak
6 gín DILMUN 2 NI kù-gi 2 *gú-li-lum*
3. níĝ-ba
$^{d}$*Aš-da-bíl*

(64)
5. 12 gín DILMUN kù:babbar
nu$_{11}$-za 1 *ḫa-bù*
7. TAR kù:babbar
šu-bal-ak
9. 6 gín DILMUN kù-gi
1 *ar-ra-sù*
11. *wa*
6 gín DILMUN 2 NI kù:babbar 2 *gú-li-lum*
13. níĝ-ba
$^{d}$*Am-rí-ig*

(65)
15. 1 ma-na kù:babbar
níĝ-ba
17. *Ba-ag-mi-su*
*Na-gàr*$^{ki}$

(66)
19. TAR kù:babbar
dumu-nita
21. en
*ʾÀ-du*$^{ki}$
23. ŠÚ+ŠA gín DILMUN kù:babbar
maškim-*sù*
25. TAR kù:babbar
*A-bù-li-um*$^{ki}$
27. 10 gín DILMUN kù:babbar
maškim-*sù*

(67)
X. 1. 10 gín DILMUN kù:babbar
níĝ-ba
3. *Mar-rúm*
EN-NE$^{ki}$

(68)
5. ŠÚ+ŠA gín DILMUN kù:babbar
*Na-ba-ti-um*$^{ki}$
7. 5 gín DILMUN kù:babbar
maškim-*sù*
9. *in* kaskal
šu-ba$_{4}$-ti

(69)
11. 3 ma-na ŠÚ+ŠA gín DILMUN kù:babbar
šu-bal-ak
13. ŠA.PI gín DILMUN kù-gi
1 dib
15. *Gi-ra-ma-lik*
lú *I-bí-šum*
17. tuš-LÚ×TIL
*Ḫal-sum*$^{ki}$

(70)
19. 15 gín DILMUN kù:babbar
šu-bal-ak
21. 3 gín DILMUN kù-gi
*ʾa$_{5}$-na-gu*
23. 1 banšur
*wa*
25. 1 kù-sal
níĝ-ba
27. *Ib-rí-um*
$^{d}$BAD
29. *Du-du-lu*$^{ki}$

(71)
6 gín DILMUN kù:babbar <šu-bal-ak>
XI. 1. 1 gín DILMUN 6 NI kù-gi

(63) 33 shekels and 3 NI of silver in exchange for 6 shekels and 2 NI of gold for 2 bracelets: gift for the god Ašdabil.
(64) 12 shekels of silver for plating 1 mace; 30 (shekels of) silver in exchange for 6 shekels of gold for its handle and 6 shekels and 2 NI of silver for 2 bracelets: gift for the god Ammarik.
(65) 1 mina of silver: gift for Baʾag-misu of the city of Nagar.
(66) 30 (shekels of) silver for the son of the king of the city of ʾAddu; 20 shekels of silver for his representative; 30 (shekels of) silver for (someone of) the city of Abulium; 10 shekels of silver for his representative.
(67) 10 shekels of silver: gift for Marrum of the city of ENNE.
(68) 20 shekels of silver for (someone of) the city of Nabatiʾum; 5 shekels of silver for his representative, received for their travels.
(69) 3;20 minas of silver in exchange for 40 shekels of gold for 1 plaque for Gira-malik, (son) of Ibišum, (who) occupied the city of Ḫalsum.
(70) 15 shekels of silver in exchange for 3 shekels of gold for the circular stand of a table and 1 buckle: gift of Ibrium for the Lord of the city of Tuttul.
(71) 6 shekels of silver <in exchange for> 1 shekel (and) 6 NI of gold for decorating with lamination 1 battle-axe for Ibrium.

*ni-zi-mu*
3. nu$_{11}$-za 1 *za-ḫa-da*
*Ib-rí-um*

(72)
5. 5 ma-na kù:babbar
kin$_5$-ak
7. 1 *gú-li-lum* ŠA.PI-II
2 *gú-li-lum* TAR-II
9. 5 *gú-li-lum* ŠÚ+ŠA-II
1 *gú-li-lum* 10-I
11. 5 ma-na kù:babbar
šu-bal-ak
13. 1 ma-na kù-gi
nu$_{11}$-za-*sù*
15. ME-sig
é
17. en

(73)
10 lá-2 ma-na 3 kù:babbar
19. *wa*
5 ma-na 55 gín DILMUN kù:babbar
21. šu-bal-ak
1 ma-na 11 gín DILMUN kù-gi
23. nu$_{11}$-za
1 ĜIŠ-gígir-II
25. 1 ĝuruš
ugula sur$_x$-BAR.AN
27. 4 BAR.AN-BAR.AN

(74)
XII. 1. ŠÚ+ŠA gín DILMUN an-na
šub *si-in* <x a-gar$_5$-gar$_5$>
3. 1 ĜIŠ-gu-kak-gíd
1 *za-ḫa-da*
5. ĜIŠ-kak-ĜIŠ-kak
4 *zi-da-nu*
7. ĜIŠ-sal
lú ĜIŠ-gígir-II
9. $^{d}$*Á-la*
*Gú-šè-bù*$^{ki}$

(75)
11. 10 gín DILMUN kù:babbar
níĝ-ba
13. *Ga-áš-ru*$_{12}$
*Na-gàr*$^{ki}$
15. DU.DU
*mi-nu*
17. Kiš$^{ki}$

(76)
1 ½ gín DILMUN an-na
19. šub *si-in*
8 gín DILMUN a-gar$_5$
21. kin$_5$-ak
1 ĝír mar-tu
23. *wa*
15 gín DILMUN kù:babbar
25. šu-bal-ak
3 gín DILMUN kù-gi
27. nu$_{11}$-za-*sù*
dumu-nita
29. en
*Ì-mar*$^{ki}$

(77)
31. 10 gín DILMUN kù:babbar
níĝ-ba 3 ĝuruš
XIII. 1. *ʾÀ-du*$^{ki}$
ḫi-mu-DU
3. maškim
*Za-ba-rúm*
5. nar

(78)
5 ma-na kù:babbar
7. šu-bal-ak
1 ma-na kù-gi 1 dib
9. TAR kù:babbar
URI
11. 1 íb-lá 1 ĝír-kun
2 ma-na TAR kù:babbar
13. šu-bal-ak
TAR kù-gi
15. nu$_{11}$-za-*sù*
Túg-du$_8$
17. lú *I-bí-zi-kir*
šu-du$_8$
19. ugula *Za-ḫi-ra-an*$^{ki}$

(72) 5 minas of silver for making 1 double bracelet of 40 (shekels), 2 double bracelets of 30 (shekels) each, 5 double bracelets of 20 (shekels) each, 1 single bracelet of 10 (shekels); 5 minas of silver in exchange for 1 mina of gold for their lamination: for the watchmen of the king's house.

(73) 8;03 minas of silver and 5;55 minas of silver in exchange for 1;11 minas of gold for plating 1 chariot for a man (who is) the overseer of a team of 4 mules.

(74) 20 shekels of tin to be melted with <x copper> for 1 spearhead, 1 battle-axe, pegs, 4 … (*zi-da-nu*), a bow of a chariot for the god Ala of the city of Gušebu.

(75) 10 shekels of silver: gift for Gašru of the city of Nagar (who) came back from the city of Kiš.

(76) 1 ½ shekel of tin to be melted with 8 shekels of copper for making 1 mar-tu dagger and 15 shekels of silver in exchange for 3 shekels of gold for its lamination for a son of the king of the city of Imar.

(77) 10 shekels of silver: gift for 3 men of the city of ʾAddu, delivered by a representative of Zabarum, the singer.

(78) 5 minas of silver in exchange for 1 mina of gold for 1 plaque; 30 (shekels of) silver for the URI-decoration of 1 belt (and) 1 dagger pendant; 2;30 minas of silver in exchange for 30 (shekels of) gold for its lamination, for Tugdu, (son) of Ibbi-zikir, (who) had captured the overseer of the city of Zaḫiran.

(79)
3 ma-na ŠA.PI gín DILMUN kù:babbar
21. šu-bal-ak
ŠA.PI 4 gín DILMUN kù-gi
23. 1 dib
2 ma-na TAR kù:babbar
XIV. 1. šu-bal-ak
TAR kù-gi 1 íb-lá 1 *si-ti-tum* 1 ĝír-kun
3. níĝ-ba
*ba-da-lum*
5. *Ḫa-ra-an*$^{ki}$

(80)
ŠA.PI gín DILMUN kù:babbar
7. 1 íb-lá 1 ĝír-kun
ŠÚ+ŠA gín DILMUN kù:babbar
9. níĝ-sa$_{10}$ 1 ĝír mar-tu ti kù-gi
*Bù-da-ì*
11. *Maš-bar-rá*$^{ki}$
tuš-LÚ×TIL
13. *Za-ḫi-ra-an*$^{ki}$
al$_6$-tuš
15. *A-la-ga*$^{ki}$

(81)
ŠA.PI gín DILMUN kù:babbar
17. 1 íb-lá 1 ĝír-kun
EN-*da-za*
19. *A-rí-gú*$^{ki}$
tuš-LÚ×TIL
21. *Nu-rí*$^{ki}$

(82)
ŠA.PI gín DILMUN kù:babbar
XV. 1. níĝ-sa$_{10}$ 2 ĝír mar-tu ti kù-gi
*Íl-zi*
3. lú *Ìr-am*$_6$*-da-mu*
*wa*
5. *Ti-ra-ì*
šeš
7. ama-gal
en

(83)
9. ŠÚ+ŠA gín DILMUN kù:babbar
níĝ-sa$_{10}$ 2 ĝír mar-tu *ba-du-u*$_9$ kù-gi
11. *En-na-ni-il*
šeš
13. *Ib-rí-um*
*wa*
15. *Na-am*$_6$-ì-ĝiš

(84)
7 gín DILMUN kù:babbar
17. níĝ-sa$_{10}$ 1 ĝír mar-tu *ba-du-u*$_9$ kù-gi
*Na-am*$_6$*-ḫa-lu*

(85)
19. 12 ½ gín DILMUN kù:babbar
šu-bal-ak
21. 2 ½ gín DILMUN kù-gi
*ni-zi-mu*
23. ⸢1⸣ [d]ib
XVI. 1. ⸢x⸣[- ]
lú nídba ì-ĝiš

(86)
3. 15 gín DILMUN kù:babbar
2 *bu*-DI
5. ama-gal
en
7. *Ra-ˀà-ak*$^{ki}$
É×PAP
9. *Ig-rí-su*
šu-mu-tak$_4$

(87)
11. 2 ma-na kù:babbar
2 ma-na an-na
13. en
*Du-gú-ra-su*$^{ki}$

(79) 3;40 minas of silver in exchange for 44 shekels of gold for 1 plaque; 2;30 minas of silver in exchange for 30 (shekels of) gold for 1 belt, 1 sheath (and) 1 dagger pendant: gift for the minister of the city of Ḫarran.
(80) 40 shekels of silver for 1 belt (and) 1 dagger pendant; 20 shekels of silver for the purchase of 1 pointed mar-tu dagger (decorated with) gold for Buda-i(l) of the city of Mašbarra, (who) occupied the city of Zaḫiran (and then) lived in the city of Alaga.
(81) 40 shekels of silver for 1 belt (and) 1 dagger pendant for ENdaza of the city of Arigu, (who) occupied the city of Nuri.
(82) 40 shekels of silver for the purchase of 2 pointed mar-tu daggers (decorated with) gold for Ilzi, (son) of Iram-damu and Tira-i(l), brother of the king's mother.
(83) 20 shekels of silver for the purchase of 2 *b.* mar-tu daggers (decorated with) gold for Ennani-il, brother of Ibrium and Naˀam-igiš.
(84) 7 shekels of silver for the purchase of 1 *b.* mar-tu dagger (decorated with) gold for Naˀam-ḫalu.
(85) 12 ½ shekels of silver in exchange for 2 ½ shekels of gold for decorating 1 [pl]aque for [...] (on the occasion) of the offering of the oil.
(86) 15 shekels of silver for 2 toggle-pins for the funerary rite of the mother of the king of the city of Raˀak, Igrisu has handed over.
(87) 2 minas of silver (and) 2 minas of tin for the king of the city of Dugurasu.

(88)

15. ŠÚ+ŠA gín DILMUN kù:babbar
ZU.PIRIG
17. útul-útul maḫ urudu
*in* ud
19. ḫúl
*Ib-rí-um*

(89)

21. 2 ma-na TAR 2 gín DILMUN kù:babbar
níĝ-sa$_{10}$ 33 túg-NI.NI
23. 3 dùl-TÚG *Ma-rí*$^{ki}$
ŠÚ+ŠA 3 gín DILMUN kù:babbar
25. níĝ-sa$_{10}$ 3 *gàr-su* si$_{4}$
XVII. 1. 4 *gàr-su* ĝi$_{6}$
ŠÚ+ŠA gín DILMUN kù:babbar
3. níĝ-sa$_{10}$ ĜIŠ-*šè-bir*$_{5}$*-gi-nu*
ĜIŠ-bar-ús
5. ki:lam$_{7}$
$^{d\text{ʾ}}$*À-da*

(90)

7. 13 gín DILMUN kù:babbar
nu$_{11}$-za 1 *ḫa-bù*
9. *ap* kù-gi sikil
ŠÚ+ŠA kù:babbar
11. *ʾa*$_{5}$*-na-gu*
si 2 gud
13. nídba
en
15. $^{d\text{ʾ}}$*À-da*
*Ḫa-lab*$_{x}^{ki}$
17. *ʾa*$_{5}$*-nun*

(91)

10 gín DILMUN kù:babbar
19. 2 *bu*-DI 4 še-šu-še-tag
níĝ-ba
21. $^{d}$*Ga-na-na*

(92)

10 lá-2 ma-na TAR kù:babbar
23. šu-bal-ak
1 ma-na ŠA.PI 2 gín DILMUN kù-gi
25. 1 íb-lá 1 *si-ti-tum* 1 ĝír-kun
1 ĜIŠ-sal
27. níĝ-[b]a
XVIII. 1. *Ib-rí-um*
10 ma-na kù:babbar
3. šu-bal-ak
2 ma-na kù-gi
5. 2 íb-lá 2 ĝír-kun
4 gín DILMUN kù:babbar
7. 2 ĜIŠ-sal-*sù*
*I-bí-zi-kir*
9. *wa*
*Ù-ti*
11. 2 dumu-nita-*sù*
*in* ud
13. ḫúl-*sù*
en
15. šu-mu-tak$_{4}$

(93)

1 ma-na ŠÚ+ŠA kù:babbar
17. níĝ-ba
diĝir-diĝir-diĝir

(94)

19. 1 ma-na ŠA.PI gín DILMUN kù:babbar
šu-bal-ak
21. ŠÚ+ŠA kù-gi 1 dib
dumu-nita
23. *ba-da-lum*
*Ḫa-ra-an*$^{ki}$

(95)

25. 15 gín DILMUN kù:babbar
*Gul-la*
27. *wa*
maškim-*sù*
29. *Na-gàr*$^{ki}$

(96)

6 kù:babbar
XIX. 1. [ḪI-]*la-um*
*Na-gàr*$^{ki}$

(88) 20 shekels of silver for the hangers of big kettles of copper on the occasion of the feast of Ibrium.

(89) 2;32 minas of silver for the purchase of 36 garments; 23 shekels of silver for the purchase of 3 red bags (and) 4 black bags; 20 shekels of silver for the purchase of a ... (ĜIŠ-*šè-bir*$_{5}$*-gi-nu*) (and) goads, at the market of the god Hadda.

(90) 13 shekels of silver for plating 1 mace, and also pure gold; 20 (shekels of) silver for the circular stand of the (4) horns of 2 bulls: offering of the king for the god Hadda of the city of Ḫalab, in month VIII.

(91) 10 shekels of silver for 2 toggle-pins (and) 4 … (še-šu-še-tag): gift for the goddess Ganana.

(92) 8;30 minas of silver in exchange for 1;42 minas of gold for 1 belt, 1 sheath (and) 1 dagger pendant, 1 … (GIŠ-sal): gi[f]t for Ibrium; 10 minas of silver in exchange for 2 minas of gold for 2 belts (and) 2 dagger pendants, 4 shekels of silver for their 2 … (GIŠ-sal) for Ibbi-zikir and Uti, 2 of his sons, on the occasion of their feast, the king has handed over.

(93) 1;20 minas of silver: gift for the gods.

(94) 1;40 minas of silver in exchange for 20 (shekels of) gold for 1 plaque for the son of the minister of the city of Ḫarran.

(95) 15 shekels of silver for Gulla and his representative of the city of Nagar.

(96) 6 (shekels of) silver for [ḪI]laʾum of the city of Nagar.

(97)

3. 12 kù:babbar
*La-zi-gú*

5. *wa*
*Bù-a-ḫu*

7. *Na-ba-ti-um*$^{ki}$

(98)

6 ma-na kù:babbar

9. níĝ-sa$_{10}$ BAR.AN.BAR.AN
*Iš*$_{11}$*-da-mu*

11. di-kud
šu-mu-tak$_4$

13. *si-in*
*Na-gàr*$^{ki}$

(99)*b)*

15. 2 kù:babbar
*ma-da-u*$_9$

17. dumu-nita
en (blank)

(100)

19. ⸢AN⸣.ŠÈ.GÚ 3 *mi-at* 74 ma-na ŠÚ+ŠA
6 gín DILMUN kù:babbar
è

21. *ap*
1 *mi-at* 60 ma-na kù:babbar

23. al$_6$-ĝál
é en

*a*) on erasure; *b*) written when the tablet was dry

(97) 12 (shekels of) silver for Lazigu and Buaḫu of the city of Nabatiʾum.
(98) 6 minas of silver for the purchase of mules: Iš-damu, the judge, has handed over to the city of Nagar.
(99) 2 (shekels of) silver for a … (*ma-da-u*$_9$) for the son of the king.
(100) Total: 374;26 minas of silver: expenditure, and also 160 minas of silver are present in the king's house.

## Commentary

This document has to be dated to the year Ibr. 16. It opens with the registration of the expenditures of 1 mina (470 g) of silver for the renewal rite concerning the city-god Kura which fell at the beginning of the new year. The 3 shekels (23 g) of silver to be given to the god in a later period of the year for a further ceremony concerning his head are registered in § 47. Tinib-dulum, a sister of the king, received in her function as priestess of the god ʾAdabal, 6;20 minas (2.977 kg) of silver, and her sister Tarib-damu, also a priestess of this god, 1 mina (470 g) of silver (§ 2).

The "expended", è, silver that year amounted to 374;26 minas (175.984 kg). The total silver "present", al$_6$-ĝál, in the king's house (i.e. the Treasury) was 160 minas (75.20 kg), (§ 100).

In order to acquire 100 (47 kg) minas of copper, 1;40 minas (783 g) of silver were expended in a ratio 1 : 60 silver – copper (§ 12).

The war against Ḫalsum, which had started the previous year, continued in this and in the following year. Gira-malik, son of Ibišum, "occupied", tuš-LÚ×TIL, the city, and received a plaque of 40 shekels (343 g) of gold (§ 69). Túg-du$_8$, a son of Ibbi-zikir, received a plaque of 1 mina (470 g) of gold, together with a belt decorated with 30 shekels of silver and plated with 30 shekels of gold, because he had captured the "overseer", ugula, of the city of Zaḫiran (§ 78). The occupation of the cities of Zaḫiran and Nuri (§§ 80, 81) must be connected to this war.

The alliance with Nagar, and its satellite kingdoms (en-en *áš-ti* en *Na-gàr*$^{ki}$), whose terms had been prepared the preceding year, was sealed by these kings in the temple of Dagan in Tuttul (§ 17). The king of Nagar received 20 minas (9.40 kg) of silver, and his sons 7 minas (3.29 kg), (§ 16). An envoy from Nagar, ḪuraNE, received 10 shekels (78 g) of silver in Tuttul (§ 18). The agreement was prepared on Ebla's side by Iš-damu, a "judge", di-kud, who had been sent to Nagar to offer the oil of the alliance, nídba ì-ĝiš (*ARET* XIV § 37), and on Nagar's side perhaps by ḪIlaʾum (see below), who received a gift of 15 shekels (117 g) of silver (§ 10). Kings who recognized Ebla's hegemony had to swear the alliance to Ebla, in the temple of the city-god Kura. Ebla and Nagar were states of equal rank; for this reason, the important temple of Dagan in Tuttul was chosen as the place to swear the alliance, as it was a city located between the area of influence of the two states. The text, however, does not mention if the king of Ebla also travelled to Tuttul. As far as relations with Mari concerned, after the war which brought about the deaths of Irkab-damu and Enna-Dagan, the kings of these two cities, new relations were sealed by exchanging a tablet decorated with silver which listed the peace clauses (see the commentary to text no. 6, above).

ḪIlaᵓum of Nagar received 5 shekels (39 g) of silver in the temple of the god Ilam (§ 56). ḪuraNE, another envoy of Nagar, received 10 shekels (78 g) of silver in Arugadu (§ 58); Baᵓag-misu: 1 mina (470 g) of silver (§ 65); and another 10 shekels were given to Gašru (also from Nagar), who came back from Kiš (§ 75). Three other officials from Nagar received silver; that is Gulla and his representative: 15 shekels (117 g), and ḪIlaᵓum: 6 shekels (47 g), (§§ 95, 96). Two envoys of Nabatiᵓum (a city belonging to Nagar) received 12 shekels (94 g) of silver (§ 97).

After a year without any diplomatic relations, Dašna and Ilum-aḫi of Mari came to Ebla, where they received 20 (157 g) shekels of silver (§ 9).

The king received a small vessel of 4 shekels (31 g) of gold (§ 37), and some pieces of equipment for the chariot decorated with 50 shekels (391 g) of gold (§ 38). The god Batum-madu, and his *paredra* Dabinadu, received two buckles in connection to the illness of the king (§ 29).

The king and Ibrium swore an "oath", nam-kud, which was registered in a tablet deposited in the temple of Hadda, presumably at Ḫalab (§ 51).

Some goods for the king's mother needed 3 shekels (23) of gold (§ 42).

Ibrium received two daggers decorated with gold valued at 2 minas (940 g) of silver "for his purification rite", in connection both with the illnesses of Ibbi-zikir and the king. That the king was ill is confirmed in § 29. The data in §§ 3–5 are of difficult interpretation. According to § 4, Ibrium received the replacement of the dagger he had given. The king performed an offering in favour of Ibrium, who also was ill. He received another dagger decorated with gold, of the same value as 1 mina (470 g) of silver, as a replacement for one of these two daggers (?), (§ 4). The king gave a clasp decorated with 1 shekel (8 g) of gold for the dagger of the god Batum-madu, in connections to Ibrium's illness of (§ 5). Ibrium and his son Ibbi-zikir's chariots needed a decoration of 3 shekels (23 g) of silver; 35 shekels (274 g) were expended for two bronze hooks (§ 22); and 6 shekels (5 g) of gold were employed for the two bows of Ibrium's chariot (§ 40). The minister further received a vessel with a lid of 40 shekels (313 g) of gold (§ 41). One and ⅙ shekel (9 g) of gold were expended for plating his battle-axe (§ 71). He also received several "large "kettles", útul, whose handles, ZU.PIRIĜ, needed 20 shekels (157 g) of silver (§ 88).

The king handed over to Ibrium, on the occasion of his "feast", húl, a belt with its ĜIŠ-sal, for which were required 1;42 minas (799 g) of gold, while Ibbi-zikir and Uti (Ibrium's sons) received a belt, for which were employed 2 minas (940 g) of gold, and 4 shekels (31 g) of silver for their ĜIŠ-sal (§ 92).

§ 6. Princess Tiša-lim, the queen of Imar, received two toggle-pins of 30 shekels (235 g) of silver, whose heads were decorated with 4 shekels (31 g) of gold.

§ 7. Five shekels (39) of silver were expended for three toggle-pins to be given to the princess Tinib-dulum; 6 shekels (47 g) of tin and 34 shekels (266 g) of copper for another object.

§ 8. Three small axes of bronze of 40 shekels (313 g) each (to be sent to Alaga), required 22 shekels of tin, and 1;38 minas of copper (18.34% of tin)

§ 11. 3 shekels (24 g) of gold were expended to replace the image of a "month", iti, "to take an omen", lú-maš, which was placed in the temple of Hadda. Thirteenth years later, according to an annual document of metal expenditures of the minister Ibbi-zikir, this month went lost, so that it had to be replaced again. This time it was specified that the temple (or chapel) of Hadda was that at the Palace, SA.ZA$_x$$^{ki}$, The use of this object is obscure (see Archi 2010c, p. 50 = 2015, pp. 692–693).

§ 21. Death of Iᵓin-Hadda, a king' son. He received as a funerary gift a belt of 30 shekels (235 g) of silver.

§ 29. Offerings to the god Batum-madu and his *paredra* Dabinadu for the illness of the king.

§ 31. Princess Tarib-damu, priestess of ᵓAdabal, received a plaque of gold of 15 shekels (117 g) of gold.

§ 32. Princess Tirin-damu received two toggle-pins of 20 shekels (157 g) of silver for her purification rite (ì-ĝiš-sag).

§ 39. Ibbi-zikir received new bridles decorated with 3 shekels (23 shekels) of gold.

§ 44. Expenditure of tin and copper, silver and gold for 100 daggers of five different shapes, to be handed over for the military review by Zarudu, a city mentioned also in *ARET* VIII 527 rev. I 27, and in TM.75.G.1451 rev. V 14. For the military reviews at Ebla, see Archi 2018a.

§ 45. Expenditure of 15 minas (7.05 kg) of tin and 120 minas (56.40 kg) of copper for four hundred daggers of different shape, whose middle weight was of 159 g. The bronze alloy always had 11.12% of tin. The first forty daggers have a decoration which required in total 1.40 minas (783 g) of gold (XVI 8). Sixty daggers required for their decoration in total 30 shekels (235 g) of gold (XVI 24). Three hundred daggers required in total 6;40 minas (3.133 kg) of silver for their decoration (XVII 17). Three hundred daggers mar-tu zú-ak valued 5 minas (2.35 minas) (XVII 26-XVIII 1). These daggers were deposited in Alaga. One handed over sixteen double bracelets of copper decorated with 2 minas (940 g) of gold; fifty double bracelets decorated with 3 minas (1.41 g) of silver; ten other double bracelets and hundred single bracelets of copper with a decoration of 3 shekels (23 g) of silver.

§ 46. Expenditure of 28;20 ⅓ minas (13.311 kg) of tin, and 208 minas (97,76 kg) of copper for six hundred sixty daggers of different shape, whose middle weight was of 166 g each, for the "men", ĝuruš-ĝuruš. The ratio of tin was around 11%. For the decoration in gold of the first eighty daggers (I 3–15) were used 8 minas (3.76 kg) of gold "delivered", mu-DU, by Kablul, (the city which delivered yearly gold, differently from the other cities which delivered silver); each dagger therefore required 6 shekels (47 g). Twenty daggers (I 23–II 5) were decorated with 4 shekels (31 g) of gold each, for a total of 1;20 minas (627 g). Ninety daggers (II 10–22) were decorated with 3 shekels (23 g) of gold each, for a total of 4;30 minas (2.11 kg). Fifty daggers (II 27–III 12) were decorated with 2 ½ shekels (20 g) of gold, for a total of 2;05 minas (980 g). Sixty daggers (III 17–IV 2) were decorated with 3 shekels of silver and ½ shekel (4 g) of gold, for a total 3 minas (1.41 kg) of silver and 30 shekels (235 g) of gold. Three hundred sixty daggers (IV 7–17) had a decoration of 1 ⅓ shekels (11 g) of silver for a total of 8 minas (3.760 kg) of silver. These daggers were delivered to the Palace.

§ 55. Three men from the city of ʾAddu received 17 shekels (133 g) of silver as a gift in Ḫalab.

§§ 57, 66. Abulium was a city ruled by a "king", en, (see also *ARET* IV 12 § 37), under the hegemony of Nagar.

§ 68. Nabatiʾum was another city of the area controlled by Nagar. His envoy received 20 shekels (157 g) of silver, and his representative 5 shekels (39 g) of silver as travel expenses.

§ 72. 5 minas (2.35 kg) of silver, and 1 mina (470 g) of gold were expended for nine bracelets of different weight, and for their decorations, for the "watchmen", ME-sig, of the "house of the king", é en.

§ 73. 8;03 minas (3.99 kg) of silver, and 1;11 (556 g) minas of gold were required for plating the chariot of an overseer of a team of mules.

§ 76. A son of the king of Imar received a dagger, which had required 8 shekels (23 g) of copper and 1 ½ shekels of tin (15.79%), besides 3 shekels (11 g) of gold for its decoration.

§ 77. Gift of 10 shekels (78 g) of silver for three men from the city of ʾAddu, which had to be brought by a representative of Zabarum, the singer.

§§ 78, 80, 81. Túg-du$_8$, a son of Ibrium, received a plaque of 1 mina (470 g) of gold, together with 1 belt decorated with 30 shekels of silver, and plated with 30 shekels of gold, because he had captured the "overseer", ugula, of the city of Zaḫiran. Buda-i(l) of the city of Mašbarra received 1 belt for which were employed 40 shekels (313 g) of silver, and a dagger whose gold decoration had the value of 20 (157 g) shekels of silver, because he had "occupied", tuš-LÚ×TIL, the city of Zaḫiran; he then resided in Alaga. The city of Nuri has to be located close to Zaḫiran: it was occupied by ENdaza of the city of Arigu. These military actions have to be connected with the war against Ḫalsum mentioned in §§ 51, 69 (see Archi 2021a, p. 207).

§ 79. The "minister", *ba-da-lum*, of Ḫarran, received a plaque of 44 shekels (345 g) of gold, and a belt, for which were employed 30 shekels (235 g) of gold.

§ 82. Ilzi, son of Iram-damu, and Tira-i(l), brother of the mother of the king, received a dagger each, decorated with gold, and valued in total 40 shekels (313 g) of silver.

§ 83. Ennani-il, a Ibrium's son, and Naʾam-ì-ĝiš, received a dagger each decorated with gold, whose value in total was 20 shekels (157 g) of silver.

§ 86. Two toggle-pins of 15 shekels (117 g) of silver were sent to the king of Raʾak for his mother's funerary rite.

§ 87. 2 minas (940 g) of silver and 2 minas of tin were sent to the king of Dugurasu.

§ 98. Iš-damu, who served as "judge", di-kud, during the last nine years of Ibrium, received 6 minas (2.82 g) of silver, which he handed over to Nagar for the purchase of mules.

§ 99. A son of the king received a *ma-da-*$u_9$ (cf. *ma-da-ḫu*) which required 2 shekels (16 g) of silver.

# 20
(Plates XXXVIII–XXXIX)

(1)
o. I. 1. [1 ma-na kù:babbar]
[saĝ kù:babbar]
3. [$^{d}$*Ku-ra*]

(2)
[x ma-na kù:babbar]
5. *Di-ni-ib-du-lum*
nin-ni
7. en
šu-ba$_4$-ti

(3)
9. 57 ma-na ŠÚ+ŠA gín DILMUN an-na
[š]ub-šub
11. *si-in*
4 *mi-at* 50 ⸢ma⸣-na a-gar$_5$[-gar$_5$]
13. kin$_5$-[ak]
3 *li-im* ĜIŠ-gu-kak-gíd zabar
15. ⸢x-x⸣-*ma*

(4)
9 gín DILMUN a-gar$_5$-gar$_5$
17. 1 gín DILMUN 5 NI an-na
⸢šub⸣
II. 1. [*si-in*]
[ ]
3. [ ]
[maškim]
5$^?$. ga:eš$_8$
*Du-du-lu*$^{ki}$

(5)
7. TAR kù:babbar
níĝ-ba
9. *Wa-ru*$_{12}$*-tum*
*Ma-rí*$^{ki}$
11. *in*
[ ]
13. [šu-b]a$_4$-ti

(6)
2 ma-na kù:babbar
15. šu-bal-ak
ŠÚ+ŠA 4 gín DILMUN kù-gi
17. kin$_5$-ak
1 ĝeštu$_x$-lá
19. *wa*
[ ]
21. ŠÚ+ŠA gín DILMUN kù:babbar
2 ⸢ĜIŠ⸣-du
23. *Tíš-ma-zi-k*[*ir*]
III. 1–5. [ ]
6$^?$. [ -*m*]*a*

(7)
7. 2 gín DILMUN an-na
šub *si-in*
9. 2 šu-i
2 gín DILMUN kù:babbar
11. [ ]
[ ]
13. *I-mar*$^{ki}$

(8)
5 gín DILMUN kù:babbar
15. nu$_{11}$-za 1 an-dùl munus
12 ½ gín DILMUN kù:babbar
17. šu-bal-ak
2 ½ gín DILMUN kù-gi
19. nu$_{11}$-za
IGI.⸢DUB⸣-*s*[*ù*]
21. [ ]
[ ]
IV. 1–5. [ ]

(9)
6$^?$. [3 gín DILMUN kù:babbar]
7. sa[ĝ kù:babbar]
$^{d}$*Ku-*[*ra*]
9. mu-t[i]-II

(1) [1 mina of silver for the silver head of the god Kura].
(2) [x minas of silver] Tinib-dulum, sister of the king, has received.
(3) 57;20 minas of tin to be melted with 450 minas of cop[per] for mak[ing] 3000 bronze spearheads for […].
(4) 9 shekels of copper (and) 1 shekel (and) 5 NI of tin to be melted [in …], [for …, the representative] of the travelling merchant of the city of Tuttul.
(5) 30 (shekels of) silver: gift for Warutum of the city of Mari, [recei]ved in the city of […].
(6) 2 minas of silver in exchange for 24 shekels of gold for making 1 earring and […]; 20 shekels of silver for 2 foot rings for Tešma-zik[ir] […].
(7) 2 shekels of tin to be melted in 2 šu-i vessels; 2 shekels of silver […] of the city of Imar.
(8) 5 shekels of silver for plating 1 female statue; 12 ½ shekels of silver in exchange for 2 ½ shekels of gold for plating i[ts] face […].
(9) [3 shekels of silver for the silver he]ad of the god Ku[ra]: second delive[ry].

(10)
TAR 3 g[ín] DILMUN 3 NI
k[ù]:babbar
11. [šu-bal-ak]
[6 gín DILMUN 2 NI kù-gi]
13. [2 *gú-li-lum*]
níĝ-ba
15. $^{d}$*Ku-ra*

(11)
3 ma-na ŠÚ+ŠA 7 gín DILMUN 3 NI
kù:babbar
17. níĝ-sa$_{10}$ 1 *mi-at* 40 lá-3 sal-TÚG
1 ⸢x⸣
19. [ ]
[ ]

(12)
V. x+1. 2 ma-n[a] 10 gín DILMUN kù-gi
kin$_{5}$-a[k]
3'. [ ]

(13)
VI. 1. [ ]⸢x⸣
[ ]⸢x⸣
3. [ ]⸢x⸣
[ ]
5. [ ]
[ ]
7. [ ]
[6 *ma-na* TAR kù:babbar]
9. šu-⸢bal⸣-ak
1 ma-na 18 gín DILMUN kù-gi
11. [
[
13. [
[
15. [
*Wa-*[*r*]*u*$_{12}$*-tum*
17. *Ma-ri*$^{ki}$

(14)
10 gín DILMUN kù:babbar
19. [n]íĝ-ba
[*I-*]*ti*
21. [*M*]*a-ri*$^{ki}$
[x]-⸢x⸣[- ]

23. [ ]
VII. 1. ⸢níĝ⸣-"mul"
*Du-li*$^{ki}$
3. àga-kár$^{!}$(ŠÈ)

(15)
10 gín DILMUN kù:babbar
5. lú ĜIŠ-nu-kiri$_{6}$
*Ìr-a-mu*
7. *Ì-mar*$^{ki}$
[šu-ba$_{4}$-ti]

(16)
9. 4 gín DILMUN kù:babbar
*ni-zi-mu*
11. 2 níĝ-anše-ak
[...]
13. [ ]
[ ]
15. [ ]
[ ]
17. [ ]
šeš
19. ama-gal
en

(17)
21. 6 gín DILMUN an-na
šub *si-in*
23. *ni-*⸢*zi*⸣*-mu*
2 níĝ-anše-ak 4 kù-sal
VIII. 1. *I-lu*$_{5}$*-za*$_{x}$*-ma-lik* "ur$_{4}$"

(18)
⸢15⸣ gín DILMUN kù:babbar
3. nu$_{11}$-za 1 *ḫa-bù*
TAR kù:babbar
5. šu-bal-ak
6 gín DILMUN ⸢kù-gi⸣
7. nu$_{11}$-za 1 *ar-ra-sù*
ŠÚ+ŠA gín DILMUN kù:babbar
9. [*ᵓa*$_{5}$*-na-gu*]
[4 si gud]
11. [nídba]
[en]
13. $^{d}$*Ra-sa-ap*
*ᵓÀ-da-ni*$^{ki}$

(10) 33 sh[ekels] (and) 3 NI of silver [in exchange for 6 shekels (and) 2 NI of gold for 2 bracelets]: gift for the god Kura.
(11) 3;27 minas (and) 3 NI of silver for the purchase of 137[(+x)] garments […].
(12) […] 2;10 min[as] of gold for making […].
(13) […] [6;30 minas of silver] in exchange for 1;18 minas of gold for […] Wa[r]utum of the city of Mari.
(14) 10 shekels of silver: [g]ift for [I]ti of [the city of M]ari [and …] (who brought) the news that the city of Duli had been vanquished.
(15) 10 shekels of silver for the gardener, Iramu of the city of Imar [has received].
(16) 4 shekels of silver for decorating 2 bridles […], the brother of the king's mother.
(17) 6 shekels of tin to be melted for decorating 2 bridles (and) 4 buckles for Iluza-malik, the collector (of goods).
(18) 15 shekels of silver for plating 1 mace; 30 (shekels of) silver in exchange for 6 shekels of gold for plating its handle; 20 shekels of silver [for the circular stand of the 4 horns of 2 bulls: offering of the king] for the god Rašap of the city of ᵓAdani.

(19)
15. 15 gín DILMUN babbar:kù
nu$_{11}$-za 1 [*ḫa-bù*]
17. *ap* kù-gi
sikil
19. nu$_{11}$[-za] 1 *ar-ra-sù*
ŠÚ+ŠA gín DILMUN kù:babbar
21. *ʾa$_5$-*[*n*]*a-gu*
4 si gud
IX. 1. nídba
en
3. $^{d}$*ʾÀ-da*
*Ḫa-lab$_x$*$^{ki}$
5. *in*
$^{d}$AMA-*ra*

(20)
7. 5 gín DILMUN kù:babbar
šu-bal-ak
9. 1 gín DILMUN kù-gi
*ni-zi-mu*
11. nu$_{11}$-za
1 *za-ḫa-da*
13. [ ]
[ ]
15. [5 gín DILMUN kù:babbar]
šu-bal-ak
17. 1 gín DILMUN kù-gi
ZU.PIRIG
19. *su-da-nu* kù-gi
BAR.AN
21. en

(21)
5 g[ín] DI[LMUN] an-na
23. šub *si-in*
1 ĜIŠ-zú
25. 1 ½ gín DILMUN kù:babbar
[ ]
27. ĜIŠ-gígir-II gibil
X. 1. *Ib-rí-um*

(22)
[(ca. 13 lines)]
15.? 1 dib-*sù*
*I-bí-zi-kir*
17. dumu-nita
*Ib-rí-um*
19. ì-na-sum

(23)
ŠÚ+ŠA 5 gín DILMUN kù:babbar
21. šu-bal-ak
5 gín DILMUN kù-gi
23. *ni-zi-mu*
1 dib
25. *Ìr-ba$_x$-zé*
[ ]

(24)
27. [ŠÚ+ŠA 5 gín DILMUN kù:babbar]
XI. 1. šu-bal-ak
[1+]4 gín DILMUN kù-gi
3. nu$_{11}$-za 1 níĝ-PA
*Ib-rí-um*

(25)
5. ŠÚ+ŠA gín DILMUN kù:babbar
[šu-bal-ak]
7. [4 gín DILMUN kù-gi]
[*z*]*i-ba-*[*d*]*u*
9. [ ]⸢x⸣[ ]
[ ]
11. [ ]

(26)
10 gín DILMUN kù:babbar 2 *bu*-DI
13. níĝ-ba
ama-gal
15. en
$^{d}$TU
17. lú *ʾÀ-da-ni*$^{ki}$

(27)
1 ma-na kù:babbar
19. 1 *gúm-a-nu*
*Ib-rí-um*

(28)
21. 5 gín DILMUN kù:babbar
šu-bal-ak
23. 1 gín DILMUN kù-gi
[ ]
25. [ ]

(19) 15 shekels of silver for plating 1 [mace], and also pure gold for pla[ting] its handle; 20 shekels of silver for the circular stand of the 4 horns of (2) bulls: offering of the king for the god Hadda of the city of Ḫalab, at the AMA-ra (festival).
(20) 5 shekels of silver in exchange for 1 shekel of gold for decorating with lamination 1 battle-axe […]; [5 shekels of silver] in exchange for 1 shekel of gold for the hangers of the … (*su-da-nu*) of gold for the mules of the king.
(21) 5 sh[ekels] of tin to be melted in 1 hook; 1 ½ shekel of silver [for …] of the new chariot for Ibrium.
(22) […] his plaque Ibbi-zikir, son of Ibrium, has given.
(23) 25 shekels of silver in exchange for 5 shekels of gold for decorating 1 plaque for Irbaze […].
(24) [25 shekels of silver] in exchange for 5 shekels of gold for plating 1 … (níĝ-PA) for Ibrium.
(25) 20 shekels of silver [in exchange for 4 shekels of gold] for the handle of […].
(26) 10 shekels of silver for 2 toggle-pins: gift of the king's mother for the goddess TU of the city of ʾAdani.
(27) 1 mina of silver for 1 *gúm-a-nu*-container for Ibrium.
(28) 5 shekels of silver in exchange for 1 shekel of gold [for …] of copper for Naʾam-ḫalu.

XII. 1. a-gar$_5$-gar$_5$
⌜*Na*⌝*-am$_6$-ḫa-lu*

(29)
3. 15 gín DILMUN kù:babbar
níĝ-sa$_{10}$ 1 ĝír mar-tu ti kù-gi
5. *Iš-má-da-mu*
lú *Bù-da-ma-lik*

(30)
7. 22 ma-na ŠÚ+ŠA gín DILMUN kù:babbar
níĝ-sa$_{10}$ 1 *li-im* 3 *mi-at* 40 ma-na a-gar$_5$-gar$_5$
9. [1+]1 ma-na kù:babbar
níĝ-sa$_{10}$ 1 *mi-at* 20 ma-na a-gar$_5$
11. 10 lá-2 ma-na ŠÚ+ŠA gín DILMUN kù:babbar
šu-bal-ak
13. 1 ma-na ŠA.PI gín DILMUN kù-gi
[ ]

XIII. 1. 8 gín DILMUN kù:babbar
*zi-du-sù*
3. ZA$_x$
en

(31)
5. 12 gín DILMUN an-na
šub *si-in*
7. 1 ma-na 8 gín DILMUN a-gar$_5$-gar$_5$
kin$_5$-ak
9. 4 ĝír 15 gín DILMUN
2 ĝír 10 gín DILMUN
11. 4 gín DILMUN kù:babbar
*zi-du-sù*
13. ZA$_x$
*Ib-rí-um*

(32)
15. 1 ma-na kù:babbar
níĝ-ba
17. *Daš-na*
*Ma-rí*$^{ki}$
19. níĝ-"mul"
*Du-li*$^{ki}$
21. šu-ba$_4$-ti

(33)
10 lá-1 ma-na ŠÚ+ŠA 5 gín DILMUN kù:babbar
23. níĝ-sa$_{10}$ 15 aktum-TÚG
40 lá-1 túg-NI.NI
25. [ ]

XIV. 1. ŠÚ+ŠA gín DILMUN kù:babbar
níĝ-sa$_{10}$ 2 *mi-at* siki na$_4$ *Ma-rí*$^{ki}$
3. 4 gín DILMUN kù:babbar
níĝ-sa$_{10}$ 33 kuš
5. Mar-tu$^{ki}$
ŠÚ+ŠA gín DILMUN kù:babbar
7. níĝ-sa$_{10}$ 2 gud
*Iš-ra*-BAD
9. lú-kar
*Kak-mi-um*$^{ki}$

(34)
11. TAR 5 gín DILMUN kù:babbar
níĝ-sa$_{10}$ raš-SAR
13. Kur$^{ki}$
ki:lam$_7$
15. *ᵓÀ-da-ni*$^{ki}$

(35)
4 ma-na kù:babbar
17. níĝ-sa$_{10}$ 2 BAR.AN
*áš-ti*
19. *Na-gàr*$^{ki}$

(36)
3 gín DILMUN kù:babbar
21. 1 šu-dub sikil
en
23. lú
ḫúl
25. [ ] (?)

XV. 1. a-mu-*sù*

(29) 15 shekels of silver for the purchase of 1 pointed mar-tu dagger (decorated with) gold for Išma-damu, (son) of Buda-malik.

(30) 22;20 minas of silver for the purchase of 1340 minas of copper; 2 minas of silver for the purchase of 120 minas of copper; 8;20 minas of silver in exchange for 1;40 minas of gold […]; 8 shekels of silver for their alloy: property of the king.

(31) 12 shekels of tin to be melted with 1;08 minas of copper for making 4 daggers of 15 shekels each, 2 daggers of 10 shekels each; 4 shekels of silver for their alloy: property of Ibrium.

(32) 1 mina of silver: gift for Dašna of the city of Mari, (who brought) the news that the city of Duli had been conquered.

(33) 9;25 minas of silver for the purchase of 54[+x] garments; 20 shekels of silver for the purchase of 200 stone weights of wool from the city of Mari; 4 shekels of silver for the purchase of 33 hides from Martu; 20 shekels of silver for the purchase of 2 oxen: Išra-BAD, trader of the city of Kakmium (has received).

(34) 35 shekels of silver for the purchase of leek from the mountain region, at the market of the city of ᵓAdani.

(35) 4 minas of silver for the purchase of 2 mules from the city of Nagar.

(36) 3 shekels of silver for 1 ring for the purification rite of the king, (on the occasion) of the feast of his ancestor.

(37)

6 ma-na ŠA.PI gín DILMUN
kù:babbar
3. šu-bal-ak
1 ma-na ŠÚ+ŠA gín DILMUN kù-gi
5. kin$_5$-ak
1 íb-lá 1 *si-ti-tum* 1 ĝír-kun
7. ŠÚ+ŠA gín DILMUN
2 *ti-gi-na*
9. ŠÚ+ŠA gín DILMUN
4 *ʾà-ra-ma-tum*
11. [ŠÚ+ŠA gín DILMUN]
ZA$_x$ saĝ
13. 10 gín DILMUN
8 ĜIŠ-ĝeštu$_x$-lá
15. 12 gín DILMUN
1 šu-dub
17. 2 gín DILMUN
[ ]
19. 2 ĜIŠ-du
*Ti-bù-da-mu*
21. *maš-ar-tum*
en

(38)

23. 3 gín DILMUN an-na
[...]
XVI. 1. 1 ĜIŠ-asari
10 gín DILMUN kù:babbar
3. šu-bal-ak
2 gín DILMUN kù-gi
5. *ʾa$_5$-na-gu*
1 ĜIŠ-asari
7. *maš-ar-tum*
en

(39)

9. 2 ma-na TAR kù:babbar
šu-bal-ak
11. 1 íb-lá 1 *si-ti-tum* 1 ĝír-kun TAR kù-gi
sikil
13. $^{d}$*ʾÀ-da*

(40)

2 [m]a[-na] TAR kù:babbar
15. šu-bal-ak
TAR kù-gi 1 íb-lá 1 *si-ti-tum* 1 ĝír-kun sikil
17. 8 gín DILMUN kù:babbar
1 íb-lá 1 *si-ti-tum* 1 ĝír-kun sikil
19. $^{d}$*ʾA$_5$-da-"bal"*
lú *Lu-ba-an*$^{ki}$
XVII. 1. *al$_6$*
tu-ra
3. *Ib-rí-um*
tak$_4$

(41)

5. ŠA.PI gín DILMUN kù:babbar
1 íb-lá 1 ĝír-kun
7. TAR 5 gín DILMUN kù:babbar
šu-bal-ak
9. 7 gín DILMUN kù-gi
maš-maš-*sù*
11. *Gi-a-da-mu*
*in* ud
13. ḫúl-*sù*
*Gi-rí*
15. dumu-nita
*Ib-rí-um*
17. šu-mu-tak$_4$

(42)

50 gín DILMUN kù:babbar
19. níĝ-sa$_{10}$ 1 ĝír mar-tu kù-gi
[ ]
21. 50 gín DILMUN babbar:kù
níĝ-sa$_{10}$ 1 ĝír mar-tu kù-gi
23. *Zi-ba-da*

(43)

r. I. 1. 2 ma-na TAR kù:babbar
šu-bal-ak
3. TAR kù-gi 1 dib
BÍL-*za-il*
5. dumu-nita
šeš
7. *Ib-rí-um*

(37) 6;40 minas of silver in exchange for 1;20 minas of gold for making 1 belt, 1 sheath (and) 1 dagger pendant; 20 shekels (of silver) for 2 torques; 20 shekels (of silver) for 4 pectorals; [20 shekels (of silver)] for ...; 10 shekels for 8 earrings; 12 shekels for 1 ring; 2 shekels [...] for 2 foot rings: for Tibu-damu, for the stele of the king.

(38) 3 shekels of tin [and x copper] for a tray; 10 shekels of silver in exchange for 2 shekels of gold for the circular stand of (this) tray, for the stele of the king.

(39) 2;30 minas of silver in exchange for 1 belt, 1 sheath (and) 1 dagger pendant of 30 (shekels of) gold for the purification rite for the god Hadda.

(40) 2;30 [m]i[nas] of silver in exchange for 30 (shekels of) gold for 1 belt, 1 sheath (and) 1 dagger pendant for the purification rite; 8 shekels of silver for 1 belt, 1 sheath (and) 1 dagger pendant for the purification rite for the god ʾAdabal of the city of Luban, to be handed over in relation to the illness of Ibrium.

(41) 40 shekels of silver for 1 belt (and) 1 dagger pendant; 35 shekels of silver in exchange for 7 shekels of gold for its striped (decoration) for Giʾa-damu, on the occasion of his feast; Giri, son of Ibrium, has handed over.

(42) 50 shekels of silver for the purchase of 1 mar-tu dagger (decorated with) gold [...]; 50 shekels of silver for the purchase of 1 mar-tu dagger (decorated with) gold for Zibada.

(43) 2;30 minas of silver in exchange for 30 (shekels of) gold for 1 plaque for BILza-il, son of the brother of Ibrium.

(44)

17 gín DILMUN an-na
9. šub *si-in*
1 ma-na ŠA.PI gín DILMUN a-gar$_5$[-gar$_5$]
11. ki[n$_5$-ak]
1 tùn tur TAR
13. 1 tùn tur ŠÚ+ŠA gín DILMUN
1 dub-nagar šu-mu-LAGAB ŠÚ+ŠA gín DILMUN
15. 1 dub-nagar 10 gín DILMUN
1 *ma-ga-za-u*$_4$ 10 gín DILMUN
17. 1 *ma-za-ḫa-rúm* 10 gín DILMUN
1 *ḫa-ra-núm* 7 gín DILMUN
19. 1 dub-nagar [10] ⸢lá-⸣2(?) gín DIL-MUN
1 UŠ×KÍD 2 gín DILMUN
21. lú kaskal
en

(45)

II. 1. ⸢TAR⸣ [a]n-na
šub *si-in*
3. 3 ma-na a-gar$_5$-gar$_5$
kin$_5$-ak
5. 6 an-zam$_x$
1 á-lá gibil
7. 7 ½ gín DILMUN kù:babbar
šu-bal-ak
9. 1 ½ gín DILMUN kù-gi
*ni-zi-mu*
11. nu$_{11}$-za
4 kù-sal
13. *Ib-rí-um*

(46)

10 gín DILMUN kù:babbar
15. šu-bal-ak
2 gín DILMUN kù-gi
17. *ni-zi-mu*
1 an-zam$_x$
19. *Ib-rí-um*

(47)

50 gín DILMUN kù:babbar
21. šu-bal-ak
10 gín DILMUN kù-gi
23. 1 pad
an-zam$_x$
25. *A-ba-ti-tum*$^{ki}$
*Ib-rí-um*

(48)

27. ŠÚ+ŠA gín DILMUN kù:babbar
III. 1. ⸢šu⸣[-bal-]ak
⸢4⸣ gín DILMUN kù-gi
3. *ni-zi-mu*
1 pad
5. *ma-da-a-um* kù-gi an-dùl
lú en
7. *ša-ti*
*Ib-rí-um*
9. mu-DU

(49)

5 gín DILMUN kù:babbar
11. šu-bal-ak
1 gín DILMUN kù-gi
13. 1 kù-sal
níĝ-ba
15. *Dar-ib-da-mu*
dumu-munus
17. en
$^{d}$BAD-munus
19. *si-in*
*Lu-ba-an*$^{ki}$
21. *in* ud
*ter*$_6$*-bí*
23. bur-KAK-*sù*
$^{dʾ}$*A*$_5$*-da-“bal”*

(50)

25. 2 ma-na TAR kù:babbar
šu-bal-ak
27. TAR kù-gi
nu$_{11}$-za 2 ĜIŠ-ban
IV. 1. [3+]3 [½ gín DILMU]N kù:babbar
šu-bal-ak

(44) 17 shekels of tin to be melted with 1;40 minas of cop[per] for m[aking] 1 small axe of 30 (shekels), 1 small axe of 20 shekels, 1 hammer with a square head of 20 shekels, 1 hammer of 10 shekels, 1 rasp of 10 shekels, 1 pliers of 10 shekels, 1 saw of 7 shekels, 1 hammer of 8 shekels, 1 blade of 2 shekels: for the journey of the king.

(45) 30 (shekels of) [t]in to be melted with 3 minas of copper for making 6 an-zam$_x$ goblets, 1 new … (á-lá); 7 ½ shekels of silver in exchange for 1 ½ shekel of gold for decorating with lamination 4 buckles for Ibrium.

(46) 10 shekels of silver in exchange for 2 shekels of gold for decorating 1 an-zam$_x$ goblet for Ibrium.

(47) 50 shekels of silver in exchange for 10 shekels of gold for 1 lid of an an-zam$_x$ goblet (in) the city of Abatitum, for Ibrium.

(48) 20 shekels of silver in ex[cha]nge for 4 shekels of gold for decorating 1 lid of a gold … (*ma-da-a-um*) of a statue of the king, which Ibrium had delivered.

(49) 5 shekels of silver in exchange for 1 shekel of gold for 1 buckle: gift of Tarib-damu, daughter of the king, for the Lady of the city of Luban, on the occasion of the elevation of her bur-KAK vessel to the god ʾAdabal.

(50) 2;30 minas of silver in exchange for 30 (shekels of) gold for plating 2 bows; 6 [½ shekels] of silver in exchange for 1 ½ shekel of gold for plating 1 side of a chariot; 10 shekels of silver in exchange for 2 shekels of gold for decorating with lamination 1 battle-axe for Ibrium.

3. 1 ½ gín DILMUN kù-gi
nu$_{11}$-za 1 zag ĜIŠ-gígir-II
5. 10 gín DILMUN kù:babbar
šu-bal-ak
7. 2 gín DILMUN [k]ù-gi
*ni-zi-mu*
9. nu$_{11}$-za
1 *za-ḫa-da*
11. *Ib-rí-um*

(51)
3 ma-na ŠÚ+ŠA gín DILMUN
kù:babbar
13. šu-bal-ak
ŠA.PI gín DILMUN kù-gi
15. 2 *ti-gi-na*
50 gí[n] DILMUN kù:babbar
17. šu-bal-ak
10 gín DILMUN kù-gi
19. *ni-zi-mu*
1 *gú-li-lum*
21. ama-gal
en

(52)
23. TAR 3 gín DILMUN 3 NI kù:babbar
šu-bal-ak
V. 1. [6 gín 2 NI DILMUN kù-gi]
[*ni-zi-mu*]
3. 2 *gú-li-lum*
níĝ-ba
5. $^{d}$*Ku-ra*

(53)
2 gín DILMUN kù:babbar
7. *ni-zi-mu*
[2 níĝ-anše-ak$^{?}$]
9. [50 gín DILMUN kù:babbar]
[šu-bal-ak]
11. 10 gín DILMUN kù-gi
*ni-zi-mu*
13. maš-maš 4 kù-sal
*I-bí-zi-kir*
15. dumu-nita
*Ib-rí-um*

(54)
17. ŠÚ+ŠA gín [DILMUN] kù:babbar
[*ni-zi-m*]*u*
19. 2 níĝ-anše-ak 4 kù-sal
*Gi-rí*
21. dumu-nita
*Ib-rí-um*

(55)
23. 7 ma-na 10 gín DILMUN kù:babbar
šu-bal-ak
25. 1 ma-na ŠÚ+ŠA 6 gín DILMUN
VI. 1. [kù-gi]
[ ]
3. 3 ma-na ŠA.PI gín DILMUN
kù:babbar
šu-bal-ak
5. ŠA.PI gín DILMUN kù-gi
2 *ti-gi-na*
7. *ma-l*[*ik-*]*tum*

(56)
1 gín DILMUN kù:babbar
9. 1 *ma-da-ḫu*
1 gín DILMUN kù:babbar
11. šu-bal-ak
5 NI gín DILMUN kù-gi
13. 1 *a-na-bù-bí-tum*
*al*$_{6}$*-sù*
15. *Ti-ra-il*
[dub-sa]r$^{?}$

(57)
17. 4 ma-na ŠÚ+ŠA 2 gín DI[LMUN]
kù:babbar
níĝ-sa$_{10}$ 1 dùl-TÚG *Ma-rí*$^{ki}$
19. 14 túg-NI.NI
1 *mi-at* 40 sal-TÚG
VII. 1. [ x kù:babbar]
níĝ-sa$_{10}$ 2 IGI.NITA u$_{5}$
3. *Bù-da-ma-lik*
[šu-ba$_{4}$-ti]
5. ki:lam$_{7}$
$^{d}$*Ga-mi-iš*

(51) 3;20 minas of silver in exchange for 40 shekels of gold for 2 torques; 50 shekels of silver in exchange for 10 shekels of gold for decorating 1 bracelet for the king's mother.
(52) 33 shekels (and) 3 NI of silver in exchange for [6 shekels (and) 2 NI of gold for decorating] 2 bracelets: gift for the god Kura.
(53) 2 shekels of silver for decorating [2 bridles; 50 shekels of silver in exchange for] 10 shekels of gold for a striped decoration of 4 buckles for Ibbi-zikir, son of Ibrium.
(54) 20 shekels of silver [for decorat]ing 2 bridles (and) 4 buckles for Giri, son of Ibrium.
(55) 7;10 minas of silver in exchange for 1;26 minas [of gold for …]; 3;40 minas of silver in exchange for 40 shekels of gold for 2 torques for the queen.
(56) 1 shekel of silver for 1 clip; 1 shekel of silver in exchange for 5 NI of gold for 1 hairpin on her (= of the queen) account: Tira-il, [the scri]be.
(57) 4;22 minas of silver for the purchase of 155 garments; [x silver] for the purchase of 2 donkeys to ride: Buda-malik [has received] at the market of the god Kamiš.

(58)
7. ŠÚ+ŠA gín DILMUN kù:babbar
*Daš-ne*
9. lú ĜIŠ-nu-kiri$_6$
*Ì-mar*$^{ki}$
11. *in*
NI-*ab*$^{ki}$
13. [šu]-ba$_4$-ti

(59)
1 ma-na kù:babbar
15. šu-bal-ak
12 gín DILMUN kù-gi
17. níĝ-ba
$^{d}$ˀ*À-d*[*a*]
19. lú *Lu-ub*$^{ki}$
*in*
21. *gi*-NI
nu$_{11}$-za ab-*sù*

(60)
23. 2 ma-na ⌜TAR⌝ kù:[b]abbar
šu-bal-ak
VIII. 1. [TA]R [kù-gi] 1 íb-lá 1 *si-ti-tum* 1 ĝír-kun
*Kùn-da-ba-an*
3. [ ]
[ ]
5. *in* ud
tuš-LÚ×TIL
7. *in*
*A-ru*$_{12}$*-ga-du*$^{ki}$

(61)
9. 1 ma-na ŠA.PI gín DILMUN kù:babbar
šu-bal-ak
11. ŠÚ+ŠA gín DILMUN kù-gi 2 *bu*-DI
*Ti-šè-li-im*
13. *ma-lik-tum*
*Ì-mar*$^{ki}$
15. *in* ud
DU.DU
17. *mi-nu*
ˀ*À-da-ni*$^{ki}$

(62)
19. TAR 3 gín DILMUN 3 NI kù:babbar
šu-bal-ak
21. 6 gín DILMUN [2] NI kù-g[i]
IX. 1. 2 *gú-li-lum*
níĝ-ba
3. [ ]
*En-na-il*
5. [ ]
$^{d}$*Am-ma-rí-ig*

(63)
7. TAR kù:babbar
níĝ-ba
9. *Wa-ru*$_{12}$*-tum*
*Ma-rí*$^{ki}$
11. e$_{11}$
*mi-nu*
13. Kiš$^{ki}$
*áš-ti*
15. *En-na-il*

(64)
10 gín DILMUN kù:babbar
17. šu-bal-ak
2 gín DILMUN kù-gi
19. [*ni-*]*zi-*[*m*]*u*
[nu$_{11}$-]za
21. [ ]
[ ]
23. lú an:zam$_x$
5 gín DILMUN kù:babbar
25. šu-bal-ak
[1] gín DILMUN [kù-gi]
X. 1. *zi-ba-du*
1 pad
3. an-zam$_x$
en

(65)
5. 10 gín DILMUN kù:babbar
2 *bu*-DI 4 *ti-ša-nu*
7. [níĝ-ba]
[$^{d}$*Ga-na-na*]
9. *in*

(58) 20 shekels of silver for Dašne, a gardener of the city of Imar, received in the city of NIab.
(59) 1 mina of silver in exchange for 12 shekels of gold: gift for the god Had[da] of the city of Lub, in month IV, for plating its (= of the temple) window.
(60) 2;30 minas of sil[v]er in exchange for [3]0 (shekels of) [gold] for 1 belt, 1 sheath (and) 1 dagger pendant for Kun-daban […] when resided in the city of Arugadu.
(61) 1;40 minas of silver in exchange for 20 shekels of gold for 2 toggle-pins for Tiša-lim, the queen of the city of Imar, when she came from the city of ˀAdani.
(62) 33 shekels (and) 3 NI of silver in exchange for 6 shekels (and) [2] NI of gol[d] for 2 bracelets: gift […] Enna-il […] for the god Ammarik.
(63) 30 (shekels of) silver: gift for Warutum of the city of Mari, who came back from the city of Kiš with Enna-il.
(64) 10 shekels of silver in exchange for 2 shekels of gold [for de]cora[tin]g with [lami]nation […] of an an-zam$_x$ goblet; 5 shekels of silver in exchange for [1] shekel [of gold] for the handle of 1 lid of the an-zam$_x$ goblet for the king.
(65) 10 shekels of silver for 2 toggle-pins (and) 4 … (*ti-ša-nu*): [gift for the goddess Ganana] (on the occasion of) the great presentation.

ĜIŠ.DUG.DU
11. maḫ

(66)
ŠA.PI kù:babbar
13. 1 íb-lá 1 ĝír-kun
TAR 5 gín DILMUN kù:babbar
15. šu-bal-ak
7 gín DILMUN kù-g[i]
17. maš-maš-*s*[*ù*]
*I-bí-zi-kir*
19. lú *I-rí-gú-nu*
[ ]-⸢x⸣
21. [ ]-⸢x⸣-*um*

(67)
10 gí[n DILMUN kù]:babbar
23. šu-bal-ak
2 gín DILMUN kù-gi 2 kù-sal
25. níĝ-ba
ama-gal
27. en
$^{d}$*Iš:šára*
29. *Zu-ra-mu*$^{ki}$
XI. 1. *wa*
$^{d}$*Iš:šára*
3. *Má*-NE$^{ki}$

(68)
12 gín DILMUN kù:babbar
5. nu$_{11}$-za 1 *ḫa-bù*
*ap* nu$_{11}$-za
7. *ar-ra-sù*
kù-gi si[kil]
9. ŠÚ+ŠA gín DILMUN kù:babbar
*ʾa*$_{5}$*-na-gu*
11. 4 si 2 gud
nídba
13. en
$^{d}$*ʾÀ-da*
15. *Ḫa-lab*$_{x}^{ki}$
iti *ʾa*$_{5}$*-nun*

(69)
17. [ ]
[ ]
19. [ ]
l[u$_{x}$]
21. UD.GÁ[NA]
ĜIŠ-sal
23. ⸢dag⸣
é
25. maḫ

(70)
5 ⸢gín DILMUN⸣ an-na
27. šu[b *s*]*i-in*
1 ĜIŠ-zú
29. 1 gín DILMUN kù:babbar
nu$_{11}$-za 1 zag ĜIŠ-gígir-II
XII. 1. *Da-bí-da-mu*
dumu-nita
3. en
*Bur-ma-an*$^{ki}$

(71)
5. ŠÚ+ŠA 5 gín DILMUN kù:babbar
šu-bal-ak
7. 5 gín DILMUN kù-gi
*ni-zi-mu*
9. 1 dib
*Gi-rí*
11. dumu-nita
*Ib-rí-um*

(72)
13. ŠA.PI gín DILMUN kù:babbar
1 íb-lá [1] ĝír-kun
15. TAR 5 gín DILMUN kù:babbar
šu-bal-ak
17. 7 gín DILMUN kù-gi
maš-maš-*sù*
19. 6 gín DILMUN kù:babbar
níĝ-sa$_{10}$ 1 ĝír mar-tu kù:babbar
21. [ ]⸢x⸣-*mi*-[ kù-g]i
[ ]-⸢x⸣
XIII. 1. [*Ig-rí-i*]*š*?
⸢É×PAP⸣

(73)
3. [x] ma-na [x 2+]6 gín DILMUN kù:babbar

(66) 40 (shekels of) silver for 1 belt (and) 1 dagger pendant; 35 shekels of silver in exchange for 7 shekels of gol[d] for it[s] striped (decoration) for Ibbi-zikir, (son) of Iri-gunu […].
(67) 10 shek[els of sil]ver in exchange for 2 shekels of gold for 2 buckles: gift of the king's mother for the goddess Išḫara of the city of Zuramu and for the goddess Išḫara of the city of MaNE.
(68) 12 shekels of silver for plating 1 mace and also for plating its handle (with) pu[re] gold; 20 shekels of silver for the circular stand of the 4 horns of 2 bulls: offering of the king for the god Hadda of the city of Ḫalab, in month VIII.
(69) […] … for the … dag (?) of the High house.
(70) 5 shekels of tin to be melted in 1 hook; 1 shekel of silver for plating a side of a chariot for Dabi-damu, son of the king of the city of Burman.
(71) 25 shekels of silver in exchange for 5 shekels of gold for decorating 1 plaque for Giri, son of Ibrium.
(72) 40 shekels of silver for 1 belt (and) [1] dagger pendant; 35 shekels of silver in exchange for 7 shekels of gold for its striped (decoration); 6 shekels of silver for the purchase of 1 mar-tu dagger (decorated with) silver […] for the funerary rite of [Igri]š.
(73) [x;x]8 minas of silver for the purchase of 39 garments; 6 shekels of silver for the purchase of GIŠ-ti-ḪAR-wood: Wabarum has received, at the market of the god Ha[dda].

níĝ-sa$_{10}$ 10 lá-1 dùl-TÚG *Ma-rí*$^{ki}$
5. 30 túg-NI.NI
6 gín DILMUN kù:babbar
7. níĝ-sa$_{10}$ ĜIŠ-ti-ḪAR
*Wa-ba-rúm*
9. šu-ba$_4$-ti
ki:lam$_7$
11. $^{d⌜?}$*À*⌝[-*da*]

(74)
ŠÚ+ŠA 5 gín DILMUN kù:babbar
13. šu-bal-ak
[2+]3 gín DILMUN kù-gi
15. nu$_{11}$-za
[*maš*-]*ar*-[*t*]*um*
17. [níĝ-]ba
[ -]*da*-[ ]
19. [ ]
[ ]
21. [ ]
XIV. 1–4. [ ]
5$^?$. [ *d*]*a*-⌜x⌝

(75)
[x g]ín [DILM]UN [an-n]a
7. [šub *si-i*]*n*
[x a-g]ar$_5$-gar$_5$
9. [*z*]*i*-⌜*ba*⌝-[*du*]
⌜útul⌝-útul maḫ urudu
11. 2 gín DILMUN kù:babbar
⌜1⌝ kù-sal
13. [ní]g-ba
[x-]GAL
15. [

(76)
XV. [(in lacuna)]
x+1. ŠA.P[I] gín DILMUN kù-gi
nu$_{11}$-za 5 *gú-li-lum* a-gar$_5$-ga[r$_5$]
TAR-II
3’. *w*[*a*]
10[(+x) *gú*]-*l*[*i-lum* ]

(77)
XVI. x+1. níĝ-⌜ba⌝
diĝir-diĝir-diĝir

(78)
3’. 1 ma-na kù:babbar
níĝ-sa$_{10}$ 1 BAR.AN
5’. *Wa-na*
šu-ba$_4$-ti
7’. (blank)

(79)
XVII. x+1. níĝ-s[a$_{10}$] 1 aktum-[TÚG] ti[-TÚG]
2 gada-[TÚG]
3’. 1 *m*[*i-at*] ⌜10⌝ [ ]
[...

XVIII. 1. (blank)

(80)
AN.ŠÈ.G[Ú] 2 [*mi-at*] 40[(+x)
m]a[-na] kù[:babbar]
3. ⌜è⌝
[*a*]*p*
5. ⌜2⌝[(+1)] *mi-at* [(x+)]⌜50⌝ [m]a-na
[kù:babbar]
[al$_6$-ĝál]
7. [é siki]

(74) 25 shekels of silver in exchange for 5 shekels of gold for plating [a ste]le: [gi]ft [for …].
(75) [x she]kels of [ti]n [to be melted] with [x cop]per for the handles of big kettles of copper; 2 shekels of silver for 1 buckle: [gi]ft [for …].
(76) […] 40 shekels of gold for plating 5 double bracelets of 30 (shekels of) copp[er] an[d] 10[(+x) bra]ce[lets …]
(77) […]: gift for the gods.
(78) 1 mina of silver for the purchase of 1 mule, Wana has received.
(79) […] for the purcha[se] of 113[+x] garments […]
(80) Tota[l] 240[(+x) m]i[nas] of sil[ver]: expenditure; [and al]so 300;50[(+x) m]inas [of silver are present in the Treasury].

## Commentary

This document has to be dated to the year Ibr. 17. It opens with the registration of the expenditures of 1 mina (470 g) of silver for the renewal rite concerning the city-god Kura which fell at the beginning of the new year. The 3 shekels (23 g) of silver to be given to the god in a later period of the year for a further ceremony concerning his head are registered in § 9. The amount of silver which Tinib-dulum, a sister of the king, had received in her function as priestess of the god ᵓAdabal, is not preserved (§ 2). Tarib-damu, one of the king's daughter, who was also a priestess of ᵓAdabal, offered a buckle of 1 shekel (8 g) of gold to the *paredra* of the god (§ 49).

The last sections of the text are badly preserved. The "expended", è, silver that year amounted to 240[+x] minas (112.80 + x kg). The total silver "present", $al_6$-ĝál, in the Treasury was ⌜300;50⌝ (?) minas (141.391 kg), (§ 80).

The king received a battle-axe, whose plating needed 1 shekel (8 g) of gold, and another shekel was employed for an element of the tack for a mule (§ 20). There was an expenditure of 22;20 minas (10.50 kg) of silver for "acquiring", níĝ-$sa_{10}$, 1,340 minas (629.80 kg) of copper, as "property" $\text{ZA}_x$, of the king. The ratio of silver to copper is 1 : 60. 1;40 minas of gold; and [x minas +] 8 shekels of silver were added in order to prepare an alloy (§ 30). Another 3 shekels (23 g) of silver were expended for jewelry for the "purification rite", sikil, of the king on the occasion of the "festival of his ancestor", ḫúl a-mu-*sù* (§ 36). An an:$zam_x$ vessel with its lid for the king required 3 shekels (23 g) of gold, (§ 64).

The queen received a piece of jewelry (the name is not preserved) for which 1;26 minas (674 g) of gold were employed, and two *ti-gi-na* of 40 shekels (313 g) of gold (§ 55).

The king's mother received a set of jewelry (two *ti-gi-na*) of 40 shekels (313 g) of gold, and a bracelet of 10 shekels (78 g) of gold (§ 51).

Five shekels (39 g) of tin and 1 ½ shekels (12 g) of silver were employed for a new chariot for Ibrium (§ 21); the plating of a níĝ-PA needed 5 shekels (39 g) of gold (§ 24), and a *gúm-a-nu* 1 mina (470 g) of silver (§ 27). Twelve shekels (94 g) of tin and 1;08 (532 g) minas of copper were needed for four daggers of 15 shekels (117 g) each, and two daggers of 10 shekels (78 g) each (with 15% of tin); 4 shekels (31 g) of silver were added to be fused with these metals, whose total was 626 g (§ 31). Ibrium received a dagger decorated with 30 shekels (235 g) of gold, and another dagger decorated with 8 shekels (63 g) of silver was given to the god ᵓAdabal for the "purification rite", sikil, of the minister on the occasion of an illness (§ 40). Thirty shekels (235 g) of tin (14.29%) and 3 minas (1.41 kg) of copper were used for six vessels, and a "new á-lá" for Ibrium, together with four buckles plated in 1 ½ shekels (12 g) of gold (§ 45). He further received another vessel of the same typology plated with 2 shekels (15 g) of gold (§ 46), and another one provided with a lid made of 10 shekels (78 g) of gold (§ 47). *A-ba-ti-tum*$^{ki}$ is perhaps another writing for *A-ba-tum*$^{ki}$. Additionally, 30 shekels (235 g) of gold were used for plating the two bows of the minister's chariot: 1 ½ shekels (12 g) for plating the edge of its box; and 2 shekels (16 g) of gold for plating a new battle-axe (§ 50).

Ibbi-zikir, Ibrium's son, received a gold plaque, whose weight is not preserved (§ 22); and bridles for which 2 shekels (16 g) of silver were employed, whose four buckles needed 10 shekels (78 g) of gold (§ 53).

Warutum of Mari received 30 shekels (235 g) of silver as a "gift", níĝ-ba, upon his first journey to Ebla (§ 5). He came to Ebla a second time (the amount of silver he received is not preserved), (§ 13). Iti of Mari, who had brought the news that the city of Duli was "vanquished", àga-kár$^!$, received 10 shekels (78 g) of silver (§ 14), and Dašna of Mari 1 mina of silver (470 g) for the same reason (§ 32). Warutum received 30 shekels (235 g) of silver as a gift, when he returned from Kiš with Enna-il (§ 63).

§ 3. Three thousand spearheads needed 57;20 minas (27.001 kg) of tin and 450 minas (211.50 kg) of copper (11.28% of tin). Each spearhead weighed 79.5 g,

§ 6. Tešma-zikir, a spouse of the king who resided in ᵓAzan, received an earring of 24 shekels (199 g) of gold, and two other objects of 20 shekels (157 g) of silver.

§ 15. Iramu, a gardener of the city of Imar, received 10 shekels (78 g) of silver (cf. § 58).

§ 33. Expenditure of 9;25 minas (4.426 kg) of silver for the purchase of garments, 20 shekels (157 g) of silver for 200 "stone (measures)", (na$_4$, of wool from Mari, and 4 shekels (31 g) of silver for thirty-one skins from Martu. Two oxen were provided by a "trader", lú-kar, from Kakmium for an expenditure of 20 shekels (157 g) of silver.

§ 35. Two mules were purchased in Nagar for 4 minas (1.128 kg) of silver.

§§ 37, 38. 1;20 minas (627 g) of gold expended for a belt, and 1;24 minas (657 g) of gold for jewels for the stele of the king: all to Tibu-damu. 3 shekels (23 g) of tin and [x] shekels of copper for a tray, 2 shekels (15 g) of gold for its circular stand, for the stele of the king.

§ 41. Giᵓa-damu, a "representative", maškim, of Ibrium, received a dagger decorated with 40 shekels (313 g) of silver and 7 shekels (55 g) of gold for its alloy, on the occasion of his "festival", ḫúl. It was Giri, a son of Ibrium, who handed over it to him.

§ 42 Zibada (whose daughter-in-law was a daughter of Ibrium) received a dagger decorated with 50 shekels (391 g) of silver and 10 shekels (78 g) of gold.

§ 43. BÍLZA-il, a son of a brother of Ibrium, received a plaque of 30 shekels (235 g) of gold.

§ 44. 1;40 (783 g) minas of copper and 17 shekels (113 g) of tin (17%) for work tools to be at disposal for a journey of the king. The two small axes weighed respectively 235 g and 157 g.

§ 48. 4 shekels (313 g) of gold for the decoration of the lid of a gold vessel of a statue of the king, which Ibrium had delivered.

§ 54. Giri, son of Ibrium, received bridles with the four buckles decorated with 20 shekels (157 g) of silver.

§ 56. The scribe Tira-il received a *ma-da-ḫu* of 1 shekel (8 g) of silver, and an *a-na-bù-bí-tum* of ⅕ (1.4 g) of gold. These two very light objects were often given to women, but sometimes also to men (see the Glossary). Tira-il was the scribe who wrote the letter to Zizi, the king of Ḫamazi (*ARET* XIII 5), and copied lexical and literary texts: the List of Geographical Names, the Tribute List, the Officials List, and the two copies of the Hymn to Ama-ušumgal hymn, *ARET* V 20, 21. In this last work he was supervised by two "experts of the tablets", dub-zu-zu: Azi and Išar (see Archi 1992, pp. 4, [no. 4], 11 [no. 13], 13 [no. 15], and 26–28 for *ARET* V 20, 21).

§ 58. Dašne, a gardener of the city of Imar, received 20 shekels (157 g) of silver (cf. § 15).

§ 61. Tiša-lim, queen of Imar, received two toggle-pins of 20 shekels (157 g) of gold, when she arrived from ᵓAdani, seat of the cult of the god Rašap.

§ 70. Dabi-damu, a son of the king of Burman, received a hook of 5 shekels (39 g) of tin, and a decoration of the box of a chariot of 1 shekel (8 g) of silver.

§ 71. Giri, a son of Ibrium, received a plaque of 5 shekels (39 g) of gold.

§ 72. Igriš(a), a "lord" mentioned in several documents of Ibrium (see *ARET* 14, p. 170) received for his "funerary rite", ⸢É×PAP⸣, a belt decorated with 40 shekels (313 g), and 7 shekels (55 g) of gold for its alloy, together with a dagger of the value of 6 shekels (47 g) of silver and a not preserved amount of gold.

§ 78. Wana, an "overseer", ugula, of mules (see the Index of the Personal Names), bought a mule of 1 mina (470 g) of silver.

# 21
## (Plates XL–XLI)

(1)
o. I. 1. 1 ma-na kù:babbar
saĝ kù:babbar
3. $^{d}$*Ku-ra*

(2)
10 lá-2 ma-na TAR kù:babbar
5. *Di-*[*ni-*]*íb-du-lum*
[nin-]ni
7. [e]n
[šu-ba$_{4}$-t]i

(3)
9. [ ]
[ ]-⌜x⌝
11. [x-N]E
[x+x$^{?}$-]*ga*
13. [x-]*ma*[-x$^{?}$]-NI
[x-]*la*

(4)
15. [x+x ma-n]a [
[

(5)
II. 1. *Gú-ra-du*$^{ki}$

(6)
7 gín DILMUN kù:babbar
3. níĝ-ba
*Ḫu-*NE*-du*
5. *wa*
*Ir*$_{11}$*-tum-a-ḫu*
7. *Sag-gar*$^{ki}$
kaskal
9. níĝ-kas$_{4}$
*Du-du-lu*$^{ki}$

(7)
11. 5 ma-na kù:babbar
šu-bal-ak
13. 1 ma-na kù-gi
nu$_{11}$-za
15. 1 ĜIŠ-gu-kak-gíd
*ap*
17. [ ]
[ ] ⌜x-x⌝
19. [1 í]b-lá [1 ĝír-k]un
[(ca. 10 lines)]

(8)
III. 1. *-sù*
*Ti-ti-nu*
3. *in* ud
ḫúl-*sù*
5. *I-bí-zi-kir*
šu-mu-tak$_{4}$

(9)
7. 2 ma-na TAR kù:babbar
šu-bal-ak
9. TAR kù-gi 1 íb-lá 1 *si-ti-tum* 1 ĝír-kun
*Za-ba-rúm*
11. É×PAP
*I-rí-ig-ì*
13. šu-mu-tak$_{4}$

(10)
4 gín DILMUN an-na
15. šub *si-in*
[*ni-zi-mu*]
17. [2 níĝ-anše-ak 4 kù-sal]
[ ]
19. [ ]
[ ]

(1) 1 mina of silver for the silver head of the god Kura.
(2) 8;30 minas of silver, Ti[ni]b-dulum, [sis]ter [of the ki]ng [has receiv]ed.
(3) […].
(4) [x min]as […]
(5) […] the city of Guradu.
(6) 7 shekels of silver: gift for ḪUNEdu and Irtum-aḫu of the city of Saggar (who) had travelled (to join) the military expedition (against) the city of Tuttul.
(7) 5 minas of silver in exchange for 1 mina of gold for plating 1 spearhead, and also […] [1 b]elt (and) [1 dagger pen]dant […].
(8) […] for Titinu on the occasion of his feast, Ibbi-zikir has handed over.
(9) 2;30 minas of silver in exchange for 30 (shekels of) gold for 1 belt, 1 sheath (and) 1 dagger pendant for the funerary rite of Zabarum; Irig-i(l) has handed over.
(10) 4 shekels of tin to be melted [for decorating 2 bridles (and) 4 buckles …] of a char[iot] for Ibbi-zikir.

21. GIŠ-gí[gir-II]
*I-bí-zi-kir*

(11)[a)]
23. ŠÚ+ŠA gín DILMUN kù:babbar
šu-bal-ak
25. 4 gín DILMUN kù-gi
*ni-zi-mu*
27. [2] níĝ-anše-ak [2+]2 k[ù-]s[al]
[(ca. 4 lines)]
IV. 1. *Ib-ri-um*

(12)
15 gín DILMUN kù:babbar
3. šu-bal-ak
3 gín DILMUN kù-gi
5. *ni-zi-mu*
2 kù-sal
7. 2 IGI.NITA
en

(13)
9. 7 gín DILMUN kù:babbar
*ni-zi-mu*
11. 4 kù-sal
TAR kù:babbar
13. šu-bal-ak
6 gín DILMUN kù-gi
15. *ni-zi-mu*
kù-sal-*sù*
17. am<a-gal>[b)]
en

(14)[c)]
19. [x g]ín [DIL]MUN} [kù:babbar]
[šu-bal-ak]
21. [x gín DILMUN kù-gi]
nu$_{11}$-za
23. [1 *za-ḫ*]*a-da*
en

(15)[d)]
25. 1 ma-na kù:babbar
níĝ-sa$_{10}$
27. ĝeštin
*Du-bí-šum*
29. šu-ba$_4$-ti

(16)
˹8˺ gín DILMUN [kù:babbar]
31. [(ca. 4 lines)]
V. 1. 5 gín DILMUN kù:babbar
šu-bal-ak
3. 1 gín DILMUN kù-gi
nu$_{11}$-za saĝ-*sù*
5. 1 ½ gín DILMUN an-na
šub *si-in*
7. 17 gín a-gar$_5$
1 dub-*sù*
9. níĝ-ba
*Ib-rí-um*
11. $^{d}$*Sa-nu-ga-ar*
*Má*-NE$^{ki}$

(17)
13. 10 gín DILMUN an-na
šub *si-in*
15. 1 ma-na a-gar$_5$-gar$_5$
{˹x˺-UŠ}
17. {gaba-ru}
{13 gín DILMUN kù:babbar}[a)]
19. [níĝ$^?$-]du$_8$[c)]
˹x-x˺

(18)
21. ŠÚ+ŠA gín DILMUN kù:babbar
[2 *bu*]-˹DI˺
23. ì-ĝiš-saĝ
[d]am
25. *ba-da-lum*
[*Ḫa-*]*ra-an*$^{ki}$

(19)
27. 3 ma-na ŠÚ+ŠA gín DILMUN kù:babbar
[ ]˹x˺
29. [ ]
VI. 1. *Iš*$_{11}$*-ru-ud*
ugula *Sal-ba*$^{ki}$

(11) 20 shekels of silver in exchange for 4 shekels of gold for decorating [2] bridles (and) 4 bu[ck]l[es] […] for Ibrium.
(12) 15 shekels of silver in exchange for 3 shekels of gold for decorating 2 buckles for 2 donkeys of the king.
(13) 7 shekels of silver for decorating 4 buckles; 30 (shekels of) silver in exchange for 6 shekels of gold for decorating the buckles, for the king's mother.
(14) [x sh]ekels [of silver in exchange for x shekels of gold] for plating [1 battle-]axe for the king.
(15) 1 mina of silver for the purchase of wine, Dubišum has received.
(16) 8 shekels of silver […]; 5 shekels of silver in exchange for 1 shekel of gold for plating its head; 1 ½ shekel of tin to be melted with 17 shekels of copper for its tablet: gift of Ibrium for the god Sanugar of the city of MANE.
(17) 10 shekels of tin to be melted with 1 mina of copper … receipt; 13 shekels of silver [as the ran]som of …
(18) 20 shekels of silver [for 2 toggle-pins] for the purification rite [for the sp]ouse of the minister of the city of [Ḫa]rran.
(19) 3;20 minas of silver […] for Išrut, the overseer of the city of Salba.

(20)

3. [x kù:babbar]
níĝ-sa$_{10}$
5. la-ḫa
lú ì-ĝiš
7. *si-in*
*A-la-ga*$^{ki}$

(21)

9. 2 ma-na TAR kù:babbar
šu-bal-ak
11. TAR kù-gi 1 dib
*Ìr-ba$_{x}$-da-mu*
13. en
*Ù-ti-ig*$^{⌜ki⌝}$

(22)

15. [20+]30 gín DILMUN kù:babbar
ZU.PIRIĜ
17. [ ]
2 gí[n] DIL[MUN] kù:babbar
19. 1 kù-sal
níĝ-ba
21. *Ib-rí-um*
$^{d}$*A-dar-a-nu*
23. [*D*]*a-na-*[*á*]*š*$^{ki}$

(23)

[1]+3 ma-na [ ]
25. [(ca. 5 lines)]
VII. 1. ki:lam$_{7}$
SA.ZA$_{x}$$^{ki}$
3. NI-*rí*$^{ki}$

(24)

⌜1⌝ *mi-at* ma-na kù:babbar
5. 10 ma-na kù:babbar
šu-bal-ak
7. 2 ma-na kù-gi
kin$_{5}$-ak
9. 1 dib
1 íb-lá 1 *si-ti-tum* 1 ĝír-kun
11. ŠA.PI gín DILMUN kù:babbar
níĝ-sa$_{10}$ 1 ĝír mar-tu kù-gi ⌜*ra*⌝-*ʾà*-[*tu*]*m*
13. [ ]
3 *z*[*ú-*]*zú-b*[*a-*]*tum*
15. ĜIŠ-gígir-II
*Ib-rí-um*
17. šu-mu-tak$_{4}$
é
19. $^{dʾ}$*À-da*

(25)

5 ma-na kù:babbar
21. [šu-ba]l-ak
[(ca. 8 lines)]
VIII. 1. *wa*
šu-mu-tak$_{4}$
3. é
$^{dʾ}$*À-da*

(26)

5. ⌜2⌝ [m]a-[n]a kù:babbar
šu-bal-ak
7. ŠÚ+ŠA 4 gín DILMUN kù-gi
1 níĝ-anše-ak 1 kù-sal
9. IGI.NITA
3 gín DILMUN an-na
11. šub *si-in*
ŠÚ+ŠA a-gar$_{5}$-gar$_{5}$
13. 1 *za-ḫa-da*
ŠA.PI gín DILMUN kù:babbar
15. šu-bal-ak
8 g[ín] DI[LMUN] kù-gi
17. n[u$_{11}$-za]-*sù*
lul-gu-ak
19. lú sikil
é
21. $^{dʾ}$*À-da*
*al*$_{6}$
23. tu-ra
*Ib-rí-um*

(27)

25. [(ca. 8 lines)]
IX. 1. nídba
en
3. $^{dʾ}$*À-da*
lú *Ḫa-lab*$_{x}$$^{ki}$

(20) [x silver] for the purchase of jars of oil for the city of Alaga.
(21) 2;30 minas of silver in exchange for 30 (shekels of) gold for 1 plaque for Irba-damu, the king of the city of Utig.
(22) [5]0 shekels of silver for the hangers of […]; 2 shek[els] of silver for 1 buckle: gift of Ibrium for the god Adaranu of [the city of D]an[a]š.
(23) 4 minas […], at the markets of the Palace (and) of the city of NIri.
(24) 100 minas of silver; 10 minas of silver in exchange for 2 minas of gold for making 1 plaque, 1 belt, 1 sheath (and) 1 dagger pendant; 40 shekels of silver for the purchase of 1 mar-tu dagger (decorated with) gold and shells […] 3 … (*zú-zú-ba-tum*) of a chariot, that Ibrium has handed over for the temple of the god Hadda.
(25) 5 minas of silver [in exchan]ge for [1 mina of gold …] and handed over in the temple of the god Hadda.
(26) 2 [m]i[n]as of silver in exchange for 24 shekels of gold for 1 bridle (and) 1 buckle of a donkey; 3 shekels of tin to be melted with 20 (shekels of) copper for 1 battle-axe; 40 shekels of silver in exchange for 8 she[kels] of gold for its la[mination], as a replacement, (given for) the purification rite for the temple of the god Hadda, in relation to the illness of Ibrium.
(27) […]: offering of the king for the god Hadda of the city of Ḫalab.

(28)
5. 2 ma-na TAR kù:babbar
níĝ-sa$_{10}$
7. 50 lá-2 DAM.KAK.UŠ tur sal

(29)
15 gín DILMUN kù:babbar
9. nu$_{11}$-za 1 *ḫa-bù*
TAR kù:babbar
11. šu-bal-ak
6 gín DILMUN kù-gi
13. nu$_{11}$-za 1 *ar-r*[*a-*]*s*[*ù*]
níĝ-ba
15. en
$^{d}$*Ra-sa-ap*
17. ⸢*ʾÀ-da*⸣-[*ni*$^{ki}$]

(30)
15 gín DILMUN kù:babbar
19. nu$_{11}$-za
1 *ḫa-bù*
21. *ap*
kù-gi
23. sikil
níĝ-ba
25. en
[(ca. 8 lines)]

(31)
X. 1. en

(32)
5 gín DILMUN kù:babbar
3. šu-bal-ak
1 gín DILMUN kù-gi
5. *ni-zi-mu*
[1 níĝ]-anše-ak
7. 2 IGI.NITA
ŠÚ+ŠA gín DILMUN kù:babbar
9. šu-bal-ak
4 gín DILMUN kù-gi
11. *ni-zi-mu*
nu$_{11}$-za
13. 2 ĜIŠ.GA[M.GAM]
ĜIŠ-gígir-II
15. en

(33)
6 ½ gín DILMUN kù:babbar
17. šu-bal-ak
1 4 NI gín DILMUN k[ù-]gi
19. *ni-zi-mu*
nu$_{11}$-za
21. 1 kun
ZA$_{x}$
23. *Ib-rí-um*

(34)
5 gín DILMUN kù:babbar
25. šu-ba[l-a]k
[1 gín DILMUN kù-gi]
[(ca. 7 lines)]
XI. 1. k[ù-]gi
en
3. *wa*
*Ib-rí-um*

(35)
5. 1 ma-na kù:[babba]r
níĝ-sa$_{10}$
7. raš-SAR

(36)
1 ma-na ŠA.PI gín DILMUN
kù:babbar
9. níĝ-ba
diĝir-diĝir-diĝir

(37)
11. 15 gín DILMUN kù:babbar
níĝ-sa$_{10}$
13. 60 íb+III-TÚG gùn
ir$_{11}$-ir$_{11}$

(38)
15. TAR 3 gín DILMUN 3 NI kù:babbar
šu-bal-ak
17. 6 gín DILMUN 2 NI kù-gi 2 *gú-li-lum*
níĝ-ba
19. $^{d}$*Ku-ra*

(28) 2;30 minas of silver for the purchase of 48 small (and) thin … (DAM.KAK.UŠ).
(29) 15 shekels of silver for plating 1 mace; 30 (shekels of) silver in exchange for 6 shekels of gold for plating it[s] hand[le]: gift of the king for the god Rašap of the city of ʾAda[ni].
(30) 15 shekels of silver for plating 1 mace, and also pure gold: gift of the king for […].
(31) […] the king.
(32) 5 shekels of silver in exchange for 1 shekel of gold for decorating [1 bri]dle of 2 donkeys; 20 shekels of silver in exchange for 4 shekels of gold for decorating with lamination 2 whe[els] of a chariot for the king.
(33) 6 ½ shekels of silver in exchange for 1 shekel (and) 4 NI of g[o]ld for decorating with lamination 1 dagger pendant: property of Ibrium.
(34) 5 shekels of silver in exch[ang]e for [1 shekel of gold …] for the king and Ibrium.
(35) 1 mina of sil[ve]r for the purchase of leek.
(36) 1;40 minas of silver: gift for the gods.
(37) 15 shekels of silver for the purchase of 60 kilts for the servants.
(38) 33 shekels (and) 3 NI of silver in exchange for 6 shekels (and) 2 NI of gold for 2 bracelets: gift for the god Kura.

(39)
AN.[Š]È.GÚ 1 *mi-at* 80 lá-1 ma-na
kù:babbar
21. lú
è
23. *in* ud
[úš] (?)
25. [*Ib-rí-um*] (?)
[(blank ?)]

(40)
XII. 1. TAR kù:babbar
níĝ-ba
3. *Ar-rúm*
ŠÚ+ŠA gín DILMUN kù:babbar
5. níĝ-ba
*Mi-su-wa-du*
7. ŠÚ+ŠA gín DILMUN kù:babbar
*En-na-Da-gan*
9. 1 ma-na TAR kù:babbar
níĝ-ba
11. ábba-ábba
*Ma-rí*$^{ki}$
13. *in* ud
nídba ì-ĝiš
15. *Ib-la*$^{ki}$
*wa*
17. *Ma-rí*$^{ki}$

(41)
ŠÚ+ŠA gín DILMUN kù:babbar
19. níĝ-du$_8$
*I-šar*
21. *Ḫa-lab*$_x^{ki}$
*áš-du*
23. *Mi-su-wa-du*
*Ma-rí*$^{ki}$

(42)
25. 5 gín DILMUN kù:babbar
lú ĜIŠ-nu-kiri$_6$
27. *in*
*A-la-ga*$^{ki}$
29. [šu-ba$_4$-ti]

(43)
[x kù:babbar]
31. [níĝ-sa$_{10}$]
XIII. 1. 14 aktum-TÚG
50 lá-2 *ʾà-da-um*-TÚG-I
3. lú *Zú-ba-an*
níĝ-sa$_{10}$
5. *in*
níĝ-kas$_4$
7. *Ma-rí*$^{ki}$

(44)
5 ma-na kù:babbar
9. šu-bal-ak
1 ma-na kù-gi
11. kin$_5$-ak
2 níĝ-anše-ak 4 kù-sal
13. *wa*
nu$_{11}$-za
15. 2 ĜIŠ.GAM.GAM
ĜIŠ-gígir-II
17. 5 gín DILMUN an-na
šub *si-in*
19. 1 ĜIŠ-zú
5 gín DILMUN kù:babbar
21. 3 *zú-zú-ba-tum*
1 ma-na 15 gín DILMUN kù:babbar
23. šu-bal-ak
15 gín DILMUN kù-gi
25. 1 níĝ-anše-ak 1 kù-sal
1 IGI.NITA
27. 10 m[a-]na [kù:babbar]
[šu-bal-ak]
29. [2 ma-na kù-gi]
XIV. 1. 1 íb-lá 1 *si-ti-tum* 1 ĝír-kun
1 dib
3. ŠA.PI gín DILMUN kù:babbar
1 á-MUŠEN
5. 1 ma-na kù:babbar

(39) Total: 179 minas of silver: expenditure, on the occasion of [the death of Ibrium].
(40) 30 (shekels of) silver: gift for Arrum; 20 shekels of silver: gift for Misuwadu; 20 shekels of silver: (gift for) Enna-Dagan; 1;30 minas of silver: gift for the Elders of the city of Mari, on the occasion of the offering of the oil of the cities of Ebla and Mari.
(41) 20 shekels of silver for the ransom of Išar of the city of Ḫalab, by Misuwadu of the city of Mari.
(42) 5 shekels of silver for the gardener, [received] in the city of Alaga.
(43) [x silver for the purchase of] 62 garments for Zuban: a purchase for the military expedition (against) the city of Mari.
(44) 5 minas of silver in exchange for 1 mina of gold for making 2 bridles (and) 4 buckles and for plating 2 wheels of a chariot; 5 shekels of tin to be melted in 1 hook; 5 shekels of silver for 3 … (*zú-zú-ba-tum*); 1;15 minas of silver in exchange for 15 shekels of gold for 1 bridle (and) 1 buckle for a donkey; 10 m[i]nas [of silver in exchange for 2 minas of gold] for 1 belt, 1 sheath, 1 dagger pendant (and) 1 plaque; 40 shekels of silver for 1 á-MUŠEN helmet; 1 mina of silver for the purchase of 1 mar-tu dagger (decorated with) shells (and) gold; 2;30 minas of silver in exchange for 30 (shekels of) gold for 1 … (*ma-da-a-um*); 30 (shekels of) silver for 1 … (*ma-da-a-um*); 30 (shekels of) silver in exchange for 6 shekels of gold for plating 1 dagger pendant; 5 minas of silver for making 1 GIŠ-šú vessel (and) 1 níg-bànda vessel for Ibrium's hands: handed over for the funerary rite [of Ibrium; (and also) 1 …] (that) Kešdut has handed over to Ibrium.

níĝ-sa$_{10}$
7. 1 ĝír mar-tu *ra-ʾà-tum* kù-gi
2 ma-na TAR kù:babbar
9. šu-bal-ak
TAR kù-gi
11. 1 *ma-da-a-um*
TAR kù:babbar
13. 1 *ma-da-a-um*
TAR kù:babbar
15. šu-bal-ak
6 gín DILMUN kù-gi
17. nu$_{11}$-za 1 kun
5 ma-na kù:babbar
19. kin$_5$-ak
1 ĜIŠ-šú 1 níĝ-bànda
21. lú 2 šu
lú *Ib-rí-um*
23. šu-mu-tak$_4$
*si-in*
25. ⌜É×PAP⌝
[ ]
27. [ ]
XV. 1. *Kéš-du-ud*
*Ib-rí-um*
3. šu-mu-tak$_4$

(45)
15 gín DILMUN kù:babbar
5. nu$_{11}$-za 1 *ḫa-bù*
TAR kù:babbar
7. šu-bal-ak
6 gín DILMUN kù-gi
9. nu$_{11}$-za 1 *ar-ra-sù*
níĝ-ba
11. $^{d?}$*À-da*
*Lu-ub*$^{ki}$
13. *in*
*gi*:NI

(46)
15. 3 ma-na ŠÚ+ŠA gín DILMUN
kù:babbar
šu-bal-ak
17. ŠA.PI gín DILMUN kù-gi
1 íb-lá 1 *si-ti-tum* 1 ĝír-kun
19. ì-ĝiš-saĝ
*I-bí-zi-kir*

(47)
21. 5 ma-na kù:babbar
šu-bal-ak
23. 1 ma-na kù-gi 2 *bu*-DI
ì-ĝiš-saĝ
25. ama-gal
en

(48)
27. 1 ma-na ⌜ŠA.PI gín⌝ [DILMUN
kù:babbar]
[šu-bal-ak]
29. [ŠÚ+ŠA gín DILMUN]
XVI. 1. kù-gi
2 *bu*-DI
3. ì-ĝiš-saĝ
*Di-ni-íb-du-lum*
5. nin-ni
en

(49)
7. 1 ma-na kù:babbar
níĝ-sa$_{10}$ 1 ĝír mar-tu kù-gi
9. en

(50)
3 ma-na ŠÚ+ŠA gín DILMUN
kù:babbar
11. šu-bal-ak
ŠA.PI gín DILMUN kù-gi 1 dib
13. *Kùn-ti-su*
*Ur-sá-um*$^{ki}$

(51)
15. 3 ma-na ŠÚ+ŠA gín DILMUN
kù:babbar
šu-bal-ak
17. ŠA.PI gín DILMUN kù-gi 1 dib
*En-na-ma-lik*
19. lú *Il-da-mu*

(52)
3 ma-na ŠÚ+ŠA gín DILMUN
kù:babbar

(45) 15 shekels of silver for plating 1 mace; 30 (shekels of) silver in exchange for 6 shekels of gold for plating its handle: gift for the god Hadda of the city of Lub, in month IV.
(46) 3;20 minas of silver in exchange for 40 shekels of gold for 1 belt, 1 sheath (and) 1 dagger pendant for the purification rite of Ibbi-zikir.
(47) 5 minas of silver in exchange for 1 mina of gold for 2 toggle-pins for the purification rite of the king's mother.
(48) 1;40 minas [of silver in exchange for 20 shekels] of gold for 2 toggle-pins for the purification rite of Tinib-dulum, sister of the king.
(49) 1 mina of silver for the purchase of 1 mar-tu dagger (decorated with) gold for the king.
(50) 3;20 minas of silver in exchange for 40 shekels of gold for 1 plaque for Kuntisu of the city of Ursaʾum.
(51) 3;20 minas of silver in exchange for 40 shekels of gold for 1 plaque for Enna-malik, (son) of Il-damu.
(52) 3;20 minas of silver in exchange for 40 shekels of gold for [1] pl[aque for …] (who) resided in the city of Mari.

21. šu-bal-ak
ŠA.PI gín DILMUN kù-gi [1] d[ib]
23. [ ]
tuš-LÚ×TIL
XVII. 1. *Ma-rí*$^{ki}$

(53)
8 gín DILMUN kù:babbar
3. níĝ-ba
NE-NE
5. *Ma-rí*$^{ki}$

(54)
5 gín DILMUN kù:babbar
7. 3 *zú-zú-ba-tum*
*I-bí-zi-kir*

(55)
9. TAR 3 3 NI gín DILMUN kù:babbar
šu-bal-ak
11. 6 2 NI gín DILMUN kù-gi 2 *gú-li-lum*
níĝ-ba
13. $^{d}$*Àš-da-bíl*

(56)
6 2 NI gín DILMUN kù:babbar
15. 2 *gú-li-lum*
$^{d}$*Am-ma-rí-ig*

(57)
17. 2 gín DILMUN kù:babbar
2 *mu-ḫar-šu*
19. en

(58)
26 ma-na kù:babbar
21. kin$_5$-ak
40 íb-lá 40 ĝír-kun
23. 6 ma-na ŠA.PI gín DILMUN
kù:babbar
[kin$_5$-ak]
25. [20 lá-2 *g*]*ú-li-lum* ŠÚ+ŠA-ŠÚ+ŠA

r. I. 1. 6 ma-na ŠA.PI gín DILMUN
kù:babbar
šu-bal-ak
3. 1 ma-na ŠÚ+ŠA gín DILMUN kù-g[i]
nu$_{11}$-za-*sù*
5. lú ĝuruš-ĝuruš
SA.ZA$_x$$^{ki}$
7. in-na-sum

(59)
TAR 3 gín DILMUN 3 NI kù:babbar
9. šu-bal-ak
6 gín DILMUN 2 NI kù-gi 2 *gú-li-lum*
11. níĝ-ba
$^{d}$*Ku-ra*

(60)
13. 15 ma-na kù:babbar
kin$_5$-ak
15. 3 ĜIŠ-šú 3 níĝ-bànda
lú diri
17. lú šu-šu
kas$_4$-kas$_4$

(61)
19. 8 ma-na TAR kù:babbar
níĝ-sa$_{10}$
21. 13 aktum-TÚG
⸢*wa*⸣
23. 35 *ʾà-da-u*[*m*]-TÚG-I
II. 1. 1 zara$_6$-TÚG
3 *mi-at* 13 íb+III-TÚG gùn
3. 60 siki na$_4$ *Ma-rí*$^{ki}$
2 gín DILMUN kù:babbar
5. níĝ-sa$_{10}$
1 ĜIŠ-*ba-rí-zú* ĜIŠ.GAM.GAM.GAM
7. 1 ma-na 8 gín DILMUN kù:babbar
níĝ-sa$_{10}$
9. 1 *mi-at* 50 ĜIŠ-ti-ḪAR
*wa*
11. níĝ-NE
*Wa-ba-rúm*

(53) 8 shekels of silver: gift for NENE of the city of Mari.
(54) 5 shekels of silver for 3 … (*zu-zu-ba-tum*) for Ibbi-zikir.
(55) 33 shekels (and) 3 NI of silver in exchange for 6 shekels (and) 2 NI of gold for 2 bracelets: gift for the god Ašdabil.
(56) 6 shekels (and) 2 NI of silver for 2 bracelets: gift for the god Ammarik.
(57) 2 shekels of silver for 2 … (*mu-ḫar-šu*) for the king.
(58) 26 minas of silver for making 40 belts (and) 40 dagger pendants; 6;40 minas of silver [for making 18 br] acelets of 20 (shekels) each; 6;40 minas of silver in exchange for 1;20 minas of gol[d] for their lamination: given to the men of the Palace.
(59) 33 shekels (and) 3 NI of silver in exchange for 6 shekels (and) 2 NI of gold for 2 bracelets: gift for the god Kura.
(60) 15 minas of silver for making 3 GIŠ-šú vessels (and) 3 níg-bànda vessels, in addition, for the hands of the messengers.
(61) 8;30 minas of silver for the purchase of 49 garments, 313 kilts (and) 60 stone weights of wool from the city of Mari; 2 shekels of silver for the purchase of 1 picket for a wheel; 1;08 minas of silver for the purchase of 150 GIŠ-ti-ḪAR-wood and … (níg-NE): Wabarum has received; 44 shekels of silver for the purchase of 9 black bags (and) 4 red bags: at the market of the god Ašdabil and at the market of the city of Šiʾam and at the m[arket] of the god Hadda.

13. šu-ba$_4^!$-ti$^!$(ŠU.BAL.AK)
ŠA.PI 4 gín DILMUN kù:babbar
15. níĝ-sa$_{10}$
10 lá-1 *gàr-su* ĝi$_6$
17. 4 *gàr-su* si$_4$-si$_4$
ki:lam$_7$
19. $^d$*Áš-da-bíl*
*wa*
21. ki:lam$_7$
*Ši-ʾà-am*$^{ki}$
23. *wa*
k[i:lam$_7$]
25. $^{dʾ}$*À-da*

(62)

III. 1. [x gín] ⌜DILMUN⌝ kù:babbar
kin$_5$-ak
3. 2 *bu*-DI 4 še-šu-tag
níĝ-ba
5. $^d$*Ga-na-na*
ĜIŠ.DUG.DU
7. maḫ

(63)

1 ma-na kù:babbar
9. šu-bal-ak
12 gín DILMUN kù-gi
11. *ni-zi-mu*
*ga-ma-a-tum*
13. ĝír mar-tu
10 gín DILMUN kù:babbar
15. *zi-ba-du*
ĝír mar-tu
17. lú *áš-du*
*A-la-ga*$^{ki}$
19. šu-ba$_4$-ti
*wa*
21. in-na-sum
SA.ZA$_x^{ki}$

(64)

23. 2 ma-na 15 gín DILMUN kù:babbar
šu-bal-ak
25. ŠÚ+ŠA 7 gín DILMUN kù-gi
*ni-zi-mu*

IV. 1. [ ]
[1 dib]
3. 1 ma-na
2 dib 50 50
5. 7 dib ŠA.PI-ŠA.PI
3 dib TAR-TAR
7. 1 dib ŠÚ+ŠA 5 gín DILMUN
1 dib ŠÚ+ŠA
9. 1 ma-na kù:babbar
*ni-zi-mu*
11. 10 lá-3 *gú-li-lum* ŠA.PI kù:babbar-gi-II
*wa*
13. 4 *gú-li-lum* TAR kù:babbar-gi
*wa*
15. 16 *gú-li-lum* ŠÚ+ŠA-ŠÚ+ŠA kù:babbar-gi-II
*wa*
17. 3 *gú-li-lum* 10 kù:babbar-gi-I
4 ma-na ŠA.PI gín DILMUN kù:babbar
19. šu-bal-ak
56 gín DILMUN kù-gi
21. *ni-zi-mu*

V. 1. [(ca. 4 lines)]
5$^?$. *ni-zi-mu*
nu$_{11}$-za
7. 11 *gú-li-lum* TAR a-gar$_5$-gar$_5$ kù-gi
*wa*
9. 10 *gú-li-lum* 15 a-gar$_5$-gar$_5$ kù-gi
8 gín DILMUN kù:babbar
11. ZU.PIRIĜ-*sù*
TAR 2 kù:babbar
13. *ni-zi-mu*
16 íb-lá 16 ĝír-kun
15. *wa*
1 á-MUŠEN kù:babbar
17. 12 gín DILMUN kù-gi
*ni-zi-mu*
19. 3 *gú-li-lum* a-gar$_5$ kù:babbar TAR-II
*wa*
21. 3 *gú-li-lum* a-gar$_5$-gar$_5$ kù:babbar 15-I
2 gín DILMUN an-na
23. šub *si-in*

(62) [x shekels] of silver for making 2 toggle-pins (and) 4 … (še-šu-tag): gift for Ganana (on the occasion of) the great presentation.

(63) 1 mina of silver in exchange for 12 shekels of gold for decorating the knobs of mar-tu daggers; 10 shekels of silver for the handles of mar-tu daggers, received from the city of Alaga and given to the Palace.

(64) 2;15 minas of silver in exchange for 27 shekels of gold for decorating […] [1 plaque] of 1 mina, 2 plaques of 50 (shekels) each, 7 plaques of 40 (shekels) each, 3 plaques of 30 (shekels) each, 1 plaque of 25 (shekels), 1 plaque of 20 (shekels); 1 mina of silver for decorating 7 double bracelets of 40 (shekels of) silver (and) gold each, and 4 bracelets of 30 (shekels of) silver (and) gold each, and 16 double bracelets of 20 (shekels of) silver (and) gold each, and 3 single bracelets of 10 (shekels of) silver (and) gold each; 4;40 minas of silver in exchange for 56 shekels of gold for decorating […] for decorating with lamination 11 bracelets of 30 (shekels of) copper (and) gold each, and 10 bracelets of 15 (shekels of) copper (and) gold each; 8 shekels of silver for their hangers; 32 (shekels of) silver for decorating 16 belts (and) 16 dagger pendants and 1 á-MUŠEN helmet of silver; 12 shekels of gold for decorating 3 double bracelets of 30 (shekels of) copper (and) silver, and 3 single bracelets of 15 (shekels of) copper (and) silver; 2 shekels of tin to be melted for decorating […]. 37 shekels of gold for decorating with lamination a mar-tu dagger: (all this) for the men of the Palace.

*ni-zi-mu*
VI. 1. [(ca. 6 lines)]
7?. TAR 7 gín DILMUN kù-gi
*ni-zi-mu*
9. nu$_{11}$-za ĝír mar-tu
ĝuruš-ĝuruš
11. SA.ZA$_{x}^{ki}$

(65)
2 gín DILMUN kù:babbar
13. *maš-da-ù*
dumu-nita
15. *Nu-ru$_{12}$-ud*

(66)
4 gín DILMUN an-na
17. šub *si-in*
ŠÚ+ŠA 4 gín DILMUN a-gar$_5$-gar$_5$
19. kin$_5$-ak
4 šu-i
21. ŠÚ+ŠA 2 ½ gín DILMUN kù:babbar
šu-bal-ak
23. 4 ½ gín DILMUN kù-gi
nu$_{11}$-za-*sù*
25. en

(67)
1 ma-na 15 gín DILMUN kù:babbar
27. šu-bal-ak
VII. 1. [15 gín DILMUN kù-gi]
[ ]
3. [ ]
[1 ma-na kù:babbar]
5. [2 *bu*-DI]
15 gín DILMUN kù:babbar
7. šu-bal-ak
3 gín DILMUN kù-gi
9. nu$_{11}$-za 2 saĝ-*sù*
ì-ĝiš-saĝ
11. *Ti-šè-li-im*
*Ì-mar*$^{ki}$

(68)
13. 1 ma-na kù:babbar
níĝ-sa$_{10}$ 1 ĝír mar-tu kù-gi
15. en
5 gín DILMUN kù:babbar
17. kin$_5$-ak
3 *zú-zú-ba-tum*
19. en

(69)
15 gín DILMUN kù:babbar
21. 1 nu$_{11}$-za *ḫa-bù*
ŠÚ+ŠA gín DILMUN kù:babbar
23. *ʾa$_5$-na-gu*
si 2 gud
25. nídba
VIII. 1. [en]
[$^{d}$*ʾÀ-da*]
3. [*in*]
[$^{d}$AMA-*ra*]

(70)
5. [x kù:babbar]
[níĝ-ba]
7. *Bar*-NE-⌜*um*⌝
*Wa-ru$_{12}$-tum*
9. $^{d}$Utu-*a-ba$_4$*
*Šu-ì*
11. *Ag-ga*
*Ma-rí*$^{ki}$

(71)
13. 2 ma-na TAR kù:babbar
šu-bal-ak
15. TAR kù-gi 1 íb-lá 1 *si-ti-tum* 1 ĝír-kun
lú en
17. sikil
$^{d}$*ʾÀ-da*
19. *al$_6$*
tu-ra
21. *I-bí-zi-kir*

(72)
5 gín DILMUN kù:babbar
23. *ni-zi-mu*
2 ĜIŠ-du
25. dam en
*ʾÀ-za-an*$^{ki}$

(65) 2 shekels of silver for the … (*maš-da-ù*) for the son of Nurut.
(66) 4 shekels of tin to be melted with 24 shekels of copper for making 4 šu-i vessels; 22 ½ shekels of silver in exchange for 4 ½ shekels of gold for their lamination, for the king.
(67) 1;15 minas of silver in exchange for [15 shekels of gold …]; [1 mina of silver for 2 toggle-pins]; 15 shekels of silver in exchange for 3 shekels of gold for plating their 2 heads, for the purification rite of Tiša-lim of the city of Imar.
(68) 1 mina of silver for the purchase of 1 mar-tu dagger (decorated with) gold for the king; 5 shekels of silver for making 3 … (*zú-zú-batum*) for the king.
(69) 15 shekels of silver for plating 1 mace; 20 shekels of silver for the circular stand of the (4) horns of 2 bulls: offering [of the king for the god Hadda, at the AMA-ra (festival)].
(70) [x silver: gift] for BarNEum, Warutum, Utu-aba, Šuʾi, (and) Agga of the city of Mari.
(71) 2;30 minas of silver in exchange for 30 (shekels of) gold for 1 belt, 1 sheath (and) 1 dagger pendant for the king (given for) the purification rite to the god Hadda, in relation to the illness of Ibbi-zikir.
(72) 5 shekels of silver for decorating 2 foot rings for the spouse of the king of the city of ʾAzan.

(73)
27. 15 gín DILMUN kù:babbar
níĝ-sa$_{10}$ 1 ĝír mar-tu *ba-du*[-*u*$_4$] kù-g[i]
IX. 1. [(ca. 5 lines)]

(74)
[x kù:babbar]
7$^{?}$. [1$^{?}$ í]b-lá [1 g]ír-kun
[2] ma-na [TAR] kù:[babbar]
9. [šu-bal-]ak
TAR kù-gi nu$_{11}$-za-*sù*
11. *Ig-na-da-ar*
lú *Mi-ga-ì*
13. *Ti-ti-nu*
šu-mu-tak$_4$
15. *in* ud
ḫúl-*sù*

(75)
17. 1 ma-na kù:babbar
kin$_5$-ak
19. 3 *gú-li-lum* ŠÚ+ŠA-ŠÚ+ŠA-II
1 ma-na TAR kù:babbar
21. šu-bal-ak
18 gín DILMUN kù-gi
23. nu$_{11}$-za-*sù*
lul-gu-ak
25. 3 *gú-li-lum*
X. 1. [(ca. 8 lines)]

(76)
9$^{?}$. [ ] ŠÚ+ŠA g[ín] DI[LMUN] kù:babbar
níĝ-kaskal
11. *Bù-gal-lu*
*Ba-zi-mu*$^{ki}$
13. DU.DU
*si-in*
15. *Ar-mi*$^{ki}$

(77)
TAR kù:babbar
17. šu-bal-ak
6 gín DILMUN kù-gi
19. lul-gu-ak
1 zi-bar
21. en
*ša-ti*
23. sikil
$^{d}$ʾ*A*$_5$-*da*-"*bal*"
25. *Lu-ba-an*$^{ki}$

(78)
3 gín DILMUN an-na
27. šub *si-in*
18 gín DILMUN a-gar$_5$-gar$_5$
29. [kin$_5$-]ak
XI. 1. [(ca. 9 lines)]

(79)
10$^{?}$. [ -]ak
11. al$_6$-tuš
$^{d}$*A-la*
13. *Gú-šè-bù*$^{ki}$

(80)
15 gín DILMUN kù:babbar
15. níĝ-ba
*Da-ti*
17. 8 gín DILMUN kù:babbar
níĝ-ba
19. *Daš-na*
3 gín DILMUN kù:babbar
21. *A-rí-su*
lú u$_5$
23. *Ma-rí*$^{ki}$

(81)
5 ma-na kù:babbar
25. šu-bal-ak
1 ma-na kù-gi
27. al$_6$-du$_{11}$-ga
lugal
XII. 1. [(ca. 8 lines)]

(82)
9$^{?}$. 1 á-MUŠEN
*wa*
11. 2 ĝír-kun
zabar
13. 3 ma-na 5 kù:babbar

(73) 15 shekels of silver for the purchase of 1 *b.* mar-tu dagger (decorated with) gol[d …].
(74) [x silver for 1 b]elt (and) [1 dagger p]endant; [2;30] minas of sil[ve]r [in exchan]ge for 30 (shekels) of silver for its lamination for Igna-dar, (son) of Miga-i(l), Titinu has handed over on the occasion of his feast.
(75) 1 mina of silver for making 3 double bracelets of 20 (shekels) each; 1;30 minas of silver in exchange for 18 shekels of gold for their lamination, as replacement of 3 bracelets […].
(76) [x+]20 sh[ekels] of silver: travel provision for Bugallu of the city of Bazimu, (who) went to the city of Armi.
(77) 30 (shekels of) silver in exchange for 6 shekels of gold, as replacement of 1 zi-bar goblet for the king that (he gave for) the purification rite to the god ʾAdabal of the city of Luban.
(78) 3 shekels of tin to be melted with 18 shekels of copper [for mak]ing […].
(79) […] (that) lies by the god Ala of the city of Gušebu.
(80) 15 shekels of silver: gift for Dati; 8 shekels of silver: gift for Dašna; 3 shekels of silver: (gift for) Arisu, (who are) couriers of the city of Mari.
(81) 5 minas of silver in exchange for 1 mina of gold, requested by the king [of the city of Mari].
(82) […] for 1 á-MUŠEN helmet and 2 dagger pendants of bronze; 3;05 minas of silver and …

wa
15. *ru*$_{12}$*-du-ga-ti-sa-nu*
TAR.TAR

(83)
17. 50 gín DILMUN kù:babbar
níĝ-sa$_{10}$
19. 1 *mi-at* íb+III-TÚG gùn
ki:lam$_7$
21. *gi-ba-i*

(84)
5 ma-na kù:babbar
23. šu-bal-ak
1 ma-na kù-gi 1 dib
25. *Ga-t*[*i*]
[ ]
XIII. 1. [(ca. 13 lines)]

(85)
14?. [20 ma-na kù:b]abbar
15. šu-bal-ak
4 ma-na kù-gi
17. 1 dib
2 *gú-li-lum*
19. *I-bí-zi-kir*

(86)
2 ma-na 5 gín DILMUN kù:babbar
21. šu-bal-ak
ŠÚ+ŠA 5 gín DILMUN kù-gi
XIV. 1. [(ca. 12 lines)]

(87)
13?. dumu-nit[a]
en
15. *si-in*
É×PAP

(88)
17. 2 gín DILMUN kù:babbar
nam-kud-nam-kud
19. en
*Ì-ra-ar*$^{ki}$
21. é
$^d$*Ku-ra*
23. (blank)
XV–XVI. (blank)

(89)[e)]
XVII. 1. [AN.ŠÈ.GÚ x *mi-at* x ma-na x kù:babbar]
⸢è⸣
3. DIŠ m[u]
úš
5. *Ib-rí-um*
*ap*
7. 4 *mi-at* [ma-n]a [x kù:babbar]
[al$_6$-ĝál]
9. [é siki]

*a*) fragment *ARET* III 433 II; *b*) three lines now missing; *c*) fragment X; *d*) fragment *ARET* III 433 II; *e*) fragment *ARET* III 436.

(83) 50 shekels of silver for the purchase of 100 kilts, at the market of the *gibalu*.
(84) 5 minas of silver in exchange for 1 mina of gold for 1 plaque for Gat[i …].
(85) [20 minas of sil]ver in exchange for 4 minas of gold for 1 plaque (and) 2 bracelets for Ibbi-zikir.
(86) 2;05 minas of silver in exchange for 25 shekels of gold […].
(87) […] for the funerary rite of a son of the king.
(88) 2 shekels of silver for the oaths of the king of the city of Irar in the temple of the god Kura.
(89) [Total: x minas of silver]: expenditure in the year of the death of Ibrium, and also 400;[xx min]as [of silver are present in the Treasury].

## Commentary

This document is dated to the year of minister Ibrium's death (Ibr. 18): DIŠ mu úš *Ib-rí-um*. It opens, as usual, with the registration of the expenditures of 1 mina (470 g) of silver for the renewal rite concerning the city-god Kura which fell at the beginning of the new year. Tinib-dulum, a sister of the king, received 8;30 minas (3.995 kg) of silver in her function as priestess of the god ᵓAdabal (§ 2).

Ibrium died around the middle of the year, and the silver expended at that time amounted to 179 minas (84.13 kg), (§ 39). The registrations from § 40 onward concern the expenditures from the months in which Ibbi-zikir replaced his father as minister (the purification rite performed by Ibbi-zikir, by king's mother, and by the priestess Tinib-dulum, are registered in §§ 46, 47, 48).

The total of the "expended", è, silver is not preserved. The silver "present", al$_6$-ĝál, in the Treasury amounted to 400;[x] minas (188.[x] kg), (§ 89).

The king received two buckles of 3 shekels (22 g) of gold for his two donkeys (§ 12), and a battle-axe decorated with gold (§ 14). 1 shekel of gold was expended for the bridles of the donkeys, and another four shekels for the decoration on the wheels of his chariot (total 39 g), (§ 32). Another expenditure for the king and Ibrium (only partially preserved) is registered in § 34. The king also received a dagger decorated with gold of the value of 1 mina (470 g) of silver (§ 49). Four šu-i vessels, for which 24 shekels (188 g) of copper and 4 shekels (31 g) of tin (11.32 %) were employed, were decorated with 4 ½ shekels (34 g) of gold (§ 66). The king received another dagger decorated with gold, of the value of 1 mina (470 g) of silver and 3 *zú-zú-ba-tum* for which 5 shekels (39 g) of silver were needed (§ 68).

The king's mother received four buckles for which 7 shekels (55 g) of silver and 6 shekels (47 g) of gold were employed (§ 13).

Ibrium received new bridles and four buckles for them, which needed 4 shekels (31 g) of gold, and some other element for his chariot (§ 11), despite the fact that he had been "ill", tu-ra, since the previous year, when an offering was dedicated to the god ᵓAdabal of Luban (no. 20 § 40). Ibrium made offerings to the gods Sanugar, Adaranu, and Hadda (§§ 16, 22, 24); in particular a "purification rite", sikil, was performed by him to the god Hadda, either at Ebla or at Ḫalab. The bridles with a buckle belonging to Hadda's chariot, together with his battle-axe, were renewed, employing 32 shekels (251 g) of gold, 20 shekels (157 g) of copper, and 3 shekels (23 g) of tin (§ 26). All in vain, as his demise was imminent. A frog decoration for another one of Ibrium's belt needed 1 ¼ shekels (10 g) of gold (§ 33), and another object was given to the king and the minister (§ 34).

The equipment for Ibrium's "funerary rite", é×pap, is registered in § 44. The bridles for two animals, with four buckles (to be deposited in the grave), and the decorations on the wheels needed 1 mina (470 g) of gold. A hook (ĝiš-zú) and three silver elements (*zú-zú-ba-tum*) for the chariot were added. Ibrium was buried like a warrior who would charge onto the battlefield with his chariot, as he had done his whole life, and his corpse, therefore, received all the trappings of a warrior: a belt with a sheath and pendant, and a plaque, of 2 minas (940 g) of gold; a helmet of 40 shekels (313 g) of silver; a dagger decorated with gold of the value of 1 mina (470 g) of silver; a *ma-da-a-um* of 30 shekels (235 g) of gold, and another one of 30 shekels of silver; and a frog of 6 shekels (47 g) of gold. He held two vessels in his hands, 1 ĝiš-šú 1 níĝ-bànda lú 2 šu, of 5 minas (2.35 kg) of silver. One presumably added also an object (in lacuna) which Kešdut, the spouse of Igriš-Ḫalab, had at its time "handed over" šu-mu-$tak_4$, to him.[1] His funerary chariot, pulled by a donkey, had a single bridle with one buckle: these and the two wheels were decorated with 15 shekels (124 g) of gold.

Ibbi-zikir, Ibrium's son and successor, received a belt decorated with 40 shekels (313 g) of gold for his "purification rite", ì-ĝiš-sag (§ 46). The king's mother and Tinib-dulum, his sister and priestess of ᵓAdabal of Luban, received two toggle-pins each, respectively of 1 mina (470 g) and 20 shekels (157 g) of gold, for the same purpose (§§ 47, 48). Tiša-lim, the queen of Imar (an Eblaite princess), also celebrated a purification rite for the death of Ibrium, receiving a piece of jewelry with 15 shekels (117 g) of gold, along with two toggle pins of 1 mina (470 g) of silver with heads decorated with 3 shekels (24 g) of gold (§ 67).

Ibbi-zikir also received 3 *zú-zú-ba-tum* of 5 shekels (39 g) for his chariot (§ 54). Having become ill, the king made an offering to the god Hadda of a belt with 30 shekels (235 g) of gold (§ 71). He received also a plaque and two bracelets of 4 minas (1.88 kg) of gold as well, presumably when he was appointed minister (§ 85).

An "offering of the oil, nídba ì-ĝiš, was performed at Ebla, and a similar rite was presumably celebrated at Mari, which closed a military confrontation. Thirty shekels (235 g) of silver were given to Arrum, the chief of the Mari delegation, and 20 shekels (157 g) to each of the other two envoys: Misuwadu and Enna-Dagan, while the Elders of Mari received 1;30 minas (705 g), (§ 40). The value of the garments provided by a certain Zuban, related to the campaign against Mari is registered in § 43.

1 On the identity of Kešdut, spouse of Irkab-damu, see Archi 2021b, pp.18 nt. 25, 30 nt. 43.

An Eblaite official, who "had resided" in Mari (presumably for sealing the peace), received a plaque of 40 shekels (313 g) of gold (§ 52), and NE-NE of Mari received 8 shekels (63 g) of silver (§ 53). A gift of silver (whose amount is not preserved) was given to five envoys from Mari: BarNEum, Warutum, ᵈUtu-aba, Šuʾì, and Agga (§ 70). Three "couriers", $u_5$, from Mari: Dati, Dašna, and Arisu, received respectively 15 (117 g), 8 (63 g), and 3 shekels (23 g) of silver (§ 80).

Two envoys from Saggar (in Nagar's territory) came to Ebla in some capacity related to the "military expedition (níg-$kas_4$) of Tuttul" (§ 6). One has to understand that Mari had moved against the Ḫabur region, which was controlled by Nagar. At this point, Ebla came to the aid of Nagar, its ally as a consequence of the treaty of year Ibr. 16 (see the commentary to text no. 19). A clash took place near Tuttul, and peace rapidly followed (see Archi 2021a, pp. 192, 194).

§ 6. Expenditure of 7 shekels (55 g) of silver for two men from Saggar (a city south of Nagar) "who had travelled (to join) the military expedition by Tuttul", kaskal níĝ-$kas_4$ *Du-du-lu*$^{ki}$

§ 8. Ibbi-zikir presented a gift (in lacuna) for Titinu, a "representative", maškim, of his father Ibrium.

§ 9. A belt decorated with 30 shekels (235 g) of gold was given for the "funerary rite", É×PAP, of Zaburum, an official mentioned in several annual documents of Ibrium (see the Index).

§ 10. Expenditure of metals for the bridles and parts of the chariot of Ibbi-zikir.

§ 18. The spouse of the "minister", *ba-da-lum*, of Ḫarran received two toggle-pins of 20 shekels (157 g) of silver for her "purification rite", ì-ĝiš-sag, presumably for the death of her husband.

§ 20. Purchase of oil for the city of Alaga.

§ 21. A plaque of 30 shekels (235 g) of gold was sent to Irba-damu, king of Utig.

§ 37. Expenditure of 15 shekels (117 g) of silver for the purchase of sixty kilts for the "servants", $ir_{11}$-$ir_{11}$.

§ 41. Išar, a man from Ḫalab, was ransomed from Misuwadu of Mari for 20 shekels (157 g) of silver.

§ 43. Purchase of 14 tunics and 48 mantles for the military expedition against Mari.

§ 50. Kuntisu, an important official from Ursaʾum, received a plaque of 40 shekels (313 g) of gold. According to *ARET* XIV 77 §§ 32–33 (year I.Z. 01), he delivered 1;55 minas (801 g) of silver, and an unnamed official delivered other 28 shekels (219 g).

§ 58. Forty belts of 26 minas (12.22 kg) of silver, and eighteen bracelets were distributed to the "men", ĝuruš-ĝuruš, of the Palace. The bracelets needed 6;40 minas (3.133 kg) of silver, together with 1;20 minas (627 g) of gold for their plating.

§ 60. 15 shekels (117 g) of silver for three ĜIŠ-šú and three níĝ-bànda vessels for the "hands of the messengers", lú šu-šu $kas_4$-$kas_4$.

§ 63. Expenditure of 12 shekels (94 g) of gold and ten shekels (78 g) of silver for the decoration of daggers first deposited to the city of Alaga and later brought to the Palace.

§ 64. Expenditures of gold and silver for fifteen plaques, more of fifty-seven bracelets, belts, helmets, and a dagger for the "men", ĝuruš-ĝuruš, of the Palace.

§§ 65, 72. Expenditure of 2 shekels (16 g) of silver for weaving the *maš-da-ù* of the new-borne son of Nurut, a spouse of the king who resided in the city of ʾAzan (*ARET* VIII rev. II 9–10). A similar passage is *ARET* I 15 § 13: *in* ud *maš-da-ù* dumu-nita-*sù* (see Archi 2021b, pp. 15–19). According to § 72, this "spouse of the king" received a pair of a jewel decorated with 5 shekels (39 g) of silver on the occasion of this birth.

## 22
(Plates XLII–XLIII)

(1)
o. I. [(ca. 4 lines in lacuna)]
5?. [e]n(?)
[ ]

(2)
7. [x m]a-[n]a [x gín DILMUN kù-gi]
gù-kak-gíd
9. dam-dam
en
11. ⸢*wa*⸣?
II. 1. [ ]
géme-gi

(3)
3. 4 ma-na kù-gi
[6] níĝ-anše-[a]k
5. 12 kù[-sal]
BAR.AN-BAR.AN
7. TAR kù-gi
2 ma-na kù:babbar
9. lú é siki

(4)
14 ma-na kù-gi
11. 10[+x] ma-[n]a kù:babbar
III. 1. [ ]
*Ar-*$ru_{12}$*-gúm*
3. *En-na-*BAD
*I-gi*
5. *Sá-gú-s*[*i*]
[ ]

(5)
7. [x ma-na kù-gi]
24 ma-n[a] kù:babbar
9. [ ]-⸢x⸣
*Ḫal-za-um*

(6)
11. 1 ma-na ŠA.PI gín DILMUN kù-gi
IV. 1. 10+⸢3⸣ ma-na 1[+x gín DILMUN kù:babbar]
*En-na-il*

(7)
3. 2 ma-na TAR 8 gín DILMUN kù-gi
17 ma-na 10 gín DILMUN kù:babbar
5. ká
*Ga-nu-lum*

(8)
7. 72 ma-na <kù:babbar>
V. 1. lú diĝir-diĝir-diĝir

(9)
[x] ma-⸢na⸣ 55 gín DILMUN kù:babbar
3. lú *En-na-ì*
di-kud

(10)
5. AN.ŠÈ.GÚ 54 ma-na 3 gín DILMUN kù-gi
1 *mi-at* 70 lá-2 ma-na ŠA.PI 5 gín DILMUN kù:babbar lú
VI. 1. *Ar-mi*$^{ki}$
in-na-sum
3. *in* ud
šu-mu-níĝin
5. SA.ZA$_{x}^{ki}$

(11)
ŠÚ+ŠA 5 gín DILMUN kù-gi 1 dib
7. *Ib-du-ma-lik*
lú *Bù-a-du*

(1) [… the ki]ng […].
(2) [x;xx m]i[n]a(s) [of gold] for neckbands for the spouses of the king and […] for the enclosed women.
(3) 4 minas of gold for [6] bridles (and) 12 buc[kles] for the mules; 30 (shekels of) gold (and) 2 minas of silver for the Treasury.
(4) 14 minas of gold (and) 10[+x] mi[n]as of silver […] for Arrukum, Enna-BAD, Igi, Sagus[i] […].
(5) [x minas of gold] (and) 24 min[as] of silver […] for Ḫalzaum.
(6) 1;40 mina of gold (and) 13;01[+x] minas [of silver] for Enna-il.
(7) 2;38 minas of gold (and) 17;10 minas of silver for the gate of Ganulum.
(8) 72 minas <of silver> for the gods.
(9) [x];55 minas of silver for Enna-i(l), the judge.
(10) Total: 54;03 minas of gold (and) 168;45 minas of silver that the city of Armi had given, on the occasion of a *journey* to the Palace.
(11) 25 shekels of gold for 1 plaque for Ibdu-malik, (son) of Buadu.

(12)
9. ŠÚ+ŠA 6 gín DILMUN kù-gi 1 dib
*ʾÀ-bí*
11. lú NI-BAD

(13)
ŠA.PI
VII. 1. [gín DILMUN kù-gi]
1 ⌜dib⌝
3. *Du-bí-zi-kir*
lú *Puzur$_4$-ra-ì*
5. lú É×PAP
en-en

(14)
7. 1 ma-na kù-gi 1 dib
*Ar-ru$_{12}$-gúm*
9. ì-na-sum
*Bur-ḫa-áš*

(15)
11. 50 gín DILMUN kù-gi 1 dib
VIII. 1. [...]
⌜i$_3$-na⌝-sum
3 *Ib-lu$_5$-zú*

(16)
1 ma-na kù-gi 1 dib
5. *En-na-*BAD
ì-na-sum
7. *In-ma-lik*
*ap*
9. ŠA.PI gín DILMUN kù-gi 1 dib
*In-ma-lik*
11. ì-na-sum
IX. 1. *I-za-iš-lu*

(17)
TAR kù-gi 1 dib
3. *Sá-gú-si*
ì-na-sum
5. *En-na-il*
lú *I-da-ni-ki-mu*

(18)
7. ŠÚ+ŠA gín DILMUN kù-gi 1 dib
*En-na-il*
9. lú *Iš-da-al$_6$*

(19)
r. I. 1. 10 gín DILMUN kù-gi 1 dib
*Nu-ba-an*$^{ki}$
3. maškim
*Sa-li-im*
5. tuš-LÚ×TIL
*in*
7. *Ar-mi*$^{ki}$

(20)
1 ma-na kù-gi sikil
9. $^{d}$*ʾÀ-da*

(21)
5 ma-na kù-gi
11. kin$_5$-ak$^!$(GÚG)
10 *gú-li-lum*
II. 1. ŠÚ+ŠA-II
*wa*
3. 10 *gú-li-lum* 10-I
1 ma-na kù-gi
5. nu$_{11}$-za-*sù*
10 *gú-li-lum* a-gar$_5$-gar$_5$ esi-II
7. *wa*
10 *gú-li-lum* a-gar$_5$-gar$_5$ 10 esi-I
9. ŠA.PI gín DILMUN kù-gi
nu$_{11}$-za-*sù*
III. 1. 10 *gú-li-lum* a-gar$_5$-gar$_5$ ŠÚ+ŠA-II
*wa*
3. 10 *gú-li-lum* a-gar$_5$-gar$_5$ 10-I
1 ma-na kù:babbar
5. nu$_{11}$-za-*sù*
ŠÚ+ŠA 4 gín DILMUN an-na
7. kin$_5$-ak
10 ĝír mar-tu
9. ŠÚ+ŠA gín DILMUN kù:babbar
*ba-du-u$_9$-sù*
IV. 1. lú *in*
šu-mu-níĝin

(12) 26 shekels of gold for 1 plaque for ʾAbi, (son) of NIBAD.
(13) 40 [shekels of gold] for 1 plaque for Dubi-zikir, (son) of Puzurra-i(l), for the funerary rite of the (former) kings.
(14) 1 mina of gold for 1 plaque for Arrukum, given by Burḫaš.
(15) 50 shekels of gold for 1 plaque [for ...] giv]en by Ibluzu.
(16) 1 mina of gold for 1 plaque for Enna-BAD, given by In-malik and also 40 shekels of gold for 1 plaque for In-malik, given by Iza-išlu.
(17) 30 (shekels of) gold for 1 plaque for Sagusi, given by Enna-il, (son) of Idani-kimu.
(18) 20 shekels of gold for 1 plaque for Enna-il, (son) of Išdaʾal.
(19) 10 shekels of gold for 1 plaque for Nuban, representative of Salim, (who) resided in the city of Armi.
(20) 1 mina of gold for a purification rite by the god Hadda.
(21) 5 minas of gold for making 10 double bracelets of 20 (shekels) each, and 10 single bracelets of 10 (shekels) each; 1 mina of gold for their lamination, 10 double bracelets of copper (and) diorite, and 10 single bracelets of 10 (shekels of) copper each (and) diorite; 40 shekels of gold for their lamination, 10 double bracelets of 20 (shekels of) copper each, and 10 single bracelets of 10 (shekels of) copper each; 1 mina of silver for their lamination; 24 shekels of tin for making 10 mar-tu daggers; 20 shekels of silver for their *b.* for the cultic journey of the Palace: supply of Bagama.

3. SA.ZA$_x$$^{ki}$
*Ba-ga-ma*
5. gaba-ru
(blank)

(22)
V. 1. 1 ma-na kù-gi
gù-kak-gíd
3. *Za-ni-ḫi-Ma-rí*$^{ki}$
é-gi
5. *Ib-ᵓà-ra*
*ᵓÀ-šu*$^{ki}$

(23)
7. TAR 4 gín DILMUN kù-gi
1 an-zam$_x$
9. *wa*
1 pad-*sù*
11. *Ib-rí-um*

(24)
[1] ma-na kù-gi
13. nu$_{11}$-za 1 [*ḫa-bù*]
níĝ-ba
VI. 1. $^{d}$BAD *Du-du-lu*$^{ki}$
6 gín DILMUN kù-gi
3. nu$_{11}$-za 1 *ar-ra-sù*
*ḫa-bù*
5. níĝ-ba
$^{d}$*Ga-mi-iš*
7. 7 gín DILMUN kù-gi
nu$_{11}$-za 1 ĜIŠ-ĝidru
9. níĝ-ba
$^{d}$*Ku-ra*
11. *Ib-rí-um*

(25)
6 gín DILMUN kù-gi
13. nu$_{11}$-za 1 [*ar-r*]*a-sù*
VII. 1. *ḫa-bù*
níĝ-ba
3. $^{dᵓ}$*A*$_5$*-da-"bal"*
*ᵓÀ-ma-du*$^{ki}$

(26)
5. ŠA.PI gín DILMUN kù-gi
*ni-zi-mu*
7. 13 dib
*Bù-da-ì*
9. *Íl-a-šar*
*Gal-za-iš-lu*
11. *Ga-du-um*
*Iš-má-da-mu*
13. *Da-da-ì*
⸢x⸣-NE-[x]
VIII. 1. *En-na-ma-lik*
*Ig-rí-iš*
3. *Gur-an-da-mu*
*Ru*$_{12}$*-zi-li-im*
5. *Iš-má-da-ba-an*
*Zé-da-mu*

(27)
7. AN.ŠÈ.GÚ 4 ma-na TAR 3 gín DILMUN kù-gi
è
9. lú mu-DU
*I*[*b-rí-*]*um*
IX. 1. *wa*
tak$_4$
3. kù-gi
É×PAP
5. en-e[n]
[ ]
7. [ ]
[ ]
9. [ ]-⸢x⸣
(blank)

(22) 1 mina of gold for a neckband for Zaneḫi-Mari, daughter-in-law of Ibᵓara of the city of ᵓAšu.
(23) 34 shekels of gold for 1 an-zam$_x$ goblet and its lid for Ibrium.
(24) [1] mina of gold for plating 1 [mace]: gift for the Lord of the city of Tuttul; 6 shekels of gold for plating its handle: gift for the god Kamiš; 7 shekels of gold for plating a scepter: gift for the god Kura by Ibrium.
(25) 6 shekels of gold for plating [the han]dle of a mace: gift for the god ᵓAdabal of the city of ᵓAmadu.
(26) 40 shekels of gold for decorating 13 plaques for Buda-i(l), Ilašar, Galzaišlu, Gadum, Išma-damu, Dada-i(l), …, Enna-malik, Igriš, Guran-damu, Ruzi-lim, Išma-daban (and) Ze-damu.
(27) Total: 4;33 minas of gold: expenditure of the delivery of Ib[ri]um and balance of the gold for the funerary rites of the kin[gs] […].

## Commentary

This document concerns some of the very last "expenditures", è, of silver and gold preceding minister Arrukum's death (he is mentioned in o. III 2, and VII 8), and those of the second part of that year, when Ibrium succeeded him as minister. For these last expenditures, gold that Ibrium himself had "delivered", mu-DU was used, according to the colophon (§ 27).

The mina (470 g) of gold for the mace of the "Lord of Tuttul", that is Dagan, and the 6 shekels (44 g) of gold for covering the handle of the mace of the god Kamiš, together with the 7 shekels (55 g) of gold for the scepter of Kura, the City-god, registered in § 24, must all be interpreted as the offerings that Ibrium dedicated to these gods when he became minister.

The registrations in §§ 1–10 concern the exceptional expenditures of 54;03 minas (26 kg) of gold and 168;45 minas (79.35 kg) of silver "which the city of Armi had given on the occasion of a *journey* to the Palace", at Ebla, lú *Ar-mi*$^{ki}$ in-na-sum *in* ud šu-mu-nígin SA.ZA$_x$$^{ki}$ (§ 10). The term šu-mu-nígin (together with *na*$_x$*-ra-mu*), usually refers to the city of Armi, and has been explained as a "circumambulation" which a delegation of this city used to perform by the Palace of Ebla with a certain regularity; this is well documented at least for the last period of the archives (Archi 2018b, pp, 36–38). These amounts of precious metals may have been given to Ebla in connection to the defeat inflicted on Abarsal by Armi (Archi 2019b, pp. 3–6).

The first delivery is not preserved. The other deliveries concern:

§ 2. [x amount of gold]: for neckbands for the spouses of the king, and other [jewels] for the "enclosed women", géme-gi (cf. ĜÁ×GÉME-gi in *ARET* XX 15 rev. VII 10; LL 1037: ĜÁ×GÉME-gi$_4$ = *a*$_5$*-za-lu-um*, *ʾasārum*).

§ 3. 4 minas (1.88 kg) of gold for three pairs of bridles, and their twelve buckles, besides 30 shekels (235 g) of gold and 2 minas (940 g) of silver, to be kept in the "Treasury", é siki.

§ 4. 14 minas (6.58 kg) of gold and 10[+x] minas of silver for Arrukum and two lords of the period of this minister: Enna-BAD, Sagusi (see the Indices in *ARET* XIV).

§ 7. The "gate" of a certain Ganulum is mentioned.

§ 8. A substantial amount of silver (72 minas, 33.84 kg) was assigned for offerings to the gods, without specifying their names.

§ 9. The judge Enna-i(l), who received an amount of silver, served from the period of Arrukum until the eleventh year of Ibrium (*ARET* XIV, pp. 141, 149).

§ 13. Dubi-zikir, son of Puzura-i(l), received a plaque of 40 shekels (313 g) for a funerary rite celebrated for the former kings (É×PAP en-en); see also § 27.

§ 14. Arrukum received a plaque of gold of 1 mina (470 g) by a certain Burḫaš.

§ 20. 1 mina (470 g) of gold for a purification rite by the god Hadda.

§ 21. 40 bracelets, some in copper, decorated with gold, 20 bracelets decorated with silver, and 10 daggers for the circumambulation of the Palace.

§ 22. A neckband of 1 mina (470 g) of gold for the princess Zaneḫi-Mari, "daughter-in-law", é-gi, of *Ib-ʾà-ra* of *ʾÀ-šu*$^{ki}$. For this lady, see the commentary of text no. 9.

§ 23. A vessel with its lid, of 34 shekels (266 g) of gold, was received by Ibrium

# 23
## (Plates XLIV–XLV)

(1)
o. I. 1. 2 ma-na ŠÚ+ŠA 3 gín DILMUN kù-gi
1 dib maḫ
lú ĜIŠ-ĝidru-ĜIŠ-ĝidru
3. in-na-sum
$^{d}$ʾ*À-da*
5. *Ḫa-lab*$_{x}^{ki}$
*in* AMA-*ra*
II. 1. en
šu-mu-tak$_4$

(2)
3. 6 2 NI gín DILMUN kù-gi
2 *gú-li-lum*
5. níĝ-ba
$^{d}$*Ku-ra*

(3)
7. 2 ma-na kù-gi
nu$_{11}$-za 1 ab
9. é
$^{d}$ʾ*À-da*
III. 1. lú *Lu-ub*$^{ki}$

(4)
6 2 NI gín DILMUN kù-gi
3. 2 *gú-li-lum*
$^{d}$*Aš-da-bíl*

(5)
5. 1 gín DILMUN kù-gi
*ni-zi-mu*
7. 1 pad an-zam$_x$
*Ib-rí-um*

(6)
9. 2 gín DILMUN kù-gi
*ni-zi-mu* <1 dib>
IV. 1. *Ib-ga-il*
*Ḫa-zu-wa-an*$^{ki}$

(7)
3. 1 gín DILMUN kù-gi
*ni-zi-mu*
5. 1 dib *Ib-bí-um*
lú *Iš-má-ga-lu*

(8)
7. 1 ½ gín DILMUN kù-gi
*ni-zi-mu*
9. 1 dib *Íl-zi*
lú *Iš*$_{11}$*-gú-nu*

(9)
V. 1. 1 gín DILMUN kù-gi
*ni-zi-mu*
3. 1 dib *Ar-si-a-ḫa*
lú NI-*na-ad*

(10)
5. 1 ½ gín DILMUN kù-gi
*ni-zi-mu*
7. 1 dib *Ḫu-ma-la*
lú NE-*ša*-LUM

(11)
9. 1 gín DILMUN kù-gi
*ni-zi-mu*
11. 1 dib *Du-bí-zi-kir*
VI. 1. lú *Áš-ba-il*

(12)
1 gín DILMUN kù-gi
3. *ni-zi-mu*
1 dib EN-*da-za*
5. *Maš-bar-rá*$^{ki}$

(13)
1 gín DILMUN kù-gi
7. *ni-zi-mu*
1 dib *A-mi-du*
9. lú *I-bí-um*

(1) 2;23 minas of gold for 1 big plaque (and) the sticks, given to the god Hadda of the city of Ḫalab, at the AMA-ra (festival), the king has handed over.
(2) 6 shekels (and) 2 NI of gold for 2 bracelets: gift for the god Kura.
(3) 2 minas of gold for plating a window for the temple of the god Hadda of the city of Lub.
(4) 6 shekels (and) 2 NI of gold for 2 bracelets: gift for the god Ašdabil.
(5) 1 shekel of gold for decorating 1 lid of an an-zam$_x$ goblet for Ibrium.
(6) 2 shekels of gold for decorating <1 plaque> for Ibga-il of the city of Ḫazuwan.
(7) 1 shekel of gold for decorating 1 plaque for Ibbium, (son) of Išma-galu.
(8) 1 ½ shekel of gold for decorating 1 plaque for Ilzi, (son) of Iš-gunu.
(9) 1 shekel of gold for decorating 1 plaque for Arsi-aḫa, (son) of NInad.
(10) 1 ½ shekel of gold for decorating 1 plaque for Ḫumala, (son) of NEšaLUM.
(11) 1 shekel of gold for decorating 1 plaque for Dubi-zikir, (son) of Ašba-il.
(12) 1 shekel of gold for decorating 1 plaque for ENdaza of the city of Mašbarra.
(13) 1 shekel of gold for decorating 1 plaque for Amidu, (son) of Ibbium.

(14)
1 ½ gín DILMUN kù-gi
11. *ni-zi-mu*
1 dib
VII. 1. *Íl-zi-ma-lik*
lú *A-dur-da-mu*

(15)
3. 1 ½ gín DILMUN kù-gi
*ni-zi-mu*
5. 1 dib *Ir-ba*$_x$*-zé*
lú *Da-si-gú-bù-ru*$_{12}$

(16)
7. ½ gín DILMUN kù-gi
*ni-zi-mu*
9. 1 dib *Íl-ba-ma-lik*
lú *I-gi*
VIII. 1. 1 ½ gín DILMUN kù-gi
*ni-zi-mu*
3. 1 dib *Ig-rí-iš*
šeš-*sù*

(17)
5. 1 gín DILMUN kù-gi
*ni-zi-mu*
7. nu$_{11}$-za 1 íb-lá 1 ĝír-kun
*Du-bí-ab*
9. *Ša-na-ru*$_{12}$*-gú*$^{ki}$

(18)
5 gín DILMUN kù-gi
11. *ni-zi-mu*
maš-maš
IX. 1. 4 íb-lá 1 ĝír-kun maš-maš
ŠÚ+ŠA 8 gín DILMUN kù-gi
3. *ni-zi-mu*
nu$_{11}$-za 2 *gú-li-lum*-II esi ŠA.PI
5. 2 *gú-li-lum*-II esi TAR.TAR
1 *gú-li-lum*-I esi ŠÚ+ŠA
7. 10 lá-1 *gú-li-lum* 10-I esi
ĝuruš-ĝuruš

(19)
X. 1. ŠÚ+ŠA 8 gín DILMUN kù-gi
*ni-zi-mu*
3. nu$_{11}$-za 7 *gú-li-lum*-II esi TAR-TAR
a-gar$_5$ 10 lá-1 *gú-li-lum*-II esi
ŠÚ+ŠA-ŠÚ+ŠA a-gar$_5$
1 *gú-li-lum*-I esi ŠÚ+ŠA a-gar$_5$
5. 2 *gú-li-lum*-I esi 10 a-gar$_5$
ĝuruš-ĝuruš
r. I. 1. SA.ZA$_x$$^{ki}$
*in* ud
3. è
níĝ-kas$_4$
5. *Gú-da-da-núm*$^{ki}$

(20)
1 gín DILMUN kù-gi
7. *zi-du*
*sa-ga-tum*
9. 1 ĝír mar-tu
*Zi-ba-da*

(21)
11. 6 gín DILMUN kù-gi
nu$_{11}$-za 1 *ar-ra-šum*
II. 1. 1 *ḫa-bù*
níĝ-ba
3. $^{d}$ʾ*À-da*
lú *Lu-ub*$^{ki}$
5. *gi*-NI

(22)
6 gín DILMUN kù-gi
7. nu$_{11}$-za 1 *ar-ra-šum*
1 *ḫa-bù*
9. níĝ-ba
$^{d}$ʾ*A*$_5$*-da-"bal"*
11. ʾ*À-ma-du*$^{ki}$
en
13. šu-mu-tak$_4$
III. 1. *in* ud
NI.DU-NI.DU

(14) 1 ½ shekel of gold for decorating 1 plaque for Ilzi-malik, (son) of Adur-damu.
(15) 1 ½ shekel of gold for decorating 1 plaque for Irba-ze, (son) of Dasi-guburu.
(16) ½ shekel of gold for decorating 1 plaque for Ilba-malik, (son) of Igi; 1 ½ shekel of gold for decorating 1 plaque for Igriš, his brother.
(17) 1 shekel of gold for decorating with lamination 1 belt (and) 1 dagger pendant for Dubi-ab of the city of Šanarugu.
(18) 5 shekels of gold for a striped decoration of 4 belts (and) 1 dagger pendant; 28 shekels of gold for decorating with lamination 2 double bracelets of 40 (shekels) each (and) diorite, 2 double bracelets of 30 (shekels) each (and) diorite, 1 single bracelet of 20 (shekels) each (and) diorite, 9 single bracelets of 10 (shekels) each (and) diorite: for the men (of the Palace).
(19) 28 shekels of gold for decorating with lamination 7 double bracelets of 30 (shekels) each (and) diorite (and) copper, 9 double bracelets of 20 (shekels) each (and) diorite (and) copper, 1 single bracelet of 20 (shekels of) copper, 2 single bracelets of 10 (shekels) each (and) diorite (and) copper: for the men of the Palace, on the occasion of the departure to the military expedition (against) the city of Gudadanum.
(20) 1 shekel of gold in alloy for the … (*sa-ga-tum*) of 1 mar-tu dagger for Zibada.
(21) 6 shekels of gold for plating the handle of 1 mace: gift for the god Hadda of the city of Lub, in month IV.
(22) 6 shekels of gold for plating the handle of 1 mace: gift for the god ʾAdabal of the city of ʾAmadu, the king has handed over in month VII.

(23)

3. 19 gín DILMUN kù-gi
*ni-zi-mu*
5. nu$_{11}$-za 1 ĝír mar-tu kù-gi
*wa*
7. *sa-ga-tum*
10 lá-1 gír mar-tu
9. ĝuruš-ĝuruš
*in* ud
11. è
níĝ-kas$_4$
13. *Gú-da-da-núm*$^{ki}$

(24)

IV. 1. 8 gín DILMUN kù-gi
nu$_{11}$-za 5 *gú-li-lum* <1> dib a-gar$_5$
3. *In-gàr*
lú-kar
5. *Ma-nu-wa-ad*$^{ki}$

(25)

6 gín DILMUN kù-gi
7. nu$_{11}$-za 1 *ar-ra-šum*
1 *ḫa-bù*
9. níĝ-ba
$^{d}$*ᵓÀ-da*
11. lú *Ḫa-lab*$_x^{ki}$
*in*
13. iti *ᵓa$_5$-nun*

(26)

V. 1. 1 gín DILMUN kù-gi
*ni-zi-mu*
3. 1 dib *A-ma*-NI
*Ma-nu-wa-ad*$^{ki}$

(27)

5. 2 gín DILMUN kù-gi
*ni-zi-mu*
7. nu$_{11}$-za <1> *gú-li-lum*
*I-lu$_5$-za$_x$-ma-lik* "ur$_4$"

(28)

9. 2 gín DILMUN kù-gi
*ni-zi-mu*
11. 1 dib *I-ib-ma-lik*
VI. 1. šeš
*Du-si-gú*

(29)

3. 2 gín DILMUN kù-gi
*ni-zi-mu*
5. 1 dib *I-bí-zi-kir*
dumu-nita
7. *Ib-rí-um*

(30)

ŠÚ+ŠA gín DILMUN kù-gi
9. nu$_{11}$-za 2 *gú-li-lum*-II esi ŠÚ+ŠA 4 a-gar$_5$ 4 *gú-li-lum*-I esi 15 a-gar$_5$ 3 *gú-li-lum*-
VII. 1. I esi ŠÚ+ŠA a-gar$_5$
1 ma-na kù-gi
3. 2 íb-lá 2 *si-ti-a-tum* 2 ĝír-kun
ME-sig é en
(blank)
VIII. (blank)

(31)

IX 1. AN.ŠÈ.GÚ 8 ma-na 3 gín DILMUN kù-gi
è
3. lú *A-da-bí-ig*$^{ki}$
(blank)

(23) 19 shekels of gold for decorating with lamination 1 mar-tu dagger (decorated with) gold and the … (*sa-ga-tum*) of 9 mar-tu daggers: for the men (of the Palace), on the occasion of the departure to the military expedition (against) the city of Gudadanum.
(24) 8 shekels of gold for plating 5 bracelets (and 1) plaque of copper for Ingar, trader of the city of Manuwat.
(25) 6 shekels of gold for plating the handle of a mace: gift for the god Hadda of the city of Ḫalab, in month VIII.
(26) 1 shekel of gold for decorating 1 plaque for AMANI of the city of Manuwat.
(27) 2 shekels of gold for decorating with lamination <1> bracelet for Iluza-malik, the collector (of goods).
(28) 2 shekels of gold for decorating 1 plaque for Iᵓib-malik, brother of Dusigu.
(29) 2 shekels of gold for decorating 1 plaque for Ibbi-zikir, son of Ibrium.
(30) 20 shekels of gold for plating 2 double bracelets of 24 (shekels) each (and) diorite (and) copper, 4 single bracelets of 15 (shekels) each (and) diorite (and) copper, 3 single bracelets of 20 (shekels) each (and) diorite (and) copper; 1 mina of gold for 2 belts, 2 sheaths (and) 2 dagger pendants: for the watchmen of the king's house.
(31) Total: 8;03 minas of gold: expenditure of the city of Adabik.

## Commentary

This is a registration of expenditures of gold for a total of 8;03 minas (3.86 kg) (§ 31). The document has already been published as *MEE* 7, 27. The "military expedition", níĝ-kas$_4$, against the city of Gudadanum (§§ 19, 23), which is mentioned in the annual text no. 11 § 31, dates this document to the year Ibr. 08.

Seven expenditures of gold were employed for objects dedicated to gods: Hadda of Ḫalab (§§ 1, 25), Kura (§ 2), Hadda of Lub (§§ 3, 21), Ašdabil (§ 4), ᵓAdabal of ᵓAmadu (§ 22).

§ 5. Ibrium received an an-zam$_x$ vessel whose lid was decorated with 1 shekel (8 g) of gold.

§ 18, 19, 23. The "men", ĝuruš-ĝuruš, of the Palace who had taken part in the expedition against Gudadanum received four belts and fourteen bracelets decorated respectively with 5 shekels (39 g) and 28 shekels (219 g) of gold (§ 18); nineteen bracelets decorated with 28 shekels (219 g) of gold (§ 19); and ten daggers which needed 19 shekels (149 g) of gold.

§§ 28, 29 A plaque decorated with 2 shekels (17 g) of gold was given to Iᵓib-malik, brother of the king's mother, and another of the same weight to Ibbi-zikir, son of Ibrium.

§ 30. Nine bracelets of copper decorated with 20 shekels (157 g) of gold and two belts with frogs decorated with 1 mina (470 g.) of gold were assigned to the watchmen of the king's house

The total in § 31 is 8;03 minas (3.75 kg); the sum gives 8;07 ⅓ minas.

List of the gold expenditures:

| | | | | | |
|---|---|---|---|---|---|
| § 1 | 2;23 | | § 18 | 0:05 | |
| § 2 | 0;06 | ⅔ | | 0:28 | |
| § 3 | 2;00 | | § 19 | 0;28 | |
| § 4 | 0:06 | ⅔ | § 20 | 0;01 | |
| § 5 | 0;01 | | § 21 | 0:06 | |
| § 6 | 0;02 | | § 22 | 0:06 | |
| § 7 | 0;01 | | § 23 | 0:19 | |
| § 8 | 0;01 | ½ | § 24 | 0:08 | |
| § 9 | 0;01 | | § 25 | 0:06 | |
| § 10 | 0;01 | ½ | § 26 | 0;01 | |
| § 11 | 0;01 | | § 27 | 0;02 | |
| § 12 | 0:01 | | § 28 | 0:02 | |
| § 13 | 0;01 | | § 29 | 0:02 | |
| § 14 | 0;01 | ½ | § 30 | 1;20 | |
| § 15 | 0;01 | ½ | | | |
| § 16 | 0;02 | | | 8;07 | ⅓ |
| § 17 | 0:01 | | | | |

# 24
(Plates XLVI–XLVII)

(1)

o. I. 1. 2 gín DILMUN kù-gi
nu$_{11}$-za
3. 1 ĝír mar-tu
*Gi-rí*

(2)

5. 2 gín DILMUN kù-gi
*ni-zi-mu*
7. 4 ĝeštu$_{x}$-lá
*Gi-rí*
9. *wa*
*Nap-ḫa-il*
11. *wa*
lul-gu-ak
13. 2 ĝeštu$_{x}$-lá
*Ir-da-mu*
15. dumu-nita
II. 1. *Ib-rí-um*

(3)

4 gín DILMUN kù-gi
3. nu$_{11}$-za 1 ĝír mar-tu
*wa*
5. 2 kù-sal
níĝ-ba
7. $^{d}$*A-na-ma-du*
*Ar-ḫa-du*$^{ki}$
9. *Bù-du-mi*
šu-mu-tak$_{4}$

(4)

11. TAR kù-gi 1 dib
*Ù-zi*
13. šeš
III. 1. *A-zú-ma*
TAR kù-gi 1 dib
3. *Iš*$_{11}$*-ru-ud*
lú *In-ma-lik*
5. tuš-LÚ×TIL
*in*
7. *U*$_{9}$*-ru*$_{12}$$^{ki}$

(5)

1 gín DILMUN kù-gi
9. *ni-zi-mu*
1 dib
11. NI-*ba-il*
lú-kar
13. *Ma-nu-wa-ad*$^{ki}$

(6)

IV. 1. 1 gín DILMUN kù-gi
*ni-zi-mu*
3. nu$_{11}$-za
1 *za-ḫa-da*
5. en

(7)

1 gín DILMUN kù-gi
7. *zi-ba-du*
1 balaĝ maḫ
9. 1 gín DILMUN kù-gi
*ni-zi-mu*
11. nu$_{11}$-za
1 *za-ḫa-da*
13. *Ib-rí-um*

(8)

16 gín DILMUN kù-gi
V. 1. nu$_{11}$-za
IGI.DUB
3. 2 an-dùl
*wa*
5. 2 šu-*sù* 2 DU-*sù*
níĝ-ba
7. *Ib-rí-um*
$^{d}$*Ra-sa-ap*
9. *wa*
$^{d}$*A-da-ma*
11. *ʾÀ-da-ni*$^{ki}$
*in*
13. *ma-ʾà-wa-tum*

(1) 2 shekels of gold for plating 1 mar-tu dagger for Giri.
(2) 2 shekels of gold for decorating 4 earrings for Giri and Napḫa-il and as replacement of 2 earrings of Irdamu, son of Ibrium.
(3) 4 shekels of gold for plating 1 mar-tu dagger and 2 buckles: gift for the god Anamadu of the city of Arḫadu, Budumi has handed over.
(4) 30 (shekels of) gold for 1 plaque for Uzi, brother of Azuma; 30 (shekels of) gold for 1 plaque for Išrut, (son) of In-malik, (who) resided in the city of Uru.
(5) 1 shekel of gold for decorating 1 plaque for NIba-il, trader of the city of Manuwat.
(6) 1 shekel of gold for decorating with lamination 1 battle-axe for the king.
(7) 1 shekel of gold for the handle of a 1 big harp; 1 shekel of gold for decorating with lamination 1 battle-axe for Ibrium.
(8) 16 shekels of gold for plating the face of 2 statues and their 2 hands and feet: gift of Ibrium for the god Rašap and the god Adamma of the city of ʾAdani, on (the occasion of) the *ma-ʾà-wa-tum* ceremony.

(9)
1 gín DILMUN kù-gi
15. nu$_{11}$-za
IGI.DUB
17. 1 an-dùl
VI. 1. níĝ-ba
*Ib-rí-um*
3. $^{d}$Nin-kar

(10)
6 gín DILMUN kù-gi
5. nu$_{11}$-za 1 *ar-ra-sù*
1 *ḫa-bù*
7. níĝ-ba
en
9. $^{d?}$*À-da-"bal"*
*A-ru*$_{12}$*-ga-du*$^{ki}$

(11)
11. 1 gín DILMUN kù-gi
kin$_{5}$-ak
13. $^{d}$*A-gi*
*Su-ti-gú*$^{ki}$

(12)
15. 1 gín DILMUN kù-gi
VII. 1. 1 kù-sal
níĝ-ba
3. *Ib-rí-um*
$^{d}$*Ba-ra-ma*
5. *in* ud
ne:saĝ-*sù*

(13)
7. 6 gín DILMUN 2 NI kù-gi 2 *gú-li-lum*
níĝ-ba
9. $^{d}$*Aš-da-bíl*

(14)
TAR kù-gi 2 *ti-gi-na*
11. TAR kù-gi 10 ĝeštu$_{x}$-lá
ŠÚ+ŠA 8 gín
VIII. 1. kù-gi
4 *ʾà-ra-ma-tum*
3. 2 buru$_{4}$-MUŠEN
13 gín DILMUN kù-gi
5. 1 *mi-at* 30 lá-3 *gur-gú-ru*$_{12}$
10 gín DILMUN kù-gi
7. 80 *du-ru*$_{12}$*-gú*
3 gín DILMUN kù-gi 2 kù-sal
9. 3 gín DILMUN kù-gi
r. I. 1. 1 šu-dub
4 gín DILMUN kù-gi
3. *ḫa-za-nu*
*wa*
5. *a-a-nu*
*gú-za-ra-tum*
7. 3 gín DILMUN kù-gi
1 [*m*]*a-ḫa-na-gúm*
9. 1 *ša-mu*
1 *a-na-bù-bí-tum*
11. 1 *ti-ba-ra-núm*
3 gín DILMUN kù-gi
II. 1. nu$_{11}$-za 2 saĝ 2 *bu*-DI
3 gín DILMUN kù-gi
3. nu$_{11}$-za 1 bur-KAK ĜIŠ-taškarin
4 gín DILMUN kù-gi
5. nu$_{11}$-za 1 *gú-li-lum* kù:babbar
*Dag-mul-da-mu*
III. 1. *Lum-na-an*$^{ki}$
šu-mu-tak$_{4}$

(15)
3. 15$^{?}$ gín DILMUN kù-gi
*ni-zi-mu*
5. 1 dib
*I-bí-zi-kir*
7. dumu-nita
*Ib-rí-um*

(16)
9. 4 gín DILMUN kù-gi
*ni-zi-mu*
11. 3 dib
*Zi-ba-da*
13. *wa*
*Íl-zi*
IV. 1. lú *En-na-ni-il*
*wa*
3. *Ma-a-bar-zú*
lú *Ig-na-da-mu*

(9) 1 shekel fo gold for plating the face of 1 statue: gift of Ibrium for the goddess Ninkar.
(10) 6 shekels of gold for plating the handle of a mace: gift of the king for the god ʾAdabal of the city of Arugadu.
(11) 1 shekel of gold for making (the statue) for the god Agi of the city of Sutigu.
(12) 1 shekel of gold for 1 buckle: gift of Ibrium for the goddess Barama, on the occasion of her first-fruit offering.
(13) 6 shekels (and) 2 NI of gold for 2 bracelets: gift for the god Ašdabil.
(14) 30 (shekels of) gold for 2 torques; 30 (shekels of) gold for 10 earrings; 28 shekels of gold for 4 pectorals (and) 2 shields; 13 shekels of gold for 127 spherical beads; 10 shekels of gold for 80 pearls; 3 shekels of gold for 2 buckles; 3 shekels of gold for 1 ring; 4 shekels of gold for beads and … of clasps; 3 shekels of gold for 1 necklace, 1 frontlet, 1 hairpin, 1 headdress; 3 shekels of gold for plating 2 heads of 2 toggle-pins; 3 shekels of gold for plating 1 bur-KAK vessel of boxwood; 4 shekels of gold for plating 1 bracelet of silver: they were handed over for Dagmul-damu of the city of Lumnan.
(15) 15 shekels of gold for decorating 1 plaque for Ibbi-zikir, son of Ibrium.
(16) 4 shekels of gold for decorating 3 plaques for Zibada, and Ilzi, (son) of Ennani-il, and Maʾabarzu, (son) of Igna-damu.

(17)

5. ŠÚ+ŠA 6 gín DILMUN kù-gi
1 *ma-da-a-um*
7. <1> an-dùl
*wa*
9. 1 pad-*s*[*ù*]
lú en
11. šu-ba$_4$-ti
(blank)
V–VII. (blank)

(18)

VIII. 1. AN.ŠÈ.GÚ 4 ma-na ŠA.PI 2 2 NI gín
DILMUN kù-gi
è
3. *ap*
5 gín DILMUN kù-gi
5. al$_6$-ĝál
é siki
7. (blank)

(17) 26 shekels of gold for 1 … (*ma-da-a-um*) for a statue and it[s] lid, that the king has received.
(18) Total: 4;42 minas (and) 2 NI of gold: expenditure, and also 5 shekels of gold are present in the Treasury.

## Commentary

This is a registration of 4;42 ⅔ minas (2.219 ⅔ kg) of gold expended for decorating objects. The leftover gold, weighing "5 shekels (39 g) was deposited in the treasury (the "House of the Wool)" (§ 18).

The jewelry "handed over" for Dagmul-damu of Lumnan needed 2;14 minas (1.050 kg) of gold (§ 14); its occasion could only have been the marriage of this princess with the king of that city. Previously (year Ibr. 01), another Eblaite princess, Dati-$^{d}$TU, who had married that same king, died in the year Ibr. 08 (see respectively the commentaries to documents XXI 2 and XXI 11). The present document must therefore be dated to the year Ibr. 09 or 10. The two ladies appear in minister's Arrukum documents, but in different clusters (*ARET* XV, 2, pp. 298–299). It could be possible that the first lady was a daughter of king Irkab-damu, and the second of his son Iš$^{c}$ar-damu..

§§ 1, 2. Giri(-malik), Napḫa-il, and Ir-damu were Ibrium's sons. For Giri, see text 12 § 6.

§ 4. The city of *U*$_9$-*ru*$_{12}$$^{ki}$ belonged to Ebla.

§ 6. The king received a battle-axe decorated with a lamination of 1 shekel of gold (8 g)

§ 7. The handle of a big harp of Ibrium was decorated with gold, and a battle-axe for him was plated with gold, for a total of 2 shekels (16 g).

§ 15. Ibbi-zikir, Ibrium's son, received a plaque decorated with 3 shekels (23 g) of gold.

List of the gold expenditures:

| | | | | |
|---|---|---|---|---|
| § 1 | 0;02 | § 11 | 0;01 | |
| § 2 | 0;02 | § 12 | 0:01 | |
| § 3 | 0;04 | § 13 | 0;06 | ⅔ |
| § 4 | 1:00 | § 14 | 2;14 | |
| § 5 | 0;01 | § 15 | 0;15 | (?) |
| § 6 | 0;01 | § 16 | 0;04 | |
| § 7 | 0;02 | § 17 | 0;26 | |
| § 8 | 0;16 | | | |
| § 9 | 0;01 | | 4:42 | ⅔ |
| § 10 | 0;06 | | | |

# 25
## (Plates XLVIII–XLIX)

(1)

o. I. 1. [x kù:babbar]
[níĝ-s]a$_{10}$
3. 72 aktum-TÚG 20 ʾà-da-um-TÚG
10 túg-NI.NI 90 lá-2 sal-TÚG 2 níĝ-lá-gaba
5. 5 *gu-zi-tum*-TÚG
ki:lam$_{7}$
7. *Im-ma-ra-an*$^{ki}$
*A-bù*-Kur$^{ki}$

(2)

9. 10 ma-na kù:babbar
II. 1. [níĝ-sa$_{10}$]
[x aktum-TÚG] 10 lá-2 túg-NI.NI 7 *ʾà-da-um*-TÚG dùl-TÚG
3. 12 gada-TÚG 94 sal-TÚG
22 íb+III-TÚG sa$_{6}$ gùn 80 íb-III-TÚG gùn
5. ki:lam$_{7}$
SA.ZA$_{x}^{ki}$
7. *wa*
$^{d}$*A-da-ma*
9. *ʾÀ-da-ni*$^{ki}$

(3)

III. 1. [x] ⸢kù:babbar⸣
níĝ-sa$_{10}$ 44 aktum-TÚG 5 zara-⸢TÚG⸣
13 *gu-zi-tum*-TÚG
3. 22 túg-NI.NI
34 íb+III-TÚG sa$_{6}$ gùn
5. 1 *mi-at* 52 íb+III-TÚG gùn
1 ĝír mar:tu ti kù:babbar
IV. 1. [ki:lam$_{7}$]
[*ʾÀ-da-ni*]⸢$^{ki}$⸣
3. AMA-*ra*

(4)

8 ma-na TAR kù:babbar
5. níĝ-sa$_{10}$ 5 *gu-zi-tum* 4 aktum-TÚG 7 túg-NI.NI
10 lá-1 *ʾà-da-um*-TÚG 60 lá-1 sal-TÚG 2 níĝ-lá-saĝ
7. 62 íb+III-TÚG (erased) 1 *mi-at* 41 íb+III-TÚG gùn
4 ma-na ŠA.PI [kù]:ba[abbar]
V. 1. [ ]
[ki:lam$_{7}$]
3. $^{d}$*Ga-mi-iš*

(5)

6 m[a-]na 2 gín DILMUN kù:babbar
5. níĝ-sa$_{10}$ 24[+1] aktum-TÚG
[x] ⸢*ʾà*⸣*-da-um*-TÚG saĝ
7. 3 túg-NI.NI 20 lá-3 sal-TÚG 27 gada-TÚG
30 íb+III-TÚG sa$_{6}$ gùn
9. [ ]
VI. 1. ⸢ki⸣:[lam$_{7}$]
SA.ZA$_{x}$<ki>

(6)

3. 8 ma-na 7 gín DILMUN kù:babbar
níĝ-sa$_{10}$ 73 *ʾà-da-um*-TÚG 11 aktum-TÚG 10 sal-TÚG
5. ki:lam$_{7}$
*Ga-ga-ba-an*$^{ki}$
7. *A-bù*-Kur$^{ki}$

(7)

5 ma-na ⸢x x⸣ [kù:babbar]
VII. 1. [níg-sa$_{10}$ ]
10 í[b-III-TÚG] sa$_{6}$ gùn 10 íb-III-TÚG babbar 2 *mi-at* íb-III-TÚG gùn
3. ki:lam$_{7}$
$^{d}$*Áš-da-bíl* {x}

(8)

5. 5 ma-na 17 ½ gín DILMUN kù:babbar
níĝ-sa$_{10}$ 13 *ʾà-da-um*-TÚG saĝ
7. [x aktum-TÚG] (?)

(1) [x silver for the purcha]se of 197 garments at the market of the city of Immaran, Abu-Kur (has received).
(2) 10 minas of silver [for the purchase of x+]121 garments (and) 102 kilts, at the markets of the Palace and of the god Adamma of the city of ʾAdani.
(3) [x] silver for the purchase of 84 garments, 186 kilts (and) 1 pointed mar-tu dagger (decorated with) silver, [at the market of the city of ʾAdani], at the AMA-ra (festival).
(4) 8;30 minas of silver for the purchase of 86 garments (and) 203 kilts; 4;40 minas [of si]l[ver …, at the market] of the god Kamiš.
(5) 6;02 m[i]nas of silver for the purchase of 72[+x] garments (and) 30[+x] kilts, at the mar[ket] of the Palace.
(6) 8;07 minas of silver for the purchase of 94 garments at the market of the city of Gagaban, Abu-Kur (has received).
(7) 5;[xx] minas [of silver for the purchase of …] (and) 220 kilts, at the market of the god Ašdabil.
(8) 5;17 ½ minas of silver for the purchase of 18+[x] garments, 2+[x] kilts, 1 mar-tu dagger of bad quality, at the market of the god Hadda and of the *gibalu* of the city of ʾAdani.

VIII. 1. [x íb-III-TÚG s]a$_6$ gùn 2 íb-III-TÚG
gùn 4 sal-TÚG
1 níĝ-lá-saĝ babbar 1 ĝír mar:tu ḫul
3. ki:lam$_7$
$^{d?}$*À-da*
5. *wa*
*gi-ba-lu*
7. *ʾÀ-da-ni*$^{ki}$

(9)
1 íb-lá ŠA.PI gín DILMUN kù:babbar
9. *En-na-il*
l[ú ]
11. [ ]

(10)
IX. 1. [ kù:babbar]
*E*[*n-na-*]*il*
3. lú *Áš-da-maḫ*

(11)
1 íb-lá TAR kù:babbar
5. *I-nu-ud-da-mu*
*Kak-mi-um*$^{ki}$
7. *in* ud
nídba ì-ĝiš
9. *Ib-la*$^{ki}$
*i*[*n*]
11. [ ]
[ ]
13. [ ]
X. (traces of signs)

(12)
r. I. x+1. 60 [ ]

(13)
II. 1. [ ]
[ ]
3. [ ]
⸢x⸣-[ ]
5. *Ì-ra-ar*$^{ki}$
*in* ud
7. DU
*M*[*a*]*-za-*⸢*tum*$^?$⸣[$^{ki}$]

(14)
9. 1 ma-na 11[+x] gí[n] DI[LMUN
kù:]babbar
2 [ ]
11. [ ]
III. 1. [ ]
l[ú] *D*[*u-si*]
3. ugula *Ib-al*$_6^{ki}$
*in* ud
5. ĜIŠ-gu-kak-gíd
šu-mu-tak$_4$

(15)
7. 1 íb-lá TAR kù:babbar
*Lu-*⸢*rí*⸣*-um*
9. *Kak-mi-um*$^{ki}$
níĝ-"mul"
11. Bàd$^{ki}$
šu-ba$_4$-⸢ti⸣

(16)
IV. 1. [ ]
[ ]-⸢*lum*⸣
3. *ba-da-lum*
*Ù-ti-gú*$^{ki}$
5. 2 maškim
*A-ag*

(17)
7. 1 ib-lá ŠA.PI kù:babbar
BÍL-*ma-lik*
9. lugal

(18)
1 íb-lá TAR ⸢kù:babbar⸣
11. ⸢x⸣-[ ]
[ ]
V. 1. [ ]
[ ]-⸢x-x⸣
3. ḫi-mu-DU
*Ma-ma*
5. (blank)

(19)
VI. 1. [ ]
še-ba diĝir-diĝir-diĝir-diĝir

(9) 1 belt of 40 shekels of silver for Enna-il, (son) o[f …],
(10) [… of silver] for E[nna-]il, son of Ašdamaḫ.
(11) 1 belt of 30 (shekels of) silver for Inud-damu of the city of Kakmium, on the occasion of the offering of the oil for the city of Ebla i[n …].
(12) 60 […].
(13) […] of the city of Irar, when went to the city of M[a]zat[um$^?$].
(14) 1;11[+x] minas of [sil]ver for 2 [… for …] (son) o[f] D[usi], the overseer of the city of Ibᶜal, when he handed over the spearheads.
(15) 1 belt of 30 (shekels of) silver for Lurium of the city of Kakmium (who brought) the news that the city of Bad had been conquered.
(16) [1 belt … for …]lum, the minister of the city of Utigu, 2 representatives of Aʾag.
(17) 1 belt of 40 (shekels of) silver for BIL-malik, the lord.
(18) 1 belt of 30 (shekels of) silver for […], Mama has delivered.
(19) [x silver] for the purchase of wheat for rations for the gods

3. níĝ-$sa_{10}$ gig
(blank)

(20)
X. 1. AN.ŠÈ.GÚ
86 ma-na 53 gín DILMUN kù:babbar
3. è
*in* ud
5. *Ib-rí-um*
(blank)

(21)
XI. 1. šu-níĝin
25 *g*[*u*]*-zi-tum*-TÚG
3. 6 *mi-at* 61 (erased) túg-túg
60 lá-1 gada-TÚG
5. 5 níĝ-lá-saĝ níĝ-lá-gaba
2 *mi-at* 23 íb-III-TÚG $sa_6$ gùn
7. 6 *mi-at* 81 íb-III-TÚG gùn
VIII–VII. (blank)

(20) Total: 86;53 minas of silver: expenditure, in the days of Ibrium.
(21) Grand total: 750 garments (and) 904 kilts.

## Commentary

The total of the expended silver amounted to 86;53 minas (40.835 kg) (§ 20), probably in a single year. The document concerns mostly expenditures made at "markets", ki-$lam_7$: two at the Palace (§§ 2, 5), three at ᵓAdani (§§ 2, 3, 8); and one at Gagaban (§ 6). Other markets take the name by gods' festivals, those of Hadda (§ 8), Ašdabil (§ 7), Kamiš (§ 4). The clothing acquired amounted to 750 garments, and 904 kilts (§ 21).

The notation "in the days of Ibrium" could mean "in the first months in which Ibrium served as minister". The conquest of a fortress of Kakmium (§ 15) however dates this document to the year Ibr. 14 (see the commentary to text 17). Inud-damu, who came to Ebla and swore the peace with the rite of the oil offering (§ 11), was an "overseer", ugula, of Kakmium, a title which he receives in no. text 8 § 8.

§ 1. The city of Immaran is also attested in *ARET* XIII 14 o. II 19, VI 7'.

§ 14. *Du-si* is a name attested at Ibᶜal, see *ARET* III 937 o. II' 12': an abbreviation for *Du-si-li-im*: VIII 527 o. X 22.

§ 16. The title *ba-da-lum*, "minister", seems not to be attested for other officials of Utig(u).

§ 17. BÍL-malik is mentioned as "lord", lugal, from the year Ibr. 07 on, see *ARET* XIV 60 § 7, and p. 170.

§ 19. A not preserved amount of silver was expended in order to "purchase wheat for rations for the gods", še-ba diĝir-diĝir-diĝir níĝ-$sa_{10}$ gig.

# List of offerings of precious objects to the gods by the central Administration in the period of minister Ibrium's mandate

Starting with the second year of Ibrium (texts no. 4 and 5), the god Kura received every year a delivery of 1 mina and 3 shekels of silver (493.5 g)[1] that served to replace the metal mask covering the face of the statue of the god kept in the temple on the northern side of the royal palace (Archi 2015, p. 501). This amount of silver could be dispensed in two shifts: a first delivery of 1 mina, followed by a second delivery (mu-ti-II) of 3 shekels (texts no. 4, 6, 8, 13–21; Ibrium 2–3, 5, 10–18). More rarely the three additional shekels of silver were already included in the first registration (texts 9–12; Ibrium 6–9). The registration of the delivery of silver for Kura opens all the annual accounts of Ibrium and Ibbi-zikir. This can only be explained as an annual ritual of renewal, that must have marked the beginning of the annual cultic cycle. Moreover, Kura received also a pair of gold bracelets, 2 *gú-li-lum*, weighing 52 g (6 gín DILMUN 2 NI kù-gi), sometimes twice a year (texts no. 2, 7, 8, 13, 15, 17–21; Ibrium 1, 4, 5, 10, 12, 14–18).

Recipients of a regular yearly offering of two gold bracelets are also the gods Ammarik and Ašdabil.

The gods Hadda of the city of Ḫalab and Hadda of the city of Lub were the recipients of regular offerings recorded in the annual accounts. However, as we can see from the table below, only from the second half of Ibrium's office these offerings were regularly recorded in the accounts. Furthermore, it should be added that in the early years of Ibrium the cult place of the deity was not always indicated.

Hadda of Ḫalab was the recipient of two regular offerings, taking place in the third and the eighth month (iti $^{d}$AMA-*ra* and iti *ʾa$_5$-nun*[2] respectively). They consisted of a mace (ešda = *ḫa-bù*) decorated with 15 shekels of silver, equipped with a handle decorated with 6 shekels of gold; four horns of a pair of oxen or bulls (4 si-si 2 gud), covered with 20 shekels of silver. Hadda of Lub, instead, received only one mace and its handle, as a regular offering in the fourth month (iti *gi*-NI).

| | | **Hadda of Ḫalab** | | **Hadda of Lub** |
|---|---|---|---|---|
| **Text** | **Year** | **iti $^{d}$AMA-*ra*** | **iti *ʾa$_5$-nun*** | **iti *gi*-NI** |
| **2** | Ibr. 1 | 1 *ḫa-bù* | | |
| **5** | Ibr. 2 | 2 gud 4 si | *ʾà-na-gu* si 2 gud | |
| **6** | Ibr. 3 | 1 *ḫa-bù* | | |
| **7** | Ibr. 4 | 1 ešda, 1 *ar-ra-sù*, *ʾa$_5$-na-gu* 4 si 2 gud | 1 ešda, *ar-ra-sù* | |
| **9** | Ibr. 6 | 1 *ḫa-bù*, *ar-ra-sa-sù*, si-si 2 gud | | |
| **10** | Ibr. 7 | 4 si-si 2 gud | | |
| **11** | Ibr. 8 | 1 ešda, 1 *ar-ra-sù*, *ʾa$_5$-na-gu* 4 si 2 gud | 1 ešda, *ʾa$_5$-na-gu* 4 si 2 gud | 1 ešda |
| **12** | Ibr. 9 | | *ʾa$_5$-na-gu* 4 si-si 2 gud | |
| **14** | Ibr. 11 | | | 1 *ḫa-bù*, 1 *ar-ra-su-sù* |
| **15** | Ibr. 12 | | 1 *ḫa-bù*, 1 *ar-ra-sù*, *ʾa$_5$-na-gu* 4 si 2 gud | 1 *ḫa-bù*, 1 *ar-ra-su-sù* |
| **16** | Ibr. 13 | 1 *ḫa-bù*, *ʾa$_5$-na-gu* si 2 gud | 1 *ḫa-bù*, *ʾa$_5$-na-gu* si 2 gud | 1 *ḫa-bù*, 1 *ar-ra-sù* |

1 In text 7 (Ibrium 4) the registration of the three shekels of gold is not preserved.

2 This is the name of the eighth month according to the "Semitic calendar", called iti nídba $^{dʾ}$*À-da* in the local calendar

| | | | | |
|---|---|---|---|---|
| **17** | Ibr. 14 | | | 1 *ḫa-bù*, 1 *ar-ra-si-sù* |
| **18** | Ibr. 15 | 1 *ḫa-bù*, *ar-ra-sù*, *ʾa*$_5$*-na-gu* si 2 gud | 1 *ḫa-bù*, *ʾa*$_5$*-na-gu* si 2 gud | 1 *ḫa-bù*, *ar-ra-sù* |
| **19** | Ibr. 16 | 1 *ḫa-bù*, *ar-ra-sù*, *ʾa*$_5$*-na-gu* si 2 gud | 1 *ḫa-bù*, *ʾa*$_5$*-na-gu* si 2 gud | 1 *ḫa-bù*, 1 *ar-ra-sù* |
| **20** | Ibr. 17 | 1 *ḫa-bù*, 1 *ar-ra-sù*, *ʾa*$_5$*-na-gu* 4 si gud | 1 *ḫa-bù*, *ar-ra-sù*, *ʾa*$_5$*-na-gu* 4 si 2 gud | nu$_{11}$-za ab-*sù* |
| **21** | Ibr. 18 | 1 *ḫa-bù*, *ʾa*$_5$*-na-gu* si 2 gud | | 1 *ḫa-bù*, 1 *ar-ra-sù* |

## Text 2 (Ibrium 1a)

| God | § | Donor | Objects | Occasion |
|---|---|---|---|---|
| $^{d}$*ʾÀ-da* | 44 | – | 1 *ḫa-bù* | níĝ-ba, $^{d}$AMA-*ra* |
| $^{d}$*ʾA*$_5$*-da-"bal" ʾÀ-ma-ad*$^{ki}$ | 9 | Ibrium | 1 *ḫa-bù* | níĝ-ba |
| $^{d}$*ʾA*$_5$*-da-"bal" La-ru*$_{12}$*-ga-du*$^{ki}$ | 54 | Ibrium | 1 banšur, 1 kù-sal | níĝ-ba |
| $^{d}$*ʾA*$_5$*-da-ra* | 28 | – | the head of his statue | – |
| $^{d}$*ʾA*$_5$*-da-ra* | 60 | – | 1 íb-la | níĝ-ba |
| $^{d}$*Á-lá Zi-ig*$^{ki}$ | 68 | king | […] | – |
| $^{d}$*Am-ma-rí-ig* | 65 | king | 1 *ḫa-bù*, 2 *gú-li-lum* | níĝ-ba |
| $^{d}$*Áš-da-bíl* | 64 | – | 2 *gú-li-lum* | níĝ-ba |
| $^{d}$*Ba-ra-ma* | 4 | king | 1 kù-sal | níĝ-ba, *in* ud ne:saĝ-*sù* |
| $^{d}$BAD *Du-du-la*$^{ki}$ | 52 | Ibrium | 1 an-dùl and its decorations | níĝ-ba |
| $^{d}$*Ì-lam* | 46 | king | 1 banšur | níĝ-ba |
| $^{d}$*Iš:šára Zi-da-ra*$^{ki}$ | 14 | Dusigu | 1 kù-sal | níĝ-ba |
| $^{d}$*Ku-ra* | 13 | Ibrium | 1 GIŠ-banšur, 1 kù-sal | níĝ-ba, *in* ud ne:saĝ-*sù* |
| $^{d}$*Ku-ra* | 25 | – | 2 *gú-li-lum* | níĝ-ba |
| $^{d}$*Ku-ra* | 40 | Ibrium | 1 *gú-li-lum*, 1 kù-sal | níĝ-ba, *in* ud lú nídba |
| $^{d}$*Ku-ra* | 53 | – | 2 *gú-li-lum* | níĝ-ba |
| $^{d}$*Ra-sa-ap ʾÀ-da-ni*$^{ki}$ | 43 | Dusigu | 1 *gú-li-lum*, 1 kù-sal | níĝ-ba |
| $^{d}$*Ra-sa-ap ʾÀ-da-ni*$^{ki}$ | 44 | – | 1 *ḫa-bù* | níĝ-ba, $^{d}$AMA-*ra* |
| $^{d}$*Ra-sa-ap ʾÀ-da-ni*$^{ki}$ | 50 | king | 4 si 2 gud | nídba, $^{d}$AMA-*ra* |
| $^{d}$*Ša-ma-gan* | 21 | king | decoration for his statue | – |
| $^{d}$Utu SA.ZA$_x$$^{ki}$ | 41 | Ibrium | 2 *ʾà-ra-ma-tum*, 2 zé | níĝ-ba |

## Text 3 (Ibrium 1b)

| God | § | Donor | Objects | Occasion |
|---|---|---|---|---|
| $^{d}$*ʾÀ-da* | 31 | – | 1 *ḫa-bù*, 1 *ar-ra-si-su* | níĝ-ba |
| $^{d}$*ʾÀ-da* lú *Du-ub*$^{ki}$ | 22 | – | 1 GIŠ-banšur, […] | níĝ-ba |
| $^{d}$*ʾA*$_5$*-da-"bal" La-ru*$_{12}$*-ga-du*$^{ki}$ | 9 | Ibrium | 1 *ḫa-bù*, 1 *ar-ra-si-su* | níĝ-ba |
| $^{d}$*ʾA*$_5$*-da-"bal" La-ru*$_{12}$*-ga-du*$^{ki}$ | 62 | Ibrium | […] | níĝ-ba |
| $^{d}$*Am-ma-rí-ig* | 25 | – | 1 an-dùl and its decoration | níĝ-ba |
| $^{d}$*Am-ma-rí-ig* | 26 | – | 2 *gú-li-lum* | níĝ-ba |
| $^{d}$*Áš-da-bíl* | 42 | – | 2 *gú-li-lum* | níĝ-ba |
| $^{d}$*Ku-ra* | 8 | – | 2 *gú-li-lum* | níĝ-ba |
| diĝir-diĝir-diĝir | 61 | – | 51 gín kb | níĝ-ba |

## Text 4 (Ibrium 2a)

| God | § | Donor | Objects | Occasion |
|---|---|---|---|---|
| $^{d}$*ʾÀ-da* | 83 | – | 1 *ḫa-bù* | níĝ-ba |
| $^{d}$*ʾÀ-da* | 110 | – | 1 *ḫa-bù* | níĝ-ba |
| $^{d}$*ʾÀ-ma-rí-ig* | 46 | – | 2 *gú-li-lum* | – |
| $^{d}$*ʾA$_{5}$-da-"bal" La-ru$_{12}$-ga-du*$^{ki}$ | 6 | – | 1 níĝ-bànda | níĝ-ba |
| $^{d}$*Á-la* | 107 | Ibrium | 1 an-dùl | níĝ-ba |
| $^{d}$*Ku-ra* | 1 | – | 1 ma-na kb saĝ kb | – |
| $^{d}$*Ku-ra* | 48 | – | 3 gín kb saĝ kb | – |
| $^{d}$*Ra-sa-ap* lú *ʾÀ-da-ni*$^{ki}$ | 83 | – | 1 *ḫa-bù* | níĝ-ba |
| $^{d}$*Ra-sa-ap ʾÀ-da-ni*$^{ki}$ | 87 | king | 2 ĜIŠ-banšur, 1 šu-dub | – |
| diĝir-diĝir-diĝir | 40 | Ibrium's daughter | several vessels | níĝ-ba |
| diĝir-diĝir-diĝir | 62 | – | 20 gín kb | níĝ-ba |
| [...] | 16 | | 3 ĜIŠ-banšur 3 ĝír mar-tu | níĝ-ba |

## Text 5 (Ibrium 2b)

| God | § | Donor | Objects | Occasion |
|---|---|---|---|---|
| $^{d}$*ʾÀ-da* | 18 | king | 2 gud 4 si | nídba, *in* AMA-*ra* |
| $^{d}$*ʾÀ-da* | 67 | king | 1 *ḫa-bù, ar-ra-su-sù, ʾà-na-gu* si 2 gud | níĝ-ba; nídba |
| $^{d}$*ʾÀ-da* | 68 | Ibrium | *ʾà-na-gu* si 2 gud | nídba, *in* iti *ʾa$_{5}$-nun* |
| $^{d}$*ʾÀ-da ʾÀ-da-ni*$^{ki}$ | 19 | king | 2 gud 4 si | nídba, *in* AMA-*ra* |
| $^{d}$*ʾA$_{5}$-da-"bal" ʾÀ-ma-du*$^{ki}$ | 77 | Ibrium | 1 ĝír mar-tu | níĝ-ba |
| $^{d}$*ʾA$_{5}$-da-"bal" La-ru$_{12}$-ga-du*$^{ki}$ | 54 | king | 1 ĜIŠ-banšur, 3 saĝ lu$_{x}$ | níĝ-ba |
| $^{d}$*ʾA$_{5}$-da-"bal" La-ru$_{12}$-ga-du*$^{ki}$ | 63 | Ibbi-zikir | 1 ĜIŠ-banšur | níĝ-ba |
| $^{d}$*ʾA$_{5}$-da-"bal" Lu-ba-an*$^{ki}$ | 50 | Ibrium | 1 ĝír mar-tu, 1 kù-sal | níĝ-ba, *in* ud ne:saĝ-*sù* |
| $^{d}$*Am-ma-rí-ig* | 62 | – | 2 *gú-li-lum* | – |
| $^{d}$*Áš-da-bíl* | 60 | – | 2 *gú-li-lum* | – |
| $^{d}$BAD *Má*-NE$^{ki}$ | 56 | Dusigu | 2 zi-bar | níĝ-ba |
| $^{d}$*Ga-na-na* | 76 | – | 2 *bu*-DI, 2 *ti-ša-na* | níĝ-ba, ĜIŠ.DUG.DU maḫ |
| $^{d}$*Gú-sar* | 72 | – | face and hands of his statue | – |
| $^{d}$[*Iš*:]*šára* ĜIŠ-kiri$_{6}$ | 16 | Ibrium | 1 ĝír mar-tu | nídba |
| $^{d}$*Ra-sa-ap ʾÀ-da-ni*$^{ki}$ | 30 | – | 1 *ḫa-bù, ar-ra-si-sù* | AMA-*ra* |
| $^{d}$*Ra-sa-ap ʾÀ-da-ni*$^{ki}$ | 78 | Ibrium | 1 ĝír mar-tu, 1 kù-sal | níĝ-ba |
| $^{d}$*Ra-sa-ap ʾÀ-da-ni*$^{ki}$ | 82 | – | *a-gú*, 3 ĜIŠ-šú, 3 níĝ-tur *in* é $^{d}$*R.* | – |
| $^{d}$*Ra-sa-ap gú-núm*$^{ki}$ | 79 | king | 1 ĝír mar-tu, 1 kù-sal | níĝ-ba, ne:saĝ-*sù* |
| diĝir-diĝir-diĝir | 85 | – | 1 ma-na TAR kb | níĝ-ba |

## Text 6 (Ibrium 3)

| God | § | Donor | Objects | Occasion |
|---|---|---|---|---|
| $^{d}$*ʾÀ-da* | 20 | – | 1 *za-ḫa-da* | níĝ-ba |
| $^{d}$*ʾÀ-da* | 31 | king | zi-du$_{8}$ | – |
| $^{d}$*ʾÀ-da* | 57 | – | 1 *ḫa-bù* | níĝ-ba, $^{d}$AMA-*ra* |

| | | | | |
|---|---|---|---|---|
| $^{dʾ}$*À-da* lú *Lu-ub*$^{ki}$ | 23 | – | 1 GIŠ-banšur | níĝ-ba |
| $^{dʾ}$*A*$_{5}$*-da-*"*bal*" *La-ru*$_{12}$*-ga*$_{x}$*-du*$^{ki}$ | 47 | – | 1 *ḫa-bù* | níĝ-ba |
| $^{d}$*Á-lá* lú *A-ra-ab*$^{ki}$ | 97 | – | head of his statue | – |
| $^{d}$*Á-lá wa* dam-*sù* lú *A-ra-ab*$^{ki}$ | 118 | – | tin for their statues | – |
| $^{d}$*A-lum A-ḫa-da-mu*$^{ki}$ | 109 | – | tin for his statue | – |
| $^{dʾ}$*À-ma-ri-ig* | 79 | – | 2 *gú-li-lum* | níĝ-ba |
| $^{d}$BAD *Ga-na-na-im* | 45 | – | 1 *ḫa-bù* | níĝ-ba |
| $^{d}$*Da-bí-na-ad* lú *A-ra-ab*$^{ki}$ | 97 | – | head of her statue | – |
| $^{d}$*Da-i-in* | 64 | – | 1 ĝír mar-tu | níĝ-ba, *in* ud en e$_{11}$ é $^{d}$*Ga-mi-iš* |
| $^{d}$*Ga-mi-iš* | 64 | – | 1 GIŠ-banšur | níĝ-ba, *in* ud en e$_{11}$ é $^{d}$*Ga-mi-iš* |
| $^{d}$*Ga-mi-iš* | 117 | king | 1 *ḫa-bù* | níĝ-ba |
| $^{d}$*Ga-na-na* | 96 | – | 2 *bu-*DI, 2 *ti-ša-na* | níĝ-ba, GIŠ.DUG.DU maḫ |
| $^{d}$*Ì-lam* lú *Za-za-u*$_{9}$ | 120 | – | tin for his statue | – |
| $^{d}$*Iš-šára Ma-*NE$^{ki}$ | 35 | – | 2 *bu-*DI, 1 an-zam$_{x}$, 1 GIŠ-banšur, 1 *ḫa-bù* | – |
| $^{d}$*Iš-šára Ma-*NE$^{ki}$ | 112 | – | 1 GIŠ-banšur | – |
| $^{d}$*Ku-ra* | 1 | – | 1 ma-na kb saĝ kb | – |
| $^{d}$*Ku-ra* | 7 | – | 3 gín kb saĝ kb 2 mu-ti | – |
| $^{d}$*Ra-sa-ap ʾÀ-da-ni*$^{ki}$ | 42 | – | 1 saĝ lu$_{5}$ GIŠ-ĝidru | – |
| $^{d}$*Ra-sa-ap ʾÀ-da-ni*$^{ki}$ | 57 | – | 1 *ḫa-bù* | níĝ-ba, $^{d}$AMA-*ra* |
| $^{d}$*Si-gar A-ḫa-da-mu*$^{ki}$ | 109 | – | tin for her statue | – |
| $^{d}$*Ša-la-ša* lú *Ga-ra-mu*$^{ki}$ | 73 | – | plating of her statue | – |
| $^{d}$*Wa-da-ʾà-an* lú *Ga-ra-mu*$^{ki}$ | 23 | – | 1 ĝír mar-tu | níĝ-ba |
| $^{d}$*Wa-da-ʾà-an* lú *Ga-ra-mu*$^{ki}$ | 73 | – | plating of his statue | – |
| diĝir-diĝir-diĝir-diĝir | 24 | – | 1 ma-na 50 kb | níĝ-ba |

## Text 7 (Ibrium 4)

| God | § | Donor | Objects | Occasion |
|---|---|---|---|---|
| $^{dʾ}$*À-da* | 39 | king | 1 ešda, 1 *ar-ra-sù*, *ʾa*$_{5}$*-na-gu* 4 si 2 gud | nídba, *in* $^{d}$AMA-*ra* |
| $^{dʾ}$*À-da* | 77 | – | 1 ešda, *ar-ra-sù* | níĝ-ba, *in* iti *ʾa*$_{5}$*-nun* |
| $^{dʾ}$*A*$_{5}$*-da-*"*bal*" *Lu-ba-an*$^{ki}$ | 68 | – | *ʾa*$_{5}$*-na-gu* 1 GIŠ-banšur, 1 kù-sal | níĝ-ba |
| $^{d}$*Am-ma-ri-ig* | 69 | – | *ʾa*$_{5}$*-na-gu* 1 GIŠ-banšur, 1 kù-sal | níĝ-ba |
| $^{d}$*Am-ma-ri-ig* | 99 | – | 2 *gú-li-lum* | níĝ-ba |
| $^{d}$*Áš-da-bíl* | 72 | – | 2 *gú-li-lum* | níĝ-ba |
| $^{d}$*Áš-da-bíl* | 73 | Ibrium | 1 ĝír mar-tu | níĝ-ba |
| $^{d}$BAD *Du-du-la*$^{ki}$ | 33 | Ibrium | [...] | níĝ-ba |
| $^{d}$*Ga-na-na* | 98 | – | 4 *ti-ša-nu*, 2 *bu-*DI | níĝ-ba, *in* ud GIŠ.DUG.DU maḫ |
| $^{d}$*Ku-ra* | 1 | – | 1 ma-na kb saĝ kb | – |
| $^{d}$*Ku-ra* | 25 | – | 2 *gú-li-lum* | níĝ-ba |
| $^{d}$*Ku-ra* | 53 | – | 2 *gú-li-lum* | níĝ-ba |
| $^{d}$*Ku-ra* | 67 | – | 1 ĝír mar-tu, 1 kù-sal | níĝ-ba |

| | | | | |
|---|---|---|---|---|
| $^{d}$Nin-kar | 10 | king's mother | 1 kù-sal | níĝ-ba |
| $^{d}$*Ra-sa-ap* | 37 | – | 1 ešda, 1 *ar-ra-sù* | níĝ-ba |
| $^{d}$*Ra-sa-ap* | 105 | king, lords | decoration of his statue | – |
| $^{d}$*Ra-sa-ap ᵓÀ-da-ni*$^{ki}$ | 38 | king | *ᵓa*$_{5}$*-na-gu* 4 si 2 gud | nídba, *in* $^{d}$AMA-*ra* |
| $^{d}$*Ra-sa-ap ᵓÀ-da-ni*$^{ki}$ | 74 | [–] | 1 kù-sal, 1 buru$_{4}$-MUŠEN | níĝ-ba, $^{d}$AMA-*ra* |
| $^{d}$*Ra-sa-ap Du-ne-ib*$^{ki}$ | 12 | Ibrium | 1 ĝír mar-tu, 1 kù-sal | níĝ-ba |
| $^{d}$*Ra-sa-ap Du-ne-ib*$^{ki}$ | 64 | – | 1 ĝír mar-tu, 1 kù-sal | níĝ-ba |
| $^{d}$*Ra-sa-ap Du-ne-ib*$^{ki}$ | 106 | king | 1 ĝír mar-tu, 1 ĜIŠ-gu-kak-gíd | – |
| $^{d}$*Sa-a-ša si-in Du-du-lu*$^{ki}$ | 34 | Ibrium | 1 an-dùl munus and its decorations | níĝ-ba |
| $^{d}$Utu SA.ZA$_{x}$$^{ki}$ | 66 | – | [1$^{?}$] *ᵓà-ra-ma-tum*, […] | níĝ-ba |
| $^{d}$*Wa-da-ᵓà-nu* lú *Ša-dab*$_{6}$$^{ki}$ | 3 | Ibrium | 1 ĝír mar-tu | níĝ-ba |
| diĝir-diĝir-diĝir | 100 | – | 2 ma-na kb | níĝ-ba |
| […] | 65 | – | 1 ĝír mar-tu, 1 kù-sal | níĝ-ba |
| […] | 70 | – | *ᵓa*$_{5}$*-na-gu* 1 ĜIŠ-banšur, 1 kù-sal | níĝ-ba |

## Text 8 (Ibrium 5)

| God | § | Donor | Objects | Occasion |
|---|---|---|---|---|
| $^{d}$*ᵓA*$_{5}$*-da-"bal" ᵓÀ-ma-du*$^{ki}$ | 20 | – | 1 ĝír mar-tu | níĝ-ba |
| $^{d}$BAD *Ga-ga-na-um* | 16 | – | 1 an-dùl | níĝ-ba |
| $^{d}$BAD *Ga-ga-na-um* | 56 | – | [1 *ḫa-bù*], *ar-ra-si-su* | – |
| $^{d}$*Ku-ra* | 1 | – | 1 ma-na kb saĝ | – |
| $^{d}$*Ku-ra* | 9 | – | [3 gín kb] saĝ | – |
| $^{d}$*Ku-ra* | 31 | – | 2 *gú-li-lum* | – |
| $^{d}$*Ku-ra* | 59 | – | 2 *gú-li-lum* | – |
| $^{d}$*Ra-sa-ap* | 36 | Ibrium | decorations for his statue | níĝ-ba |
| $^{d}$*Ra-sa-ap* [*ᵓÀ-da-ni*$^{ki}$] | 46 | king, Ibrium | 8 si 4 gud | nídba |
| $^{d}$*Ra-sa-ap ᵓÀ-da-ni*$^{ki}$ *in* SA.ZA$_{x}$$^{ki}$ | 25 | – | 1 ĝír mar-tu | – |
| diĝir-diĝir-diĝir | 21 | – | 1 ma-na 15 gín kb | níĝ-ba |

## Text 9 (Ibrium 6)

| God | § | Donor | Objects | Occasion |
|---|---|---|---|---|
| $^{d}$*ᵓÀ-da Ḫa-lab*$_{x}$$^{ki}$ | 6 | – | 1 *ḫa-bù, ar-ra-sa-sù* | níĝ-ba, AMA-*ra* |
| $^{d}$*ᵓÀ-da Ḫa-lab*$_{x}$$^{ki}$ | 8 | king | si-si 2 gud | nídba, *in* AMA-*ra* |
| $^{d}$*ᵓA*$_{5}$*-da-ra* | 62 | – | 1 an-dùl and its decorations | níĝ-ba |
| $^{d}$*Áš-da-bíl* | 33 | – | 2 *gú-li-lum* | níĝ-ba |
| $^{d}$BAD *Du-du-la*$^{ki}$ | 63 | Ibrium | 1 an-dùl | – |
| $^{d}$BAD *Ga-na-na-im* | 61 | – | 1 *ḫa-bù*, 1 *ar-ra-sù* | níĝ-ba |
| $^{d}$*Ga-mi-iš* | 56 | – | 1 *ḫa-bù* | níĝ-ba, *ḫu-ru*$_{12}$*-mu* |
| $^{d}$*Ku-ra* | 1 | – | 1 ma-na 3 gín kb saĝ kb | – |
| $^{d}$*Ku-ra* | 18 | – | 2 *gú-li-lum* | níĝ-ba |
| $^{d}$*Ra-sa-ap ᵓÀ-da-ni*$^{ki}$ | 6 | – | 1 *ḫa-bù, ar-ra-sa-sù* | níĝ-ba, AMA-*ra* |

| | | | | |
|---|---|---|---|---|
| $^{d}$*Ra-sa-ap ᵓÀ-da-ni*$^{ki}$ | 7 | king | si-si 2 gud | nídba |
| diĝir-diĝir-diĝir | 2 | – | 1 ma-na kb | níĝ-ba |

## Text 10 (Ibrium 7)

| God | § | Donor | Objects | Occasion |
|---|---|---|---|---|
| $^{d}$*ᵓÀ-da* | 16 | – | 1 *ḫa-bù*, 1 *ar-ra-sù* | níĝ-ba |
| $^{d}$*ᵓÀ-da* | 40 | king | 4 si-si 2 gud | nídba, *in* AMA-*ra* |
| $^{d}$*Á-lá* lú *Zi-ig*$^{ki}$ | 14 | – | 1 ĜIŠ-sal | – |
| $^{d}$*Am-ma-rí-ig* | 6 | – | 1 ĜIŠ-banšur and its decoration | níĝ-ba |
| $^{d}$*Ku-ra* | 1 | – | 1 ma-na 3 gín kb saĝ urudu | – |
| $^{d}$*Ku-ra* | 17 | Ibrium | 1 ĜIŠ-banšur | níĝ-ba, *in* ud ne:saĝ-*sù* |
| $^{d}$*Ku-ra* | 92 | Ibrium | 1 ĝír mar-tu, 1 kù-sal | níĝ-ba, *in* ne-saĝ-*sú* |
| $^{d}$*Ku-ra* lú *ᵓÀ-ti-ni*$^{ki}$ | 49 | – | 1 ĜIŠ-banšur, 1 ĝír mar-tu | níĝ-ba |
| $^{d}$*Ra-sa-ap gú-núm* | 57 | – | 2 si am | – |
| diĝir-diĝir-diĝir | 37 | – | 1 ma-na TAR 3 gín kb | níĝ-ba |

## Text 11 (Ibrium 8)

| God | § | Donor | Objects | Occasion |
|---|---|---|---|---|
| $^{d}$*ᵓÀ-da* (é) | 7 | Ibrium's daughter | *maš-ar-tum* | níĝ-ba |
| $^{d}$*ᵓÀ-da* | 24 | king | 1 ešda, 1 *ar-ra-sù*, *ᵓa*$_5$*-na-gu* 4 si 2 gud | nídba, *in* $^{d}$AMA-*ra* |
| $^{d}$*ᵓÀ-da* lú *Ḫa-lab*$_x$$^{ki}$ | 52 | king | 1 ešda, *ᵓa*$_5$*-na-gu* 4 si 2 gud | nídba, *in* iti *ᵓa*$_5$*-nun* |
| $^{d}$*ᵓÀ-da* lú *Lu-ub*$^{ki}$ | 37 | – | 1 ešda | níĝ-ba, *in gi*-NI |
| $^{d}$*ᵓA*$_5$*-da-"bal"* […] | 44 | – | 1 ešda | níĝ-ba, *in* ud NI.DU |
| $^{d}$*Am-rí-ig* | 39 | – | 2 *gú-li-lum* | níĝ-ba |
| $^{d}$*Am-rí-ig* | 41 | – | 1 ĝír mar-tu | níĝ-ba |
| $^{d}$BAD *Ga-na-na-im* lú *Lu-wa-šum*$^{ki}$ | 40 | – | *ᵓa*$_5$*-na-gu* 1 ĜIŠ-banšur | – |
| $^{d}$En-ki | 49 | – | *zi-du* | – |
| $^{d}$*Ku-ra* | 1 | – | 1 ma-na 3 gín kb saĝ kb | – |
| [$^{d}$*Ku-ra*] | 8 | [Ibrium$^{?}$] | 1 kù-sal, 1 ĝír mar-tu | níĝ-ba, *in* ud ne:saĝ |
| $^{d}$*Ra-sa-ap ᵓÀ-da-ni*$^{ki}$ | 23 | king | 1 ešda, 1 *ar-ra-sù*, *ᵓa*$_5$*-na-gu* 4 si 2 gud | nídba |
| $^{d}$*Ra-sa-ap Du-bí-tum*$^{ki}$ | 45 | […] | *ᵓa*$_5$*-na-gu* 1 ĜIŠ-banšur | níĝ-ba, *in* ud ḫúl é-*sù* |
| $^{d}$*Ra-sa-ap gú-núm* | 9 | Ibrium | 1 kù-sal, 1 ĝír mar-tu | níĝ-ba, *in* ud ne:saĝ |
| $^{d}$Utu lú SA.ZA$_x$$^{ki}$ | 47 | Ibrium | 2 *ᵓà-ra-ma-tum* | níĝ-ba |
| diĝir-diĝir-diĝir | 25 | – | 1 ma-na ŠA-PI gín kb | níĝ-ba |
| […] | 12 | – | 2 *gú-li-lum* | níĝ-ba |

## Text 12 (Ibrium 9)

| God | § | Donor | Objects | Occasion |
|---|---|---|---|---|
| $^{d}$*ᵓÀ-da* | 34 | – | 1 *ḫa-bù*, 1 *ar-ra-sù* | níĝ-ba |
| $^{d}$*ᵓÀ-da* | 35 | king | *ᵓa*$_5$*-na-gu* 4 si-si 2 gud | nídba, *in* iti *ᵓa*$_5$*-nun* |
| $^{d}$*ᵓA*$_5$*-da-"bal" A-ru*$_{12}$*-ga-du*$^{ki}$ | 5 | king | 2 an-dùl and their decorations | níĝ-ba, *in* […] |

| | | | | |
|---|---|---|---|---|
| $^{d}$*ʾA$_{5}$-da-"bal" Ne-a-ù*$^{ki}$ | 51 | Ibrium | 1 ĝír mar-tu, 1 kù-sal | níĝ-ba |
| $^{d}$*ʾA$_{5}$-da-ra* | 10 | Giri and Nir-damu | 1 ĝír mar-tu, 1 kù-sal | níĝ-ba, *in* ud gi$_{4}$ *mi-nu Du-du-lu*$^{ki}$ |
| $^{d}$*Am-ma-rí-ig* | 17 | – | 2 *gú-li-lum* | níĝ-ba |
| $^{d}$*Áš-da-bíl* | 15 | – | 2 *gú-li-lum* | níĝ-ba |
| $^{d}$BAD *Ar-ti-na-an*$^{ki}$ | 13 | Ibrium | 1 ĝír mar-tu | níĝ-ba |
| $^{d}$BAD *Ga-na-na-im* | 10 | Giri and Nir-damu | 1 ĝír mar-tu, 1 kù-sal | níĝ-ba, *in* ud gi$_{4}$ *mi-nu Du-du-lu*$^{ki}$ |
| $^{d}$BAD *Má*-NE$^{ki}$ | 30 | Dusigu | 1 zi-bar | níĝ-ba |
| $^{d}$BAD *Zu-ra-mu*$^{ki}$ | 30 | Dusigu | 1 zi-bar | níĝ-ba |
| $^{d}$*Ku-ra* | 1 | – | 1 ma-na 3 gín kb saĝ kb | – |
| $^{d}$*Ku-ra* | 55 | Dusigu | 2 an-dùl and their decorations | níĝ-ba, *in* ud ne:saĝ |
| $^{d}$*Ra-sa-ap Du-ne-íb*$^{ki}$ | 54 | | head and kilt of his statue | iti NI.DU |
| diĝir-diĝir-diĝir | 39 | – | TAR kb | níĝ-ba |

## Text 13 (Ibrium 10)

| God | § | Donor | Objects | Occasion |
|---|---|---|---|---|
| $^{d}$*ʾÀ-da* lú *Lu-ub*$^{ki}$ | 57 | – | [1 *ḫa-bù*] | níĝ-ba |
| $^{d}$*ʾA$_{5}$-da-"bal" A-ru$_{12}$-ga-du*$^{ki}$ | 58 | – | 1 *ḫa-bù* | níĝ-ba |
| $^{d}$*A-da-ma ʾÀ-da-ni*$^{ki}$ | 21 | Dusigu | 1 an-dùl and its decoration | níĝ-ba |
| $^{d}$*A-da-ma ʾÀ-da-ni*$^{ki}$ | 59 | Ibrium | 1 an-dùl | níĝ-ba |
| $^{d}$*A-gi Su-ti-ig*$^{ki}$ | 61 | – | [1 an-dùl] | – |
| $^{d}$*Á-lá Zi-gú*$^{ki}$ | 18 | – | 1 bur-KAK | – |
| $^{d}$*Am-ma-rí-ig* | 63 | – | 2 *gú-li-lum* | níĝ-ba |
| $^{d}$*Ga-ra-ru$_{12}$* | 25 | Ibrium | 1 ĝír mar-tu, 1 kù-sal | níĝ-ba |
| $^{d}$*Ḫa-a-ba-du* lú *Ḫa-lab$_{x}$*$^{ki}$ | 20 | Ibrium | 1 *du-rúm* | níĝ-ba |
| $^{d}$*Iš:šára Wa*-NE-*du*$^{ki}$ | 23 | Dusigu | 1 an-dùl and its decoration | níĝ-ba |
| $^{d}$*Ku-ra* | 1 | – | 1 ma-na kb saĝ kb | – |
| $^{d}$*Ku-ra* | 22 | – | 3 gín kb saĝ kb, mu-ti-II | |
| $^{d}$*Ku-ra* | 54 | – | 2 *gú-li-lum* | níĝ-ba |
| $^{d}$*Ku-ra* | 67 | – | 2 *gú-li-lum* | níĝ-ba |
| $^{d}$NE-*ti-a-du* diĝir *Du-lu*$^{ki}$ | 26 | – | 2 kù-sal | níĝ-ba |
| $^{d}$*Ra-sa-ap ʾÀ-da-ni*$^{ki}$ | 21 | Dusigu | 1 an-dùl and its decoration | níĝ-ba |
| $^{d}$*Ra-sa-ap ʾÀ-da-ni*$^{ki}$ | 31 | king | 1 *ḫa-bù*, 1 *ar-ra-sù*, *ʾa$_{5}$-na-gu* 4 si 2 gud | nídba |
| $^{d}$*Ra-sa-ap ʾÀ-da-ni*$^{ki}$ | 59 | Ibrium | 1 an-dùl | níĝ-ba |
| $^{d}$*Ra-sa-ap* $^{d}$En-ki | 14 | Ibrium | 1 ĝír mar-tu | níĝ-ba |
| [...] | 60 | [...] | 1 an-dùl | [níĝ-ba] |

## Text 14 (Ibrium 11)

| God | § | Donor | Objects | Occasion |
|---|---|---|---|---|
| $^{d}$*ʾÀ-da* | 26 | – | 1 *ḫa-bù* | – |
| $^{d}$*ʾÀ-da* lú *Lu-ub*$^{ki}$ | 55 | – | 1 *ḫa-bù*, 1 *ar-ra-su-sù* | níĝ-ba, *in* [*gi*-NI] |
| $^{d}$*ʾA$_{5}$-da-"bal" ʾÀ-ma-du*$^{ki}$ | 64 | king | 1 ĜIŠ-banšur maḫ, *ʾa$_{5}$-na-gu-sù* | [níĝ-ba] |
| $^{d}$*ʾA$_{5}$-da-"bal" Ne-a-ù*$^{ki}$ | 65 | Ibrium | 1 ĜIŠ-asari, 4 saĝ lu$_{x}$ | níĝ-ba |
| $^{d}$*Am-ma-rí-ig* | 61 | – | 2 *gú-li-lum* | [níĝ-ba] |
| $^{d}$*Áš-da-bíl* | 60 | – | [2 *gú-li-lum*] | [níĝ-ba] |

| | | | | |
|---|---|---|---|---|
| $^{d}$*Ba-ra-ma* | 4 | king's mother | 1 kù-sal | níĝ-ba |
| $^{d}$*Ga-na-na* | 66 | – | 2 *bu*-DI, 4 *ti-ša-nu* | níĝ-ba, ĜIŠ.DUG.DU maḫ |
| $^{d}$*Ku-ra* | 1 | – | 1 ma-na kb saĝ kb | – |
| $^{d}$*Ku-ra* | 17 | – | 3 gín kb saĝ kb, *in* mu-ti-II | – |
| $^{d}$*Ra-sa-ap* *ʾÀ-da-ni*$^{ki}$ | 26 | king | *ʾa*$_5$*-na-gu* 4 si 2 gud, 1 *ḫa-bù*, 1 *ar-ra-sù* | [nídba], *in* $^{d}$AMA-*ra* |
| $^{d}$*Ra-sa-ap* $^{d}$*Du-ne-íb*$^{ki}$ | 69 | king | 1 ĜIŠ-banšur, 1 kù-sal | – |
| [...] | 53 | – | 2 *gú-li-lum* | níĝ-ba |

## Text 15 (Ibrium 12)

| God | § | Donor | Objects | Occasion |
|---|---|---|---|---|
| $^{d}$*ʾÀ-da* | 54 | Ibrium | 1 ĝír mar-tu | níĝ-ba, *gi*-NI |
| $^{d}$*ʾÀ-da* | 61 | Ibrium | 1 ĝír mar-tu | sikil |
| $^{d}$*ʾÀ-da* | 71 | king | 1 *ḫa-bù*, 1 *ar-ra-sù*, *ʾa*$_5$*-na-gu* 4 si 2 gud | nídba, *in* iti *ʾa*$_5$*-nun* |
| $^{d}$*ʾÀ-da* | 79 | king | 1 dib | sikil, *al*$_6$ tu-ra ama-gal en |
| $^{d}$*ʾÀ-da* | 80 | Ibrium | 2 *gú-li-lum* | sikil, *al*$_6$ tu-ra en |
| $^{d}$*ʾÀ-da* | 81 | Ibrium | 1 dib | sikil, *al*$_6$ tu-ra en |
| $^{d}$*ʾÀ-da Lu-ub*$^{ki}$ | 49 | – | 1 *ḫa-bù*, 1 *ar-ra-su-sù* | níĝ-ba, *in gi*-NI |
| $^{d}$*ʾA*$_5$*-da-"bal" Lu-ba-an*$^{ki}$ | 37 | king | 1 ĝír mar-tu | sikil |
| $^{d}$*ʾA*$_5$*-da-"bal" Lu-ba-an*$^{ki}$ | 62 | Ibrium | 1 íb-lá 1 *si-ti-tum* 1 ĝír-kun | sikil, *al*$_6$ tu-ra *Ib-rí-um* |
| $^{d}$*ʾA*$_5$*-da-"bal" Lu-ba-an*$^{ki}$ | 79 | king | 2 *gú-li-lum* | sikil, *al*$_6$ tu-ra en |
| $^{d}$*ʾA*$_5$*-da-"bal" Lu-ba-an*$^{ki}$ | 88 | king | 1 ĝír mar-tu | sikil |
| $^{d}$*ʾA*$_5$*-da-"bal"* [...]$^{ki}$ | 7 | king | 1 *gú-li-lum a-li-iš* ĜIŠ-gu-kak-gíd | *in* ud šeš-II-ib |
| $^{d}$*A-dar-a-an Da-na-áš*$^{ki}$ | 76 | Ibrium | 1 ĝír mar-tu, 1 kù-sal | níĝ-ba |
| $^{d}$*Am-ma-rí-ig* | 58 | – | 2 *gú-li-lum* | níĝ-ba |
| $^{d}$*Áš-da-bíl* | 57 | – | 2 *gú-li-lum* | níĝ-ba |
| $^{d}$*Áš-da-bíl* | 89 | Ibrium | 1 ĝír mar-tu | sikil, *al*$_6$ tu-ra en |
| $^{d}$*Áš-da-bíl Ba-šè*$^{ki}$ | 84 | Ibrium | 1 buru$_4$-MUŠEN [...] | níĝ-ba |
| $^{d}$BAD *Du-du-lu*$^{ki}$ | 5 | Ibrium | *ʾa*$_5$*-na-gu* 1 ĜIŠ-banšur, 1 kù-sal | níĝ-ba |
| $^{d}$*Da-bi-ir* diĝir *Ib-la*$^{ki}$ | 78 | – | 1 *gú-li-lum* | – |
| $^{d}$*Ḫa-a-ba-du* | 72 | king | 1 kù-sal | níĝ-ba, *al*$_6$ tu-ra ama-gal en |
| $^{d}$*Iš:šára Má*-NE$^{ki}$ | 73 | Tabur-damu | 1 kù-sal | níĝ-ba |
| $^{d}$*Iš:šára Zi-da-ra*$^{ki}$ | 3 | Tabur-damu | 1 kù-sal | níĝ-ba |
| $^{d}$*Iš:šára Zu-ra-mu*$^{ki}$ | 73 | Tabur-damu | 1 kù-sal | níĝ-ba |
| $^{d}$*Ku-ra* | 1 | – | 1 ma-na kb saĝ kb | – |
| $^{d}$*Ku-ra* | 18 | – | 2 *gú-li-lum* | níĝ-ba |
| $^{d}$*Ku-ra* | 36 | – | 3 gín kb saĝ kb, mu-ti | – |
| $^{d}$*Ku-ra* | 38 | | 10 ma-na kg kin$_5$-ak é $^{d}$*K.* | – |
| $^{d}$*Ku-ra* | 42 | – | 2 *gú-li-lum* | níĝ-ba |

| | | | | |
|---|---|---|---|---|
| $^{d}$*Ra-sa-ap ʾÀ-da-ni*$^{ki}$ | 27 | king | 1 *ḫa-bù*, 1 *ar-ra-si-sù*, *ʾa*$_{5}$*-na-gu* 4 si 2 gud | nídba, *in* $^{d}$AMA-*ra* |
| $^{d}$*Ra-sa-ap ʾÀ-da-ni*$^{ki}$ | 31 | Dusigu | 1 kù-sal | níĝ-ba |
| $^{d}$*Ra-sa-ap ʾÀ-da-ni*$^{ki}$ | 83 | – | *ʾà-na-gu* 1 ĜIŠ-banšur, 1 kù-sal | sikil, *al*$_{6}$ ama-gal en |
| $^{d}$*Ra-sa-ap Du-ne-íb*$^{ki}$ | 65 | king | 1 ĜIŠ-banšur, 1 kù-sal | níĝ-ba |
| $^{d}$*Ra-sa-ap Du-ne-íb*$^{ki}$ | 66 | king's mother | 1 ĝír mar-tu, 1 kù-sal | níĝ-ba |
| $^{d}$*Ra-sa-ap Du-ne-íb*$^{ki}$ | 67 | Ibrium | 1 ĝír mar-tu, 1 kù-sal | níĝ-ba |
| $^{d}$*Ra-sa-ap Du-ne-íb*$^{ki}$ | 90 | | kg | – |
| $^{d}$Utu SA.ZA$_{x}^{k}$ | 59 | Tabur-damu | 1 kù-sal | níĝ-ba |
| diĝir-diĝir-diĝir | 91 | – | 1 ma-na ŠÚ+ŠA 3 gín kb | níĝ-ba-níĝ-ba |

## Text 16 (Ibrium 13)

| God | § | Donor | Objects | Occasion |
|---|---|---|---|---|
| $^{dʾ}$*À-da* | 26 | king | 1 *ḫa-bù*, *ʾa*$_{5}$*-na-gu* si 2 gud | nídba, *in* $^{d}$AMA-*ra* |
| $^{dʾ}$*À-da Ḫa-lab*$_{x}^{ki}$ | 55 | king | 1 *ḫa-bù*, *ʾa*$_{5}$*-na-gu* si 2 gud | nídba, *in* iti *ʾa*$_{5}$*-nun* |
| $^{dʾ}$*À-da Lu-ub*$^{ki}$ | 46 | – | 1 *ḫa-bù*, 1 *ar-ra-sù* | níĝ-ba, *in gi*-NI |
| $^{dʾ}$*A*$_{5}$*-da-"bal" A-ru*$_{12}$*-ga-du*$^{ki}$ | 54 | Ibrium | 1 ĝír mar-tu, 1 kù-sal | níĝ-ba |
| [$^{d}$*A-dar-a-an*] *Da-na-áš*$^{ki}$ | 23 | king | 1 kù-sal | – |
| $^{d}$*Am-rí-ig* | 43 | – | 2 *gú-li-lum* | níĝ-ba |
| $^{d}$*Áš-da-bíl* | 43 | – | 2 *gú-li-lum* | níĝ-ba |
| $^{d}$*Aš-dar*$^{?}$ | 71 | king of [...] | 1 kù-sal | níĝ-ba |
| $^{d}$BAD *Ga-na-na-im* | 11 | – | 1 an-dùl and its decoration | níĝ-ba |
| $^{d}$BAD-munus *Lu-ba-an*$^{ki}$ | 60 | [–] | 1 *ù*-NAM-*mi-lu* | sikil, *in* ud tu-da |
| $^{d}$BAD-munus *Lu-ba-an*$^{ki}$ | 63 | Ibrium | 4 útul urudu maḫ | níĝ-ba |
| $^{d}$*Iš:šára Zu-ra-mu*$^{ki}$ | 60 | [–] | 2 ĝeštu$_{x}$-lá | sikil, *in* ud tu-da |
| $^{d}$*Ku-ra* | 1 | – | 1 ma-na kb saĝ kb | – |
| $^{d}$*Ku-ra* | 12 | – | 3 gín kb saĝ kb, mu-ti-II | – |
| $^{d}$*Ku-ra* | 73 | – | 2 *gú-li-lum* | níĝ-ba |
| $^{d}$*Ra-sa-ap ʾÀ-da-ni*$^{ki}$ | 25 | king | 1 *ḫa-bù*, 1 *ar-ra-sù*, *ʾa*$_{5}$*-na-gu* si 2 gud | nídba |
| $^{d}$*Ra-sa-ap Da-ra-um*$^{ki}$ | 50 | Ibrium | 1 íb-lá 1 *si-ti-tum* 1 ĝír-kun | níĝ-ba |
| $^{d}$TU é $^{d}$*Ku-ra* | 5 | king's mother | 1 á-MUŠEN | níĝ-ba |
| diĝir-diĝir-diĝir | 72 | – | 1 ma-na [...] | níĝ-ba |
| [...] | 60 | – | 1 kù-sal | sikil, *in* ud tu-da |

## Text 17 (Ibrium 14)

| God | § | Donor | Objects | Occasion |
|---|---|---|---|---|
| $^{dʾ}$*À-da Lu-ub*$^{ki}$ | 94 | – | 1 *ḫa-bù*, 1 *ar-ra-si-sù* | níĝ-ba, *in gi*-NI |
| $^{d}$*A-da-ma gú-núm* | 96 | queen | 2 *bu*-DI | níĝ-ba, *in* ud šu-mu-níĝin é diĝir-diĝir-diĝir |
| $^{d}$*Am-ma-rí-ig* | 97 | – | 2 *gú-li-lum* | níĝ-ba |
| $^{d}$*Áš-da-bíl* | 97 | – | 2 *gú-li-lum* | níĝ-ba |

| | | | | |
|---|---|---|---|---|
| $^{d}$*Ba-ra-ma* | 101 | Tabur-damu | 1 kù-sal | níĝ-ba |
| $^{d}$*Iš:šára* en | 68 | – | 1 an-dùl and its decoration | – |
| $^{d}$*Ku-ra* | 1 | – | 1 ma-na kb saĝ kb | – |
| $^{d}$*Ku-ra* | 12 | king's daughter | 1 kù-sal 1 buru$_4$-MUŠEN | [níĝ-ba], *in* ne:saĝ-*sù* |
| $^{d}$*Ku-ra* | 29 | – | 2 *gú-li-lum* | níĝ-ba |
| $^{d}$*Ku-ra* | 37 | – | 3 gín kb saĝ kb, mu-ti | |
| $^{d}$*Ku-ra* | 67 | – | 2 *gú-li-lum* | níĝ-ba |
| $^{d}$*Ku-ra* | 70 | – | *ḫa-za-nu a-ḫa-šum* gaba | – |
| $^{d}$*Ra-sa-ap* | 96 | queen | 1 ĝír mar-tu | níĝ-ba, *in* ud šu-mu-níĝin é diĝir-diĝir-diĝir |
| $^{d}$*Ra-sa-ap* *ʾÀ-da-ni*$^{ki}$ | 63 | king | 1 *ḫa-bù*, 1 *ar-ra-si-sù*, *ʾa*$_5$*-na-gu* 4 si 2 gud | nídba, *in* $^{d}$AMA-*ra* |
| $^{d}$*Ra-sa-ap* *ʾÀ-da-ni*$^{ki}$ | 65 | king's mother | 1 kù-sal 1 buru$_4$-MUŠEN | níĝ-ba |
| diĝir-diĝir-diĝir | 117 | – | 1 ma-na 10 kb | níĝ-ba |

## Text 18 (Ibrium 15)

| God | § | Donor | Objects | Occasion |
|---|---|---|---|---|
| $^{dʾ}$*À-da Ḫa-lab*$_x$$^{ki}$ | 57 | king | 1 *ḫa-bù*, *ar-ra-sù*, *ʾa*$_5$*-na-gu* si 2 gud | nídba, *in* $^{d}$AMA-*ra* |
| $^{dʾ}$*À-da Ḫa-lab*$_x$$^{ki}$ | 105 | king | 1 *ḫa-bù*, *ʾa*$_5$*-na-gu* si 2 gud | nídba, *ʾa*$_5$*-nun* |
| $^{dʾ}$*À-da* lú *Lu-ub*$^{ki}$ | 79 | – | 1 *ḫa-bù*, *ar-ra-sù* | níĝ-ba, *in gi*-NI |
| $^{dʾ}$*A*$_5$*-da-*"*bal*" *ʾÀ-ma-du*$^{ki}$ | 30 | Ibrium | 1 *a-ba-lum* | níĝ-ba |
| $^{dʾ}$*A*$_5$*-da-*"*bal*" *ʾÀ-ma-du*$^{ki}$ | 101 | king's mother | 1 ĝír mar-tu, 1 kù-sal | níĝ-ba, NI.DU |
| $^{d}$*Am-rí-ig* | 92 | – | 2 *gú-li-lum* | níĝ-ba |
| $^{d}$*Áš-da-bíl* | 91 | – | 2 *gú-li-lum* | níĝ-ba |
| $^{d}$BAD *Du-du-lu*$^{ki}$ | 90 | – | 2 an-dùl and their ornaments, 1 banšur, 1 ĝír mar-tu | níĝ-ba |
| $^{d}$*Iš:šára Má*-NE$^{ki}$ | 82 | king's mother | 1 zi-bar | níĝ-ba |
| $^{d}$*Iš:šára U*$_9$*-gú-a-áš*$^{ki}$ | 82 | king's mother | 1 zi-bar | níĝ-ba |
| $^{d}$*Iš:šára Zi-da-ra*$^{ki}$ | 12 | king's mother | 2 *bu*-DI | níĝ-ba |
| $^{d}$*Iš:šára Zu-ra-mu*$^{ki}$ | 82 | king's mother | 1 zi-bar | níĝ-ba |
| $^{d}$*Ku-ra* | 1 | – | 1 ma-na kb saĝ kb | – |
| $^{d}$*Ku-ra* | 28 | – | 2 *gú-li-lum* | níĝ-ba |
| $^{d}$*Ku-ra* | 50 | – | 3 gín kb saĝ kb, mu-ti-II | – |
| $^{d}$*Ku-ra* | 75 | – | 2 *gú-li-lum* | níĝ-ba |
| $^{d}$*Ra-sa-ap* *ʾÀ-da-ni*$^{ki}$ | 55 | king | 1 *ḫa-bù*, 1 *ar-ra-sù*, *ʾa*$_5$*-na-gu* si 2 gud | nídba |
| $^{d}$*Ra-sa-ap* *ʾÀ-da-ni*$^{ki}$ | 56 | king's mother | 1 kù-sal buru$_4$-MUŠEN | níĝ-ba |
| $^{d}$*Ra-sa-ap Du-ne-íb*$^{ki}$ | 101 | king's mother | 1 ĝír mar-tu, 1 kù-sal | níĝ-ba, NI.DU |
| diĝir-diĝir-diĝir | 98 | – | 1 ma-na 10 kb | níĝ-ba |

## Text 19 (Ibrium 16)

| God | § | Donor | Objects | Occasion |
|---|---|---|---|---|
| $^{d}$ʾ*À-da* | 15 | Ibbi-zikir | 1 dib | sikil |
| $^{d}$ʾ*À-da Ḫa-lab*$_{x}^{ki}$ | 35 | king | 1 *ḫa-bù*, *ar-ra-sù*, ʾ*a*$_{5}$*-na-gu* si 2 gud | nídba, *in* $^{d}$AMA-*ra* |
| $^{d}$ʾ*À-da Ḫa-lab*$_{x}^{ki}$ | 90 | king | 1 *ḫa-bù*, ʾ*a*$_{5}$*-na-gu* si 2 gud | nídba, ʾ*a*$_{5}$*-nun* |
| $^{d}$ʾ*À-da* lú *Lu-ub*$^{ki}$ | 62 | – | 1 *ḫa-bù*, 1 *ar-ra-sù* | níĝ-ba, *in gi*-NI |
| $^{d}$ʾ*A*$_{5}$*-da-*"*bal*" ʾ*À-ma-du*$^{ki}$ | 36 | […] | 1 ĝír mar-tu, 1 kù-sal | níĝ-ba, *al*$_{6}$ tu-ra-*sù* |
| $^{d}$ʾ*A*$_{5}$*-da-*"*bal*" ʾ*À-ru*$_{12}$*-ga-du*$^{ki}$ | 36 | […] | 1 ĝír mar-tu, 1 kù-sal | níĝ-ba, *al*$_{6}$ tu-ra-*sù* |
| $^{d}$ʾ*A*$_{5}$*-da-*"*bal*" ʾ*À-ru*$_{12}$*-ga-du*$^{ki}$ | 61 | king's mother | 3 še-šu-še-tag, 1 buru$_{4}$-mušen | níĝ-ba |
| $^{d}$*Á-lá Gù-šè-bù*$^{ki}$ | 74 | – | pieces of equipment for his chariot | – |
| $^{d}$*Am-ri-ig* | 64 | – | 1 *ḫa-bù*, 1 *ar-ra-sù*, 2 *gú-li-lum* | níĝ-ba |
| $^{d}$*Áš-da-bíl* | 63 | – | 2 *gú-li-lum* | níĝ-ba |
| $^{d}$*Aš-dar* | 24 | Ibrium | 1 banšur, 1 kù-sal | níĝ-ba |
| $^{d}$*Ba-tum-ma-du* | 5 | king | 1 kù-sal | níĝ-ba, *al*$_{6}$ tu-ra *Ib-rí-um* |
| $^{d}$*Ba-tum-ma-du* | 29 | – | 1 kù-sal | níĝ-ba, *al*$_{6}$ tu-ra en |
| $^{d}$BAD *Du-du-lu*$^{ki}$ | 70 | Ibrium | ʾ*a*$_{5}$*-na-gu* 1 banšur, 1 kù-sal | níĝ-ba |
| $^{d}$BAD-munus *A-ru*$_{12}$*-ga-du*$^{ki}$ | 61 | king's mother | 3 še-šu-še-tag, 1 buru$_{4}$-mušen | níĝ-ba |
| $^{d}$*Da-bí-na-du* | 29 | – | 1 kù-sal | níĝ-ba, *al*$_{6}$ tu-ra en |
| $^{d}$*Ga-na-na* | 91 | | 2 *bu*-DI 4 še-šu-še-tag | níĝ-ba |
| $^{d}$*Ku-ra* | 1 | – | 1 ma-na kb saĝ kb | – |
| $^{d}$*Ku-ra* | 28 | – | 2 *gú-li-lum* | níĝ-ba |
| $^{d}$*Ku-ra* | 47 | – | 3 gín kb saĝ kb, mu-ti-II | – |
| $^{d}$*Ku-ra* | 54 | – | 2 *gú-li-lum* | níĝ-ba |
| $^{d}$*Ra-sa-ap* ʾ*À-da-ni*$^{ki}$ | 34 | king | 1 *ḫa-bù*, 1 *ar-ra-sù*, ʾ*a*$_{5}$*-na-gu* si 2 gud | nídba |
| $^{d}$*Ra-sa-ap* ʾ*À-da-ni*$^{ki}$ | 43 | king's mother | 1 kù-sal | níĝ-ba, AMA-*ra* |
| diĝir-diĝir-diĝir | 93 | – | 1 ma-na ŠÚ+ŠA kb | níĝ-ba |

## Text 20 (Ibrium 17)

| God | § | Donor | Objects | Occasion |
|---|---|---|---|---|
| $^{d}$ʾ*À-da* | 39 | – | 1 íb-lá, 1 *si-ti-tum*, 1 ĝír-kun | sikil |
| $^{d}$ʾ*À-da Ḫa-lab*$_{x}^{ki}$ | 19 | king | 1 *ḫa-bù*, 1 *ar-ra-sù*, ʾ*a*$_{5}$*-na-gu* 4 si gud | nídba, *in* $^{d}$AMA-*ra* |
| $^{d}$ʾ*À-da Ḫa-lab*$_{x}^{ki}$ | 68 | king | 1 *ḫa-bù*, *ar-ra-sù*, ʾ*a*$_{5}$*-na-gu* 4 si 2 gud | nídba, iti ʾ*a*$_{5}$*-nun* |
| $^{d}$ʾ*À-da* lú *Lu-ub*$^{ki}$ | 59 | – | plating of a window of his temple | níĝ-ba, *in gi*-NI |
| $^{d}$ʾ*A*$_{5}$*-da-*"*bal*" lú *Lu-ba-an*$^{ki}$ | 40 | – | 1 íb-lá, 1 *si-ti-tum*, 1 ĝír-kun | *al*$_{6}$ tu-ra Ibrium |
| $^{d}$*Am-ma-rí-ig* | 62 | – | 2 *gú-li-lum* | níĝ-ba |
| $^{d}$BAD-munus *si-in Lu-ba-an*$^{ki}$ | 49 | Tarib-damu | 1 kù-sal | níĝ-ba, *in* ud *ter*$_{6}$*-bí* bur-KAK-*sù* $^{d}$ʾ*A*$_{5}$*-da-*"*bal*" |

| | | | | |
|---|---|---|---|---|
| [$^{d}$*Ga-na-na*] | 65 | – | 2 *bu*-di, 4 *ti-ša-nu* | níĝ-ba, ĜIŠ.DUG.DU máḫ |
| $^{d}$*Iš:šára Má*-NE$^{ki}$ | 67 | king's mother | 1 kù-sal | níĝ-ba |
| $^{d}$*Iš:šára Zu-ra-mu*$^{ki}$ | 67 | king's mother | 1 kù-sal | níĝ-ba |
| [$^{d}$*Ku-ra*] | 1 | – | [1 ma-na kb saĝ kb] | – |
| $^{d}$*Ku-ra* | 9 | – | [3 gín kb] saĝ kb, mu-ti-II | – |
| $^{d}$*Ku-ra* | 10 | – | [2 *gú-li-lum*] | níĝ-ba |
| $^{d}$*Ku-ra* | 52 | – | 2 *gú-li-lum* | níĝ-ba |
| $^{d}$*Ra-sa-ap ʾÀ-da-ni*$^{ki}$ | 18 | [king] | 1 *ḫa-bù*, 1 *ar-ra-su*, [*ʾa*$_{5}$*-na-gu* 4 si gud] | [nídba] |
| $^{d}$TU lú *ʾÀ-da-ni*$^{ki}$ | 26 | king's mother | 2 *bu*-DI | níĝ-ba |
| diĝir-diĝir-diĝir | 77 | – | [...] | níĝ-ba |
| [...] | 8 | [...] | 1 an-dùl-munus and its decoration | [...] |

## Text 21 (Ibrium 18)

| God | § | Donor | Objects | Occasion |
|---|---|---|---|---|
| $^{d}$*ʾÀ-da* | 24 | Ibrium | 1 íb-lá, 1 *si-ti-tum*, 1 ĝír-kun, 1 ĝír mar-tu, 3 *zú-zú-ba-tum* ĜIŠ-gígir-II | – |
| $^{d}$*ʾÀ-da* | 26 | – | 1 níĝ-anše-ak, 1 kù-sal, 1 *za-ḫa-da* | sikil, *al*$_{6}$ tu-ra Ibrium |
| [*ʾÀ-da*] | 69 | [king] | 1 *ḫa-bù*, *ʾa*$_{5}$*-na-gu* si 2 gud | nídba, [*in* $^{d}$AMA-*ra*] |
| $^{d}$*ʾÀ-da* | 71 | king | 1 íb-lá, 1 *si-ti-tum*, 1 ĝír-kun | sikil, *al*$_{6}$ tu-ra Ibbi-zikir |
| $^{d}$*ʾÀ-da* lú *Ḫa-lab*$_{x}$$^{ki}$ | 27 | king | [...] | nídba |
| $^{d}$*ʾÀ-da Lu-ub*$^{ki}$ | 45 | – | 1 *ḫa-bù*, 1 *ar-ra-sù* | níĝ-ba, *in gi*-NI |
| $^{d}$*ʾA*$_{5}$*-da-"bal" Lu-ba-an*$^{ki}$ | 77 | king | 1 zi-bar | sikil |
| $^{d}$*A-dar-a-nu Da-na-áš*$^{ki}$ | 22 | Ibrium | 1 kù-sal | níĝ-ba |
| $^{d}$*Am-ma-rí-ig* | 56 | – | 2 *gú-li-lum* | níĝ-ba |
| $^{d}$*Áš-da-bíl* | 55 | – | 2 *gú-li-lum* | níĝ-ba |
| $^{d}$*Ga-na-na* | 62 | | 2 *bu*-DI 4 še-šu-tag | níĝ-ba, ĜIŠ.DUG.DU maḫ |
| $^{d}$*Ku-ra* | 1 | – | 1 ma-na kb saĝ kb | – |
| $^{d}$*Ku-ra* | 38 | – | 2 *gú-li-lum* | níĝ-ba |
| $^{d}$*Ku-ra* | 59 | – | 2 *gú-li-lum* | níĝ-ba |
| $^{d}$*Ra-sa-ap ʾÀ-da-ni*$^{ki}$ | 29 | king | 1 *ḫa-bù*, 1 *ar-ra-sù* | níĝ-ba |
| $^{d}$*Sa-nu-ga ar Má*-NE$^{ki}$ | 16 | Ibrium | 1 dub | níĝ-ba |
| diĝir-diĝir-diĝir | 36 | – | 1 ma-na ŠA.PI gín kb | níĝ-ba |
| [...] | 30 | king | 1 *ḫa-bù* | níĝ-ba |

## Text 22

| God | § | Donor | Objects | Occasion |
|---|---|---|---|---|
| $^{dʾ}$*À-da* | 20 | – | 1 ma-na kg | sikil |
| $^{dʾ}$*A*$_{5}$*-da-*“*bal*” *A-ma-du*$^{ki}$ | 25 | – | 1 *ar-ra-sù ḫa-bù* | níĝ-ba |
| $^{d}$BAD *Du-du-lu*$^{ki}$ | 24 | Ibrium | 1 [*ḫa-bù*] | níĝ-ba |
| $^{d}$*Ga-mi-iš* | 24 | Ibrium | 1 *ar-ra-sù ḫa-bù* | níĝ-ba |
| $^{d}$*Ku-ra* | 24 | Ibrium | 1 ĜIŠ-ĝidru | níĝ-ba |
| diĝir-diĝir-diĝir | 8 | – | 72 ma-na kb | – |

## Text 23

| God | § | Donor | Objects | Occasion |
|---|---|---|---|---|
| $^{dʾ}$*À-da Ḫa-lab*$_{x}^{ki}$ | 1 | en | 1 dib maḫ lú ĜIŠ-ĝidru-ĜIŠ-ĝidru | *in* AMA-*ra* |
| $^{dʾ}$*À-da* lú *Ḫa-lab*$_{x}^{ki}$ | 25 | – | 1 *ar-ra-šum*, 1 *ḫa-bù* | níĝ-ba, *in* iti *ʾa*$_{5}$*-nun* |
| $^{dʾ}$*À-da* lú *Lu-ub*$^{ki}$ | 3 | – | plating of a window of his temple | – |
| $^{dʾ}$*À-da* lú *Lu-ub*$^{ki}$ | 21 | – | 1 *ar-ra-šum*, 1 *ḫa-bù* | níĝ-ba, *gi*-NI |
| $^{dʾ}$*A*$_{5}$*-da-*“*bal*” *A-ma-du*$^{ki}$ | 22 | king | 1 *ar-ra-šum*, 1 *ḫa-bù* | níĝ-ba, *in* ud NI.DU-NI.DU |
| $^{d}$*Áš-da-bíl* | 4 | – | 2 *gú-li-lum* | níĝ-ba |
| $^{d}$*Ku-ra* | 2 | – | 2 *gú-li-lum* | níĝ-ba |

## Text 24

| God | § | Donor | Objects | Occasion |
|---|---|---|---|---|
| $^{dʾ}$*A*$_{5}$*-da-*“*bal*” *A-ru*$_{12}$*-ga-du*$^{ki}$ | 10 | king | 1 *ar-ra-sù*, 1 *ḫa-bù* | níĝ-ba |
| $^{d}$*A-da-ma ʾÀ-da-ni*$^{ki}$ | 8 | Ibrium | 1 an-dùl and its decoration | níĝ-ba, *in ma-ʾà-wa-tum* |
| $^{d}$*A-gi Su-ti-gú*$^{ki}$ | 11 | – | (a statue) | – |
| $^{d}$*A-na-ma-du Ar-ḫa-du*$^{ki}$ | 3 | – | 1 ĝír mar-tu, 2 kù-sal | níĝ-ba |
| $^{d}$*Áš-da-bíl* | 13 | – | 2 *gú-li-lum* | níĝ-ba |
| $^{d}$*Ba-ra-ma* | 12 | Ibrium | 1 kù-sal | níĝ-ba, *in* ud ne:saĝ-*sù* |
| $^{d}$Nin-kar | 9 | Ibrium | 1 an-dùl | níĝ-ba |
| $^{d}$*Ra-sa-ap ʾÀ-da-ni*$^{ki}$ | 8 | Ibrium | 1 an-dùl and its decoration | níĝ-ba, *in ma-ʾà-wa-tum* |

# Markets (ki-lam$_7$) in the period of minister Ibrium's mandate

The term ki-lam$_7$ (ki:lam$_7$), a variant of the Sumerian šakanka (KI.LAM), Akkadian *maḫīrum*, is the term for "market".[1] Markets took place in numerous locations both inside and outside the reign of Ebla and were often held on the occasion of religious festivals.[2] The term ki:lam$_7$, in fact, is usually followed by a theonym or a toponym. In some cases, the name denoting a religious ceremony (*gi-ba-lu*) or even the presence of a religious confraternity (šeš-II-ib) can specify the market.

The goods purchased at these markets were of various kinds: wool and all sorts of textiles, livestock and plant products, timber and wooden objects, bags, weapons, and so on. Sometimes the texts indicate the person in charge of the purchases, occasionally indicating their profession[3] (ur$_4$, "collector (of goods)", lú-kar, "trader").

## Gods

### $^{d}$*ʾÀ-da*

Market of the god Hadda; years 2b, 3, 4, 7, 9, 10, 12, 13, 14, 16, 17, 18 (texts no. 5, 6, 7, 10, 12, 13, 15, 16, 17, 19, 20, 21). It occurs also in text no. 25.

The month in which this market took place is only specified in text no. 5: *in* iti *ʾa$_5$-nun*, the eighth month. On two occasions the market of Hadda is mentioned together with that of the city of Šeʾamu (texts no. 13 and 21, where also the market of the god Ašdabil is recorded). This market is also mentioned together with the market of the Palace (ki:lam$_7$ SA.ZA$_x^{ki}$, no. 15).

The goods purchased are textiles (garments and kilts), wool (from the city of Mari), oxen, shells and carapaces, daggers, spearheads, bags, goads, a picket for a wheel, and other assets whose meaning is still uncertain (ĜIŠ-ti-ḪAR, níĝ-NE, ĜIŠ-*šè-bir$_5$-gi-nu*).

### $^{d}$*A-da-ma*

Market of the god Adamma, sometimes with the specification of the cult place, ki:lam$_7$ $^{d}$*A-da-ma ʾÀ-da-ni*$^{ki}$ (see below *sub ʾÀ-da-ni*$^{ki}$); years 1a, 1b, 2b, 3, 4, 8, 10, 11, 12, 15, 16 (texts no. 2, 3, 5, 6, 7, 11, 13, 14, 15, 18, 19). It occurs also in text no. 25.

On some occasions, it is mentioned together with other places, ceremonies, or functions: bàd-diĝir$^{ki}$ (text no. 3), SA.ZA$_x^{ki}$ (7 and 25), *gi-ba-lu* (11), and šeš-II-ib (13 and 15).

The goods purchased are textiles (garments and kilts), wool (from the city of Mari), oxen, daggers, myrtle, timber and wood objects (ĜIŠ-ti-ḪAR and ĜIŠ-sal).

### $^{d}$*Áš-da-bíl*

Market of the god Ašdabil; years 1a, 1b, 2b, 3, 4, 6, 8, 9, 10, 11, 14, 15, 18 (texts no. 2, 3, 5, 6, 7, 9, 11, 12, 13, 14, 17, 18, 21). It occurs also in text no. 25.

On three occasions this market is recorded together with that of the city of Šeʾamu: texts no. 7, 11 (the market of SA.ZA$_x^{ki}$ is also recorded), and 21.

In text 17 the city of Dub appears as cult center of Ašdabil (ki:lam$_7$ $^{d}$*Áš-da-bíl Du-ub*$^{ki}$ *Ìr-ku*$^{ki}$).

1 The term ki:lam$_7$ (IŠ$_{11}$.KI) has been correctly interpreted by Conti (1997, pp. 59-60, nt. 139).

2 The connection of these markets in the period of Ebla with religious festivals has been stressed by Biga 2002 and Biga 2003. Hence the choice of some scholars to translate the term ki:lam$_7$ as "fair", rather than "market". Here, however, the translation "market" will be kept.

3 On some occasions, for purchases made in the ki:lam$_7$ of the city of Mari (probably also in that of the city of Kiš, even if the term ki:lam$_7$ does not appear), dam-gàr, "merchant", is generically indicated (see texts no. 13 § 29; 14 § 16; 17 §§ 25 and 46).

The goods purchased are essentially textiles (garments and kilts), but sporadically also wool (from the city of Mari) is found, bags, one dagger, and other assets whose meaning is still uncertain (ĜIŠ-ti-ḪAR, and níĝ-NE).

**^d^*Ga-mi-iš***

Market of the god Kamiš; years 1b, 2b, 8, 9, 10, 12, 14, 15, 16, 17 (texts no. 3, 5, 11, 12, 13, 15, 17, 18, 19, 20). It occurs also in text no. 25.

In text no. 19 this market is mentioned together with that of the city of ᵓAdani (ki:lam$_7$ *ᵓÀ-da-ni wa* ^d^*Ga-mi-iš*).

The goods purchased are textiles (garments and kilts), wool (from the city of Mari), livestock (oxen and equids), leek from the mountain region, aromatic essence, daggers, helmets, chariot shafts, and ĜIŠ-ti-ḪAR.

**Other deities**

Markets named after other gods are sporadic.

- The market of ᵓAdabal of Arugadu occurs only in year 9 (text no. 12), together with that of the god Kamiš. The goods purchased are textiles (garments and kilts), equids, and leek from the mountain region.
- The market of Dagan of Tuttul occurs in year 15 (text no. 18), together with those of the gods Kamiš and Ašdabil. The goods purchased are exclusively wool (from the city of Mari) and garments.
- The market of ᵓIlam occurs in years 1a and 6 (texts no. 2 and 9); the goods purchased are oxen and leek from the mountain region.

**Festival**

The market at the festival of ^d^AMA-ra is attested in years 2b, 8, and 12 (texts no. 5, 11, and 15, where the specification of the cult place, ᵓAdani, occurs); the goods purchased are textiles (garments and kilts), lambs, GIŠ-ti-ḪAR, leek from the mountain region, and daggers.

## CITIES AND PLACES

***ᵓÀ-da-ni*^ki^**

Numerous ki:lam$_7$ took place in the city of ᵓAdani, cult place of the gods Rašap and his *paredra* Adamma. Names of deities or that of a religious ceremony are mentioned. The city was perhaps located near the estuary of the Orontes river.

**ki:lam$_7$ *ᵓÀ-da-ni*^ki^**: it is attested in years 1a, 2a, 3, 6, 10, 11, 12, 13, 14, 15, 16, and 17 (texts no. 2, 4, 6, 9, 13, 14, 15, 16, 17, 18, 19, and 20); it occurs also in text no. 25. It is sometimes specified that the market took place during the AMA-ra festival (texts no. 9, 13, 14, 16, 18, and 25). On two occasions the reference to the city of ᵓAdani is found together with that of other cities (NIab and Larugadu, text no. 6) or deities (Kamiš, text no. 19).

The goods purchased are textiles (garments and kilts), wool (from the city of Mari), livestock (oxen, lambs, and equids), hides, leek from the mountain region, goads, lapis lazuli, daggers, helmets, chariot shafts, myrtle and ĜIŠ-ti-ḪAR.

**ki:lam$_7$ ^d^*A-da-ma ᵓÀ-da-ni*^ki^**: it is attested in years 2b, 3, 8, 10, 12, 15, 16 (texts no. 5, 6, 11, 13, 15, 18, 19); it occurs also in text no. 25.

**ki:lam$_7$ *gi-ba-lu ᵓÀ-da-ni*^ki^ and *zi-ba-tum ᵓÀ-da-ni*^ki^**: the first term, and perhaps also the second one, most likely indicate religious ceremonies that took place in the city of ᵓAdani. In just one attestation (TM.75.G.1918 = ARET XXII 5 rev. XVI 17), the term *gibalu* is preceded by the AN sign, which must be considered a scribal error. That at least *gibalu* was a religious ceremony is confirmed by the fact that there are some occurrences in which the expression *in* ud *gi-ba-lu* appears (cf. ARET III o. 1'–3'; TM.75.G.2403 o. II 23, etc.).

*gi-ba-lu ʾÀ-da-ni*$^{ki}$; years 1a, 1b, 6, 7, 8 (*gi-ba-ù* [*wa*] $^{d}$*A-dam-ma ʾÀ-da-ni*$^{ki}$), 14, and 18 (*gi-ba-i*, without specification of the city) (texts no. 2, 3, 9, 10, 11, 17, and 21). It occurs also in text no. 25, mentioned together with the god Hadda: ki:lam$_7$ $^{d}$*ʾÀ-da wa gi-ba-lu ʾÀ-da-ni*$^{ki}$. The goods purchased are usually garments and kilts, with the exception of text no. 11 in which other goods appear, namely wool, daggers and oxen.

*zi-ba-tum ʾÀ-da-ni*$^{ki}$ is attested only in years 1a and 6 (texts no. 2 and 9). The goods purchased are textiles (garments and kilts), and spearheads.

**ki:lam$_7$ šeš-II-ib *ʾÀ-da-ni*$^{ki}$**: the connection between this ki:lam$_7$ and the presence of the šeš-II-ib confraternity confirms the religious context in which several markets were held by some of the most important cult centers.[4] This market is attested during the years 1b, 5, 10, 12, 13 (texts no. 3, 8, 13, 15, 16), and on two occasions the participation of the šeš-II-ib confraternity to the cult of the goddess Adamma is mentioned (ki:lam$_7$ šeš-II-ib *wa* $^{d}$*A-da-ma ʾÀ-da-ni*$^{ki}$, texts no. 13 and 15). The goods purchased are textiles (garments and kilts), wool (from the city of Mari), livestock (oxen and equids), and ĜIŠ-ti-ḪAR.

### *Ìr-ku*$^{ki}$

This town was inside the administrative horizon of Ebla, possibly not far from Emar (see Archi 2015, p. 221). Its ki:lam$_7$ is attested in years 1a, 6, 12, 14 (texts no. 2, 9, 15, 17). The passage in text no. 17 (ki:lam$_7$ $^{d}$*Áš-da-bíl Du-ub*$^{ki}$ *Ìr-ku*$^{ki}$) could be interpreted as "the market of the god Ašdabil of Dub which took place in Irku". The goods purchased are exclusively textiles (garments and kilts) and wool.

### *Ma-rí*$^{ki}$

The market of the city of Mari is attested in years 1b, 3, 10, 11, and 14 (texts no. 3, 6, 13, 14, and 17). The goods purchased are exclusively garments.

### NI-*ab*$^{ki}$

NIab was a village in close vicinity of Ebla. Its ki-lam$_7$ is attested only at the beginning of Ibrium's term, in years 1a and 3 (texts no. 2 and 6; in the latter text its reference is found together with that of the cities of ʾAdani and Larugadu). The goods purchased are textiles (garments and kilts), livestock (oxen and equids), ĜIŠ-ti-ḪAR, dyeing for fabrics, and daggers.

### SA.ZA$_x$$^{ki}$

The market of the Palace is attested in years 1a, 1b, 2b, 3, 4, 6, 8, 10, 12, 15, 16, 18 (texts no. 2, 3, 5, 6, 7, 9, 11, 13, 15, 18, 19, 21); it occurs also in text no. 25.

It is mentioned together with some deities or cities: with Adamma (texts no. 7 and 25, where it is specified Adamma of ʾAdani), with Ašdabil and the city of Šeʾamu (text no. 11), with Hadda (15), and with the city of NIri (21).

The goods purchased are textiles (garments and kilts), wool (from the city of Mari), livestock (oxen and rams), goat skins, leek from the mountain region, bags, chariot shafts, myrtle, one wooden table, and ĜIŠ-ti-ḪAR.

### *Ši-ʾà-mu*$^{ki}$

**ki:lam$_7$ *Ši(/Šè)-ʾà-mu(/am)*$^{ki}$**: it is attested in years 1a, 4, 8, 10, 18 (texts no. 2, 7, 11, 13, and 21). The market of Šeʾamu is mentioned together with two deities: Ašdabil (text no. 7 and 11—in this last text also the market of SA.ZA$_x$$^{ki}$ occurs), and Hadda (13 and 21, where also the market of Ašdabil is recorded).

4 See Biga 2002, p. 282; Biga 2003, p. 64. On the annual cultic journey of the members of the šeš-II-ib confraternity, see Archi 2002.

The goods purchased are textiles (garments and kilts), wool (from the city of Mari), oxen, bags, ĝIŠ-ti-ḪAR, and níĝ-NE.

### Other cities

Other cities are only sporadically mentioned as the seat of a market. They are:

- bàd-diĝir$^{ki}$: its market is mentioned in year 1b (text no. 3), together with that of the goddess Adamma; the goods purchased are kilts and ĝIŠ-ti-ḪAR.
- Dudulu/a (Tuttul): it is attested in years 1a and 15 (texts no. 2 and 18). In text no. 18 the market of Dagan of Tuttul is mentioned in connection with those of the gods Kamiš and Ašdabil; the goods purchased in Tuttul are exclusively wool (from the city of Mari) and garments.
- Gagaban (in the region of Nagar): it is mentioned in text no. 25; the goods purchased are garments.
- Immaran: it occurs in text no. 25; the goods purchased are garments. The market of Immaran is mentioned also in ARET XIII 14 § 24.
- Kablul (to be placed north of Karkamiš, east to the Euphrates): its market occurs only once, in year 14 (text no. 17); in this occasion two oxen are purchased.
- Kiš: it is attested only once, in year 13 (text no. 16). The term ki:lam$_7$ does not appear, but garments, wool (from the city of Mari), and shells were bought in this city.
- (L)arugadu: it occurs in years 3 and 9 (texts no. 6, together with the markets of two other cities [ʾAdani and NIab], and no. 12, as a cult place of the god ʾAdabal, together with the market of Gamiš); the goods purchased are textiles (garments and kilts), equids, leek from the mountain region, daggers, and ĝIŠ-ti-ḪAR.
- NIri: it occurs only once, in year 18 (text no. 21), in connection with the market at the Palace; the mention of purchased goods is not preserved.

## PEOPLE

Sometimes the texts inform of the identity of the people responsible for the purchases at the markets. They may have the title of ur$_4$, "collector (of goods)", or lu$_2$-kar, "trader".

### *Wa-ba-rúm*

Wabarum was certainly the most active official in acquiring goods in markets for the whole period of minister Ibrium. He is mentioned in years 1a and 1b, 2b, 3, 6, 7, 10, 11, 12, 14, 15, 16, 17, and 18 (texts no. 2, 3, 5, 6, 9, 10, 13, 14, 15, 17, 18, 19, 20, and 21). In texts no. 5 and 8 (Ibrium 2b and 5) he is identified with the title ur$_4$, "collector (of goods)". In text no. 12, §11, a certain Wabarum, travelling merchant of the city of Tuttul (ga:eš$_8$ *Du-du-lu*$^{ki}$)—perhaps to be identified with the same person—appears while handing over beer, together with his wife and son.

He made his purchases mainly at the city of ʾAdani, but he was also active in other cities, such as Larugadu, NIab, and Šeʾamu, and at the market of the Palace (SA.ZA$_x$$^{ki}$).

Wabarum went to the markets of various deities: Adamma (of ʾAdani), Ašdabil, Kamiš, and Hadda.

The commodity that he bought (almost) in every transaction is ĝIŠ-ti-ḪAR. This term seems to indicate a type of timber, perhaps sold in poles or planks, since sometimes (although very rarely) this term is preceded by a number—see for example texts no. 7 (96 ĝIŠ-ti-ḪAR), and 21 (150 ĝIŠ-ti-ḪAR *wa* níĝ-NE). Wabarum also often bought large quantities of various types of textiles, sometimes together with wool from the city of Mari. Although less frequently attested, there are also purchases of livestock (oxen, equids, and lambs) and other goods (daggers, spearheads, wooden objects, leek from the mountain region, chariot shafts, hides, etc.).

Besides Wabarum, there are other men whose names appear more than once associated with purchases made at various markets. They are, in alphabetical order:

- *A-bù*-Kur[ki], who is mentioned in texts no. 2 and 25; he bought wool and garments in three cities (Irku, Immaran, and Gagaban).
- *Bù-da-ma-lik*, mentioned in a list of ur$_4$ in ARET XIX 5 r. XIV 2–20, acquired textiles and equids at the market of Kamiš (texts no. 3, 12—where also ᵓAdabal of Arugadu is recorded—and 20).
- *Ib-bí-um*, identified as a collector of goods in text no. 4, bought ten oxen at a market whose name is not preserved (text no. 3), and also two wooden objects (2 ĜI[š-x]) at the market of the city of ᵓAdani (no. 4);
- *Ib-lu$_5$-zú*, a trader (lú-kar) of Manuwat, is mentioned in text no. 8 together with two other traders ([...-*g*]*i* and *I-za-iš-ru$_{12}$*); they bought textiles at the market of the city of ᵓAdani on the occasion of the cultic journey of the šeš-II-ib confraternity. In text 11 he bought textiles, oxen, and daggers at the market of Kamiš.
- *Na-zi*, who appears in a list of ur$_4$ in ARET XIX 5 r. XIV 2–20, was associated with the market of the city of Mari (texts no. 3 and 6), where he acquired garments and kilts.
- NI-(*l*)*a-ba-mu* is mainly active in the market of the god Hadda (texts no. 6, 7, and 10), but also went to the market in the city of Šeᵓamu (2). The goods he bought are mainly bags and garments, but also wool from the city of Mari, shells and carapaces, spearheads, daggers, and oxen.
- *Rí-ì-ma-lik*, trader of Kakmium (cf. text no. 9 § 71), bought one mule at the market of the god Kamiš (5) and ten oxen at the market of the god Adamma (14).

The following people are mentioned only once in the texts:

- BAD.MUŠ.LU$_5$, who bought wool (from the city of Mari) and ĜIŠ-ti-ḪAR at the market of the city of ᵓAdani on the occasion of the cultic journey of the šeš-II-ib confraternity (text 16);
- *Du-bí-ga-lu* acquired aromatic essence at the market of Kamiš (18);
- *Iš-ra*-BAD, trader of Kakmium, acquired garments, wool, oxen, and hides at the market of the city of ᵓAdani (20);
- *I-za-iš-ru$_{12}$*, trader of Manuwat, bought textiles at the market of the city of ᵓAdani on the occasion of the cultic journey of the šeš-II-ib confraternity, together with Ibluzu and another man (whose name has not preserved);
- *Puzur$_4$-ra-ma-lik*, trader of Kakmium (cf. text no. 13 § 52), bought textiles, equids, and leek at the market of the god Kamiš (15);
- *Rí-ì-Ḫa-lab$_x$* bought textiles, helmets, leek from the mountain region, and one mule at the market of the god Kamiš (3).

### Text 2 (Ibrium 1a)

| ki:lam$_7$ | § | Silver | Goods purchased | Buyer |
|---|---|---|---|---|
| $^d$*A-da-ma* | 24 | 1;15 | 13 kilts, ĜIŠ-sal | Wabarum |
| ᵓ*À-da-ni*$^{ki}$ | 47 | 13;14+[x] | 35 oxen, 75 garments, 84 kilts, leek from the mountain region, […], myrtle | – |
| $^d$*Áš-da-bíl* | 71 | [x]+5;10 ½ | 1 dagger, ĜIŠ-ti-ḪAR | Wabarum |
| *Du-du-la*$^{ki}$ | 70 | 3;38 | 52 garments | – |
| *gi-ba-lu* ᵓ*À-da-ni*$^{ki}$ | 15 | 1;08 | 15 garments, 1 kilt | – |
| $^d$*Ì-lam* | 51 | 3;27 | 6 oxen | – |
| *Ìr-ku*$^{ki}$ | 63 | 15;05 | 180 garments, 150 stone weights of wool | Abu-Kur |
| NI-*ab*$^{ki}$ | 55 | 24;44 | 136 garments, 23 kilts, dull red dye, ĜIŠ-ti-ḪAR, 11 oxen, 5 equids | – |
| SA.ZA$_x$$^{ki}$ | 23 | 11;38 | 410 stone weights of wool from Mari, 32 garments, 32 kilts | – |
| SA.ZA$_x$$^{ki}$ | 62 | 11;29 | 140 garments, 60 kilts, 20 stone weights of wool, 6 rams | |
| *Še-*ᵓ*à-am*$^{ki}$ | 72 | 3;35 | 56 garments, 1 bag | NI(l)abamu |
| *zi-ba-tum* ᵓ*À-da-ni*$^{ki}$ | 19 | 4;26 | 62 garments, 21 kilts | – |
| | | [x]+98;49 ½ | | |

### Text 3 (Ibrium 1b)

| ki:lam$_7$ | § | Silver | Goods purchased | Buyer |
|---|---|---|---|---|
| $^d$*A-da-ma wa* bàd-diĝir$^{ki}$ | 70 | 8;15 | 194 kilts, ĜIŠ-ti-ḪAR | Wabarum |
| $^d$*Áš-da-bíl* | 21 | 0;41 | ĜIŠ-ti-ḪAR | Wabarum |
| $^d$*Ga-mi-iš* | 13 | 12;02 | 14 garments, 140 kilts, 134 helmets, leek from the mountain region, 1 equid | Reᵓi-Ḫalab |
| $^d$*Ga-mi-iš* | 14 | 0;30 | 1 equid | Buda-malik |
| $^d$*Ga-mi-iš* | 15 | 2;00 | ĜIŠ-ti-ḪAR | Wabarum |
| *gi-ba-lu* ᵓ*À-da-ni*$^{ki}$ | 50 | 3;42 | 23 garments, 70 kilts | – |
| *Ma-rí*$^{ki}$ | 73 | 4;00 | 74 garments, 1 kilt | Nazi |
| SA.ZA$_x$$^{ki}$ | 12 | 7;40 | 25 garments, 126 kilts | – |
| šeš-II-ib ᵓ*À-da-ni*$^{ki}$ | 57 | 4;14 | 15 garments, 104 kilts, 1 equid, ĜIŠ-ti-ḪAR | Wabarum |
| […] | 37 | 1;40 | ĜIŠ-ti-ḪAR | Wabarum |
| […] | 38 | 5;00 | 10 oxen | Ibbium |
| | | 49;44 | | |

### Text 4 (Ibrium 2a)

| ki:lam$_7$ | § | Silver | Goods purchased | Buyer |
|---|---|---|---|---|
| ᵓ*À-da-ni*$^{ki}$ | 94 | 2;[xx] | 2 GI[š-x] | Ibbium, ur$_4$ |

### Text 5 (Ibrium 2b)

| ki:lam$_7$ | § | Silver | Goods purchased | Buyer |
|---|---|---|---|---|
| $^{d}$ᵓ*À-da in* iti *ᵓa$_5$-nun* | 70 | 14;14 | 5 garments, 61 oxen | – |
| $^{d}$*A-da-ma ᵓÀ-da-ni*$^{ki}$ | 1 | 17;48 | 65 garments, 210+[x] kilts, 8 daggers, 354 stone weights of wool, myrtle, ĜIŠ-ti-ḪAR | Wabarum, ur$_4$ |
| AMA-*ra* | 20 | 18;13 | 7 garments, 607 kilts, 18 daggers, ĜIŠ-ti-ḪAR, | Wabarum |
| $^{d}$*Áš-da-bíl* | 64 | 5;52 | 3 garments, 253 kilts, ĜIŠ-ti-ḪAR | Wabarum |
| $^{d}$*Ga-mi-iš* | 37 | [x] | 1 equid | Reᵓi-malik |
| $^{d}$*Ga-mi-iš* | 38 | 3;00 | ĜIŠ-ti-ḪAR | Wabarum |
| SA.ZA$_x$$^{ki}$ | 7 | 0;24 | chariot shafts, ĜIŠ-ti-ḪAR | Wabarum |
| SA.ZA$_x$$^{ki}$ | 45 | 1;56 | leek from the mountain region, 3 oxen | – |
| SA.ZA$_x$$^{ki}$ | 49 | 0;20 | 14 kilts | – |
| | | [x]+61;47 | | |

### Text 6 (Ibrium 3)

| ki:lam$_7$ | § | Silver | Goods purchased | Buyer |
|---|---|---|---|---|
| $^{d}$ᵓ*À-da* | 94 | 11;02 | 102 garments, bronze and not refined copper for 1 kettle, 1 dagger, 4 oxen, bags | NI(l)abamu |
| $^{d}$*A-da-ma ᵓÀ-da-ni*$^{ki}$ | 34 | 1;00 | GIŠ-ti-ḪAR | Wabarum |
| ᵓ*À-da-ni wa* NI-*ab*$^{ki}$ *wa La-ru$_{12}$-ga-du*$^{ki}$ | 86 | 6;16 | 35 garments, 185 kilts, 12 daggers, ĜIŠ-ti-ḪAR | Wabarum |
| $^{d}$*Áš-da-bíl* | 93 | 1;08 | 10 garments, 10 kilts | – |
| *Ma-rí*$^{ki}$ | 85 | 12;00 | 194 garments | Nazi |
| SA.ZA$_x$$^{ki}$ | 91 | 8;50 | 92 garments, 49 kilts, 1 table | – |
| | | 40;16 | | |

### Text 7 (Ibrium 4)

| ki:lam$_7$ | § | Silver | Goods purchased | Buyer |
|---|---|---|---|---|
| $^{d}$ᵓ*À-da* | 56 | 18;51 | 34 garments, 226 kilts, 2 daggers, 33 oxen | – |
| $^{d}$ᵓ*À-da* | 76 | 11;11 | 9 shells, 49 garments, 400 stone weights of wool from Mari, carapaces, 1000 spearheads, 24 bags | NIlabamu |
| $^{d}$*A-da-ma wa* SA.ZA$_x$$^{ki}$ | 28 | 11;20 | 84+[x] garments, 8 stone weights of wool from Mari, 96 ĜIŠ-ti-ḪAR | Wabarum |
| $^{d}$*A-da-ma wa* SA.ZA$_x$$^{ki}$ | 29 | 0;06 | myrtle | – |
| $^{d}$*Áš-da-bíl wa Ši-ᵓà-mu*$^{ki}$ | 75 | 7;30 | 43 garments, 265 kilts | – |
| | | 48;58 | | |

### Text 8 (Ibrium 5)

| ki:lam$_7$ | § | Silver | Goods purchased | Buyer |
|---|---|---|---|---|
| šeš-II-ib ᵓ*À-da-ni*$^{ki}$ | 15 | 4;23 | 48 garments, 48 kilts | Ibluzu, Iza-išru, traders of the city of Manuwat |
| [...]$^{ki}$ | 27 | 7;07 | 126 kilts, <ĜIŠ-ti-ḪAR> | Wabarum, ur$_4$ |
| | | 11;30 | | |

## Text 9 (Ibrium 6)

| ki:lam$_7$ | § | Silver | Goods purchased | Buyer |
|---|---|---|---|---|
| *ʾÀ-da-ni*$^{ki}$ AMA-*ra* | 17 | […] | 17 garments, 138[+x] kilts, […] | – |
| $^{d}$*Áš-da-bíl* | 34 | 4;40 | 100+[x] garments, 14 kilts | – |
| *gi-ba-lu ʾÀ-da-ni*$^{ki}$ | 47 | 1;37 | 8 garments, 68 kilts | – |
| $^{d}$*Ì-lam* | 21 | 0;10 | leek from the mountain region | – |
| *Ìr-ku*$^{ki}$ | 35 | 10;32 | 321 garments, 12 kilts | – |
| SA.ZA$_x$$^{ki}$ | 12 | 0;42 | 7 garments | – |
| *zi-ba-tum ʾÀ-da-ni*$^{ki}$ | 74 | 1;22 | 50 kilts, spearheads | Wabarum |
| | | [x]+19;03 | | |

## Text 10 (Ibrium 7)

| ki:lam$_7$ | § | Silver | Goods purchased | Buyer |
|---|---|---|---|---|
| $^{dʾ}$*À-da* | 80 | 6;40 | 76 garments, ĜIŠ-ti-ḪAR | Wabarum |
| $^{dʾ}$*À-da* | 81 | 1;00 | bags | NIlabamu |
| *gi-ba-lu ʾÀ-da-ni*$^{ki}$ | 83 | 8;20 | 100 garments, 16 kilts | – |
| | | 16;00 | | |

## Text 11 (Ibrium 8)

| ki:lam$_7$ | § | Silver | Goods purchased | Buyer |
|---|---|---|---|---|
| $^{d}$AMA-*ra* | 22 | 15;30 | 115 garments, 220+[x] kilts, leek from the mountain region | – |
| $^{d}$*Ga-mi-iš* | 30 | [x]+13;42 | 82 garments, 341 kilts, 10 daggers, 2 oxen | Ibluzu |
| *gi-ba-ù wa* $^{d}$*A-dam-ma ʾÀ-da-ni*$^{ki}$ | 6 | [x]+ 9;20 | 100 garments, 50 kilts, 93 KIN measures of wool, 7 daggers, 22 oxen | […N]E |
| SA.ZA$_x$$^{ki}$ *wa* $^{d}$*Áš-da-bíl Ši-ʾà-mu*$^{ki}$ | 33 | 14;00 | 78 garments, [x] kilts | – |
| | | [x]+52;32 | | |

## Text 12 (Ibrium 9)

| ki:lam$_7$ | § | Silver | Goods purchased | Buyer |
|---|---|---|---|---|
| $^{dʾ}$*À-da* | 38 | 13;42 | 39 garments, 18 kilts, 18 stone weights of wool from Mari, 80 oxen | – |
| $^{d}$*Áš-da-bíl* | 16 | 7;33 | 32 garments, 361 kilts | – |
| $^{d}$*Ga-mi-iš wa* $^{dʾ}$*A*$_5$-*da-"bal" A-ru*$_{12}$-*ga-du*$^{ki}$ | 2 | [x]+9;17 | 17 garments, 263 kilts, 10 […], 2 equids | Buda-malik |
| $^{d}$*Ga-mi-iš wa* $^{dʾ}$*A*$_5$-*da-"bal" A-ru*$_{12}$-*ga-du*$^{ki}$ | 3 | 0;11 | leek from the mountain region | – |
| | | [x]+30;43 | | |

### Text 13 (Ibrium 10)

| ki:lam$_7$ | § | Silver | Goods purchased | Buyer |
|---|---|---|---|---|
| *ʾÀ-da-ni*$^{ki}$ AMA-*ra* | 39 | 18;47 | [x]+135 kilts, 2 helmets, 12 oxen, ĜIŠ-ti-ḪAR, lapis lazuli | – |
| $^{d}$*Áš-da-bíl* | 62 | 12;30 | 93 garments, 512 kilts | – |
| $^{d}$*Ga-mi-iš* | 46 | 9;21 | 10 garments, 480 kilts, leek from the mountain region, 3 equids, chariot shafts | – |
| *Ma-rí*$^{ki}$ | 29 | 8;00 | 171 garments | dam-gàr |
| SA.ZA$_x$$^{ki}$ | 50 | 10;00 | 84+[x] garments | – |
| šeš-II-ib *wa* $^{d}$*A-da-ma ʾÀ-da-ni*$^{ki}$ | 15 | 14;07 | 88 kilts, 245 KIN measures of wool from Mari, 20 oxen, ĜIŠ-ti-ḪAR | Wabarum |
| *Si-ʾa-mu*$^{ki}$ *wa* $^{dʾ}$*À-da* | 74 | [x]+1;20 | 90+[x] garments, 526 kilts, 10 oxen, 22 [...] | – |
| | | 74;05 | | |

### Text 14 (Ibrium 11)

| ki:lam$_7$ | § | Silver | Goods purchased | Buyer |
|---|---|---|---|---|
| *ʾÀ-da-ni*$^{ki}$ *in* AMA-*ra* | 43 | [x]+17;44 | [x]+121 garments, 306 kilts, 5 daggers, leek from the mountain region, 11 oxen, ĜIŠ-ti-ḪAR, | Wabarum |
| $^{d}$*A-da-ma* | 81 | [...] | 10 oxen | Reʾi -malik, son of Ibbi-zim |
| $^{d}$*Áš-da-bíl* | 62 | 2;16 | [x]+39 kilts | – |
| *Ma-rí*$^{ki}$ | 16 | 11;20 | 231 garments | dam-gàr |
| | | [x]+31;20 | | |

### Text 15 (Ibrium 12)

| ki:lam$_7$ | § | Silver | Goods purchased | Buyer |
|---|---|---|---|---|
| $^{dʾ}$*À-da wa* SA.ZA$_x$$^{ki}$ | 56 | 0;48 | 18 bags | – |
| AMA-*ra ʾÀ-da-ni*$^{ki}$ | 33 | 10;55 | 171 garments, 170 kilts, 10 lambs, ĜIŠ-ti-ḪAR | Wabarum |
| $^{d}$*Ga-mi-iš* | 48 | 11;10 | 133 garments, 430 kilts, leek, 4 equids | Puzurra-malik |
| *Ìr-ku*$^{ki}$ | 22 | 1;55 | 74 garments | – |
| SA.ZA$_x$$^{ki}$ | 55 | 15;52 | 109 garments, 658 kilts, 2 goat skins | – |
| šeš-II-ib *wa* $^{d}$*A-da-ma ʾÀ-da-ni*$^{ki}$ | 19 | 12;42 | 54 garments, 166 kilts, 385 KIN measures of wool from Mari, ĜIŠ-ti-ḪAR | Wabarum |
| | | 53;22 | | |

### Text 16 (Ibrium 13)

| ki:lam$_7$ | § | Silver | Goods purchased | Buyer |
|---|---|---|---|---|
| $^{dʾ}$*À-da* | 56 | 4;09 | 32 garments, 20 KIN measures of wool from Mari, 29 bags | – |
| *ʾÀ-da-ni*$^{ki}$ AMA-*ra* | 21 | [x]+6;34 | [x+]2 equids from Nagar, 57 garments, leek from the mountain region | – |
| ⌜é⌝? *mi-i*[*š*-x] | 36 | [x]+1;43 | 6 equids, [...] | [...] |
| Kiš$^{ki}$ | 9 | 3;47 | 18 garments, 320 stone weights of wool from Mari, 65 shells | dam-gàr |
| šeš-II-ib *ʾÀ-da-ni*$^{ki}$ | 8 | 1;55 | 170 stone weights of wool from Mari, ĜIŠ-ti-ḪAR | BAD.MUŠ.LU$_5$ |
| | | [x]+18;08 | | |

### Text 17 (Ibrium 14)

| ki:lam$_7$ | § | Silver | Goods purchased | Buyer |
|---|---|---|---|---|
| $^{d}$*ˀÀ-da* | 109 | [x]+1;28 | [x]+28 garments, 49 kilts, 33 bags, goads | – |
| *ˀÀ-da-ni*$^{ki}$ | 64 | 17;10 | 265 garments, 242 kilts, 150 hides, goads | Wabarum |
| $^{d}$*Áš-da-bíl Du-ub*$^{ki}$ *Ìr-ku*$^{ki}$ | 100 | [...] | [...], 233 kilts | – |
| $^{d}$*Ga-mi-iš* | 82 | 13;25 | 194 garments, 292 kilts, leek from the mountain region, 1 ox | – |
| *gi-ba-lu* [*ˀÀ-da-ni*$^{ki}$] | 120 | [x]+1;20 | 30 kilts | – |
| *Kab-lu*$_5$*-ul*$^{ki}$ | 83 | 0;55 | 2 oxen | – |
| *Ma-rí*$^{ki}$ | 25 | 5;00 | 109 garments | dam-gàr |
| *Ma-rí*$^{ki}$ | 46 | 10;00 | 194 garments | dam-gàr |
| | | [x]+49;18 | | |

### Text 18 (Ibrium 15)

| ki:lam$_7$ | § | Silver | Goods purchased | Buyer |
|---|---|---|---|---|
| $^{d}$*A-da-ma ˀÀ-da-ni*$^{ki}$ | 23 | 4;40 | 53 garments, 100 stone weights of wool from Mari | – |
| *ˀÀ-da-ni* $^{d}$AMA-*ra* | 66 | 12;25 | 148 garments, 210 stone weights of wool from Mari, leek from the mountain region, 3 equids | – |
| $^{d}$*Ga-mi-iš* | 85 | 0;02 | aromatic essence | Dubi-galu |
| $^{d}$*Ga-mi-iš wa* $^{d}$*Áš-da-bíl wa* $^{d}$BAD *Du-du-lu*$^{ki}$ | 87 | 18;04 | 168 garments, 340 stone weights of wool from Mari | – |
| SA.ZA$_x$$^{ki}$ | 109 | 4;50 | 25 bags, 36 garments, 85 stone weights of wool from Mari, [...], ĜIŠ-ti-ḪAR | Wabarum |
| | | 40;01 | | |

### Text 19 (Ibrium 16)

| ki:lam$_7$ | § | Silver | Goods purchased | Buyer |
|---|---|---|---|---|
| $^{d}$*ˀÀ-da* | 89 | 3;15 | 36 garments, 7 bags, ĜIŠ-*šè-bir*$_5$*-gi-nu*, goads | – |
| $^{d}$*A-da-ma ˀÀ-da-ni*$^{ki}$ | 20 | 13;40 | 254 garments, 60 stone weights of wool from Mari, ĜIŠ-ti-ḪAR | – |
| *ˀÀ-da-ni wa* $^{d}$*Ga-mi-iš* | 49 | [x]+ 3;24 | 347 garments, 46 stone weights of wool from Mari, chariot shafts | Wabarum |
| SA.ZA$_x$$^{ki}$ | 48 | 0;12 | ĜIŠ-ti-ḪAR | Wabarum |
| | | [x]+20;31 | | |

### Text 20 (Ibrium 17)

| ki:lam$_7$ | § | Silver | Goods purchased | Buyer |
|---|---|---|---|---|
| $^{d}$*ˀÀ-da* | 73 | [x]+ 0;14 | 39 garments, ĜIŠ-ti-ḪAR | Wabarum |
| *ˀÀ-da-ni*$^{ki}$ | 33 | 10;09 | 54+[x] garments, 200 stone weights of wool from Mari, 33 hides from Martu, 2 oxen, | Išra-BAD, trader of Kakmium |
| *ˀÀ-da-ni*$^{ki}$ | 34 | 0;35 | leek from the mountain region | – |
| $^{d}$*Ga-mi-iš* | 57 | [x]+ 4;22 | 155 garments, 2 equids | Buda-malik |
| | | [x]+15;20 | | |

## Text 21 (Ibrium 18)

| ki:lam$_7$ | § | Silver | Goods purchased | Buyer |
|---|---|---|---|---|
| $^{d}$*Áš-da-bíl wa Ši-ʾà-am*$^{ki}$ *wa* $^{dʾ}$*À-da* | 61 | 10;24 | 49 garments, 313 kilts, 60 stone weights of wool from Mari, 1 picket for a wheel, 150 ĜIŠ-ti-ḪAR and níĝ-NE, 13 bags | Wabarum |
| *gi-ba-i* | 83 | 0;50 | 100 kilts | – |
| SA.ZA$_x$$^{ki}$ NI-*rí*$^{ki}$ | 23 | 4;[xx] | […] | |
| | | 15;14 | | |

## Text 25

| ki:lam$_7$ | § | Silver | Goods purchased | Buyer |
|---|---|---|---|---|
| $^{dʾ}$*À-da wa gi-ba-lu ʾÀ-da-ni*$^{ki}$ | 8 | 5;17 ½ | 18+[x] garments, 2+[x] kilts, 1 dagger | – |
| *ʾÀ-da-ni*$^{ki}$ AMA-*ra* | 3 | […] | 84 garments, 186 kilts, 1 dagger | – |
| $^{d}$*Áš-da-bíl* | 7 | 5;[xx] | […], 220 kilts | – |
| *Ga-ga-ba-an*$^{ki}$ | 6 | 8;07 | 94 garments | Abu-Kur |
| $^{d}$*Ga-mi-iš* | 4 | 13;10 | 86 garments, 203 kilts, […] | – |
| *Im-ma-ra-an*$^{ki}$ | 1 | […] | 197 garments | Abu-Kur |
| SA.ZA$_x$$^{ki}$ | 5 | 6;02 | 72+[x] garments, 30+[x] kilts | – |
| SA.ZA$_x$$^{ki}$ *wa* $^{d}$*A-da-ma ʾÀ-da-ni*$^{ki}$ | 2 | 10;00 | 121+[x] garments, 102 kilts | – |
| | | [x]+47;36 ½ | | |

# INDEXES

# Personal names

*ʾÀ-bí* **4** r. XV 12: [1$^{?}$] BAR.AN A-šu$^{ki}$ ʾÀ. lú $^{d}$Ra-sa-ap ŠE.SAĜ×ḪA-mul; **14** o. XIV 11: 1 dib ʾÀ. lú NI-BAD; **22** o. VI 10: 1 dib ʾÀ. lú NI-BAD.

*ʾÀ-bí-su* **10** o. III 2: (silver) níĝ-ba Wa-ru$_{12}$-tum Daš-na Iš$_{11}$-ga-um ʾÀ. Ma-rí$^{ki}$.

*ʾÀ-daš* (var. ʾÀ:daš) **4** o. XIII 13: (silver) níĝ-kaskal ʾÀ. ma-za-lum DU.DU Ar-mi$^{ki}$; **6** o. V 10: (silver) níĝ-kaskal ʾÀ. DU.DU si-in Ar-mi$^{ki}$; **17** o. XVIII 4: 1 dib … 1 ĝír mar-tu kg ʾÀ.(ʾÀ:daš) tuš-LÚ×TIL Ša-ra-bi-ig$^{ki}$; r. XIII 20: 1 íb-la 1 si-ti-tum 1 ĝír-kun níĝ-ba ʾÀ. dumu-nita A-du-ba ʾÀ-ru$_{12}$-gú$^{ki}$.

*ʾÀ-gàr* **17** o. III 23: 1 gú-li-lum a-gar$_{5}$-gar$_{5}$ 50 ʾÀ. ugula BAR.AN I-bí-zi-kir dumu-nita [Ib-rí-um šu-ba$_{4}$-ti].

*ʾÀ-la-ga-NE* **18** o. XIV 8: 1 na$_{4}$ ʾÀ. kin$_{5}$-ak 2 útul Ša-ma.

*ʾÀ-sa* **6** o. II 21: (silver) níĝ-ba A.; o. X 15: (obj. and silver) níĝ-ba Wa-ba-rúm Ma-rí$^{ki}$ (silver) níĝ-ba ʾÀ. maškim-sù; r. V 23: (silver) níĝ-ba ʾÀ. wa Gú-gi I-ku-il wa Ba-du-lum Ma-rí$^{ki}$ níĝ-“mul” Na-gàr$^{ki}$ àga-‘kar’(ŠÈ).

*ʾÀ-wa-ra* **18** o. V 19: (silver) níĝ-ba Da-a-nu Bu-si ʾÀ. Mar-tu$^{ki}$.

*A-ʾà-lu* **4** r. II 16: 1 na$_{4}$ A.; r. XII 17: (silver) [níĝ-kaskal] A. wa Ù-da-a-ḫa Ma-rí$^{ki}$ heš$_{5}$ (LÚ×KÁR) DU.DU; **6** o. XIII 5: (silver) níĝ-kaskal A. wa Ù-da-aḫ heš$_{5}$ (LÚ×KÁR) DU.DU Ma-rí$^{ki}$.

*A-a-du-LUM* **18** o. II 19: (jewels) A-ḫu-su-ub-da-mu … (jewels) A. 2 dumu-nita en; o. V 8: ma-sa-da-ù A dumu-nita en.

*A-ag* **4** r. VII 11: [ ]-⌜ig⌝ maškim A.; **18** r. II 20: (silver) níĝ-ba A. Na-gàr$^{ki}$; **25** r. IV 6: [ ]-⌜lum⌝ ba-da-lum Ù-ti-gú$^{ki}$ 2 maškim A.

*A-a-gú-nu* **15** o. XIII 12: 3 ĝír mar-tu ba-du-u$_{4}$ kb Dab-da-ar wa A. ʾÀ-su$^{ki}$ wa Ib-te-ar Su-ti-ig⌜$^{ki}$⌝.

*A-a-lu* **7** r. X 24: (silver) A. Kab-lu$_{5}$-ul$^{ki}$ al$_{6}$-tuš Mi-da-ḫi$^{ki}$.

*A-a-zi-kir* **17** r. VIII 4: 1 dib A. lú NI-wa-lum.

*A-ba-an* **18** o. XI 23: Du-bí-zi-kir lú A.

*A-ba-nu* **5** o. XIII 8: Du-bí-zi-kir lú A.

*A-ba-du* **3** r. XIII 20: (silver) níĝ-ba Daš-na A. Ma-rí$^{ki}$.

*A-ba-la* **1** o. X 18: NI-gu dumu-munus A.

*A-ba-nu* see A-ba-an.

*A-ba-rúm* **19** o. VII 27: Mu-gàr dumu-nita A.

*A-ba-ù* **17** o. XIV 3: 3 ĝír mar-tu Šu-ma-lik lú Iš$_{11}$-da-mu Iš$_{11}$-gi-da-mu A. lú NI-ti-ba$^{ki}$.

*Ab-ba* **6** o. XII 10: (silver) níĝ-ba A. Ma-rí$^{ki}$; **13** r. III 16: (silver) níĝ-ba Kùn-NE wa A. muḫaldim Ma-rí$^{ki}$ ḫi-mu-DU mè si-in Ma-nu-wa-ad$^{ki}$.

*Ab-bu$_{16}$* **12** o. VII 8: (silver) níĝ-ba A. Ma-rí$^{ki}$ níĝ-“mul” Ag-sa-gú$^{ki}$ šu-ba$_{4}$-ti.

*Ab-ra-ḫu* **14** r. XI 11: [ ] A. wa Iš$_{11}$-a-ma-lik ba-za.

*A-bu* **4** r. XV 1: 2 níĝ-anše-ak 4 kù-sal A.; **8** r. IV 5’: 1 níĝ-[anše-]a[k] A.

*A-bù-Kur$^{ki}$* **1**(b) r. II’ 2’; **2** r. XIII 12: (180 garments, 150 na$_{4}$ measures of wool) ki:lam$_{7}$ Ìr-ku$^{ki}$ A.; **3** r. VIII 14; **25** o. I 8: (197 garments) ki:lam$_{7}$ Im-ma-ra-an$^{ki}$ A.; o. VI 7: (94 garments) ki:lam$_{7}$ Ga-ga-ba-an$^{ki}$ A.

*A-bur-li-im* **12** o. XI 19: 1 ĝír mar-tu ti kg wa ʾà-lum A. lú Ig-rí-iš.

*A-bù-sa* **5** o. III 11: 2 gú-li-lum A.

*A-da-ad* **14** o. VIII 1: Zú-za-bir$_{5}$ lú A.

*A-da-mu* **2** o. XV 22: En-na-gú-nu lú A.; r. XI 6: (daggers and bracelets) Bù-da-ma-lik BÍL-ma-lik A. lú-kar Ḫa-zu-wa-an$^{ki}$.

*A-du-ba* **17** r. XIII 22: ʾÀ-daš dumu-nita A. ʾÀ-ru$_{12}$-gú$^{ki}$.

*A-dur-da-mu* **23** o. VII 2: Íl-zi-ma-lik lú A.

*A-ga-ab* **1** o. VIII 1: [ ] A. lú Ḫ[a-]zu-[ ].

*A-gàr* **6** r. IV 14: (silver) níĝ-ba A. wa Gú-zú-gú-zú Ma-rí$^{ki}$.

*Ag-ga* **18** o. XII 3: (silver) níĝ-ba A. Na-gàr$^{ki}$; r. XVII 18: (silver) A. (silver) Gul-la Ḫu-ra-NE Na-gàr$^{ki}$ in kaskal Su-da-ma-an$^{ki}$; **21** r. VIII 11: [(silver) níĝ-ba] Bar-NE-⌜um⌝ Wa-ru$_{12}$-tum $^{d}$Utu-a-ba$_{4}$ Šu-ì A. Ma-rí$^{ki}$.

*A-ḫa-ar-si* **6** o. I 18: (silver) níĝ-ba A.

*Aḫ-ra-ma-lik* **8** o. XII 17: 1 dib A. [ ]; **17** o. VI 26: I-ib-ma-lik dumu-nita A.

*A-ḫu-šu-da-mu* **15** r. IX 5: 1 dib A.dumu-nita Zé-ma-lik šeš I-nu-ud-da-mu.

*A-ḫu-su-ub-da-mu* **18** o. II 10: (jewels) A. … (jewels) A-a-du-LUM 2 dumu-nita en.

*A-ir-ra* **6** o. VIII 18: (silver) níĝ-kaskal A. wa A-zú-bù-lu [Ù-t]i-[g]ú$^{ki}$ wa A-zú DU.DU Ar-mi$^{ki}$; o. XV 2: (silver) níĝ-kaskal A. wa A-zú-bù-lu DU.DU Ar-mi$^{ki}$ maškim Ḫa-ra-il; 9 o. II 11: (silver) [níĝ-kaskal A.$^{?}$ wa A-zú-bù-lu$^{?}$] DU.DU Ar-mi$^{ki}$ maškim Ḫa-ra-ì.

*A-ku-da* **3** r. XIII 2: (silver) níĝ-ba A. wa Daš-na Ma-rí$^{ki}$.

*A-ku-$^{d}$Utu* **1** o. XIII 5’: [2 ĝí]r [mar-]tu [kg] [D]u-si wa A.

*A-lu-a-ḫa* **14** o. III 6: (silver) níĝ-ba A. Ma-rí$^{ki}$.

*A-LUM$^{ki}$* **18** o. XIV 20: níĝ-kaskal A. maškim Ḫa-ra-ì lú ĜIŠ-nu-kiri$_{6}$.

*A-LUM-mu-da* **7** o. XV 13: (silver) níĝ-ba A. Ma-r[í$^{ki}$].

*A-ma-ʾà* **5** o. XI 7: [ ] lú A.

*A-ma-NI* **13** r. VII 21: 7 gàr-su ĝi$_{6}$ Ar-wa BÍL-za-ì wa En-na-ì 2 dumu-nita šeš Ib-rí-um wa Lugal-na-⌜i⌝-iš Íl-ba-šum Íl-ba-zi-kir A. lú-kar [ ]; **23** r. V 3: 1 dib A. Ma-nu-wa-ad$^{ki}$.

*A-ma-za* **16** r. XVI 13: En-na-il lú A.

*A-mi-du* **17** r. XIX 13: 1 dib A. lú I-bí-um; **23** o. VI 8: 1 dib A. lú I-bí-um.

*Am$_{6}$-mu-tum* **11** r. IV 3: [ ] níĝ-ba Bù-za-lum A. Ma-rí$^{ki}$ ĜIŠ.DUG.D[U] izi-ĝar

*A-mu-ra* **6** o. IX 8: (tin and silver) níĝ-ba A. Du-ub$^{ki}$; **10** o. III 10: (silver) níĝ-ba A. Du-ub$^{ki}$.

*A-mur-da-mu* **14** r. VIII 13: 1 dib *A.* tuš-LÚ×TIL *Dur-zi-lum*$^{ki}$; **18** o. XV 15: *Šu*-NE-ḪAR maškim *A.* lú ĜIŠ-nu-kiri$_6$.
*A-mur-li-im* **8** r. VII 8': *Ib-dur-ti-lu* dumu-nita *A.*
*A*-NI-*ʾà* **4** r. I 20: (silver) *A. Ša-ga-bal*$^{ki}$.
*An-na-aḫ* **15** r. II 8: 2 *gú-li-lum* 50 gín D. a-gar$_5$-gar$_5$ *A.* lú-kar *Kak-mi-um*$^{ki}$.
AN-NI-NE **14** r. X 12: 1 ĝír mar-tu A.
*A-rí-su* **21** r. XI 21: (silver) *A.* lú u$_5$ *Ma-rí*$^{ki}$.
*Ar-ra-du-lum* **13** o. II 1: [1 íb-lá 1] *si-ti-tum* 1 ĝír-kun *A.* … 2 *bu*-DI dam-*sù*; **14** o. II 14: 1 ⌜ĝír⌝ mar-tu *A. Du-lu*$^{ki}$ *Ib-gi-da-mu* šu-mu-tak$_4$; r. I 11: (silver and tin) *A.* [*Du-lu*$^{ki}$] *S*[*a-m*]*u*-⌜*ù*⌝ dam-⌜gàr⌝ šu-mu-tak$_4$.
*Ar-ru*$_{12}$*-gúm* **22** o. III 2: [ ] *A.*; o. VII 8: 1 dib *A.* ì-na-sum *Bur-ḫa-áš.*
*Ar-rúm* **16** r. X 10: (silver) níĝ-ba *A. Ma-rí*$^{ki}$ (silver) maškim-*sù*; **21** o. XII 3: (silver) níĝ-ba *A.*
*Ar-ru*$_{12}$*-šum* **12** r. X 1: (silver) nam-kud *A. Na-gàr*$^{ki}$.
*Ar-si-a-ḫa* **2** o. I 6: 1 dib *A.* lú NI-*na-ad*; **3** o. VIII 22: 30 ĝír mar-tu zú-ak ì-na-sum ĝuruš-ĝuruš *A. wa* [ ]; **5** o. IV 10: 1 dib *A.* lú *Bù-lu-gú*; **13** r. VI 9: *I-ša-ni-ki-nu* šeš *A.*; **23** o. V 3: 1 dib *A.* lú NI-*na-ad.*
*Ar-wa* **13** r. VII 10: 7 *gàr-su* ĝi$_6$ *A.* BÍL-*za-ì wa En-na-ì* 2 dumu-nita šeš *Ib-rí-um wa* Lugal-*na*-⌜*i*⌝*-iš Íl-ba-šum Íl-ba-zi-kir A-ma*-NI lú-kar [ ].
*Ar-za-du* **15** o. XI 21: 10 ĝeštu$_x$-lá 2 *ti-gi-na* 62 *du-ru*$_{12}$*-gú* 1 *mi-at kur-gú-ru*$_{12}$ 2 kù-sal 1 *ma-ḫa-na-gúm ḫa-za-nu* 1 šu-dub 1 *ša-mu* 2 *ti-ba-ra-núm wa* … 2 saĝ 2 *bu*-DI … 2 *bu*-DI *A.* dumu-munus *En-na*-$^{d}$Utu; **16** r. VII 10: 1 *ma-da-ḫu A.* nin-ni en; **18** o. III 19: 2 *bu*-DI *A.* nin-ni en.
*Áš-ba-il* **23** o. VI 1: *Du-bí-zi-kir* lú *Á.*
*Áš-da-maḫ* **25** o. IX 3: [ kù:babbar] *E*[*n-na*-]*il* lú *Á.*
*Áš-da-ma-ì* **14** o. VIII 6: (silver) *Á.* maškim ga:eš$_8$ *Du-du-lu*$^{ki}$.
*A-šum* **1** o. V 13: 11 dam *A.* [šu-b]a$_4$-[ti]; **5** o. VII 6: *Bu-ra* maškim *A.*; **17** r. XIX 22: *Ib-du*-<d>*Aš-dar* dumu-nita *A.*; **19** o. VIII 1: *Mu-gàr* dumu-nita *A-ba-rúm in* ud ḫúl-*sù A.* šu-mu-tak$_4$; r. VIII 2: *Ib-du*-$^{d}$*Aš-dar* dumu-nita *A.*
*A-šu-úr-il* **9** o. XV 17: 1 ĝír mar-tu ti kg *A.* ugula šu-⌜du$_8$⌝.
*A-tar*$_x$(BAN)*-il* **4** r. II 2: (silver) *A.* SA.ZA$_x$$^{ki}$.
*A-ti* **5** o. XI 18: 1 dib *A.* [ ].
*A-za-ba* **13** o. XVI 21: (silver) níĝ-ba *A. Ir-i-tum*$^{ki}$ á-áĝ *a-dè* šir.
*A-zi-mu* **17** r. XIV 17: [10+]7 [*b*]*u*-DI [ŠÚ+Š]A-ŠÚ+ŠA [níĝ-b]a PN$_1$–PN$_8$ dam en *wa* PN$_9$–PN$_{10}$ 2 dumu-munus en *wa* ama-gal *Ib-rí-um wa A. Ti-lu-du Ti-a-da-mu Kir-su-ud* dam-*sù wa* PN$_{11}$ nin-ni *Du-si-gú* PN$_{12}$.
*A-zi-mu-tum* **16** o. XI 16: (bracelets and daggers) lú ĝuruš-ĝuruš *A.*
*A-zú* **6** o. VIII 23: (silver) níĝ-kaskal *A-ir-ra wa A-zú-bù-lu* [*Ù-t*]*i*-[*g*]*ú*$^{ki}$ *wa A.* DU.DU *Ar-mi*$^{ki}$.
*A-zú-bù-lu* **6** o. VIII 20: (silver) níĝ-kaskal *A-ir-ra wa A.* [*Ù-t*]*i*-[*g*]*ú*$^{ki}$ *wa A-zú* DU.DU *Ar-mi*$^{ki}$; o. XV 4: (silver) níĝ-kaskal *A-ir-ra wa A.* DU.DU *Ar-mi*$^{ki}$ maškim *Ḫa-ra-il*; **9** o. II 13: (silver) [níĝ-kaskal *A-ir-ra*? *wa A.*?] DU.DU *Ar-mi*$^{ki}$ maškim *Ḫa-ra-ì.*
*A-zú-gú-ra* **1** o. VI 13: *Ba-šu-rúm* lú *A.*; **14** o. XII 6: 2 *gú-li-lum* a-gar$_5$-gar$_5$ ĝuruš-I *A.* šeš *Ra-ù-tum.*
*A-zú-ma* **7** o. II 8: *Ù-zi* šeš *A.*; **24** o. III 1: *Ù-zi* šeš *A.*
*A*[- ] **10** o. XII 13.

*Ba-ag-mi-su* **19** r. IX 17: (silver) níĝ-ba *B. Na-gàr*$^{ki}$.
BAD-*da-mu* **2** o. V 13: 1 an-zam$_x$ … 1 zi-bar … 2 *bu*-DI … 2 saĝ-*sù Dar-maš-da-mu* dumu-munus en *gal-tum* B.; **10** o. VIII 15: 2 *bu*-DI dam B. *in* ud níĝ-mu-sá; **17** o. VI 14: [*Dar-maš-da-mu*] dumu-munus en é-gi B. *in* ud DU.DU nídba é diĝir en.
BAD.MUŠ.LU$_5$ **16** o. IV 4: (170 na$_4$ measures of wool) … ĜIŠ-ti-ḪAR B. šu-ba$_4$-ti ki:lam$_7$ šeš-II-ib *ʾÀ-da-ni*$^{ki}$.
BAD-*sù*-BAD **2** r. VI 13: (silver) níĝ[-ba] B. *wa Maḫ-mu M*[*a-rí*$^{ki}$].
*Ba-du-lum* **6** r. VI 3: (silver) níĝ-ba *ʾÀ-sa wa Gú-gi I-ku-il wa B. Ma-rí*$^{ki}$ níĝ-"mul" *Na-gàr*$^{ki}$ àga-"kár"(ŠÈ); **13** o. VI 18: (silver) níĝ-ba *Ib-gi-tum B. La-li I-ku*$^{!}$(DÚR)*-ku*$^{!}$(DÚR)*-tu Ma-rí*$^{ki}$; **18** o. III 3: 1 dib *B.* [dumu-nita] *Ib-rí-um.*
*Ba-ga-ar* **3** r. V 18: (silver) níĝ-ba *Iš-má-il wa B. Ma-rí*$^{ki}$.
*Ba-ga-ma* **3** r. XII 17: 2 íb-lá kg ì-ĝiš-saĝ 2 en *Ma-nu-wa-ad*$^{ki}$ *B.* šu-mu-tak$_4$ *in* ud úš *ma-lik-tum*; **5** o. III 6: 1 ĝír mar-tu kg *B.* ugula; r. IX 16: (silver) lú ĜIŠ-kiri$_6$ *B.* šu-ba$_4$-ti; **6** r. X 14: 1 ĝír mar-tu ti kg *B.* ugula sur$_x$-BAR.AN *Ib-rí-um*; r. XIV 14: 2 níĝ-anše-ak 4 kù-sal *B.* ugula SA.ZA$_x$$^{ki}$; **7** o. XVI 6: 1 dib *B.*; **10** o. XII 6: 1 zag 1 ĜIŠ-gígir-II ; **13** o. XII 6: [1 g]ír m[ar-t]u kg *Ù-zu* "ur$_4$" *Ì-mar*$^{ki}$ É×PAP *B.* šu-mu-tak$_4$; **14** o. X 16: *ʾa*$_5$*-na-gu* 4 si 2 gud … 1 *ḫa-bù* … 1 ⌜*ar*⌝*-ra*[*-sù* nídba] en $^{d}$*Ra-sa-ap* [*ʾÀ-da-ni*$^{ki}$] *in* $^{d}$AMA-*ra ap* 1 *ḫa-bù* $^{dʾ}$*À-da* kb kg sikil lú *B.* šu-ba$_4$-ti *in Ma-nu-wa-ad*$^{ki}$; **17** r. VII 24: *I-ti-ne A-da-bí-gú*$^{ki}$ maškim *B.*; **19** o. X 17: 1 zag ĜIŠ-gígir-II *B.*; **22** r. IV 4: (60 bracelets, 10 daggers) lú *in* šu-mu-níĝin SA.ZA$_x$$^{ki}$ *B.* gaba-ru.
*Ba-ḫa-ga* **5** r. IV 12: BÍL-*ma-lik* lú *B.*
*Ba-lu-zú* **2** r. I 1: *Ḫa-ra-du* lú *B.*; **6** r. VII 9: 1 íb-lá 1 *si-ti-tum* 1 ĝír-kun *B.* "ur$_4$" *Ì-mar*$^{ki}$ *in* ud ḫúl na-rú-*sù Zú-ba-núm* šu-mu-tak$_4$.
*Ba*-NE **11** o. IX 4: 1 ĝír mar-tu *ba-du-u*$_4$ kb *B.* lú-kar *A-da-bí-ig*$^{ki}$.
*Bar*-NE-*um* **21** r. VIII 7: [(silver) níĝ-ba] *B. Wa-ru*$_{12}$*-tum* $^{d}$Utu-*a-ba*$_4$ *Šu-ì Ag-ga Ma-rí*$^{ki}$.
*Bar-za-ma-li* **4** r. XII 7: 2 *gú-li-lum B.* lú *Iš-da-má.*
*Bar-za-ma-ù* **15** o. IV 6: 1 dib *B.* ugula *ʾÀ-šu*$^{ki}$ *in* ud tuš-LÚ×TIL *A-a-lu*$^{ki}$; **16** r. V 21: 1 dib *B.* ugula *A-ru*$_{12}$*-ga-du*$^{ki}$.
*Ba-sa-ḫu* **4** r. I 11: (silver) *B. Na-gàr*$^{ki}$.
*Ba-šu-rúm* **1** o. VI 12: 1 ĝír mar-tu *ba-du-u*$_4$ kbg *B.* lú *A-zú-gú-ra.*
*Ba-ti* **2** o. XV 20: *I-šar* lú *B.*
*Ba-zi-da* **1** o. VII 15: *Du-bí-šum* lú *B.*
*Ba-zú-zi* **10** o. XI 7: (silver) níĝ-ba *B. Ma-*[*r*]*í*$^{ki}$.
BÍL-*da-mu* **9** r. XIV 1: 3 *gú-li-lum* a-gar$_5$-gar$_5$ lú *Wa-su*-LUM lú *Ib-ni-ḫar wa En-nu-lum* B. *I-ti-a-gú* lú *En-na-il.*

BÍL*ma-lik* **2** r. XI 5: (daggers and bracelets) *Bù-da-ma-lik* B. *A-da-mu* lú-kar *Ḫa-zu-wa-an*$^{ki}$; **5** r. IV 11: 1 íb-lá B. lú *Ba-ḫa-ga in* ud *Gú-rá-ma-an*$^{ki}$ tuš-LÚ×TIL; **25** r. IV 8: 1 íb-lá ŠA.PI kb B. lugal.

BÍL-*za-il* **20** r. I 4: 1 dib B. dumu-nita dumu-nita šeš *Ib-rí-um*.

BÍL-*za-ì* **7** r. XIII 10: *En-na-ì* lú B.; **13** r. VII 11: 7 *gàr-su* ĝi$_6$ *Ar-wa* B. *wa En-na-ì* 2 dumu-nita šeš *Ib-rí-um wa* Lugal-*na-*⌜*i*⌝*-iš Íl-ba-šum Íl-ba-zi-kir A-ma-*NI lú-kar [ ].

*Bù-a-du* **22** o. VI 8: *Ib-du-ma-lik* lú *B.*

*Bù-a-ḫu* **19** r. XIX 6: (silver) *La-zi-gú wa B. Na-ba-ti-um*$^{ki}$.

*Bù-da-il* **5** o. XVI 10: 2 [*gú-*]*li-lum B. Ù-la-bù*$^{ki}$ *wa I-si-rúm* lú *Ib-gú-nu*.

*Bù-da-ì* **19** r. XIV 10: 1 íb-lá 1 ĝír-kun … 1 ĝír mar-tu ti kg *B. Maš-bar-rá*$^{ki}$ tuš-LÚ×TIL *Za-ḫi-ra-an*$^{ki}$ al$_6$-tuš *A-la-ga*$^{ki}$; **22** r. VII 8: 13 dib *Bù-da-ì Íl-a-šar Gal-za-iš-lu Ga-du-um Iš-má-da-mu Da-da-ì* ⌜X⌝-NE-[X] *En-na-ma-lik Ig-rí-iš Gur-an-da-mu Ru*$_{12}$*-zi-li-im Iš-má-da-ba-an Zé-da-mu*.

*Bù-da-ma-lik* **2** r. XI 4: (daggers and bracelets) *B.* BÍL-*ma-lik A-da-mu* lú-kar *Ḫa-zu-wa-an*$^{ki}$; **3** o. VII 2: 1 IGI.NITA u$_5$ *B.* šu-ba$_4$-ti … ki:lam$_7$ $^{d}$*Ga-mi-iš*; **12** o. II 2: (17 garments, 263 kilts) … 10 […] … 2 IGI.NITA *B.* šu-ba$_4$-ti … ki:lam$_7$ $^{d}$*Ga-mi-iš wa* ki:lam$_7$ $^{d}$*ʾA*$_5$*-da-*"*bal*" *A-ru*$_{12}$*-ga-du*$^{ki}$; **20** o. XII 6: *Iš-má-da-mu* lú *B.*; r. VII 3: (155 garments) … 2 IGI.NITA u$_5$ *B.* [šu-ba$_4$-ti] ki:lam$_7$ $^{d}$*Ga-mi-iš*.

*Bu-da-na-im* **2** r. XI 11: 1 ĝír mar-tu *ba-du-u*$_9$ kg *B.* dumu-nita ga-du$_8$.

*Bù-du-du* **13** r. IX 15: [ ] *B.* ugula *Ar-ʾà-mu*$^{ki}$ *in* ud *Si-da-rí-in*$^{ki}$ til.

*Bù-du-mi* **24** o. II 9: 1 ĝír mar-tu *wa* 2 kù-sal níĝ-ba $^{d}$*A-na-ma-du Ar-ḫa-du*$^{ki}$ *B.* šu-mu-tak$_4$.

*Bù-gal-lu* **21** r. X 11: (silver) níĝ-kaskal *B. Ba-zi-mu*$^{ki}$ DU.DU *si-in Ar-mi*$^{ki}$.

*Bù-lu-gú* **5** o. IV 11: *Ar-si-a-ḫa* lú *B.*

*Bu*$_x$*-ma-il* **14** o. XI 12: 2 *gú-li-lum B.* šeš *Ib-rí-um*.

*Bu*$_x$*-ma-ì* **1** o. VI 3: ⌜ĝeštin⌝ *B.*; **5** o. V 8: ĝeštin *B.* šu-ba$_4$-ti; o. VII 13: 1 gud *Ib-gi-da-mu* ugula kad$_4$-kad$_4$ *wa* šu-ba$_4$-ti *B.*; o. XIII 11: ĝeštin *B.* šu-ba$_4$-ti; **7** o. VI 17: 1 ĝír mar-tu *ba-du-u*$_4$ kbg *B.* (*Bu-*) *Gú-ra-*"*bal*"$^{ki}$; **11** o. XII 5: ĝeštin *B.* šu-ba$_4$-ti; **16** r. III 27: 1 ĝír mar-tu ti kg *B.* NE-di.

*Bu-ra* **5** o. VII 4: 2 *gú-li-lum* a-gar$_5$-gar$_5$ kg *B.* maškim *A-šum*.

*Bur-ḫa-áš* **11** r. III 21: (silver) níĝ-du$_8$ 2 dumu-nita *B.*; **22** o. VII 10: 1 dib *Ar-ru*$_{12}$*-gúm* ì-na-sum *B.*

*Bu-si* **18** o. V 18: (silver) níĝ-ba *Da-a-nu B. ʾÀ-wa-ra* Mar-tu$^{ki}$.

*Bù-sum* **7** r. XIV 19: (silver) níĝ-ba *Wa-ru*$_{12}$*-tum Da-ti B. Ma-rí*$^{ki}$; **10** o. VII 17: (silver) níĝ-ba *B. Ma-rí*$^{ki}$ ĜIŠ.DUG.DU izi-ĝar; **12** r. II 14: (silver) *B. Ma-rí*$^{ki}$; **13** o. XVII 16: (silver) níĝ-ba *B. Ma-rí*$^{ki}$; **17** r. XV 7: 1 dib *B. Ù-ti-ig*$^{ki}$.

*Bù-šu-sum* **4** r. IV 24: (silver) *B. Ma-rí*$^{ki}$.

*Bù-za-lum* **11** r. IV 2: [ ] níĝ-ba *B. Am*$_6$*-mu-tum Ma-rí*$^{ki}$ ĜIŠ.DUG.D[U] izi-ĝar.

*Da-a-nu* **18** o. V 17: (silver) níĝ-ba *D. Bu-si ʾÀ-wa-ra* Mar-tu$^{ki}$.

*Dab-da-ar* **2** r. XII 6: *Zé-da-mu* lú *D.*; **15** o. XIII 10: 3 ĝír mar-tu *ba-du-u*$_4$ kb *D. wa A-a-gú-nu ʾÀ-su*$^{ki}$ *wa Ib-te-ar Su-ti-ig*⌜$^{ki}$⌝.

*Da-bí* **10** r. V 11: 2 *bu-*DI *Sa-mu-sá-sal D.* šu-mu-tak$_4$.

*Da-bí-da-mu* **20** r. XII 1: 1 zag ĜIŠ-gígir-II *D.* dumu-nita en *Bur-ma-an*$^{ki}$.

*Da-bur-da-mu* **15** o. I 13: 1 kù-sal níĝ-ba *D.* $^{d}$*Iš:šára Zi-da-ra*$^{ki}$; r. X 11: 2 kù-sal níĝ-ba *D.* $^{d}$*Iš:šára Zu-ra-mu*$^{ki}$ *wa* $^{d}$*Iš:šára Má-*NE$^{ki}$; r. XI 13: 2 ĜIŠ-du *D.*; 17 r. XVIII 12: 1 kù-sal níĝ-ba *D. al*$_6$ *gú-a-ti* $^{d}$*Ba-ra-ma*; **18** o. X 13: 2 *ti-gi-na* … 2 ĜIŠ-du *D. ma-lik-tum*.

The queen, spouse of king Išʿar-damu, was the daughter if Iri-damu. Cousin of king Irkab-damu (see the commentary on text 15).

*Dab*$_6$*-ti* **15** o. VII 25: (silver) níĝ-ba *Iš-dub-il wa D. Ma-rí*$^{ki}$ maškim ga:eš$_8$ *Du-du-lu*$^{ki}$.

*Da-da-ì* **22** r. VII 13: 13 dib *Bù-da-ì Íl-a-šar Gal-za-iš-lu Ga-du-um Iš-má-da-mu D.* ⌜X⌝-NE-[X] *En-na-ma-lik Ig-rí-iš Gur-an-da-mu Ru*$_{12}$*-zi-li-im Iš-má-da-ba-an Zé-da-mu*.

*Da-dub* **1**(e) r. II' x+1: [ ] *D. Ìr-m*[*u-*]*da-mu* lú *Íl-zi Ìr-ga-bù* è *in* ud *Ìr-kab-da-mu si-mi* úš-*sù*; **16** o. V 3: 2 *bu-*DI *D.* dam en lú *A-ru*$_{12}$*-ga-du*$^{ki}$.

*Dag-mul-da-mu* **13** r. XI 13: 1 ĜIŠ-šú 1 níĝ-bànda … 2 *t*[*i-gi-na*] 2 ĜIŠ-du … 1 zi-bar … 1 *bu-*DI tur 1 igi-igi … *D. ma-lik-tum Lum-na-an*$^{ki}$ šu-mu-tak$_4$ (silver) géme-*sù*; **24** r. II 6: 2 *ti-gi-na* … 10 ĝeštu$_x$-lá … 4 *ʾà-ra-ma-tum* 2 buru$_4$-MUŠEN … 1 *mi-at* 30 lá-3 *gur-gú-ru*$_{12}$ … 8 *du-ru*$_{12}$*-gú* … 2 kù-sal … 1 šu-dub … *ḫa-za-nu wa a-a-nu gú-za-ra-tum* … 1 *ḫa-na-*LUM 1 *ša-mu* 1 *a-na-bù-*NE*-tum* 1 *ti-ba-ra-núm* … 2 *bu-*DI … 1 bur-KAK ĜIŠ-taškarin … 1 *gú-li-lum* kb *D. Lum-na-an*$^{ki}$ šu-mu-tak$_4$.

*Da-ḫi-ir-ma-lik* **8** r. IX 2': [ ] ⌜X-*na*⌝*-ra-tum D. maš-ar-tum*.

*Dam-da-il* **12** r. VII 3: (silver) níĝ-du$_8$ *D. Ib-su*$^{ki}$ *in* Kiš$^{ki}$ lú *Na-zu-mu* níĝ-du$_8$.

*Da-mi-gu* **18** o. XV 10: (silver) níĝ-ba *Du-tum wa D. ʾÀ-du*$^{ki}$.

*Da-mur-da-mu* **2** o. XV 5: 6 ĝeštu$_x$-lá *D.* dam *Ib-rí-um*.

*Da-*NE*-ga* **2** r. I 5: *Íl-ba-ma-lik* lú *D.*

*Da-*NE*-du* **15** r. XVI 20: 2 ma-na kb in-na-sum *si-in* šu-bal-ak kg lú $^{d}$*Ra-sa-ap Du-ne-íb*$^{ki}$ lú *D. Kab-lu*$_5$*-ul*$^{ki}$.

*Dar-ib-da-mu* **15** o. V 23: 1 dib *D.* dumu-munus en; o. X 20: 2 *ti-gi-na* 2 ĜIŠ-du 1 KA-*ḫu-a-tum D.* dumu-munus en; **16** o. I 10: (silver) [*Di-ni-i*]*b-*[*d*]*u-lum* nin-ni en šu-ba$_4$-ti (silver) *D.* nin-ni-*sù* šu-ba$_4$-ti; o. III 5: 4 ĝeštu$_x$-lá *D. wa Tíš-te-da-mu* … 2 dumu-munus en; **17** r. IV 12: 1 *zi-zi-ḫi-tum D.* dumu-munus en; **18** o. I 10: (silver) *Di-ni-íb-du-lum* nin-ni en šu-ba$_4$-ti (silver) *D.* nin-ni-*sù* šu-ba$_4$-ti; o. XVIII 8: 4 *ti-gi-na* 4 ĜIŠ-du 4 ĝeštu$_x$-lá 2 kù-sal *D. wa Tíš-te-da-mu* 2 dumu-munus en; **19** o. I 9: (silver) *Di-ne-íb-du-lum* nin-ni en (silver) *D.* [n]in-ni-*sù* šu-ba$_4$-ti; o. X 6: 1 dib *D.* dumu-munus en; **20** r. III 15: 1 kù-sal níĝ-ba

*D.* dumu-munus en $^{d}$BAD-munus *si-in Lu-ba-an*$^{ki}$ *in* ud *ter*$_6$*-bí* bur-KAK-*sù* $^{d}$ʾ*A*$_5$*-da-*"*bal*".

*Dar-maš-da-mu* **2** o. V 10: 1 an-zam$_x$ … 1 zi-bar … 2 *bu*-DI … 2 saĝ-*sù D.* dumu-munus en *gal-tum* BAD-*da-mu*; **17** o. VI 10: […] [*D.*] dumu-munus en é-gi BAD-*da-mu in* ud nídba é diĝir en.

*Da-si-gú-bù-ru*$_{12}$ **23** o. VII 6: *Ìr-ba*$_x$*-zé* lú *D.*

*Da-si*-KA **19** o. IV 17: *Ib-dur-i-šar* lú *D.*

*Daš-na* **3** o. II 19: (silver) níĝ-ba *D. wa Wa-ru*$_{12}$*-tum Ma-rí*$^{ki}$; o. XIII 15: (silver) níĝ-ba *D. wa Wa-ru*$_{12}$*-tum Ma-rí*$^{ki}$; r. XIII 4: (silver) níĝ-ba *A-ku-da wa D. Ma-rí*$^{ki}$, 19: (silver) níĝ-ba *D. A-ba-du Ma-rí*$^{ki}$; **5** o. II 16: (silver) níĝ-ba *D. wa Wa-ru*$_{12}$*-tum Ma-rí*$^{ki}$ *in Má*-NE$^{ki}$; r. V 3: (silver) níĝ-ba *D. Ma-rí*$^{ki}$ *in* níĝ-kas$_4$ *Gú-rá-ma-an*$^{ki}$ šu-ba$_4$-ti; **6** r. I 7: (silver) níĝ-ba *D. wa I-da-il Ma-rí*$^{ki}$; r. IV 3: (silver) níĝ-ba *D. wa I-da-il Ma-rí*$^{ki}$; **7** r. XIII 2: (silver) [níĝ-ba] *D. Ma-rí*$^{ki}$ níĝ-"mul" Kiš$^{ki}$ til; **8** o. III 17: (silver) *D. Ma-rí*$^{ki}$; r. III 16': (silver) níĝ-ba *D. Ma-rí*$^{ki}$; **9** o. XII 15: (silver) níĝ-ba *D. wa Šu-ga-du Ma-r*[*i*]$^{ki}$ *in Gi-da*-NE$^{ki}$ šu-ba$_4$-ti; **10** o. III 1: (silver) níĝ-ba *Wa-ru*$_{12}$*-tum D. Iš*$_{11}$*-ga-um* ʾ*À-bí-su Ma-rí*$^{ki}$; o. IV 2: (silver) níĝ-ba *D. Ma-rí*$^{ki}$; o. VIII 7: (silver) níĝ-ba *D. Ma-rí*$^{ki}$; o. XI 22: (silver) níĝ-ba *D. Wa-ru*$_{12}$*-tum Puzur-ra*-BAD *I-ti-il Ma-rí*$^{ki}$; o. XIV 12: (silver) níĝ-ba *D. Wa-ru*$_{12}$*-tum Ma-rí*$^{ki}$; r. I 2: (silver) níĝ-ba *D. Wa-ru*$_{12}$*-tum Ma-rí*$^{ki}$, 22: (silver) níĝ-ba *D. wa Wa-ru*$_{12}$*-tum Ma-rí*$^{ki}$; r. IV 4: (silver) níĝ-ba *Wa-ru*$_{12}$*-tum wa D. Ma-rí*$^{ki}$; r. VI 3: r. IV 4: (silver) níĝ-ba *Iš*$_{11}$*-ga wa D. Ma-rí*$^{ki}$; **11** o. VIII 17: (silver) níĝ-ba *Wa-ru*$_{12}$*-tum D. I-ku*$^{!}$(DÚR)*-ku*$^{!}$(DÚR)*-tu Ma-rí*$^{ki}$; **12** r. VII 20: (silver) níĝ-ba *D. Ma-rí*$^{ki}$ DU.DU *áš-da* [ ]; **13** o. XVI 15: (silver) níĝ-ba *D. wa Šu-ga-du Ma-rí*$^{ki}$; **14** o. IX 13: 1 dib *D.*; o. XIII 13: (silver) níĝ-ba *D. Ma-rí*$^{ki}$, 20: 4 ĜIŠ-gu-kak-šub lú *D. M*[*a-*]*rí*$^{⌜ki⌝}$ *i*[*n*] *Bar-ga-u*$_9$$^{ki}$ zàḫ *in* kaskal $^{d}$AMA-*ra*; **15** o. III 1: (silver) níĝ-⌜ba⌝ *D. Ma-rí*$^{ki}$ níĝ-"mul" Kiš$^{ki}$ til *wa* íb-III-TÚG šu-mu-tak$_4$; r. X 21: (silver) níĝ-ba *D. Ma-rí*$^{ki}$ níĝ-"mul" Kiš$^{ki}$ til-til; **17** r. XV 22: (silver) níĝ-ba *D. M*[*a-*]*rí*$^{ki}$; **20** o. XIII 17: (silver) níĝ-ba *D. Ma-rí*$^{ki}$ níĝ-"mul" *Du-li*$^{ki}$ šu-ba$_4$-ti; **21** r. XI 19: (silver) níĝ-ba *D.*

*Daš-ne* **20** r. VII 8: (silver) *D.* lú ĜIŠ-nu-kiri$_6$ *Ì-mar*$^{ki}$ *in* NI-*ab*$^{ki}$ šu-ba$_4$-ti.

*Da-ti* **7** o. XV 10: (silver) níĝ-ba *D.*; r. XIV 18: (silver) níĝ-ba *Wa-ru*$_{12}$*-tum D. Bù-sum Ma-rí*$^{ki}$; **13** r. I 12: (silver) níĝ-ba *D. Iš-da-maḫ Ù-lu-li* [ ]; **21** r. XI 16: (silver) níĝ-ba *D.*

*Da-ti*-$^{d}$TU **2** o. III 12: 1 bur-KAK ĜIŠ-taškarin … 2 saĝ 2 *bu*-DI … 2 *bu*-DI … 1 an-zam$_x$ … 1 zi-bar … 2 ĜIŠ-du … 1 ĜIŠ-šú 1 níĝ-bànda *D. ma-lik-tum Lum-na-an*$^{ki}$; **3** o. III 11: 10 ĝeštu$_x$-lá *D. ma-lik-tum Lum-na-an*$^{ki}$; **6** r. III 21: 4 *ba-rí-zú* im-ĝi$_6$ … 2 *bu*-DI *D. ma-lik-tum Lum-na-an*$^{ki}$; **10** o. IX 6: 2 *bu*-DI ama-gal en *Lum-na-an*$^{ki}$ *D.* šu-mu-tak$_4$; **11** o. XI 21: 1 an-zam$_x$ *D. ma-lik-tum Lum-na-an*$^{ki}$; o. XII 17: 2 *bu*-DI … 2 saĝ-*sù* … 1 kù-sal *D. ma-lik-tum Lum-na-an*$^{ki}$ É×PAP *I-šar* šu-mu-tak$_4$; **12** o. XV 3: 2 kù-sal dumu-munus *D. ma-lik-tum Lum-na-an*$^{ki}$ *Du-si-gú* šu-mu-tak$_4$.

*Da-zi-ma-ad* **7** o. V 12: 1 ĝír mar-tu ti *D.* šu-i *Ib-rí-um*; **11** o. II 7: *D.* maškim *Ìr-am*$_6$*-da-mu* [l]ú [*Í*]*l-zi.*

*D*[*a-* ] **7** o. XVI 19: (silver) níĝ-ba *D. in* NI-*rúm*$^{ki}$ šu-ba$_4$-ti.

*Di-bí-zi-kir* **4** r. VIII 20: 2 *gú-li-lum ša-ti* lú *D.*

*Dim-ma-il* **4** o. VII 3: ĝeštin-ĝeštin *D.*

*Di-ne-ib-du-lum* **2** o. I 13: 5 *zi-ba-tum D.* nin-ni en; **8** o. I 6: (silver) *Di-rín-da-mu D.* nin-ni [en]; **10** o. I 5: (silver) *D.* nin-ni en šu-ba$_4$-ti; **11** o. I 6: (silver) [*Di-rín-da-mu D.* nin-ni en]; **13** o. I 5: (silver) *D.* [ni]n-ni [e]n [šu-b]a$_4$-[t]i; **17** o. I 5: (silver) *D.* [nin-ni en] šu-ba$_4$-ti; **19** o. I 5: (silver) *D.* nin-ni en (silver) *Dar-ib-da-mu* [n]in-ni-*sù* šu-ba$_4$-ti; o. III 2: 3 *bu*-DI 2 saĝ … 1 SIG$_7$.IGI *D.* nin-ni en.

*Di-ni-íb-du-lum* **2** o. X 2: 2 ĝeštu$_x$-lá *D.* nin-ni en; **6** o. V 16: 1 an-zam$_x$ *D.* nin-ni en; **12** r. XIII 8: (silver) *D.* dam-diĝir nin-ni en šu-ba$_4$-ti; **14** o. I 5: (silver) [*D.* nin-ni en šu-ba$_4$-ti]; **15** o. I 5: (silver) *D.* nin-ni en šu-ba$_4$-ti; **16** o. I 5: (silver) *D.* nin-ni en šu-ba$_4$-ti; r. II 9: 10 ĝeštu$_x$-lá … 1 kù-sal *D.* nin-ni en; **18** o. I 5: (silver) *D.* nin-ni en šu-ba$_4$-ti; o. XVII 28: 10 lá-2 ĝeštu$_x$-lá *D.* nin-ni en; **20** o. I 5: (silver) *D.* nin-ni en šu-ba$_4$-ti; **21** o. I 5: (silver) *D.* [nin-]ni [e]n [šu-ba$_4$-t]i; o. XVI 4: 2 *bu*-DI ì-ĝiš-saĝ *D.* nin-ni en.

*Di-rín-da-mu* **8** o. I 5: (silver) *D. Di-ne-ib-du-lum* nin-ni [en]; **11** o. I 5: (silver) [*D. Di-ne-ib-du-lum* nin-ni en]; **18** r. IV 22: 2 *bu*-DI ì-ĝiš-saĝ *D.* dam-diĝir *áš-du* úš *ma-lik-tum Lum-na-an*$^{ki}$; **19** o. X 11: 1 dib ì-ĝiš-saĝ *D.* dam-diĝir *Ìr-ba*$_x$*-zé* "ur$_4$" šu-mu-tak$_4$.

*Di-rin*$_x$*-da-mu* **17** r. XXI 8: 2 *bu*-DI *D.* … 2 *bu*-DI … 2 saĝ-*sù* … 2 kù-sal *Tir*$_5$*-bù-da-mu* nin-ni-*sù.*

*Du-bí* **7** o. II 1: [ ] *D.* ugula *A-ru*$_{12}$*-lu*$^{ki}$ šu-ba$_4$-ti; **8** o. II 17: (silver) *D. wa* maškim-*sù Ma-rí*$^{ki}$; **9** r. II 13: [ ] *D.* lú *Iš-da-má* tuš-LÚ×TIL *Ar-mi*$^{ki}$ *áš-ti Gul-da-ad*$^{ki}$; **10** o. XIV 20: *En-na*-BAD *Zú-ti*$^{ki}$ maškim *D.*; **13** o. III 15: (silver) lú ĜIŠ-nu-kiri$_6$ *D.* šu-ba$_4$-ti.

*Du-bí-ab* **8** r. X 15': 1 dib *D.* [ ]; **18** o. XIV 28: 2 ĝír mar-tu ti kg *Iš*$_{11}$*-gi-bar-zú wa D.* ugula *Ti-*[*sum*]$^{ki}$; **23** o. VIII 8: 1 íb-lá 1 ĝír-kun *D. Ša-na-ru*$_{12}$*-gú*$^{ki}$.

*Du-bí-ga-lu* **17** o. XVI 16: (daggers) Lugal-*na-i-iš Íl-ba-šum D. Ša-gú-bù* dumu-nita en *Ma-nu-wa-ad*$^{ki}$; **18** r. XII 22: ĜIŠ-šim ĜÁ×LÁ ki:lam$_7$ $^{d}$*Ga-mi-iš D.*

*Du-bi-šum* **1** o. VII 14: 1 íb-lá *D.* lú *Ba-zi-da* tuš-LÚ×TIL *Kak-mi-um*$^{ki}$; (e) r. IV' 11: (silver) lú nu-kiri$_6$ *D.* ʾ*À-šu*$^{ki}$; **2** r. X 15: 1 ĝír mar-tu kg *D.* lú-kar; **9** r. III 4: *En-àr-li-im* [dumu-ni]ta *D.*; **17** o. XII 21: 1 íb-lá 1 ĝír-kun *D.* lú *Gú-ma-ni-du* maškim *I-bí-zi-kir* tuš-LÚ×TIL *Kak-mi-um*$^{ki}$ *áš-ti Šu-ra-an*$^{ki}$; **21** o. IV 28: ĝeštin *D.* šu-ba$_4$-ti.

*Du-bí-zi-kir* **3** r. XIV 2: 2 ĝír mar-tu ti kg *D. wa Íl-ba-šum* lú-kar; **4** r. XIV 12: 5 *mi-at* ĜIŠ-gu-kak-gíd … [ ] ĜIŠ-g[u-]kak-gíd … 2 níĝ-anše-ak 4 kù-sal *D.* lú *Ti-ša-rum*; **5** o. XIII 7: [ ] *D.* lú *Ab-a-nu*, 17: 1 dib *D.* lú *I-rí-ig-ma-lik*; **13** r. II 18: (silver) lul-gu-ak gur$_8$ *Puzur*$_4$*-ra-m*[*a-*]*lik* lú-kar *Kak-mi-um*$^{ki}$ KAK-*bar-zú wa D.* šu-mu-tak$_4$ *si-in* en *Kak-m*[*i-*]*u*[*m*$^{ki}$]; **18** o. XI 22: 1 dib *D.* lú *A-ba-an*; **22** o. VII 3: 1 ⌜dib⌝ *D.* lú *Puzur*$_4$*-ra-ì* lú É×PAP en-en; **23** o. V 11: 1 dib *D.* lú *Áš-ba-il.*

*Du-bù-ḫu-*$^{d}$ʾ*À-da* **15** o. V 17: 1 dib *D.* dumu-nita *I-bí-zi-kir.*

*Du-bù-uš-da-mu* **4** o. VII 14: 1 ĝír mar-tu ti kg *D. Ib-al*$_6$$^{ki}$; r. XIII 4: 4 íb-lá *si-ti-tum* ĝír-kun 4 íb-lá *si-ti-tum* ĝír-kun *D. I-ga-li-im Zú-ga-du Ì-lum-a-rí-ḫu* 4 en *Ib-al*$_6$$^{ki}$.

*Du-rí-um* **1**(a) o. II' x+1.

*Du-si* **1** o. XIII 3': [2 ĝí]r [mar-]tu [kg] *D. wa A-ku-*$^{d}$Utu; **4** r. XI 10: *Ìr-am*$_6$*-ma-lik* maškim *D.*; **25** r. III 2: [ ] l[ú] *D.* ugula *Ib-al*$_6$$^{ki}$ *in* ud GIŠ-gu-kak-gíd šu-mu-tak$_4$.

*Du-si-gú* **2** o. VI 23: 1 kù-sal níĝ-ba *D.* $^{d}$*Iš:šára Zi-da-ra*$^{ki}$; o. XIII 18: 4 ĝeštu$_x$-lá *D.*; r. III 13: 1 *gú-li-lum* 1 kù-sal níĝ-ba *D.* $^{d}$*Ra-sa-ap ʾÀ-da-ni*$^{ki}$; **3** r. IV 14: 2 *bu*-DI ama-gal ⌜*Ib-rí*⌝-[*um*] *D.* šu-mu-tak$_4$; **4** o. III 1: 2 *bu*-DI *D.* ama-gal en; o. XI 8: 4 bur-KAK-bur-KAK GIŠ-taškarin … 2 GIŠ-du *D.* ama-gal en, 15: 2 GIŠ-du *D.* ama-gal en; r. IV 11: 1 *bu*-DI sal *D.* ama-gal en; **5** o. V. 12: 2 níĝ-anše-ak 4 NE-*na-tum D.* ama-gal en; r. VI 13: 2 zi-bar níĝ-ba $^{d}$BAD *Má*-NE$^{ki}$ *D.* ì-na-sum; **6** r. V 13: ⌜2⌝ níĝ-anše-ak 4 kù-sal *D.* níĝ-ba en; r. XVI 11: 1 SIG$_7$.IGI$^{!}$(ME) *D.*; **10** r. I 13: 2 *bu*-DI *ma-lik-tum Ì-mar*$^{ki}$ *D.* [šu]-mu-tak$_4$; r. IV 17: 10 útul urudu lú *D.*; r. VIII 20; **12** o. XIV 16: 2 zi-bar níĝ-ba $^{d}$BAD *Má*-NE$^{ki}$ *wa* $^{d}$BAD *Zu-ra-mu*$^{ki}$ *D.* šu-mu-tak$_4$; o. XV 6: 2 kù-sal dumu-munus *Da-ti-*$^{d}$TU *ma-lik-tum Lum-na-an*$^{ki}$ *D.* šu-mu-tak$_4$; r. IX 17: 2 an-dùl … *ba-na-a-sa wa* 2 šu-*sù wa* 2 DU-*sù* níĝ-ba *D.* $^{d}$*Ku-ra in* ud ne:saĝ; **13** o. VIII 3: 2 an-dùl … [I]GI.DUB-*sù wa* 4 šu-*sù wa* 4 DU-*sù* níĝ-ba *D.* $^{d}$*Ra-sa-ap* $^{d}$*A-da-ma ʾÀ-da-ni*$^{ki}$, 20: 1 an-dùl … IGI.DUB-*sù* 2 šu-*sù* 2 DU-*sù* níĝ-ba *D.* $^{d}$*Iš:šára Wa*-NE-*du*$^{ki}$; **15** o. XII 4: 1 kù-sal níĝ-ba *D.* $^{d}$*Ra-sa-ap ʾÀ-da-ni*$^{ki}$; **17** r. XIV 25: [10+]7 [*b*]*u*$^{?}$-DI [ŠÚ+Š]A-ŠÚ+ŠA [níĝ-b]a PN$_1$–PN$_8$ dam en *wa* PN$_9$–PN$_{10}$ 2 dumu-munus en *wa* ama-gal *Ib-rí-um wa* PN$_{11}$–PN$_{14}$ dam-*sù wa Iš-ru*$_{12}$*-ud* nin-ni *D.* PN$_{15}$; **23** r. VI 2: *I-ib-ma-lik* šeš *D.*

*Du-tum* **2** o. VIII 7: (23 garments, 31 na$_4$ measures of wool) *áš-da D. Ma-rí*$^{ki}$; **3** r. VI 8: <1 dib> *I-ku-i-šar* en *Ma-rí*$^{ki}$ *D. Ma-rí*$^{ki}$ šu-mu-tak$_4$; **6** o. III 11: (silver) níĝ-ba *D. Ma-rí*$^{ki}$; **8** r. III 5': (silver) *D. Ma-rí*$^{ki}$; **10** o. I 11: (silver) níĝ-ba *D. Ma-rí*$^{ki}$ lú ga:eš$_8$; **18** o. XIV 14: (silver) níĝ-ba *D. wa Ìr-íb-sá-mu ʾÀ-du*$^{ki}$; o. XV 8: (silver) níĝ-ba *D. wa Da-mi-gu ʾÀ-du*$^{ki}$

*Du-ur-il* **9** r. III 17: 1 [dib] … 1 ĝír mar-tu*D. Bù-ra-tin*$^{ki}$ tuš-LÚ×TIL *Ar-mi*$^{[ki]}$ [*áš-ti*] [ $^{ki}$]; **17** o. IV 3: 2 IGI.NITA u$_5$ lú *D.*, 17: 1 íb-lá 1 ĝír-kun *D.*

*Du-ur-ì* **7** o. XI 6: 1 dib *D. Bù-ur-tin*$^{ki}$.

*En-a-mar* **3** o. II 6: še *E.*

*En-àr-li-im* **9** r. III 2: 1 dib *E.* [dumu-ni]ta *Du-*[*bí*]*-šum A-ba-ad*$^{ki}$ tuš-LÚ×TIL *Ar-mi*$^{ki}$ *áš-ti Zú-mu-šar*$^{ki}$.

EN-*da-za* **19** r. XIV 18: 1 íb-lá 1 ĝír-kun E. *A-rí-gú*$^{ki}$ tuš-LÚ×TIL *Nu-rí*$^{ki}$; **23** o. VI 4: 1 dib E. *Maš-bar-rá*$^{ki}$.

*En-gi-iš-ar* **5** r. XIII 5: 2 *gú-li-lum E.* a:zu$_5$.

EN-*mar* **3** o. XIII 6: (silver) E. *Kak-mi-um*$^{ki}$ lú GIŠ-kiri$_6$; **6** r. VI 17: 2 *bu*-DI *ma-lik-tum Ra-ʾà-ak*$^{ki}$ ÉXPAP E. šu-mu-tak$_4$; **7** o. VI 11: *Ti-ra-ì* maškim E. šu-du$_8$ *in Ma-rí*$^{ki}$; **10** o. VI 20: 4 *bu*-DI dumu-munus e[n] [*Ra-ʾà-ak*$^{ki}$] [*m*]*a-*[*li*]*k-*[*t*]*um* ⌜*A*⌝*-bar-sal*$_4$$^{ki}$ *wa ma-lik-tum Ir-i-tum* E. šu-mu-tak$_4$; **18** o. XIII 23: 1 na$_4$ E.

*En-na*-BAD **3** o. II 9: še *E.* ⌜"ur$_4$"⌝ BAD é *Ib-rí-um*; **9** o. XII 10: (silver) níĝ-kaskal *Ìr-am*$_6$*-ma-lik wa E.* DU.DU [*M*]*a-rí*$^{ki}$; **10** o. XIV 17: (silver) níĝ-kaskal *E. Zú-ti*$^{ki}$ maškim *Du-bí* DU.DU *Ar-mi*$^{ki}$; **22** o. III 3; o. VIII 5: 1 dib *E.* ì-na-sum *In-ma-lik.*

*En-na-Da-gan* **21** o. XII 8: (silver) níĝ-ba *E.*

*En-na-gú-nu* **2** o. XV 21: 10 lá-1 ĝír mar-tu zú … *E.* lú *A-da-mu.*

*En-na-il* **2** o. V 16: 1 ĝír mar-tu kg *E.* ugula *Lum-na-an*$^{ki}$; **9** o. V 5: 2 ĝír mar-tu *ba-du-u*$_4$ kb *Šè-na*$^{ki}$ šu-du$_8$ *wa E.* lú an:zam$_x$ ugula IGI.NITA; r. VII 10: 1 dib *E.* ugula *Lum-na-an*$^{ki}$; r. XIV 3: *I-ti-a-gú* lú *E.*; r. XVI 3: 1 íb-lá 1 ĝír-kun … *E.* [ ] *Rí-ì-ma-lik* lú-kar *Kak-mi-um*$^{ki}$; **14** o. VII 4: 1 íb-lá 1 ĝír-kun kg *E.* lú *Zi-ba-da*; **16** r. XVI 12: 1 dib *E.* lú *A-ma-za*; **17** o. VI 3: (silver) níĝ-kaskal *E.* [DU.DU] *si-in* Kiš$^{ki}$; r. VIII 11: 1 dib *E. Ga-sa*$^{ki}$; **19** o. IX 27: (silver) lú GIŠ-nu-kiri$_6$ *E.* ugula engar *Zú-ba-núm* šu-ba$_4$-ti; **20** r. IX 4: 2 *gú-li-lum* níĝ-ba [ ] *E.* [ ] $^{d}$*Am-ma-rí-ig*, 15: (silver) níĝ-ba *Wa-ru*$_{12}$*-tum Ma-rí*$^{ki}$ e$_{11}$ *mi-nu* Kiš$^{ki}$ *áš-ti E.*; **22** o. IV 2; o. IX 5: 1 dib *Sá-gú-si* ì-na-sum *E.* lú *I-da-ni-ki-mu*, 8: 1 dib *E.* lú *Iš-da-al*$_6$; **25** o. VIII 9: 1 íb-lá ŠA.PI gín D. kb *E.* l[ú ]; o. IX 2: [ kù:babbar] *E.* lú *Áš-da-maḫ.*

*En-na-ì* **6** r. IV 24: (silver) níĝ-kaskal *E.* lú kas$_4$-kas$_4$ DU.DU *Ma-rí*$^{ki}$; **7** r. X 13: 1 ⌜dib⌝ *E.* lú *Rí-ì-ma-lik*; r. XIII 9 and 17: 1 ĝír mar-tu *ba-du-u*$_4$ kbg *E.* lú BÍL-*za-ì* DU.DU *si-in* Ki[š$^{ki}$] [x ma-na] an-na sagi *Ma-rí*$^{ki}$ *E.* šu-mu-tak$_4$; **11** o. XI 15: 4 gud *Wa-ba-rúm E.* lú-kar *Kak-mi-um*$^{ki}$; **13** r. VII 13: 7 *gàr-su* ĝi$_6$ *Ar-wa* BÍL-*za-ì wa E.* 2 dumu-nita šeš *Ib-rí-um wa* Lugal-*na-*⌜*i*⌝*-iš Íl-ba-šum Íl-ba-zi-kir A-ma*-NI lú-kar [ ]; **14** o. XI 7: 2 níĝ-anše-ak 2[+2] kù-sal *E.* lú *Ša-ù-um*; r. IX 23: [1 íb-lá 1 ĝír-kun] e[n] *Ì-ra-ar*$^{ki}$ … 2 *bu*-DI … 2 saĝ-*sù ma-lik-tum Ì-ra-ar*$^{ki}$ *E.* [šu-mu-tak$_4$]; **15** r. X 28: (silver) níĝ-kaskal *E.* DU.DU Kiš$^{ki}$; **16** r. V 14: 1 dib *E.* lú *Rí-ì-ma-lik*; **17** r. XVII 22: 4 ĝeštu$_x$-lá *I-bi-zi-kir* dumu-nita *Ib-rí-um wa En-na-ni-il* lú *Ša-ù-um wa E.* lú *Zi-ba-da*; **18** o. XIII 8: (silver) níĝ-ba *E. Ḫa-la-bí-du*$^{ki}$ *in ʾÀ-da-ni*$^{ki}$ šu-ba$_4$-ti; **22** o. V 3: (silver) lú *E.* di-kud.

*En-na-ma-lik* **2** o. XII 11: 1 dib *E. Ma-nu-wa-ad*$^{ki}$; **4** r. IX 6: 2 *gú-li-lum*-I ĝuruš *E* lú-kar *Ma-nu-wa-ad*$^{ki}$; **5** o. IX 18: ĝeštin *E.* šu-ba$_4$-ti *in* [ ]; **21** o. XVI 18: 1 dib *E.* lú *Il-da-mu*; **22** r. VIII 1: 13 dib *Bù-da-ì Íl-a-šar Gal-za-iš-lu Ga-du-um Iš-má-da-mu Da-da-ì* ⌜x⌝-NE-[x] *E. Ig-rí-iš Gur-an-da-mu Ru*$_{12}$*-zi-li-im Iš-má-da-ba-an Zé-da-mu.*

*En-na-ni-il* **17** r. III 28: 1 dib *E.* lú *Rí-ì-ma-lik*; r. XVII 19: 4 ĝeštu$_x$-lá *I-bi-zi-kir* dumu-nita *Ib-rí-um wa E.* lú *Ša-ù-um wa En-na-ì* lú *Zi-ba-da*; **19** r. XV 11: 2 ĝír mar-tu *ba-du-u*$_9$ kg *E.* šeš *Ib-rí-um wa Na-am*$_6$-ì-ĝiš; **24** r. IV 1: *Íl-zi* lú *E.*

*En-na-*$^{d}$Utu **1** o. XI 3: *Maš-da-ru*$_{12}$ dumu-nita *E.*; **15** o. XI 23: *Ar-za-du* dumu-munus *E.*; **17** r. XIII 29: [10+]7 [*b*]*u*$^{?}$-DI [ŠÚ+Š]A-ŠÚ+ŠA [níĝ-b]a *Ra-ù-tum Kir-*[*s*]*u-*[*u*]*d* [*E.*] *Ra-ba*$_x$*-tum Maš-ga-sa-du Ma-ga-ra-du Tíš-má-da-mu Ra-ba*$_x$*-tum*-II dam en *wa* PN$_1$–PN$_2$ 2 dumu-munus en *wa* ama-gal *Ib-rí-um wa* PN$_3$–PN$_6$ dam-*sù wa* PN$_7$ nin-ni *Du-si-gú* PN$_8$.

*En-nu-lum* **9** r. XIII 21: 3 *gú-li-lum* a-gar$_5$-gar$_5$ lú *Wa-su*-LUM lú *Ib-ni-ḫar wa E.* BÍL-*da-mu I-ti-a-gú* lú *En-na-il.*

EN-*sa-rí* **8** o. II 15: *Iš-má-ga-lu* lú E.
*En-ti* **12** o. XIV 3: *Sa-mu-um* lú *E.*
E[N-]˹x-x˺-*tum* **4** r. I 7: (silver) ugula ĝiš E.
EZEN-*il* **17** o. VIII 11: (silver) níĝ[-ba] E. *Ma-rí*$^{ki}$ ḫi-mu-DU LAGAB×UD.LAGAB×UD.

*Ga-áš-ru*$_{12}$ **19** r. XII 13: (silver) níĝ-ba *G. Na-gàr*$^{ki}$ DU.DU *mi-nu* Kiš$^{ki}$.
GABA-*da-mu* **15** o. V 6: 1 dib G. lú *I-rí-ig*; **18** o. XVI 10: 1 dib G. lú *Ìr-am*$_6$*-da-mu*.
*Ga-du-um* **22** r. VII 11: 13 dib *Bù-da-ì Íl-a-šar Gal-za-iš-lu G. Iš-má-da-mu Da-da-ì* ˹x˺-NE-[x] *En-na-ma-lik Ig-rí-iš Gur-an-da-mu Ru*$_{12}$*-zi-li-im Iš-má-da-ba-an Zé-da-mu*.
*Gal-za-iš-lu* **22** r. VII 10: 13 dib *Bù-da-ì Íl-a-šar G. Ga-du-um Iš-má-da-mu Da-da-ì* ˹x˺-NE-[x] *En-na-ma-lik Ig-rí-iš Gur-an-da-mu Ru*$_{12}$*-zi-li-im Iš-má-da-ba-an Zé-da-mu*.
*Ga-nu-bù* **18** r. XVI 23: 1 ĝír mar-tu zú LAGAB×AN kg *G. Sal-ba-um*$^{ki}$ tuš-LÚ×TIL *Ḫal-sum*$^{ki}$.
*Ga-nu-lum* **22** o. IV 6: (gold and silver) ká *G.*
*Ga-ti* **21** r. XII 25: 1 dib *G.*
*Gi-a-da-mu* **2** o. XV 16: 10 lá-1 ĝír mar-tu zú *G.* …; **15** r. III 1: 1 ĝír mar-tu kg *G.*; **20** o. XVII 11: 1 íb-lá 1 ĝír-kun … maš-maš-*sù G. in* ud ḫúl-*sù Gi-rí* dumu-nita *Ib-rí-um* šu-mu-tak$_4$.
*Gi-ba-da* **15** r. VI 19: 2 *bu*-DI … 2 saĝ-*sù* níĝ-ba *Na-tum ma-lik-tum Bur-ma-an*$^{ki}$ É×PAP *G. Ib-dur-i-šar* šu-mu-tak$_4$.
*Gi-ba-rí-a* **18** r. X 20: (silver) níĝ-kaskal *G. Kab-lu*$_5$*-ul*$^{ki}$ DU.DU *si-in Ir-bí-ì-lum*$^{ki}$.
*Gi-gi* **11** o. VIII 3: *I-rí-ig-da-mu* lú *G.*
*Gi-ir-da-mu* **15** o. XVI 7: 1 íb-lá *Ir-da-mu* … 1 *si-ti-tum G.* 2 dumu-nita *Ib-rí-um*; **17** o. XI 14: 1 íb-lá 1 *si-ti-tum* 1 ĝír-kun *G.*; r. IV 6: NI-*na-du* ugula sur$_x$-BA.AN *G.* dumu-nita *Ib-rí-um*.
*Gi-ra-ma-lik* **9** r. XV 3: 1 ĝír mar-tu zú LAGAB×AN kg *G.* lú *I-b*[*í*]*-šum*; **19** r. X 15: 1 dib *G.* lú *I-bí-šum* tuš-LÚ×TIL *Ḫal-sum*$^{ki}$.
*Gi-rí* **12** o. IV 11: 1 dib *I-bí-zi-kir* dumu-nita *Ib-rí-um* … 2 ĝeštu$_x$-lá *G.* šeš-*sù*; o. VI 1: 2 ĝír mar-tu … 2 kù-sal [ní]ĝ-ba <d>BAD *Ga-na-na-im* [*w*]*a* [$^{d}$*ʾA*$_5$*-d*]*a*[*-ra*] *G. wa Ni-ir-da-mu* 2 dumu-nita *Ib-rí-um* in-na-sum *in* ud gi$_4$ *mi-nu Du-du-lu*$^{ki}$; **15** r. VI 27: 10 ˹x˺-[x] *G.*; r. VII 6: 6 ĝeštu$_x$-lá *G. wa Ir-da-mu Nap-ḫa-il* dumu-nita *Ib-rí-um*; **16** r. VI 6: 1 dib *Ir-ti* … 2 ĝeštu$_x$-lá *G.* 2 dumu-nita *Ib-rí-um*; **18** o. XI 1: 1 íb-lá 1 *si-ti-tum* 1 ĝír-kun *G. ap* 1 íb-lá 1 ĝír-kun kb … maš-maš-*sù Ir-ti* … 1 íb-lá 1 ĝír-kun *Nap-ḫa-ì* 3 dumu-nita *Ib-rí-um*; **20** o. XVII 14: 1 íb-lá 1 ĝír-kun … *Gi-a-da-mu in* ud ḫúl-*sù G.* dumu-nita *Ib-rí-um* šu-mu-tak$_4$; r. V 20: 2 níĝ-anše-ak 4 kù-sal *G.* dumu-nita *Ib-rí-um*; r. XII 1: 1 dib *G.* dumu-nita *Ib-rí-um*; **24** o. I 4: 1 ĝír mar-tu *G.*, 8: 4 ĝeštu$_x$-lá *G. wa Nap-ḫa-il wa* lul-gu-ak 2 ĝeštu$_x$-lá *Ir-da-mu* dumu-nita *Ib-rí-um*.
*Gi-ù-du* **18** r. II 25: 2 *bu*-DI ì-ĝiš-saĝ *G.* dam *Za-ba-rúm*.
*Gú-gi* **4** o. V 8: 2 *gú-li-lum G.* šu-i; **6** r. V 25: (silver) níĝ-ba *ʾÀ-sa wa G. I-ku-il wa Ba-du-lum Ma-rí*$^{ki}$ níĝ-"mul" *Na-gàr*$^{ki}$ àga-"kár"(ŠÈ).

*Gul-la* **7** r. XI 12: (silver) níĝ-ba *G.* ˹x-x-x˺ *Sa-ma-na-nu* [*S*]*i-mi*[- ] [ ] *Iš-ba-ì A-ša*$^{ki}$ *in* ud DU.DU nam-kud é $^{d}$*Ku-ra*; **10** o. XIV (silver) níĝ-ba *G.* ḫi-mu-DU 1 BAR.AN; **18** r. XVII 20: (silver) *Ag-ga* (silver) *G. Ḫu-ra*-NE *Na-gàr*$^{ki}$ *in* kaskal *Su-da-ma-an*$^{ki}$; **19** r. XVIII 26: (silver) *G. wa* maškim-*sù Na-gàr*$^{ki}$.
*Gú-ma-ni-du* **17** o. XII 22: *Du-bí-šum* lú *G.* maškim *I-bí-zi-kir*.
*Gur-an-da-mu* **22** r. VIII 3: 13 dib *Bù-da-ì Íl-a-šar Gal-za-iš-lu Ga-du-um Iš-má-da-mu Da-da-ì* ˹x˺-NE-[x] *En-na-ma-lik Ig-rí-iš G. Ru*$_{12}$*-zi-li-im Iš-má-da-ba-an Zé-da-mu*.
*Gú-sa* **18** r. XI 17: 1 *a-ba-lum* … 1 zi-bar níĝ-ba *G.* dumu-nita en *Na-gàr*$^{ki}$.
*Gú-šu* **5** r. XV 25: (silver) níĝ-ba *G.*
*Gú-zi* **2** o. XV 17: 10 lá-1 ĝír mar-tu zú … *G.* lú *Iš*$_{11}$*-gi-ba-ir*; **13** o. IV 13: *Ti-ti-nu wa G.* šu-ba$_4$-ti *in A-te-na-ad*$^{ki}$; o. VII 5: *G.* šu-mu-tak$_4$; **18** r. XV 25: 1 ĝír mar-tu *G.*
*Gú-zú-gú-zú* **6** r. IV 16: (silver) níĝ-ba *A-gàr wa G. Ma-rí*$^{ki}$.

*Ḫáb-ra-ar* **3** r. V 1: 1 ˹dib˺ *Ḫ.* ugula *ʾA*$_5$*-da-tum*$^{ki}$; **5** r. III 6: 1 ĝír mar-tu kg zú LAGAB×A *Ḫ.* lú *Ib-ga-iš-lu*; **7** o. I 17: 1 *gàr-su Ḫ.* lú ˹*Ib*˺*-ga-*[*i*]*š-lu*; o. V 22: 1 ĝír mar-tu kg *Ḫ.* [l]ú [*Ib-ga-iš-lu*]; **15** r. XV 7: 1 dib *Ḫ.* lú *Ib-ga-iš-lu*.
*Ḫáb-la-ar* **8** r. VIII 4': [x-N]E[- ] lú *Ḫ.*
*Ḫa-bù-zú* **16** r. IV 5: 1 dib *Ḫ. ʾÀ-bar-du*$^{ki}$ maškim *Za-ba-rúm* tuš-LÚ×TIL *Ḫal-sum*$^{ki}$.
*Ḫal-ba*$_x$(PÉŠ) **1**(e) r. III' 5: (silver) maškim *Ḫ. Na-am*$_6$$^{ki}$.
*Ḫal-za-um* **5** r. I 10: 1 dib *Ḫ.*; **22** o. III 10.
*Ḫa-ra-du* **2** r. I 1: 10 lá-1 ĝír mar-tu zú … *Ḫ.* lú *Ba-lu-zú*.
*Ḫa-ra-il* **3** o. II 3: še *Ḫ.*; 4 o. XIV 14: (silver) níĝ-kaskal maškim *Ḫ.*; o. XV 13: *Za-ba-ra* maškim *Ḫ.*; **6** o. XV 8: (silver) níĝ-kaskal *A-ir-ra wa A-zú-bù-lu* DU.DU *Ar-mi*$^{ki}$ maškim *Ḫ.*; **15** o. III 24: 1 dib … *Si-ti*-BAR.AN lú-kar *Kak-mi-um*$^{ki}$ [ ] *Ḫ. áš-du* 1 dib-*sù* til *in Ša-nu-gú*$^{ki}$.
*Ḫa-ra-ì* **1**(a) r. II' 2; **9** o. II 17: (silver) [níĝ-kaskal *A-ir-ra*? *wa A-zú-bù-lu*?] DU.DU *Ar-mi*$^{ki}$ maškim *Ḫ.*; **11** r. VIII 3: (silver) níĝ-kaskal *Ḫ.*; **18** o. XIV 22: (silver) níĝ-kaskal *A*-LUM$^{ki}$ maškim *Ḫ.* lú ĜIŠ-nu-kiri$_6$.
*Ḫa-zu-um* **17** o. XII 13: 1 íb-lá 1 ĝír-kun *Ḫ.* maškim *Ib-rí-um* tuš-LÚ×TIL *Ti-ma-tim*$^{ki}$ lú *Kak-mi-um*$^{ki}$; **19** r. VII 27: 1 dib *Ḫ.*
*Ḫ*[*a-*]*zu-*[ ] **1** o. VIII 3: *A-ga-ab* lú *Ḫ.*
ḪI-*ra-ù* **17** o. II 17: 2 BAR.AN Ḫ. *Na-gàr*$^{ki}$ šu-mu-tak$_4$.
ḪI-*la-um* **19** o. III 25: (silver) níĝ-ba Ḫ. *Na-gàr*$^{ki}$; r. XIX 1: (silver) Ḫ. *Na-gàr*$^{ki}$.
*Ḫu-ma-la* **23** o. V 7: 1 dib *Ḫ.* lú NE-*ša*-LUM.
*Ḫu*-NE-*du* **21** o. II 4: (silver) níĝ-ba *Ḫ. wa Ir*$_{11}$*-tum-a-ḫu Sag-gar*$^{ki}$ kaskal níĝ-kas$_4$ *Du-du-lu*$^{ki}$.
*Ḫu-ra*-NE **18** o. V 13: (silver) níĝ-ba *Ḫ. Na-gàr*$^{ki}$; r. XVII 21: (silver) *Ag-ga* (silver) *Gul-la Ḫ. Na-gàr*$^{ki}$ *in* kaskal *Su-da-ma-an*$^{ki}$; **19** o. VI 11: (silver) níĝ-ba *Ḫ. Na-gàr*$^{ki}$ *in Du-du-lu*$^{ki}$ šu-ba$_4$-ti; r. VII 17: (silver) *Ḫ. Na-gàr*$^{ki}$ *in A-ru*$_{12}$*-ga-du*$^{ki}$ šu-ba$_4$-ti.

*Ḫu-wa-sa-ra-du* **14** o. VI 16: (silver and tin) *Ḫ. Du-lu*ki ḫi-mu-DU 1 kir4-ma *wa* 10 lá-2 gada-TÚG.
*Lu-wa-sa-ra-du* **13** o. II 12: 2 íb-lá 2 *si-ti-tum* 2 ĝ[í]r-kun *Mu-zi* šeš en *wa L. Du-lu*ki.

*Ib-ʾà-ra* **9** r. IV 18: *Za-ne-ḫi-Ma-rí*ki é-gi *I. ʾÀ-šu*⌜ki⌝; r. VI 17 and VII 5: 4 *bu*-DI níĝ-ba *I. wa* nin-ni-⌜*sù*⌝ *in* ud níĝ-mu-sá ⌜*Za*⌝*-ne-ḫi-Ma-[r]í*ki é-gi *I. ʾÀ-šu*ki; **12** o. VIII 1: *Za-ne-ḫi-Ma-rí*ki dumu-munus en é-gi *I.*; **22** r. V 5: *Za-ni-ḫi-Ma-rí*ki é-gi *I. ʾÀ-šu*ki.
*I-bax-ì* **18** o. XV 19: (silver) níĝ-ba *I. Zi-rí-gú ʾÀ-du*ki *wa Ib-rí Na-gàr*ki *wa I-ku-a-ḫu Sag-gar*ki; r. XVIII 12: (silver) *I. Zi-rí-gú ʾÀ-du*ki.
*I-bax-zi-mi-nu* **7** o. III 10: 1 megida? níĝ-sikil *I.*; **16** r. II 23: še-in *I.(-ba-)* ugula ir11.
*Ib-bí-um* **3** r. II 8: 10 gud *I.* ugula é šu-ba4-ti ki:lam7 [ ]; **4** o. IV 3: ĝeštin-ĝeštin *I.* "ur4"; r. II 9: ĝeštin-ĝeštin *I.* "ur4"; r. V 4: ĝeštin-ĝeštin *I.* "ur4"; r. VII 14: 2 ĜI[š-x] *I.* "ur4" šu-ba4-ti ki:lam7 *ʾÀ-da-ni*ki; **6** o. I 8: gig *I.* šu-ba4-ti; **19** r. VI 22: ĜIŠ-sal é *A-ru12-ga-du*ki *I.* "ur4" šu-ba4-ti; **23** o. IV 5: 1 dib *I.* lú *Iš-má-ga-lu.*
*Ib-bu-tum* **8** o. III 15; o. X 3: (silver) *I.* (silver) maškim-*sù Ma-rí*ki .
*Ib-du-*d*Aš-dar* **17** r. XIX 20: 1 dib *I.* dumu-nita *A-šum*; **19** r. VII 33: 2 dib *I.* dumu-nita *A-šum wa Íl-gú-uš-ti.*
*Ib-du-*dEn-ki **7** r. V 11.
*Ib-du-ma-lik* **22** o. VI 7: 1 dib *I.* lú *Bù-a-du.*
*Ib-du-nu* **12** o. II 18: (silver) níĝ-ba *Ib-gi-tum wa Ku-tu-ʾà-bù wa I.* [ -]⌜x⌝ [ ] *Du-du-lu*ki níĝ-"mul" *Ag-sa-gú*ki šu-ba4-ti.
*Ib-dur-i-šar* **15** o. IX 3: 1 zi-bar en *Uš-ḫu-lum*ki *I.* šu-mu-tak4; r. VI 20: 2 *bu*-DI … 2 saĝ-*sù* níĝ-ba *Na-tum ma-lik-tum Bur-ma-an*ki É×PAP *Gi-ba-da I.* šu-mu-tak4; **19** o. IV 16: 2 *gú-li-lum* kb *I.* lú *Da-si*-KA.
*Ib-dur-ti-lu* **8** r. VII 6': 1 ĝír mar-tu *ba-du-u4* kg kb *I.* dumu-nita *A-mur-li-im.*
*Ib-ga-il* **15** o. XI 2: 1 *gú-li-lum* a-gar5-gar5 *I.* ugula surx-BAR.AN; **23** o. IV 1: <1 dib> *I. Ḫa-zu-wa-an*ki.
*Ib-ga-ì* **18** o. VI 18: 1 *gú-li-lum* a-gar5-gar5 *I.* ugula surx-BAR.AN en.
*Ib-ga-iš-lu* **5** r. III 7: *Ḫáb-ra-ar* lú *I.*; **7** o. I 18: *Ḫáb-ra-ar* lú *I.*; o. V 23: *Ḫáb-ra-ar* [l]ú [*I.*]; **15** r. XV 8: *Ḫáb-ra-ar* lú *I.*; **18** r. XVII 28: *Ìr-am6-ma-lik* lú *I.*
*Ib-gi-da-mu* **5** o. VII 9: 1 gud *I.* ugula kad4-kad4; **6** o. VII 13: 1 ĝír mar-tu ti kg *I.* lú *Si-gi*; r. XI 5: *Ig-rí-iš-li-im* dumu-nita *I.*; **9** o. XV 7: ĝeštin *I.* šu-ba4-ti; **14** o. II 16: 1 ⌜ĝír⌝ mar-tu *Ar-ra-du-lum Du-lu*ki *I.* šu-mu-tak4.
*Ib-gi-tum* **3** r. VIII 5: (silver) níĝ-ba *I. wa* maškim-*sù Ma-rí*ki *in Ša-dab6*ki šu-ba4-ti; r. X 13: (silver) níĝ-ba *I.* lú *I-ti Ma-rí*ki; **10** o. XVI 6: (silver) níĝ-ba *I. Ma-rí*ki níĝ-"mul" *Na-gàr*ki [t]il; r. III 19: (silver) níĝ-ba *I.*; **12** o. II 14: (silver) níĝ-ba *I. wa Ku-tu-ʾà-bù wa Ib-du-nu* [ -]⌜x⌝ [ ] *Du-du-lu*ki níĝ-"mul" *Ag-sa-gú*ki šu-ba4-ti; r. V 15: (silver) níĝ-ba *I. Ma-rí*ki ĜIŠ.DUG.DU izi-ĝar; **13** o. VI 17: (silver) níĝ-ba *I. Ba-du-lum La-li I-ku*ʾ(DÚR)*-ku*ʾ(DÚR)*-tu Ma-rí*ki; **14** o. III 16: (silver) n[íĝ-ba] *Iš-*⌜*dub*⌝*-ì wa I.* maškim ga:eš8 *Du-du-lu*ki šu-mu-tak4 *ʾà:bíl.*
*Ib-gú-nu* **5** o. XVI 14: *I-si-rúm* lú *I.*

*Ib-ḫur-ma-lik* **5** o. II 11: 1 ĝír mar-⌜tu⌝ [kb] [níĝ-ba] *I.* lú-kar *Kak-mi-um*ki; **7** o. VIII 7: 1 íb-lá 1 *si-ti-tum* 1 ĝír-kun níĝ-ba *I. Kak-mi-um*ki tuš-LÚ<×TIL> *in Ar-ḫa-du*ki
*Ib-ḫur-úr* **6** o. XII 14: (silver) níĝ-ba *I.* (silver) níĝ-ba *Sa*-NI*-gú* maškim-*sù* níĝ-"mul" *ʾÀ-du*ki àga-⌜kàr⌝(ŠÈ).
*I-bí-du-lum* **12** r. I 2: 1 íb-lá 1 *si-ti-tum* 1 ĝír-kun *I.* en *Ma-nu-wa-ad*ki *in* ud DU.DU nam-kud é d*Ku-ra.*
*I-bí-ga-lu* **4** r. XI 15: 1 dib … ì-na-sum *Ìr-am6-ma-lik* maškim *Du-si* [ ] šeš[-mu] en *Du-lu*ki *I.* šu-mu-tak4.
*I-bí-gàr-du* **6** r. II 12: 1 ĝír mar-tu kg *I.* ugula *ʾÀ-ma-du*ki.
*I-bí-iš-lu* **6** r. XV 16: 1 ma-na an-na *Na-zú-ù Ki-ma-lik wa I.* šu-mu-tak4.
*I-bí-šum* **5** o. XI 11: 1 ĝír mar-tu ti kg *I.* lú *I-gi* É×PAP; **6** r. VIII 9: 1 íb-lá 1 ĝír-kun *I.* lú *Ti-ir in* ud tuš-LÚ×TIL *Zú-ti*ki; **9** r. XV 4: [*Gi-ra*]*-m*[*a-lik*] lú *I.*; **19** r. X 16: *Gi-ra-ma-lik* lú *I.*
*I-bí-um* **3** o. IV 3: 1 dib *I.* lú *I*[*š*]*-má-ga-lu*; **7** r. X 6: 1 dib *I.* lú *Iš-má-ga-l*[*u*]; **17** r. XIX 14: *A-mi-du* lú *I.*; **23** o. VI 9: *A-mi-du* lú *I.*
*I-bí-zi-im* **14** r. XII 9: *Rí-ì-ma-lik* lú *I.*; **17** o. XIII 12: *Rí-ì-ma-lik* lú *I.*
*I-bí-zi-kir* **2** o. III 20: 1 dib *I.* dumu-nita *Ib-rí-um*; r. IV 14: 2 ĝeštux-lá *I.* dumu-nita *Ib-rí-um*; l.ed. 4: 1 íb-lá *I.* lú *I-rí-gú-nu*; **3** o. XV 17: 1 dib *I.* l[ú *Ib-rí-um*] … 1 dib *Šum*-bàdki šeš-*sù*; r. III 6: 2 níĝ-anše-ak 4 kù-sal *I.* dumu-nita *Ib-rí-um*; **5** o. VI 7: 2 *bu*-DI ama-gal *I. in* ud níĝ-mu-sá dumu-munus *Ib-rí-um Gi-ti*-NEki; r. II 2: 2 <níĝ->anše-ak 4 kù-sal … 3 *zú-zú-ba-tum I.* dumu-nita *Ib-rí-um*; r. VIII 18: 1 ĜIŠ-banšur níĝ-ba *I.* dumu-nita *Ib-rí-um* dʾ*A5-da-*"*bal*" *La-ru12-ga-du*ki; **10** o. VII 12: [ ] *I.* dumu-nita *Ib-rí-um*; **12** o IV 5: 1 dib *I.* dumu-nita *Ib-rí-um*; o. XII 5: 2 ĝeštux-lá *I.* dumu-nita *Ib-rí-um in* ud šu-du8 *in Ma-nu-wa-ad*ki, 16: 2 ĝeštux-lá *I.* lú *I-rí-gú-nu in* ud tuš-LÚ×TIL *in Ma-nu-wa-ad*ki; r. VIII 8: 1 ĝír mar-tu kg *Ib-rí-um in* ud ká-gibil lú *I.* igi-ḫi-du8; **13** o. VI 12: 1 ĜIŠ-zú … 1 zag ĜIŠ-gígir-II *I.* dumu-nita *Ib-rí-um*; **14** o. XXI 1: [ ] lú *I.*; r. IX 6: [ ] [dum]u-nita *I.* [tuš-LÚ×TIL *in*] *Ib-al6*ki; **15** o. V 19: *Du-bù-ḫu-*dʾ*À-da* dumu-nita *I.*; o. VIII 14: 1 zag ĜIŠ-gígir-II *I.* dumu-nita *Ib-rí-um*; **16** r. IX 2: 2 níĝ-anše-ak 4 kù-sal *I.* dumu-nita *Ib-rí-um in* ud tuš-LÚ×TIL *Ḫal-sum*ki; **17** o. III 25: 1 *gú-li-lum* a-gar5-gar5 50 *ʾÀ-gàr* ugula BAR.AN *I.* dumu-nita [*Ib-rí-um*] [šu-ba4-ti]; o. VII 25: *i*[*n* ud] [ ] [*I.*] [dumu-]nita *Ib-rí-um*; o. XII 24: *Du-bí-šum* lú *Gú-ma-ni-du* maškim *I.*; o. XX 12: 3 ma-na kb lul-gu-ak kb lú mu-DU *Áb-zu*ki *I.* šu-mu-tak4; r. XII 10: 1 ĝír mar-tu kg *I.* dumu-nita *Ib-rí-u*[*m*], 20: [x í]b-lá [x *si-t*]*i-*[*tu*]*m* [x ĝí]r-[ku]n … 1 ĝír mar-tu kg níĝ-ba *I. in* ud níĝ-mu-sá *ma-lik-tum*; r. XVII 15: 4 ĝeštux-lá *I.* dumu-nita *Ib-rí-um wa En-na-ni-il* lú *Ša-ù-um wa En-na-ì* lú *Zi-ba-da*; r. XX 27: 15 *ḫa-za-nu* 2 gìn-gìn 2 si4 1 šu-dub *I.*, 35: 2 banšur *maš-ar-da Ib-rí-um I.*; **18** o. VI 6: 4 kù-sal *I.* dumu-nita *Ib-rí-um*; **19** o. I 19: 2 ĝír mar-tu kg *Ib-rí-um wa* sikil-*sù al6* tu-ra *I. wa al6* tu-ra en; o. V 10: 1 dib *I.* dumu-nita *Ib-rí-um áš-du* dib-*sù* sikil dʾ*À-da*;

o. VII 19: 2 zag ĜIŠ-gígir-II … 2 ĜIŠ-zú ĜIŠ-gígir-II zú-ak *Ib-rí-um wa I.* dumu-nita-*sù*; o. XII 25: 2 [n]íĝ-anše-ak 4 kù-sal *I.*; r. XIII 17: Túg-du$_8$ lú *I.*; r. XVIII 8: 1 íb-lá 1 *si-ti-tum* 1 ĝír-kun 1 ĜIŠ-sal níĝ-[b]a *Ib-rí-um* … 2 íb-lá 2 ĝír-kun … 2 ĜIŠ-sal-*sù I. wa Ù-ti* 2 dumu-nita-*sù in* ud ḫúl-*sù* en šu-mu-tak$_4$; **20** o. X 16: [ ] 1 dib-*sù I.* dumu-nita *Ib-rí-um* ì-na-sum; r. V 14: [2 níĝ-anše-ak$^{?}$] … maš-maš 4 kù-sal *I.* dumu-nita *Ib-rí-um*; r. X 18: 1 íb-lá 1 ĝír-kun … maš-maš-*s*[*ù*] *I.* lú *I-rí-gú-nu*; **21** o. III 5: [ ]-*sù Ti-ti-nu in* ud ḫúl-*sù I.* šu-mu-tak$_4$, 22: [2 níĝ-anše-ak 4 kù-sal] […] ĜIŠ-gí[gir-II] *I.*; o. XV 20: 1 íb-lá 1 *si-ti-tum* 1 ĝír-kun ì-ĝiš-saĝ *I.*; o. XVII 8: 3 *zú-zú-ba-tum I.*; r. VIII 21: 1 íb-lá 1 *si-ti-tum* 1 ĝír-kun lú en sikil $^{d}$*ʾÀ-da al*$_6$ tu-ra *I.*; r. XIII 19: 1 dib 2 *gú-li-lum I.*; **23** r. VI 5: 1 dib *I.* dumu-nita *Ib-rí-um*; **24** r. III 6: 1 dib *I.* dumu-nita- *Ib-rí-um*.

*Ib-lu*$_5$*-zú* **5** r. XV 10: 1 dib *I.*; **7** o. II 11: 1 *gàr-su I.* lú-kar *Ma-nu-wa-ad*$^{ki}$; **8** o. V 6: (48 garments, 48 kilts) [ -g]*i I. wa I-za-iš-ru*$_{12}$ lú-kar *Ma-nu-wa-ad*$^{ki}$ ki:lam$_7$ šeš-⸢ib⸣[-II] *ʾÀ-da-ni*$^{ki}$; r. V x+1: (silver) [*I.*] *wa I-za-iš-ru*$_{12}$ [lú-k]ar *Ma-nu-wa-ad*$^{ki}$; **11** o. XIII 10: (82 garments, 341 kilts, 10 daggers) … 2 gud *I.* ki:lam$_7$ $^{d}$*Ga-mi-iš*; **22** o. VIII 3: 1 dib […] ⸢ì-na⸣-sum *I.*

*Ib-ni-ḫar* **9** r. XIII 19: 3 *gú-li-lum* a-gar$_5$-gar$_5$ lú *Wa-su*-LUM lú *I. wa En-nu-lum* BÍL-*da-mu I-ti-a-gú* lú *En-na-il*.

*Ib-rí* **18** o. XV 23: (silver) níĝ-ba *I-ba*$_x$*-ì Zi-rí-gú ʾÀ-du*$^{ki}$ *wa I. Na-gàr*$^{ki}$ *wa I-ku-a-ḫu Sag-gar*$^{ki}$.

*Ib-rí-um* **2** o. IV 2: *I-bí-zi-kir* dumu-nita *I.*, 18: 1 *ḫa-bù* … níĝ-ba *I.* $^{d}$*ʾA*$_5$*-da-"bal" ʾÀ-ma-ad*$^{ki}$; o. VI 14: 1 kù-sal níĝ-ba *I.* $^{d}$*Ku-ra in* ud ne:saĝ-*sù*; o. IX 5: 1 ĝír mar-tu kg *I.*; o. XI 21: 1 *ma-ḫa-ni-gúm I.*; o. XIII 5: 1 pad 1 an-zam$_x$ *I.*; o. XV 7: *Da-mur-da-mu* dam *I.*; r. II 3: 1 *gú-li-lum* 1 kù-sal níĝ-ba *I.* $^{d}$*Ku-ra in* ud lú nídba, 15: 2 *ʾà-ra-ma-tum* … 2 zé-*sù* níĝ-ba *I.* $^{d}$Utu SA.ZA$_x$$^{ki}$; r. IV 16: *I-bí-zi-kir* dumu-nita *I.*; r. VIII 5: 1 an-dùl … [*ba-na-a*] *wa* íb+III-TÚG níĝ-ba *I.* $^{d}$⸢BAD *Du*⸣*-du-*⸢*la*$^{ki}$⸣, 22: maš-maš 1 "KIN" siki *wa* 1 kù-sal… níĝ-ba *I.* $^{d}$*ʾA*$_5$*-da-"bal" La-ru*$_{12}$*-ga-du*$^{ki}$; r. XVI 8: 1 ĝír mar-tu *ra-ʾà-tum* kg *I.*; **3** o. II 11: *En-na*-BAD ⸢"ur$_4$"⸣ BAD é *I.*; o. III 5: 1 zag ĜIŠ-gígir-II *I.*; o. IV 21: 1 *ḫa-bù* … *ar-ra-si-su* níĝ-ba $^{d}$*ʾA*$_5$*-da-"bal" La-ru*$_{12}$*-ga-du*$^{ki}$ *I.* ì-na-sum; o. XIII 12: 1 *za-ḫa-da I.*; o. XV 18: *I-bí-zi-kir* l[ú *I.*]; r. III 8: *I-bí-zi-kir* dumu-nita *I.*; r. IV 7: 1 šu-dub *I. in* ud ḫúl na-rú-*sù*, 13: 2 *bu*-DI ama-gal *I. Du-si-gú* šu-mu-tak$_4$; r. V 13: 1 bur-KAK *na-*⸢*kar*$^{?}$*-ra*⸣*-tim I.*; r. IX 3: 2 zag 2 ĜIŠ-gígir-II *I. wa* en *Bur-ma-an*$^{ki}$; r. XI 4: […] níĝ-ba $^{d}$*ʾA*$_5$*-da-"bal" La-ru*$_{12}$*-ga-du*$^{ki}$ *I.* ì-na-sum, 22: 6 *bu*-DI níĝ-ba 3 dam *Zi-ba-da in* ud níĝ-mu-sá dumu-munus *I.*; **4** o. III 24: [1+]1 *zú-zú-ba-tum I.*; o. VI 1: 6 *bu*-D[I] 3 dam *I. Ḫa-zu-wa-an*$^{ki}$; o. IX 5: (silver) *Na-gàr*$^{ki}$ ĜIŠ.DUG.DU *I.*; o. X 21: 20 *gú-a-tum* … 1 ĜIŠ-šú 1 níĝ-bànda … 1 *mar-wa-ga-tum* … 2 *da-ni-da* … níĝ-ba diĝir-diĝir-diĝir lú dumu-munus *I.* šu-mu-tak$_4$ *si-in Ì-ra-ar*$^{ki}$; o. XIII 10: 1 zag ĜIŠ-gígir-II *I.*; r. I 4: 3 *zú-zú-ba-tum* ĜIŠ-gígir-II *I.*; r. III 12: 2 ĝír šu-du$_8$-máš lú *I.*; r. IV 4: 2 šu-i *I.*, 8: 1 *ma-ḫa-ni-gúm I.*; r. XI 2: 1 an-dùl níĝ-ba $^{d}$*Á*$^{!}$(DA)*-la I.* ì-na-sum; r. XII 14: 1 *ma-ḫa-ni-gúm I.*; r. XVI 19: [AN.ŠE.GÚ x ma-na (x)] kb è *in* ud *I.* 2 mu; **5** o. VI 11: 2 *bu*-DI ama-gal *I-bí-zi-kir in* ud níĝ-mu-sá dumu-munus *I. Gi-ti*-NE$^{ki}$, 15: 1 bur-KAK ĜIŠ-taškarin *I.*, 18: 1 ĝír mar-tu kg *I. in* ud nídba $^{d}$[*Iš*:]*šára* ĜIŠ-kiri$_6$; r. I 5: (silver) lul-gu-ak 1 *zú-zú-ba-tum* zàḫ *I.*; r. II 4: *I-bí-zi-kir* dumu-nita *I.*; r. IV 4: 1 ĝír mar-tu … 1 kù-sal níĝ-ba $^{d}$*ʾA*$_5$*-da-"bal" Lu-ba-an*$^{ki}$ *I.* ì-na-sum *in* ud ne:saĝ-*sù*; r. VIII 20: *I-bí-zi-kir* dumu-nita *I.*; r. XI 3: *ʾa*$_5$*-na-gu* si 2 gud lú *I.* nídba $^{d}$*ʾÀ-da in* iti *ʾa*$_5$*-nun*; r. XIII 24: 1 ĝír mar-tu níĝ-ba $^{d}$*ʾA*$_5$*-da-"bal" ʾÀ-ma-du*$^{ki}$ *I.* in-na-sum; r. XIV 12: 1 ĝír mar-tu … 1 kù-sal níĝ-ba $^{d}$*Ra-sa-ap ʾÀ-da-ni*$^{ki}$ *in* SA.ZA$_x$$^{ki}$ *I.*; **6** o. IX 14: 1 zag ĜIŠ-gígir-II *I.*; r. II 9: 1 ĝír mar-tu kg *I.*; r. V 20: 1 zag ĜIŠ-gígir-II *I.*; r. X 16: *Ba-ga-ma* ugula sur$_x$-BAR.AN *I.*; r. XVI 4: 2 ĜIŠ-zú 2 ĜIŠ-gígir-II *I.*, 15: 4 *ma-ḫa-ni-gi I.*; r. XVII 37: 1 šu-i *I.*; **7** o. I 13: 1 ĝír mar-tu níĝ-ba $^{d}$*Wa-da-ʾà-nu* [l]ú [*Ša-*]*dab*$^{ki}$ *I.* ì-na-sum; o. III 16: 1 ĝír mar-tu *wa* 1 kù-sal níĝ-ba *I.* $^{d}$*Ra-sa-ap Du-ne-íb*$^{ki}$; o. V 14: *Da-zi-ma-ad* šu-i *I.*; o. VII 7: 1 *za-ḫa-da I.*; o. X 1: [ ] *I.* níĝ-ba $^{d}$BAD *Du-du-lu*$^{ki}$, 14: 1 an-dùl munus … saĝ-*sù* 2 šu-*sù* DU-*sù* níĝ-ba *Sa-a-ša si-in Du-du-lu*$^{ki}$ *I.* šu-mu-tak$_4$; o. XIII 9: 4 kù-sal *I.*; o. XIV 13: 1 *za-ḫa-da I.*, 21: 1 tùn tur 1 dub-naĝar sal 1 *ma-za-ḫa-rúm* 1 UŠ×KÍD *si-in* ZA$_x$ *I.*; o. XV 19: 1 gud-I lú-gi lú ZA$_x$ *I.*; r. V 24: 1 ĝír mar-tu níĝ-ba $^{d}$*Áš-da-bíl I.* in-na-sum; r. IX 2: 1 [ĝír] mar-[tu kg] *I.*; r. XI 9: 2 *gú-li-lum I.*; **8** o. I 16: [1 ĝír mar-tu *ra-ʾà-t*]*um* [kg] [1] ĝír mar-tu kg *I.* è; o. II 2: ⸢1⸣ ĝír mar-[t]u ⸢1⸣ *r*[*a*]*-*⸢*ʾà*⸣*-tum* kg *I.* en šu-mu-tak$_4$ *in* ud ḫúl na-rú; r. II 5' [ ] *ba-na-i-sa* níĝ-ba *I.* $^{d}$*Ra-sa-ap* [ ]; r. V 15': 8 si 4 gud nídba en *wa I.* nídba $^{d}$*Ra-sa-ap* [*ʾÀ-da-ni*$^{ki}$]; r. XI 4': 1 dub ki *I.* [ ]; **9** o. V 10: 3 ĝír šu-du$_8$-m[áš] *I.*; o. XV 11: 2 ĝír mar-tu ti kg *I.* uru-bar *in* níĝ-kas$_4$ lú sikil; o. XVII 3': ⸢x⸣[ ]⸢x⸣[ ] maš[kim] *I.*; r. IX 3: 1 an-dùl lú *I.* šu-mu-tak$_4$ $^{d}$BAD *Du-du-la*$^{ki}$; r. XIII 10: [ ] *I.*; r. XVII 17: [ ] 1 ĜIŠ-gígir-II *I.*; **10** o. III 7: 2 *šu-ba*$^{?}$*-la I.*; o. IV 18: 1 *za-ḫa-da I.*; o. V 12: 1 ĜIŠ-banšur níĝ-ba $^{d}$*K. Ib-rí-um* in-na-sum *in* ud ne:s[aĝ]-*sù*; o. VII 9: 1 dub nam-kud *I.*, 14: *I-bí-zi-kir* dumu-nita *I.*; o. VIII 4: (silver) níĝ-ba *I-ti-il Ma-rí*$^{ki}$ šu-mu-tak$_4$ 1 aktum-TÚG *I.*, 22: balaĝ lú *gú-za-rí-tum* lú *I.*; o. XIII 8: 1 zag1 ĜIŠ-gígir-II *I.*; r. I 8: 1 *zú-zú-ba-tum I.*; r. III 8: 1 *ma-ḫa-ni-gúm I.*; r. X 5: 1 ĝír mar-tu 1 kù-sal níĝ-ba $^{d}$*Ku-ra I.* ì-na-sum *in* ne-saĝ-*sù*; **11** o. IV 10: *maš-ar-tum* níĝ-ba dumu-munus *I.* é-gi<-a> *Zi-ba-da* é $^{d}$*ʾÀ-da*; o. V 2: 1 kù-sal … [1 ĝ]ír mar-⸢tu⸣ níĝ-⸢ba⸣ [$^{d}$*Ku-ra*] [*I.*$^{?}$] [ì-na-sum] [*i*]*n* ⸢ud⸣ ne:saĝ, 13: 1 kù-sal … 1 ĝír mar-tu níĝ-ba *I.* $^{d}$*Ra-s*[*a-ap*] *g*[*ú-n*]*úm in* ud ne:saĝ; o. VII 4: 2 ĝír mar-tu kg *ra-ʾà-tum I.*; r. VII 3: 2 *ʾà-ra-ma-tum* … níĝ-ba *I.* $^{d}$Utu lú SA.ZA$_x$$^{ki}$; **12** o. IV 7: *I-bí-zi-kir* dumu-nita *I.*; o. VI 5: *Gi-rí wa Ni-ir-da-mu* 2 dumu-nita *I.*; o. VII 17: 1 ĝír mar-tu níĝ-ba $^{d}$BAD *Ar-ti-na-an*$^{ki}$ *I.* in-na-sum; o. IX 8: 1 ĝír mar-tu kg *I. in* ud è *si-in* níĝ-kas$_4$ *Ma-nu-wa-ad*$^{ki}$; o. XI 3: 1 ĜIŠ-gu-kak-šub sur$_x$-BAR.AN *I.*, 9: 1 ĜIŠ-zú ĜIŠ-gígir-II *I.*; o. XII 7: *I-bí-zi-kir* dumu-nita *I.*; o. XV 13: ama-gal *I.*; r. IV 4: 1 níĝ-anše-ak IGI.NITA *I.*, 7: 1 ĝír mar-tu kg *I. in* ud è *si-in* á-daḫ lú *A-te-na-ad*$^{ki}$, 15: 1 *gàr*-su gi$_6$ *I*; r. VII 15: 1 ĝír mar-tu … 1

kù-sal níĝ-ba *I.* $^{dʾ}$*A*$_5$*-da-"bal"* NE-*a-ù*$^{ki}$; r. VIII 5: 1 ĝír mar-tu kg *I. in* ud ká-gibil lú *I-bí-zi-kir* igi-ḫi-du$_8$; **13** o. V 6: 1 ĝír mar-tu níĝ-ba *I.* $^{d}$*Ra-sa-ap* $^{d}$En-ki; o. VI 14: *I-bí-zi-kir* dumu-nita *I.*; o. VII 13: 1 *du-rúm* níĝ-ba *I.* $^{d}$*Ḫa-a-ba-du* lú *Ḫa-lab*$_x$$^{ki}$; o. IX 10: 1 ĝír mar-tu 1 kù-sal níĝ-ba *I.* $^{d}$*Ga-ra-ru*$_{12}$; o. XI 18: 1 íb-lá TAR kb maš-maš kg lú mu-DU *I.*; o. XIII 11: 4 kù-sal *I.*; o. XV 10: 3 ĜIŠ-zú 3 ĜIŠ-gígir-II en *wa* ama-gal-*sù wa I.*, 17: 2 zag 2 ĜIŠ-gígir-II ama-gal en *wa I.*; o. XVI 12: 2 si [gud]-I ⌜x⌝ 1 ⌜x⌝ *I.*; r. III 6: [ ] ugula sur$_x$-BAR.AN *I.*; r. IV 2: [ ] nu$_{11}$-za-*sù I.*, 16: 2 an-dùl níĝ-ba *I.* $^{d}$*Ra-sa-ap wa* $^{d}$*A-da-ma* *ʾÀ-da-ni*$^{ki}$; r. VII 16: BÍL-*za-ì wa En-na-ì* 2 dumu-nita šeš *I.*; **14** o. VII 13: *Šum*-bàd$^{ki}$ dumu-nita *I.*; o. XI 14: *Bu*$_x$*-ma-il* šeš *I.*; o. XII 20: 4 kù-sal *I.*; o. XVI 6: [ ] é *I.* šu-ba$_4$-ti; r. III 15: *Ir-da-mu* dumu-nita *I.*; r. VII 6: 1 ĜIŠ-asar … 4 saĝ lu$_5$ *al*$_6$*-sù* níĝ-ba *ʾA*$_5$*-da-"bal"* NE-*a-ù*<$^{ki}$> *I.* šu-mu-tak$_4$; r. XII 18: 1 pad an-zam$_x$ *I.*, 26: [ ] dumu-nita *I.*; **15** o. II 7: 1 ĜIŠ-banšur *wa* 1 kù-sal níĝ-ba *I.* $^{d}$BAD *Du-du-lu*$^{ki}$; o. IV 23: 4 kù-sal … 2 níĝ-anše-ak *I.*; o. VIII 16: *I-bí-zi-kir* dumu-nita *I.*; o. XV 18: 2 ⌜ĜIŠ⌝-zú … 2 ĜIŠ-gígir-II gibil *I.*; o. XVI 9: *Ir-da-mu … Gi-ir-da-mu* 2 dumu-nita *I.*, 14: 1 ĜIŠ-šú 1 níĝ-bànda kb lú kaskal *I.*; r. II 3: 1 an-zam$_x$ *wa* 1 pad-*sù I.*; r. III 5: 1 ĝír mar-tu níĝ-ba *I.* $^{dʾ}$*À-da gi*-NI; r. V 18: 1 ĝír mar-tu kg *I.* *áš-du* ĝír mar-tu-*sù* sikil $^{dʾ}$*À-da*; r. VI 5: 1 ⌜íb⌝-lá 1 *si-ti-tum* 1 ĝír-kun sikil $^{dʾ}$*A*$_5$*-da-"bal" Lu-ba-an*$^{ki}$ *I.* šu-mu-tak$_4$ *al*$_6$ tu-ra-*sù*; r. VII 11: *Gi-rí wa Ir-da-mu Nap-ḫa-il* dumu-nita *I.*; r. VIII 9: 1 ĝír mar-tu *wa* 1 kù-sal níĝ-ba *I.* $^{d}$*Ra-sa-ap Du-ne-íb*$^{ki}$, 26: 1 an-zam$_x$ an-dùl libir lú *I.*; r. XI 5: [1 ĝír mar-tu] [*w*]*a* 1 kù-sal níĝ-ba *I.* $^{d}$*A-dar-a-an Da-na-áš*$^{ki}$; r. XII 24: 2 *gú-li-lum I. áš-du* 2 *gù-li-lum-sù* sikil $^{dʾ}$*À-da al*$_6$ tu-ra en; r. XIII 4: 1 dib *I. áš-du* 1 dib-*sù* sikil $^{dʾ}$*À-da al*$_6$ tu-ra en; r. XIV 7: 1 buru$_4$-MU[ŠEN] [ ] [níĝ-]ba $^{d}$*Áš-da-bíl Ba-šè*$^{ki}$ *I.* šu-mu-tak$_4$; r. XVI 5: [1 ĝír mar-t]u kg *I. áš-du* ĝír mar-tu-*sù* sikil $^{d}$*Áš-da-bíl al*$_6$ tu-ra en; **16** o. VI 5: 2 níĝ-anše-ak 4 kù-sal libir *I.*; o. VII 3: 2 níĝ-anše-ak 4 kù-sal gibil *I.*, 10: 2 níĝ-anše-ak 4 kù-sal 2 IGI.NITA *I.*; o. XII 18: 2 ĝír lú ZA$_x$ *I.*; r. VI 8: *Ir-ti … Gi-rí* 2 dumu-nita *I.*, 14: 1 *za-ḫa-da I.*; r. IX 4: *I-bí-zi-kir* dumu-nita *I.*, 20: 1 íb-lá 1 *si-ti-tum* 1 ĝír-kun níĝ-ba *I.* $^{d}$*Ra-sa-ap Da-ra-um*$^{ki}$; r. X 22: 1 ĝír mar-tu *wa* 1 kù-sal níĝ-ba *I.* $^{dʾ}$*A*$_5$*-da-"bal" A-ru*$_{12}$*-ga-du*$^{ki}$; r. XII 3: šum ZA$_x$ *I.*; r. XIV 27: 1 útul urudu maḫ … 3 útul urudu maḫ … [ ] níĝ[-ba] *I.* $^{d}$BAD-munus *Lu-ba-an*$^{ki}$; r. XV 21: *Ir-ti Nap-ḫa-ì* 2 dumu-nita *I.*; r. XVI 1: 2 bur-KAK ĜIŠ-⌜taškarin⌝ en *wa* 2 bur-KAK ĜIŠ-taškarin kaskal *I.*; **17** o. III 27: *I-bí-zi-kir* [dumu-nita *I.*]; o. VIII 2: [*I-bí-zi-kir* dumu-]nita *I.*; o. XI 24: [*Nap*]*-ḫa-*⌜*ì*⌝ [dumu-n]ita [*I.*]; o. XII 15: *Ḫa-zu-um* maškim *I.* tuš-LÚ×TIL *Ti-ma-tim*$^{ki}$ lú *Kak-mi-um*$^{ki}$; o. XVI 3: 1 ĝír mar-tu kg *I. in* ud è níĝ-kas$_4$ al-kur$_6$ še *Kak-mi-um*$^{ki}$; r. I 18: 2 ĜIŠ-zú … 2 zag 2 ĜIŠ-gígir-II … 3 *zú-zú-ba-tum I.*; r. III 22: maš-maš kù-sal *I.*; r. IV 8: *Gi-ir-da-mu* dumu-nita *I.*; r. VII 32: *Ti-ti-nu* maškim *I.*; r. VIII 18: *Šum*-bàd$^{ki}$ dumu-nita *I.*; r. XII 12: *I-bí-zi-kir* dumu-nita *I.*; r. XIV 15: ama-gal *I.*; r. XVII 17: *I-bí-zi-kir* dumu-nita *I.*; r. XVIII 20: ama-gal *I.*; r. XIX 6: 1 *zú-zú-ba-tum I.* zàḫ; r. XX 22: 15 *ḫa-za-nu* 2 gìn-gìn 2 si$_4$ 1 šu-dub *I.*, 34: 2 banšur *maš-ar-da I.* <*I*>*-bí-zi-kir*; r. XXII 19: 1 ĝír mar-tu kg en *Ì-mar*$^{ki}$ *I.* šu-mu-tak$_4$; **18** o. II 1: 1 *a-ba-lum wa* pad-[*s*]*ù I.*; o. III 5: *Ba-d*[*u-lum*] [dumu-nita] *I.*; o. VI 8: *I-bí-zi-kir* dumu-nita *I.*; o. XI 17: *Gi-rí … Ir-ti … Nap-ḫa-ì* 3 dumu-nita *I.*; o. XII 24: 1 *a-ba-lum* níĝ-ba $^{dʾ}$*A*$_5$*-da-"bal" ʾÀ-ma-du*$^{ki}$ *I.*; o. XVI 1: 1 *za-ḫa-da* 1 [ĜI]Š$^?$-PA-⌜x⌝-ga *I.*; o. XVII 22: 1 ĜIŠ-šú 2 níĝ-bànda kaskal-kaskal *I.*; r. I 2: 2 ĜIŠ.GAM.GAM ĜIŠ-gígir-II *I.*; r. V 15: 1 šum maḫ … 2 šum maḫ 3 *zú-zú-ba-tum* ĜIŠ-gígir-II *I.*; r. XII 16: ama-gal *I.*; r. XIII 2: 1 íb-lá 1 *si-ti-tum* 1 ĝír-kun ì-ĝiš-saĝ *I.*, 21: *Min-na-ì* ugula sur$_x$-BAR.AN *I.*; r. XVI 32: 2 šu-i … *I.*; r. XVIII 7: 1 ĝír mar-tu kg *I. áš-du* ĝír mar-tu-*sù* sikil; **19** o I 14: 2 ĝír mar-tu kg *I. wa* sikil-*sù al*$_6$ tu-ra *I-bí-zi-kir wa al*$_6$ tu-ra en, 26: 1 ĝír mar-tu kg *I.* [*áš-*]*du* [1 g]ír [mar-t]u[-*s*]*ù* sikil; o. II 14: 1 kù-sal níĝ-ba en $^{d}$*Ba-tum-ma-du áš-t*[*i*] ĝír mar-tu-*sù* šu-mu-tak$_4$ *al*$_6$ tu-ra *I.*; o. V 12: *I-bí-zi-kir* dumu-nita *I.*; o. VII 17: 2 zag ĜIŠ-gígir-II … 2 ĜIŠ-zú ĜIŠ-gígir-II zú-ak *I. wa I-bí-zi-kir* dumu-nita-*sù*; o. VIII 13: 1 banšur *wa* 1 kù-sal níĝ-ba *I.* $^{d}$*Aš-dar*; o. XIII 3: 2 ĜIŠ-ban ĜIŠ-gígir-II *I.*, 10: 1 an-zam$_x$ *wa* 1 pad-*sù I.*; r. VI 8: 1 dub lú nam-kud en *wa I.* é $^{dʾ}$*À-da*; r. X 27: 1 banšur *wa* 1 kù-sal níĝ-ba *I.* $^{d}$BAD *Du-du-lu*$^{ki}$; r. XI 4: 1 *za-ḫa-da I.*; r. XV 13: *En-na-ni-il* šeš *I.*; r. XVI 20: útul-útul maḫ urudu *in* ud ḫúl *I.*; r. XVIII 1: 1 íb-lá 1 *si-ti-tum* 1 ĝír-kun 1 ĜIŠ-sal níĝ-[b]a *I.* … 2 íb-lá 2 ĝír-kun … 2 ĜIŠ-sal-*sù I-bí-zi-kir wa Ù-ti* 2 dumu-nita-*sù in* ud ḫúl-*sù* en šu-mu-tak$_4$; **20** o. X 1: [ ] ĜIŠ-gígir-II gibil *I.*, 18: *I-bí-zi-kir* dumu-nita *I.*; o. XI 4: 1 níĝ-PA *I.*, 19: 1 *gúm-a-nu I.*; o. XIII 14: (copper) ZA$_x$ *I.*; o. XVII 3: 1 íb-lá 1 *si-ti-tum* 1 ĝír-kun sikil $^{dʾ}$*A*$_5$*-da-"bal"* lú *Lu-ba-an*$^{ki}$ *al*$_6$ tu-ra *I.* tak$_4$, 16: *Gi-rí* dumu-nita *I.*; r. I 7: BÍL-*za-il* dumu-nita šeš *I.*; r. II 13: 4 kù-sal *I.*, 19: 1 an-zam$_x$ *I.*, 26: 1 pad an-zam$_x$ *A-ba-ti-um*$^{ki}$ *I.*; r. III 8: 1 pad *ma-da-a-um* kg an-dùl lú en *ša-ti I.* mu-DU; r. IV 11: 2 ĜIŠ-ban … 1 zag ĜIŠ-gígir-II 1 *za-ḫa-da I.*; r. V 16: *I-bí-zi-kir* dumu-nita *I.*, 22: *Gi-rí* dumu-nita *I.*; r. XII 12: *Gi-rí* dumu-nita *I.*; **21** o. IV 1; o. V 10: [ ] …saĝ-*sù* … 1 dub-*sù* níĝ-ba *I.* $^{d}$*Sa-nu-ga-ar Má*-NE$^{ki}$; o. VI 21: 1 kù-sal níĝ-ba *I.* $^{d}$*A-dar-a-nu* [*D*]*a-na-*[*á*]*š*$^{ki}$; o. VII 16: 1 dib 1 íb-lá 1 *si-ti-tum* 1 ĝír-kun … 1 ĝír mar-tu kg ⌜*ra*⌝*-ʾà-*[*tu*]*m* … 3 *z*[*ú-*]*zú-b*[*a-*]*tum* ĜIŠ-gígir-II *I.* šu-mu-tak$_4$ é $^{dʾ}$*À-da*; o. VIII 24: 1 níĝ-anše-ak 1 kù-sal IGI.NITA … 1 *za-ḫa-da* … lul-gu-ak lú sikil é $^{dʾ}$*À-da al*$_6$ tu-ra *I.*; o. X 23: 1 kun ZA$_x$ *I.*; o. XI 4: [ ] en *wa I.*; o. XI 25: AN.[Š]È.GÚ 1 *mi-at* 80 lá-1 ma-na kb lú è *in* ud [úš] [*I.*]; o. XIV 22 and XV 2: (obj.) lú *I.* šu-mu-tak$_4$ *si-in* ⌜É×PAP⌝ [ ] *Kéš-du-ud I.* šu-mu-tak$_4$; r. XVII 5: [AN.ŠÈ.GÚ x *mi-at* x ma-na x kb] ⌜è⌝ DIŠ m[u] úš *I.*; **22** r. V 11: 1 an-zam$_x$ *wa* 1 pad-*sù I.*; r. VI 11: 1 [*ḫa-bù*] níĝ-ba $^{d}$BAD *Du-du-lu*$^{ki}$ … 1 *ar-ra-sù ḫa-bù* níĝ-ba $^{d}$*Ga-mi-iš* … 1 ĜIŠ-ĝidru níĝ-ba $^{d}$*Ku-ra I.*; r. VIII 10: AN.ŠÈ.GÚ 4 ma-na TAR 3 gín D. kg è lú mu-DU *I. wa* tak$_4$ kg É×PAP en-e[n]; **23** o. III 8: 1 pad an-zam$_x$ *I.*; r. VI 7: *I-bí-zi-kir* dumu-nita *I.*; **24** o. II 1: *Gi-rí wa Nap-ḫa-il wa … Ir-da-mu* dumu-nita *I.*; o. IV 13: 1 *za-ḫa-da I.*; o. V 7: IGI.DUB 2 an-dùl *wa* 2 šu-*sù* 2 DU-*sù* níĝ-ba *I.* $^{d}$*Ra-sa-ap wa* $^{d}$*A-da-ma ʾÀ-da-ni*$^{ki}$ *in* *ma-ʾà-wa-tum*; o. VI 2: IGI.DUB 1 an-dùl níĝ-ba *I.* $^{d}$Nin-kar; o. VII 3: 1 kù-sal níĝ-ba *I.* $^{d}$*Ba-ra-ma in* ud ne:saĝ-*sù*; r. III 8: *I-bí-zi-kir* dumu-nita *I.*; **25** r. X 5: AN.ŠÈ.GÚ 86 ma-na 53 gín D. kb è *in* ud *I.*

*Ib-te-ar* **15** o. XIII 15: 3 ĝír mar-tu *ba-du-u*$_4$ kb *Dab-da-ar wa A-a-gú-nu ʾÀ-su*$^{ki}$ *wa I. Su-ti-ig*$^{⌜ki⌝}$.

*Ib-u*$_9$*-mu-ud* **18** o. XIV 2: [1 na$_4$] *I.*

*Ib*[- ] **1** o. XII 4: *I-ti-ne* lú *I.*

*I-da-ad-mu* **12** o. XIV 6: lú dumu-nita *I.*

*I-da-il* **6** r. I 9: (silver) níĝ-ba *Daš-na wa I. Ma-rí*$^{ki}$; r. IV 5: (silver) níĝ-ba *Daš-na wa I. Ma-rí*$^{ki}$.

*I-dam-na* **7** o. VII 2: 2 lu$_5$ lú *I.* gud-si-dili gibil.

*I-da-ne-gi-mu* **12** r. X 10: 1 dib *I.* dumu-nita en.

*I-da-ni-ki-mu* **1** o. X 19.; 17 r. XIII 7: 6 íb-lá 6 *si-ti-tum* 6 ĝír-kun níĝ-ba *Maḫ-ra-da-mu Ì-lum-a-ḫi I. I-in-*$^{d}$*ʾÀ-da Ku-ra-da-mu* dumu-nita en *wa I-ib-ma-lik* šeš ama-gal en; **22** o. IX 6: *En-na-il* lú *I.*

*I-du-a* **17** o. IX 17: *I-šar* lú *I.*

*I-du-bù* **4** r. IX 1: (silver) *I.* tuš-LÚ×TIL *Ḫa-zu-wa-an*$^{ki}$; **5** r. XII 19: 2 *gú-li-lum I.*

*I-ga-iš-lu* **1**(e) r. III' 9: (silver) níĝ-kaskal *I.* DU.DU *si-in Ma-rí*$^{ki}$; **9** o. IX 9: (silver) *Sal-bí-um*$^{ki}$ *I.* šu-mu-tak$_4$ *si-in* NI-*rúm*$^{ki}$.

*I-ga-iš-ru*$_{12}$ **8** o. IV 14: (silver) *I-ti* ga:eš$_8$ *I.* šu-mu-tak$_4$.

*I-ga-li-im* **4** r. VI 14: 1 ĝír [m]ar-tu zú kg *I.* en *Ib-al*$_6$$^{ki}$; r. XIII 5: 4 íb-lá *si-ti-tum* ĝír-kun *Du-bù-uš-da-mu I. Zú-ga-du Ì-lum-a-rí-ḫu* 4 en *Ib-al*$_6$$^{ki}$.

*Ig-bù-ul-ma-lik* **14** o. XV 16: 1 *gú-li-lum* a-gar$_5$-gar$_5$ *I.* NE-di.

*I-gi* **1** o. VIII 16: *Ù-ra-rí* lú *I.*; **5** o. IV 17: *Íl-ba-ma-lik* lú *I.*; o. XI 12: *I-bí-šum* lú *I.*; **6** o. VII 10: *Ru*$_{12}$*-zi-ma-lik* dumu-nita *I.*; **11** o. VII 16: *Íl-gú-uš-ti* lú *I.*; **14** r. II 11: *Íl-gú-uš-ti* lú *I.*; **17** o. I 13: *Íl-gú-uš-ti* lú *I.*; **22** o. III 4; **23** o. VII 10: *Íl-ba-ma-lik* lú *I.*

*Ig-na-da-ar* **7** o. XII 21: 1 ĝír mar-tu *I.*; **14** o. XIV 15: 1 dib *ʾÀ-bí* lú NI-BAD *wa* in-na-sum *I.* lú *Mi-ga-il*, 23: 2 *gú-li-lum* kg lú *I. Mi-ga-il* ì-na-sum; **21** r. IX 11: [1$^{?}$ í]b-lá [1 g]ír-kun … *I.* lú *Mi-ga-ì Ti-ti-nu* šu-mu-tak$_4$ *in* ud ḫúl-*sù*.

*Ig-na-da-mu* **24** r. IV 4: *Ma-a-bar-zú* lú *I.*

*Ig-rí-iš* **2** r. I 19: 1 dib *I.* lú *I-rí-gú-nu*; **5** r. VII 8: 1 dib *I.* lú *I-rí-ig-gú-nu*; **7** r. XII 2: [1 ĝír mar-tu] kg *I.* lú *I-rí-ig-gú-nu* É×PAP; **12** o. XII 1: *A-bur-li-im* lú *I.*; **16** r. IX 26: 1 *gàr-su* dumu-nita *I.* šu-du$_8$ *in Ḫal-sum*$^{ki}$; **20** r. XIII 1: 1 íb-lá [1] ĝír-kun … maš-maš-*sù* … 1 ĝír mar-tu kb [ ]-⌜x⌝ *I.* ⌜É×PAP⌝; **22** r. VIII 2: 13 dib *Bù-da-ì Íl-a-šar Gal-za-iš-lu Ga-du-um Iš-má-da-mu Da-da-ì* ⌜x⌝-NE-[x] *En-na-ma-lik I. Gur-an-da-mu Ru*$_{12}$*-zi-li-im Iš-má-da-ba-an Zé-da-mu*; **23** o. VIII 3: 1 dib *Íl-ba-ma-lik* … 1 dib *I.* šeš-*sù*.

*Ig-rí-iš-li-im* **6** r. XI 3: 1 ĝír mar-tu ti kg *I.* dumu-nita *Ib-gi-da-mu*.

*Ig-rí-su* **19** r. XVI 9: 2 *bu*-DI ama-gal en *Ra-ʾà-ak*$^{ki}$ É×PAP *I.* šu-mu-tak$_4$.

*I-ib-ma-lik* **6** o. XVI 9: (silver) níĝ-kaskal *Ni-zi-ma-il wa I.* DU.DU *Ma-rí*$^{ki}$: r. I 15: (silver) níĝ-kaskal *Ìr-am*$_6$*-ma-lik wa I.* DU.DU *Ma-rí*$^{ki}$; **7** o. II 18: *Ir*-NE dumu-nita *I.*; **17** o. VI 24: 1 dib *I.* dumu-nita *Aḫ-ra-ma-lik*; o. XI 2: 1 *gàr-sù I.*; r. XIII 13: 6 íb-lá 6 *si-ti-tum* 6 ĝír-kun níĝ-ba *Maḫ-ra-da-mu Ì-lum-a-ḫi I-da-ni-ki-mu I-in-*$^{d}$*ʾÀ-da Ku-ra-da-mu* dumu-nita en *wa I.* šeš ama-gal en; 23 r. V 11: 1 dib *I.* šeš *Du-si-gú*.

*I-i-bù* **4** r. VII 7: 1 ĝír mar-tu ti kg *I.*; 6 r. VI 10: (silver) níĝ-ba *I. Ir-i-tum*$^{ki}$.

*I-in-*$^{d}$*ʾÀ-da* **13** r. VIII 6: [ ] [*Ì-lum-a-ḫi*] *wa I.* 2 dumu-nita en; **15** o. VI 5: 2 *gàr-su Ì-lum-a-ḫi wa I.* 2 dumu-nita en; **17** r. XIII 8: 6 íb-lá 6 *si-ti-tum* 6 ĝír-kun níĝ-ba *Maḫ-ra-da-mu Ì-lum-a-ḫi I-da-ni-ki-mu I. Ku-ra-da-mu* dumu-nita en *wa I-ib-ma-lik* šeš ama-gal en; **19** o. VII 5: 1 íb-lá 1 *si-ti-tum* 1 ĝír-kun *I.* dumu-nita en É×PAP.

*I-in-il* **15** o. XIII 23: 1 íb[-lá] 1 ĝír-kun … *I.* ugula *Ù-ša-li-ik*$^{ki}$ *in* ud tuš-LÚ×TIL *Kak-mi-um*$^{ki}$

*I-in-zé* **12** r. VI 19: 2 zara$_6$-TÚG … 1 níĝ-lá-gaba 3 níĝ-lá-saĝ *I. in* Kiš$^{ki}$.

*I-ku-a-ḫu* **18** o. XV 26: (silver) níĝ-ba *I-ba*$_x$*-ì Zi-rí-gú ʾÀ-du*$^{ki}$ *wa Ib-rí Na-gàr*$^{ki}$ *wa I. Sag-gar*$^{ki}$.

*I-ku-il* **5** r. II 17: (silver) níĝ-ba *I. Ma-rí*$^{ki}$; **6** r. VI 1: (silver) níĝ-ba *ʾÀ-sa wa Gú-gi I. wa Ba-du-lum Ma-rí*$^{ki}$ níĝ-"mul" *Na-gàr*$^{ki}$ âga-'kar'(ŠÈ).

*I-ku-i-šar* **3** r. VI 5: <1 dib> *I.* en *Ma-rí*$^{ki}$ *Du-tum Ma-rí*$^{ki}$ šu-mu-tak$_4$.

*I-ku*$^{!}$(DÚR)*-ku*$^{!}$(DÚR)*-tu* **11** o. VIII 18: (silver) níĝ-ba *Wa-ru*$_{12}$*-tum Daš-na I. Ma-rí*$^{ki}$; **13** o. VI 20: (silver) níĝ-ba *Ib-gi-tum Ba-du-lum La-li I. Ma-rí*$^{ki}$.

*I-ku-uḫ* **17** o. XVII 8: (silver) níĝ-ba *Wa-ru*$_{12}$*-tum wa I. Ma-rí*$^{ki}$ ḫi-mu-DU 1 az maḫ.

*Íl-a* **6** o. III 1: (silver) níĝ-ba *Í.*

*Íl-a-i-šar* **16** r. IV 16: 1 dib *Í.* di-kud.

*Íl-a-šar* **22** r. VII 9: 13 dib *Bù-da-ì Í. Gal-za-iš-lu Ga-du-um Iš-má-da-mu Da-da-ì* ⌜x⌝-NE-[x] *En-na-ma-lik Ig-rí-iš Gur-an-da-mu Ru*$_{12}$*-zi-li-im Iš-má-da-ba-an Zé-da-mu.*

*Íl-ba-da-mu* **17** o. XV 5: 1 íb-lá 1 *si-ti-tum* 1 ĝír-kun 1 dib … 1 ĝír mar-tu kg … 1 ĜIŠ-zú 1 zag ĜIŠ-gígir-II … 2 *zú-zú-ba-tum Í.* en *Kak-mi-um*$^{ki}$ *in* SA.ZA$_x$$^{ki}$ šu-ba$_4$-ti.

*Íl-ba-ma-lik* **2** r. I 4: 10 lá-1 ĝír mar-tu zú … *Í.* lú *Da*-NE-*ga*; **3** r. X 7: 1 BAR.AN *áš-ti* en *Ra-ʾà-ak*$^{ki}$ *Í.* šu-mu-tak$_4$; **5** o. IV 16: 1 dib *Í.* lú *I-gi*; **18** r. XVII 30: 2 ĝír mar-tu kg *Ìr-am*$_6$*-ma-lik* lú *Ib-ga-iš-lu wa Í.* lú *Ìr-am*$_6$*-ma-lik*; **23** o. VII 9: 1 dib *Í.* lú *I-gi.*

*Íl-ba-šum* **3** r. XIV 4: 2 ĝír mar-tu ti kg *Du-bí-zi-kir wa Í.* lú-kar; **13** r. VII 19: 7 *gàr-su* ĝi$_6$ *Ar-wa* BÍL-*za-ì wa En-na-ì* 2 dumu-nita šeš *Ib-rí-um wa* Lugal-*na-*⌜*i*⌝*-iš Í. Íl-ba-zi-kir A-ma*-NI lú-kar [ ]; **17** o. XVI 15: (daggers) Lugal-*na-i-iš Í. Du-bí-ga-lu Ša-gú-bù* dumu-nita en *Ma-nu-wa-ad*$^{ki}$.

*Íl-ba-zi-kir* **13** r. VII 20: 7 *gàr-su* gi$_6$ *Ar-wa* BIL-*za-ì wa En-na-ì* 2 dumu-nita šeš *Ib-rí-um wa* Lugal-*na-*⌜*i*⌝*-iš Íl-ba-šum Í. A-ma*-NI lú-kar [ ].

*Íl-da-ar* **2** r. X 11: 1 ĝír mar-tu kg *Í. Kak-mi-um*$^{ki}$.

*Il-da-mu* **21** o. XVI 19: *En-na-ma-lik* lú *I.*

*Íl-gú-uš-ma-lik* **17** r. III 16: *Ki-li-im* lú *Í.*

*Íl-gú-uš-ti* **11** o. VII 15: 1 dib *Í.* lú *I-gi* tuš-LÚ×TIL Kiš$^{ki}$ lú *A-bar-sal*$_4$$^{ki}$; **14** r. II 10: 1 ĝír mar-tu *Í.* lú *I-gi*; **17** o. I 12: 1 dib *Í.* lú *I-gi* tuš-LÚ×TIL *Kak-mi-um*$^{ki}$ ⌜*áš-ti*⌝ [GN]; **19** r. VIII 4: 2 dib *Ib-du-*$^{d}$*Aš-dar* dumu-nita *A-šum wa Í.*

*Il-il* **6** r. XII 5: *Du-bù-uš-da-mu wa I. Ib-al*$_6$$^{ki}$.

*Íl-mi* **5** r. XV 4: 1 dib *Í.*

*Íl-ra*-BAD **10** o. XV 19: (silver) níĝ-kaskal *Í.* maškim NI-*ba-rúm* DU.DU *si-in Ar-mi*$^{ki}$.

*Íl-ru*$_{12}$*-ga-lu* **2** o. II 13: 1 ĝír mar-tu kg *Í. Ì-ra-ar*$^{ki}$.

*Ì-lum-a-ḫa* **9** r. I 2: 1 ĝír mar-tu kg *Ì.* dumu-nita uru-bar šu-ba$_4$-ti.

*Ì-lum-a-ḫi* **13** r. VIII 4: [ ] [*Ì.*] *wa I-in-*$^{d.}$*À-da* 2 dumu-nita en; **15** o. VI 3: 2 *gàr-su Ì. wa I-in-*$^{d.}$*À-da* 2 dumu-nita en; **17** r. XIII 6: 6 íb-lá 6 *si-ti-tum* 6 ĝír-kun níĝ-ba *Maḫ-ra-da-mu Ì. I-da-ni-ki-mu I-in-*$^{d.}$*À-da Ku-ra-da-mu* dumu-nita en *wa I-ib-ma-lik* šeš ama-gal en; **19** o. III 21: (silver) *Daš-na wa Ì. Ma-rí*$^{ki}$.

*Ì-lum-a-rí-ḫu* **4** r. XIII 7: 4 íb-lá *si-ti-tum* ĝír-kun *Du-bù-uš-da-mu I-ga-li-im Zú-ga-du Ì.* 4 en *Ib-al*$_6$$^{ki}$.

*Ì-lum-na-im* **2** r. X 20: 1 ĝír mar-tu kg *Ì.* lú-kar *Ma-nu-wa-ad*$^{ki}$; 8 r. IV 8': (silver) lú ĜIŠ-kiri$_6$ *I.* šu-ba$_4$-ti.

*I-lu*$_5$*-za*$_x$*-ma-lik* **9** r. IX 9: 2 *bu*-DI *ma-lik-tum Lum-na-an*$^{ki}$ *I.* šu-mu-tak$_4$; **15** o. XII 9: 1 gín mar-tu *ba-du-u*$_4$ kb *I.* NE-*na-áš*$^{ki}$; o. XVI 26: 2 *bu*-DI … *Zi-mi-ni*-kù:babbar *ma-lik-tum Bur-ma-an*$^{ki}$ *in* ud dumu-munus tu-da *I.* [šu-mu-ta]k$_4$; r. X 17: *I.* šu-mu-tak$_4$; **17** o. II 13: 2 *bu*-[DI] … [ ] dumu[-munus] *I.* šu-mu-tak$_4$; o. XIV 7: 1 ĝír mar-tu zú kg *I. Su-ti-ig*$^{ki}$ šu-du$_8$ *in Ù-nu-bu*$^{ki}$; **20** o. VIII 1: 2 níĝ-anše-ak 4 kù-sal *I.* "ur$_4$"; **23** r. V 8: <1> *gú-li-lum I.* "ur$_4$".

*Íl-zi* **1**(e) r. II' 3': *Ìr-m*[*u-*]*da-mu* lú *Í.*; 4 o. VIII 11: *Ìr-am*$_6$*-da-mu* lú *Í.*; **9** r. XIV 17: 1 ĝír mar-tu kg *Í.* lú *Iš*$_{11}$*-gú-nu* ⌜*Ba*⌝$^?$*-sa-*⌜*rí-im*$^{ki}$⌝; **11** o. II 10: *Ìr-am*$_6$*-da-mu* [l]ú *Í.*; r. VI 17: *Ìr-am*$_6$*-da-mu* lú *Í.*; 16 r. VII 7: *Ìr-am*$_6$*-da-mu* lú *Í.*; **17** o. XVII 3: *Ìr-am*$_6$*-da-mu* lú *Í.*; **19** r. XV 2: 2 ĝír mar-tu ti kg *Í.* lú *Ìr-am*$_6$*-da-mu wa Ti-ra-ì* šeš ama-gal en; **23** o. IV 9: 1 dib *Í.* lú *Iš*$_{11}$*-gú-nu*; **24** r. III 14: 3 dib *Zi-ba-da wa Í.* lú *En-na-ni-il wa Ma-a-bar-zú* lú *Ig-na-da-mu*.

*Íl-zi-ma-lik* **23** o. VII 1: 1 dib *Í.* lú *A-dur-da-mu*.

*Ì-na-ar* **17** o. II 3: 2 *gú-li-lum* a-gar$_5$-gar$_5$ TAR 5 gín D. *sa-ḫa-wa Ì.* [*Za-*ᵓ*à-ar*]$^{ki}$.

*I-na-ni-gi* **7** r. XII 8: 26 zara$_6$-TÚG aktum-TÚG 6 níĝ-lá-DU *I. Kab-lu*$_5$*-ul*$^{[ki]}$.

*In-da-mu* **1** o. VIII 10: 2 ⌜ĜIŠ⌝ [ ] 2 ĜIŠ-⌜x⌝ dumu-nita *I.*

*In-gàr* **13** o. VII 4: ĝeštin *si-in I. Gu-zí* šu-mu-tak$_4$; o. XII 17: 2 ĝír mar-tu … *I. wa Ne-zi-ma-lik* lú-kar *Kak-mi-um*$^{ki}$; **23** r. IV 3: 5 *gú-li-lum* dib a-gar$_5$ *I.* lú-kar *Ma-nu-wa-ad*$^{ki}$.

*In-ma-lik* **22** o. VIII 7 and 10: 1 dib *En-na*-BAD ì-na-sum *I. ap* … 1 dib *I.* ì-na-sum *I-za-iš-lu*; **24** o. III 4: *Iš*$_{11}$*-ru*$_{12}$*-ud* lú *I.*

*In-ti* **1**(e) r. IV' 6: 5 IGI.NITA u$_5$ *I.*

*I-nu-ud-da-mu* **5** r. VIII 10: 1 zag ĜIŠ-gígir-II *I. Kak-mi-um*$^{ki}$; **8** o. III 6: 2 *gàr-su* gi$_6$ *I.* ugula *Kak-mi-um*⌜$^{ki}$⌝; **15** r. IX 9: *A-ḫu-šu-da-mu* dumu-nita *Zé-ma-lik* šeš *I.*; **25** o. IX 5: 1 íb-lá TAR kb *I. Kak-mi-um*$^{ki}$ *in* ud nídba ì-ĝiš *Ib-la*$^{ki}$ *i*[*n*] [ ]

*Ìr-am*$_6$*-da-mu* **1** o. VI 8: 2 níĝ-anše-ak 4 kù-sal *Ì.* lú *I-rí-gú-nu*; **4** o. VIII 9: 1 ĝír mar-tu kg *Ì.* lú *Íl-zi*; **11** o. II 9: *Da-zi-ma-ad* maškim *Ì.* [l]ú [*Í*]*l-zi*; r. VI 16: 2 níĝ-anše-ak 4 kù-sal *Ì.* lú *Íl-zi*; **16** r. VII 6: 2 níĝ-anše-ak ⌜4⌝ kù-sal *Ì.* lú *Íl-zi*; **17** o. XVII 2: 2 níĝ-anše-ak 4 kù-sal *Ì.* lú *Íl-zi*; **18** o. XVI 11: GABA-*da-mu* lú *Ì.*; **19** r. XV 3: *Íl-zi* lú *Ì.*

*Ìr-am*$_6$-kur$^{ki}$ **13** r. I 3: (silver) níĝ-ba *Ì.* sagi *Ma-rí*$^{ki}$ *in* ud kin$_5$-ak kú en.

*Ìr-am*$_6$*-ma-lik* **2** o. I 21: 1 dib *Ì. Zi-ig*$^{ki}$; **3** o. II 15: (silver) *I-ti Ma-rí*$^{ki}$ *Ì.* šu-mu-tak$_4$; **4** o. VIII 18: (silver) níĝ-kaskal *Ì.* DU.DU *Na-gàr*$^{ki}$; r. XI 8: 1 dib ĜÁ×LÁ ŠÚ+ŠA gín D. kg ì-na-sum *Ì.* maškim *Du-si*; **5** o. IV 19: (silver) níĝ-kaskal *Ì.* DU.DU *Na-gàr*$^{ki}$; **6** r. I 13: (silver) níĝ-kaskal *Ì. wa I-ib-ma-lik* DU.DU *Ma-rí*$^{ki}$; **9** o. XII 8: (silver) níĝ-kaskal *Ì. wa En-na*-BAD DU.DU [*M*]*a-rí*$^{ki}$; **14** r. X 21: (silver) níĝ-kaskal *Ì.* [ ]⌜x⌝ [DU.DU] *si-in* Kiš$^{ki}$; r. XV 14: 10 na$_4$ maḫ *Ì.*; **18** r. XVII 27 and 31: 2 ĝír mar-tu kg *Ì.* lú *Ib-ga-iš-lu wa Íl-ba-ma-lik* lú *Ì.*

*Ìr-a-mu* **20** o. VII 6: (silver) lú ĜIŠ-nu-kiri$_6$ *Ì. Ì-mar*$^{ki}$ šu-ba$_4$-ti.

*Ìr-ba*$_x$*-da-mu* **21** o. VI 12: 1 dib *Ì.* en *Ù-ti-ig*⌜$^{ki}$⌝.

*Ìr-ba-il* **17** r. XI 8: (silver) níĝ-[b]a ⌜*Ne-zi*⌝ *wa Ì. Ma-rí*$^{ki}$ maškim ga:eš$_8$ Saḫar$^{ki}$ [šu-m]u-[ta]g$_4$.

*Ìr-ba*$_x$*-zé* **10** o. X 15: 1 ĝír mar-tu níĝ-ba *Ì.* ᵓ*À-da-ni*$^{ki}$ en in-na-sum; **18** r. IV 3: 2 *bu*-DI *ma-lik-tum Lum-na-an*$^{ki}$ É×PAP *Ì.* šu-mu-tak$_4$; **19** o. X 13: 2 *bu*-DI ì-ĝiš-saĝ *Di-rín-da-mu* dam-diĝir *Ì.* "ur$_4$" šu-mu-tak$_4$; **20** o. X 25: 1 dib *Ì.* [ ]; **23** o. VII 5: 1 dib *Ì.* lú *Da-si-gú-bù-ru*$_{12}$.

*Ìr-da-ma-lik* **9** o. XVI 4': 1 ĝír mar-tu kg *Ì.* lú [ ].

*Ir-da-mu* **14** r. III 13: [1 ĝ]ír [mar-t]u [t]i *I.* dumu-nita *Ib-rí-um*; **15** o. XVI 22: 1 íb-lá *I.* … maš-maš-*sù* … 1 *si-ti-tum Gi-ir-da-mu* 2 dumu-nita *Ib-rí-um*; r. VII 8: 6 ĝeštu$_x$-lá *Gi-rí wa I. Nap-ḫa-il* dumu-nita *Ib-rí-um*; **24** o. I 14: 4 ĝeštu$_x$-lá *Gi-rí wa Nap-ḫa-il wa* lul-gu-ak 2 ĝeštu$_x$-lá *I.* dumu-nita *Ib-rí-um*.

*Ir-ti* **16** r. V 28: 1 dib *I.* … 2 ĝeštu$_x$-lá *Gi-rí* 2 dumu-nita *Ib-rí-um*; r. XV 18: 4 ĝeštu$_x$-lá *I. Nap-ḫa-ì* 2 dumu-nita *Ib-rí-um*; **18** o. XI 11: 1 íb-lá 1 *si-ti-tum* 1 ĝír-kun *Gi-rí ap* 1 íb-lá 1 ĝír-kun kb … maš-maš-*sù I.* … 1 íb-lá 1 ĝír-kun *Nap-ḫa-ì* 3 dumu-nita *Ib-rí-um*.

*Ìr-ga-bù* **1**(e) r. II' 4': [ ] *Da-d*[*ub*] *Ìr-m*[*u-*]*da-mu* lú *Íl-zi Ì.* è *in* ud *Ìr-kab-da-mu si-mi* úš-*sù*.

*Ìr-íb-sá-mu* **18** o. XIV 16: (silver) níĝ-ba *Du-tum wa Ì.* ᵓ*À-du*$^{ki}$.

*I-rí(-ig)-gú-nu* **1** o. VI 9: *Ìr-am*$_6$*-da-mu* lú *I.*; **2** r. I 20: *Ig-rí-iš* lú *I.*; l.ed. 5: *I-bí-zi-kir* lú *I.*; **5** o. X 17: *Ki-ti-ir* lú *I.* (*-ig*); r. VII 9: *Ig-rí-iš* lú *I.* (*-ig*); **7** r. XII 3: *Ig-rí-iš* lú *I.* (*-ig*); **12** o. XII 17: *I-bí-zi-kir* lú *I.*; **20** r. X 19: *I-bí-zi-kir* lú *I.*

*I-rí-ig-da-mu* **11** o. VIII 2: [1 íb-lá] 1 *si-ti-tum* 1 ĝír-kun *I.* lú *Gi-gi* šu-du$_8$ *ba-da-lum A-bar-sal*$_4$$^{ki}$.

*I-rí-ig* **2** r. I 6: 10 lá-1 ĝír mar-tu zú … *I.* lú-kar *Ḫa-zu-wa-an*$^{ki}$; **15** o. V 7: GABA-*da-mu* lú *I.*; **17** o. XIII 4: *Ru*$_{12}$*-zi-ma-lik* lú *I.* al$_6$-tuš *Ab-ra-ti-ig*$^{ki}$.

(cf. *ARET* XX 24 o. II 6–7 : GABA-*da-mu* lú *I-rí-ig-da-mu*)

*I-rí-ig-ì* **21** o. III 12: 1 íb-lá 1 *si-ti-tum* 1 ĝír-kun *Za-ba-rúm* É×PAP *I.* šu-mu-tak$_4$.

*I-rí-ig-ma-lik* **5** o. V 18: 24 íb$^?$-lá ĝír-kun *ìr-a-núm I.*; o. XIII 18: *Du-bí-zi-kir* lú *I.*; **12** o. XIV 9: 2 *gú-li-lum* kb lú *Sa-mu-um* lú *En-ti wa* lú dumu-nita *I-da-ad-mu in ìr-a-núm I.*

*Ìr-kab-ar* **1** o. V 16: (silver) níĝ[-kaskal] *Ì.* DU.DU *si-in Ar-mi*$^{ki}$.

*Ìr-kab-da-mu* **1**(e) r. II' 7': [ ] *Da-d*[*ub*] *Ìr-m*[*u-*]*da-mu* lú *Íl-zi Ìr-ga-bù* è *in* ud *Ì. si-mi* úš-*sù*.

*Ìr-mu-da-mu* **1**(e) r. II' 2': [ ] *Da-d*[*ub*] *Ì.* lú *Íl-zi Ìr-ga-bù* è *in* ud *Ìr-kab-da-mu si-mi* úš-*sù*.

*Ir*-NE **7** o. II 16: ⸢2⸣ *ti-gi-na* 2 ĜIŠ-du *I.* dumu-nita *I-ib-ma-lik*; **17** r. XIX 28: 1 dib *I.* lú *Iš*$_{11}$*-gú-ma*.

*Ìr*-NI-*ba* **4** r. III 6: 1 na$_4$(UD.NI) *Ì.*; **6** o. XVI 14: (silver) níĝ-ba *Ì. wa Sá-ba Ma-rí*$^{ki}$; **18** o. XIII 20: 1 na$_4$ *Ì.*

*Ir-ti* see *Ir-da-mu*.

*Ir*$_{11}$*-tum-a-ḫu* **21** o. II 6: (silver) níĝ-ba *Ḫu*-NE-*du wa I. Sag-gar*$^{ki}$ kaskal níĝ-kas$_4$ *Du-du-lu*$^{ki}$.

*Ir*[- ] **9** r. V 5.

*I-si-rúm* **5** o. XVI 13: 2 [*gú-*]*li-lum Bù-da-il Ù-la-bù*$^{ki}$ *wa I.* lú *Ib-gú-nu*.

*Iš*$_{11}$*-a-ma-lik* **14** r. XI 13: *Ab-ra-ḫu wa I.* ba-za.

*I-ša-ni-ki-nu* **13** r. VI 7: [ ] *Iš*$_{11}$*-la-ab* lú *Ru*$_{12}$*-zi-da-mu wa I.* šeš *Ar-si-a-ḫa* 2 lú-kar *Ma-nu-wa-ad*$^{ki}$.

*I-šar* **1**(a) o. x+I x+1: [ ] *I.* lú [ ]; **2** o. XV 19: 10 lá-1 ĝír mar-tu zú … *I.* lú *Ba-ti*; **11** o. XII 21: 2 *bu*-DI … 2 saĝ-*sù* … 1 kù-sal *Da-ti*-$^{d}$TU *ma-lik-tum Lum-na-an*$^{ki}$ É×PAP *I.* šu-mu-tak$_4$; **12** r. VI 12: (silver) níĝ-du$_8$ 1 dumu-nita *Ti-in*$^{ki}$ lú *A-da-su*$^{ki}$ *I. Da-ti-um*$^{ki}$ šu-ba$_4$-ti; **14** o. XII 10: (silver) lú *I. in Am*$_6$*-ma-šu*$^{ki}$ šu-ba$_4$-ti; **17** o. IX 16: 1 ĝír mar-tu kg *I.* lú *I-du-a*; **21** o. XII 20: (silver) níĝ-du$_8$ *I. Ḫa-lab*$_x$$^{ki}$ *áš-du Mi-su-wa-du Ma-rí*$^{ki}$.

*Iš-ba-ì* **7** r. XI 17: (silver) níĝ-ba *Gul-la* ⸢x-x-x⸣ *Sa-ma-na-nu* [*S*]*i-mi*[- ] [ ] *I. A-ša*$^{ki}$ *in* ud DU.DU nam-kud é $^{d}$*Ku-ra*.

*Iš-da-al*$_6$ **22** o. IX 9: *En-na-il* lú *I.*

*Iš-da-má* **1**(a) r. II'. 3; 4 r. XII 9: *Bar-za-ma-li* lú *I.*; **9** r. II 14: *Du-bí* lú *I.*

*Iš-da-maḫ* **13** r. I 13: (silver) níĝ-ba *Da-ti I. Ù-lu-li* [ ].

*Iš*$_{11}$*-da-mu* **7** o. XVI 16: *Puzur*$_4$*-ra-ma-lik* lú *I.*; **9** r. IV 13: *Šu-ma-lik* lú *I.*; **13** r. VIII 20: *Pu*[*zur*$_4$-]*ra*[*-ma-lik*] lú *I.*; **17** o. III 7: [2 *bu*-DI dumu-munus] en *Bur-ma-an*$^{ki}$ É×PAP é-gi en *Ra-ʾà-ak*$^{ki}$ *I.* [ ]; o. XIV 1: *Šu-ma-lik* lú *I.*; **19** r. XIX 10: BAR.AN.BAR.AN *I.* di-kud šu-mu-tak$_4$ *si-in Na-gàr*$^{ki}$.

*Iš-dub-il* **14** o. XX 2: (silver) *I.* maškim ga:eš$_8$ *Du-du-lu*$^{ki}$ šu-mu-tak$_4$ *ʾà:bíl*; r. IV 13: (silver) níĝ-ba *I.* maškim ga:eš$_8$ *Du-du-lu*$^{ki}$; **15** o. VII 23: (silver) níĝ-ba *I. wa Dab*$_6$*-ti Ma-rí*$^{ki}$ maškim ga:eš$_8$ *Du-du-lu*$^{ki}$.

*Iš-dub-ì* **7** r. VII 20: (silver) níĝ-ba *I. Ma-rí*$^{ki}$ níĝ-"mul" *Ar-ti-na-an*$^{ki}$ til; r. XIII 21: (silver) níĝ-ba *I.* maškim ga:eš$_8$ *Du-du-lu*$^{ki}$ ḫi-mu-DU mušen-babbar; **14** o. III 14: (silver) n[íĝ-ba] *I. wa Ib-gi-tum* maškim ga:eš$_8$ *Du-du-lu*$^{ki}$ šu-mu-tak$_4$ *ʾà:bíl*.

*Iš*$_{11}$*-ga-um* **10** o. III 2: (silver) níĝ-ba *Wa-ru*$_{12}$*-tum Daš-na I. ʾÀ-bí-su Ma-rí*$^{ki}$; o. XVI 18: (silver) níĝ-ba *I. Ma-rí*$^{ki}$. *Iš*$_{11}$*-ga-um* **10** o. III 2.

*Iš*$_{11}$*-ga* **10** r. VI 1: (silver) níĝ-ba *I. wa Daš-na Ma-rí*$^{ki}$.

*Iš*$_{11}$*-gi-ba-ir* **2** o. XV 18: *Gú-zi* lú *I.*

*Iš*$_{11}$*-gi-bar-zú* **15** r. XIV 14: 1 dib *I.* lú *Sá-gú-šum*; **18** o. XIV 26: 2 ĝír mar-tu ti kg *I. wa Du-bí-ab* ugula *Ti-*[*sum*]$^{ki}$.

*Iš*$_{11}$*-gi-da-mu* **17** o. XIV 2: 3 ĝír mar-tu *Šu-ma-lik* lú *Iš*$_{11}$*-da-mu I. A-ba-ù* NI-*ti-ba*$^{ki}$.

*Iš*$_{11}$*-gi-wa-aš* **2** o. IV 8: 1 dib *I. Áb-su*$^{ki}$; **4** r. VI 5: 1 ĝír mar-tu ti kg *I. Áb-su*$^{ki}$.

*Iš*$_{11}$*-gú-ma* **17** r. XIX 30: *Ir*-NE lú *I.*

*Iš*$_{11}$*-gú-nu* **9** r. XV 18: *Íl-zi* lú *I.*; **23** o. IV 10: *Íl-zi* lú *I.*

*Iš*$_{11}$*-la-ab* **13** r. VI 4: [ ] *I.* lú *Ru*$_{12}$*-zi-da-mu wa I-ša-ni-ki-nu* šeš *Ar-si-a-ḫa* 2 lú-kar *Ma-nu-wa-ad*$^{ki}$.

*Iš-má-da-ba-an* **22** r. VIII 5: 13 dib *Bù-da-ì Íl-a-šar Gal-za-iš-lu Ga-du-um Iš-má-da-mu Da-da-ì* ⸢x⸣-NE-[x] *En-na-ma-lik Ig-rí-iš Gur-an-da-mu Ru*$_{12}$*-zi-li-im I. Zé-da-mu*.

*Iš-má-da-mu* **6** r. XVI 32: (tin) en *Du-lu*$^{ki}$ *I.* šu-mu-tak$_4$; **20** o. XII 5: 1 ĝír mar-tu ti kg *I.* lú *Bù-da-ma-lik*; **22** r. VII 12: 13 dib *Bù-da-ì Íl-a-šar Gal-za-iš-lu Ga-du-um I. Da-da-ì* ⸢x⸣-NE-[x] *En-na-ma-lik Ig-rí-iš Gur-an-da-mu Ru*$_{12}$*-zi-li-im Iš-ma-da-ba-an Zé-da-mu*.

*Iš-má-ga-lu* **2** o. XIV 9: 1 dib *I.*; **3** o. IV 5: *I-bí-um* lú *I.*; 7 r. X 7: *I-bí-um* lú *I.*; **8** o. II 14: 1 ĝír mar-tu kg *I.* lú EN-*sa-rí*; **12** o. XIII 10: 1 *gú-li-lum* 15 gín D. a-gar$_5$-gar$_5$ … 2 *gú-a-zi-da-su I.* lú *Mu-gàr* NE-di; **13** o. II 4: [1 íb-lá 1] *si-ti-tum* 1 ĝír-kun *Ar-ra-du-lum* … 2 *bu*-DI dam-*sù I.* šu-mu-tak$_4$; o. IX 20: 1 kù-sal … 1 kù-sal níĝ-ba $^{d}$NE-*ti-a-du* diĝir *Du-lu*$^{ki}$ *I.* šu-mu-tak$_4$; **23** o. IV 6: *Ib-bí-um* lú *I.*

*Iš-má-il* **3** r. V 16: (silver) níĝ-ba *I. wa Ba-ga-ar Ma-rí*$^{ki}$.

*Iš-ra*-BAD **20** o. XIV 8: (54+[x] garments, 2 na$_4$ measures of wool) … 33 kuš Mar-tu$^{ki}$ … 2 gud *Iš-ra*-BAD lú-kar *Kak-mi-um*$^{ki}$ … ki:lam$_7$ *ʾÀ-da-ni*$^{ki}$

*Iš-ra-il* **14** o. XIII 8: 1 ĝír mar-tu *ba-du-u*$_4$ kb *I.* lú-kar *Kak-mi-um*$^{ki}$.

*Iš-ru*$_{12}$*-ud* **17** r. XIV 23: [10+]7 [*b*]*u*$^{?}$-DI [ŠÚ+Š]A-ŠÚ+ŠA [níĝ-b]a PN$_1$–PN$_8$ dam en *wa* PN$_9$–PN$_{10}$ 2 dumu-munus en *wa* ama-gal *Ib-rí-um wa* PN$_{11}$–PN$_{14}$ dam-*sù wa I.* nin-ni *Du-si-gú* PN$_{15}$; **18** r. VI 17: *I.* ugula *Sal-ba-ù*$^{ki}$; **21** o. VI 1: [ ] *I.* ugula *Sal-ba*$^{ki}$; **24** o. III 3: 1 dib *I.* lú *In-ma-lik* tuš-LÚ×TIL *in U*$_9$*-ru*$_{12}$$^{ki}$.

*I*[*š*- ] **10** o. XII 12.

*I-ti* **3** o. II 13: (silver) *I. Ma-rí*$^{ki}$ *Ìr-am*$_6$*-ma-lik* šu-mu-tak$_4$; r. X 14: *Ib-gi-tum* lú *I. Ma-rí*$^{ki}$; r. XI 12: *Kùn-*$^{d}$*Aš-dar* lú *I.* [*Ma-rí*$^{ki}$]; **6** o. X 19: (silver) níĝ-ba *I.* ga:eš$_8$ *Ma-rí*$^{ki}$; **8** o. IV 12: (silver) *I.* ga:eš$_8$ *I-ga-iš-ru*$_{12}$ šu-mu-tak$_4$; r. III 12': (lapis lazuli) *áš-tum I.* ga:eš$_8$ *Ma-rí*$^{ki}$; **20** o. VI 20: (silver) [n]íĝ-ba *I.* [*M*]*a-rí*$^{ki}$ [x]-⸢x⸣[- ] [ ] níĝ-"mul" *Du-li*$^{ki}$ àga-kár!(ŠÈ).

*I-ti-a-gú* **8** r. III x+1: [ ] *I.* DU.D[U] ⸢*Za*⸣*-bù-rúm*$^{ki}$; **9** r. XIV 2: 3 *gú-li-lum* a-gar$_5$-gar$_5$ lú *Wa-su*-LUM lú *Ib-ni-ḫar wa En-nu-lum* BÍL-*da-mu I.* lú *En-na-il*.

*I-ti-*$^{d}$*Aš-dar* **2** o. XII 19: maš-maš íb-lá *I.* lú nídba ì-ĝiš; **4** r. XV 7: (gold) en *Kak-mi-um*$^{ki}$ *I.* [šu-]mu-[ta]g$_4$; **18** r. VI 7: (silver) níĝ-ba *I. Ir-i-tum*$^{ki}$.

*I-ti-gi-ma-lik* **5** r. VI 7: 1 dib *I.* ugula *Mug-rí-ì*$^{ki}$.

*I-ti-il* **10** o. VII 23: (silver) níĝ-ba *I. Ma-rí*$^{ki}$ šu-mu-tak$_4$ 1 aktum-TÚG *Ib-rí-um*; o. XII 1: (silver) níĝ-ba *Daš-na Wa-ru*$_{12}$*-tum Puzur-ra*-BAD *I. Ma-rí*$^{ki}$.

*I-ti-ì* **1**(e) r. IV' 3: [ ] [*i*]*n* ud ⸢ḫi⸣-úš *I.* simug; **7** r. VIII 17: (silver) níĝ-ba *I.*

*I-ti-ki-šum* **2** r. I 10: *Mi-ga-il* lú *I.*

*I-ti-ne* **1** o. XII 2: (silver) *I.* lú *Ib*[- ]; **17** r. VII 21: 1 ĝír mar-tu zú *I. A-da-bí-gú*$^{ki}$ maškim *Ba-ga-ma.*

*I-ti-um* **7** r. XIV 26: 1 dib *I.* [*Ma-nu*]-⌜*wa*⌝-[*a*]*d*$^{ki}$.

*I-za-iš-ru*$_{12}$ **8** o. V 8: (48 garments, 48 kilts) [ -*g*]*i Ib-lu*$_5$*-zú wa I.* lú-kar *Ma-nu-wa-ad*$^{ki}$ ki:lam$_7$ šeš-⌜ib⌝[-II] *ᵓÀ-da-ni*$^{ki}$; r. V 3': (silver) [*Ib-lu*$_5$]-⌜*zú*⌝ *wa I.* [lú-k]ar *Ma-nu-wa-ad*$^{ki}$.

*I-za-iš-lu* **22** o. IX 1: 1 dib *In-ma-lik* ì-na-sum *I.*

KAK-*bar-zú* **13** r. II 16: (silver) lul-gu-ak gur$_8$ *Puzur*$_4$*-ra-m*[*a-*]*lik* lú-kar *Kak-mi-um*$^{ki}$ K. *wa Du-bí-zi-kir* šu-mu-tak$_4$.

*Kéš-du-ud* **21** o. XV 1: [ ] *K. Ib-rí-um* šu-mu-tak$_4$.

*Ki-li-im* **13** o. IV 3: (silver) nam-kud *Na-ḫal*$^{ki}$ *K.* šu-mu-tak$_4$; **17** r. III 15: 2 *gú-li-lum* kbg *K.* lú *Íl-gú-uš-ma-lik.*

*Ki-ma-lik* **6** r. XV 14: 1 ma-na an-na *Na-zú-ù K. wa I-bi-iš-lu* šu-mu-tak$_4$.

*Kir-su-ud* **9** r. VI 13: 1 *bu*-DI … 2 saĝ-*sù* níĝ-ba *K.*; **17** r. XIII 28 and XIV 20: [10+]7 [*b*]*u*$^?$-DI [ŠÚ+Š]A-ŠÚ+ŠA [níĝ-b]a *Ra-ù-tum K.* [*En-na-*$^d$Utu] *Ra-ba*$_x$*-tum Maš-ga-sa-du Ma-ga-ra-du Tiš-má-da-mu Ra-ba*$_x$*-tum*-II dam en *wa* PN$_1$–PN$_2$ 2 dumu-munus en *wa* ama-gal *Ib-rí-um wa A-zi-mu Ti-lu-du Ti-a-da-mu K.* dam-*sù wa* PN$_3$ nin-ni *Du-si-gú* PN$_4$.

*Ki-sa-du* **6** r. I 24: 3 útul-útul$^!$ urudu maḫ … 10 lá-2 ĝeštu$_x$ *K.* ga-du$_8$ en; **17** r. XIV 26: [10+]7 [*b*]*u*$^?$-DI [ŠÚ+Š]A-ŠÚ+ŠA [níĝ-b]a PN$_1$–PN$_8$ dam en *wa* PN$_9$–PN$_{10}$ 2 dumu-munus en *wa* ama-gal *Ib-rí-um wa* PN$_{11}$–PN$_{14}$ dam-*sù wa* PN$_{15}$ nin-ni *Du-si-gú K.*

*Ki-ti-ir* **4** r. II 12: (silver) *K. La-ru*$_{12}$*-ga-du*$^{ki}$; **5** o. X 16: 1 dib *K.* lú *I-rí-ig-gú-nu.*

*Ku-a*-NE **18** r. IV 14: (silver) [n]íĝ-du$_8$ 1 dumu-nita *K.* lú NE-*da-mu* SA.ZA$_x$$^{ki}$ *áš-ti Ìr-ku*$^{ki}$

*Kùn-*$^d$*Aš-dar* **3** r. XI 11: (silver) níĝ-ba *K.* lú ⌜*I*⌝*-ti* [*Ma-rí*$^{ki}$].

*Kùn-da-ba-an* **20** r. VIII 2: 1 íb-lá 1 *si-ti-tum* 1 ĝír-kun *K.* [ ] *in* ud tuš-LÚ×TIL *in A-ru*$_{12}$*-ga-du*$^{ki}$.

*Kùn-i-šar* **18** r. II 13: (silver) níĝ-ba *K. ᵓÀ-du*$^{ki}$ *in Ša-dab*$_6$$^{ki}$ šu-ba$_4$-ti.

*Kùn*-NE **13** r. III 14: (silver) níĝ-ba *K. wa Ab-ba* muḫaldim *Ma-rí*$^{ki}$ ḫi-mu-DU mè *si-in Ma-nu-wa-ad*$^{ki}$.

*Kùn-ti-su* **21** o. XVI 13: 1 dib *K. Ur-sá-um*$^{ki}$.

*Ku-ra-da-mu* **17** r. XIII 9: 6 íb-lá 6 *si-ti-tum* 6 ĝír-kun níĝ-ba *Maḫ-ra-da-mu Ì-lum-a-ḫi I-da-ni-ki-mu I-in-*$^{d}$*ᵓÀ-da K.* dumu-nita en *wa I-ib-ma-lik* šeš ama-gal en.

Ku-tu **4** r. I 14: (silver) K. *A-bù-li-um*$^{ki}$.

Ku-tu-*ᵓà-bù* **12** o. II 16: (silver) níĝ-ba *Ib-gi-tum wa* K. *wa Ib-du-nu* [ -]⌜x⌝ [ ] *Du-du-lu*$^{ki}$ níĝ-"mul" *Ag-sa-gú*$^{ki}$ šu-ba$_4$-ti.

*La-a-na-ma* **4** r. I 17: (silver) *L.* [*G*]*a-ga-*[*b*]*a-an*$^{ki}$; **6** o. XIII 20: (silver) *L. Ga-ga-ba-an*$^{ki}$.

*Lá-da* **7** o. V 17: 1 ĝír mar-tu kg *L.* lú-kar *A-da-bí-ig*$^{ki}$.

*La-da-da-áš* **3** r. V 8: 1 dib *Ḫáb-ra-ar* ugula *ᵓA*$_5$*-da-tum*$^{ki}$ ... 1 dib *L.* šeš-*sù.*

*Lá-da-il* **4** o. V 4: (silver) ì-na-sum *Zi-rí-gú* níĝ-du$_8$ dumu-nita *L. Ma-rí*$^{ki}$.

*La-gi* **15** o. IV 13: 1 dib *Bar-za-ma-ù* ugula *ᵓÀ-šu*$^{ki}$ …1 ĝír mar-tu *ba-du-u*$_4$ kb *L.* maškim-*sù.*

*La-la*-LUM **10** o. XII 16: (silver) ⌜níĝ⌝-ba *L.*

*La-li* **13** o. VI 19: (silver) níĝ-ba *Ib-gi-tum Ba-du-lum L. I-ku*$^!$(DÚR)*-ku*$^!$(DÚR)*-tu Ma-rí*$^{ki}$.

*La-sa-nu* **10** r. III 15: (silver) níĝ-ba *L. Ḫa-ra-an*$^{ki}$.

*La-zi-gú* **19** r. XIX 4: (silver) *L. wa Bù-a-ḫu Na-ba-ti-um*$^{ki}$.

Lugal-*na-i-iš* **13** r. VII 18: 7 *gàr-su* ĝi$_6$ *Ar-wa* BÍL-*za-ì wa En-na-ì* 2 dumu-nita šeš *Ib-rí-um wa* L. *Íl-ba-šum Íl-ba-zi-kir A-ma*-NI lú-kar [ ]; **17** o. XVI 14: (daggers) L. *Íl-ba-šum Du-bí-ga-lu Ša-gú-bù* dumu-nita en *Ma-nu-wa-ad*$^{ki}$.

*Lu-rí-um* **25** r. III 8: 1 íb-lá TAR kb *L. Kak-mi-um*$^{ki}$ níĝ-"mul" Bàd$^{ki}$ šu-ba$_4$-⌜ti⌝.

*Lu-wa-sa-ra-du* see *Ḫu-wa-sa-ra-du.*

*Ma-a-bar-zú* **24** r. IV 3: 3 dib *Zi-ba-da wa Íl-zi* lú *En-na-ni-il wa M.* lú *Ig-na-da-mu.*

*Ma-gal-lu* **2** r. I 11: 10 lá-1 ĝír mar-tu zú … *M.* lú [ ]; **6** r. VIII 5: 1 íb-lá *si-ti-tum* ĝír-kun kb maš-maš kg *Na-bù-mu* … 1 íb-lá *si-ti-tum* ĝír-kun maš-maš kg *M.* 2 lú-kar.

*Ma-ga-ra-du* **17** r. XIV 2: [10+]7 [*b*]*u*$^?$-DI [ŠÚ+Š]A-ŠÚ+ŠA [níĝ-b]a *Ra-ù-tum Kir-*[*s*]*u-*[*u*]*d* [*En-na-*$^d$Utu] *Ra-ba*$_x$*-tum Maš-ga-sa-du M. Tiš-má-da-mu Ra-ba*$_x$*-tum*-II dam en *wa* PN$_1$–PN$_2$ 2 dumu-munus en *wa* ama-gal *Ib-rí-um wa* PN$_3$–PN$_6$ dam-*sù wa* PN$_7$ nin-ni *Du-si-gú* PN$_8$.

*Maḫ-mu* **3** r. VI 15: (silver) níĝ[-ba] BAD-*sù*-BAD *M. M*[*a-rí*$^{ki}$].

*Maḫ-ra-da-mu* **9** r. XVII 9: 1 dib *M.* dumu-nita en; **17** r. XIII 5: 6 íb-lá 6 *si-ti-tum* 6 ĝír-kun níĝ-ba *M. Ì-lum-a-ḫi I-da-ni-ki-mu I-in-*$^{d}$*ᵓÀ-da Ku-ra-da-mu* dumu-nita en *wa I-ib-ma-lik* šeš ama-gal en.

*Ma-li-gú* **9** r. XVII 20: 1 ĝír mar-tu ti kg *M. Ga-rí-*⌜*u*$_9$⌝$^{[ki]}$.

*Ma-ma* **25** r. V 4: [ ]-⌜x-x⌝ ḫi-mu-DU *M.*

*Mar-rúm* **19** r. X 3: (silver) níĝ-ba *M.* EN-NE$^{ki}$.

*Maš-da-ru*$_{12}$ **1** o. XI 1: (silver) *M.* dumu-nita *En-na-*$^d$Utu.

*Maš-ga-sa-du* **17** r. XIV 2: [10+]7 [*b*]*u*$^?$-DI [ŠÚ+Š]A-ŠÚ+ŠA [níĝ-b]a *Ra-ù-tum Kir-*[*s*]*u-*[*u*]*d* [*En-na-*$^d$Utu] *Ra-ba*$_x$*-tum M. Ma-ga-ra-du Tiš-má-da-mu Ra-ba*$_x$*-tum*-II dam en *wa* PN$_1$–PN$_2$ 2 dumu-munus en *wa* ama-gal *Ib-rí-um wa* PN$_3$–PN$_6$ dam-*sù wa* PN$_7$ nin-ni *Du-si-gú* PN$_8$.

*Ma-ù-ud* **17** r. XIV 9: [10+]7 [*b*]*u*$^?$-DI [ŠÚ+Š]A-ŠÚ+ŠA [níĝ-b]a PN$_1$–PN$_8$ dam en *wa M. Za-ni-ḫi-Ma-rí*$^{ki}$ 2 dumu-munus en *wa* ama-gal *Ib-rí-um wa* PN$_9$–PN$_{12}$ dam-*sù wa* PN$_{13}$ nin-ni *Du-si-gú* PN$_{14}$.

*Ma-za-a-du* **4** o. VII 9: 2 *bu*-DI 10 lá-2 ĝeštu$_x$-lá 30 *du-ru*$_{12}$*-gú* 1 *gu-za*$_x$*-gú* 1 šu-dub 1 *ma-ḫa-na-gúm M. ma-lik-tum Ib-al*$_6$$^{ki}$.

*Ma-za-um* **12** o. XI 15: 1 níĝ-saĝšu lú *M.*

*Ma-zú-ru*$_{12}$ **8** r. VII 2': 1 ĝ[ír] mar-t[u] *ba-du-*[*u*$_4$] kg kb *M.*

*Ma*[- ] **4** o. XIV 2.

*Mi-ga-il* **2** r. I 9: 10 lá-1 ĝír mar-tu zú … *M.* lú *I-ti-ki-šum*; **14** o. XIV 16: *Ig-na-da-ar* lú *M.*; o. XV 1: 2 *gú-li-lum* kg lú *I*[*g-n*]*a-*[*da-ar*] *M.* ì-na-sum.

*Mi-ga-ì* **16** r. II 18: (silver) níĝ-du$_8$ 3 *na-se*$_{11}$ *Ib-la*$^{ki}$ *áš-ti Ir-i-tum*$^{ki}$ *M.* lú gud-gud [šu]-ba$_4$-ti; **21** r. IX 12: *Ig-na-da-ar* lú *M.*

*Min-na-ì* **18** r. XIII 19: 1 ĝír mar-tu *ba-du-u*$_4$ kbg *M.* ugula sur$_x$-BAR.AN *Ib-rí-um.*

*Mi-su-wa-du* **4** o. VI 4: (silver) *M. Ma-rí*$^{ki}$; **21** o. XII 6: (silver) níĝ-ba *M.*, 23: (silver) níĝ-du$_8$ *I-šar Ḫa-lab*$_x$$^{ki}$ *áš-du M. Ma-rí*$^{ki}$.

*Mu-gàr* **4** r. IX 13: [1 *gú-*]*li-lum* dumu-nita *M.* NE-di; **12** o. XIII 11: *Iš-má-ga-lu* lú *M.* NE-di; **19** o. VII 25: 1 íb-lá 1 *si-ti-tum* 1 ĝír-kun *M.* dumu-nita *A-ba-rúm in* ud ḫúl-*sù A-šum* šu-mu-tak$_4$.

*Mu*-NE-*a-du* **13** o. II 16: 1 íb-lá 1 *si-ti-tum* 1 ĝír-kun *M.* ugula *Ar-ḫa-du*$^{ki}$ *in* ud DU.DU nam-kud é $^{d}$*Ku-ra*; **14** o. V 2: (silver) *M.* ugula *Ar-ḫa-du*$^{ki}$ *Puzur*$_4$*-ra-ma-lik* lú kas$_4$-kas$_4$ šu-mu-tak$_4$.

*Mu-zi* **13** o. II 8: 2 íb-lá 2 *si-ti-tum* 2 ĝ[í]r-kun *M.* šeš en *wa Lu-wa-sa-ra-du Du-lu*$^{ki}$.

*Na-am*$_6$*-ḫa-lu* **18** r. V 21: 2 šu-i *N.*; **19** r. XV 18: 1 ĝír mar-tu *ba-du-u*$_9$ kg *N.*; **20** o. XII 2.

*Na-am*$_6$-ì-ĝiš **19** r. XV 15: 2 ĝír mar-tu *ba-du-u*$_9$ kg *En-na-ni-il* šeš *Ib-rí-um wa N.*

*Na-bù-mu* **6** r. VIII 2: 1 íb-lá *si-ti-tum* ĝír-kun kb maš-maš kg *N.* … 1 íb-lá *si-ti-tum* ĝír-kun maš-maš kg *Ma-gal-lu* 2 lú-kar.

*Na-mi-ir* **11** r. III 13: (silver) níĝ-ba en *Ša-bir*$_5$*-ti-du*$^{ki}$ (silver) *N.* maskim-*sù.*

*Na-na-tum* **12** o. VI 18: (silver) níĝ-ba *Wa-ba-rúm* ga:eš$_8$ *Du-du-lu*$^{ki}$ (silver) níĝ-ba *N.* dam-*sù.*

*Na*-NE **1** o. VI 16: (silver) níĝ-kaskal *N. Na-gàr*$^{ki}$ DU.DU *si-in Ar-mi*$^{ki}$; **5** o. X 4: (silver) *N. wa* ⌜Šubur⌝ *Na-gàr*$^{ki}$ *in* níĝ-kas$_4$ *A-da-*[*bí-*]⌜*ig*⌝$^{ki}$ šu-ba$_4$-ti; **6** o. XIII 17: (silver) *N. Na-gàr*$^{ki}$; r. III 15: (silver) níĝ-ba *N. Na-gàr*$^{ki}$; **8** o. VI 15: (silver) *N. Na-gàr*$^{ki}$; **10** r. III 11: (silver) níĝ-ba *N. Na-gàr*$^{ki}$; r. IX 3: (silver) níĝ-ba *N. wa* maškim-*sù Na-gàr*$^{ki}$.

*Nap-ḫa-il* **7** o. XVII 16: (silver) níĝ-kaskal *N.* DU.DU *si-in Ma-rí*$^{ki}$; **15** r. VII 9: 6 ĝeštu$_x$-lá *Gi-rí wa Ir-da-mu N.* dumu-nita *Ib-rí-um*; **24** o. I 10: 4 ĝeštu$_x$-lá *Gi-rí wa N. wa* lul-gu-ak 2 ĝeštu$_x$-lá *Ir-da-mu* dumu-nita *Ib-rí-um.*

*Nap-ḫa-ì* **16** r. XV 19: 4 ĝeštu$_x$-lá *Ir-ti N.* 2 dumu-nita *Ib-rí-um*; **17** o. XI 22: 1 íb-lá 1 ĝír-kun … [*ba-d*]*u-u*$_4$ [1] ĝír [mar-]tu *N.* [dumu-n]ita [*Ib-rí-u*]*m*; **18** o. XI 15: 1 íb-lá 1 *si-ti-tum* 1 ĝír-kun *Gi-rí ap* 1 íb-lá 1 ĝír-kun kb … maš-maš-*sù Ir-ti* … 1 íb-lá 1 ĝír-kun *N.* 3 dumu-nita *Ib-rí-um.*

*Na-tum* **15** r. VI 15: 2 *bu*-DI … 2 saĝ-*sù* níĝ-ba *N. ma-lik-tum Bur-ma-an*$^{ki}$ É×PAP *Gi-ba-da Ib-dur-i-šar* šu-mu-tak$_4$.

*Na-zi* **3** r. XIV 12: (74 garments, 1 kilt) ⌜ki:lam$_7$⌝ *Ma-rí*$^{ki}$ *N.*; **6** o. XV 16: (silver) níĝ-ba *Puzur*$_4$*-ra-*$^{d}$Utu *Ma-rí*$^{ki}$ šu-mu-tak$_4$ túg-túg *áš-da N.*; r. IX 5: (194 garments) ki:lam$_7$ *Ma-rí*$^{ki}$ *N.*

*Na-zu-mu* **12** r. VII 8: (silver) níĝ-du$_8$ *Dam-da-il Ib-su*$^{ki}$ *in* Kiš$^{ki}$ lú *N.* níĝ-du$_8$; **13** r. I 20: [ ] ḫi-mu-DU 1 BAR.AN *N.* zàḫ; r. VI 14: 1 ĝír mar-tu kg *N. in* ud níĝ-kas$_4$ *si-in* Kiš$^{ki}$; **15** o. XVII 8: (silver) níĝ-ba *Wa-ru*$_{12}$*-tum Ma-rí*$^{ki}$ e$_{11}$ *áš-ti N. mi-nu* Kiš$^{ki}$.

*Na-zú-ù* **6** r. XV 13: 1 ma-na an-na *N. Ki-ma-lik wa I-bí-iš-lu* šu-mu-tak$_4$.

*N*[*a-* ] **7** o. XVIII 15.

NE-*a-da-nu* **7** o. I 6: (silver) níĝ-ba N. *ʾÀ-du*$^{ki}$.

NE-*a-du* **1**(e) r. III' 16: (silver) N.

NE-*da*-ḪI **10** o. XIII 3: (silver) níĝ-ba N. *Na-gàr*$^{ki}$.

NE-*da-mu* **18** r. IV 15: *Ku-a*-NE lú NE-*da-mu.*

NE-*iš-da-ar* **19** o. VIII 17: (silver) níĝ-kaskal N. *Kab-lu*$_5$*-ul*$^{ki}$ DU.DU *si-in Ar-mi*$^{ki}$.

NE-NE **21** o. XVII 4: (silver) níĝ-ba N. *Ma-rí*$^{ki}$.

NE-*ša*-LUM **23** o. V 8: *Ḫu-ma-la* lú N.

*Ne-zi* **17** r. XI 6: (silver) níĝ-[b]a *N. wa Ìr-*[*b*]*a-il Ma-rí*$^{ki}$ maškim ga:eš$_8$ Saḫar$^{ki}$ [šu-m]u-[ta]g$_4$.

*Ne-zi-ma-ì* see *Ni-zi-ma-il.*

*Ne-zi-ma-lik* **7** r. XV 6: 1 dib *N.* lú-kar *Kak-mi-um*$^{ki}$; **13** o. XII 19: 2 ĝír mar-tu … *In-gàr wa N.* lú-kar *Kak-mi-um*$^{ki}$.

NI-*a-ba-mu* see NI-*la-ba-mu.*

NI-BAD **14** o. XIV 12: *ʾÀ-bí* lú N.; 22 o. VI 11: *ʾÀ-bí* lú N.

NI-*ba-il* **24** o. III 11: 1 dib N. lú-kar *Ma-nu-wa-ad*$^{ki}$.

NI-*ba-rúm* **10** o. XV 21: *Íl-ra*-BAD maškim N.

NI-*dim* **18** o. IV 17: (silver) níĝ-ba lú N. "ur$_4$" *Na-gàr*$^{ki}$.

NI-*gi* **3** o. IX 9: 1 ĝír mar-tu ti kg N. saĝ-du$_8$ lú-kar *A-da-bí-ig*$^{ki}$ … 1 ĝír mar-tu *ba-du-u*$_4$ kb kg *Ù-ra*-AN maškim-*sù*; **8** r. VI 10': 7 *mi-at* 80 <GIŠ->gu-kak-gíd … 2 si dàra … 1 ĝír mar-tu zú LAGAB×AN.A N. *A-da-bí-ig*$^{ki}$.

NI-*gu* **1** o. X 16: 1 *gú-li-lum* … *wa* [1] kù-sal N. dumu-munus *A-ba-la I-da-ni-ki-mu.*

*Ni-ir-da-mu* **12** o. VI 3: 2 ĝír mar-tu … 2 kù-sal [ní]ĝ-ba <$^{d}$>BAD *Ga-na-na-im* [*w*]*a* [$^{d}$*ʾA*$_5$*-d*]*a*[*-ra*] *Gi-rí wa N.* 2 dumu-nita *Ib-rí-um* in-na-sum *in* ud gi$_4$ *mi-nu Du-du-lu*$^{ki}$.

NI-*la-ba-mu* **3** r. VIII 1: 4 GIŠ-šú 1 níĝ-bànda l[ú 2 šu] … 20 *gàr-su* N. šu-ba$_4$-ti; **7** r. VII 11: 1 *li-im* GIŠ-gu-kak-gíd … 24 *gàr-su Ì.* šu-ba$_4$-ti ki:lam$_7$ $^{d}$*ʾÀ-da*; **10** r. VI 15: *gàr-su* N. [šu-ba$_4$-ti] … *in* ⌜ki⌝:lam$_7$ $^{d}$*ʾÀ-da.*

NI-*a-ba-mu* **2** o. VII 9: *gàr-su* N. šu-ba$_4$-ti; r. XVII 13: (56 garments) … 1 *gàr-su* N. ki:lam$_7$ *Šè-ʾà-am*$^{ki}$; **6** r. XIII 11: (102 garments) … 1 útul tur … 1 ĝír kg … 4 gud … *gàr-su* N. šu-ba$_4$-ti ki:lam$_7$ $^{d}$*ʾÀ-da.*

NI-*má-ti* **4** r. VI 9: 1 ĝír mar-tu] ⌜ti⌝ kg N. lú-kar *Kak-mi-um*$^{ki}$.

NI-*na-ad* **2** o. I 7: *Ar-si-a-ḫa* lú N.; **23** o. V 4: *Ar-si-a-ḫa* lú N.

NI-*na-du* **17** r. IV 4: 1 ĝír mar-tu *ba-du-u*$_4$ kg N. ugula sur$_x$-BAR.AN *Gi-ir-da-mu* dumu-nita *Ib-rí-um.*

NI-*wa-lum* **17** r. VIII 5: *A-a-zi-kir* lú N.

*Ni-zi-ma-il* **4** o. II 19: (silver) níĝ-kaskal *N.* DU.DU *Na-gàr*$^{ki}$; o. XIV 20: (silver) níĝ-kaskal *N.* DU.DU *Na-gàr*$^{ki}$; r. VIII 3: 20 ma-na kb en *Na-gàr*$^{ki}$ *N.* šu-mu-tak$_4$, 7: (silver) níĝ-kaskal *N.* DU.DU *Na-gàr*$^{ki}$; **6** o. XI 20: (silver) níĝ-kaskal *N.* DU.DU *Ma-rí*$^{ki}$; o. XVI 7: (silver) níĝ-kaskal *N. wa I-ib-ma-lik* DU.DU *Ma-rí*$^{ki}$.

*Ne-zi-ma-ì* **1** o. VII 6: (silver) níĝ-kaskal *N. Puzur*$_4$*-ra-a-gú* DU.DU *si-in Na-gàr*$^{ki}$.

*Ni-zi-ma-ì* **18** o. XIV 5: 1 na$_4$ *N.*

*Nu-ru$_{12}$-ud* **21** r. IV 15: dumu-nita *N.*

*Puzur$_4$-ra-a-gú* **1** o. VII 7: (silver) níĝ-kaskal *Ne-zi-ma-ì P.* DU.DU *si-in Na-gàr*$^{ki}$.

*Puzur$_4$-ra-*BAD **10** o. XI 24: (silver) níĝ-ba *Daš-na Wa-ru$_{12}$-tum P. I-ti-il Ma-rí*$^{ki}$.

*Puzur$_4$-ra-ḫa-al$_6$* **3** o. I 17: še *P.*; **12** o. III 9: 2 an-dùl *ap* kg lú dib *P.*

*Puzur$_4$-ra-il* **5** r. XII 4: 43 *ʾà-da-um-*TÚG-I *in Ša-bir$_5$-ti-um*$^{ki}$ *P. Na-gàr*$^{ki}$.

*Puzur$_4$-ra-ì* **22** o. VII 4: *Du-bí-zi-kir* lú *P.*

*Puzur$_4$-ra-ma-lik* **4** r. III 3: 1 na$_4$(UD.NI) *P.*; **7** o. XVI 15: 1 ĝír mar-tu kg *P.* lú *Iš$_{11}$-da-mu*; **13** r. II 13: (silver) lul-gu-ak gur$_8$ *P.* lú-kar *Kak-mi-um*$^{ki}$ KAK-*bar-zú wa Du-bí-zi-kir* šu-mu-tak$_4$; r. VIII 19: [ ] *P.* lú *Iš$_{11}$-da-mu*; 14 o. V 4: (silver) *Mu-*NE*-a-du* ugula *Ar-ḫa-du*$^{ki}$ *P.* lú kas$_4$-kas$_4$ šu-mu-tak$_4$; **15** o. XVII 21: (133 garments, 430 kilts) … raš-SAR … 4 IGI.N[ITA] *P.* ki:lam$_7$ $^{d}$*Ga-mi-iš.*

*Puzur$_4$-ra-*$^{d}$Utu **6** o. XV 11: (silver) níĝ-ba *P. Ma-rí*$^{ki}$ šu-mu-tak$_4$ túg-túg *áš-da Na-zi.*

*Ra-ba$_x$-tum* **17** r. XIV 1 and 5: [10+]7 [*b*]*u*$^?$-DI [ŠÚ+Š]A-ŠÚ+ŠA [níĝ-b]a *Ra-ù-tum Kir-*[*s*]*u-*[*u*]*d* [*En-na-*$^{d}$Utu] *R. Maš-ga-sa-du Ma-ga-ra-du Tiš-má-da-mu R.*-II dam en *wa* PN$_1$–PN$_2$ 2 dumu-munus en *wa* ama-gal *Ib-rí-um wa* PN$_3$–PN$_6$ dam-*sù wa* PN$_7$ nin-ni *Du-si-gú* PN$_8$.

*Ra-ù-tum* **14** o. XII 8: *A-zú-gú-ra* šeš *R.*; **17** r. XIII 27: [10+]7 [*b*]*u*$^?$-DI [ŠÚ+Š]A-ŠÚ+ŠA [níĝ-b]a *R. Kir-*[*s*]*u-*[*u*]*d* [*En-na-*$^{d}$Utu] *Ra-ba$_x$-tum Maš-ga-sa-du Ma-ga-ra-du Tiš-má-da-mu Ra-ba$_x$-tum-*II dam en *wa* PN$_1$–PN$_2$ 2 dumu-munus en *wa* ama-gal *Ib-rí-um wa* PN$_3$–PN$_6$ dam-*sù wa* PN$_7$ nin-ni *Du-si-gú* PN$_8$.

*Rí-dam-ma-lik* **2** o. XIV 2: 1 dib *R.* ugula *Šu-ti-gú*$^{ki}$; **13** o. IV 7: 1 ĝír mar-tu *ba-du-u$_4$* kb *R.* ugula *Su-ti-gú*$^{ki}$.

*Rí-ì-Ḫa-lab$_x$* **3** o. VI 11: (14 garments, 140 kilts) … 134 níĝ-saĝšu … raš-SAR Kur$^{ki}$ …1 BAR.AN *R.* šu-ba$_4$-ti … ki:lam$_7$ $^{d}$*Ga-mi-iš.*

*Rí-ì-ma-lik* **1** o. X 6: dumu-nita *R.*; **3** o. I 3: še *R.* ugula *A-da-*⸢*áš*⸣$^{ki}$, 7: še *R.* ugula *Ig-du-ra*$^{ki}$; **5** o. XV 11: 1 BAR.AN *R.* šu-ba$_4$-ti … ki:lam$_7$ $^{d}$*Ga-mi-iš*; **7** r. X 14: *En-n*[*a-*]⸢*ì*⸣ lú *R.*; **9** r. XVI 5: 1 ĝír mar-tu kg … 1 dib … 1 íb-lá 1 ĝír-kun … *En-na-*⸢*il*⸣ [ ] *R.* lú-kar *Kak-mi-um*$^{ki}$; **14** r. XII 8: 10 gud *R.* lú *I-bí-zi-im*; **16** r. V 15: *En-na-ì* lú *R.*; **17** o. XIII 11: 2 gud *in R.* 1 SA.ZA$_x$$^{ki}$ *I-bí-zi-im*; r. IV 1: *En-na-ni-il* lú *R.*

*Ru$_{12}$-zi-da-mu* **3** o. VII 15: (silver) lú nu-kiri$_6$ DU.DU *al$_6$* dumu-nita *R. Ma-nu-wa-ad*$^{ki}$; **13** r. VI 5: *Iš$_{11}$-la-ab* lú *R.*; **16** o. I 16: 1 dib *R.* en *Ì-mar*$^{ki}$.

*Ru$_{12}$-zi-li-im* **22** r. VIII 4: 13 dib *Bù-da-ì Íl-a-šar Gal-za-iš-lu Ga-du-um Iš-má-da-mu Da-da-ì* ⸢x⸣-NE-[x] *En-na-ma-lik Ig-rí-iš Gur-an-da-mu R. Iš-ma-da-ba-an Zé-da-mu.*

*Ru$_{12}$-zi-lum* **10** o. X 10: (silver) n[íĝ-]ba *Šu-ga-du R. Ma-rí*$^{ki}$.

*Ru$_{12}$-zi-ma-lik* **6** o. VII 8: 1 ĝír mar-tu ti kg *R.* dumu-nita *I-gi*; **17** o. XIII 3: 1 ĝír mar-tu zú kg *R.* lú *I-rí-ig* al$_6$-tuš *Ab-ra-ti-ig*$^{ki}$.

*Ru$_{12}$-zu-il* **6** r. X 10: 1 ĝír mar-tu kg *R.*ugula sur$_x$-BAR.AN.

*Ru$_{12}$-zu-mu* **3** o. I 11: še *R.*

*Sá-ba* **6** o. XVI 16: (silver) níĝ-ba *Ìr-*NI*-ba wa S. Ma-rí*$^{ki}$.

*Sa-d*[*a-* ] **14** r. III 20: 3 ĝír lú *S.* [ ].

*Sag-da-mu* **3** o. I 14: še *S.*

*Sá-gú-si* **22** o. III 5; o. IX 3: 1 dib *S.* ì-na-sum *En-na-il* lú *I-da-ni-ki-mu.*

*Sá-gú-šum* **4** o. V 19: 1 zag ĜIŠ-gígir-II *S*; o. VIII 6: 4 ĝír-ĝír šu-du$_8$-máš … 1 ĝír mar-tu kg *S.*; r. X 9: 2 níĝ-anše-ak 4 kù-sal *S.*; **6** o. XII 6: 1 íb-lá *si-ti-tum* ĝír-⸢kun⸣ *S.* É×PAP; **15** r. XIV 16: *Iš$_{11}$-gi-bar-zú* lú *S.*

*Sa-ḫa-a* **4** r. VII 3: 1 ĝír mar-tu ti kg *S.* ugula *Ù-si-gú*$^{ki}$; 14 r. XIX x+1: […] ⸢*S.*⸣ ugula *Ù-si-gú*$^{ki}$.

*Sa-li-im* **22** r. I 4: *Nu-ba-an*$^{ki}$ maškim *S.*

*Sa-ma-na-nu* **7** r. XI 14: (silver) níĝ-ba *Gul-la* ⸢x-x-x⸣ *S.* [*S*]*i-mi*[*-* ] [ ] *Iš-ba-ì A-ša*$^{ki}$ *in* ud DU.DU nam-kud é $^{d}$*Ku-ra.*

*Sa-mu-sá-sal* **10** r. V 10: 2 *bu-*DI *S. Da-bí* šu-mu-tak$_4$.

*Sa-mu-ù* **13** r. II 7: (silver) lul-gu-ak gur$_8$ *S.* dam-gàr *Ga-ra-ma-an*$^{ki}$; **14** r. I 13: (silver and tin) *Ar-ra-du-lum* [*Du-lu*$^{ki}$] *S.* dam-⸢gàr⸣ šu-mu-tak$_4$.

*Sa-mu-um* **12** o. XIV 2: 2 *gú-li-lum* kb lú *S.* lú *En-ti wa* lú dumu-nita *I-da-ad-mu in ìr-a-núm I-rí-ig-ma-lik.*

*Sa-*NI*-gú* **6** o. XII 17: (silver) níĝ-ba *Ib-ḫur-úr* (silver) níĝ-ba *S.* maškim-*sù* níĝ-"mul" *ʾÀ-du*$^{ki}$ àga-⸢kàr⸣(ŠÈ).

*Si-gi* **6** o. VII 14: *Ib-gi-da-mu* lú *S.*

*Si-mi*[*-* ] **7** r. XI 15: (silver) níĝ-ba *Gul-la* ⸢x-x-x⸣ *Sa-ma-na-nu S.* [ ] *Iš-ba-ì A-ša*$^{ki}$ *in* ud DU.DU nam-kud é $^{d}$*Ku-ra.*

*Si-ti-*BAR.AN **15** o. III 20: 1 íb-lá 1 ĝír-kun … 1 dib …1 ĝír-mar-tu kg *S.* lú-kar *Kak-mi-um*$^{ki}$.

*Ša-gú-bù* **17** o. XVI 17: (daggers) Lugal-*na-i-iš Íl-ba-šum Du-bí-ga-lu Š.* dumu-nita en *Ma-nu-wa-ad*$^{ki}$.

*Ša-ma* **3** r. VIII 17: 2 na$_4$ *Š.* simug; **18** o. XIV 11: 1 na$_4$ *ʾÀ-la-ga-*NE kin$_5$-ak 2 útul *Š.*

*Ša-ù-um* **14** o. XI 8: *En-na-í* lú *Š.*; **17** r. XVII 20: *En-na-ni-il* lú *Ša-ù-um.*

*Šu-a-ḫa* **14** o. II 20: (silver) níĝ-ba *Š.* maškim ga:eš$_8$ *Du-du-lu*$^{ki}$.

Šubur **4** o. II 2: (silver) Š. *Na-gàr*$^{ki}$ ḫi-mu-DU 2 *na-se$_{11}$ Ma-rí*$^{ki}$; o. XII 19: 1 na na$_4$ 12 ma-na kb en *Na-gàr*$^{ki}$ Š. [šu-mu-tak$_4$]; r. IX 16: (silver) Š. *Na-gàr*$^{ki}$ šu-mu-tak$_4$ íb+III-TÚG babbar *Ma-rí*$^{ki}$ *wa* til-*sù*; **5** o. X 4: (silver) *Na-*NE *wa* Š. *Na-gàr*$^{ki}$ *in* níĝ-kas$_4$ *A-da-*[*bí-*]⸢*ig*⸣$^{ki}$ šu-ba$_4$-ti; **14** r. VII 17: (silver) níĝ-ba Š. *Du*<*-lu*>$^{ki}$ kin$_5$-ak *šè-li.*

*Šu-ga-du* **9** o. XI 12: (silver) *Š. in An-ga-li-lu*$^{ki}$ šu-ba$_4$-ti; o. XII 17: (silver) níĝ-ba *Daš-na wa Š. Ma-r*[*í*]$^{ki}$ *in Gi-da-*NE$^{ki}$ šu-ba$_4$-ti; **10** o. X 9: (silver) n[íĝ-]ba *Š. Ru$_{12}$-zi-lum Ma-rí*$^{ki}$; **13** o. V 1: (silver) níĝ-ba *Wa-ru$_{12}$-tum wa Š. Ma-rí*$^{ki}$; o. XVI 17: (silver) níĝ-ba *Daš-na wa Š. Ma-rí*$^{ki}$.

*Šu-ì* **21** r. VIII 10: [(silver) níĝ-ba] *Bar*-NE-⌜*um*⌝ *Wa-ru*$_{12}$*-tum* $^{d}$Utu-*a-ba*$_{4}$ *Š. Ag-ga Ma-rí*$^{ki}$.

*Šu-ma-lik* **9** r. IV 11: 1 ĝír mar-tu kg *Š.* lú *Iš*$_{11}$*-da-mu*; **17** o. XIII 24: 3 ĝír mar-tu *Š.* lú *Iš*$_{11}$*-da-mu Iš*$_{11}$*-gi-da-mu A-ba-ù* NI-*ti-ba*$^{ki}$.

*Šum*-bàd$^{ki}$ **3** r. I 3: 1 dib *I-bí-zi-kir* l[ú *Ib-rí-um*] … 1 dib *Š.* šeš-*sù*; **14** o. VII 11: 1 dib *Š.* dumu-nita *Ib-rí-um*; **17** r. VIII 16: 2 níĝ-anše-ak 4 kù-sal *Š.* dumu-nita *Ib-rí-um*.

*Šu-mi-nu* **17** o. III 15: 10 na$_{4}$ *Š.* kin$_{5}$-ak 2 útul urudu.

*Šu*-NE **6** r. X 19: 1 ĝír mar-tu *ba-du-u*$_{9}$ kb kg *Š.* ugula sur$_{x}$-BAR.AN en.

*Šu*-NE-ḪAR **18** o. XV 13: (silver) *Š.* maškim *A-mur-da-mu* lú ĜIŠ-nu-kiri$_{6}$.

*Tal-du-du* **18** o. XVII 6: 2 *ti-gi-na* 10 lá-2 ĝeštu$_{x}$-lá 92 *gur-gú-ru*$_{12}$ 3 *mi-at* 60 *ḫa-za-nu* 1 šu-dub 1 *ma-ḫa-na-gúm* 2 kù-sal 1 *a-a-nu* 2 ĜIŠ-du *T.* dam en.

*Ti-a-da-mu* **17** r. XIV 19: [10+]7 [*b*]*u*-DI [ŠÚ+Š]A-ŠÚ+ŠA [níĝ-b]a PN$_{1}$–PN$_{8}$ dam en *wa* PN$_{9}$–PN$_{10}$ 2 dumu-munus en *wa* ama-gal *Ib-rí-um wa A-zi-mu Ti-lu-du T. Kir-su-ud* dam-*sù wa* PN$_{11}$ nin-ni *Du-si-gú* PN$_{12}$.

*Ti-bù-da-mu* **20** o. XIV 20: 1 íb-lá 1 *si-ti-tum* 1 ĝír-kun … 2 *ti-gi-na* … 4 *ʾà-ra-ma-tum* … 8 ĜIŠ-ĝeštu$_{x}$-lá … 1 šu-dub … 2 ĜIŠ-du *T. maš-ar-tum* en.

*Ti-ir* **6** r. VIII 10: *I-bí-šum* lú *T.*

*Ti-lu-du* **17** r. XIV 18: [10+]7 [*b*]*u*-DI [ŠÚ+Š]A-ŠÚ+ŠA [níĝ-b]a PN$_{1}$–PN$_{8}$ dam en *wa* PN$_{9}$–PN$_{10}$ 2 dumu-munus en *wa* ama-gal *Ib-rí-um wa A-zi-mu T. Ti-a-da-mu Kir-su-ud* dam-*sù wa* PN$_{11}$ nin-ni *Du-si-gú* PN$_{12}$.

*Ti-ra-il* **20** r. VI 15: 1 *ma-da-ḫu* … 1 *a-na-bù-bí-tum al*$_{6}$*-sù T.* [dub-sa]r.

*Ti-ra-ì* **7** o. VI 9: 1 ĝír mar-tu ti kg *T.* maškim *En-mar* šu-du$_{8}$ *in Ma-rí*$^{ki}$; **13** o. X 2: [ ] *T. A-da-bí-ig*$^{ki}$; **19** r. XV 5: 2 ĝír mar-tu ti kg *Íl-zi* lú *Ìr-am*$_{6}$*-da-mu wa T.* šeš ama-gal en.

*Tir*$_{5}$*-bù-da-mu* **17** r. XXI 16: 2 *bu*-DI *Di-rin*$_{x}$*-da-mu* … 2 *bu*-DI … 2 saĝ-*sù* … 2 kù-sal *T.* nin-ni-*sù*.

*Ti-ša-li-im* **17** o. VII 20: 2 *bu*-DI níĝ-ba *T. ma-lik-tum Ì-mar*⌜$^{ki}$⌝ *i*[*n* ud] [ ] [*I-bí-zi-kir* dumu-]nita *Ib-rí-um*; r. V 26: 2 *bu*-DI *T. ma-lik-tum Ì-mar*$^{ki}$ *in* ud DU.DU *mi-nu ʾÀ-da-ni*$^{ki}$; r. IX 31: 2 *bu*-DI *T. ma-lik-tum Ì-mar*$^{ki}$ *in* ud DU.DU *mi-nu* NI-*ab*$^{ki}$ *si-in* SA.ZA$_{x}$$^{ki}$.

*Ti-šè-li-im* **13** o. XIV 1: 1 dib ì-ĝiš-saĝ en *Ì-mar*$^{ki}$ … 2 *bu*-DI … 2 saĝ-*sù* ì-ĝiš-saĝ *T.* ama-gal-*sù*; o. XV 25: 2 *bu*-DI … 2 saĝ-*sù* níĝ-ba *T. ma-lik-tum Ì-mar*$^{ki}$ *in* ud DU.DU *si-in* SA.ZA$_{x}$$^{ki}$ tak$_{4}$ AMA-*ra*; **19** o. II 22: 2 *bu*-DI … 2 saĝ-*sù* níĝ-ba *T. ma-lik-tum Ì-mar*$^{ki}$; **20** r. VIII 12: 2 *bu*-DI *T. ma-lik-tum Ì-mar*$^{ki}$ *in* ud DU.DU *mi-nu ʾÀ-da-ni*$^{ki}$; **21** r. VII 11: [2 *bu*-DI] … 2 saĝ-*sù* ì-ĝiš-saĝ *T. ma-lik-tum Ì-mar*$^{ki}$.

*Ti-ša-rum* **4** r. XIV 14: *Du-bí-zi-kir* lú *T.*

*Tíš-má-da-mu* **3** o. XI 16: 2 *bu*-DI ì-ĝiš-saĝ *T.* dam en; **17** r. XIV 4: [10+]7 [*b*]*u*$^{?}$-DI [ŠÚ+Š]A-ŠÚ+ŠA [níĝ-b]a *Ra-ù-tum Kir-*[*s*]*u-*[*u*]*d* [*En-na-*$^{d}$Utu] *Ra-ba*$_{x}$*-tum Maš-ga-sa-du Ma-ga-ra-du T. Ra-ba*$_{x}$*-tum-*II dam en *wa* PN$_{1}$–PN$_{2}$ 2 dumu-munus en *wa* ama-gal *Ib-rí-um wa* PN$_{3}$–PN$_{6}$ dam-*sù wa* PN$_{7}$ nin-ni *Du-si-gú* PN$_{8}$.

*Tíš-ma-zi-kir* **20** o. II 23: 2 ⌜ĜIŠ⌝-du *T.*

*Tíš-te-da-mu* **16** o. III 7 and 12: 4 ĝeštu$_{x}$-lá *Dar-ib-da-mu wa T.* … 2 kù-sal *T.* 2 dumu-munus en; **18** o. XVIII 10: 4 *ti-gi-na* 4 ĜIŠ-du 4 ĝeštu$_{x}$-lá 2 kù-sal *Dar-ib-da-mu wa T.* 2 dumu-munus en.

*Ti-ti-nu* **13** o. IV 11: (silver) lú ĜIŠ-nu-kiri$_{6}$ *T. wa Gú-zi* šu-ba$_{4}$-ti *in A-te-na-ad*$^{ki}$; **17** r. VII 30: 1 dib *T.* maškim *Ib-rí-um*; **21** o. III 2: [ ]-*sù T. in* ud ḫúl-*sù I-bí-zi-kir* šu-mu-tak$_{4}$; r. IX 13: [1$^{?}$ í]b-lá [1 g]ír-kun … *Ig-na-da-ar* lú *Mi-ga-ì T.* šu-mu-tak$_{4}$ *in* ud ḫúl-*sù*.

Túg-du$_{8}$ **19** r. XIII 16: 1 dib … 1 íb-lá 1 ĝír-kun … T. lú *I-bí-zi-kir* šu-du$_{8}$ ugula *Za-ḫi-ra-an*$^{ki}$.

*Ù-ba-nu* **10** o. XV 12: (silver) níĝ-du$_{8}$ *Ù.* KAR kù-gi en *Ma-nu-wa-ad*$^{ki}$.

*Ù-da-aḫ* **3** r. XII 6: (silver) níĝ-ba *Ù. Ma-rí*$^{ki}$ kuš$_{7}$; **6** r. XIII 7: (silver) níĝ-kaskal *A-ʾà-lu wa Ù.* heš$_{5}$ (LÚ×KÁR) DU.DU *Ma-rí*$^{ki}$; **10** o. XIV 8: (silver) níĝ-ba *Ù. Na-gàr*$^{ki}$.

*Ù-da-a-ḫa* **4** r. XII 19: (silver) [níĝ-kaskal] *A-ʾà-lu wa Ù. Ma-rí*$^{ki}$ heš$_{5}$ (LÚ×KÁR) DU.DU.

*U*$_{9}$*-da-ar* **4** r. II 19: [1 n]a$_{4}$ *U*$_{9}$.

*Ù-da-sa* **8** r. VIII 7': 1 ĝír mar-tu *ba-du-u*$_{4}$ kg kb *Ù.* di-kud.

*Ù-ḫa* **4** o. III 17: (silver) *Ù.* ⌜*ʾÀ*.$^{?}$⌝-*ma*$^{ki}$ [šu-]ba$_{4}$-ti *in* [ ].

*Ù-li-li* **14** r. X 15: (silver) níĝ-ba *Ù.* maškim [ga:eš$_{8}$] [*Du-du-lu*]$^{ki}$.

*Ù-rí-rí* **17** o. VII 2: [ ] ⌜níĝ-ba⌝ *Ù* maškim ga:eš$_{8}$ *in* kaskal é $^{d}$BAD *Ga-na-na*.

*Ù-lu-li* **13** r. I 14: (silver) níĝ-ba *Da-ti Iš-da-maḫ Ù.* [ ].

*Ú-mu-*⌜*ti*⌝ **13** r. XII 1.

*Ù*-NE-NE **6** o. XV 19: (silver) níĝ-ba *Ù. Ma-rí*$^{ki}$.

*Ù-ra*-AN **3** o. IX 15: 1 ĝír mar-tu ti kg NI-*gi* saĝ-du$_{8}$ lú-kar *A-da-bí-ig*$^{ki}$ … 1 ĝír mar-tu *ba-du-u*$_{4}$ kb kg *Ù.* maškim-*sù*.

*Ù-ra-rí* **1** o. VIII 15: 2 ĝeštu$_{x}$-lá *Ù.* lú *I-gi*.

Ur-é(-gal) **11** o. II 3: kb X U. (cf. TM.75.G.1233 r. IX 10: Ur-é; ARET VII 18 r. IV 1: Ur-é-gal).

*Ù-rí-rí* see *Ù-li-li*.

*Uš-ga* **11** r. V 10: 1 na$_{4}$ maḫ *áš-ti U.* "ur$_{4}$" *A-da-bí-ig*$^{ki}$

*Ù-ti* **15** r. XIII 17: 1 dib *Ù.*; **16** r. XII 7: 2 níĝ-anše-ak 4 kù-sal *Ù.*; **19** r. XVIII 10: 1 íb-lá 1 *si-ti-tum* 1 ĝír-kun 1 ĜIŠ-sal níĝ-[b]a *Ib-rí-um* … 2 íb-lá 2 ĝír-kun … 2 ĜIŠ-sal-*sù I-bí-zi-kir wa Ù.* 2 dumu-nita-*sù in* ud ḫúl-*sù* en šu-mu-tak$_{4}$.

$^{d}$Utu-*a-ba*$_{4}$ **21** r. VIII 9: [(silver) níĝ-ba] *Bar*-NE-⌜*um*⌝ *Wa-ru*$_{12}$*-tum* $^{d}$U. *Šu-ì Ag-ga Ma-rí*$^{ki}$.

*Ù-zi* **7** o. II 6: 1 *gàr-su Ù.* šeš *A-zú-ma*; **24** o. II 12: 1 dib *Ú.* šeš *A-zú-ma*.

*Ù-zu* **13** o. XII 3: [1 g]ír m[ar-t]u kg *Ù.* "ur$_{4}$" *Ì-mar*$^{ki}$ É×PAP *Ba-ga-ma* šu-mu-tak$_{4}$.

*Wa-ba-rúm* **1** o. IX 14: 1 íb-lá 1 *si-ti-tum* 1 ĝír-kun en *Ì-ra-ar*$^{ki}$ *W.* šu-mu-tak$_{4}$ É×PAP; **2** o. X 16: (13 kilts) … ĜIŠ-sal *W.* šu-ba$_{4}$-ti ki:lam$_{7}$ $^{d}$*A-da-ma*; r. XVII 5: [ ] 1 ĝír mar-tu kg … ĜIŠ-ti-ḪAR *W.* ki:lam$_{7}$ $^{d}$*Áš-da-bíl*; **3** o. VII 6: ĜIŠ-ti-ḪAR *W.* šu-ba$_{4}$-

ti ki:⸢lam$_7$⸣ $^{d}$*Ga-mi-iš*; o. X 3': ĜIŠ-ti-ḪAR *W.* šu-ba$_4$-ti ki:lam$_7$ $^{d}$*Áš-da-bíl*; r. II 4: ĜIŠ-ti-ḪAR *W.* šu-ba$_4$-ti … ki:lam$_7$ [ ]; r. IX 14: (15 garments, 104 kilts) … 1 BAR.AN … ĜIŠ-ti-ḪAR *W.* šu-ba$_4$-ti ki:lam$_7$ šeš-II-ib *ʾÀ-da-ni*$^{ki}$; r. XIII 11: (104 kilts) … ĜIŠ-ti-ḪAR *W.* ki:lam$_7$ $^{d}$*A-da-ma wa* ki:lam$_7$ bàd-diĝir$^{ki}$; **5** o. II 3: (65 garments, 210+[x] kilts, 8 daggers, 354 na$_4$ measures of wool) … ĜIŠ-ti-ḪAR ĜIŠ-ád *W.* "ur$_4$" šu-ba$_4$-ti ki:lam$_7$ <$^{d}$>*A-da-ma ʾÀ-da-ni*$^{ki}$; o. IV 2: ĜIŠ-má-gíd … ĜIŠ-ti-ḪAR *W.* šu-ba$_4$-ti ki:lam$_7$ SA.ZA$_x$$^{ki}$; o. IX 6: (7 garments, 607 kilts, 18 daggers) … ĜIŠ-ti-ḪAR *W.* šu-ba$_4$-ti ki:lam$_7$ AMA-*ra*; o. XV 14: ĜIŠ-ti-ḪAR *W.* šu-ba$_4$-ti ki:lam$_7$ $^{d}$*Ga-mi-iš*; r. IX 10: (3 garments, 253 kilts) … ĜIŠ-ti-ḪAR *W.* šu-ba$_4$-ti ki:lam$_7$ $^{d}$*Áš-da-bíl*; **6** o. X 11: ĝír mar-tu kg (silver) níĝ-ba *W. Ma-rí*$^{ki}$ (silver) níĝ-ba *ʾÀ-sa* maškim-*sù*; o. XI 6: ĜIŠ-ti-ḪAR ki:lam$_7$ $^{d}$*A-da-ma ʾÀ-da-ni*$^{ki}$ *W.* šu-ba$_4$-ti; r. IX 16: (35 garments, 185 kilts, 12 daggers) … ĜIŠ-ti-ḪAR *W.* šu-ba$_4$-ti ki:lam$_7$ *ʾÀ-da-ni*$^{ki}$ *wa* NI-*ab*$^{ki}$ *wa La-ru*$_{12}$*-ga-du*$^{ki}$; **7** o. IX 4: (84+[x] garments, 8 na$_4$ measures of wool) … ĜIŠ-ti-ḪAR *W.* šu-ba$_4$-ti … ki:lam$_7$ $^{d}$*A-da-ma wa* SA.ZA$_x$$^{ki}$; **8** o XI 8: (126 kilts) … <ĜIŠ-ti-ḪAR> *W.* "ur$_4$" [šu]-⸢ba$_4$⸣-[ti] [ki:lam$_7$] [ ]$^{ki}$; r. IV 12': ĜIŠ-ti-ḪAR *W.* "ur$_4$" šu-ba$_4$-ti; **9** r. VI 2: ĜIŠ-ti-ḪAR *W.* šu-ba$_4$-ti *in* ud šu-mu-níĝin SA.ZA$_x$$^{ki}$; r. XVI 12: (50 kilts) … ĜIŠ-gu-kak-gíd *W.* ⸢šu⸣-ba$_4$-ti ki:⸢lam$_7$⸣ *zi-ba-tum ʾÀ-da-ni*$^{ki}$; **10** o. IX 20: (silver) níĝ-ba *W. Ma-rí*$^{ki}$ *in* ud di-kud DU.DU; r. VI 11: (76 garments) … ĜIŠ-ti-ḪAR *W.* šu-ba$_4$-ti … *in* ⸢ki⸣:lam$_7$ $^{d}$*ʾÀ-da*; **11** o. XI 14: 4 gud *W. En-na-ì* lú-kar *Kak-mi-um*$^{ki}$; **12** o. VI 13: (silver) níĝ-ba *W.* ga:eš$_8$ *Du-du-lu*$^{ki}$ (silver) níĝ-ba *Na-na-tum* dam-*sù* (silver) níĝ-ba dumu-nita-*sù* šu-mu-tak$_4$ ŠE+TIN (silver) níĝ-ba 2 maškim-*sù in Sa-gàr-du*$^{ki}$ šu-ba$_4$-ti; o. X 17: 2 *ma-ga-za-ʾà* zabar gibil 2 zú naĝar *W.* šu-ba$_4$-ti; r. X 5: ĜIŠ-*šè-bir*$_5$*-gi-nu W.* šu-ba$_4$-ti; r. XIII 5: [ ]⸢x⸣ 5 buluĝ$_4$-buluĝ$_4$ gibil lú ĜIŠ-taškarin *W.* šu-ba$_4$-ti; **13** o. V 17: (88 kilts, 245 KIN measures of wool) … 20 gud … ĜIŠ-ti-ḪAR *W.* šu-ba$_4$-ti ki:lam$_7$ šeš-II-ib *wa* $^{d}$*A-da-ma ʾÀ-da-ni*$^{ki}$; **14** o. XVII 8: (121+[x] garments, 306 kilts, 5 daggers) … raš-SAR Kur$^{ki}$ … 11 gud en … ĜIŠ-ti-ḪAR *W.* šu-ba$_4$-ti ki:lam$_7$ *ʾÀ-da-ni*$^{ki}$ *in* $^{d}$AMA-*ra*; r. XII 4: [ ] *W.* [šu-ba$_4$-ti]; **15** o. VII 5: (54 garments, 166 kilts, 385 KIN measures of wool) … ĜIŠ-ti-ḪAR *W.* šu-ba$_4$-ti ki:lam$_7$ šeš-II-ib *wa* $^{d}$*A-da-ma ʾÀ-da-ni*$^{ki}$; o. XIII 3: (171 garments, 170 kilts) … 10 sila$_4$ sa$_6$ … ĜIŠ-ti-ḪAR *W.* ki:lam$_7$ $^{d}$AMA-*ra ʾÀ-da-ni*$^{ki}$; **17** r. V 14: (265 garments, 242 kilts, 150 hides) … ĜIŠ-bar-ús *W.* <ki:lam$_7$> *ʾÀ-da-ni*$^{ki}$; **18** r. XIX 8: 25 *gàr-su* … (36 garments, 85 na$_4$ measures of wool) … ĜIŠ-ti-ḪAR <ki:lam$_7$> SA.ZA$_x$$^{ki}$ *W.* šu-ba$_4$-ti; **19** r. V 4: ĜIŠ-ti-ḪAR ki:lam$_7$ SA.ZA$_x$$^{ki}$ *W.* šu-ba$_4$-ti, 16: (347 garments, 46 na$_4$ measures of wool) … ĜIŠ-ma-dul$_{10}$ *W.* šu-ba$_4$-ti ki:lam$_7$ *ʾÀ-da-ni*$^{ki}$ *wa* $^{d}$*Ga-mi-iš*; **20** r. XIII 8: (39 garments) … ĜIŠ-ti-ḪAR *W.* šu-ba$_4$-ti ki:lam$_7$ $^{d}$⸢*ʾÀ*⸣[*-da*]; **21** r. II 12: (49 garments, 313 kilts, 60 na$_4$ measures of wool) … 1 ĜIŠ-*ba-ri-zú* ĜIŠ.GAM.GAM.GAM … 1 *mi-at* 50 ĜIŠ-ti-ḪAR *wa* níĝ-NE *W.* šu-ba$_4$!-ti!(ŠU.BAL.AK) … ki:lam$_7$ $^{d}$*Áš-da-bíl wa* ki:lam$_7$ *Ši-ʾà-am*$^{ki}$ *wa* k[i:lam$_7$] $^{d}$*ʾÀ-da*.

(see the commentary on text no. 12)

*Wa-na* **7** o. VI 5: 1 dib *W.* ugula BAR.AN-BAR.AN; **8** o. XII 10: 2 *gú-li-lum W.* ugula sur$_x$-BAR.AN; r. V 10: še-in *W.* ugula BAR.AN šu-ba$_4$-ti; **16** r. XV 3: 3 *zú-zú-ba-tum* ĜIŠ-gígir-II *W.*, 11: 5 tùn gal TAR.TAR 5 dub-naĝar šu-mu-LAGAB 15 5 dub-naĝar 10 sal *W.* ugula *A-la-ga*$^{ki}$; r. XVI 19: 1 dib *W.* ugula *A-la-ga*$^{ki}$; **17** o. VIII 7: BAR.AN *áš-ti A-ša*$^{ki}$ *W.* šu-ba$_4$-ti; **20** r. XVI 5': 1 BAR.AN *W.* šu-ba$_4$-ti.

*Wa-ra-núm* **4** o. IV. 6: (silver) *W. Ma-rí*$^{ki}$.

*Wa-ru*$_{12}$*-tum* **3** o. II 21: (silver) níĝ-ba *Daš-na W. Ma-rí*$^{ki}$; o. XIII 17: (silver) níĝ-ba *Daš-na wa W. Ma-rí*$^{ki}$; **4** r. X 17: [ ] níĝ-"mul" àga-"kár"(ŠÈ) *Ma-rí*$^{ki}$ *wa* til *W.*; **5** o. II 18: (silver) níĝ-ba *Daš-na wa W. Ma-rí*$^{ki}$ *Má*-NE$^{ki}$; r. II 7: (silver) níĝ-ba *W. Ma-rí*$^{ki}$; r. IV 18: (silver) níĝ-ba *W. wa* maškim *Ma-rí*$^{ki}$; r. XV 28: (silver) níĝ-ba *W. Ma-rí*$^{ki}$ šu-mu-tak$_4$; **7** o. XV 22: (silver) níĝ-ba *W.* [*Ma-rí*$^{ki}$]; r. X 17: (silver) níĝ-ba *W. Ma-rí*$^{ki}$; r. XIV 17: (silver) níĝ-ba *W. Da-ti Bù-sum Ma-rí*$^{ki}$; **9** o. XII 23: (silver) *W. Ma-rí*$^{ki}$; **10** o. II 13: (silver) níĝ-ba *W. Daš-na Iš*$_{11}$*-ga-um ʾÀ-bí-su Ma-rí*$^{ki}$; o. XI 23: (silver) níĝ-ba *Daš-na W. Puzur-ra-*BAD *I-ti-il Ma-rí*$^{ki}$; o. XIV 13: (silver) níĝ-ba *Daš-na W. Ma-rí*$^{ki}$; r. I 4: (silver) níĝ-ba *Daš-na W. Ma-rí*$^{ki}$; r. II 2: (silver) níĝ-ba *Daš-na wa W. Ma-rí*$^{ki}$; r. IV 2: (silver) níĝ-ba *W. wa Daš-na Ma-rí*$^{ki}$; **11** o. VIII 16: (silver) níĝ-ba *W. Daš-na I-ku*!(DÚR)*-ku*!(DÚR)*-tu Ma-rí*$^{ki}$; **12** o. IX 16: (silver) níĝ-ba *W. Ma-rí*$^{ki}$ níĝ-"mul" *Ag-sa-gú*$^{ki}$ šu-ba$_4$-ti; **13** o. IV 22: (silver) níĝ-ba *W. wa Šu-ga-du Ma-rí*$^{ki}$; **14** r. V 12: (silver) [níĝ-ba] *W. Ma-rí*$^{ki}$ níĝ-"mul" Kiš$^{ki}$ til-til; **15** o. VII 14: (silver) níĝ-ba *W. Ma-rí*$^{ki}$ níĝ-"mul" *in* uru$^{ki}$-uru$^{ki}$ Kiš$^{ki}$ šu-ba$_4$-ti; o. XVII 4: (silver) níĝ-ba *W. Ma-rí*$^{ki}$ e$_{11}$ *áš-ti Na-zu-mu mi-nu* Kiš$^{ki}$; **16** o. XIV 18: (silver) níĝ-ba *W. Ma-rí*$^{ki}$ šu-mu-tak$_4$ igi-du$_8$; **17** o. XVII 6: (silver) níĝ-ba *W. wa I-ku-uḫ Ma-rí*$^{ki}$ ḫi-mu-DU 1 az maḫ; **20** o. II 9: (silver) níĝ-ba *W. Ma-rí*$^{ki}$ *in* [ ] [šu-b]a$_4$-ti; o. V 16: [ ] *W. Ma-rí*$^{ki}$; r. IX 9: (silver) níĝ-ba *W. Ma-rí*$^{ki}$ e$_{11}$ *mi-nu* Kiš$^{ki}$ *áš-ti En-na-il*; **21** r. VIII 8: [(silver) níĝ-ba] *Bar*-NE-⸢*um*⸣ *W.* $^{d}$Utu-*a-ba*$_4$ *Šu-ì Ag-ga Ma-rí*$^{ki}$.

*Wa-su*-LUM **9** r. XIII 18: 3 *gú-li-lum* a-gar$_5$-gar$_5$ lú *W.* lú *Ib-ni-ḫar wa En-nu-lum* BÍL-*da-mu I-ti-a-gú* lú *En-na-il*.

*Za-a-ti* **6** o. XVI 3: 4 ĝír šu-du$_8$-máš … 3 *zú-zú-ba-tum* en *Gú-da-da-núm*$^{ki}$ *Z.* šu-mu-tak$_4$; **16** r. VI 17: (silver) lú ĜIŠ-nu-kiri$_6$ *Z.* šu-ba$_4$-ti *in Ša-dab*$_6$$^{ki}$.

*Za-ba-ra* **4** o. XV 11: (silver) níĝ-kaskal *Z.* maškim *Ḫa-ra-il*.

*Za-ba-rúm* **5** r. VII 2: še ĝuruš-ĝuruš-*sù wa* da[m]-*sù Z.* še-<SAĜ×>ḪA-mul; **9** r. XIV 12: (silver) *Z.* šu-ba$_4$-ti níĝ-sa$_{10}$ še-še; **15** o. II 14: (silver) níĝ-du$_8$ 1 dumu-nita *A-ba-ti-lum*$^{ki}$ maškim *Za-ba-rúm áš-ti Ìr-ku*$^{ki}$; **16** r. IV 8: *Ḫa-bù-zú ʾÀ-bar-du*$^{ki}$ maškim *Z.*; **18** o. V 26: la-ḫa ĝeštin en *Gú-da-da-núm*$^{ki}$ *Z.* šu-ba$_4$-ti; r. III 1: *Gi-ù-du* dam *Z.*; **19** r. XIII 4: (silver) níĝ-ba 3 ĝuruš *ʾÀ-du*$^{ki}$ ḫi-mu-DU maškim *Z.* nar; **21** o. III 10: 1 íb-lá 1 *si-ti-tum* 1 ĝír-kun *Z.* É×PAP *I-rí-ig-ì* šu-mu-tak$_4$.

*Za-gàr* **6** r. II 3: (silver) níĝ-kaskal *Z. A-dar-ki-zú*$^{ki}$ DU.DU *Ar-mi*$^{ki}$.

*Za-gi-ti-ma* **8** o. II 12.

*Za-ne-ḫi-Ma-rí*$^{ki}$ **9** r. IV 16: 2 *bu*-DI *Z.* é-gi *Ib-ʾà-ra ʾÀ-šu*$^{⸢ki⸣}$; r. VII 3: 4 *bu*-DI níĝ-ba *Ib-ʾà-ra wa* nin-ni-⸢*sù*⸣ *in* ud níĝ-mu-sá *Z.* é-gi *Ib-ʾà-ra ʾÀ-šu*$^{ki}$; **12** o. VII 20: 2 *bu*-DI *Z.* dumu-munus en é-gi *Ib-ʾà-ra.*

*Za-ni-ḫi-Ma-rí*$^{ki}$ **17** r. XIV 10: [10+]7 [*b*]*u*-DI [ŠÚ+Š]A-ŠÚ+ŠA [níĝ-b]a PN$_1$–PN$_8$ dam en *wa Ma-ù-ud Z.* 2 dumu-munus en *wa* ama-gal *Ib-rí-um wa* PN$_9$–PN$_{12}$ dam-*sù wa* PN$_{13}$ nin-ni *Du-si-gú* PN$_{14}$; 22 r. V 3: 1 ma-na kg gù-kak-gíd *Z.* é-gi *Ib-ʾà-ra ʾÀ-šu*$^{ki}$.

*Za-rí-ba* **17** o. IX 1: *Z.* (silver) níĝ-kaskal-*sù.*

*Za-za-u*$_9$ **6** l.ed. 4: 1 ŠA.PI an-na kin$_5$-ak $^{d}$*Ì-lam* lú *Z.*

*Za-zú* **1** o. IX 18: (silver) *Z. Ga-ga-ba-an*$^{ki}$.

*Zé-ba-da-ar* **9** o. XIII 9: 1 dib *Z.* l[ú]-ka[r].

*Zé-da-ar* **5** r. VII 14: 1 dib *Z.* lú-kar.

*Zé-da-mu* **2** r. XII 5: 1 dib *Z.* lú *Dab-da-ar*; **22** r. VIII 6: 13 dib *Bù-da-ì Íl-a-šar Gal-za-iš-lu Ga-du-um Iš-má-da-mu Da-da-ì* ⸢X⸣-NE-[X] *En-na-ma-lik Ig-rí-iš Gur-an-da-mu Ru*$_{12}$*-zi-li-im Iš-ma-da-ba-an Z.*

*Zé-ma-lik* **15** r. IX 7: *A-ḫu-šu-da-mu* dumu-nita *Z.* šeš *I-nu-ud-da-mu.*

*Zi-ba-da* **3** o. XII 5: 1 dib *Z.*; r. XI 18: 6 *bu*-DI níĝ-ba 3 dam *Z. in* ud níĝ-mu-sá dumu-munus *Ib-rí-um*; **8** o. XIII 9: 1 íb-lá 1 kun *Z.*; **11** o. IV 12: *maš-ar-tum* níĝ-ba dumu-munus [*I*]*b-rí-*[*u*]*m* é-gi<-a> *Z.* é $^{d}$*ʾÀ-da*; **13** o. XIII 5: 4 kù-sal *al*$_6$ kù-sal *Z.*; **14** o. VII 5: *En-na-il* lú *Z.*; **17** r. XVII 23: *En-na-ì* lú *Z.*; **19** o. VIII 29: 4 kù-sal *a-li-iš* kù-sal-kù-sal *Z.*; **20** o. XVII 23: 1 ĝír mar-tu kg *Z.*; **23** r. I 10: 1 ĝír mar-tu *Z.*; **24** r. III 12: 3 dib *Z. wa Íl-zi* lú *En-na-ni-il wa Ma-a-bar-zú* lú *Ig-na-da-mu.*

*Zi-ir-a-ḫu* **11** r. VII 18: 1 íb-lá 1 ĝír-kun … maš-[maš-*sù*] … 1 dib … 1 ĝír mar-tu kg *Z.* ugula *A-bar-sal*$_4^{ki}$ *in* ud šu-du$_8$.

*Zi-la-da-mu* **11** r. IV 16: (silver) lú ĜIŠ-kiri$_6$ *Z.* šu-ba$_4$-ti; **12** o. V 7: (silver) lú ĜIŠ-kiri$_6$ *Z.* ugula kas$_4$ šu-ba$_4$-ti; **14** o. III 3: (silver) lú ĜIŠ-kiri$_6$ *Z.* šu-ba$_4$-ti.

*Zi-mi-ni*-kù:babbar **13** o. IX 4: 4 *ʾà-ra-ma-tum Z. ma-lik-tum Bur-ma-an*$^{ki}$; **15** o. XVI 20: 2 *bu*-DI … *Z. ma-lik-tum Bur-ma-an*$^{ki}$ *in* ud dumu-munus tu-da *I-lu*$_5$*-za*$_x$*-ma-lik* [šu-mu-ta]g$_4$.
(see the commentary on text no. 13)

*Zi-rí-gú* **4** o. V 1: (silver) ì-na-sum *Z.* níĝ-du$_8$ dumu-nita *Lá-da-il Ma-rí*$^{ki}$; **18** o. XV 20: (silver) níĝ-ba *I-ba*$_x$*-ì Z. ʾÀ-du*$^{ki}$ *wa Ib-rí Na-gàr*$^{ki}$ *wa I-ku-a-ḫu Sag-gar*$^{ki}$; r. XVIII 13: (silver) *I-ba*$_x$*-ì Z. ʾÀ-du*$^{ki}$.

*Zú-ba-an* **21** o. XIII 3: (62 garments) lú *Z.* níĝ-sa$_{10}$ *in* níĝ-kas$_4$ *Ma-rí*$^{ki}$.

*Zú-ba-núm* **6** r. VII 14: 1 íb-lá 1 *si-ti-tum* 1 ĝír-kun *Ba-lu-zù* "ur$_4$" *Ì-mar*$^{ki}$ *in* ud ḫúl na-rú-*sù Z.* šu-mu-tak$_4$; **14** o. V 13: 2 *bu*-DI dumu-munus en *Ì-ra-ar*$^{ki}$ É×PAP *Z.* šu-mu-tak$_4$; **16** o. XIII 4: [ -]*ma*-[x] ugula sur$_x$-B[AR.AN] *Z. in Na-gàr*$^{ki}$; **19** o. IX 29: (silver) lú ĜIŠ-nu-kiri$_6$ *En-na-il* ugula engar *Z.* 2 šu-ba$_4$-ti.

*Zú-ga-du* **4** r. XIII 6: 4 íb-lá *si-ti-tum* ĝír-kun *Du-bù-uš-da-mu I-ga-li-im Z. Ì-lum-a-rí-ḫu* 4 en *Ib-al*$_6^{ki}$.

*Zú-gú-uš* **6** o. IV 1: (silver) níĝ-ba *Z. Na-gàr*$^{ki}$; r. XVII 7: (tin) *Z. Na-gàr*$^{ki}$

*Zú-za-bir*$_5$ **14** o. VII 20: 1 íb-lá 1 ĝír-kun … maš-maš-*sù Z.* lú *A-da-ad* tuš-LÚ×TIL *in Am*$_6$*-ʾà-rúm*$^{ki}$.

*Zú-zu* **3** o. VII 20; **4** r. II 5: (silver) *Z. Ir-i-tum*$^{ki}$; **10** o. VI 5: (silver) níĝ-ba *Z. Ir-i-tum*$^{ki}$ *in A-bí-na-du*$^{ki}$ šu-ba$_4$-ti.

[ -*g*]*i* **8** o. V 5: (48 garments, 48 kilts) X. *Ib-lu*$_5$*-zú wa I-za-iš-ru*$_{12}$ lú-kar *Ma-nu-wa-ad*$^{ki}$ ki:lam$_7$ šeš-⸢ib⸣[-II] *ʾÀ-da-ni*$^{ki}$.

[ ]-⸢*ig*⸣ **4** r. VII 9: X. maškim *A-ag.*

[ -]*il* **9** o. XVIII x+1: [ ] X. šu-ba$_4$-ti.

[ ]-⸢*lum*⸣ **25** r. IV 2: X. *ba-da-lum Ù-ti-gú*$^{ki}$ 2 maškim *A-ag.*

[ -]*ma*-[x] **16** o. XIII 2: [ ] X. ugula sur$_x$-B[AR.AN] *Zú-ba*[*-núm*] *in Na-gàr*$^{ki}$.

⸢x-x⸣-*ma* **20** o. I 15: 3 *li-im* ĜIŠ-gu-kak-gíd zabar X.

⸢x-*na*⸣-*ra-tum* **8** r. IX x+1: [ ] X. *Da-ḫi-ir-ma-lik maš-ar-tum.*

[ -N]E$^?$-[N]E **13** r. XII 12: [ ] X *Ma-rí*$^{ki}$ *in* ⸢x⸣-[x-]*ma*-⸢x⸣ šu-ba$_4$-ti.

⸢X⸣-NE-[X] **22** r. VII 14: 13 dib *Bù-da-ì Íl-a-šar Gal-za-iš-lu Ga-du-um Iš-má-da-mu Da-da-ì* X. *En-na-ma-lik Ig-rí-iš Gur-an-da-mu Ru*$_{12}$*-zi-li-im Iš-ma-da-ba-an Zé-da-mu.*

[X-N]E[- ] **8** r. VIII 3': 1 ĝír mar-tu *ba-du-u*$_4$ kg X. lú *Ḫáb-la-ar.*

[ -]N[E] **11** o. III 10: (100 garments, 50 kilts, 93 KIN measures of wool, 7 daggers) … 22 gud-gud [ ] X šu-ba$_4$-ti ki:lam$_7$ *gi-ba-ù* [*wa*] $^{d}$*A-d*[*am-*]*ma ʾÀ-da-ni*$^{ki}$.

⸢X-X-X⸣ **7** r. XI 13: (silver) níĝ-ba *Gul-la* X. *Sa-ma-na-nu* [*S*]*i-mi*[- ] [ ] *Iš-ba-ì A-ša*$^{ki}$ *in* ud DU.DU nam-kud é $^{d}$*Ku-ra.*

⸢X⸣[- ] **19** r. XVI 1: ⸢1⸣ [d]ib X. lú nídba ì-ĝiš; **25** r. II 4: [ ] X. *Ì-ra-ar*$^{ki}$ *in* ud DU *M*[*a*]*-za-t*[*um*$^{?ki}$]

# Divine names

$^{d}$*ʾÀ-da* **2** r. IV 8: 2 *ḫa-bù* ... níĝ-ba $^{d}$*Ra-sa-ap ʾÀ-da-ni*$^{ki}$ *wa* $^{d}$*ʾÀ*. $^{d}$AMA-*ra*; **3** o. XI 11: 1 ĜIŠ-banšur ... [níĝ-ba] $^{[d]}$*ʾÀ*. lú *Du-ub*$^{ki}$; o. XIV 5: [1 *ḫa-*]*b*[*ù*] ... níĝ-ba $^{d}$*ʾÀ*.; **4** r. IV 22: 2 *ḫa-bù* níĝ-ba $^{d}$*Ra-sa-ap* lú *ʾÀ-da-ni*$^{ki}$ *wa* $^{d}$*ʾÀ*.; r. XII 3: níĝ-ba $^{d}$*ʾÀ*.; **5** o. VII 20: 1 gud ... 1 gud ... nídba en $^{d}$*ʾÀ*. ... 4 si-*sù in* AMA-*ra*; o. VIII 8: 2 gud nídba en $^{d}$*ʾÀ*. *ʾÀ-da-ni*$^{ki}$ ... 4 si-*sù in* AMA-*ra*; r. X 13 and 15: 1 *ḫa-bu* ... níĝ-ba $^{d}$*ʾÀ*. ... *ʾà-na-gu* si 2 gud lú en nídba $^{d}$*ʾÀ*.; r. XI 5: *ʾà-na-gu* si 2 gud lú *Ib-rí-um* nídba $^{d}$*ʾÀ*. *in* iti *ʾa*$_5$-nun, 19: (5 garments) … 61 gud ki:lam$_7$ $^{d}$*ʾÀ*. *in* iti *ʾa*$_5$*-nun*; **6** o. VII 4: 1 *za-ḫa-da ra-ʾà-tum* kg níĝ-ba $^{d}$*ʾÀ*. ì-na-sum; o. VIII 3: 1 ĜIŠ-banšur níĝ-ba $^{d}$*ʾÀ*. lú *Lu-ub*$^{ki}$; o. X 5: zi-du$_8$ en $^{d}$*ʾÀ*.; r. I 3: 2 *ḫa-bù* níĝ-ba $^{d}$*Ra-sa-ap ʾÀ-da-ni*$^{ki}$ *wa* $^{d}$*ʾÀ*. $^{d}$AMA-*ra*; r. XIII 14: (102 garments) … 1 útul tur … 1 ĝír kg … 4 gud … *gàr-su* NI-*a-ba-mu* šu-ba$_4$-ti ki:lam$_7$ $^{d}$*ʾÀ*.; **7** o. XII 13: 1 ešda ... *ʾa*$_5$*-na-gu* 4 si 2 gud nídba en $^{d}$*ʾÀ*. *in* $^{d}$AMA-*ra*; o. XVII 13: (34 garments, 226 kilts, 2 daggers) … 33 gud-gud ki:lam$_7$ $^{d}$*ʾÀ*.; o. XVIII 6: 1 g[ír] mar[-tu] kg $^{d}$*ʾÀ*.(?); r. VII 14: (9 shells, 49 garments, 400 na$_4$ measures of wool, carapaces) … 1 *li-im* ĜIŠ-gu-kak-gíd … 24 *gàr-su* NI-*la-ba-mu* šu-ba$_4$-ti ki:lam$_7$ $^{d}$*ʾÀ*.; r. VIII 5: 1 ešda ... níĝ-ba $^{d}$*ʾÀ*. *in* iti *ʾa*$_5$*-nun*; **9** o. III 19: [ ] [*a*]*r-ra-sa-su* níĝ-ba $^{d}$*Ra-sa-ap ʾÀ-da-ni*$^{ki}$ *wa* $^{d}$*ʾÀ*. *Ḫa-lab*$_x^{ki}$ AMA-*ra*; o. IV 11: si-si 2 gud nídba en $^{d}$*ʾÀ*. [*Ḫ*]*a-lab*$_x^{ki}$ [*i*]*n* AMA-*ra*; **10** o. V 7: 1 *ḫa-bù* … 1 *ar-ra-sù* níĝ-ba $^{d}$*ʾÀ*.; o. XI 14: 4 si-si 2 gud lú en nídba $^{d}$*ʾÀ*. *in* AMA-*ra*; r. VII 5: (76 garments) … ĜIŠ-ti-ḪAR *Wa-ba-rúm* šu-ba$_4$-ti … *gàr-su* NI-*la-ba-mu* [šu-ba$_4$-ti] … (gold) en *A-la-u*$_9^{[ki]}$ *in* ⸢ki⸣:lam$_7$ $^{d}$*ʾÀ*.; **11** o. IV 14: *maš-ar-tum* níĝ-ba dumu-munus [*I*]*b-rí-*[*u*]*m* é-gi *Zi-ba-da* é $^{d}$*ʾÀ*.; o. XI 6: [1 *ar-r*]*a-*[*sù*] … *ʾa*$_5$*-na-gu* 4 si 2 gud nídba en $^{d}$*ʾÀ*. *in* AMA-*ra*; r. IV 10: 1 ešda níĝ-ba $^{d}$*ʾÀ*. lú *Lu-ub*$^{ki}$ *in gi*-NI; r. VIII 16: 1 ešda … *ʾa*$_5$*-n*[*a-gu*] 1[+3 si 2 gud] ⸢nídba⸣ en $^{d}$*ʾÀ*. lú *Ḫa-lab*$_x^{ki}$ *in* iti *ʾa*$_5$*-nun*; **12** r. I 16: 1 *ḫa-*⸢*bù*⸣ … 1 *ar-ra-sù* níĝ-ba $^{d}$*ʾÀ*.; r. II 5: *ʾa*$_5$*-na-gu* 4 si-si 2 gud nídba en $^{d}$*ʾÀ*. *in* iti *ʾa*$_5$*-nun*; r. III 10: (39 garments, 18 kilts, 18 na$_4$ measures of wool) … 80 gud-gud ki:lam$_7$ $^{d}$*ʾÀ*.; **13** r. IV 6: [1 *ḫa-bù*] níĝ[-ba] $^{d}$*ʾÀ*. lú *Lu-ub*$^{ki}$; r. X 14: (90+[x] garments, 526 kilts) … 10 gud … 22 [ ] [ki:]⸢lam$_7$⸣ *Si-*⸢*ʾà*⸣*-mu*$^{ki}$ *wa* ki:lam$_7$ $^{d}$*ʾÀ*.; **14** o. X 13: 1 *ḫa-bù* $^{d}$*ʾÀ*.; r. II 20: 1 *ḫa-bù* … 1 *ar-ra-su-sù* níĝ-ba $^{d}$*ʾÀ*. lú *Lu-ub*$^{ki}$ [*i*]*n* [*gi*-NI]; **15** r. I 12: 1 *ḫa-bù* … 1 ⸢*ar*⸣*-ra-su*[*-su*] níĝ-ba $^{d}$*ʾÀ*. *Lu-u*[*b*$^{ki}$] [*i*]*n g*[*i*-NI]; r. III 6: 1 ĝír mar-tu níĝ-ba *Ib-rí-um* $^{d}$*ʾÀ*. *gi*-NI; r. IV 4: 10 *gàr-su* ki:lam$_7$ $^{d}$*ʾÀ*. *wa* 10 lá-2 *gàr-su* ki:lam$_7$ SA.ZA$_x^{ki}$; r. V 22: 1 ĝír mar-tu kg *Ib-rí-um áš-du* ĝír mar-tu-*sù* sikil $^{d}$*ʾÀ*.; r. IX 21: 1 *ḫa-bù* … 1 *ar-ra-sù* kg sikil … *ʾa*$_5$*-na-gu* 4 si 2 gud nídba en $^{d}$*ʾÀ*. *in* iti *ʾa*$_5$*-nun*; r. XII 7: 2 *gú-li-lum* …1 dib en *áš-du* dib-*sù* sikil $^{d}$*ʾÀ*. *al*$_6$ tu-ra ama-gal-*sù*, 28: 2 *gú-li-lum Ib-rí-um áš-du* 2 *gù-li-lum-sù* sikil $^{d}$*ʾÀ*. *al*$_6$ tu-ra en; r. XIII 8: 1 dib *Ib-rí-um áš-du* 1 dib-*sù* sikil $^{d}$*ʾÀ*. *al*$_6$ tu-ra en; **16** r. I 20: 1 *ḫa-bù ap* kg ⸢sikil⸣ … *ʾa*$_5$*-na-gu* si 2 gud [níd]ba en $^{d}$*ʾÀ*. *in* $^{d}$AMA-*ra*; r. VII 22: 1 *ḫa-bù* … 1 *ar-ra-sù* níĝ-ba $^{d}$*ʾÀ*. lú *Lu-ub*$^{ki}$ *in gi*-NI; r. XI 9: 1 *ḫa-bù ap* kg sikil … *ʾa*$_5$*-na-gu* si 2 gud nídba en $^{d}$*ʾÀ*. *Ḫa-lab*$_x^{ki}$ *in* iti *ʾa*$_5$*-nun*, 21: (32 garments, 20 KIN measures of wool) … 29 *gàr-su* ki:lam$_7$ $^{d}$*ʾÀ*.; **17** r. XV 16: 1 *ḫa-bù* … 1 *ar-ra-si-sù* níĝ-ba $^{d}$*ʾÀ*. lú *Lu-ub*$^{ki}$ *in gi*-NI; r. XX 17: (28+[x] garments, 49 kilts) … 33 *gàr-su* … ĜIŠ-bar-ús ki:lam$_7$ $^{d}$*ʾÀ*.; **18** o. XIX 22: 1 *ḫa-bù ap* kg sikil … *ar-ra-sù* … *ʾa*$_5$*-na-gu* si 2 gud nídba en $^{d}$*ʾÀ*. *Ḫa-lab*$_x^{ki}$ *in* $^{d}$AMA-*ra*; r. XI 8: 1 *ḫa-bù* … *ar-ra-sù* níĝ-ba $^{d}$*ʾÀ*. lú *Lu-ub*$^{ki}$ *in gi*-NI; r. XVIII 2: 1 *ḫa-bù ap* kg sikil … *ʾa*$_5$*-na-gu* si 2 gud nídba en $^{[d]}$*ʾÀ*. *Ḫa-lab*$_x^{ki}$ *ʾa*$_5$*-nun*; **19** o. IV 6: (gold) lul-gu-ak 1 iti lú é $^{d}$*ʾÀ*. lú-máš; o. V 16: 1 *li-im* ĜIŠ-gu-kak-g[íd] zabar … 1 ĜIŠ-gu-kak-gíd … 1 dib *I-bí-zi-kir* dumu-nita *Ib-rí-um áš-du* dib-*sù* sikil $^{d}$*ʾÀ*.; o. XI 16: 1 *ḫa-bù ap* … *ar-ra-sù* kg sikil … *ʾa*$_5$*-na-gu* si 2 gud nídba $^{d}$*ʾÀ*. *Ḫa-lab*$_x^{ki}$ *in* $^{d}$AMA-*ra*; r. VI 10: 1 dub lú nam-kud en *wa Ib-rí-um* é $^{d}$*ʾÀ*., 16: 1 dub *ma-lik-*[*t*]*um* [ ] ⸢é⸣ $^{d}$⸢*ʾÀ*⸣.; r. VIII 27: 1 *ḫa-bù* … 1 *ar-ra-sù* níĝ-ba $^{d}$*ʾÀ*. lú *Lu-ub*$^{ki}$ *in gi*-NI; r. XVII 6: (36 garments) … 7 *gàr-su* … ĜIŠ-*šè-bir*$_5$*-gi-nu* ĜIŠ-bar-ús ki:lam$_7$ $^{d}$*ʾÀ*., 15: 1 *ḫa-bù ap* kg sikil … *ʾa*$_5$*-na-gu* si 2 gud nídba en $^{d}$*ʾÀ*. *Ḫa-lab*$_x^{ki}$ *ʾa*$_5$*-nun*; **20** o. IX 3: 1 [*ḫa-bù*] … 1 *ar-ra-sù* … *ʾa*$_5$*-*[*n*]*a-gu* 4 si gud nídba en $^{d}$*ʾÀ*. *Ḫa-lab*$_x^{ki}$ *in* AMA-*ra*; o. XVI 13: 1 íb-lá 1 *si-ti-tum* 1 ĝír-kun TAR kg sikil $^{d}$*ʾÀ*.; r. VII 18: níĝ-ba $^{d}$*ʾÀ*. lú *Lu-ub*$^{ki}$ *in gi*-NI nu$_{11}$-za ab-*sù*; r. XI 14: 1 *ḫa-bù ap* … *ar-ra-sù* kg si[kil] … *ʾa*$_5$*-na-gu* 4 si 2 gud nídba en $^{d}$*ʾÀ*. *Ḫa-lab*$_x^{ki}$ iti *ʾa*$_5$*-nun*; r. XIII 11: (39 garments) … ĜIŠ-ti-ḪAR *Wa-ba-rúm* šu-ba$_4$-ti ki:lam$_7$ $^{d}$*ʾÀ*.; **21** o. VII 19: 1 dib 1 íb-lá 1 *si-ti-tum* 1 ĝír-kun … 1 ĝír mar-tu kg ⸢*ra*⸣*-ʾà-*[*tu*]*m* … 3 *z*[*ú-*]*zú-b*[*a-*]*tum* ĜIŠ-gígir-II *Ib-rí-um* šu-mu-tak$_4$ é $^{d}$*ʾÀ*.; o. VIII 4: [ ] *wa* šu-mu-tak$_4$ é $^{d}$*ʾÀ*., 21: 1 níĝ-anše-ak 1 kù-sal IGI.NITA … 1 *za-ḫa-da* … lul-gu-ak lú sikil é $^{d}$*ʾÀ*. *al*$_6$ tu-ra *Ib-rí-um*; o. IX 3: [ ] níd-ba en $^{d}$*ʾÀ*. lú *Ḫa-lab*$_x^{ki}$; o. XV 11: 1 *ḫa-bù* … 1 *ar-ra-sù* níĝ-ba $^{d}$*ʾÀ*. *Lu-ub*$^{ki}$ *in gi*:NI; r. II 25: (49 garments, 313 kilts, 60 na$_4$ measures of wool) … 1 ĜIŠ-*ba-ri-zú* ĜIŠ.GAM.GAM.GAM … 1 *mi-at* 50 ĜIŠ-ti-ḪAR *wa* níĝ-NE *Wa-ba-rúm* šu-ba$_4$$^{!}$-ti$^{!}$(ŠU.BAL.AK) … 13 *gàr-su* ki:lam$_7$ $^{d}$*Áš-da-bíl wa* ki:lam$_7$ *Ši-ʾà-am*$^{ki}$ *wa* k[i:lam$_7$] $^{d}$*ʾÀ*.; r. VIII 2: 1 nu$_{11}$-za *ḫa-bù* … *ʾa*$_5$*-na-gu* si 2 gud nídba [en $^{d}$*ʾÀ*. *in* $^{d}$AMA-*ra*], 18: 1 íb-lá 1 *si-ti-tum* 1 ĝír-kun lú en sikil $^{d}$*ʾÀ*. *al*$_6$ tu-ra *I-bí-zi-kir*; **22** r. I 9: 1 ma-na kg sikil $^{d}$*ʾÀ*.; **23** o. I 4: 1 dib maḫ lú ĜIŠ-ĝidru-ĜIŠ-ĝidru in-na-sum $^{d}$*ʾÀ*. *Ḫa-lab*$_x^{ki}$ *in* AMA-*ra* en šu-mu-tak$_4$; o. II 10: 1 ab é $^{d}$*ʾÀ*. lú *Lu-ub*$^{ki}$; r. II 3: 1 *ar-ra-šum* 1 *ḫa-bù* níĝ-ba $^{d}$*ʾÀ*. lú *Lu-ub*$^{ki}$ *gi*-NI; r. IV 7: 1 *ar-ra-šum* 1 *ḫa-bù* níĝ-ba $^{d}$*ʾÀ*. lú *Ḫa-lab*$_x^{ki}$ *in* iti *ʾa*$_5$*-nun*; **25** o. VIII 4: (18+[x] garments, 2+[x] kilts, 1 dagger) ki:lam$_7$ $^{d}$*ʾÀ*. *wa gi-ba-lu ʾÀ-da-ni*$^{ki}$.

$^{d}$*ʾA*$_5$*-da-"bal"* **2** o. IV 19: 1 *ḫa-bù* ... níĝ-ba *Ib-rí-um* $^{d}$*ʾA*$_5$. *ʾÀ-ma-ad*$^{ki}$; r. VIII 23: maš-maš 1 "KIN" siki wa 1 kù-sal ... níĝ-ba *Ib-rí-um* $^{d}$*ʾA*$_5$. *La-ru*$_{12}$*-ga-du*$^{ki}$;

**3** o. IV 19: 1 *ḫa-bù* ... níĝ-ba $^{d}$ʾA$_5$. *La-ru*$_{12}$*-ga-du*$^{ki}$ *Ib-rí-um* ì-na-sum; r. XI 2: [ ] níĝ-ba $^{d}$ʾA$_5$. *La-ru*$_{12}$*-ga-du*$^{ki}$ *Ib-rí-um* ì-na-sum; **4** o. II 15: 1 c [níĝ-ba] [$^{d}$]⌜ʾA$_5$⌝. *L*[*a-r*]*u*$_{12}$*-ga*[*-du*]$^{ki}$; **5** r. IV 2: 1 ĝír mar-tu ... 1 kù-sal níĝ-ba $^{d}$ʾA$_5$. *Lu-ba-an*$^{ki}$ *Ib-rí-um* ì-na-sum *in* ud ne:saĝ-*sù*; r. V 20: 1 ĜIŠ-banšur ... 3 saĝ lu$_x$ ... urudu-*sù* níĝ-b[a] $^{d}$ʾA$_5$. *La-ru*$_{12}$*-ga-du*$^{ki}$ en ì-na-sum; r. IX 1: 1 ĜIŠ-banšur níĝ-ba *I-bí-zi-kir* dumu-nita *Ib-rí-um* $^{d}$ʾA$_5$. *La-ru*$_{12}$*-ga-du*$^{ki}$; r. XIII 22: 1 ĝír mar-tu níĝ-ba $^{d}$ʾA$_5$. *ʾÀ-ma-du*$^{ki}$ *Ib-rí-um* ì-na-sum; **6** o. XIV 15: 1 *ḫa-bù* níĝ-ba $^{d}$ʾA$_5$. *La-ru*$_{12}$*-zàr-du*$^{ki}$; **7** r. IV 9: [1 ĜIŠ-banšur] ... 1 kù-sal níĝ-ba $^{d}$ʾA$_5$. [*Lu-b*]*a-an*$^{[ki]}$; **8** o. VII 5: 1 ĝír mar-tu níĝ-ba $^{d}$ʾA$_5$. *ʾÀ-ma-du*$^{ki}$; **11** r. V 19: 1 ešda níĝ-ba $^{d}$ʾA$_5$. [ ] *in* ud NI.DU; **12** o. II 10: (17 garments, 263 kilts) … 10 […] … 2 IGI.NITA *Bù-da-ma-lik* šu-ba$_4$-ti … raš-SAR Kur$^{ki}$ ki:lam$_7$ $^{d}$*Ga-mi-iš* *wa* ki:lam$_7$ $^{d}$ʾA$_5$. *A-ru*$_{12}$*-ga-du*$^{ki}$; o. III 17: *ba-na-i-su-ma* *wa* 2 šu-šu-*sù* 2 DU.DU-*sù* níĝ-ba $^{d}$ʾA$_5$. [*A-*]*ru*$_{12}$-[*ga-d*]*u*$^{ki}$ [e]n [*i*]*n* [ ]; r. VII 16: 1 ĝír mar-tu … 1 kù-sal níĝ-ba *Ib-rí-um* $^{d}$ʾA$_5$. *Ne-a-ù*$^{ki}$; **13** r. IV 11: 1 *ḫa-bù* níĝ-ba $^{d}$ʾA$_5$. *A-ru*$_{12}$*-ga-du*$^{ki}$; **14** r. VI 11: 1 ĜIŠ-banšur maḫ … urudu-*sù* … *ʾa*$_5$*-na-gu-sù* [níĝ-ba] $^{d}$ʾA$_5$. *A-ma-du*$^{ki}$ en šu-mu-tak$_4$; r. VII 4: 1 ĜIŠ-asar … 4 saĝ lu$_x$ *al*$_6$*-sù* níĝ-ba $^{d}$ʾA$_5$. *Ne-a-ù*$^{<ki>}$ *Ib-rí-um* šu-mu-tak$_4$; **15** o. II 23: 1 *gú-li-lum a-li-iš* ĜIŠ-gu-kak-gíd $^{d}$ʾA$_5$. [ ]$^{ki}$ en ì-na-sum *in* ud šeš-II-ib; o. XIV 11: 1 ĝír mar-tu kg en *áš-du* 1 ĝír mar-tu-*sù* sikil $^{d}$ʾA$_5$. *Lu-ba-an*$^{ki}$; r. VI 3: 1 ⌜íb⌝-lá 1 *si-ti-tum* 1 ĝír-kun sikil $^{d}$ʾA$_5$. *Lu-ba-an*$^{ki}$ *Ib-rí-um* šu-mu-tak$_4$ *al*$_6$ tu-ra-*sù*; r. XII 15: 2 *gú-li-lum-sù* sikil $^{d}$ʾA$_5$. *Lu-ba-an*$^{ki}$ *al*$_6$ tu-ra-*sù*; r. XVI 1: 1 *gú-bù* kg libir … 1 ĝír mar-tu kg en *áš-du* ĝír mar-tu-*sù* sikil $^{d}$ʾA$_5$. *Lu-ba-an*$^{ki}$; **16** r. X 23: 1 ĝír mar-tu *wa* 1 kù-sal níĝ-ba *Ib-rí-um* $^{d}$ʾA$_5$. *A-ru*$_{12}$*-ga-du*$^{ki}$; **18** o. XII 22: 1 *a-ba-lum* níĝ-ba $^{d}$ʾA$_5$. *ʾÀ-ma-du*$^{ki}$ *Ib-rí-um*; r. XVII 5: 2 ĝír mar-tu … 2 kù-sal níĝ-ba ama-gal en $^{d}$*Ra-sa-ap Du-ne-íb*$^{ki}$ *wa* $^{d}$ʾA$_5$. *ʾÀ-ma-du*$^{ki}$ NI.DU; **19** o. XI 27 and 30: 2 gí[r] mar-tu *wa* 2 kù-sal níĝ-ba $^{d}$ʾA$_5$. *A-ru*$_{12}$*-ga-du*$^{ki}$ *wa* $^{d}$ʾA$_5$. *ʾÀ-ma-du*$^{ki}$ [ ]-⌜x⌝ [šu-m]u-tak$_4$ *al*$_6$ tu-ra-*sù*; r. VIII 13: 6 še-šu-še-tag *wa* 1 buru$_4$-MUŠEN níĝ-ba $^{d}$ʾA$_5$. *wa* $^{d}$BAD-munus *A-ru*$_{12}$*-ga-du*$^{ki}$ ama-gal en šu-mu-tak$_4$; **20** o. XVI 19: 1 íb-lá 1 *si-ti-tum* 1 ĝír-kun sikil $^{d}$ʾA$_5$. lú *Lu-ba-an*$^{ki}$ *al*$_6$ tu-ra *Ib-rí-um* tak$_4$; r. III 24: 1 kù-sal níĝ-ba *Dar-ib-da-mu* dumu-munus en $^{d}$BAD-munus *si-in Lu-ba-an*$^{ki}$ *in* ud *ter*$_6$*-bí* bur-KAK-*sù* $^{d}$ʾA$_5$.; **21** r. X 24: (gold) lul-gu-ak 1 zi-bar en *ša-ti* sikil $^{d}$ʾA$_5$. *Lu-ba-an*$^{ki}$; **22** r. VII 3: 1 [*ar-r*]*a-sù ḫa-bù* níĝ-ba $^{d}$ʾA$_5$. *ʾÀ-ma-du*$^{ki}$; **23** r. II 10: 1 *ar-ra-šum* 1 *ḫa-bù* níĝ-ba $^{d}$ʾA$_5$. *ʾÀ-ma-du*$^{ki}$ en šu-mu-tak$_4$ *in* ud NI.DU-NI.DU; **24** o. VI 9: 1 *ar-ra-sù* 1 *ḫa-bù* níĝ-ba en $^{d}$ʾA$_5$. *A-ru*$_{12}$*-ga-du*$^{ki}$.

$^{d}$ʾ*A*$_5$*-da-ra* **2** o. XII 5: saĝ $^{d}$ʾA$_5$; r. XI 19: 1 íb-lá níĝ-ba $^{d}$ʾA$_5$; **9** r. VIII 17: *ba-na-ʾà-sa wa* íb+III-TÚG [*w*]*a* an-zam$_x$ *wa* 2 *gú-li-lum-su* níĝ-ba $^{d}$ʾA$_5$.; **12** o. V 20: 2 kù-sal [ní]g-ba $^{<d>}$BE *Ga-na-na-im* [*w*]*a* $^{d}$ʾA$_5$.

$^{d}$*A-da-ma* **2** o. XI 2: (13 kilts) … ĜIŠ-sal [*Wa-ba-*]*rúm* šu-ba$_4$-ti ki:lam$_7$ $^{d}$*A*.; **3** r. XIII 13: (194 kilts) … ĜIŠ-ti-ḪAR *Wa-ba-rúm* ki:lam$_7$ $^{d}$*A*. *wa* ki:lam$_7$ bàd-diĝir$^{ki}$; **5** o. II 6: (65 garments, 210+[x] kilts, 8 daggers, 354 na$_4$ measures of wool) … ĜIŠ-ti-ḪAR ĜIŠ-ád *Wa-ba-rúm* "ur$_4$" šu-ba$_4$-ti ki:lam$_7$ $^{<d>}$*A*. *ʾÀ-da-ni*$^{ki}$; **6** o. XI 4: ĜIŠ-ti-ḪAR ki:lam$_7$ $^{d}$*A*. *ʾÀ-da-ni*$^{ki}$ *Wa-ba-rúm* šu-ba$_4$-ti; **7** o. IX 9: (84+[x] garments, 8 na$_4$ measures of wool) … 96 ĜIŠ-ti-ḪAR *Wa-ba-rúm* šu-ba$_4$-ti … ĜIŠ-ád ki:lam$_7$ $^{d}$*A*. *wa* SA.ZA$_x$$^{ki}$; **13** o. VI 4: (88 kilts, 245 KIN measures of wool) … 20 gud … ĜIŠ-ti-ḪAR *Wa-ba-rúm* šu-ba$_4$-ti ki:lam$_7$ šeš-II-ib *wa* $^{d}$*A*. *ʾÀ-da-ni*$^{ki}$; o. VIII 5: 2 an-dùl … [I]GI.DUB-*sù wa* 4 šu-*sù* 4 DU-*sù* níĝ-ba *Du-si-gú* $^{d}$*Ra-sa-ap* $^{d}$*A*. *ʾÀ-da-ni*$^{ki}$; r. IV 19: 2 an-dùl níĝ-ba *Ib-rí-um* $^{d}$*Ra-sa-ap wa* $^{d}$*A*. *ʾÀ-da-ni*$^{ki}$; **14** r. XII 11: 10 gud *Rí-ì-ma-lik* lú *I-bí-zi-im* ki:lam$_7$ $^{d}$*A*.; **15** o. VII 10: (54 garments, 166 kilts, 385 KIN measures of wool) … ĜIŠ-ti-ḪAR *Wa-ba-rúm* šu-ba$_4$-ti ki:lam$_7$ šeš-II-ib *wa* $^{d}$*A*. *ʾÀ-da-ni*$^{ki}$; **17** r. XVI 7: 2 *bu*-DI níĝ-ba $^{d}$*A*. *gú-núm ma-lik-tum* ì-na-sum *in* ud šu-mu-níĝin é diĝir-diĝir-diĝir; 18 o. X 1: (53 garments, 100 na$_4$ measures of wool) ki:lam$_7$ $^{d}$*A*. *ʾÀ-da-ni*$^{ki}$; **19** o. VII 1: (254 garments, 60 na$_4$ measures of wool) … ĜIŠ-ti-ḪAR ki:lam$_7$ $^{d}$*A*. *ʾÀ-da-ni*$^{ki}$; **24** o. V 10: IGI.DUB 2 an-dùl *wa* 2 šu-*sù* 2 DU-*sù* níĝ-ba *Ib-rí-um* $^{d}$*Ra-sa-ap wa* $^{d}$*A*. *ʾÀ-da-ni*$^{ki}$ *in ma-ʾà-wa-tum*; **25** o. II 8: (121+[x] garments, 102 kilts) ki:lam$_7$ SA.ZA$_x$$^{ki}$ *wa* $^{d}$*A*. *ʾÀ-da-ni*$^{ki}$.

$^{d}$*A-dam-ma* **11** o. IV 2: (100 garments, 50 kilts, 93 KIN measures of wool, 7 daggers) … 22 gud-gud [ ] [ -]N[E] šu-ba$_4$-ti ki:lam$_7$ *gi-ba-ù* [*wa*] $^{d}$*A*. *ʾÀ-da-ni*$^{ki}$.

$^{d}$*A-dar-a-an* **15** r. XI 6: [1 ĝír mar-tu] [*w*]*a* 1 kù-sal níĝ-ba *Ib-rí-um* $^{d}$*A*. *Da-na-áš*$^{ki}$; **16** o. XIV 12: 1 kù-sal [$^{d}$*A*.] *Da-na-áš*$^{ki}$ en šu-mu-tak$_4$.

$^{d}$*A-dar-a-nu* **21** o. VI 22: 1 kù-sal níĝ-ba *Ib-rí-um* $^{d}$*A*. [*D*]*a-na-*[*á*]*š*$^{ki}$.

$^{d}$*A-gi* **13** r. V 6: [ ] kin$_5$-ak $^{d}$*A*. *Su-ti-ig*$^{ki}$; **24** o. VI 13: (gold) kin$_5$-ak $^{d}$*A*. *Su-ti-gú*$^{ki}$.

$^{d}$*Á-la* **2** r. XVI 3: [ ] nu$_{11}$-za-*sù* en $^{d}$*Á Zi-ig*$^{ki}$; **4** r. XI 1: 1 an-dùl níĝ-ba $^{d}$*Á*$^{!}$(DA). *Ib-rí-um* ì-na-sum; **6** r. XIV 7: saĝ $^{d}$*Á*. *wa Da-bí-na-ad* lú *A-ra-ab*$^{ki}$; r. XVII 30: $^{d}$*Á*. *wa* dam-*sù* lú *A-ra-ab*$^{ki}$; **10** o. IV 13: lú DU.DU lu$_x$ tuš $^{d}$*Á*. lú *Zi-ig*$^{ki}$; **13** o. VI 25: $^{d}$*Á*. *Zi-gú*$^{ki}$; **19** r. XII 9: lú ĜIŠ-gígir-II $^{d}$*Á*. *Gú-šè-bù*$^{ki}$; **21** r. XI 12: [ -]ak al$_6$-tuš $^{d}$*Á*. *Gú-šè-bù*$^{ki}$.

$^{d}$*A-lum* **6** r. XVI 21: (tin) $^{d}$*A*. *wa* $^{d}$*Si-gar A-ḫa-da-mu*$^{ki}$.

$^{d}$*Am-ma-rí-ig* **2** r. XIV 8: 1 *ḫa-bù* ... 2 *gú-li-lum* níĝ-ba en $^{d}$*A*.; **3** o. XII 16: 1 an-dùl ... níĝ-ba $^{d}$*A*., 20: ⌜2⌝ [*gú-*]*l*[*i-lum*] níĝ-b[a] $^{d}$*A*.; **5** r. VIII 14: 2 *gú-li-lum* $^{c}$*A*.; **7** r. IV 19: 1 ĜIŠ-banšur ... 1 kù-sal níĝ-ba $^{d}$*A*.; r. XIV 11: 2 *gú-li-lum* níĝ-ba $^{d}$*A*.; **10** o. II 10: 1 ĜIŠ-banšur … 1 saĝ ⌜lu$_x$⌝ 1 ĜIŠ-banšur níĝ-ba $^{d}$*A*.; **12** o. IX 2: 2 *gú-li-lum* níĝ-ba $^{d}$*A*.; **13** r. V 18: 2 *gú-li-lum* níĝ-ba $^{d}$*A*.; **14** r. V 4: [2] *gú-*[*l*]*i-lum* [níĝ-ba] $^{d}$*A*.; **15** r. IV 18: 2 *gú-li-lum* níĝ-ba $^{d}$*A*.; **17** r. XVI 24: 2 *gú-li-lum* níĝ-ba $^{d}$*A*.; **20** r. IX 6: 2 *gú-li-lum* níĝ-ba [ ] *En-na-il* [ ] $^{d}$*A*.; **21** o. XVII 16: 2 *gú-li-lum* níĝ-ba $^{d}$*A*.

$^{d}$ʾ*À-ma-rí-ig* **4** o. XII 13: 2 *gù-li-lum* $^{d}$ʾ*À*.; **6** r. VI 22: 2 *gú-li-lum* níĝ-ba $^{d}$ʾ*À*.;

$^{d}$*Am-rí-ig* **11** r. IV 21: 2 *gú-li-lum* níĝ-ba $^{d}$*A*.; r. V 6: 1 ĝír mar-tu níĝ-ba $^{d}$*A*.; **16** r. VII 2: 2 *gú-li-lum* níĝ-ba $^{d}$*A*.; **18** r. XV 19: 2 *gú-li-lum* $^{d}$*A*.; **19** r. IX 14: 1 *ḫa-bù* … 1 *ar-ra-sù wa* … 2 *gú-li-lum* níĝ-ba $^{d}$*A*.

$^{d}$*A-na-ma-du* **24** o. II 7: 1 ĝír mar-tu *wa* 2 kù-sal níĝ-ba $^{d}$*A. Ar-ḫa-du*$^{ki}$ *Bù-du-mi* šu-mu-tak$_4$.

$^{d}$*Áš-da-bíl* **2** r. XIII 18: 2 *gú-li-lum* níĝ-ba $^{d}$*Á.*; r. XVII 7: [ ] 1 ĝír mar-tu kg … ĜIŠ-ti-ḪAR *Wa-ba-rúm* ki:lam$_7$ $^{d}$*Á.*; **3** o. X 6': ĜIŠ-ti-ḪAR *Wa-ba-rúm* šu-ba$_4$-ti ki:lam$_7$ $^{d}$*Á.*; r. IV 3: 2 *gú-li-lum* níĝ-ba $^{d}$*Á.*; **5** r. VIII 3: 2 *gú-li-lum* $^{d}$*Á.*; r. IX 13: (3 garments, 253 kilts) … ĜIŠ-ti-ḪAR *W.* šu-ba$_4$-ti ki:lam$_7$ $^{d}$*Á.*; **6** r. XII 12: (10 garments, 10 kilts) ki:lam$_7$ $^{d}$*Á.*; **7** r. V 17: 2 *gú-li-lum* [ní]g-ba $^{d}$*Á.*, 23: 1 ĝír mar-tu níĝ-ba $^{d}$*Á. Ib-rí-um* in-na-sum; r. VI 18: (43 garments, 265 kilts) ki:lam$_7$ $^{d}$*Á. wa* [*Ši-*]⌜*ʾà*⌝*-mu*$^{ki}$; **9** o. XIII 16: 2 *gú-li-lum* níĝ-⌜ba⌝ $^{d}$*Á.*; o. XIV 7: (100+[x] garments, 14 kilts) ki:lam$_7$ $^{d}$*Á.*; **11** r. III 6: (78 garments, [x] kilts) ki:lam$_7$ SA.ZA$_x$$^{ki}$ $^{d}$*Á. Ši-ʾà-mu*$^{ki}$; **12** o. VIII 7: 2 *gú-li-lum* níĝ-ba $^{d}$*Á.*, 14: (32 garments, 361 kilts) ki:lam$_7$ $^{d}$*Á.*; **13** r. V 15: (93 garments, 512 kilts) ki:lam$_7$ $^{d}$*Á.*; **14** r. V 1: [2 *gú-li-lum* níĝ-ba $^{d}$*Á.*], 8: (39 kilts) [ ] [ki:lam$_7$] $^{d}$*Á.*; **15** r. IV 14: 2 *gú-li-lum* níĝ-ba $^{d}$*Á.*; r. XIV 5: 1 buru$_4$-MU[ŠEN] [ ] [níĝ-]ba $^{d}$*Á. Ba-šè*$^{ki}$ *Ib-rí-um* šu-mu-tak$_4$; r. XVI 9: [1 ĝír mar-t]u kg *Ib-rí-um áš-du* ĝír mar-tu-*sù* sikil $^{d}$*Á. al*$_6$ tu-ra en; **16** r. VI 25: 2 *gú-li-lum* níĝ-ba $^{d}$*Á.*; **17** r. XVI 20: 2 *gú-li-lum* níĝ-ba $^{d}$*Á.*; r. XVIII 5: ([…] garments, 233 kilts) ki:lam$_7$ $^{d}$*Á. Du-ub*$^{ki}$ *Ìr-ku*$^{ki}$; **18** r. XIII 13: (168 garments, 340 na$_4$ measures of wool) ki:lam$_7$ $^{d}$*Ga-mi-iš wa* $^{d}$*Á. wa* $^{d}$BAD *Du-du-lu*$^{ki}$; r. XV 17: 2 *gú-li-lum* níĝ-ba $^{d}$*Á.*; **19** r. IX 4: 2 *gú-li-lum* níĝ-ba $^{d}$*Á.*; **21** o. XVII 13: 2 *gú-li-lum* níĝ-ba $^{d}$*Á.*; r. II 19: (49 garments, 313 kilts, 60 na$_4$ measures of wool) … 1 ĜIŠ-*ba-ri-zú* ĜIŠ.GAM.GAM.GAM … 1 *mi-at* 50 ĜIŠ-ti-ḪAR *wa* níĝ-NE *Wa-ba-rúm* šu-ba$_4$$^{!}$-ti$^{!}$(ŠU.BAL.AK) … 13 *gàr-su* ki:lam$_7$ $^{d}$*Á. wa* ki:lam$_7$ *Ši-ʾà-am*$^{ki}$ *wa* k[i:lam$_7$] $^{dʾ}$*À-da*; **23** o. III 4: 2 *gú-li-lum* $^{d}$*Á.*; **24** o. VII 9: 2 *gú-li-lum* níĝ-ba $^{d}$*Á.*; **25** o. VII 4: ([…] garments, 220 kilts) ki:lam$_7$ $^{d}$*Á.*

$^{d}$*Aš-dar* **16** r. XVII 10: 1 kù-sal níĝ-ba $^{d}$*A.* en [x-g]*a*-[x]$^{ki}$; **19** o. VIII 14: 1 banšur *wa* 1 kù-sal níĝ-ba *Ib-rí-um* $^{d}$*A.*

$^{d}$BAD **2** r. VIII 6: 1 an-dùl ... [*ba-na-a*] *wa* íb+III-TÚG níĝ-ba *Ib-rí-um* $^{d}$B. ⌜*Du*⌝*-du-*⌜*la*$^{ki}$⌝; **5** r. VI 12: 2 zi-bar níĝ-ba $^{d}$B. *Má*-NE$^{ki}$ *Du-si-gú* ì-na-sum; **6** o. XIV 2: 1 *ḫa-bù* níĝ-ba $^{d}$B. *Ga-na-na-im*; 7 o. X 3: [ ] *Ib-rí-um* níĝ-ba $^{d}$B. *Du-du-lu*$^{ki}$; **8** o. VI 8: 1 an-dùl níĝ-ba $^{d}$B. *Ga-na-na-um*; r. IX 10': [1 *ḫa-bù*] … *ar-ra-si-su* $^{d}$B. *Ga-na-na-um*; **9** r. VIII 2: 1 *ḫa-bù* … 1 *ar-ra-sù* [níĝ-b]a$^{?}$ $^{d}$B. *Ga-*[*na-*]*na-im*; r. IX 5: 1 an-dùl lú *Ib-rí-um* šu-mu-tak$_4$ $^{d}$B. *Du-du-la*$^{ki}$; **11** r. IV 25: [$^{d}$B.] *Ga-na-na-im* lú *Lu-wa-šum*$^{ki}$; **12** o. V 18: 2 kù-sal [ní]ĝ-ba $^{d}$B.*Ga-na-na-im* [*w*]*a* [$^{d}$NI-*d*]*a*[*-la*]; o. VII 16: 1 ĝír mar-tu níĝ-ba $^{d}$B. *Ar-ti-na-an*$^{ki}$; o. XIV 13 and 15: 2 zi-bar níĝ-ba $^{d}$B. *Má*-NE$^{ki}$ *wa* $^{d}$B. *Zu-ra-mu*$^{ki}$ *Du-si-gú* šu-mu-tak$_4$; **15** o. II 8: 1 ĜIŠ-banšur *wa* 1 kù-sal níĝ-ba *Ib-rí-um* $^{d}$B. *Du-du-lu*$^{ki}$; **16** o. V 18: 1 an-dùl … IGI.DUB-*sù wa* 2 DU-*sù wa* 2 šu-*sù* níĝ-ba $^{d}$B. *Ga-na-na-im*; **17** o. VII 7: *in* kaskal é $^{d}$B. *Ga-na-na*; **18** r. XIII 15: (168 garments, 340 na$_4$ measures of wool) ki:lam$_7$ $^{d}$*Ga-mi-iš wa* $^{d}$*Áš-da-bíl wa* $^{d}$B. *Du-du-lu*$^{ki}$; r. XV 12: 1 an-dùl munus … IGI.DUB-*sa* 2 šu 2 DU-*sù* … 1 an-dùl nita … IGI.DUB-*sù wa* íb-lá *si-ti-tum* íb+III-TÚG … 1 banšur 1 ĝír mar-tu-*sù* níĝ-ba $^{d}$B. *Du-du-lu*$^{ki}$; **19** o. VI 7: níĝ-ba en-en lú *áš-ti* en *Na-gàr*$^{ki}$ DU.DU nam-kud é $^{d}$B. *Du-du-lu*$^{ki}$, **20**: níĝ-ba *ʾÀ-du*$^{ki}$ é $^{d}$B. *Ga-na-na-im* šu-ba$_4$-ti; r. X 28: *ʾa*$_5$*-na-gu* 1 banšur *wa* 1 kù-sal níĝ-ba *Ib-rí-um* $^{d}$B. *Du-du-lu*$^{ki}$; **22** r. VI 1: 1 [*ḫa-bù*] níĝ-ba $^{d}$B. *Du-du-lu*$^{ki}$ … *Ib-rí-um*.

$^{d}$BAD-munus **16** r. XIII 19: 1 *ù*-NAM-*mi-lu* 8 gín D. sikil $^{d}$B. *Lu-ba-an*$^{ki}$; r. XIV 28: 1 šùr dub maḫ … [ ] níĝ[-ba] *Ib-rí-um* $^{d}$B. *Lu-ba-an*$^{ki}$; **19** r. VIII 15: 6 še-šu-še-tag *wa* 1 buru$_4$-MUŠEN níĝ-ba $^{dʾ}$*A*$_5$*-da-"bal"* *wa* $^{d}$B. *A-ru*$_{12}$*-ga-du*$^{ki}$ ama-gal en šu-mu-tak$_4$; **20** r. III 18: 1 kù-sal níĝ-ba *Dar-ib-da-mu* dumu-munus en $^{d}$B. *si-in Lu-ba-an*$^{ki}$ *in* ud *ter*$_6$*-bí* bur-KAK-*sù* $^{dʾ}$*A*$_5$*-da-"bal"*.

$^{d}$*Ba-li-ḫa* **6** r. IV 20: $^{d}$*B.*-II lú 8 bàd$^{ki}$.

$^{d}$*Ba-ra-ma* **2** o. II 7: 1 kù-sal níĝ-ba en $^{d}$*B. in* ud ne:saĝ-*sù*; **14** o. II 8: 1 kù-sal níĝ-ba ama-gal en $^{d}$*B.* [ ]; **17** r. XVIII 115: 1 kù-sal níĝ-ba *Da-bur-da-mu al*$_6$ *gú-a-ti* $^{d}$*B.*; **24** o. VII 4: 1 kù-sal níĝ-ba *Ib-rí-um* $^{d}$*B. in* ud ne:saĝ-*sù*.

$^{d}$*Ba-tum-ma-du* **19** o. II 8: 1 kù-sal níĝ-ba en $^{d}$*B. áš-t*[*i*] ĝír mar-tu-*sù* šu-mu-tak$_4$ *al*$_6$ tu-ra *Ib-rí-um*; o. IX 17: 2 kù-sal níĝ-ba $^{d}$*B. wa* $^{d}$*Da-bí-na-du áš-ti* 2 ĝír mar-tu kg *al*$_6$ tu-ra en.

$^{d}$*Da-bí-ir* **15** r. XI 18: $^{d}$*D.* diĝir *Ib-la*$^{ki}$.

$^{d}$*Da-bí-na-ad* **6** r. XIV 9: saĝ $^{d}$*Á-la wa* $^{d}$*D.* lú *A-ra-ab*$^{ki}$.

*Da-bí-na-du* **19** o. IX 19: 2 kù-sal níĝ-ba $^{d}$*Ba-tum-ma-du wa* $^{d}$*D. áš-ti* 2 ĝír mar-tu kg *al*$_6$ tu-ra en.

$^{d}$*Da-i-in* **6** r. II 17: 1 ĝír mar-tu níĝ-ba $^{d}$*D.* ... *in* ud en e$_{11}$ é $^{d}$*Ga-mi-iš*.

$^{d}$En-ki **11** r. VII 24; **13** o. V 7: 1 ĝír mar-tu níĝ-ba *Ib-rí-um* $^{d}$*Ra-sa-ap* $^{d}$E.

(Enki is associated with Rašap also in the offering list TM.75.10103 o. III 14–17: 2 udu $^{d}$*Ra-sa-ap* $^{d}$En-ki 2 udu $^{d}$*Ra-sa-ap gú-nu*. Enki receives offerings "in the garden", *in* ĜIŠ-nu-kiri$_6$ and Rašap is sometimes qualified with the term *gú-nu*, which has been interpreted as a kind of garden, see Archi 2010a, pp. 31–33).

$^{d}$*Ga-mi-iš* **3** o. VII 9: (14 garments, 140 kilts) … 134 níĝ-saĝšu … raš-SAR Kur$^{ki}$ … 1 BAR.AN *Rí-ì-Ḫa-lab*$_x$ šu-ba$_4$-ti … 1 IGI.NITA u$_5$ *Bù-da-ma-lik* šu-ba$_4$-ti … ĜIŠ-ti-ḪAR *Wa-ba-rúm* šu-ba$_4$-ti ki:⌜lam$_7$⌝ $^{d}$*G.*; **5** o. XV 17: 1 BAR.AN *Rí-ì-ma-lik* šu-ba$_4$-ti … ĜIŠ-ti-ḪAR *Wa-ba-rúm* šu-ba$_4$-ti ki:lam$_7$ $^{d}$*G.*; **6** r. III 2 and 7: 1 ĜIŠ-banšur níĝ-ba $^{d}$*G. in* ud en e$_{11}$ é $^{d}$*G.*; r. XVII 25: 1 *ḫa-bù* níĝ-ba $^{d}$*G.* en ì-na-sum; **9** r. V 16: 1 *ḫa-bù* níĝ-ba $^{d}$*G.*; **11** o. XIII 12: (82 garments, 341 kilts, 10 daggers) … 2 gud *Ib-lu*$_5$*-zú* ki:lam$_7$ $^{d}$*G.*; **12** o. II 7: (17 garments, 263 kilts) … 10 […] … 2 IGI.NITA *Bù-da-ma-lik* šu-ba$_4$-ti … raš-SAR Kur$^{ki}$ ki:lam$_7$ $^{d}$*G. wa* ki:lam$_7$ $^{dʾ}$*A*$_5$*-da-"bal" A-ru*$_{12}$*-ga-du*$^{ki}$; **13** o. XVII 13: (10 garments, 480 kilts) … raš-SAR Kur$^{ki}$ … 3 IGI.NITA u$_5$ en … ĜIŠ-ma-dul$_{10}$ ki:lam$_7$ $^{d}$*G.*; **15** r. I 2: (133 garments, 430 kilts) … raš-SAR … 4 IGI.N[ITA] *Puz*[*ur*$_4$*-ra*]*-ma-l*[*ik*] ki:lam$_7$ $^{d}$*G.*; **17** r. X 17: (194 garments, 292 kilts) … raš-SAR Kur$^{ki}$ … 1 gud ki:lam$_7$ $^{d}$*G.*; **18** r. XII 21: ĜIŠ-šim ĜÁ×LÁ ki:lam$_7$ $^{d}$*G. Du-bí-ga-lu*; r. XIII 11: (168 garments, 340 na$_4$ measures of wool) ki:lam$_7$ $^{d}$*G. wa* $^{d}$*Áš-da-bíl* *wa* $^{d}$BAD *Du-du-lu*$^{ki}$; **19** r. V 21: (347 garments, 46 na$_4$ measures of wool) … ĜIŠ-ma-dul$_{10}$ *Wa-ba-rúm* šu-ba$_4$-ti ki:lam$_7$ *ᵓÀ-da-ni*$^{ki}$ *wa* $^{d}$*G.*, 25: (silver) *si-in* al$_6$-tuš $^{d}$*G.* en ì-na-sum; **20** r. VII 6: (155 garments) … 2 IGI.NITA u$_5$ *Bù-da-ma-lik* [šu-ba$_4$-ti] ki:lam$_7$ $^{d}$*G.*; **22** r. VI 6: 1 *ar-ra-sù ḫa-bù* níĝ-ba $^{d}$*G.* … *Ib-rí-um*; **25** o. V 3: (86 garments, 203 kilts) [ ] [ki:lam$_7$] $^{d}$*G.*

$^{d}$*Ga-na-na* **5** r. XIII 15: 2 *bu*-DI 2 *ti-ša-na* níĝ-ba $^{d}$*G.* ĜIŠ.DUG.DU maḫ; **6** r. XIV 3: 2 *bu*-DI 2 *ti-ša-na* níĝ-ba $^{d}$*G.* ĜIŠ.DUG.DU maḫ; **7** r. XIV 4: [ ] níĝ-ba $^{d}$*G. in* ud ĜIŠ.DUG.DU maḫ; **14** r. VII 13: [2 *b*]*u*-DI 4 *ti-ša-na* níĝ-ba $^{d}$*G.* ĜIŠ.DUG.DU maḫ; **19** r. XVII 21: 2 *bu*-DI 4 še-šu-še-tag níĝ-ba $^{d}$*G.*; **20** r. X 8: 2 *bu*-DI 4 *ti-ša-na* [níĝ-ba $^{d}$*G.*] *in* ĜIŠ.DUG.DU maḫ; **21** r. III 5: 2 *bu*-DI 4 še-šu-tag níĝ-ba $^{d}$*G.* ĜIŠ.DUG.DU maḫ.

$^{d}$*Ga-ra-ru*$_{12}$ **13** o. IX 11: 1 ĝír mar-tu 1 kù-sal níĝ-ba *Ib-rí-um* $^{d}$*G.*

$^{d}$*Gú-šar* **5** r. XII 11: *ba-na-a* $^{d}$*G.*

$^{d}$*Ḫa-a-ba-du* **13** o. VII 14: 1 *du-rúm* níĝ-ba *Ib-rí-um* $^{d}$*Ḫ.* lú *Ḫa-lab*$_x$$^{ki}$; **15** r. X 3: 1 kù-sal [níĝ-b]a en $^{d}$*Ḫ.* *al*$_6$ tu-ra ama-gal-*sù*.

$^{d}$*Ì-lam* **2** r. VI 26: maš-maš 1 "KIN" siki ... níĝ-ba en $^{d}$*Ì.*; r. VII 14: 6 gud-gud ki:lam$_7$ $^{d}$*Ì.*; **6** l.ed. 3: (tin) $^{d}$*Ì.* lú *Za-za-u*$_9$; **9** o. IX 18: ⸢raš⸣-SAR Kur⸢ki⸣ ki:lam$_7$ $^{d}$*Ì.*; **19** r. VII 11: é $^{d}$*Ì.* šu-ba$_4$-ti.

$^{d}$*Iš:šára* **2** o. VI 24: 1 kù-sal níĝ-ba *Du-si-gú* $^{d}$*I. Zi-da-ra*$^{ki}$; **5** o. VII 1: 1 ĝír mar-tu kg *Ib-rí-um in* ud nídba $^{d}$<*Iš-*>*šára* ĜIŠ-kiri$_6$; **6** o. XI 16: 2 *bu*-DI ... 1 an-zam$_x$ ... 1 ĜIŠ-banšur *wa* 1 *ḫa-bù* $^{d}$*I.* [*Má-*]NE$^{ki}$; r. XVII 4: 1 ĜIŠ-banšur $^{d}$*I. Má*-NE$^{ki}$; **13** o. VIII 21: 1 an-dùl … IGI.DUB-*sù* 2 šu-*sù* 2 DU-*sù* níĝ-ba *Du-si-gú* $^{d}$*I. Wa*-NE-*du*$^{ki}$; **15** o. I 14: 1 kù-sal níĝ-ba *Da-bur-da-mu* $^{d}$*I. Zi-da-ra*$^{ki}$; r. X 12 and 15: 2 kù-sal níĝ-ba *Da-bur-da-mu* $^{d}$*I. Zu-ra-mu*$^{ki}$ *wa* $^{d}$*I. Má*-NE$^{ki}$ *I-lu*$_5$*-za*$_x$*-ma-lik* šu-mu-tak$_4$; **16** r. XIII 14: 2 ĝeštu$_x$-lá 15 sikil $^{d}$*I. Zu-ra-mu*$^{ki}$; **17** r. VI 14: 1 an-dùl $^{d}$*I.* en … *ba-na-i-sù wa* íb-lá-*sù wa* šu-kešda-gùn-*sù*; **18** o. V 4: 2 *bu*-DI níĝ-ba ama-gal en $^{d}$*I. Zi-da-ra*$^{ki}$; r. XI 30: 3 zi-bar níĝ-ba ama-gal en $^{d}$*I. Má*-NE$^{ki}$ *Ù-gú-a-áš*$^{ki}$ *wa Zu-ra-mu*$^{ki}$; **20** r. X 28 and XI 2: 2 kù-sal níĝ-ba ama-gal en $^{d}$*I. Zu-ra-mu*$^{ki}$ *wa* $^{d}$*I. Má*-NE$^{ki}$.

$^{d}$*Ku-ra* 1(c) r. x+I 3; **2** o. VI 15: 1 ĜIŠ-banšur *wa* 1 kù-sal níĝ-ba *Ib-rí-um* $^{d}$*K. in* ud ne:saĝ-*sù*; o. XI 8: 2 *gú-li-lum* níĝ-ba $^{d}$*K.*; r. II 4: 1 *gú-li-lum* 1 kù-sal níĝ-ba *Ib-rí-um* $^{d}$*K. in* ud lú nídba; r. VIII 12: 2 *gú-li-lum* níĝ-ba $^{d}$*K.*; **3** o. IV 11: 2 *gú-li-lum* níĝ-ba $^{d}$*K.*; **4** o. I 3: saĝ kb $^{d}$*K.*; o. XIII 4: saĝ kb $^{d}$*K.*, 21: nam-kud *Ì-ra-ar*$^{ki}$ é $^{d}$*K.*; **6** o. I 3: saĝ kb $^{d}$*K.*; o. II 14: saĝ kb $^{d}$*K.* 2 mu-ti; o. III 22: 1 dub lú nam-kud *Ib-la*$^{ki}$ *wa Ma-ri*$^{ki}$ é $^{d}$*K.*; **7** o. I 3: [s]ag kb $^{d}$*K.*; o. VII 18: 2 *gú-li-lum* níĝ-ba $^{d}$*K.*; o. XVI 12: [2 *gú-l*]*i-*[*lu*]*m* [níĝ-]ba $^{d}$*K.*; r. III 20: 1 ĝír mar-tu ... 1 kù-sal níĝ-ba $^{d}$*K.*; r. XI 23: *Gul-la* ⸢x-x-x⸣ *Sa-ma-na-nu* [*S*]*i-mi*[- ] [ ] *Iš-ba-ì A-ša*$^{ki}$ *in* ud DU.DU nam-kud é $^{d}$*K.*; **8** o. I 3: saĝ $^{d}$*K.*; o. III 13: saĝ $^{d}$*K.*; o. XIII 5: 2 *gú-li-lum* $^{d}$*K.*; r. X 9': 2 *gú-li-lum* $^{d}$*K.*; **9** o. I 3: saĝ kb $^{d}$*K.*; o. VIII 15: 2 *gú-li-lum* níĝ-ba $^{d}$*K.*; r. V 11: nam-kud en *Bur-ma-an*$^{ki}$ é $^{d}$*K.*; **10** o. I 3: saĝ urudu $^{d}$*K.*; o. V 11: 1 ĜIŠ-banšur níĝ-ba $^{d}$*K. Ib-rí-um* in-na-sum *in* ud ne:s[ag]-*sù*; o. XIII 15: 1 [ĜIŠ]-⸢banšur⸣ *wa* nu$_{11}$-za 1 ĝír mar-tu níĝ-ba $^{d}$*K.* lú *ᵓÀ-ti-ni*$^{ki}$; r. X 4: 1 ĝír mar-tu 1 kù-sal níĝ-ba $^{d}$*K. Ib-rí-um* ì-na-sum *in* ne-saĝ-*sù*; **11** o. I 3: saĝ kb $^{d}$*K.*; o. V 1: 1 kù-sal … [1 g]ír mar-⸢tu⸣ níĝ-⸢ba⸣ [$^{d}$*K.*] [*Ib-rí-um*?] [ì-na-sum] [*i*]*n* ⸢ud⸣ ne:saĝ; **12** o. I 3: saĝ kb $^{d}$*K.*; o. IV 18: nam-kud en *Ì-ra-ar*$^{ki}$ é $^{d}$*K.*; *I-bí-du-lum* en *Ma-nu-wa-ad*$^{ki}$ *in* ud DU.DU nam-kud é $^{d}$*K.*; r. IX 18: 2 an-dùl … *ba-na-a-sa wa* 2 šu-šu *wa* 2 DU-*sù* níĝ-ba *Du-si-gú* $^{d}$*K. in* ud ne:saĝ; **13** o. I 3: saĝ kb $^{d}$*K.*; o. II 22: nam-kud é $^{d}$*K.*; o. VIII 9: saĝ kb $^{d}$*K.* mu-ti-II; r. III 11: 2 *gú-li-lum* níĝ-ba $^{d}$*K.*; r. VII 7: 2 *gú-li-lum* níĝ-ba $^{d}$*K.*; **14** o. I 3: saĝ kb $^{d}$*K.*; o. VI 11: saĝ kb $^{d}$*K. in* mu-ti-II; **15** o. I 3: saĝ kb $^{d}$*K.*; o. VI 15: 2 *gú-li-lum* níĝ-ba $^{d}$*K.*; o. XIV 3: saĝ kb $^{d}$*K.* mu-ti, 18: (silver) kin$_5$-ak é $^{d}$*K.*; o. XV 9: 2 *gú-li-lum* níĝ-ba $^{d}$*K.*; **16** o. I 3: saĝ kb $^{d}$*K.*; o. II 17: 1 á-MUŠEN … saĝ-*sù* níĝ-ba ama-gal en $^{d}$TU é $^{d}$*K.*; o. V 21: saĝ kb $^{d}$*K. in* mu-ti-II; o. XII 11; r. XVII 19: 2 *gú-li-lum* níĝ-]ba $^{d}$*K.*; **17** o. I 3: saĝ kb $^{d}$*K.*; o. V 3: 1 kù-sal 1 buru$_4$-MUŠEN [níĝ-ba] dumu-munus en $^{d}$*K.* ì-na-sum *in* ne:saĝ-*sù*; o. XI 8: 2 *gú-li-lum* níĝ-ba $^{d}$*K.*; o. XIII 15: saĝ kb $^{d}$*K.* mu-ti; r. VI 12: 2 *gú-li-lum* níĝ-ba $^{d}$*K.*; r. VII 3: *ḫa-za-nu a-ḫa-šum* gaba $^{d}$*K. wa* en; r. XI 1; **18** o. I 3: saĝ kb $^{d}$*K.*; o. XII 10: 2 *gú-li-lum* níĝ-ba $^{d}$*K.*; o. XVII 11: saĝ kb $^{d}$*K.* mu-ti-II; r. VI 14: 2 *gú-li-lum* níĝ-ba $^{d}$*K.*; **19** o. I 3: saĝ kb $^{d}$*K.*; o. IX 11: 2 *gú-li-lum* níĝ-ba $^{d}$*K.*; r. IV 26: saĝ kb $^{d}$*K.* mu-ti-II; r. VI 29: 2 *gú-li-lum* níĝ-ba $^{d}$*K.*; **20** o. I 3: [saĝ kb $^{d}$*K.*]; o. IV 8: sa[g kb] $^{d}$*K.* mu-t[i]-II, 15: [2 *gú-li-lum*] níĝ-ba $^{d}$*K.*; r. V 5: 2 *gú-li-lum* níĝ-ba $^{d}$*K.*; **21** o. I 3: saĝ kb $^{d}$*K.*; o. XI 19: 2 *gú-li-lum* níĝ-ba $^{d}$*K.*; r. I 12: 2 *gú-li-lum* níĝ-ba $^{d}$*K.*; r. XIV 22: nam-kud-nam-kud en *Ì-ra-ar*$^{ki}$ é $^{d}$*K.*; **22** r. VI 10: 1 ĜIŠ-ĝidru níĝ-ba $^{d}$*K. Ib-rí-um*; **23** o. II 6: 2 *gú-li-lum* níĝ-ba $^{d}$*K.*

$^{d}$NE-*ti-a-du* **13** o. IX 18: 1 kù-sal … 1 kù-sal níĝ-ba $^{d}$N. diĝir *Du-lu*$^{ki}$.

$^{d}$Nin-kar **7** o. III 7: 1 kù-sal níĝ-ba ama-gal en $^{d}$N.; **24** o. VI 3: IGI.DUB 1 an-dùl níĝ-ba *Ib-rí-um* $^{d}$N.

$^{d}$*Ra-sa-ap* **2** r. III 14: 1 *gú-li-lum* 1 kù-sal níĝ-ba *Du-si-gú* $^{d}$*R. ᵓÀ-da-ni*$^{ki}$; r. IV 5: 2 *ḫa-bù* ... níĝ-ba $^{d}$*R. ᵓÀ-da-ni*$^{ki}$ *wa* $^{d}$*ᵓÀ-da* $^{d}$AMA-*ra*; r. VII 8: 2 gud ... 4 si-*sù* nídba en $^{d}$*R. ᵓÀ-da-ni*$^{ki}$ $^{d}$AMA-*ra*; **4** r. IV 18: 2 *ḫa-bù* níĝ-ba $^{d}$*R.* lú *ᵓÀ-da-ni*$^{ki}$ *wa* $^{d}$*ᵓÀ-da*; r. V 18: 2 ĜIŠ-banšur kg ... 1 šu-dub sikil lú en $^{d}$*R. ᵓÀ-da-ni*$^{ki}$; r. XV 14: *ᵓÀ-bí* lú $^{d}$*R.* ŠE.SAĜ×ḪA-bul$_x$; **5** o. XII 13: 1 *ḫa-bù* ... $^{d}$*Ra-sa-ap ᵓÀ-da-ni*$^{ki}$ AMA-*ra*; r. XIV 8: 1 ĝír mar-tu ... 1 kù-sal níĝ-ba $^{d}$*R. ᵓÀ-da-ni*$^{ki}$ *in* SA.ZA$_x$$^{ki}$ *Ib-rí-um*, 19: 1 ĝír mar-tu ... 1 kù-sal níĝ-ba $^{d}$*R. gú-núm*$^{ki}$ en in-na-sum ne-saĝ-*sù*; r. XV 20: *a-gú* ... 3 ĜIŠ-šú 3 níĝ-bànda ... *in* é $^{d}$*R. ᵓÀ-da-ni*$^{ki}$ SA.ZA$_x$$^{ki}$; **6** o. XIII 14: 1 saĝ lu$_5$ ... $^{d}$*R. ᵓÀ-da-ni*$^{ki}$; o. XIV 11: 2 ĜIŠ-DU en *in* ud SIG$_7$ è *si-in* ki $^{d}$*R.*; o. XVI 27: 2 *ḫa-bù* níĝ-ba $^{d}$*R. ᵓÀ-da-ni*$^{ki}$ *wa* $^{d}$*ᵓÀ-da* $^{d}$AMA-*ra*; **7** o. III 17: 1 ĝír mar-tu *wa* 1 kù-sal níĝ-ba *Ib-rí-um* $^{d}$*R. Du-ne-íb*$^{ki}$; o. XI 15: 1 ešda ... níĝ-ba $^{d}$*R.*, 21: *ᵓa*$_5$*-na-gu* 4 si 2 gud nídba en [$^{d}$*R. ᵓÀ-da-ni*$^{ki}$ *in*] $^{d}$AMA-*ra*; r. II 13: 1 ĝír mar-tu ... [1 k]ù-sal níĝ-ba $^{d}$*R. Du-ne-íb*$^{ki}$; r. VI 7: 1 kù-sal 1 buru$_4$-MUŠEN [níĝ-ba] [ ] [$^{d}$*R.*] *ᵓÀ-da-ni*$^{ki}$ šu-mu-tak$_4$ $^{d}$AMA-*ra*; r. XV 14: nu$_{11}$-za $^{d}$*R. Du-ne-íb*$^{ki}$, 25: [nu$_{11}$-z]a [$^{d}$*R.*]; r. XVI 5: [1 ĝí]r mar-[t]u kg [1 ĜIŠ]-gu-kak-gíd $^{d}$*R. Du-ne-íb*$^{ki}$ en in-na-sum; **8** o. X 9: 1 ⸢ĝír mar⸣-[tu] [$^{d}$*R.*] [*ᵓÀ-d*]*a-*[*n*]*i*$^{ki}$ *in* SA.ZA$_x$$^{ki}$; r. II 6': *ba-na-i-sa* níĝ-ba *Ib-rí-um* $^{d}$*R.*; r. V 17': 8 si 4 gud nídba en *wa Ib-rí-um* nídba $^{d}$*R.* [*ʾÀ-da-ni*$^{ki}$]; **9** o. III 16: [ ] [*a*]*r-ra-sa-su* níĝ-ba $^{d}$*R. ʾÀ-da-ni*$^{ki}$ *wa* $^{d}$*ʾÀ-da Ḫa-lab*$_{x}^{ki}$ AMA-*ra*; o. IV 4: [x kb] [nu$_{11}$-za si-si] 2 gud nídba en $^{d}$*R. ʾÀ-da-ni*$^{ki}$; o. VIII 7: [$^{d}$*R.*] *ʾÀ-da-ni*$^{ki}$ AMA-*ra*; **10** o. XV 8: 2 si am lú $^{d}$*R. gú-núm*; **11** o. V 14: 1 ĝír mar-tu níĝ-ba *Ib-rí-um* $^{d}$*R. g*[*ú-n*]*úm in* ud ne:saĝ; o. X 16: 1 ešda … 1 *ar-ra-sù* … *ʾa*$_5$*-na-gu* 4 si 2 gud nídba en $^{d}$*R. ʾÀ-da-ni*$^{ki}$; r. VI 7: 1 ĜIŠ-banšur níĝ-ba $^{d}$*R. Du-bí-tum*$^{ki}$ [ ]⌜x⌝ [*in*] ud ḫúl é-*sù*; **12** r. VIII 15: saĝ $^{d}$*R. Du-ne-íb*$^{ki}$ *wa* nu$_{11}$-za íb+III-TÚG-*sù*; **13** o. V 7: 1 ĝír mar-tu níĝ-ba *Ib-rí-um* $^{d}$*R.* $^{d}$En-ki; o. VIII 4: 2 an-dùl … [I]GI.DUB-*sù wa* 4 šu-*sù* 4 DU-*sù* níĝ-ba *Du-si-gú* $^{d}$*R.* $^{d}$*A-da-ma ʾÀ-da-ni*$^{ki}$; o. XI 13: 1 *ḫa-bù* … 1 *ar-ra-sù* … *ʾa*$_5$*-na-gu* 4 si 2 gud nídba en $^{d}$*R. ʾÀ-da-ni*$^{ki}$; r. IV 17: 2 an-dùl níĝ-ba *Ib-rí-um* $^{d}$*R. wa* $^{d}$*A-da-ma ʾÀ-da-ni*$^{ki}$; **14** o. X 7: *ʾa*$_5$*-na-gu* 4 si 2 gud … 1 *ḫa-bù* … 1 ⌜*ar*⌝*-ra*[*-sù* nídba] en $^{d}$*R.* [*ʾÀ-da-ni*$^{ki}$] *in* $^{d}$AMA-*ra*; r. VIII 6: [1 ĜIŠ-ba]nšur [*wa*] 1 kù-sal $^{d}$*R. Du-ne-íb*$^{ki}$ en šu-mu-tak$_4$; **15** o. X 11: 1 *ḫa-bù* … 1 *ar-ra-si-su* …*ʾa*$_5$*-na-gu* 4 si 2 gud nídba en $^{d}$*R. ʾÀ-da-ni*$^{ki}$ *in* $^{d}$AMA-*ra*; o. XII 5: 1 kù-sal níĝ-ba *Du-si-gú* $^{d}$*R. ʾÀ-da-ni*$^{ki}$; r. VIII 10: 1 ĝír mar-tu *wa* 1 kù-sal níĝ-ba *Ib-rí-um* $^{d}$*R. Du-ne-íb*$^{ki}$; r. XIII 29: *ʾa*$_5$*-na-gu* 1 ĜIŠ-banšur *wa* 1 kù-sal sikil *al*$_6$ ama-gal en $^{d}$*R. ʾÀ-da-ni*$^{ki}$; r. XVI 18: 2 ma-na kb in-na-sum *si-in* šu-bal-ak kg lú $^{d}$*R. Du-ne-íb*$^{ki}$ lú *Da-*NE*-du Kab-lu*$_5$*-ul*$^{ki}$; **16** r. I 9: 1 *ḫa-bù* … 1 *ar-ra-sù* … *ʾa*$_5$*-na-gu* si 2 gud nídba en $^{d}$*R. ʾÀ-da-ni*$^{ki}$; r. IX 21: 1 íb-lá 1 *si-ti-tum* 1 ĝír-kun níĝ-ba *Ib-rí-um* $^{d}$*R. Da-ra-um*$^{ki}$; **17** r. IV 26: 1 *ḫa-bù* … 1 *ar-ra-si-sù* … *ʾa*$_5$*-na-gu* 4 si 2 gud nídba en $^{d}$*R. ʾÀ-da-ni*$^{ki}$ *in* $^{d}$AMA-*ra*; r. V 23: 1 kù-sal 1 buru$_4$-MUŠEN níĝ-ba ama-gal en $^{d}$*R. ʾÀ-da-ni*$^{ki}$; r. XVI 3: 1 ĝír mar-tu níĝ-ba $^{d}$*R.*; **18** o. XVIII 24: 1 *ḫa-bù* … 1 *ar-ra-sù* … *ʾa*$_5$*-na-gu* si 2 gud nídba en $^{d}$*R. ʾÀ-da-ni*$^{ki}$; o. XIX 7: 1 kù-sal buru$_4$-MUŠEN níĝ-ba ama-gal en $^{d}$*R. ʾÀ-da-ni*$^{ki}$; r. XVII 2: 2 ĝír mar-tu … 2 kù-sal níĝ-ba ama-gal en $^{d}$*R. Du-ne-íb*$^{ki}$ *wa* $^{dʾ}$*A*$_5$*-da-"bal" ʾÀ-ma-du*$^{ki}$ NI.DU; **19** o. XI 3: 1 *ḫa-bù* … 1 *ar-ra-sù* … *ʾa*$_5$*-na-gu* si 2 gud nídba en $^{d}$*R. ʾÀ-da-ni*$^{ki}$; o. XIII 25: 1 kù-sal níĝ-ba ama-gal en $^{d}$*R. ʾÀ-da-ni*$^{ki}$ AMA-*ra*; **20** o. VIII 13: 1 *ḫa-bù* … 1 *ar-ra-sù* … [*ʾa*$_5$*-na-gu* 4 si gud nídba en] $^{d}$*R. ʾÀ-da-ni*$^{ki}$; **21** o. IX 16: 1 *ḫa-bù* … 1 *ar-r*[*a-*]*s*[*ù*] níĝ-ba en $^{d}$*R.* ⌜*ʾÀ-da*⌝-[*ni*$^{ki}$]; **24** o. V 8: IGI.DUB 2 an-dùl *wa* 2 šu-*sù* 2 DU-*sù* níĝ-ba *Ib-rí-um* $^{d}$*R. wa* $^{d}$*A-da-ma ʾÀ-da-ni*$^{ki}$ *in ma-ʾà-wa-tum*.

$^{d}$*Sa-a-ša* **7** o. X 11: 1 an-dùl sal ... níĝ-ba $^{d}$*S. si-in Du-du-lu*$^{ki}$ *Ib-rí-um* šu-mu-tak$_4$.

(cf. $^{d}$*Ša-la-ša*; see Archi 1995 p. 2 = Archi 2015, p. 633)

$^{d}$*Sa-nu-ga-ar* **21** o. V 11: [ ] … saĝ-*sù* … 1 dub-*sù* níĝ-ba *Ib-rí-um* $^{d}$*S. Má-*NE$^{ki}$.

$^{d}$*Si-gar* **6** r. XVI 23: (tin) $^{d}$*A-lum wa* $^{d}$*S. A-ḫa-da-mu*$^{ki}$.

$^{d}$*Ša-la-ša* **6** r. V 8: nu$_{11}$-za $^{d}$*Wa-da-ʾà-an wa* $^{d}$*Š.* lú *Ga-ra-mu*$^{ki}$.

$^{d}$*Ša-ma-gan* **2** o. IX 13: *ba-na-a wa* íb+III-TÚG $^{d}$*Š.* en ... saĝ-*sù*.

$^{d}$*Šára* see $^{d}$*Iš:šára*.

$^{d}$TU **16** o. II 15: 1 á-MUŠEN … saĝ-*sù* níĝ-ba ama-gal en $^{d}$T. é $^{d}$*Ku-ra*; **20** o. XI 16: 2 *bu-*DI níĝ-ba ama-gal en $^{d}$T. lú *ʾÀ-da-ni*$^{ki}$.

$^{d}$Utu **2** r. II 16: 2 *ʾà-ra-ma-tum* ... 2 zé-*sù* níĝ-ba *Ib-rí-um* $^{d}$U. SA.ZA$_{x}^{ki}$; **7** r. III 11: [x] ⌜*ʾà-ra*⌝*-ma-tum* ... [ ] [níĝ-ba] $^{d}$U. SA.ZA$_{x}^{ki}$; **11** r. VII 4: 2 *ʾà-ra-ma-tum* … nu$_{11}$-za-*sù* níĝ-ba *Ib-rí-um* $^{d}$U. lú SA.ZA$_{x}^{ki}$; **15** r. V 1: 1 kù-sal níĝ-ba *Da-bur-da-mu* $^{d}$U. SA.ZA$_{x}^{ki}$.

$^{d}$*Wa-da-ʾà-an* **6** o. VIII 8: 1 ĝír mar-tu níĝ-ba $^{d}$*W.* lú *Ga-ra-mu*$^{ki}$; r. V 6: nu$_{11}$-za $^{d}$*W. wa* $^{d}$*Ša-la-ša* lú *Ga-ra-mu*$^{ki}$; **7** o. I 11: 1 ĝír mar-tu níĝ-ba $^{d}$*W.* [l]ú [*Ša-*]*dab*$^{ki}$ *Ib-rí-um* in-na-sum.

[$^{d}$X] **13** r. IV 25: ⌜1⌝ an-dùl [níĝ-ba] [ ] [$^{d}$X].

# Geographical names

*ʾÀ-bar-du*$^{ki}$ **16** r. IV 6: *Ḫa-bù-zú ʾÀ.* maškim *Za-ba-rúm* tuš-LÚ×TIL *Ḫal-sum*$^{ki}$.

*ʾÀ-bí-gú*$^{ki}$ **11** o. VIII 11: šeš *Ti-la-rí-im*$^{ki}$ *ʾÀ. áš-da Tar$_5$-ḫa-um*$^{ki}$.

*ʾÀ-da-ni*$^{ki}$ **2** o. VII 6: (15 garments, 1 kilt) ki:lam$_7$ *gi-ba-lu ʾÀ.*; o. IX 2: (62 garments, 21 kilts) ki:lam$_7$ *zi-ba-tum ʾÀ.*; r. III 15: níg-ba *Du-si-gú* $^{d}$*Ra-sa-ap ʾÀ.*; r. IV 6: níĝ-ba $^{d}$*Ra-sa-ap ʾÀ.*; r. VI 5: 35 gud-gud … (75 garments, 84 kilts) … raš-SAR Kur$^{ki}$ [ ] ĜIŠ-ád ki:lam$_7$ *ʾÀ.*, 11: en *Ma-nu-wa-ad*$^{ki}$ *in ʾÀ.* šu-ba$_4$-ti; r. VII 9: nídba en $^{d}$*Ra-sa-ap ʾÀ.* $^{d}$AMA-*ra*; **3** r. VII 5: (23 garments, 70 kilts) ki:lam$_7$ *gi-ba-lu ʾÀ.*; r. X 1: (15 garments, 104 kilts) … 1 BAR.AN … ĜIŠ-ti-ḪAR *Wa-ba-rúm* šu-ba$_4$-ti ki:lam$_7$ šeš-II-ib *ʾÀ.*; **4** r. IV 20: níĝ-ba $^{d}$*Ra-sa-ap* lú *ʾÀ.*; r. V 19: $^{d}$*Ra-sa-ap ʾÀ.*; r. VII 17: 2 ĜI[Š-x] *Ib-bí-um* “ur$_4$” šu-ba$_4$-ti ki:lam$_7$ *ʾÀ.*; **5** o. II 7: (65 garments, 210+[x] kilts, 8 daggers, 354 na$_4$ measures of wool) … ĜIŠ-ti-ḪAR ĜIŠ-ád *Wa-ba-rúm* “ur$_4$” šu-ba$_4$-ti ki:lam$_7$ <$^{d}$>*A-da-ma ʾÀ.*; o. VIII 9: nídba en $^{dʾ}$*À-da ʾÀ.*; o. IX 14: *in ʾÀ.* šu-ba$_4$-ti; o. XII 14: $^{d}$*Ra-sa-ap ʾÀ.* AMA-*ra*; r. XIV 9: níĝ-ba $^{d}$*Ra-sa-ap ʾÀ. in* SA.ZA$_x$$^{ki}$; r. XV 21: *in* é $^{d}$*Ra-sa-ap ʾÀ.* SA.ZA$_x$$^{ki}$; **6** o. XI 5: ĜIŠ-ti-ḪAR ki:lam$_7$ $^{d}$*A-da-ma ʾÀ. Wa-ba-rúm* šu-ba$_4$-ti; o. XIII 15: $^{d}$*Ra-sa-ap ʾÀ.*; r. I 1: níĝ-ba $^{d}$*Ra-sa-ap ʾÀ.*; r. X 3: (35 garments, 185 kilts, 12 daggers) … ĜIŠ-ti-ḪAR *Wa-ba-rúm* šu-ba$_4$-ti ki:lam$_7$ *ʾÀ. wa* NI-*ab*$^{ki}$ *wa La-ru$_{12}$-ga-du*$^{ki}$; **7** o. XI 22: nídba en [$^{d}$*Ra-sa-ap ʾÀ. in*] $^{d}$AMA-*ra*; r. VI 8: [níĝ-ba] [ ] [$^{d}$*Ra-sa-*]*a*[*p*] *ʾÀ.* šu-mu-tak$_4$ $^{d}$AMA-*ra*; **8** o. VI 1: (48 garments, 48 kilts) [ -*g*]*i Ib-lu$_5$-zú wa I-za-iš-ru$_{12}$* lú-kar *Ma-nu-wa-ad*$^{ki}$ ki:lam$_7$ šeš-⸢ib⸣[-II] *ʾÀ.*; o. X 10: [$^{d}$*Ra-sa-ap*] [*ʾÀ.*] *in* [SA.]ZA$_x$$^{ki}$; r. V 18’: nídba en *wa Ib-rí-um* nídba $^{d}$*Ra-sa-ap* [*ʾÀ.*]; **9** o. III 17: níĝ-ba $^{d}$*Ra-sa-ap ʾÀ. wa* $^{dʾ}$*À-da Ḫa-lab$_x$*$^{ki}$ AMA-*ra*; o. IV 5: nídba en $^{d}$*Ra-sa-ap ʾÀ.*; o. VIII 7: (17 garments, 138[+x] kilts, …) [ki:lam$_7$] *ʾÀ.* AMA-*ra*; r. II 1: (8 garments, 68 kilts) ki:lam$_7$ *gi-*[*ba-lu*] *ʾÀ.*; r. XVI 16: (50 kilts) … ĜIŠ-gu-kak-gíd *Wa-ba-rúm* ⸢šu⸣-ba$_4$-ti ki:⸢lam$_7$⸣ *zi-ba-tum ʾÀ.*; **10** o. X 16: níĝ-ba *Ìr-ba$_x$-zé ʾÀ.*; r. VII 13: (100 garments, 16 kilts) ki:lam$_7$ *gi-ba-lu ʾÀ.*; **11** o. IV 3: (100 garments, 50 kilts, 93 KIN measures of wool, 7 daggers) … 22 gud-gud [ ] [ -]N[E] šu-ba$_4$-ti ki:lam$_7$ *gi-ba-ù* [*wa*] $^{d}$*A-d*[*am-*]*ma ʾÀ.*; o. X 17: nídba en $^{d}$*Ra-sa-ap ʾÀ.*; **13** o. VI 5: (88 kilts, 245 KIN measures of wool) … 20 gud … ĜIŠ-ti-ḪAR *Wa-ba-rúm* šu-ba$_4$-ti ki:lam$_7$ šeš-II-ib *wa* $^{d}$*A-da-ma ʾÀ.*; o. VIII 6: níĝ-ba *Du-si-gú* $^{d}$*Ra-sa-ap* $^{d}$*A-da-ma ʾÀ.*; o. X 14: nídba en $^{d}$*Ra-sa-ap ʾÀ.*; o. XIV 16: (135+[x] kilts, 2 helmets) … 12 gud … ĜIŠ-ti-ḪAR … ki:lam$_7$ *ʾÀ.* AMA-*ra*; r. IV 20: níĝ-ba *Ib-rí-um* $^{d}$*Ra-sa-ap wa* $^{d}$*A-da-ma ʾÀ.*; **14** o. X 8: [nídba] en $^{d}$*Ra-sa-ap* [*ʾÀ.*] *in* $^{d}$AMA-*ra*; o. XVII 11: (121+[x] garments, 306 kilts, 5 daggers) … raš-SAR Kur$^{ki}$ … 11 gud en … ĜIŠ-ti-ḪAR *Wa-ba-rúm* šu-ba$_4$-ti ki:lam$_7$ *ʾÀ. in* $^{d}$AMA-*ra*; **15** o. VII 11: (54 garments, 166 kilts, 385 KIN measures of wool) … ĜIŠ-ti-ḪAR *Wa-ba-rúm* šu-ba$_4$-ti ki:lam$_7$ šeš-II-ib *wa* $^{d}$*A-da-ma ʾÀ.*; o. X 12: nídba en $^{d}$*Ra-sa-ap ʾÀ. in* $^{d}$AMA-*ra*; o. XII 6: níĝ-ba *Du-si-gú* $^{d}$*Ra-sa-ap ʾÀ.*; o. XIII 6: (171 garments, 170 kilts) … 10 sila$_4$ sa$_6$ … ĜIŠ-ti-ḪAR *Wa-ba-rúm* ki:lam$_7$ $^{d}$AMA-*ra ʾÀ.*; r. XIII 30: $^{d}$*Ra-sa-ap ʾÀ.*; **16** o. IV 8: (170 na$_4$ measures of wool) … ĜIŠ-ti-ḪAR BAD.MUŠ.LU$_5$ šu-ba$_4$-ti ki:lam$_7$ šeš-II-ib *ʾÀ.*; o. XIII 19: [x$^{?}$+]2 BAR.AN *Na-gàr*$^{ki}$ … (57 garments) … raš-SAR Kur$^{ki}$ ki:lam$_7$ *ʾÀ.* $^{d}$AMA-*ra*; r. I 10: nídba en $^{d}$*Ra-sa-ap ʾÀ.*; **17** r. IV 27: nídba en $^{d}$*Ra-sa-ap ʾÀ. in* $^{d}$AMA-*ra*; r. V 15: (265 garments, 242 kilts, 150 hides) … ĜIŠ-bar-ús *Wa-ba-rúm* <ki:lam$_7$> *ʾÀ.*, 24: níĝ-ba ama-gal en $^{d}$*Ra-sa-ap ʾÀ.*; r. VI 6: *Ti-ša-li-im ma-lik-tum Ì-mar*$^{ki}$ *in* ud DU.DU *mi-nu ʾÀ.*; r. XXII 29: (30 kilts) ki:[la]m$_7$ [*g*]*i-*⸢*ba*⸣*-lu* [*ʾÀ.*]; **18** o. X 2: (53 garments, 100 na$_4$ measures of wool) ki:lam$_7$ $^{d}$*A-da-ma ʾÀ.*; o. XIII 11: níĝ-ba *En-na-ì Ḫa-la-bí-du*$^{ki}$ *in ʾÀ.* šu-ba$_4$-ti; o. XVIII 25: nídba en $^{d}$*Ra-sa-ap ʾÀ.*; o. XIX 8: níĝ-ba ama-gal en $^{d}$*Ra-sa-ap ʾÀ.*; r. III 15: (148 garments, 210 na$_4$ measures of wool) … raš-SAR Kur$^{ki}$ … 3 IGI.NITA u$_5$ en ki:lam$_7$ *ʾÀ.* $^{d}$AMA-*ra*; **19** o. VII 2: (254 garments, 60 na$_4$ measures of wool) … ĜIŠ-ti-ḪAR ki:lam$_7$ $^{d}$*A-da-ma ʾÀ.*; o. XI 4: nídba en $^{d}$*Ra-sa-ap ʾÀ.*; o. XIII 26: níĝ-ba ama-gal en $^{d}$*Ra-sa-ap ʾÀ.* AMA-*ra*; r. V 19: (347 garments, 46 na$_4$ measures of wool) … ĜIŠ-ma-dul$_{10}$ *Wa-ba-rúm* šu-ba$_4$-ti ki:lam$_7$ *ʾÀ. wa* $^{d}$*Ga-mi-iš*; **20** o. VIII 14: [ ] $^{d}$*Ra-sa-ap ʾÀ.*; o. XI 17: níĝ-ba ama-gal en $^{d}$TU lú *ʾÀ.*; o. XIV 15: (54+[x] garments, 2 na$_4$ measures of wool) … 33 kuš … 2 gud *Iš-ra-*BAD lú-kar *Kak-mi-um*$^{ki}$ … raš-SAR Kur$^{ki}$ ki:lam$_7$ *ʾÀ.*; r. VIII 18: *Ti-šè-li-im ma-lik-tum Ì-mar*$^{ki}$ *in* ud DU.DU *mi-nu ʾÀ.*; **21** o. IX 17: níĝ-ba en $^{d}$*Ra-sa-ap ʾÀ.*; **24** o. V 11: níĝ-ba *Ib-rí-um* $^{d}$*Ra-sa-ap wa* $^{d}$*A-da-ma ʾÀ. in ma-ʾà-wa-tum*; **25** o. II 9: (121+[x] garments, 102 kilts) ki:lam$_7$ SA.ZA$_x$$^{ki}$ *wa* $^{d}$*A-da-ma ʾÀ.*; o. IV 2: (84 garments, 186 kilts, 1 dagger) [ki:lam$_7$] [*ʾÀ.*] AMA-*ra*; o. VIII 7: (18+[x] garments, 2+[x] kilts, 1 dagger) ki:lam$_7$ $^{dʾ}$*À-da wa gi-ba-lu ʾÀ.*

*ʾA$_5$-da-tum*$^{ki}$ **3** r. V 2: *Ḫáb-ra-ar* ugula *ʾA$_5$*.

*ʾÀ-du*$^{ki}$ **3** r. XI 8; 4 o. VIII 15; r. X 19; **6** o. XIII 1: níĝ-“mul” *ʾÀ.* àga-“kàr”(ŠÈ); **7** o. I 7: NE-*a-da-nu ʾÀ.*; **8** o. VII 1; **10** r. IX 9: níĝ-ba *ʾÀ.*; **16** r. XVI 24; **18** o. XIV 17: níĝ-ba *Du-tum wa Ìr-íb-sá-mu ʾÀ.*; o. XV 11: níĝ-ba *Du-tum wa Da-mi-gu ʾÀ.*, 21: níĝ-ba *I-ba$_x$-ì Zi-rí-gú ʾÀ.*; r. II 14: níĝ-ba *Kùn-i-šar ʾÀ. in Ša-dab$_6$*$^{ki}$ šu-ba$_4$-ti; r. XVI 2; r. XVIII 14: *I-ba$_x$-ì Zi-rí-gú ʾÀ.*; **19** o. VI 18: níĝ-ba *ʾÀ.* é $^{d}$BAD *Ga-na-na-im* šu-ba$_4$-ti; r. VII 3: níĝ-ba 3 guruš *ʾÀ. in Ḫa-lab$_x$*$^{ki}$ šu-ba$_4$-ti; r. IX 22: dumu-nita en *ʾÀ.*; r. XIII 1: níĝ-ba 3 guruš *ʾÀ.* ḫi-mu-DU maškim *Za-ba-rúm* nar.

*ʾÀ-lu*$^{ki}$ **18** r. XIX 15: (silver) níĝ-ba *Gú-ra-du*$^{ki}$ (silver) níĝ-ba *ʾÀ. in Ša-dab$_6$*$^{ki}$ šu-ba$_4$-ti.

*ʾÀ-ma* **4** o. III 18: *Ù-ḫa ʾÀ.* [šu-]ba$_4$-ti *in* [ ].

*ʾÀ-ma-ad*$^{ki}$ **2** o. IV 20: níĝ-ba $^{dʾ}$*A$_5$-da-“bal” ʾÀ.*

*ʾÀ-ma-du*$^{ki}$ **5** r. XIII 23: níĝ-ba $^{d}$*ʾA*$_5$*-da-"bal"* *ʾÀ*.; **6** r. II 13: *I-bí-gàr-du* ugula *ʾÀ*.; **8** o. VII 6: níĝ-ba $^{d}$*ʾA*$_5$*-da-"bal"* *ʾÀ*.; **14** r. VI 12: [níĝ-ba] *ʾA*$_5$*-da-"bal"* *ʾÀ*.; **18** o. XII 23: níĝ-ba $^{d}$*ʾA*$_5$*-da-"bal"* *ʾÀ*. *Ib-rí-um*; r. XVII 6: níĝ-ba ama-gal en $^{d}$*Ra-sa-ap Du-ne-ib*$^{ki}$ *wa* $^{d}$*ʾA*$_5$*-da-"bal"* *ʾÀ*.; **19** o. XI 31: níĝ-ba $^{d}$*ʾA*$_5$*-da-"bal"* *A-ru*$_{12}$*-ga-du*$^{ki}$ *wa* $^{d}$*ʾA*$_5$*-da-"bal"* *ʾÀ*.; **22** r. VII 4: níĝ-ba $^{d}$*ʾA*$_5$*-da-"bal"* *ʾÀ*.; **23** r. II 11: níĝ-ba $^{d}$*ʾA*$_5$*-da-"bal"* *ʾÀ*.

*ʾÀ-su*$^{ki}$ **1**(e) r. IV' 12: *Du-bí-šum* *ʾÀ*.; **4** r. XV 11; **15** o. IV 7: *Bar-za-ma-ù* ugula *ʾÀ*.; o. XIII 13: *Dab-da-ar wa A-a-gú-nu* *ʾÀ*.

*ʾÀ-šu*$^{ki}$ **9** r. IV 19: *Za-ne-ḫi-Ma-rí*$^{ki}$ é-gi *Ib-ʾà-ra* *ʾÀ*.; r. VII 6: *in* ud níĝ-mu-sá ⸢*Za*⸣*-ne-ḫi-Ma-*[*r*]*í*$^{ki}$ é-gi *Ib-ʾà-ra* *ʾÀ*.; **22** r. V 6: *Za-ni-ḫi-Ma-rí*$^{ki}$ é-gi *Ib-ʾà-ra* *ʾÀ*.

*ʾÀ-ti-ni*$^{ki}$ **10** o. XIII 17: níĝ-ba $^{d}$*Ku-ra* lú *ʾÀ*.

*ʾÀ-za-an*$^{ki}$ **21** r. VIII 26: dam en *ʾÀ*.

*A-a-lu*$^{ki}$ **15** o. IV 10: *Bar-za-ma-ù* ugula *ʾÀ-šu*$^{ki}$ *in* ud tuš-LÚ×TIL *A*.

*A-ba-ad*$^{ki}$ **9** r. III 5: *En-àr-li-im* [dumu-ni]ta *Du-*[*bí*]*-šum A*.

*A-bar-sal*$_4$$^{ki}$ **10** o. VI 16: dumu-munus e[n *Ra-ʾà-ak*$^{ki}$ *m*]*a-*[*li*]*k-*[*t*]*um A*. *wa ma-lik-tum Ir-i-tum*; **11** o. VII 19: *Íl-gú-uš-ti* lú *I-gi* tuš-LÚ×TIL Kiš$^{ki}$ lú *A*.; o. VIII 6: *ba-da-lum A*.; r. VII 19: *Zi-ir-a-ḫu* ugula *A*.; **13** r. XII 21: *ba-da-lum A*.

*A-ba-ti-lum*$^{ki}$ **15** o. II 12: níĝ-du$_8$ 1 dumu-nita *A*. maškim *Za-ba-rúm áš-ti Ìr-ku*$^{ki}$.

*A-ba-ti-tum*$^{ki}$ **20** r. II 25: 1 pad an-zam$_x$ *A*. *Ib-rí-um*.

*A-bí-na-du*$^{ki}$ **10** o. VI 8: *Zú-zú Ir-i-tum*$^{ki}$ *in A*. šu-ba$_4$-ti.

*Ab-ra-ti-ig*$^{ki}$ **17** o. XIII 6: *Ru*$_{12}$*-zi-ma-lik* lú *I-rí-ig* al$_6$-tuš *A*.

*Ab-ru*$_{12}$*-ti-um*$^{ki}$ **3** r. VII 10: ÚR *áš-ti Ir-i-tum*$^{ki}$.

*Áb-su*$^{ki}$ **2** o. IV 9: *Iš*$_{11}$*-gi-wa-aš Á*.; **4** r. VI 6: *Iš*$_{11}$*-gi-wa-aš Á*.

*Áb-zu*$^{ki}$ **17** o. XX 11: kb lú mu-DU *Á*. *I-bí-zi-kir* šu-mu-tak$_4$.

*A-bù-li-um*$^{ki}$ **4** o. VI 13; r. I 15: *Ku-tu A*.; **6** o. IV 6; **16** r. XVI 26; **18** r. XV 29; **19** r. VII 15: *Š*[*u-*/*D*[*a-* ] *A*.; r. IX 26.

*Áb-zu*$^{ki}$ see *Áb-su*$^{ki}$

*A-da-áš*$^{ki}$ **3** o. I 4: *Rí-ì-ma-lik* ugula *A*.

*A-da-bí-ig*$^{ki}$ **3** o. IX 12: lú-kar *A*.; **5** o. X 10: *in* níĝ-kas$_4$ *A*.; **7** o. V 19: *Lá-da* lú-kar *A*.; **8** r. VII 11': NI-*gi A*.; **10** o. XVI 12: *A*. ì-ti *mi-nu Ar-mi*$^{ki}$; **11** o. IX 6: *Ba*-NE lú-kar *A*.; r. V 11: *Uš-ga* "ur$_4$" *A*.; **13** o. X 3: *Ti-ra-ì A*.; **23** r. IX 3: AN.ŠÈ.GÚ 8 ma-na 3 gín D. kg è lú *A*.

*A-da-bí-gú*$^{ki}$ **17** r. VII 22: *I-ti-ne A*.

*A-dar*-KA*-mu*$^{ki}$ **10** o. II 1: [(níĝ-)]kaskal *A*.

*A-dar-ki-zú*$^{ki}$ **6** r. II 4: níĝ-kaskal *Za-gàr A*. DU.DU *Ar-mi*$^{ki}$.

*A-da-su*$^{ki}$ **12** r. VI 11: níĝ-du$_8$ 1 dumu-nita *Ti-in*$^{ki}$ lú *A*.

*A-daš*$^{ki}$ **18** r. II 3: (silver) níĝ-ba *A*.; r. XI 24: níĝ-ba en *A*.

*Ag-sa-gú*$^{ki}$ **12** o. III 3: níĝ-ba *Ib-gi-tum wa Ku-tu-ʾà-bù wa Ib-du-nu* [ -]⸢x⸣ [ ] *Du-du-lu*$^{ki}$ níĝ-"mul" *A*. šu-ba$_4$-ti; o. VII 11: níĝ-ba *Ab-bu*$_{16}$ *Ma-rí*$^{ki}$ níĝ-"mul" *A*. šu-ba$_4$-ti; o. X 1: níĝ-ba *Wa-ru*$_{12}$*-tum Ma-rí*$^{ki}$ níĝ-"mul" *A*. šu-ba$_4$-ti.

*A-ḫa-da-mu*$^{ki}$ **6** r. XVI 24: $^{d}$*A-lum wa* $^{d}$*Si-gar A*.

*A-ḫa-za-ni-ig*$^{ki}$ **17** o. XX 6: *in* ud níĝ-kas$_4$ *A*.

*A-la-ga*$^{ki}$ **16** r. XV 12: *Wa-na* ugula *A*.; r. XVI 20: *Wa-na* ugula *A*.; **18** o. IV 14; o. XV 5: 1 *mi-at* sal-TÚG *si-in A*.; **19** o. III 14 and 17: 3 tùn tur ŠA.PI-ŠA.PI lú šu-mu-tak$_4$ *si-in A*. *in* ud igi-ḫi-du$_8$$^{!}$(šu-du$_8$) *A*.; o. XVIII 19: (703 daggers, 176 bracelets) lú šu-mu-tak$_4$ *si-in A*.; r. XIV 15: *Bù-da-ì Maš-bar-rá*$^{ki}$ tuš-LÚ×TIL *Za-ḫi-ra-an*$^{ki}$ al$_6$-tuš *A*.; **21** o. VI 8: la-ḫa lú ì-ĝiš *si-in A*.; o. XII 28: (silver) lú ĜIŠ-nu-kiri$_6$ *in A*. [šu-ba$_4$-ti]; r. III 18: (daggers) lú *áš-du A*. šu-ba$_4$-ti *wa* in-na-sum SA.ZA$_x$$^{ki}$.

*A-la-u*$_9$$^{ki}$ **10** r. VII 2: en *A*. *in* ⸢ki⸣:lam$_7$ $^{d}$*ʾÀ-da*.

*Am*$_6$*-ʾà-rúm*$^{ki}$ **14** o. VIII 4: *Zú-za-bir*$_5$ lú *A-da-ad* tuš-LÚ×TIL *in A*.

*Am*$_6$*-ma-šu*$^{ki}$ **5** r. XI 11: lú ĜIŠ-sar *in A*. [šu]-ba$_4$-ti; **14** o. XII 12: lú *I-šar in A*. šu-ba$_4$-ti.

*An-ga-li-lu*$^{ki}$ **9** o. XI 14: *Šu-ga-du in A*. šu-ba$_4$-ti.

*Ar-ʾà-mu*$^{ki}$ **13** r. IX 16: *B*[*ù-*]*du-d*[*u*] ugula *A*.

*A-ra-ab*$^{ki}$ **6** r. XIV 10: saĝ $^{d}$*Á-la wa* $^{d}$*Da-bí-na-ad* lú *A*.; r. XVII 34: $^{d}$*Á-la wa dam-sù* lú *A*.

*Ar-ḫa-du*$^{ki}$ **7** o. VIII 11: *Ib-ḫur-ma-lik Kak-mi-um*$^{ki}$ tuš-LÚ<×TIL> *in A*.; **13** o. II 17: *Mu*-NE*-a-du* ugula *A*.; **14** o. V 2: *Mu*-NE*-a-du* ugula *A*.; **24** o. II 8: níĝ-ba $^{d}$*A-na-ma-du A*.

*A-rí-gú*$^{ki}$ **19** r. XIV 19: EN*-da-za A*. tuš-LÚ×TIL *Nu-rí*$^{ki}$.

*Ar-mi*$^{ki}$ **1** o. V 19: *Ìr-kab-ar* DU.DU *si-in A*.; o. VII 3: níĝ-kaskal *Na*-NE *Na-gàr*$^{ki}$ DU.DU *si-in A*.; **4** o. XIII 16: níĝ-kaskal *ʾÀ-daš ma-za-lum* DU.DU *A*.; r. VIII 15: [ ] *wa ma-z*[*a-*]*lum* DU.DU *A*.; **6** o. V 13: níĝ-kaskal *ʾÀ-daš* DU.DU *si-in A*.; o. IX 2: níĝ-kaskal *A-ir-ra wa A-zú-bù-lu* [*Ù-t*]*i-*[*g*]*ú*$^{ki}$ *wa A-zú* DU.DU *A*.; o. XV 6: níĝ-kaskal *A-ir-ra wa A-zú-bù-lu* DU.DU *A*. maškim *Ḫa-ra-ì*; r. II 6: níĝ-kaskal *Za-gàr A-dar-ki-zú*$^{ki}$ DU.DU *A*.; r. IV 11: níĝ-kaskal *Ḫar-zàr-du*$^{ki}$ DU.DU *A*.; **9** o. II 8: níĝ-kaskal *Gi-li-ti-um*$^{ki}$ DU.DU *A*., 15: [níĝ-kaskal *A-ir-ra*$^{?}$ *wa A-zú-bù-lu*$^{?}$] DU.DU *A*. maškim *Ḫa-ra-ì*; r. II 16: *Du-bí* lú *Iš-da-má* tuš-LÚ×TIL *A*.; r. III 7: *En-àr-li-im* [dumu-ni]ta *Du-*[*bí*]*-šum A-ba-ad*$^{ki}$ tuš-LÚ×TIL *A*. *áš-ti Zú-mu-šar*$^{ki}$; r. IV 3: *Du-ur-il Bù-ra-tin*$^{ki}$ tuš-LÚ×TIL *A*. [*áš-ti*] [ $^{ki}$]; **10** o. XIV 22: níĝ-kaskal *En-na*-BAD *Zú-ti*$^{ki}$ maškim *Du-bí* DU.DU *A*.; o. XVI 3: níĝ-kaskal *Íl-ra*-BAD maškim NI*-ba-rúm* DU.DU *si-in A*., 15: *A-da-bí-ik*$^{ki}$ ì-ti *mi-nu A*.; **11** r. VIII 8: níĝ-kaskal *Kab-lu*$_5$*-ul*$^{ki}$ DU.DU *A*.; **19** o. VIII 21: níĝ-kaskal NE*-iš-da-ar Kab-lu*$_5$*-ul*$^{ki}$ DU.DU *A*.; **21** r. X 15: níĝ-kaskal *Bù-gal-lu Ba-zi-mu*$^{ki}$ DU.DU *si-in A*.; **22** o. VI 1: (silver) lú *A*. in-na-sum *in* ud šu-mu-níĝin SA.ZA$_x$$^{ki}$; r. I 7: *Nu-ba-an*$^{ki}$ maškim *Sa-li-im* tuš-LÚ×TIL *in A*.

*Ar-ti-na-an*$^{ki}$ **7** r. VIII 23: níĝ-"mul" *A*. til; **12** o. VII 16: $^{d}$BAD *A*.

*A-ru*$_{12}$*-ga-du*$^{ki}$ see *La-ru*$_{12}$*-ga-du*$^{ki}$

*À-ru*$_{12}$*-gú*$^{ki}$ **17** r. XIII 23: níĝ-ba *ʾÀ-daš* dumu-nita *A-du-ba* *ʾÀ*.

*A-ru*$_{12}$*-lu*$^{ki}$ **7** o. II 2: *Du-bí* ugula *A*. šu-ba$_4$-ti.

*A-ša*$^{ki}$ **7** r. XI 17: *Gul-la* ⸢x-x-x⸣ *Sa-ma-na-nu* [*S*]*i-mi*[- ] [ ] *Iš-ba-ì A. in* ud DU.DU nam-kud é $^{d}$*Ku-ra*; **17** o. VIII 6: BAR.AN *áš-ti A. Wa-na* šu-ba$_{4}$-ti.

*Áš-da-ti-um*$^{ki}$ **4** o. II 11: (silver) níĝ-sa$_{10}$ 1 *mi-at* 20 ḪU.UD-ḪU.UD *áš-ti Á.*; o. V 14: (silver) níĝ-sa$_{10}$ [1 *mi-a*]*t* 30 ḪU.UD-ḪU.UD *áš-ti Á.*

*A-te-na-ad*$^{ki}$ **12** r. IV 12: *in* ud è *si-in* á-daḫ lú *A.*; **13** o. IV 16: *Ti-ti-nu wa Gú-zi* šu-ba$_{4}$-ti *in A.*

*A-zú*$^{ki}$ **4** o. XIV 17: níĝ-kaskal *A.*

*Ba-ḫa-ni-um*$^{ki}$ **1** o. V 5: (gold) níĝ-sa$_{10}$ 1 BAR.AN *B.*

*Ba-na-i-um*$^{ki}$ **7** o. IX 14: *B. in* níĝ-kas$_{4}$ *Ma-rí*$^{ki}$; **10** o. III 17: níĝ-ba *B.*; **12** r. V 6: níĝ-du$_{8}$ 1 guruš *Lu-wa-šum*$^{ki}$ *áš-ti B.*

*Bar-ga-u*$_{9}$$^{ki}$ **14** o. XIV 2: lú *Daš-na M*[*a-*]*rí*⸢$^{ki}$⸣ *i*[*n*] *B.* zàḫ *in* kaskal $^{d}$AMA-*ra.*

*Ba-sa-ḫi-um*$^{ki}$ **6** o. IV 12.

*Ba-sa-rí-im*$^{ki}$ **9** r. XV 19: *Íl-zi* lú *Iš*$_{11}$*-gú-nu B.*

*Ba-šè*$^{ki}$ **15** r. XIV 6: [níĝ-]ba $^{d}$*Áš-da-bíl B.*

*Ba-zi-mu*$^{ki}$ **21** r. X 12: níĝ-kaskal *Bù-gal-lu B.* DU.DU *si-in Ar-mi*$^{ki}$.

*Bù-ra*(/*ur*)*-tin*$^{ki}$ **7** o. XI 7: *Du-ur-ì B.*(-*ur*); 9 r. IV 1: *Du-ur-il B.*

*Bur-ma-an*$^{ki}$ **3** r. IX 6: *Ib-rí-um wa* en *B.*; **9** r. V 9: nam-kud en *B.* é $^{d}$*Ku-ra*; **13** o. IX 6: *Zi-mi-ni-*kù:babbar *ma-lik-tum B.*; **15** o. XVI 22: *Zi-mi-ni-*kù:babbar *ma-lik-tum B.*; r. VI 17: *Na-tum ma-lik-tum B.*; **17** o. III 2: [dumu-munus] en *B.* É×PAP é-gi en *Ra-ʾà-ak*$^{ki}$; **20** r. XII 4: *Da-bí-da-mu* dumu-nita en *B.*

*Da-na-áš*$^{ki}$ **15** r. XI 7: níĝ-ba *Ib-rí-um* $^{d}$*A-dar-a-an D.*; **16** o. XIV 13: [$^{d}$*A-dar-a-an*] *D.* en šu-mu-tak$_{4}$; **21** o. VI 23: níĝ-ba *Ib-rí-um* $^{d}$*A-dar-a-nu D.*

*Da-ra-um*$^{ki}$ **16** r. IX 22: níĝ-ba *Ib-rí-um* $^{d}$*Ra-sa-ap D.*

*Da-rí-íb*$^{ki}$ **4** o. XII 6: ĝuruš-ĝuruš *D.*

*Da-ti-um*$^{ki}$ **12** r. VI 13: *I-šar D.* šu-ba$_{4}$-ti.

DU$^{ki}$ **18** r. XVI 9: lú ĜIŠ-nu-kiri$_{6}$ D.

*Du-bí-tum*$^{ki}$ **11** r. VI 8: níĝ-ba $^{d}$*Ra-sa-ap D.*

*Du-du-lu*$^{ki}$ **7** o. V 6: lú ì-na-sum SA.ZA$_{x}$$^{ki}$ *in D. in* níĝ-kas$_{4}$ *Ma-rí*$^{ki}$; o. VIII 4: [ ] tuš-LÚ<×TIL> *Ma-rí*$^{ki}$ *áš-ti D.*; o. X 3: *Ib-rí-um* níĝ-ba $^{d}$BAD *D.*, 13: níĝ-ba $^{d}$*Sa-a-ša si-in D. Ib-rí-um* šu-mu-tak$_{4}$; r. XIII 24: níĝ-ba *Iš-dub-ì* maškim ga:eš$_{8}$ *D.*; **12** o. III 1: níĝ-ba *Ib-gi-tum wa Ku-tu-ʾà-bù wa Ib-du-nu* [ -]⸢x⸣ [ ] *D.* níĝ-"mul" *Ag-sa-gú*$^{ki}$ šu-ba$_{4}$-ti; o. VI 10: *Gi-rí wa Ni-ir-da-mu* 2 dumu-nita *Ib-rí-um* in-na-sum *in* ud gi$_{4}$ *mi-nu D.*, 15: *Wa-ba-rúm* ga:eš$_{8}$ *D.*; **14** o. II 23: *Šu-a-ḫa* maškim ga:eš$_{8}$ *D.*; o. III 19: *Iš-*⸢*dub*⸣*-ì wa Ib-gi-tum* maškim ga:eš$_{8}$ *D.*; o. VIII 9: *Áš-da-ma-ì* maškim ga:eš$_{8}$ *D.*; o. XIX 20; o. XX 5: *Iš-dub-il* maškim ga:eš$_{8}$ *D.*; r. IV 16: níĝ-ba *Iš-dub-il* maškim ga:eš$_{8}$ *D.*; r. X 18: *Ù-li-li* maškim [ga:eš$_{8}$ *D.*]; **15** o. II 8: níĝ-ba *Ib-rí-um* $^{d}$BAD *D.*; o. VIII 4: níĝ-ba *Iš-dub-il wa Dab*$_{6}$*-ti Ma-rí*$^{ki}$ maškim ga:eš$_{8}$ *D.*; **18** r. XIII 16: ki:lam$_{7}$ $^{d}$*Ga-mi-iš wa* $^{d}$*Áš-da-bíl wa* $^{d}$BAD *D.*; r. XV 13: níĝ-ba $^{d}$BAD *D.*; **19** o. VI 8: é $^{d}$BAD *D.*, 14: níĝ-ba *Ḫu-ra-*NE *Na-gàr*$^{ki}$ *in D.* šu-ba$_{4}$-ti; r. X 29: níĝ-ba *Ib-rí-um* $^{d}$BAD *D.*; 20 o. II 6: [ ] [maškim] ga:eš$_{8}$ *D.*; **21** o. II 10: níĝ-ba *Ḫu-*NE*-du wa Ir*$_{11}$*-tum-a-ḫu Sag-gar*$^{ki}$ kaskal níĝ-kas$_{4}$ *D.*; **22** r. VI 1: níĝ-ba $^{d}$BAD *D.*

*Du-du-la*$^{ki}$ **2** r. VIII 6: níĝ-ba *Ib-rí-um* $^{d}$BAD *D.*; r. XVI 13: (52 garments) ki:lam$_{7}$ *D.*; **9** r. IX 5: *Ib-rí-um* šu-mu-tak$_{4}$ $^{d}$BAD *D.*; r. XIII 5.

*Du-gú-ra-su*$^{ki}$ **10** o. VI 2: [ ] DU.DU *D.*; 17 r. VIII 26: ugula *Ib-al*$_{6}$$^{ki}$ DU.DU *D.*; **19** r. XVI 14: en *D.*

*Du-li*$^{ki}$ **20** o. VII 2: [n]íĝ-ba [*I-*]*ti* [*M*]*a-rí*$^{ki}$ [x]-⸢x⸣[- ] [ ] níĝ-"mul" *D.* àga-kár$^{!}$(ŠÈ); o. XIII 20: níĝ-ba *Daš-na Ma-rí*$^{ki}$ níĝ-"mul" *D.* šu-ba$_{4}$-ti.

*Du-lu*$^{ki}$ **4** r. XI 14: en *D.*; **6** r. XVI 31: en *D.*; **10** o. X 6: en *D.*; **13** o. I 11: [e]n *D.*, 17: [*m*]*a-lik-*[*t*]*um D.*; o. II 13: *Mu-zi* šeš en *wa Lu-wa-sa-ra-du D.*; o. IX 19: níĝ-ba $^{d}$NE*-ti-a-du* diĝir *D.*; **14** o. VI 17: *Ḫu-wa-sa-ra-du*$^{\{ki\}}$ *D.*; r. I 12: *Ar-ra-du-lum* [*D.*]; r. VII 18: níĝ-ba Šubur *D.*

*Du-ne-ib*$^{ki}$ **7** o. III 18: níĝ-ba *Ib-rí-um* $^{d}$*Ra-sa-ap D.*; r. II 14: níĝ-ba $^{d}$*Ra-sa-ap D.*; r. XV 15: nu$_{11}$-za $^{d}$*Ra-sa-ap D.*; r. XVI 6: $^{d}$*Ra-sa-ap D.*; **12** r. VIII 16: $^{d}$*Ra-sa-ap D.*; **14** r. VIII 6: $^{d}$*Ra-sa-ap D.*; **15** r. VIII 11: níĝ-ba *Ib-rí-um* $^{d}$*Ra-sa-ap D.*; r. XVI 19: lú $^{d}$*Ra-sa-ap D.*; **18** r. XVII 3: níĝ-ba ama-gal en $^{d}$*Ra-sa-ap D. wa* $^{dʾ}$*A*$_{5}$*-da-"bal" ʾÀ-ma-du*$^{ki}$.

*Du-nu*$^{ki}$ **4** o. XIV 7: níĝ-kaskal *D.*

*Dur-zi-lum*$^{ki}$ **14** r. VIII 15: *A-mur-da-mu* tuš-LÚ×TIL *D.*

*Du-ub*$^{ki}$ **3** o. XI 12: [níĝ-ba] $^{[d]ʾ}$*À-da* lú *D.*; **6** o. IX 9: níĝ-ba *A-mu-ra D.*; **10** o. III 11: níĝ-ba *A-mu-ra D.*; r. XI 16; **17** r. XVIII 6: ([…] garments, 233 kilts) ki:lam$_{7}$ $^{d}$*Áš-da-bíl D. Ìr-ku*$^{ki}$.

EN-NE$^{ki}$ **4** o. XIII 6; **6** o. XIV 19; **18** r. XVI 6; **19** r. X 4: níĝ-ba *Mar-rúm* E.

*Ga-ga-ba-an*$^{ki}$ **1** o. IX 19: *Za-zú G.*; **4** o. VI 9: (silver) *G.* (silver) maškim-*sù*; r. I 18: *La-*⸢*a*⸣*-*[*na-ma*] *G.*; **5** r. XVI 4; **6** o. IV 4; o. XIII 21: *La-a-na-ma G.*; **9** o. XI 19: *Na-gàr*$^{ki}$ *wa G. in* [ $^{ki}$] šu-ba$_{4}$-ti; **10** o. XV 4: níĝ-ba *G.*; **25** o. VI 6: (94 garments) ki:lam$_{7}$ *G. A-bù-*Kur$^{ki}$.

*Ga-na-na* **17** o. VII 7: $^{d}$BAD *G.*

*Ga-na-na-im* **6** o. XIV 2: $^{d}$BAD *G.*; **9** r. VIII 2: $^{d}$BAD *G.*; **12** o. V 18: $^{d}$BAD *G.*; **16** o. V 18: $^{d}$BAD *G.*; **19** o. VI 20: $^{d}$BAD *G.*

*Ga-na-na-um* **8** o. VI 8: $^{d}$BAD *G.*; r. IX 10': $^{d}$BAD *G.*

*Ga-ra-ma-an*$^{ki}$ **3** o. VIII 15: *in* ud dumu-nita en *Ḫa-zu-wa-an*$^{ki}$ ḫi-úš *in G.* lú *Ḫar-sum*$^{ki}$; **13** r. II 9: ⸢*Sa-mu-ù*⸣ dam-gàr *G.*

*Ga-ra-mu*$^{ki}$ **6** o. VIII 10: níĝ-ba $^{d}$*Wa-da-ʾà-an* lú *G.*; r. V 10: $^{d}$*Wa-da-ʾà-an wa* $^{d}$*Ša-la-ša* lú *G.*

*Ga-rí-u*$_{9}$$^{ki}$ **9** r. XVII 21: *Ma-li-gú G.*

*Ga-sa*$^{ki}$ **9** o. X 14: lú simug *G.*; **17** r. VIII 12: *En-na-il G.*

*Ga-wa-na*$^{ki}$ **15** r. V 15: *ma-lik-tum Ì-ra-ar*$^{ki}$ … *in* ud DU.DU *G.*

*Ga-zú-wa-ti-um*$^{ki}$ **4** o. XIV 10: níĝ-kaskal *G.*

*Gi-da-*NE$^{ki}$ **9** o. XII 20: *Daš-na wa Šu-ga-du Ma-r*[*i*]$^{ki}$ *in G.* šu-ba$_{4}$-ti.

*Gi-ti-*NE$^{ki}$ **5** o. VI 12: *in* ud níĝ-mu-sá dumu-munus *Ib-rí-um G.*

*Gi-li-ti-um*$^{ki}$ **9** o. II 6: níĝ-kaskal *G.* DU.DU *[A]r-mi*$^{ki}$.

*Gú-da-da-núm*$^{ki}$ **6** o. XVI 2: en *G.*; **11** r. II 9: *in* ud è níĝ-kas$_4$ *G.*; **18** o. V 25: la-ḫa ĝeštin en *G. Za-ba-rúm* šu-ba$_4$-ti; **23** r. I 5: *in* ud è níĝ-kas$_4$ *G.*; r. III 13: *in* ud è níĝ-kas$_4$ *G.*

*Gul-da-ad*$^{ki}$ **9** r. II 18: *áš-ti G.*

*Gú-ra-*BÀD$^{ki}$ **8** r. VII 11': 1 ĝír mar-tu kg *G.*

*Gú-ra-"bal"*$^{ki}$ **7** o. VI 18: *Bu-ma-ì G.*

*Gur-ad*$^{ki}$ **11** o. IX 1: [ ] lú *G.*

*Gú-ra-du*$^{ki}$ **16** r. XVI 27; **18** r. XIX 12: (silver) níĝ-ba *G.* (silver) níĝ-ba *ʾÀ-lu*$^{ki}$ *in Ša-dab*$_6$$^{ki}$ šu-ba$_4$-ti; **21** o. II 1.

*Gú-rá-ma-an*$^{ki}$ **5** r. IV 14: BÍL-*ma-lik* lú *Ba-ḫa-ga in* ud *G.* tuš-LÚ×TIL; r. V 7: níĝ-ba *Daš-na Ma-rí*$^{ki}$ *in* níĝ-kas$_4$ *G.* šu-ba$_4$-ti.

*Gú-šè-bù*$^{ki}$ **19** r. XII 10: $^{d}$*Á-la G.*; **21** r. XI 13: $^{d}$*Á-la G.*

*Ḫa-lab*$_x$$^{ki}$ **9** o. III 20: níĝ-ba $^{d}$*Ra-sa-ap ʾÀ-da-ni*$^{ki}$ *wa* $^{dʾ}$*À-da Ḫ.* AMA-*ra*; o. IV 12: nídba en $^{dʾ}$*À-da Ḫ.*; **11** r. VIII 17: ⸢nídba⸣ en $^{dʾ}$*À-da* lú *Ḫ.*; **13** o. VII 15: $^{d}$ *Ḫa-a-ba-du* lú *Ḫ.*; **16** r. XI 10: nídba en $^{dʾ}$*À-da Ḫ.*; **18** o. XIX 23: nídba en $^{dʾ}$*À-da Ḫ. in* $^{d}$AMA-*ra*; r. XVIII 3: nídba en $^{[d]ʾ}$*À-da Ḫ. ʾa*$_5$*-nun*; **19** o. XI 17: nídba $^{dʾ}$*À-da Ḫ. in* $^{d}$AMA-*ra*; r. VII 5: níĝ-ba 3 guruš *ʾÀ-du*$^{ki}$ *in Ḫ.* šu-ba$_4$-ti; r. XVII 16: nídba en $^{dʾ}$*À-da Ḫ. ʾa*$_5$*-nun*; **20** o. IX 4: nídba en $^{dʾ}$*À-da Ḫ. in* AMA-*ra*; r. XI 15: nídba en $^{dʾ}$*À-da Ḫ.* iti *ʾa*$_5$*-nun*; **21** o. IX 4: nídba en $^{dʾ}$*À-da* lú *Ḫ.*; o. XII 21: níĝ-du$_8$ *I-šar Ḫ. áš-du Mi-su-wa-du Ma-rí*$^{ki}$; **23** o. I 5: $^{dʾ}$*À-da Ḫ. in* AMA-*ra*; r. IV 11: níĝ-ba $^{dʾ}$*À-da* lú *Ḫ. in* iti *ʾa*$_5$*-nun.*

*Ḫa-la-bí-du*$^{ki}$ **18** o. XIII 9: níĝ-ba *En-na-ì Ḫ. in ʾÀ-da-ni*$^{ki}$ šu-ba$_4$-ti.

*Ḫal-sum*$^{ki}$ **16** r. IV 10: *Ḫa-bù-zú ʾÀ-bar-du*$^{ki}$ maškim *Za-ba-rúm* tuš-LÚ×TIL *Ḫ.*; r. VIII 22: *in* maškim *Ḫ.*; r. IX 7: *I-bí-zi-kir* dumu-nita *Ib-rí-um in* ud tuš-LÚ×TIL *Ḫ.*; r. IX 29: dumu-nita *Ig-rí-iš* šu-du$_8$ *in Ḫ.*; **18** r. XVI 26: *Ga-nu-bù Sal-ba-um*$^{ki}$ tuš-LÚ×TIL *Ḫ.*; **19** r. X 18: *Gi-ra-ma-lik* lú *I-bí-šum* tuš-LÚ×TIL *Ḫ.*

*Ḫar-sum*$^{ki}$ **3** o. VIII 17: *in* ud dumu-nita en *Ḫa-zu-wa-an*$^{ki}$ ḫi-úš *in Ga-ma-ra-an*$^{ki}$ lú *Ḫ.*

*Ḫa-ra-an*$^{ki}$ **3** r. X 10; **10** r. III 16: níĝ-ba *La-sa-nu Ḫ.*; **13** o. XI 1: *ba-da-lum Ḫ.*; **16** r. X 7: níĝ-ba *ba-da-lum Ḫ.*; **18** o. XIII 5: *ba-da-lum Ḫ.*; **19** r. XIV 5: níĝ-ba *ba-da-lum Ḫ.*; r. XVIII 24: dumu-nita *ba-da-lum Ḫ.*; **21** o. V 26: [2 *bu*]-⸢DI⸣ ì-ĝiš-saĝ *ba-da-lum Ḫ.*

*Ḫar-zàr-du*$^{ki}$ **6** r. IV 9: níĝ-kaskal *Ḫ.* DU.DU *Ar-mi*$^{ki}$.

*Ḫa-zu-wa-an*$^{ki}$ **2** r. I 8: *I-rí-ig* lú-kar *Ḫ.*; r. XI 8: *Bù-da-ma-lik* BÍL-*ma-lik A-da-mu* lú-kar *Ḫ.*; **3** o. VIII 12: *in* ud dumu-nita en *Ḫ.* ḫi-úš *in Ga-ma-ra-an*$^{ki}$ lú *Ḫar-sum*$^{ki}$; **4** o. VI 2: 3 dam *Ib-rí-um Ḫ.*; r. IX 3: *I-du-bù* tuš-LÚ×TIL *Ḫ.*; **23** o. IV 2: *Ib-ga-il Ḫ.*

*Ḫi-la-zi-um*$^{ki}$ **6** o. IV 16.

*Ḫi-la-zu*$^{ki}$ **1** o. X 21.

*Ib-al*$_6$$^{ki}$ **3** o. VIII 8: [ ] níĝ-kas$_4$ nu-du$_{11}$-nu-du$_{11}$ šu-ba$_4$-ti *si-in I.*; **4** o. VII 11: *Ma-za-a-du ma-lik-tum I.*, 15: *Du-bù-uš-da-mu I.*; r. VI 16: *I-ga-li-im* en *I.*; r. XIII 9: *Du-bù-uš-da-mu I-ga-li-im Zú-ga-du Ì-lum-a-rí-ḫu* 4 en *I. in* ud [nídba ì-ĝiš]; **6** r. XII 6: *Du-bù-uš-da-mu wa Il-il I.*; **14** r. IX 9: [ ] [dum]u-nita *I-bí-zi-kir* [tuš-LÚ×TIL *in*] *I.*; **17** r. VIII 24: ugula *I.* DU.DU *Du-gú-ra-su*$^{ki}$; **25** r. III 3: [ ] l[ú] *D[u-si]* ugula *I.*

*Ib-la*$^{ki}$ **6** o. III 18: 1 dub lú nam-kud *I. wa Ma-rí*$^{ki}$ é $^{d}$*Ku-ra*; **15** r. XI 19: $^{d}$*Da-bí-ir* diĝir *I.*; **16** r. II 15: níĝ-du$_8$ 3 *na-se*$_{11}$ *I. áš-ti Ir-i-tum*$^{ki}$; **21** o. XII 15: níĝ-ba ábba-ábba *Ma-rí*$^{ki}$ *in* ud nídba ì-ĝiš *I. wa Ma-rí*$^{ki}$; **25** o. IX 9: 1 íb-lá TAR kb *I-nu-ud-da-mu Kak-mi-um*$^{ki}$ *in* ud nídba ì-ĝiš *I. i[n]* [ ].

*Ib-su*$^{ki}$ **12** r. VII 4: níĝ-du$_8$ *Dam-da-il I.*

*I-bu*$_{16}$*-bù*$^{ki}$ **5** r. XVI 19: siki *I.*

*Ig-du-ra*$^{ki}$ **3** o. I 8: *Rí-ì-ma-lik* ugula *I.*

*Ì-la-ar*$^{ki}$ see *Ì-ra-ar*$^{ki}$.

*Ì-mar*$^{ki}$ **2** o. XI 15: en *Ì.*; **5** o. III 2: lú *Ì.* šu-ba$_4$-ti; **6** r. VII 10: *Ba-lu-zú* "ur$_4$" *Ì.*; **7** r. VIII 12: *in Ša-dab*$_6$$^{ki}$ ⸢lú⸣ *Ì.* ⸢*wa*⸣ [ ]⸢$^{ki}$⸣; **10** r. I 12: *ma-lik-tum Ì.*; **13** o. XII 4: *Ù-zu* "ur$_4$" *Ì.*; o. XIII 17: ì-ĝiš-saĝ en *Ì.*; o. XVI 1: *Ti-šè-li-im ma-lik-tum Ì.*; **16** o. I 18: *Ru*$_{12}$*-zi-da-mu* en *Ì.*; **17** o. VII 22: níĝ-ba *Ti-ša-li-im ma-lik-tum Ì.*; r. VI 2: *Ti-ša-li-im ma-lik-tum Ì.*; r. IX 33: *Ti-ša-li-im ma-lik-tum Ì.*; r. XXII 18: en *Ì. Ib-rí-um* šu-mu-tak$_4$; **18** r. XIV 15: en *I.*; **19** o. II 24: níĝ-ba *Ti-šè-li-im ma-lik-tum Ì-mar*$^{ki}$; r. XII 30: dumu-nita en *Ì.*; **20** o. III 13; o. VII 7: *Ìr-a-mu Ì.* šu-ba$_4$-ti; r. VII 10: *Dašne* lú ĜIŠ-nu-kiri$_6$ *Ì.*; r. VIII 14: *Ti-šè-li-im ma-lik-tum Ì.*; **21** r. VII 12: *Ti-šè-li-im ma-lik-tum Ì.*

*Im-ma-ra-an*$^{ki}$ **25** o. I 7: (197 garments) ki:lam$_7$ *I. A-bù-*Kur$^{ki}$.

*Ì-ra-ar*$^{ki}$ **1** o. IX 13: en *Ì. Wa-ba-rúm* šu-mu-tak$_4$ É×PAP; **2** o. II 14: *Íl-ru*$_{12}$*-ga-lu Ì.*; **3** o. XIII 4: en *Ì.*; **4** o. IX 15: níĝ-ba 4 dam *Ì.*; o. X 1 and 4: níĝ-ba guruš-guruš *Ì. in* ud *ma-lik-tum Ì.* DU.DU, 24: níĝ-ba diĝir-diĝir-diĝir lú dumu-munus *Ib-rí-um* šu-mu-tak$_4$ *si-in Ì.*; o. XIII 19: nam-kud *Ì.* é $^{d}$*Ku-ra*; **9** o. VI 11: e[n] *Ì.*; **12** o. IV 16: nam-kud en *Ì.* é ⸢$^{d}$⸣*Ku-ra*; **13** o. III 22: en *Ì.*; **14** o. V 11: dumu-munus en *Ì.*; r. IX 15: e[n] *Ì.*, 22: *ma-lik-tum Ì.*; **15** r. V 9: *ma-lik-tum Ì.* ama-gal en šu-mu-tak$_4$ *in* ud DU.DU *Ga-wa-na*$^{ki}$; **21** r. XIV 20: (silver) nam-kud-nam-kud en *Ì.* é $^{d}$*Ku-ra*; **25** r. II 5: ⸢x⸣-[ ] *Ì. in* ud DU *M[a]-za-t[um*$^{?ki}$].

*Ì-la-ar*$^{ki}$ **5** o. IX 12: *ma-lik-tum Ì. in ʾÀ-da-ni*$^{ki}$ šu-ba$_4$-ti.

(see the commentary on text no. 4)

*Ir-bí-ì-lum*$^{ki}$ **18** r. X 24: níĝ-kaskal *Gi-ba-rí-a Kab-lu*$_5$*-ul*$^{ki}$ DU.DU *si-in I.*

*Ir-i-tum*$^{ki}$ **3** r. VII 12: *áš-ti I.*; **4** r. II 6: *Zú-zu I.*; **6** r. VI 11: níĝ-ba *I-i-bù I.*; **10** o. VI 6: *Zú-zú I. in A-bí-na-du*$^{ki}$ šu-ba$_4$-ti, 19: dumu-munus e[n *Ra-ʾà-ak*$^{ki}$ *m*]*a-[li]k-[t]um* ⸢*A*⸣*-bar-sal*$_4$$^{ki}$ *wa ma-lik-tum I.*; o. XI 19: níĝ-ba *I.*; **13** o. XVI 22: níĝ-ba *A-za-ba I.*; **16** r. II 17: níĝ-du$_8$ 3 *na-se*$_{11}$ *Ib-la*$^{ki}$ *áš-ti I.*; **18** r. VI 8: níĝ-ba *I-ti-*$^{d}$*Aš-dar I.*

*Ìr-ku*$^{ki}$ **2** r. XIII 11: (180 garments, 150 na$_4$ measures of wool) ki:lam$_7$ *Ì. A-bù-*Kur$^{ki}$; **9** o. XIV 17: (321 garments, 12 kilts) ki:lam$_7$ *Ì.*; **15** o. II 16: níĝ-du$_8$ 1 dumu-nita *A-ba-ti-lum*$^{ki}$ maškim *Za-ba-rúm áš-ti Ì.*; o. VIII 10: (74 garments) ki:lam$_7$ *Ì.*; **17** r. XVIII 7: ([...], 233 kilts) ki:lam$_7$ $^{d}$*Áš-da-bíl Du-ub*$^{ki}$ *Ì.*; **18** r. IV 18: [n]íĝ-du$_8$ 1 dumu-nita *Ku-a-*NE lú NE-*da-mu* SA.ZA$_x$$^{ki}$ *áš-ti Ì.*

*Kab-lu*$_5$*-ul*$^{ki}$ **4** o. IX 4: *in* mè *K.*; **6** o. IX 20: en *K.*; r. XVII 13: en *K.*; **7** r. XI 1: *A-a-lu K.* al$_6$-tuš *Mi-da-ḫi*$^{ki}$; r. XII 9: *I-na-ni-gi K.*; **8** o. XI 3: en *K.*; **11** r. III 17: níĝ-kaskal *K.*; r. VIII 6: níĝ-kaskal *K.* DU.DU *Ar-mi*$^{ki}$; **15** r. XVI 21: lú *Da-*NE*-du K.*; **17** r. X 21: 2 gud ki:lam$_7$ *K.* šu-mu-tak$_4$ ⌜$^d$*Ku-ra*⌝; **18** r. X 21: níĝ-kaskal *Gi-ba-rí-a K.* DU.DU *si-in Ir-bí-ì-lum*$^{ki}$; **19** o. VIII 18: níĝ-kaskal NE*-iš-da-ar K.* DU.DU *si-in Ar-mi*$^{ki}$; o. XIV 2: (daggers) *ap* 2 ma-na kg lú mu-DU *K. zi-du-sù*; r. I 8: (daggers) *ap* 10 lá-2 ma-na kg *zi-du-sù* lú mu-DU *K.*

*Kak-mi-um*$^{ki}$ **1** o. VII 17: *Du-bí-šum* lú *Ba-zi-da* tuš-LÚ×TIL *K.*; **2** r. X 12: *Íl-da-ar K.*; **3** o. XIII 7: EN*-mar* lú *K.*; **4** r. VI 11: NI*-má-ti* lú-kar *K.*; r. XV 6: en *K.*; **5** o. II 13: *Ib-ḫur-ma-lik* lú-kar *K.*; r. VIII 11: *I-nu-ud-da-mu K.*; **6** o. II 2: en *K.*; o. XVI 23: dumu-nita *Ù-du-bù*$^{ki}$ *áš-ti K.*; r. XV 11: en *K.*; **7** o. VIII 8: *Ib-ḫur-ma-lik K.* tuš-LÚ<×TIL> *in Ar-ḫa-du*$^{ki}$; r. XV 9: *Ne-zi-ma-lik* lú-kar *K.*; **8** o. III 7: *I-nu-ud-da-mu* ugula *K.*; o. XII 4: lú ĜIŠ-kiri$_6$ *K.*; r. X x+1; 9 r. XVI 7: *En-na-*⌜*il*⌝ [ ] *Rí-ì-ma-lik* lú-kar *K.*; **10** o. I 16: lú ĜIŠ-kiri$_6$ *K.*; o. VII 5: lú ĜIŠ-kiri$_6$ *K.*; **11** o. XI 17: *Wa-ba-rúm En-na-ì* lú-kar *K.*; **13** o. XII 21: *In-gàr wa Ne-zi-ma-lik* lú-kar *K.*; r. II 13: *Puzur*$_4$*-ra-m*[*a-*]*lik* lú-kar *K.*, 22: *si-in* en *K.*; **14** o. IV 12: *in* níĝ-kas$_4$ *K.*; o. XIII 10: *Iš-ra-il* lú-kar *K.*; **15** o. III 22: *Si-ti-*BAR.AN lú-kar *K.*; o. XIII 27: *I-in-il* ugula *Ù-ša-li-ik*$^{ki}$ *in* ud tuš-LÚ×TIL *K.*; r. II 10: *An-na-aḫ* lú-kar *K.*; **17** o. I 15: *Íl-gú-uš-ti* lú *I-gi* tuš-LÚ×TIL *K.* ⌜*áš-ti*⌝ [GN]; o. XII 18: *Ḫa-zu-um* maškim *Ib-rí-um* tuš-LÚ×TIL *Ti-ma-tim*$^{ki}$ lú *K.*, 26: *Du-bí-šum* lú *Gú-ma-ni-du* maškim *I-bí-zi-kir* tuš-LÚ×TIL *K. áš-ti Šu-ra-an*$^{ki}$; o. XVI 9: *in* ud è níĝ-kas$_4$ al-kur$_6$ še *K.*; **20** o. XIV 10: *Iš-ra-*BAD lú-kar *K.*; **25** o. IX 6: *I-nu-ud-da-mu K. in* ud nídba ì-ĝiš *Ib-la*$^{ki}$ *i*[*n*] [ ]; r. III 9: *Lu-*⌜*rí*⌝*-um K.* níĝ-"mul" Bàd$^{ki}$ šu-ba$_4$-⌜ti⌝.

Kiš$^{ki}$ **7** r. XIII 5: níĝ-"mul" K. til, 13: *En-na-ì* lú BÍL*-za-ì* DU.DU *si-in* K.; **11** o. VII 18: *Íl-gú-uš-ti* lú *I-gi* tuš-LÚ×TIL *K.* lú *A-bar-sal*$_4$$^{ki}$; **12** r. VI 21: *I-in-zé in* K.; r. VII 6: níĝ-du$_8$ *Dam-da-il Ib-su*$^{ki}$ *in* K.; **13** r. VI 18: *in* ud níĝ-kas$_4$ *si-in* K.; r. VII 1; **14** r. V 15: [níĝ-ba] *Wa-ru*$_{12}$*-tum Ma-rí*$^{ki}$ níĝ-"mul" K. til-til; r. X 25: níĝ-kaskal [*Í*]*r-am*$_6$*-*[*m*]*a-lik* [ ]⌜x⌝ [DU.DU] *si-in* K.; **15** o. III 4: níĝ-⌜ba⌝ *Daš-na Ma-rí*$^{ki}$ níĝ-"mul" K. til; o. VII 19: níĝ-ba *Wa-ru*$_{12}$*-tum Ma-rí*$^{ki}$ níĝ-"mul" in uru$^{ki}$-uru$^{ki}$ K. šu-ba$_4$-ti; o. XVII 10: e$_{11}$ *áš-ti Na-zu-mu mi-nu* K.; r. X 24: níĝ-ba *Daš-na Ma-rí*$^{ki}$ níĝ-"mul" K. til-til, 30: níĝ-kaskal *En-na-ì* DU.DU K.; **16** o. IV 17: *in* K. dam-gàr; **17** o. VI 6: níĝ-kaskal *En-na-il* [DU.DU] *si-in* K.; **19** r. XII 17: níĝ-ba *Ga-áš-ru*$_{12}$ *Na-gàr*$^{ki}$ DU.DU *mi-nu* K.; **20** r. IX 13: níĝ-ba *Wa-ru*$_{12}$*-tum Ma-rí*$^{ki}$ e$_{11}$ *mi-nu* K. *áš-ti En-na-il.*

*Kul-ba-an*$^{ki}$ **14** o. XX 12: ugula *K.* ga:eš$_8$ šu-ba$_4$-ti.

Kur$^{ki}$ **2** r. V 13: raš-SAR K.; **3** o. VI 8: raš-SAR K.; **4** r. XI 18: raš-SAR K.; **5** r. II 10: raš-SAR K.; **7** o. IX 19: raš-SAR K.; **9** o. IX 16: ⌜raš⌝-SAR K.; **11** o. X 2: raš-SAR K.; **12** o. II 5: raš-SAR K.; **13** o. XVII 6: raš-SAR K.; **14** o. XVII 2: raš-SAR K.; **16** o. XIII 17: raš-SAR K.; **17** r. X 13: raš-SAR K.; **18** r. III 10: raš-SAR K.; **20** o. XIV 13: raš-SAR K.

*La-dab*$_6$*-bí-um*$^{ki}$ **6** o. IV 10.

*La-ru*$_{12}$*-ga-du*$^{ki}$ **2** r. IX 1: $^{d}$*ʾA*$_5$*-da-"bal" L.*; **3** o. IV 20: $^{d}$*ʾA*$_5$*-da-"bal" L.*; r. XI 3: $^{d}$*ʾA*$_5$*-da-"bal" L.*; **4** o. II 16: [$^d$]⌜*ʾA*$_5$⌝*-da-*["*ba*]*l" L.*; r. II 13: *Ki-ti-ir L.*; **5** r. VI 1: níĝ-b[a] $^{d}$*ʾA*$_5$*-da-"bal" L.*; r. IX 2: níĝ-ba *I-bí-zi-kir* dumu-nita *Ib-rí-um* $^{d}$*ʾA*$_5$*-da-"bal" L.*; **6** o. XIV 16: níĝ-ba $^{d}$*ʾA*$_5$*-da-"bal" L.*(*-ga*$_x$-); r. X 7: (35 garments, 185 kilts, 12 daggers) … ĜIŠ-ti-ḪAR *Wa-ba-rúm* šu-ba$_4$-ti ki:lam$_7$ *ʾÀ-da-ni*$^{ki}$ *wa* NI*-ab*$^{ki}$ *wa L.*

*A-ru*$_{12}$*-ga-du*$^{ki}$ **12** o. II 11: $^{d}$*ʾA*$_5$*-da-"bal" A.*; o. III 18: níĝ-ba ⌜$^d$⌝*ʾA*$_5$*-da-*["*b*]*al" A.*; **13** r. IV 12: níĝ-ba $^{d}$*ʾA*$_5$*-da-"bal" A.*; **15** o. XIV 21: lú ĜIŠ-nu-kiri$_6$ *A.*; **16** o. V 6: *Da-dub* dam en lú *A.*; r. V 22: *Bar-za-ma-ù* ugula *A.*; r. X 24: níĝ-ba *Ib-rí-um* $^{d}$*ʾA*$_5$*-da-"bal" A.*; **19** o. XI 28: níĝ-ba $^{d}$*ʾA*$_5$*-da-"bal" A. wa* $^{d}$*ʾA*$_5$*-da-"bal" ʾÀ-ma-du*$^{ki}$; r. VI 21: é *A.*; r. VII 20: *Ḫu-ra-*NE *Na-gàr in A.* šu-ba$_4$-ti; r. VIII 16: níĝ-ba $^{d}$*ʾA*$_5$*-da-"bal" wa* $^{d}$BAD-munus *A.*; **20** r. VIII 8: *Kùn-da-ba-an* [ ] *in* ud tuš-LÚ×TIL *in A.*; **24** o. VI 10: níĝ-ba $^{d}$*ʾA*$_5$*-da-"bal" A.*

*Lu-a-tum*$^{ki}$ **4** r. XII 26.

*Lu-ba-an*$^{ki}$ **5** r. IV 3: níĝ-ba $^{d}$*ʾA*$_5$*-da-"bal" L.*; **7** r. IV 10: níĝ-ba $^{d}$*ʾA*$_5$*-da-"bal" L.*; **15** o. XIV 12: sikil $^{d}$*ʾA*$_5$*-da-"bal" L.*; r. VI 4: sikil $^{d}$*ʾA*$_5$*-da-"bal" L.*; r. XII 16: sikil $^{d}$*ʾA*$_5$*-da-"bal" L.*; r. XVI 2: sikil $^{d}$*ʾA*$_5$*-da-"bal" L.*; **16** r. XIII 20: sikil $^{d}$BAD-munus *L.*; r. XIV 29: níĝ[-ba] *Ib-rí-um* $^{d}$BAD-munus *L.*; **20** r, III 20: níĝ-ba *Dar-ib-da-mu* dumu-munus en $^{d}$BAD-munus *si-in L.*; **21** r. X 25: sikil $^{d}$*ʾA*$_5$*-da-"bal" L.*

*Lum-na-an*$^{ki}$ **2** o. III 14: *Da-ti-*$^{d}$TU *ma-lik-tum L.*; o. V 17: *En-na-il* ugula *L.*; **3** o. III 13: *Da-ti-*$^{d}$TU *ma-lik-tum L.*; **6** r. III 23: *Da-ti-*$^{d}$TU *ma-lik-tum L.*; **9** r. VII 11: *En-na-il* ugula *L.*; r. IX 8: *ma-lik-tum L.*; **10** o. IX 5: ama-gal en *L.*; **11** o. XII 2: *Da-ti-*$^{d}$TU *ma-lik-tum L.*, 19: *Da-ti-*$^{d}$TU *ma-lik-tum L.* É×PAP; **12** o. XV 5: *Da-ti-*$^{d}$TU *ma-lik-tum L.*; **13** r. XI 15: *Dag-*⌜*mul*⌝*-da-mu ma-lik-tum L.*; **17** o. XII 1: *ma-lik-tum L.* ama-gal en šu-mu-tak$_4$ *in* ud DU.DU *si-in U*$_9$*-gú-a-aš*$^{ki}$; **18** r. IV 1: *ma-lik-tum L.* É×PAP, 27: ì-ĝiš-saĝ *Di-rín-da-mu* dam-diĝir *áš-du* úš *ma-lik-tum L.*; **24** r. III 1: *Dag-mul-da-mu L.*

*Lu-ub*$^{ki}$ **6** o. VIII 4: níĝ-ba $^{d}$*ʾÀ-da L.*; **11** r. IV 11: níĝ-ba $^{d}$*ʾÀ-da* lú *L.*; **13** r. IV 7: níĝ-ba $^{d}$*ʾÀ-da* lú *L.*; **14** r. II 21: níĝ-ba $^{d}$*ʾÀ-da* lú *L.*; **15** r. I 13: níĝ-ba $^{d}$*ʾÀ-d*[*a*] lú *L.*; **16** r. VII 23: níĝ-ba $^{d}$*ʾÀ-da* lú *L.*; **17** r. XV 17: níĝ-ba $^{d}$*ʾÀ-da* lú *L.*; **18** r. XI 9: níĝ-ba $^{d}$*ʾÀ-da* lú *L.*; **19** r. VIII 28: níĝ-ba $^{d}$*ʾÀ-da* lú *L. in gi-*NI; **20** r. VII 19: : níĝ-ba $^{d}$*ʾÀ-d*[*a*] lú *L. in gi-*NI; **21** o. XV 12: níĝ-ba $^{d}$*ʾÀ-da* lú *L. in gi*:NI; **22** o. III 1: é $^{d}$*ʾÀ-da* lú *L.*; **23** r. II 4: níĝ-ba $^{d}$*ʾÀ-da* lú *L. gi-*NI;

*Lu-wa-šum*$^{ki}$ **11** r. V 2: [$^{d}$BAD] *Ga-na-na-im* lú *L.*; **12** r. V 4: níĝ-du$_8$ 1 ĝuruš *L. áš-ti Ba-na-i-um*$^{ki}$.

*Má-*NE$^{ki}$ **5** o. III 1: *Daš-na wa Wa-ru*$_{12}$*-tum Ma-rí*$^{ki}$ *in M.*; r. VI 12: níĝ-ba $^{d}$BAD *M.*; **6** o. XI 17: $^{d}$*Iš:šára M.*; r. XVII 5: $^{d}$*Iš:šára M.*; **12** o. XIV 13: níĝ-ba $^{d}$BAD *M. wa* $^{d}$BAD *Zu-ra-mu*$^{ki}$; **15** r. X 16: níĝ-ba *Da-bur-da-mu* $^{d}$*Iš:šára Zu-ra-mu*$^{ki}$ *wa* $^{d}$*Iš:šára M.*; **18** r. XI 31: níĝ-ba ama-gal en $^{d}$*Iš:šára M. U*$_9$*-gú-a-áš*$^{ki}$ *wa Zu-ra-mu*$^{ki}$; **20** r. XI 3: níĝ-ba ama-gal en $^{d}$*Iš:šára*

Zu-ra-mu$^{ki}$ wa $^{d}$Iš:šára M.; **21** o. V 12: níĝ-ba Ib-rí-um $^{d}$Sa-nu-ga-ar M.

Ma-nu-wa-ad$^{ki}$ **2** o. XII 12: En-na-ma-lik M.; r. VI 10: en M. in ʾÀ-da-ni$^{ki}$ šu-ba$_4$-ti; r. X 22: Ì-lum-na-im lú-kar M.; **3** o. VII 16: Ru$_{12}$-zi-da-mu M.; r. XII 16: 2 en M.; **4** r. IX 8: En-na-ma-lik lú-kar M.; **6** o. I 14: en M.; **7** o. II 13: Ib-lu$_5$-zú lú-kar M.; r. XV 1: I-ti-um M.; **8** o. V 9: [ -g]i Ib-lu$_5$-zú wa I-za-iš-ru$_{12}$ lú-kar M.; r. V 5': [Ib-lu$_5$]-⸢zú⸣ wa I-za-iš-ru$_{12}$ [lú-k]ar M.; **9** o. IV 22: Ma-gal-lu lú M.; **10** o. XV 16: en M.; **12** o. IX 13: in ud è si-in níĝ-kas$_4$ M.; o. XII 11: in ud šu-du$_8$ in M.; o. XIII 2: I-bí-zi-kir lú I-rí-gú-nu in ud tuš-LÚ×TIL in M.; r. I 4: I-bí-du-lum en M.; **13** r. III 22: ḫi-mu-DU mè si-in M.; r. VI 11: Iš$_{11}$-la-ab lú Ru$_{12}$-zi-da-mu wa I-ša-ni-ki-nu šeš Ar-si-a-ḫa 2 lú-kar M.; **14** o. X 19: lú Ba-ga-ma šu-ba$_4$-ti in M.; **17** o. XVI 20: Lugal-na-i-iš Il-ba-šum Du-bi-ga-lu Ša-gú-bù dumu-nita en M.; **23** r. IV 5: In-gàr lú M.; r. V 4: A-ma-NI M.; **24** o. III 13: NI-ba-il lú-kar M.

Mar-da-ma-LUM$^{ki}$ **10** o. IX 17: níĝ-ba "ur$_4$" M.

Ma-ri$^{ki}$ **1**(e) r. III' 12: níĝ-kaskal I-ga-iš-lu DU.DU si-in M.; **2** o. VIII 5: 31 siki na$_4$ M., 8: Du-tum M.; **3** o. II 14: I-ti M., 22: Daš-na wa Wa-ru$_{12}$-tum M.; o. XIII 18: Daš-na wa Wa-ru$_{12}$-tum M.; r. VI 1: Iš-má-il wa Ba-ga-ar M., 7 and 9: I-ku-i-šar en M. Du-tum M. šu-mu-tak$_4$, 16: BAD-sù-BAD wa Maḫ-mu M.; r. VIII 8: Ib-gi-tum wa maškim-sù M. in Ša-dab$_6$$^{ki}$ šu-ba$_4$-ti; r. X 15: Ib-gi-tum lú I-ti M.; r. XI 13: Kùn-$^{d}$Aš-dar lú ⸢I⸣-ti [M.]; r. XII 3: áš-da M., 7: Ù-da-aḫ M. kuš$_7$; r. XIII 5: A-ku-da wa Daš-na M., 21: Daš-na wa A-ba-du M.; r. XIV 11: (74 garments, 1 kilt) ⸢ki:lam$_7$⸣ M. Na-zi; **4** o. II 6: 2 na-se$_{11}$ M.; o. IV 7: Wa-ra-núm M.; o. V 5: dumu-nita Lá-da-il M.; o. VI 5: Mi-su-wa-du M.; r. V 1: Bù-šu-sum M.; r. IX 20: M. wa til-sù; r. X 14: níĝ-"mul" àga-ʿkàr'(ŠÈ) wa til Wa-ru$_{12}$-tum; r. XII 20: [níĝ-kaskal] A-ʾà-⸢lu⸣ wa Ù-da-a-ḫa M. heš$_5$ (LÚ×KÁR) DU.DU; **5** o. II 19: Daš-na wa Wa-ru$_{12}$-tum M. in Má-NE$^{ki}$; r. II 8: níĝ-ba Wa-ru$_{12}$-tum M., 18: níĝ-ba I-ku-il M.; r. IV 21: níĝ-ba Wa-ru$_{12}$-tum wa maškim M.; r. V 4: níĝ-ba Daš-na M. in níĝ-kas$_4$ Gú-rá-ma-an$^{ki}$ šu-ba$_4$-ti; r. XVI 1: níĝ-ba Wa-ru$_{12}$-tum M.; **6** o. II 11: 2 dam túg-nu-tag M.; o. III 5 and 8: guruš-guruš maškim-sù M. in ud nídba ì-ĝiš M., 12: Du-tum M., 20: 1 dub lú nam-kud Ib-la$^{ki}$ wa M. é $^{d}$Ku-ra; o. X 12: níĝ-ba Wa-ba-rúm M., 21: níĝ-ba I-ti ga:eš$_8$ M.; o. XII 1: níĝ-kaskal Ni-zi-ma-il DU.DU M., 11: níĝ-ba Ab-ba M.; o. XIII 10: níĝ-kaskal A-ʾà-lu wa Ù-da-aḫ heš$_5$ (LÚ×KÁR) DU.DU M.; o. XV 12: níĝ-ba Puzur$_4$-ra-$^{d}$Utu M., 20: níĝ-ba Ù-NE-NE M.; o. XVI 11: níĝ-kaskal Ni-zi-ma-il wa I-ib-ma-lik DU.DU M., 17: níĝ-ba Ìr-NI-ba wa Sá-ba M.; r. I 10: níĝ-ba Daš-na wa I-da-il M., 17: níĝ-kaskal Ìr-am$_6$-ma-lik wa I-ib-ma-lik DU.DU M.; r. IV 6: níĝ-ba Daš-na wa I-da-il M., 17: níĝ-ba A-gàr wa Gú-zú-gú-zú M.; r. V 3: níĝ-kaskal En-na-ì lú kas$_4$-kas$_4$ DU.DU M.; r. VI 4: níĝ-ba ... I-ku-il wa Ba-du-lum M.; r. IX 4: (194 garments) ki:lam$_7$ M. Na-zi; r. XVII 16: en M.; **7** o. V 9: lú ì-na-sum SA.ZA$_x$$^{ki}$ in Du-du-lu$^{ki}$ in níĝ-kas$_4$ M.; o. VI 14: Ti-ra-ì maškim EN-mar šu-du$_8$ in M.; o. VIII 2: [ ] tuš-LÚ<×TIL> M. áš-ti Du-du-lu$^{ki}$, 15: 1 dùl-TÚG M.; o. IX 1: 10 lá-2 na$_4$ siki M., 17: Ba-na-i-um$^{ki}$ in níĝ-kas$_4$ M.; o. XV 14: níĝ-ba A-LUM-mu-d[a] M., 23: níĝ-ba ⸢Wa⸣-[r]u$_{12}$[-tum M.]; o. XVIII 3: níĝ-kaskal Nap⸣-ḫ[a-il] DU.DU si-in M.; r. VII 5: 4 mi-at na$_4$ siki M.; r. VIII 21: níĝ-ba Iš-dub-ì M.; r. X 18: níĝ-ba Wa-ru$_{12}$-tum M.; r. XIII 2: [níĝ-ba] Daš-na M. níĝ-"mul" Kiš$^{ki}$ til, 16: [1 ma-na] an-na M. En-na-ì šu-mu-tak$_4$; r. XIV 20: níĝ-ba Wa-ru$_{12}$-tum Da-ti Bù-sum M.; **8** o. III 3: Du-bí wa maškim-sù M.; o. IV 1: Daš-na M.; o. X 6: Ib-bu-tum … maškim-sù M.; r. III 6': Du-tum M., 13': I-ti ga:eš$_8$ M., 17': Daš-na M.; **9** o. XI 7: [ ] M. in Zi-ma-du$^{ki}$ šu-ba$_4$-ti; o. XII 12: níĝ-kaskal Ìr-am$_6$-ma-lik wa En-na-BAD DU.DU M., 18: Daš-na wa Šu-ga-du M. in Gi-da-NE$^{ki}$ šu-ba$_4$-ti, 24: Wa-ru$_{12}$-tum M.; **10** o. I 12: Du-tum M. lú ga:eš$_8$; o. III 4: níĝ-ba Wa-ru$_{12}$-tum Daš-na Iš$_{11}$-ga-um ʾÀ-bí-su M.; o. IV 3: níĝ-ba Daš-na M.; o. VII 18: níĝ-ba Bù-sum M.; o. VIII 1: níĝ-ba I-ti-il M., 8: níĝ-ba Daš-na M.; o. IX 21: níĝ-ba Wa-ba-rúm M.; o. X 11: n[íg-]ba Šu-ga-du Ru$_{12}$-zi-lum M.; o. XI 8: níĝ-ba Ba-zú-zi M.; o. XII 2: níĝ-ba Daš-na Wa-ru$_{12}$-tum Puzur$_4$-ra-BAD I-ti-il M.; o. XIV 14: níĝ-ba Daš-na Wa-ru$_{12}$-tum M.; o. XVI 7: níĝ-ba Ib-gi-tum M., 19: níĝ-ba Iš$_{11}$-ga-um M.; r. I 5: níĝ-ba Daš-na Wa-ru$_{12}$-tum M.; r. II 3: níĝ-ba Daš-na wa Wa-ru$_{12}$-tum M.; r. IV 5: níĝ-ba Wa-ru$_{12}$-tum wa Daš-na M.; r. VI 4: níĝ-ba Iš$_{11}$-ga wa Daš-na M.; r. XII 8: en M.; **11** o. VII 7: níĝ-ba M. níĝ-"mul" Na-gàr$^{ki}$ til; o. VIII 19: níĝ-ba Wa-ru$_{12}$-tum Daš-na I-ku$^{!}$(DÚR)-ku$^{!}$(DÚR)-tu M.; r. IV 4: níĝ-ba Bù-za-lum Am$_6$-mu-tum M. ĜIŠ.DUG.D[U] izi-ĝar; **12** o. VII 9: Ab-bu$_{16}$ M.; o. IX 17: níĝ-ba Wa-ru$_{12}$-tum M. níĝ-"mul" Ag-sa-gú$^{ki}$ šu-ba$_4$-ti; r. III 6: 18 siki na$_4$ M.; r. VII 21: níĝ-ba Daš-na M.; **13** o. IV 19: sagi M.; o. V 2: níĝ-ba Wa-ru$_{12}$-tum wa Šu-ga-du M., 12: 2 mi-at 45 "KIN" siki M.; o. VI 21: níĝ-ba Ib-gi-tum Ba-du-lum La-li I-ku$^{!}$(DÚR)-ku$^{!}$(DÚR)-tu M.; o. X 11: 20 dùl-TÚG M., 13: (171 garments) ki:lam$_7$ M. dam-gàr; o. XVI 18: níĝ-ba Daš-na wa Šu-ga-du M.; o. XVII 17: níĝ-ba Bù-sum M.; r. I 5: níĝ-ba Ìr-am$_6$-kur$^{ki}$ sagi M.; r II 1: 24 dùl-TÚG M.; r. III 18: níĝ-ba Kùn-NE wa Ab-ba muḫaldim M. ḫi-mu-DU mè si-in Ma-nu-wa-at$^{ki}$; r. XII 13: [ -N]E$^{?}$-[N]E M.; r. XIII 16: [ -]⸢X⸣ DU.DU M.; **14** o. III 7: níĝ-ba A-ku-a-ḫa M.; o. VI 8: (231 garments) ki:lam$_7$ M. dam-gàr; o. XIII 14: níĝ-ba Daš-na M., 21: lú Daš-na M. i[n] Bar-ga-u$_9$$^{ki}$ zàḫ in kaskal $^{d}$AMA-ra; r. V 13: [níĝ-ba] Wa-ru$_{12}$-tum M. níĝ-"mul" Kiš$^{ki}$ til-til; **15** o. III 2: níĝ-⸢ba⸣ Daš-na M. níĝ-"mul" Kiš$^{ki}$ til; o. VII 2: 3 mi-at 85 "KIN" siki M.; o. VIII 1: níĝ-ba Iš-dub-il wa Dab$_6$-ti M.; o. XII 18: íb+III-TÚG M.; o. XVII 5: níĝ-ba Wa-ru$_{12}$-tum M.; r. III 9: 6 dùl-TÚG M.; r. X 22: níĝ-ba Daš-na M. níĝ-"mul" Kiš$^{ki}$ til-til; **16** o. IV 10: 1 túg-NI.NI M., 13: 3 mi-at 20 siki na$_4$ M.; o. XIV 19: níĝ-ba Wa-ru$_{12}$-tum M. šu-mu-tak$_4$ igi-du$_8$; r. X 11: níĝ-ba Ar-rúm M.; r. XI 15: 4 dùl-TÚG M., 16: 20 "KIN" siki M.; **17** o. VIII 12: níĝ-ba EZEN-il M. ḫi-mu-DU LAGAB×UD.LAGAB×UD; o. IX 7: (109 garments) ki:lam$_7$ M. dam-gàr [šu-]mu-[t]ak$_4$; o. X 4: 3 mi-at 80 siki na$_4$ M.; o. XVII 9: níĝ-ba Wa-ru$_{12}$-tum wa I-ku-uḫ M., 18: (194 garments) ki:lam$_7$ M. dam-gàr; r. IV 6: 1 dùl-TÚG M.; r. X 8: 6 dùl-TÚG M.; r. XI 9: níĝ-[b]a ⸢Ne-zi⸣

*wa Ìr-[b]a-il M.* maškim ga:eš$_8$ Saḫar$^{ki}$; r. XV 23: níĝ-ba *Daš-na M.*; **18** o. IX 15: 4 dùl-TÚG *M.*, 17: 1 *mi-at* siki na$_4$ *M.*; r. III 6: 4 dùl-TÚG *M.*, 8: 2 *mi-at* 10 siki na$_4$ *M.*; r. XIII 4: 72 dùl-TÚG *M.*, 9: 3 *mi-at* 40 siki na$_4$ *M.*; r. XVIII 31: 85 siki na$_4$ *M.*; **19** o. III 22: *Daš-na wa Ì-lum-a-ḫi M.*; o. VI 26: 60 siki na$_4$ *M.*; r. V 9: 46 siki na$_4$ *M.*; r. XVI 23: 3 dùl-TÚG *M.*; **20** o. II 10: níĝ-ba *Wa-ru$_{12}$-tum M.*; o. V 17: *Wa-[r]u$_{12}$-tum M.*; o. VI 21: [n]íg-ba *[I-]ti M.*; o. XIII 18: níĝ-ba *Daš-na M.* níĝ-"mul" *Du-li*$^{ki}$ šu-ba$_4$-ti; o. XIV 2: 2 *mi-at* siki na$_4$ *M.*; r. VI 18: 1 dùl-TÚG *M.*; r. IX 10: níĝ-ba *Wa-ru$_{12}$-tum M.* e$_{11}$ *mi-nu* Kiš$^{ki}$ *áš-ti En-na-il*; r. XIII 4: 10 lá-1 dùl-TÚG *M.*; **21** o. XII 12 and 17: níĝ-ba ábba-ábba *M. in* ud nídba ì-ĝiš *Ib-la*$^{ki}$ *wa M.*, 24: níĝ-du$_8$ *I-šar Ḫa-lab*$_x^{ki}$ *áš-du Mi-su-wa-du M.*; o. XIII 7: (garm.) lú *Zú-ba-an* níĝ-sa$_{10}$ *in* níĝ-kas$_4$ *M.*; o. XVII 1: [ ] tuš-LÚ×TIL *M.*, 5: níĝ-ba NE-NE *M.*; r. II 3: 60 siki na$_4$; r. VIII 12: [(silver) níĝ-ba] *Bar*-NE-⸢*um*⸣ *Wa-ru$_{12}$-tum* $^{d}$Utu-*a-ba$_4$ Šu-ì Ag-ga M.*

Mar-tu$^{ki}$ **18** o. V 20: níĝ-ba *Da-a-nu Bu-si ʾÀ-wa-ra* M.; **20** o. XIV 5: 33 kuš M.

*Maš-a*$^{ki}$ **12** r. II 21: ga:eš$_8$ *in M.*

*Maš-bar-rá*$^{ki}$ **19** r. XIV 11: *Bù-da-ì M.* tuš-LÚ×TIL *Za-ḫi-ra-an*$^{ki}$ al$_6$-tuš *A-la-ga*$^{ki}$; **23** o. VI 5: EN-*da-za M.*

*Maš-ga-du*$^{ki}$ **7** r. XV 11: kg sikil lú *M.*

*M[a]-za-t[um*$^{?ki}$] **25** r. II 8: ⸢x⸣-[ ] *Ì-ra-ar*$^{ki}$ *in* ud DU *M.*

*Mi-da-ḫi*$^{ki}$ **7** r. XI 3: *A-a-lu Kab-lu$_5$-ul*$^{ki}$ al$_6$-tuš *M.*

*Mi-na-i-um*$^{ki}$ **4** r. VI 2.

*Mug-ri-ì*$^{ki}$ **5** r. VI 8: *I-ti-gi-ma-lik* ugula *M.*

*Na-am$_6$*$^{ki}$ **1**(e) r. III' 6: *Ḫal-ba*$_x$(PÉŠ) *N.*

*Na-ba-ti-um*$^{ki}$ **4** o. VI 15; **6** o. IV 8; **19** r. X 6: (silver) *N.* (silver) maškim-*sù in* kaskal šu-ba$_4$-ti; r. XIX 7: *La-zi-gú wa Bù-a-ḫu N.*

*Na-gàr*$^{ki}$ **1** o. VI 17: níĝ-kaskal *Na*-NE *N.* DU.DU *si-in Ar-mi*$^{ki}$; o. VII 10: níĝ-kaskal *Ne-zi-ma-ì Puzur$_4$-ra-a-gú* DU.DU *si-in N.*; **4** o. II 3: Šubur *N.* ḫi-mu-DU, 21: níĝ-kaskal *Ni-zi-ma-il* DU.DU *N.*; o. III 12: *N.* šu-ba$_4$-ti *in* ⸢*Za*$^?$*-ù*$^{?}$⸣$^{ki}$; o. VI 7; o. VIII 13; o. IX 1: níĝ-kaskal *Ìr-a[m$_6$-]ma-lik* DU.DU *N.*, 3: *N.* ĜIŠ.DUG.DU *I.*; o. XII 18: en *N.*; o. XIV 4, 22: níĝ-kaskal *Ni-zi-ma-il* DU.DU *N.*; r. I 12: *Ba-sa-ḫu N.*; r. VIII 2: en *N.*, 9: níĝ-kaskal *Ni-zi-ma-il* DU.DU *N.*; r. IX 17: Šubur *N.* šu-mu-tak$_4$; r. XIII 18; **5** o. X 7: *Na*-NE *wa* ⸢Šubur⸣ *N.*; r. XII 5: *in Ša-bir$_5$-ti-um*$^{ki}$ *Puzur$_4$-ra-il N.*; **6** o. IV 2: *Zú-gú-uš N.*, 21: níĝ-kaskal *Ìr-am$_6$-ma-lik* DU.DU *N.*; o. XIII 18: *Na*-NE *N.*; r. III 16: níĝ-ba *Na*-NE *N.*; r. VI 6: níĝ-"mul" *N.* àga-⸢kar'(ŠÈ); r. XVII 8: *Zú-gú-uš N.*; **8** o. VI 16: *Na*-NE *N.*; **9** o. VIII 18: níĝ-ba *N. wa* [ ]; o. XI 17: *N. wa Ga-ga-ba-an*$^{ki}$ *in* [ $^{ki}$] šu-ba$_4$-ti; 10 o. XIII 4: níĝ-ba NE-*da*-ḪI *N.*; o. XIV 9: níĝ-ba *Ù-da-aḫ N.*; o. XV 1; o. XVI 9: níĝ-ba *Ib-gi-tum Ma-rí*$^{ki}$ níĝ-"mul" *N.* [t]il; r. I 16: *N. in* ⸢kaskal⸣ šu-ba$_4$-ti; r. III 12: níĝ-ba *Na*-NE *N.*; r. IX 6: níĝ-ba *Na*-NE *wa* maškim-*sù N.*; **11** o. VII 9: níĝ-ba *Ma-rí*$^{ki}$ níĝ-"mul" *N.* til; **12** r. X 2: *Ar-ru$_{12}$-šum N.*; **16** o. XIII 6: *Zú-ba[-núm] in N.*, 9: [x$^?$+]2 BAR.AN *N.*; r. XVI 22; **17** o. II 18: ḪI-*ra-ù N.* šu-mu-tak$_4$; **18** o. IV 18: níĝ-ba lú NI-*dim* "ur$_4$" *N.*; o. V 14: níĝ-ba *Ḫu-ra*-NE *N.*; o. XII 4: níĝ-ba *Ag-ga N.*; o. XV 24: níĝ-ba … *Ib-rí N.*; o. XVII 14: (silver) *N. in Sal-ba-ù*$^{ki}$ šu-ba$_4$-ti; r. II 21: níĝ-ba *A-ag N.*; r. XI 20: níĝ-ba *Gú-sa* dumu-nita en *N.*; r. XV 27; r. XVII 22: *Ag-ga … Gul-la Ḫu-ra*-NE *N. in* kaskal *Su-da-ma-an*$^{ki}$; **19** o. III 26: níĝ-ba ḪI-*la-um N.*; o. V 20: níĝ-ba en *N.* … níĝ-ba dumu-nita-dumu-nita-*sù*; o. VI 3: níĝ-ba en-en lú *áš-ti* en *N.* DU.DU nam-kud é $^{d}$BAD *Du-du-lu*$^{ki}$, 12: níĝ-ba *Ḫu-ra*-NE *N. in Du-du-lu*$^{ki}$ šu-ba$_4$-ti; r. VII 9: ḪI-*la-um N.* é $^{d}$*Ì-lam* šu-ba$_4$-ti, 18: *Ḫu-ra*-NE *N. in A-ru$_{12}$-ga-du*$^{ki}$ šu-ba$_4$-ti; r. IX 18: níĝ-ba *Ba-ag-mi-su N.*; r. XII 14: níĝ-ba *Ga-áš-ru$_{12}$ N.* DU.DU *mi-nu* Kiš$^{ki}$; r. XVIII 29: *Gul-la wa* maškim-*sù N.*; r. XIX 2: [ḪI-]*la-um N.*, 14: BAR.AN.BAR.AN *Iš$_{11}$-da-mu* di-kud šu-mu-tak$_4$ *si-in N.*; **20** o. XIV 19: 2 BAR.AN *áš-ti N.*

*Na-ḫal*$^{ki}$ **13** o. IV nam-kad *N.*

*Ne-a-ù*$^{ki}$ **12** r. VII 17: $^{d}$*ʾA$_5$-da-"bal" N.*; **14** r. VII 5: $^{d}$*ʾA$_5$-da-"bal" N.*
(see the commentary to text no. 12)

NE-*na-áš*$^{ki}$ **15** o. XII 10: *I-lu$_5$-za$_x$-ma-lik* N.; **17** r. VI 32: 1 an-dùl *sa-du* en *wa ma-lik-tum si-in* N.; r. VII 11: 1 *gú-li-lum* ùz-sal a:tu$_{22}$ é *ma-tim* N. *ma-lu-gi-iš* en.

NI-*ab*$^{ki}$ **2** r. X 7: (136 garments, 23 kilts) … ú-ḫáb … ĜIŠ-ti-ḪAR … 11 gud … 1 BAR.NITA … 4 IGI.NITA u$_5$ ki:lam$_7$ N.; **6** r. X 5: (35 garments, 185 kilts, 12 daggers) … ĜIŠ-ti-ḪAR *Wa-ba-rúm* šu-ba$_4$-ti ki:lam$_7$ *ʾÀ-da-ni*$^{ki}$ *wa* N. *wa La-ru$_{12}$-ga-du*$^{ki}$; 17 r. X 1: *Ti-ša-li-im ma-lik-tum Ì-mar*$^{ki}$ *in* ud DU.DU *mi-nu* N. *si-in* SA.ZA$_x^{ki}$; 20 r. VII 12: *Daš-ne* lú ĜIŠ-nu-kiri$_6$ *Ì-mar*$^{ki}$ *in* N. šu-ba$_4$-ti.

NI-*rí*$^{ki}$ **21** o. VII 3: [ ] ki:lam$_7$ SA.ZA$_x^{ki}$ N.

NI-*rúm*$^{ki}$ **7** o. XVII 2: níĝ-ba *D[a-* ] *in* N. šu-ba$_4$-ti; **9** o. IX 12: (silver) *Sal-bí-um*$^{ki}$ *I-ga-iš-lu* šu-mu-tak$_4$ *si-in* N.

NI-*ti-ba*$^{ki}$ **17** o. XIV 4: *Šu-ma-lik* lú *Iš$_{11}$-da-mu Iš$_{11}$-gi-da-mu A-ba-ù* N.

*Nu-ba-an*$^{ki}$ **22** r. I 2: 1 dib *N.* maškim *Sa-li-im* tuš-LÚ×TIL *in Ar-mi*$^{ki}$.

*Nu-rí*$^{ki}$ **19** r. XIV 21: EN-*da-za A-rí-gú*$^{ki}$ tuš-LÚ×TIL *N.*

*Ra-ʾà-ak*$^{ki}$ **3** r. X 6: *áš-ti* en *R.*; **4** r. V 11: *áš-ti R.*; **6** r. VI 15: *ma-lik-tum R.* É×PAP; **10** o. VI 14: dumu-munus e[n *R. m*]*a-[li]k-[t]um* ⸢*A*⸣*-bar-sal$_4$*$^{ki}$ *wa ma-lik-tum Ir-i-tum*$^{ki}$; **17** o. III 6: É×PAP é-gi en *R.*; **19** r. XVI 7: ama-gal en *R.* É×PAP.

*Sa-gàr-du*$^{ki}$ **12** o. VII 4: *in S.* šu-ba$_4$-ti.

*Sag-gar*$^{ki}$ **18** o. XV 27: níĝ-ba … *I-ku-a-ḫu S.*; r. XVI 4; **21** o. II 7: níĝ-ba *Ḫu*-NE-*du wa Ir$_{11}$-tum-a-ḫu S.*

Saḫar$^{ki}$ **17** r. XI 12: ⸢*Ne-zi*⸣ *wa Ìr-[b]a-il Ma-rí*$^{ki}$ maškim ga:eš$_8$ S.

*Sa-ḫa-ru$_{12}$*$^{ki}$ see *Ša-ḫa-ru$_{12}$*$^{ki}$.

*Sal-ba*$^{ki}$ **21** o. VI 2: *Iš$_{11}$-ru-ud* ugula *S.*

*Sal-ba-ù*$^{ki}$ **18** o. XVII 16: (silver) *Na-gàr*$^{ki}$ *in S.* šu-ba$_4$-ti; r. VI 18: *Iš$_{11}$-ru-ud* ugula *S.*

*Sal-ba-um*$^{ki}$ **18** r. XVI 24: *Ga-nu-bù S.* tuš-LÚ×TIL *Ḫal-sum*$^{ki}$.

*Sal-bí-um*$^{ki}$ **9** o. IX 8: (silver) *S. I-ga-iš-lu* šu-mu-tak$_4$ *si-in* NI-*rúm*$^{ki}$; **18** o. VI 11: (silver) níĝ-ba *S.*
*Sa-ma-rí*$^{ki}$ **14** o. XVI 12: 2 íb+III-TÚG **L.**
*Sa-nap-zu-gúm*$^{ki}$ see *Ša-nap-zu-gúm*$^{ki}$.
*Si-*ʾ*à-mu*$^{ki}$ see *Ši-à-mu*$^{ki}$.
*Si-da-rí-in*$^{ki}$ **13** r. IX 18: *in* ud *S.* til.
*Si-*NE*-su*$^{ki}$ **1**(d) r. x+I x+1.
*Si-zú*$^{ki}$ **4** o. XII 8.
*Su-da-ma-an*$^{ki}$ **18** r. XVII 24: *Ag-ga … Gul-la Ḫu-ra-*NE *Na-gàr*$^{ki}$ *in* kaskal *S.*
*Su-ti-gú*$^{ki}$ see *Šu-ti-gú*$^{ki}$.
*Su-ti-ig*$^{ki}$ see *Šu-ti-gú*$^{ki}$.

*Ša-bir*$_5$*-ti-du*$^{ki}$ **11** r. III 11: en *Š.*; r. V 15: en *Š.*
*Ša-bir*$_5$*-ti-(t)um*$^{ki}$ **5** r. X 5: en *Š.*; r. XII 3: *in Š. Puzur*$_4$*-ra-il Na-gàr*$^{ki}$; **6** r. XVII 19: en *Š.* (*-tum*); **17** r. XXII 24: *áš-ti Š.*
*Ša-dab*$_6$$^{ki}$ **3** r. VIII 10: *Ib-gi-tum wa* maškim-*sù Ma-rí*$^{ki}$ *in Š.* šu-ba$_4$-ti; **7** o. I 12: $^{d}$*Wa-da-*ʾ*à-nu* lú *Š.*; r. VIII 11: *in Š.* ⌜lú *Ì*⌝-[*m*]*ar*$^{ki}$ ⌜*wa*⌝ [ ]⌜ki⌝; **8** o. VI 12: [ ] *in Š.* šu-ba$_4$-ti; **16** r. VI 20: *Za-a-ti* šu-ba$_4$-ti *in Š.*; **18** r. II 16: níĝ-ba *Kùn-i-šar* ʾ*À-du*$^{ki}$ *in Š.* šu-ba$_4$-ti; r. XIX 17: (silver) níĝ-ba *Gú-ra-du*$^{ki}$ (silver) níĝ-ba ʾ*À-lu*$^{ki}$ *in Š.* šu-ba$_4$-ti.
*Ša-ga-bal*$^{ki}$ **4** r. I 21: *A-*NI*-*ʾ*à Š.*
*Ša-ḫa-ru*$_{12}$$^{ki}$ **12** r. II 12: (gold) níĝ-ba *Š.*
*Sa-ḫa-ru*$_{12}$$^{ki}$ **12** o. V 4: en *S.*
*Ša-nap-zu-gúm*$^{ki}$ **10** o. III 14: níĝ-ba *Š.*
*Sa-nap-zu-gúm*$^{ki}$ **14** o. III 11: en *S.*; **15** o. VI 10.
*Ša-na-ru*$_{12}$*-gú*$^{ki}$ **23** o. VIII 9: *Du-bí-ab Š.*
*Ša-nu-gú*$^{ki}$ **15** o. IV 2: [ ] *Ḫa-ra-il áš-du* 1 dib-*sù* til *in Š.*
*Ša-ra-bí-ig*$^{ki}$ **17** o. XVIII 6: ʾ*À:daš* tuš-LÚ×TIL *Š.*
*Šè-*ʾ*à-am*$^{ki}$ see *Ši-*ʾ*à-mu*$^{ki}$
*Šè-na(-um)*$^{ki}$ **8** r. XI 12': [ ] lú an-zam$_x$ šu-du$_8$ *Š.*(*-um*$^{ki}$); **9** o. V 2: *Š.* šu-du$_8$ *wa En-na-il* lú an:zam$_x$.
*Ši-*ʾ*à-mu*$^{ki}$ **7** r. VI 20: (43 garments, 265 kilts) ki:lam$_7$ $^{d}$*Áš-da-bil wa Š.*; **11** r. III 7: (78 garments, [x] kilts) ki:lam$_7$ SA.ZA$_x$$^{ki}$ $^{d}$*Áš-da-bíl Š.*
*Si-*ʾ*à-mu*$^{ki}$ **13** r. X 11: (90+[x] garments, 526 kilts) … 10 gud … 22 [ ] [ki:]⌜lam$_7$⌝ *S. wa* ki:lam$_7$ $^{d}$ʾ*À-da.*
*Šè-*ʾ*à-am*$^{ki}$ **2** r. XVII 15: (56 garments) … 1 *gàr-su* NI*-a-ba-mu* ki:lam$_7$ *Š.*
*Ši-*ʾ*à-am*$^{ki}$ **21** r. II 22: (49 garments, 313 kilts, 60 na$_4$ measures of wool) … 1 ĜIŠ-*ba-ri-zú* ĜIŠ.GAM.GAM.GAM … 1 *mi-at* 50 ĜIŠ-ti-ḪAR *wa* níĝ-NE *Wa-ba-rúm* šu-ba$_4$!-ti!(ŠU.BAL.AK) … 13 *gàr-su* ki:lam$_7$ $^{d}$*Áš-da-bíl wa* ki:lam$_7$ *Š. wa* k[i:lam$_7$] $^{d}$ʾ*À-da.*
*Šu-ra-an*$^{ki}$ **17** o. XII 28: *Du-bí-šum* lú *Gú-ma-ni-du* maškim *I-bí-zi-kir* tuš-LÚ×TIL *Kak-mi-um*$^{ki}$ *áš-ti Š.*
*Šu-ti-gú*$^{ki}$ **2** o. XIV 3: *Rí-dam-ma-lik* ugula *Š.*
*Su-ti-gú*$^{ki}$ **13** o. IV 8: [*Rí-*]*dam-ma-lik* ugula *S.*; **24** o. VI 14: $^{d}$*A-gi S.*
*Su-ti-ig*$^{ki}$ **13** r. V 7: $^{d}$*A-gi S.*; 15 o. XIII 16: *Ib-te-ar S.*; **17** o. XIV 8: *I-lu*$_5$*-za*$_x$*-ma-lik S.*

*Tar*$_5$*-ḫa-um*$^{ki}$ **1**(e) r. III' 14; **11** o. VIII 13: šeš *Ti-la-rí-im*$^{ki}$ ʾ*À-bí-gú*$^{ki}$ *áš-da T.*
*Ti-in*$^{ki}$ **12** r. VI 10: níĝ-du$_8$ 1 dumu-nita *T.* lú *A-da-su*$^{ki}$.
*Ti-la-rí-im*$^{ki}$ **11** o. VIII 10: šeš *T.* ʾ*À-bí-gú*$^{ki}$ *áš-da Tar*$_5$*-ḫa-um*$^{ki}$.
*Ti-ma-ti-im*$^{ki}$ **17** o. XII 17: *Ḫa-zu-um* maškim *Ib-rí-um* tuš-LÚ×TIL *T.* lú *Kak-mi-um*$^{ki}$.
*Ti-sum*$^{ki}$ **18** o. XV 1: *Iš*$_{11}$*-gi-bar-zú wa Du-bí-ab* ugula *T.*

*Ù-du-bù*$^{ki}$ **6** o. XVI 21: dumu-nita *Ù. áš-ti Kak-mi-um*$^{ki}$.
*U*$_9$*-gú-a-aš*$^{ki}$ **17** o. XII 8: *ma-lik-tum Lum-na-an*$^{ki}$ ama-gal en šu-mu-tak$_4$ *in* ud DU.DU *si-in U*$_9$; **18** r. XII 1: níĝ-ba ama-gal en $^{d}$*Iš:šára Má-*NE$^{ki}$ *U*$_9$. *wa Zu-ra-mu*$^{ki}$.
*Ù-la-bù*$^{ki}$ **5** o. XVI 11: *Bù-da-il Ù.*
*Ù-nu-bu*$^{ki}$ **17** o. XIV 11: *I-lu*$_5$*-za*$_x$*-ma-lik Su-ti-ig*$^{ki}$ šu-du$_8$ *in Ù.*
*Ur-sá-um*$^{ki}$ **7** r. XI 26: níĝ-kaskal *U.*; **21** o. XVI 14: *Kùn-ti-su U.*
*U*$_9$*-ru*$_{12}$$^{ki}$ **24** o. III 7: *Iš*$_{11}$*-ru-ud* lú *In-ma-lik* tuš-LÚ×TIL *in U*$_9$.
*Ù-si-gú*$^{ki}$ **4** r. VII 4: *Sa-ḫa-a* ugula *Ù.*; 14 r. XIX x+2: ⌜*Sa*⌝[*-ḫa-a*] ugula *Ù.*
*Ù-ša-li-ik*$^{ki}$ **15** o. XIII 24: *I-in-il* ugula *Ù.*
*Uš-ḫu-lum*$^{ki}$ **15** o. I 20: en *U.*; o. IX 2: en *U.*
*Ù-ti-gú*$^{ki}$ **6** o. VIII 21: *A-ir-ra wa A-zú-bù-lu Ù.*; **25** r. IV 4: [ ]-⌜*lum*⌝ *ba-da-lum Ù.* 2 maškim *A-ag.*
*Ù-ti-ig*$^{ki}$ **17** r. XV 8: *Bù-sum Ù.*; **21** o. VI 14: *Ìr-ba*$_x$*-da-mu* en *Ù.*

*Wa-*NE*-du*$^{ki}$ **13** o. VIII 22: níĝ-ba *Du-si-gú* $^{d}$*Iš:šára W.*

*Za-*ʾ*à-ar*$^{ki}$ **17** o. II 4: *Ì-na-ar* [*Z.*]
*Za-bù-rúm*$^{ki}$ **8** r. III 3': *I-t*[*i*]*-a-gú* DU.D[U] *Z.*
*Za-ḫi-ra-an*$^{ki}$ **19** r. XIII 19: šu-du$_8$ ugula *Z.*; r. XIV 13: *Bù-da-ì Maš-bar-rá*$^{ki}$ tuš-LÚ×TIL *Z.* al$_6$-tuš *A-la-ga*$^{ki}$.
*Zàr-*ʾ*à-*NI*-um*$^{ki}$ **6** o. IV 14.
*Za-ru*$_{12}$*-du*$^{ki}$ **19** o. XV 33: (104 daggers) lú tak$_4$ igi-ḫi-du$_8$ *Z.*(<ki>).
*Za-ù*$^{ki}$ **4** o. III 15: *Na-gàr*$^{ki}$ šu-ba$_4$-ti *in Z.*
*Zi-da-ra*$^{ki}$ **2** o. VII 1: níĝ-ba *Du-si-gú* $^{d}$*Iš:šára Z.*; **15** o. I 15: níĝ-ba *Da-bur-da-mu* $^{d}$*Iš:šára Z.*; **18** o. V 5: níĝ-ba ama-gal en $^{d}$*Iš:šára Z.*
*Zi-gú*$^{ki}$ **13** o. VI 26: $^{d}$*Á-la Z.*
*Zi-ig*$^{ki}$ **2** o. I 22: *Ìr-am*$_6$*-ma-lik Z.*; r. XVI 4: en $^{d}$*Á-la Z.*; **10** o. IV 14: $^{d}$*Á-la Z.*
*Zi-ma-du*$^{ki}$ **9** o. XI 9: [ ] *Ma-rí*$^{ki}$ *in Z.* šu-ba$_4$-ti.
*Zi-ti-ru*$_{12}$$^{ki}$ **10** r. IX 12: níĝ-ba *Z.*
*Zú-mu-šar*$^{ki}$ **9** r. III 9: *En-àr-li-im* [dumu-ni]ta *Du-*[*bí*]*-šum A-ba-ad*$^{ki}$ tuš-LÚ×TIL *Ar-mi*$^{ki}$ *áš-ti Z.*

*Zu-ra-mu*$^{ki}$ **12** o. XIV 15: níĝ-ba $^{d}$BAD *Má*-NE$^{ki}$ *wa* $^{d}$BAD *Z.*; **15** r. X 13: níĝ-ba *Da-bur-da-mu* $^{d}$*Iš:šára Z. wa* $^{d}$*Iš:šára Má*-NE$^{ki}$; **16** r. XII 15: sikil $^{d}$*Iš:šára Z.*; **18** r. XII 3: níĝ-ba ama-gal en $^{d}$*Iš:šára Má*-NE$^{ki}$ *U*$_{9}$*-gú-a-áš*$^{ki}$ *wa Z.*; **20** r. X 29: níĝ-ba ama-gal en $^{d}$*Iš:šára Z. wa* $^{d}$*Iš:šára Má*-NE$^{ki}$.

*Zú-ti*$^{ki}$ **6** r. VIII 13: *I-bi-šum* lú *Ti-ir in* ud tuš-LÚ×TIL *Z.*; **10** o. XIV 18: *En-na*-BAD *Z.*

[x-*g*]*a*-[x]$^{ki}$ **16** r. XVII 12: níĝ-ba ⸢d⸣[*Aš-d*]*ar*$^{?}$ en X.

[ ]-⸢x⸣$^{ki}$ **10** r. XII: [x-(x-)n]a X. ḫi-mu-DU ⸢ĜIŠ⸣-ti-ḪAR; **13** r. IX 10.

[ ]$^{ki}$ **7** r. VIII 14: *in Ša-dab*$_{6}$$^{ki}$ ⸢lú *Ì*⸣-[*m*]*ar*$^{ki}$ ⸢*wa*⸣ X.; **15** o. II 24: $^{d?}$*A*$_{5}$*-da-“bal”* X.

# Glossary

## A

*ʾà-bíl* (*ʾà:bíl*) «food provision (?)» **14** o. III 21: (silver) n[íg-ba] *Iš-⌜dub⌝-ì wa Ib-gi-tum* maškim ga:eš$_8$ *Du-du-lu*$^{ki}$ šu-mu-tak$_4$ **L.**; o. XX 7: (silver) *Iš-dub-il* maškim ga:eš$_8$ *Du-du-lu*$^{ki}$ šu-mu-tak$_4$ **L.**

*ʾà-da-um*-TÚG «mantle (simple:-I / double: -II)» **2** o. VII 3; o. VIII 4, 15; o. X 8; r. V 7; r. IX 6; r. XII 10; r. XVI 10; **3** o. V 10, 11; o. VI 2; r. VI 18; r. IX 8; r. XIV 7; **5** o. I 2; o. VIII 15; o. XIV 7: r. IX 5; r. XII 1; **6** r. IX 7; r. XI 10; r. XII 15; **7** o. VIII 16; o. XVII 6; r. VII 3; **8** o. V 1; **9** o. VII 13; o. XIV 10, 12; **10** r. VI 7; r. VII 9; **11** o. II 15; o. IX 8, 9; o. XIII 3, 4; r. II 16; **12** r. III 1; **13** r. V 11; r. X 1, 2; **14** o. VI 4; **15** o. VI 17; o. XII 14; o. XVII 13; r. III 10; **16** o. IV 11; **17** o. VIII 18; o. XVII 16; r. V 5; r. X 6; r. XX 4; **18** r. III 5; r. XIII 5; r. XVIII 29; **21** o. XIII 2; r. I 23; **25** o. I 3; o. II 2: 7 **L.** dùl-TÚG; o. IV 6; o. V 6: [x] **L.** saĝ; o. VI 4; o. VII 6: 13 **L.** saĝ.

*ʾà-lum* **12** o. XI 18: 1 ĝír mar-tu ti kg *wa* **L.**; **17** r. XII 7: 1 šu-dub *ma-lik-tum* **L.**; **18** r. VIII 1: 20 ĝír mar-tu ti kg **L.**; **19** o. XIV 15: 20 ĝír mar-tu ti kg **L.**; r. I 19: 20 ĝír mar-tu ti kg **L.**

*ʾa$_5$-na-gu* «circular edge» **5** r. XI 1: ŠÚ+ŠA 5 gín D. kb **L.** si 2 gud; **7** o. XI 17: ŠÚ+ŠA gín D. kb **L.** 4 si 2 gud; o XII 9: ŠÚ+ŠA gín D. kb **L.** 4 si 2 gud; r. IV 2: ½ gín D. [kb **L.** 1 ĜIŠ-banšur], 12: ½ g[ín] D. kb **L.** 1 ĜIŠ-banšur, 21: ½ gín D. kb **L.** 1 ĜIŠ-banšur; **11** o. X 12: ŠÚ+ŠA gín D. kb **L.** 4 si 2 gud; o. XI 2: ŠÚ+ŠA gín D. kb **L.** 4 si 2 gud; r. IV 23: 1 gín D. kb **L.** 1 ĜIŠ-banšur; r. VI 4: 1 gín D. kb **L.** 1 ĜIŠ-banšur; r. VIII 12: ŠÚ+ŠA gín D. kb **L.** 1[+3 si 2 gud]; **12** r. I 18: ŠÚ+ŠA gín D. kb **L.** 4 si-si 2 gud; **13** o. XI 9: ŠÚ+ŠA gín D. kb **L.** 4 si 2 gud; **14** o. IX 19: ŠÚ+ŠA gín D. kb **L.** 4 si 2 gud; r. VI 9: 1 ĜIŠ-banšur maḫ … 9 gín D. kg **L.**-*sù*; **15** o. II 2: 3 ½ kg **L.** 1 ĜIŠ-banšur *wa* 1 kù-sal; o. X 7: ŠÚ+ŠA gín D. kb **L.** 4 si 2 gud; r. VII 15: 3 gín D. kg **L.** 1 ĜIŠ-banšur *wa* 1 kù-sal; r. IX 17: ŠÚ+ŠA gín D. kb **L.** 4 si 2 gud; r. XIII 21: 5 gín D. kg **L.** 1 ĜIŠ-banšur *wa* 1 kù-sal; **16** o. XIV 8: [ ] **L.**-*sù*; r. I 5: ŠÚ+ŠA gín D. kb **L.** si 2 gud, 16: ŠÚ+ŠA gín D. kb **L.** si 2 gud; r. XI 5: ŠÚ+ŠA gín D. kb **L.** si 2 gud; **17** r. IV 22: ŠÚ+ŠA gín D. kb **L.** 4 si 2 gud; r. XX 31: 4 ½ kg **L.** 2 banšur *maš-ar-da Ib-rí-um* <*I*->*bí-zi-kir*; **18** o. XVIII 20: ŠÚ+ŠA gín D. kb **L.** si 2 gud; o. XIX 18: ŠÚ+ŠA gín D. kb **L.** si 2 gud; r. XVII 37: ŠÚ+ŠA kb **L.** si 2 gud; **19** o. X 26: ŠÚ+ŠA gín D. kb **L.** si 2 gud; o. XI 12: ŠÚ+ŠA gín D. kb **L.** si 2 gud; r. X 22: 3 gín D. kg **L.** 1 banšur *wa* 1 kù-sal; r. XVII 11: ŠÚ+ŠA kb **L.** si 2 gud; **20** o. VIII 9: ŠÚ+ŠA gín D. kb [**L.** 4 si gud], 21: ŠÚ+ŠA gín D. kb **L.** 4 si gud; o. XVI 5: 2 gín D. kg **L.** 1 ĜIŠ-asari; r. XI 10: ŠÚ+ŠA gín D. kb **L.** 4 si 2 gud; **21** r. VII 23: ŠÚ+ŠA gín D. kb **L.** si 2 gud.

*ʾa$_5$-nun* see iti.

*ʾà-ra-ma-tum* «pectoral» **2** o. II 8: ŠÚ+ŠA gín D. kb 2 **L.**; **7** r. III 5; **11** r. VI 19: ŠÚ+ŠA gín D. kb 2 **L.**; **13** o. IX 3: 4 gín D. kg *ni-zi-mu* 4 **L.**; **20** o. XV 10: 1 ma-na ŠÚ+ŠA gín D. kg kin$_5$-ak … 4 **L.** [ŠÚ+ŠA gín D.]; **24** o. VIII 2: ŠÚ+ŠA 8 kg 4 **L.** 2 buru$_4$-MUŠEN.

á-âĝ «to give instructions (for singing)» **13** o. XVI 23: (silver) níĝ-ba *A-za-ba Ir-i-tum*$^{ki}$ **L.** *a-dè* šir.

*a-a-nu* (a jewel) **18** o. XVII 2: 1 ma-na TAR kg kin$_5$-ak … 1 **L.**; **24** r. I 5: 4 gín D. kg *ḫa-za-nu wa* **L.** *gú-za-ra-tum*.

ab «window» **20** r. VII 22: 12 gín D. kg níĝ-ba $^{d}$*ʾÀ-d[a]* lú *Lu-ub*$^{ki}$ … nu$_{11}$-za **L.**-*sù*; **23** o. II 8: 2 ma-na kg nu$_{11}$-za 1 **L.** é $^{d}$*ʾÀ-da* lú *Lu-ub*$^{ki}$.

*a-ba-lum* (a vessel) **18** o. I 21: ŠA.PI gín D. kg 1 **L.** *wa* pad-[*s*]*ù*; o. XII 20: 12 gín D. kg 1 **L.**; r. XI 13: ŠÚ+ŠA gín D. kb 1 **L.**

ábba «elder» **21** o. XII 11: (silver) níĝ-ba **L.** *Ma-rí*$^{ki}$ *in* ud nídba ì-ĝiš *Ib-la*$^{ki}$ *wa Ma-rí*$^{ki}$.

á-daḫ «to help» **12** r. IV 11: *in* ud è *si-in* **L.** lú *A-te-na-ad*$^{ki}$.
(cf. AN.Á.DAḪ)

*a-dè* (preposition) «for, as a replacement for» **12** r. II 16: 6 gín D. kb *Bù-sum Ma-rí*$^{ki}$ **L.** túg-*sù*; **13** o. XVI 24: á-âĝ **L.** šir; **17** r. VI 25: ŠA.PI lá-1 gín D. kb **L.** 1 an-dùl.

àga-kár (written àga-ŠÈ) «to vanquish, to raid» **4** r. X 13: níĝ-"mul" **L.** *Ma-rí*$^{ki}$ *wa* til *Wa-ru*$_{12}$*-tum*; **6** o. XIII 2: níĝ-"mul" *ʾÀ-du*$^{ki}$ **L.**; r. VI 7: níĝ-"mul" *Na-gàr*$^{ki}$ **L.**; **20** o. VII 3: níĝ-"mul" *Du-lí*$^{ki}$ **L.**

a-gar$_5$ «copper» **2** o. XIV 19: 5 *gú-li-lum* **L.**; r. III 2: 3 *gú-li-lum* **L.** TAR-II esi, 3: 2 *gú-li-lum* **L.** ŠÚ+ŠA-II esi, 4: 20 *gú-li-lum* **L.** 10-I esi; r. XI 3: 3 *gú-li-lum* **L.** kg; r. XIV 11: 10 *gú-li-lum* **L.** ŠÚ+ŠA-II esi, 13: 20 *gú-li-lum* **L.** 10-I esi; **3** r. VIII 13; **18** r. XIV 8; **19** o. XIII 30; o. XIV 13, 21; o. XV 5, 13, 23; o. XVII 3, 20; o. XVIII 6: 16 *gú-li-lum* TAR-II **L.**, 13: 1 *mi-at gú-li-lum* 11 **L.**; r. II 16; r. III 25; r. XII 20; **20** o. XII 10; **21** o. V 7; r. V 19: 3 *gú-li-lum* **L.** kb TAR-II; **23** o. X 3: 7 *gú-li-lum*-II esi TAR.TAR **L.** 10 lá-1 *gú-li-lum*-II esi ŠÚ+ŠA-ŠÚ+ŠA **L.**, 4: 1 *gú-li-lum*-I esi ŠÚ+ŠA **L.**, 5: 2 *gú-li-lum*-I esi 10 **L.**; r. IV 2: 5 *gú-li-lum* dib **L.**; r. VI 9: 2 *gú-li-lum*-II esi ŠÚ+ŠA 4 **L.** 4 *gú-li-lum*-I esi 15 **L.**; r. VII 1: 3 *gú-li-lum*-I esi ŠÚ+ŠA **L.**

a-gar$_5$-gar$_5$ **5** o IV 19: 3 *gú-li-lum*-II **L.**, 20: 10 *gú-li-lum*-I esi **L.**; o. VII 3: 2 *gú-li-lum* **L.** kg; **6** o. V 4: 23 dib **L.** kg; o. X 1; **9** r. X 10: 1 dib **L.**, 12: 1 dib **L.**; r. XI 2: 15 *gú-li-lum* **L.**-II esi, 4: 2 *gú-li-lum* **L.** *sa-ḫ[a-]wa*-II esi ĜÁ×LÁ TAR, 6: 1$^{?}$ *gú-li-lum* **L.** *sa-ḫa-wa* 20 esi, 7: 12 *gú-li-lum* **L.** *sa-ḫa-wa* 12 esi, 11: 1 *gú-li-lum* **L.**-II esi, 13: 4 *gú-li-lum* **L.**[-I] esi; r. XIII 17: 3 *gú-li-lum* **L.**; **10** r. II 15: ⌜5⌝ *gú-li-lum* **L.**-II esi; **12** o. X 6; o. XIII 7: o. XIII 7: 1 *gú-li-lum* 15 gín D. **L.**; r. XI 10; r. XII 10; **13** o. X 6; r. III 3: 1 *gú-li-*

*lum* **L.** kg; **14** o. IV 19: 2 *gú-li-lum*-I **L.** kg esi ⌜x⌝; o. XII 5: 2 *gú-li-lum*-I **L.** esi; o. XIII 17; o. XV 15: 1 *gù-li-lum* **L.**; o. XVIII 8: 10 *gú-li-lum*-II lú TAR.TAR **L.**, 10: 10 *gú-li-lum* **L.**-II ⌜lú⌝ [ŠÚ+ŠA-ŠÚ+ŠA], 12: 10 *gú-li-lum* **L.**-I lú 15 10; o. XIX 1: 10 *gú-li-lum* **L.**-II ⌜lú⌝ TAR.TAR, 3: 4 *gú-li-lum* **L.**-II lú ŠÚ+ŠA-ŠÚ+ŠA, 5: 20 *gú-li-lum* **L.**-I lú 15 10; r. VI 4, 18; r. VII 24; r. XIV 10': 2 *gú-li-lum* **L.** lú ŠA.PI-ŠA.PI-II, 12': 1 *gú-li-lum* **L.** lú ŠÚ+ŠA-I *sa-ḫa-wa*, 15': 1 *gú-li-lum* **L.** [ ]; **15** o. XI 1: 1 *gú-li-lum* **L.**; o. XV 12; r. II 7: 2 *gú-li-lum* 50 gín D. **L.**, 15; **16** o. II 5; o. X 4: 6 *gú-li-lum* **L.** TAR-II, 5: 14 *gú-li-lum* **L.** ŠÚ+ŠA-II, 6: 5 *gú-li-lum* **L.** 10-I, 10: 3 *gú-li-lum* **L.** 10-I; o. XI 3; r. V 3; r. XII 1: 15 *gú-li-lum* **L.** 15-I, 3: 14 *gú-li-lum* **L.** 12-I; r. XV 6; r. XVI 4; **17** o. II 2: 2 *gú-li-lum* **L.** TAR 5 gín D. *sa-ḫa-wa*; o. III 22: 1 *gú-li-lum* **L.** 50; o. V 18; o. XIII 10; o. XIV 19; o. XV 14: 5 *gú-li-lum* **L.** TAR-II, 15: 10 *gú-li-lum* **L.** ŠÚ+ŠA ŠÚ+ŠA-II, 16: 5 *gú-li-lum* **L.** 15-I, 17: 10 *gú-li-lum* **L.** 10-I; o. XVIII 20; o. XIX 16; o. XX 15, 20; r. VIII 20; r. IX 4; r. XXI 19; **18** o. IV 4:, 7; o. VI 17: 1 *gú-li-lum* **L.**; o. VII 9: 12 *gú-li-lum* **L.**, 11: 12 *gú-li-lum* **L.** ŠÚ+ŠA-ŠÚ+ŠA-II; o. VIII 7: 20 *gú-li-lum* **L.** lú TAR-II, 10: 20 *gú-li-lum* **L.** lú 12-I; o. IX 1, 9; o. XVI 3: 14 ma-na kb níĝ-sa$_{10}$ 980 ma-na **L.**; r. II 7; r. V 3, 8, 18; r. VI 1; r, VII 1, 9, 19; r. VIII 7, 17; r. IX 7, 15; r. X 5; r. XV 8; r. XVI 29; r. XVIII 17; **19** o. II 29; o. III 7; o. IV 9: 1 ma-na ŠA.PI gín D. kb níĝ-sa$_{10}$ 1 *mi-at* ma-na **L.**, 20; o. V 4; o. VII 14; o. IX 2; o. XIV 5, 28; o. XVI 3, 19; o. XVII 13; o. XVIII 8: 50 *gú-li-lum* 10 (-I) **L.**, 11: 10 *gú-li-lum* TAR 2 **L.**; r. I 1, 10, 18, 26; r. II 8, 25; r. III 15; r. IV 5; **20** o. I 12, 18; o. XII 1, 8; o. XIII 7; r. I 10; r. II 3; r. XIV 8; r. XV 2': 5 *gú-li-lum* **L.** TAR-II; **21** o. V 15; o. VIII 12; r. V 7: 11 *gú-li-lum* TAR **L.** kg, 9: 10 *gú-li-lum* 15 **L.** kg, 21: 3 *gú-li-lum* **L.** kb 15-I; r. VI 18; r, X 28; **22** r. II 6: 10 *gú-li-lum*-II **L.** esi, 8: 10 *gú-li-lum*-I **L.** 10 esi; r. III 1: 10 *gú-li-lum* **L.** ŠÚ+ŠA-II, 3: 10 *gú-li-lum* **L.** 10-I.

*a-gú* «antimony paste» **5** r. XV 12: 1 ½ gín d. kb níĝ-sa$_{10}$ **L.**
(see Archi 2003, pp. 29–30)

*a-ḫa-šum* **17** r. VII 1: 2 gín D. kb *ḫa-za-nu* **L.** gaba $^{d}$*Ku-ra wa* en.

aktum-TÚG «tunic» **2** o VII 3; o. VIII 2, 13; o. X 7; r. V 5; r. IX 3; r. XII 8; r. XIII 4, 5 (-II); r. XVI 11; r. XVII 9; **3** o. V 12; r. VI 19; **5** o. I 4; o. XIV 8; **6** r. VIII 15; r. IX 8; r. XI 7; r. XII 8, 14; **7** o. VIII 13: 12 **L.** ti-TÚG; r. VI 12; r. VII 4; r. XII 6; **8** o. V 1; **10** o. VIII 3; r. VI 8; r. VII 8; **11** o. III 1; o. IX 10: **L.** ti-TÚG; **13** o. X 11; r. V 10; r. X 3; **14** o. VI 5; o. XVI 10; **16** o. IV 10; **17** o. VIII 16; o. IX 5; o. XVII 13; r. V 2; r. XX 5; **18** r. XIII 7: 2 **L.** ti-TÚG; **20** o. XIII 23; r. XVII x+1: 1 **L.** ti[-TÚG]; 21 o. XIII 1; r. I 21; **25** o. I 3; o. II 2; o. III 2; o. IV 5; o. V 5; o. VI 4; o. VII 7;

*al$_6$* (preposition) «on, above; debited to; on account of» **3** o. VII 13; **12** r. IX 3; **13** o. XIII 3; **14** r. VII 2; **15** r. VI 7; r. X 4; r. XII 8, 17, 29; r. XIII 9, 26; r. XIV 26; r. XVI 10; **17** r. XVIII 13; **19** o. I 17, 21; o. IX 22; o. XII 3; **20** o. XVII 1; r. VI 14; **21** o. VIII 22; r. VIII 19.

*a-lu-nu* (preposition) «on, above» **6** o. II 7: *a-<lu->nu* ĝiš ba:tuš; **16** r. XVII 5: ḫúb-ki ba:tuš **L.** ĝiš.
(variant of *al$_6$*, *a-lu* ĝiš: to be connected to *al$_6$*, see Archi 2002a, p. 2 = 2015a, p. 52)

á-lá (see *PSD* A/1, p. 103) **20** r. II 6: ⌜TAR⌝ [a]n-na šub *si-in* 3 ma-na a-gar$_5$-gar$_5$ kin$_5$-ak 6 an-zam$_x$ 1 **L.** gibil.

A.LAGAB×ḪAL see *s.v.* zú

al$_6$-du$_{11}$-ga «request» **21** r. XI 27: 1 ma-na kg **L.** lugal [ ].

al$_6$-ĝál «(to be) present» **3** l.ed. 3; **8** o. VII 11; **12** r. XV 5; **15** r. XVIII 6; **16** r. XVII 24; **17** l.ed. x+4; **18** l.ed. 5; **19** r. XIX 23; **20** r. XVIII 6; **21** r. XVII 8; **24** r. VIII 5.

*a-li-iš* (preposition) «on, above» **15** o. II 21: 1 *gú-li-lum* **L.** ĜIŠ-gu-kak-gíd; **19** o. VIII 27: 4 kù-sal **L.** kù-sal-kù-sal.

al-kur$_6$ «to uproot (the crop)» **17** o. XVI 7: *in* ud è níĝ-kas$_4$ **L.** še *Kak-mi-um*$^{ki}$.

al$_6$-tuš (var. tuš) «to reside; to stay; resident» **7** r. XI 2: *A-a-lu Kab-lu$_5$-ul*$^{ki}$ **L.** *Mi-da-ḫi*$^{ki}$; **10** o. IV 12: 1 ĜIŠ-sal lú DU.DU lu$_5$ **L.** (tuš) $^{d}$*Á-la* lú *Zi-ig*$^{ki}$; **17** o. XIII 5: *Ru$_{12}$-zi-ma-lik* lú *I-ri-ig* **L.** *Ab-ra-ti-ig*$^{ki}$; **19** r. V 24: (silver) *si-in* **L.** $^{d}$*Ga-mi-iš* en ì-na-sum; r. XIV 14: *Bù-da-ì Maš-bar-rá*$^{ki}$ tuš-LÚ×TIL *Za-ḫi-ra-an*$^{ki}$ **L.** *A-la-ga*$^{ki}$; **21** r. XI 11: [ -]ak **L.** $^{d}$*Á-la Gú-šè-bù*$^{ki}$.

*a-lu-nu* see *al$_6$*

am «elephant» **10** o. XV 7: 2 ma-na ŠA.PI gín D. kb nu$_{11}$-za 2 si **L.**

ama-gal «mother» **3** r. IV 12: 2 *bu*-DI **L.** ⌜*Ib-rí*⌝-[*um*] *Du-si-gú* šu-mu-tak$_4$; **4** o. III 2: 2 *bu*-DI *Du-si-gú* **L.** en; o IV 10: 2 *bu*-DI [ ]; o. XI 9: 4 bur-KAK-bur-KAK ĜIŠ-taškarin … 2 ĜIŠ-du *Du-si-gú* **L.** en, 16: 2 ĜIŠ-du *Du-si-gú* **L.** en; r. IV 12: 1 *bu*-DI sal *Du-si-gú* **L.** en; **5** o. V 13: 2 níĝ-anše-ak 4 NE-*na-tum Du-si-gú* **L.** en; o. VI 7: 2 *bu*-DI **L.** *I-bi-zi-kir in* ud níĝ-mu-sá dumu-munus *Ib-rí-um Gi-ti*-NE$^{ki}$; **7** o. III 6: 1 kù-sal níĝ-ba **L.** en $^{d}$Nin-kar; **10** o. IX 3: 2 *bu*-DI **L.** en *Lum-na-an*$^{ki}$ *Da-ti*-$^{d}$TU šu-mu-tak$_4$; **12** o. XV 12: 10 geštu$_x$-lá **L.** *Ib-rí-um*; r. XI 5: 2 níĝ-anše-ak sur$_x$-BAR.AN **L.** en; **13** o. XIV 2: 1 dib ì-ĝiš-saĝ en *Ì-mar*$^{ki}$ … 2 *bu*-DI … 2 saĝ-*sù* ì-ĝiš-saĝ *Ti-šè-li-im* **L.**-*sù*; o. XV 8: 3 ĜIŠ-zú 3 ĜIŠ-gígir-II en *wa* **L.**-*sù wa Ib-rí-[u]m*, 14: 2 zag 2 ĜIŠ-gígir-II **L.** en *wa Ib-rí-um*; r. VIII 13: 4 *bu*-DI **L.** en; **14** o. II 6: 1 kù-sal níĝ-ba **L.** en $^{d}$*Ba-ra-ma* [ ]; o. XIII 5: ĜIŠ-taškarin lú en *wa* **L.**-*sù*; **15** o. V 12: 2 ĜIŠ-ĝidru 2 šu-dub **L.** en; r. V 10: 2 *bu*-DI … 2 saĝ-*sù ma-lik-tum Ì-ra-ar*$^{ki}$ **L.** en šu-mu-tak$_4$; r. VII 28: 1 ĝír mar-tu *wa* 1 kù-sal níĝ-ba **L.** [e]n; r. X 6: 1 kù-sal [níĝ-b]a en $^{d}$*Ḫa-a-ba-du al$_6$* tu-ra **L.**-*sù*; r. XII 10: 1 dib en *áš-du* dib-*sù* sikil $^{dʾ}$*À-da al$_6$* tu-ra **L.**-*sù*; r. XIII 27: 1 ĜIŠ-banšur *wa* 1 kù-sal sikil *al$_6$* **L.** en $^{d}$*Ra-sa-ap ʾÀ-da-ni*$^{ki}$; **16** o. II 1: 1 ĜIŠ-šú 1 níĝ-bànda **L.** en, 13: 1 á-MUŠEN … saĝ-*sù* níĝ-ba **L.** en $^{d}$TU é $^{d}$*Ku-ra*, 24: 6 *da-ne-a-tum si-ti-tum* **L.** en; r. III 12: maš-maš kù-sal **L.** en; r. IX 13: 1 šu-dub **L.** en; **17** o. VII 14: 2 níĝ-anše-ak 4!(2) kù-sal 2 IGI.NITA **L.** en; o. XII 2: [2 *b*]*u*-DI *ma-lik-tum Lum-na-an*$^{ki}$ **L.** en šu-mu-tak$_4$ *in* ud DU.DU *si-in U$_9$-gú-a-aš*$^{ki}$; r. III 7: *kam$_4$-ma-a-tum* zàḫ *ša-ti* kù-sal

**L.** en; r. V 21: 1 kù-sal 1 buru$_4$-MUŠEN níĝ-ba **L.** en $^{d}$*Ra-sa-ap ʾÀ-da-ni*$^{ki}$; r. XIII 15: *I-ib-ma-lik* šeš **L.** en; r. XIV 14: 10+]7 [*b*]*u*-DI [ŠÚ+Š]A-ŠÚ+ŠA [níĝ-b]a PN$_1$–PN$_8$ dam en *wa* PN$_9$–PN$_{10}$ 2 dumu-munus en *wa* **L.** *Ib-rí-um wa* PN$_{11}$–PN$_{14}$ dam-*sù wa* PN$_{15}$ nin-ni *Du-si-gú* PN$_{16}$; r. XVIII 19: 2 *bu*-DI **L.** *Ib-rí-um*; **18** o. III 15: 1 zi-bar **L.** en; o. V 2: 2 *bu*-DI níĝ-ba **L.** en $^{d}$*Iš:šára Zi-da-ra*$^{ki}$; o. XIX 5: 1 kù-sal buru$_4$-MUŠEN níĝ-ba **L.** en $^{d}$*Ra-sa-ap ʾÀ-da-ni*$^{ki}$; r. XI 28: 3 zi-bar níĝ-ba **L.** en $^{d}$*Iš:šára Má*-NE$^{ki}$ *U*$_9$*-gú-a-áš*$^{ki}$ *wa Zu-ra-mu*$^{ki}$; r. XII 15: 2 *bu*-DI ... 2 saĝ-*sù* **L.** *Ib-rí-um* É×PAP; r. XVI 16: 1 ĝír ... **L.** en, 39: 2 ĝír mar-tu ... 2 kù-sal níĝ-ba **L.** en *Ra-sa-ap Du-ne-ib*$^{ki}$ *wa* $^{dʾ}$*A*$_5$*-da-"bal" À-ma-du*$^{ki}$ NI.DU; **19** o. XIII 17: ZA$_x$ *a-si-ga-tim* **L.** en, 23: 1 kù-sal níĝ-ba **L.** en $^{d}$*Ra-sa-ap ʾÀ-da-ni*$^{ki}$ AMA-*ra*; r. VIII 17: 6 še-šu-še-tag *wa* 1 buru$_4$-MUŠEN níĝ-ba $^{dʾ}$*A*$_5$*-da-"bal" wa* $^{d}$BAD-munus *A-ru*$_{12}$*-ga-du*$^{ki}$ **L.** en šu-mu-tak$_4$; r. XV 7: *Ti-ra-ì* šeš **L.** en; r. XVI 5: 2 *bu*-DI **L.** en *Ra-ʾà-ak*$^{ki}$ É×PAP *Ig-rí-su* šu-mu-tak$_4$; **20** o. VII 19: [ ] šeš **L.** en; o. XI 14: 2 *bu*-DI níĝ-ba **L.** en $^{d}$TU lú *ʾÀ-da-ni*$^{ki}$; r. IV 21: 2 *ti-gi-na* ... 1 *gú-li-lum* **L.** en; r. X 26: 2 kù-sal níĝ-ba **L.** en $^{d}$*Iš:šára Zu-ra-mu*$^{ki}$ *wa* $^{d}$*Iš:šára Má*-NE$^{ki}$; **21** o. IV 17: 4 kù-sal ... **L.** en; o. XV 25: 2 *bu*-DI ì-ĝiš-saĝ **L.** en.

$^{(d)}$AMA-ra (a festival in month III, named according to the Local Calendar) *see* iti

a-mu «father, ancestor» **20** o. XV 1: 1 šu-dub sikil en lú ḫúl [ ] **L.**-*sù*.

á-MUŠEN «(a type of) helmet» (see *ARET* XII, p. 515) **4** r. XVI 1: ŠA.PI gín D. kb 1 **L.** níĝ-saĝšu; **11** r. II 4: [ ] 80 í[b-lá] 80 ĝír m[ar-tu] 21 **L.** zabar; **16** o. II 7: 2 gín D. kb 1 **L.**; o. VIII 12: 10 gín D. kb *ni-zi-mu* 8 **L.**, 13: 15 gín D. kb ZU.PIRIĜ 13 **L.** zabar, 17: TAR an-na SUD.PA.SIKIL 5 íb-lá 20 ĝír-kun zabar 35 **L.** zabar; **21** o. XIV 4: ŠA.PI gín D. kb 1 **L.**; r. V 16: TAR 2 kb *ni-zi-mu* 16 íb-lá 6 ĝír-kun *wa* 1 **L.** kb; r. XII 9: [ ] 1 **L.** *wa* 2 ĝír-kun zabar;

*a-na-bù-bi-tum* «harpin» **20** r. VI 13: 5 NI gín D. kg 1 **L.** *al*$_6$*-sù Ti-ra-il* [dub-sa]r; **24** r. I 10: 3 gín D. kg 1 [*m*]*a-ḫa-na-gúm* 1 *ša-mu* 1 **L.** 1 *ti-ba-ra-núm*.

AN.Á.DAḪ **7** o. IV 2: [...] nu$_{11}$-za **L.** diĝir-diĝir.

an-dùl «statue(tte)» **2** r. VII 16: 15 gín D. kb nu$_{11}$-za 1 **L.**; r. XV 12: 7 gín D. kb nu$_{11}$-za 1 **L.**; **3** o. XII 7: TAR 5 gín D. kb nu$_{11}$-za 1 **L.**; **4** r. X 22: 8 gín D. kb nu$_{11}$-za$^!$(KUR) 1 **L.**; **7** o. X 5: ŠA.PI gín D. kb nu$_{11}$-za 1 **L.** munus; **8** o. VI 6: TAR kg daḫ nu$_{11}$-za 1 **L.**; **9** r. VIII 4: ŠÚ+ŠA 6 gín D. nu-za$_{11}$ 1 an-dùl; r. IX 1: 5 ma-na 5 gín ⌜D.⌝ [kb] nu$_{11}$-za 1 **L.**; **12** o. III 6: 1 ma-na kb nu$_{11}$-za 2 **L.**; r. IX 7: TAR 3 gín D. kb nu$_{11}$-za 2 **L.**; **13** o. VII 17: ŠA.PI 3 gín D. kb nu$_{11}$-za 2 **L.**; o. VIII 12: 12 3 gín D. kb nu$_{11}$-za 1 **L.**; r. IV 14: TAR 4 gín D. kb nu$_{11}$-za 2 **L.**; **15** r. VIII 24: 7 gín D. kg *ni-zi-mu* 1 an-zam$_x$ **L.** libir lú *Ib-rí-um*; **16** o. V 8: 7 ma-na TAR kb nu$_{11}$-za 1 **L.**; **17** r. VI 14: 10 gín D. kb nu$_{11}$-za 1 **L.** $^{d}$*Iš:šára* en, 25: ŠA.PI lá-1 gín D. kb *a-dè* 1 **L.** *sa-du* en *wa ma-lik-tum si-in* NE-*na-áš*$^{ki}$; **18** r. XIV 19: 4 ma-na TAR kb nu$_{11}$-za 1 **L.** munus, 26: 4 ma-na ŠÚ+ŠA kb nu$_{11}$-za 1 **L.** nita; **20** o. III 15: 5 gín D. kb nu$_{11}$-za 1 **L.** munus; r. III 5: 1 pad *ma-da-a-um* kg **L.** lú en *ša-ti Ib-rí-um* mu-DU; **24** o. V 3: 16 gín D. kg nu$_{11}$-za IGI.DUB 2 **L.** *wa* 2 šu-*sù* 2 DU-*sù*, 17: 1 gín D. kg nu$_{11}$-za IGI.DUB 1 **L.**; r. IV 7: ŠÚ+ŠA 6 gín D. kg 1 *ma-da-a-um* <1> **L.** *wa* 1 pad-*s*[*ù*].

AN.LAGAB×A, AN.LAGAB×AN see *s.v.* zú

an-na «tin» **4** r. III 15; r. XIII 20; r. XIV 7; **5** o. XII 18; r. V 15; r. VIII 4; **6** o. I 12, 17: o. IX 5; r. XV 1, 6, 9, 12, 18; r. XVI 5, 9, 12, 16, 19, 25, 29; r. XVII 2, 6, 9, 14, 17, 20, 28, 35, l.ed. 1, 8: AN.ŠÈ.GÚ ... 23 ma-na 12 gín D. **L.** è, 10: šu-nígin 1 *mi-at* 98 ma-na kb **L.**; **7** o. VI 19; o. VII 8; o. XIV 14; r. XIII 14; **9** r. XVII 11; **10** r. XI 2, 5; r. XII 6; r. XIII x+1, 4; **11** o. V 18; **12** o. IX 3; o. X 3, 10, 19; o. XI 4, 10; r. XI 7; r. XII 7; **13** o. I 19; o. III 9, 18; o. IV 17; o. VI 6; o. X 4; o. XII 8; o. XV 2; r. III 23; **14** o. III 22; o. IV 13; o. VI 15; o. XIII 15; o. XV 18; o. XX 15; r. I 10; r. III 16; r. VI 2, 15; r. VII 21; **15** o. XIV 22; o. XV 10; r. II 13; **16** o. III 15; o. VI 14; o. X 14; o. XI 1, 17; r. V 1; r. XIV 15; r. XV 4; r. XVI 2; **17** o. V 17; o. XIV 18; o. XVIII 7, 15, 19; o. XIX 15; o. XX 14, 19; r. I 9; r. VIII 19; r. IX 3; r. XI 23; r. XXI 18; **18** o. IV 1, 9; o. VIII 16; o. IX 7; r. II 4; r. V 1, 6, 16, 22; r. VI 19; r. VII 11, 16; r. VIII 9, 14; r. IX 8, 13; r. X 7; r. XI 21; r. XVI 27; r. XVIII 15; **19** o. II 27; o. III 5; o. IV 18; o. V 2; o. VII 12; o. VIII 30; o. XIII 28; o. XIV 6, 11, 22, 26; o. XV 11, 24; o. XVI 1, 12, 17; o. XVII 4, 11, 21; o. XVIII 20; r. I 11, 16; r. II 1, 6, 18, 23; r. III 8, 13, 26; r. IV 3, 13; r. XII 1, 18; r. XVI 12; **20** o. I 9, 17; o. III 7; o. VII 21; o. IX 22; o. XIII 5; o. XV 23; r. I 8; r. II 1; r. XI 26; r. XIV 6; **21** o. III 14; o. V 5, 13; o. VIII 10; o. XIII 17; r. V 22; r. VI 16; r. X 26.

AN.ŠÈ.GÚ «(partial) total» **2** l.ed. 11: **L.** 1 *mi-at* 97 ma-na 50 gín D. kb è; **3** r. XV 2: **L.** 1 *mi-at* 56$^!$ ma-na TAR 4 gín D.$^!$(NI) kb è; **4** r. XVI 16: [**L.** x ma-na (x)] kb è; **5** r. XVII 1: **L.** 1 *mi-at* 32 ma-na 50 gín D. kb è 2 mu 2 dub; **6** l.ed. 6: **L.** 1 *mi-at* 74 ma-na ŠA.PI 8 gín D. kb è 23 ma-na 12 gín D. an-na è; **7** r. XVI 10: **L.** 1 *mi-at* 50 lá-1 ma-na kb è; **10** r. XVI 1: **L.** 90 ma-na ŠÚ+ŠA 6 gín D. kb ⌜è⌝; **11** r. XI 1: [**L.** x *m*]*i-at* [x+]4 m[a-]n[a ]; **12** r. XV 1: [**L.** x kb] è *ap* 3 *mi-at* 1 ma-na kb [al$_6$-ĝál]; **13** r. XVII 1: **L.** 1 *mi-at* 70 m[a-]n[a] 40[+x] g[ín D. kb]; **15** r. XVIII 1: **L.** 2 ⌜*mi-at*⌝ 32 ma-na kb è 1 mu ⌜*ap* 3⌝ *mi-at* 50 ma-na kb al$_6$-ĝál; **16** r. XVII 20: **L.** ⌜1⌝[+1$^?$] *mi-at* 97 ma-na 10 kb è *ap* ⌜2⌝ *m*[*i-at* x ma-na x kb] [al$_6$-ĝál] [é siki]; **17** l.ed. x+1: **L.** 2 *mi-at* 65 ma-na 4 gín D. kb è [(1+$^?$)]1 *mi-at* 10 lá-2 ma-na š[a-pi] gí[n] D. kb al$_6$-ĝál lú diri; **18** l.ed. 1: **L.** 2 *mi-at* 80 lá-3 ma-na ŠA.PI 6 gín D. kb è *ap* 4 *mi-at* 40 lá-3 ma-na kb al$_6$-ĝál; **19** r. XIX 19: **L.** 3 *mi-at* 74 ma-na ŠÚ+ŠA 6 gín D. kb è *ap* 1 *mi-at* 60 ma-na kb al$_6$-ĝál é en; **20** r. XVIII 2: **L.** 2 [*mi-at*] 40[(+x) m]a[-na] k[b] ⌜è⌝ [*a*]*p* ⌜2⌝[(+1)] *mi-at* [(x+)]⌜50⌝ [m]a-na [kb] [al$_6$-ĝál é siki]; **21** o. XI 20: **L.** 1 *mi-at* 80 lá-1 ma-na kb lú è *in* ud [úš *Ib-rí-um*]; r. XVII 1: [**L.** x *mi-at* x ma-na kb] ⌜è⌝ DIŠ m[u] úš *Ib-rí-um ap* 4 *mi-at* [ma-n]a [x kb] [al$_6$-ĝál é siki]; **22** o. V 5: **L.** 54 ma-na 3 gín D. kg; r. VIII 7: **L.** 4 ma-na TAR 3 gín D. kg è lú mu-DU *I*[*b-rí-*]*um wa* tak$_4$ kg É×PAP en-e[n] [ ]; **23** r. IX 1: **L.** 8 ma-na 3 gín D. kg è lú *A-da-bí-ig*$^{ki}$; **24** r. VIII 1: **L.** 4 ma-na ŠA.PI 2 2 NI gín D. kg è *ap* 5 gín D. kg al$_6$-ĝál é siki; **25** r. X 1: **L.** 86 ma-na 53 gín D. kb è *in* ud *Ib-rí-um*.

an-zam$_x$ «(a kind of) glass» (a small vessel) **2** o. III 5: 10 gín D. kb 1 **L.**; o. V 1: 10 gín D. kb 1 **L.**; o. XIII 4: 4 gín D. kg *ni-zi-mu* 1 pad 1 **L.**; **4** r. XVI 13: ŠÚ+ŠA gín D. kg 1 **L.**; **6** o. V 15: 17 gín D. kb 1 **L.**; o. XI 11: 10 gín D. kb 1 **L.**; **8** r. XI 9': [ ] lú **L.** *wa* šu-du$_8$ *Šè-na-um*$^{ki}$; **9** o. V 6: *Šè-na*$^{ki}$ šu-du$_8$ *wa En-na-il* lú **L.** ugula IGI.NITA; r. VIII 13: 6 gín D. kg nu$_{11}$-za *ba-na-ʾà-sa wa* íb+III-TÚG [*w*]*a* **L.** 2 *gú-li-lum-sù*; **10** r. VII 18: [ ] *ni-zi-mu* [1] **L.**; r. VIII 5: 10 gín D. kg 1 pad **L.**; **11** o. XI 20: 2 gín D. kg *ni-zi-mu* 1 **L.**; **14** r. XII 17: 1 kg 1 pad **L.**; **15** r. I 19: ŠA.PI gín D. kg kin$_5$-ak 1 **L.** *wa* 1 pad-*sù*; r. VIII 16: 50 gín D. kg kin$_5$-ak 1 **L.** *wa* 1 pad-*sù*, 24: 7 gín D. kg *ni-zi-mu* 1 **L.** an-dùl libir lú *Ib-rí-um*; **18** o. III 9: ŠÚ+ŠA 3 gín D. kg 1 **L.** ĜIŠ-ĝidru; **19** o. XII 9: 4 gín D. kg *ni-zi-mu* 1 **L.**; o. XIII 7: ŠA.PI gín D. kg 1 **L.** *wa* 1 pad-*sù*; **20** r. II 5: ⌜TAR⌝ [a]n-na šub *si-in* 3 ma-na a-gar$_5$-gar$_5$ kin$_5$-ak 6 **L.** 1 á-lá gibil, 18: 2 gín D. kg *ni-zi-mu* 1 **L.**, 24: 10 gín D. kg 1 pad **L.**; r. IX 23: [ ] lú **L.**(an:zam$_x$); r. X 3: [1] gín D. [kg] *zi-ba-du* 1 pad **L.**; **22** r. V 8: TAR 4 gín D. kg 1 **L.** *wa* 1 pad-*sù*; **23** o. III 7: 1 gín D. kg *ni-zi-mu* 1 pad **L.**

*ap* (conjunction) «and also; that is» **3** l.ed. 1; **12** o. III 7; r. XV 3; **13** o. XI 19; **14** o. X 11; **15** r. IX 12; r. XVIII 4; **16** r. I 13; r. XI 2; r. XVII 22; **18** o. XI 2; o. XIX 12; r. VII 8; r. VIII 6; r. IX 6; r. X 4; r. XVII 34; l.ed. 3; **19** o. XI 7; o. XIII 33; o. XIV 4, 20; o. XV 4, 22, 29; o. XVI 10; o. XVII 2, 19; r. I 4, 9, 25; r. II 15; r. III 6, 24; r. IV 11; r. XVII 9; r. XIX 21; **20** o. VIII 17; r. XI 6; r. XVIII 4; **21** o. II 16; o. IX 21; r. XVII 6; **22** o. VIII 8; **24** r. VIII 3.

*ar-ra* «haft» **7** o. XI 13: 1 ešda … 6 gín D. kg nu$_{11}$-za 1 **L.**-*sù*; o. XII 7: 1 ešda … 6 gín D. kg nu$_{11}$-za 1 **L.**-*sù*; r. I 13: 1 e[šda] … [6 gín D. kg] 1 **L.**-*sù*; r. VIII 3: 1 ešda … 6 gín D. kg [nu$_{11}$-]za **L.**-*sù*; **9** r. VII 17: 1 *ḫa-bù* … 6 gín D. kg nu$_{11}$-za 1 **L.**-*sù*; **10** o. V 5: 1 *ḫa-bù* … 6 gín D. kg nu$_{11}$-za 1 **L.**-*sù*; **11** o. X 10: 1 ešda … 6 gín D. kg nu$_{11}$-za 1 **L.**-*sù*, 23: 1 ešda … 6 gín D. kg nu$_{11}$-za [1 **L.**-*sù*]; **12** r. I 14: 1 *ḫa-bù* … 6 gín D. kg nu$_{11}$-za 1 **L.**-*sù*; **13** o. XI 7: 1 *ḫa-bù* … 6 gín D. kg nu$_{11}$-za 1 **L.**-*sù*; **14** o. X 4: 1 *ḫa-bù* … 6 gín D. kg nu$_{11}$-za 1 **L.**[-*sù*]; **15** r. IX 14: 12 gín D. kb nu$_{11}$-za 1 *ḫa-bù ap* nu$_{11}$-za 1 **L.**-*sù* kg sikil; **16** r. I 3: 1 *ḫa-bù* … 6 gín D. kg nu$_{11}$-za 1 **L.**-*sù*; r. VII 20: 1 *ḫa-bù* … 6 gín D. kg nu$_{11}$-za 1 **L.**-*sù*; **18** o. XVIII 18: 1 *ḫa-bù* … 6 gín D. kg nu$_{11}$-za 1 **L.**-*sù*; o. XIX 16: 1 *ḫa-bù* … kg sikil nu$_{11}$-za **L.**-*sù*; r. XI 6: 1 *ḫa-bù* … 6 gín D. kg nu$_{11}$-za 1 **L.**-*sù*; **19** o. X 24: 1 *ḫa-bù* … 6 gín D. kg nu$_{11}$-za 1 **L.**-*sù*; o. XI 9: 1 *ḫa-bù* … 15 gín D. kb nu$_{11}$-za 1 *ḫa-bù ap* nu$_{11}$-za **L.**-*sù*; r. VIII 25: 1 *ḫa-bù* … 6 gín D. kg nu$_{11}$-za 1 **L.**-*sù*; r. IX 10: 1 *ḫa-bù* … 6 gín D. kg 1 **L.**; **20** o. VIII 7: 1 *ḫa-bù* … 6 gín D. ⌜kg⌝ nu$_{11}$-za 1 **L.**-*sù*, 19: [1 *ḫa-bù*] … 15 gín D. kb nu$_{11}$-za 1 [*ḫa-bù*] *ap* kg sikil nu$_{11}$[-za] 1 **L.**-*sù*; r. XI 7: 1 *ḫa-bù* … 12 gín D. kb nu$_{11}$-za 1 *ḫa-bù ap* nu$_{11}$-za **L.**-*sù* kg si[kil]; **21** o. IX 13: 1 *ḫa-bù* … 6 gín D. kg nu$_{11}$-za 1 **L.**-*sù*; o. XV 9: 6 gín D. kg nu$_{11}$-za 1 **L.**-*sù*; **22** r. VI 3: 1 *ḫa-bù* … 6 gín D. kg nu$_{11}$-za 1 **L.**-*sù ḫa-bù*, 13: 6 gín D. kg nu$_{11}$-za 1 **L.**-*sù ḫa-bù*; **24** o. VI 5: 6 gín D. kg nu$_{11}$-za 1 **L.**-*sù* 1 *ḫa-bù*.

*ar-ra-sa* **9** o. III 14: 2 *ḫa-bù* … [ ] **L.**-*sù*

*ar-ra-si* **5** o. XII 12: 1 *ḫa-bù* … 6 gín D. kg nu$_{11}$-za 1 **L.**-*sù*; **17** r. IV 20: 1 *ḫa-bù* … 6 gín D. kg nu$_{11}$-za 1 **L.**-*sù*; r. XV 14: 1 *ḫa-bù* … 6 gín D. kg nu$_{11}$-za **L.**-*sù*.

*ar-ra-si-su* **3** o. IV 17: 1 *ḫa-bù* … 5 gín D. kg nu$_{11}$-za **L.**; o. XIV 3: [1 *ḫa-*]*b*[*ù*] … 6 gín D. kg nu$_{11}$-za 1 **L.**; **8** r. IX 9': [1 *ḫa-bù*] … 6 gín D. kg nu$_{11}$-za 1 **L.**; **15** o. X 5: 1 *ḫa-bù* … 6 gín D. kg nu$_{11}$-za 1 **L.**

*ar-ra-su* **5** r. X 11: 1 *ḫa-bù* … 6 gín D. kg nu$_{11}$-za **L.**-*sù*; **14** r. II 18: 1 *ḫa-bù* … 6 gín D. kg nu$_{11}$-za 1 **L.**-*sù*; **15** r. I 10: 1 *ḫa-bù* … 4 gín D. kg nu$_{11}$-za **L.**[-*sù*].

*ar-ra-šum* **23** r. I 12: 6 gín D. kg nu$_{11}$-za 1 **L.** 1 *ḫa-bù*; r. II 7: 6 gín D. kg nu$_{11}$-za 1 **L.** 1 *ḫa-bù*; r. IV 7: 6 gín D. kg nu$_{11}$-za 1 **L.** 1 *ḫa-bù*.

asari see ĜIŠ-asari.

*a-si-ga-tim* **19** o. XIII 16: 3 gín D. kg kin$_5$-ak ZA$_x$ **L.** ama-gal en.

cf. *ARET* XXII 5 r. VII 23–27: 10 gín D. kb ZA$_x$ *la-si-ga-tum* 2 *lum-a-núm* en *I-bí-zi-kir*, "10 shekels of silver belonging to the *l.* of two *l.* of the king (and) Ibbi-zikir"; XXII 6 r. XVI 21–XVII 1: 1 ma-na 7 gín D. kg 1 *lum-a-núm wa* ZA$_x$ *a-si-ga-tum-sù* en *áš-du* 1 *lum-a-núm-sù* lú kb *ma-lik-tum* in-na-sum 1 ma-na 5 gín D. kb 1 *lum-a-núm wa a-si-ga-tum-sù I-bí-zi-kir*, "1;07 minas of gold (for) a *l.* and its belonging of the *a.* of the king together with a *l.* of silver given by the queen; 1;05 minas of silver (for) a *l.* and its *a.* of Ibbi-zikir".

*áš-da* (preposition) «from; with; by» **2** o. VIII 6; **3** r. XII 2; **6** o. XV 15; **11** o. VIII 12; **12** r. VII 23.

*áš-du* (preposition) «from; as a replacement for» (locative and temporal) **15** o. III 25; o. XIV 8; r. V 19; r. XII 4, 25; r. XIII 5; r. XV 17; **18** r. IV 24; r. XVIII 8; **19** o. I 27; o. V 13; **21** o. XII 22; r. III 17.

*áš-tum* **8** r. III 10'.

aš-ḫal «filter (?)» **4** r. XV 23: 1 bur-KAK **L.** ì-ĝiš; **6** r. VII 4: 2 bur-KAK **L.** ì-ĝiš; **8** o. VII 11: 1 **L.** 1 LAGAB al$_6$-ĝál.

(cf. Akk. *šaḫālum*)

*áš-ti* (preposition) «from; by; with» **3** r. VII 11; r. X 4; **4** o. II 10; o. V 13; r. V 10; **6** o. XVI 22; **7** o. VIII 3; **9** r. II 17; r. III 8; r. IV 4; **11** r. V 9; **12** r. VI 5; **15** o. II 15; o. XVII 7; **16** r. II 16; **17** o. I 16; o. VIII 5; o. XII 27; r. XXII 23; **18** r. IV 17; **19** o. II 9; o. VI 1; o. IX 20; **20** o. XIV 18; r. IX 14.

*áš-tum* see *áš-du*

a-tu$_{22}$ (a:tu$_{22}$) «lustration» **17** r. VII 9: 1 *gú-li-lum* ùz-munus **L.** é *ma-ti-im* NE-*na-áš*$^{ki}$ *ma-lu-gi-iš* en.

az «bear» **17** o. XVII 11: *Wa-ru*$_{12}$*-tum wa I-ku-uḫ Ma-rí*$^{ki}$ ḫi-mu-DU 1 **L.**! maḫ.

a-zu$_5$ «physician» **5** r. XIII 6: *En-gi-iš-ar* **L.**

## B

ba «carapace (of a turtle)»

ba-ba **7** r. VII 6

babbar «white» **15** r. III 17: 2 kuš **L.** ùz-nita; **25** o. VIII 2: 1 níg-lá-saĝ **L.**

see íb+III-TÚG babbar and íb+III-TÚG babbar gíd s.v. íb(+II/III/IV/V-)TÚG.

BAD «majordomo» **3** o. II 10: *En-na*-BAD ⸢"ur$_4$"⸣ **L.** é *Ib-rí-um*.

bàd$^{ki}$ «fortress» **6** r. IV 21: $^{d}$*Ba-li-ḫa*-II lú 8 **L.**; **25** r. III 11: *Lu-*⸢*rí*⸣*-um Kak-mi-um*$^{ki}$ níĝ-"mul" **L.** šu-ba$_4$-⸢ti⸣.

*ba-da-lum* «minister» **11** o. VIII 5: [1 íb-lá] 1 *si-ti-tum* 1 ĝír-kun *I-rí-ig-da-mu* lú *Gi-gí* šu-du$_8$ **L.** *A-bar-sal*$_4$$^{ki}$; **13** o. X 17: 1 ĝír mar-tu kg **L.** ⸢*Ḫa*⸣*-ra-a*[*n*$^{ki}$]; r. XII 20: (gold) **L.** *A-bar-sal*$_4$$^{ki}$ šu-du$_8$ *in* [ ]; **16** r. X 6: 1 dib níĝ-ba **L.** *Ḫa-ra-an*$^{ki}$; **18** o. XIII 4: (gold) **L.** *Ḫa-ra-an*$^{ki}$; **19** r. XIV 4: 1 íb-lá 1 *si-ti-tum* 1 ĝír-kun níĝ-ba **L.** *Ḫa-ra-an*$^{ki}$; r. XVIII 23: 1 dib dumu-nita **L.** *Ḫa-ra-an*$^{ki}$; **21** o. V 25: [2 *bu*]-⸢DI⸣ ì-ĝiš-saĝ [d]am **L.** [*Ḫa-*]*ra-an*$^{ki}$; **25** r. IV 3: [ ] [ ]-⸢*lum*⸣ **L.** *Ù-ti-gú*$^{ki}$.

bàd-diĝir$^{ki}$ **3** r. XIII 16: (104 kilts) … ĜIŠ-ti-ḪAR *Wa-ba-rúm* ki:lam$_7$ $^{d}$*A-da-ma wa* ki:lam$_7$ **L.**

*ba-du-u*$_4$(/*u*$_9$) (an element which qualifies a dagger) **17** o. XI 20: [x] gín D. kg **L.** [1] ĝír [mar-]tu; o. XIX 13: 7 gín D. kb **L.** 3 ĝír mar-tu-*sù*; **22** r. III 10: 10 ĝír mar-tu ŠÚ+ŠA gín D. kb **L.**-*sù*.
 see ĝír mar-tu.

*ba-ga-ne-su* «*clasp*» **10** o. XIII 20: 3 gín D. kb 2 ĝeštu$_x$-lá 2[+2] **L.**

*ba-ga-ni-sa* **3** o. XIV 14: [ ] *ni-zi-mu* 2 **L.**

balaĝ «harp» **10** o. VIII 20: 8 gín D. kb nu$_{11}$-za **L.** lú *gú-za-rí-tum* lú *Ib-rí-um*; **14** o. XV 8: [2 gín D. k]g *zi-ba-tum* 1 **L.** zabar lú en; **16** r. XII 20: 4 gín D. kg *ni-zi-mu* nu$_{11}$-za 1 **L.** nar; **24** o. IV 8: 1 gín D. kg *zi-ba-du* 1 **L.** maḫ.
 (Civil 2008, pp. 99–100, suggests "drum")

*ba-na-ù* «face; front side»

*ba-na-a*/(-*ʾà*) **2** o. IX 10: 1 gín D. kg nu$_{11}$-za **L.** *wa* íb+III-TÚG; r. VIII 1: 1 an-dùl … 5 gín D. kg nu$_{11}$-za [**L.**] *wa* íb+III-TÚG; r. XV 17:1 an-dùl … ½ gín D. kg nu$_{11}$-za **L.**-*ša*; **3** o. XII 12:1 an-dùl … 6 gín D. kg nu$_{11}$-za **L.**(-⸢*ʾà*⸣) *wa* 2 šu 2 DU-*sù*; **5** r. XII 10: 5 gín D. kg nu$_{11}$-za **L.** $^{d}$*Gú-šar*; **9** r. VIII 9:1 an-dùl … 6 gín D. kg nu$_{11}$-za **L.** (-⸢*ʾà*⸣)-*sa wa* íb+III-TÚG [*w*]*a* an-zam$_x$ *wa* 2 *gù-li-lum-sù*; **12** o. XI 13: 7 gín D. an-na šub *si-in* **L.** 1 níĝ-saĝšu; r. IX 11: 2 an-dùl … 8 gín D. kg nu$_{11}$-za **L.**-*sa wa* 2 šu-*sù wa* 2 DU-*sù*.

*ba-na-i* **8** r. II 3': [ ] 4 gín D. kg nu$_{11}$-za **L.**-*sa*; **12** o. III 12: 2 an-dùl …ŠÚ+ŠA 2 gín D. kg nu$_{11}$-za **L.**-*su-ma wa* 2 šu-šu-*sù* 2 DU.DU-*sù*; **17** r. VI 19: 1 an-dùl … 1 gín 3 NI kg nu$_{11}$-za **L.**-*sù wa* íb-lá-*sù wa* šu-kešda gùn-*sù*.

IGI.DUB **13** o. VII 21: 2 an-dùl … 10 gín D. kg nu$_{11}$-za **L.**-*sù wa* 4 šu-*sù* 4 DU-*sù*; o. VIII 17: 1 an-dùl … 3 gín D. kg nu$_{11}$-za **L.**-*sù* 2 šu-*sù* 2 DU-*sù*; o. X 8: 3 ma-na an-na šub *si-in* 24 ma-na a-gar$_5$-gar$_5$ kin$_5$-ak **L.** 40 níĝ-saĝšu; **14** o. IV 16: 4 ma-na TAR an-na šub *si-in* kin$_5$-ak **L.** 60 níĝ-saĝšu; **16** o. V 12: 1 an-dùl … 2 ma-na 5 gín D. kg nu$_{11}$-za **L.**-*sù wa* 2 DU-*sù wa* 2 šu-*sù*; **18** r. XIV 23: 1 an-dùl munus … ⸢1⸣ ma-na 14 gín kg nu$_{11}$-za **L.**-*sa* 2 šu 2 DU-*sù*; r. XV 2: 1 an-dùl nita … 2 ma-na 12 kg nu$_{11}$-za **L.**-*sù wa* íb-lá *si-ti-tum* íb+III-TÚG; **20** o. III 20: 1 an-dùl munus … 2 ½ gín D. kg nu$_{11}$-za **L.**-*s*[*ù*]; **24** o. V 2: 16 gín D. kg nu$_{11}$-za **L.** 2 an-dùl *wa* 2 šu-*sù* 2 DU-*sù*, 16: 1 gín D. kg nu$_{11}$-za **L.** 1 an-dùl.

banšur see ĜIŠ-banšur.

BAR.AN «mule» **1**(e) r. III' 17: 1 ma-na 10 gín kb NE-a-*du* 2 **L.** [ ]⸢x⸣[ ]; **2** o. VIII 10: 1 ma-na kb níĝ-sa$_{10}$ 1 **L.** *Sag-gar*$^{ki}$; **3** o. VI 10: 1 ma-na TAR kb níĝ-sa$_{10}$ 1 **L.**; r. IX 11: 1 m[a-]na 10 [gín D. kb] níĝ-sa$_{10}$ 1 **L.**; r. X 3: 4 ma-na kb níĝ-sa$_{10}$ 1 **L.** *áš-ti* en *Ra-ʾà-ak*$^{ki}$ *Íl-ba-ma-lik* šu-mu-tak$_4$; **4** r. V 7: 1 ma-na TAR kb níĝ-sa$_{10}$ 1 **L.** lú [ ] *áš-ti Ra-ʾà-ak*$^{ki}$; r. VI 1: 1 ma-na ŠÚ+ŠA 5 gín D. kb níĝ-sa$_{10}$ 1 **L.** *Mi-na-i-um*$^{ki}$; r. XV 10: [x m]a-na kb [níĝ-]sa$_{10}$ [1$^?$] **L.** *A-šu*$^{ki}$ *ʾÀ-bí* lú $^{d}$*Ra-sa-ap* ŠE.SAĜ×ḪA-mul; **5** o. XV 10: [x kb] níĝ-sa$_{10}$ 1 **L.** *Rí-ì-ma-lik* šu-ba$_4$-ti; **6** o. XIV 18: 2 ma-na kb níĝ-sa$_{10}$ 1 **L.** EN-NE$^{ki}$; **7** o. IX 13: 2 ma-na kb níĝ-sa$_{10}$ 1 **L.** *Ba-na-i-um*$^{ki}$ *in* níĝ-kas$_4$ *Ma-rí*$^{ki}$; **10** o. XIV 5: 10 gín D. kb níĝ-ba *Gul-la* ḫi-mu-DU 1 **L.**; **13** r. I 19: ŠA.PI gín D. kb níĝ-ba PN$_1$–PN$_3$ [ ] ḫi-mu-DU 1 **L.** *Na-zu-mu* zàḫ; **16** o. XIII 8: 6 ma-na kb [ní]ĝ-sa$_{10}$ [x$^?$+]2 **L.** *Na-gàr*$^{ki}$; **17** o. II 16: 6 ma-na kb níĝ-sa$_{10}$ 2 **L.** ḪI-*ra-ù Na-gàr*$^{ki}$ šu-mu-tak$_4$; o. VIII 4: 5 ma-na kb níĝ-sa$_{10}$ **L.** *áš-ti A-ša*$^{ki}$ *Wa-na* šu-ba$_4$-ti; 20 o. IX 20: *su-da-nu* kg **L.** en; o. XIV 17: 4 ma-na kb níĝ-sa$_{10}$ 2 **L.** *áš-ti Na-gàr*$^{ki}$; r. XVI 4': 1 ma-na kb níĝ-sa$_{10}$ 1 **L.** *Wa-na* šu-ba$_4$-ti.

BAR.AN-BAR.AN **19** r. XI 27: 1 ĜIŠ-gígir-II 1 guruš ugula sur$_x$-BAR.AN 4 .; r. XIX 9: 6 ma-na kb níĝ-sa$_{10}$ **L.** *Iš*$_{11}$*-da-mu* di-kud šu-mu-tak$_4$ *si-in Na-gàr*$^{ki}$; **22** o. II 6: [6] níĝ-anše-[a]k 12 kù[-sal] **L.**

ugula BAR.AN «overseer of the mules» **12** r. V 11: *Wa-na* **L.**; **17** o. III 24: *ʾÀ-gàr* **L.**

ugula BAR.AN-BAR.AN **7** o. VI 6: *Wa-na* **L.**

*ba-rí-zú* (a container; unit of measurement of capacity: ½ of a gú-bar) **6** r. III 18: 4 **L.** im-gi$_6$.

BAR.NITA «onagre» **2** r. X 3: 55 gín D. kb 1 **L.**

bar-ús see ĜIŠ-bar-ús.

ba-tuš (ba:tuš) «to reside, to stay» **6** o. II 9: (silver) níĝ-ba ḫúb-ki *in* ud *a-*<*lu*->*nu* ĝiš **L.**; **16** r. XVII 4: (silver) níĝ-ba ḫúb-ki **L.** *a-lu-nu* ĝiš.

ba-za «dwarf» **14** r. XI 14: *Ab-ra-ḫu wa Iš*$_{11}$*-a-ma-lik* **L.**

*bu*-DI «toggle-pin» **2** o. III 1: 3 gín D. kg nu$_{11}$-za 2 saĝ 2 **L.**; o. V 5: ŠÚ+ŠA gín D. kb 2 **L.**; **3** o. XI 14: 10 gín D. kb 2 **L.**; r. IV 11: ŠÚ+ŠA 2 gín D. <kb> 2 **L.**; r. XI 15: 53 gín D. kb 6 **L.**; **4** o. II 23: 6 gín D. kb 2 **L.**; o. IV 9: TAR kb 2 **L.**; o. V 21: 1 ma-na 10 gín kb 6 **L.**; o. VII 6: 2 **L.**; o. IX 12: 1 ma-na ŠÚ+ŠA gín D. kb 10 lá-2 **L.**; r. IV 10: 2 NI g[ín D. kb] 1 **L.** sal; **5** o. VI 6: ŠÚ+ŠA gín D. kb 2 **L.**; o. IX 10: ŠÚ+ŠA gín D. kb **L.**; r. XIII 12: 10 gín D. kb 2 **L.** 2 *ti-ša-na*; **6** o. XI 9: ŠA.PI gín D. kb 2 **L.**; r. III 20: ŠÚ+ŠA gín D. kb 2 **L.**; r. VI 13: ŠÚ+ŠA gín D. kb 2 **L.**; r. XIV 1: 10 gín D. kb 2 **L.** 2 *ti-ša-na*; **7** r. XIV 2: 10 gín D. kb [ ] 4 *ti-ša-nu* 2 **L.**; **9** o. VI 12: ŠÚ+ŠA gín D. kb 2 **L.**; r. IV 15: TAR kb 2 **L.**; r. VI 7: TAR kb 1 **L.**, 15: ŠÚ+ŠA gín D. kb 4 **L.**; r. IX 6: ŠÚ+ŠA ⸢gín⸣ [D.] kb 2 **L.**; **10** o. VI 11: ŠA.PI gín D. kb 4 **L.**; o. VIII 13: ŠÚ+ŠA gín D. kb 2 **L.**; o. IX 2: 10 gín D. kb 2 **L.**; r. I 10: TAR kb 2 **L.**; r. V 9: ŠÚ+ŠA gín D. kb 2 **L.**; **11** o. XII 8: ŠÚ+ŠA gín D. kb 2 **L.**; **12** o. VII 19: ŠÚ+ŠA gín D. kb 2 **L.**; **13** o. I 15: [2] **L.**; o. II 2: ŠÚ+ŠA gín D. kb 2 **L.**; TAR [x] gí[n] D. kb *ni-zi-mu* nu$_{11}$-za 1 **L.**; o. XIII 19: 1 ma-na kb 2 **L.** … 2 saĝ-*sù* ì-ĝiš-saĝ *Ti-šè-li-im* ama-gal-*sù*; o. XV

19: TAR kb 2 **L.** … 2 saĝ-*sù*; r. VIII 12: 4 gín D. kg nu$_{11}$-za saĝ 4 **L.**; r. XI 7: 2 gín D. kb 1 **L.** tur; **14** o. V 8: ŠÚ+ŠA gín D. kb 2 **L.**; r. VII 9: 10 gín D. kb [2] **L.** *wa* 4 *ti-ša-nu*; r. IX 16: TAR kb 2 **L.** … 2 saĝ-*sù*; **15** o. XI 19: 1 ma-na 14 gín D. kg kin$_5$-ak … *wa* nu$_{11}$-za 2 saĝ 2 **L.**, 20: TAR kb 2 **L.**; o. XVI 15: ŠÚ+ŠA gín D. kb 2 **L.**; r. V 3: ŠÚ+ŠA gín D. kb 2 **L.**; r. VI 9: ŠÚ+ŠA gín D. kb 2 **L.**; **16** o. V 2: ŠÚ+ŠA gín D. kb 2 **L.**; **17** o. II 6: ŠÚ+ŠA gín D. kb 2 **L.**, 21: ŠÚ+ŠA gín D. k[b 2 **L.**]; o. VII 18: [ŠÚ+Š]A gín D. kg 2 **L.**; o. XI 26: [ ] 2 **L.**; r. V 25: TAR kb 2 **L.**; r. IX 29: ŠÚ+ŠA gín D. kb 2 **L.**; r. XIII 25: 5 ma-na ŠA.PI kb [10+]7 **L.** [ŠÚ+Š]A-ŠÚ+ŠA; r. XIV 29: 50 gín D. kb kin$_5$-ak 2 **L.**, 33: [ ] [x] **L.**; r. XVI 5: 10 gín D. kb 2 **L.**; r. XVIII 18: TAR kg 2 **L.**; r. XXI 7: TAR kg 2 **L.**, ŠÚ+ŠA kb 2 **L.**; **18** o. III 18: ŠÚ+ŠA gín D. kb 2 **L.**; o. IV 19: 2 gín D. kb 2 **L.**; r. II 23: ŠÚ+ŠA gín D. kb 2 **L.**; r. III 18: ŠÚ+ŠA gín D. kb 2 **L.**; r. IV 20: ŠÚ+ŠA gín D. kb 2 **L.**; r. XII 10: ŠÚ+ŠA gín D. kb 2 **L.**; **19** o. II 15: TAR kb 2 **L.**, 26: 5 gín D. kb 3 **L.** 2 saĝ; o. X 9: ŠÚ+ŠA gín D. kb 2 **L.**; r. XVI 4: 15 gín D. kb 2 **L.**; r. XVII 19: 10 gín D. kb 2 *bu*-DI 4 še-šu-še-tag; **20** o. XI 12: 10 gín D. kb 2 **L.**; r. X 6: 10 gín D. kb 2 **L.** 4 *ti-ša-nu*; **21** o. V 21: ŠÚ+ŠA gín D. kb [2 **L.**]; o. XV 23: 1 ma-na kg 2 **L.**; o. XVI 2: [ŠÚ+ŠA gín D.] kg 2 **L.**; r. III 3: [x gín] ⸢D.⸣ kb kin$_5$-ak 2 **L.** 4 še-šu-tag; r. VII 5: [1 ma-na kb 2 **L**]; **24** r. II 1: 3 gín D. kg nu$_{11}$-za 2 saĝ 2 **L.**

bulug$_4$ «chisel; seal pin» **12** o. X 16: 2 zú **L.**

bulug$_4$-bulug$_4$ **12** r. XII 6: 6 **L.** gibil lú ĜIŠ-gígir-II; r. XIII 4: 5 **L.** gibil lú ĜIŠ-taškarin.

bur-KAK (a bowl for oil, in boxwood, decorated with gold, also used for the marriage ritual) **2** o. II 19: 6 gín D. kg nu$_{11}$-za 1 **L.** ĜIŠ-taškarin; **3** r. V 11: 6 gín D. kg nu$_{11}$-za 1 **L.** *na-kar*$^{?}$*-ra-tim*; **4** r. XV 22: 5 kb 1 **L.** *aš-ḫal* ì-ĝiš; **5** o. VI 14: 5 gín D. kg nu$_{11}$-za 1 **L.** ĜIŠ-taškarin; **6** r. VII 3: ŠÚ+ŠA gín D. kb 2 **L.** *aš-ḫal* ì-ĝiš; **13** o. VI 24: TAR [x] gí[n] D. kb nu$_{11}$-za 1 **L.**; **16** r. XII 25: 1 gín D. kg *ni-zi-mu* nu$_{11}$-za 1 **L.** ga:eš$_8$; r. XV 25 and 29: ŠA.[PI 1+]⸢1⸣ gín D. kg nu$_{11}$-za 2 **L.** ĜIŠ-⸢taškarin⸣ kaskal en *wa* 2 **L.** ĜIŠ-taškarin kaskal ⸢*Ib*⸣*-rí-um*; **20** r. III 23: níĝ-ba *Dar-ib-da-mu* dumu-munus en $^{d}$BAD-munus *si-in Lu-ba-an*$^{ki}$ *in* ud *ter*$_6$*-bí* **L.**-*sù* $^{d?}$*A*$_5$*-da-*"*bal*"; **24** r. II 3: 3 gín D. kg nu$_{11}$-za 1 **L.** ĜIŠ-taškarin.

bur-KAK-bur-KAK **4** o. XI 5: TAR kg nu$_{11}$-za$^{!}$(KUR) 4 **L.** ĜIŠ-taškarin.

buru$_4$-MUŠEN «shield; hawk» **7** r. VI 4: 1 gín D. kg 1 kù-sal 1 **L.**; **15** r. XIV 2: 2 gín D. kb 1 **L.**; **17** o. IV 20: 1 gín D. kg 1 kù-sal 1 **L.**; r. V 19: 1 gín D. kg 1 kù-sal 1 **L.**; **18** o. XIX 3: 1 kg 1 kù-sal **L.**; **19** r. VIII 11: 6 gín D. ½ kg kin$_5$-ak 6 še-šu-še-tag *wa* 1 **L.**; **24** o. VIII 3: ŠÚ+ŠA 8 kg 4 *ˀà-ra-ma-tum* 2 **L.**

## D

daḫ «to add» **7** r. XV 19: ŠÚ+ŠA 4 gín D. kg **L.** kg lú en *wa* [l]ugal-[lu]gal [ì-n]a-sum; **8** o. VI 5: TAR kg **L.** nu$_{11}$-za 1 an-dùl; **12** r. VI 1: 5 gín D. kg **L.** níg-du$_8$ 1 ĝuruš.

daḫ$_x$(MU.MU.MU) **14** r. XIV 7': 10 gín D. kg **L.** *ni-zi-mu* nu$_{11}$-za-*sù*; **17** r. XVIII 22: ŠÚ+ŠA kb **L.** ⸢níĝ⸣-sa$_{10}$ [ ]; **18** o. IX 2: 11 ma-na an-na šub *si-in* 6 *mi-at* ma-na a-gar$_5$-gar$_5$ **L.** kin$_5$-ak 2 útul gibil.

dam «woman, wife; working woman» **1** o. V 12: 2 ma-na 10 gín D. kb níĝ-sa$_{10}$ 11 **L.** [*A*-]*šum* [šu-b]a$_4$-[ti]; o. XV 6: *Da-mur-da-mu* **L.** *Ib-rí-um*; **3** r. XI 17: 6 *bu*-DI níĝ-ba 3 **L.** *Zi-ba-da*; **4** o. V 22: 6 *bu*-DI 3 **L.** *Ib-rí-um Ḫa-zu-wa-an*$^{ki}$; o. IX 14: 10 lá-2 *bu*-DI níĝ-ba 4 **L.** *Ì-ra-ar*$^{ki}$; **5** r. VII 1: še ĝuruš-ĝuruš-*sù wa* **L.**-*sù Za-ba-rúm* še-<SAĜ×>ḪA-mul; **6** o. II 11: ŠÚ+ŠA gín D. kb níĝ-sa$_{10}$ 2 **L.** túg-nu-tag *Ma-rí*$^{ki}$; r. XVII 32: 1 ma-na an-na kin$_5$-ak $^{d}$*Á-la wa* **L.**-*sù* lú *A-ra-ab*$^{ki}$; **8** r. V 8': (silver) [*Ib*-lu$_5$]-⸢*zú*⸣ *wa I-za-iš-ru*$_{12}$ [lú-k]ar *Ma-nu-wa-ad*$^{ki}$ … 1 gu-dùl-TÚG gi$_6$ **L.**-*sù*; **10** o. VIII 14: 2 *bu*-DI **L.** BAD-*da-mu*; r. IV 12: ⸢10⸣ útul$^{!}$ urudu$^{!}$ lú **L.** lú ĜIŠGAL-titab(MUNU$_4$.A); **12** o. VI 19: (silver) níĝ-ba *Wa-ba-rúm* … (silver) níĝ-ba *Na-na-tum* **L.**-*sù*; **13** o. II 3: [1 íb-lá 1] *si-ti-tum* 1 ĝír-kun … *Ar-ru-du-lum* … 2 *bu*-DI **L.**-*sù*; **17** r. XIV 21: [10+]7 [*b*]*u*-DI [ŠÚ+Š]A-ŠÚ+ŠA [níĝ-b]a … ama-gal *Ib-rí-um wa A-zi-mu Ti-lu-du Ti-a-da-mu Kir-su-ud* **L.**-*sù*; **18** r. II 26: 2 *bu*-DI ì-ĝiš-saĝ *Gi-ù-du* **L.** *Za-ba-rúm*; **21** o. V 24: [2 *bu*]-⸢DI⸣ ì-ĝiš-saĝ **L.** *ba-da-lum* [*Ḫa*-]*ra-an*$^{ki}$.

dam en «spouse of the king» **3** o. XI 17: ⸢2⸣ *bu*-DI ì-ĝiš-saĝ *Tíš*-⸢*má*⸣*-da-mu* **L.**; **16** o. V 4: 2 *bu*-DI *Da-dub* **L.** lú *A-ru*$_{12}$*-ga-du*$^{ki}$; **17** r. XIV 5: [10+]7 [*b*]*u*-DI [ŠÚ+Š]A-ŠÚ+ŠA [níĝ-b]a *Ra-ù-tum Kir-*[*s*]*u-*[*u*]*d* [*En-na-*$^{d}$Utu] *Ra-ba*$_x$*-tum Maš-ga-sa-du Ma-ga-ra-du Tíš-ma-da-mu Ra-ba*$_x$*-tum*-II **L.**; **18** o. XVII 7: 2 *ti-gi-na* 10 lá-2 ĝeštu$_x$-lá 92 *gur-gú-ru*$_{12}$ 3 *mi-at* 60 *ḫa-za-nu* 1 šu-dub 1 *ma-ḫa-na-gúm* 2 kù-sal 1 *a-a-nu* 2 ĜIŠ-du *Tal-du-du* **L.**; **21** r. VIII 25: 2 ĜIŠ-du **L.** *ˀÁ-za-an*$^{ki}$.

dam-dam en **22** o. I 9: gù-kak-gíd **L.** ⸢*wa*⸣ [ ] géme-gi.

dam-diĝir «priestess» **12** r. XIII 9: (silver) *Di-ni-íb-du-lum* **L.** nin-ni en šu-ba$_4$-ti; **18** r. IV 23: 2 *bu*-DI ì-ĝiš-saĝ *Di-rín-da-mu* **L.** *áš-du* úš *ma-lik-tum Lum-na-an*$^{ki}$; **19** o. X 12: 2 *bu*-DI ì-ĝiš-saĝ *Di-rín-da-mu* **L.** *Ìr-ba*$_x$*-zé* "ur$_4$" šu-mu-tak$_4$.

dam-gàr «merchant» **13** o. X 14: (171 garments) ki:lam$_7$ *Ma-rí*$^{ki}$ **L.**; r. II 8: ⸢*Sa-mu-ù*⸣ **L.** *Ga-ra-ma-an*$^{ki}$; **14** o. VI 8: (231 garments) ki:lam$_7$ *Ma-rí*$^{ki}$ **L.**; r. I 14: *S*[*a-m*]*u-*⸢*ù*⸣ **L.**; **16** o. IV 18: (18 garments, 320 na$_4$ measures of wool, 65 shells) *in* Kiš$^{ki}$ **L.**; **17** o. IX 8: (109 garments) ki:lam$_7$ *Ma-rí*$^{ki}$ **L.** [šu-]mu-[t]ak$_4$; o. XVII 19: (194 garments) ki:lam$_7$ *Ma-rí*$^{ki}$ **L.**

DAM.KAK.UŠ **21** o. IX 7: 50 lá-2 **L.** tur sal.

*da-ne-a-tum* (a decoration: cf. *da-ni-da*) **16** o. II 22: 1 ½ gín D. kg kin$_5$-ak 6 **L.** *si-ti-tum*.

*da-ni-da* (a form of a jewel) **4** o. X 15: 3 gín D. kb *ḫa-za-nu* 2 **L.**

dàra «(toggle-pin in the shape of a) mountain goat» **5** o. V 5: 3 gín D. kb **L.**-*sù*; **8** r. VI 7': 2 si **L.**

dib «plaque» **2** o. I 5: [1] gín D. kg *ni-zi-mu* 1 **L.**, 20: 1 gín D. kg *ni-zi-mu* 1 **L.**; o. III 19: 1 gín D. kg *ni-zi-mu* 1 **L.**; o. IV 7: 11 gín D. kg *ni-zi-mu* 1 **L.**; o. XII 10: 1 gín D. kg *ni-zi-mu* 1 **L.**; o. XIV 1: 2 gín D.

kg *ni-zi-mu* 1 **L.**, 8: 2 gín D. kg *ni-zi-mu* 1 **L.**; r. I 18: 2 gín D. kg *ni-zi-mu* 1 **L.**; r. VI 17 and 19: ŠA.PI 3 gín D. kg kin$_5$-ak 1 **L.** lú ĜIŠ-ĝeštin *wa* 1 **L.**-II ŠA.PI gín D. kg; r. XII 4: 3 gín D. kg *n[i-z]i-⌜mu⌝* 1 **L.**; **3** o. IV 2: 2 gín D. kg *ni-zi-mu* 1 **L.**; o. XII 4: 8 gín D. kg *ni-zi-mu* 1 **L.**; o. XIV 19: ŠÚ+ŠA gín [D. kg] 1 **L.**; o. XV 6: [ŠÚ+ŠA 5 gín D. kg] [1 **L.**], 16: [ ] *n[i-zi-]m[u]* 1 **L.**; r. I 2: ŠÚ+ŠA gín D. kg 1 **L.**; r. IV 18: ŠA.PI gín D. kg 1 **L.**; r. V 5: TAR kg 1 **L.**; r. VI 4: TAR kg <1 **L.**>; **4** r. XI 6: 1 **L.** ĜÁ×LÁ ŠÚ+ŠA gín D. kg; r. XII 25: 4 gín D. kb ZU.PIRIĜ 2 **L.**; **5** o. IV 9: ½ gín D. kg *ni-zi-mu* 1 **L.**, 15: 1 gín D. kg *ni-zi-mu* 1 **L.**; o. X 16: 5 gín D. kg *ni-zi-mu* 1 **L.**, 22: 2 gín D. kg *ni-zi-mu* 1 **L.**; o. XI 18: 2 gín D. kg *ni-zi-mu* 1 **L.**; o. XIII 17: 2 gín D. kg *ni-zi-mu* 1 **L.**; r. I 10: 1 gín D. kg *ni-zi-mu* 1 **L.**; r. VI 7: ŠÚ+ŠA 2 gín D. kg 1 **L.**; r. VII 8: 2 gín D. kg 1 **L.**, 14: ½ gín D. kg 1 **L.**; r. X 3: ŠÚ+ŠA 4 gín D. kg <1 **L.**>; r. XV 3: 3 gín D. kg *ni-zi-mu* 1 **L.**, 9: 2 kg *ni-zi-mu* 1 **L.**; **6** o. V 4: 23 **L.** a-gar$_5$-gar$_5$ kg; **7** o. VI 4: ŠA.PI gín D. kg 1 **L.**; o. XI 5: ½ gín D. kg *ni-zi-mu* 1 **L.**; o. XVI 5: 2 ½ gín D. kg *ni-zi-mu* 1 **L.**; r. IX 19: ŠÚ+ŠA gín D. kg *ni-zi-mu* 1 **L.**; r. X 5: 1 gín D. kg *ni-zi-mu* 1 **L.**, 12: [1] gín D. kg *ni-zi-mu* 1 **L.**; r. XIV 25: 1 gín D. kg *ni-zi-mu* 1 **L.**; r. XV 5: TAR kg 1 **L.**; **8** o. XII 16: 4 gín D. kg *ni-zi-mu* 1 **L.**; r. X 14': ½ gín D. kg *ni-zi-mu* 1 **L.**; **9** o. IV 19: 2 gín D. kg *ni-zi-mu* 1 **L.**; o. XIII 8: ŠÚ+ŠA 5 gín D. kg 1 **L.**; r. III 1: TAR kg 1 **L.**, 12: [2 ma-na 6 gín D.] kg 1 [**L.**]; r. IV 8: TAR kg 1 **L.**; r. VII 9: TAR kg 1 **L.**; r. X 10: 1 ma-na ŠÚ+ŠA 6 gín D. kg *ni-zi-mu* nu$_{11}$-za ḫaš-ḫaš 1 **L.** a-gar$_5$-gar$_5$ lú 4 *gú-li-lum*; 12: 1 **L.** a-gar$_5$-gar$_5$; r. XV 9: 50 gín D. kg 1 **L.**; r. XVII 8: 1 gín D. kg *ni-zi-mu* 1 **L.**; **11** o. VII 14: TAR kg 1 **L.**; r. VII 15: TAR kg 1 **L.**; **12** o. III 8: *ap* kg lú **L.**; o. IV 4: 50 gín D. kg 1 **L.**; r. X 9: TAR 7 gín D. kg 1 **L.**; **13** o. XIII 14: TAR kg 1 **L.**; r. IX 3: [š]a-pi g[ín D. kg] 1 **L.**; **14** o. VII 10: 8 gín D. kg *ni-zi-mu* 1 **L.**; o. IX 12: 2 gín D kg *ni-zi-mu* 1 **L.**; o. XIV 10: ⌜1⌝ gín D. kg [*ni-*]*zi-mu* 1 **L.**; r. VIII 12: ŠA.PI gín D. kg 1 **L.**; **15** o. III 17: TAR kg 1 **L.**, 26: [ ] *Ḫa-ra-il áš-du* 1 **L.**-*sù* til *in Ša-nu-gú*$^{ki}$; o. IV 5: ŠÚ+ŠA gín D. kg 1 **L.**; o. V 5: 3 gín D. kg *ni-zi-mu* 1 **L.**, 16: 10 gín D. kg 1 **L.**, 22: 10 gín D. kg 1 **L.**; r. IX 4: ŠA.PI gín D. kg 1 **L.**; r. XII 2 and 5: 1 ma-na ša[-pi gín D. kg] 1 **L.** en *áš-du* **L.**-*sù* sikil $^{d}$ʾ*À-da al*$_6$ tu-ra ama-gal-*sù*; r. XIII 3 and 6: 2 ma-na k[g] 1 **L.** *Ib-rí-um áš-du* **L.**-*sù* sikil $^{d}$ʾ*À-da al*$_6$ tu-ra en, 16: 1 gín D. kg *ni-zi-mu* 1 **L.**; r. XIV 13: 1 gín D. kg *ni-zi-mu* 1 **L.**; r. XV 6: 50 gín D. kg 1 **L.**; **16** o. I 15: 1 ma-na 12 gín D. kg 1 **L.**; o. VII 15–19: TAR 1 gín D. kg *ni-zi-mu* 2 **L.** lú <1> ma-na 3 **L.** lú 50 gín D. 8 **L.** lú ŠA.PI gín D. 3 **L.** lú TAR.TAR 3 **L.** lú ŠÚ+ŠA gín D; r. IV 4: ŠÚ+ŠA gín D. kg 1 **L.**, 15: ŠÚ+ŠA 2 gín D. kg *ni-zi-mu* 1 **L.**; r. V 13: 2 gín D. kg *ni-zi-mu* 1 **L.**, 20: 1 gín D. kg *ni-zi-mu* 1 **L.**, 27: 2 gín D. kg *ni-zi-mu* 1 **L.**; r. X 4: 50 gín D. kg 1 **L.**; r. XVI 11: 10 kg *ni-zi-mu* 1 **L.**, 18: 10 kg *ni-zi-mu* 1 **L.**; **17** o. I 11: ŠA.PI gín D. kg 1 **L.**; o. VI 23: ⌜20⌝ gín D. kg 1 **L.**; o. XIV 15: 2 ma-na kg 1 íb-lá 1 *si-ti-tum* 1 ĝír-kun 1 **L.**; o. XVIII 1: TAR kg 1 **L.**; r. I 6: ŠA.PI gín D. kg 1 **L.**, 23: TAR kg *ni-zi-mu* 1 **L.**; r. III 27: 1 gín D. 3 NI kg *ni-zi-mu* 1 **L.**; r. VII 29: 1 gín D. kg *ni-zi-mu* 1 **L.**; r. VIII 3: TAR kg 1 **L.**, 10: ½ gín D. kg *ni-zi-mu* 1 **L.**; r. XV 6: 10 gín D. kg *ni-zi-mu* 1 **L.**; r. XIX 12: ½ kg *ni-zi-mu* 1 **L.**, 19: 10 kg *ni-zi-mu* 1 **L.**, 27: 1 kg *ni-zi-mu* 1 **L.**, 35: 1 ½ kg *ni-zi-m[u]* 1 **L.**; **18** o. III 2: ŠÚ+ŠA gín D. kg 1 **L.**; o. XI 21: 1 gín D. kg *ni-zi-mu* 1 **L.**; o. XVI 9: TAR kg 1 **L.**; **19** o. V 9 and 14: 1 ma-na ŠA.PI gín D. kg 1 **L.** *I-bí-zi-kir* dumu-nita *Ib-rí-um áš-du* **L.**-*sù* sikil $^{d}$ʾ*À-da*; o. X 5: 15 gín D. kg 1 **L.**; r. VII 26: 2 gín D. kg *ni-zi-mu* 1 **L.**, 32: 2 gín D. kg *ni-zi-mu* 2 **L.**; r. X 14: ŠA.PI gín D. kg 1 **L.**; r. XIII 8: 1 ma-na kg 1 **L.**, 23: ŠA.PI 4 gín D. kg 1 **L.**; r. XV 23: 2 ½ gín D. kg *ni-zi-mu* 1 **L.**; r. XVIII 21: ŠÚ+ŠA kg 1 **L.**; **20** o. X 15: [ ] 1 **L.**-*sù*, 24: 5 gín D. kg *ni-zi-mu* 1 **L.**; r. I 3: TAR kg 1 **L.**; r. XII 9: 5 gín D. kg *ni-zi-mu* 1 **L.**; **21** o. VI 11: TAR kg 1 **L.** *Ìr-ba*$_x$-*da-mu* en *Ù-ti-ig*$^{ki}$; o. VII 9: 2 ma-na kg kin$_5$-ak 1 **L.** 1 íb-lá 1 *si-ti-tum* 1 ĝír-kun; o. XIV 2: [2 ma-na kg] 1 íb-lá 1 *si-ti-tum* 1 ĝír-kun 1 **L.**; o. XVI 12: ŠA.PI gín D. kg 1 **L.**, 17: ŠA.PI gín D. kg 1 **L.**, 22: ŠA.PI gín D. kg [1] **L.**; r. IV 4–8: [1 **L.**] 1 ma-na 2 **L.** 50 50 7 **L.** ŠA.PI-ŠA.PI 3 **L.** TAR-TAR 1 **L.** ŠÚ+ŠA 5 gín D. 1 **L.** ŠÚ+ŠA; r. XII 24: 1 ma-na kg 1 **L.**; r. XIII 17: 4 ma-na kg 1 **L.** 2 *gú-li-lum*; **22** o. VI 6: ŠÚ+ŠA 5 gín D. kg 1 **L.**, 9: ŠÚ+ŠA 6 gín D. kg 1 **L.**; o. VII 2: ŠA.PI [gín D. kg] 1 **L.**, 7: 1 ma-na kg 1 **L.**, 11: 50 gín D. kg 1 **L.**; o. VIII 4: 1 ma-na kg 1 **L.**, 9: ŠA.PI gín D. kg 1 **L.**; o. IX 2: TAR kg 1 **L.**, 7: ŠÚ+ŠA 5 gín D. kg 1 **L.**; r. I 1: 10 gín D. kg 1 **L.**; r. VII 7: ŠA.PI gín D. kg *ni-zi-mu* 13 **L.**; **23** o. I 1: 2 ma-na ŠÚ+ŠA 3 gín D. kg 1 **L.** maḫ lú ĜIŠ-ĝidru-ĜIŠ-ĝidru in-na-sum; o. III 10: 2 gín D. kg *ni-zi-mu* <1 **L.**>; o. IV 5: 1 gín D. kg *ni-zi-mu* 1 **L.**, 9: 1 ½ gín D. kg *ni-zi-mu* 1 **L.**; o. V 3: 1 gín D. kg *ni-zi-mu* 1 **L.**, 7: 1 ½ gín D. kg *ni-zi-mu* 1 **L.**, 11: 1 gín D. kg *ni-zi-mu* 1 **L.**; o. VI 4: 1 gín D. kg *ni-zi-mu* 1 **L.**, 8: 1 gín D. kg *ni-zi-mu* 1 **L.**, 12: 1 ½ gín D. kg *ni-zi-mu* 1 **L.**; o. VII 5: 1 ½ gín D. kg *ni-zi-mu* 1 **L.**, 9: ½ gín D. kg *ni-zi-mu* 1 **L.**; o. VIII 3: 1 ½ gín D. kg *ni-zi-mu* 1 **L.**; r. IV 2: 8 gín D. kg nu$_{11}$-za 5 *gú-li-lum* **L.** a-gar$_5$; r. V 3: 1 gín D. kg *ni-zi-mu* 1 **L.**, 11: 2 gín D. kg *ni-zi-mu* 1 **L.**; r. VI 5: 2 gín D. kg *ni-zi-mu* 1 **L.**; **24** o. II 11: TAR kg 1 **L.** *Ù-zi* šeš *A-zú-ma*; o. III 2: TAR kg 1 **L.**, 10: 1 gín D. kg *ni-zi-mu* 1 **L.**; r. III 5: 13$^?$ gín D. kg *ni-zi-mu* 1 **L.**, 11: 4 gín D. kg *ni-zi-mu* 3 **L.**

di-kud «judge» **8** r. VIII 8': 1 ĝír mar-tu *ba-du-u*$_4$ kg kb *Ù-da-sa* **L.**; **10** o. X 2: (silver) níĝ-ba *Wa-ba-rúm Ma-rí*$^{ki}$ *in* ud **L.** DU.DU; **16** r. IV 17: 1 dib *Íl-a-i-šar* **L.**; **19** r. XIX 11: BAR.AN.BAR.AN *Iš*$_{11}$-*da-mu* **L.** šu-mu-tak$_4$ *si-in Na-gàr*$^{ki}$; **22** o. V 4: (silver) lú *En-na-ì* **L.**

diĝir «god» **13** o. IX 19: 1 kù-sal … 1 kù-sal níĝ-ba $^{d}$NE-*ti-a-du* **L.** *Du-lu*$^{ki}$; **15** r. XI 19: 1 *gú-li-lum* $^{d}$*Da-bi-ir* **L.** *Ib-la*$^{ki}$; **17** o. VI 19: nídba é **L.**

diĝir-diĝir **7** o. IV 2: […] nu$_{11}$-za AN.Á.DAḪ

diĝir-diĝir-diĝir **3** r. X 18: (silver) níĝ-ba **L.**; **4** o. XV 16: (silver) níĝ-ba **L.**; **5** r. XVI 7: (silver) níĝ-ba **L.**; **7** r. V 8: šu-mu-t[ak$_4$] diri **L.**; r. XIV 14: (silver) níĝ-ba **L.**; **8** o. VII 9: (silver) níĝ-ba **L.**; **9** o. II 3: (silver) níĝ-ba **L.**; **10** o. X 21: (silver) níĝ-ba **L.**; **11** o. XI 11: (silver) níĝ-ba **L.**; **12** r. III 13: (silver) níĝ-ba **L.**; **14** r. XIX 2: 2 [ ] **L.**; **15** r. XVII 2: (silver) níĝ-ba-níĝ-ba **L.**; **16** r. XVII 15: (silver) [níĝ-]ba **L.**; **17** r. XVI 14: *in* ud šu-mu-nígin é **L.**; r.

XXII 14: (silver) ⌜níĝ-ba⌝ **L.**; **18** r. XVI 20: (silver) níĝ-ba **L.**; **19** r. XVIII 18: (silver) níĝ-ba **L.**; **20** r. XVI 2': (15+[x] bracelets) níĝ-⌜ba⌝ **L.**; **21** o. XI 10: (silver) níĝ-ba **L.**; **22** o. V 1: 70 ma-na lú **L.**

diĝir-diĝir-diĝir-diĝir **6** o. VIII 13: (silver) níĝ-ba **L.**; **25** r. VI 2: [ ] še-ba **L.** níĝ-sa$_{10}$ gig.

DILMUN «weighed, standard (shekel)» *passim.*

diri «surplus; remainder» **3** o. V 3: 40[+x] **L.** ĝír mar-tu; r. III 12: [ ] **L.** ĝír mar-tu; **7** r. V 76: šu-mu-t[ak$_4$] **L.** diĝir-diĝir-diĝir; **12** r. XV 7: [AN.ŠÈ.GÚ x kb] [è] *ap* 3 *mi-at* 1 ma-na kb [al$_6$-ĝá]l é en **L.**; **17** l.ed. x+5: AN.ŠÈ.GÚ 2 *mi-at* 65 ma-na 4 gín D. kb è [(1+$^?$)]1 *mi-at* 10 lá-2 ma-na š[a-pi] gí[n] D. kb al$_6$-ĝál lú **L.**; **21** r. I 16: 3 ĜIŠ-šú 3 níĝ-bànda lú **L.** lú šu-šu kas$_4$-kas$_4$.

DU «foot» **3** o. XII 14: 6 gín D. kg nu$_{11}$-za *ba-na-⌜ʾà⌝ wa* 2 šu 2 **L.**-*sù*; **7** o. X 9: 17 gín D. kb nu$_{11}$-za saĝ-*sù* 2 šu-*sù* **L.**-*sù*; **12** r. IX 15: 2 an-dùl … 8 gín D. kg nu$_{11}$-za *ba-na-a-sa wa* 2 šu-*sù wa* 2 **L.**-*sù*; **13** o. VIII 1: 2 an-dùl … 10 gín D. kg nu$_{11}$-za [I]GI.DUB-*sù wa* 4 šu-*sù* 4 **L.**-*sù*, 18: 1 an-dùl … 3 gín D. kg nu$_{11}$-za IGI.DUB-*sù* 2 šu-*sù* 2 **L.**-*sù*; **16** o. V 14: 1 an-dùl … 2 ma-na 5 gín D. kg nu$_{11}$-za IGI.DUB-*sù wa* 2 **L.**-*sù wa* 2 šu-*sù*; **18** r. XIV 24: 1 an-dùl munus … ⌜1⌝ ma-na 14 gín kg nu$_{11}$-za IGI.DUB-*sa* 2 šu 2 -*sù*; **24** o. V 5: 16 gín D. kg nu$_{11}$-za IGI.DUB 2 an-dùl *wa* 2 šu-*sù* 2 -*sù*.

DU.DU **10** o. IV 10: 1 ĜIŠ-sal lú **L.** lu$_5$ tuš $^d$*Á-la* lú *Zi-ig*$^{ki}$; **12** o. III 15: ŠÚ+ŠA 2 gín D. kg nu$_{11}$-za *ba-na-i-su-ma wa* 2 šu-šu-*sù* 2 **L.**-*sù*.

DU «to go; departure» **25** r. II 7: ⌜x⌝-[ ] *Ì-ra-ar*$^{ki}$ *in* ud **L.** *M*[*a*]*-za-t*[*um*$^{?ki}$].

DU.DU **1** o. V 17: *Ìr-kab-ar* **L.** *si-in Ar-mi*$^{ki}$; o. VII 1: *Na*-N[E] *Na-gà*[*r*$^{ki}$] **L.** *si-in Ar-mi*$^{ki}$, 8: *Ne-zi-ma-ì* ⌜*Puzur*$_4$⌝*-ra-a-gú* **L.** *si-in Na-gàr*$^{ki}$; (e) r. III' 10: *I-ga-iš-lu* **L.** *si-in Ma-rí*$^{ki}$; **3** o. VII 12: lú nu-kiri$_6$ **L.** *al*$_6$ dumu-nita *Ru*$_{12}$*-zi-da-mu Ma-nu-wa-ad*$^{ki}$; **4** o. II 20: *Ni-zi-ma-il* **L.** *Na-gàr*$^{ki}$, o. VIII 19: *Ìr-a*[*m*$_6$-]*ma-lik* **L.** *Na-gàr*$^{ki}$; o. X 5: *in* ud *ma-lik-tum Ì-ra-ar*$^{ki}$ **L.**; o. XIII 15: *ʾÀ-daš ma-za-lum* **L.** *Ar-mi*$^{ki}$; o. XIV 21: *Ni-zi-ma-il* **L.** *Na-gàr*$^{ki}$; r. VIII 8: *Ni-zi-ma-il* **L.** *Na-gàr*$^{ki}$, 14: [PN] *wa ma-z*[*a-*]*lum* **L.** *Ar-mi*$^{ki}$; r. XII 22: *A-ʾà-*⌜*lu*⌝ *wa Ù-da-a-ḫa Ma-rí*$^{ki}$ LÚ×KÁR **L.**; **6** o. IV 20: *Ìr-am*$_6$*-ma-lik* **L.** *Na-gàr*$^{ki}$; o. V 11: *ʾÀ-daš* **L.** *si-in Ar-mi*$^{ki}$; o. IX 1: *A-ir-ra wa A-zú-bù-lu* [*Ù-t*]*i-*[*g*]*ú*$^{ki}$ [*w*]*a A-zú* **L.** *Ar-mi*$^{ki}$; o. XI 21: *Ni-zi-ma-il* **L.** *Ma-rí*$^{ki}$; o. XIII 9: *A-ʾà-lu wa Ù-da-aḫ* LÚ×KÁR **L.** *Ma-rí*$^{ki}$; o. XV 5: *A-ir-ra wa A-zú-bù-lu* **L.** *Ar-mi*$^{ki}$; o. XVI 10: *Ni-zi-ma-il wa I-ib-ma-lik* **L.** *Ma-rí*$^{ki}$; r. I 16: *Ìr-am*$_6$*-ma-lik wa I-ib-ma-lik* **L.** *Ma-rí*$^{ki}$; r. II 5: *Za-gàr A-dar-ki-zú*$^{ki}$ **L.** *Ar-mi*$^{ki}$; r. IV 10: *Ḫar-zàr-du*$^{ki}$ **L.** *Ar-mi*$^{ki}$; r. V 2: *En-na-ì* lú kas$_4$-kas$_4$ **L.** *Ma-rí*$^{ki}$; **7** o. XVIII 1: ⌜*Nap*⌝*-ḫ*[*a-il*] **L.** *si-in Ma-rí*$^{ki}$; r. XI 20: *Gul-la* ⌜x-x-x⌝ *Sa-ma-na-nu* [*S*]*i-mi*[- ] *Iš-ba-ì A-ša*$^{ki}$ *in* ud **L.** nam-kud é $^d$*Ku-ra*; r. XII 14: maškim:<e>-gi$_4$ **L.**; r. XIII 11: *En-na-ì* lú BÍL-*za-ì* **L.** *si-in* Ki[š$^{ki}$]; **8** r. II 2': *I-t*[*i*]*-a-gú* **L.** ⌜*Za*⌝*-bù-rúm*$^{ki}$; **9** o. II 7: *Gi-li-ti-um*$^{ki}$ **L.** [*A*]*r-mi*$^{ki}$, 14: [*A-ir-ra wa A-zú-bù-lu*] **L.** *Ar-mi*$^{ki}$; o. XII 11: *Ìr-am*$_6$*-ma-lik wa En-na-*BAD **L.** [*M*]*a-rí*$^{ki}$; **10** o. VI 1: [ ] **L.** *Du-gú-ra-su*$^{ki}$; o. X 3: *Wa-ba-rúm Ma-rí*$^{ki}$ *in* ud di-kud **L.**; o. XIV 21: *En-na-*BAD *Zú-ti*$^{ki}$ maškim *Du-bí* **L.** *Ar-mi*$^{ki}$; o. XVI 1: *Íl-ra-*BAD maškim NI-*ba-rúm* **L.** *si-in Ar-mi*$^{ki}$; **11** r. VIII 7: *Kab-lu*$_5$*-ul*$^{ki}$ **L.** *Ar-mi*$^{ki}$; **12** r. I 6: *I-bí-du-lum* en *Ma-nu-wa-ad*$^{ki}$ *in* ud nam-kud é $^d$*Ku-ra*; r. VII 22: *Daš-na Ma-rí*$^{ki}$ **L.** *áš-da* [ ]; **13** o. II 19: *Mu-*NE*-a-du* ugula *Ar-ḫa-du*$^{ki}$ *in* ud nam-kud é $^d$*Ku-ra*; o. XVI 3: *Ti-šè-li-im ma-lik-tum Ì-mar*$^{ki}$ *in* ud **L.** *si-in* SA.ZA$_x$$^{ki}$; r. XIII 15: [ -]⌜x⌝ **L.** *Ma-rí*$^{ki}$; **14** r. X 23: [*Ì*]*r-am*$_6$-[*m*]*a-lik* [ ]⌜x⌝ [] *si-in* Kiš$^{ki}$; **15** r. V 14: *ma-lik-tum Ì-ra-ar*$^{ki}$ … *in* ud **L.** *Ga-wa-na*$^{ki}$; r. X 29: *En-na-ì* **L.** Kiš$^{ki}$; **17** o. VI 4: *En-na-il* [**L.**] *si-in* Kiš$^{ki}$, 16: [*Dar-maš-da-mu*] dumu-munus en é-gi BAD-*da-mu in* ud nídba é diĝir en; o. XII 6: *ma-lik-tum Lum-na-an*$^{ki}$ … *in* ud **L.** *si-in U*$_9$*-gú-a-aš*$^{ki}$; r. VI 4: *Ti-ša-li-im ma-lik-tum Ì-mar*$^{ki}$ *in* ud **L.** *mi-nu ʾÀ-da-ni*$^{ki}$; ugula *Ib-al*$_6$$^{ki}$ **L.** *Du-gú-ra-su*$^{ki}$ šu-mu-tak$_4$; r. IX 35: *Ti-ša-li-im ma-lik-tum Ì-mar*$^{ki}$ *in* ud **L.** *mi-nu* NI-*ab*$^{ki}$ *si-in* SA.ZA$_x$$^{ki}$; **18** r. X 22: *Gi-ba-rí-a Kab-lu*$_5$*-ul*$^{ki}$ **L.** *si-in Ir-bí-ì-lum*$^{ki}$; **19** o. VI 4: en-en lú *áš-ti* en *Na-gàr*$^{ki}$ nam-kud é $^d$BAD *Du-du-lu*$^{ki}$; o. VIII 19: NE-*iš-da-ar Kab-lu*$_5$*-ul*$^{ki}$ *si-in Ar-mi*$^{ki}$; r. XII 15: *Ga-áš-ru*$_{12}$ *Na-gàr*$^{ki}$ **L.** *mi-nu* Kiš$^{ki}$; *Ti-šè-li-im ma-lik-tum Ì-mar*$^{ki}$ *in* ud **L.** *mi-nu ʾÀ-da-ni*$^{ki}$; **21** r. X 13: *Bù-gal-lu Ba-zi-mu*$^{ki}$ *si-in Ar-mi*$^{ki}$.

dub «tablet, document» **3** r. XV 4: AN.ŠÈ.GÚ 1 *mi-at* 56$^!$ ma-na TAR 4 gín D. kb è 2 **L.**; **5** r. XVII 4: AN.ŠÈ.GÚ 1 *mi-at* 32 ma-na 50 gín D. kb è 2 mu 2 **L.**; **6** o. III 15: 50 gín D. kb nu$_{11}$-za 1 **L.** lú nam-kud *Ib-la*$^{ki}$ *wa Ma-rí*$^{ki}$ é $^d$*Ku-ra*; **10** o. VII 7: 50 gín D. kb nu$_{11}$-za 1 **L.** nam-kud *Ib-rí-um*; **19** r. VI 4: 10 gín D. kb nu$_{11}$-za 1 **L.** lú nam-kud en *wa Ib-rí-um* é $^{dʾ}$*À-da*, 12: 10 gín D. kb nu$_{11}$-za 1 **L.** *ma-lik-*[*t*]*um* [ ] ⌜é⌝ $^{d⌜ʾ}$*À*⌝[*-da*]; 21 o. V 8: 1 ½ gín D. an-na šub *si-in* 17 gín a-gar$_5$ 1 **L.**-*sù*.

dub-naĝar «hammer» **7** o. XIV 16: 8 gín D. an-na šub *si-in* … 1 **L.** sal …; **12** r. XI 14 and 16: 1 ma-na ŠÚ+ŠA 3 gín D. an-na šub *si-in* 9 ma-na TAR gín D. a-gar$_5$-gar$_5$ kin$_5$-ak … 6 **L.** sal lú 15 gín D. 6 **L.** sal 10 …; r. XII 4: 6 **L.** tur 5, 13 and 14: 57 gín D. an-na šub *si-in* 6 ma-na ŠA.PI 6 gín D. a-gar$_5$-gar$_5$ kin$_5$-ak … 5 **L.** sal 15 5 **L.** sal 10 …; **16** r. XV 10: TAR an-na šub *si-in* 4 ma-na ŠÚ+ŠA a-gar$_5$-gar$_5$ kin$_5$-ak … 5 **L.** 10 sal; **20** r. I 15 and 19: 17 gín D. an-na šub *si-in* 1 ma-na ŠA.PI gín D. a-gar$_5$[-gar$_5$] kin$_5$-ak … 1 **L.** 10 gín D. … 1 **L.** [10] ⌜lá-⌝2(?) gín D.

dub-naĝar šu-mu-LAGAB «hammer with a square head» **12** r. XI 13: 1 ma-na ŠÚ+ŠA 3 gín D. an-na šub *si-in* 9 ma-na TAR gín D. a-gar$_5$-gar$_5$ kin$_5$-ak … 6 **L.** ŠÚ+ŠA-ŠÚ+ŠA …; **16** r. XV 9: TAR an-na šub *si-in* 4 ma-na ŠÚ+ŠA a-gar$_5$-gar$_5$ kin$_5$-ak …5 **L.** 15; **20** r. I 14: 17 gín D. an-na šub *si-in* 1 ma-na ŠA.PI gín D. a-gar$_5$[-gar$_5$] kin$_5$-ak … 1 **L.** ŠÚ+ŠA gín D.

dub-sar «scribe» **20** r. VI 16: *Ti-ra-il* **L.**

dùl-TÚG (a kind of cloak) **6** r. IX 1; **7** o. VIII 15: 1 **L.** *Ma-rí*$^{ki}$; **13** o. X 11: **L.** *Ma-rí*$^{ki}$; r. II 1: **L.** *Ma-rí*$^{ki}$; **14** o. VI 4; **15** r. III 9: 6 **L.** *Ma-rí*$^{ki}$; **16** r. XI 15: 4 **L.** *Ma-rí*$^{ki}$; **17** r. V 6: 1 **L.** *Ma-rí*$^{ki}$; r. X 8: 6 **L.** *Ma-rí*$^{ki}$; **18** o. IX 15: 4 **L.** *Ma-rí*$^{ki}$; r. III 6: 4 **L.** *Ma-rí*$^{ki}$; r. XIII 4: 72 **L.** *Ma-rí*$^{ki}$; **19** r. XVI 23: 3 **L.** *Ma-rí*$^{ki}$; **20** r. VI 18: 1 **L.** *Ma-rí*$^{ki}$; r. XIII 4: 10 lá-1 **L.** *Ma-rí*$^{ki}$; **25** o. II 2: 7 *ʾà-da-um-*TÚG **L.**

dumu-munus «daughter» **1** o. X 17: NI-*gu* **L.** *A-ba-la*; **3** r. XI 21: *in* ud níĝ-mu-sá **L.** *Ib-rí-um*; **4** o. VI 18: 1 dumu-nita 1 **L.** [x-]*da*[- ]; o. X 20: 20 *gú-a-tum* … 1 ĜIŠ-šú 1 níĝ-bànda … 1 *mar-wa-ga-tum* … *ḫa-za-nu* 2 *da-ni-da* … níĝ-ba diĝir-diĝir-diĝir lú **L.** *Ib-rí-um* šu-mu-tak$_4$ *si-in Ì-ra-ar*$^{ki}$; **5** o. VI 9: *in* ud níĝ-mu-sá **L.** *Ib-rí-um Gi-ti-*NE$^{ki}$; **11** o. IV 9: *maš-ar-tum* níĝ-ba **L.** [*I*]*b-rí-*[*u*]*m* é-gi<-a> *Zi-ba-da* é $^{d}$ʾ*À-da*; **12** o. XV 2: 2 kù-sal **L.** *Da-ti-*$^{d}$TU *ma-lik-tum Lum-na-an*$^{ki}$ *Du-si-gú* šu-mu-tak$_4$; **15** o. XI 22: 10 ĝeštu$_x$-lá 2 *ti-gi-na* 62 *du-ru*$_{12}$*-gú* 1 *mi-at kur-gú-ru*$_{12}$ 2 kù-sal 1 *ma-ḫa-na-gúm ḫa-za-nu* 1 šu-dub 1 *ša-mu* 2 *ti-ba-ra-núm wa* … 2 saĝ 2 *bu-*DI … 2 *bu-*DI *Ar-za-du* **L.** *En-na-*$^{d}$Utu; o. XVI 24: 2 *bu-*DI … 2 saĝ-*sù Zi-mi-ni-*kù:babbar *ma-lik-tum Bur-ma-an*$^{ki}$ *in* ud **L.** tu-da; **17** o. II 12: [ ] **L.** *I-l*[*u*$_5$-]*-z*[*a*$_x$]-⌜*ma*⌝-*lik* šu-mu-tak$_4$.

dumu-munus en «daughter of the king» **2** o. V 11: 1 an-zam$_x$ … 1 zi-bar … 2 *bu-*DI … 2 saĝ-*sù Dar-maš-da-mu* **L.** *gal-tum* BAD-*da-mu*; **10** o. VI 12: 4 *bu-*DI **L.** [*Ra-*ʾ*à-ak*$^{ki}$] [*m*]*a-*[*li*]*k-*[*t*]*um* ⌜*A*⌝*-bar-sal*$_4$$^{ki}$ *wa ma-lik-tum Ir-i-tum*$^{ki}$ EN-*mar* šu-mu-tak$_4$; **12** o. VII 21: 2 *bu-*DI *Za-ne-ḫi-Ma-rí*$^{ki}$ **L.** é-gi *Ib-*ʾ*à-ra*; 14 o. V 9: 2 *bu-*DI **L.** *Ì-ra-ar*$^{ki}$ É×PAP *Zú-ba-núm* šu-mu-tak$_4$; **15** o. V 24: 1 dib *Dar-ib-da-mu* **L.**; o. X 21: 2 *ti-gi-na* 2 ĜIŠ-du 1 KA-*ḫu-a-tum Dar-ib-da-mu* **L.**; **16** o. III 13: 4 ĝeštu$_x$-lá *Dar-ib-da-mu wa Tiš-te-da-mu* … 2 **L.**; **17** o. II 22: [2 *bu-*DI **L.**] *Bur-ma-an*$^{ki}$ É×PAP é-gi en *Ra-*ʾ*à-ak*$^{ki}$; o. V 1: (obj.) [níĝ-ba] […] **L.** $^{d}$*Ku-ra* ì-na-sum *in* ne:saĝ-*sù*; o. VI 11: [*Dar-maš-da-mu*] **L.** é-gi BAD-*da-mu in* ud DU.DU nídba é diĝir en; r. IV 13: 1 *zi-zi-ḫi-tum Dar-ib-da-mu* **L.**; r. XIV 11: [10+]7 [*b*]*u*?-DI [ŠÚ+Š]A-ŠÚ+ŠA [níĝ-b]a PN$_1$–PN$_8$ dam en *wa Ma-ù-ud Za-ni-ḫi-Ma-rí*$^{ki}$ 2 **L.** *wa* ama-gal *Ib-rí-um wa* PN$_9$–PN$_{12}$ dam-*sù wa* PN$_{13}$ nin-ni *Du-si-gú* PN$_{14}$; **18** o. XVIII 11: 4 *ti-gi-na* 4 ĜIŠ-du 4 ĝeštu$_x$-lá 2 kù-sal *Dar-ib-da-mu wa Tiš-te-da-mu* 2 **L.**; r. XII 7: 4 níĝ-bànda 2 dumu-nita 2 **L.**; **19** o. X 7: 1 dib *Dar-ib-da-mu* **L.**; **20** r. III 16: 1 kù-sal níĝ-ba *Dar-ib-da-mu* **L.** $^{d}$BAD-munus *si-in Lu-ba-an*$^{ki}$.

dumu-munus tur en **17** r. XXI 3: [ ] **L.**

dumu-nita «son» **1** o. VIII 9: 2 ⌜ĜIŠ⌝ [ ] 2 ĜIŠ-⌜x⌝ **L.** *In-da-mu*; o. X 5: **L.** ⌜*Rí*⌝*-ì*[*-ma-lik*]; o. XI 2: (silver) *Maš-da-ru*$_{12}$ **L.** *En-na-*$^{d}$Utu; **2** o. IV 1: 1 dib *I-bí-zi-kir* **L.** *Ib-rí-um*; r. IV 15: 2 ĝeštu$_x$-lá *I-bí-zi-kir* **L.** *Ib-rí-um*; r. XI 12: 1 ĝír mar-tu *ba-du-u*$_9$ kg *Bu-da-na-im* **L.** ga-du$_8$; **3** o. VII 14: (silver) lú nu-kiri$_6$ DU.DU **L.** *Ru*$_{12}$*-zi-da-mu Ma-nu-wa-ad*$^{ki}$; r. III 7: 2 níĝ-anše-ak 4 kù-sal *I-bí-zi-kir* **L.** *Ib-rí-um*; **4** o. V 3: (silver) níĝ-du$_8$ **L.** *Lá-da-il Ma-rí*$^{ki}$; o. VI 18: 1 **L.** 1 dumu-munus [x-]*da*[- ]; r. IX 12: [1 *gú-*]*li-lum* **L.** *Mu-gàr* NE-di; **5** r. II 3: 3 *zú-zú-ba-tum I-bí-zi-kir* **L.** *Ib-rí-um*; r. VIII 19: 1 ĜIŠ-banšur níĝ-ba *I-bí-zi-kir* **L.** *Ib-rí-um* $^{d}$ʾ*A*$_5$*-da-*"*bal*" *La-ru*$_{12}$*-ga-du*$^{ki}$; **6** o. VII 9: 1 ĝír mar-tu ti kg *Ru*$_{12}$*-zi-ma-lik* **L.** *I-gi*; o. XVI 20: (silver) níĝ-du$_8$ **L.** *Ù-du-bù*$^{ki}$ *áš-ti Kak-mi-um*$^{ki}$; r. XI 4: 1 ĝír mar-tu ti kg *Ig-rí-iš-li-im* **L.** *Ib-gi-da-mu*; **7** o. II 17: ⌜2⌝ *ti-gi-na* 2 ĜIŠ-du *Ir-*NE **L.** *I-ib-ma-lik*; **8** r. VII 7': 1 ĝír mar-tu *ba-du-u*$_4$ kg kb *Ib-dur-ti-lu* **L.** *A-mur-li-im*; **9** r. I 3: 1 ĝír mar-tu kg *Ì-lum-a-ḫa* **L.** uru-bar; r. III 3: 1 dib *En-àr-li-im* **L.** *Du-*[*bí*]*-šum A-ba-ad*$^{ki}$ tuš-LÚ×TIL *Ar-mi*$^{ki}$; **10** o. VII 13: *I-bí-zi-kir* **L.** *Ib-rí-um*; **11** r. III 20: (silver) níĝ-du$_8$ 2 **L.** *Bur-ḫa-áš*; **12** o. IV 6: 1 dib *I-bí-zi-kir* **L.** *Ib-rí-um*; o. VI 4: 2 kù-sal [ní]ĝ-ba $^{d}$BAD *Ga-na-na-im* [*w*]*a* [$^{d}$ʾ*A*$_5$*-d*]*a*[*-ra*] Gi-*rí wa Ni-ir-da-mu* 2 **L.** *Ib-rí-um* in-na-sum *in* ud gi$_4$ *mi-nu Du-du-lu*$^{ki}$, 22: (silver) níĝ-ba *Wa-ba-rúm* … (silver) níĝ-ba **L.**-*sù*; o. XII 6: 2 ĝeštu$_x$-lá *I-bí-zi-kir* **L.** *Ib-rí-um in* ud šu-du$_8$ *in Ma-nu-wa-ad*$^{ki}$; o. XIV 5: 2 *gú-li-lum* kb lú *Sa-mu-um* lú *En-ti wa* lú **L.** *I-da-ad-mu in ìr-a-núm I-rí-ig-ma-lik*; r. VI 9: (silver) níĝ-du$_8$ 1 **L.** *Ti-in*$^{ki}$ lú *A-da-su*$^{ki}$; **13** o. VI 13: 1 zag ĜIŠ-gígir-II *I-bí-zi-kir* **L.** *Ib-rí-um*; r. VII 14: 7 *gàr-su* gi$_6$ … BÍL-*za-ì wa En-na-ì* 2 **L.** šeš *Ib-rí-um*; **14** o. VII 12: 1 dib *Šum-*bàd$^{ki}$ **L.** *Ib-rí-um*; r. III 14: 1 g]ír [mar-t]u [t]i *Ir-da-mu* **L.** *Ib-rí-um*; r. IX 5: [ ] **L.** *I-bí-zi-kir* [tuš-LÚ×TIL *in*] *Ib-al*$_6$$^{ki}$; r. XII 25: [ ] **L.** *Ib-rí-um*; **15** o. II 11: (silver) níĝ-du$_8$ 1 **L.** *A-ba-ti-lum*$^{ki}$ maškim *Za-ba-rúm*; o. V 18: 1 dib *Du-bù-ḫu-*$^{d}$ʾ*À-da* **L.** *I-bí-zi-kir*; o. VIII 15:1 zag ĜIŠ-gígir-II *I-bí-zi-kir* **L.** *Ib-rí-um*; o. XVI 8: 1 íb-lá *Ir-da-mu* … 1 *si-ti-tum Gi-ir-da-mu* 2 **L.** *Ib-rí-um*; r. VII 10: 6 ĝeštu$_x$-lá *Gi-rí wa Ir-da-mu Nap-ḫa-il* **L.** *Ib-rí-um*; r. IX 6: 1 dib *A-ḫu-šu-da-mu* **L.** *Zé-ma-lik* šeš *I-nu-ud-da-mu*; **16** r. VI 7: 1 dib *Ir-ti* … 2 ĝeštu$_x$-lá *Gi-rí* 2 **L.** *Ib-rí-um*; r. IX 3: 2 níĝ-anše-ak 4 kù-sal *I-bí-zi-kir* **L.** *Ib-rí-um*, 25: 1 *gàr-su* **L.** *Ig-rí-iš* šu-du$_8$ *in Ḫal-sum*$^{ki}$; r. XV 20: 4 ĝeštu$_x$-lá *Ir-ti Nap-ḫa-ì* 2 **L.** *Ib-rí-um*; **17** o. III 26: 1 *gú-li-lum* a-gar$_5$-gar$_5$ 50 ʾ*À-gàr* ugula BAR.AN *I-bí-zi-kir* **L.** [*Ib-rí-um*] [šu-ba$_4$-ti]; o. VI 25: 1 dib *I-ib-ma-lik* **L.** *Aḫ-ra-ma-lik*; o. VIII 1: *i*[*n* ud] [ ] [*I-bí-zi-kir*] **L.** *Ib-rí-um*; o. XI 23: [1] ĝír [mar-]tu [*Nap*]*-ḫa-*⌜*ì*⌝ **L.** [*Ib-rí-u*]*m*; r. IV 7: NI-*na-du* ugula sur$_x$-BAR.AN *Gi-ir-da-mu* **L.** *Ib-rí-um*; r. VIII 17: 2 níĝ-anše-ak 4 kù-sal *Šum-*bàd$^{ki}$ **L.** *Ib-rí-um*; r. XII 11: 1 ĝír mar-tu kg *I-bí-zi-kir* **L.** *Ib-rí-u*[*m*]; r. XIII 21: 1 íb-lá 1 *si-ti-tum* 1 ĝír-kun níĝ-ba ʾ*À-daš* **L.** *A-du-ba* ʾ*À-ru*$_{12}$*-gú*$^{ki}$; r. XVII 16: 4 ĝeštu$_x$-lá *I-bí-zi-kir* **L.** *Ib-rí-um*; r. XIX 21: 1 dib *Ib-du-*$^{<d>}$*Aš-dar* **L.** *A-šum*; **18** o. III 4: 1 dib *Ba-d*[*u-lum* **L.**] *Ib-rí-um*; o. VI 7: 4 kù-sal *I-bí-zi-kir* **L.** *Ib-rí-um*; o. XI 16: 1 íb-lá 1 *si-ti-tum* 1 ĝír-kun *Gi-rí* … 1 íb-lá 1 ĝír-kun kb … maš-maš-*sù Ir-ti* … 1 íb-lá 1 ĝír-kun *Nap-ḫa-ì* 3 **L.** *Ib-rí-um*; r. IV 13: (silver) níĝ-du$_8$ 1 **L.** *Ku-a-*NE lú NE-*da-mu* SA.ZA$_x$$^{ki}$ *áš-ti Ìr-ku*$^{ki}$; **19** o. V 11: 1 dib *I-bí-zi-kir* **L.** *Ib-rí-um*; o. VII 20: 2 ĜIŠ-zú ĜIŠ-gígir-II zú-ak *Ib-rí-um wa I-bí-zi-kir* **L.**-*sù*, 26: 1 íb-lá 1 *si-ti-tum* 1 ĝír-kun *Mu-gàr* **L.** *A-ba-rúm in* ud ḫúl-*sù*; r. VIII 1: 2 dib *Ib-du-*$^{d}$*Aš-dar* **L.** *A-šum wa Ìl-gú-uš-ti*; r. XVIII 11: 1 íb-lá 1 *si-ti-tum* 1 ĝír-kun 1 ĜIŠ-sal níĝ-[b]a *Ib-rí-um* … 2 íb-lá 2 ĝír-kun 2 ĜIŠ-sal-*sù I-bí-zi-kir wa Ù-ti* 2 **L.**-*sù in* ud ḫúl-*sù* en šu-mu-tak$_4$, 22: 1 dib **L.** *ba-da-lum Ḫa-ra-an*$^{ki}$; **20** o. X 17: 1 dib-*sù I-bí-zi-kir* **L.** *Ib-rí-um*; o. XVII 15: 1 íb-lá 1 ĝír-kun … *Gi-a-da-mu in* ud ḫúl-*sù Gi-rí* **L.** *Ib-rí-um* šu-mu-tak$_4$; r. I 5: 1 dib BÍL-*za-il* **L.** šeš *Ib-rí-um*; r. V 15: 4 kù-sal *I-bí-zi-kir* **L.** *Ib-rí-um*, 21: 2 níĝ-anše-ak 4 kù-sal *Gi-rí* **L.** *Ib-rí-um*; r. XII 11: 1 dib *Gi-rí* **L.** *Ib-rí-um*; **21** r. VI 14: **L.** *Nu-ru*$_{12}$*-ud*; **23** r. VI 6: 1 dib *I-bí-zi-kir* **L.** *Ib-rí-um*; **24** o. I

15: 4 ĝeštu$_x$-lá *Gi-rí wa Nap-ḫa-il wa* … 2 ĝeštu$_x$-lá *Ir-da-mu* **L.** *Ib-rí-um*; r. III 7: 1 dib *I-bí-zi-kir* **L.** *Ib-rí-um*.

dumu-nita-dumu-nita **10** o. IX 13: 20 íb-lá 20 ĝír-kun in-na-sum 1 é-duru$_5^{ki}$ **L.**; **19** o. V 23: (silver) níĝ-ba en *Na-gàr*$^{ki}$ (silver) níĝ-ba **L.**-*sù*.

dumu-nita-dumu-nita NE-di «young dancers» **10** o. XIII 21–22.

dumu-nita en «son of the king» **3** o. VIII 10: [ ] níĝ-kas$_4$ nu-du$_{11}$-nu-du$_{11}$ šu-ba$_4$-ti *si-in Ib-al*$_6^{ki}$ *in* ud **L.** *Ḫa-zu-wa-an*$^{ki}$ ḫi-úš *in Ga-ra-ma-an*$^{ki}$ lú *Ḫar-sum*$^{ki}$; **9** r. XVII 10: 1 dib *Maḫ-ra-da-mu* **L.**; **12** r. X 11: 1 dib *I-da-ne-gi-mu* **L.**; **13** r. VIII 7: [*Ì-lum-a-ḫi*] *wa I-in-*$^{d}$*ʾÀ-da* 2 **L.**; **15** o. VI 6: 2 *gàr-su Ì-lum-a-ḫi wa I-in-*$^{d}$*ʾÀ-da* 2 **L.**; **17** o. XVI 18: (4 daggers) Lugal-*na-i-iš Íl-ba-šum Du-bí-ga-lu Ša-gú-bù* **L.** *Ma-nu-wa-ad*$^{ki}$; r. XIII 10: 6 íb-lá 6 *si-ti-tum* 6 ĝír-kun níĝ-ba *Maḫ-ra-da-mu Ì-lum-a-ḫi I-da-ni-ki-mu I-in-*$^{d}$*ʾÀ-da Ku-ra-da-mu* **L.** *wa I-ib-ma-lik* šeš ama-gal en; **18** o. II 20: 2 *gú-li-lum wa* 2 *ti-gi-na wa* 2 ĜIŠ-du *A-ḫu-su-ub-da-mu* … 2 *gú-li-lum wa* 2 *ti-gi-na wa* 2 ĜIŠ-du *A-a-du*-LUM 2 **L.**; o. V 9: *ma-sa-da-ù A-a-du*-LUM **L.**; r. XI 18: 1 *a-ba-lum* … 1 zi-bar níĝ-ba *Gú-sa* **L.** *Na-gàr*$^{ki}$; r. XII 6: 4 níĝ-bànda 2 **L.** 2 dumu-munus en; **19** o. VII 6: 1 íb-lá 1 *si-ti-tum* 1 ĝír-kun *I-in-*$^{d}$*ʾÀ-da* **L.** É×PAP; r. IX 20: (silver) **L.** *ʾÀ-du*$^{ki}$ (silver) maškim-*sù*; r. XII 28: 1 ĝír mar-tu… **L.** *Ì-mar*$^{ki}$; r. XIX 17: *ma-da-u*$_9$ **L.**; **20** r. XII 2: 1 ĜIŠ-zú … 1 zag ĜIŠ-gígir-II *Da-bí-da-mu* **L.** *Bur-ma-an*$^{ki}$; **21** r. XIV 13: [ ] **L.** *si-in* É×PAP.

dur «chain» **17** r. IX 24: 3 NI kb 1 bar:ús lú **L.** 2 si-dù en *wa ma-lik-tum*.

*du-ru*$_{12}$*-gú* (a kind of pearl) **4** o. VII 6: TAR 7 10 gín D. kb 2 *bu*-DI 10 lá-2 ĝeštu$_x$-lá 30 **L.**; **15** o. XI 10: 1 ma-na 14 gín D. kg kin$_5$-ak … 62 **L.**; **24** o. VIII 7: 10 gín D. kg 80 **L.**

*du-rúm* (a kind of band of metal) **13** o. VII 11: 3 gín D. kg kin$_5$-ak 1 **L.**

## E

é «house » **1** o. V 10: ⌜ME⌝-sig **L.**; **3** r. II 9: ugula **L.**; **5** o. III 16: ME-sig **L.**; **16** r. IV 25: 6 IGI.NITA u$_5$ […] ki:lam$_7$ **L.** *mi-i*[*š-x*].

é DN «temple» **4** o. XIII 20: **L.** $^{d}$*Ku-ra*; **5** r. XV 19: *in* **L.** *Ra-sa-ap ʾÀ-da-ni*$^{ki}$ SA.ZA$_x^{ki}$; **6** o. III 21: **L.** $^{d}$*Ku-ra*; r. III 6: **L.** $^{d}$*Ga-mi-iš*; **7** r. XI 22: **L.** $^{d}$*Ku-ra*; **9** r. V 10: **L.** $^{d}$*Ku-ra*; **11** o. IV 13: **L.** $^{d}$*ʾÀ-da*; r. VI 12: níĝ-ba $^{d}$*Ra-sa-ap Du-bí-tum*$^{ki}$ [ ]⌜x⌝ [*in*] ud ḫúl **L.**-*sù*; **12** o. IV 17: **L.** ⌜$^{d}$⌝*Ku-ra*; r. I 8: **L.** $^{d}$*Ku-ra*; **13** o. II 21: **L.** $^{d}$*Ku-ra*; **15** o. XIV 17: **L.** $^{d}$*Ku-ra*; **16** o. II 16: **L.** $^{d}$*Ku-ra*; **17** o. VI 18: **L.** diĝir; o. VII 6: **L.** $^{d}$BAD *Ga-na-na*; r. XVI 13: **L.** diĝir-diĝir-diĝir; **19** o. IV 5: **L.** $^{d}$*ʾÀ-da*; o. VI 6: **L.** $^{d}$BAD *Du-du-lu*$^{ki}$, 19: **L.** $^{d}$BAD *Ga-na-na-im*; r. VI 9: **L.** $^{d}$*ʾÀ-da*, 15: **L.** $^{d}$⌜*ʾÀ*⌝[*-da*], 20: **L.** *A-ru*$_{12}$*-ga-du*$^{ki}$; r. VII 10: **L.** $^{d}$*Ì-lam*; **21** o. VII 18: **L.** $^{d}$*ʾÀ-da*; o. VIII 3: **L.** $^{d}$*ʾÀ-da*, 20: **L.** $^{d}$*ʾÀ-da*; r. XIV 21: **L.** $^{d}$*Ku-ra*; 23 o. II 9: **L.** $^{d}$*ʾÀ-da* lú *Lu-ub*$^{ki}$.

é PN **3** o. II 10: **L.** *Ib-rí-um*; **14** o. XVI 5: **L.** *Ib-rí-um*.

é en **2** r. III 6: gaba-ru **L.**; r. XV 10: gaba-ru **L.**; **3** r. III 1; **4** o. XII 1: sagi kas$_4$-kas$_4$ **L.**; o. XV 20: gaba-ru **L.**; r. XIII 16: gaba-ru **L.**; **5** o. V 3: ME-sig **L.**; r. XIII 10: ME-sig **L.**; r. XVI 20: ugula **L.**; **6** o. V 6: ME-sig **L.**; **7** r. IX 13: ME-sig **L.**; **10** o. VII 2: ME-sig **L.**; r. III 3: gaba-ru **L.**; **12** r. XV 6: 3 *mi-at* 1 ma-na kb [al$_6$-gá]l **L.** diri; **13** r. XV 2: ME-sig **L.**; **16** r. XIII 5: ME-sig **L.**; **17** o. XV 21: ME-sig **L.**; **18** o. VIII 14: ME-sig **L.**; **19** r. XI 16: ME-sig **L.**; r. XIX 24: 1 *mi-at* 60 ma-na kb al$_6$-ĝál **L.**; **23** r. VII 4: ME-sig **L.**

é maḫ «High house» (a Palace sector) **20** r. XI 24: ĜIŠ-sal ⌜dag⌝ **L.**

é *ma-tim* «mausoleum» **17** r. VII 10: 1 *gú-li-lum* ùz-munus a:tu$_{22}$ **L.** NE-*na-áš*$^{ki}$ *ma-lu-gi-iš* en.

é siki «treasury; (lit.) wool warehouse» **8** o. VII 12: 1 aš-ḫal 1 LAGAB al$_6$-ĝál **L.**; **16** r. XVII 25: ⌜2⌝ *m*[*i-at* x ma-na x kb] [al$_6$-ĝál] [**L.**]; **20** r. XVIII 7: ⌜2⌝[(+1)] *mi-at* [(x+)]⌜50⌝ [m]a-na [kb] [al$_6$-ĝál] [**L.**]; **21** r. XVII 9: 4 *mi-at* [ma-n]a [x kb] [al$_6$-ĝál] [**L.**]; **22** o. II 9: TAR kg 2 ma-na kb lú **L.**; **24** r. VIII 6: 5 gín D. kg al$_6$-ĝál **L.**

è «expenditure» **1**(e) r. II' 5': PN$_1$–PN$_3$ **L.** *in* ud *Ìr-kab-da-mu si-mi* úš-*sù*; **2** l.ed. 13; **3** r. XV 3; **4** r. XVI 17; **5** r. XVII 2: (silver) **L.** 2 mu 2 dub; **6** o. XIV 8: *in* ud SIG$_7$ **L.** *si-in* ki $^{d}$*Ra-sa-ap*; r. l.ed. 7, 9; **7** r. XVI 11; **8** o. I 17; **9** r. XVIII 5: **L.** [DI]š mu; **10** r. XVI 3; **12** r. XV 2; **14** r. XX x+1: **L.** *ni-zi-mu* ZA$_x$ ĝuruš-ĝuruš; **15** r. XVIII 2: (silver) **L.** 1 mu; **16** r. XVII 21; **18** l.ed. 2; **19** r. XIX 20; **20** r. XVIII 3; **21** o. XI 22; r. XVII 2; **22** r. VIII 8; **23** r. IX 2; **24** r. VIII 2; **25** r. X 3.

è «departure» **11** r. II 7: *in* ud **L.** níĝ-kas$_4$ *Gú-da-da-núm*$^{ki}$; **12** o. IX 10: *in* ud **L.** *si-in* níĝ-kas$_4$ *Ma-nu-wa-ad*$^{ki}$; r. IV 9: *in* ud **L.** *si-in* á-daḫ lú *A-te-na-ad*$^{ki}$; **17** o. XVI 5: *in* ud **L.** níĝ-kas$_4$ al-kur$_6$ še *Kak-mi-um*$^{ki}$; **23** r. I 3: *in* ud **L.** níĝ-kas$_4$ *Gú-da-da-núm*$^{ki}$; r. III 11: *in* ud **L.** níĝ-kas$_4$ *Gú-da-da-núm*$^{ki}$.

e$_{11}$ «to exit, to rise» **6** r. III 5: *in* ud en **L.** é $^{d}$*Ga-mi-iš*; **15** o. XVII 6: *Wa-ru*$_{12}$*-tum Ma-rí*$^{ki}$ **L.** *áš-ti Na-zu-mu mi-nu* Kiš$^{ki}$; **20** r. IX 11: *Wa-ru*$_{12}$*-tum Ma-rí*$^{ki}$ **L.** *mi-nu* Kiš$^{ki}$ *áš-ti En-na-il*.

é-duru$_5^{ki}$ «team (of 20 workmen)» **10** o. IX 12: 20 íb-lá 20 ĝír-kun in-na-sum 1 **L.** dumu-nita-dumu-nita; **17** o. X 7: 26 gu-dù[l]-TÚG m[aḫ] lú **L.**; r. XX 8: 3 gu-dùl-TÚG **L.**; r. XXII 22: 2 gu-dùl-TÚG **L.** *áš-ti Ša-bir*$_5$*-ti-um*$^{ki}$.

é-gi(-a) «daughter-in-law» **9** r. IV 17: *Za-ne-ḫi-Ma-rí*$^{ki}$ **L.** *Ib-ʾà-ra ʾÀ-šu*$^{⌜ki⌝}$; r. VII 4: *Za-ne-ḫi-Ma-rí*$^{ki}$ **L.** *Ib-ʾà-ra ʾÀ-šu*$^{ki}$; **11** o. IV 11: *maš-ar-tum* níĝ-ba dumu-munus [*I*]*b-rí-*[*u*]*m* **L.** *Zi-ba-da* é $^{d}$*ʾÀ-da*; **12** o. VII 23: *Za-ne-ḫi-Ma-rí*$^{ki}$ dumu-munus en **L.** *Ib-ʾà-ra*; **17** o. III 4: É×PAP **L.**. en *Ra-ʾà-ak*$^{ki}$; o. VI 13: [*Dar-maš-da-mu*] dumu-munus en **L.** BAD-*da-mu*; **22** r. V 4: *Za-ni-ḫi-Ma-rí*$^{ki}$ **L.** *Ib-ʾà-ra ʾÀ-šu*$^{ki}$.

eme «blade» **17** r. I 6: ĜIŠ-kak-ĜIŠ-kak **L.** gud-si-dili.

en «king» **1** o. IX 12: 1 íb-lá 1 *si-ti-tum* 1 ĝír-kun **L.** *Ì-ra-ar*$^{ki}$ *Wa-ba-rúm* šu-mu-tak$_4$; **2** o. I 15: *Di-ne-íb-du-lum* nin-ni **L.**; o. II 6: 1 kù-sal níĝ-ba **L.** $^{d}$*Ba-*

*ra-ma in* ud ne:saĝ-*sù*; o. V 11: *Dar-maš-da-mu* dumu-munus **L.**; o. VI 5: 2 *ti-ki-na* **L.**; o. IX 14: *ba-na-a wa* íb+III-TÚG $^{d}$*Ša-ma-gan* **L.**; o. X 4: *Di-ne-ib-du-lum* nin-ni **L.**; o. XI 14: 1 ĝír mar-tu *ra-ʾà-tum* tur **L.** *Ì-mar*$^{ki}$; o. XIII 12: ĜIŠ-sur$_{x}$ ĜIŠ-gígir-II!(III) **L.**; r. III 7: (25+[x] bracelets) gaba-ru é **L.**; r. IV 25 maš-maš 1 "KIN" siki … maš-maš-*sù* níĝ-ba **L.** $^{d}$*Ì-lam*; r. VI 9: 1 íb-lá ĝír-kun **L.** *Ma-nu-wa-ad*$^{ki}$ *in ʾÀ-da-ni*$^{ki}$ šu-ba$_{4}$-ti; r. VII 7: 2 gud … 4 si-*sù* nídba **L.** $^{d}$*Ra-sa-ap ʾÀ-da-ni*$^{ki}$ $^{d}$AMA-*ra*; r. XIV 7: 1 *ḫa-bù* … 2 *gú-li-lum* níĝ-ba **L.** $^{d}$*Am-ma-rí-ig*; r. XV 10: (45 bracelets) gaba-ru é **L.**; r. XVI 2: [ ] nu$_{11}$-za-*sù* **L.** $^{d}$*Á-la Zi-ig*$^{ki}$; **3** o. III 19: 6 ĜIŠ-kak-ĜIŠ-kak lú ĜIŠ-asari kaskal **L.**; o. XI 18: *Tiš-⌜má⌝-da-mu* dam **L.**; o. XIII 3: [1 za]g ĜIŠ-gígir-II **L.** *Ì-ra-ar*$^{ki}$; o. XIV 15: [ ] 2 *ba-ga-ni-sa* **L.**; r. III 2: [ ] é **L.**; r. VI 6: <1 dib> *I-ku-i-šar* **L.** *Ma-rí*$^{ki}$ *Du-tum Ma-rí*$^{ki}$ šu-mu-tak$_{4}$; r. IX 5: 2 zag 2 ĜIŠ-gígir-II *Ib-rí-um wa* **L.** *Bur-ma-an*$^{ki}$; r. X 5: 1 BAR.AN *áš-ti* **L.** *Ra-ʾà-ak*$^{ki}$ *Íl-ba-ma-lik* šu-mu-tak$_{4}$; r. XII 15: 2 íb-lá kg ì-ĝiš-saĝ 2 **L.** *Ma-nu-wa-ad*$^{ki}$ *Ba-ga-ma* šu-mu-tak$_{4}$ *in* ud úš *ma-lik-tum*; **4** o. I 17: [ ] [x g]*ú*-[*l*]*i*-[*lum* x gí]n [D.] [ì]-na-sum SA.ZA$_{x}$$^{ki}$ *in* zar$^{ki}$ **L.**; o. III 3: *Du-si-gú* ama-gal **L.**; o. XI 10: *Du-si-gú* ama-gal **L.**, 17: *Du-si-gú* ama-gal **L.**; o. XII 1: 12 zi-bar tur lú sagi kas$_{4}$-kas$_{4}$ é **L.**, 17: 1 na na$_{4}$ 12 ma-na kb **L.** *Na-gàr*$^{ki}$ Šubur [ ]; o. XV 20: (20 bracelets) gaba-ru é **L.** tak$_{4}$ igi-igi; r. IV 13: *Du-si-gú* ama-gal **L.**; r. V 17: 2 ĜIŠ-banšur kg … 1 šu-dub sikil lú **L.** $^{d}$*Ra-sa-ap ʾÀ-da-ni*$^{ki}$; r. VI 15: 1 ĝír [m]ar-tu zú kg *I-ga-li-im* **L.** *Ib-al*$_{6}$$^{ki}$; r. VIII 1: 20 ma-na kb **L.** *Na-gàr*$^{ki}$ *Ni-zi-ma-il* šu-mu-tak$_{4}$; r. X 5:6 *zú-zú-ba-tum* 2 ĜIŠ-gígir-II **L.**; r. XI 13: [PN] šeš[-mu] **L.** *Du-lu*$^{ki}$; r. XIII 8: 4 íb-lá *si-ti-tum* ĝír-kun *Du-bù-uš-da-mu I-ga-li-im Zú-ga-du Ì-lum-a-rí-ḫu* 4 **L.** *Ib-al*$_{6}$$^{ki}$ *in* ud [nídba ì-ĝiš], 16: 4 íb-lá gaba-ru é **L.**; r. XV 5: 1 ⌜ma-na⌝ [kg] **L.** *Kak-mi-um*$^{ki}$ ⌜*I*⌝-*ti*-[$^{d}$]*Aš-dar* [šu-]mu-[ta]g$_{4}$; **5** o. V 3: ME-sig é **L.**, 13: *Du-si-gú* ama-gal **L.**; o. VII 19: 1 gud *Ib-gi-da-mu* ugula kad$_{4}$-kad$_{4}$ *wa* šu-ba$_{4}$-ti *Bu*$_{x}$-*ma-ì* níĝ-sa$_{10}$ … 1 gud maškim-*sù* nídba **L.** $^{d}$*ʾÀ-da* … 4 si-*sù in* AMA-*ra*; o. VIII 7: 2 gud nídba **L.** $^{d}$*ʾÀ-da ʾÀ-da-ni*$^{ki}$ … 4 si-*sù in* AMA-*ra*; r. III 3: (86 garments) ir$_{11}$-ir$_{11}$ **L.**; r. VI 2: 1 ĜIŠ-banšur … 3 saĝ lu$_{5}$ … URUDU-*sù* níĝ-b[a] $^{d}$*ʾA*$_{5}$-*da*-"*bal*" *La-ru*$_{12}$-*ga-du*$^{ki}$ **L.** ì-na-sum; r. X 4: <1 dib> **L.** *Ša-bir*$_{5}$-*ti-um*$^{ki}$, 17: 1 *ḫa-bu* … níĝ-ba $^{d}$*ʾÀ*. … *ʾà-na-gu* si 2 gud lú **L.** nídba $^{d}$*ʾÀ-da*; r. XIII 10: ME-sig! é **L.**; r. XIV 21: 1 ĝír mar-tu … 1 kù-sal níĝ-ba $^{d}$*Ra-sa-ap gú-núm*$^{ki}$ **L.** in-na-sum ne:saĝ-*sù*; r. XVI 21 ugula é **L.**; **6** o. I 13: 3 ma-na an-na **L.** *Ma-nu-wa-ad*$^{ki}$; o. II 1: 1 ma-na an-na **L.** *Kak-mi-um*$^{ki}$; o. V 7: ME-sig é **L.**, 18: *Di-ni-íb-du-lum* nin-ni **L.**; o. IX 19: 1 zag ĜIŠ-gígir-II **L.** *Kab-lu*$_{5}$-*ul*$^{ki}$; o. X 4: 10 ma-na kb zi-du$_{8}$ **L.** $^{d}$*ʾÀ-da*; o. XIV 5: 2 ĜIŠ-DU **L.** *in* ud SIG$_{7}$ è *si-in* ki $^{d}$*Ra-sa-ap*; o. XVI 1: 4 ĝír šu-du$_{8}$-máš … 3 *zú-zú-ba-tum* **L.** *Gú-da-da-núm*$^{ki}$ *Za-a-ti* šu-mu-tak$_{4}$; r. I 26: *Ki-sa-du* ga-du$_{8}$ **L.**; r. III 4: 1 ĝír mar-tu níĝ-ba $^{d}$*Da-i-in wa* maš-maš 1 ĜIŠ-banšur níĝ-ba $^{d}$*Ga-mi-iš in* ud **L.** e$_{11}$ é $^{d}$*Ga-mi-iš*; 12: 6 ĜIŠ-kak-ĜIŠ-kak 2 ĜIŠ-banšur kaskal **L.**; r. V 15: ⌜2⌝ níĝ-anše-ak 4 kù-sal *Du-si-gú* níĝ-ba **L.**; r. VII 6: 2 bur-KAK aš-gal ì-ĝiš kaskal **L.**; r. X 21: *Šu*-NE ugula sur$_{x}$-BAR.AN **L.**; r. XIII 18: 1 ĜIŠ-šú 1 níĝ-bànda lú šu-šu **L.**; r. XV 10: 1 ma-na an-na **L.** *Kak-mi-um*$^{ki}$; r. XVI 8: 2 ĜIŠ-zú ĜIŠ-gígir-II **L.**; r. XVII 12: 1 ĜIŠ-zú 2 ĜIŠ-gígir-II **L.** *Kab-lu*$_{5}$-*ul*$^{ki}$, 15: 1 ma-na an-na **L.** *Ma-rí*$^{ki}$, 18: TAR an-na **L.** *Ša-bir*$_{5}$-*ti-tum*$^{ki}$, 26: 1 *ḫa-bù* níĝ-ba $^{d}$*Ga-mi-iš* **L.** ì-na-sum; **7** o. III 6: ama-gal **L.**; o. XI 20: *ʾa*$_{5}$-*na-gu* 4 si 2 gud nídba **L.** [$^{d}$*Ra-sa-ap*] [*ʾÀ-da-ni*$^{ki}$] [*in*] $^{d}$AMA-*ra*; o. XII 12: 1 ešda … *ʾa*$_{5}$-*na-gu* 4 si 2 gud nídba **L.** $^{d}$*ʾÀ-da in* $^{d}$AMA-*ra*; o. XIII 15: 1 ĝír **L.**, 21: 2 *za-ḫa-da* **L.**; o. XIV 8: ĜIŠ-bar-ús … lú 2 ĜIŠ-gígir-II ; r. IX 14: ME-sig é **L.**, 20; r. X 22: 2 *zú-zú-ba-tum* **L.**; r. XII 20: 1 ĝír mar-tu **L.**; r. XV 21: (gold) daḫ(MU.MU) kg lú **L.** *wa* [l]ugal-[lu]gal [ì-n]a-sum [nu$_{11}$-z]a [$^{d}$*Ra-s*]*a-ap*; r. XVI 7: [1 gí]r mar-[t]u kg [1 ĜIŠ]-gu-kak-gíd $^{d}$*Ra-sa-ap Du-ne-íb*$^{ki}$ **L.** in-na-sum; **8** o. I 8: *Di-ne-ib-du-lum* nin-ni [**L.**]; o. II 3: ⌜1⌝ ĝír mar-[t]u ⌜1⌝ *r*[*a*]-⌜*ʾà*⌝-*tum* kg *Ib-rí-um* **L.** šu-mu-tak$_{4}$ *in* ud ḫúl na-rú; o. XI 2: [ ] **L.** *Kab-lu*$_{5}$-*ul*$^{ki}$ šu-ba$_{4}$-ti; o. XIV 11: 4 s[ag ] 4 *zi*-[*kir-*]*ra-tu*[*m*] **L.**; o. XV 4: 10 lá-2 kù-sal 2 níĝ-anše-ak lú **L.**; r. V 13': 8 si 4 gud nídba **L.** *wa Ib-rí-um* nídba $^{d}$*Ra-sa-ap* [*ʾÀ-da-ni*$^{ki}$]; r. VI 3': ⌜18⌝ gud **L.**; **9** o. III 4: 7 sila$_{4}$ ḪI.DIM lú níĝ-lá-gaba **L.** sikil; o. IV 3: [si-si] 2 gud nídba **L.** $^{d}$*Ra-sa-ap ʾÀ-da-ni*$^{ki}$, 10: si-si 2 gud nídba **L.** $^{d}$*ʾÀ-da* [*Ḫ*]*a-lab*$_{x}$$^{ki}$ [*i*]*n* AMA-*ra*; o. VI 10: **L.** *Ì-ra-ar*$^{ki}$; r. V 8: (silver) nam-kud **L.** *Bur-ma-an*$^{ki}$ é $^{d}$*Ku-ra*; r. XVII 10: *Maḫ-ra-da-mu* dumu-nita **L.**; **10** o. I 7: *Di-ne-ib-du-lum* nin-ni **L.**; o. IV 7: *iš-ki-lum* **L.**; o. VI 13: dumu-munus **L.** [*Ra-ʾà-ak*$^{ki}$]; o. VII 2: ME-sig é **L.**; o. IX 4: ama-gal **L.** *Lum-na-an*$^{ki}$; o. X 5: (silver) **L.** *Du-lu*$^{ki}$, 17: 1 ĝír mar-tu níĝ-ba *Ìr-ba*$_{x}$-*zé ʾÀ-da-ni*$^{ki}$ **L.** in-na-sum; o. XI 4: 1 ĜIŠ-šú lú šu-šu **L.**, 12: 4 si-si 2 gud lú **L.** nídba $^{d}$*ʾÀ-da in* AMA-*ra*; o. XV 15: (silver) níĝ-du$_{8}$ *Ù-ba-nu* KAR kg **L.** *Ma-nu-wa-ad*$^{ki}$; r. II 7: 1 *mar-wa-ga*$_{x}$(ZÀR)-*tum* šu-šu **L.**; r. III 4: 4 *gú-li-lum*-I esi gaba-ru é **L.**; r. V 7: 3 ĝír mar-tu **L.**; r. VII 1: (gold) **L.** *A-la-u*$_{9}$[$^{ki}$] *in* ⌜ki⌝:lam$_{7}$ $^{d}$*ʾÀ-da*, 19: [1] an-zam$_{x}$ **L.**; r. VIII 6: 1 pad an-zam$_{x}$ **L.**, 11: 1 zi-bar **L.**; r. XII 7: 1 ma-na ⌜an⌝-na **L.** *Ma-rí*$^{ki}$; **11** o. I 8: [*Di-rín-da-mu Di-ne-ib-du-lum* nin-ni **L.**]; o. VI 8: 1 *mar-wa-ga-tum* lú 2 šu **L.**, 21: 2 níĝ-anše-ak 2 kù-sal lú 2 IGI.NITA ; o. X 15: 1 ešda … 1 *ar-ra-sù* … *ʾa*$_{5}$-*na-gu* 4 si 2 gud nídba **L.** $^{d}$*Ra-sa-ap ʾÀ-da-ni*$^{ki}$; o. XI 5: [1 *ar-r*]*a*-[*sù*] … *ʾa*$_{5}$-*na-gu* 4 si 2 gud nídba **L.** $^{d}$*ʾÀ-da in* $^{d}$AMA-*ra*; r. III 10: (silver) níĝ-ba **L.** *Ša-bir*$_{5}$-*ti-du*$^{ki}$ (silver) *Na-mi-ir* maškim-*sù*; r. V 14: 1 ĝír mar-tu kg **L.** *Ša-bir*$_{5}$-*ti-du*$^{ki}$; r. VIII 15: 1 ešda … *ʾa*$_{5}$-*n*[*a-gu*] 1[+3 si 2 gud] ⌜nídba⌝ **L.** $^{d}$*ʾÀ-da* lú *Ḫa-lab*$_{x}$$^{ki}$ *in* iti *ʾa*$_{5}$-*nun*; **12** o. III 19: *ba-na-i-su-ma wa* 2 šu-šu-*sù* 2 DU.DU-*sù* níĝ-ba ⌜$^{d}$⌝*ʾA*$_{5}$-*da*-["*b*]*al*" [*A*-]*ru*$_{12}$-[*ga-d*]*u*$^{ki}$ **L.** [*i*]*n* [ ]; o. IV 15: (silver) nam-kud **L.** *Ì-ra-ar*$^{ki}$ é ⌜$^{d}$⌝*Ku-ra*; o. V 3: (gold) **L.** *Sa-ḫa-ru*$_{12}$$^{ki}$; o. VII 22: *Za-ne-ḫi-Ma-rí*$^{ki}$ dumu-munus **L.**; r. I 3: 1 íb-lá 1 *si-ti-tum* 1 ĝír-kun *I-bí-du-lum* **L.** *Ma-nu-wa-ad*$^{ki}$ *in* ud DU.DU nam-kud é $^{d}$*Ku-ra*; r. II 4: *ʾa*$_{5}$-*na-gu* 4 si-si 2 gud nídba **L.** $^{d}$*ʾÀ-da in* iti *ʾa*$_{5}$-*nun*; r. V 7: 2 *gú-li-lum* **L.**; r X 11: *I-da-ne-gi-mu* dumu-nita **L.**; r. XI 6: [am]a-gal **L.**; r. XIII 11: *Di-ni-íb-du-lum* dam-diĝir nin-ni **L.**; r. XV 6: 3 *mi-at* 1 ma-na kb [al$_{6}$-ĝá]l é **L.** diri; **13** o. I 7: [*Di-n*]*e*-[*í*]*b*-[*du-*]*lum* [ni]n-ni **L.**, 10:

[x í]b-lá [x *si-*]*ti-tum* [x gí]r-kun **L.** [*Du-*]*lu*$^{ki}$; r. II 10: *Mu-zi* šeš **L.**; o. III 13: 2 ĜIŠ.GAM.GAM … 1 zag … 1 ĜIŠ-zú ĜIŠ-gígir-II **L.**, 21: 1 ĜIŠ-gu-kak-šub **L.** *Ì-ra-ar*$^{ki}$; o. XI 12: 1 *ḫa-bù* … 1 *ar-ra-sù* … *ʾa$_5$-na-gu* 4 si 2 gud nídba **L.** $^{d}$*Ra-sa-ap ʾÀ-da-ni*$^{ki}$; o. XIII 16: 1 dib ì-ĝiš-saĝ **L.** *Ì-mar*$^{ki}$; o. XV 6: 3 ĜIŠ-zú 3 ĜIŠ-gígir-II **L.** *wa* ama-gal-*sù wa Ib-rí-*[*u*]*m*, 15: ama-gal **L.**; o. XVII 9: 3 IGI.NITA u$_5$ **L.**; r. I 9: (silver) níĝ-ba *Ìr-am$_6$*-kur$^{ki}$ sagi *Ma-rí*$^{ki}$ *in* ud kin$_5$-ak kú **L.**; r. II 21: (silver) lul-gu-ak gur$_8$ *Puzur$_4$-ra-m*[*a-*]*lik* lú-kar *Kak-mi-um*$^{ki}$ KAK-*bar-zú wa Du-bí-zi-kir* šu-mu-tak$_4$ *si-in* **L.** *Kak-m*[*i-*]*u*[*m*$^{ki}$]; r. VIII 8: [*Ì-lum-a-ḫi*] *wa I-in-*$^{d}$*ʾÀ-da* 2 dumu-nita **L.**, 14: ama-gal **L.**; r. XV 3: ME-sig é [**L.**]; **14** o. I 7: [*Di-ni-íb-du-lum* nin-ni **L.**], 19: 1 *mu-ḫar-tim* … 1 ĝír mar-tu **L.**; o. II 7: ama-gal **L.**; o. III 10: 1 *gàr-su* **L.** *Sa-nap-zu-gúm*$^{ki}$; o. V 10: dumu-munus **L.** *Ì-ra-ar*$^{ki}$; o. VIII 16: 4 ĜIŠ-ban 2 ĜIŠ-gígir-II **L.**; o. IX 7: 2 zag 2 ĜIŠ-gígir-II … 2 ĜIŠ-bar-ús ĜIŠ-gígir-II **L.**; o. X 6: *a$_5$-na-gu* 4 si 2 gud … 1 *ḫa-bù* … 1 ⸢*ar*⸣*-ra*[*-sù*] [nídba] **L.** $^{d}$*Ra-sa-ap* [*ʾÀ-da-ni*$^{ki}$] *in* $^{d}$AMA-*ra*; o. XIII 3: ⸢LUM⸣?-[ ] ĜIŠ-taškarin lú **L.** *wa* ama-gal-*sù*; o. XV 9: 1 balaĝ zabar lú **L.**; o. XVI 1: 2 ĜIŠ-gu-kak-gíd **L.**; o. XVII 5: 11 gud **L.**; r. VI 13: 1 ĜIŠ-banšur maḫ … urudu-*sù* … *ʾa$_5$-na-gu-sù* [níĝ-ba] $^{d}$*ʾA$_5$-da-"bal" ʾÀ-ma-du*$^{ki}$ **L.** šu-mu-tak$_4$; r. VII 27: ĜIŠ-bar-ús **L.**; r. VIII 8: [1 ĜIŠ-ba]nšur [*wa*] 1 kù-sal $^{d}$*Ra-sa-ap Du-ne-íb*$^{ki}$ **L.** šu-mu-tak$_4$; r. IX 14: [1 íb-lá 1 ĝír-kun] **L.** *Ì-ra-ar*$^{ki}$; r. XIII 7: 1 níĝ-anše-ak 1 kù-sal 1 IGI.NITA **L.**; **15** o. I 7: *Di-ni-íb-du-lum* nin-ni **L.**, 19: (gold) **L.** *Uš-ḫu-lum*$^{ki}$; o. II 25: 1 *gú-li-lum a-li-iš* ĜIŠ-gu-kak-gíd $^{d}$*ʾA$_5$-da-"bal"* [ ]$^{ki}$ **L.** ì-na-sum *in* ud šeš-II-ib; o. V 13: ama-gal **L.**, 25: *Dar-ib-da-mu* dumu-munus **L.**; o. VI 7: *Ì-lum-a-ḫi wa I-in-*$^{d}$*ʾÀ-da* 2 dumu-nita **L.**; o. VIII 20: 1 *zú-zú-ba-tum* **L.** zàḫ; o. IX 1: 1 zi-bar **L.** *Uš-ḫu-lum*$^{ki}$, 22: 2 ĜIŠ-ban ĜIŠ-gígir-II lú *ra-ʾà-tum ša-ti* **L.**; o. X 10: 1 *ḫa-bù* … 1 *ar-ra-si-su* …*ʾa$_5$-na-gu* 4 si 2 gud nídba **L.** $^{d}$*Ra-sa-ap ʾÀ-da-ni*$^{ki}$ *in* $^{d}$AMA-*ra*, 22: *Dar-ib-da-mu* dumu-munus **L.**; o. XIV 7: 1 ĝír mar-tu kg **L.** *áš-du* 1 ĝír mar-tu-*sù* sikil $^{d}$*ʾA$_5$-da-"bal" Lu-ba-an*$^{ki}$; r. II 20: 1 *ma-ḫa-ni-gúm wa* 1 tùn gal **L.**; r. III 19: 2 níĝ-anše-ak kg maḫ? **L.**; r. V 11: ama-gal **L.**; r. VII 20: 1 ĜIŠ-banšur *wa* 1 kù-sal níĝ-ba **L.**; r. VIII 1: ⸢ama⸣-gal **L.**, 19: 1 an-zam$_x$ *wa* 1 pad-*sù* **L.**; r. IX 20: 1 *ḫa-bù* … 1 *ar-ra-sù* kg sikil … *ʾa$_5$-na-gu* 4 si 2 gud nídba **L.** $^{d}$*ʾÀ-da in* iti *ʾa$_5$-nun*; r. X 2: 1 kù-sal [níĝ-b]a **L.** $^{d}$*Ḫa-a-ba-du al$_6$* tu-ra ama-gal-*sù*; r. XII 3: 1 dib **L.** *áš-du* dib-*sù* sikil $^{d}$*ʾÀ-da al$_6$* tu-ra ama-gal-*sù wa* 2 *gú-li-lum-sù* sikil $^{d}$*ʾA$_5$-da-"bal" Lu-ba-an*$^{ki}$ *al$_6$* tu-ra-*sù*, 31: 2 *gù-li-lum Ib-rí-um áš-du* 2 *gù-li-lum-sù* sikil $^{d}$*ʾÀ-da al$_6$* tu-ra **L.**; r. XIII 11: 1 dib *Ib-rí-um áš-du* 1 dib-*sù* sikil $^{d}$*ʾÀ-da al$_6$* tu-ra **L.**, 28: ama-gal **L.**; r. XV 2: 4 sur$_x$-lu$_x$ lú *al$_6$* ĜIŠ-ĝidru-ĜIŠ-ĝidru ĜIŠ-uštin **L.**, 16: 1 ĝír mar-tu kg **L.** *áš-du* ĝír mar-tu-*sù* sikil $^{d}$*ʾA$_5$-da-"bal" Lu-ba-an*$^{ki}$; r. XVI 12: [1 ĝír mar-t]u kg *Ib-rí-um áš-du* ĝír mar-tu-*sù* sikil $^{d}$*Áš-da-bíl al$_6$* tu-ra **L.**; **16** o. I 7: [*Di-ni-í*]*b-*[*d*]*u-lum* nin-ni **L.**, 17: 1 dib *Ru$_{12}$-zi-da-mu* **L.** *Ì-mar*$^{ki}$; o. II 2: ama-gal **L.**, 14: ama-gal **L.**, 25: ama-gal **L.**; o. V 5: *Da-dub* dam **L.** lú *A-ru$_{12}$-ga-du*$^{ki}$; o. XIV 14: 1 kù-sal [$^{d}$*A-dar-a-an*] *Da-na-áš*$^{ki}$ **L.** šu-mu-tak$_4$; r. I 8: 1 *ḫa-bù* … 1 *ar-ra-sù* … *ʾa$_5$-na-gu* si 2 gud nídba **L.** $^{d}$*Ra-sa-ap ʾÀ-da-ni*$^{ki}$, 19: 1 *ḫa-bù ap* kg ⸢sikil⸣ … *ʾa$_5$-na-gu* si 2 gud [níd]ba **L.** $^{d}$*ʾÀ-da in* $^{d}$AMA-*ra*; r. II 11: *Di-ni-íb-du-lum* nin-ni **L.**; r. III 6: *su-da-*⸢*nu*⸣ *wa* 4 kù-sal-*sù* **L.**, 13: ama-gal **L.**, 24: *ma-wa-lu* ĜIŠ-bar-ús ĜIŠ-gígir-II **L.**; r. V 8: 6 ĜIŠ-kak-ĜIŠ-kak lú 2 asari kaskal **L.**; r. VII 12: *Ar-za-du* nin-ni **L.**; r. IX 14: ama-gal **L.**; r. XI 8: 1 *ḫa-bù ap* kg sikil … *ʾa$_5$-na-gu* si 2 gud nídba **L.** $^{d}$*ʾÀ-da Ḫa-lab$_x$*$^{ki}$ *in* iti *ʾa$_5$-nun*; r. XIII 6: ME-sig é **L.**; r. XIV 6: 1 zag-*sù* kg **L.**; r. XV 27: 2 bur-KAK ĜIŠ-⸢taškarin⸣ kaskal **L.**; r. XVII 11: 1 kù-sal níĝ-ba ⸢d⸣[*Aš-d*]*ar*(?) **L.** [x-*g*]*a-*[x]$^{ki}$; *Di-ne-íb-du-lum* [nin-ni **L.**]; **17** o. III 1–6: [2 *bu-*DI dumu-munus] **L.** *Bur-ma-an*$^{ki}$ É×PAP é-gi **L.** *Ra-ʾà-ak*$^{ki}$; o. V 2: dumu-munus **L.**, 16: 2 šu-i … **L.**; o. VI 12 and 20: [*Dar-maš-da-mu*] dumu-munus **L.** é-gi BAD-*da-mu in* ud DU.DU nídba é diĝir **L.**; o. VII 15: ama-gal **L.**; o. XII 3: ama-gal **L.**; o. XV 6: 1 íb-lá 1 *si-ti-tum* 1 ĝír-kun 1 dib … 1 ĝír mar-tu kg … 1 ĜIŠ-zú 1 zag ĜIŠ-gígir-II … 2 *zú-zú-ba-tum Ìl-ba-da-mu* **L.** *Kak-mi-um*$^{ki}$ *in* SA.ZA$_x$$^{ki}$ šu-ba$_4$-ti, 22: ME-sig é **L.**; o. XVI 19: dumu-nita **L.** *Ma-nu-wa-ad*$^{ki}$; r. I 24: 1 dib **L.**; r. II 9: ĜIŠ-bar-ús *wa* … 1 *za-ḫa-da* **L.**, 22: 1 níĝ-anše-ak 1 kù-sal 2 IGI.NITA **L.**, 30: 1 ĜIŠ-gu-kak-šub **L.**; r. III 8: ama-gal **L.**; r. IV 14: *Dar-ib-da-mu* dumu-munus **L.**, 25: 1 *ḫa-bù* … 1 *ar-ra-si-sù* … *ʾa$_5$-na-gu* 4 si 2 gud nídba **L.** $^{d}$*Ra-sa-ap ʾÀ-da-ni*$^{ki}$ *in* $^{d}$AMA-*ra*; r. V 22: ama-gal **L.**; r. VI 15: 1 an-dùl $^{d}$*Iš:šára* **L.**, 28: 1 an-dùl *sa-du* **L.** *wa ma-lik-tum si-in* NE-*na-áš*$^{ki}$; r. VII 5: *ḫa-za-nu a-ḫa-šum* gaba $^{d}$*Ku-ra wa* **L.**, 13: 1 *gú-li-lum* ùz-munus a:tu$_{22}$ é *ma-tim* NE-*na-áš*$^{ki}$ *ma-lu-gi-iš* **L.**; r. IX 18: šu-dub **L.** *wa ma-lik-tum*, 26: 1 bar:ús lú dur 2 si-dù **L.** *wa ma-lik-tum*; r. XI 20: 2 šu-dub **L.** *wa ma-lik-tum*; r. XIII 11 and 16: *Maḫ-ra-da-mu Ì-lum-a-ḫi I-da-ni-ki-mu I-in-*$^{d}$*ʾÀ-da Ku-ra-da-mu* dumu-nita **L.** *wa I-ib-ma-lik* šeš ama-gal **L.**; r. XIV 7 and 12: *Ra-ù-tum Kir-*[*s*]*u-*[*u*]*d* [*En-na-*$^{d}$Utu] *Ra-ba$_x$-tum Maš-ga-sa-du Ma-ga-ra-du Tíš-má-da-mu Ra-ba$_x$-tum*-II dam **L.** *wa Ma-ù-ud Za-ni-ḫi-Ma-rí*$^{ki}$ 2 dumu-munus **L.**; r. XVII 9: 1 *mu-rúm wa* 1 *gúm-a-nu* ⸢*wa*⸣ 2 ĜIŠ.ALAM *su-da$_5$-lik* **L.**; r. XXI 4: dumu-munus tur **L.**; r. XXII 11: 2 ĜIŠ-gu-kak-šub 2 gu-x šub 8 **L.**, 17: 1 ĝír mar-tu kg **L.** *Ì-mar*$^{ki}$ *Ib-rí-um* šu-mu-tak$_4$; **18** o. I 7: *Di-ni-íb-du-lum* nin-ni **L.**; o. II 21: *A-ḫu-su-ub-da-mu* … *A-a-du-*LUM 2 dumu-nita **L.**; o III 16: ama-gal **L.**, 21: *Ar-za-du* nin-ni **L.**; o. V 3: ama-gal **L.**, 10: *A-a-du-*LUM dumu-nita **L.**, 24: la-ḫa ĝeštin **L.** *Gú-da-da-núm*$^{ki}$; o. VI 20: ugula sur$_x$-BAR.AN **L.**; o. VII 5: 15 ĜIŠ-kak-ĜIŠ-kak *ša-ti* 5 ĜIŠ-asari kaskal **L.**; o. VIII 15: ME-sig é **L.**; o. XII 16: 2 KA-si **L.**; o. XVI 6: 1 ĝír mar-tu kg **L.**; o. XVII 8: *Tal-du-du* dam **L.**; o. XVII 30: *Di-ni-íb-du-lum* nin-ni **L.**; o. XVIII 12: *Dar-ib-da-mu wa Tíš-te-da-mu* 2 dumu-munus **L.**, 23: 1 *ḫa-bù* … 1 *ar-ra-sù* … *ʾa$_5$-na-gu* si 2 gud nídba **L.** $^{d}$*Ra-sa-ap ʾÀ-da-ni*$^{ki}$; o. XIX 6: ama-gal **L.**, 21: 1 *ḫa-bù ap* kg sikil … *ar-ra-sù* … *ʾa$_5$-na-gu* si 2 gud nídba **L.** $^{d}$*ʾÀ-da Ḫa-lab$_x$*$^{ki}$ *in* $^{d}$AMA-*ra*; r. I 12: 2 níĝ-anše-ak 2 kù-sal 2 IGI.NITA *wa su-da-nu* kù-sal **L.**, 22: ĜIŠ-bar-ús ĜIŠ-gígir-II **L.**, 28: 1 *za-ḫa-da* **L.**; r. III 13: 3 IGI.NITA u$_5$ **L.**; r. IV 10:

1 níĝ-PA **L.**; r. VI 4: bar-ús **L.**; r. XI 19: *Gú-sa* dumu-nita **L.** *Na-gàr*$^{ki}$, 23: 2 ma-na an-na níĝ-ba **L.** *A-daš*$^{ki}$, 29: ama-gal **L.**; r. XII 8: 2 dumu-nita 2 dumu-munus **L.**; r. XIV 14: 1 ĜIŠ-zú … 1 zag ĜIŠ-gígir-II **L.** *Ì-mar*$^{ki}$; r. XVI 17: ama-gal **L.**; r. XVII 1: ama-gal **L.**, 16: 2 ĜIŠ.GAM.GAM ĜIŠ-gígir-II *ra-ᵓà-tum* **L.**; r. XVIII 1: 1 *ḫa-bù ap* kg sikil … *ᵓa*$_5$*-na-gu* si 2 gud nídba **L.** $^{[d]}$*ᵓÀ-da Ḫa-lab*$_x$$^{ki}$ *ᵓa*$_5$*-nun*, 24: 2 ĝír … **L.**; **19** o. I 7: *Di-ne-íb-du-lum* nin-ni **L.**, 23: 2 ĝír mar-tu kg *Ib-ri-um wa* sikil-*sù al*$_6$ tu-ra *I-bí-zi-kir wa al*$_6$ tu-ra **L.**; o. II 7: 1 kù-sal níĝ-ba **L.** $^{d}$*Ba-tum-ma-du áš-t*[*i*] ĝír mar-tu-*sù* šu-mu-tak$_4$ *al*$_6$ tu-ra *Ib-rí-um*; o. III 4: *Di-ne-íb-du-lum* nin-ni **L.**; o. V 19: (silver) níĝ-ba **L.** *Na-gàr*$^{ki}$ (silver) níĝ-ba dumu-nita-dumu-nita-*sù*; o. VI 2: (silver) níĝ-ba en-en lú *áš-ti* **L.** *Na-gàr*$^{ki}$ LU.DU nam-kud é $^{d}$BAD *Du-du-lu*$^{ki}$; o. VII 7: *I-in-*$^{d}$*ᵓÀ-da* dumu-nita **L.**; o. IX 24: 2 kù-sal … *áš-ti* 2 ĝír mar-tu kg *al*$_6$ tu-ra **L.**; o. X 8: *Dar-ib-da-mu* dumu-munus **L.**; o. XI 2: 1 *ḫa-bù* … 1 *ar-ra-sù* … *ᵓa*$_5$*-na-gu* si 2 gud nídba **L.** $^{d}$*Ra-sa-ap ᵓÀ-da-ni*$^{ki}$; o. XII 10: 1 an-zam$_x$ **L.**, 19: sur$_x$-BAR.AN **L.**; o. XII 18: ama-gal **L.**, 24: ama-gal **L.**; r. V 26: (silver) *si-in* al$_6$-tuš $^{d}$*Ga-mi-iš* **L.** ì-na-sum; r. VI 6: 1 dub lú nam-kud **L.** *wa Ib-rí-um* é $^{d}$*ᵓÀ-da*; r. VIII 18: ama-gal **L.**; r. XI 17: ME-sig é **L.**; r. XII 29: dumu-nita **L.** *Ì-mar*$^{ki}$; r. XV 8: ama-gal **L.**; r. XVI 6: ama-gal **L.** *Ra-ᵓà-ak*$^{ki}$, 13: (silver and tin) **L.** *Du-gú-ra-su*$^{ki}$; r. XVII 14: 1 *ḫa-bù ap* kg sikil … *ᵓa*$_5$*-na-gu* si 2 gud nídba **L.** $^{d}$*ᵓÀ-da Ḫa-lab*$_x$$^{ki}$ *ᵓa*$_5$*-nun*; r. XVIII 14: 2 íb-lá 2 ĝír-kun … 2 ĜIŠ-sal-*sù I-bí-zi-kir wa Ù-ti* 2 dumu-nita-*sù in* ud ḫúl-*sù* **L.** šu-mu-tak$_4$; r. XIX 18: dumu-nita **L.**; **20** o. I 7: *Di-ni-íb-du-lum* nin-ni **L.**; o. VII 20: ama-gal **L.**; o. VIII 12: 1 *ḫa-bù* … 1 *ar-ra-sù* … [*ᵓa*$_5$*-na-gu* 4 si gud nídba **L.**] $^{d}$*Ra-sa-ap ᵓÀ-da-ni*$^{ki}$; o. IX 2: 1 [*ḫa-bù*] … 1 *ar-ra-sù* … *ᵓa*$_5$-[*n*]*a-gu* 4 si gud nídba **L.** $^{d}$*ᵓÀ-da Ḫa-lab*$_x$$^{ki}$ *in* $^{d}$AMA-*ra*, 21: BAR.AN **L.**; o. XI 15: ama-gal **L.**; o. XIII 4: ZA$_x$ **L.**; o. XIV 22: 1 šu-dub sikil **L.** lú ḫúl [ ] a-mu-*sù*; o. XV 22: *maš-ar-tum* **L.**; o. XVI 8: *maš-ar-tum* **L.**; r. I 22: (9 tools) lú kaskal **L.**; r. III 6: 1 pad *ma-da-a-um* kg an-dùl lú **L.** *ša-ti Ib-rí-um* mu-DU; r. IV 22: ama-gal **L.**; r. X 4: 1 pad an-zam$_x$ **L.**, 27: ama-gal **L.**; r. XI 13: 1 *ḫa-bù ap* … *ar-ra-sù* kg si[kil] … *ᵓa*$_5$*-na-gu* 4 si 2 gud nídba **L.** $^{d}$*ᵓÀ-da Ḫa-lab*$_x$$^{ki}$ iti *ᵓa*$_5$*-nun*; r. XII 3: *Da-bí-da-mu* dumu-nita **L.** *Bur-ma-an*$^{ki}$; **21** o. I 7: *Di-*[*ni-*]*íb-du-lum* [nin-]ni **L.**; o. IV 8: 2 kù-sal 2 IGI.NITA **L.**, 18: am<a-gal> **L.**, 24: [1 *za-ḫ*]*a-da* **L.**; o. VI 13: *Ìr-ba*$_x$*-da-mu* **L.** *Ù-ti-ig*$^{ki}$; o. IX 2: [ ] nídba **L.** $^{d}$*ᵓÀ-da* lú *Ḫa-lab*$_x$$^{ki}$, 15: 1 *ḫa-bù* … 1 *ar-r*[*a-*]*s*[*ù*] níĝ-ba **L.** $^{d}$*Ra-sa-ap* ⸢*ᵓÀ-da*⸣-[*ni*$^{ki}$], 25: 1 *ḫa-bù ap* kg sikil níĝ-ba **L.**; o. X 1, 15: [1 níĝ]-anše-ak 2 IGI.NITA … 2 ĜIŠ.GA[M.GAM] ĜIŠ-gígir-II **L.**; o. XI 2: [ ] **L.** *wa Ib-rí-um*; o. XV 26: ama-gal **L.**; o. XVI 6: *Di-ni-íb-du-lum* nin-ni **L.**, 9: 1 ĝír mar-tu kg **L.**; o. XVII 19: 2 *mu-ḫar-šu* **L.**; r. VI 25: 4 šu-i … **L.**; r. VII 15: 1 ĝír mar-tu kg **L.**, 19: 3 *zú-zú-ba-tum* **L.**; r. VIII 1: 1 nu$_{11}$-za *ḫa-bù* … *ᵓa*$_5$*-na-gu* si 2 gud nídba [**L.**] [$^{d}$*ᵓÀ-da in* $^{d}$AMA-*ra*], 16: 1 íb-lá 1 *si-ti-tum* 1 ĝír-kun lú **L.** sikil $^{d}$*ᵓÀ-da al*$_6$ tu-ra *I-bí-zi-kir*, 25: dam **L.** *ᵓÀ-za-an*$^{ki}$; r. X 21: 1 zi-bar **L.** *ša-ti* sikil $^{d}$*ᵓA*$_5$*-da-"bal" Lu-ba-an*$^{ki}$; r. XIV 14: [ ] dumu-nita **L.**, 19: (silver) nam-kud-nam-kud **L.** *Ì-ra-ar*$^{ki}$ é $^{d}$*Ku-ra*; **22** o. I 5, 10: dam-dam **L.**; **23** o. II 1: 1 dib maḫ lú ĜIŠ-ĝidru-ĜIŠ-ĝidru in-na-sum $^{d}$*ᵓÀ-da Ḫa-lab*$_x$$^{ki}$ *in* AMA-*ra* **L.** šu-mu-tak$_4$; r. II 12: 1 *ar-ra-šum* 1 *ḫa-bù* níĝ-ba $^{d}$*ᵓA*$_5$*-da-"bal" ᵓÀ-ma-du*$^{ki}$ **L.** šu-mu-tak$_4$ *in* ud NI.DU-NI.DU; r. VII 4: ME-sig é **L.**; **24** o. IV 5: 1 *za-ḫa-da* **L.**; o. VI 8: 1 *ar-ra-sù* 1 *ḫa-bù* níĝ-ba **L.** $^{d}$*ᵓA*$_5$*-da-"bal" A-ru*$_{12}$*-ga-du*$^{ki}$; r. IV 10: 1 *ma-da-a-um* <1> an-dùl *wa* 1 pad-*s*[*ù*] lú **L.** šu-ba$_4$-ti.

en-en **19** o. V 26: (silver) níĝ-ba **L.**; **22** o. VII 6: 1 ⸢dib⸣ *Du-bí-zi-kir* lú *Puzur*$_4$*-ra-ì* lú É×PAP **L.**; r. IX 5: tak$_4$ kg É×PAP **L.**

engar «farmer»

ugula engar «overseer of the farmers» **19** o. IX 28: (silver) lú ĜIŠ-nu-kiri$_6$ *En-na-il* **L.** *Zú-ba-núm* 2 šu-ba$_4$-ti.

É×PAP «funeral rite» **1** o. IX 16: 1 ĝír ⸢mar⸣[-tu] … 1 íb-lá 1 *si-ti-tum* 1 ĝír-kun en *Ì-ra-ar*$^{ki}$ *Wa-ba-rúm* šu-mu-tak$_4$ **L.**; **5** o. XI 13: 1 ĝír mar-tu ti kg *I-bí-šum* lú *I-gi* **L.**; **6** o. XII 7: 1 íb-lá *si-ti-tum* ĝír-⸢kun⸣ *Sá-gú-šum* **L.**; r. VI 16: 2 *bu*-DI *ma-lik-tum Ra-ᵓà-ak*$^{ki}$ **L.** EN-*mar* šu-mu-tak$_4$; **7** r. XII 4: 1 ĝír mar]-tu kg *Ig-rí-iš* lú *I-rí-ig-gú-nu* **L.**; **11** o. XII 20: 2 *bu*-DI … 2 saĝ-*sù* … 1 kù-sal *Da-ti-*$^{d}$TU *ma-lik-tum Lum-na-an*$^{ki}$ **L.** *I-šar* šu-mu-tak$_4$; **13** o. XII 5: [1 g]ír m[ar-t]u kg *Ù-zu* "ur$_4$" *Ì-mar*$^{ki}$ **L.** *Ba-ga-ma* šu-mu-tak$_4$; **14** o. V 12: 2 *bu*-DI dumu-munus en *Ì-ra-ar*$^{ki}$ **L.** *Zú-ba-núm* šu-mu-tak$_4$; **15** r. VI 18: 2 *bu*-DI … 2 saĝ-*sù* níĝ-ba *Na-tum ma-lik-tum Bur-ma-an*$^{ki}$ **L.** *Gi-ba-da Ib-dur-i-šar* šu-mu-tak$_4$; **17** o. III 3: [2 *bu*-DI dumu-munus] en *Bur-ma-an*$^{ki}$ **L.** é-gi en *Ra-ᵓà-ak*$^{ki}$; **18** r. IV 2: 2 *bu*-DI *ma-lik-tum Lum-na-an*$^{ki}$ **L.** *Ìr-ba*$_x$*-zé* šu-mu-tak$_4$; r. XII 17: 2 *bu*-DI … 2 saĝ-*sù* ama-gal *Ib-rí-um* **L.**; **19** o. VII 8: 1 íb-lá 1 *si-ti-tum* 1 ĝír-kun *I-in-*$^{d}$*ᵓÀ-da* dumu-nita en **L.**; r. XVI 8: 2 *bu*-DI ama-gal en *Ra-ᵓà-ak*$^{ki}$ **L.** *Ig-rí-su* šu-mu-tak$_4$; **20** r. XIII 2: [*Ig-rí-i*]*š*$^{?}$ **L.**; **21** o. III 11: 1 íb-lá 1 *si-ti-tum* 1 ĝír-kun *Za-ba-rúm* **L.** *I-rí-ig-ì* šu-mu-tak$_4$; o. XIV 25: (obj.) lú *Ib-rí-um* šu-mu-tak$_4$ *si-in* **L.**; r. XIV 16: [ ] dumu-nita en *si-in* **L.**; **22** o. VII 5: 1 ⸢dib⸣ *Du-bí-zi-kir* lú *Puzur*$_4$*-ra-ì* lú **L.** en-en; r. IX 4: tak$_4$ kg **L.** en-e[n] [ ].

esi «diorite» **2** r. III 2–4: 3 *gú-li-lum* TAR-II **L.** 2 *gú-li-lum*-II ŠÚ+ŠA **L.** 20 *gú-li-lum*-I 10 **L.**; r. XIV 11: 10 *gú-li-lum*-II a-gar$_5$-gar$_5$ ŠÚ+ŠA **L.**, 13: 20 *gú-li-lum*-I a-gar$_5$-gar$_5$ 10 **L.**, 16: 5 *gú-li-lum*-II TAR **L.**, 18: 5 *gú-li-lum*-II ŠÚ+ŠA **L.**; r. XV 4: 5 *gú-li-lum*-I 10 **L.**; **4** r. IX 5: 2 *gú-li-lum*-I **L.**; **5** o. III 15: 3 *gú-li-lum*-II **L.** 10 *gú-li-lum*-I **L.**; o. V 1: 10 *gú-li-lum*-I **L.** a-gar$_5$-gar$_5$; **6** o. VI 8: 10 *gú-li-lum*-II **L.** TAR, 10: 10 *gú-li-lum*-II **L.** ŠÚ+ŠA, 12: 20 *gú-li-lum*-I 10 **L.**; **9** r. X 1: 7 *gú-li-lum*-II ⸢kb⸣ **L.** GÁ×LÁ TAR-*su*, 3–4: 10 *gú-li-lum*-II kb esi GÁ×LÁ ŠÚ+ŠA gín DILMUN 1 *gú-li-lum*-I kb **L.** 1 gín DILMUN ĜÁ×LÁ-*sù*; r. XI 2: 15 *gú-li-lum*-II a-gar$_5$-gar$_5$ **L.**, 4: 2 *gú-li-lum*-II a-gar$_5$-gar$_5$ *sa-ḫ*[*a-*]*wa* **L.** ĜÁ×LÁ TAR, 6–7: 1$^{?}$ *gú-li-lum* a-gar$_5$-gar$_5$ *sa-ḫa-wa* 20 **L.** 12 *gú-li-lum* a-gar$_5$-gar$_5$ *sa-ḫa-wa* 12 **L.**, 11: 1 *gú-li-lum*-II a-gar$_5$-gar$_5$ **L**, 13: 4 *gú-li-lum*[-I] [a-]gar$_5$-gar$_5$ **L.**; **10** r. II 12: 4 *gú-li-lum*[-II] **L**[-**L.**], 15: ⸢5⸣ *gú-li-lum*-II a-gar$_5$-gar$_5$ **L.**;

r. III 1: 4 *gú-li-lum*-I **L.**; **14** o. IV 19: 2 *gú-li-lum*-I a-gar$_5$-gar$_5$ kg **L.** ⸢x⸣; o. XII 5: 2 *gú-li-lum*-I a-gar$_5$-gar$_5$ **L.**; **22** r. II 6: 10 *gú-li-lum*-II a-gar$_5$-gar$_5$ **L.**, 8: 10 *gú-li-lum*-I a-gar$_5$-gar$_5$ 10 **L.**; **23** o. IX 4–7: 2 *gú-li-lum*-II **L.** ŠA.PI 2 *gú-li-lum*-II **L.** TAR.TAR 1 *gú-li-lum*-I **L.** ŠÚ+ŠA 10 lá-1 *gú-li-lum* 10-I **L.**; o. X 3–5: 7 *gú-li-lum*-II **L.** TAR-TAR a-gar$_5$ 10 lá-1 *gú-li-lum*-II **L.** ŠÚ+ŠA-ŠÚ+ŠA a-gar$_5$ 1 *gú-li-lum*-I **L.** ŠÚ+ŠA a-gar$_5$ 2 *gú-li-lum*-I **L.** 10 a-gar$_5$; r. VI 9–VII 1: 2 *gú-li-lum*-II **L.** ŠÚ+ŠA 4 a-gar$_5$ 4 *gú-li-lum*-I **L.** 15 a-gar$_5$ 3 *gú-li-lum*-I **L.** ŠÚ+ŠA a-gar$_5$.

ešda «mace» (/*ḫa-bù*) **7** o. XI 9: 15 gín D. kb nu$_{11}$-za 1 **L.**; o. XII 3: 15 gín D. kb nu$_{11}$-za 1 **L.**; r. I 11: 10[+x] gí[n] D. kb nu$_{11}$-za 1 **L.**; r. VII 16: 15 gín D. kb nu$_{11}$-za 1 **L.**; **11** o. X 6: 13 gín D. kb nu$_{11}$-za 1 **L.**, 19: 13 gín D. kb nu$_{11}$-za 1 **L.**; r. IV 8: 13 gín D. kb nu$_{11}$-za 1 **L.**; r. V 17: 13 gín D. kb nu$_{11}$-za 1 **L.**; r. VIII 10: 15 gín D. kb nu$_{11}$-za 1 **L.**

## G

gaba «breast strap» **17** r. VII 2: 2 gín D. kb *ḫa-za-nu a-ḫa-šum* **L.** $^{d}$*Ku-ra wa* en.

gaba-ru «supply» **2** r. III 5: (25+[x] bracelets) **L.** é en; r. XV 9: (45 bracelets) **L.** é en; **4** o. XV 19: (20 bracelets) **L.** é en tak$_4$ igi-igi; r. XIII 15: 4 íb-lá **L.** é en; **10** r. III 2: (4 bracelets) **L.** é en; **12** r. V 1: 8 *gàr-su* gi$_6$ si$_4$-si$_4$ lú **L.**; **21** o. V 17: {⸢x⸣-UŠ} ; **22** r. IV 5: (60 bracelets and 10 daggers) lú *in* šu-mu-níĝin SA.ZA$_x^{ki}$ *Ba-ga-ma* **L.**

gada-TÚG «linen cloth» **2** o. VII 3; r. XII 12; **3** o. V 13; o. VI 3; r. XIV 9; **5** o. I 3; o. XIV 8; r. XI 15; **6** r. VIII 17; r. IX 10; r. XI 11; r. XII 9, 16; **8** r. X 3'; **9** o. V 12; o. VII 14; r. I 14; **11** o. III 2; **12** o. VIII 10; r. III 2: 23 **L.** mu$_4^{mu}$, 3: 10 **L.** ḫul, 4: 4 **L.** *kir-na-nu*; **14** o. VI 21: 1 kir$_4$-ma *wa* 10 lá-2 **L.**; **15** o. VI 19; **16** o. XIII 14; **17** r. V 7; r. X 9; r. XX 6; **18** o. IX 16; r. III 7; **19** o. VI 25; **20** r. XVII 2'; **25** o. II 3; o. V 7; r. IX 4: šu-níĝin … 60 lá-1 **L.**

gada-TÚG-gada-TÚG **14** r. XI 16; **15** r. III 13.

ga-du$_8$ «wet-nurse» **2** r. XI 13: *Bu-da-na-im* dumu-nita **L.**; **6** r. I 25: 10 lá-2 ĝeštu$_x$-lá *Ki-sa-du* **L.** en.

ga-eš$_8$ (GA:RAŠ) «travelling merchant» **6** o. X 20: (silver) níĝ-ba *I-ti* **L.** *Ma-rí*$^{ki}$; **7** r. XIII 23: (silver) níĝ-ba *Iš-dub-ì* maškim **L.** *Du-du-lu*$^{ki}$; **8** o. IV 13: (silver) *I-ti* **L.** *I-ga-iš-ru*$_{12}$ šu-mu-tak$_4$; r. III 12': (silver) *áš-tum I-ti* **L.** *Ma-rí*$^{ki}$; **10** o. I 13: (silver) níĝ-ba *Du-tum Ma-rí*$^{ki}$ lú **L.**; **12** o. VI 14: (silver) níĝ-ba *Wa-ba-rúm* **L.** *Du-du-lu*$^{ki}$; r. II 19: (silver) *Bù-sum Ma-rí*$^{ki}$ *a-dè* túg-*sù* ugula ki:lam$_7$ **L.** *in Maš-a*$^{ki}$; **14** o. II 22: (silver) níĝ-ba *Šu-a-ḫa* maškim **L.** *Du-du-lu*$^{ki}$; o. III 18: (silver) n[íĝ-ba] *Iš-*⸢*dub*⸣*-ì wa Ib-gi-tum* maškim **L.** *Du-du-lu*$^{ki}$; o. VIII 8: (silver) *Áš-da-ma-ì* maškim **L.** *Du-du-lu*$^{ki}$; o. XX 4: (silver) *Iš-dub-il* maškim **L.** *Du-du-lu*$^{ki}$, 13: [ ] ugula *Kul-ba-an*$^{ki}$ **L.** šu-ba$_4$-ti; r. IV 15: (silver) níĝ-ba *Iš-dub-il* maškim **L.** *Du-du-lu*$^{ki}$; r. X 17: (silver) níĝ-ba *Ù-li-li* maškim [**L.** *Du-du-lu*]$^{ki}$; **15** o. VIII 3: (silver) níĝ-ba *Iš-dub-il wa Dab*$_6$*-ti Ma-rí*$^{ki}$ maškim **L.** *Du-du-lu*$^{ki}$; **16** r. XII 25: 1 bur-KAK **L.**; **17** o. VII 4: [silver] níĝ-ba *Ù-ri-rí* maškim **L.** *in* kaskal é $^{d}$BAD *Ga-na-na*; r. XI 11: (silver) níĝ-[b]a ⸢*Ne-zi*⸣ *wa Ìr-[b]a-il Ma-rí*$^{ki}$ maškim **L.** Saḫar$^{ki}$ [šu-m]u-[ta]g$_4$; **20** o. II 5: [ ] [maškim] **L.** *Du-du-lu*$^{ki}$.

gal «big»
see tùn gal s.v. tùn.

*gal-tum* «daughter-in-law» **2** o. V 12: *Dar-maš-da-mu* dumu-munus en **L.** BAD-*da-mu*.

*ga-ma-a-tum* «knob» **7** o. IV 15: 20 ĝír mar-tu ti kb … 6 gín D. kg **L.**-*sù*; **8** o. IX 2: 10 ĝír [ ] **L.**; **14** o. IV 6: 2 *mi-at* ĝír mar-tu … 4 ma-na ŠÚ+ŠA 7 gín D. kb kin$_5$-ak **L.**-⸢*sù*⸣; **18** r. X 3: 2 *mi-at* 52 ĝír ma[r-tu] š[A.PI(?)] kb 5 ma-na ŠÚ+ŠA 2 gín D. 2 NI kb **L.**-*sù*; **19** o. XV 21: 12 ĝír mar-tu zú AN.LAGAB×A … 17 gín D. ½ kg nu$_{11}$-za *ša-ga-tum-sù wa* **L.**; o. XVII 18: 3 *mi-at* ĝír [ma]r-tu *ga-me-ù* kb 6 ma-na ŠA.PI gín D. kb **L.**-*sù*, 25: 1 ĝír mar-tu 1 3 NI kb **L.**-*sù*; r. IV 10: 3 *mi-at* 60 ĝír mar-tu *ga-mi-ù* kb 10 lá-2 ma-na kb **L.**, 17: 1 ĝír mar-tu 1 gín D. 3 NI kb **L.**; **21** r. III 12: 12 gín D. kg *ni-zi-mu* **L.** ĝír mar-tu.

*ga-ma-tum* **16** r. VIII 3: 10 gín D. kb *ni-zi-mu* nu$_{11}$-za … **L.** 17 ĝír mar-tu, 16: 12 gín D. kg *ni-zi-mu* nu$_{11}$-za … **L.** 5 ĝír mar-tu kb.

*kam*$_4$*-ma-a-tum* **2** o. XV 14: 10 gín D. kg [ ] *sa-ga-tum wa* **L.** 10 lá-1 ĝír mar-tu zú; **13** o. XII 16: 2 ĝír mar-tu … 3 NI gín D. kg **L.**-*sù*; **14** r. XIII 14: 3 kb *zi-ba-tum wa* **L.** 16 ĝír mar-tu kg 10 ⸢10⸣ ĝír ⸢mar⸣-tu ti kg 15 g[ír] mar-tu zú AN.LAGAB×AN 2 ĝír mar-tu *ba-du-u*$_4$ kg 6 ĝír mar-tu kb; **15** o. XV 2: 27 gín D. kb **L.** 20 ĝír mar-tu; **17** o. XVIII 14: 3 *mi-at* ĝír mar-tu zabar … 6 ma-na TAR kb kin$_5$-ak **L.**-*sù*; o. XIX 11: 17 ĝír mar-tu zú *wa* 3 ĝír mar-tu *ba-du-u*$_4$ kbg … TAR kg nu$_{11}$-za *šu-ga-tum-sù wa* **L.**-*sù*; o. XX 1: 1 *mi-at* ĝír mar-tu ti{-la} 2 ma-na 10 gín D. kb **L.**-*sù*; r. III 3: 2 gín D. kb kin$_5$-ak **L.** zàḫ *ša-ti* kù-sal ama-gal en; **18** r. X 11: 1 ĝír mar-tu 1 gín D. 3 NI kb **L.**

*gàr-su* «bag» **2** o. VII 8; r. XVII 12; **3** r. VII 18; **6** r. XIII 10; **7** o. I 16; o. II 5, 10; r. VII 10; **8** o. III 5: 2 **L.** ĝi$_6$; **10** r. VI 14; **12** r. IV 14: 1 **L.** gi$_6$, 17: 8 **L.** ĝi$_6$ si$_4$-si$_4$; **13** r. VII 9: 7 **L.** ĝi$_6$; **14** o. III 9; **15** o. VI 2; r. IV 2, 6; **16** r. IX 24; r. XI 18: 15 si$_4$ **L.**, 19: 14 ĝi$_6$ **L.**; **17** o. XI 1; r. XX 12: 10 lá-1 **L.** ĝi$_6$, 13: 24 **L.** si$_4$-si$_4$; **18** r. XVIII 26: 10 lá-1 **L.** ĝi$_6$, 27: 16 **L.** si$_4$; **19** r. XVI 25: 3 **L.** si$_4$; r. XVII 1: 4 **L.** ĝi$_6$; **21** r. II 16: 10 lá-1 **L.** ĝi$_6$, 17: 4 **L.** si$_4$-si$_4$.

géme «maidservant» **13** r. XI 18: 1 ĜIŠ-šú 1 níĝ-bànda … 2 *t*[*i-gi-na*] 2 ĜIŠ-du ... 1 zi-bar … 1 *bu*-DI tur 1 igi-igi … *Dag-*⸢*mul*⸣*-da-mu ma-lik-tum Lum-na-an*$^{ki}$ šu-mu-tak$_4$ (silver) **L.**-*sù*.

géme-gi «enclosed woman» **22** o. II 2: gù-kak-gíd dam-dam en ⸢*wa*⸣ [ ] **L.**

gi$_4$ «to return; to refund» **12** o. VI 8: 2 ĝír mar-tu … 2 kù-sal [ní]g-ba $^{d}$BAD *Ga-na-na-im* [*w*]*a* [$^{d}$NI-*d*]*a-la Gi-ri wa Ni-ir-da-mu* 2 dumu-nita *Ib-rí-um* in-na-sum *in* ud **L.** *mi-nu Du-du-lu*$^{ki}$.

*gi-ba-lu* (a religious ceremony) **2** o. VII 5: (15 garments, 1 kilt) ki:lam$_7$ **L.** *ʾÀ-da-ni*$^{ki}$; **3** r. VII 4: (23 garments, 70 kilts) ki:lam$_7$ **L.** *ʾÀ-da-ni*$^{ki}$; **9** r. I 17: (8 garments, 68 kilts) ki:lam$_7$ **L.** *ᵓÀ-da-ni*$^{ki}$; **10** r. VII 12: (100 garments, 16 kilts) ki:lam$_7$ **L.** ⸢*ᵓÀ*⸣*-da-*[*ni*]$^{ki}$; **17** r. XXII 28: (30 kilts) ki:[la]m$_7$ **L.** [*ᵓÀ-da-ni*$^{ki}$]; **25** o. VIII 6: (18+[x] garments, 2+[x] kilts, 1 dagger) ki:lam$_7$ $^{d}$*ᵓÀ-da wa* **L.** *ᵓÀ-da-ni*$^{ki}$.

*gi-ba-i* **21** r. XII 21: ki:lam$_7$ **L.**

*gi-ba-ù* **11** o. III 13: (100 garments, 50 kilts, 93 KIN measures of wool, 7 daggers) … 22 gud-gud [ ] [ -]N[E] šu-ba$_4$-ti ki:lam$_7$ **L.** [*wa*] $^{d}$*A-d*[*am-*]*ma ᵓÀ-da-ni*$^{ki}$.

gibil «new» **7** o. VII 3: gud-si-dili **L.**; **12** o. X 14: 2 *ma-ga-za-ᵓà* zabar **L.**; r. VIII 7: ká **L.**; r. XII 6: 6 bulug$_4$-bulug$_4$ **L.** lú ĜIŠ-gígir-II; r. XIII 4: 5 bulug$_4$-bulug$_4$ **L.** lú ĜIŠ-taškarin; **15** o. XV 17: 2 ĜIŠ-gígir-II **L.**; **16** o. VII 2: 2 níĝ-anše-ak 4 kù-sal **L.**; r. XVI 6: 3 útul urudu maḫ **L.**; **17** r. XXI 22: 1 *mi-at* 10 ĝír **L.**; **18** o. IX 4: 2 útul **L.**; **19** o. IX 5: 2 útul urudu **L.** maḫ; **20** o. IX 27: ĜIŠ-gígir-II **L.**; r. II 6: 1 á-lá **L.**

gíd «long»

see íb+III-TÚG babbar gíd s.v. íb(+II/III/IV/V-)TÚG.

gíd-TÚG «long garment» **14** o. VI 3; **15** o. VI 21; **17** o. XVII 15; r. XX 3 (gíd:TÚG).

gig «wheat» **6** o. I 7; **25** r. VI 3.

gín «shekel» *passim.*

gìn-gìn see za-gìn.

*gi*-NI see iti.

*gi-zu* (a vessel) **5** r. XVI 14: 5 gín D. kg *ni-zi-mu* 1 *zi-ru*$_{12}$ *wa* 2 **L.** *wa* LAGAB-LAGAB.

*gú-a-tum* (a vessel) **4** o. X 8: ŠÚ+ŠA gín D. kb nu$_{11}$-za$^{!}$(KUR) 20 **L.**

*gú-a-ti* **17** r. XVIII 14: 1 kù-sal níĝ-ba *Da-bur-da-mu al*$_6$ **L.** $^{d}$*Ba-ra-ma.*

*gú-a-zi-da-su* **12** o. XIII 9: 1 gín D. kb 2 **L.**

*gú-bù* (a vessel) **15** r. XV 13: 10 gín D. kg *zi-ba-du* 1 **L.** kg libir.

gud «ox» **2** r. VII 3; r. X 1; **3** r. II 7; **5** o. VII 8, 16; o. VIII 5; r. II 12; r. X 16: ŠÚ+ŠA 5 gín D. kb *ᵓa*$_5$*-na-gu* si 2 **L.**; r. XI 2: ŠÚ+ŠA 5 gín D. kb *ᵓa*$_5$*-na-gu* si 2 **L.**, 17; **6** r. XIII 8; **7** o. XI 18: ŠÚ+ŠA gín D. kb *ᵓa*$_5$*-na-gu* 4 si 2 **L.**; o. XII 10: ŠÚ+ŠA gín D. kb *ᵓa*$_5$*-na-gu* 4 si 2 **L.**; r. VIII 9; **8** r. V 11': 1 ma-na kb nu$_{11}$-za 8 si 4 **L.**; r. VI 2'; **9** o. IV 1: [1 ma-na kb] [nu$_{11}$-za si-si] 2 **L.**, 8: 1 ma-na kb nu$_{11}$-za si-si 2 **L.**; **10** o. XI 11: 1 ma-na kb nu$_{11}$-za 4 si-si 2 **L.**; **11** o. X 13: ŠÚ+ŠA gín D. kb *ᵓa*$_5$*-na-gu* 4 si 2 **L.**; o. XI 3: ŠÚ+ŠA gín D. kb *ᵓa*$_5$*-na-gu* 4 si 2 **L.**, 13; o. XIII 9; r. VIII 13: ŠÚ+ŠA gín D. kb *ᵓa*$_5$*-n*[*a-gu*] 1[+3 si 2 **L.**]; **12** r. II 2: ŠÚ+ŠA gín D. kb *ᵓa*$_5$*-na-gu* 4 si-si 2 **L.**; **13** o. V 14; o. XI 10: ŠÚ+ŠA gín D. kb *ᵓa*$_5$*-na-gu* 4 si 2 **L.**; o. XIV 9; o. XVI 10: 1 gín D. kb nu$_{11}$-za 2 si [**L.**]-I; r. X 7; **14** o. IX 20: ŠÚ+ŠA gín D. kb *ᵓa*$_5$*-na-gu* 4 si 2 **L.**; o. XVII 4; r. XII 7; **15** o. X 8: ŠÚ+ŠA gín D. kb *ᵓa*$_5$*-na-gu* 4 si 2 **L.**; r. IX 18: ŠÚ+ŠA gín D. kb *ᵓa*$_5$*-na-gu* 4 si 2 **L.**; **16** r. I 6: ŠÚ+ŠA gín D. kb *ᵓa*$_5$*-na-gu* si 2 **L.**, 17: ŠÚ+ŠA gín D. kb *ᵓa*$_5$*-na-gu* si 2 **L.**; r. XI 6: ŠÚ+ŠA gín D. kb *ᵓa*$_5$*-na-gu* si 2 **L.**; **17** o. XIII 8; r. IV 23: ŠÚ+ŠA gín D. kb *ᵓa*$_5$*-na-gu* 4 si 2 **L.**; r. X 15, 19; **18** o. XVIII 21: ŠÚ+ŠA gín D. kb *ᵓa*$_5$*-na-gu* si 2 **L.**; o. XIX 19: ŠÚ+ŠA gín D. kb *ᵓa*$_5$*-na-gu* si 2 **L.**; r. XVII 38: ŠÚ+ŠA kb *ᵓa*$_5$*-na-gu* si 2 **L.**; **19** o. X 27: ŠÚ+ŠA gín D. kb *ᵓa*$_5$*-na-gu* si 2 **L.**; o. XI 13: ŠÚ+ŠA gín D. kb *ᵓa*$_5$*-na-gu* si 2 **L.**; r. XVII 12: ŠÚ+ŠA kb *ᵓa*$_5$*-na-gu* si 2 **L.**; **20** o. VIII 10: ŠÚ+ŠA gín D. kb [*ᵓa*$_5$*-na-gu* 4 si **L.**], 22: ŠÚ+ŠA gín D. kb *ᵓa*$_5$*-*[*n*]*a-gu* 4 si **L.**; o. XIV 7; r. XI 11: ŠÚ+ŠA kb *ᵓa*$_5$*-na-gu* 4 si 2 **L.**; **21** r. VII 24: ŠÚ+ŠA gín D. kb *ᵓa*$_5$*-na-gu* si 2 **L.**

gud-gud **2** r. V 2; r. VII 12; **7** o. XVII 11; **11** o. III 7; **12** r. III 8; **16** r. II 19: *Mi-ga-ì* lú **L.**

gud-si-dili «battering ram» **7** o. VII 3: 2 lu$_5$ lú *I-dam-na* **L.** gibil; o. XV 16: 2[+x$^{?}$ gín] ⸢D.⸣ kb nu$_{11}$-za 1 **L.**-I (gud-<si->dili); **17** o. XX 18: 6 *ḫar-ᵓà-ru*$_{12}$ maḫ lú **L.**; r. I 2: 6 ĜIŠ-kak-ĜIŠ-kak eme **L.**

(see Steinkeller 1987, and Pasquali 2004)

gu-dùl-TÚG (a clothing) **5** o. I 5; **8** r. V 7': 1 **L.** gi$_6$; **14** o. XXI 6; **17** o. X 6: 26 **L.** m[aḫ]; r. XX 7: 3 **L.** é-duru$_5$$^{ki}$; r. XXII 22: 2 **L.** é-duru$_5$$^{ki}$ *áš-ti Ša-bir*$_5$*-ti-um*$^{ki}$.

gù-kak-gíd «neckband; collar» **22** o. I 8: [x m]a-[n]a [x gín D. kg] **L.** dam-dam en; r. V 2: 1 ma-na kg **L.** *Za-ni-ḫi-Ma-rí*$^{ki}$ é-gi *Ib-ᵓà-ra ᵓÀ-šu*$^{ki}$.

gukkal «fat-tailed sheep» **14** r. XV 11.

*gú-la-zi-na-tum* **9** r. XIII 16: 5 gín D. kb **L.** 3 *gú-li-lum* a-gar$_5$-gar$_5$.

*gú-li-lum* «bracelet» **1** o. X 9: [x] gín D. kb 1 **L.**; (d) r. II' x+1; **2** o. XI 6: 6 gín D. 2 NI kg 2 **L.**; r. I 25: 2 gín D. kg kin$_5$-ak 1 **L.** 1 kù-sal; r. III 1: 55 gín D. kg nu$_{11}$-za [x **L.**] 10 ⸢gín⸣ kb, 11: 2 ½ gín D. kg 1 **L.** 1 kù-sal, r. VIII 10: 6 2 NI gín D. kg 2 **L.**; r. XIII 16: 6 gín D. 2 NI kg 2 **L.**; r. XIV 5: 6 2 NI gín D. kb 2 **L.**, 16 and 18: 4 ma-na 10 gín D. kb kin$_5$-ak 5 **L.**-II TAR esi *wa* 5 **L.**-II ŠÚ+ŠA esi; r. XV 4: 50 gín D. kb kin$_5$-ak 5 **L.**-I 10 esi; **3** o. IV 9: 6 gín D. 2 NI kg 2 **L.**; o. XII 17: 6 gín D. 2 NI kb 2 **L.**; r. I 10: ŠÚ+ŠA gín D. kg *ni-zi-mu* ḫaš-ḫaš **L.**; r. IV 1: 6 gín D. [2 NI] kg 2 **L.**; **4** o. I 12: [x] **L.** [x gí]n [D.]; o. III 7: 10 ½ gín D. kb ZU.PIRIĜ kin$_5$-ak **L.** *wa* níĝ-anše-ak kù-sal SA.ZA$_x$$^{ki}$; o. V 7: ŠA.PI gín D. kb 2 **L.**; o. XII 4: 8 gín D. kb *ni-zi-mu* 10 lá-2 **L.**, 12: 6 2 NI gín D. kb 2 **L.**; o. XV 18: 3 ma-na ŠÚ+ŠA gín D. kb kin$_5$-ak 20 **L.**; r. VIII 18: 2 gín D. kb *ni-zi-mu* 2 **L.**; r. IX 5: TAR kb 2 **L.**-I esi, 11: 5 gín D. kb [kin$_5$-ak] [1 **L.**]; r. XII 6: 2 gín D. kb *ni-zi-mu* 2 **L.**; **5** o. III 10: 8 gín D. kg nu$_{11}$-za 2 **L.**, 15: ŠÚ+ŠA 2 gín D. kg nu$_{11}$-za 3 **L.**-II esi 10 **L.**-I esi; o. VI 4: 2 ½ gín D. kg *ni-zi-mu* nu$_{11}$-za **L.** *ìr-a-núm-sù*; o. XVI 9: 2 **L.**; r. VIII 2: 6 2 NI gín D. kg 2 **L.**, 13: 6 2 NI gín D. kb 2 **L.**; r. XII 18: 3 gín D. kg *ni-zi-mu* nu$_{11}$-za 2 **L.**; r. XIII 4: 1 ½ gín D. kg *ni-zi-mu* nu$_{11}$-za 2 **L.**, 8: ŠA.PI gín D. kb nu$_{11}$-za 20 **L.**; **6** o. VI 8, 10 and 12: 11 ma-na ŠA.PI kb kin$_5$-ak 10 **L.**-II esi TAR *wa* 10 **L.**-II esi ŠÚ+ŠA *wa* 20 **L.**-I 10 esi; r. VI 20: 6 2 NI gín D. kb 2 **L.**; **7** o. VII 16: 6 gín D. 2 NI kg 2 **L.**; o. XVI 10: 8 gín D. 2 NI kg 2 **L.**; r. V 15: ⸢6⸣ gín D. [1+]1 NI kg 2 **L.**; r. XI 8: 6 gín D. kg *ni-zi-mu* 2 **L.**; r. XIV 9: 6 gín 2 NI kb 2 **L.**; **8** o. XII 9: 2 gín D. kg *ni-zi-mu* 2 **L.**; o. XIII 4: 6 2 NI gín D. kg 2 **L.**; r. X 8': 6 2 NI gín D. kg 2 **L.**; **9** o. VIII 13: [6 g]ín D. [3 N]I kg 2 **L.**; o. XIII 14: 6 gín D. 2 NI kg 2 **L.**; r. VIII 15: 6 gín D. kg nu$_{11}$-za *ba-na-ᵓà-sa wa* íb+III-TÚG [*w*]*a* an-zam$_x$ *wa* 2 **L.**-*sù*; r. X 10: 1 ma-na ŠÚ+ŠA 6 gín D. kg *ni-zi-mu* nu$_{11}$-za ḫaš-ḫaš 1 dib a-gar$_5$-gar$_5$ lú 4 **L.**; r. XIV 8: [ ] ki[n$_5$-ak] **L.** ĝuruš-ĝuruš SA.ZA$_x$$^{ki}$; **10** r. II 11: 5 gín D. kb *ni-zi-mu* nu$_{11}$-za 4 **L.**[-II] esi, 18: [ša]-pi gín D. kb kin$_5$-ak 4 **L.** I:esi; **11** o. VI 12: 6 gín D. 2

NI kg 2 **L.**; r. IV 19: 6 2 NI gín D. kb 2 **L.**; **12** o. VIII 5: 6 gín D. 2 NI kg 2 **L.**, 16: 6 gín D. 2 NI kg 2 **L.**; r. V 6: ŠA.PI 2 gín D. kg *ni-zi-mu* 2 **L.**; r. III 9: 6 gín D. 2 NI kg 2 **L.**; r. V 16: 6 gín D. 2 NI kb 2 **L.**; r. VII 5: [6 gín D. 2 NI kg] 2 **L.**; r. XIII 19–20: 2 ma-na kb kin$_5$-ak 2 **L.**-II ŠÚ+ŠA 2 **L.**-I 10; **14** o. XI 11: 10 gín D. kb *ni-zi-mu* 2 **L.**; o. XVII 15–17: 5 m[a-]na ⌜TAR⌝ [kb] 1 **L.**-II lú TAR 5 **L.**-II lú ŠÚ+ŠA-ŠÚ+ŠA 20 **L.**-I lú 10 10; r. II 1: 6 gín D. ⌜2⌝ NI kg 2 **L.**; r. IV 20: [6 gín D. 2 NI kg 2 **L.**]; r. V 2: 6 gín D. 2 NI kg 2 **L.**; **15** o. II 20: 3 gín D. kg 1 **L.** *a-li-iš* ĜIŠ-gu-kak-gíd; o. VI 13: 6 gín D. 2 NI kg 2 **L.**; o. XV 7: 6 gín D. 2 NI kg 2 **L.**; r. IV 12: 6 gín D. 2 NI kg 2 **L.**, 16: 6 gín D. 2 NI kb 2 **L.**; r. XI 17: 3 NI kg 1 **L.** $^{d}$*Da-bí-ir* diĝir *Ib-la*$^{ki}$, 24: 2 ma-na kg kin$_5$-ak 2 **L.** … en *áš-du* … 2 **L.**-*sù* sikil $^{d?}$*A*$_5$*-da-*"*bal*" *Lu-ba-an*$^{ki}$; r. XII 23 and 26: 2 ma-na kg kin$_5$-ak 2 **L.** *Ib-rí-um áš-du* 2 **L.**-*sù* sikil $^{d?}$*À-da*; **16** o. XIII 12: 6 gín D. 2 NI kg 2 **L.**; r. VI 23: 6 gín D. 2 NI kg 2 **L.**, 26: 6 gín D. 2 NI kb 2 **L.**; r. XVII 17: [6] gín D. 2 NI kg 2 **L.**; **17** o. XI 6: 6 gín D. 2 NI kg 2 **L.**; r. VI 9: 6 gín D. 2 NI kg 2 **L**; r. VII 7: 1 gín D. kb 1 **L.** ùz-munus; r. XVI 18: 6 gín D. 2 NI kg 2 **L.**, 22: 6 gín D. 2 NI kb 2 **L.**; **18** o. II 5: 14 gín D. kg 2 **L.** *wa* 2 *ti-gi-na wa* 2 ĜIŠ-du, 14: 14 gín D. kg 2 **L.** *wa* 2 *ti-gi-na wa* 2 ĜIŠ-du; o. VII 14 and 16: 5 ma-na ŠÚ+ŠA gín D. kb kin$_5$-ak 10 **L.**-II lú ŠÚ+ŠA-ŠÚ+ŠA *wa* 12 **L.**-I lú 20; o. VIII 9: 3 ma-na kb nu$_{11}$-za … 40 **L.**-I lú 15; o. XII 8: 6 2 NI gín D. kg 2 **L.**; r. VI 12: 6 gín D. 2 NI kg 2 **L.**; r. XV 16: 6 2 NI kg 2 **L.**, 18: 6 2 NI kb 2 **L.**; **19** o. IX 9: 6 gín D. 2 NI kg 2 **L**; r. VI 27: 6 gín D. 2 NI kg 2 **L.**; r. IX 2: 6 gín D. 2 NI kg 2 **L.**, 12: 6 gín D. 2 NI kg 2 **L.**; r. XI 7–10: 5 ma-na kb kin$_5$-ak 1 **L.**-II ŠA.PI 2 **L.**-II TAR 5 **L.**-II ŠÚ+ŠA 1 **L.**-I 10; **20** o. IV 13: 6 gín D. 2 NI kg 2 **L.**; r. IV 20: 10 gín D. kg *ni-zi-mu* 1 **L.**; r. V 3: [6 gín D. 2 NI kg] 2 **L.**; r. VIII 21: 6 gín D. [2] NI kg 2 **L.**; r. XV 4: ša-p[i] gín D. kg nu$_{11}$-za 5 **L.**-II a-gar$_5$-ga[r$_5$] TAR *wa* 10[(+x)] **L.**; 20 o. IV 13: [6 gín D. 2 NI kg] [2 **L.**]; **21** o. XI 17: 6 gín D. 2 NI kg 2 **L.**; o. XVII 11: 6 2 NI gín D. kg 2 **L.**, 6 2 NI gín D. kg 2 **L.**; o. XVII 25: 6 ma-na ŠA.PI gín D. kb [kin$_5$-ak 20 lá-2] **L.** ŠÚ+ŠA-ŠÚ+ŠA; r. I 10: 6 gín D. 2 NI kg 2 **L.**; r. IX 19–25: 1 ma-na kb kin$_5$-ak 3 **L.**-II ŠÚ+ŠA-ŠÚ+ŠA … lul-gu-ak 3 **L.** [ ]; r. XIII 18: 4 ma-na kg 1 dib 2 **L.**; **22** r. I 12 and II 3: 5 ma-na kg kin$_5$-ak$^{!}$(GÚG) 10 **L.** ŠÚ+ŠA-II *wa* 10 **L.** 10-I; **23** o. II 4: 6 2 NI gín D. kg 2 **L.**; o. III 3: 6 2 NI gín D. kg 2 **L.**; o. IX 4–7: ŠÚ+ŠA 8 gín D. kg *ni-zi-mu* nu$_{11}$-za 2 **L.**-II esi ŠA.PI 2 **L.**-II esi TAR.TAR 1 **L.**-I esi ŠÚ+ŠA 10 lá-1 **L.** 10-I esi ĝuruš-ĝuruš; r. V 7: 2 gín D. kg *ni-zi-mu* nu$_{11}$-za <1> **L.**; **24** o. VII 7: 6 gín D. 2 NI kg 2 **L.**

*gú-li-lum-gú-li-lum* **11** r. II 12: 5 gín D. kg ZU.PIRIĜ **L.** ĝuruš-ĝuruš.

*gú-li-lum* a-gar$_5$ **23** o. X 3–5: ŠÚ+ŠA 8 gín D. kg *ni-zi-mu* nu$_{11}$-za 7 **L.**-II esi TAR.TAR a-gar$_5$ 10 lá-1 **L.**-II esi ŠÚ+ŠA-ŠÚ+ŠA a-gar$_5$ 1 **L.**-I esi ŠÚ+ŠA a-gar$_5$ 2 **L.**-I esi 10 a-gar$_5$ ĝuruš-ĝuruš SA.ZA$_x^{ki}$; r. IV 2: 8 gín D. kg nu$_{11}$-za 5 **L.** dib a-gar$_5$; r. VI 9–VII 1: ŠÚ+ŠA gín D. kg nu$_{11}$-za 2 **L.**-II esi ŠÚ+ŠA 4 a-gar$_5$ 4 **L.**-I esi 15 a-gar$_5$ 3 **L.**-I esi ŠÚ+ŠA a-gar$_5$.

*gú-li-lum* a-gar$_5$-gar$_5$ **2** o. XIV 19: 9 gín D. kg *ni-zi-mu* nu$_{11}$-za … ḫaš-ḫaš 5 **L.** lú ĝuruš-ĝuruš SA.ZA$_x^{ki}$; r. III 2–4: 55 gín D. kg nu$_{11}$-za … 3 **L.**-II TAR esi 2 **L.**-II ŠÚ+ŠA esi 20 **L.**-I 10 esi gaba-ru é en; r. XIV 11 and 13: 1 ma-na kb nu$_{11}$-za 10 **L.**-II ŠÚ+ŠA esi *wa* 20 **L.**-I 10 esi; **5** o. IV 19: ŠA.PI 6 gín D. kb nu$_{11}$-za 3 **L.**-II 10 *gú-li-lum*-I esi a-gar$_5$-gar$_5$; **7** r. IX 6–9: 1 ma-[n]a 5 gín D. kg nu$_{11}$-za 10 **L.**-II TAR 5 **L.**-II ŠÚ+ŠA 10 **L.**-I ⌜15?⌝ 10 **L.** 10-I 10-I; **9** r. XI 2–7: [ ] 15 **L.**-II esi *wa* 2 **L.** *sa-ḫ*[*a-*]*wa*-II esi ĜÁ×LÁ TAR *wa* 1? **L.** *sa-ḫa-wa* 20 esi 12 **L.** *sa-ḫa-wa* 12 esi, 11–13: 5 gín D. kb *ni-zi-mu* nu$_{11}$-za ḫaš-ḫaš 1 **L.**-II esi *wa* 4 **L.**[-I] esi; r. XIII 17: 5 gín D. *gú-la-*⌜*zi*⌝*-na-tum* 3 **L.**; **10** r. II 15: ⌜4⌝ gín D. kb ZU.PIRIĜ ⌜5⌝ **L.** II:esi; **12** o. XIII 7: 1 ½ gín D. kg *ni-zi-mu* nu$_{11}$-za 1 **L.** 15 gín D. a-gar$_5$-gar$_5$; **13** r. XIV 18: ŠA.PI gín D. kb nu$_{11}$-za 5 **L.** TAR *wa* 5 **L.** ŠÚ+ŠA; **14** o. XII 5: 2 gín D. kg *ni-zi-mu* nu$_{11}$-za 2 **L.**-I esi; o. XV 15: 1 gín D. kg *ni-zi-mu* nu$_{11}$-za 1 **L.**; o. XVIII 8–12: 1 ma-na ŠÚ+ŠA 7 ½ gín D. kg [nu$_{11}$-za] 10 **L.**-II lú TAR.TAR a-gar$_5$-gar$_5$ *wa* 10 **L.**-II ⌜lú⌝ [ŠÚ+ŠA-ŠÚ+ŠA] [*wa*] 10 **L.**-I lú 15 10, 15–o. XIX 5: 10 ma-na ŠÚ+ŠA 7 gín D. kb nu$_{11}$-za 10 **L.**-II ⌜lú⌝ TAR.TAR *wa* 4 **L.**-II lú ŠÚ+ŠA-ŠÚ+ŠA *wa* 20 **L.**-I lú 15 10; r. XIV 10'–15': 10 gín D. kg daḫ$_x$(MU.MU.MU) *ni-zi-mu* nu$_{11}$-za-*sù* 2 **L.**-II lú ŠA.PI-ŠA.PI *wa* 1 **L.**-I lú ŠÚ+ŠA *sa-ḫa-wa wa* 1 **L.** [ ]; **15** o. XI 1: 2 D. kg *ni-zi-mu* 1 **L.**; r. II 7: 10 gín D. kg nu$_{11}$-za 2 **L.** 50 gín D. a-gar$_5$-gar$_5$; **16** o. X 4–6: TAR 2 gín D. kg *ni-zi-mu* nu$_{11}$-za 6 **L.**-II TAR 14 **L.**-II ŠÚ+ŠA 5 **L.**-I 10, 10: 2 gín D. kb *ni-zi-mu* nu$_{11}$-za 3 **L.**-I 10; r. XIII 1 and 3: [50 g]ín [D. k]g nu$_{11}$-za 15 **L.**-I 15 *wa* 14 **L.**-I 12; **17** o. II 2: 2 **L.** TAR 5 gín D. *sa-ḫa-wa*; o. III 22: 5 gín D. kg *ni-zi-mu* nu$_{11}$-za 1 **L.** 50; o. XV 14–17: 1 ma-na 15 gín D. kg nu$_{11}$-za 5 **L.**-II TAR 10 **L.**-II ŠÚ+ŠA ŠÚ+ŠA 5 **L.**-I 15 10 **L.**-I 10; **18** o. VI 17: 1 gín D. kg *ni-zi-mu* nu$_{11}$-za 1 **L.**; o. VII 9 and 11: 1 ma-na ŠÚ+ŠA 4 gín D. kg nu$_{11}$-za 12 **L.** *wa* 12 **L.**-II ŠÚ+ŠA-ŠÚ+ŠA; o. VIII 7 and 9: 3 ma-na kb nu$_{11}$-za 20 **L.**-II lú TAR *wa* … 20 **L.**-I lú 12; **19** o. XVIII 6 and 8: 2 ma-na kg nu$_{11}$-za 16 **L.** TAR 2 a-gar$_5$ *wa* 50 **L.** 10 10 a-gar$_5$-gar$_5$, 11 and 13: 3 ma-na kb nu$_{11}$-za 10 **L.** TAR 2 a-gar$_5$-gar$_5$ *wa* 1 *mi-at* **L.**-I 10 a-gar$_5$; **20** r. XV 2': ŠA.P[I] gín D. kg nu$_{11}$-za 5 **L.**-II TAR *wa* 10[(+x) *gú*]-*l*[*i-lum* ]; **22** r. II 6 and 8: 10 **L.**-II esi *wa* 10 **L.**-I 10 esi; r. III 1 and 3: 10 **L.**-II ŠÚ+ŠA *wa* 10 **L.**-I 10.

*gú-li-lum* a-gar$_5$-gar$_5$ kù:babbar **21** r. V 19–21: 12 gín D. kg *ni-zi-mu* 3 **L.**-II TAR *wa* 3 **L.**-I 15.

*gú-li-lum* a-gar$_5$-gar$_5$ kù-gi **5** o. VII 3; **6** r. VII 18; **13** r. III 3: [ ] 1 ĝír mar-tu ti kg *wa* 1 **L.**; **14** o. IV 19: 2 **L.**-I esi ⌜x⌝; **21** r. V 7–9: [ ] *ni-zi-mu* nu$_{11}$-za 11 **L.** TAR a-gar$_5$-gar$_5$ kg *wa* 10 **L.** 15 a-gar$_5$-gar$_5$ kg.

*gú-li-lum* kù:babbar **2** o. XIV 16: 9 gín D. kg *ni-zi-mu* nu$_{11}$-za ḫaš-ḫaš 4 **L.**; **9** r. IX 15–X 4: 1 ma-na TAR kg *ni-zi-mu* 7 **L.**-II esi ĜÁ×LÁ TAR-*sù wa* 10 **L.**-II esi ĜÁ×LÁ ŠÚ+ŠA gín D. 1 **L.**-I esi 1 gín D. ĜÁ×LÁ-*sù*; **12** o. XIV 1: 2 gín D. kg *ni-zi-mu* nu$_{11}$-za 1 **L.**; **14** r. XIV x+1: [x] **L.**-II [T]AR.TAR, 2': 10 lá-1 **L.**-II ŠÚ+ŠA-ŠÚ+ŠA; **16** o. IX 4–7: 10 gín D. kb *ni-zi-mu* 3 **L.**-II ŠA.PI 2 **L.**-II TAR 15 **L.**-II ŠÚ+ŠA 7 **L.** 11 kb; **19** o. IV 15: 1 ½ gín D. kg *ni-zi-mu* nu$_{11}$-za 2 **L.**; **24** r. II 5: 4 gín D. kg nu$_{11}$-za 1 **L.**

*gú-li-lum* kù:babbar-gi **17** r. III 14: 1 gín D. kg *ni-zi-mu* $nu_{11}$-za 2 **L.**; **21** r. IV 11–17: 1 ma-na kb *ni-zi-mu* 10 lá-3 **L.**-II ŠA.PI kbg *wa* 4 **L.** TAR kbg *wa* 16 **L.**-II ŠÚ+ŠA-ŠÚ+ŠA kbg *wa* 3 **L.**-I 10 kbg.

*gú-li-lum* kù-gi **14** o. XIV 21: 2 gín D. kg *ni-zi-mu* $nu_{11}$-za 2 **L.**

*gúm-a-nu* (a container, cf. *gú-mi-a-nu*) **17** r. XVII 5: [ ] $kin_5$-ak 1 *mu-rúm wa* 1 **L.** *wa* 2 ĜIŠ-alam *su-da₅-lik* en; **20** o. XI 19: 1 ma-na kb 1 **L.**

gu-mug-TÚG (a kind of cloak) **9** o. XIV 14.

gùn «multicoloured» **17** r. VI 23: 1 an-dùl … 1 gín 3 NI kg $nu_{11}$-za *ba-na-i-sù wa* íb-lá-*sù wa* šu-kešda **L.**-*sù*

see íb+III-TÚG ($sa_6$) gùn.

gùn «dyer»

gùn-gùn **4** o. XV 7: 1 útul urudu lú **L.** íb+III-TÚG.

*gú-núm* (epithet of the god Rašap)

$^{d}$*A-da-ma gú-núm* **17** r. XVI 8.

$^{d}$*Ra-sa-ap gú-núm* **5** r. XIV 20 (*gú-núm*$^{ki}$); **10** o. XV 9; **11** o. V 15.

gu-X **17** r. XXII 10: 2 ĜIŠ-gu-kak-šub 2 **L.** šub 8 en.

$gur_8$ «raft, platform» **13** r. II 6: 1 ma-na 2 gín D. kb lul-gu-ak **L.**, 12: 10 gín D. kb lul-gu-ak **L.**; **16** r. XIV 8: 4 gín D. kb **L.** má-gal-má-gal mu-DU *na-se*$_{11}$-*na-se*$_{11}$ *in* ud [ ]; **17** o. XVII 21: 10 gín D. kb **L.** ĜIŠ-gígir-sum šu-mu-$tak_4$ túg-túg.

*gur-gú-ru*$_{12}$ «spherical bead» **18** o. XVI 18: 1 ma-na TAR kg $kin_5$-ak … 92 **L.**; **24** o. VIII 5: 13 gín D. kg 1 *mi-at* 30 lá-3 **L.**

*gu-za*$_x$*-gú* **4** o. VII 7: TAR 7 10 gín D. kb 2 *bu*-DI 10 lá-2 $\hat{g}e\check{s}tu_x$-lá 30 *du-ru*$_{12}$*-gú* 1 **L.** 1 šu-dub 1 *ma-ḫa-na-gúm.*

*gú-za-ra-tum* «clasp (of a necklace)» **24** r. I 6: 4 gín D. kg *ḫa-za-nu wa a-a-nu* **L.**

*gú-za-rí-tum* **10** o. VIII 21: 8 gín D. kb $nu_{11}$-za balaĝ lú **L.** lú *Ib-rí-um.*

*gú-za-ru*$_{12}$*-tum* **10** r. V 15: 3 gín D. kb $nu_{11}$-za **L.** lú [x]-˹x-x˺.

(this lemma is attested also in *ARET* XXII 12 r. XX 25: 1 *gú-li-lum* kù-gi 12 ½ 1 *gú-za-ra-tum* 5 *zu-lu-mu Za-a-šè* "a bracelet of 12 ½ (shekels of gold, and) a *g.* of 5 (shekels of gold) for Zaʾaše (minister of Ibbi-zikir's daughter) for (her) consent (to marry the prince Irʾak-damu) (see Archi 2021b, p. 27).

*gu-zi-tum*-TÚG (a cloak) **2** r. XII 9; **3** o. VI 1; **5** r. XI 14; **8** o. V 2; **25** o. I 5; o. III 2; o. IV 5; r. IX 2: šu-níĝin 25 **L.**

## Ĝ

ĜÁ×LÁ «weight» **4** o. IX 18: 3 íb<-lá> **L.** ŠA.PI; **9** r. X 1: 7 *gú-li-lum* kb˺-II esi TAR-*sù*, 3: 10 *gú-li-lum* kb-II esi ŠÚ+ŠA gín D., 4: 1 *gú-li-lum* kb-I esi 1 gín D. -*sù*; r. XI 4: 2 *gú-li-lum* $a\text{-}gar_5\text{-}gar_5$ *sa-ḫ*[*a*-]*wa*-II esi TAR; **18** r. XII 19: ĜIŠ-šim **L.**

ĝeštin «wine» **1** o. VI 2; 5 o. V 7; o. IX 17; o. XIII 10; **9** o. XV 6; **11** o. XII 4; **13** o. VII 2: **18** o. V 23: la-ḫa **L.** en *Gú-da-da-núm*$^{ki}$; **21** o. IV 27.

ĝeštin-ĝeštin **4** o. IV 2; o. VII 2; r. II 8; r. V 3.

ĝeštu «ear» (a kind of handle)

ĝeštu-ĝeštu **10** o. XI 1: 5 gín D. kb **L.** 1 ĜIŠ-šú.

$\hat{g}e\check{s}tu_x$-lá «earring» **1** o. VIII 14: 1 gín D. kg 2 **L.**; **2** o. X 1: 1 gín D. kg *ni-zi-mu* 2 **L.**; o. XIII 17: 2 gín D. 2 NI kg *ni-zi-mu* 4 **L.**; o. XV 4: 2 gín D. kg *ni-zi-mu* 6 **L.**; r. IV 13: 2 gín D. kg 2 **L.**; **3** o. III 10: 4 gín D. kg *ni-zi-mu* 10 **L.**; **4** o. VII 6: 10 lá-2 **L.**; **6** r. I 23: 4 gín D. kb $kin_5$-ak 10 lá-2 **L.**; **10** o. XIII 19: 3 gín D. kb 2 **L.** 2[+2] ˹*ba*˺*-ga-ne-su*; **12** o. IV 10: 2 gín D. kg 2 **L.**; o. XII 4: 2 gín D. kg 2 **L.**, 15: 2 gín D. kg 2 **L.**; o. XV 11: ŠÚ+ŠA gín D. kg. 10 **L.**; **13** r. XIII 1: [x gín D. kb] 4 **L.**; **15** o. XI 8: 1 ma-na 14 gín D. kg $kin_5$-ak 10 **L.** r. VII 5: 2 gín D. kg *ni-zi-mu* 6 **L.**; **16** o. III 4: 3 gín D. kg 4 **L.**; r. II 3: 10 gín D. kb *ni-zi-mu* 10 **L.**; r. XIII 12: ŠÚ+ŠA 6 gín D. kg $kin_5$-ak lul-gu-ak 2 **L.** 15; r, XV 17: ½ kg *ni-zi-mu* 4 **L.**; **17** r. XVII 14: 3 gín D. 2 NI kg $kin_5$-ak 4 **L.**; **18** o. XVI 17: 1 ma-na TAR kg $kin_5$-ak … 10 lá-2 **L.**; o. XVII 27: 6 gín D. kg *ni-zi-mu* 10 lá-2 **L.**; o. XVIII 6: 8 gín D. kg *ni-zi-mu* 4 *ti-gi-na* 4 ĜIŠ-du 4 **L.** 2 kù-sal; 20 o. II 18: ŠÚ+ŠA 4 gín D. kg $kin_5$-ak 1 **L.** *wa* [ ]; **24** o. I 7 and 13: 2 gín D. kg *ni-zi-mu* 4 **L.** *Gi-rí wa Nap-ḫa-il wa* lul-gu-ak 2 **L.** *Ir-da-mu* dumu-nita *Ib-rí-um*; o. VII 11: TAR kg 10 **L.**

ĜIŠ-$\hat{g}e\check{s}tu_x$-lá **20** o. XV 14: 10 gín D. 8 **L.**

$\hat{g}i_6$ «black» **8** o. III 5: 2 *gàr-su* **L.**; r. V 7': 1 gu-dùl-TÚG **L.**; **12** r. IV 14: 1 *gàr-su* **L.**, 17: 8 *gàr-su* **L.** $si_4$-$si_4$; **13** r. VII 9: 7 *gàr-su* **L.**; **16** r. XI 19: 14 **L.** *gàr-su*; **17** r. V 11: 1 *mi-at* 50 kuš-kuš $sa_6$ **L.**; r. XX 12: 10 lá-1 *gàr-su* **L.**; **18** r. XVIII 26: 10 lá-1 *gàr-su* **L.**; **19** r. XVII 1: 4 *gàr-su* **L.**; **21** r. II 16: 10 lá-1 *gàr-su* **L.**

ĝír «dagger» **1**(b) r. x+1 3'; **4** r. III 10: 4 g[ín D. kb] [*n*]*i-zi-mu* $nu_{11}$-za!(KUR) 2 **L.** šu-$du_8$-máš; **5** o. I 9: 4 **L.** zú-ak; o. IX 3: 1 **L.** zú-ak; **6** o. XV 22: 8 gín D. kb $nu_{11}$-za 4 **L.** šu-$du_8$-máš; r. XIII 6: 1 **L.** kg; r. XVI 18: 4 an-na $kin_5$-ak 4 **L.** šu-$du_8$-máš; **7** o. IX 21; o. XIII 14: ½ gín D. kg *ni-zi-mu* $nu_{11}$-za 1 **L.**; o. XVII 2 **L.** zabar; **8** o. VIII 7: 10 **L.** [ ]; **9** o. V 9: 3 **L.** šu-$du_8$-m[áš]; **14** r. III 18: [x g]ín D. an-na šub *si-in* 3 **L.**; **16** o. VIII 23: 52 gín D. kb *ni-zi-mu* 32 **L.** 55 íb-lá kb; o. XII 16: 1 gín D. kg *ni-zi-mu* $nu_{11}$-za 2 **L.** lú $ZA_x$ *Ib-rí-um*; **17** r. IX 10: 5 gín D. kb $kin_5$-ak 1 **L.**; r. XXI 22: 3 ma-na ŠÚ+ŠA an-na šub *si-in* 26 ma-na ŠÚ+ŠA $a\text{-}gar_5\text{-}gar_5$ $kin_5$-ak 1 *mi-at* 10 **L.** gibil, 28; **18** r. XVI 11: 2 ½ kb 1 **L.**; r. XVIII 19: 2 an-na šub *si-in* 10 $a\text{-}gar_5\text{-}gar_5$ $kin_5$-ak 2 **L.**; **20** o. XIII 9–10: 12 gín D. an-na šub *si-in* 1 ma-na 8 gín D. $a\text{-}gar_5\text{-}gar_5$ $kin_5$-ak 4 **L.** 15 gín D. 2 **L.** 10 gín D.

ĝír-ĝír **4** o. VIII 3: 8 gín D. kb *zi-tum* 4 **L.** šu-$du_8$-máš.

ĝír mar-tu (a type of dagger) **1** o. IX 6: [1 gín] ˹kg˺ $nu_{11}$-za *sa-ga-ti* 1 **L.**; o. XIII 2': [2] **L.** [kg]; (e) r. x+I x+1: [x] **L.** kg; **2** o. II 12: 1 **L.** kg; o. V 15: 1 **L.** kg; o. IX 4: 1 **L.** kg; r. X 10: 1 **L.** kg, 14: 1 **L.** kg, 19: 1 **L.** kg; r. XVII 2: 1 **L.** kg; 2 o. XI 13: 3 gín D. kg $nu_{11}$-za 1 **L.** *ra-ʾà-tum* tur; r. XVI 7: 1 **L.** *ra-ʾà-tum* kg; **3** o. V 3: 40[+x] diri **L.**, 7: 60 **L.** SA.$ZA_x$$^{ki}$; r. III 13: [ ] diri **L.**; **4** o. IV 15: 12 gín D. kb $nu_{11}$-za!(KUR) 3 ĜIŠ-banšur 3 **L.**; o. VIII 5: 1 **L.** kg, 8: 1 **L.** kg; **5** o.

II 9; o. III 6: 1 **L.** kg; o. VI 17: 1 **L.** kg; o. XIV 13: 4 **L.** kb; r. III 14: 3 gín D. kb nu$_{11}$-za 1 **L.**; r. XIII 20: 3 gín D. kg nu$_{11}$-za 1 **L.**; r. XIV 3: 2 gín D. kb nu$_{11}$-za 1 **L.**, 14: 2 gín D. kb nu$_{11}$-za 1 **L.**; **6** o. V 20: 20 **L.** kg; o. VIII 6: nu$_{11}$-za 1 **L.**; o. X 8: 10 gín D. kb *ru$_{12}$-du-ga-tum* **L.** kg; o. XII 3: 1 *mi-at* si-si **L.** kg; r. II 11: 1 **L.** kg, 15: 10 gín D. kb nu$_{11}$-za 1 **L.**; r. IX 13: 12 **L.** ḫul; r. X 9: 1 **L.** kg; r. XV 3: 40 **L.** kg; **7** o. I 9: 2 gín D. kb nu$_{11}$-za 1 **L.**; o. III 12: 3 gín D. kb nu$_{11}$-za 1 **L.** *wa* 1 kù-sal; 20: [x **L.** (x) kg]; o. V 16: 1 **L.** kg, 21: 1 **L.** kg; o. X 17: 3 gín D. kb nu$_{11}$-za 1 **L.**; o. XII 20: 2 gín D. kg *ni-zi-mu* nu$_{11}$-za 1 **L.**; o. XVI 14: ŠA.PI gín D. kb 1 **L.** kg; o. XVIII 5: 1 **L.** kg; r. II 7: 2 g[ín D.] kb nu$_{11}$-za 1 **L.**, 16: 2 gín D. kb nu$_{11}$-za 1 **L.**; r. III 14: 2 gín D. kb nu$_{11}$-za 1 **L.**; r. V 21: 2 gín D. kg nu$_{11}$-za 1 **L.**; r. IX 1: 1 **L.** kg; r. XII 1: [1 **L.**] kg, 19: 7 gín D. kg *zi-du* 1 **L.**; r. XVI 3: [1] **L.** kg; **8** o. I 14: [1 **L.** *ra-ʾà-t*]*um* kg, 15: 1 **L.** kg, 18: ⸢1⸣ **L.** ⸢1⸣ *r*[*a*]-⸢*ʾà*⸣-*tum* kg; o. II 13: 1 **L.** kg; o. VII 3: 4 gín D. kb nu$_{11}$-za 1 **L.**; o. X 8: 4 gín D. kb nu$_{11}$-za 1 **L.**; r. VII 10': 1 **L.** kg; **9** o. X 8: 40 si-si **L.**, 11: 1 ma-na ŠÚ+ŠA gín D. kb *zi-du* [20?]+10? **L.**; o. XVI 3': 1 **L.** kg; o. XVII 5': 1 **L.** kg; r. I 2: 1 **L.** kg; r. III 16: [x] gín D. kg nu$_{11}$-za 1 **L.**; r. IV 10: 1 **L.** kg; r. XII 6: ŠÚ+ŠA gín D. kg *ni-zi-mu* nu$_{11}$-za 10 **L.** kg; r. XIV 16: 1 **L.** kg; r. XV 6: 1 **L.** kg; **10** o. X 13: 3 gín D. kb nu$_{11}$-za 1 **L.**; o. XIII 13: 5 gín D. kb maš-maš 1 [ĜIŠ]-⸢banšur⸣ *wa* nu$_{11}$-za 1 **L.**; r. V 1: 10 gín D. kb *ma-za-um* **L.**, 6: TAR 7 gín D. kg *ma-za-um* 3 **L.**; r. X 1: 3 gín D. kb nu$_{11}$-za 1 **L.** 1 kù-sal; r. XIV: 8 **L.** guruš-guruš SA.ZA$_{x}^{ki}$; **11** o. IV 20: 2 gín D. kb nu$_{11}$-za [1] **L.**; o. V 11: 2 gín D. kb nu$_{11}$-za 1 **L.**; o. VII 2: 2 **L.** kg *ra-ʾà-tum Ib-rí-um*; o. XIII 7: 10 **L.** ḫul; r. II 3: [ ] 80 í[b-lá] 80 **L.** 21 á-MUŠEN zabar; r. V 4: 2 gín D. kb nu$_{11}$-za 1 **L.**, 13: 1 **L.** kg; r. VII 17: 1 **L.** kg; **12** o. V 12: 4 gín D. kb nu$_{11}$-za 2 **L.**; o. VII 14: 2 gín D. kb nu$_{11}$-za 1 **L.**; r. IV 6: 1 **L.** kg; r. VII 11: 2 gín D. kb nu$_{11}$-za 1 **L.**; r. VIII 4: 1 **L.** kg; **13** o. V 4: 2 gín D. kb nu$_{11}$-za 1 **L.**; o. IX 8: 2 ½ gín D. kb nu$_{11}$-za 1 **L.** 1 kù-sal; o. X 16: 1 **L.** kg; o. XII 2: 1 **L.** kg, 10: 4 gín D. an-na šub *si-in* 2 **L.**; r. VI 13: 1 **L.** kg; **14** o. I 18: 7 gín D. kg *zi-tum* 1 **L.** en; o. II 13: 7 gín D. kg *zi-tum* 1 **L.**; o. IV 3: 6 ma-na ŠA.PI gín D. an-na šub-šub *si-in* kin$_5$-ak 2 *mi-at* **L.**; r. II 9: 1 gín D. kg *ni-zi-mu* [nu$_{11}$-za] 1 **L.**; r. X 11: [x kg] nu$_{11}$-za 1 **L.**; r. XIII 15: 16 **L.** kg, 19: 6 **L.** kb; **15** o. III 19: 1 **L.** kg; o. XIV 6 and 9: 1 **L.** kg en *áš-du* 1 **L.**-*sù*; o. XV 3: 27 gín D. kb *kam$_4$-ma-a-tum* 20 **L.**; r. II 22: 1 **L.** kg; r. III 3: 2 gín D. [kb] nu$_{11}$-za 1 **L.**; r. V 17 and 20: 1 **L.** kg *Ib-rí-um áš-du* 1 **L.**-*sù*; r. VII 24: 2 gín D. 2 NI kg nu$_{11}$-za 1 **L.** *wa* 1 kù-sal; r. VIII 5: 3 gín D. kg nu$_{11}$-za 1 **L.** *wa* 1 kù-sal; r. XI 1: 2 ½ gín D. kb nu$_{11}$-za [1 **L.**] [*w*]*a* 1 kù-sal; r. XV 15 and 18: 1 ma-na kb níĝ-sa$_{10}$ 1 **L.** kg en *áš-du* **L.**-*sù*; r. XVI 4 and 7: [1 **L.**] kg *Ib-rí-um áš-du* **L.**-*sù*; **16** o. XI 8: TAR[(+x)] kg *zi-ba-d*[*u*] 14 **L.** kg, 14: 6 gín D. kb *ni-zi-mu* nu$_{11}$-za 12 **L.** kb; r. VII 29 and r. VIII 4: 10 gín D. kb *ni-zi-mu* nu$_{11}$-za 2 **L.** kb … *wa ga-ma-tum* 17 **L.**; r. VIII 10 and 17: 12 gín D. kg *ni-zi-mu* nu$_{11}$-za 4 **L.** kg ... *wa ga-ma-tum* 5 **L.** kb; r. X 18: 4 gín D. kg nu$_{11}$-za 1 **L.** *wa* 1 kù-sal; **17** o. IX 15: 1 gín D. kg *zi-du ša-ga-tum* 1 **L.** kg; o. XI 21: [x] gín D. kg [*ba-d*]*u-u$_4$* [1] **L.**; o. XIII 23: 3 gín D. kg *ni-zi-mu zi-du* 3 *ša-ga-tum* 3 **L.**; o. XIV 17: 1 **L.** kg; o. XVI 2: 1 **L.** kg; o. XVIII 3: 1 **L.** kg; o. XIX 14: 7 gín D. kb *ba-du-u$_4$* 3 **L.**-*sù*; r. VIII 23: 10 gín D. an-na šub *si-in* 1 ma-na 10 gín D. a-gar$_5$-gar$_5$ kin$_5$-ak 3 **L.**; r. XII 9: 1 **L.** kg, 18: 1 **L.** kg; r. XVI 1: [ ] ⸢nu$_{11}$-za⸣ 1 **L.**; r. XXII 16: 1 **L.** kg; **18** o. IV 11 and 13: 17 gín D. a-gar$_5$-gar$_5$ *wa* 1 gín D. an-na kin$_5$-ak 1 **L.** *mu-lu-iš* 1 *li-im* **L.** *A-la-ga*$^{ki}$; o. XVI 5: 1 **L.** kg; r. VI 16: 1 **L.** kg; r. VII 3: 1 ma-na ŠA.PI 6 gín D. 2 NI an-na šub *si-in* 12 ma-na ŠÚ+ŠA gín D. a-gar$_5$-gar$_5$ kin$_5$-ak 40 **L.** kg, 13: ŠÚ+ŠA gín D. a-gar$_5$-gar$_5$ *wa* 2 gín D. 2 NI an-na kin$_5$-ak 1 **L.**; r. VIII 11: 18 gín D. a-gar$_5$-gar$_5$ *wa* 2 ½ gín D. an-na kin$_5$-ak 1 **L.**; r. IX 10: 17 a-gar$_5$-gar$_5$ 2 gín D. 3 NI an-na kin$_5$-ak 1 **L.**, 17: 10 lá-1 ma-na ŠÚ+ŠA 6 gín D. an-na šub *si-in* 75 ma-na TAR 6 a-gar$_5$-gar$_5$ kin$_5$-ak 2 *mi-at* 52 **L.** š[a-pi(?)] kb; r. X 9: [TA]R 8 ⸢a⸣-gar$_5$-gar$_5$ *wa* 2 4 NI an-na kin$_5$-ak 1 **L.**, 15: 90 lá-2 **L.** zú-ak lú *ma-lu-iš* **L.** ĝuruš-ĝuruš; r. XV 10: 6 an-na šub *si-in* ŠA.PI a-gar$_5$-gar$_5$ 1 banšur 1 **L.**-*sù*, 24: 1 kg *ni-zi-mu* nu$_{11}$-za 1 **L.**; r. XVI 34: 6 gín kb nu$_{11}$-za 2 **L.**; r. XVII 26: 2 **L.** kg; r. XVIII 6 and 9: 1 **L.** kg *Ib-rí-um áš-du* **L.**-*sù* sikil; **19** o. I 13: 2 **L.** kg, 25 and 27: 1 **L.** kg *Ib-rí-um* [*áš-*]*du* [1] **L.**[-*sù*] sikil; o. II 10: 1 kù-sal níĝ-ba en $^{d}$*Ba-tum-ma-du áš-t*[*i*] **L.**-*sù*; o. IX 21: 2 kù-sal … *áš-ti* 2 **L.** kg *al$_6$* tu-ra en; o. XI 23: 8 gín D. kg nu$_{11}$-za 2 **L.** *wa* 2 kù-sal; o. XIII 32: 53 gín D. 3 NI an-na šub *si-in* 6 ma-na ŠA.PI a-gar$_5$ kin$_5$-ak 20 **L.** kg; o. XIV 8: ŠÚ+ŠA a-gar$_5$-gar$_5$ 2 an-na 2 NI kin$_5$-ak 1 **L.**, 24: 19 a-gar$_5$ 2 ½ an-na kin$_5$-ak 1 **L.**; o. XV 8: 18 a-gar$_5$ 2 4 NI kin$_5$-ak 1 **L.**, 26: 18 a-gar$_5$ 2 ½ an-na kin$_5$-ak 1 **L.**; o. XVI 14: 18 a[-gar$_5$] [x an-na] kin$_5$-ak 1 **L.**; o. XVII 6: 18 a-gar$_5$ 2 4 NI an-na kin$_5$-ak 1 **L.**, 23: 18 a-gar$_5$ 2 an-na 4 NI kin$_5$-ak 1 **L.**; r. I 3: 3 ma-na TAR 3 gín D. 2 NI an-na 26 ma-na ŠA.PI gín D. a-gar$_5$-gar$_5$ kin$_5$-ak 80 **L.** kg, 13: ŠÚ+ŠA a-gar$_5$-gar$_5$ 2 gín D. 2 NI an-na kin$_5$-ak 1 **L.**; r. II 3: 19 gín D. a-gar$_5$-gar$_5$ 3? an-na kin$_5$-ak 1 **L.** 4 gín kg *zi-du-sù*, 20: 18 a-gar$_5$ *wa* 2 gín D. 4 NI an-na kin$_5$-ak 1 **L.**; r. III 10: 18 a-gar$_5$ 2 gín D. 4 NI an-na kin$_5$-ak 1 **L.**, 28: 18 a-gar$_5$ 2 gín D. 4 NI an-na kin$_5$-ak 1 **L.**; r. IV 15: 18 a-gar$_5$ 2 gín D. 4 NI an-na kin$_5$-ak 1 **L**; r. XII 22: 1 ½ gín D. an-na šub *si-in* 8 gín D. a-gar$_5$ kin$_5$-ak 1 **L.**; **20** o. XVII 19: 1 **L.** kg, 22: 1 **L.** kg; r. XII 20: 1 **L.** kg; 21 o. VII 12: 1 **L.** kg ⸢*ra*⸣-*ʾà*-[*tu*]*m*; o. XIV 7: 1 **L.** *ra-ʾà-tum* kg; o. XVI 8: 1 **L.** kg en; r. III 13: 12 gín D. kg *ni-zi-mu ga-ma-a-tum* **L.**, 16: 10 gín D. kb *zi-ba-du* **L.**; r. VI 9: TAR 7 gín D. kg *ni-zi-mu* nu$_{11}$-za **L.** guruš-guruš SA.ZA$_{x}^{ki}$; r. VII 14: 1 **L.** kg en; **22** r. III 8: ŠÚ+ŠA 4 gín D. an-na kin$_5$-ak 10 **L.**; **23** r. I 9: 1 gín D. kg *zi-du sa-ga-tum* 1 **L.** *Zi-ba-da*; r. III 5 and 8: 19 gín D. kg *ni-zi-mu* nu$_{11}$-za 1 **L.** kg *wa sa-ga-tum* 10 lá-1 **L.** gurus-guruš; **24** o. I 3: 2 gín D. kg nu$_{11}$-za 1 **L.**; o. II 3: 4 gín D. kg nu$_{11}$-za 1 **L.** *wa* 2 kù-sal; 25 o. VIII 2: 1 **L.** ḫul.

ĝír mar-tu *ba-du-u$_4$* **1** o. VI 11: 1 **L.** kbg; **3** o. IX 14: 1 **L.** kbg; **7** o. VI 16: 1 **L.** kbg; **14** o. XIII 7: 1 **L.** kb; r. XIII 18: 2 **L.** kg; 15 o. IV 12: 1 **L.** kb; o. XII 8: 1 **L.** kb; o. XIII 8: 3 **L.** kb; **16** r. VIII 14: 12 gín D. kg *ni-zi-mu* nu$_{11}$-za … 5 **L.** kg; 17 o. XVI 11: 2 **L.** kg, 13: 1 **L.** kbg; o. XVIII 9: 10 ma-na an-na kin$_5$-ak 3 *mi-at* **L.** zabar; o. XIX 4: 56 gín D. an-na šub *si-in* 5 ma-na ŠA.PI gín D. a-gar$_5$-gar$_5$ kin$_5$-ak 17 ĝír mar-tu zú *wa* 3 **L.** kbg; r. IV 3: 1 **L.** kb; **18** r. XIII 18: 1 **L.** kbg; **21** r. VIII 28: 1 **L.** kg.

ĝír mar-tu *ba-du-u*$_9$ **2** r. XI 2: 1 **L.** kg, 9: 1 **L.** kg; **6** o. VI 2: 20 **L.** kbg; r. X 18: 1 **L.** kbg; r. XV 5: 20 **L.** kbg; **8** r. VII x+1: 1 **L.** kg kb, 5': 1 **L.** kg kb; r. VIII 2': 1 **L.** kg, 6': 1 **L.** kg kb; r. XI 15': 1 *mi-at* **L.** kb; **9** o. V 1: 2 **L.** kb; r. XII 9: 6 **L.** kg, 13: 3 gín D. kb *ni-zi-mu zi-tum* 4 **L.** kb; **11** o. IX 3: 1 **L.** kb; **13** o. IV 6: 1 **L.** kb; **19** o. XVI 5: 1 ma-na TAR an-na šub *si-in* 12 ma-na a-gar$_5$-gar$_5$ kin$_5$-ak 40 **L.** kg, 21: 2 ma-na 15 gín an-na šub *si-in* 20 lá-2 ma-na a-gar$_5$-gar$_5$ kin$_5$-ak 60 **L.** kbg; r. II 27: 1 ma-na 52 [g]ín D. an-na šub *si-in* 15 ma-na a-gar$_5$-gar$_5$ kin$_5$-ak 50 **L.** kg; r. III 17: 2 ma-na 15 gín D. an-na šub *si-in* 20 lá-2 ma-na a-gar$_5$-gar$_5$ kin$_5$-ak 60 **L.** kbg, r. XV 10: 2 **L.** kg, 17: 1 **L.** kg.

ĝír mar-tu *ga-me*(*/mi*)*-ù* «m.-dagger with a (knob shaped like a) fungus» **19** o. XVII 15–16: 11 ma-na 15 gín D. an-na šub *si-in* 90 ma-na a-gar$_5$-gar$_5$ kin$_5$-ak 3 *mi-at* **L.** kb; r. IV 7–8: 13 ma-na TAR an-na šub *si-in* 1 *mi-at* 10 lá-2 ma-na a-gar$_5$-gar$_5$ kin$_5$-ak 3 *mi-at* 60 **L.**(*-mi-*) kb.

ĝír mar-tu ti «pointed m.-dagger» **1**(e) r. x+I 2': 1 **L.** kg.; r. XI 2: 2 **L.** kg; **3** o. IX 8: 1 **L.** kg; r. XIV 1: 2 **L.** kg; **4** o. VII 13: 1 **L.** kg; r. VI 4: 1 **L.** kg, 8: 1 **L.** kg; r. VII 2: 1 **L.** kg, 6: 1 **L.** kg; **5** o. XI 10: 1 **L.** kg; **6** o. VII 7: 1 **L.** kg, 12: 1 **L.** kg; r. X 13: 1 **L.** kg; r. XI 2: 1 **L.** kg; **7** o. IV 4: 10 lá-2 **L.** kg, 9: TAR kg *zi-du* 10 **L.** kg, 11: ŠA.PI gín D. kb nu$_{11}$-za 20 **L.** kb; o. V 11: 2 gín D. kb nu$_{11}$-za 1 **L.**; o. VI 8: 1 **L.** kg; **8** o. VIII 5: 20 **L.** kg; **9** o. XV 10: 2 **L.** kg, 16: 1 **L.** kg; r. XII 7: 2 **L.** kg; r. XVII 19: 1 **L.** kg; **12** o. IX 7: 1 **L.** kg; o. XI 17: 1 **L.** kg *wa ʾà-lum*; **13** r. III 1: [ ] 1 **L.** kg *wa* 1 *gú-li-lum* a-gar$_5$-gar$_5$ kg; **14** r. III 12: 1 gín D. kg nu$_{11}$-za [1] **L.**; r. XIII 16: 10 **L.** kg; **16** o. XI 8: TAR[(+x)] kg *zi-ba-d*[*u*] … 7 **L.** kg; r. III 26: 1 **L.** kg; r. VIII 1: 10 gín D. kb *ni-zi-mu* nu$_{11}$-za … 3 **L.** kb, 12: 12 gín D. kg *ni-zi-mu* nu$_{11}$-za … 4 **L.** kg; **17** o. XIX 19: 1 ma-na ŠA.PI gín D. an-na šub *si-in* 26 ma-na ŠA.PI a-gar$_5$-gar$_5$ kin$_5$-ak 1 *mi-at* **L.**; **18** o. XIV 25: 2 **L.** kg; r. VIII 1: 50 gín D. an-na šub *si-in* 6 ma-na ŠÚ+ŠA gín D. a-gar$_5$-gar$_5$ kin$_5$-ak 20 **L.** kg *ʾà-lum*; r. IX 1: 1 ma-na 52 ½ gín D. an-na šub *si-in* 15 ma-na a-gar$_5$-gar$_5$ kin$_5$-ak 50 **L.** kg; **19** o. XIV 15: 50 gín D. an-na šub *si-in* 6 ma-na ŠÚ+ŠA a-gar$_5$ kin$_5$-ak 20 **L.** kg *ʾà-lum*, 30: 1 [m]a-na TAR an-na šub *si-in* 12 ma-na a-gar$_5$-gar$_5$ kin$_5$-ak 40 **L.** kg; r. I 20: 50 gín D. an-na šub *si-in* 6 ma-na ŠÚ+ŠA gín D. a-gar$_5$-gar$_5$ kin$_5$-ak 20 **L.** kg *ʾà-lum*; r. II 10: 3 ma-na ŠÚ+ŠA gín D. an-na šub *si-in* 34 ma-na a-gar$_5$-gar$_5$ kin$_5$-ak 90 **L.** kg; r. XIV 9: 1 **L.** kg; r. XV 1: 2 **L.** kg; **20** o. XII 4: 1 **L.** kg; **25** o. III 6: 1 **L.** kb.

ĝír mar-tu zú-ak «serrated dagger» **5** o. I 8; o. IX 3; 11 o. III 5: 10 lá-3 **L.**; **14** o. XVI 17: 5 **L.**; **17** o. XVIII 18: 1 ma-na ŠA.PI gín an-na šub *si-in* kin$_5$-ak 1 *mi-at* **L.**; **18** o. IV 6: 3 ma-na ŠÚ+ŠA gín D. an-na šub *si-in* 56 ma-na ŠA.PI gín D. a-gar$_5$-gar$_5$ kin$_5$-ak 2 *mi-at* **L.**; r. X 13: 90 lá-2 **L.** lú *ma-lu-iš* ĝír mar-tu ĝuruš-ĝuruš; **19** o. XVIII 1; r. IV 20.

ĝír mar-tu zú **2** o. XV 15: 10 lá-1 **L.**; **3** o. VIII 19: 30 **L.**; **4** r. VI 13: 1 **L.** kg; **6** r. XV 4: 20 **L.**; **17** o. XIII 2: 1 **L.** kg; o. XIV 6: 1 **L.** kg; o. XVI 12: 1 **L.** kg; o. XIX 2: 56 gín D. an-na šub *si-in* 5 ma-na ŠA.PI gín D. a-gar$_5$-gar$_5$ kin$_5$-ak 17 **L.** *wa* 3 ĝír mar-tu *ba-du-u*$_4$ kbg; r. VII 20: 2 NI gín D. kg *ni-zi-mu* nu$_{11}$-za *ša-ga-ti* 1 **L.**

ĝír mar-tu zú A.LAGAB×ḪAL **3** r. III 10.

ĝír mar-tu zú AN.LAGAB×A **19** o. XV 15: TAR an-na šub *si-in* 3 ma-na TAR 5 a-gar$_5$ kin$_5$-ak 12 **L.**, 30: 10 lá-2 **L.** kg.

ĝír mar-tu zú AN.LAGAB×AN **14** r. XIII 17.

ĝír mar-tu zú LAGAB×A **5** r. III 5; **16** o. XI 10: TAR[(+x)] kg *zi-ba-d*[*u*] … 17 **L.** kg.

ĝír mar-tu zú LAGAB×AN **9** r. XII 8; r. XV 2; **18** r. XVI 22: 1 **L.** kg.

ĝír mar-tu zú LAGAB×AN.A **8** o. XIV 2; r. VI 9'.

ĝír-kun «pendant (carrying the dagger)» **1** o. V 8: 10 ma-na kb kin$_5$-ak 17 íb-lá 17 *si-ti-tum* 17 **L.**; o. VII 20: TAR kb [*ni*]*-zi-mu* 1 íb-lá [1] *si-ti*[*-tum* 1 **L.**]; o. IX 11: ŠÚ+ŠA gín D. kg 1 íb-lá 1 *si-ti-tum* 1 **L.**; r. VI 8: TAR kg 1 íb-lá **L.**; **4** o. I 6: 3 ma-na 7 gín D. kb *ni-zi-mu* 20 íb-lá *si-ti-tum* **L.**; o. IX 19: 7 íb-lá *si-ti-tum* **L.**; r. I 8: 3 íb-lá *si-ti-tum* **L.**; r. XIII 3: 4 íb-lá *si-ti-tum* **L.**; **5** o. V 16: 10 gín D. kb *ni-zi-mu* 24 íb-lá **L.**; **6** o. VI 5: 13 ma-na ŠÚ+ŠA gín D. kb kin$_5$-ak 20 íb-lá 20 **L.** ĜÁ×LÁ ŠA.PI; o. XII 5: 50 gín D. kb 1 íb-lá *si-ti-tum* **L.**; r. VII 8: 1 ma-na kb 1 íb-lá 1 *si-ti-tum* 1 **L.**, 21: ŠA.PI kb 1 íb-lá *si-ti-tum* **L.** kb maš-maš kg; r. VIII 4: ŠA.PI gín D. kb 1 íb-lá *si-ti-tum* **L.** maš-maš kg, 8: ŠA.PI gín D. kb 1 íb-lá 1 **L.**; **7** o. VIII 5: TAR kb 1 íb-lá 1 *si-ti-tum* 1 **L.**; **9** r. XV 12: TAR kb URI 1 íb-lá 1 **L.**; **10** o. IX 10: 13 m[a-]n[a] šú[+ŠA gí]n [D.] kb kin$_5$-ak 20 íb-lá 20 **L.**; **11** o. VIII 1: [TAR kg 1 íb-lá] 1 *si-ti-tum* 1 **L.**; r. VII 7: ŠA.PI gín D. kb 1 íb-lá 1 **L.**; **12** r. I 1: ŠA.PI gín D. kg 1 íb-lá 1 *si-ti-tum* 1 **L.**; **13** o. I 9: [x m]a-na [kb x í]b-lá [x *si-*]*ti-tum* [**L.** gí]r-kun, 18: [š]a-pi gín D. kb [1 íb-lá 1] *si-ti-tum* 1 **L.**; o. II 7: 2 ma-na kb 2 íb-lá 2 *si-ti-tum* 2 **L.**, 15: 1 ma-na kb 1 íb-lá 1 *si-ti-tum* 1 **L.**; o. XI 21: 10 gín D. kb 1 **L.**; r. IX 6: TAR kg 1 íb-lá 1 *si-ti-tum* 1 **L.**; **14** o. VII 2: TAR kb URI 1 íb-lá 1 **L.** kg, 15: ŠA.PI gín D. kg 1 íb-lá 1 **L.**; r. VIII 17: ŠA.PI gín D. kg 1 íb-lá 1 **L.**; r. VIII 13: [TAR kg 1 íb-lá 1 **L.**]; r. XIII 23: 1 ma-na 16 kb *ni-zi-mu* URI 10 lá-2 íb-lá 5 **L.** kb maš-maš; **15** o. III 10: ŠA.PI gín D. kb 1 íb-lá 1 **L.**; o. XIII 18: TAR [k]b 1 íb[-lá] 1 **L.**; r. VI 1: TAR kb 1 ⸢íb⸣-lá 1 *si-ti-tum* 1 **L.**; **16** o. VIII 2: 6 gín D. kb *ni-zi-mu* 7 íb-lá 5 **L.** lú URI lú kg; o. X 16: TAR an-na SUD.PA.SIKIL 5 íb-lá 20 **L.** zabar 35 á-MUŠEN zabar; o. XIII 21: TAR kb 1 íb-lá 1 *si-ti-tum* 1 **L.**; r. IX 18: 1 gín D. kg 1 íb-lá 1 *si-ti-tum* 1 **L.**; **17** o. IV 16: [ ] lul-gu-ak 1 íb-lá 1 **L.**; o. XI 13: 2 gín D. kg *ni-zi-mu* 1 íb-lá 1 *si-ti-tum* 1 **L.**, 16: 12 gín D. kb 1 íb-lá 1 **L.**; o. XII 12: ŠA.PI gín D. kb 1 íb-lá 1 **L.**; o. XIV 14: 2 ma-na kg 1 íb-lá 1 *si-ti-tum* 1 **L.** 1 dib; r. XII 16: [x ma-na kg x í]b-lá [x *si-t*]*i-*[*tu*]*m* [x] **L.**; r. XIII 3: 3 ma-na kg kin$_5$-ak 6 íb-lá 6 *si-ti-tum* 6 **L.**, 18: TAR kb kin$_5$-ak 1 íb-lá 1 *si-ti-tum* 1 **L.**; r. XXI 26: 2 ma-na kg kin$_5$-ak 2 íb-lá 2 *si-ti-tum* 2 **L.**; **18** o. X 18: [10 gín D. kg] 1 íb-lá 1 *si-ti-tum* 1 **L.**; o. XI 5: 7 gín D. kb *ni-zi-mu* 1 íb-lá

1 **L.** kb, 14: 8 gín D. kb *ni-zi-mu* 1 íb-lá 1 **L.**; r. XII 26: 1 ma-na kg 1 íb-lá 1 *si-ti-tum* 1 **L.**; **19** o. VII 4: TAR kb 1 íb-lá 1 *si-ti-tum* 1 **L.**, 24: TAR kg 1 íb-lá 1 *si-ti-tum* 1 **L.**; r. XIII 11: TAR kb URI 1 íb-lá 1 **L.**; r. XIV 2: TAR kg 1 íb-lá 1 *si-ti-tum* 1 **L.**, 7: ŠA.PI gín D. kb 1 íb-lá 1 **L.**, ŠA.PI gín D. kb 1 íb-lá 1 **L.**; r. XVII 25: 1 ma-na ŠA.PI 2 gín D. kg 1 íb-lá 1 *si-ti-tum* 1 **L.** 1 ĜIŠ-sal; r. XVIII 5: 2 ma-na kg 2 íb-lá 2 **L.**; **20** o. XV 6: 1 ma-na ŠÚ+ŠA gín D. kg kin$_{5}$-ak 1 íb-lá 1 *si-ti-tum* 1 **L.** ŠÚ+ŠA gín D.; o. XVI 11: 1 íb-lá 1 *si-ti-tum* 1 **L.** TAR kg sikil, 16: TAR kg 1 íb-lá 1 *si-ti-tum* 1 **L.** sikil, 18: 8 gín D. kb 1 íb-lá 1 *si-ti-tum* 1 **L.** sikil; o. XVII 6: ŠA.PI gín D. kb 1 íb-lá 1 **L.**; r. VII 1: [TA]R [kg] 1 íb-lá 1 *si-ti-tum* 1 **L.** *Kùn-da-ba-an*; r. X 13: ŠA.PI kb 1 íb-lá 1 **L.**; r. XII 14: ŠA.PI kb 1 íb-lá [1] **L.**; **21** o. II 19: [ ] ⸢x-x⸣ [1 í]b-lá 1 **L.**; o. III 9: TAR kg 1 íb-lá 1 *si-ti-tum* 1 **L.**; o. VII 10: 2 ma-na kg kin$_{5}$-ak 1 dib 1 íb-lá 1 *si-ti-tum* 1 **L.**; o. XIV 1: [2 ma-na kg] 1 íb-lá 1 *si-ti-tum* 1 **L.** 1 dib; o. XV 18: ŠA.PI gín D. kb 1 íb-lá 1 *si-ti-tum* 1 **L.**; o. XVII 22: 26 ma-na kb kin$_{5}$-ak 40 íb-lá 40 **L.**; r. V 14: TAR 2 kb *ni-zi-mu* 16 íb-lá 6 **L.** *wa* 1 á-MUŠEN kb; r. VIII 15: TAR kg 1 íb-lá 1 *si-ti-tum* 1 **L.**; r. IX 7: [ ] [1? í]b-lá [1] **L.**; r, XII 11: [ ] á-MUŠEN *wa* 2 **L.** zabar; **23** o. VIII 7: 1 gín D. kg *ni-zi-mu* nu$_{11}$-za 1 íb-lá 1 **L.**; o. IX 1: 5 gín D. kg *ni-zi-mu* maš-maš 4 íb-lá 1 **L.** maš-maš; r. VII 3: 1 ma-na kg 2 íb-lá 2 *si-ti-a-tum* 2 **L.**

ĝiš «wood, grove» **6** o. II 8: (silver) níĝ-ba ḫúb-ki *in* ud *a-*<*lu*->*nu* **L.** ba:tuš; **16** r. XVII 6: (silver) níĝ-ba ḫúb-ki ba:tuš *a-lu-nu* **L.**

ugula ĝiš **4** r. I 6: (silver) **L.** E[N-]⸢x-x⸣-*tum* 3 íb-lá *si-ti-tum* ĝír-kun lú ĝuruš-ĝuruš.

ĜIŠ-ád «buckthorn; myrtle» **2** r. VI 3; **5** o. II 2: ĜIŠ-ti-ḪAR ; **7** o. IX 7; **15** o. VI 9.

(*LLE*,I no. 430: ĜIŠ-ád(ĜÍR-*gunû*) = *a-da-tum*. Civil 2008, p. 104 refers to Akkadian *eddetu*, "boxthorn", adding: "but more pertinent to the present context is $^{\text{ĝiš šim}}$ád = *asu*, 'myrtle'")

ĜIŠ-alam «statue» **17** r. XVII 7: [ ] kin$_{5}$-ak 1 *mu-rúm wa* 1 *gúm-a-nu* ⸢*wa*⸣ 2 **L.** *su-da$_{5}$-lik* en.

ĜIŠ-asari «tray» **3** o. III 17: 6 ĜIŠ-kak-ĜIŠ-kak lú **L.** kaskal en; **14** o. V 20: 11 *ra-ʾà-tum* … LAGAB×UD-LAGAB×UD kin$_{5}$-ak **L.** sagi; r. VI 19: 1 ma-na 54 gín D. a-gar$_{5}$-g[ar$_{5}$] nu$_{11}$-za 1 **L.**; **18** o. VII 3: 15 ĜIŠ-kak-ĜIŠ-kak *ša-ti* 5 kaskal ⸢en⸣; **20** o. XVI 1: 3 gín D. an-na [ ] 1 **L.**, 6: 2 gín D. kg *ʾa$_{5}$-na-gu* 1 **L.** *maš-ar-tum* en.

asari **16** r. V 6: 6 ĜIŠ-kak-ĜIŠ-kak lú 2 **L.** kaskal en.

ĜIŠ-ban «bow» **14** o. VIII 14: 9 gín D. kg *ni-zi-mu* 4 **L.** 2 ĜIŠ-gígir-II en; **15** o. IX 19: 10 gín D. kg *ni-zi-mu* nu$_{11}$-za 2 **L.** ĜIŠ-gígir-II lú *ra-ʾà-tum ša-ti* en; **19** o. XIII 1: 6 gín D. kg *ni-zi-mu* nu$_{11}$-za 2 ĜIŠ-gígir-II; **20** r. III 28: TAR kg nu$_{11}$-za 3 **L.**

ĜIŠ-banšur «table» **1**(c) r x+I 2': **L.** $^{d}$*Ku-ra*; **2** o. VI 10: 2 gín D. kg maš-maš 1 **L.** *wa* 1 kù-sal; **3** o. XI 5: 2 gín D. kb maš-maš 1 **L.**; **4** o. IV 15: 12 gín D. kb nu$_{11}$-za!(KUR) 3 **L.** 3 ĝír mar-tu; r. V 13: 2 **L.** kg; **5** o. XII 17: 3 ma-na kb nu$_{11}$-za 1 **L.**; r. V 10: 1 ma-na ŠÚ+ŠA 5 gín D. kb nu$_{11}$-za 1 **L.**; r. VIII 16; **6** o. VIII 1: 5 gín D. kb nu$_{11}$-za 1 **L.**; o. XI 13: 50 gín D. kb nu$_{11}$-za 1 **L.** *wa* 1 *ḫa-bù*; r. II 19: maš-maš 1 **L.**; r. III 10: 11 gín D. kb 6 ĜIŠ-kak-ĜIŠ-kak 2 **L.**; r. XI 13: 1 **L.** kg; r. XVII 3: 3 an-na 1 **L.**; r. IV 3: ½ gín D. [kb *ʾa$_{5}$-na-gu* 1 **L.**], 13: ½ g[ín] D. kb *ʾa$_{5}$-na-gu* 1 **L.**, 22: ½ gín D. kb *ʾa$_{5}$-na-gu* 1 **L.**; **10** o. II 8: 2 ma-na kb nu$_{11}$-za 1 **L.**, 8: ŠÚ+ŠA gín D. kg nu$_{11}$-za 1 saĝ ⸢lu$_{5}$⸣ 1 **L.**; o. XIII 11: 5 gín D. kb maš-maš 1 **L.** *wa* nu$_{11}$-za 1 ĝír mar-tu; r. X 12: 2 gín D. kg maš-maš 1 **L.** *wa* [x] kù-sal; **11** r. IV 24: 1 gín D. kb *ʾa$_{5}$-na-gu* 1 **L.**; r. VI 5: 1 gín D. kb *ʾa$_{5}$-na-gu* 1 **L.**; **14** r. VI 1: 50 gín D. kb nu$_{11}$-za 1 **L.** maḫ; r. VIII 3: [4 gín D. kg kin$_{5}$-ak 1 **L.** *wa*] 1 kù-sal; **15** o. II 3: 3 ½ kg *ʾa$_{5}$-na-gu* 1 **L.** *wa* 1 kù-sal; r. VII 16: 3 gín D. kg *ʾa$_{5}$-na-gu* 1 **L.** *wa* 1 kù-sal; r. XIII 22: 5 gín D. kg *ʾa$_{5}$-na-gu* 1 **L.** *wa* 1 kù-sal sikil *al$_{6}$* ama-gal en.

banšur **17** r. XX 32: 4 ½ kg *ʾa$_{5}$-na-gu* 2 **L.** *maš-ar-da Ib-rí-um* <*I*->*bí-zi-kir*; **18** r. XV 9: 6 an-na šub *si-in* ŠA.PI a-gar$_{5}$-gar$_{5}$ 1 **L.** 1 ĝír mar-tu-*sù*; **19** o. VIII 9: [3 gín D. kg] *wa* 2 gín D. kb ì-na-sum 1 **L.** *wa* 1 kù-sal ; r. X 23: 3 gín D. kg *ʾa$_{5}$-na-gu* 1 *wa* 1 kù-sal.

ĜIŠ-*ba-rí-zú* (a kind of picket) **21** r. II 6: 1 **L.** ĜIŠ. GAM.GAM.GAM.

ĜIŠ-bar-ús «goad» **7** o. XIV 2: [x] g[ín D. kb] *ni-zi-mu* maš-maš **L.**; o. XV 4: 6 *zú-zú-ba-tum* **L.** zú-ak 2 ĜIŠ-gígir-II; **14** o. IX 5: 2 NI gín D. kg *ni-zi-mu ma-wa-ù* 2 **L.** ĜIŠ-gígir-II e[n]; 14 r. VII 26: 2 gín D. an-na šub *si-in* 16 gín D. a-⸢gar$_{5}$⸣-gar$_{5}$ kin$_{5}$-ak **L.** en; **16** r. III 22: 2 gín D. kg *ni-zi-mu ma-wa-lu* **L.** ĜIŠ-gígir-II en; **17** r. II 5: 2 NI gín D. kg *ni-zi-mu ma-wa-lu* **L.**; r. V 13; r. XX 15; **18** r. I 20: 1 gín D. kg *wa* 1 gín D. kb *ni-zi-mu ma-wa-*⸢*lu*⸣ **L.** ĜIŠ-gígir-II en; **19** r. XVII 4: ĜIŠ-*šè-bir$_{5}$-gi-nu* **L.**

bar-ús **18** r. VI 3: 4 gín D. an-na šub *si-in* ŠÚ+ŠA 6 a-gar$_{5}$-gar$_{5}$ kin$_{5}$-ak **L.** en.

bar:ús **17** r. IX 22: 3 NI kb 1 **L.** lú dur 2 si-dù en *wa ma-lik-tum*.

ĜIŠ-du «foot ring (?)» **2** o. III 9: 16 gín D. kb 2 **L.**; **4** o. XI 7: TAR kb 2 **L.**, 14: ŠA.PI 2 gín D. kg 2 **L.**; **6** o. XIV 4: 10 gín D. kb 2 **L.**; **7** o. II 15: 10 gín D. kb ⸢2⸣ *ti-gi-na* 2 **L.**; **13** r. XI 1: TAR kb 2 *t*[*i-gi-na*] 2 **L.**; **15** o. X 18: 14 gín D. kg 2 *ti-gi-na* 2 **L.** 1 KA-*ḫu-a-tum*; r. XI 12: 2 gín D. kg *ni-zi-mu* 2 **L.**; **18** o. II 9: 14 gín D. kg 2 *gú-li-lum wa* 2 *ti-gi-na wa* 2 **L.**, 18: 14 gín D. kg 2 *gú-li-lum wa* 2 *ti-gi-na wa* 2 **L.**; o. X 12: 2 gín D. kg *ni-zi-mu* 2 ; o. XVII 3: 1 ma-na TAR kg kin$_{5}$-ak … 2 , 5: TAR kb 2 **L.**; o. XVIII 5: 8 gín D. kg *ni-zi-mu* 4 *ti-gi-na* 4 **L.** 4 ĝeštu$_{x}$-lá 2 kù-sal; **20** o. II 22: ŠÚ+ŠA gín D. kb 2 **L.**; o. XV 19: [ ] 2 **L.**; **21** r. VIII 24: 5 gín D. kg *ni-zi-mu* 2 **L.**

ĜIŠ.DUG.DU «to arrive, to come back; arrival» **4** o. IX 4: (silver) *Na-gàr*$^{ki}$ **L.** *Ib-rí-um*; **5** r. XIII 16: 2 *bu*-DI 2 *ti-ša-na* níĝ-ba $^{d}$*Ga-na-na* **L.** maḫ; **6** r. XIV 4: 2 *bu*-DI 2 *ti-ša-na* níĝ-ba $^{d}$*Ga-na-na* **L.** maḫ; **7** r. XIV 6: 4 *ti-ša-nu* 2 *bu*-DI níĝ-ba $^{d}$*Ga-na-na in* ud **L.** maḫ; **10** o. VII 19: (silver) níĝ-ba *Bù-sum Ma-rí*$^{ki}$ **L.** izi-ĝar; **11** r. IV 5: [silver] níĝ-ba *Bù-za-lum Am$_{6}$-mu-tum Ma-rí*$^{ki}$ **L.** izi-ĝar; **12** r. V 17: (silver) níĝ-ba *Ib-gi-tum Ma-rí*$^{ki}$ **L.** izi-ĝar; **14** r. VII 14: [2 *b*]*u*-DI *wa* 4 *ti-ša-nu* níĝ-ba $^{d}$*Ga-na-na* **L.** maḫ; **20** r. X 10: *in* **L.** maḫ; **20** r. X 10: 2 *bu*-DI 4 *ti-ša-nu* [níĝ-ba]

[$^{d}$*Ga-na-na*] *in* **L.** maḫ; **21** r. III 6: 2 *bu*-DI 4 še-šu-tag níĝ-ba $^{d}$*Ga-na-na* **L.** maḫ.

ĜIŠ.GAM.GAM «wheel» **13** o. III 4: TAR 2 gín D. kg nu$_{11}$-za 2 **L.**; **16** o. VI 9: ŠÚ+ŠA 7 gín D. kg nu$_{11}$-za 2 **L.**; **18** r. I 1: 2 gín D. kg *ni-zi-mu* nu$_{11}$-za 2 **L.** ĜIŠ-gígir-II; r. XVII 13: 10 kg *ni-zi-mu* nu$_{11}$-za 2 **L.** ĜIŠ-gígir-II *ra-ʾà-tum*; **21** o. X 13: 4 gín D. kg *ni-zi-mu* nu$_{11}$-za 2 **L.** ĜIŠ-gígir-II; o. XIII 15: 1 ma-na kg kin$_5$-ak 2 níĝ-anše-ak 4 kù-sal *wa* nu$_{11}$-za 2 ĜIŠ-gígir-II.

ĜIŠ.GAM.GAM.GAM **21** r. II 6: 1 ĜIŠ-*ba-rí-zú* **L.**

ĜIŠ.GAM-ĜIŠ.GAM **18** r. XIV 1: TAR kg nu$_{11}$-za 2 **L.** ĜIŠ-gígir-II;

ĜIŠ-gígir-II «two wheels chariot» **2** o. XIII 11: ĜIŠ-sur$_x$ **L.** en; **3** o. III 4: 1 zag *Ib-rí-um*; o. XIII 2: [1 za]g? **L.** en *Ì-ra-ar*$^{ki}$; r. IX 2: 2 zag 2 **L.** *Ib-rí-um wa* en *Bur-ma-an*$^{ki}$; **4** o. V 18: 1 zag ; o. XIII 9: 1 zag *Ib-rí-um*; r. I 3: 3 *zú-zú-ba-tum* **L.** *Ib-rí-um*; r. X 4: 6 *zú-zú-ba-tum* 2 **L.** en; **5** r. VIII 9: 1 zag *I-nu-ud-da-mu Kak-mi-um*$^{ki}$; **6** o. IX 13: 1 zag *Ib-rí-um*, 18: 1 zag en *Kab-lu$_5$-ul*$^{ki}$; r. V 19: 1 zag . *Ib-rí-um*; r. XVI 3: 2 ĜIŠ-zú 2 **L.** *Ib-rí-um*, 7: 2 ĜIŠ-zú **L.** en; r. XVII 11: 2 ĜIŠ-zú 1 **L.** en *Kab-lu$_5$-ul*$^{ki}$; **7** o. XIV 7: maš-maš-*sù* 2 **L.** en; o. XV 6: 6 *zú-zú-ba-tum* ĜIŠ-bar-ús zú-ak 2 **L.** en; **9** r. XVII 16: [ ] 1 **L.** *Ib-rí-um*; **10** o. XII 5: 1 zag 1 . *Ba-ga-ma*; o. XIII 7: 1 zag 1 *Ib-rí-um*; o. XI 7: 1 ĜIŠ-zú **L.** *Ib-rí-um*; r. XII 6: 6 bulug$_4$-bulug$_4$ gibil lú **L.**; **13** o. III 12: 1 ĜIŠ-zú **L.** en; o. VI 11: 1 zag *I-bí-zi-kir* dumu-nita *Ib-rí-um*; o. XV 5: 3 ĜIŠ-zú 3 **L.** en *wa* ama-gal-*sù wa Ib-rí-[u]m*, 13: 2 zag 2 **L.** ama-gal en *wa Ib-rí-um*; **14** o. VIII 15: 4 ĜIŠ-ban 2 **L.** en, 22: 2 zag 2 ; o. IX 6: 2 ĜIŠ-bar-ús **L.** e[n]; **15** o. VIII 13: 1 zag **L.** *I-bí-zi-kir* dumu-nita *Ib-rí-um*; o. IX 20: 2 ĜIŠ-ban **L.** lú *ra-ʾà-tum ša-ti* en; o. XV 17: 3 gín D. kb nu$_{11}$-za 2 **L.** gibil *Ib-rí-um*; **16** o. VI 17: 1 ĜIŠ-zú 1 **L.**; r. III 23: ĜIŠ-bar-ús **L.** en; r. XV 2: 3 *zú-zú-ba-tum* **L.** *Wa-na*; **17** o. XV 2: 1 zag **L.** … *Íl-ba-da-mu* en *Kak-mi-um*$^{ki}$; r. I 14: 2 zag 2 **L.** … *Ib-rí-um*; **18** r. I 1: 2 ĜIŠ.GAM.GAM **L.** *Ib-rí-um*, 21: ĜIŠ-bar-ús **L.** en; r. V 14: 3 *zú-zú-ba-tum Ib-rí-um*; r. XIV 1: 2 ĜIŠ.GAM-ĜIŠ.GAM **L.**, 13: 1 kg nu$_{11}$-za 1 zag **L.** en *Ì-mar*$^{ki}$; r. XVII 14: 2 ĜIŠ.GAM.GAM **L.** *ra-ʾà-tum* en; **19** o. VII 11: 2 zag **L.**, 15: 2 ĜIŠ-zú **L.** zú-ak *Ib-rí-um wa I-bi-zi-kir* dumu-nita-*sù*; o. X 16: 1 zag **L.** *Ba-ga-ma*; o. XIII 2: 2 ĜIŠ-ban *Ib-rí-um*; r. XI 24: 1 ma-na 11 gín D. kg nu$_{11}$-za 1 **L.** 1 ĝuruš ugula sur$_x$-BAR.AN 4 BAR.AN-BAR.AN; r. XII 8: ŠÚ+ŠA gín D. an-na šub *si-in* <x a-gar$_5$-gar$_5$> 1 ĜIŠ-gu-kak-gíd 1 *za-ḫa-da* ĜIŠ-kak-ĜIŠ-kak 4 *zi-da-nu* ĜIŠ-sal lú $^{d}$*Á-la Gú-šè-bù*$^{ki}$; **20** o. IX 27: [ ] **L.** gibil *Ib-rí-um*; r. IV 4: 1 zag **L.**; r. XI 30: 1 zag **L.** *Da-bí-da-mu* dumu-nita en *Bur-ma-an*$^{ki}$; **21** o. III 21: […] **L.** *I-bi-zi-kir*; o. VII 15: 3 *z[ú-]zú-b[a-]tum* **L.** *Ib-rí-um* šu-mu-tak$_4$ é $^{dʾ}$*À-da*; o. X 14: 2 ĜIŠ.GA[M.GAM] **L.** en; o. XIII 16: 2 ĜIŠ.GAM.GAM ĜIŠ-gígir-sum «wagon» **17** o. XVII 22: 10 gín D. kb gur$_8$ **L.** šu-mu-tak$_4$ túg-túg.

ĜIŠ-gu-kak-gíd «spearhead; goad» **4** r. XIV 4: 50 ma-na zabar kin$_5$-ak 5 *mi-at* **L.**, 9: 5 ma-na TAR 3 3 NI an-na kin$_5$-ak [ ] **L.**; **6** r. XV 8: 11 ma-na 6 gín D. an-na kin$_5$-ak 1 *li-im* **L.** zabar; **7** r. VII 8; r. XVI 4; **8** r. VI 5': 7 *mi-at* 80 L. (<ĜIŠ->); 9 r. XVI 11; **12** o. IX 5: 11 ma-na 10 gín D. an-na kin$_5$-ak 1 *li-im* **L.** zabar; **14** o. XV 20: 3 gín D. an-na šub *s[i-]in* 2 **L.** en; **15** o. II 22: 1 *gù-li-lum a-li-iš* **L.**; **19** o. IV 22: 20 lá-1 ma-na ŠÚ+ŠA 7 gín D. an-na šub *si-in* 1 *mi-at* 50 ma-na a-gar$_5$-gar$_5$ kin$_5$-ak 1 *li-im* . zabar; o. V 5: 1 gín D. 6 NI an-na šub *si-in* 9 gín D. a-gar$_5$-gar$_5$ 1 **L.**; r. XII 3: ŠÚ+ŠA gín D. an-na šub *si-in* <x a-gar$_5$-gar$_5$> 1 **L.**; **20** o. I 14: 57 ma-na ŠÚ+ŠA gín D. an-na šub-šub *si-in* 4 *mi-at* 50 ⌜ma⌝-na a-gar$_5$[-gar$_5$] kin$_5$-ak 3 *li-im* **L.** zabar; **21** o. II 15: 1 ma-na kg nu$_{11}$-za 1 **L.** *ap* [ ]; **25** r. III 5: [ ] l[ú] *D[u-si]* ugula *Ib-al$_6$*$^{ki}$ *in* ud **L.** šu-mu-tak$_4$.

ĜIŠ-gu-kak-šub **12** o. XI 1: 3 ½ gín D. an-na šub *si-in* 1 **L.** sur$_x$-BAR.AN; **13** o. III 20: 3 gín D. an-na šub *si-in* 1 **L.**; **14** o. XIII 19: [x] gí[n] D. a-gar$_5$-gar$_5$ lul-gu-ak 4 .; **17** r. II 29: 5 gín D. kg *ni-zi-mu* nu$_{11}$-za *si-gi* 1 **L.** en; r. XXII 9: 2 **L.**

ĜIŠ-ĝeštin «(bead in a shape of a) grape» **2** r. VI 17: ŠA.PI 3 gín D. kg kin$_5$-ak 1 dib lú

ĜIŠ-ĝeštu$_x$-lá see ĝeštu$_x$-lá.

ĜIŠ-ĝidru «stick, sceptre» **6** o. XIII 13: 5 gín D. kb nu$_{11}$-za 1 saĝ lu$_5$ **L.**; **15** o. V 10: 3 gín D. kg 2 **L.** 2 šu-dub; **18** o. III 9: ŠÚ+ŠA 3 gín D. kg 1 an-zam$_x$ **L.** *ma-lik-tum*; **22** r. VI 8: 7 gín D. kg nu$_{11}$-za 1

ĜIŠ-ĝidru-ĜIŠ-ĝidru **15** r. XIV 27: 4 sur$_x$-lu$_x$ lú *al$_6$* **L.** ĜIŠ-uštin en; **23** o. I 2: 1 dib maḫ lú **L.** in-na-sum $^{dʾ}$*À-da Ḫa-lab$_x$*$^{ki}$ *in* AMA-*ra*.

ĜIŠ-kak «peg»

ĜIŠ-kak-ĜIŠ-kak **3** o. III 16; **6** r. III 9: 11 gín D. kb 6 **L.** 2 ĜIŠ-banšur; **16** r. V 5: 3 gín D. an-na šub *si-in* 17 gín D. a-gar$_5$-gar$_5$ kin$_5$-ak 6 **L.** lú 2 asari kaskal en; **17** o. XX 23: 10 gín D. an-na šub *si-in* 10 lá-2 ma-na a-gar$_5$-gar$_5$ kin$_5$-ak 6 **L.** eme gud-si-dili; **18** o. VII 1: TAR 6 gín D. kb kin$_5$-ak 15 **L.** *ša-ti* 5 ĜIŠ-asari kaskal ⌜en⌝; **19** r. XII 5: ŠÚ+ŠA gín D. an-na šub *si-in* <x a-gar$_5$-gar$_5$> …

ĜIŠ-kiri$_6$ «garden» **3** o. XIII 8: (silver) EN-*mar Kak-mi-um*$^{ki}$ lú **L.**; **5** o. VII 1: $^{d}$<*Iš-*>*šára* ; r. IX 15: (silver) lú **L.** *Ba-ga-ma* šu-ba$_4$-ti; r. XI 9: (silver) lú **L.** *in Am$_6$-ma-šu*$^{ki}$ [šu]-ba$_4$-ti; **8** o. XII 3: (silver) lú **L.** *Kak-mi-um*$^{ki}$; r. IV 7': (silver) lú **L.** *I-lum-na-im* šu-ba$_4$-ti; **10** o. I 15: (silver) lú **L.** *Kak-mi-um*$^{ki}$; o. VII 4: lú **L.** *Kak-mi-um*$^{ki}$; **11** r. IV 15: (silver) lú **L.**

ĜIŠ-ma-dul$_{10}$ «beam (of the chariot)» **4** o. XII 10; **5** o. III 18; **13** o. XVII 11; **19** r. V 15.

ĜIŠ-MUNŠUB **17** r. I 30: 2 gín D. kb *ni-zi-mu* nu$_{11}$-⌜za⌝ 1 *za-⌜ḫa⌝-d[a] wa* 1 **L.**

(*LLE*,I no. 483: ĜIŠ-MUNŠUB = *uš-du-bù*)

ĜIŠ-nu-kiri$_6$ «gardener» **3** o. VII 11: (silver) lú **L.** DU.DU *al$_6$* dumu-nita *Ru$_{12}$-zi-da-mu Ma-nu-wa-ad*$^{ki}$; **12** o. V 6: (silver) lú **L.** *Zi-la-da-mu* ugula kas$_4$ šu-ba$_4$-ti; **13** o. III 15: (silver) lú **L.** *Du-bí* šu-ba$_4$-ti; o. IV 10: (silver) lú **L.** *Ti-ti-nu wa Gú-zi* šu-ba$_4$-ti *in A-te-na-ad*$^{ki}$; **14** o. III 1: (silver) lú **L.** *Zi-la-da-mu* šu-ba$_4$-ti; **15** o. XIV 20: (silver) lú **L.** *A-ru$_{12}$-ga-du*$^{ki}$; **16** r. VI 16: (silver) lú **L.** *Za-a-ti* šu-ba$_4$-ti *in Ša-dab$_6$*$^{ki}$; **18** o. XIV 23: (silver) níĝ-kaskal *A*-LUM$^{ki}$ maškim *Ḫa-ra-ì* lú **L.**; o. XV 16: (silver) *Šu*-NE-ḪAR maškim *A-mur-da-mu* lú **L.**; r. XVI 8: (silver) lú **L.** DU$^{ki}$; **19** o. IX 26: (silver) lú **L.** *En-na-il* ugula engar *Zú-ba-núm* 2 šu-ba$_4$-ti; **20** o. VII 5: (silver) lú **L.** *Ìr-*

*a-mu Ì-mar*$^{ki}$ [šu-ba$_4$-ti]; r. VII 9: (silver) *Daš-ne* lú **L.** *Ì-mar*$^{ki}$ *in* NI-*ab*$^{ki}$ [šu]-ba$_4$-ti 21 o. XII 26: (silver) lú **L.** *in A-la-ga*$^{ki}$ [šu-ba$_4$-ti].

nu-kiri$_6$ **1**(e) r. IV' 10: (silver) lú **L.** [*Du-*]*bí-šum ʾÀ-šu*$^{ki}$.

[ĜI]Š$^?$-PA-⸢X⸣-ga **18** o. XV 34: 3 kg *ni-zi-mu* nu$_{11}$-za 1 *za-ḫa-da* 1 **L.** *Ib-rí-um*.

ĜIŠ-sal (a jewel) **2** o. X 15; **10** o. IV 9: 10 gín D. kb nu$_{11}$-za 1 **L.**; **19** r. VI 19: **L.** é *A-ru*$_{12}$*-ga-du*$^{ki}$ *Ib-bí-um* "ur$_4$" šu-ba$_4$-ti; r. XII 7: ŠÚ+ŠA gín D. an-na šub *si-in* 1… ; r. XVII 26: 1 ma-na ŠA.PI 2 gín D. kg 1 íb-lá 1 *si-ti-tum* 1 ĝír-kun 1 **L.**; r. XVIII 7: 2 íb-lá 2 ĝír-kun 4 gín D. kb 2 **L.**-*sù*; **20** r. XI 22: **L.** ⸢dag⸣ é maḫ.

ĜIŠ-sur$_x$ «double yoke» **2** o. XIII 10: 3 gín D. kg *ni-zi-mu* nu$_{11}$-za **L.** ĝiš-gígir-II$^!$(III).

ĜIŠ-*šè-bir*$_5$*-gi-nu* (a tool belonging to the chariot) **12** r. X 4; **19** r. XVII 3: **L.** ĜIŠ-bar-ús. (cf. *ARET* III 185 o.$^?$ I 2': ĜIŠ-gígir-II *ša-bir*$_5$*-gi-nu*)

ĜIŠ-šim (an aromatic essence) **18** r. XII 19: **L.** ĜÁ×LÁ.

ĜIŠ-šú (a vessel) **2** o. III 11: 2 ma-na kb 1 **L.** 1 níĝ-bànda; **3** r. VII 15: 8 gín D. kb *zi-ba-tum* 4 **L.** 1 níĝ-bànda l[ú 2 šu]; **4** o. X 10: 4 ma-na TAR kb 1 **L.** 1 níĝ-bànda; **5** r. XV 15: TAR 5 gín D. kb *ni-zi-mu* 3 **L.** 3 níĝ-bànda; **6** r. XIII 16: 3 ma-na ŠÚ+ŠA kb 1 **L.** 1 níĝ-bànda; **10** o. XI 2: 5 gín D. kb ĝeštu-ĝeštu 1 **L.** lú šu-šu; o. XII 9: 3 gín D. kb [ZU.]PIRIĜ níĝ-bànda šu-šu; **13** r. X 16: 2 ma-na kb 1 **L.** 1 níĝ-bànda lú 2 šu; **15** o. XVI 12: 2 gín kb *zi-ba-du* 1 **L.** 1 níĝ-bànda kb lú kaskal *Ib-rí-um*; **16** o. I 20: 10 ma-na TAR kb 1 **L.** 1 níĝ-bànda 10 kb kg; **18** o. XVII 20: 7 gín D. kb *zi-ba-du* 1 **L.** 2 níĝ-bànda kaskal-kaskal *Ib-rí-um*; **21** o. XIV 20: 5 ma-na kb kin$_5$-ak 1 **L.** 1 níĝ-bànda lú 2 šu; r. I 15: 15 ma-na kb kin$_5$-ak 3 3 níĝ-bànda lú diri lú šu-šu kas$_4$-kas$_4$.

ĜIŠ-taškarin «boxwood» **2** o. II 19: 6 gín D. kg nu$_{11}$-za 1 bur-KAK **L.**; **4** o. XI 5: TAR kg nu$_{11}$-za$^!$(KUR) 4 bur-KAK-bur-KAK **L.**; **5** o. VI 14: 5 gín D. kb nu$_{11}$-za 1 bur-KAK **L.**; **12** r. XIII 4: 5 bulug$_4$-bulug$_4$ gibil lú **L.**; **14** o. XIII 2: 3 gín D. kb *mu-sa-du* ⸢LUM⸣$^?$-[ ] **L.**; **16** r. XV 25 and 29: ŠA.[PI 1+]⸢1⸣ gín D. kg nu$_{11}$-za 2 bur-KAK **L.** kaskal en *wa* 2 bur-KAK **L.** kaskal ⸢*Ib*⸣*-rí-um*; 24 r. II 3: 3 gín D. kg nu$_{11}$-za 1 bur-KAK **L.**
(Steinkeller 2021, pp. 182–183 has suggested that the ĜIŠ-taškarin which Gudea imported from the Amanus region should be identified with Cilician fir because of its dimension: "from the mountain range of the Amanus, he (cut) cedars (ĜIŠ-eren) of sixty and fifty cubits [length] and ([ĜIŠ-]taškarin) of twenty-five cubits length" (Statue B V 28–32). Neo-Assyrian inscriptions of Tiglath-pileser I and Tiglath-pileser III also mention the importation of ĜIŠ-taškarin logs. Boxwood usually reaches two meters high, but in some areas even twelve meters (and more), with a diameter of the trunk of more than fourteen centimeters. It is an ideal wood for carving small size objects. In the case of Gudea, one could also take in account a wrong teminilogical use of this term. The list of the objects made of ĜIŠ-taškarin registered in the Ebla texts, instead, confirms that at Ebla this term had the meaning of "boxwood". The list includes ĜIŠ-ná, "beds", ĜIŠ-uštin, "seats", ĜIŠ-banšur, "tables", ĜIŠ-asari, "trays", ĜIŠ-šú, "bowls", and in particular bur-KAK, the "bowl" for the oil used in the wedding ritual (see *ARET* XX, p. 257), sometimes decorated with gold. Fir wood absorbs liquids. A "statuette", an-dùl, of the goddess Išḫara made of this wood, was requested by the ritual for the royal wedding, *ARET* XI § 101. The work of this wood was entrusted to special craftsmen: naĝar-naĝar ĜIŠ-taškarin. This documentation, collected by Catagnoti (2016), agrees with the use of *taskarinnu* as decorative material, well documented by the Akkadian sources (see CAD T, pp. 281–282).

ĜIŠ-ti-ḪAR (a kind of timber/log) **2** r. IX 14; r. XVII 4; **3** o. VII 5; o. X 2'; r. II 3; r. IX 13; r. XIII 10; **5** o. II 2; o. IV 1; o. IX 5; o. XIV 13; r. IX 9; **6** o. XI 2; r. IX 15; **7** o. IX 3: 2 ma-na kb 96 **L.**; **8** r. IV 11'; **9** r. VI 1; **10** r. VI 10; r. XII 5; **13** o. V 16; o. XIV 11; **14** o. XVII 7; r. I 2; **15** o. VII 4; o. XIII 2; **18** r. XIX 6: **L.** SA.ZA$_x$$^{ki}$; **19** o. VI 28; r. V 1; **20** r. XIII 7; **21** r. II 9.

ĜIŠ-uštin «seat, throne» **15** r. XV 1: 4 sur$_x$-lu$_x$ lú *al*$_6$ ĜIŠ-ĝidru-ĜIŠ-ĝidru **L.** en.

ĜIŠ-zú «hook (also as a part of the wagon)» **5** r. VIII 6: 4 gín D. an-na šub **L.**; **6** r. XVI 2: 13 gín D. an-na šub-šub 2 **L.** 2 ĜIŠ-gígir-II, 6: 13 an-na šub 2 **L.** ĜIŠ-gígir-II; r. XVII 11: 3 an-na 2 **L.** 1 ĜIŠ-gígir-II; **12** o. XI 7: 5 gín D. an-na šub *si-in* 1 **L.** ĜIŠ-gígir-II; **13** o. III 11: 5 gín D. an-na šub *si-in* 1 **L.** ĜIŠ-gígir-II; o. VI 8: 4 gín D. an-na šub *si-in* 1 **L.**; o. XV 4: 16 gín D. an-na šub *si-in* 3 **L.** 3 ĜIŠ-gígir-II; **15** o. XV 14: 12 gín D. an-na šub *si-in* 1 ma-na 10 a-gar$_5$-gar$_5$ kin$_5$-ak 2 **L.**; **16** o. VI 16: 5 gín D. an-na šub *si-in* 1 **L.** 1 ĜIŠ-gígir-II; **17** o. XIV 20: ŠÚ+ŠA 6 a-gar$_5$-gar$_5$ 1 **L.**; r. I 11: 10 gín D. an-na šub *si-in* 2 **L.**; **18** r. XIV 9: 5 an-na šub *si-in* TAR a-gar$_5$ 1 **L.**; **19** o. VII 15: 10 gín D. an-na šub *si-in* 1 ma-na a-gar$_5$-gar$_5$ 2 **L.** ĜIŠ-gígir-II zú-ak; **20** o. IX 24: 5 g[ín] D. an-na šub *si-in* 1 **L.**; r. XI 28: 5 ⸢gín D. an-na šu[b *s*]*i-in* 1 **L.**; **21** o. XIII 19: 5 gín D. an-na šub *si-in* 1 ĜIŠ-[ ] **4** r. VII 13; **11** o. VIII 21; **14** r. XII 23: 1 kb 1 **L.**; **21** o. III 21.

ĝuruš «male worker, man» **12** r. VI 3: (silver) níĝ-du$_8$ 1 **L.** *Lu-wa-šum*$^{ki}$ *áš-ti Ba-na-i-um*$^{ki}$; **19** r. VII 2: (silver) níĝ-ba 3 **L.** *ʾÀ-du*$^{ki}$ *in Ḫa-lab*$_x$$^{ki}$ šu-ba$_4$-ti; r. XI 25: 1 ĜIŠ-gígir-II 1 **L.** ugula sur$_x$-BAR.AN 4 BAR.AN-BAR.AN; r. XII 32: (silver) níĝ-ba 3 **L.** *ʾÀ-du*$^{ki}$ ḫi-mu-DU maškim *Za-ba-rúm* nar.

ĝuruš-ĝuruš **2** o. XIV 20: (9 bracelets) lú **L.** SA.ZA$_x$$^{ki}$; **3** o. V 4: 40[+x] diri ĝír mar-tu **L.**; o. VIII 21: 30 ĝír mar-tu zú-ak ì-na-sum **L.**; r. III 14: 1 ĝír mar-tu zú A.LAGAB×ḪAL [ ] diri ĝír mar-tu **L.** *in* ud igi-ḫi-du$_8$ SA.ZA$_x$$^{ki}$; **4** o. I 7: 20 íb-lá *si-ti-tum* ĝír-kun lú **L.** SA.ZA$_x$$^{ki}$; o. IX 20: 3 íb<-lá> ĜÁ×LÁ ŠA.PI 7 íb-lá *si-ti-tum* ĝír-kun níĝ-ba **L.** *Ì-ra-ar*$^{ki}$ *in* ud *ma-lik-tum Ì-ra-ar*$^{ki}$ DU.DU; o. XII 5: 10 lá-2 *gú-li-lum* **L.**; r. I 9: 3 íb-lá *si-ti-tum* ĝír-kun lú **L.**; **5** r. VI 17: še **L.**-*sù wa* da[m]-*sù Za-ba-rúm* še-<SAĜ×>ḪA-mul; **6** o. III 4: (silver) níĝ-ba **L.** maškim-*sù Ma-rí*$^{ki}$; **9** r. XII 15: (53 bracelets, 2 plaques, 22[+x] daggers) lú [**L.**] [SA.]ZA$_x$$^{ki}$; **10** r. II 12: 4 *gú-li-lum* **L.**; r. XIV 2: 8 ĝír mar-tu **L.** SA.ZA$_x$$^{ki}$; **11** r. II 13: *gú-li-lum-gú-li-*

*lum* **L.**; **14** o. IV 8: 2 *mi-at* ĝír mar-tu … ì-na-sum **L.** SA.ZA$_{x}$$^{ki}$ *in* níĝ-kas$_{4}$ *Kak-mi-um*$^{ki}$; r. XI 1: (silver) níĝ-kaskal **L.**; r. XX 4': ⌜è⌝ *ni-zi-mu* ZA$_{x}$ **L.**; **16** o. XI 15: (19 plaques, 84 belts, 25 pendants, 56 helmets, 82 daggers, 55 bracelets) lú **L.** *A-zi-mu-tum*; r. VIII 18: (40 daggers) lú **L.** ḫaš-ḫaš *in* maškim *Ḫal-sum*$^{ki}$; **18** r. X 16: 90 lá-2 ĝír mar-tu zú-ak lú *mu-lu-iš* ĝír mar-tu **L.**; **19** r. IV 21: (706 daggers) lú **L.** SA.ZA$_{x}$$^{ki}$ in-na-sum; **21** r. I 5: (40 belts, 40 pendants, 18 bracelets) lú **L.** SA.ZA$_{x}$$^{ki}$ in-na-sum; r. VI 10: (14 plaques, 57 bracelets, 16 belts, 6 pendants, 1 helmet, 1 dagger) **L.** SA.ZA$_{x}$$^{ki}$; **23** o. IX 8: (14 bracelets) **L.**; o. X 6: (19 bracelets) **L.** SA.ZA$_{x}$$^{ki}$ *in* ud è níĝ-kas$_{4}$ *Gú-da-da-núm*$^{ki}$; r. III 9: (10 daggers) **L.** *in* ud è níĝ-kas$_{4}$ *Gú-da-da-núm*$^{ki}$.

## Ḫ

*ḫa-bù* «mace» (/ešda/) **2** o. IV 14: 6 gín D. kg nu$_{11}$-za 1 **L.**; r. III 17: TAR kb nu$_{11}$-za 2 **L.**; r. XIII 21: 15 gín D. kb nu$_{11}$-za 1 **L.**; **3** o. IV 13: 13 gín D. kb nu$_{11}$-za 1 **L.**; o. XIII 20: 15 gín D. kb nu$_{11}$-za 1 **L.**; **4** r. IV 16: TAR kb nu$_{11}$-za!(KUR) 2 **L.**; **5** o. XII 8: 13 gín D. kb nu$_{11}$-za 1 **L.**; r. X 7: 15 gín D. kb nu$_{11}$-za 1 **L.**; **6** o. XI 15: 50 gín D. kb nu$_{11}$-za 1 ĜIŠ-banšur *wa* 1 **L.**; o. XIII 23: 15 gín D. kb nu$_{11}$-za 1 **L.**; o. XIV 13: 15 gín D. kb nu$_{11}$-za 1 **L.**; o. XVI 25: TAR kb nu$_{11}$-za 2 **L.**; r. XVII 23: 15 an-na šub-šub nu$_{11}$-za 1 **L.**; **8** r. IX 5': 10? gín D. kb [nu$_{11}$-za 1L.]; **9** o. III 7: TAR kb nu$_{11}$-za 2 **L.**; r. V 14: 12 gín D. kb nu$_{11}$-za 1 **L.**; r. VI 13: 13 gín D. kb nu$_{11}$-za 1 **L.**; **10** o. V 1: 15 gín D. [kb] nu$_{11}$-za 1 **L.**; **12** r. I 11: 15 gín D. kb nu$_{11}$-za 1 **L.**; **13** r. IV 4: [13 g]ín [D. kb nu$_{11}$-za 1 **L.**], 9: 13 gín D. kb nu$_{11}$-za 1 **L.**; **14** o. IX 23: 15 gín D. kb nu$_{11}$-za 1 **L.**; o. X 12: *ap* 1 **L.** $^{d}$*ʾÀ-da* kb-kg sikil; r. II 14: 13 gín D. kb nu$_{11}$-za 1 **L.**; **15** o. X 1: 15 gín D. kb nu$_{11}$-za 1 **L.**; r. I 6: 13 gín D. kb nu$_{11}$-za 1 **L.**; r. IX 11: 12 gín D. kb nu$_{11}$-za 1 **L.** *ap* nu$_{11}$-za 1 *ar-ra-sù* kg sikil; **16** o. XIV 24: 13 gín D. kb nu$_{11}$-za 1 **L.**; r. I 12: 13 gín D. kb nu$_{11}$-za 1 **L.**; r. VII 15: 12 gín D. kb nu$_{11}$-za 1 **L.**; r. XI 1: 12 gín D. kb nu$_{11}$-za 1 **L.**; **17** r. IV 16: 15 gín D. kb nu$_{11}$-za 1 **L.**; r. XV 10: 15 gín D. kb nu$_{11}$-za 1 **L.**; **18** o. XVIII 14: 15 gín D. kb nu$_{11}$-za 1 **L.**; o. XIX 11: 15 gín D. kb nu$_{11}$-za 1 **L.**; r. XI 2: 15 gín D. kb nu$_{11}$-za 1 **L.**; r. XVII 33: 15 kb nu$_{11}$-za 1 **L.**; **19** o. X 19: 13 gín D. kb nu$_{11}$-za 1 **L.**; o. XI 6: 15 gín D. kb nu$_{11}$-za 1 **L.** *ap* nu$_{11}$-za *ar-ra-sù*; r. VIII 21: 12 gín D. kb nu$_{11}$-za 1 **L.**; r. IX 6: 12 gín D. kb nu$_{11}$-za 1 **L.**; r. XVII 8: 13 gín D. kb nu$_{11}$-za 1 **L.**; **20** o. VIII 3: ⌜15⌝ gín D. kb nu$_{11}$-za 1 **L.**, 16: 15 gín D. kb nu$_{11}$-za 1 [**L.**]; r. XI 5: 12 gín D. kb nu$_{11}$-za 1 **L.**; **21** o. IX 9: 15 gín D. kb nu$_{11}$-za 1 **L.**, 20: 15 gín D. kb nu$_{11}$-za 1 **L.** *ap* kg sikil; o. XV 5: 15 gín D. kb nu$_{11}$-za 1 **L.**; r. VII 21: 15 gín D. kb nu$_{11}$-za 1 **L.**; **22** r. V 13: [1] ma-na kg nu$_{11}$-za 1 [**L.**]; r. VI 4: 6 gín D. kg nu$_{11}$-za 1 *ar-ra-sù* **L.**; r. VII 1: 6 gín D. kg nu$_{11}$-za 1 *ar-ra-sù* **L.**; **23** r. II 1: 6 gín D. kg nu$_{11}$-za 1 *ar-ra-šum* 1 **L.**, 8: 6 gín D. kg nu$_{11}$-za 1 *ar-ra-šum* 1 **L.**; r. IV 8: 6 gín D. kg nu$_{11}$-za 1 *ar-ra-šum* 1 **L.**

*ḫar-ʾà-ru*$_{12}$ (an element of the battering ram) **17** o. XX 17: 1 ma-na ŠÚ+ŠA 4 gín D. an-na šub *si-in* 11 ma-na a-gar$_{5}$-gar$_{5}$ kin$_{5}$-ak 6 **L.** maḫ lú gud-si-dili.

*ḫa-ra-nu* «saw (with semi-circular hand)» **12** r. XII 2–3: 1 ma-na ŠÚ+ŠA 3 gín D. an-na šub *si-in* 9 ma-na TAR gín D. a-gar$_{5}$-gar$_{5}$ kin$_{5}$-ak … 6 **L.** 10 6 gín **L.** 5 gín.

*ḫa-ra-núm* **20** r. I 18: 17 gín D. an-na šub *si-in* 1 ma-na ŠA.PI gín D. a-gar$_{5}$[-gar$_{5}$] kin$_{5}$-ak 1 **L.** 7 gín D.

ḫaš-ḫaš «granulation» **2** o. XIV 15: nu$_{11}$-za **L.** 4 *gú-li-lum* kb, 18: **L.** 5 *gú-li-lum* a-gar$_{5}$-gar$_{5}$; **3** r. I 9: *ni-zi-mu* **L.** *gú-li-lum* ⌜x⌝ [ ]; **9** r. IX 14: nu$_{11}$-za **L.** 7 *gú-li-lum* ⌜kb⌝-II esi ĜÁ×LÁ TAR-*sù wa* 10 *gú-li-lum* kb-II esi ĜÁ×LÁ ŠÚ+ŠA gín D. 1 *gú-li-lum* kb-I esi 1 gín D. ĜÁ×LÁ-*sù*; r. X 9: nu$_{11}$-za **L.** 1 dib a-gar$_{5}$-gar$_{5}$ lú 4 *gú-li-lum* [ ] 1 dib a-gar$_{5}$-gar$_{5}$ [ ] 15 *gú-li-lum* a-gar$_{5}$-gar$_{5}$-II esi *wa* 2 *gú-li-lum* a-gar$_{5}$-gar$_{5}$ *sa-ḫ*[*a*-]*wa*-II esi ĜÁ×LÁ TAR *wa* 1? *gú-li-lum* a-gar$_{5}$-gar$_{5}$ *sa-ḫa-wa* 20 esi 12 *gú-li-lum* a-gar$_{5}$-gar$_{5}$ *sa-ḫa-wa* 12 esi; r. XI 10: nu$_{11}$-za **L.** 1 *gú-li-lum* a-gar$_{5}$-gar$_{5}$-II esi *wa* 4 *gú-li-lum* [a-]gar$_{5}$-gar$_{5}$[-I] esi; **16** r. VIII 19: ĝír mar-tu kb lú ĝuruš-ĝuruš **L.** *in* maškim *Ḫal-sum*$^{ki}$.

*ḫa-za-nu* «(bead in the shape of a) clove» **4** o. X 14: 3 gín D. kb **L.** 2 *da-ni-da*; **15** o. XI 14: 1 *ma-ḫa-na-gúm* **L.**; **17** r. VI 33: 2 gín D. kb **L.** *a-ḫa-šum* gaba $^{d}$*Ku-ra wa* en; r. XI 18: [x g]ín D. k[b] kin$_{5}$-ak **L.** 2 šu-dub; r. XX 19: 5 kb 15 **L.** 2 gìn-gìn 2 si$_{4}$ 1 šu-dub, 24: 4 kb 15 **L.** 2 gìn-gìn 2 si$_{4}$ 1 šu-dub; **18** o. XVI 19: 1 ma-na TAR kg kin$_{5}$-ak … 3 *mi-at* 60 **L.**; **24** r. I 3: 4 gín D. kg **L.** *wa a-a-nu gú-za-ra-tum*.

ḫeš$_{5}$ (LÚ×KÁR) «prisoner» **4** r. XII 21: (silver) [níĝ-kaskal] *A-ʾà-lu wa Ù-da-a-ḫa Ma-ri*$^{ki}$ **L.** DU.DU; **6** o. XIII 8: (silver) níĝ-kaskal *A-ʾà-lu wa Ù-da-aḫ* **L.** DU.DU *Ma-ri*$^{ki}$.

ḪI.DIM **9** o. III 1: […] níĝ-sa$_{10}$ 7 sila$_{4}$ **L.**

ḫi-mu-DU «to deliver; delivery» **4** o. II 4; **7** r. XIII 25; **10** o. XIV 4; r. XII 4; **13** r. I 18; **14** o. VI 18; **17** o. VIII 13; o. XVII 10; **19** r. XIII 2; **25** r. V 3.

ḫi-úš «to die» **1**(e) r. IV' 2: *in* ud **L.** *I-ti-ì* simug; **3** o. VIII 13: *in* ud dumu-nita en *Ḫa-zu-wa-an*$^{ki}$ **L.** *in Ga-ra-ma-an*$^{ki}$.

ḫúb-ki «dancer, acrobat» **6** o. II 5: (silver) níĝ-ba **L.** *in* ud *a-*<*lu-*>*nu* ĝiš ba:tuš; **16** r. XVII 3: (silver) níĝ-ba **L.** ba:tuš *a-lu-nu* ĝiš.

(ḫúb = Akk. *ḫuppûm*, see Catagnoti 1997)

*ḫu-bù* **4** o. XV 2: 2 gín D. kb ZU.PIRIĜ 2 **L.**

ḫul «bad; poor quality» **2** r. V 8: 1 túg-NI.NI **L.**; r. XII 12: 7 túg-NI.NI **L.**; r. XIII 6: 14 túg-NI.NI **L.**; r. XVII 10: 1 túg-NI.NI **L.**; **6** r. IX 13: 12 ĝír mar-tu **L.**; **11** o. XIII 7: 10 ĝír mar-tu **L.**; **12** r. III 3: 10 gada-TÚG **L.**; **25** o. VIII 2: 1 ĝír mar:tu **L.**

ḫúl «feast» **3** r. IV 9: 1 šu-dub *Ib-rí-um in* ud **L.** na-rú-*sù*; **6** r. VII 12: 1 íb-lá 1 *si-ti-tum* 1 ĝír-kun *Ba-lu-zú* "ur$_{4}$" *Ì-mar*$^{ki}$ *in* ud **L.** na-rú-*sù*; **8** o. II 6: ⌜1⌝ ĝír mar-[t]u ⌜1⌝ *r*[*a*]-⌜*ʾà*⌝-*tum* kg *Ib-rí-um* en šu-mu-tak$_{4}$ *in* ud **L.** na-rú [ ]; **11** r. VI 11: 1 ĜIŠ-banšur níĝ-ba $^{d}$*Ra-sa-ap Du-bí-tum*$^{ki}$ [ ]⌜x⌝ [*in*] ud **L.** é-*sù*; **19** o. VII 29: 1 íb-lá 1 *si-ti-tum* 1 ĝír-kun *Mu-gàr* dumu-nita *A-ba-rúm in* ud **L.**-*sù*; r. XVI 19:

útul-útul maḫ urudu *in* ud **L.** *Ib-rí-um*; r. XVIII 13: 2 íb-lá 2 ĝír-kun … 2 ĜIŠ-sal-*sù I-bí-zi-kir wa Ù-ti* 2 dumu-nita-*sù in* ud **L.**-*sù*; **20** o. XIV 24: 1 šu-dub sikil en lú **L.**; o. XVII 13: 1 íb-lá 1 ĝír-kun … *Gi-a-da-mu in* ud **L.**-*sù*; **21** o. III 4: [ ] *Ti-ti-nu in* ud **L.**-*sù*; r. IX 16: 1? í]b-lá [1 g]ír-kun … *Ig-na-da-ar* lú *Mi-ga-ì Ti-ti-nu* šu-mu-tak₄ *in* ud **L.**-*sù*.

*ḫu-ru₁₂-mu* see iti.

ḪU.UD **7** r. XIII 26: ḫi-mu-DU **L.**

ḪU.UD-ḪU.UD **4** o. II 9: 1 *mi-at* 20 **L.** *áš-ti Áš-da-ti-u*[*m*]⌜ki⌝; o. V 12: [1 *mi-a*]*t* 30 **L.** *áš-ti Áš-da-ti-um*ki; **6** o. I 5: 1 *mi-at* 20 **L.**

(see *LLE*,I no. 758: UD.ḪU = *ḫa-ḫa-tum*; the city of origin of this good does not seem to be attested in other documents)

## I

íb-lá «belt (for weapon)» **1** o. V 8: 10 ma-na kb kin₅-ak 17 **L.** 17 *si-ti-tum* 17 ĝír-kun; o. VII 13: 15 gín D. kb *ni-zi-mu* 1 **L.**, 20: TAR kb [*ni*]-*zi-mu* 1 **L.** [1] *si-ti*[-*tum* 1 ĝír-kun]; o. IX 11: ŠÚ+ŠA gín D. kg 1 **L.** 1 *si-ti-tum* 1 ĝír-kun; o. XII 18: 2 gín D. kg *ni-zi-mu* maš-maš **L.**; r. VI 8: TAR kg 1 **L.** ĝír-kun; r. XI 17: 10 gín D. kg 1 **L.**; l.ed. 3: TAR kg 1 **L.**, 8: 1 ma-na kg 2 **L.**; **3** r. XII 13: [1 ma-na] kg kin₅-ak 2 **L.** kg; **4** o. I 6: 3 ma-na 7 gín D. kb *ni-zi-mu* 20 **L.** *si-ti-tum* ĝír-kun; o. IX 18–19: 5 ma-na TAR kb kin₅-ak 3 **L.**(<-lá>) ĜÁ×LÁ ŠA.PI 7 **L.** *si-ti-tum* ĝír-kun; r. I 8: 3 **L.** *si-ti-tum* ĝír-kun; r. XIII 3: 4 **L.** *si-ti-tum* ĝír-kun, 14: 4 **L.** gaba-ru é en; **5** o. I 4: 1 **L.** saĝ; o. V 16: 10 gín D. kb *ni-zi-mu* 24 **L.** ĝír-kun; o. XI 8: TAR kb **L.**; r. IV 10: TAR kg **L.**; **6** o. VI 5: 13 ma-na ŠÚ+ŠA gín D. kb kin₅-ak 20 **L.** 20 ĝír-kun ĜÁ×LÁ ŠA.PI; o. XII 5: 50 gín D. kb 1 **L.** *si-ti-tum* ĝír-⌜kun⌝; r. VII 8: 1 ma-na kb 1 **L.** 1 *si-ti-tum* 1 ĝír-kun, 21: ŠA.PI kb 1 **L.** *si-ti-tum* ĝír-kun kb maš-maš kg; r. VIII 4: ŠA.PI gín D. kb 1 **L.** *si-ti-tum* ĝír-kun maš-maš kg, 8: ŠA.PI gín D. kb 1 **L.** 1 ĝír-kun; r. XIV 17: 50 kb 1 **L.** kb maš-maš kg, 20: ŠA.PI kb 1 **L.** maš-maš kg; **7** o. VIII 5: TAR kb 1 **L.** 1 *si-ti-tum* 1 ĝír-kun; **8** o. IX 4: 20 **L.** 20 kun ŠA.PI; o. XIII 8: ŠA.PI gín D. kb URI 1 **L.** 1 kun; **9** r. XV 12: TAR kb URI 1 **L.** 1 ĝír-kun; **10** o. IX 10: 13 m[a-]n[a] ŠÚ[+ŠA gí]n [D.] kb kin₅-ak 20 **L.** 20 ĝír-kun; **11** o. VII 23: [TAR kg 1 **L.**] 1 *si-ti-tum* 1 ĝír-kun; r. II 3: [ ] 80 **L.** 80 ĝír m[ar-tu] 21 á-MUŠEN zabar; r. VII 7: ŠA.PI gín D. kb 1 **L.** 1 ĝír-kun; **12** r. I 1: ŠA.PI gín D. kg 1 **L.** 1 *si-ti-tum* 1 ĝír-kun; **13** o. I 9: [x m]a-na [kb x] **L.** [x *si-*]*ti-tum* [x gí]r-kun, 18: [š]a-pi gín D. kb [1 **L.** 1] *si-ti-tum* 1 ĝír-kun; o. II 7: 2 ma-na kb 2 **L.** 2 *si-ti-tum* 2 g[í]r-kun, 15: 1 ma-na kb 1 **L.** 1 *si-ti-tum* 1 ĝír-kun; o. XI 15: 1 **L.** TAR kb; r. IX 6: TAR kg 1 **L.** 1 *si-ti-tum* 1 g[ír-kun]; **14** o. VII 2: TAR kb URI 1 **L.** 1 ĝír-kun kg, 15: ŠA.PI gín D. kg 1 **L.** 1 ĝír-kun; r. VIII 17: ŠA.PI gín D. kb 1 **L.** 1 ĝír-kun; r. IX 13: [TAR kg 1 **L.** 1 ĝír-kun]; r. XIII 23: 1 ma-na 16 kb *ni-zi-mu* URI 10 lá-2 **L.** 5 g[ír-kun] kb maš-maš; **15** o. III 10: ŠA.PI gín D. kb 1 **L.** 1 ĝír-kun; o. XIII 18: TAR [k]b 1 **L.** 1 ĝír-kun; o. XV 21: 2 gín D. kb *ni-zi-mu* 1 **L.**; r. VI 1: TAR kb 1 **L.** 1 *si-ti-tum* 1 ĝír-kun; **16** o. VIII 2: 6 gín D. kb *ni-zi-mu* 7 **L.** 5 ĝír-kun lú URI lú kg, 15: 12 gín D. kb *ni-zi-mu* 17 **L.** maš-maš kg; o. IX 1: 52 gín D. kb *ni-zi-mu* 32 ĝír 55 **L.** kb; o. X 16: TAR an-na SUD.PA.SIKIL 5 **L.** 20 ĝír-kun zabar 35 á-MUŠEN zabar; o. XIII 21: TAR kb 1 **L.** 1 *si-ti-tum* 1 ĝír-kun; r. IX 18: 1 gín D. kg 1 **L.** 1 *si-ti-tum* 1 ĝír-kun; **17** o. IV 16: [ ] lul-gu-ak 1 **L.** 1 ĝír-kun; o. XI 13: 2 gín D. kg *ni-zi-mu* 1 **L.** 1 *si-ti-tum* 1 ĝír-kun, 16: 12 gín D. kb 1 **L.** 1 ĝír-kun; o. XII 12: ŠA.PI gín D. kb 1 **L.** 1 ĝír-kun; o. XIV 14: 2 ma-na kg 1 **L.** 1 *si-ti-tum* 1 ĝír-kun 1 dib; r. VI 21: 1 an-dùl … 1 gín 3 NI kg nu₁₁-za *ba-na-i-sù wa* **L.**-*sù wa* šu-kešda gùn-*sù*; r. XII 16: [x ma-na kg x] **L.** [x *si-t*]*i*-[*tu*]*m* [x gí]r-[ku]n; r. XIII 3: 3 ma-na kg kin₅-ak 6 **L.** 6 *si-ti-tum* 6 ĝír-kun, 18: TAR kb kin₅-ak 1 **L.** 1 *si-ti-tum* 1 ĝír-kun; r. XXI 26: 2 ma-na kg kin₅-ak 2 **L.** 2 *si-ti-tum* 2 ĝír-kun; **18** o. X 18: [10 gín D. kg] 1 **L.** 1 *si-ti-tum* 1 ĝír-kun; o. XI 5: 7 gín D. kb *ni-zi-mu* 1 **L.** 1 ĝír-kun kb, 14: 8 gín D. kb *ni-zi-mu* 1 **L.** 1 ĝír-kun; r. XII 26: 1 ma-na kg 1 **L.** 1 *si-ti-tum* 1 ĝír-kun ì-ĝiš-saĝ *Ib-rí-um*; r. XV 4: 2 ma-na 12 kg nu₁₁-za IGI.DUB-*sù wa* **L.** *si-ti-tum* íb+III-TÚG; **19** o. VII 4: TAR kb 1 **L.** 1 *si-ti-tum* 1 ĝír-kun, 24: TAR kg 1 **L.** 1 *si-ti-tum* 1 ĝír-kun; r. XIII 11: TAR kb URI 1 **L.** 1 ĝír-kun; r. XIV 2: TAR kg 1 **L.** 1 *si-ti-tum* 1 ĝír-kun, 7: ŠA.PI gín D. kb 1 **L.** 1 ĝír-kun, 17: ŠA.PI gín D. kb 1 **L.** 1 ĝír-kun; r. XVII 25: 1 ma-na ŠA.PI 2 gín D. kg 1 **L.** 1 *si-ti-tum* 1 ĝír-kun 1 ĜIŠ-sal; r. XVIII 5: 2 ma-na kg 2 **L.** 2 ĝír-kun; **20** o. XV 6: 1 ma-na ŠÚ+ŠA gín D. kg kin₅-ak 1 **L.** 1 *si-ti-tum* 1 ĝír-kun ŠÚ+ŠA gín D.; o. XVI 11: 1 **L.** 1 *si-ti-tum* 1 ĝír-kun TAR kg sikil, 16: TAR kg 1 **L.** 1 *si-ti-tum* 1 ĝír-kun sikil; 18: 8 gín D. kg 1 **L.** 1 *si-ti-tum* 1 ĝír-kun sikil; o. XVII 6: ŠA.PI gín D. kb 1 **L.** 1 ĝír-kun; r. VIII 1: [TA]R [kg] 1 **L.** 1 *si-ti-tum* 1 ĝír-kun; r. X 13: ŠA.PI kb 1 **L.** 1 ĝír-kun; r. XII 14: ŠA.PI kb 1 **L.** [1] ĝír-kun; **21** o. II 19: [ ] ⌜x-x⌝ [1] **L.** [1 ĝír-k]un; o. III 9: TAR kg 1 **L.** 1 *si-ti-tum* 1 ĝír-kun; o. VII 10: 2 ma-na kg kin₅-ak 1 dib 1 **L.** 1 *si-ti-tum* 1 ĝír-kun; o. XIV 1: [2 ma-na kg] 1 **L.** 1 *si-ti-tum* 1 ĝír-kun 1 dib; o. XV 18: ŠA.PI gín D. kb 1 **L.** 1 *si-ti-tum* 1 ĝír-kun; o. XVII 22: 26 ma-na kb kin₅-ak 40 **L.** 40 ĝír-kun; r. V 14: TAR 2 kb *ni-zi-mu* 16 **L.** 6 ĝír-kun *wa* 1 á-MUŠEN kb; r. VIII 15: TAR kg 1 **L.** 1 *si-ti-tum* 1 ĝír-kun; r. IX 7: [ ] [1?] **L.** [1 g]ír-kun; **23** o. VIII 7: 1 gín D. kg *ni-zi-mu* nu₁₁-za 1 **L.** 1 ĝír-kun; o. IX 1: 5 gín D. kg *ni-zi-mu* maš-maš 4 **L.** 1 ĝír-kun maš-maš; r. VII 3: 1 ma-na kg 2 **L.** 2 *si-ti-a-tum* 2 ĝír-kun; **25** o. VIII 8: 1 **L.** ŠA.PI gín D. kb; o. IX 4: 1 **L.** TAR kb; r. III 7: 1 **L.** TAR kb; r. IV 7: 1 **L.** ŠA.PI kb, 10: 1 **L.** TAR ⌜kb⌝.

íb(+II/III/IV/V-)TÚG «kilt, waistband» **2** o. IX 12: 1 gín D. kg nu₁₁-za *ba-na-a wa* **L.**; r. VIII 3: 5 gín D. kg nu₁₁-za [*ba-na-a*] *wa* **L.**; r. VIII 3: 1 an-dùl … 5 gín D. kg nu₁₁-za [ ] *wa* **L.**; **4** o. XV 8: 1 útul urudu lú gùn-gùn **L.**; **5** r. XVI 3 (silver) níĝ-ba *Wa-ru₁₂-tum Ma-rí*ki šu-mu-tak₄ **L.** *Ga-ga-ba-an*ki; **9** r. VIII 11: 6 gín D. kg nu₁₁-za *ba-na-ʾà-sa wa* **L.** [*w*]*a* an-zamₓ *wa* 2 *gú-li-lum-sù*; **12** r. IX 1: ŠÚ+ŠA 6 gín D. kg kin₅-ak saĝ d*Ra-sa-ap Du-ne-íb*ki *wa* nu₁₁-za **L.**-*sù*; **14** o. XVI 12: 2 **L.** *Sa-ma-rí*ki; **15** o. III 7: (silver) níĝ-ba *Daš-na Ma-rí*$^{ki}$ … *wa* **L.** šu-mu-tak$_4$; o. XII 18: 3 **L.** *Ma-rí*$^{ki}$; **18** r. XV 5: 2 ma-na 12 kg nu$_{11}$-za IGI.DUB-*sù wa* íb-lá *si-ti-tum* **L.**; **25** o. IV 7.

íb+III-TÚG babbar **1**(a) r. x+I x+1; **2** o. X 9; r. V 11; r. IX 10; **4** r. IX 19; **5** r. III 1; **9** o. XIV 15; **25** o. VII 2.

íb+III-TÚG babbar gíd **2** o. VIII 3; r. V 6; r. IX 8; **3** o. V 14; r. XIV 8; **8** o. XI 6.

íb+III-TÚG gíd **2** r. XII 13.

íb(+I/II/III/IV/V-)TÚG gùn **1**(e) r. x+I 3'; **2** o. VIII 17; r. XII 16; **3** o. V 16; o. VI 4; r. VII 2; r. IX 9; r. XIII 8; **5** o. I 7; o. IX 1; o. XIV 9; r. III 10; r. IX 7; **6** r. IX 12; **7** o. XVII 8; r. VI 16; **8** o. V 3; o. XI 6; **9** o. XIV 5; r. I 15; r. XVI 9; **11** o. IX 12; o. XIII 6; **12** o. I 7; o. VIII 12; **13** o. V 11; o. XIV 6; o. XVII 4; r. V 13; r. X 5; **14** o. XVI 16; o. XXI 9; **15** o. VII 1; o. XII 17; o. XVII 16; r. III 16; **17** o. X 3; r. V 10; r. X 11; r. XVIII 3; r. XX 10; **21** o. XI 13: 60 **L.** ir$_{11}$-ir$_{11}$; r. II 2; r. XII 19; **25** o. II 4; o. III 5; o. IV 7; o. VII 2; o. VIII 1; r. IX 7: šu-níĝin … 6 *mi-at* 81 **L.**

íb(+I/II/III/IV/V-)TÚG sa$_6$ gùn **1**(e) r. x+I 4'; **2** o. VII 3; o. VIII 16; o. X 13; r. V 10; r. IX 9; r. XII 15; **3** o. V 15; o. VI 4; r. XIII 7; **5** o. I 6; o. VIII 16; o. XIV 9; r. III 9; r. IX 6; **6** r. IX 11; r. XI 12; r. XII 10; **7** o. XVII 7; r. VI 15; **8** o. V 2; o. XI 6; **9** o. VII 15; **10** r. VII 10; **11** o. III 3; o. IX 11; o. XIII 5; r. II 17; **12** o. I 6; o. VIII 11; r. III 5; **13** o. V 10; o. XIV 5; o. XVII 3; r. V 12; r. X 4; **14** o. XVI 15; o. XXI 7; r. V 6; **15** o. VI 22; o. XII 16; o. XVII 15; r. III 15; **17** o. X 2; r. V 9; r. X 10; r. XVIII 2; r. XX 9; r. XXII 26; **25** o. II 4; o. III 4; o. V 8; o. VII 2; o. VIII 1; r. IX 6: šu-níĝin … 2 *mi-at* 23 **L.**

igi «eye»

igi-igi «pair of eyes» **13** r. XI 11: [x gín D. a]n-na šub *si-in* 1 **L.**

igi «provision»

igi-igi **4** o. XV 22: (20 bracelets) gaba-ru é en tak$_4$ **L.**

(see *ARET* XI, p. 153)

igi-du$_8$ «present» **16** o. XIV 21: (silver) níĝ-ba *Wa-ru$_{12}$-tum Ma-rí*$^{ki}$ šu-mu-tak$_4$ **L.**

IGI.DUB see *ba-na-ù*

igi-ḫi-du$_8$ «review, parade» **3** r. III 16: *in* ud **L.** SA.ZA$_x$$^{ki}$; **8** o. IX : *in* **L.** *in* ud ⌜nídba⌝ [ ]; o. XIV 5: *in* **L.**; **12** r. VIII 9: *in* ud ká gibil lú *I-bí-zi-kir* **L.**; **19** o. III 16: *in* ud **L.**(šu-du$_8$) *A-la-ga*$^{ki}$; o. XV 32: (104 daggers) lú tak$_4$ **L.** *Za-ru$_{12}$-du*$^{\langle ki\rangle}$.

IGI.NITA «donkey» **1**(e) r. IV' 6: 2 ma-na kb níĝ-sa$_{10}$ 5 **L.** u$_5$; **2** r. X 5:2 ma-na 2 kb níĝ-sa$_{10}$ 4 **L.** u$_5$; **3** o. VII 1: TAR kb 1 **L.** u$_5$; **11** o. VI 20: 2 níĝ-anše-ak 2 kù-sal lú 2 **L.** en; **12** o. II 1: [ ] níĝ-sa$_{10}$ 2 **L.**; r. IV 3: 1 níĝ-anše-ak **L.**; **13** o. XVII 8: 1 ma-na 1 gín D. kb níĝ-sa$_{10}$ **3 L.** u$_5$; **14** r. XIII 6: 1 níĝ-anše-ak 1 kù-sal 1 **L.** en; **15** o. XVII 20: 1 ma-na ŠÚ+ŠA 5 gín D. kb níĝ-sa$_{10}$ 4 **L.**; **16** o. VII 9: 2 níĝ-anše-ak 4 kù-sal 2 **L.** *Ib-rí-um*; r. IV 19: 1 ma-na ŠA.PI 1 gín D. kb níĝ-sa$_{10}$ 6 **L.** u$_5$; **17** o. IV 2: [x ma-na x] gín D. kb níĝ-sa$_{10}$ 2 **L.** u$_5$; o. VII 13: 2 níĝ-anše-ak 4!(2) kù-sal lú 2 **L.** ama-gal en; r. II 21: 1 níĝ-anše-ak 1 kù-sal 2 **L.** en; **18** r. I 8: 2 níĝ-anše-ak 2 kù-sal 2 *wa su-da-nu* kù-sal en; r. III 12: 55 gín D. kb níĝ-sa$_{10}$ 3 **L.** u$_5$ en; **21** o. IV 7: 2 kù-sal 2 **L.** en; o. VIII 9: 1 níĝ-anše-ak 1 kù-sal ; o. X 7: [1 níĝ]-anše-ak 2 **L.**; o. XIII 26: 1 níĝ-anše-ak 1 kù-sal 1 **L.**

ugula IGI.NITA **9** o. V 7.

ì-ĝiš «oil» **4** r. XV 24: 1 bur-KAK *aš-ḫal* **L.**; **6** r. VII 4: 2 bur-KAK *aš-ḫal* **L.**; **21** o. VI 6: la-ḫa lú **L.** *si-in A-la-ga*$^{ki}$.

see nídba ì-ĝiš.

ì-ĝiš-saĝ «purification ceremony (for a death)» **3** o. XI 15: 2 *bu*-DI **L.** *Tíš-*⌜*má*⌝*-da-mu* dam en; r. XII 14: 2 íb-lá kg **L.** 2 en *Ma-nu-wa-ad*$^{ki}$; **13** o. XIII 15 and 24: 1 dib **L.** en *Ì-mar*$^{ki}$ … 2 *bu*-DI … 2 saĝ-*sù* **L.** *Ti-šè-li-im* ama-gal-*sù*; **18** r. II 24: 2 *bu*-DI **L.** *Gi-ù-du* dam *Za-ba-rúm*; r. IV 21: 2 *bu*-DI **L.** *Di-rín-da-mu* dam-diĝir *áš-du* úš *ma-lik-tum Lum-na-an*$^{ki}$; r. XIII 1: 1 íb-lá 1 *si-ti-tum* 1 ĝír-kun **L.** *Ib-rí-um*; **19** o. X 10: 2 *bu*-DI **L.** *Di-rín-da-mu* dam-diĝir; **21** o. V 23: [2 *bu*]-⌜DI⌝ **L.** [d]am *ba-da-lum* [*Ḫa*-]*ra-an*$^{ki}$; o. XV 19: 1 íb-lá 1 *si-ti-tum* 1 ĝír-kun **L.** *I-bí-zi-kir*, 24: 2 *bu*-DI **L.** ama-gal en; o. XVI 3: 2 *bu*-DI **L.** *Di-ni-íb-du-lum* nin-ni en; r. VII 10: [2 *bu*-DI] … 2 saĝ-*sù* **L.** *Ti-šè-li-im Ì-mar*$^{ki}$.

im-ĝi$_6$ «black clay» **6** r. III 18: 4 *ba-rí-zú* **L.**

*in* (preposition) 1) «in» (locative); 2) for» (temporal); 3) «for» (final).

1) *in* GN *passim.*

2) **5** o. VIII 2: **L.** AMA-*ra*, 12: **L.** AMA-*ra*; r. XI 6: **L.** iti *ᵓa$_5$-nun*, 20: **L.** iti *ᵓa$_5$-nun*; **7** o. XII 1: **L.** $^{d}$AMA-*ra*, 15: **L.** $^{d}$AMA-*ra*; r. VIII 6: **L.** iti *ᵓa$_5$-nun*; **9** o. IV 13: **L.** AMA-*ra*; 10 o. XI 15: **L.** AMA-*ra*; **11** o. XI 8: **L.** $^{d}$AMA-*ra*; r. IV 12: **L.** *gi*-NI; r. VIII 18: **L.** iti *ᵓa$_5$-nun*; **12** o. III 20: **L.** [ ]; r. II 7: **L.** iti *ᵓa$_5$-nun*; **14** o. VI 12: **L.** mu-ti-II; o. X 9: **L.** $^{d}$AMA-*ra*; o. XVII 12: **L.** $^{d}$AMA-*ra*; r. II 22: **L.** [*gi*-NI]; **15** o. X 13: **L.** $^{d}$AMA-*ra*; r. I 14: **L.** *g*[*i*-NI]; r. IX 22: **L.** iti *ᵓa$_5$-nun*; **16** r. I 21: **L.** $^{d}$AMA-*ra*; r. VII 24: **L.** *gi*-NI; r. XI 11: **L.** iti *ᵓa$_5$-nun*; **17** r. IV 28: **L.** $^{d}$AMA-*ra*; r. XV 18: **L.** *gi*-NI; **18** o. XIX 24: **L.** $^{d}$AMA-*ra*; r. XI 10: **L.** *gi*-NI; **19** o. XI 18: **L.** $^{d}$AMA-*ra*; **20** r. VII 20: **L.** *gi*-NI; **21** o. XV 13: **L.** *gi*:NI; r. VIII 3: [**L.**] [$^{d}$AMA-*ra*]; **23** o. I 6: **L.** AMA-*ra*; r. IV 12: **L.** iti *ᵓa$_5$-nun*; **24** o. V 12: **L.** *ma-ᵓà-wa-tum.*

3) **4** o. IX 8: **L.** mè *Kab-lu$_5$-ul*$^{ki}$; **5** o. X 8: **L.** níĝ-kas$_4$ *A-da-*[*bí*-]⌜*ik*⌝$^{ki}$; r. V 5: **L.** níĝ-kas$_4$ *Gú-rá-ma-an*$^{ki}$; r. XV 18: **L.** é $^{d}$*Ra-sa-ap ᵓÀ-da-ni*$^{ki}$ SA.ZA$_x$$^{ki}$; **7** o. V 7: **L.** níĝ-kas$_4$ *Ma-rí*$^{ki}$; o. IX 15: **L.** níĝ-kas$_4$ *Ma-rí*$^{ki}$; **8** o. IX 7: **L.** igi-ḫi-du$_8$; o. XIV 4: **L.** igi-ḫi-du$_8$; **9** o. XV 13: **L.** níĝ-kas$_4$ lú sikil; **10** r. I 17: **L.** ⌜kaskal⌝; r. X 7: **L.** ne-saĝ-*sù*; **14** o. IV 10: **L.** níĝ-kas$_4$ *Kak-mi-um*$^{ki}$; **16** r. VIII 20: **L.** maškim *Ḫal-sum*$^{ki}$; **17** o. V 5: **L.** ne-saĝ-*sù*; **18** r. XVII 23: **L.** kaskal *Su-da-ma-an*$^{ki}$; **19** r. X 9: **L.** kaskal; **21** o. XIII 5: **L.** níĝ-kas$_4$ *Ma-rí*$^{ki}$; **22** r. IV 1: **L.** šu-mu-níĝin SA.ZA$_x$$^{ki}$.

ì-na-sum «to give» **3** o. IV 22; o. VIII 20; r. XI 5; **4** o. I 13; o. IV 21; r. XI 3, 7; **5** r. IV 5; r. VI 3, 14; **6** o. VII 5; r. XVII 27; **7** o. V 3; r. XV 13, 24; **8** o. IX 5; o. XIV 3; **10** r. X 6; **11** o. V 3; **14** o. IV 7; o. XV 2; **15** o. II 26; **17** o. V 4; r. XVI 10; **19** o. VIII 8; r. VI 1; **20** o. X 19; **22** o. VII 9; o. VIII 2, 6, 11; o. IX 4.

see also in-na-sum **5** r. XIV 1, 22; **7** o. I 14; r. V 25; r. XVI 8; **10** o. V 13; o. IX 11; o. X 18; **12** o. VI 6; o. VII 18; **14** o. XIV 14; **15** r. XVI 14; **17** o. XX 2;

**18** r. X 17; **19** r. IV 23; **21** r. I 7; r. III 21; **22** o. VI 2; **23** o. I 3.

*in* ud (conjunction) «when, on the occasion of» **1**(e) r. II' 6': [ ] è **L.** *Ìr-kab-da-mu si-mi* úš-*sù*; r. IV' 1: **L.** ⌜ḫi⌝-úš *I-ti-ì* simug; **2** o. II 8: 1 kù-sal níĝ-ba en $^{d}$*Ba-ra-ma* **L.** ne:saĝ-*sù*; o. VI 16: 1 ĜIŠ-banšur *wa* 1 kù-sal níĝ-ba *Ib-rí-um* $^{d}$*Ku-ra* **L.** ne:saĝ-*sù*; r. II 5: 1 *gú-li-lum* 1 kù-sal níĝ-ba *Ib-rí-um* $^{d}$*Ku-ra* **L.** lú nídba; **3** o. VIII 9: **L.** dumu-nita en *Ḫa-zu-wa-an*$^{ki}$ ḫi-úš *in Ga-ra-ma-an*$^{ki}$ lú *Ḫar-sum*$^{ki}$; r. III 15: 1 ĝír mar-tu zú A.LAGAB×ḪAL [ ] diri ĝír mar-tu ĝuruš-ĝuruš **L.** igi-ḫi-du$_{8}$ SA.ZA$_{x}^{ki}$; r. IV 8: 1 šu-dub *Ib-rí-um* **L.** ḫúl na-rú-*sù*; r. XI 19: 6 *bu*-DI níĝ-ba 3 dam *Zi-ba-da* **L.** níĝ-mu-sá dumu-munus *Ib-rí-um*; r. XII 19: 2 íb-lá kg ì-ĝiš-saĝ 2 en *Ma-nu-wa-ad*$^{ki}$ *Ba-ga-ma* šu-mu-tak$_{4}$ **L.** úš *ma-lik-tum*; **4** o. X 2: 3 íb<-lá> ĜÁ×LÁ ŠA.PI 7 íb-lá *si-ti-tum* ĝír-kun níĝ-ba ĝuruš-ĝuruš *Ì-ra-ar*$^{ki}$ **L.** *ma-lik-tum Ì-ra-ar*$^{ki}$ DU.DU; r. XIII 10: 4 íb-lá *si-ti-tum* ĝír-kun PN$_{1}$–PN$_{4}$ 4 en *Ib-al*$_{6}^{ki}$ **L.** [nídba ì-ĝiš]; r. XVI 18:[ AN.ŠE.GÚ x ma-na (x)] kb è **L.** *Ib-rí-um* 2 mu; **5** o. VI 8: 2 *bu*-DI ama-gal *I-bí-zi-kir* **L.** níĝ-mu-sá dumu-munus *Ib-rí-um Gi-ti*-NE$^{ki}$, 19: 1 ĝír mar-tu kg *Ib-rí-um* **L.** nídba $^{d}$<*Iš*->*šára* ĜIŠ-kiri$_{6}$; r. IV 6: 1 ĝír mar-tu … 1 kù-sal níĝ-ba $^{dʾ}$*A*$_{5}$*-da-"bal" Lu-ba-an*$^{ki}$ *Ib-rí-um* ì-na-sum **L.** ne:saĝ-*sù*, 13: íb-lá BÍL-*ma-lik* lú *Ba-ḫa-ga* **L.** *Gú-rá-ma-an*$^{ki}$ tuš-LÚ×TIL; **6** o. II 6: (silver) níĝ-ba ḫúb-ki **L.** *a*-<*lu*->*nu* ĝiš ba:tuš; o. III 6: (silver) níĝ-ba ĝuruš-ĝuruš maškim-*sù Ma-ri*$^{ki}$ **L.** nídba ì-ĝiš *Ma-ri*$^{ki}$; o. XIV 6: 2 ĜIŠ-DU en **L.** SIG$_{7}$ è *si-in* ki $^{d}$*Ra-sa-ap*; r. III 3: 1 ĝír mar-tu níĝ-ba $^{d}$*Da-i-in wa* maš-maš 1 ĜIŠ-banšur níĝ-ba $^{d}$*Ga-mi-iš* **L.** en e$_{11}$ é $^{d}$*Ga-mi-iš*; r. VII 11: 1 íb-lá 1 *si-ti-tum* 1 ĝír-kun *Ba-lu-zú* "ur$_{4}$" *Ì-mar*$^{ki}$ **L.** ḫúl na-rú-*sù*; r. VIII 11: 1 íb-lá 1 ĝír-kun *I-bí-šum* lú *Ti-ir* **L.** tuš-LÚ×TIL *Zú-ti*$^{ki}$; **7** r. XI 19: (silver) níĝ-b]a PN$_{1}$-PN$_{4}$ *A-ša*$^{ki}$ **L.** DU.DU nam-kud é $^{d}$*Ku-ra*; r. XIV 5: 4 *ti-ša-nu* 2 *bu*-DI níĝ-ba $^{d}$*Ga-na-na* **L.** ĜIŠ.DUG.DU maḫ; **8** o. II 5: ⌜1⌝ ĝír mar-[t]u ⌜1⌝ *r*[*a*]-⌜*ʾà*⌝-*tum* kg *Ib-rí-um* en šu-mu-tak$_{4}$ **L.** ḫúl na-rú [ ]; o. IX 9: 20 íb-lá 20 kun ŠA.PI ì-na-sum SA.ZA$_{x}^{ki}$ *in* igi-ḫi-du$_{8}$ **L.** ⌜nídba⌝ [ ]; **9** r. VI 4: ĜIŠ-ti-ḪAR *Wa-ba*-⌜*rúm*⌝ šu-ba$_{4}$-ti **L.** šu-mu-níĝin SA.ZA$_{x}^{ki}$; r. VII 1: 4 *bu*-DI níĝ-ba *Ib-ʾà-ra wa* nin-ni-⌜*sù*⌝ **L.** níĝ-mu-sá ⌜*Za*⌝-*ne-ḫi-Ma*-[*r*]*i*$^{ki}$ é-gi *Ib-ʾà-ra ʾÀ-šu*$^{ki}$; **10** o. V 14: 1 ĜIŠ-banšur níĝ-ba $^{d}$*Ku-ra Ib-rí-um* in-na-sum **L.** ne:s[aĝ]-*sù*; o. VIII 16: 2 *bu*-DI dam BAD-*da-mu* **L.** níĝ-mu-sá; o. X 1: (silver) níĝ-ba *Wa-ba-rúm Ma-ri*$^{ki}$ **L.** di-kud DU.DU; **11** o. V 4: 1 kù-sal … [1 g]ír mar-⌜tu⌝ níĝ-⌜ba⌝ [$^{d}$*Ku-ra*] [*Ib-rí-um*$^{?}$] [ì-na-sum] **L.** ne:saĝ, 16: 1 kù-sal … 1 ĝír mar-tu níĝ-ba *Ib-ri-um* $^{d}$*Ra-s*[*a-ap*] *g*[*ú-n*]*úm* **L.** ne:saĝ; r. II 6: 80 í[b-lá] 80 ĝír m[ar-tu] 21 á-MUŠEN zabar SUD. SI.PA.SAL-*sù* **L.** è níĝ-kas$_{4}$ *Gú-da-da-núm*$^{ki}$; r. VI 1: 1 ešda níĝ-ba [$^{dʾ}$*A*$_{5}$*-d*]*a-"bal"* [ ] **L.** NI.DU, 10: 1 ĜIŠ-banšur níĝ-ba $^{d}$*Ra-sa-ap Du-bí-tum*$^{ki}$ [ ]⌜x⌝ **L.** ḫúl é-*sù*; r. VII 20: 1 íb-lá 1 ĝír-kun … maš-[maš-*sù*] … 1 dib … 1 ĝír mar-tu kg *Zi-ir-a-ḫu* ugula *A-bar-sal*$_{4}^{ki}$ **L.** šu-du$_{8}$; **12** o. VI 7: 2 ĝír mar-tu … 2 kù-sal [ní]ĝ-ba $^{d}$BAD *Ga-na-na-im* [*w*]*a* [$^{dʾ}$*A*$_{5}$*-d*]*a*[*-ra*] *Gi-rí wa Ni-ir-da-mu* 2 dumu-nita *Ib-rí-um* in-na-sum **L.** gi$_{4}$ *mi-nu Du-du-lu*$^{ki}$; o. IX 9: 1 *li-im* ĜIŠ-gu-kak-gíd zabar … 1 ĝír mar-tu kg *Ib-rí-um* **L.** è *si-in* níĝ-kas$_{4}$ *Ma-nu-wa-ad*$^{ki}$; o. XII 8: 2 ĝeštu$_{x}$-lá *I-bí-zi-kir* dumu-nita *Ib-rí-um* **L.** šu-du$_{8}$ *in Ma-nu-wa-ad*$^{ki}$, 18: 2 ĝeštu$_{x}$-lá *I-bí-zi-kir* lú *I-rí-gú-nu* **L.** tuš-LÚ×TIL *in Ma-nu-wa-ad*$^{ki}$; r. I 5: 1 íb-lá 1 *si-ti-tum* 1 ĝír-kun *I-bí-du-lum* en *Ma-nu-wa-ad*$^{ki}$ **L.** DU.DU nam-kud é $^{d}$*Ku-ra*; r. IV 8: 1 ĝír mar-tu kg *Ib-rí-um* **L.** è *si-in* á-daḫ lú *A-te-na-ad*$^{ki}$; r. VIII 6: 1 ĝír mar-tu kg *Ib-rí-um* **L.** ká gibil lú *I-bí-zi-kir* igi-ḫi-du$_{8}$; r. IX 19: 2 an-dùl … *ba-na-a-sa wa* 2 šu-*sù wa* 2 DU-*sù* níĝ-ba *Du-si-gú* $^{d}$*Ku-ra* **L.** ne:saĝ; **13** o. II 18: 1 íb-lá 1 *si-ti-tum* 1 ĝír-kun *Mu*-NE-*a-du* ugula *Ar-ḫa-du*$^{ki}$ **L.** DU.DU nam-kud é $^{d}$*Ku-ra*; o. XVI 2: 2 *bu*-DI … 2 saĝ-*sù* níĝ-ba *Ti-šè-li-im ma-lik-tum Ì-mar*$^{ki}$ **L.** DU.DU *si-in* SA.ZA$_{x}^{ki}$ tak$_{4}$ AMA-*ra*; r. I 6: (silver) níĝ-ba *Ìr-am*$_{6}$-kur$^{ki}$ sagi *Ma-ri*$^{ki}$ **L.** kin$_{5}$-ak kú en; r. VI 15: 1 ĝír mar-tu kg *Na-zu-mu* **L.** níĝ-kas$_{4}$ *si-in* Kiš$^{ki}$; r. IX 17: [ ] *B*[*ù*-]*du-d*[*u*] ugula *Ar-ʾà-mu*$^{ki}$ **L.** *Si-da-rí-in*$^{ki}$ til; **15** o. II 27: 1 *gú-li-lum a-li-iš* ĜIŠ-gu-kak-gíd $^{dʾ}$*A*$_{5}$*-da-"bal"* [ ]$^{ki}$ en ì-na-sum **L.** šeš-II-ib; o. IV 8: 1 dib *Bar-za-ma-ù* ugula *ʾÀ-šu*$^{ki}$ **L.** tuš-LÚ×TIL *A-a-lu*$^{ki}$; o. XIII 25: 1 íb[-lá] 1 ĝír-kun … *I-in-il* ugula *Ù-ša-li-ik*$^{ki}$ **L.** tuš-LÚ×TIL *Kak-mi-um*$^{ki}$; o. XVI 23: 2 *bu*-DI … 2 saĝ-*sù Zi-mi-ni*-kù:babbar *ma-lik-tum Bur-ma-an*$^{ki}$ **L.** dumu-munus tu-da; r. V 13: 2 *bu*-DI … 2 saĝ-*sù ma-lik-tum Ì-ra-ar*$^{ki}$ ama-gal en šu-mu-tak$_{4}$ **L.** DU.DU *Ga-wa-na*$^{ki}$; **16** r. IX 5: 2 níĝ-anše-ak 4 kù-sal *I-bí-zi-kir* dumu-nita *Ib-rí-um* **L.** tuš-LÚ×TIL *Ḫal-sum*$^{ki}$; r. XIII 27: 2 ĝeštu$_{x}$-lá 15 sikil $^{d}$*Iš:šára Zu-ra-mu*$^{ki}$ *wa* 1 *ù*-NAM-*mi-lu* 8 gín D. sikil $^{d}$BAD-munus *Lu-ba-an*$^{ki}$ *wa* 1 kù-sal 4 gín D. sikil [ ]⌜x⌝ [ ] s[ikil] **L.** tu-da; r. XIV 12: gur$_{8}$ má-gal-má-gal mu-DU *na-se*$_{11}$*-na-se*$_{11}$ **L.** [ ]; **17** o. VI 15: [*Dar-maš-da-mu*] dumu-munus en é-gi BAD-*da-mu* **L.** DU.DU nídba é diĝir en; o. VII 23: 2 *bu*-DI níĝ-ba *Ti-ša-li-im ma-lik-tum Ì-mar*$^{ki}$ **L.** [ ] [*I-bí-zi-kir*] [dumu-]nita *Ib-rí-um*; o. XII 5: [2 *b*]*u*-DI *ma-lik-tum Lum-na-an*$^{ki}$ ama-gal en šu-mu-tak$_{4}$ **L.** DU.DU *si-in U*$_{9}$*-gú-a-aš*$^{ki}$; o. XVI 4: 1 ĝír mar-tu kg *Ib-rí-um* **L.** è níĝ-kas$_{4}$ al-kur$_{6}$ še *Kak-mi-um*$^{ki}$; o. XX 4: (daggers) in-na-sum SA.ZA$_{x}^{ki}$ **L.** níĝ-kas$_{4}$ *A-ḫ*[*a-za*-]*ni-ig*$^{⌜ki⌝}$; r. VI 3: 2 *bu*-DI *Ti-ša-li-im ma-lik-tum Ì-mar*$^{ki}$ **L.** DU.DU *mi-nu ʾÀ-da-ni*$^{ki}$; r. IX 34: 2 *bu*-DI *Ti-ša-li-im ma-lik-tum Ì-mar*$^{ki}$ **L.** DU.DU *mi-nu* NI-*ab*$^{ki}$ *si-in* SA.ZA$_{x}^{ki}$; r. XII 21: [x í]b-lá [x *si-t*]*i-*[*tu*]*m* [x gí]r-[ku]n … 1 ĝír mar-tu kg níĝ-ba *Ib-rí-um* **L.** níĝ-mu-sa *ma-lik-tum*; r. XVI 11: 2 *bu*-DI níĝ-ba $^{d}$*A-da-ma gú-núm ma-lik-tum* ì-na-sum **L.** šu-mu-níĝin é diĝir-diĝir-diĝir; **18** o. I 16: 3 útul maḫ urudu **L.** *ir-me*; **19** o. III 15: 3 tùn tur ŠA.PI-ŠA. PI lú šu-mu-tak$_{4}$ *si-in A-la-ga*$^{ki}$ **L.** igi-ḫi-du$^{!}$(šu-du$_{8}$) *A-la-ga*$^{ki}$; o. VII 28: 1 íb-lá 1 *si-ti-tum* 1 ĝír-kun *Mu-gàr* dumu-nita *A-ba-rúm* **L.** ḫúl-*sù*; r. XVI 18: útul-útul maḫ urudu **L.** ḫúl *Ib-rí-um*; r. XVIII 12: 1 íb-lá 1 *si-ti-tum* 1 ĝír-kun 1 ĜIŠ-sal níĝ-[b]a *Ib-rí-um* … 2 íb-lá 2 ĝír-kun … 2 ĜIŠ-sal-*sù I-bí-zi-kir wa Ù-ti* 2 dumu-nita-*sù* **L.** ḫúl-*sù*; **20** o. XVII 12: 1 íb-lá 1 ĝír-kun … maš-maš-*sù Gi-a-da-mu* **L.** ḫúl-*sù*; r. III 21: 1 kù-sal níĝ-ba *Dar-ib-da-mu* dumu-munus en $^{d}$BAD-munus *si-in Lu-ba-an*$^{ki}$ **L.** *ter*$_{6}$*-bí* bur-KAK-*sù* $^{dʾ}$*A*$_{5}$*-da-"bal"*; r. VIII 5: 1 íb-lá 1 *si-ti-tum* 1 ĝír-kun

*Kùn-da-ba-an* [ ] **L.** tuš-LÚ×TIL *in A-ru$_{12}$-ga-du*$^{ki}$, 15: 2 *bu-*DI *Ti-šè-li-im ma-lik-tum Ì-mar*$^{ki}$ **L.** DU.DU *mi-nu ʾÀ-da-ni*$^{ki}$; **21** o. III 3: [ ]-*sù Ti-ti-nu* **L.** ḫúl-*sù*; o. XI 23: AN.[Š]È.GÚ 1 *mi-at* 80 lá-1 ma-na kb lú è **L.** [úš *Ib-rí-um*]; o. XII 13: (silver) níĝ-ba ábba-ábba *Ma-rí*$^{ki}$ **L.** nídba ì-ĝiš *Ib-la*$^{ki}$ *wa Ma-rí*$^{ki}$; r. IX 15: [1$^{?}$ í]b-lá [1 g]ír-kun ... *Ig-na-da-ar* lú *Mi-ga-ì Ti-ti-nu* šu-mu-tak$_4$ **L.** ḫúl-*sù*; **22** o. VI 3: (silver) lú *Ar-mi*$^{ki}$ in-na-sum **L.** šu-mu-níĝin SA.ZA$_x$$^{ki}$; **23** r. I 2: (19 bracelets) ĝuruš-ĝuruš SA.ZA$_x$$^{ki}$ **L.** è níĝ-kas$_4$ *Gú-da-da-núm*$^{ki}$; r. III 1: 1 *ar-ra-šum* 1 *ḫa-bù* níĝ-ba $^{d}$*ʾA$_5$-da-"bal" ʾÀ-ma-du*$^{ki}$ en šu-mu-tak$_4$ **L.** NI.DU-NI.DU; r. III 10: (10 daggers) ĝuruš-ĝuruš **L.** è níĝ-kas$_4$ *Gú-da-da-núm*$^{ki}$; **24** o. VII 5: 1 kù-sal níĝ-ba *Ib-rí-um* $^{d}$*Ba-ra-ma* **L.** ne:saĝ-*sù*; **25** o. IV 2: (270 garments, 1 dagger) [ ] **L.** AMA-*ra*; o. IX 7: 1 íb-lá TAR kb *I-nu-ud-da-mu Kak-mi-um*$^{ki}$ **L.** nídba ì-ĝiš *Ib-la*$^{ki}$ *i*[*n*] [ ]; r. II 6: ⸢x⸣-[ ] *Ì-ra-ar*$^{ki}$ **L.** DU *M*[*a*]-*za-t*[*um*$^{?ki}$]; r. III 4: [ ] l[ú] *D*[*u-si*] ugula *Ib-al*$_6$$^{ki}$ **L.** ĜIŠ-gu-kak-gíd šu-mu-tak$_4$; r. X 4: AN.ŠÈ.GÚ 86 ma-na 53 gín D. kb è **L.** *Ib-rí-um.*

ir$_{11}$ «servant»

ir$_{11}$-ir$_{11}$ **5** r. III 2: 85[+1] íb+II-TÚG babbar **L.** en; **21** o. XI 14: 60 íb+III-TÚG gùn **L.**

ugula ir$_{11}$ **16** r. II 24: *I-ba-zi-mi-nu* **L.**

*ìr-a-núm* «work gang» **5** o. V 17–VI 5: 24 íb$^{?}$-lá ĝír-kun **L.** *I-rí-ig-ma-lik* ... 2 ½ gín D. kg *ni-zi-mu* nu$_{11}$-za *gú-lilum* **L.**-*sù*; **12** o. XIV 8: 2 *gú-li-lum* kb lú *Sa-mu-um* lú *En-ti wa* lú dumu-nita *I-da-ad-mu in* **L.** *I-rí-ig-ma-lik.*

*ir-me* (a feast in month IX) **18** o. I 17: 3 útul maḫ urudu *in* ud **L.**

*iš-ki-lum* **10** o. IV 6: 10 gín D. kb *ni-zi-mu* **L.** en

iti «month» **19** o. IV 3: 3 gín D. kg lul-gu-ak 1 **L.** lú é $^{d}$*ʾÀ-da* lú-máš.

$^{d}$AMA-*ra* **2** r. IV 9; r. VII 10; **6** r. I 4; **7** o. XII 1: *in* **L.**, 15: *in* **L.**; r. VI 10; **11** o. X 4: (115 garments, 220+[x] kilts) ... raš-SAR Kur$^{ki}$ ki:lam$_7$ **L.**; o. XI 8: *in* **L.**; **14** o. X 10: *in* **L.**; o. XIV 5; o. XVII 13: (121+[x] garments, 306 kilts, 5 daggers) ... raš-SAR Kur$^{ki}$ ... 11 gud en ... ĜIŠ-ti-ḪAR *Wa-ba-rúm* šu-ba$_4$-ti ki:lam$_7$ *ʾÀ-da-ni*$^{ki}$ *in* **L.**; **15** o. X 14: *in* **L.**; o. XIII 5: (171 garments, 170 kilts) ... 10 sila$_4$ sa$_6$ ... ĜIŠ-ti-ḪAR *Wa-ba-rúm* ki:lam$_7$ **L.** *ʾÀ-da-ni*$^{ki}$; **16** o. XIII 20: [x$^{?}$+]2 BAR.AN *Na-gàr*$^{ki}$ ... (57 garments) ... raš-SAR Kur$^{ki}$ ki:lam$_7$ *ʾÀ-da-ni*$^{ki}$ **L.**; r. I 22: *in* **L.**; **17** r. IV 29: *in* **L.**; **18** o. XIX 25: *in* **L.**; r. III 16: (148 garments, 210 na$_4$ measures of wool) ... raš-SAR Kur$^{ki}$ ... 3 IGI.NITA u$_5$ en ki:lam$_7$ *ʾÀ-da-ni*$^{ki}$ **L.**; **19** o. XI 19: *in* **L.**; **20** o. IX 6: *in* **L.**; **21** r. VIII 4: [*in*] [**L.**].

AMA-*ra* **5** o. VIII 3: *in* **L.**, 13: *in* **L.**; o. IX 9: (7 garments, 607 kilts, 18 daggers) ... ĜIŠ-ti-ḪAR *Wa-ba-rúm* šu-ba$_4$-ti ki:lam$_7$ **L.**; o. XII 15; **9** o. III 21; o. IV 14: [*i*]*n* **L.**; o. VIII 9: (17 garments, 38 kilts) [... ki:lam$_7$] *ʾÀ-da-ni*$^{ki}$; **10** o. XI 16: *in* **L.**; **13** o. XV 1: (135+[x] kilts, 2 helmets) ... 12 gud ... ĜIŠ-ti-ḪAR ... ki:lam$_7$ *ʾÀ-da-ni*$^{ki}$; o. XVI 7; **19** o. XIII 27; **22** o. I 6: *in* **L.**; **25** o. IV 3: (84 garments, 186 kilts, 1 dagger) [ki:lam$_7$] [*ʾÀ-da-ni*]⸢$^{ki}$⸣ **L.**

iti *ʾa$_5$-nun* **5** r. XI 7: *in* **L.**, 21: *in* **L.**; **7** r. VIII 7: *in* **L.**; **11** r. VIII 19: *in* **L.**; **12** r. II 7: *in* **L.**; **15** r. IX 23: *in* **L.**; **16** r. XI 12: *in* **L.**; **19** r. XVII 17 (<iti>); **20** r. XI 16; **23** r. IV 13: *in* **L.**

*gi-*NI **11** r. IV 13: *in* **L.**; **14** r. II 23: [*i*]*n* [**L.**]; **15** r. I 15: *i*[*n*] **L.**; r. III 7; **16** r. VII 25: *in* **L.**; **17** r. XV 19: *in* **L.**; **18** r. XI 11: *in* **L.**; **19** r. VIII 30: *in* **L.**; **20** r. VII 21: *in* **L.**; **21** o. XV 14: *in* **L.**; **23** r. II 5.

*ḫu-ru$_{12}$-mu* **9** r. V 17.

iti NI.DU **11** r. VI 2: *in* ud **L.**(<iti>); **12** r. IX 4–5: *al$_6$* **L.**; **18** r. XVII 7 (<iti>).

NI.DU-NI.DU **23** r. III 2: *in* ud **L.**

ì-ti «to attend; to be available» **10** o. XVI 13: (silver) *A-da-bí-ig*$^{ki}$ **L.** *mi-nu Ar-mi*$^{ki}$.

izi-ĝar «brazier» (feast of the braziers) **10** o. VII 20: ĜIŠ.DUG.DU **L.**; **11** r. IV 6: ĜIŠ.DUG.D[U] **L.**; **12** r. V 18: ĜIŠ.DUG.DU **L.**

## K

ká «gate (administrative district constituted by villages under the authority of an overseer, ugula)» **12** r. VIII 7: *in* ud **L.** gibil lú *I-bí-zi-kir* igi-ḫi-du$_8$; **22** o. IV 5: (gold and silver) **L.** *Ga-nu-lum.*

kad$_4$ (a kind of craft)

kad$_4$-kad$_4$ **5** o. VII 10: *Ib-gi-da-mu* ugula **L.**

KA-*ḫu-a-tum* **15** o. X 19: 14 gín D. kg 2 *ti-gi-na* 2 ĜIŠ-du 1 **L.**

*kam$_4$-ma-a-tum* see *s.v. ga-ma-a-tum*

kar «to hand over» **10** o. XV 13: (silver) níĝ-du$_8$ *Ù-ba-nu* **L.** kg en *Ma-nu-wa-ad*$^{ki}$.

kas$_4$ «messenger» **12** o. V 9: *Zi-la-da-mu* ugula **L.**

kas$_4$-kas$_4$ **4** o. XI 23: 12 zi-bar tur lú sagi **L.** é en; **6** r. V 1: (silver) níĝ-kaskal *En-na-ì* lú **L.** DU.DU *Ma-rí*$^{ki}$; **14** o. V 5: (silver) *Mu-*NE*-a-du* ugula *Ar-ḫa-du*$^{ki}$ *Puzur$_4$-ra-ma-lik* lú **L.** šu-mu-tak$_4$; **21** r. I 18: 3 ĜIŠ-šú 3 níĝ-bànda lú diri lú šu-šu **L.**

KA-si (an ornament of the harness) **18** o. XII 15: TAR kg *zi-ba-tum* 2 **L.** en.

kaskal «journey, expedition» **3** o. III 18: 6 ĜIŠ-kak-ĜIŠ-kak lú ĜIŠ-asari **L.** en; **6** r. III 11: 6 ĜIŠ-kak-ĜIŠ-kak 2 ĜIŠ-banšur **L.** en; r. VII 5: 2 bur-KAK aš-ḫal ì-ĝiš **L.** en; **10** r. I 18: (silver) *Na-gàr*$^{ki}$ *in* **L.**; **14** o. XIV 4: 4 ĜIŠ-gu-kak-šub lú *Daš-na M*[*a-*]*rí*⸢$^{ki}$⸣ *i*[*n*] *Bar-ga-u$_9$*$^{ki}$ zàḫ *in* **L.** $^{d}$AMA-*ra*; **15** o. XVI 13: 1 ĜIŠ-šú 1 níĝ-bànda kb lú **L.** *Ib-rí-um*; **16** r. V 7: 6 ĜIŠ-kak-ĜIŠ-kak lú 2 asari **L.** en; r. XV 26 and 30: 2 bur-KAK ĜIŠ-⸢taškarin⸣ **L.** en *wa* 2 bur-KAK ĜIŠ-taškarin **L.** ⸢*Ib*⸣*-rí-um*; **17** o. VII 5: [silver] ⸢níĝ-ba⸣ *Ù-ri-rí* maškim ga:eš$_8$ *in* **L.** é $^{d}$BAD *Ga-na-na*; **18** o. VII 4: 15 ĜIŠ-kak-ĜIŠ-kak *ša-ti* 5 ĜIŠ-asari **L.** ⸢en⸣; r. XVII 23: (silver) *Ag-ga* (silver) *Gul-la Ḫu-ra-*NE *Na-gàr*$^{ki}$ *in* **L.** *Su-da-ma-an*$^{ki}$; **19** r. X 9: (silver) *Na-ba-ti-um*$^{ki}$ (silver) maškim-*sù in* **L.** šu-ba$_4$-ti; **20** r. I 21: (9 tools) lú **L.** en; **21** o. II 8: (silver) níĝ-ba *Ḫu-*NE*-du wa Ir$_{11}$-tum-a-ḫu Sag-gar*$^{ki}$ **L.** níĝ-kas$_4$ *Du-du-lu*$^{ki}$.

kaskal-kaskal **18** o. XVII 21: 1 ĜIŠ-šú 2 níĝ-bànda **L.** *Ib-rí-um.*

ki «landed property» **6** o. XIV 10: *in* ud SIG$_7$ è *si-in* **L.** $^{d}$*Ra-sa-ap*; 8 r. XI 3': 1 dub **L.** *Ib-rí-um.*

ki-lam$_7$ (ki:lam$_7$) «market» **1**(a) r. x+I 2'; **2** o. VII 4: **L.** *gi-ba-lu ʾÀ-da-ni*$^{ki}$; o. VIII 18: **L.** *zi-ba-tum ʾÀ-da-ni*$^{ki}$; o. X 10: **L.** SA.ZA$_x^{ki}$; o. XI 1: **L.** $^{d}$*A-da-ma*; r. VI 4: **L.** *ʾÀ-da-ni*$^{ki}$; r. VII 13: **L.** $^{d}$*Ì-lam*; r. X 6: **L.** NI-*ab*$^{ki}$; r. XII 21: **L.** SA.ZA$_x^{ki}$; r. XIII 10: **L.** *Ìr-ku*$^{ki}$ *A-bù*-Kur$^{ki}$; r. XVI 12: **L.** *Du-du-la*$^{ki}$; r. XVII 6: **L.** $^{d}$*Áš-da-bíl*, 14: **L.** *Šè-ʾà-am*$^{ki}$; **3** o. V 17: **L.** SA.ZA$_x^{ki}$; o. VII 8: **L.** $^{d}$*Ga-mi-iš*; o. X 5': **L.** $^{d}$*Áš-da-bíl*; r. II 11; r. VII 3: **L.** *gi-ba-lu ʾÀ-da-ni*$^{ki}$; r. IX 16: **L.** šeš-II-ib *ʾÀ-da-ni*$^{ki}$; r. XIII 12 and 15: **L.** $^{d}$*A-da-ma wa* **L.** bàd-diĝir$^{ki}$; r. XIV 10: **L.** *Ma-rí*$^{ki}$ *Na-zi*; **4** r. VII 16: **L.** *ʾÀ-da-ni*$^{ki}$; **5** o. II 5: **L.** <$^{d}$>*A-da-ma ʾÀ-da-ni*$^{ki}$; o. IV 4: **L.** SA.ZA$_x^{ki}$; o. IX 8: **L.** AMA-*ra*; o. XV 16: **L.** $^{d}$*Ga-mi-iš*; r. II 13: **L.** SA.ZA$_x^{ki}$; r. III 11: **L.** SA.ZA$_x^{ki}$; r. IX 12: **L.** $^{d}$*Áš-da-bíl*; r. XI 18: **L.** $^{dʾ}$*À-da*; **6** o. XI 3: **L.** $^{d}$*A-da-ma ʾÀ-da-ni*$^{ki}$; r. IX 3: **L.** *Ma-rí*$^{ki}$ *Na-zi*; r. X 2: **L.** *ʾÀ-da-ni*$^{ki}$ *wa* NI-*ab*$^{ki}$ *wa La-ru*$_{12}$*-ga-du*$^{ki}$; r. XI 14: **L.** SA.ZA$_x^{ki}$; r. XII 11: **L.** $^{d}$*Áš-da-bíl*; r. XIII 13: **L.** $^{dʾ}$*À-da*; **7** o. IX 8: **L.** $^{d}$*A-da-ma wa* SA.ZA$_x^{ki}$; o. XVII 12: **L.** $^{dʾ}$*À-da*; r. VI 17: **L.** $^{d}$*Áš-da-bíl wa* [*Ši-*]⌜*ʾà*⌝*-mu*$^{ki}$; r. VII 13: **L.** $^{dʾ}$*À-da*; **8** o. V 10: **L.** šeš-⌜ib⌝[-II] *ʾÀ-da-ni*$^{ki}$; o. XI 10: [**L.**] [ ]$^{ki}$; **9** o. V 13: **L.** SA.ZA$_x^{ki}$; o. VIII 7: [**L.**] *ʾÀ-da-ni*$^{ki}$ $^{d}$AMA-*ra*; o. IX 17: **L.** $^{d}$*Ì-lam*; o. XIV 6: **L.** $^{d}$*Áš-da-bíl*, 16: **L.** *Ìr-ku*$^{ki}$; r. I 16: **L.** *gi-*[*ba-lu*] *ʾÀ-da-ni*$^{ki}$; r. XVI 14: **L.** *zi-ba-tum ʾÀ-da-ni*$^{ki}$; **10** r. VII 4: *in* **L.** $^{dʾ}$*À-da*, 11: **L.** *gi-ba-lu* ⌜*ʾÀ*⌝*-da-*[*ni*]$^{ki}$; **11** o. III 12: **L.** *gi-ba-ù* [*wa*] $^{d}$*A-d*[*am-*]*ma ʾÀ-da-ni*$^{ki}$; o. X 3: **L.** $^{d}$AMA-*ra*; o. XIII 11: *Ib-lu*$_5$*-zú* **L.** $^{d}$*Ga-mi-iš*; r. III 4: **L.** SA.ZA$_x^{ki}$ $^{d}$*Áš-da-bíl Ši-ʾà-mu*$^{ki}$; **12** o. II 6 and 9: **L.** *Ga-mi-iš wa* **L.** $^{dʾ}$*A*$_5$*-da-"bal" A-ru*$_{12}$*-ga-du*$^{ki}$; o. VIII 13: **L.** $^{d}$*Áš-da-bíl*; r. II 18: ugula **L.**; r. III 9: **L.** $^{dʾ}$*À-da*; **13** o. VI 1: **L.** šeš-II-ib *wa* $^{d}$*A-da-ma ʾÀ-da-ni*$^{ki}$; o. X 12: **L.** *Ma-rí*$^{ki}$ dam-gàr; o. XIV 15: **L.** *ʾÀ-da-ni*$^{ki}$ AMA-*ra*; o. XVII 12: **L.** $^{d}$*Ga-mi-iš*; r. II 2: **L.** SA.ZA$_x^{ki}$; r. V 14: **L.** $^{d}$*Áš-da-bíl*; r. X 10 and 13: **L.** *Si-*⌜*ʾà*⌝*-mu*$^{ki}$ *wa* **L.** $^{dʾ}$*À-da*; **14** o. VI 6: **L.** *Ma-rí*$^{ki}$ dam-gàr; o. XVII 10: **L.** *ʾÀ-da-ni*$^{ki}$ *in* AMA-*ra*; r. V 8: [**L.**] $^{d}$*Áš-da-bíl*; r. XII 10: **L.** [$^{d}$*A-*]*da-ma*; **15** o. VII 7: **L.** šeš-II-ib *wa* $^{d}$*A-da-ma ʾÀ-da-ni*$^{ki}$; o. VIII 9: **L.** *Ìr-ku*$^{ki}$; o. XIII 4: *Wa-ba-rúm* **L.** $^{d}$AMA-*ra ʾÀ-da-ni*$^{ki}$; r. I 1: *Puz*[*ur*$_4$*-ra*]*-ma-l*[*ik*] **L.** $^{d}$*Ga-mi-iš*; r. III 20: en **L.** SA.ZA$_x^{ki}$; r. IV 3: **L.** $^{dʾ}$*À-da*, 7: **L.** SA.ZA$_x^{ki}$; **16** o. IV 6: **L.** šeš-II-ib *ʾÀ-da-ni*$^{ki}$; o. XIII 18: **L.** *ʾÀ-da-ni*$^{ki}$ $^{d}$AMA-*ra*; r. IV 24: **L.** ⌜é⌝? *mi-i*[*š*-x]; r. XI 20: **L.** $^{dʾ}$*À-da*; **17** o. IX 6: **L.** *Ma-rí*$^{ki}$ dam-gàr [šu-]mu-[tak$_4$]; o. XVII 17: **L.** *Ma-rí*$^{ki}$ dam-gàr; r. X 16: **L.** $^{d}$*Ga-mi-iš*, 20: **L.** *Kab-lu*$_5$*-ul*$^{ki}$; r. XVIII 4: **L.** $^{d}$*Áš-da-bíl Du-ub*$^{ki}$ *Ìr-ku*$^{ki}$; r. XX 16: **L.** $^{dʾ}$*À-da*; r. XXII 27: **L.** [*g*]*i-*⌜*ba*⌝*-lu* [*ʾÀ-da-ni*$^{ki}$]; **18** o. IX 18: **L.** $^{d}$*A-da-ma ʾÀ-da-ni*$^{ki}$; r. III 14: **L.** *ʾÀ-da-ni*$^{ki}$ $^{d}$AMA-*ra*; r. XII 20: **L.** $^{d}$*Ga-mi-iš Du-bí-ga-lu*; r. XIII 10: **L.** $^{d}$*Ga-mi-iš wa* $^{d}$*Áš-da-bíl wa* $^{d}$BAD *Du-du-lu*$^{ki}$; **19** o. VI 29: **L.** $^{d}$*A-da-ma ʾÀ-da-ni*$^{ki}$; r. V 2: **L.** SA.ZA$_x^{ki}$, 18: **L.** *ʾÀ-da-ni*$^{ki}$ *wa* $^{d}$*Ga-mi-iš*; r. XVII 5: **L.** $^{dʾ}$*À-da*; **20** o. XIV 14: **L.** *ʾÀ-da-ni*$^{ki}$; r. VII 5: **L.** $^{d}$*Ga-mi-iš*; r. XIII 10: **L.** $^{d}$⌜*ʾÀ*⌝[*-da*]; **21** o. VII 1: **L.** SA.ZA$_x^{ki}$ NI-*rí*$^{ki}$; r. II 18–25: **L.** $^{d}$*Áš-da-bíl wa* **L.** *Ši-ʾà-am*$^{ki}$ *wa* **L.** $^{dʾ}$*À-da*; r. XII 20: **L.** *gi-ba-i*; **25** o. I 6: **L.** *Im-ma-ra-an*$^{ki}$ *A-bù*-Kur$^{ki}$; o. II 5: **L.** SA.ZA$_x^{ki}$ *wa* $^{d}$*A-da-ma ʾÀ-da-ni*$^{ki}$; o. IV 1: [**L.**] [*ʾÀ-da-ni*]⌜$^{ki}$⌝ AMA-*ra*; o. V 2: [**L.**] $^{d}$*Ga-mi-iš*; o. VI 1: **L.** SA.ZA$_x^{\langle ki\rangle}$, 5: **L.** *Ga-ga-ba-an*$^{ki}$ *A-bù*-Kur$^{ki}$; o. VII 3: **L.** $^{d}$*Áš-da-bíl*; o. VIII 3: **L.** $^{dʾ}$*À-da wa gi-ba-lu ʾÀ-da-ni*$^{ki}$.

"KIN" (a measure of the wool) see siki.

kin$_5$-ak «to make, to work» **1** o. V 7: 10 ma-na kb **L.** 17 íb-lá 17 *si-ti-tum* 17 ĝír-kun; **2** o. I 11: 1 gín D. kg **L.** 5 *zi-ba-tum*; o. II 3: 1 gín D. kg **L.** 1 kù-sal; o. VI 3: ŠÚ+ŠA gín D. kg **L.** 2 *ti-ki-na*; o. IX 16: 3 gín D. kb **L.** saĝ-*sù*; o. XII 3: 10 gín D. kg **L.** saĝ $^{dʾ}$*A*$_5$*-da-ra*; r. I 24: 2 gín D. kg **L.** 1 *gú-li-lum* 1 kù-sal; r. XIV 15: 4 ma-na 10 gín D. kb **L.** 5 *gú-li-lum* TAR-II esi *wa* 5 *gú-li-lum* ŠÚ+ŠA-II esi; r. XV 3: 50 gín D. kb **L.** 5 *gú-li-lum* 10-I esi; **3** o. III 15: 15 gín D. kb **L.** 6 ĜIŠ-kak-ĜIŠ-kak; r. IV 5: 4 gín D. kb **L.** 1 šu-dub; r. XII 12: [1 ma-na] kg **L.** 2 íb-lá kg; **4** o. III 6: 10 ½ gín D. kb ZU.PIRIĜ **L.** *gú-li-lum wa* níĝ-anše-ak kù-sal; o. IX 17: 5 ma-na TAR kb **L.** 3 íb<-lá> ĜÁ×LÁ ŠA.PI 7 íb-lá *si-ti-tum* ĝír-kun; o. XI 19: 1 ma-na kb **L.** 12 zi-bar tur; o. XV 17: 3 ma-na ŠÚ+ŠA gín D. kb **L.** 20 *gú-li-lum*; r. I 1: 7 gín D. kb **L.** 3 *zú-zú-ba-tum* ĜIŠ-gígir-II; r. III 16: 1 ma-na 53 an-na **L.** níĝ-anše-ak kù-sal; r. IX 10: 5 gín D. kb [**L.**] [ *gú-*]*li-lum*; r. X 2: 10 gín D. kb **L.** 6 *zú-zú-ba-tum* 2 ĜIŠ-gígir-II, 7: 2 ma-na kb **L.** 2 níĝ-anše-ak 4 kù-sal; r. XIII 2: 1 ma-na 12 gín D. kb **L.** 4 íb-lá *si-ti-tum* ĝír-kun, 13: [x gín D. kb] **L.** 4 íb-lá; r. XIV 3: 50 ma-na zabar **L.** 5 *mi-at* ĜIŠ-gu-kak-gíd, 8: 5 ma-na TAR 3 3 NI an-na **L.** [ ] ĜIŠ-g[u-]kak-gíd; **5** r. I 20: [x gín D. kb **L.**] 3 *zú-zú-ba-tum*; **6** o. V 3: TAR kb ZU.PIRIĜ **L.** 23 dib a-gar$_5$-gar$_5$ kg; o. VI 4: 13 ma-na ŠÚ+ŠA gín D. kb **L.** 20 íb-lá 20 ĝír-kun ĜÁ×LÁ ŠA.PI, 7: 11 ma-na ŠA.PI kb **L.** 10 *gú-li-lum*-II esi TAR *wa* 10 *gú-li-lum*-II esi ŠÚ+ŠA *wa* 20 *gú-li-lum* 10-I esi; r. I 22: 4 gín D. kb **L.** 10 lá-2 ĝeštu$_x$-lá; r. VII 2: ŠÚ+ŠA gín D. kb **L.** 2 bur-KAK *aš-ḫal* ì-ĝiš; r. XV 2: 3 ma-na ŠA.PI gín D. an-na **L.** 40 ĝír mar-tu kg 20 ĝír mar-tu zú 20 ĝír mar-tu *ba-du-u*$_9$ kbg, 7: 11 ma-na 6 gín D. an-na **L.** 1 *li-im* ĜIŠ-gu-kak-gíd zabar; r. XVI 17: 4 an-na **L.** 4 ĝír šu-du$_8$-máš, 20: ŠÚ+ŠA an-na **L.** $^{d}$*A-lum wa* $^{d}$*Si-gar A-ḫa-da-mu*$^{ki}$; r. XVII 29: 1 ma-na an-na **L.** $^{d}$*Á-la wa* dam-*sù* lú *A-ra-ab*$^{ki}$; l.ed. 2: ŠA.PI an-na **L.** $^{d}$*Ì-lam* lú *Za-za-u*$_9$; **7** o. V 2: [ ] šub *si-in* **L.**-*sù*; o. XV 2: [x ma-na x] gín D. kb **L.** 6 *zú-zú-ba-tum* ĜIŠ-bar-ús zú-ak 2 ĜIŠ-gígir-II en; **8** o. IX 4: 13 ma-na ŠÚ+ŠA gín D. kb **L.** 20 íb-lá 20 kun ŠA.PI; o. XIV 9: 2 ma-na TAR 2 gín D. kg **L.** 4 s[ag ] 4 *zi-*[*kir-*]*ra-tu*[*m*]; **9** r. XIV 7: [ ] **L.** *gú-li-lum* ĝuruš-ĝuruš SA.ZA$_x^{ki}$; **10** o. IX 9: 13 m[a-]n[a] ŠÚ[+ŠA gí]n [D.] kb **L.** 20 íb-lá 20 ĝír-kun; r. II 17: [ša]-pi gín D. kb **L.** 4 *gú-li-lum*-I esi; **12** o. IX 4: 11 ma-na 10 gín D. an-na **L.** 1 *li-im* ĜIŠ-gu-kak-gíd zabar; r. VIII 13: ŠÚ+ŠA 6 gín D. kb **L.** saĝ $^{d}$*Ra-sa-ap Du-ne-íb*$^{ki}$ *wa* nu$_{11}$-za íb+III-TÚG-*sù* lú *al*$_6$ [ ] NI-du$_8$; r. XI 2: ŠA.PI gín D. kg **L.** 2 níĝ-anše-ak, 11: 1 ma-na ŠÚ+ŠA 3 gín D. an-na šub *si-in* 9 ma-na TAR gín D. a-gar$_5$-gar$_5$ **L.** 6 tùn-tur lú TAR.TAR 6 dub-naĝar šu-mu-LAGAB ŠÚ+ŠA-ŠÚ+ŠA 6 dub-naĝar sal lú 15 gín D. 6 dub-naĝar sal 10 6 *ma-za-ḫa-ru*$_{12}$ 10 6 *ḫa-ra-nu* 10 6 *ḫa-ra-nu* 5 6 dub-naĝar tur 5 12 ⌜UŠ×KÍD⌝; r. XII 11: 57 gín D. an-na šub *si-in* 6 ma-na ŠA.PI 6 gín D. a-gar$_5$-gar$_5$ **L.** 5 tùn tur TAR.TAR 5 dub-naĝar sal 15 5 dub-naĝar sal 10 5 *ma-ga-za-u*$_9$ 10 5 *ma-za-ḫa-ru*$_{12}$ TAR [ ]; **13** o. VII 10: 3 gín D. kg **L.** 1 *du-rúm*; o. X 7: 3 ma-na an-na šub *si-in* 24 ma-na a-gar$_5$-gar$_5$ **L.** IGI.DUB 40 níĝ-saĝšu; r. I 7: *in* ud **L.** kú en; r. V 5: [ ] **L.** $^d$*A-gi Su-ti-ig*$^{ki}$; r. XIII 18: 2 ma-na kb **L.** 2 *gú-li-lum*-II ŠÚ+ŠA 2 *gú-li-lum*-I 10; **14** o. I 12: [x] gín D. [k]g **L.** 1 *mu-ḫar-tim*; o. IV 2: 6 ma-na ŠA.PI gín D. an-na šub-šub *si-in* **L.** 2 *mi-at* ĝír mar-tu, 5: 4 ma-na ŠÚ+ŠA 7 gín D. kb **L.** *kam*$_4$*-ma-a-tum-*⸢*sù*⸣, 15: 4 ma-na TAR an-na šub *si-in* **L.** IGI.DUB 60 níĝ-saĝšu; o. V 19: 11 *ra-ʾà-tum* … LAGAB×UD-LAGAB×UD **L.** ĜIŠ-asari sagi; r. VII 19: 9 gín D. kb … **L.** *šè-li*, 25: 2 gín D. an-na šub *si-in* 16 gín D. a-⸢gar$_5$⸣-gar$_5$ **L.** ĜIŠ-bar-ús en; r. VIII 2: [4 gín D. kg **L.** 1 ĜIŠ-ba]nšur [*wa*] 1 kù-sal; r. XI 4: 2 gín D. kb **L.** [ ]; **15** o. XI 7: 1 ma-na 14 gín D. kg **L.** 10 ĝeštu$_x$-lá 2 *ti-gi-na* 62 *du-ru*$_{12}$*-gú* 1 *mi-at kur-gú-ru*$_{12}$ 2 kù-sal 1 *ma-ḫa-na-gúm ḫa-za-nu* 1 šu-dub 1 *ša-mu* 2 *ti-ba-ra-núm wa* nu$_{11}$-za 2 saĝ 2 *bu*-DI; o. XIV 16: 10 ma-na kg **L.** é $^d$*Ku-ra*; o. XV 13: 12 gín D. an-na šub *si-in* 1 ma-na 10 a-gar$_5$-gar$_5$ **L.** 2 ⸢ĜIŠ⸣-zú; r. I 19: ŠA.PI gín D. kg **L.** 1 an-zam$_x$ *wa* 1 pad-*sù*; r. II 16: 1 ma-na a-gar$_5$-gar$_5$ **L.** 1 *ma-ḫa-ni-gúm wa* 1 tùn gal; r. VIII 15: 50 gín D. kg **L.** 1 an-zam$_x$ *wa* 1 pad-*sù*; r. XI 23: 2 ma-na kg **L.** 2 *gù-li-lum*; r. XII 22: 2 ma-na kg **L.** 2 *gù-li-lum*; r. XIV 19: 10 gín D. kb ZU.PIRIĜ **L.** 3 útul urudu maḫ; **16** o. II 21: 1 ½ gín D. kg L. 6 *da*-NE-*a-tum si-ti-tum*; o. VI 21: 2 ma-na TAR kg **L.** 2 níĝ-anše-ak 4 kù-sal gibil; r. V 4: 3 gín D. an-na šub *si-in* 17 gín D. a-gar$_5$-gar$_5$ **L.** 6 ĜIŠ-kak-ĜIŠ-kak lú 2 asari; r. VIII 25: 1 ma-na kg **L.** 2 níĝ-anše-ak 4 kù-sal; r. XIII 10: ŠÚ+ŠA 6 gín D. kg **L.** lul-gu-ak 2 ĝeštu$_x$-lá 15; r. XV 7: TAR an-na šub *si-in* 4 ma-na ŠÚ+ŠA a-gar$_5$-gar$_5$ **L.** 5 tùn gal TAR.TAR 5 dub-naĝar šu-mu-LAGAB 15 5 dub-naĝar 10 sal; r. XVI 5: 13 ma-na ŠÚ+ŠA an-na šub *si-in* 4 *mi-at* ma-na a-gar$_5$-gar$_5$ **L.** 2 útul urudu maḫ gibil; **17** o. VII 11: 50 gín D. kg **L.** 2 níĝ-anše-ak 4!(2) kù-sal 2 IGI.NITA; o. XVIII 8: 10 ma-na an-na **L.** 3 *mi-at* ĝír mar-tu zabar, 13: 6 ma-na TAR kb **L.** *kam*$_4$*-ma-a-tum-sù*, 17: 1 ma-na ŠA.PI gín an-na šub *si-in* **L.** 1 *mi-at* ĝír mar-tu zú-ak; o. XIX 2: 56 gín D. an-na šub *si-in* 5 ma-na ŠA.PI gín D. a-gar$_5$-gar$_5$ **L.** 17 ĝír mar-tu zú *wa* 3 ĝír mar-tu *ba-du-u*$_4$ kbg, 18: 1 ma-na ŠA.PI gín D. an-na šub *si-in* 26 ma-na ŠA.PI a-gar$_5$-gar$_5$ **L.** 1 *mi-at* ĝír mar-tu ti{-la}, 21: 2 ma-na 10 gín D. kb **L.** *kam*$_4$*-ma-a-tum-sù*; o. XX 17: 1 ma-na ŠÚ+ŠA 4 gín D. an-na šub *si-in* 11 ma-na a-gar$_5$-gar$_5$ **L.** 6 *ḫar-ʾà-ru*$_{12}$ maḫ lú gud-si-dili, 22: 10 gín D. an-na šub *si-in* 10 lá-2 ma-na a-gar$_5$-gar$_5$ **L.** 6 ĜIŠ-kak-ĜIŠ-kak eme gud 1 si; r. I 16: 5 gín D. kb **L.** 3 *zú-zú-ba-tum*; r. III 2: 2 gín D. kb **L.** *kam*$_4$*-ma-a-tum* zàḫ *ša-ti* kù-sal ama-gal en; r. IV 10: 5 gín D. kb **L.** 1 *zi-zi-ḫi-tum*; r. VIII 22: 10 gín D. an-na šub *si-in* 1 ma-na 10 gín D. a-gar$_5$-gar$_5$ **L.** 3 ĝír mar-tu; r. IX 9: 5 gín D. kb **L.** 1 ĝír; r. XI 17: [x g]ín D. k[b] **L.** [*ḫ*]*a-za-nu* 2 šu-dub, 30: ŠÚ+ŠA gín D. kg **L.** 2 šu-dub; r. XII 4: 12[(+x)] gín D. kg **L.** 1 šu-dub; r. XIII 2: 3 ma-na kg **L.** 6 íb-lá 6 *si-ti-tum* 6 ĝír-kun, 18: TAR kb **L.** 1 íb-lá 1 *si-ti-tum* 1 ĝír-kun; r. XIV 28: 50 gín D. kb **L.** 2 *bu*-DI; r. XVII 2: [ ] **L.** 1 *mu-rúm wa* 1 *gúm-a-nu* ⸢*wa*⸣ 2 ĜIŠ-alam *su-da*$_5$*-lik* en, 13: 3 gín D. 2 NI kg **L.** 4 geštu$_x$-lá; r. XXI 21: 3 ma-na ŠÚ+ŠA an-na šub *si-in* 26 ma-na ŠÚ+ŠA a-gar$_5$-gar$_5$ **L.** 1 *mi-at* ĝír gibil, 26: 2 ma-na kg **L.** 2 íb-lá 2 *si-ti-tum* 2 ĝír-kun; **18** o. IV 5: 3 ma-na ŠÚ+ŠA gín D. an-na šub *si-in* 56 ma-na ŠA.PI gín D. a-gar$_5$-gar$_5$ **L.** 2 *mi-at* ĝír mar-tu zú-ak, 10: 17 gín D. a-gar$_5$-gar$_5$ *wa* 1 gín D. an-na **L.** 1 ĝír mar-tu *mu-lu-iš* 1 *li-im* ĝír mar-tu *A-la-ga*$^{ki}$; o. VI 22: TAR gín D. kb **L.** 15 ĜIŠ-kak-ĜIŠ-kak *ša-ti* 5 ĜIŠ-asari; o. VII 13: 5 ma-na ŠÚ+ŠA gín D. kb **L.** 10 *gú-li-lum* lú ŠÚ+ŠA-ŠÚ+ŠA-II *wa* 12 *gú-li-lum* lú 20-I; o. IX 3: 11 ma-na an-na šub *si-in* 6 *mi-at* ma-na a-gar$_5$-gar$_5$ daḫ$_x$(MU.MU.MU) **L.** 2 útul gibil, 10 and 12: 2 ma-na 12 gín D. an-na šub *si-in* 13 ma-na TAR a-gar$_5$-gar$_5$ **L.** 10 lá-1 *ma-ba-ra-zú* **L.**-*sù*; o. XIII 16: 10 na$_4$ PN **L.** 2 útul urudu; o. XIV 9: 1 na$_4$ PN **L.** 2 útul; o. XVI 15: 1 ma-na TAR kg **L.** 2 *ti-gi-na* 10 lá-2 ĝeštu$_x$-lá 92 *gur-gú-ru*$_{12}$ 3 *mi-at* 60 *ḫa-za-nu* 1 šu-dub 1 *ma-ḫa-na-gúm* 2 kù-sal 1 *a-a-nu* 2 ĜIŠ-du; r. V 4: TAR 3 gín D. an-na šub *si-in* 24 ma-na a-gar$_5$-gar$_5$ **L.** 1 šum maḫ, 9: 6 gín D. an-na šub *si-in* 5 ma-na a-gar$_5$-gar$_5$ **L.** 2 šum maḫ, 12: 5 gín D. **L.** 3 *zú-zú-ba-tum* ĜIŠ-gígir-II, 19: 2 gín D. an-na šub *si-in* 10 gín D. a-gar$_5$-gar$_5$ **L.** 2 šu-i; r. VI 2: 4 gín D. an-na šub *si-in* ŠÚ+ŠA 6 a-gar$_5$-gar$_5$ **L.** bar-ús; r. VII 2: 1 ma-na ŠA.PI 6 gín D. 2 NI an-na šub *si-in* 12 ma-na ŠÚ+ŠA gín D. a-gar$_5$-gar$_5$ **L.** 40 ĝír mar-tu kg, 12: ŠÚ+ŠA gín D. a-gar$_5$-gar$_5$ *wa* 2 gín D. 2 NI an-na **L.** 1 ĝír mar-tu, 20: 50 gín D. an-na šub *si-in* 6 ma-na ŠÚ+ŠA gín D. a-gar$_5$-gar$_5$ **L.** 20 ĝír mar-tu ti kg *ʾà-lum*; r. VIII 10: 18 gín D. a-gar$_5$-gar$_5$ *wa* 2 ½ gín D. an-na **L.** 1 ĝír mar-tu, 18: 1 ma-na 52 ½ gín D. an-na šub *si-in* 15 ma-na a-gar$_5$-gar$_5$ **L.** 50 ĝír mar-tu ti kg; r. IX 9: 17 a-gar$_5$-gar$_5$ 2 gín D. 3 NI an-na **L.** 1 ĝír mar-tu, 16: 10 lá-1 ma-na ŠÚ+ŠA 6 gín D. an-na šub *si-in* 75 ma-na TAR 6 a-gar$_5$-gar$_5$ **L.** 2 *mi-at* 52 ĝír ma[r-tu] Š[A.PI(?)] kb; r. X 8: [TA]R 8 ⸢a⸣-gar$_5$-gar$_5$ *wa* 2 4 NI an-na **L.** 1 ĝír mar-tu; r. XVIII 18: 2 an-na šub *si-in* 10 a-gar$_5$-gar$_5$ **L.** 2 ĝír; **19** o. III 8: ŠÚ+ŠA 2 gín D. an-na šub *si-in* 1 m[a-]na TAR [4+]4 gín D. a-gar$_5$-gar$_5$ **L.** 3 tùn tur ŠA.PI-ŠA.PI; o. IV 21: 20 lá-1 ma-na ŠÚ+ŠA 7 gín D. an-na šub *si-in* 1 *mi-at* 50 ma-na a-gar$_5$-gar$_5$ **L.** 1 *li-im* ĜIŠ-gu-kak-g[íd] zabar; o. IX 3: 10 lá-1 ma-na 20 gín D. an-na šub *si-in* 2 *mi-at* 17 ma-na a-gar$_5$-g[ar$_5$] **L.** sig$_4$-KI 2 útul urudu gibil maḫ; o. XIII 14: 3 gín D. kg **L.** ZA$_x$, 31: 53 gín D. 3 NI an-na šub *si-in* 6 ma-na ŠA.PI a-gar$_5$ **L.** 20 ĝír mar-tu kg; o. XIV 7: ŠÚ+ŠA a-gar$_5$-gar$_5$ 2 an-na 2 NI **L.** 1 ĝír mar-tu, 14: 50 gín D. an-na šub *si-in* 6 ma-na ŠÚ+ŠA a-gar$_5$ **L.** 20 ĝír mar-tu ti kg *ʾà-lum*, 23: 19 a-gar$_5$ 2 ½ an-na **L.** 1 ĝír mar-tu, 29: 1 [m]a-na TAR an-na šub *si-in* 12 ma-na a-gar$_5$-gar$_5$ **L.** 40 ĝír mar-tu ti kg; o. XV 7: 18 a-gar$_5$ 2 4 NI **L.** 1 ĝír mar-tu, 14: TAR an-na šub *si-in* 3 ma-na TAR 5 a-gar$_5$ **L.** 12 ĝír mar-tu zú AN.LAGAB×A, 25: 18 a-gar$_5$ 2 ½ an-na **L.** 1 ĝír mar-tu; o. XVI 4: 1 ma-na TAR an-na šub *si-in* 12 ma-na a-gar$_5$-gar$_5$ **L.** 40 ĝír mar-tu *ba-du-u*$_9$ kg, 13: 18 a[-gar$_5$] [x an-na] **L.** 1 ĝír mar-tu, 20: 2 ma-na 15 gín an-na šub *si-in* 20 lá-2 ma-na a-gar$_5$-gar$_5$ **L.** 60 ĝír mar-tu *ba-du-u*$_9$ kbg; o. XVII 5: 18 a-gar$_5$ 2 4 NI an-na **L.** 1 ĝír mar-tu, 14: 11 ma-na 15 gín D. an-na šub *si-in* 90 ma-na a-gar$_5$-gar$_5$ **L.** 3 *mi-at* ĝír [ma]r-tu *ga-me-ù* kb, 22: 18 a-gar$_5$ 2 an-na 4 NI **L.** 1 ĝír mar-tu; r. I 2: 3 ma-na TAR 3 gín D. 2 NI an-na šub *si-in* 26 ma-na ŠA.PI gín D. a-gar$_5$-gar$_5$ **L.** 80 ĝír mar-tu kg, 12: ŠÚ+ŠA a-gar$_5$-gar$_5$ 2 gín D. 2 NI an-na **L.** 1 ĝír mar-tu, 19: 50 gín D. an-na šub *si-in* 6 ma-na ŠÚ+ŠA gín D. a-gar$_5$-gar$_5$ **L.** 20 ĝír mar-tu ti kg *ʾà-lum*; r. II 2: 19 gín D. a-gar$_5$-gar$_5$ 3$^?$ an-na **L.** 1 ĝír mar-tu 4 gín kg *zi-du-sù*, 9: 3 ma-na ŠÚ+ŠA gín D. an-na šub *si-in* 34 ma-na a-gar$_5$-gar$_5$ **L.** 90 ĝír mar-tu ti kg, 19: 18 a-gar$_5$ *wa* 2 gín D. 4 NI an-na **L.** 1 ĝír mar-tu, 26: 1 ma-na 52 [g]ín D. an-na šub *si-in* 15 ma-na a-gar$_5$-gar$_5$ **L.** 50 ĝír mar-tu *ba-du-u$_9$* kg; r. III 9: 18 a-gar$_5$ 2 gín D. 4 NI an-na **L.** 1 ĝír mar-tu, 16: 2 ma-na 15 gín D. an-na šub *si-in* 20 lá-2 ma-na a-gar$_5$-gar$_5$ **L.** 60 ĝír mar-tu *ba-du-u$_9$* kbg, 27: 18 a-gar$_5$ 2 gín D. 4 NI an-na **L.** 1 ĝír mar-tu; r. IV 6: 13 ma-na TAR an-na šub *si-in* 1 *mi-at* 10 lá-2 ma-na a-gar$_5$-gar$_5$ **L.** 3 *mi-at* 60 ĝír mar-tu *ga-mi-ù* kb, 14: 18 a-gar$_5$ 2 gín D. 4 NI an-na **L.** 1 ĝír mar-tu; r. VIII 8: 6 gín D. ½ kg **L.** 6 še-šu-še-tag *wa* 1 buru$_4$-MUŠEN; r. XI 6: 5 ma-na kb **L.** 1 *gú-li-lum* ŠA.PI-II 2 *gú-li-lum* TAR-II 5 *gú-li-lum* ŠÚ+ŠA-II 1 *gú-li-lum* 10-I; r. XII 21: 1 ½ gín D. an-na šub *si-in* 8 gín D. a-gar$_5$ **L.** 1 ĝír mar-tu; **20** o. I 13: 57 ma-na ŠÚ+ŠA gín D. an-na šub-šub *si-in* 4 *mi-at* 50 ⸢ma⸣-na a-gar$_5$[-gar$_5$] **L.** 3 *li-im* ĜIŠ-gu-kak-gíd zabar; o. II 17: ŠÚ+ŠA 4 gín D. kg **L.** 1 ĝeštu$_x$-lá *wa* [ ]; o. V 2': 2 ma-n[a] 10 gín D. kg **L.** [ ]; o. XIII 8: 12 gín D. an-na šub *si-in* 1 ma-na 8 gín D. a-gar$_5$-gar$_5$ **L.** 4 ĝír 15 gín D. 2 ĝír 10 gín D.; o. XV 5: 1 ma-na ŠÚ+ŠA gín D. kg **L.** 1 íb-lá 1 *si-ti-tum* 1 ĝír-kun ŠÚ+ŠA gín D. 2 *ti-gi-na* ŠÚ+ŠA gín D. 4 *ʾà-ra-ma-tum* [ŠÚ+ŠA gín D.]; r. I 11: 17 gín D. an-na šub *si-in* 1 ma-na ŠA.PI gín D. a-gar$_5$[-gar$_5$] **L.** 1 tùn tur TAR 1 tùn tur ŠÚ+ŠA gín D. 1 dub-naĝar šu-mu-LAGAB ŠÚ+ŠA gín D. 1 dub-naĝar 10 gín D. 1 *ma-ga-za-u$_4$* 10 gín D. 1 *ma-za-ḫa-rúm* 10 gín D. 1 *ḫa-ra-núm* 7 gín D. 1 dub-naĝar ⸢4⸣ gín D. 1 UŠ×KÍD 2 gín D.; r. II 4: ⸢TAR⸣ [a]n-na šub *si-in* 3 ma-na a-gar$_5$-gar$_5$ **L.** 6 an-zam$_x$ 1 á-lá gibil; **21** o. VII 8: 2 ma-na kg **L.** 1 dib 1 íb-lá 1 *si-ti-tum* 1 ĝír-kun; o. XIII 11: 1 ma-na kg **L.** 2 níĝ-anše-ak 4 kù-sal *wa* nu$_{11}$-za 2 ĜIŠ.GAM.GAM ĜIŠ-gígir-II; o. XIV 19: 5 ma-na kb **L.** 1 ĜIŠ-šú 1 níĝ-bànda lú 2 šu; o. XVII 21: 26 ma-na kb **L.** 40 íb-lá 40 ĝír-kun, 24: 6 ma-na ŠA.PI gín D. kb [**L.** 20 lá-2 g]*ú-li-lum* ŠÚ+ŠA-ŠÚ+ŠA; r. I 14: 15 ma-na kb **L.** 3 ĜIŠ-šú 3 níĝ-bànda; r. III 2: [x gín] ⸢D.⸣ kb **L.** 2 *bu*-DI 4 še-šu-tag; r. VI 19: 4 gín D. an-na šub *si-in* ŠÚ+ŠA 4 gín D. a-gar$_5$-gar$_5$ **L.** 4 šu-i; r. VII 17: 5 gín D. kb **L.** 3 *zú-zú-ba-tum*; r. IX 18: 1 ma-na kb **L.** 3 *gú-li-lum* ŠÚ+ŠA-ŠÚ+ŠA-II; r. X 29: 3 gín D. an-na šub *si-in* 18 gín D. a-gar$_5$-gar$_5$ **L.** [ ]; **22** r. I 11: 5 ma-na kg **L.** 10 *gú-li-lum*-II ŠÚ+ŠA *wa* 10 *gú-li-lum*-I 10 … 10 *gú-li-lum*-II a-gar$_5$-gar$_5$ esi *wa* 10 *gú-li-lum*-I a-gar$_5$-gar$_5$ 10 esi … 10 *gú-li-lum*-II a-gar$_5$-gar$_5$ ŠÚ+ŠA *wa* 10 *gú-li-lum*-I a-gar$_5$-gar$_5$ 10; r. III 7: ŠÚ+ŠA 4 gín D. an-na **L.** 10 ĝír mar-tu; **24** o. VI 12: 1 gín D. kg **L.** $^{d}$*A-gi Su-ti-gú*$^{ki}$.

kir$_{11}$ «female lamb» **6** o. VIII 15: 1 **L.** sa$_6$ siki.

kir$_4$-ma «monkey» **14** o. VI 19: *Ḫu-wa-sa-ra-du*$^{\{ki\}}$ *Du-lu*$^{ki}$ ḫi-mu-DU 1 **L.** *wa* 10 lá-2 gada-TÚG.

*kir-na-nu* (a linen cloth) **12** r. III 4: 4 gada-TÚG **L.**

kú «food» **13** r. I 8: (silver) níĝ-ba *Ìr-am$_6$*-kur$^{ki}$ sagi *Ma-rí*$^{ki}$ *in* ud kin$_5$-ak **L.** en.

kù-babbar (kù:babbar) «silver» **1** o. V 1, 6, 11, 14; o. VI 5, 10, 14; o. VII 4, 11, 18; o. VIII 4, 11, 17; o. IX 1, 8, 17; o. X 1, 8, 10, 20, 22; o. XI 4; o. XII 1; o. XIII x+1; (b) r. x+I 2'; r. II' 3'; (c) r. II' x+1; (d) r. x+I 2; (e) r. II' 10'; r. III' 3, 7, 13, 15; r. IV' 5, 9, 13; **2** o. I 1, 8, 16, 23; o. II 10, 15, 20; o. III 2, 4, 6, 8, 10, 15; o. IV 3, 10, 15, 21; o. V 2, 4, 6, 14, 18; o. VI 6, 18; o. VII 2, 7, 11, 14; o. VIII 9, 12; o. IX 3, 6, 15, 18; o. X 5, 12, 14; o. XI 3, 9, 16, 22; o. XII 6, 13, 22; o. XIII 6, 13, 19; o. XIV 4, 10, 16: 4 *gú-li-lum* **L.**, 22; o. XV 8; r. I 14, 21; r. II 7, 9, 18; r. III 1: [x *gú-li-lum*] 10 ⸢gín⸣ **L.**, 8, 16, 18; r. IV 10, 17, 20; r. V 1, 3, 12, 14; r. VI 2, 6, 13; r. VII 2, 4, 11, 15, 17; r. VIII 7, 13, 19; r. IX 2, 11, 13, 15; r. X 2, 4, 8, 13, 17; r. XI 1, 9, 14, 20; r. XII 7, 18; r. XIII 2, 13, 19, 22; r. XIV 4, 9, 14, 19; r. XV 2, 5, 11, 13; r. XVI 5, 9, 14; r. XVII 3, 8, 11, 16; l.ed. 1, 6, 11: AN.ŠÈ.GÚ 1 *mi-at* 97 ma-na 50 gín D. **L.**; **3** o. I 1, 5, 9, 12, 15; o. II 1, 4, 7, 12, 17, ; o. III 1,6, 14, 20; o. IV 6, 12, 14; o. V 1, 5, 9, 19; o. VI 5, 9, 13; o. VII 4, 10, 17; o. VIII 18; o. IX 7, 13, 17; o. X x+1; o. XI 4, 6, 13, 19; o. XII 6, 8, 17, 21; o. XIII 5, 9, 13, 19, 21; o. XIV 16; o. XV 3, 19; r. I 5; r. II 1, 6; r. III 9, 18; r. IV 4, 11, 16; r. V 3, 8, 14; r. VI 2, 11, 17; r. VII 6, 13, 17; r. VIII 3, 12, 15, 19; r. IX 7, 10, 12; r. X 2, 9, 11, 16, 19; r. XI 6, 9, 14, 23; r. XII 4, 9, 22; r. XIII 6, 9, 17, 22; r. XIV 6; r. XV 2: AN.ŠÈ.GÚ 1 *mi-at* 55 ma-na TAR 4 gín D. **L.**; l.ed. 2: 2 dub *ab* 4 *mi-at* 83 ma-na **L.** al$_6$-ĝál; **4** o. I 1, 2: saĝ **L.** $^{d}$*Ku-ra*, 4, 9; o. II 1, 7, 12, 17, 22; o. III 4, 11, 16; o. IV 1, 5, 8, 13, 17, 20; o. V 6, 10, 15, 20; o. VI 3, 6, 8, 10, 12, 14, 16; o. VII 1, 5, 12; o. VIII 1, 4, 7, 12, 14, 16; o. IX 2, 6, 11, 16; o. X 6, 9, 11, 13, 16; o. XI 1, 6, 11, 18; o. XII 2, 7, 9, 11, 14, 16; o. XIII 2, 3: saĝ **L.** $^{d}$*Ku-ra*, 5, 7, 11, 17, 22; o. XIV 3, 5, 8, 11, 15, 18, 23; o. XV 4, 9, 14, 17, 23; r. I 5, 10, 13, 16, 19; r. II 1, 4, 7, 11, 14, 17; r. III 1, 4, 7, 13; r. IV 1, 5, 9, 14, 23; r. V 2, 6, 12, 14, 20: r. VI 3, 7, 12; r. VII 1, 5, 12, 18; r. VIII 5, 10, 16, 21; r. IX 4, 9, 15; r. X 1, 6, 10, 18, 20; r. XI 4, 17, 19; r. XII 4, 10, 15, 23; r. XIII 1, 12, 17, 19; r. XIV 5, 10, 15; r. XV 2, 9, 16, 21, 25; r. XVI 2, 11, 16: [AN.ŠE.GÚ x ma-na (x)] **L.** è; **5** o. I 1; o. II 1, 8, 14; o. III 4, 7, 12, 17, 19; o. IV 8, 12, 18; o. V 4, 6, 10, 14, 19; o. VI 6, 13, 16; o. VII 2, 7, 15, 21; o. VIII 4, 10, 14; o. IX 4, 10, 16; o. X 3, 12, 18; o. XI 8, 9, 14; o. XII 7, 9, 16; o. XIII 9, 13, 19; o. XIV 6, 10, 12; o. XV 8, 13, 18; o. XVI 15; r. I 1, 6, 11, 14, 19; r. II 5, 9, 11, 15, 19; r. III 4, 8, 13, 15; r. IV 8, 16; r. V 1, 9, 11; r. VI 4, 15; r. VII 4, 10, 16; r. VIII 7, 12, 15; r. IX 3, 8, 14; r. X 1, 6, 8 ,14, 20; r. XI 8, 13, 16, 22; r. XII 6, 12, 14, 20; r. XIII 7, 11, 17; r. XIV 2, 4, 13, 15, 24; r. XV 5, 11, 13, 16, 23, 26; r. XVI 5, 8, 17; r. XVII 1: AN.ŠÈ.GÚ 1 *mi-at* 32 ma-na 50 gín D. **L.** è; **6** o. I 1, 2: saĝ **L.** $^{d}$*Ku-ra*, 4, 6, 10, 15; o. II 3, 10, 12, 13: saĝ **L.** $^{d}$*Ku-ra* 2 mu-ti, 16, 19, 22; o. III 2, 9, 13, 23; o. IV 3, 5, 7, 9, 11, 13, 15, 17; o. V 1, 8, 14, 19, 21; o. VI 3, 6; o. VII 1, 6, 11, 15; o. VIII 11, 14, 16; o. IX 3, 6, 10, 15, 21; o. X 2, 6, 9, 13, 17; o. XI 1, 8, 10, 12, 18; o. XII 2, 4, 8, 12, 15; o. XIII 3, 11, 16, 19, 22; o. XIV 3, 12, 17, 20, 22; o. XV 9, 17, 21, 23; o. XVI

5, 12, 18, 24; r. I 5, 11, 18, 21; r. II 1, 7, 10, 14; r. III 8, 13, 17, 19; r. IV 1, 7, 12, 18, 22; r. V 4, 11, 16, 21; r. VI 8, 12, 19; r. VII 1, 7, 16, 20, 21: 1 íb-lá *si-ti-tum* ĝír-kun **L.**; r. VIII 3, 7, 14; r. IX 6, 14; r. X 8, 12, 17; r. XI 6, 12; r. XII 7, 13; r. XIII 1, 5, 7, 9, 15, 19; r. XIV 5, 11, 16, 17: 1 íb-lá **L.**, 19; l.ed. 6: AN.ŠÈ.GÚ 1 *mi-at* 74 ma-na ŠA.PI 8 gín D. **L.** è, 10: šu-níĝin 1 *mi-at* 98 ma-na **L.** an-na; **7** o. I 1, 2: [s]aĝ **L.** [$^{d}$*K*]*u-ra*, 4, 8, 15, 19; o. II 4, 9, 14, 19; o. III 1, 8, 11, 19; o. IV 3, 5, 10, 11: 20 ĝír mar-tu ti **L.**, 12, 16; o. V 10, 15, 20; o. VI 1, 7, 15; o. VII 4, 13, 19; o. VIII 5, 12; o. IX 2, 6, 12, 18, 20; o. X 4, 6, 16; o. XI 1, 8, 10, 16; o. XII 2, 4, 8, 16; o. XIII 1, 4, 10, 16, 22; o. XIV 3, 9; o. XV 1, 8, 11, 15, 20; o. XVI 1, 7, 13, 17; o. XVII 4, 10, 14; o. XVIII 4, 10, 12; o. XIX 2; r. I 10, 12, 14; r. II 6, 8, 15, 17; r. III 6, 13, 15; r. IV 1, 4, 11, 14, 20, 23; r. V 9, 12, 18; r. VI 1, 11; r. VII 1, 7, 9, 15, 17; r. VIII 8, 15, 18, 25; r. IX 3, 10, 15; r. X 1, 8, 15, 19, 23; r. XI 4, 10, 24, 27; r. XII 5, 15, 21; r. XIII 7, 19; r. XIV 1, 8, 12, 15, 21; r. XV 2, 9, 16; r. XVI 1, 10: AN.ŠÈ.GÚ 1 *mi-at* 50 lá-1 ma-na **L.** è; **8** o. I 1, 4; o. II 16; o. III 4, 11, 14, 16; o. IV 2, 6, 11, 16; o. VI 2, 9, 14, 17; o. VII 2, 7, 10, 13; o. VIII 2; o. IX 3; o. X 2, 4, 7; o. XI 5, 7; o. XII 2, 5, 12; o. XIII 1, 6, 10; o. XIV 6, 12; o. XV 1, 5; r. III 4', 7', 14'; r. IV 2', 6', 10', 14'; r. V 6', 9'; r. VI x+1, 4', 6', 8'; o. VII x+1, 4', 9'; o. VIII x+1, 5', 9'; r. IX 4', 6', 11'; r. X 2', 5', 10'; r. XI x+1, 13', 15': 1 *mi-at* ĝír mar-tu *ba-du-*$u_4$ **L.**; **9** o. I 1, 2: saĝ **L.** $^{d}$*Ku-ra*; o. II 1, 4, 9, 18; o. III 6, 8, 22; o. IV 6, 15; o. V 1: 2 ĝír mar-tu *ba-du-*$u_4$ **L.**, 8, 11, 15; o. VI 12, 13; o. VIII 10, 16; o. IX 7, 13; o. X 7, 9; o. XI 11, 16, 23; o. XII 6, 13, 22; o. XIII 5, 11, 17; o. XIV 8; o. XV 5, 9, 15; o. XVI 2'; o. XVII 4'; o. XVIII 3'; r. I 6, 13; r. II 2, 19; r. III 10, 13; r. IV 6, 9, 14; r. V 1, 6, 12, 18; r. VI 7, 8, 14; r. VII 7, 12, 14; r. VIII 5, 18; r. IX 6, 11; r. X 1: 7 *gú-li-lum* **L.**-II esi ĜÁ×LÁ TAR-*sù*, 3: 10 *gú-li-lum* **L.**-II esi ĜÁ×LÁ ŠÚ+ŠA gín D., 4: 1 *gú-li-lum* **L.**-I esi 1 gín D. ĜÁ×LÁ-*sù*, 5; r. XI 8; r. XII 1, 10, 13: 4 ĝír mar-tu *ba-du-*$u_4$ **L.**; r. XIII 6, 11; r. XIV 11, 15; r. XV 1, 5, 7, 10, 13; r. XVI 8, 10, 17; r. XVII 5, 18; r. XVIII 7; **10** o. I , 4, 9, 14, 17; o. II 2, 4, 11; o. III 5, 8, 12, 15, 18; o. IV 4, 8, 15, 19; o. V 2, 8, 16; o. VI 3, 10; o. VII 3, 6, 15, 21; o. VIII 5, 9, 12, 18; o. IX 1, 8, 14, 18; o. X 4, 7, 12, 19, 22; o. XI 5, 9, 17, 20; o. XII 3, 7, 11, 14; o. XIII 1, 5, 9, 18; o. XIV 1, 6, 10, 15, 23; o. XV 2, 5, 10, 17; o. XVI 4, 16, 20; r. I 6, 9, 15, 20; r. II 4, 8, 13, 16; r. III 5, 9, 13, 17, 20; r. IV 6, 9, 18; r. V 2, 8, 13, 18; r. VI 5, 9, 13, 17; r. VII 6; r. VIII 1, 7, 12; r. IX 1, 7, 10, 13, 21; r. X 9; r. XII 1; r. XVI 2: AN.ŠÈ.GÚ 90 ma-na ŠÚ+ŠA 6 gín D. **L.**; **11** o. I 1, 2: saĝ **L.** $^{d}$*K*[*u-ra*], 4; o. II 2, 4, 11, 14; o. III 6, 8; o. IV 4, 15, 19; o. V 6, 10; o. VI 2, 9, 15; o. VII 1, 5, 20; o. VIII 7, 14, 20; o. IX 2, 3: 1 ĝír mar-tu *ba-du-*$u_4$ **L.**, 7; o. X 1, 5, 7, 11, 18, 20; o. XI 1, 9, 12, 18; o. XII 3, 7, 9, 13; o. XIII 1, 8; r. II 10, 14; r. III 8, 15, 18; r. IV 7, 14, 18, 22; r. V 3, 7, 12, 16; r. VI 3, 13, 18, 20; r. VII 6, 8, 12, 16, 22; r. VIII 1, 4, 9, 11; **12** o. I 1, 2: saĝ **L.** $^{d}$*Ku-ra*, 4, 8, 10; o. II 4, 12; o. III 5; o. IV 1, 8, 13, 19; o. V 5, 11, 13; o. VI 11, 16, 20, 25; o. VII 6, 13, 19; o. VIII 2, 8, 15; o. IX 6, 14; o. XI 16; o. XII 2, 12; o. XIII 3, 8, 13; o. XIV 1: 2 *gú-li-lum* **L.**, 10, 18; o. XV 8, 14; r. I 10, 12, 17; r. II 8, 13, 22; r. III 7, 11, 14; r. IV 5, 13, 16; r. V 2, 8, 13, 19; r. VI 7, 15, 17; r. VII 1, 10, 12, 18; r. VIII 3, 10; r. IX 6, 8, 21; r. X 3, 7, 12; r. XIII 7; r. XIV 1 and 4: [AN.ŠÈ.GÚ x **L.** è] *ap* 3 *mi-at* 1 ma-na **L.** [al$_6$-ĝá]l; **13** o. I 1, 2: saĝ **L.** $^{d}$*Ku-ra*, 4, 9, 12, 18; o. II 6, 14; o. III 1, 5, 14, 23; o. IV 5, 6: 1 ĝír mar-tu *ba-du-*$u_4$ **L.**, 9, 20; o. V 3, 9, 13, 15; o. VI 9, 15, 22; o. VII 1, 7, 16, 18; o. VIII 7, 8: saĝ **L.** $^{d}$*Ku-ra* mu-ti-II, 11, 13, 23; o. IX 7, 12, 15, 21; o. X 1, 10, 15; o. XI 2, 8, 15, 20; o. XII 1, 11, 13, 22; o. XIII 6, 12, 18, 20; o. XIV 3, 8, 12; o. XV 11, 18, 20; o. XVI 8, 13, 19; o. XVII 1, 5, 7, 10, 14; r. I 1, 10, 22; r. II 4, 10, 23; r. III 7, 12; r. IV 3, 8, 13, 21; r. V 1, 8, 16; r. VI 1, 12, 19; r. VII 2, 8, 24; r. VIII 9, 15, 21; r. IX 4, 11, 20; r. X 6, 8, 15, 18; r. XI 2, 4, 6, 12, 17, 19; r. XII 17, 25; r. XIII 17; r. XIV 16; r. XVII 1: AN.ŠÈ.GÚ 1 *mi-at* 70 m[a-]n[a] 40[+x] g[ín D. **L.**]; **14** o. I 1, 2: saĝ **L.** $^{d}$*Ku-ra*, 4, 9, 14; r. II 1, 11, 18, 24; r. III 4, 8, 12; r. IV 4, 18; r. V 7, 15, 17; r. VI 1, 9, 10: saĝ **L.** $^{d}$*Ku-ra in* mu-ti-II, 14, 22; o. VII 6, 14, 16; o. VIII 5, 10, 17, 23; o. IX 8, 14, 18, 21; o. X 1, 20, 21; o. XI 4, 9, 15, 20; o. XII 9, 14, 21; o. XIII 6, 7: 1 ĝír mar-tu *ba-du-*$u_4$ **L.**, 11; o. XIV 6, 17; o. XV 4, 10; o. XVI 8; o. XVII 1, 3, 6, 14, 18; o. XVIII 4, 13; o. XIX 6; o. XX 1, 8; o. XXI 2, 10; r. I 1, 5, 9, 16; r. II 4, 12, 15; r. III 1, 9; r. IV 11, 17; r. V 5, 10, 20; r. VI 6, 20; r. VII 8, 15, 28; r. VIII 10, 12, 16; r. IX 10, 16; r. X 7, 13, 19, 26; r. XI 3, 15, 23; r. XII 6, 12, 19, 23; r. XIII 1, 8, 11, 19: 6 ĝír mar-tu **L.**, 20, 23; r. XIV x+1: [x *g*]*ú-li-lum* **L.** [T]AR.TAR-II, 2': 10 lá-1 *gú-li-lum* **L.** ŠÚ+ŠA-ŠÚ+ŠA-II, 4'; r. XV 10, 12, 16; r. XVIII 3; r. XIX 3; **15** o. I 1, 2: saĝ **L.** $^{d}$*Ku-ra*, 4, 9, 16, 21; o. II 9, 17, 29; o. III 9, 11, 15, 18; o. IV 3, 11, 12: 1 ĝír mar-tu *ba-du-*$u_4$ **L.**, 15, 17, 20; o. V 1, 8, 14, 20; o. VI 1, 8, 11, 16; o. VII 3, 12, 21; o. VIII 5, 11, 17, 22; o. IX 5, 10, 15, , 23; o. X 2, 6, 15, 23; o. XI 4, 20, 24; o. XII 7, 8: 1 ĝír mar-tu *ba-du-*$u_4$ **L.**, 11, 19; o. XIII 1, 7, 9: 1 ĝír mar-tu *ba-du-*$u_4$ **L.**, 17, 19; o. XIV 1, 2: saĝ **L.** $^{d}$*Ku-ra* mu-ti, 5, 13, 19; o. XV 1, 5, 15, 19, 23; o. XVI 2, 10, 12: 1 ĜIŠ-šú 1 níĝ-bànda **L.**, 15, 16; o. XVII 2, 11, 17, 19; r. I 3, 5, 7, 16; r. II 4, 11, 21; r. III 2, 8; r. IV 1, 9, 15, 19; r. V 3, 4, 16, 23; r. VI 9, 10, 22; r. VII 1, 12, 21; r. VIII 2, 12, 20; r. IX 1, 10, 16, 24; r. X 7, 19, 26, 31; r. XI 8, 14, 20, 25; r. XII 19, 32; r. XIII 12, 18; r. XIV 1, 9, 17, 21; r. XV 3, 9, 14; r. XVI 3, 13, 22; r. XVIII 1 and 5: AN.ŠÈ.GÚ 2 ⌜*mi-at*⌝ 32 ma-na **L.** è 1 mu ⌜*ap*⌝ ⌜3⌝ *mi-at* 50 ma-na **L.** al$_6$-gál; **16** o. I 1, 2: saĝ **L.** $^{d}$*Ku-ra*, 4, 9, 13, 19; o. II 3, 6, 8, 18; o. III 1, 8, 19, 21; o. IV 2, 9, 14; o. V 1, 7, 9, 19, 23; o. VI 6, 10, 18; o. VII 4, 11, 20; o. VIII 5, 10, 12: 8 á-MUŠEN **L.**, 13, 16, 21; o. IX 1: 50 íb-lá **L.**, 2, 4: 3 *gú-li-lum* **L.** ŠA.PI-II, 5: 2 *gú-li-lum* **L.** TAR-II, 6: 15 *gú-li-lum* **L.** ŠÚ+ŠA-II, 7: 7 *gú-li-lum* 11 **L.**, 8, 13; o. X 7, 11; o. XI 4, 11, 14; o. XII 12, 19; o. XIII 7, 10, 16, 21; o. XIV 9, 16, 22, 25; r. I 4, 11, 15; r. II 1, 4, 12, 21, 25; r. III 7, 14, 17, 25; r. IV 1, 11, 18, 20; r. V 9, 16, 23; r. VI 1, 9, 15, 21, 26; r. VII 3, 8, 13, 16, 26, 29: 2 ĝír mar-tu **L.**; r. VIII 1: 3 ĝír mar-tu ti **L.**, 5, 17: 5 ĝír mar-tu **L.**, 23; r. IX 8, 15, 23, 30; r. X 2, 8, 12, 15, 25; r. XI 4, 13, 17, 22; r. XII 4, 8, 13, 15, 21, 26; r. XIII 7; r. XIV 1, 7, 19, 30; r. XV 13, 22; r. XVI 7, 14, 21, 23, 25, 27; r. XVII 1, 7, 16, 20: AN[.ŠÈ].GÚ ⌜1⌝[+1?] *mi-at*

97 ma-na 10 **L.** è *ap* ⸢2⸣ *m*[*i-at* x ma-na x **L.**] [al$_6$-ĝál é siki]; **17** o. I 1, 2: saĝ **L.** $^d$*Ku-ra*, 4, 9, 18; o. II 1, 5, 15, 20; o. III 17; o. IV 1, 18; o. V 12, 21; o. VI 1, 21; o. VII 8, 16; o. VIII 3, 9, 15; o. IX 2, 4, 10; o. X 5, 8, 10; o. XI 3, 9, 15, 17; o. XII 9, 11, 19; o. XIII 1, 7, 13, 14: saĝ **L.** $^d$*Ku-ra* mu-ti, 17; o. XIV 5, 12, 16, 21; o. XV 3, 11, 18; o. XVI 1, 10, 21; o. XVII 4, 12, 20, 25; o. XVIII 2, 10, 12; o. XIX 5, 12, 20; o. XX 7, 9; r. I 3, 12, 15, 19, 25, 31; r. II 10, 16, 23; r. III 1, 9, 17, 23; r. IV 2, 3: 1 ĝír mar-tu *ba-du-u*$_4$ **L.**, 9, 15, 17, 21; r. V 1, 12, 16, 25; r. VI 7, 13, 16, 24, 33; r. VII 6, 14, 25; r. VIII 1, 6, 13; r. IX 1, 8, 11, 21, 29; r. X 4, 12, 14, 18; r. XI 4, 16, 27; r. XII 1, 8, 13, 17, 24; r. XIII 17, 24; r. XIV 27; r. XV 2, 9, 11, 20; r. XVI 4, 15, 21; r. XVII 10; r. XVIII 8, 16, 21; r. XIX 3, 8, 15, 23, 31; r. XX 11, 14, 18, 23, 28, 36; r. XXI 5, 9, 10, 13, 23, 27; r. XXII 12, 15, 21; l.ed. x+1 and x+3: AN.ŠÈ.GÚ 2 *mi-at* 65 ma-na 4 gín D. **L.** è [(1+$^?$)]1 *mi-at* 10 lá-2 ma-na š[A.PI] gí[n] D. **L.** al$_6$-ĝál lú diri; **18** o. I 1, 2: saĝ **L.** $^d$*Ku-ra*, 4, 9, 13, 18; o. II 2, 11, 22; o. III 6, 11, 17; o. IV 15, 19; o. V 6, 11, 15, 21; o. VI 1, 9, 12, 21; o. VII 6, 12; o. VIII 5, 11; o. IX 5, 13; o. X 3, 8, 15; o. XI 3, 5: 1 íb-lá 1 ĝír-kun **L.**, 6, 12, 18; o. XII 1, 5, 11, 17; o. XIII 1, 13, 18, 21, 24; o. XIV 3, 6, 12, 18, 24; o. XV 2, 6, 12, 17, 28; o. XVI 2, 4, 7, 12; o. XVII 4, 9, 10: saĝ **L.** $^d$*Ku-ra* mu-ti-II, 13, 18, 23, 31; o. XVIII 13, 15, 19, 26; o. XIX 9, 17, 26; r. I 3, 5, 13, 17, 23; r. II 1, 11, 18, 22; r. III 2, 9, 11, 17; r. IV 5, 11, 19; r. VI 5, 9; r. VII 4; r. VIII 2; r. IX 2; r. X 1: 2 *mi-at* 52 ĝír ma[r-tu] š[A.PI(?)] **L.**, 2, 10, 18; r. XI 1, 3, 12, 14, 25; r. XII 4, 9, 11, 18, 23; r. XIII 3, 8, 17, 22; r. XIV 2, 10, 16, 18, 20, 25, 27; r. XV 14, 18, 20, 26, 28, 30; r. XVI 1, 3, 5, 7, 10, 12, 18, 21, 31, 33, 35; r. XVII 8, 17, 19, 25, 32, 36; r. XVIII 5, 11, 20, 25, 28, 30; r. XIX 5, 10, 13; l.ed. 1: AN.ŠÈ.GÚ 2 *mi-at* 80 lá-3 ma-na ŠA.PI 6 gín D. **L.** è *ap* 4 *mi-at* 40 lá-3 ma-na **L.** al$_6$-ĝál; **19** o. I 1, 2: saĝ **L.** $^d$*Ku-ra*, 4, 8. 12; o. II 3, 15, 16, 25; o. III 18, 23, 27; o. IV 8, 10, 15: 2 *gú-li-lum* **L.**; o. V 6, 17, 21, 24; o. VI 9, 16, 22, 27; o. VII 3, 9, 21; o. VIII 3, 7, 15, 22; o. IX 6, 12, 25; o. X 2, 9, 15, 18, 20, 25; o. XI 5, 11, 20; o. XII 5, 11, 20, 26; o. XIII 4, 11, 19; o. XIV 16, 31; o. XV 16; o. XVI 6, 22, 25; o. XVII 7, 16: 3 *mi-at* ĝír [ma]r-tu *ga-me-ù* **L.**, 17, 24, 26; o. XVIII 2, 9, 14; r. I 21; r. II 11; r. III 18, 22, 29; r. IV 8: 3 *mi-at* 60 ĝír mar-tu *ga-mi-ù* **L.**, 9, 16, 19, 24, 25: saĝ **L.** $^d$*Ku-ra* mu-ti-II, 28; r. V 6, 10, 22; r. VI 2, 11, 17, 24, 30; r. VII 7, 16, 22, 28; r. VIII 5, 20, 22, 31; r. IX 5, 7, 12, 15, 19, 23, 25, 27; r. X 1, 5, 7, 11, 19, 30; r. XI 5, 11, 18, 20; r. XII 11, 24, 31; r. XIII 6, 9, 12, 20, 24; r. XIV 6, 8, 16, 22; r. XV 9, 16, 19; r. XVI 3, 11, 15, 21, 24; r. XVII 2, 7, 10, 18, 22; r. XVIII 2, 6, 16, 19, 25, 30; r. XIX 3, 8, 15, 19 and 22: ⸢AN⸣.ŠÈ.GÚ 3 *mi-at* 74 ma-na ŠÚ+ŠA 6 gín D. **L.** è *ap* 1 *mi-at* 60 ma-na **L.** al$_6$-ĝál é en; **20** o. I 1, 2: [saĝ **L.** $^d$*Ku-ra*], 4; o. II 7, 14, 21; o. III 10, 14, 16; o. IV 6, 7: sa[ĝ **L.**] $^d$*Ku-*[*ra*] mu-t[i]-II, 10, 16; o. VI 8, 18; o. VII 4, 9; o. VIII 2, 4, 8, 15, 20; o. IX 7, 15, 25; o. X 20, 27; o. XI 5, 12, 18, 21; o. XII 3, 7, 9, 11; o. XIII 1, 11, 15, 22; o. XIV 1, 3, 6, 11, 16, 20; o. XV 2; o. XVI 2, 9, 14, 17; o. XVII 5, 7, 18, 21; r. I 1; r. II 7, 14, 20, 27; r. III 10, 25; r. IV 1, 5, 12, 16, 23; r. V 6, 9, 17, 23; r. VI 3, 8, 10, 17; r. VII 1, 7, 14, 23; r. VIII 9, 19; r. IX 7, 16, 24; r. X 5, 12, 14, 22; r. XI 4, 9, 29; r. XII 5, 13, 15, 19, 20: 1 ĝír mar-tu **L.**, r. XIII 3, 6, 12; r. XIV 11; r. XVI 3'; r. XVIII 2 and 5: AN.ŠÈ.G[Ú] 2 [*mi-at*] 40[(+x) m]a[-na] **L.** ⸢è⸣ [*a*]*p* ⸢2⸣[(+1)] *mi-at* [(x+)]⸢50⸣ [m]a-na [**L.** al$_6$-ĝál é siki]; **21** o. I 1, 2: saĝ **L.** $^d$*Ku-ra*, 4; o. II 2, 11; o. III 7, 23; o. IV 2, 9, 12, 19, 25, 30; o. V 1, 18, 21, 27; o. VI 3, 9, 15, 18; o. VII 4, 11, 20; o. VIII 5, 14; o. IX 5, 8, 10, 18; o. X 2, 8, 16, 24; o. XI 5, 8, 11, 15, 20: AN.[Š]È.GÚ 1 *mi-at* 80 lá-1 ma-na **L.** lú è *in* ud [úš] [*Ib-ri-um*]; o. XII 1, 4, 7, 9, 18, 25, 30; o. XIII 8, 20, 27; o. XIV 3, 5, 8, 12, 14, 18; o. XV 4, 6, 15, 21, 27; o. XVI 7, 10, 15, 20; o. XVII 2, 6, 9, 14, 17, 20, 23; r. I 1, 8, 13, 19; r. II 4, 7, 14; r. III 1, 8, 14, 23; r. IV 9, 18; r. V 10, 12, 16: 1 á-MUŠEN **L.**, 19–21: 3 *gú-li-lum* a-gar$_5$ **L.** TAR-II *wa* 3 *gú-li-lum* a-gar$_5$-gar$_5$ **L.** 15-I; r. VI 12, 21, 26; r. VII 4, 6, 13, 16, 20, 22; r. VIII 5, 13, 22, 27: r. IX 6, 8, 17, 20; r. X 9, 16; r. XI 14, 17, 20, 24; r. XII 13, 17, 22; r. XIII 14, 20; r. XIV 17; r. XVII 1 and 7: [AN.ŠÈ.GÚ x *mi-at* x ma-na x **L.**] ⸢è⸣ DIŠ m[u] úš *Ib-rí-um ap* 4 *mi-at* [ma-n]a [x **L.**] [al$_6$-ĝál é siki]; **22** o. II 8, 11; o. III 8; o. IV 1, 4; o. V 2, 6; r. III 4, 9; **25** o. I 1, 9; o. III 1, 6: 1 ĝír mar:tu **L.**; o. IV 4, 8; o. V 4; o. VI 3, 8; o. VII 5; o. VIII 8; o. IX 3; r. II 9; r. III 7; r. IV 7, 10; r. X 2: AN.ŠÈ.GÚ 86 ma-na 53 gín D. **L.** è *in* ud *Ib-rí-um*.

kù-babbar kù-gi (kù:babbar-gi) «silver and gold» **1** o. VI 11: 1 ĝír mar-tu *ba-du-u*$_4$ **L.**; **3** o. IX 14: 1 ĝír mar-tu *ba-du-u*$_4$ **L.**; **6** o. VI 2: 20 ĝír mar-tu *ba-du-u*$_9$ **L.**; r. X 18: 1 ĝír mar-tu *ba-du-u*$_9$ **L.**; r. XV 5: 20 ĝír mar-tu *ba-du-u*$_9$ **L.**; **7** o. VI 16: 1 ĝír mar-tu *ba-du-u*$_4$ **L.**; r. XIII 8: 1 ĝír mar-tu *ba-du-u*$_4$ **L.**; **14** o. X 14: 1 *ḫa-bù* $^{d?}$*À-da* **L.** sikil; **16** o. I 20: 1 ĜIŠ-šú 1 níĝ-bànda 10 **L.**; **17** o. XVI 1 ĝír mar-tu *ba-du-u*$_4$ **L.**; o. XIX 4: 3 ĝír mar-tu *ba-du-u*$_4$ **L.**; r. III 14: 2 *gú-li-lum* **L.**; **19** o. XVI 21: 60 ĝír mar-tu *ba-du-u*$_9$ **L.**; r. III 17: 60 ĝír mar-tu *ba-du-u*$_9$ **L.**; 21 r. IV 11–17: 10 lá-3 *gú-li-lum* ŠA.PI **L.**-II *wa* 4 *gú-li-lum* TAR **L.** *wa* 16 *gú-li-lum* ŠÚ+ŠA-ŠÚ+ŠA **L.**-II *wa* 3 *gú-li-lum* 10 **L.**-I.

kù-gi kù:babbar **8** r. VII x+1: 1 g[ír] mar-t[u] *ba-du-*[*u*$_4$] **L.**, 5': 1 ĝír mar-tu *ba-du-u*$_4$ **L.**; r. VIII 6': 1 ĝír mar-tu *ba-du-u*$_4$ **L.**

kù-gi «gold» **1** o. V 3; o. VIII 6, 13, 19; o. IX 3, 10; o. X 3, 12; o. XI 8; o. XIII 2': [2 gí]r [mar-]tu **L.**; (a) r. II' 1; (b) r. x+I x+1; (c) r. III' x+1; (e) r. x+I x+1: [x ĝír] ma[r-tu] **L.**, 2': 1 ĝír mar-⸢tu⸣ ti **L.**; **2** o. I 3, 10, 18; o. II 2, 12: 1 ĝír mar-tu **L.**, 17, 22; o. III 17; o. IV 5, 12; o. V 8, 15: 1 ĝír mar-tu **L.**; o. VI 2, 8, 20; o. IX 4: 1 ĝír mar-tu **L.**, 8, 20; o. XI 5, 11, 18; o. XII 2, 8, 15; o. XIII 1, 8, 15, 21; o. XIV 6, 12; o. XV 2, 10; r. I 16, 23; r. II 11, 20; r III 10; r. IV 2, 12, 22; r. VI 8, 15, 19: 1 dib lú ĜIŠ-ĝeštin *wa* 1 dib-II ŠA.PI gín D. **L.**; r. VII 19; r. VIII 9, 15; r. X 10: 1 ĝír mar-tu **L.**, 14: 1 ĝír mar-tu **L.**, 19: 1 ĝír mar-tu **L.**; r. XI 2: 2 ĝír mar-tu ti **L.** 1 ĝír mar-tu *ba-du-u*$_9$ **L.**, 3: 3 *gú-li-lum* a-gar$_5$-gar$_5$ **L.**, 10: 1 ĝír mar-tu *ba-du-u*$_9$ **L.**, 16; r. XII 2; r. XIII 15; r. XIV 2, 21; r. XV 7, 15; r. XVI 7: 1 ĝír mar-tu *ra-ʾà-tum* **L.**; r. XVII 1: 1 ĝír mar-tu **L.**, 18; l.ed. 3: TAR **L.** 1 íb-lá, 8: 1 ma-na **L.** 2 íb-lá; **3** o. III 8, 22; o. IV 8, 16; o. VII 19; o. VIII 9: 1 ĝír mar-tu ti **L.**; o. XI 8; o. XII 2, 10; o. XIV 2, 18; o. XV 5; r. I 2, 7; r. III 20; r. IV 18; r. V 5, 10; r. VI 4; r. XII 11, 13: 2 íb-lá **L.**; r. XIV 1: 2 ĝír mar-tu ti **L.**; **4** o. XI 3, 13; r. XV 4; r. XVI 13; **5** o. III 5: 1 ĝír mar-tu **L.**, 9, 14; o. IV 8, 14; o. VI 2, 16: 1 ĝír mar-tu **L.**; o. VII 3: 2 *gú-li-lum* a-gar$_5$-gar$_5$ **L.**; o. X 14, 20; o. XI 10: 1 ĝír mar-tu ti **L.**, 16; o. XII 11; o. XIII 15; o. XVI 17; r. I 8, 16; r. III 5: 1 ĝír mar-tu **L.** zú LAGAB×A, 17; r. IV 10; r. V 13; r. VI 6, 9; r. VII 6, 12; r. VIII 1; r. X 3, 10; r. XII 8, 16; r. XIII 1, 19; r. XIV 6, 17; r. XV 1, 7; r. XVI 10; **6** o. V 4: 23 dib a-gar$_5$-gar$_5$ **L.**, 20: 20 ĝír mar-tu **L.**; o. VII 2: 1 *za-ḫa-da ra-ʾà-tum* **L.**, 7: 1 ĝír mar-tu ti **L.**, 12: 1 ĝír mar-tu ti **L.**; o. X 8: ĝír mar-tu **L.**; o. XII 3: 1 *mi-at* si-si ĝír mar-tu **L.**; r. II 8: 1 ĝír mar-tu **L.**, 11: 1 ĝír mar-tu **L.**; r. VII 18: 1 *gú-li-lum* a-gar$_5$-gar$_5$ **L.**; r. VIII 1: maš-maš **L.**; r. X 9: 1 ĝír mar-tu **L.**, 13: 1 ĝír mar-tu ti **L.**; r. XI 2: 1 ĝír mar-tu ti **L.**, 13: 1 ĜIŠ-banšur **L.**; r. XII 2; r. XIII 6: 1 ĝír **L.**; r. XIV 17: 1 íb-lá kb maš-maš **L.**, 20: 1 íb-lá maš-maš **L.**; r. XV 3: 40 ĝír mar-tu **L.**; **7** o. III 3, 20: [x ĝír mar-t]u [(x) **L.**]; o. IV 4: 10 lá-2 ĝír mar-tu ti **L.**, 7, 9: 10 ĝír mar-tu ti **L.**; 14; o. V 16: 1 ĝír mar-tu ti **L.**, 21: 1 ĝír mar-tu **L.**; o. VI 3, 8: 1 ĝír mar-tu ti **L.**; o. VII 15, 21; o. X 8; o. XI 3, 12; o. XII 6, 18; o. XIII 6, 12, 18; o. XIV 5, 11; o. XVI 3, 9, 14: 1 ĝír mar-tu **L.**; o. XVIII 5: 1 g[ír] mar[-tu] **L.**, 14; r. I 12, 16; r. II 10, 19; r. III 8, 17; r. IV 6, 16; r. V 1, 14, 20; r. VI 3; r. VIII 2; r. IX 1: 1 [ĝír] mar-[tu **L.**], 5, 17; r. X 3, 10; r. XI 6; r. XII 1: [1 ĝír mar]-tu **L.**, 17; r. XIV 23; r. XV 4, 10: **L.** sikil, 18, 20; r. XVI 3: [1 gí]r mar-[t]u **L.**; **8** o. I 14: [1 ĝír mar-tu 1 *ra-ʾà-t]um* **L.**, 15: [1] ĝír mar-tu **L.**; o. II 1: ⌜1⌝ ĝír mar-[t]u ⌜1⌝ *r[a]-⌜ʾà⌝-tum* **L.**, 13: 1 ĝír mar-tu **L.**; o. VI 4; o. VIII 4, 5: 20 ĝír mar-tu ti **L.**; o. XII 7, 14; o. XIII 3, 12; o. XIV 8; r. II 2'; r. VII 10': 1 ĝír mar-tu **L.**; r. VIII 2': 1 ĝír mar-tu *ba-du-u$_4$* **L.**, 11'; r. IX 8', 13'; r. X 7', 12'; **9** o. III 10; o. IV 17; o. VI 1, 15; o. VIII 12; o. XIII 7, 13; o. XV 10: 2 ĝír mar-tu ti **L.**, 16: 1 ĝír mar-tu ti **L.**; o. XVI 3': 1 ĝír mar-tu **L.**; o. XVII 5': 1 ĝír mar-tu **L.**; r. I 1: 1 ĝír mar-tu **L.**; r. II 4; r. III 1, 12, 15; r. IV 8, 10: 1 ĝír mar-tu **L.**; r. VI 10; r. VII 9, 16; r. VIII 7; r. IX 12; r. X 7; r. XII 3, 6: 1 ĝír mar-tu **L.**, 7: [x] ĝír mar-tu ti **L.**, 9: 6 ĝír mar-tu *ba-du-u$_4$* **L.**; r. XIV 16: 1 ĝír mar-tu **L.**; r. XV 2: 1 ĝír mar-tu zú LAGAB×AN **L.**, 6: 1 ĝír mar-tu **L.**, 9; r. XVI 1; r. XVII 6, 19: 1 ĝír mar-tu ti **L.**; **10** o. II 6; o. V 4; o. XV 14; r. V 4; r. VI 19; r. VIII 3, 14; r. X 11; **11** o. II 6; o. IV 4, 17; o. V 8; o. VI 4, 11, 17; o. VII 2: 2 ĝír mar-tu **L.**, 13, 22; o. X 9, 22; o. XII 11, 15; r. V 13: 1 ĝír mar-tu **L.**; r. VI 22; r. VII 10, 14, 17: 1 ĝír mar-tu **L.**; **12** o. III 7: *ap* **L.** lú dib, 10; o. IV 3, 10; o. V 2, 15; o. VIII 4; o. IX 7: 1 ĝír mar-tu **L.**; o. XI 17: 1 ĝír mar-tu ti **L.**; o. XII 4, 14; o. XIII 5, 15; o. XV 1, 10, 16; r. I 14; r. II 10; r. III 16; r. IV 6: 1 ĝír mar-tu **L.**; r. V 4; r. VIII 4: 1 ĝír mar-tu **L.**, 12; r. IX 10; r. X 9; r. XI 1; **13** o. III 3, 7; o. VII 9, 20; o. VIII 15; o. IX 1, 14; o. X 16: 1 ĝír mar-tu **L.**; o. XI 6, 16: maš-maš **L.**, 24; o. XII 2: [1 g]ír m[ar-t]u **L.**, 15; o. XIII 1, 8, 14, 22; o. XV 22; r. III 1: 1 ĝír mar-tu ti **L.**, 3: 1 *gú-li-lum* a-gar$_5$-gar$_5$ **L.**, 9; r. VI 13: 1 ĝír mar-tu **L.**; r. VII 4; r. VIII 1, 11; r. IX 2, 6, 13; r. XII 19; **14** o. I 11, 16; o. II 3; o. IV 19: 2 *gú-li-lum*-I a-gar$_5$-gar$_5$ **L.** esi ⌜x⌝; o. VII 3: 1 íb-lá 1 ĝír-kun **L.**, 8, 18; o. VIII 12, 19; o. IX 2, 10; o. X 3, 23; o. XI 17; o. XII 2, 16; o. XIV 8, 19, 21: 2 *gù-li-lum* **L.**; o. XV 6, 12; o. XVIII 2, 6; r. I 18; r. II 6, 17; r. III 11; r. IV 19; r. V 2; r. VI 8; r. VIII 1, 12, 20; r. IX 12, 19; r. X 9; r. XII 14, 20; r. XIII 3, 10, 15: 16 ĝír mar-tu **L.**, 16: ⌜10⌝ ĝír ⌜mar⌝-tu ti **L.**, 18: 2 ĝír mar-tu *ba-du-u$_4$* **L.**; r. XIV 6'; r. XVII x+1; r. XVIII 5; r. XIX 5; **15** o. I 11, 18; o. II 1, 19; o. III 13, 17, 19: 1 ĝír mar-tu **L.**; o. IV 5, 17; o. V 3, 10, 16, 22; o. VI 13; o. VIII 24; o. IX 7, 12, 17; o. X 4, 17, 25; o. XI 6; o. XII 2; o. XIII 21; o. XIV 2: 1 ĝír mar-tu **L.**, 15; o. XV 7, 25; o. XVI 4, 18; r. I 9, 18; r. II 6, 22: 1 ĝír mar-tu **L.**; r. III 18: 2 níĝ-anše-ak **L.** maḫ?; r. IV 10, 21; r. V 6, 17: 1 ĝír mar-tu **L.**; r. VI 12, 24; r. VII 3, 14, 23; r. VIII 4, 14, 22; r. IX 3, 15: 1 *ar-ra-sù* **L.** sikil, 26; r. X 9; r. XI 10, 16, 22; r. XII 1, 21; r. XIII 2, 14, 20; r. XIV 11, 23; r. XV 5, 11, 13: 1 *gú-bù* **L.** libir, 15: 1 ĝír mar-tu **L.**; r. XVI 4: [1 ĝír mar-t]u **L.**, 17; **16** o. I 15; o. II 10, 20; o. III 3, 10; o. V 11; o. VI 2, 8, 12, 20; o. VII 6, 13; o. VIII 4: 7 íb-lá lú URI lú **L.**, 7, 15: 17 íb-lá maš-maš **L.**, 18; o. IX 10; o. X 1; o. XI 6, 8: 14 ĝír mar-tu **L.**, 9: 7 ĝír mar-tu ti **L.**, 10: 17 ĝír mar-tu zú LAGAB×A **L.**; o. XII 14; o. XIII 12; o. XIV 11; r. I 1, 14: 13 gín D. kb nu$_{11}$-za 1 *ḫa-bù* ap **L.** ⌜sikil⌝; r. II 6; r. III 1, 9, 19, 26: 1 ĝír mar-tu ti **L.**; r. IV 3, 13; r. V 11, 18, 25; r. VI 3, 11, 23; r. VII 18; r. VIII 7, 10: 4 ĝír mar-tu **L.**, 12: 4 ĝír mar-tu ti **L.**, 14: 5 ĝír mar-tu *ba-du-u$_4$* **L.**, 25; r. IX 10, 17; r. X 4, 17; r. XI 3: 12 gín D. kb nu$_{11}$-za 1 *ḫa-bù ap* **L.** sikil, 24; r. XII 10, 17, 23, 28; r. XIII 9; r. XIV 3, 24; r. XV 15, 24; r. XVI 9, 16; r. XVII 17; **17** o. I 11, 20; o. III 19; o. IV 20; o. V 14, 23; o. VI 23; o. VII 10, 18; o. IX 12; o. XI 5, 11, 19; o. III 2: 1 ĝír mar-tu zú **L.**, 19; o. XIV 6: 1 ĝír mar-tu zú **L.**, 14, 17: 1 ĝír mar-tu **L.**; o. XV 13; o. XVI 2: 1 ĝír mar-tu **L.**, 11: 1 ĝír mar-tu *ba-du-u$_4$* **L.**, 12: 1 ĝír mar-tu zú **L.**; o. XVII 27; o. XVIII 3: 1 ĝír mar-tu **L.**; o. XIX 7; r. I 5, 21; r. II 2, 12, 18, 25; r. III 11, 19, 25; r. IV 19; r. V 18; r. VI 9, 18; r. VII 16, 27; r. VIII 3, 8; r. IX 13; r. XI 29; r. XII 3, 9: 1 ĝír mar-tu **L.**, 15, 18: 1 ĝír mar-tu **L.**; r. XIII 1; r. XV 4, 13; r. XVI 17; r. XVII 12; r. XVIII 10, 18; r. XIX 10, 17, 25, 33; r. XX 30; r. XXI 7, 12, 15, 25; r. XXII 16: 1 ĝír mar-tu **L.**; **18** o. I 20; o. II 4, 13; o. III 2, 8, 13; o. VI 3, 14; o. VII 8; o. VIII 3; o. X 5, 10, 17; o. XI 8, 19; o. XII 7, 13, 19; o. XIII 3; o. XIV 25: 2 ĝír mar-tu ti **L.**; o. XV 30; o. XVI 5: 1 ĝír mar-tu **L.**, 9, 14; o. XVII 25; o. XVIII 2, 17; o. XIX 2, 13: 15 gín D. kb nu$_{11}$-za 1 *ḫa-bù ap* **L.** sikil, 28; r. I 5, 15, 25; r. IV 7; r. VI 11, 16: 1 ĝír mar-tu **L.**; r. VII 3: 40 ĝír mar-tu **L.**, 6, 14; r. VIII 1: 20 ĝír mar-tu ti **L.** *ʾà-lum*, 4, 12; r. IX 1: 50 ĝír mar-tu ti **L.**, 4, 11; r. XI 5; r. XII 13, 25; r. XIII 24; r. XIV 4, 12, 22; r. XV 1, 16, 22; r. XVI 14, 22: 1 ĝír mar-tu zú LAGAB×A **L.**, 37; r. XVII 10, 26: 2 ĝír mar-tu **L.**, 35: 15 kb nu$_{11}$-za 1 *ḫa-bù ap* **L.** sikil; r. XVIII 6: 1 ĝír mar-tu **L.**, 22; **19** o. I 13: 2 ĝír mar-tu **L.**, 25: 1 ĝír mar-tu **L.**; o. II 5, 18; o. IV 1, 12; o. V 8; o. VII 23; o. VIII 5, 24; o. IX 8, 14, 21: 2 ĝír mar-tu **L.**; o. X 4, 22; o. XI 10: **L.** sikil, 22; o. XII 7, 13, 22, 28; o. XIII 6, 13, 21, 32 and 33: 20 ĝír mar-tu **L.** *ap* 2 ma-na **L.**; o. XIV 9, 15: 20 ĝír mar-tu ti **L.** *ʾà-lum*,

18, 25, 30: 40 ĝír mar-tu ti **L.**; o. XV 2, 9, 18, 27, 30: 10 lá-2 ĝír mar-tu zú AN.LAGAB×A **L.**; o. XVI 5: 40 ĝír mar-tu *ba-du-u*$_9$ **L.**, 8, 15, 24; o. XVII 9; o. XVIII 4; r. I 3: 80 ĝír mar-tu **L.**, 5, 14, 20: 20 ĝír mar-tu ti **L.** *ʾà-lum*, 23; r. II 4, 10: 90 ĝír mar-tu ti **L.**, 13, 21; r. III 1: 50 ĝír mar-tu *ba-du-u*$_9$ **L.**, 4, 11, 20; r. IV 1; r. VI 26; r. VII 13, 24, 30; r. VIII 7, 24; r. IX 2, 9; r. X 13, 21; r. XI 1, 13, 22; r. XII 26; r. XIII 8, 14, 22; r. XIV 2, 9: 1 ĝír mar-tu ti **L.**; r. XV 1: 2 ĝír mar-tu ti **L.**, 10: 2 ĝír mar-tu *ba-du-u*$_9$ **L.**, 17: 1 ĝír mar-tu *ba-du-u*$_9$ **L.**, 21; r. XVII 9: 13 gín D. kb nu$_{11}$-za 1 *ḫa-bù ap* **L.** sikil, 24; r. XVIII 4, 21; **20** o. II 16; o. III 18; o. IV 12; o. V x+1; o. VI 10; o. VIII 6, 17: 15 gín D. kb nu$_{11}$-za 1 [*ḫa-bù*] *ap* **L.** sikil; o. IX 9, 17; o. X 22; o. XI 2, 7, 23; o. XII 4: 1 ĝír mar-tu **L.**, 13; o. XV 4; o. XVI 4, 11, 16; o. XVII 9, 19: 1 ĝír mar-tu **L.**, 22: 1 ĝír mar-tu **L.**; r. I 3; r. II 9, 16, 22; r. III 2, 5: 1 pad *ma-da-a-um* **L.** an-dùl, 12, 27; r. IV 3, 7, 14, 18; r. V 1, 11; r. VI 1, 5, 12; r, VII 16; r. VIII 1, 11, 21; r. IX 18; 26; r. X 16, 24; r. XI 8: 12 gín D. kb nu$_{11}$-za 1 *ḫa-bù ap* nu$_{11}$-za *ar-ra-sù* **L.** si[kil]; r. XII 7, 17, 21; r. XIII 14; r. XV x+1; **21** o. II 13; o. III 9, 25; o. IV 4, 14, 21; o. V 3; o. VI 11; o. VII 7, 12: 1 ĝír mar-tu **L.** *⌜ra⌝-ʾà-[tu]m*; o. VIII 7, 16; o. IX 12, 22: 15 gín D. kb nu$_{11}$-za 1 *ḫa-bù ap* **L.** sikil; o. X 4, 10, 18, 26; o. XI 1, 17; o. XIII 10, 24, 29; o. XIV 7: 1 ĝír mar-tu *ra-ʾà-tum* **L.**, 10, 16; o. XV 8, 17, 23; o. XVI 1, 8: 1 ĝír mar-tu **L.**, 12, 17, 22; o. XVII 11; r. I 3, 10; r. III 10, 25; r. IV 20; r. V 7: 11 *gú-li-lum* TAR a-gar$_5$-gar$_5$ **L.**, 9: 10 *gú-li-lum* 15 a-gar$_5$-gar$_5$ **L.**, 17; r. VI 7, 23; r. VII 1, 8, 14: 1 ĝír mar-tu **L.**; r. VIII 15, 28: 1 ĝír mar-tu *ba-du*[*-u*$_4$] **L.**; r. IX 10, 22; r. X 18; r. XI 26; r. XII 24; r. XIII 16, 22; **22** o. II 3, 7, 10; o. III 7, 11; o. IV 3; o. V 5: AN.ŠÈ.GÚ 54 ma-na 3 gín D. **L.**; o. VI 6, 9; o. VII 1, 7, 11; o. VIII 4, 9; o. IX 2, 7; r. I 1, 8; r. II 4, 9; r. V 1, 7, 12; r. VI 2, 7, 12; r. VII 5; r. VIII 7 and IX 3: AN.ŠÈ.GÚ 4 ma-na TAR 3 gín D. **L.** è lú mu-DU *I*[*b-rí-*]*um wa* tak$_4$ **L.** É×PAP en-e[n]; **23** o. I 1; o. II 3, 7; o. III 2, 5, 9; o. IV 3, 7; o. V 1, 5, 9; o. VI 2, 6, 10; o. VII 3, 7; o. VIII 1, 5, 10; o. IX 2; o. X 1; r. I 6, 11; r. II 6; r. III 3, 5: 1 ĝír mar-tu **L.**; r. IV 1, 6; r. V 1, 5, 9; r. VI 3, 8; r. VII 2; r. IX 1: AN.ŠÈ.GÚ 8 ma-na 3 gín D. **L.** è lú *A-da-bí-ig*$^{ki}$; **24** o. I 1, 5; o. II 2, 11; o. III 2, 8; o. IV 1, 6, 9, 14; o. V 14; o. VI 4, 11, 15; o. VII 7, 10, 11; o. VIII 1, 4, 6, 8, 9; r. I 7, 12; r. II 2, 4; r. III 3, 9; r. IV 5; r. VIII 1 and 4: AN.ŠÈ.GÚ 4 ma-na ŠA.PI 2 2 NI gín D. **L.** è *ap* 5 gín D. **L.** al$_6$-ĝál é siki.

kun «tail; rear part (of a throne); frog (of a belt)» **8** o. IX 4: 13 ma-na ŠÚ+ŠA gín D. kb kin$_5$-ak 20 íb-lá 20 **L.** ŠA.PI; o. XIII 8: ŠA.PI gín D. kb URI 1 íb-lá 1 **L.**; **21** o. X 21: 1 4 NI gín D. kg *ni-zi-mu* nu$_{11}$-za 1 **L.** ZA$_x$ *Ib-rí-um*; o. XIV 17: 6 gín D. kg nu$_{11}$-za 1 **L.**

*kur-gú-ru*$_{12}$ «spherical bead» **15** o. XI 11: 1 ma-na 14 gín D. kg kin$_5$-ak … 1 *mi-at* **L.**

kù-sal «buckle» **1** o. VI 7: 1 ma-na ŠÚ+ŠA gín D. kb *ni-zi-mu* 2 níĝ-anše-ak 4 **L.**; o. X 15: 3 gín D. kg nu$_{11}$-za-*sù wa* [1] **L.**; **2** o. II 4: 1 gín D kg kin$_5$-ak 1 **L.**; o. VI 12: 2 gín D. kg maš-maš 1 ĜIŠ-banšur *wa* 1 **L.**, 21: 1 ½ gín D. kg 1 **L.**; r. II 1: 2 gín D. kg kin$_5$-ak 1 *gú-li-lum* 1 **L.**; r. III 11: 2 ½ gín D. kg 1 *gú-li-lum* 1 **L.**; r. VIII 18: 1 gín D. kg maš-maš 1 “KIN” siki *wa* 1 **L.**; **3** r. III 5: 56 gín D. kb *ni-zi-mu* 2 níĝ-anše-ak 4 **L.**; **4** o. III 9: 10 ½ gín D. kb ZU.PIRIĜ kin$_5$-ak *gú-li-lum wa* níĝ-anše-ak **L.** SA.ZA$_x^{ki}$; r. III 17: 1 ma-na 53 an-na kin$_5$-ak níĝ-anše-ak **L.**; r. X 8: 2 ma-na kb kin$_5$-ak 2 níĝ-anše-ak 4 **L.**; r. XIV 11: 1 ma-na ŠÚ+ŠA gín D. kb 2 níĝ-anše-ak 4 **L.**, 16: 1 ma-na ŠÚ+ŠA gín D. kb 2 níĝ-anše-ak 4 **L.**; **5** r. I 13: 8 gín D. kb *ni-zi-mu* 2 <níĝ->anše-ak 4 **L.**; r. III 17: 1 gín D. kg 1 **L.**; r. XIV 6: ½ gín D. kg 1 **L.**, 17: ½ kg 1 **L.**; r. V 12: 1 ma-na ŠÚ+ŠA gín D. kb 2 níĝ-anše-ak 4 **L.**; r. XIV 13: 1 ma-na ŠÚ+ŠA kb 2 níĝ-anše-ak 4 **L.**; **7** o. III 4: 1 gín D. kg 1 **L.**, 14: 3 gín D. kb nu$_{11}$-za 1 ĝír mar-tu *wa* 1 **L.**; o. XIII 3: [ ] kb *ni-zi-mu* 2 níĝ-anše-ak 1 **L.**, 8: 2 gín D. kg *ni-zi-mu* maš-maš 4 **L.**; r. II 11: ½ gín D. kg [1] **L.**, 20: ½ g[ín D.] kg 1 **L.**; r. III 18: 2 NI gín D. kg 1 **L.**; r. IV 7: 2 N[I gín] D. kg 1 **L.**, 17: 2 NI gín D. kg 1 **L.**; r. V 2: [½ gín d. kg] [1 **L.**]; r. VI 4: 1 gín D. kg 1 **L.** 1 buru$_4$-MUŠEN; **8** o. XV 3: 6 gín D. kb *ni-zi-mu* 10 lá-2 **L.** 2 níĝ-anše-ak; **10** r. X 2: 3 gín D. kb nu$_{11}$-za 1 ĝír mar-tu 1 **L.**, 14: 2 gín D. kg maš-maš 1 ĜIŠ-banšur *wa* [x] **L.**; **11** o. IV 18: [½ gí]n [D.] kg 1 **L.**; o. V 9: ½ gín D. kg 1 **L.**; o. VI 19: 4 gín D. kg *ni-zi-mu* 2 níĝ-anše-ak 2 **L.**; o. XII 16: 1 ½ gín D. kg 1 **L.**; r. VI 15: 15 gín D. kg *ni-zi-mu* 2 níĝ-anše-ak 4 **L.**; **12** o. V 16: 1 ½ gín D. kg 2 **L.**; o. XV 1: 1 ½ gín D. kg 2 **L.**; r. VII 13: ½ gín D. kb 1 **L.**; **13** o. IX 8: 2 ½ gín D. kb nu$_{11}$-za 1 ĝír mar-tu 1 **L.**, 14: ½ gín D. kg 1 **L.**, 16: 1 gín D. kb 1 **L.**; o. XIII 2 and 4: 4 gín D. kg 4 **L.** *al*$_6$ **L.** *⌜Zi⌝-ba-⌜da⌝*, 10: 1 ½ gín D. kg *ni-zi-mu* maš-maš 4 **L.**; 14 o. II 4: 1 gín D. kb 1 **L.**; **14** o. XI 6: [1] ma-na ŠÚ+ŠA gín D. kb *n*[*i-zi-*]*m*[*u*] 2 níĝ-anše-ak 2[+2] **L.**; o. XII 19: [½ gín D. kg] *ni-zi-mu* maš-maš 4 **L.**; r. VIII 5: [4 gín D. kg kin$_5$-ak 1 ĜIŠ-ba]nšur [*wa*] 1 **L.**; r. XIII 5: 1 ½ kg *ni-zi-mu* 1 níĝ-anše-ak 1 **L.** 1 IGI.NITA en; **15** o. I 11: 1 gín D. kg 1 **L.**; o. II 5: 3 ½ kg *ʾa*$_5$*-na-gu* 1 ĜIŠ-banšur *wa* 1 **L.**; o. IV 19: 2 gín D. kg *ni-zi-mu* nu$_{11}$-za 4 **L.**; o. IX 14: ŠA.PI 8 gín D. kg *ni-zi-mu* 4 **L.**-*sù*; o. XI 12: 1 ma-na 14 gín D. kg kin$_5$-ak … 2 **L.**; o. XII 2: 1 gín D. kg 1 **L.**; r. IV 21: 1 gín D. kg 1 **L.**; r. VII 18: 3 gín D. kg *ʾa*$_5$*-na-gu* 1 ĜIŠ-banšur *wa* 1 **L.**, 26: 2 gín D. 2 NI kg nu$_{11}$-za 1 ĝír mar-tu *wa* 1 **L.**; r. VIII 7: 3 gín D. kg nu$_{11}$-za 1 ĝír mar-tu *wa* 1 **L.**; r. IX 26: 1 kg 1 **L.**; r. X 9: 2 gín D. kg 2 **L.**; r. XI 3: 2 ½ gín D. kb nu$_{11}$-za [1 ĝír mar-tu] [*w*]*a* 1 **L.**; r. XIII 24: 5 gín D. kg *ʾa*$_5$*-na-gu* 1 ĜIŠ-banšur *wa* 1 **L.** sikil *al*$_6$ ama-gal en; **16** o. III 11: 2 gín D. kg 2 **L.**; o. VI 4: ŠÚ+ŠA 5 gín D. kg *ni-zi-mu* 2 níĝ-anše-ak 4 **L.** libir *Ib-rí-um*; o. VII 1: 2 ma-na TAR kg kin$_5$-ak 2 níĝ-anše-ak 4 **L.** gibil *Ib-rí-um*, 8: 2 gín D. kg *ni-zi-mu* 2 níĝ-anše-ak 4 **L.** 2 IGI.NITA *Ib-rí-um*; o. XIV 11: ½ gín kg 1 **L.**; r. II 8: 1 gín kg *ni-zi-mu* 1 **L.**; r. III 5: [ŠÚ+ŠA k]g *ni-zi-mu su-da-⌜nu⌝*? *wa* 4 **L.**-*sù*, 11: 1 gín D. kg *ni-zi-mu* maš-maš **L.**; r. VII 5: 10 gín D. kb *ni-zi-mu* 2 níĝ-anše-ak ⌜4⌝ **L.**; r. IX 1: 1 ma-na kg kin$_5$-ak 2 níĝ-anše-ak 4 **L.**; r. X 20: 4 gín D. kg nu$_{11}$-za 1 ĝír mar-tu *wa* 1 **L.**; r. XII 6: 5 gín D. kg *ni-zi-mu* 2 níĝ-anše-ak 4 **L.**; r. XIII 22: ŠÚ+ŠA 6 gín D. kg kin$_5$-ak lul-gu-ak … 1 **L.** 4 gín D. [ ]⌜x⌝; r. XVII 8: 1 kb 1 **L.**; **17** o. IV 20: 1 gín D. kg 1 **L.** 1 buru$_4$-MUŠEN; o. VII 12: 50 gín D. kg kin$_5$-ak 2 níĝ-anše-ak 4!(2) **L.** 2 IGI.NITA; o.

XVII 1: ŠÚ+ŠA 2 gín D. kb *ni-zi-mu* 2 níĝ-anše-ak 4 **L.**; r. II 14: 3 gín D. kg *ni-zi-mu* 2 níĝ-anše-ak 4 **L.** sur$_x$-BAR.AN, 20: 2 gín D. kg *ni-zi-mu* 1 níĝ-anše-ak 1 **L.** 2 IGI.NITA; r. III 6: 2 gín D. kb kin$_5$-ak *kam$_4$-ma-a-tum* zàḫ *ša-ti* **L.** ama-gal en, 21: 3 gín D. kg *ni-zi-mu* maš-maš **L.** *Ib-rí-um*; r. V 19: 1 gín D. kg 1 **L.** 1 buru$_4$-MUŠEN; r. VIII 15: 5 gín D. kb *ni-zi-mu* 2 níĝ-anše-ak 4 **L.**; r. XVIII 10: 1 kg 1 **L.**; r. XXI 15: 4 kg 2 **L.**; **18** o. VI 5: 10 gín D. kg *ni-zi-mu* 4 **L.**; o. XVII 1: 1 ma-na TAR kg kin$_5$-ak … 2 **L.**; o. XVIII 7: 8 gín D. kg *ni-zi-mu* 4 *ti-gi-na* 4 ĜIŠ-du 4 ĝeštu$_x$-lá 2 **L.**; o. XIX 2: 1 kg 1 **L.** buru$_4$-MUŠEN; r. I 7 and 11: 3 gín D. kg *ni-zi-⌈mu⌉* 2 níĝ-anše-ak 2 **L.** 2 IGI.NITA *wa su-da-nu* **L.** en; r. XIV 5: 2 ma-na kg 2 níĝ-anše-ak 4 **L.**; r. XVI 37: 2 kg 2 **L.**; **19** o. II 5: 1 gín D. kg 1 **L.**; o. VIII 11: [3 gín D. kg] *wa* 2 gín D. kb ì-na-sum 1 banšur *wa* 1 **L.**, 26: 1 gín D. kg *ni-zi-mu* 4 **L.** *a-li-iš* kù-sal-kù-sal *Zi-ba-da*; o. IX 15: 2 gín D. kg 2 **L**; o. XI 25: 8 gín D. kg nu$_{11}$-za 2 gí[r] mar-tu *wa* 2 **L.**; o. XII 17: 50 gín D. kg *ni-zi-mu su-da-nu wa* **L.** sur$_x$-BAR.AN en, 24: 3 gín D. kg *ni-zi-mu* 2 [n]íĝ-anše-ak 4 **L.** *I-bí-zi-kir*; o. XIII 21: 1 gín D. kg 1 **L.**; r. X 25: 3 gín D. kg *ᵓa$_5$-na-gu* 1 banšur *wa* 1 **L.**; **20** o. VII 24: 6 gín D. an-na šub *si-in ni-⌈zi⌉-mu* 2 níĝ-anše-ak 4 **L.**; r. II 12: 1 ½ gín D. kg *ni-zi-mu* nu$_{11}$-za 4 **L.** *Ib-rí-um*; r. III 13: 1 gín D. kg 1 **L.**; r. V 13: 10 gín D. kg *ni-zi-mu* maš-maš 4 **L.** *I-bí-zi-kir* dumu-nita *Ib-rí-um*, 19: ŠÚ+ŠA gín [D.] kb [*ni-zi-m*]*u* 2 níĝ-anše-ak 4 **L.** *Gi-rí* dumu-nita *Ib-rí-um*; r. X 24: 2 gín D. kg 2 **L.**; r. XIV 12: 2 gín D. kb ⌈1⌉ **L.**; **21** o. III 17: 4 gín D. an-na šub *si-in* [*ni-zi-mu* 2 níĝ-anše-ak 4 **L.**], 27: 4 gín D. kg *ni-zi-mu* [2] níĝ-anše-ak [2+]2 **L.**; o. IV 6: 3 gín D. kg *ni-zi-mu* 2 **L.** 2 IGI.NITA en, 11: 7 gín D. kb *ni-zi-mu* 4 **L.**, 16: 6 gín D. kg *ni-zi-mu* **L.**-*sù* am<a-gal> en; o. VI 19: 2 gí[n] D. kb 1 **L.**; o. VIII 8: ŠÚ+ŠA 4 gín D. kg 1 níĝ-anše-ak 1 **L.** 1 IGI.NITA; o. XIII 12: 1 ma-na kg kin$_5$-ak 2 níĝ-anše-ak 4 **L.** *wa* nu$_{11}$-za 2 ĜIŠ.GAM.GAM ĜIŠ-gígir-II, 25: 15 gín D. kg 1 níĝ-anše-ak 1 **L.** 1 IGI.NITA; **22** o. II 5: 4 ma-na kg [6] níĝ-anše-[a]k 12 **L.** BAR.AN-BAR.AN; 24 o. II 5: 4 gín D. kg nu$_{11}$-za 1 ĝír mar-tu *wa* 2 **L.**; o. VII 1: 1 gín D. kg 1 **L.**; o. VIII 8: 3 gín D. kg 2 **L.**

kù-sal-kù-sal **19** o. VIII 28.

kuš «hide, leather» **15** r. III 17: 2 **L.** babbar ùz-nita lú 2 níĝ-anše-ak kg maḫ; **20** o. XIV 4: 33 **L.** Mar-tu$^{ki}$.

kuš-kuš **17** r. V 11: 1 *mi-at* 50 **L.** sa$_6$ ĝi$_6$.

kuš$_7$ (a high official) **3** r. XII 8: *Ù-da-aḫ Ma-rí*$^{ki}$ **L.**

# L

LAGAB «block» **8** o. VII 11: 3 ma-na 50 gín D. [kb] 1 aš-ḫal 1 **L.** al$_6$-ĝál é siki.

LAGAB-LAGAB **5** r. XVI 16: 5 gín D. kg *ni-zi-mu* 1 *zi-ru$_{12}$ wa* 2 *gi-zu wa* **L.**

LAGAB×A, LAGAB×AN, LAGAB×AN.A see *s.v.* zú

LAGAB×UD «ostrich shell»

LAGAB×UD-LAGAB×UD **14** o. V 18: **L.** kin$_5$-ak ĜIŠ-asari sagi; **17** o. VIII 14: EZEN-*il Ma-rí*$^{ki}$ ḫi-mu-DU la-ḫa «jar» **18** o. V 22: **L.** ĝeštin en *Gú-da-da-núm*$^{ki}$; **21** o. VI 5: **L.** lú ì-ĝiš *si-in A-la-ga*$^{ki}$.

libir «previous, precedent» **15** r. VIII 25: 1 an-zam$_x$ an-dùl **L.** lú *Ib-rí-um*; r. XV 13: 1 *gú-bù* kg **L.**; **16** o. VI 4: 2 níĝ-anše-ak 4 kù-sal **L.**

lú (determinative-relative pronoun) *passim*.

lu$_5$ «androcephalus bull» **5** r. V 14: ŠÚ+ŠA gín D. kg nu$_{11}$-za 3 saĝ **L.**; **6** o. XIII 12: 5 gín D. kb nu$_{11}$-za 1 saĝ **L.** ĜIŠ-ĝidru; **7** o. VII 1: [ ] 2 **L.**; **10** o. II 7: ŠÚ+ŠA gín D. kg nu$_{11}$-za 1 saĝ **L.**; o. IV 11: 1 ĜIŠ-sal lú DU.DU **L.** tuš $^{d}$*À-la* lú *Zi-ig*$^{ki}$; **14** r. VII 1: 6 gín D. kb nu$_{11}$-za 4 saĝ **L.** *al$_6$-sù*; **20** r. XI 20: [ ] **L.** UD.GÁ[NA] ĜIŠ-sal.

lugal 1) «lord» (title of the Eblaite highest officials); 2) «king» (title of the rulers of Mari and Kish).

**25** r. IV 9: 1 ib-lá ŠA.PI kb BÍL-*ma-lik* **L.**

lugal-lugal **7** r. XV 23: ŠÚ+ŠA 4 gín D. kg daḫ(MU.MU) kg lú en *wa* **L.** [ì-n]a-sum [nu$_{11}$-z]a$^?$ [$^{d}$*Ra-s*]*a-ap*.

2) **21** r. XI 28: 1 ma-na kg al$_6$-du$_{11}$-ga **L.** [ ].

lú-kar «trader» **2** r. I 7: *I-rí-ig* **L.** *Ḫa-zu-wa-an*$^{ki}$; r. X 16: *Du-bí-šum* **L.**, 21: *Ì-lum-na-im* **L.** *Ma-nu-wa-ad*$^{ki}$; r. XI 7: *Bù-da-ma-lik* BÍL-*ma-lik A-da-mu* **L.** *Ḫa-zu-wa-an*$^{ki}$; **3** o. IX 11: **L.** *A-da-bí-ig*$^{ki}$; r. XIV 5: *Du-bí-zi-kir wa Íl-ba-šum* **L.**; **4** r. VI 10: NI-*má-ti* **L.** *Kak-mi-um*$^{ki}$; r. IX 7: *En-na-ma-lik* **L.** *Ma-nu-wa-ad*$^{ki}$; **5** o. II 12: *Ib-ḫur-ma-lik* **L.** *Kak-mi-um*$^{ki}$; r. VII 15: *Zé-da-ar* **L.**; **6** r. VIII 6: *Na-bù-mu* … *Ma-gal-lu* 2 **L.**; **7** o. II 12: *Ib-lu$_5$-zú* **L.** *Ma-nu-wa-ad*$^{ki}$; o. V 18: *Lá-da* **L.** *A-da-bí-ig*$^{ki}$; r. XV 7: *Ne-zi-ma-lik* **L.** *Kak-mi-um*$^{ki}$; **8** o. V 9: *Ib-lu$_5$-zú wa I-za-iš-ru$_{12}$* **L.** *Ma-nu-wa-ad*$^{ki}$; r. V 4': [*Ib-lu$_5$*]-⌈*zú*⌉ *wa I-za-iš-ru$_{12}$* **L.** *Ma-nu-wa-ad*$^{ki}$; **9** o. XIII 10: *Zé-ba-da-ar* **L.**; r. XVI 6: *En-na-⌈il⌉* [ ] *Rí-ì-ma-lik* **L.** *Kak-mi-um*$^{ki}$; **11** o. IX 5: *Ba-*NE **L.** *A-da-bí-ig*$^{ki}$; o. XI 16: *Wa-ba-rúm En-na-ì* **L.** *Kak-mi-um*$^{ki}$; **13** o. XII 20: *In-gàr wa Ne-zi-ma-lik* **L.** *Kak-mi-um*$^{ki}$; r. II 14: *Puzur$_4$-ra-m*[*a-*]*lik* **L.** *Kak-mi-um*$^{ki}$; r. VI 10: *Iš$_{11}$-la-ab* … *wa I-ša-ni-ki-mu* … 2 **L.** *Ma-nu-wa-ad*$^{ki}$; r. VII 22: Lugal-*na-⌈i⌉-iš Íl-ba-šum Íl-ba-zi-kir A-ma-*NI **L.** [ ]; **14** o. XIII 9: *Iš-ra-il* **L.** *Kak-mi-um*$^{ki}$; **15** o. III 21: *Si-ti-*BAR.AN **L.** *Kak-mi-um*$^{ki}$; r. II 9: *An-na-aḫ* **L.** *Kak-mi-um*$^{ki}$; **20** o. XIV 9: *Iš-ra-*BAD **L.** *Kak-mi-um*$^{ki}$; **23** r. IV 4: *In-gàr* **L.** *Ma-nu-wa-ad*$^{ki}$; **24** o. III 12: NI-*ba-il* **L.** *Ma-nu-wa-ad*$^{ki}$.

lul-gu-ak «replacement» **5** o. V 11: 1 ma-na 20 gín D. kb **L.** 2 níĝ-anše-ak 4 NE-*na-tum*; r. I 2: ⌈x⌉ g[ín] D. kb **L.** 1 *zú-zú-ba-tum* zàḫ; **13** r. II 5: 1 ma-na 2 gín D. kb **L.** gur$_8$; **14** o. XIII 18: [x] gí[n] D. a-gar$_5$-gar$_5$ **L.** 4 ĜIŠ-gu-kak-šub; **15** o. VIII 18: 2 gín D. kb **L.** 1 *zú-zú-ba-tum* en zàḫ; **16** r. IV 4: 2 gín D. kg **L.** 2 ĝeštu$_x$-lá; r. XIII 11: ŠÚ+ŠA 6 gín D. kg kin$_5$-ak **L.** 2 ĝeštu$_x$-lá 15; **17** o. IV 15: [ ] **L.** 1 íb-lá 1 ĝír-kun; o. XX 8: 3 ma-na kb **L.** kb lú mu-DU *Áb-zu*$^{ki}$; r. XIX 4: 10 kb **L.** 1 *zú-zú-ba-tum Ib-rí-um* zàḫ; **19** o. IV 2: 3 gín D. kg **L.** 1 iti lú é $^{dᵓ}$*À-da* lú-máš; **21** o. VIII 18: 1 *za-ḫa-da* … **L.** lú sikil é $^{dᵓ}$*À-da al$_6$* tu-ra *Ib-rí-um*; r. IX 24: 3 *gú-li-lum* ŠÚ+ŠA-ŠÚ+ŠA-II … **L.** 3 *gú-li-lum* [ ]; r. X 19: 6 gín D. kg **L.** 1 zi-bar en; **24** o. I 12: 4 ĝeštu$_x$-lá … *wa* **L.** 2 ĝeštu$_x$-lá.

lú-máš «to take an omen» **19** o. IV 7: (gold) lul-gu-ak 1 iti lú é $^{d}$ʾ*À-da* **L.**

# M

*ma-ʾà-wa-tum* (a ceremony) **24** o. V 13: IGI.DUB 2 an-dùl *wa* 2 šu-*sù* 2 DU-*sù* níĝ-ba *Ib-rí-um* $^{d}$*Ra-sa-ap wa* $^{d}$*A-da-ma* ʾ*À-da-ni*$^{ki}$ *in* **L.**

*ma-ba-ra-zú* **18** o. IX 11: 2 ma-na 12 gín D. an-na 13 ma-na TAR a-gar$_5$-gar$_5$ kin$_5$-ak 10 lá-1 **L.**
(*LLE*,I no. 747: GIG$_4$-BAR = *ma-ba-ra-zu-um*)

*ma-da-a-um* **20** r. III 5: ⌜4⌝ gín D. kg *ni-zi-mu* 1 pad **L.** kg an-dùl lú en; **21** o. XIV 11: TAR kg 1 **L.**, 13: TAR kb 1 **L.**; **24** r. IV 6: ŠÚ+ŠA 6 gín D. kg 1 **L.** <1> an-dùl *wa* 1 pad-*s*[*ù*].
*ma-da-u*$_9$ **19** r. XIX 16: 2 kb **L.**

*ma-da-ḫu* «clip» **16** r. VII 9: 2 gín D. kb 1 **L.**; **20** r. VI 9: 1 gín D. kb 1 **L.**
(see Waetzoldt, *MEE* 12, pp. 387–388)

má-gal «large ship»
má-gal-má-gal **16** r. XIV 9: 4 gín D. kb gur$_8$ **L.** mu-DU *na-se*$_{11}$-*na-se*$_{11}$ *in* ud [ ].

*ma-ga-um* **10** r. XI 7: 5 gín D. an-na šub 1 **L.** zabar.
(*LLE*,I no. 1227: EDEN-ĜISAL = *ma-ga-um*)

*ma-ga-za-u*$_4$(/*u*$_9$) «rasp» **12** r. XII 15: 1 ma-na ŠÚ+ŠA 3 gín D. an-na šub *si-in* 9 ma-na TAR gín D. a-gar$_5$-gar$_5$ … 5 **L.**(-*u*$_9$) 10; **20** r. I 16: 17 gín D. an-na šub *si-in* 1 ma-na ŠA.PI gín D. a-gar$_5$[-gar$_5$] kin$_5$-ak … 1 **L.** 10 gín D.
*ma-ga-za-*ʾ*à* **12** o. X 13: 7 gín D. an-na šub *si-in* 2 **L.** zabar gibil.

maḫ «large» **4** o. IX 7: 1 na$_4$ **L.**; **5** r. XIII 16: ĜIŠ.DUG.DU **L.**; **6** r. I 20: 3 útul-útul urudu **L.**; r. XIV 4: ĜIŠ.DUG.DU **L.**; **7** r. XIV 7: ĜIŠ.DUG.DU **L.**; **11** r. V 8: 1 na$_4$ **L.**; **14** r. VI 1: 1 ĜIŠ-banšur **L.**; r. VII 14: ĜIŠ.DUG.DU **L.**; r. XV 13: 10 na$_4$ **L.**; **15** r. III 18: 2 níĝ-anše-ak kg **L.**; r. XIV 20: 3 útul urudu **L.**; **16** o. III 18: 1 útul urudu **L.**; r. XIV 18: 1 útul urudu **L.**, 21: 3 útul urudu **L.**; r. XVI 6: 2 útul urudu **L.** gibil; **17** o. X 6: 26 gu-dù[l]-TÚG **L.**; o. XVII 11: 1 az$^!$ **L.**; o. XX 17: 6 *ḫar-*ʾ*à-ru*$_{12}$ **L.**; r. IX 7: 1 šum **L.**; **18** o. I 15: 3 útul **L.** urudu; r. V 5: 1 šum **L.**, 10: 2 šum **L.**; **19** o. IX 5: 2 útul urudu gibil **L.**; r. XVI 17: útul-útul **L.** urudu; **20** r. X 11: *in* ĜIŠ.DUG.DU **L.**; r. XIV 10: útul-útul **L.** urudu; **21** r. III 7: ĜIŠ.DUG.DU **L.**; **23** o. I 1: 1 dib **L.**; **24** o. IV 8: 1 balaĝ **L.**

*ma-ḫa-na-gúm* «(neck)lace» **4** o. VII 8: TAR 7 10 gín D. kb 2 *bu*-DI 10 lá-2 ĝeštu$_x$-lá 30 *du-ru*$_{12}$-*gú* 1 *gu-za*$_x$-*gú* 1 šu-dub 1 **L.**; **15** o. XI 13: 1 ma-na 14 gín D. kg kin$_5$-ak … 1 **L.** *ḫa-za-nu*; **18** o. XVI 21: 1 ma-na TAR kg kin$_5$-ak … 1 **L.**; **24** r. I 8: 3 gín D. kg 1 **L.** 1 *ša-mu* 1 *a-na-bù-bí-tum* 1 *ti-ba-ra-núm*.
*ma-ḫa-ni-gi* **6** r. XVI 14: TAR an-na šub 4 **L.**
*ma-ḫa-ni-gúm* **2** o. XI 20: 2 gín D. kg nu$_{11}$-za 1 **L.**; **4** r. IV 7: 5 2 NI g[ín D. kb] nu$_{11}$-za 1 **L.** *Ib-rí-um*; r. XII 13: 2 gín D. kb *ni-zi-mu* nu$_{11}$-za$^!$(KUR) 1 **L.** *Ib-rí-um*; 10 r. III 7: 2 gín D. kb nu$_{11}$-za 1 **L.** *Ib-rí-um*; **15** r. II 17: 10 gín D. an-na šub *si-in* 1 ma-na a-gar$_5$-gar$_5$ kin$_5$-ak 1 **L.** *wa* 1 tùn gal en.

*ma-lik-tum* «queen» **2** o. III 13: 1 bur-KAK ĜIŠ-taškarin … 2 saĝ 2 *bu*-DI … 2 *bu*-DI … 1 an-zam$_x$ … 1 zi-bar … 2 ĜIŠ-du … 1 ĜIŠ-šú 1 níĝ-bànda *Da-ti-*$^{d}$TU **L.** *Lum-na-an*$^{ki}$; **3** o. III 12: 10 ĝeštu$_x$-lá *D. ma-lik-tum Lum-na-an*$^{ki}$: r. XII 21: 2 íb-lá kg ì-ĝiš-saĝ 2 en *Ma-nu-wa-ad*$^{ki}$ *Ba-ga-ma* šu-mu-tak$_4$ *in* ud úš **L.**; **4** o. VII 10: 2 *bu*-DI 10 lá-2 ĝeštu$_x$-lá 30 *du-ru*$_{12}$-*gú* 1 *gu-za*$_x$-*gú* 1 šu-dub 1 *ma-ḫa-na-gúm Ma-za-a-du* **L.** *Ib-al*$_6$$^{ki}$; o. X 3: 3 íb<-lá> GÁ×LÁ ŠA.PI 7 íb-lá *si-ti-tum* ĝír-kun níĝ-ba guruš-guruš *Ì-ra-ar*$^{ki}$ *in* ud **L.** *Ì-ra-ar*$^{ki}$ DU.DU; 5 o. IX 11: <2> *bu*-DI **L.** *Ì-la-ar*$^{ki}$ *in* ʾ*À-da-ni*$^{ki}$ šu-ba$_4$-ti; **6** r. III 22: 4 *ba-rí-zú* im-ĝi$_6$ … 2 *bu*-DI *Da-ti-*$^{d}$TU **L.** *Lum-na-an*$^{ki}$; r. VI 14: 2 *bu*-DI **L.** *Ra-*ʾ*à-ak*$^{ki}$ É×PAP EN-*mar* šu-mu-tak$_4$; **9** r. IX 7: 2 *bu*-DI **L.** *Lum-na-an*$^{ki}$ *I-lu*$_5$-*za*$_x$-*ma-lik* šu-mu-tak$_4$; **10** o. VI 15 and 18: 4 *bu*-DI dumu-munus e[n] [*Ra-*ʾ*à-ak*$^{ki}$] **L.** ⌜*A*⌝-*bar-sal*$_4$$^{ki}$ *wa* **L.** *Ir-i-tum*$^{ki}$ EN-*mar* šu-mu-tak$_4$; r. I 11: 2 *bu*-DI **L.** *Ì-mar*$^{ki}$ *Du-si-*⌜*gú*⌝ [šu]-mu-tak$_4$; **11** o. XII 1: 1 an-zam$_x$ *Da-ti-*$^{d}$TU **L.** *Lum-na-an*$^{ki}$, 18: 2 *bu*-DI … 2 saĝ-*sù* … 1 kù-sal *Da-ti-*$^{d}$TU **L.** *Lum-na-an*$^{ki}$; **12** o. XV 4: 2 kù-sal dumu-munus *Da-ti-*$^{d}$TU **L.** *Lum-na-an*$^{ki}$; **13** o. I 16: [2 *b*]*u*-DI **L.** [*D*]*u-lu*$^{ki}$; o. IX 5: 4 ʾ*à-ra-ma-tum Zi-mi-ni*-kù:babbar **L.** *Bur-ma-an*$^{ki}$; o. XV 26: 2 *bu*-DI … 2 saĝ-*sù* níĝ-ba *Ti-šè-li-im* **L.** *Ì-mar*$^{ki}$; r. XI 14: 1 ĜIŠ-šú 1 níĝ-bànda … 2 *t*[*i-gi-na*] 2 ĜIŠ-du ... 1 zi-bar … 1 *bu*-DI tur 1 igi-igi … *Dag-*⌜*mul*⌝-*da-mu* **L.** *Lum-na-an*$^{ki}$ šu-mu-tak$_4$ (silver) géme-*sù*; **14** r. IX 21: 2 *bu*-DI … 2 saĝ-*sù* **L.** *Ì-ra-ar*$^{ki}$ *En-na-ì* [šu-mu-tak$_4$]; **15** o. XVI 21: 2 *bu*-DI … *Zi-mi-ni*-kù:babbar **L.** *Bur-ma-an*$^{ki}$ *in* ud dumu-munus tu-da *I-lu*$_5$-*za*$_x$-*ma-lik* [šu-mu-ta]g$_4$; r. V 8: 2 *bu*-DI … 2 saĝ-*sù* **L.** *Ì-ra-ar*$^{ki}$ ama-gal en šu-mu-tak$_4$ *in* ud DU.DU *Ga-wa-na*$^{ki}$; **17** o. VII 21: 2 *bu*-DI *Ti-ša-li-im* **L.** *Ì-mar*⌜$^{ki}$⌝ *i*[*n* ud] [ ] [*I-bí-zi-kir* dumu-]nita *Ib-rí-um*; o. XI 27: [2 *b*]*u*-DI **L.** *Lum-na-an*$^{ki}$ ama-gal en šu-mu-tak$_4$ *in* ud DU.DU *si-in U*$_9$-*gú-a-aš*$^{ki}$; r. I 8: 1 dib NI.GI **L.**; r. VI 1: 2 *bu*-DI *Ti-ša-li-im* **L.** *Ì-mar*$^{ki}$ *in* ud DU.DU *mi-nu* ʾ*À-da-ni*$^{ki}$, 30: 1 an-dùl *sa-du* en *wa* **L.** *si-in* NE-*na-áš*$^{ki}$; r. IX 20: šu-dub en *wa* **L.**, 28: 1 bar:ús lú dur 2 si-dù en *wa* **L.**, 32: 2 *bu*-DI *Ti-ša-li-im* **L.** *Ì-mar*$^{ki}$ *in* ud DU.DU *mi-nu* NI-*ab*$^{ki}$ *si-in* SA.ZA$_x$$^{ki}$; r. XI 22: 2 šu-dub en *wa* **L.**, 26: 1 sig$_7$-igi **L.**, 34: 2 šu-dub en *wa* **L.** sikil; r. XII 6: 1 šu-dub **L.** ʾ*à-lum*, 23: [x í]b-lá [x *si-t*]*i-*[*tu*]*m* [x gí]r-[ku]n … 1 ĝír mar-tu kg níĝ-ba *Ib-rí-um in* ud níĝ-mu-sá **L.**; r. XVI 9: 1 ĝír mar-tu níĝ-ba $^{d}$*A-da-ma gú-núm* **L.** ì-na-sum *in* ud šu-mu-níĝin é diĝir-diĝir-diĝir; **18** o. III 10: 1 an-zam$_x$ ĜIŠ-ĝidru **L.**; o. X 14: 2 *ti-gi*-na … 2 ĜIŠ-du *Da-bur-da-mu* **L.**; r. III 19: 2 *bu*-DI **L.** *Lum-na-an*$^{ki}$ É×PAP *Ìr-ba*$_x$-*zé* šu-mu-tak$_4$; r. IV 26: 2 *bu*-DI ì-ĝiš-saĝ *Di-rín-da-mu* dam-diĝir *áš-du* úš **L.** *Lum-na-an*$^{ki}$; **19** o. II 23: 2 *bu*-DI … 2 saĝ-*sù* níĝ-ba *Ti-šè-li-im* **L.** *Ì-mar*$^{ki}$; r. VI 13: 1 dub **L.** [ ] ⌜é⌝ $^{d}$⌜ʾ*À*⌝[-*da*]; 20 r. VI 7: 2 *ti-gi-na* **L.**; r. VIII 13: 2 *bu*-DI *Ti-šè-li-im* **L.** *Ì-mar*$^{ki}$ *in* ud DU.DU *mi-nu* ʾ*À-da-ni*$^{ki}$.

*ma-lu-gi-iš* «enthroning» **17** r. VII 12: 1 *gú-li-lum* ùz-munus a:tu$_{22}$ é *ma-tim* NE-*na-áš*$^{ki}$ **L.** en.
("king's enthroning", see Fronzaroli 1992, p. 184)

ma-na «mina» *passim*.

mar-tu see ĝír mar-tu s.v. ĝír.

*mar-wa-ga-tum* «drinking cane (?)» **4** o. X 12: 5 gín D. kb 1 **L.**; **10** o. X 12: 5 gín D. kb 1 **L.**(-*ga*$_x$-) šu-šu en; **11** o. VI 6: 2 gín D. kg *ni-zi-mu* 1 **L.** lú 2 šu en.

(cf. Akk. *râqum*, "to become empty". This term occurs in general in the following context: 1 níĝ-bànda 1 GIŠ-šú 1 *m.* lú 2 šu en. See also *ARET* XXII 4 o. XXVIII 15–16; 8 o. XXVIII 1–3)

*ma-sa-da-ù* «*pallium*» **18** o. V 7: 2 gín D. kb **L.**

*maš-da-ù* **4** o. VI 17: 2 gín D. kb **L.** 1 dumu-nita 1 dumu-munus; **21** r. VI 13: 2 gín D. kb **L.** dumu-nita PN.

(variants of *maš-da-bù*, the garment for the consecration of a newborn, see Archi 2021b, pp. 19, 25)

maš «striped decoration»

maš-maš **2** o. VI 9: 2 gín D. kg **L.** 1 GIŠ-banšur *wa* 1 kù-sal; o. XII 17: 2 gín D. kg *ni-zi-mu* **L.** íb-lá; r. IV 18: 1 ½ kb **L.** 1 "KIN" siki, 23: ½ kg **L.**-*sù*; r. VIII 16: 1 gín D. kg **L.** 1 "KIN" siki *wa* 1 kù-sal, 20: 1 gín D. kb **L.**-*sù*; **3** o. XI 4: 2 gín D. kb **L.** 1 GIŠ-banšur; **6** r. II 19: **L.** 1 GIŠ-banšur; r. VIII 1: 1 íb-lá *si-ti-tum* ĝír-kun kb **L.** kg, 4: 1 íb-lá *si-ti-tum* ĝír-kun **L.** kg; r. XIV 17: 1 íb-lá kb **L.** kg, 20: 1 íb-lá **L.** kg; **7** o. XIII 8: 2 gín D. kg *ni-zi-mu* **L.** 4 kù-sal; o. XIV 2: [x] g[ín D. kb] *ni-zi-mu* **L.** GIŠ-bar-ús, 6: 3 gín D. kg **L.**-*sù* lú 2 GIŠ-gígir-II; **10** o. XIII 10: 5 gín D. kb **L.** 1 [GIŠ]-⌜banšur⌝ *wa* nu$_{11}$-za 1 ĝír mar-tu; r. X 12: 2 gín D. kg **L.** 1 GIŠ-banšur *wa* [x] kù-sal; **11** r. VII 11: 1 íb-lá 1 ĝír-kun … 8 gín D. kg **L.**[-*sù*]; **13** o. XI 16: **L.** kg, 24: 1 ĝír-kun … 1 gín D. kg **L.**-*sù*; o. XIII 10: 1 ½ gín D. kg *ni-zi-mu* **L.** 4 kù-sal; **14** o. VII 19: 1 íb-lá 1 ĝír-kun … 7 gín D. kg **L.**-*sù*; o. XII 18: [½ gín D. kg] *ni-zi-mu* **L.** 4 kù-sal; r. III 8: [ ] **L.**-*sù*; r. VIII 21: 1 íb-lá 1 ĝír-kun … [7 gín D. kg **L.**-*sù*]; r. XIII 24: 10 lá-2 íb-lá 5 g[ír-kun] kb **L.**; **15** o. III 14: 1 íb-lá 1 ĝír-kun … 7 gín D. kg **L.**-*sù*; o. XVI 1: 1 íb-lá … ½ kg *ni-zi-mu* **L.**-*sù*; **16** o. VIII 15: 12 gín D. kb *ni-zi-mu* 17 íb-lá **L.** kg, 20: 2 gín D. kg *ni-zi-mu* **L.**-*sù*; r. III 11: 1 gín D. kg *ni-zi-mu* **L.** kù-sal; r. XII 12: 2 níĝ-anše-ak 4 kù-sal … 2 gín D. kg *ni-zi-mu* **L.**-*sù*; **17** r. III 21: 3 gín D. kg *ni-zi-mu* **L.** kù-sal; **18** o. XI 10: 1 íb-lá 1 ĝír-kun kb … 1 gín D. kg *ni-zi-mu* **L.**-*sù*; **20** o. XVII 10: 1 íb-lá 1 ĝír-kun 7 gín D. kg **L.**-*sù*; r. V 13: 10 gín D. kg *ni-zi-mu* **L.** 4 kù-sal; r. X 17: 1 íb-lá 1 ĝír-kun … 7 gín D. kg **L.**-*s*[*ù*]; r. XII 18: 1 íb-lá [1] ĝír-kun … 7 gín D. kg **L.**-*sù*; **23** o. VIII 12 and IX 1: 5 gín D. kg *ni-zi-mu* **L.** 4 íb-lá 1 ĝír-kun **L.**

(see Waetzoldt, *MEE* 12, pp. 346–347)

*maš-ar-da* see *maš-ar-tum*

*maš-ar-tum* «stele» **8** r. IX 3': [ ] ⌜x-*na*⌝-*ra-tum Da-ḫi-ir-ma-lik* **L.**; **11** o. IV 7: 3 gín D. kg nu$_{11}$-za **L.**; **20** o. XV 21: 1 íb-lá 1 *si-ti-tum* 1 ĝír-kun … 2 *ti-gi-na* … 4 *ʾà-ra-ma-tum* … 8 GIŠ-ĝeštu$_x$-lá … 1 šu-dub … 2 GIŠ-du *Ti-bù-da-mu* **L.** en; o. XVI 1 GIŠ-asari **L.** en; r. XIII 16: [2+]3 gín D. kg nu$_{11}$-za **L.**

*maš-ar-da* **17** r. XX 33: 4 ½ kg *ʾa*$_5$-*na-gu* 2 banšur **L.** *Ib-rí-um* <*I*->*bí-zi-kir*.

*maš-da-ù* see *ma-sa-da-ù*.

maškim «delegate, representative» **1**(e) r. III' 4: (silver) **L.** *Ḫal-ba*$_x$(PÉŠ) *Na-a*[*m*$_6$]$^{ki}$; **3** o. IX 16: 1 ĝír mar-tu ti kg NI-*gi* saĝ-du$_8$ lú-kar *A-da-bí-ig*$^{ki}$ … 1 ĝír mar-tu *ba-du-u*$_4$ kbg *Ù-ra*-AN **L.**-*sù*; **4** o. VI 11: (silver) *Ga-ga-ba-an*$^{ki}$ (silver) **L.**-*sù*; o. XIV 13: (silver) níĝ-kaskal **L.** *Ḫa-ra-il*; o. XV 12: (silver) níĝ-kaskal *Za-ba-ra* **L.** *Ḫa-ra-il*; r. VII 10: [ ]-⌜*ig*⌝ **L.** *A-ag*; r. XI 9: *Ìr-am*$_6$-*ma-lik* **L.** *Du-si*; **5** o. VII 5: (silver) níĝ-sa$_{10}$ 2 *gú-li-lum* a-gar$_5$-gar$_5$ kg *Bu-ra* **L.** *A-šum*, 17: 1 gud *Ib-gi-da-mu* ugula kad$_4$-kad$_4$ ... 1 gud **L.**-*sù*; r. IV 20: (silver) níĝ-ba *Wa-ru*$_{12}$-*tum wa* **L.** *Ma-rí*$^{ki}$; **6** o. III 4: (silver) níĝ-ba ĝuruš-ĝuruš **L.**-*sù Ma-rí*$^{ki}$; o. X 16: (silver) níĝ-ba *Wa-ba-rúm Ma-rí*$^{ki}$ (silver) níĝ-ba *ʾÀ-sa* **L.**-*sù*; o. XII 18: (silver) níĝ-ba *Ib-ḫur-úr* (silver) níĝ-ba *Sa*-NI-*gú* **L.**-*sù*; o. XV 7: (silver) níĝ-kaskal *A-ir-ra wa A-zú-bù-lu* DU.DU *Ar-mi*$^{ki}$ **L.** *Ḫa-ra-il*; **7** o. VI 10: 1 ĝír mar-tu ti kg *Ti-ra-ì* **L.** EN-*mar*; r. XIII 22: (silver) níĝ-ba *Iš-dub-ì* **L.** ga:eš$_8$ *Du-du-lu*$^{ki}$; **8** o. III 2: (silver) *Du-bí wa* **L.**-*sù Ma-rí*$^{ki}$; o. X 5: (silver) *Ib-bu-tum* (silver) **L.**-*sù Ma-rí*$^{ki}$; **9** o. II 16: [(silver) níĝ-kaskal *A-ir-ra*$^?$ *wa A-zú-bù-lu*$^?$] DU.DU *Ar-mi*$^{ki}$ **L.** *Ḫa-ra-ì*; o. XVII 2': ⌜x⌝[ ]⌜x⌝[ ] **L.** *Ib-rí-um*; **10** o. XIV 19: (silver) níĝ-kaskal *En-na*-BAD *Zú-ti*$^{ki}$ **L.** *Du-bí* DU.DU *Ar-mi*$^{ki}$; o. XV 20: (silver) níĝ-kaskal *Íl-ra*-BAD **L.** NI-*ba-rúm* DU.DU *si in Ar-mi*$^{ki}$; r. IX 5: (silver) níĝ-ba *Na*-NE *wa* **L.**-*sù Na-gàr*$^{ki}$; **11** o. II 8: *Da-zi-ma-ad* **L.** *Ìr-am*$_6$-*da-mu* [l]ú [*Í*]*l-zi*; r. III 14: (silver) níĝ-ba en *Ša-bir*$_5$-*ti-du*$^{ki}$ (silver) *Na-mi-ir* **L.**-*sù*; **12** o. VII 2: (silver) níĝ-ba *Wa-ba-rúm* … (silver) níĝ-ba 2 **L.**-*sù*; **14** o. II 21: (silver) níĝ-ba *Šu-a-ḫa* **L.** ga:eš$_8$ *Du-du-lu*$^{ki}$; o. III 17: (silver) n[íĝ-ba] *Iš*-⌜*dub*⌝-*ì wa Ib-gi-tum* **L.** ga:eš$_8$ *Du-du-lu*$^{ki}$; o. VIII 7: *Áš-da-ma-ì* **L.** ga:eš$_8$ *Du-du-lu*$^{ki}$; o. XX 3: *Iš-dub-il* **L.** ga:eš$_8$ *Du-du-lu*$^{ki}$; r. IV 14: (silver) níĝ-ba *Iš-dub-il* **L.** ga:eš$_8$ *Du-du-lu*$^{ki}$; r. X 16: (silver) níĝ-ba *Ù-li-li* **L.** [ga:eš$_8$] [*Du-du-lu*]$^{ki}$; **15** o. II 13: (silver) níĝ-du$_8$ 1 dumu-nita *A-ba-ti-lum*$^{ki}$ **L.** *Za-ba-rúm*; o. IV 14: 1 dib *Bar-za-ma-ù* ugula *ʾÀ-šu*$^{ki}$ … 1 ĝír mar-tu *ba-du-u*$_4$ kb *La-gi* **L.**-*sù*; o. VIII 2: (silver) níĝ-ba *Iš-dub-il wa Dab*$_6$-*ti Ma-rí*$^{ki}$ **L.** ga:eš$_8$ *Du-du-lu*$^{ki}$; **16** r. IV 7: *Ḫa-bù-zú ʾÀ-bar-du*$^{ki}$ **L.** *Za-ba-rúm* tuš-LÚ×TIL *Ḫal-sum*$^{ki}$; r. VIII 21: (40 daggers) lú ĝuruš-ĝuruš ḫaš-ḫaš *in* **L.** *Ḫal-sum*$^{ki}$; r. X 14: (silver) níĝ-ba *Ar-rúm Ma-rí*$^{ki}$ (silver) níĝ-ba **L.**-*sù*; **17** o. VII 3: [silver] níĝ-ba *Ù-rí-rí* **L.** ga:eš$_8$ *in* kaskal é $^{d}$BAD *Ga-na-na*; o. XII 14: *Ḫa-zu-um* **L.** *Ib-rí-um* tuš-LÚ×TIL *Ti-ma-tim*$^{ki}$ lú *Kak-mi-um*$^{ki}$, 23: *Du-bí-šum* lú *Gú-ma-ni-du* **L.** *Ib-rí-um* tuš-LÚ×TIL *Kak-mi-um*$^{ki}$ *áš-ti Šu-ra-an*$^{ki}$; r. VII 23: *I-ti-ne A-da-bí-gú*$^{ki}$ **L.** *Ba-ga-ma*, 31: *Ti-ti-nu* **L.** *Ib-rí-um*; r. XI 10: (silver) níĝ-[b]a ⌜*Ne-zi*⌝ *wa Ìr*-[*b*]*a-il Ma-rí*$^{ki}$ **L.** ga:eš$_8$ Saḫar$^{ki}$ [šu-m]u-[ta]g$_4$; **18** o. XIV 21: (silver) níĝ-kaskal *ma-ra-* **L.** *Ḫa-ra-ì* lú GIŠ-nu-kiri$_6$; o. XV 14: (silver) *Šu*-NE-ḪAR **L.** *A-mur-da-mu* lú GIŠ-nu-kiri$_6$; **19** r. IX 24: (silver) dumu-nita en *ʾÀ-du*$^{ki}$ (silver) **L.**-*sù*, 28: (silver) *A-bù-li-um*$^{ki}$ (silver) **L.**-*sù*; r. X 8: (silver) *Na-ba-ti-um*$^{ki}$ (silver) **L.**-*sù in* kaskal šu-ba$_4$-ti; r. XIII 3: (silver) níĝ-ba 3 guruš *ʾÀ-du*$^{ki}$ ḫi-mu-DU **L.** *Za-ba-rúm* nar; r. XVIII 28: (silver) *Gul-la wa* **L.**-*sù Na-gàr*$^{ki}$; **20** o. II 4: [ ] [**L.**] ga:eš$_8$ *Du-du-lu*$^{ki}$; **22** r. I 3: 1 dib *Nu-ba-an*$^{ki}$ **L.** *Sa-li-im* tuš-LÚ×TIL *in Ar-mi*$^{ki}$; **25** r. IV 5: [ ]-⌜*lum*⌝ *ba-da-lum U-ti-gú*$^{ki}$ 2 **L.** *A-ag*.

maškim:e-gi$_4$ «travelling representative» **7** r. XII 13: *I-na-ni-gi Kab-lu$_5$-ul*$^{[ki]}$ [ ] [ ] *wa* **L.**(<e>) DU.DU.

*ma-tim* see é *ma-tim* s.v. é.

*ma-wa-lu* (an element of the goad) **16** r. III 16: 2 gín D. kb *ni-zi-mu* **L.**, 21: 2 gín D. kg *ni-zi-mu* **L.** ĜIŠ-bar-ús ĜIŠ-gígir-II en; **17** r. II 4: 2 NI gín D. kg *ni-zi-mu* **L.** ĜIŠ-bar-ús; **18** r. I 19: 1 gín D. kg *wa* 1 gín D. kb *ni-zi-mu* **L.** ĜIŠ-bar-ús ĜIŠ-gígir-II en

*ma-wa-ù* **14** o. IX 4: 2 NI gín D. kg *ni-zi-mu* **L.** 2 ĜIŠ-bar-ús ĜIŠ-gígir-II e[n].

*ma-za-ḫa-ru*$_{12}$ «pliers» **12** r. XII 1 and 16: 1 ma-na ŠÚ+ŠA 3 gín D. an-na šub *si-in* 9 ma-na TAR gín D. a-gar$_5$-gar$_5$ … 6 **L.** 10 … 5 **L.** TAR.

*ma-za-ḫa-rúm* **7** o. XIV 17; **20** r. I 17: 17 gín D. an-na šub *si-in* 1 ma-na ŠA.PI gín D. a-gar$_5$[-gar$_5$] kin$_5$-ak … 1 **L.** 10 gín D.

*ma-za-lum* «courier; messenger» **4** o. XIII 14: (silver) níĝ-kaskal *ʾÀ-daš* **L.** DU.DU *Ar-mi*$^{ki}$; r. VIII 13: (silver) [PN] *wa* **L.**[-*sù*] DU.DU *Ar-mi*$^{ki}$; **14** o. XX 9: (silver) **L.** [ ] [ ] ugula *Kul-ba-an*$^{ki}$ ga:eš$_8$.

*ma-za-um* **10** r. IV 19: 10 gín D. kb **L.** ĝír mar-tu; r. V 5: TAR 7 gín D. kg **L.** 3 ĝír mar-tu.

mè «battle» **4** o. IX 9: 1 na$_4$ maḫ *in* **L.** *Kab-lu$_5$-ul*$^{ki}$; **13** r. III 20: *Kùn*-NE *wa Ab-ba* muḫaldim *Ma-rí*$^{ki}$ ḫi-mu-DU **L.** *si-in Ma-nu-wa-ad*$^{ki}$.

megida «sow» **7** o. III 9: 1 **L.**$^?$ níĝ-sikil.

ME-sig «custodian, watchman» (defective writing for igi-sig; Fronzaroli 1997, p. 4; Catagnoti 2019) **1** o. V 9: 17 íb-lá 17 *si-ti-tum* 17 ĝír-kun **L.** é; 2 l.ed. 9: 2 íb-lá **L.**; **5** o. III 16: (10 bracelets) **L.** é; o. V 2: (13 bracelets) **L.** é en; r. XIII 9: 20 *gú-li-lum* **L.** é en; **6** o. V 5: 23 dib a-gar$_5$-gar$_5$ kg **L.** é en; **7** r. IX 12: (35 bracelets) **L.** é en; **10** o. VII 1: [ ] **L.** é en; **13** r. XV 1: (10 bracelets) [ ] **L.** é [en]; **15** o. XV 4: 20 ĝír mar-tu **L.**; **16** r. XIII 4: (29 bracelets) **L.** é en; **17** o. XV 20: (30 bracelets) **L.** é en; **18** o. VIII 13: (126 bracelets) **L.** é en; **19** r. XI 15: (9 bracelets) **L.** é en; **23** r. VII 4: (9 bracelets, 2 belts, 2 sheaths, 2 pendants) **L.** é en.

*mi-nu* (preposition) «from» **10** o. XVI 14: *A-da-bí-ig*$^{ki}$ ì-ti **L.** *Ar-mi*$^{ki}$; **12** o. VI 9: *in* ud gi$_4$ **L.** *Du-du-lu*$^{ki}$; **15** o. XVII 9: *Wa-ru*$_{12}$*-tum Ma-rí*$^{ki}$ e$_{11}$ *áš-ti Na-zu-mu* **L.** Kiš$^{ki}$; **17** r. VI 5: *in* ud DU.DU **L.** *ʾÀ-da-ni*$^{ki}$; r. IX 36: *in* ud DU.DU **L.** NI-*ab*$^{ki}$ *si-in* SA.ZA$_x$$^{ki}$; **19** r. XII 16: *Ga-áš-ru*$_{12}$ *Na-gàr*$^{ki}$ DU.DU **L.** Kiš$^{ki}$; **20** r. VIII 17: *in* ud DU.DU **L.** *ʾÀ-da-ni*$^{ki}$; r. IX 12: *Wa-ru*$_{12}$*-tum Ma-rí*$^{ki}$ e$_{11}$ **L.** Kiš$^{ki}$ *áš-ti En-na-il.*

mu «year» **4** r. XVI 20: *in* ud *Ib-rí-um* 2 **L.**; **5** r. XVII 3: è 2 **L.** 2 dub; **9** r. XVIII 6: è [DI]š **L.**; **15** r. XVIII 3: è 1 **L.**; **21** r. XVII 3: ⌜è⌝ DIŠ **L.** úš *Ib-rí-um.*

mu-DU «delivery (by someone to); has delivered» **13** o. XI 17: 1 íb-lá TAR kb maš-maš kg lú **L.** *Ib-rí-um*; **16** r. XIV 10: gur$_8$ má-gal-má-gal **L.** *na-se*$_{11}$*-na-se*$_{11}$ *in* ud [ ]; **17** o. XX 10: 3 ma-na kb lul-gu-ak kb lú **L.** *Ab-zu*$^{ki}$; **19** o. XIV 1: 2 ma-na kg lú **L.** *Kab-lu$_5$-ul*$^{ki}$ *zi-du-sù*; r. I 7: 10 lá-2 ma-na kg *zi-du-sù* lú **L.** *Kab-lu$_5$-ul*$^{ki}$; **20** r. III 9: 1 pad *ma-da-a-um* kg an-dùl lú en *ša-ti Ib-rí-um* **L.**; **22** r. VIII 9: AN.ŠÈ.GÚ 4 ma-na TAR 3 gín D. kg è lú **L.** *I*[*b-rí-*]*um.*

muḫaldim «cook» **13** r. III 17: *Kùn*-NE *wa Ab-ba* **L.** *Ma-rí*$^{ki}$ ḫi-mu-DU mè *si-in Ma-nu-wa-ad*$^{ki}$.

*mu-ḫar-šu* **21** o. XVII 18: 2 gín D. kb 2 **L.** en.

*mu-ḫar-tum* **17** r. XX 37: 2 kb **L.**

*mu-ḫar-tim* **14** o. I 13: [x] gín D. [k]g kin$_5$-ak 1 **L.**

mu$_4$$^{mu}$ «to dress» **12** r. III 2: 23 gada-TÚG **L.**

*mu-lu-iš* «until the height of; to reach» **18** o. IV 12: 1 ĝír mar-tu **L.** 1 *li-im* ĝír mar-tu *A-la-ga*$^{ki}$; r. X 14: 90 lá-2 ĝír mar-tu zú-ak lú **L.** ĝír mar-tu ĝuruš-ĝuruš.

munus «female; woman» **7** o. X 5: 1 an-dùl **L.**; **18** r. XIV 19: 1 an-dùl **L.**; **20** o. III 15: 1 an-dùl **L.**

*mu-rúm* (a container for ointments) **17** r. XVII 3: [ ] kin$_5$-ak 1 **L.** *wa* 1 *gúm-a-nu wa* 2 ĜIŠ.ALAM *su-da$_5$-lik* en.

*mu-sa-du* **14** o. XII 22: 3 gín D. kb **L.** ⌜LUM⌝$^?$-[ ] ĜIŠ-taškarin.

mu-ti «at disposition, received» **6** o. II 15: 2 **L.**; **13** o. VIII 10: **L.**-II; **14** o. VI 13: *in* **L.**-II; **15** o. XIV 4; **17** o. XIII 16; **18** o. XVII 12: **L.**-II; **19** r. IV 27: **L.**-II; **20** o. IV 9: **L.**-II.

## N

na «palette» **4** o. XII 15: 1 ½ gín D. kb 1 **L.** na$_4$ (see Civil 2008, p. 77)

na$_4$ «stone; stone weight» **3** r. VIII 16; **4** o. IX 7: 1 **L.** maḫ; o. XII 15; r. II 15, 18; r. III 2, 5; **11** r. V 8: 1 **L.** maḫ; **14** r. XV 3: 10 **L.** maḫ; **16** r. X 1: 2 **L.** 3; **18** o. XIII 14: 10 **L.**, 19, 22; o. XIV 1, 4, 7.

(a measure of the wool: ½ di 1 "KIN") see siki.

naĝar «carpenter» **6** r. XVI 28: TAR an-na *ni-zi-mu* ZA$_x$ **L.**; **7** o. VII 12: ŠA.PI gín D. an-na *ni-zi-mu* ZA$_x$ **L.**

naĝar-naĝar **11** o. VI 1: 1 ma-na an-na šub *si-in ni-zi-mu* ZA$_x$ **L.**; **12** o. X 9: ŠA.PI 4 gín D. an-na šub *si-in* 6 ma-na 10 gín D. a-gar$_5$-gar$_5$ *ni-zi-mu* ZA$_x$ **L.**; **15** o. XIV 26: 1 ma-na gín D. an-na šub *si-in ni-zi-mu* ZA$_x$ **L.**; **16** o. XII 5: 1 ma-na 50 gín D. <an-na> šub *si-in* 3[+x ma-n]a [T]AR gín D. ⌜a⌝-gar$_5$-gar$_5$ *ni-zi-mu* ZA$_x$-ZA$_x$ **L.**; **18** r. II 10: 2 ma-na an-na šub *si-in* 12 ma-na a-gar$_5$-gar$_5$ *ni-zi-mu* ZA$_x$-ZA$_x$ **L.**

*na-kar-ra-tim* **3** r. V 12: nu$_{11}$-za 1 bur-KAK **L.**

nam-kud «oath» **4** o. XIII 18: (silver) **L.** *Ì-ra-ar*$^{ki}$ é $^d$*Ku-ra*; **6** o. III 17: 1 dub lú **L.** *Ib-la*$^{ki}$ *wa Ma-rí*$^{ki}$ é $^d$*Ku-ra*; **7** r. XI 21: *Gul-la* ⌜x-x-x⌝ *Sa-ma-na-nu* [*S*]*i-mi*[- ] [ ] *Iš-ba-ì A-ša*$^{ki}$ in ud DU.DU **L.** é $^d$*Ku-ra*; **9** r. V 7: (silver) **L.** en *Bur-ma-an*$^{ki}$ é $^d$*Ku-ra*; **10** o. VII 8: 1 dub **L.** *Ib-rí-um* [ ]; **12** o. IV 14: (silver) **L.** en *Ì-ra-ar*$^{ki}$ é ⌜$^d$⌝*Ku-ra*; r. I 7: *I-bí-du-lum en Ma-nu-wa-ad*$^{ki}$ *in* ud DU.DU **L.** é $^d$*Ku-ra*; r. IX 22: (silver) **L.** *Ar-ru*$_{12}$*-šum Na-gàr*$^{ki}$; **13** o. II 20: *Mu*-NE-*a-du* ugula *Ar-ḫa-du*$^{ki}$ *in* ud DU.DU **L.** é $^d$*Ku-ra*; o. IV 1: (silver) **L.** *Na-ḫal*$^{ki}$ *Ki-li-im* šu-mu-tak$_4$; **19** o. VI 5: en-en lú *áš-ti* en *Na-gàr*$^{ki}$ DU.DU **L.** é $^d$BAD *Du-du-lu*$^{ki}$; r. VI 5: 1 dub lú **L.** en *wa Ib-rí-um* é $^{dʾ}$*À-da.*

nam-kud-nam-kud **21** r. XIV 18: (silver) **L.** en *Ì-ra-ar*$^{ki}$ é $^d$*Ku-ra.*

*nap-ḫu* «rock crystal; vitreus paste» **15** r. I 4.
nar «singer» **16** r. XII 20: 1 balaĝ **L.**; **19** r. XIII 5: *Za-ba-rúm* **L.**
na-rú «stele» **3** r. IV 10: *Ib-rí-um in* ud ḫúl **L.**-*sù*; **6** r. VII 13: *Ba-lu-zú* "ur$_4$" *Ì-mar*$^{ki}$ *in* ud ḫúl **L.**-*sù*; **8** o. II 7: *Ib-rí-um* … *in* ud ḫúl **L.** [ ].
*na-se*$_{11}$ «people» **4** o. II 5: 2 **L.** *Ma-rí*$^{ki}$; **16** r. II 14: (silver) níĝ-du$_8$ 3 **L.** *Ib-la*$^{ki}$ *áš-ti Ir-i-tum*$^{ki}$.
*na-se*$_{11}$-*na-se*$_{11}$ **16** r. XIV 11: gur$_8$ má-gal-má-gal mu-DU **L.** *in* ud [ ].
NE-di «dancer» **4** r. IX 14: *Mu-gàr* **L.**; **12** o. XIII 12: *Mu-gàr* **L.**; **14** o. XV 17: *Ig-bù-ul-ma-lik* **L.**; **16** r. III 28: *Bu*$_x$-*ma-ì* **L.**
see *s.v.* dumu-nita-dumu-nita NE-di
NE-*na-tum* **5** o. V 11: 1 ma-na 20 gín D. kb lul-gu-ak 2 níĝ-anše 4 **L.**
ne-saĝ «first-fruit (offering)» **2** o. II 9: 1 kù-sal níĝ-ba en $^{d}$*Ba-ra-ma in* ud **L.**-*sù*; o. VI 17: 1 ĜIŠ-banšur *wa* 1 kù-sal níĝ-ba *Ib-rí-um* $^{d}$*Ku-ra in* ud **L.**-*sù*; **5** r. IV 7: 1 ĝír mar-tu ... 1 kù-sal níĝ-ba $^{d}$ʾ*A*$_5$-*da*-"*bal*" *Lu-ba-an*$^{ki}$ *Ib-rí-um* ì-na-sum *in* ud **L.**-*sù*, 23: 1 ĝír mar-tu ... 1 kù-sal níĝ-ba $^{d}$*Ra-sa-ap gú-núm*$^{ki}$ en in-na-sum **L.**-*sù*; **10** o. V 15: 1 ĜIŠ-banšur níĝ-ba $^{d}$*Ku-ra Ib-rí-um* in-na-sum *in* ud **L.**-*sù*; r. X 8: 1 ĝír mar-tu 1 kù-sal níĝ-ba $^{d}$*Ku-ra Ib-rí-um* ì-na-sum *in* **L.**-*sù*; **11** o. V 5: 1 kù-sal … [1 g]ír mar-⸢tu⸣ níĝ-ba [$^{d}$*Ku-ra*] [*Ib-rí-um*$^{?}$] [ì-na-sum] [*i*]*n* ⸢ud⸣ **L.**, 17: 1 kù-sal … 1 ĝír mar-⸢tu⸣ níĝ-ba *Ib-rí-um* $^{d}$*Ra-s*[*a-ap*] *g*[*ú-n*]*úm in* ud **L.**; **12** r. IX 20: 2 an-dùl … *ba-na-a-sa wa* 2 šu-*sù wa* 2 DU-*sù* níĝ-ba *Du-si-gú* $^{d}$*Ku-ra in* ud **L.**; **17** o. V 6: 1 kù-sal 1 buru$_4$-MUŠEN [níĝ-ba] […] dumu-munus en $^{d}$*Ku-ra* ì-na-sum *in* **L.**-*sù*; **24** o. VII 6: 1 kù-sal níĝ-ba *Ib-rí-um* $^{d}$*Ba-ra-ma in* ud **L.**-*sù*.
NI (fraction of a shekel) *passim*.
nídba «(sacrificial) offering» **2** r. II 6: 1 *gú-li-lum* 1 kù-sal níĝ-ba *Ib-rí-um* $^{d}$*Ku-ra in* ud lú **L.**; r. VII 6: 2 gud 1 ma-na kb nu$_{11}$-⸢za⸣ 4 si-*sù* **L.** en $^{d}$*Ra-sa-ap* ʾ*À-da-ni*$^{ki}$ $^{d}$AMA-*ra*; **5** o. VI 20: 1 ĝír mar-tu kg *Ib-rí-um in* ud **L.** $^{d}$<*Iš-*>*šára* ĜIŠ-kiri$_6$; o. VII 18: 1 gud *Ib-gi-da-mu* ugula kad$_4$-kad$_4$ … 1 gud maškim-*sù* **L.** en $^{d}$ʾ*À-da*; o. VIII 6: 2 gud **L.** en $^{d}$ʾ*À-da* ʾ*À-da-ni*$^{ki}$ 1 ma-na kb nu$_{11}$-za **4** si-*sù in* AMA-*ra*; r. X 18: ŠÚ+ŠA 5 gín D. kb ʾ*a*$_5$-*na-gu* si 2 gud lú en **L.** $^{d}$ʾ*À-da*; r. XI 4: ŠÚ+ŠA 5 gín D. kb ʾ*a*$_5$-*na-gu* si 2 gud lú *Ib-rí-um* **L.** $^{d}$ʾ*À-da in* iti ʾ*a*$_5$-*nun*; **7** o. XI: ŠÚ+ŠA gín D. kb ʾ*a*$_5$-*na-gu* 4 si 2 gud **L.** en [$^{d}$*Ra-sa-ap* ʾ*À-da-ni*$^{ki}$ *in*] $^{d}$AMA-*ra*; o. XII 11: ŠÚ+ŠA gín D. kb ʾ*a*$_5$-*na-gu* 4 si 2 gud **L.** en $^{d}$ʾ*À-da in* $^{d}$AMA-*ra*; **8** o. IX 10: *in* ud **L.** [ ]; r. V 12' and 16': 8 si 4 gud **L.** en *wa Ib-rí-um* **L.** $^{d}$*Ra-sa-ap* [ʾ*À-da-ni*$^{ki}$]; **9** o. IV 1: [ ] 2 gud **L.** en $^{d}$*Ra-sa-ap* ʾ*À-da-ni*$^{ki}$; **10** o. XI 13: 4 si-si 2 gud lú en **L.** $^{d}$ʾ*À-da in* AMA-*ra*; **11** o. X 14: 13 gín D. kb nu$_{11}$-za 1 ešda … 6 gín D. kg nu$_{11}$-za 1 *ar-ra-sù* ŠÚ+ŠA gín D. kb ʾ*a*$_5$-*na-gu* 4 si 2 gud **L.** en $^{d}$*Ra-sa-ap* ʾ*À-da-ni*$^{ki}$; o. XI 4: 13 gín D. kb nu$_{11}$-za 1 ešda … 6 gín D. kg nu$_{11}$-za [1 *ar-r*]*a*-[*sù*] ŠÚ+ŠA gín D. kb ʾ*a*$_5$-*na-gu* 4 si 2 gud **L.** en $^{d}$ʾ*À-da in* $^{d}$AMA-*ra*; r. VIII 14: 15 gín D. kb nu$_{11}$-za 1 ešda ŠÚ–ŠA gín D. kb ʾ*a*$_5$-*n*[*a-gu*] 1[+3 si 2 gud] **L.** en $^{d}$ʾ*À-da* lú *Ḫa-lab*$_x^{ki}$ *in* iti ʾ*a*$_5$-*nun*; **12** r. II 3: ŠÚ+ŠA gín D. kb ʾ*a*$_5$-*na-gu* 4 si-si 2 gud **L.** en $^{d}$ʾ*À-da in* iti ʾ*a*$_5$-*nun*; **13** o. XI 11: 15 gín D. kb nu$_{11}$-za 1 *ḫa-bù* … 6 gín D. kg nu$_{11}$-za 1 *ar-ra-sù* ŠÚ+ŠA gín D. kb ʾ*a*$_5$-*na-gu* 4 si 2 gud **L.** en $^{d}$*Ra-sa-ap* ʾ*À-da-ni*$^{ki}$; **14** o. X 5: ŠÚ+ŠA gín D. kb ʾ*a*$_5$-*na-gu* 4 si 2 gud 15 gín D. kb nu$_{11}$-za 1 *ḫa-bù* … 6 gín D. kg nu$_{11}$-za 1 ⸢*ar*⸣-*ra*[-*sù*] [**L.**] en $^{d}$*Ra-sa-ap* [ʾ*À-da-ni*$^{ki}$] *in* $^{d}$AMA-*ra*; **15** o. X 9: 15 gín D. kb nu$_{11}$-za 1 *ḫa-bù* … 6 gín D. kg 1 *ar-ra-si-su* ŠÚ+ŠA gín D. kb ʾ*a*$_5$-*na-gu* 4 si 2 gud **L.** en $^{d}$*Ra-sa-ap* ʾ*À-da-ni*$^{ki}$ *in* $^{d}$AMA-*ra*; r. IX 19: 12 gín D. kb nu$_{11}$-za 1 *ḫa-bù ap* nu$_{11}$-za 1 *ar-ra-sù* kg sikil ŠÚ+ŠA gín D. kb ʾ*a*$_5$-*na-gu* 4 si 2 gud **L.** en $^{d}$ʾ*À-da in* iti ʾ*a*$_5$-*nun*; **16** r. I 7: 13 gín D. kb nu$_{11}$-za 1 *ḫa-bù* … 6 gín D. kg nu$_{11}$-za 1 *ar-ra-sù* ŠÚ+ŠA gín D. kb ʾ*a*$_5$-*na-gu* si 2 gud **L.** en $^{d}$*Ra-sa-ap* ʾ*À-da-ni*$^{ki}$, 18: 13 gín D. kb nu$_{11}$-za 1 *ḫa-bù ap* kg ⸢sikil⸣ ŠÚ+ŠA gín D. kb ʾ*a*$_5$-*na-gu* si 2 gud **L.** en $^{d}$ʾ*À-da in* $^{d}$AMA-*ra*; r. XI 7: 12 gín D. kb nu$_{11}$-za 1 *ḫa-bù ap* kg sikil ŠÚ+ŠA gín D. kb ʾ*a*$_5$-*na-gu* si 2 gud **L.** en $^{d}$ʾ*À-da Ḫa-lab*$_x^{ki}$ *in* iti ʾ*a*$_5$-*nun*; **17** o. VI 17: *in* ud DU.DU **L.** é diĝir en; r. IV 24: 15 gín D. kb nu$_{11}$-za 1 *ḫa-bù* … 6 gín D. kg nu$_{11}$-za 1 *ar-ra-si-sù* ŠÚ+ŠA gín D. kb ʾ*a*$_5$-*na-gu* 4 si 2 gud **L.** en $^{d}$*Ra-sa-ap* ʾ*À-da-ni*$^{ki}$ *in* $^{d}$AMA-*ra*; **18** o. XVIII 22: 15 gín D. kb nu$_{11}$-za 1 *ḫa-bù* … 6 gín D. kg nu$_{11}$-za 1 *ar-ra-sù* ŠÚ+ŠA gín D. kb ʾ*a*$_5$-*na-gu* si 2 gud **L.** en $^{d}$*Ra-sa-ap* ʾ*À-da-ni*$^{ki}$; o. XIX 20: 15 gín D. kb nu$_{11}$-za 1 *ḫa-bù ap* kg sikil nu$_{11}$-za 1 *ar-ra-sù* ŠÚ+ŠA gín D. kb ʾ*a*$_5$-*na-gu* si 2 gud **L.** en $^{d}$ʾ*À-da Ḫa-lab*$_x^{ki}$ *in* $^{d}$AMA-*ra*; r. XVII 39: 15 kb nu$_{11}$-za 1 *ḫa-bù ap* kg sikil ŠÚ+ŠA kb ʾ*a*$_5$-*na-gu* si 2 gud **L.** en $^{[d]}$ʾ*À-da Ḫa-lab*$_x^{ki}$ ʾ*a*$_5$-*nun*; **19** o. XI 1: 13 gín D. kb nu$_{11}$-za 1 *ḫa-bù* … 6 gín D. kg nu$_{11}$-za 1 *ar-ra-sù* ŠÚ+ŠA gín D. kb ʾ*a*$_5$-*na-gu* si 2 gud **L.** en $^{d}$*Ra-sa-ap* ʾ*À-da-ni*$^{ki}$, 14: 15 gín D. kb nu$_{11}$-za 1 *ḫa-bù ap* nu$_{11}$-za *ar-ra-sù* kg sikil ŠÚ+ŠA gín D. kb ʾ*a*$_5$-*na-gu* si 2 gud **L.** en $^{d}$ʾ*À-da Ḫa-lab*$_x^{ki}$ *in* $^{d}$AMA-*ra*; r. XVII 13: 13 gín D. kb nu$_{11}$-za 1 *ḫa-bù ap* kg sikil ŠÚ+ŠA kb ʾ*a*$_5$-*na-gu* si 2 gud **L.** en $^{d}$ʾ*À-da Ḫa-lab*$_x^{ki}$ ʾ*a*$_5$-*nun*; **20** o. VIII 11: 15 gín D. kb nu$_{11}$-za 1 *ḫa-bù* … 6 gín D. kg nu$_{11}$-za 1 *ar-ra-sù* ŠÚ+ŠA gín D. kb [ʾ*a*$_5$-*na-gu* 4 si gud **L.** en] $^{d}$*Ra-sa-ap* ʾ*À-da-ni*$^{ki}$; o. IX 1: 15 gín D. kb nu$_{11}$-za 1 [*ḫa-bù*] *ap* kg sikil nu$_{11}$[-za] 1 *ar-ra-sù* ŠÚ+ŠA gín D. kb ʾ*a*$_5$-[*n*]*a-gu* 4 si gud **L.** en $^{d}$ʾ*À-da Ḫa-lab*$_x^{ki}$ *in* $^{d}$AMA-*ra*; r. XI 12: 12 gín D. kb nu$_{11}$-za 1 *ḫa-bù ap* nu$_{11}$-za *ar-ra-sù* kg si[kil] ŠÚ+ŠA gín D. kb ʾ*a*$_5$-*na-gu* 4 si 2 gud **L.** en $^{d}$ʾ*À-da Ḫa-lab*$_x^{ki}$ iti ʾ*a*$_5$-*nun*; **21** o. IX 1: [ ] **L.** en $^{d}$ʾ*À-da* lú *Ḫa-lab*$_x^{ki}$; r. VII 25: 15 gín D. kb nu$_{11}$-za 1 *ḫa-bù* ŠÚ+ŠA gín D. kb ʾ*a*$_5$-*na-gu* si 2 gud **L.** [en $^{d}$ʾ*À-da in* $^{d}$AMA-*ra*].
nídba ì-ĝiš **2** o. XII 21: maš-maš íb-lá *I-ti-aš-dar* lú **L.**; **4** r. XIII 11: 4 íb-lá *si-ti-tum* ĝír-kun *Du-bù-uš-da-mu I-ga-li-im Zú-ga-du Ì-lum-a-rí-ḫu* 4 en *Ib-al*$_6^{ki}$ *in* ud [**L.**]; **6** o. III 7: (silver) níĝ-ba ĝuruš-ĝuruš maškim-*sù Ma-rí*$^{ki}$ *in* ud **L.** *Ma-rí*$^{ki}$; **19** r. XVI 2: 1 [d]ib ⸢x⸣[- ] lú **L.**; **21** o. XII 14: (silver) níĝ-ba *Ar-rúm* (silver) níĝ-ba *Mi-su-wa-du* (silver) *En-na-Da-gan* (silver) níĝ-ba ábba-ábba *Ma-rí*$^{ki}$ in ud **L.** *Ib-la*$^{ki}$ *wa Ma-rí*$^{ki}$; **25** o. IX 8: 1 íb-lá TAR kb *I-nu-ud-da-mu Kak-mi-um*$^{ki}$ *in* ud *Ib-la*$^{ki}$ *i*[*n*] [ ].
NI.DU see iti.
NI.GI **17** r. I 7: 1 dib **L.** *ma-lik-tum*.
(*LLE*,I no. 865: NI.GI = *sa-gúm*/*gu-um*)

níĝ «goods» **4** r. XIV 1: an-na PA **L.**-*sù*-**L.**-*sù*.

níĝ-anše-ak «harness» **1** o. VI 7: 1 ma-na ŠÚ+ŠA gín D. kb *ni-zi-mu* 2 **L.** 4 kù-sal; **3** r. III 5: 56 gín D. kb *ni-zi-mu* 2 **L.** 4 kù-sal; **4** o. III 9: 10 ½ gín D. kb ZU.PIRIĜ kin$_5$-ak *gú-li-lum wa* **L.** kù-sal SA.ZA$_x$$^{ki}$; r. III 17: 1 ma-na 53 an-na kin$_5$-ak **L.** kù-sal; r. X 8: 2 ma-na kb kin$_5$-ak 2 **L.** 4 kù-sal; r. XIV 11: 1 ma-na ŠÚ+ŠA gín D. kb 2 **L.** 4 kù-sal, 16: 1 ma-na ŠÚ+ŠA gín D. kb 2 **L.** 4 kù-sal; **5** o. V 11: 1 ma-na 20 gín D. kb lul-gu-ak 2 **L.** 4 NE-*na-tum*; r. I 13: 8 gín D. kb 2 **L.** 4 kù-sal; **6** r. V 12: 1 ma-na ŠÚ+ŠA gín D. kb 2 **L.** 4 kù-sal; r. XIV 12: 1 ma-na ŠÚ+ŠA kb 2 **L.** 4 kù-sal; **7** o. XIII 3: [ ] kb *ni-zi-mu* 2 **L.** 1 kù-sal; **8** o. XV 3: 6 gín D. kb *ni-zi-mu* 10 lá-2 kù-sal 2 **L.**; r. IV 4': 2 gín D. ⌜kb⌝ *ni*-⌜*zi*⌝-*mu* 1 **L.**; **11** o. VI 19: 4 gín D. kg *ni-zi-mu* 2 **L.** 2 kù-sal lú 2 IGI.NITA; r. VI 15: 15 gín D. kg *ni-zi-mu* 2 **L.** 4 kù-sal; **12** r. IV 2: 1 gín D. kg *ni-zi-mu* 1 **L.** IGI.NITA; r. XI 3: ŠA.PI gín D. kg kin$_5$-ak 2 **L.** sur$_x$-BAR.AN [am]a-gal en; **14** o. XI 6: [1] ma-na ŠÚ+ŠA gín D. kb *n*[*i-zi-*]*m*[*u*] 2 **L.** 2[+2] kù-sal; r. XIII 5: 1 ½ kg *ni-zi-mu* 1 **L.** 1 kù-sal 1 IGI.NITA en; **15** o. IV 22: 5 gín D. kb *ni-zi-mu* 2 **L.**; r. III 18: 2 kuš babbar ùz-nita lú 2 **L.** kg maḫ$^?$; **16** o. VI 4: ŠÚ+ŠA 5 gín D. kg *ni-zi-mu* 2 **L.** 4 kù-sal libir *Ib-rí-um*; o. VII 1: 2 ma-na TAR kg kin$_5$-ak 2 **L.** 4 kù-sal gibil *Ib-rí-um*, 8: 2 gín D. kg *ni-zi-mu* 2 **L.** 4 kù-sal 2 IGI.NITA *Ib-rí-um*; r. VII 5: 10 gín D. kb *ni-zi-mu* 2 **L.** ⌜4⌝ kù-sal; r. IX 1: 1 ma-na kg kin$_5$-ak 2 **L.** 4 kù-sal; r. XII 6: 5 gín D. kg *ni-zi-mu* 2 **L.** 4 kù-sal; 17 o. VII 12: 50 gín D. kg kin$_5$-ak 2 **L.** 4!(2) kù-sal 2 IGI.NITA; o. XVII 1: ŠÚ+ŠA 2 gín D. kb *ni-zi-mu* 2 **L.** 4 kù-sal; r. II 14: 3 gín D. kg *ni-zi-mu* 2 **L.** 4 kù-sal sur$_x$-BAR.AN, 20: 2 gín D. kg *ni-zi-mu* 1 **L.** 1 kù-sal 2 IGI.NITA; r. VIII 15: 5 gín D. kb *ni-zi-mu* 2 **L.** 4 kù-sal; **18** r. I 7: 3 gín D. kg *ni-zi-*⌜*mu*⌝ 2 **L.** 2 kù-sal 2 IGI.NITA *wa su-da-nu* kù-sal en; r. XIV 5: 2 ma-na kg 2 **L.** 4 kù-sal; **19** o. XII 24: 3 gín D. kg *ni-zi-mu* 2 **L.** 4 kù-sal *I-bí-zi-kir*; **20** o. VII 11: 4 gín D. kb *ni-zi-mu* 2 **L.**, 24: 6 gín D. an-na šub *si-in ni-*⌜*zi*⌝*-mu* 2 **L.** 4 kù-sal; r. V 8: 2 gín D. kb *ni-zi-mu* [2 **L.**], 19: ŠÚ+ŠA gín [D.] kb [*ni-zi-m*]*u* 2 **L.** 4 kù-sal; **21** o. III 17: 4 gín D. an-na šub *si-in* [*ni-zi-mu* 2 **L.** 4 kù-sal], 27: 4 gín D. kg *ni-zi-mu* [2] **L.** [2+]2 k[ù-]s[al]; o. VIII 8: ŠÚ+ŠA 4 gín D. kg 1 **L.** 1 kù-sal IGI.NITA; o. X 6: 1 gín D. kg *ni-zi-mu* [1] **L.** 2 IGI.NITA; o. XIII 12: 1 ma-na kg kin$_5$-ak 2 **L.** 4 kù-sal *wa* nu$_{11}$-za 2 ĜIŠ.GAM.GAM ĜIŠ-gígir-II, 25: 15 gín D. kg 1 **L.** 1 kù-sal 1 IGI.NITA; **22** o. II 4: 4 ma-na kg [6] **L.** 12 kù[-sal] BAR.AN-BAR.AN.

níĝ-ba «gift» **2** o. II 5: 1 gín D. kg kin$_5$-ak 1 kù-sal **L.** en $^d$*Ba-ra-ma in* ud ne:saĝ-*sù*; o. IV 17: 6 gín D. kg nu$_{11}$-za 1 *ḫa-bù* 15 gín D. kb nu$_{11}$-za-*sù* **L.** *Ib-rí-um* $^{d}$*ʾA$_5$-da-"bal" ʾÀ-ma-ad*$^{ki}$; o. VI 13: 2 gín D. kg maš-maš 1 ĜIŠ-banšur *wa* 1 kù-sal **L.** *Ib-rí-um* $^d$*Ku-ra in* ud ne:saĝ-*sù*, 22: 1 ½ gín D. kg 1 kù-sal **L.** *Du-si-gú Iš:šára*: *Zi-da-ra*$^{ki}$; o. XI 7: 6 gín D. 2 NI kg 2 *gú-li-lum* **L.** $^d$*Ku-ra*; r. II 2: 2 gín D. kg kin$_5$-ak 1 *gú-li-lum* 1 kù-sal **L.** *Ib-rí-um* $^d$*Ku-ra in* ud lú nídba, 14: 3 gín D. kg nu$_{11}$-za 2 zé-*sù* **L.** *Ib-rí-um* $^d$Utu SA.ZA$_x$$^{ki}$; r. III 12: 2 ½ gín D. kg 1 *gú-li-lum* 1 kù-sal **L.** *Du-si-gú* $^d$*Ra-sa-ap ʾÀ-da-ni*$^{ki}$; r. IV 4: TAR kb nu$_{11}$-za 2 *ḫa-bù* ... [ŠÚ+ŠA] g[ín D.] kg nu$_{11}$-za-*sù* **L.** $^d$*Ra-sa-ap* ⌜*ʾÀ-da*⌝*-ni*$^{ki}$ *wa* $^{d}$*ʾÀ-da* $^d$AMA-*ra*; r. IV 24: 1 ½ kb maš-maš 1 "KIN" siki ... ½ kg maš-maš-*sù* **L.** en $^d$*Ì-lam*; r. VIII 4: 15 gín D. kb nu$_{11}$-za 1 an-dùl ... 5 gín D. kg nu$_{11}$-za [*ba-na-a*] *wa* íb+III-TÚG **L.** *Ib-rí-um* $^{d}$⌜BAD⌝ ⌜*Du*⌝*-du-*⌜*la*$^{ki}$⌝, 11: 6 2 NI gín D. kg 2 *gú-li-lum* **L.** $^d$*Ku-ra*, 21: 1 gín D. kg maš-maš 1 "KIN" siki *wa* 1 kù-sal 1 gín D. kb maš-maš-*sù* **L.** *Ib-rí-um* $^{d}$*ʾA$_5$-da-"bal" La-ru$_{12}$-ga-du*$^{ki}$; r. XI 18: 10 gín D. kg 1 íb-lá **L.** $^{d}$*ʾA$_5$-da-ra*; r. XIII 17: 6 gín D. 2 NI kg 2 *gú-li-lum* **L.** $^d$*Áš-da-bíl*; r. XIV 6: 15 gín D. kb nu$_{11}$-za 1 *ḫa-bù* ... 6 gín D. kg nu$_{11}$-za-*sù* 6 2 NI gín D. kb 2 *gú-li-lum* **L.** en $^d$*Am-ma-rí-ig*; r. XV 18; **3** o. II 18: 10 gín D. kb **L.** *Daš-na wa Wa-ru$_{12}$-tum Ma-rí*$^{ki}$; o. IV 10: 6 gín D. 2 NI kg 2 *gú-li-lum* **L.** $^d$*Ku-ra*, 18: 13 gín D. kb nu$_{11}$-za 1 *ḫa-bù* ... 5 gín D. kg nu$_{11}$-za *ar-ra-si-su* **L.** $^{d}$*ʾA$_5$-da-"bal" La-ru$_{12}$-ga-du*$^{ki}$ *Ib-rí-um* ì-na-sum; o. XI 10: 2 gín D. kb maš-maš 1 ĜIŠ-banšur ... 2 ½ gín D. kg [ ]⌜x⌝ **L.** $^{[d]}$*ʾÀ-da* lú *Du-ub*$^{ki}$; o. XII 15: TAR 5 gín D. kb nu$_{11}$-za 1 an-dùl ... 6 gín D. kg nu$_{11}$-za *ba-na-*⌜*ʾà*⌝ *wa* 2 šu 2 DU-*sù* **L.** $^d$*Am-ma-rí-ig*, 19: 6 gín D. 2 NI kb ⌜2⌝ [*gú-*]*l*[*i-lum*] **L.** $^d$*Am-ma-rí-ig*; o. XIII 14: 13 gín D. kb **L.** *Daš-na wa Wa-ru$_{12}$-tum Ma-rí*$^{ki}$; o. XIV 4: 15 gín D. kb [nu$_{11}$-za 1 *ḫa-*]*b*[*ù*] ... 6 gín D. kg nu$_{11}$-za 1 *ar-ra-si-su* **L.** $^{d}$*ʾÀ-da*; r. IV 2: 6 gín D. [2 NI] kg 2 *gú-li-lum* **L.** $^d$*Áš-da-bíl*; r. V 15: ŠÚ+ŠA gín D. kb **L.** *Iš-má-il wa Ba-ga-ar Ma-rí*$^{ki}$; r. VI 12: ŠA.PI gín D. kb **L.** BAD-*sù*-BAD *wa Maḫ-mu M*[*a-rí*$^{ki}$]; r. VIII 4: 1 ma-na 2 gín D. kb **L.** *Ib-gi-tum wa* maškim-*sù Ma-rí*$^{ki}$; r. X 12: 4 gín D. kb **L.** *Ib-gi-tum* lú *I-ti Ma-rí*$^{ki}$, 17: 51 gín D. kb **L.** diĝir-diĝir-diĝir; r. XI 1: 4 gín D. kb [ ] **L.** $^{d}$*ʾA$_5$-da-"bal" La-ru$_{12}$-ga-du*$^{ki}$ *Ib-rí-um* ì-na-sum, 7: 10 gín D. kb **L.** *ʾÀ-du*$^{ki}$, 10: ŠÚ+ŠA gín D. kb **L.** *Kùn-*$^d$*Aš-dar*, 16: 53 gín D. kb 6 *bu-*DI **L.** 3 dam *Zi-ba-da in* ud níĝ-mu-sá dumu-munus *Ib-rí-um*; r. XII 5: 1 ma-na kb **L.** *Ù-da-aḫ Ma-rí*$^{ki}$ kuš$_7$; r. XIII 1: ŠÚ+ŠA gín D. kb **L.** *A-ku-da wa Daš-na Ma-rí*$^{ki}$, 18: ŠÚ+ŠA gín D. kb **L.** *Daš-na wa A-ba-du Ma-rí*$^{ki}$; **4** o. II 14: 5 gín D. kb 1 níĝ-bànda [**L.**] [$^d$]⌜*ʾA$_5$*⌝*-da-*[*"ba*]*l" L*[*a-r*]*u$_{12}$-ga*[*-du*]$^{ki}$; o. IV 16: 12 gín D. kb nu$_{11}$-za!(KUR) 3 ĜIŠ-banšur 3 ĝír mar-tu **L.**, 18: ŠA.PI gín D. kb **L.** [DN]; o. IX 13: 1 ma-na ŠÚ+ŠA gín D. kb 10 lá-2 *bu-*DI **L.** 4 dam *Ì-ra-ar*$^{ki}$, 20: 5 ma-na TAR kb kin$_5$-ak 3 íb<-lá> ĜÁ×LÁ ŠA.PI 7 íb-lá *si-ti-tum* ĝír-kun **L.** ĝuruš-ĝuruš *Ì-ra-ar*$^{ki}$; o. X 17: 20 *gú-a-tum* ... 1 ĜIŠ-šú 1 níĝ-bànda ... 1 *mar-wa-ga-tum* ... 2 *da-ni-da* 8 gín D. kb **L.** diĝir-diĝir-diĝir; o. XV 15: ŠÚ+ŠA gín D. kb **L.** diĝir-diĝir-diĝir; r. IV 17: TAR kb nu$_{11}$-za!(KUR) 2 *ḫa-bù* **L.** $^d$*Ra-sa-ap* lú *ʾÀ-da-ni*$^{ki}$ *wa* $^{d}$*ʾÀ-da*; r. X 23: 8 gín D. kb nu$_{11}$-za!(KUR) 1 an-dùl **L.** $^d$*Á*!(DA)*-la*; r. XII 2: 15 gín D. kb nu$_{11}$-za!(KUR) 1 *ḫa-bu* **L.** $^{d}$*ʾÀ-da*; **5** o. II 10: 1 ĝír mar-⌜tu⌝ [kb(?)] [**L.**] *Ib-ḫur-ma-lik* lú-kar *Kak-mi-um*$^{ki}$, 15: TAR kb **L.** *Daš-na wa Wa-ru$_{12}$-tum Ma-rí*$^{ki}$; r. II 6: 15 gín D. kb **L.** *Wa-ru$_{12}$-tum Ma-rí*$^{ki}$; 16: 5 gín D. kb **L.** *I-ku-il Ma-rí*$^{ki}$; r. IV 1: 3 gín D. kb nu$_{11}$-za 1 ĝír mar-tu ... 1 gín D. kg 1 kù-sal **L.** $^{d}$*ʾA$_5$-da-"bal" Lu-ba-an*$^{ki}$ *Ib-rí-um* ì-na-sum, 17: 10 gín D. kb **L.** *Wa-ru$_{12}$-tum wa* maškim *Ma-rí*$^{ki}$; r. V 2: 5 gín D. kb **L.** *Daš-na Ma-rí*$^{ki}$, 19: 1 ma-na ŠÚ+ŠA 5 gín D. kb nu$_{11}$-za 1 ĜIŠ-banšur ... ŠÚ+ŠA gín D. kg nu$_{11}$-za 3 saĝ lu$_5$ 10 gín D. an-na šub *si-in* URUDU-*sù* **L.** $^{d}$*ʾA$_5$-da-*

"*bal*" *La-ru*$_{12}$*-ga-du*$^{ki}$ en ì-na-sum; r. VI 11: 8 gín D. kb 2 zi-bar **L.** $^{d}$BAD *Má*-NE$^{ki}$ *Du-si-gú* ì-na-sum; r. VIII 17: 1 ĜIŠ-banšur **L.** *I-bí-zi-kir* dumu-nita *Ib-rí-um* $^{d}$*ʾA*$_{5}$*-da-*"*bal*" *La-ru*$_{12}$*-ga-du*$^{ki}$; r. X 12: 15 gín D. kb nu$_{11}$-za 1 *ḫa-bù* ... 6 gín D. kg nu$_{11}$-za *ar-ra-si-sù* **L.** $^{d}$*ʾÀ-da*; r. XIII 14: 10 gín D. kb 2 *bu*-DI 2 *ti-ša-na* **L.** $^{d}$*Ga-na-na* ĜIŠ.DUG.DU maḫ, 21: 3 gín D. kg nu$_{11}$-za 1 ĝír mar-tu **L.** $^{d}$*ʾA*$_{5}$*-da-*"*bal*" *ʾÀ-ma-du*$^{ki}$ *Ib-rí-um* in-na-sum; r. XIV 7: 2 gín D. kb nu$_{11}$-za 1 ĝír mar-tu ... ½ gín D. kg 1 kù-sal **L.** $^{d}$*Ra-sa-ap ʾÀ-da-ni*$^{ki}$ *in* SA.ZA$_{x}$$^{ki}$ *Ib-rí-um*, 18: 2 gín D. kb nu$_{11}$-za 1 ĝír mar-tu ... ½ gín D. kg 1 kù-sal **L.** $^{d}$*Ra-sa-ap gú-núm*$^{ki}$ en in-na-sum; r. XV 24: 1 ma-na kb **L.** *Gú-šu*, 27: 10 gín D. kb **L.** *Wa-ru*$_{12}$*-tum Ma-rí*$^{ki}$; r. XVI 6: 1 ma-na TAR kb **L.** diĝir-diĝir-diĝir; **6** o. II 4: 1 ma-na kb **L.** ḫúb-ki, 17: 5 ma-na kb **L.** *A-ḫa-ar-si*, 20: 3 ma-na kb **L.** *ʾÀ-sa*, 23: 2 ma-na kb **L.** *Íl-a*; o. III 3: 1 ma-na kb **L.** ĝuruš-ĝuruš maškim-*sù Ma-rí*$^{ki}$, 10: 10 gín D. kb **L.** *Du-tum Ma-rí*$^{ki}$, 23: 5 ma-na kb **L.** *Zú-gú-uš Na-gàr*$^{ki}$; o. VII 3: 2 ma-na kb níĝ-sa$_{10}$ 1 *za-ḫa-da ra-ʾà-tum* kg **L.** $^{d}$*ʾÀ-da* ì-na-sum; o. VIII 2 and 7: 5 gín D. kb nu$_{11}$-za 1 ĜIŠ-banšur **L.** $^{d}$*ʾÀ-da* lú *Lu-ub*$^{ki}$ *wa* nu$_{11}$-za 1 ĝír mar-tu **L.** $^{d}$*Wa-da-ʾà-an* lú *Ga-ra-mu*$^{ki}$, 12: 1 ma-na 50 kb **L.** diĝir-diĝir-diĝir-diĝir; o. IX 7: 1 ma-na an-na 5 gín D. kb **L.** *A-mu-ra Du-ub*$^{ki}$; o. X 10 and 14: 3 ma-na kb **L.** *Wa-ba-rúm Ma-rí*$^{ki}$ 1 ma-na kb **L.** *ʾÀ-sa* maškim-*sù*, 18: 2 ma-na kb **L.** *I-ti* ga:eš$_{8}$ *Ma-rí*$^{ki}$; o. XII 9: 2 ma-na kb **L.** *Ab-ba Ma-rí*$^{ki}$, 13 and 16: 1 ma-na kb **L.** *Ib-ḫur-úr* 5 gín D. kb **L.** *Sa*-NI-*gú* maškim-*sù*; o. XIV 1: 15 gín D. kb nu$_{11}$-za 1 *ḫa-bù* **L.** $^{d}$BAD *Ga-na-na-im*, 14: 15 gín D. kb nu$_{11}$-za 1 *ḫa-bù* **L.** $^{d}$*ʾA*$_{5}$*-da-*"*bal*" *La-ru*$_{12}$*-ga*$_{x}$(ZÀR)*-du*$^{ki}$; o. XV 10: 10 gín D. kb **L.** *Puzur*$_{4}$*-ra-*$^{d}$Utu *Ma-rí*$^{ki}$ šu-mu-tak$_{4}$, 18: 15 gín D. kb **L.** *Ù*-NE-NE *Ma-rí*$^{ki}$; o. XVI 13: 10 gín D. kb **L.** *Ìr*-NI-*ba wa Sá-ba Ma-rí*$^{ki}$, 26: TAR kb nu$_{11}$-za 2 *ḫa-bù* **L.** $^{d}$*Ra-sa-ap ʾÀ-da-ni*$^{ki}$ *wa* $^{d}$*ʾÀ-da* $^{d}$AMA-*ra*; r. I 6: 10 gín D. kb **L.** *Daš-na wa I-da-il Ma-rí*$^{ki}$; r. II 16 and r. III 1: 10 gín D. kb nu$_{11}$-za 1 ĝír mar-tu **L.** $^{d}$*Da-i-in wa* maš-maš 1 ĜIŠ-banšur **L.** $^{d}$*Ga-mi-iš*; r. III 14: 5 gín D. kb **L.** *Na*-NE *Na-gàr*$^{ki}$; r. IV 2: ŠÚ+ŠA gín D. kb **L.** *Daš-na wa I-da-il Ma-rí*$^{ki}$, 13: 10 gín D. kb **L.** *A-gàr wa Gú-zú-gú-zú Ma-rí*$^{ki}$; r. V 14: 1 ma-na ŠÚ+ŠA gín kb ⌜2⌝ níĝ-anše-ak 4 kù-sal *Du-si-gú* **L.** en, 22: 1 ma-na kb **L.** *ʾÀ-sa wa Gú-gi I-ku-il wa Ba-du-lum Ma-rí*$^{ki}$; r. VI 9: 5 gín D. kb **L.** *I-i-bù Ir-i-tum*$^{ki}$, 21: 6 2 NI gín D. kb 2 *gú-li-lum* **L.** $^{d}$*ʾÀ-ma-rí-ig*; r. XIV 2: 10 gín D. kb 2 *bu*-DI 2 *ti-ša-na* **L.** $^{d}$*Ga-na-na* ĜIŠ.DUG.DU maḫ; r. XVII 24: 15 an-na šub-šub nu$_{11}$-za 1 *ḫa-bù* **L.** $^{d}$*Ga-mi-iš* en ì-na-sum; **7** o. I 5: 10 gín D. kb **L.** NE-*a-da-nu ʾÀ-du*$^{ki}$, 10: 2 gín D. kb nu$_{11}$-za 1 ĝír mar-tu **L.** $^{d}$*Wa-da-ʾà-nu* [l]ú [*Ša-*]*dab*$^{ki}$ *Ib-rí-um* in-na-sum; o. III 5: 1 gín D. kg 1 kù-sal **L.** ama-gal en $^{d}$Nin-kar; 15: 3 gín D. kb nu$_{11}$-za 1 ĝír mar-tu *wa* 1 kù-sal **L.** *Ib-rí-um* $^{d}$*Ra-sa-ap Du-ne-íb*$^{ki}$; o. VII 17: 6 gín D. 2 NI kg 2 *gú-li-lum* **L.** $^{d}$*Ku-ra*; o. VIII 6: TAR kb 1 íb-lá 1 *si-ti-tum* 1 ĝír-kun **L.** *Ib-ḫur-ma-lik Kak-mi-um*$^{ki}$ tuš-LÚ<×TIL> *in Ar-ḫa-du*$^{ki}$; o. X 2: [ ] *Ib-rí-um* **L.** $^{d}$BAD *Du-du-lu*$^{ki}$, 10: ŠA.PI gín D. kb nu$_{11}$-za 1 an-dùl munus ... 17 gín D. kg nu$_{11}$-za saĝ-*sù* 2 šu-*sù* DU-*sù* **L.** $^{d}$*Sa-a-ša si-in Du-du-lu*$^{ki}$ *Ib-rí-um* šu-mu-tak$_{4}$; o. XI 14: 15 gín D. kb nu$_{11}$-za 1 ešda ... 6 gín D. kg nu$_{11}$-za 1 *ar-ra-sù* **L.** $^{d}$*Ra-sa-ap*; o. XV 9: ŠÚ+ŠA gín D. kb **L.** *Da-ti*, 12: 5 gín D. kb **L.** *A*-LUM-*mu-d*[*a*] *Ma-r*[*í*$^{ki}$], 21: 10 gín D. kb **L.** ⌜*Wa*⌝-[*r*]*u*$_{12}$[*-tum Ma-rí*$^{ki}$]; o. XVI 11: 8 gín D. 2 NI kg [2 *gú-l*]*i*-[*lu*]*m* **L.** [$^{d}$*K*]*u-ra*, 18: 15 gín D. kb **L.** *D*[*a-* ]; r. II 12: 3 [gín D.] kb nu$_{11}$-z[a] 1 ĝír mar-tu ... ½ gín D. kg [1 k]ù-sal **L.** $^{d}$*Ra-sa-ap Du-ne-íb*$^{ki}$, 21: 2 gín D. kb nu$_{11}$-za 1 ĝír mar-tu ... ½ g[ín D.] kg 1 kù-s[al] **L.** [$^{d}$ ]; r. III 10: [ ] [x] ⌜*ʾà-ra*⌝*-ma-tum* ... 2 gín D. kg n[u$_{11}$]-za [ **L.**] $^{d}$Utu SA.ZA$_{x}$$^{ki}$, 19: 2 gín D. kb nu$_{11}$-za 1 ĝír mar-tu ... 2 NI gín D. kg 1 kù-sal **L.** $^{d}$*Ku-ra*; r. IV 8: ½ gín D. [kb *ʾa*$_{5}$*-na-gu* 1 ĜIŠ-banšur] ... 2 N[I gín] D. kg 1 kù-sal **L.** $^{d}$*ʾA*$_{5}$*-da-*"*bal*" [*Lu-b*]*a-an*$^{[ki]}$, 18: ½ g[ín] D. kb *ʾa*$_{5}$*-na-gu* 1 ĜIŠ-banšur ... 2 NI gín D. kg 1 kù-sal **L.** $^{d}$*Am-ma-rí-ig*; r. V 3: ½ gín D. kb *ʾa*$_{5}$*-na-gu* 1 ĜIŠ-banšur ... [½ gín D. kg] [1 kù-sal] [**L.**] ⌜$^{d}$⌝[ ], 16: ⌜6⌝ gín D. [1+]1 NI kg 2 *gú-li-lum* **L.** $^{d}$*Áš-da-bil*, 22: 2 gín D. kg nu$_{11}$-za 1 ĝír mar-tu **L.** $^{d}$*Áš-da-bíl*; r. VI 5: 1 gín D. kg 1 kù-sal 1 buru$_{4}$-MUŠEN [**L.**] [ ] [$^{d}$*Ra-sa-*]*a*[*p*] *ʾÀ-da-ni*$^{ki}$; r. VIII 4: 15 gín D. kb nu$_{11}$-za 1 ešda ... 6 gín D. kg [nu$_{11}$-]za *ar-r*[*a-*]*sù* **L.** $^{d}$*ʾÀ-da in* iti *ʾa*$_{5}$*-nun*, 16: ŠA.PI gín D. kb **L.** *I-ti-ì*, 19: 10 gín D. kb **L.** *Iš-dub-ì Ma-rí*$^{ki}$ níĝ-"mul" *Ar-ti-na-an*$^{ki}$ til; r. X 16: 14 gín D. kb **L.** *Wa-ru*$_{12}$*-tum Ma-rí*$^{ki}$; r. XI 11: 50 gín D. kb **L.** *Gul-la* ⌜x-x-x⌝ *Sa-ma-na-nu* [*S*]*i-mi*[- ] [ ] *Iš-ba-ì A-ša*$^{ki}$ *in* ud DU.DU nam-kud é $^{d}$*Ku-ra*; r. XIII 1: 1 ma-na kb [**L.**] *Daš-na Ma-rí*$^{ki}$ níĝ-"mul" Kiš$^{ki}$ til, 20: 10 gín D. kb **L.** *Iš-dub-ì* maškim ga:eš$_{8}$ *Du-du-lu*$^{ki}$ ḫi-mu-DU ḪU.UD; r. XIV 3: 10 gín D. kb [ ] 4 *ti-ša-nu* 2 *bu*-DI **L.** $^{d}$*Ga-na-na in* ud ĜIŠ.DUG.DU maḫ, 10: 6 gín 2 NI kb 2 *gú-li-lum* **L.** $^{d}$*Am-ma-rí-ig*, 13: 2 ma-na kb **L.** diĝir-diĝir-diĝir, 16: 2 [ma-n]a kb **L.** *Wa-ru*$_{12}$*-tum Da-ti Bù-sum Ma-rí*$^{ki}$; **8** o. VI 7: TAR kg daḫ nu$_{11}$-za 1 an-dùl **L.** $^{d}$BAD *Ga-na-na-um*; o. VII 4: 4 gín D. kb nu$_{11}$-za 1 ĝír mar-tu **L.** $^{d}$*ʾA*$_{5}$*-da-*"*bal*" *ʾÀ-ma-du*$^{ki}$, 8: 1 ma-na 15 gín D. kb **L.** diĝir-diĝir-diĝir; r. II 4': 4 gín D. kb nu$_{11}$-za *ba-na-i-sa* **L.** *Ib-rí-um* $^{d}$*Ra-sa-ap*; r. III 15': 10 gín D. kb **L.** *Daš-na Ma-rí*$^{ki}$ [ ]; **9** o. II 2: 1 ma-na kb **L.** diĝir-diĝir-diĝir; o. III 15: [ ] [*a*]*r-ra-sa-sù* L. $^{d}$*Ra-sa-ap ʾÀ-da-ni*$^{ki}$ *wa* $^{d}$*ʾÀ-da Ḫa-lab*$_{x}$$^{ki}$ AMA-*ra*; o. IV 9: 1 ma-na kb nu$_{11}$-za si-si 2 gud **L.** en $^{d}$*ʾÀ-da* [*Ḫ*]*a-lab*$_{x}$$^{ki}$ [*i*]*n* AMA-*ra*; o. VIII 14: [6 g]ín D. [3 N]I [kg] 2 *gú-li-lum* **L.** $^{d}$*Ku-*[*ra*], 17: ŠÚ+ŠA gín D. kb **L.** *Na-gàr*$^{ki}$ *wa* [ ]; o. XII 14: ŠÚ+ŠA gín D. kb **L.** *Daš-na wa Šu-ga-du Ma-r*[*í*]$^{ki}$; o. XIII 15: 6 gín D. 2 NI kg 2 *gú-li-lum* **L.** $^{d}$*Áš-da-bíl*; r. V 15: 12 gín D. kb nu$_{11}$-za 1 *ḫa-bù* **L.** $^{d}$*Ga-mi-iš ḫu-ru*$_{12}$-⌜*mu*⌝; r. VI 12: 2 gín D. kg nu$_{11}$-za 2 saĝ-*sù* **L.** *Kir-su-ut*, 16: ŠÚ+ŠA gín D. kb 4 *bu*-DI **L.** *Ib-ʾà-ra wa* nin-ni-⌜*sù*⌝ *in* ud níĝ-mu-sá ⌜*Za*⌝*-ne-ḫi-Ma-*[*r*]*í*$^{ki}$ é-gi *Ib-ʾà-ra ʾÀ-šu*$^{ki}$; r. VIII 1: 13 gín D. kb nu$_{11}$-za 1 *ḫa-bù* ... 6 gín D. kg nu$_{11}$-za 1 *ar-ra-sù* [**L.**] $^{d}$BAD *Ga-*[*na-*]*na-im*, 16: 6 gín D. kg nu$_{11}$-za *ba-na-ʾà-sa wa* íb+III-TÚG [*w*]*a* an-zam$_{x}$ *wa* 2 *gú-li-lum-sù* **L.** $^{d}$*ʾA*$_{5}$*-da-ra*; **10** o. I 10: TAR kb L. *Du-tum Ma-rí*$^{ki}$ lú ga:eš$_{8}$; o. II 9: 2 ma-na kb nu$_{11}$-za 1 ĜIŠ-banšur ... ŠÚ+ŠA gín D. kg nu$_{11}$-za 1 saĝ ⌜lu$_{5}$⌝ 1 ĜIŠ-banšur **L.** $^{d}$*Am-ma-rí-ig*, 12: 1 ma-na ŠÚ+ŠA gín D. kb **L.** *Wa-ru*$_{12}$*-tum Daš-na Iš*$_{11}$*-ga-um ʾÀ*-NE-*su Ma-rí*$^{ki}$; o. III 9: ⌜5⌝ gín D. kb **L.** *A-mu-ra Du-ub*$^{ki}$, 13: 5 gín D. kb

**L.** *Ša-nap-zu-gúm*$^{ki}$, 16: 10 gín D. kb **L.** *Ba-na-⌜i⌝-um*$^{ki}$; o. IV 1: 10 gín D. kb **L.** *Daš-na Ma-rí*$^{ki}$; o. V 6: 15 gín D. [kb] nu$_{11}$-za 1 *ḫa-bù* … 6 gín D. kg nu$_{11}$-za 1 *ar-ra-sù* **L.** $^{dʾ}$*À-da*, 10: 10 gín D. kb nu$_{11}$-za 1 ĜIŠ-banšur **L.** $^{d}$*Ku-ra Ib-rí-um* in-na-sum *in* ud ne:s[aĝ]-*sù*; o. VI 4: 10 gín D. kb **L.** *Zú-zú Ir-i-tum*$^{ki}$; o. VII 16: TAR kb **L.** *Bù-sum Ma-rí*$^{ki}$, 22: 10 gín D. kb **L.** *I-ti-il Ma-rí*$^{ki}$; o. VIII 6: 10 gín D. kb **L.** *Daš-na Ma-rí*$^{ki}$; o. IX 15: 10 gín D. kb **L.** "ur$_4$" *Mar-da-ma-*LUM$^{ki}$, 19: 4 ma-na kb **L.** *Wa-ba-rúm Ma-rí*$^{ki}$; o. X 8: 10 gín [D. kb] **L.** *Šu-ga-du Ru$_{12}$-zi-lum Ma-rí*$^{ki}$, 14: 3 gín D. kb nu$_{11}$-za 1 ĝír mar-tu **L.** *Ìr-ba$_x$-zé ʾÀ-da-ni*$^{ki}$, 20: 1 ma-na TAR 3 gín D. kb **L.** diĝir-diĝir-diĝir; o. XI 6: 15 gín D. kb **L.** *Ba-zú-zi Ma-[r]í*$^{ki}$, 18: 5 gín D. kb **L.** *Ir-i-tum*$^{ki}$, 21: 1 ma-na kb **L.** *Daš-na Wa-ru$_{12}$-tum Puzur$_4$-ra-*BAD *I-ti-il Ma-rí*$^{ki}$; o. XII 15: [x+]1 [gí]n D. kb **L.** *[L]a$^?$-la-*LUM; o. XIII 2: [x gí]n D. kb **L.** NE-*da-*ḪI *Na-gàr*$^{ki}$, 14: 5 gín D. kb maš-maš 1 [ĜIŠ]-⌜banšur⌝ *wa* nu$_{11}$-za 1 ĝír mar-tu **L.** $^{d}$*Ku-ra* lú *ʾÀ-ti-ni*$^{ki}$; o. XIV 2: 10 gín D. kb **L.** *Gul-la* ḫi-mu-DU 1 BAR.AN, 7: 10 gín D. kb **L.** *Ù-da-aḫ Na-gàr*$^{ki}$, 11: ŠÚ+ŠA gín D. kb **L.** *Daš-na Wa-ru$_{12}$-tum Ma-rí*$^{ki}$; o. XV 3: 5 gín D. kb **L.** *Ga-ga-ba-an*$^{ki}$; o. XVI 5: 1 [ma-]na kb **L.** *Ib-gi-tum Ma-rí*$^{ki}$ níĝ-"mul" *Na-gàr*$^{ki}$ [t]il, 17: ŠÚ+ŠA gín D. kb **L.** *Iš$_{11}$-ga-um Ma-rí*$^{ki}$; r. I 1: ŠÚ+ŠA gín D. kb **L.** *Daš-na wa Wa-ru$_{12}$-tum Ma-rí*$^{ki}$, 21: TAR kb **L.** *Daš-na wa Wa-ru$_{12}$-tum Ma-rí*$^{ki}$; r. III 10: 10 gín D. kb **L.** *Na-*NE *Na-gàr*$^{ki}$, 14: [x] gín D. kb **L.** *La-sa-nu Ḫa-ra-an*$^{ki}$, 18: ŠA.PI gín D. kb **L.** *Ib-gi-tum*; r. IV 1: ŠÚ+ŠA gín D. kb **L.** *Wa-ru$_{12}$-tum wa Daš-na Ma-rí*$^{ki}$; r. V 19: 1 ma-na kb **L.** *Iš$_{11}$-ga wa Daš-na Ma-rí*$^{ki}$; r. IX 2: ŠÚ+ŠA gín D. kb **L.** *Na-*NE *wa* maškim-*sù Na-gàr*$^{ki}$, 8: ŠÚ+ŠA gín D. kb **L.** *ʾÀ-du*$^{ki}$, 11: 5 gín D. kb **L.** *Zi-ti-ru$_{12}$*$^{ki}$; r. X 3: 3 gín D. kb nu$_{11}$-za 1 ĝír mar-tu 1 kù-sal **L.** $^{d}$*Ku-ra Ib-rí-um* ì-na-sum *in* ne-saĝ-*sù*; **11** o. IV 8: 3 gín D. kg nu$_{11}$-za *maš-ar-tum* **L.** dumu-munus *[I]b-rí-[u]m* é-gi<-a> *Zi-ba-da* é $^{dʾ}$*À-da*, 21: [½ gí]n [D.] kg 1 kù-sal 2 gín D. kb nu$_{11}$-za [1 g]ír mar-tu **L.** [$^{d}$*Ku-ra*] [*Ib-rí-um*$^?$] [ì-na-sum] [*i*]*n* ⌜ud⌝ ne:saĝ; o. V 12: ½ gín D. kg 1 kù-sal 2 gín D. kb nu$_{11}$-za 1 ĝír mar-tu **L.** *Ib-rí-um* $^{d}$*Ra-s[a-ap] g[ú-n]úm in* ud ne:saĝ; o. VI 13: 6 gín D. 2 NI kg 2 *gú-li-lum* **L.** ⌜$^{d}$⌝[ ]; o. VII 6: ŠÚ+ŠA gín D. kb **L.** *Ma-rí*$^{ki}$; o. VIII 15: TAR kb **L.** *Wa-ru$_{12}$-tum Daš-na I-ku$^!$-*KU$^!$-TU; o. XI 10: 1 ma-na ŠA.PI gín D. kb **L.** diĝir-diĝir-diĝir; r. III 9: 2 ma-na kb **L.** en *Ša-bir$_5$-ti-du*$^{ki}$ 16 gín D. kb *Na-mi-ir* maškim-*sù*; r. IV 1: [ ] **L.** *Bù-za-lum Am$_6$-mu-tum Ma-rí*$^{ki}$ ĜIŠ.DUG.D[U] izi-ĝar, 9: 13 gín D. kb nu$_{11}$-za 1 ešda **L.** $^{dʾ}$*À-da* lú *Lu-ub*$^{ki}$ *in gi-*NI, 20: 6 2 NI gín D. kb 2 *gú-li-lum* **L.** $^{d}$*Am-rí-ig*; r. V 5: 2 gín D. kb nu$_{11}$-za 1 ĝír mar-tu **L.** $^{d}$*Am-rí-ig*, 18: 13 gín D. kb nu$_{11}$-za 1 ešda **L.** [$^{dʾ}$*A$_5$-d*]*a-*"*bal*" [ ] *in* ud NI.DU; r. VI 6: 1 gín D. kb *ʾa$_5$-na-gu* 1 ĜIŠ-banšur **L.** $^{d}$*Ra-sa-ap Du-bí-tum*$^{ki}$ [ ]⌜x⌝ [*in*] ud ḫúl é-*sù*; r. VII 2: ŠÚ+ŠA gín D. kb 2 *ʾà-ra-ma-tum* … ŠÚ+ŠA kg nu$_{11}$-za-*sù* **L.** *Ib-rí-um* $^{d}$Utu lú SA.ZA$_x$$^{ki}$; **12** o. II 13: ŠÚ+ŠA 5 gín D. kb **L.** *Ib-gi-tum wa Ku-tu-ʾà-bù wa Ib-du-nu* [ -]⌜x⌝ [ ] *Du-du-lu*$^{ki}$ níĝ-"mul" *Ag-sa-gú*$^{ki}$ šu-ba$_4$-ti; o. III 16: ŠÚ+ŠA 2 gín D. kg nu$_{11}$-za *ba-na-i-su-ma wa* 2 šu-šu-*sù* 2 DU.DU-*sù* **L.** ⌜$^{d}$⌝*ʾA$_5$-da-*["*b*]*al*" [*A-*]*ru$_{12}$-*[*ga-d*]*u*$^{ki}$ [e]n [*i*]*n* [ ]; o. V 17: 4 gín D. kb nu$_{11}$-za 2 ĝír mar-tu … 1 ½ gín D. kg 2 kù-sal **L.** $^{d}$BAD *Ga-na-na-im* [*w*]*a* [$^{dʾ}$*A$_5$-d*]*a*[*-ra*]; o. VI 12: 4 ma-na kb **L.** *Wa-ba-rúm* ga:eš$_8$ *Du-du-lu*$^{ki}$, 17: 2 ma-na kb **L.** *Na-na-tum* dam-*sù*, 21: 1 ma-na kb **L.** dumu-nita-*sù*; o. VII 1: 1 ma-na kb **L.** maškim-*sù*, 7: 2 ma-na kb **L.** *Ab-bu$_{16}$ Ma-rí*$^{ki}$ níĝ-"mul" *Ag-sa-gú*$^{ki}$ šu-ba$_4$-ti, 15: 2 gín D. kb nu$_{11}$-za 1 ĝír mar-tu **L.** $^{d}$BAD *Ar-ti-na-an*$^{ki}$ *Ib-rí-um* in-na-sum; o. VIII 6: 6 gín D. 2 NI kg 2 *gú-li-lum* **L.** $^{d}$*Áš-da-bíl*; o. IX 1: 6 gín D. 2 NI kg 2 *gú-li-lum* **L.** $^{d}$*Am-ma-rí-ig*, 15: 1 ma-na kb L. *Wa-ru$_{12}$-tum Ma-rí*$^{ki}$ níĝ-"mul" *Ag-sa-gú*$^{ki}$ šu-ba$_4$-ti; o. XIV 12: 2 gín D. kb 2 zi-bar **L.** $^{d}$BAD *Má-*NE$^{ki}$ *wa* $^{d}$BAD *Zu-ra-mu*$^{ki}$ *Du-si-gú* šu-mu-tak$_4$; r. I 15: 15 gín D. kb nu$_{11}$-za 1 *ḫa-⌜bù⌝* … 6 gín D. kg nu$_{11}$-za 1 *ar-ra-sù* **L.** $^{dʾ}$*À-da*; r. II 11: 5 gín D kg **L.** *Ša-ḫa-ru$_{12}$*$^{ki}$; r. III 12: TAR kb **L.** diĝir-diĝir-diĝir; r. V 14: 1 ma-na kb **L.** *Ib-gi-tum Ma-rí*$^{ki}$ ĜIŠ.DUG.DU izi-ĝar; r. VII 14: 2 gín D. kb nu$_{11}$-za 1 ĝír mar-tu ½ gín D. kb 1 kù-sal **L.** *Ib-rí-um* $^{dʾ}$*A$_5$-da-*"*bal*" NE-*a-ù*$^{ki}$, 19: 1 ma-na kb **L.** *Daš-na* DU.DU *Ma-rí*$^{ki}$ *áš-da* [ ]; r. IX 16: TAR 3 gín D. kb nu$_{11}$-za 2 an-dùl … 8 gín D. kg nu$_{11}$-za *ba-na-a-sa wa* 2 šu-*sù wa* 2 DU-*sù* **L.** *Du-si-gú* $^{d}$*Ku-ra in* ud ne:saĝ; **13** o. IV 21: ŠÚ+ŠA gín D. kb **L.** *Wa-ru$_{12}$-tum wa Šu-ga-du Ma-rí*$^{ki}$; o. V 5: 2 gín D. kb nu$_{11}$-za 1 ĝír mar-tu **L.** *Ib-rí-um* $^{d}$*Ra-sa-ap* $^{d}$En-ki; o. VI 16: TAR kb **L.** *Ib-gi-tum ba-da-lum La-li I-ku$^!$*(DÚR)-*ku$^!$*(DÚR)-*tu Ma-rí*$^{ki}$; o. VII 12: 3 gín D. kg kin$_5$-ak 1 *du-rúm* **L.** *Ib-rí-um* $^{d}$*Ḫa-a-ba-du* lú *Ḫa-lab$_x$*$^{ki}$; o. VIII 2: ŠA.PI 3 gín D. kb nu$_{11}$-za 2 an-dùl … 10 gín D. kg nu$_{11}$-za [I]GI.DUB-*sù wa* 4 šu-*sù* 4 DU-*sù* **L.** *Du-si-gú* $^{d}$*Ra-sa-ap A-da-ma ʾÀ-da-ni*$^{ki}$, 19: 12 gín D. kb nu$_{11}$-za 1 an-dùl … 3 gín D. kg nu$_{11}$-za IGI.DUB-*sù* 2 šu-*sù* 2 DU-*sù* **L.** *Du-si-gú* $^{d}$*Iš:šára Wa-*NE-*du*$^{ki}$; o. IX 9: 2 ½ gín D. kb nu$_{11}$-za 1 ĝír mar-tu 1 kù-sal **L.** *Ib-rí-um* $^{d}$*Ga-ra-ru$_{12}$*, 17: 1 kù-sal … 1 kù-sal **L.** $^{d}$NE-*ti-a-du* diĝir *Du-lu*$^{ki}$; o. XV 24: TAR kb 2 *bu-*DI … 3 gín D. kg nu$_{11}$-za 2 saĝ-*sù* **L.** *Ti-šè-li-im ma-lik-tum Ì-mar*$^{ki}$; o. XVI 14: 50 gín D. kb **L.** *Daš-na wa Šu-ga-du Ma-rí*$^{ki}$, 20: 3 gín D. kb **L.** *A-za-ba Ir-i-tum*$^{ki}$; o. XVII 15: ŠÚ+ŠA gín D. kb **L.** *Bù-sum Ma-rí*$^{ki}$; r. I 2: 2 ma-na kb **L.** *Ìr-am$_6$-*kur$^{ki}$ sagi *Ma-rí*$^{ki}$, 11: ŠA.PI gín D. kb **L.** *Da-ti Iš-da-maḫ Ù-lu-li* [ ]; r. III 10: 6 gín D. 2 NI kg 2 *gú-li-lum* **L.** $^{d}$*Ku-ra*, 13: 2 ma-na kb **L.** *Kùn-*NE *wa Ab-ba* muḫaldim *Ma-rí*$^{ki}$; r. IV 5:[13 g]ín [D. kb nu$_{11}$-za 1 *ḫa-bù*] **L.** $^{dʾ}$*À-da* lú *Lu-ub*$^{ki}$, 10: 13 gín D. kb nu$_{11}$-za 1 *ḫa-bù* **L.** $^{dʾ}$*A$_5$-da-*"*bal*" *A-ru$_{12}$-ga-du*$^{ki}$, 15: TAR 4 gín D. kb nu$_{11}$-za 2 an-dùl **L.** *Ib-rí-um* $^{d}$*Ra-sa-ap wa* $^{d}$*A-da-ma ʾÀ-da-ni*$^{ki}$, 23: 5 gín D. kb nu$_{11}$-za ⌜1⌝ an-dùl [**L.**] [ ] [$^{d}$X]; r. V 17: 6 gín D. 2 NI kb 2 *gú-li-lum* **L.** $^{d}$*Am-ma-⌜rí⌝*[*-ig*]; r. VII 6: 6 gín D. 2 NI kg 2 *gú-li-lum* **L.** $^{d}$*Ku-ra*; **14** o. II 5: 1 kù-sal **L.** ama-gal en $^{d}$*Ba-ra-ma* [ ], 19: 5 gín D. kb **L.** *Šu-a-ḫa* maškim ga:eš$_8$ *Du-du-lu*$^{ki}$; o. III 5: 5 gín D. kb **L.** *A-ku-a-ḫa Ma-rí*$^{ki}$, 13: 10 gín D. kb **L.** *Iš-⌜dub⌝-ì wa Ib-gi-tum* maškim ga:eš$_8$ *Du-du-lu*$^{ki}$; o. XIII 12: ŠÚ+ŠA gín D. kb **L.** *Daš-na Ma-rí*$^{ki}$; r. II 2: 6 gín D. ⌜2⌝ NI kg 2 *gú-li-lum* **L.** [ ], 19: 13 gín D. kb nu$_{11}$-za 1 *ḫa-bù* … 6 gín D. kg nu$_{11}$-za 1 *ar-ra-su-sù* **L.** $^{dʾ}$*À-da* lú *Lu-ub*$^{ki}$ [*i*]*n* [*gi-*NI]; r. IV 12: [ k]b **L.** *Iš-dub-il* maškim ga:eš$_8$ *Du-du-lu*$^{ki}$,

21: [6 gín D. 2 NI kg 2 *gú-li-lum* **L.** $^{d}$*Áš-da-b*]*il*; r. V 3: 6 gín D. 2 NI kg [2] *gú-*[*l*]*i-lum* [**L.**] $^{d}$*Am-ma-rí-ig*, 11: 1 ma-na kb [**L.**] *Wa-ru*$_{12}$*-tum Ma-rí*$^{ki}$ níĝ-"mul" Kiš$^{ki}$ til-til; r. VI 10: 50 gín D. kb nu$_{11}$-za 1 ĜIŠ-banšur maḫ … [x gín D. a-ga]r$_{5}$-gar$_{5}$ URUDU-*sù* … 9 gín D. kg *ᵓa*$_{5}$*-na-gu-sù* [**L.**] $^{d}$*ᵓA*$_{5}$*-da-"bal" ᵓÀ-ma-du*$^{ki}$ en šu-mu-tak$_{4}$; r. VII 3: 1 ma-na 54 gín D. a-gar$_{5}$-g[ar$_{5}$] nu$_{11}$-za 1 ĜIŠ-asari 6 gín D. kb nu$_{11}$-za 4 saĝ lu$_{5}$ *al*$_{6}$*-sù* **L.** $^{d}$*ᵓA*$_{5}$*-da-"bal"* NE-*a-ù*<ki> *Ib-rí-um* šu-mu-tak$_{4}$, 12: 10 gín D. kb [2 *b*]*u*-DI *wa* 4 *ti-ša-nu* **L.** $^{d}$*Ga-na-na* ĜIŠ.DUG.DU maḫ, 16: 9 gín D. kb **L.** Šubur *Du*<-*lu*>$^{ki}$ kin$_{5}$-ak *šè-li*; r. X 14: 4 gín D. kb **L.** *Ù-li-li* maškim [ga:eš$_{8}$ *Du-du-lu*]$^{ki}$; **15** o. I 12: 1 gín D. kg 1 kù-sal **L.** *Da-bur-da-mu* $^{d}$*Iš:šára Zi-da-ra*$^{ki}$; o. II 6: 3 ½ gín kg 1 ĜIŠ-banšur *wa* 1 kù-sal **L.** *Ib-rí-um* $^{d}$BAD *Du-du-lu*$^{ki}$, 30: TAR kb **L.** *Daš-na Ma-rí*$^{ki}$ níĝ-"mul" Kiš$^{ki}$ til; o. VI 14: 6 gín D. 2 NI kg 2 *gú-li-lum* **L.** $^{d}$*Ku-ra*; o. VII 13: TAR kb **L.** *Wa-ru*$_{12}$*-tum Ma-rí*$^{ki}$ níĝ-"mul" *in* uru$^{ki}$-uru$^{ki}$ Kiš$^{ki}$ šu-ba$_{4}$-ti, 22: 6 gín D. kb **L.** *Iš-dub-il wa Dab*$_{6}$*-ti Ma-rí*$^{ki}$ maškim ga:eš$_{8}$ *Du-du-lu*$^{ki}$; o. XII 3: 1 gín D. kg 1 kù-sal **L.** *Du-si-gú* $^{d}$*Ra-sa-ap ᵓÀ-da-ni*$^{ki}$; o. XV 8: 6 gín D. 2 NI kg 2 *gú-li-lum* **L.** $^{d}$*Ku-ra*; o. XVII 3: ŠÚ+ŠA gín D. kb **L.** *Wa-ru*$_{12}$*-tum Ma-rí*$^{ki}$ e$_{11}$ *áš-ti Na-zu-mu mi-nu* Kiš$^{ki}$; r. I 11: 13 gín D. kb nu$_{11}$-za 1 *ḫa-bù* … 4 gín D. kg nu$_{11}$[-za] 1 ⸢*ar*⸣*-ra-su*[*-sù*] **L.** $^{d}$*ᵓÀ-d*[*a*] *Lu-u*[*b*$^{ki}$] *i*[*n*] *g*[*i*-NI]; r. III 4: 2 gín D. [kb] nu$_{11}$-za 1 ĝír mar-tu L. *Ib-rí-um* $^{d}$*ᵓÀ-da gi*-NI; r. IV 13: 6 gín D. 2 NI kg 2 *gú-li-lum* **L.** $^{d}$*Áš-da-bíl*, 17: 6 gín D. 2 NI kb 2 *gú-li-lum* **L.** $^{d}$*Am-ma-rí-ig*, 22: 1 gín D. kg 1 kù-sal **L.** *Da-bur-da-mu* $^{d}$Utu SA.ZA$_{x}$$^{ki}$; r. VI 14: ŠÚ+ŠA gín D. kb 2 *bu*-DI … 3 gín D. kg nu$_{11}$-za 2 saĝ-*sù* **L.** *Na-tum ma-lik-tum Bur-ma-an*$^{ki}$; r. VII 19: 3 gín D. kg *ᵓa*$_{5}$*-na-gu* 1 ĜIŠ-banšur *wa* 1 kù-sal **L.** en, 27: 2 gín D. 2 NI kg nu$_{11}$-za 1 ĝír mar-tu *wa* 1 kù-sal **L.** ⸢ama⸣-gal en; r. VIII 8: 3 gín D. kg nu$_{11}$-za 1 ĝír mar-tu *wa* 1 kù-sal **L.** *Ib-rí-um* $^{d}$*Ra-sa-ap Du-ne-íb*$^{ki}$; r. X 1: 1 kg 1 kù-sal **L.** en $^{d}$*Ḫa-a-ba-du al*$_{6}$ tu-ra ama-gal-*sù*, 10: 2 gín D. kg 2 kù-sal L. *Da-bur-da-mu* $^{d}$*Iš:šára Zu-ra-mu*$^{ki}$ *wa* $^{d}$*Iš:šára Má*-NE$^{ki}$, 20: 1 ma-na kb **L.** *Daš-na Ma-rí*$^{ki}$ níĝ-"mul" Kiš$^{ki}$ til-til; r. XI 4: 2 ½ gín D. kb nu$_{11}$-za [1 ĝír mar-tu] [*w*]*a* 1 kù-sal **L.** *Ib-rí-um* $^{d}$*A-dar-a-an Da-na-áš*$^{ki}$; r. XIV 4: 2 gín D. kb 1 buru$_{4}$-MU[ŠEN] [ ] **L.** $^{d}$*Áš-da-bíl Ba-šè*$^{ki}$ *Ib-rí-um* šu-mu-tak$_{4}$; **16** o. II 12: 2 gín D. kb 1 á-MUŠEN … 5 NI kg saĝ-*sù* **L.** ama-gal en $^{d}$TU é $^{d}$*Ku-ra*; o. V 17: 7 ma-na TAR kb nu$_{11}$-za 1 an-dùl … 2 ma-na 5 gín D. kg nu$_{11}$-za IGI.DUB-*sù wa* 2 DU-*sù wa* 2 šu-*sù* **L.** $^{d}$BAD *Ga-na-na-im*; r. VI 24: 6 gín D. 2 NI kg 2 *gú-li-lum* **L.** $^{d}$*Áš-da-bíl*; r. VII 1: 6 gín D. 2 NI kb 2 **L.** $^{d}$*Am-rí-ig*, 21: 12 gín D. kb nu$_{11}$-za 1 *ḫa-bù* … 6 gín D. kg nu$_{11}$-za 1 *ar-ra-sù* **L.** $^{d}$*ᵓÀ-da* lú *Lu-ub*$^{ki}$ *in gi*-NI; r. IX 19: 1 gín D. kg 1 íb-lá 1 *si-ti-tum* 1 ĝír-kun **L.** *Ib-rí-um* $^{d}$*Ra-sa-ap Da-ra-um*$^{ki}$; r. X 5: 50 gín D. kg 1 dib **L.** *ba-da-lum Ḫa-ra-an*$^{ki}$, 9 and 13: 5 ma-na kb **L.** *Ar-rúm Ma-rí*$^{ki}$ 1 ma-na kb **L.** maškim-*sù*, 21: 4 gín D. kg nu$_{11}$-za 1 ĝír mar-tu *wa* 1 kù-sal **L.** *Ib-rí-um* $^{d}$*ᵓA*$_{5}$*-da-bal A-ru*$_{12}$*-ga-du*$^{ki}$; r. XIV 26: 6 gín D. an-na šub *si-in zi-ba-du* 1 útul urudu maḫ 15 gín D. kb ZU.PIRIĜ 3 útul urudu maḫ … [2 g]ín D. kg **L.** *Ib-rí-um* $^{d}$BAD-munus *Lu-ba-an*$^{ki}$; r. XVII 2: [x m]a-[n]a kb **L.** ḫúb-ki ba:tuš *a-lu-nu* ĝiš, 9: 1 kb 1 kù-sal **L.** ⸢$^{d}$⸣[*Aš-d*]*ar*(?) en [x-*g*]*a*-[x]$^{ki}$,14: 1[+x] ma-na [ ] **L.** [diĝir-diĝir]-diĝir, 18: [6] gín D. 2 NI kg 2 *gú-li-lum* **L.** $^{d}$*Ku-ra*; **17** o. IV 21: 1 gín D. kg 1 kù-sal 1 buru$_{4}$-MUŠEN [**L.**] dumu-munus en $^{d}$*Ku-ra* í-na-sum *in* ne:saĝ-*sù*; o. VII 1: [ ] **L.** *Ù-rí-rí* maškim ga:eš$_{8}$ *in* kaskal é $^{d}$BAD *Ga-na-na*, 19: [ŠÚ+Š]A gín D. kg 2 *bu*-DI **L.** *Ti-ša-li-im ma-lik-tum Ì-mar*$^{ki}$; o. VIII 10: [x ma-n]a [kb] **L.** EZEN-*il Ma-rí*$^{ki}$; o. XI 7: 6 gín D. 2 NI kg 2 *gú-li-lum* **L.** $^{d}$*Ku-ra*; o. XVII 5: TAR kb **L.** *Wa-ru*$_{12}$*-tum wa I-ku-uḫ Ma-rí*$^{ki}$ ḫi-mu-DU 1 az$^{!}$ maḫ; r. V 20: 1 gín D. kg 1 kù-sal 1 buru$_{4}$-MUŠEN **L.** ama-gal en $^{d}$*Ra-sa-ap ᵓÀ-da-ni*$^{ki}$; r. VI 11: 6 gín D. 2 NI kg 2 *gú-li-lum* **L.** $^{d}$*Ku-ra*; r. XI 5: [ ] k[b] **L.** ⸢*Ne-zi*⸣ *wa Ìr-*[*b*]*a-il Ma-rí*$^{ki}$ maškim ga:eš$_{8}$ Saḫar$^{ki}$; r. XII 19: [x í]b-lá [x *si-t*]*i-*[*tu*]*m* [x ĝí]r-[ku]n … 1 ĝír mar-tu kg **L.** *Ib-rí-um in* ud níĝ-mu-sá *ma-lik-tum*; r. XIII 4: 3 ma-na kg kin$_{5}$-ak 6 íb-lá 6 *si-ti-tum* 6 ĝír-kun **L.** PN$_{1}$–PN$_{5}$ dumu-nita en *wa* PN$_{6}$ šeš ama-gal en, 19: TAR kb kin$_{5}$-ak 1 íb-lá 1 *si-ti-tum* 1 ĝír-kun **L.** *ᵓÀ-daš* dumu-nita *A-du-ba ᵓÀ-ru*$_{12}$*-gú*$^{ki}$, 26: 5 ma-na ŠA.PI kb [10+]7 [*b*]*u*$^{?}$-DI [ŠÚ+Š]A-ŠÚ+ŠA **L.** FPN$_{1}$–FPN$_{8}$ dam en *wa* FPN$_{9}$–FPN$_{10}$ 2 dumu-munus en *wa* ama-gal *Ib-rí-um wa* FPN$_{11}$–FPN$_{14}$ dam-*sù wa Iš-ru*$_{12}$*-ud* nin-ni *Du-si-gú Ki-sa-du*; r. XV 15: 15 gín D. kb nu$_{11}$-za 1 *ḫa-bu* … 6 gín D. kg nu$_{11}$-za *ar-ra-si-sù* **L.** $^{d}$*ᵓÀ-da* lú *Lu-ub*$^{ki}$ *in gi*-NI, 21: 10 gín D. kb **L.** *Daš-na Ma-rí*$^{ki}$; r. XVI 2: [ ] ⸢nu$_{11}$-za⸣ 1 ĝír mar-tu **L.** $^{d}$*Ra-sa-ap*, 6: 10 gín D. kb 2 *bu*-DI **L.** $^{d}$*A-da-ma gú-núm ma-lik-tum* ì-na-sum *in* ud šu-mu-níĝin é diĝir-diĝir-diĝir, 19: 6 gín D. 2 NI kg 2 *gú-li-lum* **L.** $^{d}$*Áš-da-bíl*, 23: 6 gín D. 2 NI kb 2 *gú-li-lum* **L.** $^{d}$*Am-ma-rí-ig*; r. XVIII 11: 1 kg 1 kù-sal **L.** *Da-bur-da-mu al*$_{6}$ *gú-a-ti* $^{d}$*Ba-ra-ma*; r. XXII 13: 1 ma-na 10 kb **L.** diĝir-diĝir-diĝir; **18** o. IV 16: 1 ma-na kb **L.** lú NI-*dim* "ur$_{4}$" *Na-gàr*$^{ki}$; o. V 1: 2 gín D. kb 2 *bu*-DI **L.** ama-gal en $^{d}$*Iš:šára Zi-da-ra*$^{ki}$, 12: 10 gín D. kb **L.** *Ḫu-ra*-NE *Na-gàr*$^{ki}$, 16: 10 gín D. kb **L.** *Da-a-nu Bu-si ᵓÀ-wa-ra* Mar-tu$^{ki}$; o. VI 10: 5 gín D. kb **L.** *Sal-bí-um*$^{ki}$; o. XII 2: 10 gín D. kb **L.** *Ag-ga Na-gàr*$^{ki}$, 9: 6 2 NI gín D. kg 2 *gú-li-lum* **L.** $^{d}$*Ku-ra*, 21: 12 gín D. kg 1 *a-ba-lum* **L.** $^{d}$*ᵓA*$_{5}$*-da-"bal" ᵓÀ-ma-du*$^{ki}$ *Ib-rí-um*; o. XIII 7: 5 gín D. <kb> **L.** *En-na-ì Ḫa-la-bí-du*$^{ki}$; o. XIV 13: 10 gín D. kb **L.** *Du-tum wa Ìr-bí-sá-mu ᵓÀ-du*$^{ki}$; o. XV 7: 10 gín D. kb **L.** *Du-tum wa Da-mi-gu ᵓÀ-du*$^{ki}$, 18: ŠÚ+ŠA gín D. kb **L.** *I-ba*$_{x}$*-ì Zi-rí-gú ᵓÀ-du*$^{ki}$ *wa Ib-rí Na-gàr*$^{ki}$ *wa I-ku-a-ḫu Sag-gàr*$^{ki}$; o. XIX 4: 1 kg 1 kù-sal buru$_{4}$-MUŠEN **L.** ama-gal en $^{d}$*Ra-sa-ap ᵓÀ-da-ni*$^{ki}$; r. II 2: 5 gín D. kb **L.** *A-daš*$^{ki}$, 12: 10 gín D. kb **L.** *Kùn-i-šar ᵓÀ-du*$^{ki}$, 19: 5 gín D. kb **L.** *A-ag Na-gàr*$^{ki}$; r. VI 6: 2 gín D. kb **L.** *I-ti-*$^{d}$*Aš-dar Ir-i-tum*$^{ki}$, 13: 6 gín D. 2 NI kg 2 *gú-li-lum* **L.** $^{d}$*Ku-ra*; r. XI 7: 15 gín D. kb nu$_{11}$-za 1 *ḫa-bu* … 6 gín D. kg nu$_{11}$-za *ar-ra-sù* **L.** $^{d}$*ᵓÀ-da* lú *Lu-ub*$^{ki}$ *in gi*-NI, 16: ŠÚ+ŠA gín D. kb 1 *a-ba-lum* 5 gín D. kb 1 zi-bar **L.** *Gú-sa* dumu-nita en *Na-gàr*$^{ki}$, 22: 2 ma-na an-na **L.** en *A-daš*$^{ki}$, 27: 10 gín D. kb 3 zi-bar **L.** ama-gal en $^{d}$*Iš:šára Má*-NE$^{ki}$ *U*$_{9}$*-gú-a-áš*$^{ki}$ *wa Zu-ra-mu*$^{ki}$; r. XV 11: 4 ma-na TAR kb nu$_{11}$-za 1 an-dùl munus … ⸢1⸣ ma-na 14 gín kg IGI.DUB-*sa* 2 šu 2 DU-*sù* 4 ma-na ŠÚ+ŠA kb 1 an-dùl nita … 2 ma-na 12 kg nu$_{11}$-za IGI.

DUB-*sù wa* íb-lá *si-ti-tum* íb+III-TÚG 6 an-na šub *si-in* ŠA.PI a-gar$_5$-gar$_5$ 1 banšur 1 ĝír mar-tu-*sù* **L.** $^{d}$BAD *Du-du-lu*$^{ki}$; r. XVI 19: 1 ma-na kb **L.** diĝir-diĝir-diĝir, 38: 6 gín kb nu$_{11}$-za 2 ĝír mar-tu … 2 kg 2 kù-sal **L.** ama-gal en $^{d}$*Ra-sa-ap Du-ne-íb*$^{ki}$ *wa* $^{d}$*ʾA$_5$-da-"bal" ʾÀ-ma-du*$^{ki}$ NI.DU; r. XIX 11: ŠÚ+ŠA kb **L.** *Gú-ra-du*$^{ki}$, 14: 10 kb **L.** *ʾÀ-lu*$^{ki}$; **19** o. II 6: 1 gín D. kg 1 kù-sal **L.** en $^{d}$*Ba-tum-ma-du*, 21: TAR kb 2 *bu*-DI … 4 gín D. kg nu$_{11}$-za 2 saĝ-*sù* **L.** *Ti-šè-li-im ma-lik-tum Ì-mar*$^{ki}$; o. III 24: 15 gín D. kb **L.** ḪI-*la-um Na-gàr*$^{ki}$; o. V 18 and 22: 20 ma-na kb **L.** en *Na-gàr*$^{ki}$ 7 ma-na kb **L.** dumu-nita-dumu-nita-*sù*, 25: 5 ma-na kb **L.** en-en lú *áš-ti* en *Na-gàr*$^{ki}$ DU.DU nam-kud é $^{d}$BAD *Du-du-lu*$^{ki}$; o. VI 10: 10 gín D. kb **L.** *Ḫu-ra*-NE *Na-gàr*$^{ki}$ *in Du-du-lu*$^{ki}$ šu-ba$_4$-ti, 17: ŠÚ+ŠA gín D. kb **L.** *ʾÀ-du*$^{ki}$ é $^{d}$BAD *Ga-na-na-im* šu-ba$_4$-ti; o. VIII 12: [3 gín D. kg] *wa* 2 gín D. kb 1 banšur *wa* 1 kù-sal **L.** *Ib-rí-um* $^{d}$*Áš-dar*; o. IX 10: 6 gín D. 2 NI kg 2 *gú-li-lum* **L.** $^{d}$*Ku-ra*, 16: 2 gín D. kg 2 kù-sal **L.** $^{d}$*Ba-tum-ma-du wa* $^{d}$*Da-bí-na-du áš-ti* 2 ĝír mar-tu kg *al$_6$* tu-ra en; o. XI 26: 8 gín D. kg nu$_{11}$-za 2 ĝí[r] mar-tu *wa* 2 kù-sal **L.** $^{d}$*ʾA$_5$-da-"bal" A-ru$_{12}$-ga-du*$^{ki}$ *wa* $^{d}$*ʾA$_5$-da-"bal" ʾÀ-ma-du*$^{ki}$ [ ]-⌜x⌝ [šu-m]u-tak$_4$ *al$_6$* tu-ra-*sù*; o. XIII 22: 1 gín D. kg 1 kù-sal **L.** ama-gal en $^{d}$*Ra-sa-ap ʾÀ-da-ni*$^{ki}$ AMA-*ra*; r. VI 28: 6 gín D. 2 NI kg 2 *gú-li-lum* **L.** $^{d}$*Ku-ra*; r. VII 1: 17 gín D. kb **L.** 3 ĝuruš *ʾÀ-du*$^{ki}$ *in Ḫa-lab$_x$*$^{ki}$ šu-ba$_4$-ti; r. VIII 12: 6 gín D. ½ kg kin$_5$-ak 6 še-šu-še-tag *wa* 1 buru$_4$-MUŠEN **L.** $^{d}$*ʾA$_5$-da-"bal" wa* $^{d}$BAD-munus *A-ru$_{12}$-ga-du*$^{ki}$ ama-gal en šu-mu-tak$_4$, 26: 12 gín D. kb nu$_{11}$-za 1 *ḫa-bù* … 6 gín D. kg nu$_{11}$-za 1 *ar-ra-sù* **L.** $^{d}$*ʾÀ-da* lú *Lu-ub*$^{ki}$ *in gi*-NI; r. IX 3: 6 gín D. 2 NI kg 2 *gú-li-lum* **L.** $^{d}$*Áš-da-bíl*, 13: 12 gín D. kb nu$_{11}$-za 1 *ḫa-bù* … 6 gín D. kg 1 *ar-ra-sù wa* 6 gín D. 2 NI kb 2 *gú-li-lum* **L.** $^{d}$*Am-rí-ig*, 16: 1 ma-na kb **L.** *Ba-ga-ma Na-gàr*$^{ki}$; r. X 2: 10 gín D. kb **L.** *Mar-rúm* EN-NE$^{ki}$, 26: 3 gín D. kg *ʾa$_5$-na-gu* 1 banšur *wa* 1 kù-sal **L.** *Ib-rí-um* $^{d}$BAD *Du-du-lu*$^{ki}$; r. XII 12: 10 gín D. kb **L.** *Ga-áš-ru$_{12}$ Na-gàr*$^{ki}$ DU.DU *mi-nu* Kiš$^{ki}$, 32: 10 gín D. kb **L.** 3 ĝuruš *ʾÀ-du*$^{ki}$; r. XIV 3: ŠA.PI 4 gín D. kg 1 dib … TAR kg 1 íb-lá 1 *si-ti-tum* 1 ĝír-kun **L.** *ba-da-lum Ḫa-ra-an*$^{ki}$; r. XVII 18: 10 gín D. kb 2 *bu*-DI 4 še-šu-še-tag **L.** $^{d}$*Ga-na-na*, 27: 1 ma-na ŠA.PI 2 gín D. kg 1 íb-lá 1 *si-ti-tum* 1 ĝír-kun 1 ĜIŠ-sal **L.** *Ib-rí-um*; r. XVIII 17: 1 ma-na ŠÚ+ŠA kb **L.** diĝir-diĝir-diĝir; **20** o. II 8: TAR kb **L.** *Wa-ru$_{12}$-tum Ma-rí*$^{ki}$; o. IV 14: [6 gín D. 2 NI kg 2 *gú-li-lum*] **L.** $^{d}$*Ku-ra*; o. VI 19: 10 gín D. kb **L.** [*I*-]*ti Ma-rí*$^{ki}$; o. XI 13: 10 gín D. kb 2 *bu*-DI **L.** ama-gal en $^{d}$TU lú *ʾÀ-da-ni*$^{ki}$; o. XIII 16: 1 ma-na kb **L.** *Daš-na Ma-rí*$^{ki}$; r. III 14: 1 gín D. kg 1 kù-sal **L.** *Dar-ib-da-mu* dumu-munus en $^{d}$BAD-munus *si-in Lu-ba-an*$^{ki}$; r. V 4: [6 gín D. 2 NI kg] 2 *gú-li-lum* **L.** $^{d}$*Ku-ra*; r. VII 17: 12 gín D. kg **L.** $^{d}$*ʾÀ-d*[*a*] lú *Lu-ub*$^{ki}$ *in gi*-NI nu$_{11}$-za ab-*sù*; r. IX 1: 6 gín D. [2] NI kg 2 *gú-li-lum* **L.** [ ] *En-na-il* [ ] $^{d}$*Am-ma-rí-ig*, 8: TAR kb **L.** *Wa-ru$_{12}$-tum Ma-rí*$^{ki}$; r. X 7: 10 gín D. kb 2 *bu*-DI 4 *ti-ša-nu* [**L.**] [$^{d}$*Ga-na-na*] *in* ĜIŠ.DUG.DU maḫ, 25: 2 gín D. kg 2 kù-sal **L.** ama-gal en $^{d}$*Iš:šára Zu-ra-mu*$^{ki}$ *wa* $^{d}$*Iš:šára Má*-NE$^{ki}$; r. XIII 17: [2+]3 gín D. kg nu$_{11}$-za [*maš*-]*ar*-[*t*]*um* **L.** [ -]*da*-[ ]; r. XIV 13: 2 gín D. kb ⌜1⌝ kù-sal **L.** [x-]GAL; r. XVI x+1: ŠA.P[I] gín D. kg nu$_{11}$-za 5 *gú-li-lum* a-gar$_5$-ga[r$_5$] TAR-II *w*[*a*] 10[(+x) *gú*]-*l*[*i-lum* ] **L.** diĝir-diĝir-diĝir; **21** o. II 3: 7 gín D. kb *Ḫu*-NE-*du wa Ir$_{11}$-tum-a-ḫu Sag-gar*$^{ki}$; o. V 9: [ ] 1 gín D. kg nu$_{11}$-za 1 saĝ-*sù* 1 ½ gín D. an-na šub *si-in* 17 gín a-gar$_5$ 1 dub-*sù* **L.** *Ib-rí-um* $^{d}$*Sa-nu-ga-ar Má*-NE$^{ki}$; o. VI 20: [20+]30 gín D. kb ZU.PIRIĜ [ ] 2 gín D. kb 1 kù-sal **L.** *Ib-rí-um* $^{d}$*A-dar-a-nu* [*D*]*u-na-*[*á*]*š*$^{ki}$; o. IX 14: 15 gín D. kb nu$_{11}$-za 1 *ḫa-bù* … 6 gín D. kg nu$_{11}$-za 1 *ar-r*[*a*-]*s*[*ù*] **L.** en $^{d}$*Ra-sa-ap* ⌜*ʾÀ-da*⌝-[*ni*$^{ki}$]; o. XI 9: 1 ma-na ŠA.PI gín D. kb **L.** diĝir-diĝir-diĝir, 18: 6 gín D. 2 NI kg 2 *gú-li-lum* **L.** $^{d}$*Ku-ra*; o. XII 2: TAR kb **L.** *Ar-rúm*, 5: ŠÚ+ŠA gín D. kb **L.** *Mi-su-wa-du*, 10: 1 ma-na TAR kb **L.** ábba-ábba *Ma-rí*$^{ki}$; o. XV 10: 15 gín D. kb nu$_{11}$-za 1 *ḫa-bù* … 6 gín D. kg nu$_{11}$-za 1 *ar-ra-sù* **L.** $^{d}$*ʾÀ-da Lu-ub*$^{ki}$ *in gi*:NI; o. XVII 3: 8 gín D. kb **L.** NE-NE *Ma-rí*$^{ki}$, 12: 6 2 NI gín D. kg 2 *gú-li-lum* **L.** $^{d}$*Áš-da-bíl*; r. I 11: 6 gín D. 2 NI kg 2 *gú-li-lum* **L.** $^{d}$*Ku-ra*; r. III 4: [x gín] ⌜D.⌝ kb kin$_5$-ak 2 *bu*-DI 4 še-šu-tag **L.** $^{d}$*Ga-na-na* ĜIŠ.DUG.DU maḫ; r. VIII 6: [x kù:babbar] [**L.**] *Bar*-NE-⌜*um*⌝ *Wa-ru$_{12}$-tum* $^{d}$Utu-*a-ba$_4$ Šu-ì Ag-ga Ma-rí*$^{ki}$ r. XI 15: 15 gín D. kb **L.** *Da-ti*, 18: 8 gín D. kb **L.** *Daš-na*; **22** r. V 14: [1] ma-na kg nu$_{11}$-za 1 [*ḫa-bù*] **L.** $^{d}$BAD *Du-du-lu*$^{ki}$; r. VI 5: 6 gín D. kg nu$_{11}$-za 1 *ar-ra-sù ḫa-bù* **L.** $^{d}$*Ga-mi-iš*, 9: 7 gín D. kg nu$_{11}$-za 1 ĜIŠ-ĝidru **L.** $^{d}$*Ku-ra Ib-rí*-um; r. VII 2: 6 gín D. kg nu$_{11}$-za 1 *ar-ra-sù ḫa-bù* **L.** $^{d}$*ʾA$_5$-da-"bal" ʾÀ-ma-du*$^{ki}$; **23** o. II 5: 6 2 NI gín D. kg 2 *gú-li-lum* **L.** $^{d}$*Ku-ra*; r. II 2: 6 gín D. kg nu$_{11}$-za 1 *ar-ra-šum* 1 *ḫa-bù* **L.** $^{d}$*ʾÀ-da* lú *Lu-ub*$^{ki}$ *gi*-NI, 9: 6 gín D. kg nu$_{11}$-za 1 *ar-ra-šum* 1 *ḫa-bù* **L.** $^{d}$*ʾA$_5$-da-"bal" ʾÀ-ma-du*$^{ki}$ en šu-mu-tak$_4$ *in* ud NI.DU-NI.DU; r. IV 9: 6 gín D. kg nu$_{11}$-za 1 *ar-ra-šum* 1 *ḫa-bù* **L.** $^{d}$*ʾÀ-da* lú *Ḫa-lab$_x$*$^{ki}$ *in* iti *ʾa$_5$-nun*; **24** o. II 6: 4 gín D. kg nu$_{11}$-za 1 ĝír mar-tu *wa* 2 kù-sal **L.** $^{d}$*A-na-ma-du Ar-ḫa-du*$^{ki}$; o. V 6: 16 gín D. kg nu$_{11}$-za IGI.DUB 2 an-dùl *wa* 2 šu-*sù* 2 DU-*sù* **L.** *Ib-rí-um* $^{d}$*Ra-sa-ap wa* $^{d}$*A-da-ma ʾÀ-da-ni*$^{ki}$ *in ma-ʾà-wa-tum*; o. VI 1: 1 gín D. kg nu$_{11}$-za IGI.DUB 1 an-dùl **L.** *Ib-rí-um* $^{d}$Nin-kar, 7: 6 gín D. kg nu$_{11}$-za 1 *ar-ra-sù* 1 *ḫa-bù* **L.** en $^{d}$*ʾA$_5$-da-"bal" A-ru$_{12}$-ga-du*$^{ki}$; o. VII 2: 1 gín D. kg 1 kù-sal **L.** *Ib-rí-um* $^{d}$*Ba-ra-ma*, 8: 6 gín D. 2 NI kg 2 *gú-li-lum* **L.** $^{d}$*Áš-da-bíl*.

níĝ-ba-níĝ-ba **15** r. XVII 1: 1 ma-na ŠÚ+ŠA 3 gín D. kb **L.** diĝir-diĝir-diĝir.

níĝ-bànda (a vessel) **2** o. III 11: 2 ma-na kb 1 ĜIŠ-šú 1 **L.**; **3** r. VII 15: 8 gín D. kb *zi-ba-tum* 4 ĜIŠ-šú 1 **L.** l[ú 2 šu]; **4** o. II 13: 5 gín D. kb 1 **L.**; o. X 10: 4 ma-na TAR kb 1 ĜIŠ-šú 1 **L.**; **5** r. XV 15: TAR 5 gín D. kb *ni-zi-mu* 3 ĜIŠ-šú 3 **L.**; **6** r. XIII 16: 3 ma-na ŠÚ+ŠA kb 1 ĜIŠ-šú 1 **L.**; **10** o. XII 9: 3 gín D. kb [ZU.]PIRIĜ ĜIŠ-šú **L.** šu-šu; **13** r. X 16: 2 ma-na kb 1 ĜIŠ-šú 1 **L.** lú 2 šu; **15** o. XVI 12: 2 gín kb *zi-ba-du* 1 ĜIŠ-šú 1 **L.** kb lú kaskal *Ib-rí-um*; **16** o. I 20: 10 ma-na TAR kb 1 ĜIŠ-šú 1 **L.** 10 kb kg; **18** o. XVII 20: 7 gín D. kb *zi-ba-du* 1 ĜIŠ-šú 2 **L.** kaskal-kaskal *Ib-rí-um*; r. XII 5: 16 gín D. kb 4 **L.** 2 dumu-nita 2 dumu-munus en; **21** o. XIV 20: 5 ma-na kb kin$_5$-ak 1 ĜIŠ-šú 1 **L.** lú 2 šu; r. I 15: 15 ma-na kb kin$_5$-ak 3 ĜIŠ-šú 3 **L.** lú diri lú šu-šu kas$_4$-kas$_4$.

níĝ-du$_8$ «exchange value; ransom» **3** r. VII 7: 12 gín D. kb **L.** 1 lú úr *Ab-ru$_{12}$-ti-um*$^{ki}$ *áš-ti Ir-i-tum*$^{ki}$; **4**

o. V 2: 6 gín D. kb ì-na-sum *Zi-rí-gú* **L.** dumu-nita *Lá-da-il Ma-rí*$^{ki}$; **6** o. XVI 19: 3 gín D. kb **L.** dumu-nita *Ù-du-bù*$^{ki}$ *áš-ti Kak-mi-um*$^{ki}$; **10** o. XV 11: 2 gín D. kb **L.** *Ù-ba-nu* KAR kg en *Ma-nu-wa-ad*$^{ki}$; **11** o. VIII 8: 15 gín D. kb **L.** šeš *Ti-la-rí-im*$^{ki}$ *ʾÀ-bí-gú*$^{ki}$ *áš-da Tar*$_5$*-ḫa-um*$^{ki}$; r. III 19: 5 gín D. kb **L.** 15 gín D. kb **L.** 2 dumu-nita *Bur-ḫa-áš*; **12** r. VI 2: 5 gín D. kb daḫ **L.** 1 ĝuruš *Lu-wa-šum*$^{ki}$ *áš-ti Ba-na-i-um*$^{ki}$, 8: 3 gín D. kb **L.** 1 dumu-nita *Ti-in*$^{ki}$ lú *A-da-su*$^{ki}$; r. VII 2 and 9: ŠÚ+ŠA gín D. kb **L.** *Dam-da-il Ib-su*$^{ki}$ *in* Kiš$^{ki}$ lú *Na-zu-mu* **L.**; **15** o. II 10: 15 gín D. kb **L.** 1 dumu-nita *A-ba-ti-lum*$^{ki}$ maškim *Za-ba-rúm áš-ti Ìr-ku*$^{ki}$; **16** r. II 13: ŠÚ+ŠA gín D. kb **L.** 3 *na-se*$_{11}$ *Ib-la*$^{ki}$ *áš-ti Ir-i-tum*$^{ki}$; **18** r. IV 12: 10 gín D. kb **L.** 1 dumu-nita *Ku-a-*NE lú NE-*da-mu* SA.ZA$_x^{ki}$ *áš-ti Ìr-ku*$^{ki}$; **21** o. V 19: {13 gín D. kb} **L.** ˹x-x˺; o. XII 19: ŠÚ+ŠA gín D. kb **L.** *I-šar Ḫa-lab*$_x^{ki}$ *áš-du Mi-su-wa-du Ma-rí*$^{ki}$.

níĝ-gaba see níĝ-lá-gaba.

níĝ-kas$_4$ «military expedition» **3** o. VIII 4: [ ] **L.** nu-du$_{11}$-nu-du$_{11}$ šu-ba$_4$-ti *si-in Ib-al*$_6^{ki}$; **5** o. X 9: (silver) *Na-*NE *wa* ˹Šubur˺ *Na-gàr*$^{ki}$ *in* **L.** *A-da-[bí-]˹ig˺*$^{ki}$ šu-ba$_4$-ti; r. V 6: (silver) níĝ-ba *Daš-na Ma-rí*$^{ki}$ *in* **L.** *Gú-rá-ma-an*$^{ki}$ šu-ba$_4$-ti; **7** o. V 8: (38 daggers) lú ì-na-sum SA.ZA$_x^{ki}$ *in Du-du-lu*$^{ki}$ *in* **L.** *Ma-rí*$^{ki}$; o. IX 16: 1 BAR.AN *Ba-na-i-um*$^{ki}$ *in* **L.** *Ma-rí*$^{ki}$; **9** o. XV 13: 2 ĝír mar-tu ti kg *Ib-rí-um* uru-bar *in* **L.** lú sikil; **11** r. I 8: (80 belts, 80 daggers, 21 helmets) *in* ud è **L.** *Gú-da-da-núm*$^{ki}$; **12** o. IX 12: 1 *li-im* ĜIŠ-gu-kak-gíd zabar … 1 ĝír mar-tu kg *Ib-rí-um in* ud è *si-in* **L.** *Ma-nu-wa-ad*$^{ki}$; **13** r. VI 16: 1 ĝír mar-tu kg *Na-zu-mu in* ud **L.** *si-in* Kiš$^{ki}$; **14** o. IV 11: 2 *mi-at* ĝír mar-tu … ì-na-sum ĝuruš-ĝuruš SA.ZA$_x^{ki}$ *in* **L.** *Kak-mi-um*$^{ki}$; **17** o. XVI 6: 1 ĝír mar-tu kg *Ib-rí-um in* ud è **L.** al-kur$_6$ še *Kak-mi-um*$^{ki}$; o. XX 5: (523 daggers) in-na-sum SA.ZA$_x^{ki}$ *in* ud **L.** *A-ḫ[a-za-]ni-ig*˹$^{ki}$˺; **21** o. II 9: (silver) níĝ-ba *Ḫu-*NE*-du wa Ir*$_{11}$*-tum-a-ḫu Sag-gar*$^{ki}$ kaskal **L.** *Du-du-lu*$^{ki}$; o. XIII 6: (62 garments) lú *Zú-ba-an* níĝ-sa$_{10}$ *in* **L.** *Ma-rí*$^{ki}$; **23** r. I 4: (19 bracelets) ĝuruš-ĝuruš SA.ZA$_x^{ki}$ *in* ud è **L.** *Gú-da-da-núm*$^{ki}$; r. III 12: (10 daggers) guruš-guruš *in* ud è **L.** *Gú-da-da-núm*$^{ki}$.

níĝ-kaskal «travel provisions» **1** o. V 15: [x gín D. kb] **L.** *Ìr-kab-ar* DU.DU *si-in Ar-mi*$^{ki}$; o. VI 15: ŠÚ+ŠA g[ín D.] kb **L.** *Na-*N[E] *Na-gà[r*$^{ki}$] DU.DU *si-in Ar-mi*$^{ki}$; o. VII 5: 6 gín D. kb **L.** *Ne-zi-ma-ì* ˹*Puzur*$_4$˺*-ra-a-gú* DU.DU *si-in Na-gàr*$^{ki}$; (e) r. III' 8: 3 gín D. kb **L.** *I-ga-iš-lu* DU.DU *si-in Ma-rí*$^{ki}$; **4** o. II 18: 3 gín D. kb **L.** *Ni-zi-ma-il* DU.DU *Na-gàr*$^{ki}$; o. VIII 17: 3 gín D. kb **L.** *Ìr-a[m*$_6$*-]ma-lik* DU.DU *Na-gàr*$^{ki}$; o. XIII 12: ŠÚ+ŠA gín D. kb **L.** *ʾÀ-daš ma-za-lum* DU.DU *Ar-mi*$^{ki}$; o. XIV 6: 5 gín D. kb **L.** *Du-nu*$^{ki}$, 9: 15 gín D. kb **L.** *Ga-zú-wa-ti-um*$^{ki}$, 12: 4 gín D. kb **L.** maškim *Ḫa-ra-il*, 16: 4 gín D. kb **L.** *A-zú*$^{ki}$, 19: 3 gín D. kb **L.** *Ni-zi-ma-il* DU.DU *Na-gàr*$^{ki}$; o. XV 10: 6 gín D. kb **L.** *Za-ba-ra* maškim *Ḫa-ra-il*; r. VIII 6: 3 gín D. kb **L.** *Ni-zi-ma-il* DU.DU *Na-gàr*$^{ki}$; r. XII 16: ŠÚ+ŠA gín D. kb [**L.**] *A-ʾà-*˹*lu*˺ *wa Ù-da-a-ḫa Ma-rí*$^{ki}$ LÚ×KÁR DU.DU; **6** o. IV 18: 2 gín D. kb **L.** *Ìr-am*$_6$*-ma-lik* DU.DU *Na-gàr*$^{ki}$; o. V 9: 15 gín D. kb **L.** *ʾÀ-daš* DU.DU *si-in Ar-mi*$^{ki}$; o. VIII 17: 5 gín D. kb **L.** *A-ir-ra wa A-zú-bù-lu* [*Ù-t*]*i-*[*g*]*ú*$^{ki}$ [*w*]*a A-zú* DU.DU *Ar-mi*$^{ki}$; o. XI 19: 5 gín D. kb **L.** *Ni-zi-ma-il* DU.DU *Ma-rí*$^{ki}$; o. XIII 4: 10 gín D. kb **L.** *A-ʾà-lu wa Ù-da-aḫ* LÚ×KÁR DU.DU *Ma-rí*$^{ki}$; o. XV 1: 5 gín D. kb **L.** *A-ir-ra wa A-zú-bù-lu* DU.DU *Ar-mi*$^{ki}$; o. XVI 6: 4 gín D. kb **L.** *Ni-zi-ma-il wa I-ib-ma-lik* DU.DU *Ma-rí*$^{ki}$; r. I 12: 5 gín D. kb **L.** *Ìr-am*$_6$*-ma-lik wa I-ib-ma-lik* DU.DU *Ma-rí*$^{ki}$; r. II 2: 5 gín D. kb **L.** *Za-gàr A-dar-ki-zú*$^{ki}$ DU.DU *Ar-mi*$^{ki}$; r. IV 8: 10 gín D. kb **L.** *Ḫar-zàr-du*$^{ki}$ DU.DU *Ar-mi*$^{ki}$, 23: 2 gín D. kb **L.** *En-na-ì* lú kas$_4$-kas$_4$ DU.DU *Ma-rí*$^{ki}$; **7** o. XVII 15: 10 gín D. kb **L.** ˹*Nap*˺*-ḫ*[*a-il*] DU.DU *si-in Ma-rí*$^{ki}$; r. XI 25: 5 gín D. kb **L.** *Ur-sá-um*$^{ki}$; **9** o. II 5: 8 gín D. kb **L.** *Gi-li-ti-um*$^{ki}$ DU.DU [*A*]*r-mi*$^{ki}$, 10: [x gí]n [D. kb **L.** *A-ir-ra*? *wa A-zú-bù-lu*?] DU.DU *Ar-mi*$^{ki}$; o. XII 7: 5 gín D. kb **L.** *Ìr-am*$_6$*-ma-lik wa En-na-*BAD DU.DU [*M*]*a-rí*$^{ki}$; **10** o. I 18: 10 gín D. kb **L.** *A-dar-*KA*-mu*$^{ki}$; o. XIV 16: 14 gín D. kb **L.** *En-na-*BAD *Zú-ti*$^{ki}$ maškim *Du-bí* DU.DU *Ar-mi*$^{ki}$; o. XV 18: 5 gín D. kb **L.** *Íl-ra-*BAD maškim NI-*ba-rúm* DU.DU *si-in Ar-mi*$^{ki}$; **11** r. III 16: TAR kb **L.** *Kab-lu*$_5$*-ul*$^{ki}$; r. VIII 2: [x] gín D. kb **L.** *Ḫa-ra-ì*, 5: 5 gín D. kb **L.** *Kab-lu*$_5$*-ul*$^{ki}$ DU.DU *Ar-mi*$^{ki}$; **14** r. X 20: 5 gín D. kb **L.** [*Ì*]*r-am*$_6$*-*[*m*]*a-lik* [ ]˹x˺ [DU.DU] *si-in* Kiš$^{ki}$, 26: 1 ma-na kb **L.** ĝuruš-ĝuruš; **15** r. X 27: 5 gín D. kb **L.** *En-na-ì* DU.DU Kiš$^{ki}$; **17** o. VI 2: 5 gín D. kb **L.** *En-na-il* [DU.DU] *si-in* Kiš$^{ki}$; o. IX 3: [ ] *Za-rí-ba* 2 gín D. kb **L.**-*sù*; r. IX 2: (daggers) ugula *Ib-al*$_6^{ki}$ DU.DU *Du-gú-ra-su*$^{ki}$ šu-mu-tak$_4$ ŠÚ+ŠA 5 gín D. kb **L.**-*sù*; **18** o. XIV 19: 10 gín D. kb **L.** *A-*LUM$^{ki}$ maškim; r. X 19: TAR kb **L.** *Gi-ba-rí-a Kab-lu*$_5$*-ul*$^{ki}$ DU.DU *si-in Ir-bí-ì-lum*$^{ki}$; **19** o. VIII 16: ŠÚ+ŠA gín D. kb **L.** NE-*iš-da-ar Kab-lu*$_5$*-ul*$^{ki}$ DU.DU *si-in Ar-mi*$^{ki}$; **21** r. X 10: [ ] ŠÚ+ŠA g[ín] D. kb **L.** *Bù-gal-lu Ba-zi-mu*$^{ki}$ DU.DU *si-in Ar-mi*$^{ki}$.

níĝ-lá-DU «feet-band» **7** r. XII 7.

níĝ-lá-gaba «breast-band» **2** r. V 9; r. XIII 8; **3** r. VII 1; **9** o. III 3; **12** o. I 5; r. VI 18; **15** r. III 14; **16** o. IV 12; o. XIII 15; **17** r. XI 14; **25** o. I 4; r. IX 5: šu-níĝin … 5 níĝ-lá-saĝ **L.**

níĝ-lá-saĝ «headband» **2** r. XII 14; **6** r. IX 2; r. XII 18; **7** r. VI 14; **11** o. IX 11; **12** r. VI 18; **15** o. XII 13; **17** r. XI 14; **25** o. IV 6; o. VIII 2: 1 **L.** babbar; r. IX 5: šu-níĝin … 5 **L.** níĝ-lá-gaba.

níĝ-"mul" «news» **4** r. X 12: **L.** àga-"kár"(ŠÈ) *Ma-rí*$^{ki}$ *wa Wa-ru*$_{12}$*-tum*; **6** o. XII 19: **L.** *ʾÀ-du*$^{ki}$ àga-"kár"(ŠÈ); r. VI 5: **L.** *Na-gàr*$^{ki}$ àga-"kár"(ŠÈ); **7** r. VIII 22: **L.** *Ar-ti-na-an*$^{ki}$ til; r. XIII 4: **L.** Kiš$^{ki}$ til; **10** o. XVI 8: **L.** *Na-gàr*$^{ki}$ [t]il; **11** o. VII 8: **L.** *Na-gàr*$^{ki}$ til; **12** o. III 2: **L.** *Ag-sa-gú*$^{ki}$ šu-ba$_4$-ti; o. VII 10: **L.** *Ag-sa-gú*$^{ki}$ šu-ba$_4$-ti; o. IX 18: **L.** *Ag-sa-gú*$^{ki}$ šu-ba$_4$-ti; **14** r. V 14: **L.** Kiš$^{ki}$ til-til; **15** o. III 3: **L.** Kiš$^{ki}$ til; o. VII 16: **L.** *in* uru$^{ki}$-uru$^{ki}$ Kiš$^{ki}$ šu-ba$_4$-ti; r. X 23: **L.** Kiš$^{ki}$ til-til; **20** o. VII 1: **L.** *Du-li*$^{ki}$ àga-"kár"(ŠÈ); o. XIII 19: **L.** *Du-li*$^{ki}$ šu-ba$_4$-ti; **25** r. III 10: **L.** Bàd$^{ki}$ šu-ba$_4$-˹ti˺.

níĝ-mu-sá «wedding (by payment of the bride-price)» **3** r. XI 20: *in* ud **L.** dumu-munus *Ib-rí-um*; **5** o. VI 9: *in* ud **L.** dumu-munus *Ib-rí-um Gi-ti-*NE$^{ki}$; **9** r. VII 2: *in* ud **L.** ˹*Za*˺*-ne-ḫi-Ma-*[*r*]*í*$^{ki}$ é-gi *Ib-ʾà-ra ʾÀ-šu*$^{ki}$; **10** o. VIII 17: *in* ud **L.**; **17** r. XII 22: *in* ud **L.** *ma-lik-tum*

níĝ-NE **18** r. XIV 17: 11 ½ kb níĝ-sa$_{10}$ 75 ma-na **L.**; **21** r. II 11: 1 ma-na 8 gín D. kb níĝ-sa$_{10}$ 1 *mi-at* 50 ĜIŠ-ti-ḪAR *wa* **L.**
(see *LLE*,I no. 34: NÍĜ.NE)

níĝ-PA **18** r. IV 9: 3 gín D. kg *ni-zi-mu* nu$_{11}$-za 1 **L.** en; **20** o. XI 3: [1+]4 gín D. kg nu$_{11}$-za 1 **L.** *Ib-rí-um*.

níĝ-sa$_{10}$ «purchase price, value» **1** o. V 4: 10 gín D. kg **L.** 1 BAR.AN, 12: 2 ma-na 10 gín D. kb **L.** 11 dam; o. VI 2: 50 gín D. <kb> **L.** ĝeštin, 11: 7 gín D. kb **L.** 1 ĝír mar-tu *ba-du-u*$_4$ kbg; o. XIII 2': [x gín D.] kb **L.** [2 ĝí]r [mar-]tu kg; (b) r. x+I 3': 50 gín D. kb **L.** 20 ⸢ĝír⸣; r. II' 4': 10 lá-1 ma-na ŠÚ+ŠA 2 kb **L.** ⸢x-x⸣; (e) r. IV' 6: 2 ma-na kb **L.** 5 IGI.NITA u$_5$; **2** o. II 11: 50 gín D. kb **L.** 1 ĝír mar-tu kg; o. V 15: 50 gín D. kb **L.** 1 ĝír mar-tu kg; o. VII 3: 1 ma-na 8 gín D. kb **L.** 6 *ʾà-da-um*-TÚG 6 aktum-TÚG 3 gada-TÚG 1 íb+III-TÚG sa$_6$ gùn, 8: ŠÚ+ŠA 7 gín D. kb **L.** *gàr-sù*, 15: 4 ma-na 11 gín D. kb **L.** 6 zara$_6$-TÚG 11 aktum-TÚG 1 íb+III-TÚG babbar gíd 5 *ʾà-da-um*-TÚG-I 31 siki na$_4$ *Ma-rí*$^{ki}$; o. VIII 10: 1 ma-na kb **L.** 1 BAR.AN, 13: 4 ma-na ŠÚ+ŠA 6 gín D. kb **L.** 42 aktum-TÚG 15 sal-TÚG 5 *ʾà-da-um*-TÚG-I 10 íb+III-TÚG sa$_6$ gùn 11 íb+III-TÚG gùn; o. IX 4: 1 ma-na kb **L.** 1 ĝír mar-tu kg; o. X 6: 11 ma-na TAR 8 gín D. kb **L.** 4 *mi-at* 10 siki na$_4$ *Ma-rí*$^{ki}$ 10 lá-2 aktum-TÚG 24 *ʾà-da-um*-TÚG-I 32 íb+III-TÚG babbar, 13: ŠA.PI 5 gín D. kb **L.** 13 íb+III-TÚG sa$_6$ gùn, 15: TAR kb **L.** ĜIŠ-sal; r. V 2: [x ma-na] 5 gín D. kb **L.** 35 gud-gud, 4: 10 ma-na 7 gín D. kb **L.** 10 lá-2 zara$_6$-TÚG 44 aktum-TÚG 2 íb+III-TÚG babbar gíd 1 túg-NI.NI ḫul 2 níĝ-<lá>-gaba 75 íb+III-TÚG sa$_6$ gùn 7 íb+III-TÚG babbar, 13: 55 gín D. kb **L.** raš-SAR Kur$^{ki}$, 15: 2 ma-na 7 gín D. kb **L.** [...]; r. VI 3: [x gín D.] kb **L.** ĜIŠ-ád; r. VII 3: 1 ma[-na] TAR kb **L.** 2 gud, 12: 3 ma-na ŠÚ+ŠA 7 gín D. kb **L.** 6 gud-gud; r. IX 3: 11 ma-na TAR 3 gín D. kb **L.** 95 aktum-TÚG 20 lá-2 túg-NI.NI ḫul 4 zara$_6$-TÚG 10 lá-2 *ʾà-da-um*-TÚG-I 11 sal-TÚG 2 íb+III-TÚG babbar gíd 16 íb+III-TÚG sa$_6$ gùn 5 íb+III-TÚG babbar, 11: 8 gín D. kb **L.** ú-ḫáb, 14: 4 ma-na kb **L.** ĜIŠ-ti-ḪAR; r. X 1: 6 ma-na 6 gín D. kb **L.** 11 gud, 3: 55 gín D. kb **L.** 1 BAR.NITA, 5: 2 ma-na 2 kb **L.** 4 IGI.NITA u$_5$, 9: ŠA.PI gín D. kb **L.** 1 ĝír mar-tu kg, 14: TAR 5 gín D. kb **L.** 1 ĝír mar-tu kg, 18: ŠA.PI kb **L.** 1 ĝír mar-tu kg; r. XI 2: 1 ma-na ŠÚ+ŠA 5 gín D. kb **L.** 2 ĝír mar-tu ti kg 1 ĝír mar-tu *ba-du-u*$_9$ kg 3 *gú-li-lum* a-gar$_5$-gar$_5$ kg, 10: 10 gín D. kb **L.** 1 ĝír mar-tu *ba-du-u*$_9$ kg; r. XII 8: 11 ma-na 11 gín D. kb **L.** 76 aktum-TÚG 3 *gu-zi-tum*-TÚG 20 lá-1 *ʾà-da-um*-TÚG-I 7 túg-NI.NI ḫul 31 gada-TÚG íb+III-TÚG gíd 4 níĝ-lá-saĝ 30 íb+III-TÚG sa$_6$ gùn 30 íb+III-TÚG gùn 20 siki na$_4$ sa$_6$, 19: 18 gín D. kb **L.** 6 udu-nita sa$_6$; r. XIII 3: 15 ma-na 5 gín D. kb **L.** 10 lá-1 zara$_6$-TÚG 90 aktum-TÚG 52 aktum-TÚG-II 14 túg-NI.NI ḫul 7 sal-TÚG 10 lá-2 níĝ-<lá>gaba 1 *mi-at* 50 siki na$_4$ sa$_6$; r. XVI 6: 1 ma-na kb **L.** 1 ĝír mar-tu *ra-ʾà-tum* kg, 10: 3 ma-na TAR 8 gín D. kb **L.** 20 lá-2 *ʾa-da-um*-TÚG-I 34 aktum-TÚG; r. XVII 1: **L.** 1 ĝír mar-tu kg, 4: 1 ma-na ŠA.PI ½ gín D. kb **L.** ĜIŠ-ti-ḪAR, 12: ⸢2⸣? kb **L.** 1 gàr-*sù*; **3** o. I 2: ⸢5⸣ ma-na kb **L.** še, 6: 5 ma-na kb **L.** še, 10: 5 ma-na kb **L.** še, 13: 5 ma-na kb **L.** še, 16: 7 ma-na kb **L.** še; o. II 2: 5 ma-na kb **L.** še, 5: 5 ma-na kb **L.** še, 8: 5 ma-na kb **L.** še; o. V 2: ŠÚ+ŠA gín D. kb **L.** 40[+x] diri ĝír mar-tu, 10: 7 ma-na ŠA.PI gín D. kb **L.** 2 *ʾà-da-um*-TÚG-II 1 *ʾà-da-um*-TÚG-I 14 aktum-TÚG 8 gada-TÚG 1 íb+III-TÚG gíd babbar 1 *mi-at* 20 íb+III-TÚG sa$_6$ gùn 5 íb+III-TÚG gùn; o. VI 1: 10 ma-na 6 gín D. kb **L.** 10 lá-1 *gu-zi-tum*-TÚG 1 *ʾà-da-um*-TÚG-I 4 gada-TÚG 1 *mi-at* íb+III-TÚG sa$_6$ gùn 40 íb+III-TÚG gùn, 6: 13 gín D. kb **L.** 1 *mi-at* 34 níĝ-saĝšu, 8: 3 gín D. kb **L.** raš-SAR Kur$^{ki}$, 10: 1 ma-na TAR kb **L.** 1 BAR.AN, 14: TAR kb **L.** 1 IGI.NITA u$_5$; o. VII 5: 2 ma-na kb **L.** ĜIŠ-ti-ḪAR; o. VIII 19: ŠA.PI 6 gín D. kb **L.** 30 ĝír mar-tu zú-ak; o. IX 8: ŠÚ+ŠA [+x] gín D. kb **L.** 1 ĝír mar-tu ti kg, 14: 8 gín D. kb **L.** 1 ĝír mar-tu *ba-du-u*$_4$ kbg; o. X 2': ša-p[i] 1 gín D. kb **L.** ĜIŠ-ti-ḪAR; r. II 2: 1 ma-na ŠA.PI gín D. kb **L.** ĜIŠ-ti-ḪAR, 7: 5 ma-na kb **L.** 10 gud; r. III 10: 17 gín D. kb **L.** 1 ĝír mar-tu zú ⸢A.LAGAB×ḪAL⸣; r. VI 18: 3 ma-na ŠA.PI 2 gín D. kb **L.** 16 *ʾà-da-um*-TÚG-I 6 aktum-TÚG 1 níĝ-lá-gaba 70 íb+III-TÚG gùn; r. VII 18: 1 ma-na TAR 1 gín D. kb **L.** 20 *gàr-su*; r. VIII 13: 5 ma-na kb **L.** (blank) a-gar$_5$-gar$_5$, 16: 16 gín D. kb **L.** 2 na$_4$; r. IX 8: 2 ma-na ŠA.PI 4 gín D. kb **L.** 15 *ʾà-da-um*-TÚG-I 1 *mi-at* 4 íb+III-TÚG gùn, 11: 1 m[a-]na 10 [gín D. kb] **L.** 1 BAR.AN, 13: ŠÚ+ŠA gín D. kb **L.** ĜIŠ-ti-ḪAR; r. X 3: 4 ma-na kb **L.** 1 BAR.AN; r. XII 1: ŠA.PI gín D. kb **L.** 40 siki na$_4$ *áš-da Ma-rí*$^{ki}$; r. XIII 7: 3 ma-na 55 gín D. kb **L.** 27 íb+III-TÚG sa$_6$ gùn 1 *mi-at* 67 íb+III-TÚG gùn, 10: 4 ma-na ŠÚ+ŠA gín kb **L.** ĜIŠ-ti-ḪAR; r. XIV 1: 50 gín D. kb **L.** 2 ĝír mar-tu ti kg, 7: 4 ma-na kb **L.** 71 *ʾà-da-um*-TÚG-I 1 íb+III-TÚG gíd babbar 3 gada-TÚG; **4** o. II 8: TAR kb **L.** 1 *mi-at* 20 ḪU.UD-ḪU.UD; o. IV 2: 2 ma-na kb **L.** ĝeštin-ĝeštin; o. V 11: TAR kb **L.** [1 *mi-a*]*t* 30 ḪU.UD-ḪU.UD; o. VII 2: 50 gín D. kb **L.** ĝeštin-ĝeštin, 13: ŠÚ+ŠA 7 gín D. kb **L.** 1 ĝír mar-tu ti kg; o. VIII 5: 1 ma-na kb **L.** 1 ĝír mar-tu kg, 8: 1 ma-na kb **L.** 1 ĝír mar-tu kg; o. IX 7: 17 gín D. kb **L.** 1 na$_4$ maḫ; o. XII 10: TAR kg **L.** 30 lá-2 ĜIŠ-ma-dul$_{10}$, 15: 1 ½ gín D. kb **L.** 1 na na$_4$; r. II 8: 4 ma-na kb **L.** ĝeštin-ĝeštin, 15: 8 gín D. kb **L.** 1 na$_4$, 18: 4 gín D. kb **L.** [1 n]a$_4$; r. III 2: 3 gín D. kb **L.** 1 na$_4$(UD.NI), 5: 3 gín D. kb **L.** 1 na$_4$(UD.NI); r. V 3: 1 ma-na kb **L.** ĝeštin-ĝeštin, 7: 1 ma-na TAR kb **L.** 1 BAR.AN, 13: 1 ma-na kb **L.** 2 ĜIŠ-banšur kg; r. VI 1: 1 ma-na ŠÚ+ŠA 5 gín D. kb **L.** 1 BAR.AN, 4: TAR kb **L.** 1 ĝír mar-tu ti kg, 8: TAR kb **L.** [1 ĝír mar-tu] ⸢ti⸣ kg, 13: ŠÚ+ŠA gín D. kb **L.** 1 ĝír [m]ar-tu zú kg; r. VII 2: TAR kb **L.** 1 ĝír mar-tu ti kg, 6: TAR kb **L.** 1 ĝír mar-tu ti kg, 13: 2 ma-na [x g]ín D. [kb] **L.** 2 ĜI[Š-x]; r. XI 18: 14 gín D. kb **L.** raš-SAR Kur$^{ki}$; r. XV 10: [x m]a-na kb **L.** [1?] BAR.AN; **5** o. I 1: 14 ma-na ŠÚ+ŠA 7 gín D. kb **L.** 27 *ʾà-da-um*-TÚG-I 34 gada-TÚG 1 aktum-TÚG 1 túg-NI.NI 1 íb-lá-saĝ 1 gu-dùl-TÚG [x íb+III-TÚG] sa$_6$ gùn 2 *mi-at* 10 íb+III-TÚG gùn 4 ĝír mar-tu zú-ak 4 ĝír zú-ak 3 *mi-at* 54 na$_4$ siki sa$_6$; o. II 1: 3 ma-na ŠÚ+ŠA 1 gín D. kb **L.** ĜIŠ-ti-ḪAR ĜIŠ-ád, 8: 8 gín D. kb **L.** 1 ĝír mar-⸢tu⸣ [kb(?)]; o. III 5: 1 ma-na kb **L.** 1 ĝír mar-tu kg, 17: 10 gín D. kb **L.** ĜIŠ-má-dul$_{10}$, 19: 10 gín D. kb **L.** ĜIŠ-ti-ḪAR; o. V 7: 10 gín D. kb **L.** ĝeštin; o. VI 17: 1 ma-na kb **L.** 1 ĝír mar-tu kg; o. VII 3: 1 ma-na ŠA.PI gín D. kb **L.** 2 *gú-li-lum* a-gar$_5$-gar$_5$ kg, 8: TAR kb **L.** 1 gud, 14, 16: ŠÚ+ŠA 5 gín D. kb **L.** 1 gud; o. VIII 5: 1 ma-na

13 gín D. kb **L.** 2 gud, 14: 14 ma-na 13 gín D. kb **L.** 7 *ʾà-da-um* 1 *mi-at* 33 íb+III-TÚG sa$_6$ gùn 4 *mi-at* 74 íb+III-TÚG gùn 17 ĝír mar-tu zú-ak 1 ĝír zú-ak; o. IX 5: 4 ma-na kb **L.** ĜIŠ-ti-ḪAR; o IX 17: 6 gín D. kb **L.** ĝeštin; o. XI 9: ŠÚ+ŠA gín D. kb **L.** 1 ĝír mar-tu ti kg; o. XIII 10: TAR kb **L.** ĝeštin; o. XIV 6: [x kb **L.** x *ʾà-da-um*-TÚG-I] 2 gada-TÚG 4 aktum-TÚG 40 lá-2 íb+III-TÚG sa$_6$ gùn 3 *mi-at* 70 íb+III-TÚG gùn, 11: 10 gín D. kb **L.** ú-ḫáb, 12: 13 gín D. kb **L.** 4 ĝír mar-tu kb; o. XV 9: [x kb] **L.** 1 BAR.AN, 13: 3 ma-na kb **L.** ĜIŠ-ti-ḪAR; o. XVI 9: [ ] [**L.**] 2 [*gú-*]*li-lum*; r. II 10: ŠÚ+ŠA gín D. kb **L.** raš-SAR Kur$^{ki}$, 12: 1 ma-na TAR 6 gín D. kb **L.** 3 gud, 20: ŠÚ+ŠA gín D. kb **L.** 85[+1] íb+II-TÚG babbar; r. III 5: 17 gín D. kb **L.** 1 ĝír mar-tu kg zú LAGAB×A, 9: ŠÚ+ŠA gín D. kb **L.** 7 íb+II-TÚG sa$_6$ gùn 7 íb+II-TÚG gùn; r. VI 16: 4 ma-na kb **L.** še; r. VIII 16: 3 gín D. kb **L.** 1 ĜIŠ-banšur; r. IX 4: 4 ma-na 52 gín D. kb **L.** 3 *ʾà-da-um*-TÚG-I 22 íb+II-TÚG sa$_6$ gùn 2 *mi-at* 31 íb+II-TÚG gùn, 9: 1 ma-na kb **L.** ĜIŠ-ti-ḪAR; r. XI 14: 14 gín D. kb **L.** 1 *gu-zi-tum*-TÚG 4 gada-TÚG, 17: 14 ma-na kb **L.** 61 gud; r. XII 1: 1 ma-na ŠA.PI 8 gín D. kb **L.** 43 *ʾà-da-um*-TÚG-I; r. XV 12: 1 ½ gín D. kb **L.** *a-gú*, 17: 10 gín D. kb **L.**; r. XVI 18: 1 ma-na kb **L.** siki; **6** o. I 5: TAR kb **L.** 1 *mi-at* 20 ḪU.UD-ḪU.UD, 7: 4 ma-na kb **L.** gig; o. II 11: ŠÚ+ŠA gín D. kb **L.** 2 dam túg-nu-tag *Ma-ri*$^{ki}$; o. V 20: 10 ma-na kb **L.** 20 ĝír mar-tu kg; o. VII 2: 2 ma-na kb **L.** 1 *za-ḫa-da ra-ʾè-tum* kg, 7: ŠÚ+ŠA 5 gín D. kb **L.** 1 ĝír mar-tu ti kg, 12: TAR kb **L.** 1 ĝír mar-tu ti kg; o. VIII 15: 2 ½ gín D. kb **L.** 1 kir$_{11}$-sa$_6$ siki; o. IX 22: 10 ma-na kb **L.** 5 *mi-at* ma-na a-gar$_5$-gar$_5$; o. XI 2: 1 ma-na kb **L.** ĜIŠ-ti-ḪAR; o. XII 3: 1 ma-na ŠA.PI gín D. kb **L.** 1 *mi-at* si-si ĝír mar-tu kg; o. XIV 18: 2 ma-na kb **L.** 1 BAR.AN, 21: ŠÚ+ŠA gín D. kb **L.** raš-SAR; r. II 8: 1 ma-na kb **L.** 1 ĝír mar-tu kg, 11: ŠA.PI gín D. kb **L.** 1 ĝír mar-tu kg; r. III 18: 4 gín D. kb **L.** 4 *ba-ri-zú* im-ĝi$_6$; r. VII 17: 13 gín D. kb **L.** 1 *gú-li-lum* a-gar$_5$-gar$_5$ kg; r. VIII 15: 12 ma-na kb **L.** 1 *mi-at* 62 aktum-TÚG 15 zara$_6$-TÚG 1 gada-TÚG 11 dùl-TÚG 5 níĝ-lá-saĝ; r. IX 7: 5 ma-na 16 gín D. kb **L.** 10 *à-da-um*-TÚG-II ⌜10⌝?+1 aktum-TÚG 10 túg-NI.NI 4 gada-TÚG 40 íb+III-TÚG sa$_6$ gùn 1 *mi-at* 45 íb+III-TÚG gùn 12 ĝír mar-tu ḫul, 15: 1 ma-na kb **L.** ĜIŠ-ti-ḪAR; r. X 9: ŠA.PI gín D. kb **L.** 1 ĝír mar-tu kg, 13: TAR kb **L.** 1 ĝír mar-tu ti kg, 18: 17 gín D. kb **L.** 1 ĝír mar-tu *ba-du-u*$_9$ kbg; r. XI 2: [ ] **L.** 1 ĝír mar-tu ti kg, 7: 8 ma-na 50 gín D. kb **L.** 31 aktum-TÚG 2 sal-TÚG 2 túg-NI.NI 10 *ʾà-da-um*-TÚG-I 47 gada-TÚG 50 lá-1 íb+III-TÚG sa$_6$ gùn 1 ĜIŠ-banšur kg; r. XII 8: 1 ma-na 8 gín D. kb **L.** 3 aktum-TÚG 7 gada-TÚG 10 íb+III-TÚG sa$_6$ gùn, 14: 7 ma-na TAR 3 gín D. kb **L.** 50 lá-3 aktum-TÚG 25 *ʾà-da-um*-TÚG-I 15 gada-TÚG 12 sal-TÚG 3 níĝ-lá-saĝ; r. XIII 2: ŠA.PI 7 gín D. kb **L.** 5 ma-na ŠA.PI zabar 2 ma-na TAR urudu 1 útul tur, 6: 6 gín D. kb **L.** 1 ĝír kg, 8: 2 ma-na kb **L.** 4 gud, 10: TAR 6 gín D. kb **L.** *gàr-su*; **7** o. I 16: 5 gín D. kb **L.** 1 *gàr-su*; o. II 5: 5 gín D. kb **L.** 1 *gàr-su*, 10: 4 gín D. kb **L.** 1 *gàr-su*; o. III 9: 12 gín D. kb **L.** 1 megida? níĝ-sikil, 20: 5 ma-na kb **L.** [x ĝír mar-t]u [(x) kg]; o. IV 4: 3 ma-na ŠA.PI gín D. kb **L.** 10 lá-2 ĝír mar-tu ti kg; o. V 16: ŠA.PI gín D. kb **L.** 1 ĝír mar-tu kg, 21: ŠA.PI gín D. kb **L.** 1 ĝír mar-tu kg; o. VI 8: ŠÚ+ŠA 5 gín D. kb **L.** 1 ĝír mar-tu ti kg, 16: 5 gín D. kb **L.** 1 ĝír mar-tu *ba-du-u*$_4$ kbg; o. VIII 13: 10 lá-1 ma-na ŠÚ+ŠA gín D. kb **L.** 12 aktum-TÚG ti-TÚG 12 túg-NI.NI 1 dùl-TÚG *Ma-ri*$^{ki}$ 26 *ʾà-da-um*-TÚG-I 33 [ -TÚG] [ ] 10 lá-2 na$_4$ siki *Ma-ri*$^{ki}$; o. IX 7: 6 gín D. kb **L.** ĜIŠ-ád, 13: 2 ma-na kb **L.** 1 BAR.AN, 19: TAR kb **L.** raš-SAR Kur$^{ki}$, 21: [1 ma-na] kb **L.** 10 g[ír ]; o. XVII 5: 6 ma-na ŠA.PI gín D. kb **L.** 33 túg-NI.NI 1 *ʾà-da-um*-TÚG-II 24[+2?] íb[+III]-TÚG sa$_6$ [gùn] 2 *m*[*i-at*] íb[+III-TÚG] gùn 2 ĝír zabar, 11: 12 ma-na 11 gín D. kb **L.** 33 gud-gud; o. XVIII 5: ŠA.PI gín D. kb **L.** 1 ĝ[ír] mar[-tu] kg; r. VI 12: 10 lá-3 ma-na TAR kb **L.** 3 zara$_6$-TÚG 2 aktum-TÚG 40 lá-3 túg-NI.NI 1 níĝ-lá-saĝ 20 lá-2 íb+III-TÚG sa$_6$ gùn 2 *mi-at* 50 lá-3 íb+IV-TÚG gùn; r. VII 2: 10 lá-2 ma-na ŠÚ+ŠA 5 gín D. kb **L.** [10? l]á-1 ⌜*ra*⌝[-*ʾà*]-*tum* 3 *ʾà-da-um*-TÚG-I 46 aktum-TÚG 4 *mi-at* na$_4$ siki *Ma-ri*$^{ki}$, 8: 1 ma-na ŠA.PI gín D. [kb] **L.** 1 *li-im* ĜIŠ-gu-kak-gíd, 10: 1 ma-na 6 gín D. kb **L.** 24 *gàr-su*; r. VIII 9: 6 ma-na 10 gín D. kb **L.** 40 lá-2 gud, 26: 1 ma-na kb **L.** 1 [ĝír] mar-[tu kg]; r. XI 28: TAR kb **L.** [1 ĝír mar]-tu kg; r. XII 6: 10 ma-na kb **L.** 26 zara$_6$-TÚG aktum-TÚG 6 níĝ-lá-du; r. XIII 8: 10 gín D. kb **L.** 1 vír mar-tu *ba-du-u*$_4$ kbg; r. XVI 2: [x ma-na x gí]n D. kb **L.** [1 gí]r mar-[t]u kg [1 ĜIŠ]-gu-kak-gíd; **8** o. III 5: 12 gín D. kb **L.** 2 *gàr-su* ĝi$_6$; o. V 1: 4 ma-na ŠÚ+ŠA 3 gín D. [kb] **L.** 33 aktum-TÚG 14 *ʾà-da-um*-TÚG-I 1 *gu-zi-tum* 10 íb+III-TÚG sa$_6$ gùn 40 lá-2 íb+III-TÚG gùn; o. XI 6: 3 ma-na 57 gín D. kb **L.** 2 íb+III-TÚG babbar gíd 65 íb+III-TÚG sa$_6$ gùn 60 lá-1 [íb+III-TÚG gùn]; r. IV 11’: 2 ma-na ŠÚ+ŠA gín D. kb **L.** ĜIŠ-ti-ḪAR; r. V 7’: 6 gín D. kb **L.** 1 gu-dùl-TÚG ĝi$_6$; r. VI 2’: [x ma-na x gín] ⌜D⌝ kb **L.** ⌜18⌝ gud, 5’: 53 gín D. kb **L.** 7 *mi-at* 80 <ĜIŠ->gu-kak-gíd, 7’: 1 gín D. kb **L.** 2 si dàra, 9’: 15 gín D. kb **L.** 1 ĝír mar-tu zú LAGAB×AN.A; r. VII 5’: 9 gín D. kb **L.** 1 ĝír mar-tu *ba-du-u*$_4$ kg kb, 10’: ŠA.PI gín D. kb **L.** 1 ĝír mar-tu kg; r. VIII 2’: 10 gín D. kb **L.** 1 ĝír mar-tu *ba-du-u*$_4$ kg, 6’: 8 gín D. kb **L.** 1 ĝír mar-tu *ba-du-u*$_4$ kg kb; **9** o. III 1: [ ] **L.** 7 sila$_4$ ḪI.DIM; o. V 1: **L.** 2 ĝír mar-tu *ba-du-u*$_4$ kb, 12: ŠA.PI 2 gín D. kb **L.** 7 gada-TÚG; o. VII 13: [ ] **L.** 10 *ʾà-da-um*-TÚG-I 7 gada-TÚG 40 lá-2 íb+III-TÚG sa$_6$ gùn 1 *mi-at* [ ]; o. IX 14: 10 gín D. kb **L.** ⌜raš⌝-SAR Kur⌜$^{ki}$⌝; o. X 8: ŠÚ+ŠA gín D. kb **L.** 40 si-si ĝír mar-tu; o. XIII 18: 4 ma-na ŠA.PI gín D. kb **L.** 1 *mi-at* sal-TÚG [ ] 14 íb+III-TÚG gùn; o. XIV 9: 10 ma-na TAR 2 gín D. kb **L.** 3 [ ] ⌜x⌝ 1 túg-NI.NI sa$_6$ 40 *ʾà-da-um*-TÚG-I 10 túg-NI.NI 40 *ʾà-da-um*-TÚG-I 1 *mi-at* 15 sal-TÚG 1 *mi-at* 12 gu-mug-TÚG 12 íb+III-TÚG babbar; o. XV 6: TAR kb L. ĝeštin, 10: 5 kb L. 2 ĝír mar-tu ti kg, 16: ŠÚ+ŠA 5 gín [D.] kb **L.** 1 ĝír mar-tu ti kg; o. XVI 3’: ŠA.PI gín D. kb **L.** 1 ĝír mar-tu kg; o. XVII 5’: 1 ma-na kb **L.** 1 ĝír mar-tu kg; o. XVIII 4’: TAR 5 gín D. kb **L.** 1 ĝír mar-tu kg; r. I 14’: 1 ma-na TAR 7 gín D. kb **L.** 8 gada-TÚG 68 íb+III-TÚG gùn; r. IV 10: TAR kb **L.** 1 ĝír mar-tu kg; r. V 19: ŠÚ+ŠA gín D. kb **L.** ĜIŠ-ti-ḪAR; r. XIV 14: 3 ma-na kb … **L.** še-še, 16: ŠA.PI gín D. kb **L.** 1 ĝír mar-tu kg; r. XV 2: ⌜15⌝ gín D. kb **L.** 1 ĝír mar-tu zú LAGAB×AN kg, 6: ŠA.PI gín D. kb **L.** 1 ĝír mar-tu kg; r. XVI 9: 50 gín D. kb **L.** 50 íb+III-TÚG gùn, 11: TAR

2 gín D. kb **L.** ĜIŠ-gu-kak-gíd; r. XVII 19: ŠÚ+ŠA kb **L.** 1 ĝír mar-tu ti kg; r. XVIII 8: [x+]2 kb **L.** [ ]; **10** r. IV 7: 1 ma-na 15 gín D. kb **L.** 3 *mi-at* ma-na níĝ-saĝ; r. VI 6: 5 ma-na kb **L.** 66 *ʾà-da-um*-TÚG-I 10 aktum-TÚG, 10: ⌜1⌝$^?$ ma-na ša-⌜pi⌝ gín D. kb **L.** ĜIŠ-ti-ḪAR, 14: 1 ma-na kb **L.** *gàr-sù*; r. VII 7: 8 ⌜ma⌝-na ŠÚ+Š[A] gín D. kb **L.** 80 aktum-TÚG 20 *ʾà-da-um*-TÚG-I 16 íb+III-TÚG sa$_6$ gùn; r. IX 14: 50 gín D. kb **L.** [ ]; **11** o. II 12: [x g]ín D. k[b] **L.** [1] sila$_4$ lú šu-du$_8$-máš, 15: [x kb] **L.** 10 lá-2 *ʾà-da-um*-TÚG-II 31 *ʾà-da-um*-TÚG-I 3 zara$_6$-TÚG 14 aktum-TÚG 44 gada-TÚG 50 íb+IV-TÚG sa$_6$ gùn 93 "KIN" siki sa$_6$ 10 lá-3 ĝír mar-tu zú[-ak]; o. III 7: 10 lá-2 ma-na TAR kb **L.** 22 gud-gud; o. VII 2: 2 ma-na kb **L.** 2 ĝír mar-tu kg *ra-ʾà-tum*; o. VIII 21: 2 gín D. kb **L.** 1 ĜIŠ-⌜x-x⌝; o. IX 3: 5 gín D. kb **L.** 1 ĝír mar-tu *ba-du-u$_4$* kb, 8: 14 ma-na ŠA.PI 4 gín D. kb **L.** 35 *ʾà-da-um*-TÚG-II 25 *ʾà-da-um*-TÚG-I 52 aktum-TÚG ti-TÚG 3 níĝ-lá-saĝ 20 íb+IV-TÚG sa$_6$ gùn 2 *mi-at* [(x) íb+IV-TÚG gùn]; o. X 2: [ša-]pi 6 k[b] **L.** raš-SAR Kur$^{ki}$; o. XI 13: 1 ma-na kb **L.** 4 gud; o. XII 4: 1 ma-na TAR kb **L.** ĝeštin; o. XIII 2: 13 ma-na [x] gín D. kb **L.** 53 zara$_6$-TÚG 13 *ʾà-da-um*-TÚG-II 16 *ʾà-da-um*-TÚG-I 35 íb+IV-TÚG sa$_6$ gùn 3 *mi-at* 6 íb+IV-TÚG gùn 10 ĝír mar-tu ḫul, 9: ŠA.PI 2 gín D. kb **L.** 2 gud; r. II 15: 14 ma-na kb **L.** 26 túg-NI.NI 52 *ʾà-da-um*-TÚG-I [x í]b[+III]-TÚG-sa$_6$-gùn [ ]; r. V 8: 1 ⌜ma-na kb⌝ **L.** 1 na$_4$ maḫ, 13: ŠA.PI gín D. kb **L.** 1 ĝír mar-tu kg; r. VII 17: TAR kb **L.** 1 ĝír mar-tu kg; **12** o. I 5: 6 ma-na TAR 4 gín D. kb **L.** 1 zara$_6$-TÚG 14 túg-NI.NI 2 níĝ-lá-gaba 53 íb+III-TÚG sa$_6$ gùn 2 *mi-at* 10 íb+III-TÚG gùn, 9: 2 ma-na [x+]3 [g]ín D. [k]b **L.** 10 [ ]; o. II 1: [ ] **L.** 2 IGI.NITA, 5: 11 gín D. kb **L.** raš-SAR Kur$^{ki}$; o. VIII 9: 7 ma-na TAR 3 gín D. kb **L.** 31 túg-NI.NI 1 gada-TÚG 10 lá-2 íb+III-TÚG sa$_6$ gùn 3 *mi-at* 53 íb+III-TÚG gùn; o. IX 7: 1 ma-na kb **L.** 1 ĝír mar-tu kg; o. XI 17: TAR 5 gín D. kb **L.** 1 ĝír mar-tu ti kg *wa ʾà-lum*; r. II 23: 2 ma-na 50 gín D. kb **L.** 2 *ʾà-da-um*-TÚG-I 23 gada-TÚG mu$_4$$^{mu}$ 10 gada-TÚG ḫul 4 gada-TÚG *kir-na-nu* 18 íb+III-TÚG sa$_6$ gùn 18 siki na$_4$ *Ma-rí*$^{ki}$; r. III 8: 10 ma-na 52 gín D. kb **L.** 80 gud-gud; r. IV 6: 1 ma-na kb **L.** 1 ĝír mar-tu kg, 14: 4 gín D. kb **L.** 1 *gàr-su* gi$_6$, 17: ŠÚ+ŠA 4 gín D. kb **L.** 8 *gàr-su* gi$_6$ si$_4$-si$_4$ lú gaba-ru; r. V 9: 10 gín D. kb **L.** še-in; r. VI 16: TAR kb **L.** 2 zara$_6$-TÚG, 18: ŠA.PI gín D. kb **L.** 1 níĝ-lá-gaba 3 níĝ-lá-saĝ; r. VIII 4: 50 gín D. kb **L.** 1 ĝír mar-tu kg; r. X 4: [x] gín D. kb **L.** ĜIŠ-*šè-bir$_5$-gi-nu*; **13** o. IV 6: 4 gín D. kb **L.** 1 ĝír mar-tu *ba-du-u$_4$* kb; o. V 10: 7 ma-na TAR 4 gín D. kb **L.** 60 lá-2 íb+III-TÚG sa$_6$ gùn 30 íb+III-TÚG gùn 2 *mi-at* 45 "KIN" siki *Ma-rí*$^{ki}$, 14: 5 ma-na TAR 3 gín D. kb **L.** 20 gud, 16: 1 ma-na kb **L.** ĜIŠ-ti-ḪAR; o. VII 2: 1 ma-na kb **L.** ĝeštin; o. X 11: 10 lá-2 ma-na kb **L.** 1 *mi-at* 50 aktum-TÚG 1 zara$_6$-TÚG 20 dùl-TÚG *Ma-rí*$^{ki}$, 16: ŠA.PI gín D. kb **L.** 1 ĝír mar-tu kg; o. XII 2: [ kb] **L.** [1 ĝ]ír m[ar-t]u kg; o. XIV 4: 2 ma-na 50 gín D. kb [**L.**] [x *mi-at*] 30+[3(?)+]2 íb+III-TÚG sa$_6$ gùn 1 *mi-at* íb+III-TÚG gùn 2 níĝ-saĝšu, 9: 3 ma-na ŠÚ+ŠA 4 gín D. kb **L.** 12 gud, 11: 13 gín D. kb **L.** ĜIŠ-ti-ḪAR; o. XVII 2: 7 ma-na ŠA.PI 2 gín D. kb **L.** 10 túg-NI.NI 40 íb+III-TÚG sa$_6$-gùn 4 *mi-at* 40 íb+III-TÚG gùn, 6: ŠÚ+ŠA gín D. kb **L.** raš-SAR Kur$^{ki}$, 8: 1 ma-na 1 gín D. kb **L.** 3 IGI.NITA u$_5$, 11: 18 gín D. kb **L.** ĜIŠ-ma-dul$_{10}$; r. I 23: 10 m[a-]na kb **L.** 60 [ ] [ ] 24 dùl-TÚG *Ma-rí*$^{ki}$; r. V 9: 12 ma-na TAR kb **L.** 42 túg-NI.NI 35 aktum-TÚG 16 *ʾà-da-um*-TÚG 40 íb+III-TÚG sa$_6$ gùn 4 *mi-at* 72 íb+III-TÚG gùn; r. VI 13: ŠA.PI gín D. kb **L.** 1 ĝír mar-tu kg; r. VII 9: 16 gín D. kb **L.** 7 *gàr-su* ĝi$_6$; r. IX 21: [x kb **L.**] ⌜10⌝[+x *ʾà-da-um*-TÚG-II] [x *ʾà*]*-da-*[*u*]*m*-TÚG-I 80 aktum-TÚG 30 íb+III-TÚG sa$_6$ gùn 4 *mi-at* 96 íb+III-TÚG gùn, 7: ŠÚ+ŠA g[ín] D. kb **L.** 10 gud, 9: 1 ma-na kb **L.** 22 [ ]; **14** o. III 9: 4 gín D. kb **L.** 1 *gàr-su*; o. IV 19: 1 ma-na kb **L.** 2 *gú-li-lum*-I a-gar$_5$-gar$_5$ kg esi ⌜x⌝; o. V 16: 11 gín D. kb **L.** 11 *ra-ʾà-tum*, 18: 10 gín D. kb **L.** LAGAB×UD-LAGAB×UD; o. VI 2: 11 [ma-na] ŠÚ+ŠA gín D. kb **L.** 8 zara$_6$-TÚG 7 gíd-TÚG 30 lá-2 *ʾà-da-um*-TÚG-I dùl-TÚG-I 1 *mi-at* 90 lá-2 aktum-TÚG; o. IX 15: 18 gín D. kb **L.** 1 [ ]; o. XIII 7: 4 gín D. kb **L.** 1 ĝír mar-tu *ba-du-u$_4$* kb; o. XVI 9: 13 ma-na [x] gín D. kb **L.** 96 aktum-TÚG 3 zara$_6$-TÚG 2 íb+III-TÚG *Sa-ma-rí*$^{k}$ 22 túg-NI.NI [ ] 54 íb+III-TÚG sa$_6$ gùn 2 *mi-at* 50 íb+III-TÚG gùn 5 ĝír mar-tu zú-ak; o. XVII 2: ŠA.PI [gín D.] kb **L.** raš-SAR Kur$^{ki}$, 4: 3 ma-na TAR 4 gín D. kb **L.** 11 gud, 7: TAR kb **L.** ĜIŠ-ti-ḪAR; o. XXI 3: 6 ma-na ŠÚ+ŠA 2 ½ gín D. kb **L.** 34 túg-NI.NI *wa* 6 zara$_6$-TÚG 1 gu-dù[l-TÚG] [x í]b+III-TÚG [s]a$_6$ gùn *wa* 2 *mi-at* 60 íb+III-TÚG gùn; r. I 2: TAR kb **L.** ĜIŠ-ti-ḪAR, 6: 9 gín D. kb **L.** [siki$^?$] ⌜si$_4$$^?$ x⌝ [siki *ba-r*]*a-i*; r. V 6: 2 ma-na 16 gín D. kb **L.** 40 lá-1 íb+III-TÚG sa$_6$ gùn [ ]; r. XI 16: 6 m[a-]na TAR [k]b **L.** 43 gada-TÚG-gada-TÚG [ ], 24: [x gín D.] k[b] **L.** zú AN.LAGAB×AN; r. XII 7: [x ma-na kb] **L.** 10 gud; r. XV 11: 3 gín D. kb **L.** 13 gukkal$^?$, 13: ŠÚ+ŠA gín D. kb **L.** 10 na$_4$ maḫ; r. XVIII x+1; **15** o. III 19: TAR kb **L.** 1 ĝír-mar-tu kg; o. IV 12: 4 gín D. kb **L.** 1 ĝír mar-tu *ba-du-u$_4$* kb; o. VI 2: 6 gín D. kb **L.** 2 *gàr-su*, 9: 1 gín D. kb **L.** ĜIŠ-ád *Sa-nap-zu-gúm*$^{ki}$, 17: 1 ma-na ŠA.PI 2 gín D. kb **L.** 1 *ʾà-da-um*-TÚG-II 2 zara$_6$-TÚG 30 gada-TÚG 16 sal-TÚG 5 gíd-TÚG 20 íb+III-TÚG sa$_6$ ⌜gùn⌝ 1 *mi-at* 46 íb+III-TÚG gùn 3 *mi-at* 85 "KIN" siki *Ma-rí*$^{ki}$; o. VII 4: 2 ma-na kb **L.** ĜIŠ-ti-ḪAR; o. VIII 6: 1 ma-na 55 gín D. kb **L.** 10 lá-1 túg-NI.NI 1 túg-NI.NI sa$_6$ 64 sal-TÚG; o. XII 8: 4 gín D. kb **L.** 1 ĝír mar-tu *ba-du-u$_4$* kb, 12: 10 lá-1 ma-na 5 gín D. kb **L.** 5 túg-NI.NI 3 níĝ-lá-saĝ 10 *ʾà-da-um*-TÚG 1 *mi-at* 53 sal-TÚG 50 lá-3 íb+III-TÚG sa$_6$ gùn 1 *mi-at* 20 íb+III-TÚG gùn 3 íb+III-TÚG *Ma-rí*$^{ki}$, 20: 10 gín D. kb **L.** 10 sila$_4$ sa$_6$; o. XIII 2: 1 ma-na TAR kb **L.** ĜIŠ-ti-ḪAR, 8: 12 gín D. kb **L.** 3 ĝír mar-tu *ba-du-u$_4$* kb; o. XIV 6: 1 ma-na kb **L.** 1 ĝír mar-tu kg; o. XVII 12: 10 lá-1 ma-na 12 gín D. kb **L.** 10 lá-2 túg-NI.NI 15 *ʾà-d*[*a-*]*um*-TÚG[-II$^?$] 1 *mi*[*-at*] 10 sal-TÚG 30 íb+III-TÚG sa$_6$ gùn 4 *mi-at* íb+III-TÚG gùn, 18: TAR 3 gín D. kb **L.** raš-SAR, 20: 1 ma-na ŠÚ+ŠA 5 gín D. kb **L.** 4 IGI.N[ITA]; r. I 4: 10 gín D. kb **L.** 1 ma-na 7 gín D. *nap-ḫu*; r. II 22: ŠA.PI gín D. kb **L.** 1 ĝír mar-tu kg; r. III 9: 15 ma-na 22 gín D. kb **L.** 6 dùl-TÚG *Ma-rí*$^{ki}$ 4 *ʾà-da-um*-TÚG-II 11 túg-NI.NI 46 sal-TÚG 40 gada-TÚG-gada-TÚG 2 níĝ-lá-gaba 80 lá-2 íb+III-TÚG sa$_6$ gùn 5 *mi-at* 80 íb+III-TÚG gùn 2 kuš babbar ùz-nita lú 2 níĝ-anše-ak kg maḫ$^?$; r. IV 2: ŠA.PI 8 gín D. kb **L.** *gàr-su*; r. V 17: 1 ma-na kb **L.** 1 ĝír mar-tu kg; r. XVI 4: 1

[ma-]n[a] kb [**L.** 1 ĝír mar-t]u kg; **16** o. II 4: 20 ma-na kb **L.** ⌜x⌝ *li-im* 2 *mi-at* ma-na a-gar$_5$-gar$_5$; o. III 22: 1 ma-na ŠÚ+ŠA 5 gín D kb **L.** 1 *mi*-at 70 siki na$_4$ *Ma-rí*$^{ki}$; o. IV 3: TAR kb **L.** ĜIŠ-ti-ḪAR, 10: 3 ma-na TAR 2 gín D kb **L.** 12 aktum<-TÚG> 1 zara$_6$-TÚG 1 túg-NI.NI *Ma-rí*$^{ki}$ 2 *ʾà-da-um*-TÚG-I 2 níĝ-lá-gaba 3 *mi-at* 20 siki na$_4$ *Ma-rí*$^{ki}$, 15: 15 gín D kb **L.** 65 *ra-ʾà-tum*; o. XII 20: 7 ma-na 10 gín D kb **L.** [ ]; o. XIII 8: 6 ma-na kb **L.** [x$^?$+]2 BAR.AN *Na-gàr*$^{ki}$, 13: <x gín D. kb> **L.** 24 túg-NI.NI 30 gada-TÚG 3 níĝ-lá-gaba, 17: TAR 4 gín D. kb **L.** raš-SAR Kur$^{ki}$; r. II 22: 10 gín D kb **L.** še-in; r. III 26: 17 gín D kb **L.** 1 ĝír mar-tu ti kg; r. IV 19: 1 ma-na ŠA.PI 1 gín D kb **L.** 6 IGI.NITA u$_5$$^!$; r. IX 24: 3 gín D kb **L.** 1 *gár-su*; r. X 1: 11 gín D. kb **L.** 2 na$_4$ 3; r. XI 14: 2 ma-na ŠA.PI 6 gín D kb **L.** 30 lá-2 túg-NI.NI 4 dùl-TÚG *Ma-rí*$^{ki}$ 20 "KIN" siki *Ma-rí*$^{ki}$, 18: 1 ma-na ŠÚ+ŠA 3 gín D. kb **L.** 15 si$_4$ *gàr-su* 14 gi$_6$ *gàr-su*; **17** o. II 2: TAR kb **L.** 2 *gú-li-lum* a-gar$_5$-gar$_5$ TAR 5 gín D. *sa-ḫa-wa*, 16: 6 ma-na kb **L.** 2 BAR.AN; o. IV 2: [ ma-na x] gín D. kb **L.** 2 IGI.NITA u$_5$; o. VIII 4: 5 ma-na kb **L.** BAR.AN, 16: 4 ma-na kb **L.** 34 aktum-TÚG 2 zara$_6$-TÚG 5 *ʾà-da-um*-TÚG-I [ ]; o. IX 5: 5 ma-na kb **L.** 1 *mi-at* 10 lá-2 aktum-TÚG 1 zara$_6$-TÚG; o. X 6: 1 ma-na kb **L.** 26 gu-dù[l]-TÚG m[aḫ] lú é-duru$_5$⌜$^{ki}$⌝, 9: 6 gín D. kb **L.** 25[(+x) *ra-*]*ʾà-t*[*um*]; o. XII 10: 1 ma-na kb **L.** 50 ma-na a-gar$_5$-gar$_5$; o. XIII 2: 12 gín D. kb **L.** 1 ĝír mar-tu zú kg, 8: ŠA.PI gín D. kb **L.** 2 gud; o. XIV 6: 8 gín D. kb **L.** 1 ĝír mar-tu zú kg, 17: 50 gín D. kb **L.** 1 ĝír mar-tu kg; o. XVI 2: 1 ma-na kb **L.** 1 ĝír mar-tu kg, 11: ŠA.PI 5 gín D. kb **L.** 2 ĝír mar-tu *ba-du-u*$_4$ kg 1 ĝír mar-tu zú kg 1 ĝír mar-tu *ba-du-u*$_4$ kbg; o. XVII 13: 10 ma-na kb **L.** 1 *mi-at* 46 aktum-TÚG 10 lá-2 zara$_6$-TÚG 7 gíd-TÚG 33 *ʾà-da-um*-TÚG-I; o. XVIII 3: TAR kb **L.** 1 ĝír mar-tu kg, 11: 1 ma-na 10 gín D. kb **L.** si-si-*sù*; r. IV 3: 4 gín D. kb **L.** 1 ĝír mar-tu *ba-du-u*$_4$ kb; r. V 2: TAR kb **L.** 1 *mi-at* aktum-TÚG 5 zara$_6$-TÚG 30 lá-1 túg-NI.NI 80 *ʾà-da-um*-TÚG-I 1 dùl-TÚG *Ma-rí*$^{ki}$ 4 gada-TÚG 4 sal-TÚG 62 íb+III-TÚG sa$_6$ gùn 1 *mi-at* 80 íb+III-TÚG gùn 1 *mi-at* 50 kuš-kuš sa$_6$ gi$_6$, 13: ŠA.PI gín D. kb **L.** ĜIŠ-bar-ús; r. X 5: 12 ma-na kb **L.** 30 lá-1 túg-NI.NI 60 *ʾà-da-um*-TÚG-I 82 sal-TÚG 6 dùl-TÚG *Ma-rí*$^{ki}$ 17 gada-TÚG 52 íb+III-TÚG sa$_6$ gùn 2 *mi-at* 40 íb+III-TÚG gùn, 13: 1 ma-na kb **L.** raš-SAR Kur$^{ki}$, 15: ŠÚ+ŠA 5 gín D. kb **L.** 1 gud, 19: 55 gín D. kb **L.** 2 gud; r. XII 9: 50 gín D. kb **L.** 1 ĝír mar-tu kg, 18: ⌜56⌝ gín D. kb **L.** 1 ĝír mar-tu kg; r. XVIII 23: ŠÚ+ŠA kb daḫ$_x$(MU.MU.MU) **L.** [ ]; r. XX 12: 1 ma-na ŠÚ+ŠA kb **L.** 10 lá-1 *gàr-su* gi$_6$ 24 *gàr-su* si$_4$-si$_4$, 15: 8 kb **L.** ĜIŠ-bar-ús; r. XXI 28: 1 ma-na TAR kb **L.** 2 ⌜ĝír⌝ [ ]; r. XXII 16: 1 ma-na kb **L.** 1 ĝír mar-tu kg, 22: 1 ma-na TAR kb **L.** 2 gu-dùl-TÚG é-duru$_5$$^{ki}$, 26: 1 ma-na 20[+x **L.** [20+]10 íb+III-TÚG sa$_6$ gùn; **18** o. V 20: 1 ma-na kb **L.** la-ḫa ĝeštin; o. IX 14: 4 ma-na ŠA.PI gín D. kb **L.** 23 túg-NI.NI 4 dùl-TÚG *Ma-rí*$^{ki}$ 26 gada-TÚG 1 *mi-at* siki na$_4$ *Ma-rí*$^{ki}$; o. XIII 14: ŠÚ+ŠA 4 gín D. kb **L.** 10 na$_4$, 19: 10 gín D. kb **L.** 1 na$_4$, 22: 12 gín D. kb **L.** 1 na$_4$, 24: 13 gín D. kb **L.** 1 na$_4$; o. XIV 4: 3 gín D. kb **L.** 1 na$_4$, 7: 5 gín D. kb **L.** 1 na$_4$, 25: ŠA.PI gín D. kb **L.** 2 ĝír mar-tu ti kg; o. XV 3: 2 ma-na 10 gín D. kb **L.** 1 *mi-at* sal-TÚG *si-in A-la-ga*$^{ki}$; o. XVI 3: 14 ma-na kb **L.** 9 *mi-at* 80 ma-na a-gar$_5$-gar$_5$, 5: 1 ma-na kb **L.** 1 ĝír mar-tu kg; r. III 3: 11 ma-na 10 gín D. kb **L.** 50 túg-NI.NI 2 zara$_6$-TÚG 22 *ʾà-da-um*-TÚG-I 4 4 dùl-TÚG *Ma-rí*$^{ki}$ 70 gada-TÚG 2 *mi-at* 10 siki na$_4$ *Ma-rí*$^{ki}$, 10: ŠÚ+ŠA gín D. kb **L.** raš-SAR Kur$^{ki}$, 12: 55 gín D. kb **L.** 3 IGI.NITA u$_5$; r. VI 16: TAR kb **L.** 1 ĝír mar-tu kg; r. X 13: 1 ma-na TAR kb **L.** 90 lá-2 ĝír mar-tu zú-ak; r. XII 19: 2 gín D. kb **L.** ĜIŠ-šim ĜÁ×LÁ; r. XIII 4: 13 ma-na ŠÚ+ŠA kb **L.** 72 dùl-TÚG *Ma-rí*$^{ki}$ 60 lá-3 *ʾà-da-um*-TÚG-I 40 lá-3 túg-NI.NI 2 aktum-TÚG ti-TÚG, 9: 4 ma-na ŠA.PI 4 kb **L.** 3 *mi-at* 40 siki na$_4$ *Ma-rí*$^{ki}$, 18: [ ] kb **L.** 1 ĝír mar-tu *ba-du-u*$_4$ kbg; r. XIV 17: 11 ½ kb **L.** 75 ma-na níĝ-NE; r. XVI 22: 15 kb **L.** 1 ĝír mar-tu LAGAB×A kg; r. XVII 26: 1 ma-na 10 kb **L.** 2 ĝír mar-tu kg; r. XVIII 6: 1 ma-na kb **L.** 1 ĝír mar-tu kg, 26: 1 ma-na TAR 3 kb **L.** 10 lá-1 *gàr-su* ĝi$_6$ 16 *gàr-su* si$_4$, 29: 2 ma-na 6 kb **L.** 36 *ʾà-da-um*-TÚG-I, 31: 1 ma-na 4 kb **L.** 85 siki na$_4$ *Ma-rí*<$^{ki}$>; r. XIX 6: 7 kb **L.** ĜIŠ-ti-ḪAR SA.ZA$_x$$^{ki}$; **19** o. I 13: 2 ma-na kb **L.** 2 ĝír mar-tu kg, 25: 1 ma-na kb **L.** 1 ĝír mar-tu kg; o. IV 9: 1 ma-na ŠA.PI gín D. kb **L.** 1 *mi-at* ma-na a-gar$_5$-gar$_5$; o. VI 23: 11 ma-na ŠA.PI gín D. kb **L.** 30 lá-2 túg-NI.NI 1 *mi-at* 46 sal-TÚG 80 gada-TÚG 60 siki na$_4$ *Ma-rí*$^{ki}$, 28: 2 ma-na kb **L.** ĜIŠ-ti-ḪAR; o. XVII 26: 5 ma-na kb **L.** 3 *mi-at* ĝír mar-tu zú-ak; r. IV 20: 1[+x$^?$ ma-na k]b **L.** 40 ĝír mar-tu zú-ak; r. V 1: 12 gín D. kb **L.** ĜIŠ-ti-ḪAR, 7: 1 ma-na ŠA.PI 4 gín D. kb **L.** 70 lá-3 túg-NI.NI 2 *mi-at* 80 sal-TÚG 46 siki na$_4$ *Ma-rí*$^{ki}$; r. VI 18: 12 gín D. kb **L.** ĜIŠ-sal é *A-ru*$_{12}$*-ga-du*$^{ki}$; r. XIV 9: ŠÚ+ŠA gín D. kb **L.** 1 ĝír mar-tu ti kg; r. XV 1: ŠA.PI gín D. kb **L.** 2 ĝír mar-tu ti kg, 10: ŠÚ+ŠA gín D. kb **L.** 2 ĝír mar-tu *ba-du-u*$_9$ kg, 17: 7 gín D. kb **L.** 1 ĝír mar-tu *ba-du-u*$_9$ kg; r. XVI 22: 2 ma-na TAR 2 gín D. kb **L.** 33 túg-NI.NI 3 dùl-TÚG *Ma-rí*$^{ki}$, 25: ŠÚ+ŠA 3 gín D. kb **L.** 3 *gàr-su* si$_4$ 4 *gàr-su* gi$_6$; r. XVII 3: ŠÚ+ŠA gín D. kb **L.** ĜIŠ-*šè-bir*$_5$*-gi-nu* ĜIŠ-bar-ús; r. XIX 9: 6 ma-na kb **L.** BAR.AN.BAR.AN; **20** o. IV 17: 3 ma-na ŠÚ+ŠA 7 gín D. 3 NI kb **L.** 1 *mi-at* 40 lá-3 sal-TÚG 1 ⌜x⌝ [ ]; o. XII 4: 15 gín D. kb **L.** 1 ĝír mar-tu ti kg, 8: 22 ma-na ŠÚ+ŠA gín D. kb **L.** 1 *li-im* 3 *mi-at* 40 ma-na a-gar$_5$-gar$_5$, 10: 1 ma-na kb **L.** 1 *mi-at* 20 ma-na a-gar$_5$; o. XIII 23: 10 lá-1 ma-na ŠÚ+ŠA gín D. kb **L.** 15 aktum-TÚG 40 lá-1 túg-NI.NI [ ]; o. XIV 2: ŠÚ+ŠA gín D. kb **L.** 2 *mi-at* siki na$_4$ *Ma-rí*$^{ki}$, 4: 4 gín D. kb **L.** 33 kuš Mar-tu$^{ki}$, 7: ŠÚ+ŠA gín D. kb **L.** 2 gud, 12: TAR 5 gín D. kb **L.** raš-SAR Kur$^{ki}$, 17: 4 ma-na kb **L.** 2 BAR.AN;] *áš-ti Na-gàr*$^{ki}$; o. XVII 19: 50 gín D. kb **L.** 1 ĝír mar-tu kg, 22: 50 gín D. kb **L.** 1 ĝír mar-tu kg; r. VI 18: 4 ma-na ŠÚ+ŠA 2 gín D. kb **L.** 1 dùl-TÚG *Ma-rí*$^{ki}$ 14 túg-NI.NI 1 *mi-at* 40 sal-TÚG; r. VII 2: [ kb] **L.** 2 IGI.NITA u$_5$; r. XII 20: 6 gín D. kb **L.** 1 ĝír mar-tu kg; r. XIII 4: [x] ma-na [x 2+]6 gín D. kb **L.** 10 lá-1 dùl-TÚG *Ma-rí*$^{ki}$ 30 túg-NI.NI, 7: 6 gín D. kb **L.** ĜIŠ-ti-ḪAR; r. XVI 4': 1 ma-na kb **L.** 1 BAR.AN; r. XVII x+1: [ ] **L.** 1 aktum-[TÚG] ti[-TÚG] 2 gada-[TÚG]; **21** o. IV 26: 1 ma-na kb **L.** ĝeštin; o. VI 4: [x kb] **L.** la-ḫa lú i-ĝiš; o. VII 12: ŠA.PI gín D. kb **L.** 1 ĝír mar-tu kg ⌜*ra*⌝*-ʾà-*[*tu*]*m* [ ] 3 *z*[*ú-*]*zú-b*[*a-*]*tum* ĜIŠ-gígir-II; o. IX 6: 2 ma-na TAR kb **L.** 50 lá-2 DAM.KAK.UŠ tur sal; o. XI 6: 1 ma-na kb **L.** raš-SAR, 12: 15 gín D. kb **L.** 60 íb+III-TÚG gùn;

o. XII 31 and XIII 4: [x kb **L.**] 14 aktum-TÚG 50 lá-2 ᵓà-da-um-TÚG-I lú *Zú-ba-an* **L.** *in* níĝ-kas$_4$ *Ma-rí*$^{ki}$; o. XIV 6: 1 ma-na kb **L.** 1 ĝír mar-tu *ra-ᵓà-tum* kg; o. XVI 8: 1 ma-na kb **L.** 1 ĝír mar-tu kg; r. I 20: 8 ma-na TAR kb **L.** 13 aktum-TÚG ⌜*wa*⌝ 35 *ᵓà-da-u*[*m*]-TÚG-I 1 zara$_6$-TÚG 3 *mi-at* 13 íb+III-TÚG gùn 60 siki na$_4$ *Ma-rí*$^{ki}$; r. II 5: 2 gín D. kb **L.** 1 ĜIŠ-*ba-ri-zú* ĜIŠ. GAM.GAM.GAM, 8: 1 ma-na 8 gín D. kb **L.** 1 *mi-at* 50 ĜIŠ-ti-ḪAR *wa* níĝ-NE, 15: ŠA.PI 4 gín D. kb **L.** 10 lá-1 *gàr-su* gi$_6$ 4 *gàr-su* si$_4$-si$_4$; r. VII 14: 1 ma-na kb **L.** 1 ĝír mar-tu kg; r. VIII 28: 15 gín D. kb **L.** 1 ĝír mar-tu *ba-du*[*-u*$_4$] kg; r. XII 18: 50 gín D. kb **L.** 1 *mi-at* íb+III-TÚG gùn; **25** o. I 2: [x kb] **L.** 72 aktum-TÚG 20 *ᵓà-da-um*-TÚG 10 túg-NI.NI 90 lá-2 sal-TÚG 2 níĝ-lá-gaba 5 *gu-zi*-mug-TÚG; o. II 1: 10 ma-na kb **L.** [x aktum-TÚG] 10 lá-2 túg-NI.NI 7 *ᵓà-da-um*-TÚG dùl-TÚG 12 gada-TÚG 94 sal-TÚG 22 íb+III-TÚG sa$_6$ gùn 80 íb-III-TÚG gùn; o. III 2: [x] ⌜kb⌝ **L.** 44 aktum-TÚG 5 zara-⌜TÚG⌝ 13 *gu-zi-tum*-TÚG 22 túg-NI.NI 34 íb+III-TÚG sa$_6$ gùn 1 *mi-at* 52 íb+III-TÚG gùn 1 ĝír mar:tu ti kb; o. IV 5: 8 ma-na TAR kb **L.** 5 *gu-zi-tum* 4 aktum-TÚG 7 túg-NI.NI 10 lá-1 *ᵓà-da-um*-TÚG 60 lá-1 sal-TÚG 2 níĝ-lá-saĝ 62 íb+III-TÚG 1 *mi-at* 41 íb+III-TÚG gùn; o. V 5: 6 m[a-]na 2 gín D. kb **L.** 24[+1] aktum-TÚG [x] ⌜*ᵓà*⌝*-da-um*-TÚG saĝ 3 túg-NI. NI 20 lá-3 sal-TÚG 27 gada-TÚG 30 íb+III-TÚG sa$_6$ gùn; o. VI 4: 8 ma-na 7 gín D. kb **L.** 73 *ᵓà-da-um*-TÚG 11 aktum-TÚG 10 sal-TÚG; o. VII 1: 5 ma-na ⌜x x⌝ [kb] [**L.**] [ ] 10 í[b-III-TÚG] sa$_6$ gùn 10 íb-III-TÚG babbar 2 *mi-at* íb-III-TÚG gùn, 6: 5 ma-na 17 ½ gín D. kb **L.** 13 *ᵓà-da-um*-TÚG saĝ [x aktum-TÚG] [x íb-III-TÚG s]a$_6$ gùn 2 íb-III-TÚG gùn 4 sal-TÚG 1 níĝ-lá-saĝ babbar 1 ĝír mar:tu ḫul; r. VI 3: [ ] še-ba diĝir-diĝir-diĝir-diĝir **L.** 10 gig.

níĝ-saĝ **10** r. IV 8: 1 ma-na 15 gín D. kb níĝ-sa$_{10}$ 3 *mi-at* ma-na **L.**
(*LLE*,I no. 36: NÍĜ.SAĜ)

níĝ-saĝšu «helmet (*ARET* XX, p. 271); a capacity measure (*ARET* IX, p. 401)» **3** o. VI 6; 4 r. XVI 1: 1 á-MUŠEN **L.**; **12** o. XI 14: 7 gín D. an-na šub *si-in ba-na-a* 1 **L.**; **13** o. X 9: 3 ma-na an-na šub *si-in* 24 ma-na a-gar$_5$-gar$_5$ kin$_5$-ak IGI.DUB 40 **L.**; o. XIV 7; **14** o. IV 17: 4 ma-na TAR an-na šub *si-in* kin$_5$-ak IGI. DUB 60 **L.**

níĝ-sikil «purification» **7** o. III 9: 1 megida? **L.**

níĝ-*sù*
níĝ?-*sù*-níĝ?-*sù* **4** r. XIV 1: 1 ma-na ŠA.PI gín D. kb šu-bal-ak an-na PA **L.**

níĝ-[ ] **16** r. I 24: ŠÚ+ŠA 5 gín D. nu$_{11}$-[za] 6 **L.**

nin-ni «sister» **2** o. I 14: 5 *zi-ba-tum Di-ne-ib-du-lum* **L.** en.; o. X 3: 2 ĝeštu$_x$-lá *Di-ne-íb-du-lum* **L.** en; **6** o. V 17: 1 an-zam$_x$ *Di-ni-íb-du-lum* **L.** en; **8** o. I 7: (silver) *Di-rín-da-mu Di-ne-íb-du-lum* **L.** [en]; **9** r. VI 19: 4 *bu*-DI níĝ-ba *Ib-ᵓà-ra wa* **L.**-⌜*sù*⌝ *in* ud níĝ-mu-sá ⌜*Za*⌝*-ne-ḫi-Ma-*[*r*]*í*$^{ki}$ é-gi *Ib-ᵓà-ra ᵓÀ-šu*$^{ki}$; **10** o. I 6: (silver) *Di-ne-íb-du-lum* **L.** en; **11** o. I 7: (silver) [*Di-rín-da-mu Di-ne-íb-du-lum* **L.** en]; **12** r. XIII 10: (silver) *Di-ni-íb-du-lum* dam-diĝir **L.** en šu-ba$_4$-ti; **13** o. I 6: (silver) [*Di-n*]*e-*[*í*]*b-*[*du-*]*lum* **L.** [e]n [šu-b]a$_4$-[t]i; **14** o. I 6: (silver) [*Di-ni-íb-du-lum* **L.** en šu-ba$_4$-ti]; **15** o. I 6: (silver) *Di-ni-íb-du-lum* **L.** en šu-ba$_4$-ti; **16** o. I 6: (silver) [*Di-ni-í*]*b-*[*d*]*u-lum* **L.** en ⌜šu⌝-ba$_4$-ti (silver) *Dar-ib-da-mu* **L.**-*sù* ⌜šu⌝-ba$_4$-ti; r. II 10: 10 ĝeštu$_x$-lá … 1 kù-sal *Di-ni-íb-du-lum* **L.** en; r. VII 11: 1 *ma-da-ḫu Ar-za-du* **L.** en; **17** o. I 6: (silver) *Di-ne-íb-du-lum* [**L.** en] šu-ba$_4$-ti; r. XIV 24: [10–]7 [*b*]*u*?-DI [ŠÚ+Š]A-ŠÚ+ŠA [níĝ-b]a PN$_1$–PN$_8$ dam en *wa* PN$_9$–PN$_{10}$ 2 dumu-munus en *wa* ama-gal *Ib-rí-um wa* PN$_{11}$–PN$_{14}$ dam-*sù wa Iš-ru*$_{12}$*-ud* **L.** *Du-si-gú* PN$_{15}$; r. XXI 17: 2 *bu*-DI *Di-rin*$_x$*-da-mu* … 2 *bu*-DI … 2 saĝ-*sù* … 2 kù-sal *Tir*$_5$*-bù-da-mu* **L.**-*sù*; **18** o. I 6 and 11: (silver) *Di-ni-íb-du-lum* **L.** en šu-ba$_4$-ti (silver) *Dar-ib-da-mu* **L.**-*sù* šu-ba$_4$-ti; o. III 20: 2 *bu*-DI *Ar-za-du* **L.** en; o. XVII 29: 10 lá-2 ĝeštu$_x$-lá *Di-ni-íb-du-lum* **L.** en.; **19** o. I 6 and 10: (silver) *Di-ne-íb-du-lum* **L.** en (silver) *Dar-ib-da-mu* **L.**-*sù* šu-ba$_4$-ti; o. III 3: 3 *bu*-DI 2 saĝ … 1 sig$_7$-igi *Di-ne-íb-du-lum* **L.** en; **20** o. I 6: (silver) *Di-ni-íb-du-lum* **L.** en šu-ba$_4$-ti; **21** o. I 6: (silver) *Di-*[*ni-*]*íb-du-lum* **L.** [e]n [šu-ba$_4$-t]i; o. XVI 5: 2 *bu*-DI ì-ĝiš-saĝ *Di-ni-íb-du-lum* **L.** en.

nita «male; man» **18** r. XIV 26: 1 an-dùl **L.**

*ni-zi-mu* «decoration» **1** o. VI 6: 1 ma-na ŠÚ+ŠA gín D. kb **L.** 2 níĝ-anše-ak 4 kù-sal; o. VII 12: 15 gín D. kb **L.** 1 íb-lá, 19: TAR kb **L.** 1 íb-lá [1] *si-ti*[*-tum* 1 ĝír-kun]; o. VIII 7: 3 gín D. kg **L.** 2 ⌜ĜIŠ⌝ [ ] 2 ĜIŠ-⌜x⌝; **2** o. I 4: [1] gín D. kg **L.** 1 dib, 19: 1 gín D. kg **L.** 1 dib; o. III 18: 1 gín D. kg **L.** 1 dib; o. IV 6: 11 gín D. kg **L.** 1 dib; o. IX 21: 1 gín D. kg **L.** 2 ĝeštu$_x$-lá; o. XII 9: 1 gín D. kg **L.** 1 dib, 16: 2 gín D. kg **L.** maš-maš íb-lá; o. XIII 2: 4 gín D. kg **L.** 1 pad 1 an-zam$_x$, 9: 3 gín D. kg **L.** nu$_{11}$-za ĜIŠ-sur$_x$ ĜIŠ-gígir-II!(III), 16: 2 gín D. 2 NI kg **L.** 4 ĝeštu$_x$-lá, 22: 2 gín D. kg **L.** 1 dib; o. XIV 7: 2 gín D. kg **L.** 1 dib, 13: 9 gín D. kg **L.** nu$_{11}$-za ḫaš-ḫaš 4 *gú-li-lum* kb *wa* ḫaš-ḫaš 5 *gú-li-lum* a-gar$_5$-gar$_5$; o. XV 3: 2 gín D. kg **L.** 6 ĝeštu$_x$-lá; r. I 17: 2 gín D. kg **L.** 1 dib; r. XII 3: 3 gín D. kg **L.** 1 dib; **3** o. III 9: 4 gín D. kg **L.** 10 ĝeštu$_x$-lá; o. IV 1: 2 gín D. kg **L.** 1 dib; o. XII 3: 8 gín D. kg **L.** 1 dib; o. III 10: 1 gín D. kb **L.** nu$_{11}$-za 1 *za-ḫa-da*; o. XIV 13: [ ] **L.** 2 *ba-ga-ni-sa*; o. XV 15: [ ] **L.** 1 dib; r. I 8: ŠÚ+ŠA gín D. kg **L.** ḫaš-ḫaš *gú-li-lum*; r. III 4: 56 gín D. kb **L.** 2 níĝ-anše-ak 4 kù-sal; **4** o. I 5: 3 ma-na 7 gín D. kb **L.** 20 íb-lá *si-ti-tum* ĝír-kun; o. XII 3: 8 gín D. kb **L.** 10 lá-2 *gú-li-lum*; r. III 8: 4 g[ín D. kb] **L.** nu$_{11}$-za!(KUR) 2 ĝír šu-du$_8$-máš; r. VIII 17: 2 gín D. kb **L.** 2 *gú-li-lum*; r. XII 5: 2 gín D. kb **L.** 2 *gú-li-lum*, 11: 2 gín D. kb **L.** nu$_{11}$-za!(KUR) 1 *ma-ḫa-ni-gúm*; **5** o. IV 9: ½ gín D. kg **L.** 1 dib, 15: 1 gín D. kg **L.** 1 dib; o. V 15: 10 gín D. kb **L.** 24 íb?-lá ĝír-kun; o. VI 3: 2 ½ gín D. kg **L.** nu$_{11}$-za *gú-li-lum*; o. X 15: 5 gín D. kg **L.** 1 dib, 21: 2 gín D. kg **L.** 1 dib; o. XI 17: 2 gín D. kg **L.** 1 dib; o. XIII 16: 2 gín D. kg **L.** 1 dib; o. XVI 18: 2 gín D. kg **L.** nu$_{11}$-za-*sù*; r. I 9: 1 gín D. kg **L.** 1 dib, 12: 8 gín D. kb **L.** 2 <níĝ->anše-ak 4 kù-sal, 17: 2 gín D. kg **L.** nu$_{11}$-z[a-]*sù*; r. VII 7: 2 gín D. kg **L.** 1 dib, 13: ½ gín D. kg **L.** 1 dib; r. XII 17: 3 gín D. kg **L.** nu$_{11}$-za 2 *gú-li-lum*; r. XIII 2: 1 ½ gín D. kg **L.** nu$_{11}$-za 2 *gú-li-lum*; r. XV 2: 3 gín D. kg **L.** 1 dib, 8: 2 kg **L.** 1 dib, 14: TAR 5 gín D. kb **L.** 3 ĜIŠ-šú 3 níĝ-bànda; r. XVI 11: 5 gín D. kg **L.** 1 *zi-ru*$_{12}$ *wa* 2 *gi-zu wa* níĝin-níĝin; **6** r. XVI 26: TAR an-na **L.** ZA$_x$ naĝar; **7** o. VII

6: 1 gín D. kb **L.** nu$_{11}$-za 1 *za-ḫa-da*, 10: ŠA.PI gín D. an-na šub *si-in* **L.** ZA$_x$ naĝar; o. XI 4: ½ gín D. kg **L.** 1 dib; o. XII 19: 2 gín D. kg **L.** nu$_{11}$-za 1 ĝír mar-tu; o. XIII 2 [...] kb **L.** 2 níĝ-anše-ak 1 kù-sal, 7: 2 gín D. kg **L.** maš-maš 4 kù-sal, 13: ½ gín D. kg **L.** nu$_{11}$-za 1 ĝír, 19: 2 gín D. kg **L.** nu$_{11}$-za 2 *za-ḫa-da*; o. XIV 1: [x] g[ín D. kb] **L.** maš-maš ĜIŠ-bar-ús; o. XVI 4: 2 ½ gín D. kg **L.** 1 dib; r. IX 18: ŠÚ+ŠA gín D. kg **L.** 1 dib; r. X 4: 1 gín D. kg **L.** 1 dib, 11: [1] gín D. kg **L.** 1 dib, 20: 2 gín D. kb **L.** 2 *zú-zú-ba-tum*; r. XI 7: 6 gín D. kg **L.** 2 *gú-li-lum*; r. XIV 24: 1 gín D. kg **L.** 1 dib; **8** o. XII 8: 2 gín D. kg **L.** 2 *gú-li-lum*, 15: 4 gín D. kg **L.** 1 dib; o. XV 2: 6 gín D. kb **L.** 10 lá-2 kù-sal 2 níĝ-anše-ak; r. IV 3': 2 gín D. ⌜kb⌝ **L.** 1 níĝ-[anše-]a[k]; r. IX 14': 1 gín D. kg **L.** [ ]; r. X 13': ½ gín D. kg **L.** 1 dib; **9** o. IV 18: 2 gín D. kg **L.** 1 dib; r. IX 13: 1 ma-na TAR kg **L.** nu$_{11}$-za ḫaš-ḫaš 7 *gú-li-lum* ⌜kb⌝-II esi ĜÁ×LÁ TAR-*sù wa* 10 *gú-li-lum* kb-II esi ĜÁ×LÁ ŠÚ+ŠA gín D. 1 *gú-li-lum* kb-I esi 1 gín D. ĜÁ×LÁ-*sù*; r. X 8: 1 ma-na ŠÚ+ŠA 6 gín D. kg **L.** nu$_{11}$-za ḫaš-ḫaš 1 dib a-gar$_5$-gar$_5$ lú 4 *gú-li-lum* [ ] 1 dib a-gar$_5$-gar$_5$ [ ] 15 *gú-li-lum* a-gar$_5$-gar$_5$-II esi *wa* 2 *gú-li-lum* a-gar$_5$-gar$_5$ *sa-ḫ[a-]wa*-II esi ĜÁ×LÁ TAR *wa* 1? *gú-li-lum* a-gar$_5$-gar$_5$ *sa-ḫa-wa* 20 esi 12 *gú-li-lum* a-gar$_5$-gar$_5$ *sa-ḫa-wa* 12 esi; r. XI 9: 5 gín D. kb **L.** nu$_{11}$-za ḫaš-ḫaš 1 *gú-li-lum* a-gar$_5$-gar$_5$-II esi *wa* 4 *gú-li-lum* [a-]gar$_5$-gar$_5$[-I] esi; r. XII 4: ŠÚ+ŠA gín D. kg **L.** nu$_{11}$-za 10 ĝír mar-tu kg 2 ĝír mar-tu ti kg [x] ĝír mar-tu zú LAGAB×AN 6 ĝír mar-tu *ba-du-u$_4$* kg, 11: 3 gín D. kb **L.** *zi-tum* 4 ĝír mar-tu *ba-du-u$_4$* kb; r. XVII 7: 1 gín D. kg **L.** 1 dib; **10** o. IV 5: 10 gín D. kb **L.** *iš-ki-lum* en, 16: 2 gín D. kb **L.** nu$_{11}$-za 1 *za-ḫa-da*; r. II 9: 5 gín D. kb **L.** nu$_{11}$-za 4 *gú-li-lum*; r. VII 17: [ ] **L.** [1] an-zam$_x$; **11** o. V 20: 1 ma-na an-na šub *si-in* **L.** ZA$_x$ naĝar-naĝar; o. VI 5: 2 gín D. kg **L.** 1 *mar-wa-ga-tum*, 18: 4 gín D. kg **L.** 2 níĝ-anše-ak 2 kù-sal; o. XI 19: 2 gín D. kg **L.** 1 an-zam$_x$; r. VI 14: 15 gín D. kg **L.** 2 níĝ-anše-ak 4 kù-sal; **12** o. X 7: 6 ma-na 10 gín D. a-gar$_5$-gar$_5$ **L.** ZA$_x$ naĝar-naĝar; o. XIII 6: 1 ½ gín D. kg **L.** nu$_{11}$-za 1 *gú-li-lum* 15 gín D. a-gar$_5$-gar$_5$, 16: 2 gín D. kg **L.** nu$_{11}$-za 1 *gú-li-lum* kb; r. IV 1: 1 gín D. kg **L.** 1 níĝ-anše-ak; r. V 5: ŠA.PI 2 gín D. kg **L.** 2 *gú-li-lum*; **13** o. VI 23: TAR [x] gí[n] D. kb **L.** nu$_{11}$-za 1 bur-KAK; o. IX 2: 4 gín D. kg **L.** 4 *ʾà-ra-ma-tum*; o. XIII 9: 1 ½ gín D. kg **L.** maš-maš 4 kù-sal; r. VIII 2: 3 gín D. kg **L.** [ ]; **14** o. VII 9: 8 gín D. kg **L.** 1 dib. o. VIII 13: 9 gín D. kg **L.** 4 ĜIŠ-ban 2 ĜIŠ-gígir-II en, 20: ½ gín D. kg **L.** nu$_{11}$-za 2 zag 2 ĜIŠ-gígir-II; o. IV 3: 2 NI gín D. kg **L.** *ma-wa-ù* 2 ĜIŠ-bar-ús ĜIŠ-gígir-II e[n], 11: 2 gín D. kg **L.** 1 dib; o. X 24: ½ gín D. kg **L.** nu$_{11}$-za [ ]; o. XI 5: [1] ma-na ŠÚ+ŠA gín D. kb **L.** 2 níĝ-anše-ak 2[+2] kù-sal, 10: 10 gín D. kb **L.** 2 *gú-li-lum*, 18: 4 ½ gín D. kg **L.** nu$_{11}$-za-*sù*; o. XII 3: 2 gín D. kg **L.** nu$_{11}$-za 2 *gú-li-lum* a-gar$_5$-gar$_5$ esi-I, 17: [½ gín D. kg] **L.** maš-maš 4 kù-sal; o. XIV 9: ⌜1⌝ gín D. kg **L.** 1 dib, 20: 2 gín D. kg **L.** nu$_{11}$-za 2 *gú-li-lum* kg; o. XV 13: 1 gín D. kg **L.** nu$_{11}$-za 1 *gú-li-lum* a-gar$_5$-gar$_5$; r. II 7: 1 gín D. kg **L.** [nu$_{11}$-za] 1 ĝír mar-tu; r. XII 15: 1 kg **L.** 1 pad an-zam$_x$; r. XIII 4: 1 ½ kg **L.** 1 níĝ-anše-ak 1 kù-sal 1 IGI.NITA en, 21: 1 ma-na 16 kb **L.** URI 10 lá-2 íb-lá 5 ĝ[ír-kun] kb maš-maš; r. XIV 8': 10 gín D. kg daḫ$_x$(MU.MU.MU) **L.** nu$_{11}$-za-*sù* 2 *gú-li-lum* a-gar$_5$-gar$_5$ lú ŠA.PI-ŠA.PI-II *wa* 1 *gú-li-lum* a-gar$_5$-gar$_5$ lú ŠÚ+ŠA-I *sa-ḫa-wa wa* 1 *gú-li-lum* a-gar$_5$-gar$_5$ [ ]; r. XX 2': è **L.** ZA$_x$ ĝuruš-ĝuruš; **15** o. IV 18: 2 gín D. kg **L.** nu$_{11}$-za 4 kù-sal, 21: 5 gín D. kb **L.** 2 níĝ-anše-ak; o. V 4: 3 gín D. kg **L.** 1 dib; o. IX 8: 2 ma-na kg **L.** 4 *su-da-ni*, 13: ŠA.PI 8 gín D. kg **L.** 4 kù-sal-*sù*, 18: 10 gín D. kg **L.** nu$_{11}$-za 2 ĜIŠ-ban ĜIŠ-gígir-II lú *ra-ʾà-tum ša-ti* en; o. XIV 24: 1 ma-na 10 gín D. an-na šub *si-in* **L.** ZA$_x$ naĝar-naĝar; o. XV 20: 2 gín D. kb **L.** 1 íb-lá, 26: ½ kg **L.** maš-maš-*sù*; o. XVI 5: ½ gín D. kg **L.** 1 *si-ti-tum*; r. VI 23: 6 gín D. kg **L.** 10 ⌜x⌝-[x]; r. VII 4: 2 gín D. kg **L.** 6 ĝeštu$_x$-lá; r. VIII 23: 7 gín D. kg **L.** 1 an-zam$_x$ an-dùl libir; r. XI 11: 2 gín D. kg **L.** 2 ĜIŠ-du; r. XIII 15: 1 gín D. kg **L.** 1 dib; r. XIV 12: 1 gín D. kg **L.** 1 dib; **16** o. VI 3: ŠÚ+ŠA 5 gín D. kg **L.** 2 níĝ-anše-ak 4 kù-sal libir; o. VII 7: 2 gín D. kg **L.** 2 níĝ-anše-ak 4 kù-sal, 14: TAR 1 gín D. kg **L.** 2 dib lú <1> ma-na 3 dib lú 50 gín D. 8 dib 3 lú ŠA.PI gín D. 3 dib lú TAR. TAR 3 dib ŠÚ+ŠA gín D.; o. VIII 1: 6 gín D. kb **L.** 7 íb-lá 5 ĝír-kun lú URI lú kg, 8: 5 gín D. kg **L.** nu$_{11}$-za-*sù*, 11: 10 gín D. kb **L.** 8 á-MUŠEN kb, 14: 12 gín D. kb **L.** 17 íb-lá maš-maš kg, 19: 2 gín D. kg **L.** maš-maš-*sù*, 22: 52 gín D. kb **L.** 32 ĝír 55 íb-lá kb; o. IX 3: 10 gín D. kb **L.** 3 *gú-li-lum* kb ŠA.PI-II 2 *gú-li-lum* kb TAR-II 15 *gú-li-lum* kb ŠÚ+ŠA-II 7 *gú-li-lum* 11 kb, 11: TAR 7 gín D. kg **L.** nu$_{11}$-za-*sù*; o. X 2: TAR 2 gín D. kg **L.** nu$_{11}$-za 6 *gú-li-lum* a-gar$_5$-gar$_5$ TAR-II 14 *gú-li-lum* a-gar$_5$-gar$_5$ ŠÚ+ŠA-II 5 *gú-li-lum* a-gar$_5$-gar$_5$ 10-I, 8: 2 gín D. kb **L.** nu$_{11}$-za 3 *gú-li-lum* a-gar$_5$-gar$_5$ 10-I; o. XI 12: 6 gín D. kb **L.** nu$_{11}$-za 12 ĝír mar-tu kb; o. XII 3: 1 ma-na 50 gín D. <an-na> šub *si-in* 3[+x ma-n]a [T]AR gín D. ⌜a⌝-gar$_5$-gar$_5$ **L.** ZA$_x$-ZA$_x$ naĝar-naĝar, 15: 1 gín D. kg **L.** nu$_{11}$-za 2 ĝír lú ZA$_x$ *Ib-rí-um*; r. II 2: 10 gín D. kb **L.** 10 ĝeštu$_x$-lá, 7: 1 gín D. kg **L.** 1 kù-sal; r. III 2: [ŠÚ+ŠA k]g **L.** *su-da-⌜nu⌝*? *wa* 4 kù-sal-*sù*, 10: 1 gín D. kg **L.** maš-maš kù-sal, 15: 2 gín D. kb **L.** *ma-wa-lu*, 20: 2 gín D. kg **L.** *ma-wa-lu* ĜIŠ-bar-ús ĜIŠ-gígir-II; r. IV 14: ŠÚ+ŠA 2 gín D. kg **L.** 1 dib; r. V 12: 2 gín D. kg **L.** 1 dib, 19: 1 gín D. kg **L.** 1 dib, 26: 2 gín D. kg **L.** 1 dib; r. VI 12: 1 gín D. kg **L.** nu$_{11}$-za 1 *za-ḫa-da*; r. VII 4: 10 gín D. kb **L.** 2 níĝ-anše-ak ⌜4⌝ kù-sal, 27: 10 gín D. kb **L.** nu$_{11}$-za 2 ĝír mar-tu kb *wa* 3 ĝír mar-tu ti kb *wa ga-ma-tum* 17 ĝír mar-tu; r. VIII 8: 12 gín D. kg **L.** nu$_{11}$-za 4 ĝír mar-tu kg *wa* 4 ĝír mar-tu ti kg *wa* 5 ĝír mar-tu *ba-du-u$_4$* kg *wa ga-ma-tum* 5 ĝír mar-tu kb; r. IX 11: 1 gín D. kg **L.** 1 šu-dub; r. XI 25: 1 gín kg **L.** nu$_{11}$-za šum; r. XII 5: 5 gín D. kb **L.** 2 níĝ-anše-ak 4 kù-sal, 11: 2 gín D. kg **L.** maš-maš-*sù*, 18: 4 gín D. kg **L.** nu$_{11}$-za 1 balaĝ nar, 24: 1 gín D. kg **L.** nu$_{11}$-za 1 bur-KAK ga:eš$_8$; r. XV 16: ½ kg **L.** 4 ĝeštu$_x$-lá; r. XVI 10: 10 kg **L.** 1 dib, 17: 10 kg **L.** 1 dib; **17** o. III 20: 5 gín D. kg **L.** nu$_{11}$-za 1 *gú-li-lum* a-gar$_5$-gar$_5$ 50; o. XI 12: 2 gín D. kg **L.** 1 íb-lá 1 *si-ti-tum* 1 ĝír-kun; o. XIII 20: 3 gín D. kg **L.** *zi-du* 3 *ša-ga-tum* 3 ĝír mar-tu; o. XVI 22: ŠÚ+ŠA 2 gín D. kb **L.** 2 níĝ-anše-ak 4 kù-sal; r. I 22: TAR kg **L.** 1 dib, 26: 2 gín D. kb **L.** nu$_{11}$-⌜za⌝ 1 *za-⌜ḫa⌝-d[a]* *wa* 1 ĜIŠ-MUNŠUB; r. II 3: 2 NI gín D. kg **L.** *ma-wa-lu* ĜIŠ-bar-ús, 13: 3 gín D. kg **L.** 2 níĝ-anše-ak 4 kù-sal sur$_x$-BAR.AN, 19: 2 gín D. kg **L.** 1 níĝ-anše-ak 1 kù-sal 2 IGI.NITA, 26: 5 gín D. kg **L.** nu$_{11}$-za *si-gi* 1 ĜIŠ-gu-kak-šub; r. III 12: 1 gín D. kg **L.** nu$_{11}$-za 2 *gú-li-lum* kbg, 20: 3 gín D. kg **L.** maš-maš kù-sal, 26: 1 gín D. 3 NI kg **L.** 1 dib; r. VII 17: 2 NI gín D. kg **L.** nu$_{11}$-za *ša-ga-ti* 1 ĝír mar-tu zú, 28: 1 gín D. kg **L.** 1 dib; r. VIII 9: ½ gín D. kg **L.** 1 dib, 14: 5 gín D. kb **L.** 2 níĝ-anše-ak 4 kù-sal; r. XV 5: 10 gín D. kg **L.** 1 dib; r. XIX 11: ½ kg **L.** 1 dib, 18: 10 kg **L.** 1 dib, 26: 1 kg **L.** 1 dib, 34: 1 ½ kg **L.** 1 di[b]; **18** o. VI 4: [10+]4 [gín D. kg] **L.** 4 kù-sal, 15: 1 gín D. kg **L.** nu$_{11}$-za 1 *gú-li-lum* a-gar$_5$-gar$_5$; o. X 6: 15 gín D. kg **L.** 2 *ti-gi-na*, 11: 2 gín D. kg **L.** 2 ĜIŠ-du; o. XI 4: 7 gín D. kb **L.** 1 íb-lá 1 ĝír-kun kb, 9: 1 gín D. kg **L.** maš-maš-*sù*, 13: 8 gín D. kb **L.** 1 íb-lá 1 ĝír-kun, 20: 1 gín D. kg **L.** 1 dib; o. XV 31: 3 kg **L.** nu$_{11}$-za 1 *za-ḫa-da* 1 [ĜI]Š?-PA-⸢x⸣-ga; o. XVII 26: 6 gín D. kg **L.** 10 lá-2 ĝeštu$_x$-lá; o. XVIII 3: 8 gín D. kg **L.** 4 *ti-gi-na* 4 ĜIŠ-du 4 ĝeštu$_x$-lá 2 kù-sal; o. XIX 29: 2 gín D. kg **L.** nu$_{11}$-za 2 ĜIŠ.GAM.GAM ĜIŠ-gígir-II; r. I 6: 3 gín D. kg **L.** 2 níĝ-anše-ak 2 kù-sal 2 IGI.NITA *wa su-da-nu* kù-sal, 18: 1 gín D. kg *wa* 1 gín D. kb **L.** *ma-wa-⸢lu⸣* ĜIŠ-bar-ús ĜIŠ-gígir-II, 26: 6 g[ín] D. kg **L.** nu$_{11}$-za 1 *za-ḫa-da*; r. II 8: 2 ma-na an-na šub *si-in* 12 ma-na a-gar$_5$-gar$_5$ **L.** ZA$_x$-ZA$_x$ naĝar-naĝar; r. IV 8: 3 gín D. kg **L.** nu$_{11}$-za 1 níĝ-PA; r. XV 23: 1 kg **L.** nu$_{11}$-za 1 ĝír mar-tu; r. XVII 11: 10 kg **L.** nu$_{11}$-za 2 ĜIŠ.GAM.GAM ĜIŠ-gígir-II *ra-ʾà-tum*; **19** o. IV 13: 1 ½ gín D. kg **L.** nu$_{11}$-za 2 *gú-li-lum* kb; o. VIII 25: 1 gín D. kg **L.** 4 kù-sal; o. XII 8: 4 gín D. kg **L.** 1 an-zam$_x$ en, 14: 50 gín D. kg **L.** *su-da-nu wa* kù-sal, 23: 3 gín D. kg **L.** 2 [n]íĝ-anše-ak 4 kù-sal, 29: 6 gín D. kg **L.** nu$_{11}$-za 2 ĜIŠ-ban ĜIŠ-gígir-II; r. VII 25: 2 gín D. kg **L.** 1 dib, 31: 2 gín D. kg **L.** 2 dib; r. XI 2: 1 gín D. 6 NI kg **L.** nu$_{11}$-za 1 *za-ḫa-da*; r. XV 22: 2 ½ gín D. kg **L.** ⸢1⸣ [d]ib; **20** o. VII 10: 4 gín D. kb **L.** 2 níĝ-anše-ak, 23: 6 gín D. an-na šub *si-in* **L.** 2 níĝ-anše-ak 4 kù-sal; o. IX 10: 1 gín D. kg **L.** nu$_{11}$-za 1 *za-ḫa-da*; o. X 23: 5 gín D. kg **L.** 1 dib; r. II 10: 1 ½ gín D. kg **L.** nu$_{11}$-za 4 kù-sal, 17: 2 gín D. kg **L.** 1 an-zam$_x$; r. III 3: ⸢4⸣ gín D. kg **L.** 1 pad *ma-da-a-um* kg an-dùl; r. IV 8: 2 gín D. [k]g **L.** nu$_{11}$-za 1 *za-ḫa-da*, 19: 10 gín D. kg **L.** 1 *gú-li-lum*; r. V 7: 2 gín D. kb **L.** [2 níĝ-anše-ak?], 12: 10 gín D. kg **L.** maš-maš 4 kù-sal, 18: ŠÚ+ŠA gín [D.] kb **L.** 2 níĝ-anše-ak 4 kù-sal; r. IX 19: 2 gín D. kg **L.** [nu$_{11}$-]za [ ]; r. XII 8: 5 gín D. kg **L.** 1 dib; **21** o. III 16: 4 gín D. an-na šub *si-in* [**L.** 2 níĝ-anše-ak 4 kù-sal], 26: 4 gín D. kg **L.** [2] níĝ-anše-ak [2+]2 k[ù-]s[al]; o. IV 5: 3 gín D. kg **L.** 2 kù-sal, 10: 7 gín D. kb **L.** 4 kù-sal, 15: 6 gín D. kg **L.** kù-sal-*sù*; o. X 5: 1 gín D. kg **L.** [1 níĝ]-anše-ak, 11: 4 gín D. kg **L.** nu$_{11}$-za 2 ĜIŠ.GA[M.GAM] ĜIŠ-gígir-II, 19: 1 4 NI gín D. kg **L.** nu$_{11}$-za 1 kun; r. III 11: 12 gín D. kg **L.** *ga-ma-a-tum* ĝír mar-tu, 26: ŠÚ+ŠA 7 gín D. kg **L.** [ ]; r. IV 10: 1 ma-na kb **L.** 10 lá-3 *gú-li-lum* ŠA.PI kbg-II *wa* 4 *gú-li-lum* TAR kbg *wa* 16 *gú-li-lum* ŠÚ+ŠA-ŠÚ+ŠA kbg-II *wa* 3 *gú-li-lum* 10 kbg-I, 21: 56 gín D. kg **L.** [ ]; r. V 5: [ ] **L.** nu$_{11}$-za 11 *gú-li-lum* TAR a-gar$_5$-gar$_5$ kg *wa* 10 *gú-li-lum* 15 a-gar$_5$-gar$_5$ kg, 13: TAR 2 kb **L.** 16 íb-lá 6 ĝír-kun *wa* 1 á-MUŠEN kb, 18: 12 gín D. kg **L.** 3 *gú-li-lum* a-gar$_5$ kb TAR-II *wa* 3 *gú-li-lum* a-gar$_5$-gar$_5$ kb 15-I, 24: 2 gín D. an-na šub *si-in* **L.** [ ]; r. VI 8: TAR 7 gín D. kg **L.** nu$_{11}$-za ĝír mar-tu; r. VIII 23: 5 gín D. kb **L.** 2 ĜIŠ-du; **22** r. VII 6: ŠA.PI gín D. kg **L.** 13 dib; **23** o. III 6: 1 gín D. kg **L.** 1 pad an-zam$_x$, 10: 2 gín D. kg **L.** <1 dib>; o. IV 4: 1 gín D. kg **L.** 1 dib, 8: 1 ½ gín D. kg **L.** 1 dib; o. V 2: 1 gín D. kg **L.** 1 dib, 6: 1 ½ gín D. kg **L.** 1 dib, 10: 1 gín D. kg **L.** 1 dib; o. VI 3: 1 gín D. kg **L.** 1 dib, 7: 1 gín D. kg **L.** 1 dib, 11: 1 ½ gín D. kg **L.** 1 dib; o. VII 4: 1 ½ gín D. kg **L.** 1 dib, 8: ½ gín D. kg **L.** 1 dib; o. VIII 2: 1 ½ gín D. kg **L.** 1 dib, 6: 1 gín D. kg **L.** nu$_{11}$-za 1 íb-lá 1 ĝír-kun, 11: 5 gín D. kg **L.** maš-maš 4 íb-lá 1 ĝír-kun maš-maš; o. IX 3: ŠÚ+ŠA 8 gín D. kg **L.** nu$_{11}$-za 2 *gú-li-lum*-II esi ŠA.PI 2 *gú-li-lum*-II esi TAR.TAR 1 *gú-li-lum*-I esi ŠÚ+ŠA 10 lá-1 *gú-li-lum* 10-I esi; o. X 2: ŠÚ+ŠA 8 gín D. kg **L.** nu$_{11}$-za 7 *gú-li-lum*-II esi TAR-TAR a-gar$_5$ 10 lá-1 *gú-li-lum*-II esi ŠÚ+ŠA-ŠÚ+ŠA a-gar$_5$ 1 *gú-li-lum*-I esi ŠÚ+ŠA a-gar$_5$ 2 *gú-li-lum*-I esi 10 a-gar$_5$; r. III 4: 19 gín D. kg **L.** nu$_{11}$-za 1 ĝír mar-tu kg *wa sa-ga-tum* 10 lá-1 ĝír mar-tu; r. V 2: 1 gín D. kg **L.** 1 dib, 6: 2 gín D. kg **L.** nu$_{11}$-za <1> *gú-li-lum*, 10: 2 gín D. kg **L.** 1 dib; r. VI 4: 2 gín D. kg **L.** 1 dib; **24** o. I 6: 2 gín D. kg **L.** 4 ĝeštu$_x$-lá; o. III 9: 1 gín D. kg **L.** 1 dib; o. IV 2: 1 gín D. kg **L.** nu$_{11}$-za 1 *za-ḫa-da*, 10: 1 gín D. kg **L.** nu$_{11}$-za 1 *za-ḫa-da*; r. III 4: 13? gín D. kg **L.** 1 dib, 10: 4 gín D. kg **L.** 3 dib.

nu-du$_{11}$ «without authorization»

nu-du$_{11}$-nu-du$_{11}$ **3** o. VIII 5: [ ] níĝ-kas$_4$ **L.** šu-ba$_4$-ti *si-in Ib-al*$_6^{ki}$ *in* ud dumu-nita en *Ḫa-zu-wa-an*$^{ki}$ ḫi-úš *in Ga-ra-ma-an*$^{ki}$ lú *Ḫar-sum*$^{ki}$.

nu-kiri$_6$ see ĜIŠ-nu-kiri$_6$.

nu$_{11}$-za «plating, lamination, metal leaf; to plate» **1** o. IX 4: [1 gín] kg **L.** *sa-ga-ti* 1 ĝír ⸢mar⸣[-tu]; o. X 4: 2 gín D. kg **L.**-*sù*, 13: 3 gín D. kg **L.**-*sù wa* [1] kù-sal; o. XI 9: 12 gín D. kg **L.** 2 ⸢x⸣; **2** o. II 18: 6 gín D. kg **L.** 1 bur-KAK ĜIŠ-taškarin; o. III 1: 3 gín D. kg **L.** 2 saĝ 2 *bu*-DI; 6 gín D. kg **L.** 1 *ḫa-bù*, 16: 15 gín D. kb **L.**-*sù*; o. V 9: 3 gín D. kg **L.** 2 saĝ-*sù*; o. IX 9: 1 gín D. kg **L.** *ba-na-a wa* íb+III-TÚG; o. XI 12: 3 gín D. kg **L.** 1 ĝír mar-tu *ra-ʾà-tum* tur, 19: 2 gín D. kg **L.** 1 *ma-ḫa-ni-lum*; o. XIII 10: 3 gín D. kg *ni-zi-mu* **L.** ĜIŠ-sur$_x$ ĜIŠ-gígir-II!(III); o. XIV 14: 9 gín D. kg *ni-zi-mu* **L.** ḫaš-ḫaš 4 *gú-li-lum* kb *wa* ḫaš-ḫaš 5 *gú-li-lum* a-gar$_5$-gar$_5$; r. II 12: 3 gín D. kg **L.** 2 zé-*sù*, 21: 55 gín D. kg **L.** [x *gú-li-lum*] 10 ⸢gín⸣ kb 3 *gú-li-lum*-II a-gar$_5$-gar$_5$ TAR esi 2 *gú-li-lum*-II a-gar$_5$-gar$_5$ ŠÚ+ŠA esi 20 *gú-li-lum*-I a-gar$_5$-gar$_5$ 10 esi; r. III 17: TAR kb **L.** 2 *ḫa-bù*; r. IV 3: [ŠÚ+ŠA] g[ín D.] kg **L.**-*sù*; r. VII 5: 1 ma-na kb **L.** 4 si-*sù*, 16: 15 gín D. kb **L.** 1 an-dùl, 20: 5 gín D. kg **L.** [ ]; r. XIII 20: 15 gín D. kb **L.** 1 *ḫa-bù*; r. XIV 3: 6 gín D. kg **L.**-*sù*, 10: 1 ma-na kb **L.** 10 *gú-li-lum*-II a-gar$_5$-gar$_5$ ŠÚ+ŠA esi *wa* 20 *gú-li-lum*-I a-gar$_5$-gar$_5$ 10 esi; r. XV 1: [52] gín D. kg **L.**-*sù*, 8: 10 gín D. kg **L.**-*sù*, 12: 7 gín D. kb **L.** 1 an-dùl, 16: ½ gín D. kg **L.** *ba-na-a-ša*; r. XVI 1: **L.**-*sù*; **3** o. III 2: 1 ½ gín D. kb **L.** 1 zag ĜIŠ-gígir-II; o. IV 13: 13 gín D. kb **L.** 1 *ḫa-bù*, 17: 5 gín D. kg **L.** *ar-ra-si-su*; o. XII 7: TAR 5 gín D. kb **L.** 1 an-dùl, 11: 6 gín D. kg **L.** *ba-na-⸢ʾà⸣ wa* 2 šu 2 DU-*sù*; o. XIII 11: 1 gín D. kb *ni-zi-nu* **L.** 1 *za-ḫa-da*, 20: 15 gín D. kb [**L.** 1 *ḫa-*]*b*[*ù*]; o. XIV 3: 6

gín D. kg **L.** 1 *ar-ra-si-su*; r. V 11: 6' gín D. kg **L.** 1 bur-KAK *na-*⸢*kar*⸣$^?$-⸢*ra*⸣*-tim*; r. IX 1: 3 gín D. kb **L.** 2 zag 2 ĜIŠ-gígir-II; **4** o. IV 14: 12 gín D. kb **L.** 3 ĜIŠ-banšur 3 ĝír mar-tu; o. V 16: 1 ½ gín D. kb **L.** 1 zag ĜIŠ-gígir-II; o. X 7: ŠÚ+ŠA gín D. kb **L.** 20 *gú-a-tum*; o. XI 4: TAR kg **L.** 4 bur-KAK-bur-KAK ĜIŠ-taškarin; o. XIII 8: 1 ½ gín D. kb **L.** 1 zag ĜIŠ-gígir-II; r. III 9: 4 g[ín D. kb] [*n*]*i-zi-mu* **L.** 2 ĝír šu-du$_8$-máš; r. IV 2: 1 gín D. kb **L.** 2 šu-i *Ib-rí-um*, 6: 5 2 NI g[ín D. kb] **L.** 1 *ma-ḫa-ni-gúm*; r. X 21: 8 gín D. kb **L.** 1 an-dùl; r. XI 20: 15 gín D. kb **L.** 1 *ḫa-bu*; r. XII 12: 15 gín D. kb *ni-zi-mu* **L.** 1 *ma-ḫa-ni-gúm*; **5** o. III 10: 8 gín D. kb **L.** 2 *gú-li-lum*, 15: ŠÚ+ŠA 2 gín D. kg **L.** 3 *gú-li-lum*-II esi 10 *gú-li-lum*-I esi; o. IV 19: ŠA.PI 6 gín D. kg **L.** 3 *gú-li-lum*-II a-gar$_5$-gar$_5$ 10 *gú-li-lum*-I esi a-gar$_5$-gar$_5$; o. VI 4: 2 ½ gín D. kg *ni-zi-mu* **L.** *gú-li-lum*, 14: 5 gín D. kg **L.** 1 bur-KAK ĜIŠ-taškarin; o. VIII 1: 1 ma-na kb **L.** 4 si-*sù in* AMA-*ra*, 11: 1 ma-na kb **L.** 4 si-*sù in* AMA-*ra*; o. XII 8: 13 gín D. kb **L.** 1 *ḫa-bù*, 12: 6 gín D. kg **L.** *ar-ra-si-sù*, 17: 3 ma-na kb **L.** ĜIŠ-banšur; o. XVI 19: 2 gín D. kg *ni-zi-mu* **L.**-*sù*; r. I 18: 2 gín D. kg *ni-z*[*i*-]*m*[*u*] **L.**-*sù*; r. III 14: 3 gín D. kb **L.** 1 ĝír mar-tu; r. V 10: 1 ma-na ŠÚ+ŠA 5 gín D. kb **L.** 1 ĜIŠ-banšur, 14: ŠÚ+ŠA gín D. kg **L.** 3 saĝ lu$_5$; r. VIII 8: 1 gín D. kb 1 zag ĝIŠ-gígir-II; r. X 7: 15 gín D. kb **L.** 1 *ḫa-bù*, 11: 6 gín D. kg **L.** *ar-ra-si-sù*; r. XII 9: 5 gín D. kg **L.** *ba-na-a*, 13: ŠÚ+ŠA 3 gín D. kb **L.** 2 šu-*sù*, 18: 3 gín D. kg *ni-zi-mu* **L.** 2 *gú-li-lum*; r. XIII 3: 1 ½ gín D. kg *ni-zi-mu* **L.** 2 *gú-li-lum*, 8: ŠA.PI gín D. kb **L.** 20 *gú-li-lum*, 20: 3 gín D. kg **L.** 1 ĝír mar-tu; r. XIV 14: 2 gín D. kb **L.** 1 ĝír mar-tu; r. XV 14: TAR 5 gín D. kb **L.** 3 ĜIŠ-šú 3 níĝ-bànda; **6** o. III 14: 50 gín D. kb **L.** 1 dub; o. VIII 1 and 6: 5 gín D. kb **L.** 1 ĜIŠ-banšur ... *wa* **L.** 1 ĝír mar-tu; o. IX 11: 2 gín D. kb 1 zag ĝIŠ-gígir-II, 16: 1 ½ gín D. kb 1 zag ĜIŠ-gígir-II; o. XI 13: 50 gín D. kb 1 ĜIŠ-banšur *wa* 1 *ḫa-bù*; o. XIII 12: 5 gín D. kb **L.** 1 saĝ lu$_5$ ĜIŠ-ĝidru, 23: 15 gín D. kb **L.** 1 *ḫa-bù*; o. XIV 13: 15 gín D. kb **L.** 1 *ḫa-bù*; o. XV 22: 8 gín D. kb **L.** 4 ĝír šu-du$_8$-máš; o. XVI 25: TAR kb **L.** 2 *ḫa-bù*; r. II 15: 10 gín D. kb **L.** 1 ĝír mar-tu; r. IV 19: TAR 2 gín D. kb **L.** $^{d}$*Ba-li-ḫa*-II; r. V 5: TAR kb **L.** $^{d}$*Wa-da-ʾà-an wa* $^{d}$*Ša-la-ša* lú *Ga-ra-mu*$^{ki}$, 17: 2 gín D. kb **L.** 1 zag ĜIŠ-gígir-{II-}II; r. XVII 22: 15 an-na šub-šub **L.** 1 *ḫa-bù*; **7** o. I 9: 2 gín D. kb **L.** 1 ĝír mar-tu; o. III 12: 3 gín D. kb **L.** 1 ĝír mar-tu *wa* 1 kù-sal; o. IV 1: [ ] **L.** AN.Á.DAH diĝir-diĝir, 11: ŠA.PI gín D. kb **L.** 20 ĝír mar-tu ti kb; o. V 11: 2 gín D. kb **L.** 1 ĝír mar-tu ti; o. VII 6: 1 gín D. kb *ni-zi-mu* **L.** 1 *za-ḫa-da*; o. X 5: ŠA.PI gín D. kb **L.** 1 an-dùl munus, 9: 17 gín D. kg **L.** saĝ-*sù* 2 šu-*sù* DU-*sù*, 17: 3 gín D. kb **L.** 1 ĝír mar-tu; o. XI 9: 15 gín D. kb **L.** 1 ešda, 13: 6 gín D. kg **L.** 1 *ar-ra-sù*; o. XII 3: 15 gín D. kb **L.** 1 ešda, 7: 6 gín D. kg **L.** 1 *ar-ra-sù*, 20: 2 gín D. kg *ni-zi-mu* **L.** 1 ĝír mar-tu; o. XIII 14: ½ gín D. kg *ni-zi-mu* **L.** 1 ĝír, 20: 2 gín D. kg *ni-zi-mu* **L.** 2 *za-ḫa-da*; o. XIV 12: 8 gín D. kg **L.** 1 *za-ḫa-da*; o. XV 16: 2[+x$^?$ gín] ⸢D.⸣ kb **L.** 1 gud-I; r. I 11: 10[+x] gí[n] D. kb **L.** 1 ešda; r. II 7: 2 g[ín D.] kb **L.** 1 ĝír mar-tu, 16: 2 gín D. kb **L.** 1 ĝír mar-tu; r. III 9: 2 gín D. kg **L.** [ ], 14: 2 gín D. kg **L.** 1 ĝír mar-tu; r. V 21: 2 gín D. kg **L.** 1 ĝír mar-tu; r. VII 16: 15 gín D. kb **L.** 1 ešda; r. VIII 3: 6 gín D. kg **L.** *ar-r*[*a*-]*sù*; r. IX 6: 1 ma-[n]a 5 gín D. kg **L.** 10 *gú-li-lum*-II a-gar$_5$-gar$_5$ TAR 5 *gú-li-lum*-II a-gar$_5$ ŠÚ+ŠA 10 *gú-li-lum*-I ⸢a⸣-gar$_5$-gar$_5$ ⸢15$^?$⸣ 10 *gú-l*[*i*]*-lum*-I a-gar$_5$-gar$_5$ 10 10; r. XV 14: 10 ma-na kb ŠÚ+ŠA 7 gín D. kg sikil lú *Maš-ga-du*$^{ki}$ *wa* ì-na-sum **L.** $^{d}$*Ra-sa-ap Du-ne-íb*$^{ki}$, 25: ŠÚ+ŠA 4 gín D. kg daḫ kg lú en *wa* [l]ugal-[lu]gal [ì-n]a-sum [**L.** $^{d}$*Ra-s*]*a-ap*; **8** o. VI 6: TAR kg daḫ **L.** 1 an-dùl; o. VII 3: 4 gín D. kb **L.** 1 ĝír mar-tu; o. X 8: 4 gín D. kb **L.** 1 ⸢ĝír mar⸣-[tu]; r. V 10': 1 ma-na kb **L.** 8 si 4 gud; r. IX 5': 10$^?$ gín D. kb [**L.** 1 *ḫa-bù*], 9': 6 gín D. kg **L.** *ar-ra-si-su*; r. XI 2': [x] g[ín] ⸢D⸣ kb **L.** 1 dub; **9** o. III 7: TAR kb **L.** 2 *ḫa-bù*, 23: [1 ma-na kb] [**L.** si-si] 2 gud; o. IV 7: 1 ma-na kb **L.** si-si 2 gud; o. V 9: 3 gín D. kb **L.** 3 ĝír šu-du$_8$-m[áš]; r. III 16: [x] gín D. kg **L.** 1 ĝír mar-tu; r. V 13: 12 gín D. kb **L.** 1 *ḫa-bù*; r. VI 11: 2 gín D. kg **L.** 2 saĝ-*sù*; r. VII 13: 13 gín D. kb **L.** 1 *ḫa-bù*, 17: 6 gín D. ⸢kg⸣ **L.** 1 *ar-ra-sù*; r. VIII 4: ŠÚ+ŠA 6 gín D. **L.** 1 an-dùl, 8: 6 gín D. kg **L.** *ba-na-ʾà-sa wa* íb+III-TÚG [*w*]*a* an-zam$_x$ *wa* 2 *gú-li-lum-sù*; r. IX 1: 5 ma-na 5 gín ⸢D.⸣ [kb] **L.** 1 an-dùl, 14: 1 ma-na TAR kg *ni-zi-mu* **L.** ḫaš-ḫaš 7 *gú-li-lum*-II ⸢kb⸣ esi GÁ×LÁ TAR-*sù wa* 10 *gú-li-lum*-II kb esi GÁ×LÁ ŠÚ+ŠA gín D. 1 *gú-li-lum*-I kb esi 1 gín D. GÁ×LÁ-*sù*; r. X 9: 1 ma-na ŠÚ+ŠA 6 gín D. kg *ni-zi-mu* **L.** ḫaš-ḫaš 1 dib a-gar$_5$-gar$_5$ lú 4 *gú-li-lum* [ ] 1 dib a-gar$_5$-gar$_5$ [ ] 15 *gú-li-lum*-II a-gar$_5$-gar$_5$ esi *wa* 2 *gú-li-lum*-II a-gar$_5$-gar$_5$ *sa-ḫ*[*a*-]*wa* esi GÁ×LÁ TAR *wa* 1$^?$ *gú-li-lum* a-gar$_5$-gar$_5$ *sa-ḫa-wa* 20 esi 12 *gú-li-lum* a-gar$_5$-gar$_5$ *sa-ḫa-wa* 12 esi; r. XI 10: 5 gín D. kb *ni-zi-mu* **L.** ḫaš-ḫaš 1 *gú-li-lum*-II a-gar$_5$-gar$_5$ esi *wa* 4 *gú-li-lum*[-I] [a-]gar$_5$-gar$_5$ esi; r. XII 5: ŠÚ+ŠA gín D. kg *ni-zi-mu* **L.** 10 ĝír mar-tu kg 2 ĝír mar-tu ti kg [x] ĝír mar-tu zú LAGAB×AN 6 ĝír mar-tu *ba-du-u*$_4$ kg; r. XIII 7: 1 gín D. kb **L.** [ ]x; r. XVI 2: [TAR] kg **L.**-*sù*; **10** o. II 3: 2 ma-na kb **L.** 1 ĜIŠ-banšur; o. IV 9: 10 gín D. kb **L.** 1 ĜIŠ-sal, 17: 2 gín D. kb *ni-zi-mu* **L.** 1 *za-ḫa-da*; o. V 1: 15 gín D. [kb] **L.** 1 *ḫa-bù*, 5: 6 gín D. kg **L.** 1 *ar-ra-sù*; o. VII 7: 50 gín D. kb **L.** 1 dub; o. VIII 19: 8 gín D. kb **L.** balaĝ; o. X 13: 3 gín D. kb **L.** 1 ĝír mar-tu; o. XI 10: 1 ma-na kb **L.** 4 si-si 2 gud; o. XII 4: 1 gín D. kb **L.** 1 zag 1 ĜIŠ-gígir-II; o. XIII 6: 1 ½ gín D. kb **L.** 1 zag 1 ĜIŠ-gígir-II, 13: 5 gín D. kb maš-maš 1 [ĜIŠ]-⸢banšur⸣ *wa* **L.** 1 ĝír mar-tu; o. XV 6: 2 ma-na ŠA.PI gín D. kb **L.** 2 si am; r. II 10: 5 gín D. kb *ni-zi-mu* **L.** 4 *gú-li-lum*; r. III 6: 6 gín D. kb **L.** 1 *ma-ḫa-ni-gúm*; r. V 14: 3 gín D. kb **L.** *gú-za-ru*$_{12}$*-tum* lú ⸢gi⸣; r. X 1: 3 gín D. kb **L.** 1 ĝír mar-tu 1 kù-sal; **11** o. IV 7: 3 gín D. kg **L.** *maš-ar-tum*; o. IV 20: 2 gín D. kb **L.** [1 g]ír mar-tu; V 11: 2 gín D. kb **L.** 1 ĝír mar-tu; o. X 6: 13 gín D. kb **L.** 1 ešda, 10: 6 gín D. kg **L.** 1 *ar-ra-sù*, 19: 13 gín D. kb **L.** 1 ešda, 23: 6 gín D. kg **L.** [1 *ar-r*]*a-*[*sù*]; o. XII 12: 2 gín D. kg **L.** 2 saĝ-*sù*; r. IV 8: 13 gín D. kb **L.** 1 ešda; r. V 4: 2 gín D. kg **L.** 1 ĝír mar-tu, 17: 13 gín D. kb **L.** 1 ešda; r. VII 1: 2 *ʾà-ra-ma-tum* … ŠÚ+ŠA kg **L.**-*sù*; **12** o. III 6: 1 ma-na kb **L.** 2 an-dùl, 11: ŠÚ+ŠA 2 gín D. kg **L.** *ba-na-i-su-ma wa* 2 šu-šu-*sù* 2 DU.DU-*sù*; o. V 12: 4 gín D. kb **L.** 2 ĝír mar-tu; o. VII 14: 2 gín D. kb **L.** 1 ĝír mar-tu; o. XIII 7: 1 ½ gín D. kg *ni-zi-mu* **L.** 1 *gú-li-lum*

15 gín D. a-gar$_5$-gar$_5$, 17: 2 gín D. kg *ni-zi-mu* **L.** 1 *gú-li-lum* kb; r. I 11: 15 gín D. kb **L.** 1 *ḫa-*˹*bù*˺, 14: 6 gín D. kg **L.** 1 *ar-ra-sù*; r. VII 11: 2 gín D. kb **L.** 1 ĝír mar-tu; r. VIII 18: ŠÚ+ŠA 6 gín D. kg kin$_5$-ak saĝ $^{d}$*Ra-sa-ap Du-ne-íb*$^{ki}$ *wa* **L.** íb+III-TÚG-*sù*; r. IX 7 and 11: TAR 3 gín D. kb **L.** 2 an-dùl … 8 gín D. kg **L.** *ba-na-a-sa wa* 2 šu-*sù wa* 2 DU-*sù*; **13** o. III 4: TAR 2 gín D. kg **L.** 2 ĜIŠ.GAM.GAM, 8: 2 gín D. kg **L.** 1 zag; o. V 4: 2 gín D. kb **L.** 1 ĝír mar-tu; o. VI 10: 1 gín D. kb **L.** 1 zag ĜIŠ-gígir-II, 24: TAR [x] gí[n] D. kb *ni-zi-mu* **L.** 1 bur-KAK; o. VII 17: ŠA.PI 3 gín D. kb **L.** 2 an-dùl, 21: 10 gín D. kg **L.** [I]GI.DUB-*sù wa* 4 šu-*sù* 4 DU-*sù*; o. VIII 12: 12 gín D. kb **L.** 1 an-dùl, 16: 3 gín D. kg **L.** IGI.DUB-*sù* 2 šu-*sù* 2 DU-*sù*; o. IX 8: 2 ½ gín D. kb **L.** 1 ĝír mar-tu 1 kù-sal; o. XI 3: 15 gín D. kb **L.** 1 *ḫa-bù*, 7: 6 gín D. kg **L.** 1 *ar-ra-sù*; o. XII 12: 2 ĝír mar-tu 4 gín D. kb **L.**-*sù*; o. XIII 23: 2 *bu*-DI … 3 gín D. kg **L.** 2 saĝ-*sù*; o. XV 12: 3 gín D. kb **L.** 2 zag 2 ĜIŠ-gígir-II, 23: 2 *bu*-DI … 3 gín D. kg **L.** 2 saĝ-*sù*; o. XVI 9: 1 gín D. kb **L.** 2 si [gud]-I; r. IV 1: [ ] **L.**-*sù*, 4: [13 g]ín [D. kb **L.** 1 *ḫa-bù*], 9: 13 gín D. kb **L.** 1 *ḫa-bù*, 14: TAR 4 gín D. kb **L.** 2 an-dùl, 22: 5 gín D. kb **L.** ˹1˺ an-dùl; r. VIII 12: 4 gín D. kg **L.** saĝ 4 *bu*-DI; r. XIV 17: ŠA.PI gín D. kb **L.** 5 *gú-li-lum*-II a-gar$_5$-gar$_5$ TAR *wa* 5 *gú-li-lum*-II a-gar$_5$-gar$_5$ ŠÚ+ŠA; **14** o. VIII 21: ½ gín D. kg *ni-zi-mu* **L.** 2 zag 2 ĜIŠ-gígir-II; o. IX 22: 15 gín D. kb **L.** 1 *ḫa-bù*; o. X 4: 6 gín D. kg **L.** 1 ˹*ar*˺-*ra*[-*sù*], 25: ½ gín D. kg *ni-zi-mu* **L.** [ ]; o. XI 19: 2 *gú-li-lum* … 4 ½ gín D. kg *ni-zi-mu* **L.**-*sù*; o. XII 4: 2 gín D. kg *ni-zi-mu* **L.** 2 *gú-li-lum*-I a-gar$_5$-gar$_5$ esi; o. XIV 21: 2 gín D. kg *ni-zi-mu* **L.** 2 *gú-li-lum* kg; o. XV 14: 1 gín D. kg *ni-zi-mu* **L.** 1 *gú-li-lum* a-gar$_5$-gar$_5$; o. XVIII 3: … *gú-li-lum* … 1 ma-na 6 gín D. kg **L.**-*sù*, 7: 1 ma-na ŠÚ+ŠA 7 ½ gín D. kg [**L.**] 10 *gú-li-lum*-II lú TAR.TAR a-gar$_5$-gar$_5$ *wa* 10 *gú-li-lum*-II a-gar$_5$-gar$_5$ ˹lú˺[ŠÚ+ŠA-ŠÚ+ŠA] [*wa*] 10 *gú-li-lum*-I a-gar$_5$-gar$_5$ lú 15 10, 14: 10 ma-na ŠÚ+ŠA 7 gín D. kb **L.** 10 *gù-li-lum*-II a-gar$_5$-g[ar$_5$] ˹lú˺ TAR.TAR *wa* 4 *gú-li-lum*-II a-gar$_5$-gar$_5$ lú ŠÚ+ŠA-ŠÚ+ŠA *wa* 20 *gú-li-lum*-I a-gar$_5$-gar$_5$ lú 15 10; r. II 8: 1 gín D. kg *ni-zi-mu* [**L.**] 1 ĝír mar-tu, 13: 13 gín D. kb **L.** 1 *ḫa-bù*, 18: 6 gín D. kg **L.** 1 *ar-ra-su-sù*; r. III 12: 1 gín D. kg **L.** [1 ĝ]ír [mar-t]u [t]i; r. V 20: 50 gín D. kb **L.** 1 ĜIŠ-banšur maḫ; r. VI 19: 1 ma-na 54 gín D. a-gar$_5$-g[ar$_5$] **L.** 1 ĜIŠ-asari, 21: 6 gín D. kb **L.** 4 saĝ lu$_5$ *al*$_6$-*sù*; r. IX 20: 2 *bu*-DI … 3 gín D. kg **L.** 2 saĝ-*sù*; r. X 10: [x kg] **L.** 1 ĝír mar-tu; r. XIV 9': 10 gín D. kg daḫ$_x$(MU.MU.MU) *ni-zi-mu* **L.**-*sù* 2 *gú-li-lum*-II a-gar$_5$-gar$_5$ lú ŠA.PI-ŠA.PI *wa* 1 *gú-li-lum*-I a-gar$_5$-gar$_5$ lú ŠÚ+ŠA *sa-ḫa-wa wa* 1 *gú-li-lum* a-gar$_5$-gar$_5$ [ ]; **15** o. IV 19: 2 gín D. kg *ni-zi-mu* **L.** 4 kù-sal; o. VIII 12: 1 gín D. kb **L.** 1 zag ĜIŠ-gígir-II; o. IX 19: 10 gín D. kg *ni-zi-mu* **L.** 2 ĜIŠ-ban ĜIŠ-gígir-II lú *ra-ʾà-tum ša-ti* en; o. X 1: 15 gín D. kb **L.** 1 *ḫa-bù*, 5: 6 gín D. kg **L.** 1 *ar-ra-si-su*; o. XI 19: 1 ma-na 14 gín D. kg kin$_5$-ak … *wa* **L.** 2 saĝ 2 *bu*-DI; o. XIII 22: 1 íb[-lá] 1 ĝír-kun … TAR kg **L.**-*sù*; o. XV 16: 3 gín D. kb **L.** 2 ĜIŠ-gígir-II gibil; o. XVI 19: 3 gín D. kg **L.** 2 saĝ-*sù*; r. I 6: 13 gín D. kb **L.** 1 *ḫa-bù*, 10: 4 gín D. kg **L.** 1 ˹*ar*˺-*ra-su*[-*sù*]; r, II 7: 10 gín D. kg **L.** 2 *gú-li-lum* 50 gín D. a-gar$_5$-gar$_5$; r. III 3: 2 gín D. [kb] **L.** 1 ĝír mar-tu; r. V 7: 3 gín D. kg **L.** 2 saĝ-*sù*; r. VI 13: 3 gín D. kg **L.** 2 saĝ-*sù*; r. VII 24: 2 gín D. 2 NI kg **L.** 1 ĝír mar-tu *wa* 1 kù-sal; r. VIII 5: 3 gín D. kg **L.** 1 ĝír mar-tu *wa* 1 kù-sal; r. IX 11 and 13: 12 gín D. kb **L.** 1 *ḫa-bù ap* **L.** 1 *ar-ra-sù* kg sikil; r. X 32: 2 ½ gín D. kb **L.** [1 ĝír mar-tu] [*w*]*a* 1 kù-sal; r. XIV 24: 18 gín D. kg **L.** 4 sur$_x$-lu$_x$ lú *al*$_6$ ĜIŠ-ĝidru-ĜIŠ-ĝidru ĜIŠ-uštin en; **16** o. V 8 and 12: 7 ma-na TAR kb **L.** 1 an-dùl … 2 ma-na 5 gín D. kg **L.** IGI.DUB-*sù wa* 2 DU-*sù wa* 2 šu-*sù*; o. VI 9: ŠÚ+ŠA 7 gín D. kg **L.** 2 ĜIŠ.GAM.GAM, 13: 1 ½ gín D. kg **L.** 1 zag; o. VIII 9: 5 gín D. kg *ni-zi-mu* **L.**-*sù*; o. IX 12: TAR 7 gín D. kg *ni-zi-mu* **L.**-*sù*; o. X 3: TAR 2 gín D. kg *ni-zi-mu* **L.** 6 *gú-li-lum* a-gar$_5$-gar$_5$ TAR-II 14 *gú-li-lum*-II a-gar$_5$-gar$_5$ ŠÚ+ŠA 5 *gú-li-lum*-I a-gar$_5$-gar$_5$ 10, 9: 2 gín D. kb *ni-zi-mu* **L.** 3 *gú-li-lum*-I a-gar$_5$-gar$_5$ 10; o. XI 13: 6 gín D. kb *ni-zi-mu* **L.** 12 ĝír mar-tu kb; o. XII 16: 1 gín D. kg *ni-zi-mu* **L.** 2 ĝír lú ZA$_x$ *Ib-rí-um*; o. XIV 23: 13 gín D. kb **L.** 1 *ḫa-bù*; r. I 2: 6 gín D. kg **L.** 1 *ar-ra-sù*, 12: 13 gín D. kb **L.** 1 *ḫa-bù*, 24: ŠÚ+ŠA 5 gín D. **L.** 6 níĝ-[ ]; r. VI 13: 1 gín D. kg *ni-zi-mu* **L.** 1 *za-ḫa-da*; r. VII 14: 12 gín D. kb **L.** 1 *ḫa-bù*, 19: 6 gín D. kg **L.** 1 *ar-ra-sù*, 28: 10 gín D. kb *ni-zi-mu* **L.** 2 ĝír mar-tu kb *wa* 3 ĝír mar-tu ti kb *wa ga-ma-tum* 17 ĝír mar-tu; r. VIII 9: 12 gín D. kg *ni-zi-mu* **L.** 4 ĝír mar-tu kg *wa* 4 ĝír mar-tu ti kg *wa* 5 ĝír mar-tu *ba-du-u*$_4$ kg *wa ga-ma-tum* 5 ĝír mar-tu kb; r. X 18: 4 gín D. kg **L.** 1 ĝír mar-tu *wa* 1 kù-sal; r. XI 1: 12 gín D. kb **L.** 1 *ḫa-bù*, 26: 1 gín kg *ni-zi-mu* **L.** šum; r. XII 19: 4 gín D. kg *ni-zi-mu* **L.** 1 balaĝ, 25: 1 gín D. kg *ni-zi-mu* **L.** 1 bur-KAK; r. XIII 1: [50 g]ín [D. k]g **L.** 15 *gú-li-lum*-I a-gar$_5$-gar$_5$ 15 *wa* 14 *gú-li-lum*-I a-gar$_5$-gar$_5$ 12; r. XV 25: ŠA.[PI 1+]˹1˺ gín D. kg **L.** 2 bur-KAK ĜIŠ-˹taškarin˺ … *wa* 2 bur-KAK ĜIŠ-taškarin; **17** o. III 21: 5 gín D. kg *ni-zi-mu* **L.** 1 *gú-li-lum* a-gar$_5$-gar$_5$ 50; o. V 15: 2 šu-i … 5 gín D. kg **L.**-*sù*, 24: [ ] … 1 ½ gín D. kg **L.**-*sù*; o. XIV 22: 1 gín D. kb **L.** 1 zag ĜIŠ-gígir-II; o. XV 14: 1 ma-na 15 gín D. kg **L.** 5 *gú-li-lum*-II a-gar$_5$-gar$_5$ TAR 10 *gú-li-lum*-II a-gar$_5$-gar$_5$ ŠÚ+ŠA ŠÚ+ŠA 5 *gú-li-lum*-I a-gar$_5$-gar$_5$ 15 10 *gú-li-lum*-I a-gar$_5$-gar$_5$ 10; o. XIX 8: TAR kg **L.** *ša-ga-tum-sù wa kam*$_4$-*ma-a-tum-sù*; r. I 13: 3 gín D. kb **L.** 2 zag 2 ĜIŠ-gígir-II, 27: 2 gín D. kb *ni-zi-mu* **L.** 1 *za-*˹*ḫa*˺-*d*[*a*] *wa* 1 ĜIŠ-MUNŠUB; r. II 7: 2 NI gín D. kg … **L.** 1 *za-ḫa-da*, 27: 5 gín D. kg *ni-zi-mu* **L.** *si-gi* 1 ĜIŠ-gu-kak-šub; r. III 13: 1 gín D. kg *ni-zi-mu* **L.** 2 *gú-li-lum* kbg; r. IV 16: 15 gín D. kb **L.** 1 *ḫa-bù*; r. VI 14: 10 gín D. kb **L.** 1 an-dùl $^{d}$*Iš:šára* en, 19: 1 gín 3 NI kg **L.** *ba-na-i-sù wa* íb-lá-*sù wa* šu-kešda gùn-*sù*; r. VII 18: 2 NI gín D. kg *ni-zi-mu* **L.** *ša-ga-ti* 1 ĝír mar-tu zú; r. IX 14: 1 gín D. kg **L.**-*sù* lú TAR *sa* šu-dub en *wa ma-lik-tum*; r. XV 10: 15 gín D. kb **L.** 1 *ḫa-bu*, 14: 6 gín D. kg **L.** *ar-ra-si-sù*; r. XVI 1: [ ] **L.** 1 ĝír mar-tu; r. XXI 12: 3 kg **L.** 2 saĝ-*sù*; **18** o. VI 16: 1 gín D. kg *ni-zi-mu* **L.** 1 *gú-li-lum* a-gar$_5$-gar$_5$; o. VII 8: 1 ma-na ŠÚ+ŠA 4 gín D. kg **L.** 12 *gú-li-lum* a-gar$_5$-gar$_5$ *wa* 12 *gú-li-lum*-II a-gar$_5$-gar$_5$ ŠÚ+ŠA-ŠÚ+ŠA; o. VIII 6: 3 ma-na kb **L.** 20 *gú-li-lum*-II a-gar$_5$-gar$_5$ lú TAR *wa* 40 *gú-li-lum*-I lú 15 20 *gú-li-lum*-I a-gar$_5$-gar$_5$ lú 12; o. XV 32: 3 kg *ni-zi-mu* **L.** 1 *za-ḫa-da* 1 [ĜI]Š$^?$-PA-˹x˺-ga; o. XVIII 14: 15 gín D. kb

L. 1 *ḫa-bù*, 18: 6 gín D. kg L. 1 *ar-ra-sù*; o. XIX 10: 15 gín D. kb L. 1 *ḫa-bù*, 15: kg sikil L. *ar-ra-sù*, 30: 2 gín D. kg *ni-zi-mu* L. 2 ĜIŠ.GAM.GAM ĜIŠ-gígir-II; r. I 27: 6 g[ín] D. kg *ni-zi-mu* L. 1 *za-ḫa-da*; r. IV 9: 3 gín D. kg *ni-zi-mu* L. 1 níĝ-PA; r. XI 6: 6 gín D. kg L. 1 *ar-ra-sù*; r. XII 14: 3 gín D. kg L. 2 saĝ-*sù*; r. XIV 1: TAR kg L. 2 ĜIŠ.GAM-ĜIŠ.GAM ĜIŠ-gígir-II, 13: 1 kg L. 1 zag ĜIŠ-gígir-II, 19: 4 ma-na tar kb L. 1 an-dùl munus, 23: ⌜1⌝ ma-na 14 gín kg L. IGI.DUB-*sa* 2 šu 2 DU-*sù*, 26: 4 ma-na ŠÚ+ŠA kb L. 1 an-dùl nita; r. XV 2: 2 ma-na 12 kg L. IGI.DUB-*sù wa* íb-lá *si-ti-tum* íb+III-TÚG, 24: 1 kg *ni-zi-mu* L. 1 ĝír mar-tu; r. XVI 15: 1 ĝír … 2 kg L.-*sù*, 31: 2 šu-i 2 kb L.-*sù*, 34: 6 gín kb L. 2 ĝír mar-tu; r. XVII 12: 10 kg *ni-zi-mu* L. 2 ĜIŠ.GAM.GAM ĜIŠ-gígir-II *ra-ʾà-tum*, 33: 15 kb L. 1 *ḫa-bù*; r. XVIII 23 2 ĝír … 3 kg L.-*sù*; **19** o. II 19: 2 *bu*-DI … 4 gín D. kg L. 2 saĝ-*sù*; o. IV 14: 1 ½ gín D. kg *ni-zi-mu* L. 2 *gú-li-lum* kb; o. VII 10: 3 gín D. kb L. 2 zag ĜIŠ-gígir-II; o. X 16: 1 gín D. kb L. 1 zag ĜIŠ-gígir-II, 19: 13 gín D. kb L. 1 *ḫa-bù*, 23: 6 gín D. kg L. 1 *ar-ra-sù*; o. XI 6 and 8: 15 gín D. kb L. 1 *ḫa-bù ap* L. *ar-ra-sù* kg sikil, 23: 8 gín D. kg L. 2 ĝí[r] mar-tu *wa* 2 kù-sal; o. XII 30: 6 gín D. kg *ni-zi-mu* L. 2 ĜIŠ-ban ĜIŠ-gígir-II; o. XIV 19: 20 ĝír mar-tu ti kù-gi *ʾà-lum* … 1 ma-na kg L.-*sù*, 25: 1 ĝír mar-tu 3 kg L.-*sù*; o. XV 19: 12 ĝír mar-tu zú AN.LAGAB×A … 17 gín D. ½ kg L. *ša-ga-tum-sù wa ga-ma-a-tum*, 28: 1 ĝír mar-tu 1 ½ kg L.-*sù*; o. XVIII 5: 2 ma-na kg L. 16 *gú-li-lum* TAR-II a-gar$_5$ *wa* 50 *gú-li-lum* 10-I a-gar$_5$-gar$_5$, 10: 3 ma-na kb L. 10 *gú-li-lum* TAR-II a-gar$_5$-gar$_5$ *wa* 1 *mi-at gú-li-lum* 11 a-gar$_5$; r. VI 3: 10 gín D. kb L. 1 dub, 12: 10 gín D. kb L. 1 dub; r. VIII 21: 12 gín D. kb L. 1 *ḫa-bù*, 25: 6 gín D. kg L. 1 *ar-ra-sù*; r. IX 6: 12 gín D. kb L. 1 *ḫa-bù*; r. XI 3: 1 gín D. 6 NI kg *ni-zi-mu* L. 1 *za-ḫa-da*, 14: (bracelets) 1 ma-na kg L.-*sù*, 23: 1 ma-na 11 gín D. kg L. 1 ĜIŠ-gígir-II; r. XII 27: 1 ĝír mar-tu *wa* …15 gín D. kg L.-*sù*; r. XIII 15: 1 íb-lá 1 ĝír-kun … TAR kg L.-*sù*; r. XVII 8: 13 gín D. kb L. 1 *ḫa-bù*; **20** o. III 15: 5 gín D. kb L. 1 an-dùl munus, 19: 2 ½ gín D. kg L. IGI.⌜DUB⌝-*s*[*ù*]; o. VIII 3: ⌜15⌝ gín D. kb L. 1 *ḫa-bù*, 7: 6 gín D. ⌜kg⌝ L. 1 *ar-ra-sù*, 16 and 19: 15 gín D. kb L. 1 [*ḫa-bù*] *ap* kg sikil L. 1 *ar-ra-sù*; o. IX 11: 1 gín D. kg *ni-zi-mu* L. 1 *za-ḫa-da*; o. XI 3: [1+]4 gín D. kg L. 1 níĝ-PA; r. II 11: 1 ½ gín D. kg *ni-zi-mu* L. 4 kù-sal; r. III 28: TAR kg L. 2 ĜIŠ-ban; r. IV 4: 1 ½ gín D. kg L. 1 zag ĜIŠ-gígir-II, 9: 2 gín D. [k]g *ni-zi-mu* L. 1 *za-ḫa-da*; r. VII 22: 12 gín D. kg … L. ab-*sù*; r. IX 20: 2 gín D. kg [*ni*-]*zi*-[*mu*] L. [ ]; r. XI 5–6: 12 gín D. kb L. 1 *ḫa-bù ap* L. *ar-ra-sù* kg si[kil], 30: 1 gín D kb L. 1 zag ĜIŠ-gígir-II; r. XIII 15: [2+]3 gín D. kg L. [*maš*-]*ar*-[*t*]*um*; r. XV 2': ša-p[i] gín D. kg L. 5 *gú-li-lum*-II a-gar$_5$-ga[r$_5$] TAR *w*[*a*] 10[(+x) *gú*]-*l*[*i-lum* ]; **21** o. II 14: 1 ma-na kg L. 1 ĜIŠ-gu-kak-gíd *ap* [ ]; o. IV 22: [x gín D. kg] L. [1 *za-ḫ*]*a-da*; o. V 4: 1 gín D. kg L. saĝ-*sù*; o. VIII 17: 1 *za-ḫa-da* … 8 g[ín] D. kg L.-*sù*; o. IX 9: 15 gín D. kb L. 1 *ḫa-bù*, 13: 6 gín D. kg L. 1 *ar-ra-sù*; o. X 12: 4 gín D. kg *ni-zi-mu* L. 2 ĜIŠ.GA[M.GAM] ĜIŠ-gígir-II, 20 <gín>: 1 4 NI gín D. kg *ni-zi-mu* L. 1 kun; 1 ma-na kg kin$_5$-ak … L. 2 ĜIŠ.GAM.GAM ĜIŠ-gígir-II; o. XIV 17: 6 gín D. kg L. 1 kun; o. XV 5: 15 gín D. kb L. 1 *ḫa-bù*, 9: 6 gín D. kg L. 1 *ar-ra-sù*; r. I 4: 2 *gú-li-lum* … 1 ma-na ŠÚ+ŠA gín D. kg L.-*sù*; r. V 6: [ ] *ni-zi-mu* L. 11 *gú-li-lum* TAR a-gar$_5$-gar$_5$ kg *wa* 10 *gú-li-lum* 15 a-gar$_5$-gar$_5$ kg; r. VI 9: TAR 7 gín D. kg *ni-zi-mu* L. ĝír mar-tu, 24: 4 šu-i … 4 ½ gín D. kg L.-*sù*; r. VII 9: 3 gín D. kg L. 2 saĝ-*sù*; r. IX 10: TAR kg L.-*sù*, 23: 3 *gú-li-lum* ŠÚ+ŠA-ŠÚ+ŠA-II … 18 gín D. kg L.-*sù*; **22** r. II 5: (20 bracelets) 1 ma-na kg L.-*sù*, 10: (20 bracelets) ŠA.PI gín D. kg L.-*sù*; r. III 5: (20 bracelets) 1 ma-na kb L.-*sù*; r. V 13: [1] ma-na kg L. 1 [*ḫa-bù*]; r. VI 3: 6 gín D. kg L. 1 *ar-ra-sù ḫa-bù*, 8: 7 gín D. kg L. 1 ĜIŠ-ĝidru, 13: 6 gín D. kg L. 1 [*ar-r*]*a-sù ḫa-bù*; **23** o. II 8: 2 ma-na kg L. 1 ab; o. VIII 7: 1 gín D. kg *ni-zi-mu* L. 1 íb-lá 1 ĝír-kun; o. IX 4: ŠÚ+ŠA 8 gín D. kg *ni-zi-mu* L. 2 *gú-li-lum*-II esi ŠA.PI 2 *gú-li-lum*-II esi TAR.TAR 1 *gú-li-lum*-I esi ŠÚ+ŠA 10 lá-1 *gú-li-lum* 10-I esi; o. X 3: ŠÚ+ŠA 8 gín D. kg *ni-zi-mu* L. 7 *gú-li-lum*-II esi TAR-TAR a-gar$_5$ 10 lá-1 *gú-li-lum*-II esi ŠÚ+ŠA-ŠÚ+ŠA a-gar$_5$ 1 *gú-li-lum*-I esi ŠÚ+ŠA a-gar$_5$ 2 *gú-li-lum*-I esi 10 a-gar$_5$; r. I 12: 6 gín D. kg L. 1 *ar-ra-šum* 1 *ḫa-bù*; r. II 7: 6 gín D. kg L. 1 *ar-ra-šum* 1 *ḫa-bù*; r. III 5: 19 gín D. kg *ni-zi-mu* L. 1 ĝír mar-tu kg *wa sa-ga-tum* 10 lá-1 ĝír mar-tu; r. IV 2: 8 gín D. kg L. 5 *gú-li-lum* dib a-gar$_5$, 7: 6 gín D. kg L. 1 *ar-ra-šum* 1 *ḫa-bù*; r. V 7: 2 gín D. kg *ni-zi-mu* L. <1> *gú-li-lum*; r. VI 9: ŠÚ+ŠA gín D. kg L. 2 *gú-li-lum*-II esi ŠÚ+ŠA 4 a-gar$_5$ 4 *gú-li-lum*-I esi 15 a-gar$_5$ 3 *gú-li-lum*-I esi ŠÚ+ŠA a-gar$_5$; **24** o. I 2: 2 gín D. kg L. 1 ĝír mar-tu; o. II 3: 4 gín D. kg L. 1 ĝír mar-tu *wa* 2 kù-sal; o. IV 3: 1 gín D. kg *ni-zi-mu* L. 1 *za-ḫa-da*, 11: 1 gín D. kg *ni-zi-mu* L. 1 *za-ḫa-da*; o. V 1: 16 gín D. kg L. IGI.DUB 2 an-dùl *wa* 2 šu-*sù* 2 DU-*sù*, 15: 1 gín D. kg L. IGI.DUB 1 an-dùl; o. VI 5: 6 gín D. kg L. 1 *ar-ra-sù* 1 *ḫa-bù*; r. II 1: 3 gín D. kg L. 2 saĝ 2 *bu*-DI, 3: 3 gín D. kg L. 1 bur-KAK ĜIŠ-taškarin, 5: 4 gín D. kg L. 1 *gú-li-lum* kb.

## P

PA **4** r. XIV 1: L. níĝ-*sù*-níĝ-*sù*.

pad «lid» **2** o. XIII 3: 4 gín D. kg *ni-zi-mu* 1 L. 1 an-zam$_x$; **10** r. VIII 4: 10 gín D. kg 1 L. an-zam$_x$; **14** r. XII 16: 1 kg *ni-zi-mu* 1 L. an-zam$_x$; **15** r. II 2: ŠA.PI gín D. kg kin$_5$-ak 1 an-zam$_x$ *wa* 1 L.-*sù Ib-rí-um*; r. VIII 18: 50 gín D. kg kin$_5$-ak 1 an-zam$_x$ *wa* 1 L.-*sù* en; **18** o. I 23: ŠA.PI gín D. kg 1 *a-ba-lum wa* L.-[*s*]*ù Ib-rí-um*; **19** o. XIII 9: ŠA.PI gín D. kg 1 an-zam$_x$ *wa* 1 L.-*sù Ib-rí-um*; **20** r. II 23: 10 gín D. kg 1 L. an-zam$_x$ *A-ba-ti-um*$^{ki}$ *Ib-rí-um*; r. III 4: ⌜4⌝ gín D. kg *ni-zi-mu* 1 L. *ma-da-a-um* kg an-dùl; r. X 2: [1] gín D. [kg] *zi-ba-du* 1 L. an-zam$_x$; **22** r. V 10: TAR 4 gín D. kg 1 an-zam$_x$ *wa* 1 L.-*sù Ib-rí-um*; **23** o. III 7: 1 gín D. kg *ni-zi-mu* 1 L. an-zam$_x$ *Ib-rí-um*; **24** r. IV 9: ŠÚ+ŠA gín D. kg 1 *ma-da-a-um* <1> an-dùl *wa* 1 L.-*s*[*ù*].

## R

*ra-ˀà-tum* «shell» **2** o. XI 13: 3 gín D. kg nu$_{11}$-za 1 ĝír mar-tu **L.** tur; r. XVI 7: 1 ĝír mar-tu **L.** kg; **7** r. VII 2; 14 o. V 16: 11 **L.** … LAGAB×UD-LAGAB×UD kin$_{5}$-ak ĜIŠ-asari sagi; **8** o. I 14: [1 ĝír mar-tu **L.**] kg, 18: ⌜1⌝ ĝír mar-tu ⌜1⌝ **L.** kg; **11** o. VII 3: 2 ĝír mar-tu kg **L.** *Ib-ri-um*; **15** o. IX 20: 2 ĝiš-ban ĜIŠ-gígir-II lú **L.** *ša-ti* en; **16** o. IV 15; **17** o. X 9; **18** r. XVII 15: 10 kg *ni-zi-mu* nu$_{11}$-za 2 ĜIŠ.GAM.GAM ĜIŠ-gígir-II **L.** en; **21** o. VII 12: 1 ĝír mar-tu kg **L.**; o. XIV 7: 1 ĝír mar-tu **L.** kg.

see *za-ḫa-da ra-ˀà-tum* s.v. *za-ḫa-da*.

raš-SAR «leek» **2** r. V 7: **L.** Kur$^{ki}$; **3** o. VI 8: **L.** Kur$^{ki}$; **4** r. XI 18: **L.** Kur$^{ki}$; **5** r. II 10: **L.** Kur$^{ki}$; **6** o. XIV 21; **7** o. IX 19: **L.** Kur$^{ki}$; **9** o. IX 15: **L.** Kur⌜$^{ki}$⌝; **11** o. X 2: **L.** Kur$^{ki}$; **12** o. II 5: **L.** Kur$^{ki}$; **13** o. XVII 6: **L.** Kur$^{ki}$; **14** o. XVII 2: **L.** Kur$^{ki}$; **15** o. XVII 18; **16** o. XIII 17: **L.** Kur$^{ki}$; **17** r. X 13: **L.** Kur$^{ki}$; **18** r. III 10: **L.** Kur$^{ki}$; **20** o. XIV 12: **L.** Kur$^{ki}$; **21** o. XI 7.

*ru$_{12}$-du-ga-tum* (a kind of binding) **6** o. X 7: 10 gín D. kb **L.** ĝír mar-tu kg.

*ru$_{12}$-du-ga-ti-sa-nu* **21** r. XII 15: 3 ma-na 5 kb *wa* **L.** TAR.TAR.

## S

sa$_{6}$ «good» **2** r. XII 17: 20 siki na$_{4}$ **L.**, 20: 6 udu-nita **L.**; r. XIII 9: 1 *mi-at* 50 siki na$_{4}$ **L.**; **5** o. I 10: 3 *mi-at* 54 na$_{4}$ siki **L.**; **6** o. VIII 15: 1 kir$_{11}$ **L.** siki; **9** o. XIV 10: 1 túg-NI.NI **L.**; **11** o. III 4: 93 "KIN" siki **L.**; **15** o. VIII 7: 1 túg-NI.NI **L.**; o. XII 20: 10 sila$_{4}$ **L.**; **17** r. V 11: 1 *mi-at* 50 kuš-kuš **L.** gi$_{6}$.

(see íb+III-TÚG sa$_{6}$ gùn)

sada(ĜIŠGAL)-titab(MUNU$_{4}$.GÚG) (a kind of malt) **4** r. XV 20: 1 útul urudu lú **L.**

sada(ĜIŠGAL)-titab(MUNU$_{4}$.A) **10** r. IV 13: 10 útul! urudu! lú dam lú **L.**

(see Archi 1986, p. 203; Milano 1990, *ARET* IX, pp. 387–388)

*sa-du* «protective spirit» **17** r. VI 27: 1 an-dùl **L.** en *wa ma-lik-tum si-in* NE-*na-áš*$^{ki}$.

(see Fronzaroli 1988, p. 27; *ARET* XI, p. 51)

*sa-ga-tum* (a part of the dagger) **2** o. XV 12: 10 gín D. kg nu$_{11}$-za **L.** *wa kam$_{4}$-ma-a-tum* 10 lá-1 ĝír mar-tu zú; **8** o. XIV 1: 13 2 NI gín D. ⌜kg⌝ [ ] **L.** 10 ĝír mar-tu zú LAGAB×AN.A; **23** r. I 8: 1 gín D. kg *zi-du* **L.** 1 ĝír mar-tu; r. III 7: 19 gín D. kg *ni-zi-mu* nu$_{11}$-za 1 ĝír mar-tu kg *wa* **L.** 10 lá-1 ĝír mar-tu.

*sa-ga-ti* **1** o. IX 5: [1 gín] kg nu$_{11}$-za **L.** 1 ĝír ⌜mar⌝[-tu].

*ša-ga-tum* **17** o. IX 14: 1 gín D. kg *zi-du* **L.** 1 ĝír mar-tu kg; o. XIII 22: 3 gín D. kg *ni-zi-mu zi-du* 3 **L.** 3 ĝír mar-tu; o. XIX 9: 17 ĝír mar-tu zú *wa* 3 ĝír mar-tu *ba-du-u$_{4}$* kbg … TAR kg nu$_{11}$-za **L.**-*sù wa kam$_{4}$-ma-a-tum-sù*; **19** o. XV 19: 12 ĝír mar-tu zú AN.LAGAB×A … 17 gín D. ½ kg nu$_{11}$-za **L.**-*sù wa ga-ma-a-tum.*

*ša-ga-ti* **17** r. VII 19: 2 NI gín D. kg *ni-zi-mu* nu$_{11}$-za **L.** 1 ĝír mar-tu zú.

sagi «steward» **4** o. XI 22: 12 zi-bar tur lú **L.** kas$_{4}$-kas$_{4}$ é en; **7** r. XIII 15: [x ma-na] an-na **L.** *Ma-rí*$^{ki}$ *En-na-ì* šu-mu-tak$_{4}$; **13** o. IV 18: 1 ma-na an-na **L.** *Ma-rí*$^{ki}$; r. I 4: (silver) níĝ-ba *Ìr-am$_{6}$*-kur$^{ki}$ **L.** *Ma-rí*$^{ki}$ *in* ud kin$_{5}$-ak kú en; **14** o. V 21: LAGAB×UD-LAGAB×UD kin$_{5}$-ak ĜIŠ-asari **L.**

(see *ARET* XVI, p. 261)

saĝ «head» **2** o. III 1: 3 gín D. kg nu$_{11}$-za 2 **L.** 2 *bu*-DI, 3: ŠÚ+ŠA gín D. kb 2 **L.**; o. V 9: 3 gín D. kg nu$_{11}$-za 2 **L.**-*sù*; o. IX 17: $^{d}$*Ša-ma-gan* en 3 gín D. kb kin$_{5}$-ak **L.**-*sù*; o. XII 4: 10 gín D. kg kin$_{5}$-ak **L.** $^{d}$*ˀA$_{5}$-da-ra*; **4** o. I 2: 1 ma-na kb **L.** kb $^{d}$*Ku-ra*; o. XIII 3: 3 g[ín D. kb] **L.** kb $^{d}$*Ku-ra*; **5** r. V 14: ŠÚ+ŠA gín D. kg 3 **L.** lu$_{5}$; **6** o. I 2: 1 ma-na kb **L.** kb $^{d}$*Ku-ra*; o. II 13: 3 gín D. kb **L.** kb $^{d}$*Ku-ra* 2 mu-ti; o. XIII 12: 5 gín D. kb nu$_{11}$-za 1 **L.** lu$_{5}$ ĜIŠ-ĝidru; r. XIV 6: 8 gín D. kb **L.** $^{d}$*Á-la wa* $^{d}$*Da-bí-na-ad* lú *A-ra-ab*$^{ki}$; **7** o. I 2: [1 m]a-[n]a kb **L.** kb [$^{d}$*K*]*u-ra*; o. X 9: 17 gín D. kb nu$_{11}$-za **L.**-*sù* 2 šu-*sù* DU-*sù*; **8** o. I 2: 1 ma-na kb **L.** $^{d}$*Ku-ra*; o. III 12: [3 gín D. kb] **L.** $^{d}$*Ku-ra*; o. XIV 10: 4 **L.** 4 *zi-*[*kir-*]*ra-tu*[*m*] en; **9** o. I 2: 1 ma-na 3 gín kb **L.** kb $^{d}$*Ku-ra*; r. VI 11: 2 gín kg nu-za$_{11}$ 2 **L.**-*sù*; **10** o. I 2: 1 ma-na 3 gín D. kb **L.** urudu $^{d}$*Ku-ra*; o. II 7: ŠÚ+ŠA gín D. kg nu$_{11}$-za 1 **L.** ⌜lu$_{5}$⌝; **11** o. I 2: 1 ma-na 3 gín D. kb **L.** [k]b $^{d}$*K*[*u-ra*]; o. XII 12: 2 gín D. kg nu$_{11}$-za 2 **L.**-*sù*; **12** o. I 2: 1 ma-na 3 gín D. kb **L.** kb $^{d}$*Ku-ra*; r. VIII 14: ŠÚ+ŠA 6 gín D. kg kin$_{5}$-ak **L.** $^{d}$*Ra-sa-ap Du-ne-íb*$^{ki}$; **13** o. I 2: 1 ma-na kb **L.** kb $^{d}$*Ku-ra*; o. VIII 8: 3 gín D. kb **L.** kb $^{d}$*Ku-ra* mu-ti-II; o. XIII 23: 2 *bu*-DI … 3 gín D. kg nu$_{11}$-za 2 **L.**-*sù* ì-ĝiš-saĝ *Ti-šè-li-im* ama-gal-*sù*; o. XV 23: 2 *bu*-DI … 3 gín D. kg nu$_{11}$-za 2 **L.**-*sù*; r. VIII 12: 4 gín D. kg nu$_{11}$-za **L.** 4 *bu*-DI; **14** o. I 2: 1 ma-na kb **L.** kb $^{d}$*Ku-ra*; o. VI 10: 3 gín kb **L.** kb $^{d}$*Ku-ra in* mu-ti-II; r. VI 21: 6 gín D. kb nu$_{11}$-za 4 **L.** lu$_{5}$ *al$_{6}$-sù*; r. IX 20: 2 *bu*-DI … 3 gín D. kg nu$_{11}$-za 2 **L.**-*sù*; **15** o. I 2: 1 ma-na kb **L.** kb $^{d}$*Ku-ra*; o. XI 19: 1 ma-na 14 gín D. kg kin$_{5}$-ak … *wa* nu$_{11}$-za 2 **L.** 2 *bu*-DI; o. XIV 2: [3 g]ín D. k[b] **L.** kb $^{d}$*Ku-ra* mu-ti; o. XVI 19: 2 *bu*-DI … 3 gín D. kg nu$_{11}$-za 2 **L.**-*sù*; r. V 7: 2 *bu*-DI … 3 gín D. kg nu$_{11}$-za 2 **L.**-*sù*; r. VI 13: 2 *bu*-DI … 3 gín D. kg nu$_{11}$-za 2 **L.**-*sù*; **16** o. I 2: [1] ma-na kb **L.** kb $^{d}$*Ku-ra*; o. II 11: 1 á-MUŠEN … 5 NI kg **L.**-*sù*; o. V 20: 3 gín D. kb **L.** kb $^{d}$*Ku-ra* mu-ti-II; **17** o. I 2: 1 ma-na kb **L.** kb $^{d}$*Ku-ra*; o. XIII 14: 3 gín D. kb **L.** kb $^{d}$*Ku-ra* mu-ti; r. XXI 12: 2 *bu*-DI … 3 kg nu$_{11}$-za 2 **L.**-*sù*; **18** o. I 2: 1 ma-na kb **L.** kb $^{d}$*Ku-ra*; o. XVII 10: 3 gín D. kb **L.** kb $^{d}$*Ku-ra* mu-ti-II; r. XII 14: 2 *bu*-DI … 3 gín D. kg nu$_{11}$-za 2 **L.**-*sù*; **19** o. I 2: 1 ma-na kb **L.** kb $^{d}$*Ku-ra*; o. II 20: 2 *bu*-DI … 4 gín D. kg nu$_{11}$-za 2 **L.**-*sù*, 26: 5 gín D. kb 3 *bu*-DI 2 **L.**; r. IV 25: 3 gín D. kb **L.** kb $^{d}$*Ku-ra* mu-ti-II; **20** o. I 2: [1 ma-na kb **L.** kb $^{d}$*Ku-ra*]; o. IV 7: [3 gín D. kb] **L.** [kb] $^{d}$*Ku-*[*ra*] mu-t[i]-II; o. XV 12: 4 *ˀà-ra-ma-tum* … ZA$_{x}$ **L.**; **21** o. I 2: 1 ma-na kb **L.** kb $^{d}$*Ku-ra*; o. V 4: [ ] 1 gín D. kg nu$_{11}$-za **L.**-*sù*; r. VII 9: [2 *bu*-DI] … 3 gín D. kg nu$_{11}$-za 2 **L.**-*sù*; **24** r. II 1: 3 gín D. kg nu$_{11}$-za 2 **L.** 2 *bu*-DI.

saĝ «of superior quality» **5** o. I 4: 1 íb-lá **L.**; **25** o. VII 6: 13 *ˀà-da-um*-TÚG **L.**

saĝ-du$_{8}$ «to make available» **3** o. IX 10: 1 ĝír mar-tu ti kg NI-*gi* **L.** lú-kar *A-da-bí-ig*$^{ki}$.

*sa-ḫa-wa* «pendant»
see *gú-li-lum*.

sal «thin, fine» **4** r. IV 10: 1 *bu*-DI **L.**; **7** o. XIV 16: 1 dub-naĝar **L.**; **12** r. XI 14: 6 dub-naĝar **L.** lú 15 gín D., 16: 6 dub-naĝar **L.** 10; r. XII 13: 5 dub-naĝar **L.** 15, 14: 5 dub-naĝar **L.** 10; **16** r. XV 10: 5 dub-naĝar 10 **L.**; **21** o. IX 7: 50 lá-2 DAM.KAK.UŠ tur **L.**

sal-TÚG (a garment) **2** o. VIII 14; r. XIII 7; **6** r. XI 8; r. XII 17; **9** o. XIII 18; o. XIV 13; **15** o. VI 20; o. VIII 8; o. XII 15; o. XVII 14; r. III 12; **17** r. V 8; r. X 7; **19** o. VI 24; r. V 8; **20** o. IV 17; r. VI 20; **25** o. I 4; o. II 3; o. IV 6; o. V 7; o. VI 4.

SA.ZA$_x^{ki}$ «the royal Palace» **2** o. X 11: (410 na$_4$ measures of wool, 32 garments, 32 kilts) ki:lam$_7$ **L.**; o. XIV 21: (9 bracelets) lú ĝuruš-ĝuruš **L.**; r. II 17: 2 *ʾà-ra-ma-tum* … 2 zé-*sù* níĝ-ba *Ib-rí-um* $^{d}$Utu **L.**; r. XIII 1: (140 garments, 60 kilts, 20 na$_4$ measures of wool) … 6 udu-nita sa$_6$ ki:lam$_7$ **L.**; **3** o. V 8: 60 ĝír mar-tu **L.**, 18: (25 garments, 126 kilts) ki:lam$_7$ **L.**; r. III 17: 1 ĝír mar-tu zú A.LAGAB×ḪAL [ ] diri ĝír mar-tu ĝuruš-ĝuruš *in* ud igi-ḫi-du$_8$ **L.**; **4** o. I 8: 20 íb-lá *si-ti-tum* ĝír-kun lú ĝuruš-ĝuruš **L.**, 14: [x g]*ú*-[*l*]*i*-[*lum* x gí]n [D.] ì-na-sum **L.** *in* zar$^{ki}$ en; o. III 10: *gú-li-lum wa* níĝ-anše-ak kù-sal **L.**; r. II 3: (silver) *A-tar*$_x$(BAN)-*il* **L.**; r. III 19: níĝ-anše-ak kù-sal 10 u$_5$ **L.**; **5** o. IV 5: ĜIŠ-ma-dul$_{10}$ … ĜIŠ-ti-ḪAR *Wa-ba-rúm* šu-ba$_4$-ti ki:lam$_7$ **L.**; r. II 14: raš-SAR Kur$^{ki}$ … 3 gud ki:lam$_7$ **L.**; r. III 12: (14 kilts) ki:lam$_7$ **L.**; r. XIV 11: 1 ĝír mar-tu … 1 kù-sal níĝ-ba *Ra-sa-ap ʾÀ-da-ni*$^{ki}$ *in* **L.** *Ib-rí-um*; r. XV 22: *a-gú* … 3 ĜIŠ-šú 3 níĝ-bànda … *in* é $^{d}$*Ra-sa-ap ʾÀ-da-ni*$^{ki}$ **L.**; **6** r. XI 15: (92 garments, 49 kilts) … 1 ĜIŠ-banšur kg ki:lam$_7$ **L.**; r. XIV 15: *Ba-ga-ma* ugula **L.**; **7** o. V 4: (38 daggers) lú ì-na-sum **L.** *in Du-du-lu*$^{ki}$ *in* níĝ-kas$_4$ *Ma-rí*$^{ki}$; o. IX 11: (84+[x] garments, 8 na$_4$ measures of wool) … 96 ĜIŠ-ti-ḪAR *Wa-ba-rúm* šu-ba$_4$-ti … ĜIŠ-ád ki:lam$_7$ $^{d}$*A-da-ma wa* **L.**; r. III 12: [ ] [x] ⌜*ʾà-ra*⌝-*ma-tum* … [níĝ-ba] $^{d}$Utu **L.**; **8** o. IX 6: (30[+x] daggers, 20 belts, 20 frogs) ì-na-sum **L.** *in* igi-ḫi-du$_8$ *in* ud ⌜nídba⌝ [ ]; o. X 12: 1 ⌜ĝír mar⌝-[tu] [$^{d}$*Ra-sa-ap*] [*ʾÀ-d*]*a*-[*n*]*i*$^{ki}$ *in* **L.**; **9** o. V 14: 7 gada-TÚG ki:lam$_7$ **L.**; r. VI 6: ĜIŠ-ti-ḪAR *Wa-ba-*⌜*rúm*⌝ šu-ba$_4$-ti *in* ud šu-mu-níĝin **L.**; r. XIII 1: (53 bracelets, 2 plaques, 22[+x] daggers) lú [ĝuruš-ĝuruš] **L.**; **10** r. XIV 3: 8 ĝír mar-tu ĝuruš-ĝuruš **L.**; **11** r. III 5: (78 garments, [x kilts]) ki:lam$_7$ **L.** $^{d}$*Áš-da-bil Ši-ʾà-mu*$^{ki}$; r. VII 5: 2 *ʾà-ra-ma-tum* … níĝ-ba *Ib-rí-um* $^{d}$Utu lú **L.**; **13** o. XVI 5: 2 *bu*-DI … 2 saĝ-*sù* níĝ-ba *Ti-šè-li-im ma-lik-tum Ì-mar*$^{ki}$ *in* ud DU.DU *si-in* **L.** tak$_4$ AMA-*ra*; r. II 3: (84[+x] garments) ki:lam$_7$ **L.**; **14** o. IV 9: 2 *mi-at* ĝír mar-tu … ì-na-sum ĝuruš-ĝuruš **L.** *in* níĝ-kas$_4$ *Kak-mi-um*$^{ki}$; **15** r. III 21: (109 garments, 658 kilts, 2 hides) ki:lam$_7$ **L.**; r. IV 8: 10 *gàr-su* ki:lam$_7$ $^{d}$*ʾÀ-da wa* 10 lá-2 *gàr-su* ki:lam$_7$ **L.**; r. V 2: 1 kù-sal níĝ-ba *Da-bur-da-mu* $^{d}$Utu **L.**; **17** o. XIII 10: 2 gud *in* **L.** *Rí-ì-ma-lik I-bí-zi-im*; o. XV 9: 1 íb-lá 1 *si-ti-tum* 1 ĝír-kun 1 dib … 1 ĝír mar-tu kg … 1 ĜIŠ-zú … 1 zag ĜIŠ-gígir-II … 2 *zú-zú-ba-tum Íl-ba-da-mu* en *Kak-mi-um*$^{ki}$ *in* šu-ba$_4$-ti; o. XX 3: (523 daggers) in-na-sum **L.** *in* ud níĝ-kas$_4$ *A-ḫ*[*a-za-*]*ni-ig*⌜$^{ki}$⌝; r. X 3: 2 *bu*-DI *Ti-ša-li-im ma-lik-tum Ì-mar*$^{ki}$ *in* ud DU.DU *mi-nu* NI-*ab*$^{ki}$ *si-in* ; **18** r. XIX 7: 25 *gàr-su* … (36 garments, 85 na$_4$ measures of wool) … ĜIŠ-ti-ḪAR <ki:lam$_7$> *Wa-ba-rúm* šu-ba$_4$-ti; **19** r. IV 22: (706 daggers) lú ĝuruš-ĝuruš **L.** in-na-sum; r. V 3: ĜIŠ-ti-ḪAR ki:lam$_7$ **L.** *Wa-ba-rúm* šu-ba$_4$-ti; **21** o. VII 2: [ ] ki:lam$_7$ **L.** NI-*rí*$^{ki}$; r. I 6: (40 belts, 40 pendants, 18 bracelets) lú ĝuruš-ĝuruš **L.** in-na-sum; r. III 22: (daggers) lú *áš-du A-la-ga*$^{ki}$ šu-ba$_4$-ti *wa* in-na-sum **L.**; r. VI 11: (14 plaques, 57 bracelets, 16 belts, 6 pendants, 1 helmet, 1 dagger) ĝuruš-ĝuruš ; **22** o. VI 5: (silver) lú *Ar-mi*$^{ki}$ in-na-sum in ud šu-mu-níĝin ; r. IV 3: (60 bracelets, 10 daggers) lú *in* šu-mu-níĝin **L.** *Ba-ga-ma* gaba-ru; **23** r. I 1: (19 bracelets) ĝuruš-ĝuruš **L.** *in* ud è níĝ-kas$_4$ *Gú-da-da-núm*$^{ki}$; **25** o. II 6: (121+[x] garments, 102 kilts) ki:lam$_7$ *wa* $^{d}$*A-da-ma ʾÀ-da-ni*$^{ki}$; o. VI 2: (72+[x] garments; 30+[x] kilts) ⌜ki⌝:[lam$_7$] **L.**

si «horn; tusk; ivory» **2** r. VII 5: 1 ma-na kb nu$_{11}$-za 4 **L.**-*sù*; 5 o. VIII 1: 1 ma-na kb nu$_{11}$-za 4 **L.**-*sù in* AMA-*ra*, 11: 1 ma-na kb nu$_{11}$-za 4 **L.**-*sù in* AMA-*ra*; r. X 16: ŠÚ+ŠA 5 gín D. kb *ʾa*$_5$-*na-gu* **L.** 2 gud; r. XI 2: ŠÚ+ŠA 5 gín D. kb *ʾa*$_5$-*na-gu* **L.** 2 gud; **7** o. XI 18: ŠÚ+ŠA gín D. kb *ʾa*$_5$-*na-gu* 4 **L.** 2 gud; o. XII 10: ŠÚ+ŠA gín D. kb *ʾa*$_5$-*na-gu* 4 **L.** 2 gud; **8** r. V 10': 1 ma-na kb nu$_{11}$-za 8 **L.** 4 gud; r. VI 7': 2 **L.** dàra; **10** o. XV 6: 2 ma-na ŠA.PI gín D. kb nu$_{11}$-za 2 **L.** am; **11** o. X 13: ŠÚ+ŠA gín D. kb *ʾa*$_5$-*na-gu* 4 **L.** 2 gud; o. XI 3: ŠÚ+ŠA gín D. kb *ʾa*$_5$-*na-gu* 4 **L.** 2 gud; r. VIII 13: ŠÚ+ŠA gín D. kb *ʾa*$_5$-*n*[*a-gu*] 1[+3 **L.** 2 gud]; **13** o. XI 10: ŠÚ+ŠA gín D. kb *ʾa*$_5$-*na-gu* 4 **L.** 2 gud; o. XVI 9: 1 gín D. kb nu$_{11}$-za 2 **L.** [gud]-I; **15** r. IX 18: ŠÚ+ŠA gín D. kb *ʾa*$_5$-*na-gu* 4 **L.** 2 gud; **16** r. I 6: ŠÚ+ŠA gín D. kb *ʾa*$_5$-*na-gu* **L.** 2 gud, 17: ŠÚ+ŠA gín D. kb *ʾa*$_5$-*na-gu* **L.** 2 gud; r. XI 6: ŠÚ+ŠA gín D. kb *ʾa*$_5$-*na-gu* **L.** 2 gud; **17** r. IV 23: ŠÚ+ŠA gín D. kb *ʾa*$_5$-*na-gu* 4 **L.** 2 gud; **18** o. XVIII 21: ŠÚ+ŠA gín D. kb *ʾa*$_5$-*na-gu* **L.** 2 gud; o. XIX 19: ŠÚ+ŠA gín D. kb *ʾa*$_5$-*na-gu* **L.** 2 gud; r. XVII 38: ŠÚ+ŠA kb *ʾa*$_5$-*na-gu* **L.** 2 gud; **19** o. X 27: ŠÚ+ŠA gín D. kb *ʾa*$_5$-*na-gu* **L.** 2 gud; o. XI 13: ŠÚ+ŠA gín D. kb *ʾa*$_5$-*na-gu* **L.** 2 gud; r. XVII 12: ŠÚ+ŠA kb *ʾa*$_5$-*na-gu* **L.** 2 gud; **20** o. VIII 10: ŠÚ+ŠA gín D. kb [*ʾa*$_5$-*na-gu* 4 **L.** gud], 22: ŠÚ+ŠA gín D. kb *ʾa*$_5$-[*n*]*a-gu* 4 **L.** gud; r. XI 11: ŠÚ+ŠA gín D. kb *ʾa*$_5$-*na-gu* 4 **L.** 2 gud; **21** r. VII 24: ŠÚ+ŠA gín D. kb *ʾa*$_5$-*na-gu* **L.** 2 gud.

si-si **6** o. XII 3: 1 *mi-at* **L.** ĝír mar-tu kg; **9** o. III 23: [1 ma-na kb] [nu$_{11}$-za **L.**] 2 gud; o. IV 7: 1 ma-na kb nu$_{11}$-za **L.** 2 gud; o. X 8: 40 **L.** ĝír mar-tu; **10** o. XI 10: 1 ma-na kb nu$_{11}$-za 4 **L.** 2 gud; **12** r. II 1: ŠÚ+ŠA gín D. kb *ʾa*$_5$-*na-gu* 4 **L.** 2 gud; **14** o. IX 20: ŠÚ+ŠA gín D. kb *ʾa*$_5$-*na-gu* 4 **L.** 2 gud; **17** o. XVIII 11: 3 *mi-at* ĝír mar-tu zabar … **L.**-*sù*.

si$_4$ «red» **16** r. XI 18: 15 **L.** *gàr-su*; **18** r. XVIII 27: 16 *gàr-su* **L.**; **19** r. XVI 25: 3 *gàr-su* **L.**

si$_4$-si$_4$ **12** r. IV 17: 8 *gàr-su* gi$_6$ **L.**; **17** r. XX 13: 24 *gàr-su* **L.**; **21** r. II 17: 4 *gàr-su* **L.**

si$_4$ «carnelian» **17** r. XX 20: 5 kb 15 *ḫa-za-nu* 2 gìn-gìn 2 **L.** 1 šu-dub *Ib-rí-um*, 25: 4 kb 15 *ḫa-za-nu* 2 gìn-gìn 2 **L.** 1 šu-dub *I-bí-zi-kir*.

si-dù «betyl» **17** r. IX 25: 1 bar:ús lú dur 2 **L.** en *wa ma-lik-tum*.
(see Fronzaroli 2022)

SIG$_7$ **6** o. XIV 7: 2 ĜIŠ-DU en *in* ud **L.** è *si-in* ki $^{d}$*Ra-sa-ap*.

sig$_{17}$ «yellow stone» **7** o. XV 17: 2[+x$^?$ gín] ⌜D.⌝ kb nu$_{11}$-za 1 gud-I lú **L.** lú ZA$_x$ *Ib-rí-um*.

*si-gi* (preposition) «together» **17** r. II 28: 5 gín D. kg *ni-zi-mu* nu$_{11}$-za **L.** 1 ĜIŠ-gu-kak-šub en.

sig$_7$-igi «eyebrow (decoration)» **6** r. XVI 10: 5 an-na 1 **L.** *Du-si-gú*; **17** r. XI 25: 5 gín D. an-na šub *si-in* 1 **L.** *ma-lik-tum*; **19** o. III 1: 6 gín D. an-na šub *si-in* TAR a-gar$_5$-gar$_5$ 1 **L.** *Di-ne-íb-du-lum* nin-ni en.

sig$_4$-KI **19** o. IX 4: 10 lá-1 ma-na 20 gín D. an-na šub *si*-in 2 *mi-at* 17 ma-na a-gar$_5$-g[ar$_5$] [k]in$_5$-ak **L.** 2 útul urudu gibil maḫ.

*si-in* (preposition) 1) «to, towards» (locative), 2) «for» (final)

1) *si-in* GN **1** o. V 18; o. VII 2, 9; (e) r. III' 11; **3** o. VIII 7; **4** o. X 23; **6** o. V 12; **7** o. X 12; o. XVIII 2; r. XIII 12; **9** o. IX 11; **10** o. XVI 2; **13** o. XVI 4; r. III 21; r. VI 17; **14** r. X 24; **17** o. VI 5; o. XII 7; r. VI 31; r. X 2; **18** o. XV 4; r. X 23; **20** r. III 19; **21** o. VI 7; r. X 14.

2) **1**(e) r. IV' 14; **5** r. V 17: 10 gín D. an-na **L.** URUDU-*sù*; **6** o. XIV 9: *in* ud SIG$_7$ è **L.** ki $^{d}$*Ra-sa-ap*; **7** o. VII 9: ŠA.PI gín D. an-na **L.** *ni-zi-mu* ZA$_x$ naĝar; o. XIV 15 and 19: 8 gín D. an-na **L.** 1 tùn tur 1 dub-naĝar sal 1 *ma-za-ḫa-rúm* 1 UŠ×KÍD **L.** ZA$_x$ ⌜*Ib*⌝-[*r*]*í-um*; 12 o. IX 11: **L.** níĝ-kas$_4$ *Ma-nu-wa-ad*$^{ki}$; r. IV 10: *in* ud è **L.** á-daḫ lú *A-te-na-ad*$^{ki}$; **13** o. VII 3: **L.** PN; r. II 20: **L.** en *Kak-m*[*i-*]*u*[*m*$^{ki}$]; **15** r. XVI 15: 2 ma-na kb in-na-sum **L.** šu-bal-ak kg; **19** o. III 13: 3 tùn tur ŠA.PI-ŠA.PI lú šu-mu-tak$_4$ **L.** *A-la-ga*$^{ki}$; o. XVIII 18: (703 daggers, 176 bracelets) lú šu-mu-tak$_4$ **L.** *A-la-ga*$^{ki}$; r. V 23: 10 gín D. kb **L.** al$_6$-tuš $^{d}$*Ga-mi-iš*; r. XIX 13: BAR.AN.BAR.AN *Iš*$_{11}$*-da-mu* di-kud šu-mu-tak$_4$ **L.** *Na-gàr*$^{ki}$; **21** r. XIV 15: [ ] dumu-nit[a] en **L.** É×PAP.

see also *s.v.* šub.

siki «wool» **5** o. XVI 18: **L.** *I-bu*$_{16}$*-bù*$^{ki}$; **6** o. VIII 15: 1 kir$_{11}$ sa$_6$ **L.**

Measures:

"KIN" siki **2** r. IV 19; r. VIII 16; **11** o. III 4: 93 **L.** sa$_6$; **13** o. V 12: 2 *mi-at* 45 **L.** *Ma-rí*$^{ki}$; **15** o. VII 2: 3 *mi-at* 85 **L.** *Ma-rí*$^{ki}$; **16** r. XI 16: 20 **L.** *Ma-rí*$^{ki}$.

siki na$_4$ **2** o. VIII 5: 31 **L.** *Ma-rí*$^{ki}$; o. X 6: **L.** *Ma-rí*$^{ki}$; r. XII 17: 20 **L.** sa$_6$; r. XIII 9: 1 *mi-at* 50 **L.** sa$_6$; **3** r. XII 1: 40 **L.** *áš-da Ma-rí*$^{ki}$; **5** o. I 10: 3 *mi-at* 54 **L.** (na$_4$ siki) sa$_6$; 7 o. IX 1: 10 lá-2 **L.** (na$_4$ siki) *Ma-rí*$^{ki}$; r. VII 5: 4 *mi-at* **L.** (na$_4$ siki) *Ma-rí*$^{ki}$; **12** r. III 6: 18 **L.** *Ma-rí*$^{ki}$; **16** o. IV 1: 1 *mi-at* 70 gín D. kb **L.** *Ma-rí*$^{ki}$, 13: 3 *mi-at* 20 **L.** *Ma-rí*$^{ki}$; **17** o. X 4: 3 *mi-at* 80 **L.** *Ma-rí*$^{ki}$; **18** o. IX 17: 1 *mi-at* **L.** *Ma-rí*$^{ki}$; r. III 8: 2 *mi-at* 10 **L.** *Ma-rí*$^{ki}$; r. XIII 9: 3 *mi-at* 40 **L.** *Ma-rí*$^{ki}$; r. XVIII 31: 85 **L.** *Ma-rí*$^{<ki>}$; **19** o. VI 26: 60 **L.** *Ma-rí*$^{ki}$; r. V 9: **L.** *Ma-rí*$^{ki}$; **20** o. XIV 2: 2 *mi-at* **L.** *Ma-rí*$^{ki}$; **21** r. II 3: 60 **L.** *Ma-rí*$^{ki}$.

Qualifications:

siki *ba-ra-i* **14** r. I 6.

siki si$_4$ **14** r. I 6.

sikil «pure; purification» **4** r. V 16: 2 ĜIŠ-banšur kg … 1 šu-dub **L.** lú en $^{d}$*Ra-sa-ap* ᵓ*À-da-ni*$^{ki}$; **7** r. XV 10: (silver and gold) **L.** lú *Maš-ga-du*$^{ki}$ *wa* ì-na-sum nu$_{11}$-za $^{d}$*Ra-sa-ap Du-ne-íb*$^{ki}$; **9** o. III 5: 7 sila$_4$ ḪI.DIM lú níĝ-lá-gaba en **L.**; o. XV 14: 2 ĝír mar-tu ti kg *Ib-rí-um* uru-bar *in* níĝ-kas$_4$ lú **L.**; **14** o. X 15: 1 *ḫa-bù* $^{dᵓ}$*À-da* kb kg **L.**; **15** o. XIV 10: 1 ĝír mar-tu kg en *áš-du* 1 ĝír mar-tu-*sù* **L.** $^{dᵓ}$*A*$_5$*-da-"bal" Lu-ba-an*$^{ki}$; r. V 21: 1 ĝír mar-tu kg *Ib-rí-um áš-du* ĝír mar-tu-*sù* **L.** $^{dᵓ}$*À-da*; r. VI 2: 1 ⌜íb⌝-lá 1 *si-ti-tum* 1 ĝír-kun **L.** $^{dᵓ}$*A*$_5$*-da-"bal" Lu-ba-an*$^{ki}$ *Ib-rí-um* šu-mu-tak$_4$ *al*$_6$ tu-ra-*sù*; r. IX 15: 1 *ar-ra-sù* kg **L.**; r. XII 6 and 14: 1 dib en *áš-du* dib-*sù* **L.** $^{dᵓ}$*À-da al*$_6$ tu-ra ama-gal-*sù wa* 2 *gú-li-lum-sù* **L.** $^{dᵓ}$*A*$_5$*-da-"bal" Lu-ba-an*$^{ki}$ *al*$_6$ tu-ra-*sù*, 27: 2 *gú-li-lum Ib-rí-um áš-du* 2 *gú-li-lum-sù* **L.** $^{dᵓ}$*À-da al*$_6$ tu-ra en; r. XIII 7: 1 dib *Ib-rí-um áš-du* 1 dib-*sù* **L.** $^{dᵓ}$*À-da al*$_6$ tu-ra en, 25: 1 ĜIŠ-banšur *wa* 1 kù-sal **L.** *al*$_6$ ama-gal en $^{d}$*Ra-sa-ap* ᵓ*À-da-ni*$^{ki}$; r. XV 19: 1 ĝír mar-tu kg en *áš-du* ĝír mar-tu-*sù* **L.** $^{dᵓ}$*A*$_5$*-da-"bal" Lu-ba-an*$^{ki}$; r. XVI 8: [1 ĝír mar-t]u kg *Ib-rí-um áš-du* ĝír mar-tu-*sù* **L.** $^{d}$*Áš-da-bíl al*$_6$ tu-ra en; **16** r. I 14: 1 *ḫa-bù ap* kg **L.**; r. XI 3: 1 *ḫa-bù ap* kg **L.**; r. XIII 13–23: 2 ĝeštu$_x$-lá 15 **L.** $^{d}$*Iš*:*šára Zu-ra-mu*$^{ki}$ *wa*: 1 *ù*-NAM-*mi-lu* 8 gín D. **L.** $^{d}$BAD-munus *Lu-ba-an*$^{ki}$ *wa* 1 kù-sal 4 gín D. **L.** [ ]⌜x⌝ [ ] **L.** *in* ud tu-da; **18** o. XIX 14: 1 *ḫa-bù ap* kg **L.**; r. XVII 35: 1 *ḫa-bù ap* kg **L.**; r. XVIII 10: 1 ĝír mar-tu kg *Ib-rí-um áš-du* ĝír mar-tu-*sù* **L.**; **19** o. I 16: 2 ĝír mar-tu kg *Ib-rí-um wa* **L.**-*sù al*$_6$ tu-ra *I-bí-zi-kir wa al*$_6$ tu-ra en; o. II 2: 1 ĝír mar-tu kg *Ib-rí-um* [*áš-*]*du* [1 ĝ]ír [mar-t]u[-*s*]*ù* **L.**; o. V 15: 1 dib *I-bí-zi-kir* dumu-nita *Ib-rí-um áš-du* dib-*sù* **L.** $^{dᵓ}$*À-da*; o. XI 10: 1 *ḫa-bù ap* … *ar-ra-sù* kg **L.**; r. XVII 9: 1 *ḫa-bù ap* kg **L.**; **20** o. VIII 18: 1 [*ḫa-bù*] *ap* kg **L.**; o. XIV 21: 1 šu-dub **L.** en lú ḫúl [ ] a-mu-*sù*; o. XVI 12: 1 íb-lá 1 *si-ti-tum* 1 ĝír-kun TAR kg **L.** $^{dᵓ}$*À-da*, 16: 1 íb-lá 1 *si-ti-tum* 1 ĝír-kun **L.**, 18: 1 íb-lá 1 *si-ti-tum* 1 ĝír-kun **L.** ᵓ*A*$_5$*-da-"bal"* lú *Lu-ba-an*$^{ki}$ *al*$_6$ tu-ra *Ib-rí-um* tak$_4$; r. XI 8: 1 *ḫa-bù ap* … *ar-ra-sù* kg **L.**; **21** o. VIII 19: 1 *za-ḫa-da* … lul-gu-ak lú **L.** é $^{dᵓ}$*À-da al*$_6$ tu-ra *Ib-rí-um*; o. IX 23: 1 *ḫa-bù ap* kg **L.**; r. VIII 17: 1 íb-lá 1 *si-ti-tum* 1 ĝír-kun lú en **L.** $^{dᵓ}$*À-da al*$_6$ tu-ra *I-bí-zi-kir*; r. X 23: (silver) lul-gu-ak 1 zi-bar en *ša-ti* **L.** $^{dᵓ}$*A*$_5$*-da-"bal" Lu-ba-an*$^{ki}$; **22** r. I 8: 1 ma-na kg **L.** $^{dᵓ}$*À-da*.

sila$_4$ «lamb» **9** o. III 1: 7 **L.** ḪI.DIM; **11** o. II 12: [x] **L.** lú šu-du$_8$-máš; **15** o. XII 20: 10 **L.** sa$_6$.

*si-mi* «to establish» **1**(e) r. II' 8': *Da-d*[*ub*] *Ìr-m*[*u-*]*da-mu* lú *Íl-zi Ìr-ga-bù* è in ud *Ìr-kab-da-mu* **L.** úš-*sù*.

simug «smith, metalworker» **1**(e) r. IV' 4: [ ] [*i*]*n* ud ⌜ḫi⌝-úš *I-ti-ì* **L.**; **3** r. VIII 18: 2 na$_4$ *Ša-ma* **L.**; **9** o. X 13: (70$^?$ daggers) lú **L.** *Ga-sa*$^{ki}$.

*si-ti-tum* «sheath» **1** o. V 8: 10 ma-ba kb kin$_5$-ak 17 íb-lá 17 **L.** 17 ĝír-kun; o. VII 20: TAR kb [*ni*]*-zi-mu* 1 íb-lá [1] **L.** [1 ĝír-kun]; o. IX 11: ŠÚ+ŠA gín D. kg 1 íb-lá 1 **L.** 1 ĝír-kun; **4** o. I 6: 3 ma-na 7 gín D. kb *ni-zi-mu* 20 íb-lá **L.** ĝír-kun; o. IX 19: 7 íb-lá **L.** ĝír-kun; r. I 8: 3 íb-lá **L.** ĝír-kun; r. XIII 3: 4 íb-lá **L.** ĝír-kun; **6** o. XII 5: 50 gín D. kb 1 íb-lá **L.** ĝír-⌜kun⌝; r. VII 8: 1 ma-na kb 1 íb-lá 1 **L.** 1 ĝír-kun, 21: ŠA.PI kb 1 íb-lá **L.** ĝír-kun kb maš-maš kg; r. VIII 4: ŠA.PI gín D. kb 1 íb-lá **L.** ĝír-kun maš-maš kg; **7** o. VIII 5: TAR kb 1 íb-lá 1 **L.** 1 ĝír-kun; **11** o. VIII 1: [TAR kg 1 íb-lá] 1 **L.** 1 ĝír-kun; **12** r. I 1: ŠA.PI gín D. kg 1 íb-lá 1 **L.** 1 ĝír-kun; **13** o. I 9: [x m]a-na [kb x í]b-lá [x] **L.** [x ĝí]r-kun, 18: [š]a-pi gín D. kb [1 íb-lá 1] **L.** 1 ĝír-kun; o. II 7: 2 ma-na kb 2 íb-lá 2 **L.** 2 ĝ[í]r-kun, 15: 1 ma-na kb 1 íb-lá 1 **L.** 1 ĝír-kun; r. IX 6: TAR kg 1 íb-lá 1 **L.** 1 ĝ[ír-kun]; **15** o. XVI 6: ½ gín D. kg *ni-zi-mu* 1 **L.**; r. VI 1: TAR kb 1 ⌜íb⌝-lá 1 **L.** 1 ĝír-kun; **16** o. II 23: 1 ½ gín D. kg kin$_5$-ak 6 *da-ne-a-tum* **L.**; o. XIII 21: TAR kb 1 íb-lá 1 **L.** 1 ĝír-kun; **17** o. XI 13: 2 gín D. kg *ni-zi-mu* 1 íb-lá 1 **L.** 1 ĝír-kun; o. XIV 14: 2 ma-na kg 1 íb-lá 1 **L.** 1 ĝír-kun 1 dib; r. XII 16: [x ma-na kg x í]b-lá [x] **L.** [x gí]r-[ku]n; r. XIII 3: 3 ma-na kg kin$_5$-ak 6 íb-lá 6 **L.** 6 ĝír-kun, 18: TAR kb kin$_5$-ak 1 íb-lá 1 **L.** 1 ĝír-kun; r. XXII 26: 2 ma-na kg kin$_5$-ak 2 íb-lá 2 **L.** 2 ĝír-kun; **18** o. X 18: [10 gín D. kg] 1 íb-lá 1 **L.** 1 ĝír-kun; r. XII 26: 1 ma-na kg 1 íb-lá 1 **L.** 1 ĝír-kun ì-ĝiš-saĝ *Ib-rí-um*; r. XV 4: 2 ma-na 12 kg nu$_{11}$-za IGI.DUB-*sù wa* íb-lá **L.** íb+III-TÚG; **19** o. VII 4: TAR kb 1 íb-lá 1 **L.** 1 ĝír-kun, 24: TAR kg 1 íb-lá 1 **L.** 1 ĝír-kun; r. XIV 2: TAR kg 1 íb-lá 1 **L.** 1 ĝír-kun; r. XVII 25: 1 ma-na ŠA.PI 2 gín D. kg 1 íb-lá 1 **L.** 1 ĝír-kun 1 ĜIŠ-sal; **20** o. XV 6: 1 ma-na ŠÚ+ŠA gín D. kg kin$_5$-ak 1 íb-lá 1 **L.** 1 ĝír-kun ŠÚ+ŠA gín D.; o. XVI 11: 1 íb-lá 1 **L.** 1 ĝír-kun TAR kg sikil, 16: TAR kg 1 íb-lá 1 **L.** 1 ĝír-kun sikil, 18: 8 gín D. kb 1 íb-lá 1 **L.** 1 ĝír-kun sikil; r. VIII 1: [TA]R [kg] 1 íb-lá 1 **L.** 1 ĝír-kun; **21** o. III 9: TAR kg 1 íb-lá 1 **L.** 1 ĝír-kun; o. VII 10: 2 ma-na kg kin$_5$-ak 1 dib 1 íb-lá 1 **L.** 1 ĝír-kun; o. XIV 1: [2 ma-na kg] 1 íb-lá 1 **L.** 1 ĝír-kun 1 dib; o. XV 18: ŠA.PI gín D. kb 1 íb-lá 1 **L.** 1 ĝír-kun ì-ĝiš-saĝ *I-bí-zi-kir*; r. VIII 15: TAR kg 1 íb-lá 1 **L.** 1 ĝír-kun.

*si-ti-a-tum* **23** r. VII 3: 1 ma-na kg 2 íb-lá 2 **L.** 2 ĝír-kun.

-*sù* (suffix personal pronoun III person) *passim.*

*su-da$_5$-lik* «(/šutallik malikim/ (king's) attaining to sovereignty » **17** r. XVII 8: 1 *mu-rúm wa* 1 *gúm-a-nu* ⌜*wa*⌝ 2 ĜIŠ.ALAM **L.** en.
(see Fronzaroli 1992, p. 184 nt. 75)

*su-da-nu* (a decoration) **16** r. III 3: [ŠÚ+ŠA k]g *ni-zi-mu* **L.** *wa* 4 kù-sal-*sù*; **18** r. I 10: 2 níĝ-anše-ak 2 kù-sal 2 IGI.NITA *wa* **L.** kù-sal en; **19** o. XII 15: 50 gín D. kg *ni-zi-mu* **L.** *wa* kù-sal sur$_x$-BAR.AN en; **20** o. IX 19: 1 gín D. kg ZU.PIRIĜ **L.** kg BAR.AN en.

*su-da-ni* **15** o. IX 9: 2 ma-na kg *ni-zi-mu* 4 **L.**

SUD.PA.SIKIL (a bronze accessory of belt and dagger) **16** o. X 15: TAR an-na **L.** 5 íb-lá 20 ĝír-kun zabar 35 á-MUŠEN zabar.

SUD.SI.PA.SAL **11** r. II 5: 80 í[b-lá] 80 ĝír m[ar-tu] 21 á-MUŠEN zabar **L.**-*sù in* ud è níĝ-kas$_4$ *Gú-da-da-núm*$^{ki}$.
(PA-sikil-SUD in *ARET* XX 9 r. IV 3, and SUD*gunû*(LAK233).X.PA.SIKIL in *ARET* XX 15 r. VI 10 qualify a category of women for the service of the Palace; see Conti 2003, pp. 134–135)

-*su-ma* (suffix personal pronoun III dual person) **12** o. III 12: *ba-na-i*-**L.**

sur$_x$-BAR.AN «pair of mules» **12** o. XI 2: 1 ĜIŠ-gu-kak-šub **L.** *Ib-rí-um*; r. XI 4: 2 níĝ-anše-ak **L.** [am]a-gal en; **17** r. II 15: 2 níĝ-anše-ak 4 kù-sal **L.**; **19** o. XII 18: *su-da-nu wa* kù-sal **L.** en.

ugula sur$_x$-BAR.AN «overseer of the mule teams» **6** r. X 11: *u*$_{12}$-*zu-il* **L.**, 15: *Ba-ga-ma* **L.** *Ib-rí-um*, 20: *Šu*-NE **L.** en; **8** o. XII 11: *Wa-na* **L.**; **13** r. III 5: [ ] **L.** *Ib-rí-um*; **15** o. XI 3: *Ib-ga-il* **L.**; **16** o. XIII 3: [ -]*ma*-[x] **L.**; **17** r. IV 5: NI-*na-du* **L.** *Gi-ir-da-mu* dumu-nita *Ib-rí-um*; **18** o. VI 19: *Ib-ga-ì* **L.** en; r. XIII 20: *Min-na-ì* **L.** *Ib-rí-um*; **19** r. XI 26: 1 ĜIŠ-gígir-II 1 guruš **L.** 4 BAR.AN-BAR.AN.

sur$_x$-lu$_x$ «pair of androcephalus bulls» **15** r. XIV 25: 18 gín D. kg nu$_{11}$-za 4 **L.** lú *al*$_6$ ĜIŠ-ĝidru-ĜIŠ-ĝidru ĜIŠ-uštin en.

## Š

*ša* (relative pronoun)

*ša-ti* **4** r. VIII 19: 2 *gú-li-lum* **L.** lú *Di-bí-zi-kir*; **15** o. IX 21: 2 ĜIŠ-ban ĜIŠ-gígir-II lú *ra-ʾà-tum* **L.** en; **17** r. III 5: *kam*$_4$-*ma-a-tum* zàḫ **L.** kù-sal ama-gal-en; **18** o. VII 2: 15 ĜIŠ-kak-ĜIŠ-kak **L.** 5 ĜIŠ-asari kaskal ⌜en⌝; **20** r. III 7: 1 pad *ma-da-a-um* kg an-dùl lú en **L.** *Ib-rí-um* mu-DU; **21** r. X 22: 1 zi-bar en **L.** sikil $^{dʾ}$*A*$_5$-*da-"bal" Lu-ba-an*$^{ki}$.

*šu-ti* **9** r. II 20: (silver) **L.** (gold) 1 dib *En-àr-li-im* [dumu-n]ita *Du-*[*bí*]*-šum A-ba-ad*$^{ki}$.

*ša-ga-tum/ti* see *sa-ga-tum.*

*ša-mu* «frontlet» **15** o. XI 16: 1 ma-na 14 gín D. kg kin$_5$-ak … 1 **L.**; **24** r. I 9: 3 gín D. kg 1 [*m*]*a-ḫa-na-gúm* 1 **L.** 1 *a-na-bù-bí-tum* 1 *ti-ba-ra-núm.*

ŠA.PI «⅔ of a mina» (= 40 shekels) *passim.*

*ša-ti* (relative pronoun) see *ša.*

še «barley» **3** o. I 2, 6, 10, 13, 16; o. II 2, 5, 8; **5** r. VII 16; **17** o. XVI 8: al-kur$_6$ **L.** *Kak-mi-um*$^{ki}$.

še-še **9** r. XIV 14.

še-ba «barley ration» **25** r. VI 2: [ ] **L.** diĝir-diĝir-diĝir-diĝir níĝ-sa$_{10}$ gig.

še-in «straw» **12** r. V 9; **16** r. II 22.

*šè-li* «(an object in) malachite» **14** r. VII 20: 9 gín D. kb kin$_5$-ak **L.**

ŠE.SAĜ×ḪA-mul (debt with interest) **4** r. XV 15: [1?] BAR.AN *A-šu*$^{ki}$ *ʾÀ-bí* lú $^{d}$*Ra-sa-ap* **L.**; **5** r. VII 3: še ĝuruš-ĝuruš-*sù wa* da[m]-*sù Za-ba-rúm* **L.**
(cf. Archi 2002a, p. 95 = 2015, p. 225)

šeš(-mu) «brother» **3** r. I 4: 1 dib *I-bí-zi-kir* l[ú *Ib-rí-um*] … 1 dib *Šum*-bàd$^{ki}$ **L.**-*sù*; r. V 7: 1 ⌜dib⌝ *Ḫáb-ra-ar* ugula *ʾA*$_5$-*da-tum*$^{ki}$ … 1 dib *La-da-da-áš* **L.**-*sù*; **4** r. XI 12: [PN] **L.**(-mu) en *Du-lu*$^{ki}$; **7** o. II 7: 1 *gàr-su Ù-zi* **L.** *A-zú-ma*; **11** o. VIII 9: (silver) níĝ-du$_8$ **L.** *Ti-la-rí-im*$^{ki}$ *ʾÀ-bí-gú*$^{ki}$ *áš-da Tar*$_5$-*ḫa-um*$^{ki}$; **12** o. IV 12: 1 dib *I-bí-zi-kir* dumu-nita *Ib-rí-um* … 2 ĝeštu$_x$-lá *Gi-rí* **L.**-*sù*; **13** o. II 9: 2 íb-lá 2 *si-ti-tum* 2 ĝ[í]r-kun *Mu-zi* **L.** en *wa Lu-wa-sa-ra-du Du-lu*$^{ki}$; r. VI 8: *Iš*$_{11}$-*la-ab* lú *Ru*$_{12}$-*zi-da-mu wa I-ša-ni-ki-mu* **L.** *Ar-si-a-ḫa* 2 lú-kar *Ma-nu-wa-ad*$^{ki}$; r. VII 15: BÍL-*za-ì wa En-na-ì* 2 dumu-nita **L.** *Ib-rí-um*; **14** o. XI 13: 2 *gú-li-lum Bu*$_x$-*ma-il* **L.** *Ib-rí-um*; o. XII 7: 2 *gú-li-lum* … *A-zú-gú-ra* **L.** *Ra-ù-tum*; **15** r. IX 8: 1 dib *A-ḫu-šu-da-mu* dumu-nita *Zé-ma-lik* **L.** *I-nu-ud-da-mu*; **17** r. XIII 14: *I-ib-ma-lik* **L.** ama-gal en; **19** r. XV 6: 2 ĝír mar-tu ti kg *Íl-zi* lú *Ìr-am*$_6$-*da-mu* *wa Ti-ra-ì* **L.** ama-gal en, 12: 2 ĝír mar-tu *ba-du-u*$_{9}$ kg *En-na-ni-il* **L.** *Ib-rí-um wa Na-am*$_{6}$-ì-ĝiš; **20** o. VII 18: [ ] **L.** ama-gal en; r. I 6: 1 dib BÍL-*za-il* dumu-nita **L.** *Ib-rí-um*; **23** o. VIII 4: 1 dib *Íl-ba-ma-lik* lú *I-gi* … 1 dib *Ig-rí-iš* **L.**-*sù*; r. VI 1: 1 dib *I-ib-ma-lik* **L.** *Du-si-gú*; **24** o. II 13: 1 dib *Ù-zi* **L.** *A-zú-ma*.

šeš-II-ib (member of a religious confraternity) **3** r. IX 17: (15 garments, 104 kilts) … 1 BAR.AN … ĜIŠ-ti-ḪAR *Wa-ba-rúm* šu-ba$_{4}$-ti ki:lam$_{7}$ **L.** *ʾÀ-da-ni*$^{ki}$; **8** o. V 11: (48 garments, 48 kilts) [ -g]*i Ib-lu*$_{5}$-*zú wa I-za-iš-ru*$_{12}$ lú-kar *Ma-nu-wa-ad*$^{ki}$ ki:lam$_{7}$ **L.**(šeš-ib-[II]) *ʾÀ-da-ni*$^{ki}$; **13** o. VI 2: (88 kilts, 245 KIN measures of wool) … 20 gud … ĜIŠ-ti-ḪAR *Wa-ba-rúm* šu-ba$_{4}$-ti ki:lam$_{7}$ **L.** *wa* $^{d}$*A-da-ma ʾÀ-da-ni*$^{ki}$; **15** o. II 28: 1 *gú-li-lum a-li-iš* ĜIŠ-gu-kak-gíd $^{dʾ}$*A*$_{5}$-*da-"bal"* [ ]$^{ki}$ en ì-na-sum *in* ud **L.**; o. VII 8: (54 garments, 166 kilts, 385 KIN measures of wool) … ĜIŠ-ti-ḪAR *Wa-ba-rúm* šu-ba$_{4}$-ti ki:lam$_{7}$ **L.** *wa* $^{d}$*A-da-ma ʾÀ-da-ni*$^{ki}$; **16** o. IV 7: (170 na$_{4}$ measures of wool) … ĜIŠ-ti-ḪAR BAD.MUŠ.LU$_{5}$ šu-ba$_{4}$-ti ki:lam$_{7}$ **L.** *ʾÀ-da-ni*$^{ki}$.

še-šu-še-tag **19** r. VIII 9: 6 gín D. kg kin$_{5}$-ak 6 **L.** *wa* 1 buru$_{4}$-MUŠEN; r. XVII 19: 10 gín D. kb 2 *bu*-DI 4 **L.**

še-šu-tag **21** r. III 3: [x gín] ⌜D.⌝ kb kin$_{5}$-ak 2 *bu*-DI 4

(an object. *LLE*,I no. 583: ŠE.ŠU.TAG / ŠE.BAD = *za-a-bù-um*. The offering of this object was the occasion of a ceremony—see TM.75.G.10103 o. VI 22–24: nídba in ud še-šu-tag—on which some sheep were sacrificed, ibid. V 21–23: 2 udu še-šu-tag $^{dʾ}$*A*$_{5}$-*da-"bal"*)

ŠE+TIN «beer» **12** o. VI 24: (silver) níĝ-ba *Wa-ba-rúm* ga:eš$_{8}$ *Du-du-lu*$^{ki}$ (silver) níĝ-ba *Na-na-tum* dam-*sù* (silver) níĝ-ba dumu-nita-*sù* šu-mu-tak$_{4}$ **L.**

šir «song» **13** o. XVI 25: (silver) níĝ-ba *A-za-ba Ir-i-tum*$^{ki}$ á-âĝ *a-dè* **L.**

šitim «builder» **3** r. VII: (silver) níĝ-du$_{8}$ 1 lú **L.** *Ab-ru*$_{12}$-*ti-um*$^{ki}$ *áš-ti Ir-i-tum*$^{ki}$.

šu «hand» **3** o. XII 14: 6 gín D. kg nu$_{11}$-za *ba-na-*⌜*ʾà*⌝ *wa* 2 **L.** 2 DU-*sù*; r. VII 16: 4 ĜIŠ-šú 1 níĝ-bànda l[ú 2 **L.**]; **5** r. XII 13: ŠÚ+ŠA 3 gín D. kb nu$_{11}$-za 2 **L.**-*sù*; **7** o. X 9: 17 gín D. kb nu$_{11}$-za saĝ-*sù* 2 **L.**-*sù* DU-*sù*; **11** o. VI 7: 1 *mar-wa-ga-tum* lú 2 **L.** en; **12** r. IX 13: 2 an-dùl … 8 gín D. kg nu$_{11}$-za *ba-na-a-sa wa* 2 **L.**-*sù wa* 2 DU-*sù*; **13** o. VII 23: 2 an-dùl … 10 gín D. kg nu$_{11}$-za [I]GI.DUB-*sù wa* 4 **L.**-*sù* 4 DU-*sù*; o. VIII 18: 1 an-dùl … 3 gín D. kg nu$_{11}$-za IGI.DUB-*sù* 2 **L.**-*sù* 2 DU-*sù*; r. X 17: 1 ĜIŠ-šú 1 níĝ-bànda lú 2 **L.**; **16** o. V 16: 1 an-dùl … 2 ma-na 5 gín D. kg nu$_{11}$-za IGI.DUB-*sù wa* 2 DU-*sù wa* 2 **L.**-*sù*; **18** r. XIV 24: 1 an-dùl munus … ⌜1⌝ ma-na 14 gín kg nu$_{11}$-za IGI.DUB-*sa* 2 **L.** 2 DU-*sù*; **21** o. XIV 21: 5 ma-na kb kin$_{5}$-ak 1 ĜIŠ-šú 1 níĝ-bànda lú 2 **L.**; **24** o. V 5: 16 gín D. kg nu$_{11}$-za IGI.DUB 2 an-dùl *wa* 2 **L.**-*sù* 2 DU-*sù*.

šu-šu **6** r. XIII 17: 1 ĜIŠ-šú 1 níĝ-bànda lú **L.** en; **10** o. XI 3: 1 ĜIŠ-šú lú **L.** en; o. XII 10: 3 gín D. kb [ZU.]PIRIĜ ĜIŠ-šú níĝ-bànda **L.**; r. II 6: 1 *mar-wa-ga*$_{x}$(ZÀR)-*tum* **L.** en; **12** o. III 14: ŠÚ+ŠA 2 gín D. kg nu$_{11}$-za *ba-na-i-su-ma wa* 2 **L.**-*sù* 2 DU.DU-*sù*; **21** r. I 17: 3 ĜIŠ-šú 3 níĝ-bànda lú diri lú **L.** kas$_{4}$-kas$_{4}$.

šub «to melt» **5** o. XII 18: 15 gín D. an-na **L.** [ ]; r. V 16: 10 gín D. an-na **L.** *si-in* URUDU-*sù*; **6** r. XVI 5: 13 an-na **L.** 2 ĜIŠ-zú ĜIŠ-gígir-II, 13: TAR an-na **L.** 4 *ma-ḫa-ni-gi*; r. XVII 36: 2 an-na **L.** 1 šu-i; **7** o. V 1: [ ] **L.** *si-in* kin$_{5}$-ak-*sù*; o. VI 20: 50 gín D. an-na **L.** *s*[*i-in* ]; o. VII 9: ŠA.PI gín D. an-na **L.** *si-in ni-zi-mu* ZA$_{x}$ naĝar; o. XIV 15: 8 gín D. an-na **L.** *si-in* 1 tùn tur 1 dub-naĝar sal 1 *ma-za-ḫa-rúm* 1 UŠ×KÍD *si-in* ZA$_{x}$ *Ib-rí-um*; **9** r. XVII 12: ŠA.PI 7 gín D. an-na **L.** [*si-i*]*n* [ ] x [ ]; **10** r. XI 3: 1 ma-na an-na **L.** 30 tùn ⌜gal⌝ urudu, 6: 5 gín D. an-na **L.** 1 *ma-ga-um* zabar; r. XIII 5: 7 gín D. an-na **L.** [ ]; **11** o. V 19: 1 ma-na an-na **L.** *si-in ni-zi-mu* ZA$_{x}$ naĝar-naĝar; **12** o. X 4: ŠA.PI 4 gín D. an-na **L.** *si-in* 6 ma-na 10 gín D. a-gar$_{5}$-gar$_{5}$ *ni-zi-mu* ZA$_{x}$ naĝar, 11: 7 gín D. an-na **L.** *si-in* 2 *ma-ga-za-ʾà* zabar gibil 2 zú naĝar, 20: 3 ½ gín D. an-na **L.** *si-in* 1 ĜIŠ-gu-kak-šub sur$_{x}$-BAR.AN; o. XI 5: 5 gín D. an-na **L.** *si-in* 1 ĜIŠ-zú ĜIŠ-gígir-II *Ib-rí-um*, 11: 7 gín D. an-na **L.** *si-in ba-na-a* 1 níĝ-saĝšu; r. XI 8: 1 ma-na ŠÚ+ŠA 3 gín D. an-na **L.** *si-in* 9 ma-na TAR gín D. a-gar$_{5}$-gar$_{5}$; r. XII 8: 57 gín D. an-na **L.** *si-in* 6 ma-na ŠA.PI 6 gín D. a-gar$_{5}$-gar$_{5}$; **13** o. III 10: 5 gín D. an-na **L.** *si-in* 1 ĜIŠ-zú ĜIŠ-gígir-II, 19: 3 gín D. an-na **L.** *si-in* 1 ĜIŠ-gu-kak-šub; o. VI 7: 4 gín D. an-na **L.** *si-in* 1 ĜIŠ-zú; o. X 5: 3 ma-na an-na **L.** *si-in* 24 ma-na a-gar$_{5}$-gar$_{5}$; o. XII 9: 4 gín D. an-na **L.** *si-in* 2 ĝír mar-tu; o. XV 3: 16 gín D. an-na **L.** *si-in* 3 ĜIŠ-zú 3 ĜIŠ-gígir-II; r. XI 10: [x gín D. a]n-na **L.** *si-in* 1 igi-igi; **14** o. IV 14: 4 ma-na TAR an-na **L.** *si-in* kin$_{5}$-ak IGI.DUB 60 níĝ-saĝšu; o. XIII 16: ⌜2⌝ gín [D. an-n]a [**L.** *si-in*] [x] gí[n] D. a-gar$_{5}$-gar$_{5}$ lul-gu-ak 4 ĜIŠ-gu-kak-šub; o. XV 19: 3 gín D. an-na **L.** *si-in* 2 ĜIŠ-gu-kak-gíd; r. III 17: [x g]ín D. an-na **L.** *si-in* 3 ĝír; r. VI 3: 10 gín D. an-na [**L.** *si-in* x gín D. a-ga]r$_{5}$-gar$_{5}$, 16: 16 gín D. an-na **L.** *si-in* 1 ma-na 54 gín D. a-gar$_{5}$-g[ar$_{5}$]; r. VII 22: 2 gín D. an-na **L.** *si-in* 16 gín D. a-⌜gar$_{5}$⌝-gar$_{5}$; **15** o. XIV 23: 1 ma-na 10 gín D. an-na **L.** *si-in ni-zi-mu* ZA$_{x}$ naĝar-naĝar; r. II 14: 10 gín D. an-na **L.** *si-in* 1 ma-na a-gar$_{5}$-gar$_{5}$; **16** o. III 16: 11 gín D. an-na **L.** *si-in zi-ba-ti* 1 útul urudu maḫ; o. VI 15: 5 gín D. an-na **L.** *si-in* 1 ĜIŠ-zú 1 ĜIŠ-gígir-II; o. XI 2: 1 ma-na TAR an-na **L.** *si-in* [x ma-na (x gín D.) a-gar$_{5}$-gar$_{5}$]; r. V 2: 3 gín D. an-na **L.** *si-in* 17 gín D. a-gar$_{5}$-gar$_{5}$; r. XIV 16: 6 gín D. an-na **L.** *si-in zi-ba-du* 1 útul urudu maḫ; r. XV 5: TAR an-na **L.** *si-in* 4 ma-na ŠÚ+ŠA a-gar$_{5}$-gar$_{5}$; r. XVI 3: 13 ma-na ŠÚ+ŠA an-na **L.** *si-in* 4 *mi-at* ma-na a-gar$_{5}$-gar$_{5}$; **17** o. V 18: 1 gín D. an-na **L.** *si-in* 5 gín D. a-gar$_{5}$-gar$_{5}$; o. XIV 19: 4 gín D. an-na **L.** *si-in* ŠÚ+ŠA 6 a-gar$_{5}$-gar$_{5}$; o. XVIII 16: 1 ma-na ŠA.PI gín an-na **L.** *si-in* kin$_{5}$-ak 1 *mi-at* ĝír mar-tu zú-ak, 20: 56 gín D. an-na **L.** *si-in* 5 ma-na ŠA.PI gín D. a-gar$_{5}$-gar$_{5}$; o. XIX 16: 1 ma-na ŠA.PI gín D. an-na **L.** *si-in* 26 ma-na ŠA.PI a-gar$_{5}$-gar$_{5}$; o. XX 15: 1 ma-na ŠÚ+ŠA 4 gín D. an-na **L.** *si-in* 11 ma-na a-gar$_{5}$-gar$_{5}$, 20: 10 gín D. an-na **L.** *si-in* 10 lá-2 ma-na a-gar$_{5}$-gar$_{5}$; r. I 10: 10 gín D. an-na **L.** *si-in* 2 ĜIŠ-zú; r. VIII 20: 10 gín D. an-na **L.** *si-in* 1 ma-na 10 gín D. a-gar$_{5}$-gar$_{5}$; r. IX 4: ŠÚ+ŠA gín D. an-na **L.** *si-in* 20 lá-2 ma-na a-gar$_{5}$-gar$_{5}$; r. XI 24: 5 gín D. an-na **L.** *si-in* 1 SIG$_{7}$.IGI *ma-lik-tum*; r. XXI 19: 3 ma-na ŠÚ+ŠA an-na **L.** *si-in* 26 ma-na ŠÚ+ŠA a-gar$_5$-gar$_5$; **18** o. IV 2: 3 ma-na ŠÚ+ŠA gín D. an-na **L.** *si-in* 56 ma-na ŠA.PI gín D. a-gar$_5$-gar$_5$; o. VIII 17: 11 ma-na an-na **L.** *si-in* 3! *mi-at* ma-na a-gar$_5$-gar$_5$ daḫ$_x$(MU.MU.MU); o. IX 8: 2 ma-na 12 gín D. an-na **L.** *si-in* 13 ma-na TAR a-gar$_5$-gar$_5$; r. II 5: 2 ma-na an-na **L.** *si-in* 12 ma-na a-gar$_5$-gar$_5$; r. V 2: TAR 3 gín D. an-na **L.** *si-in* 24 ma-na a-gar$_5$-gar$_5$, 7: 6 gín D. an-na **L.** *si-in* 5 ma-na a-gar$_5$-gar$_5$, 17: 2 gín D. an-na **L.** *si-in* 10 gín D. a-gar$_5$-gar$_5$, 23: 4 gín D. an-na **L.** *si-in* ŠÚ+ŠA 6 a-gar$_5$-gar$_5$; r. VI 20: 1 ma-na ŠA.PI 6 gín D. 2 NI an-na **L.** *si-in* 12 ma-na ŠÚ+ŠA gín D. a-gar$_5$-gar$_5$; r. VII 17: 50 gín D. an-na **L.** *si-in* 6 ma-na ŠÚ+ŠA gín D. a-gar$_5$-gar$_5$; r. VIII 15: 1 ma-na 52 ½ gín D. an-na **L.** *si-in* 15 ma-na a-gar$_5$-gar$_5$; r. IX 14: 10 lá-1 ma-na ŠÚ+ŠA 6 gín D. an-na **L.** *si-in* 75 ma-na TAR 6 a-gar$_5$-gar$_5$; r. XIV 7: 5 an-na **L.** *si-in* TAR a-gar$_5$; r. XV 7: 6 an-na **L.** *si-in* ŠA.PI a-gar$_5$-gar$_5$; r. XVI 28: 2 an-na **L.** *si-in* 10 a-gar$_5$-gar$_5$; r. XVIII 16: 2 an-na **L.** *si-in* 10 a-gar$_5$-gar$_5$; **19** o. II 28: 6 gín D. an-na **L.** *si-in* TAR a-gar$_5$-gar$_5$; o. III 6: ŠÚ+ŠA 2 gín D. an-na **L.** *si-in* 1 m[a-]na TAR [4+]4 gín D. a-gar$_5$-gar$_5$; o. IV 19: 20 lá-1 ma-na ŠÚ+ŠA 7 gín D. an-na **L.** *si-in* 1 *mi-at* 50 ma-na a-gar$_5$-gar$_5$; o. V 3: 1 gín D. 6 NI an-na **L.** *si-in* 9 gín D. a-gar$_5$-gar$_5$; o. VII 13: 10 gín D. an-na **L.** *si-in* 1 ma-na a-gar$_5$-gar$_5$; o. IX 1: 10 lá-1 ma-na 20 gín D. an-na **L.** *si-in* 2 *mi-at* 17 ma-na a-gar$_5$-g[ar$_5$]; o. XIII 29: 53 gín D. 3 NI an-na **L.** *si-in* 6 ma-na ŠA.PI a-gar$_5$; o. XIV 12: 50 gín D. an-na **L.** *si-in* 6 ma-na ŠÚ+ŠA a-gar$_5$, 27: 1 [m]a-na TAR an-na **L.** *si-in* 12 ma-na a-gar$_5$-gar$_5$; o. XV 12: TAR an-na **L.** *si-in* 3 ma-na TAR 5 a-gar$_5$; o. XVI 2: 1 ma-na TAR an-na **L.** *si-in* 12 ma-na a-gar$_5$-gar$_5$, 18: 2 ma-na 15 gín an-na **L.** *si-in* 20 lá-2 ma-na a-gar$_5$-gar$_5$; o. XVII 12: 11 ma-na 15 gín D. an-na **L.** *si-in* 90 ma-na a-gar$_5$-gar$_5$; o. XVIII 21: 3 ma-na TAR 3 gín D. 2 NI an-na **L.** *si-in* 26 ma-na ŠA.PI gín D. a-gar$_5$-gar$_5$; r. I 17: 50 gín D. an-na **L.** *si-in* 6 ma-na ŠÚ+ŠA gín D. a-gar$_5$-gar$_5$; r. II 7: 3 ma-na ŠÚ+ŠA gín D. an-na **L.** *si-in* 34 ma-na a-gar$_5$-gar$_5$, 24: 1 ma-na 52 [g]ín D. an-na **L.** *si-in* 15 ma-na a-gar$_5$-gar$_5$; r. III 14: 2 ma-na 15 gín D. an-na **L.** *si-in* 20 lá-2 ma-na a-gar$_5$-gar$_5$; r. IV 4: 13 ma-na TAR an-na **L.** *si-in* 1 *mi-at* 10 lá-2 ma-na a-gar$_5$-gar$_5$; r. XII 2: ŠÚ+ŠA gín D. an-na **L.** *si-in* <x a-gar$_5$-gar$_5$>, 19: 1 ½ gín D. an-na **L.** *si-in* 8 gín D. a-gar$_5$; **20** o. I 18: 9 gín D. a-gar$_5$-gar$_5$ 1 gín D. 5 NI an-na **L.** [*si-in* ]; o. III 8: 2 gín D. an-na **L.** *si-in* 2 šu-i; o. VII 22: 6 gín D. an-na **L.** *si-in ni-⌜zi⌝-mu* 2 níĝ-anše-ak 4 kù-sal; o. IX 23: 5 g[ín] D. an-na **L.** *si-in* 1 ĜIŠ-zú; o XIII 6: 12 gín D. an-na **L.** *si-in* 1 ma-na 8 gín D. a-gar$_5$-gar$_5$; r. I 9: 17 gín D. an-na **L.** *si-in* 1 ma-na ŠA.PI gín D. a-gar$_5$[-gar$_5$]; r. II 2: ⌜TAR⌝ [a]n-na **L.** *si-in* 3 ma-na a-gar$_5$-gar$_5$; r. XI 27: 5 ⌜gín D. an-na **L.** [*s*]*i-in* 1 ĜIŠ-zú; r. XIV 7: [x g]ín [D.] [an-n]a [**L.** *si-i*]*n* [x a-g]ar$_5$-gar$_5$; **21** o. III 15: 4 gín D. an-na **L.** *si-in* [*ni-zi-mu* 2 níĝ-anše-ak 4 kù-sal]; o. V 6: 1 ½ gín D. an-na **L.** *si-in* 17 gín a-gar$_5$, 14: 10 gín D. an-na **L.** *si-in* 1 ma-na a-gar$_5$-gar$_5$; o. VIII 11: 3 gín D. an-na **L.** *si-in* ŠÚ+ŠA a-gar$_5$-gar$_5$; o. XIII 18: 5 gín D. an-na **L.** *si-in* 1 ĜIŠ-zú; r. VI 17: 4 gín D. an-na **L.** *si-in* ŠÚ+ŠA 4 gín D. a-gar$_5$-gar$_5$; r. X 27: 3 gín D. an-na **L.** *si-in* 18 gín D. a-gar$_5$-gar$_5$.

šub-šub **6** r. XVI 1: 13 gín D. an-na **L.** 2 ĜIŠ-zú 2 ĜIŠ-gígir-II; r. XVII 21: 15 an-na **L.** nu$_{11}$-za 1 *ḫa-bù*; **14** o. III 23: 6 ma-na ŠA.PI gín D. an-na **L.** *si-in* kin$_5$-ak 2 *mi-at* ĝír mar-tu; **20** o. I 10: 57 ma-na ŠÚ+ŠA gín D. an-na **L.** *si-in* 4 *mi-at* 50 ⌜ma⌝-na a-gar$_5$[-gar$_5$].

*šu-ba-la* **10** o. III 6: ŠA.PI gín D. kb 2 **L.**

šu-bal-ak «to exchange» **1** o. V 2; o. VIII 5, 12, 18; o. IX 2, 9; o. X 2, 11; o. XI 7; **2** o. I 2, 9, 17; o. II 1, 16, 21; o. III 16; o. IV 4, 11; o. V 7; o. VI 1, 7, 19; o. VII 12; o. IX 7, 19; o. XI 4, 10, 17; o. XII 1, 7, 14, 23; o. XIII 7, 14, 20; o. XIV 5, 11; o. XV 1, 9; r. I 15, 22; r. II 10, 19; r. III 9; r. IV 1, 11, 21; r. VI 7, 14; r. VII 18; r. VIII 8, 14; r. XI 15; r. XII 1; r. XIII 14; r. XIV 1, 20; r. XV 6, 14; r. XVII 17; l.ed. 2, 7; **3** o. III 7, 21; o. IV 7, 15; o. VII 18; o. XI 7; o. XII 1, 9; o. XIV 1, 17; o. XV 4; r. I 1, 6; r. III 19; r. IV 17; r. V 4, 9; r. VI 3; r. XII 10; **4** o. XI 2, 12; r. III 14; r. XI 5; r. XIII 20; r. XIV 6; r. XV 3; r. XVI 12; **5** o. III 8, 13; o. IV 7, 13; o. VI 1; o. X 13, 19; o. XI 15; o. XII 10; o. XIII 14; o. XVI 16; r. I 7, 15; r. III 16; r. IV 9; r. V 12; r. VI 5; r. VII 5, 11, 17; r. X 2, 9; r. XII 7, 15, 21; r. XIII 18; r. XIV 5, 16, 25; r. XV 6; r. XVI 9; **6** o. I 11, 16; o. IX 4, r. XII 1; **7** o. III 2; o. IV 6, 13; o. VI 2; o. VII 14, 20; o. X 7; o. XI 2, 11; o. XII 5, 17; o. XIII 5, 11, 17; o. XIV 4, 10; o. XVI 2, 8; o. XVIII 13; r. I 15; r. II 9, 18; r. III 7, 16; r. IV 5, 15, 24; r. V 13, 19; r. VI 2; r. VIII 1; r. IX 4, 16; r. X 2, 9; r. XI 5; r. XII 16; r. XIV 22; r. XV 3, 17; **8** o. VI 3; o. VIII 3; o. XII 6, 13; o. XIII 2, 11; o. XIV 7, 13; r. II x+1; r. III 8'; r. VIII 10'; r. IX 7', 12'; r. X 6', 11'; **9** o. III 9; o. IV 16; o. VI 14; o. XIII 6, 12; r. II 3; r. III 11; r. IV 7; r. VI 9; r. VII 8, 15; r. VIII 6; r. IX 12; r. X 6; r. XII 2; r. XV 8, 14; r. XVII 5; **10** o. II 5; o. V 3; r. V 3; r. VI 18; r. VIII 2, 8, 13; r. X 10; **11** o. II 5; o. IV 5, 16; o. V 7; o. VI 3, 10, 16; o. VII 12, 21; o. X 8, 21; o. XII 10, 14; r. VI 21; r. VII 9, 13; **12** o. IV 2, 9; o. V 1, 14; o. VIII 3; o. XII 3, 13; o. XIII 4, 14; o. XIV 19; o. XV 9, 15; r. I 13; r. II 9; r. III 15; r. V 3; r. VIII 11; r. IX 9; r. X 8, 13; **13** o. III 2, 6; o. VII 8, 19; o. VIII 14, 24; o. IX 13; o. XI 5, 23; o. XII 14, 23; o. XIII 7, 13, 21; o XIV 13; o. XV 21; r. III 8; r. VII 3, 25; r. VIII 10; r. IX 1, 12; r. XII 18; **14** o. I 10, 15; o. II 2; o. VII 7, 17; o. VIII 11, 18; o. IX 1, 9; o. X 2, 22; o. XI 16; o. XII 1, 15; o. XIV 7, 18; o. XV 5, 11; o. XVIII 1, 5; r. I 17; r. II 5, 16; r. III 10; r. IV 18; r. VI 7; r. VII 29; r. VIII 11, 19; r. IX 11, 18; r. X 8; r. XII 13, 20; r. XIII 2, 9; r. XIV 5'; r. XVIII 4; r. XIX 4; **15** o. I 10, 17, 22; o. II 18; o. III 12, 16; o. IV 4, 16; o. V 2, 9, 15, 21; o. VI 12; o. VIII 23; o. IX 6, 11, 16; o. X 3, 16, 24; o. XI 5; o. XII 1; o. XIII 20; o. XIV 14; o. XV 6, 24; o. XVI 3, 17; r. I 8, 17; r. II 5; r. IV 10, 20; r. V 5; r. VI 11, 23; r. VII 2, 13, 22; r. VIII 3, 13, 21; r. IX 2, 25; r. X 8; r. XI 9, 15, 21, 26; r. XII 20; r. XIII 1, 13, 19; r. XIV 10, 22; r. XV 4, 10; r. XVI 16; **16** o. I 14; o. II 9, 19; o. III 2, 9; o. V 10; o. VI 1, 7, 11, 19; o. VII 5, 12; o. VIII 6, 17; o. IX 9, 14; o. XI 5; o. XII 13; o. XIII 11; o. XIV 10, 26; r. II 5, 26; r. III 18; r. IV 2, 12; r. V 10, 17, 24; r. VI 2, 10, 22; r. VII 17; r. VIII 6, 24; r. IX 9, 16; r. X 3, 16; r. XI 23; r. XII 9, 16, 22, 27; r. XIII 8; r. XIV 2, 23; r. XV 14, 23; r. XVI 8, 15; **17** o. I 10, 19; o. III

18; o. IV 19; o. V 13, 22; o. VI 22; o. VII 9, 17; o. IX 11; o. XI 4, 10, 18; o. XIII 18; o. XIV 13; o. XV 12; o. XVII 26; o. XIX 6; r. I 4, 20; r. II 1, 11, 17, 24; r. III 10, 18, 24; r. IV 18; r. V 17; r. VI 8, 17; r. VII 15, 26; r. VIII 2, 7; r. IX 12; r. XI 28; r. XII 2, 14, 25; r. XV 3, 12; r. XVI 16; r. XVII 11; r. XVIII 9, 17; r. XIX 9, 16, 24, 32; r. XX 29; r. XXI 6, 11, 14, 24; **18** o. I 19; o. II 3, 12; o. III 1, 7, 12; o. VI 2, 13; o. VII 7; o. VIII 2; o. X 4, 9, 16; o. XI 7; o. XII 6, 12, 18; o. XIII 2; o. XV 29; o. XVI 8, 13; o. XVII 23; o. XVIII 1, 16; o. XIX 1, 27; r. I 4, 14, 24; r. IV 6; r. VI 10; r. VII 5; r. VIII 3; r. IX 3; r. XI 4, ; r. XII 12, 24; r. XIII 23; r. XIV 3, 11, 21, 28; r. XV 15, 21; r. XVI 13, 36; r. XVII 9; r. XVII 21; **19** o. II 4, 17; o. III 28; o. IV 11; o. V 7; o. VII 22; o. VIII 4, 23; o. IX 7, 13; o. X 3, 21; o. XI 21; o. XII 6, 12, 21, 27; o. XIII 5, 12, 20; o. XIV 17; o. XV 1, 17; o. XVI 7, 23; o. XVIII 3; r. I 22; r. II 12; r. III 3, 19; r. VI 25; r. VII 23, 29; r. VIII 6, 23; r. IX 1, 8; r. X 12, 20; r. XI 12, 21; r. XII 25; r. XIII 7, 13, 21; r. XIV 1; r. XV 20; r. XVII 23; r. XVIII 3, 20; **20** o. II 15; o. III 17; o. IV 11; o. VI 9; o. VIII 5; o. IX 8, 16; o. X 21; o. XI 1, 6, 22; o. XII 12; o. XV 3; o. XVI 3, 10, 15; o. XVII 8; r. I 2; r. II 8, 15, 21; r. III 1, 11, 26; r. IV 2, 6, 13, 17, 24; r. V 10, 24; r. VI 4, 11; r. VII 15, 24; r. VIII 10, 20; r. IX 17, 25; r. X 15, 23; r. XII 6, 16; r. XIII 13; **21** o. II 12; o. III 8, 24; o. IV 3, 13, 20; o. V 2; o. VI 10; o. VII 6, 21; o. VIII 6, 15; o. IX 11; o. X 3, 9, 17, 25; o. XI 16; o. XIII 9, 23, 28; o. XIV 9, 15; o. XV 7, 16, 22, 28; o. XVI 11, 16, 21; o. XVII 10; r. I 2, 9; r. II 13; r. III 9, 24; r. VI 22, 27; r. VII 7; r. VIII 14; r. IX 9, 21; r. X 17; r. XI 25; r. XII 23; r. XIII 15, 21.

šu-ba$_4$-ti «to receive; receipt; to be conquered (said of a town)» **1** o. V 14; o. VI 4; (e) r. III' 2; r. IV' 8; **2** o. VII 10; o. X 17; r. VI 12; **3** o. VI 12; o. VII 3, 7; o. VIII 6; o. X 4'; r. II 5, 10; r. VIII 2, 11; r. IX 15; **4** o. III 13, 19; o. IV 4; o. VII 4; r. II 10; r. V 5; r. VII 15; **5** o. II 4; o. III 3; o. IV 3; o. V 9; o. VII 12; o. IX 7, 15, 19; o. X 11; o. XIII 12; o. XV 12, 15; r. V 8; r. IX 11, 17; r. XI 12; r. XVI 22; **6** o. I 9; o. XI 7; r. X 1, r. XIII 12; **7** o. II 3; o. IX 5; o. XVII 3; r. VII 12; **8** o. VI 13; o. XI 4, 9; r. IV 9', 13'; **9** o. XI 10, 15, 22; o. XII 21; o. XV 8; o. XVIII 2'; r. I 5; r. VI 3; r. XIII 14; r. XIV 13; r. XVI 13; **10** o. I 8; o. VI 9; r. I 19; r. VI 12, 16; r. XII 19; **11** o. III 11; o. XII 6; r. IV 17; **12** o. II 3; o. III 3; o. V 10; o VII 5, 12; o. X 2, 18; r. V 12; r. VI 14; r. X 6; r. XIII 6, 12; **13** o. I 8; o. III 17; o. IV 14; o. V 18; r. XII 16; **14** o. I 8; o. III 3; o. X 17; o. XII 13; o. XVI 7; o. XVII 9; o. XX 14; r. XII 5; **15** o. I 8; o. VII 6, 20; **16** o. I 8, 12; o. IV 5; r. II 20; r. IV 23; r. VI 18; **17** o. I 8; o. III 28; o. VIII 8; o. XV 10; r. XV 1; **18** o. I 8, 12; o. V 27; o. XIII 12; o. XVII 17; **19** o. I 11; o. VI 15, 21; o. X 1; r. V 5, 17; r. VI 23; r. VII 6, 12, 21; r. X 10; **20** o. I 8; o. II 13; o. VII 8; o. XIII 21; r. VII 13; r. XIII 9; r. XVI 6'; **24** r. IV 11; **25** r. III 12.

šu-du$_8$ «to take possession of» **7** o. VI 12; **8** r. XI 11'; **9** o. V 3; o. XVI x+1; **11** o. VIII 4; r. VII 21; **12** o. XII 9; **13** r. XII 22; **16** r. IX 27; **17** o. XIV 9; **19** r. XIII 18.

šu-dub «ring» **3** r. IV 6: 4 gín D. kb kin$_5$-ak 1 **L.**; **4** o. VII 8: TAR 7 10 gín D. kb 2 *bu*-DI 10 lá-2 ĝeštu$_x$-lá 30 *du-ru$_{12}$-gú* 1 *gu-za$_x$-gú* 1 **L.** 1 *ma-ḫa-na-gúm*; r. V 15: 1 ½ gín D. kb 1 **L.**; **15** o. V 11: 3 gín D. kg 2 ĜIŠ-ĝidru 2 **L.**; o. XI 15: 1 ma-na 14 gín D. kg kin$_5$-ak … 1 **L.**; **16** r. IX 12: 1 gín D. kg *ni-zi-mu* 1 **L.**; **17** r. IX 17: 1 gín D. kg nu$_{11}$-za-*sù* lú TAR *sa* **L.** en *wa ma-lik-tum*; r. XI 15, 19: [x g]ín D. k[b] kin$_5$-ak [*ḫ*]*a-za-nu* 2 **L.** en *wa ma-lik-tum*; r. XII 5: 12[(+x)] gín D. kg kin$_5$-ak 1 **L.** *ma-lik-tum ʾà-lum*; r. XX 21: 5 kb 15 *ḫa-za-nu* 2 gìn-gìn 2 si$_4$ 1 **L.**, 24: 4 kb 15 *ḫa-za-nu* 2 gìn-gìn 2 si$_4$ 1 **L.**; **18** o. XVI 20: 1 ma-na TAR kg kin$_5$-ak … 1 **L.**; **20** o. XIV 21: 3 gín D. kb 1 **L.** sikil en lú ḫúl; o. XV 16: 12 gín D. 1 **L.**; **24** r. I 1: 3 gín D. kg 1 **L.**

šu-du$_8$-máš «to take an omen» **4** o. VIII 3: 4 ĝír-ĝír **L.**; r. III 10: 2 ĝír **L.**; **6** o. XV 22: 4 ĝír **L.**; r. XVI 18: 4 ĝír **L.**; **9** o. V 9: 3 ĝír **L.**; **11** o. II 13: [x] sila$_4$ lú **L.**

šu-i «barber» **4** o. V 9; **7** o. V 13: *Da-zi-ma-ad* **L.** *Ib-ri-um*.

šu-i (a vessel) **4** r. IV 3: 1 gín D. kb nu$_{11}$-za!(KUR) 2 **L.** *Ib-rí-um*; **6** r. XVII 36: 2 an-na šub 1 **L.** *Ib-rí-um*; **17** o. V 11: 2 **L.** … 5 gín D. kg nu$_{11}$-za-*sù* en; **18** r. V 20: 2 gín D. an-na šub *si-in* 10 gín D. a-gar$_5$-gar$_5$ kin$_5$-ak 2 **L.**; r. XVI 30: 2 an-na šub *si-in* 10 a-gar$_5$-gar$_5$ 2 **L.** 2 kb nu$_{11}$-za-*sù Ib-rí-um*; **20** o. III 9: 2 gín D. an-na šub *si-in* 2 **L.**; **21** r. VI 20: 4 gín D. an-na šub *si-in* ŠÚ+ŠA 4 gín D. a-gar$_5$-gar$_5$ kin$_5$-ak 4 **L.** … nu$_{11}$-za-*sù* en.

šu-kešda «*pair of gloves*» **17** r. VI 23: 1 an-dùl … 1 gín 3 NI kg nu$_{11}$-za *ba-na-i-sù wa* íb-lá-*sù wa* **L.** gùn-*sù*.

šum «saw» **16** r. XII 1: 1 gín kg *ni-zi-mu* nu$_{11}$-za **L.** ZA$_x$ *Ib-rí-um*; **17** r. IX 7: ŠÚ+ŠA gín D. an-na šub *si-in* 20 lá-2 ma-na a-gar$_5$-gar$_5$ kin$_5$-ak 1 **L.** maḫ; **18** r. V 5: TAR 3 gín D. an-na šub *si-in* 24 ma-na a-gar$_5$-gar$_5$ kin$_5$-ak 1 **L.** maḫ, 10: 6 gín D. an-na šub *si-in* 5 ma-na a-gar$_5$-gar$_5$ kin$_5$-ak 2 **L.** maḫ.

šu-mu-LAGAB see s.v. dub-naĝar.

šu-mu-níĝin «procession, cultic journey» **9** r. VI 5: ĜIŠ-ti-ḪAR *Wa-ba-*⌈*rúm*⌉ šu-ba$_4$-ti *in* ud **L.** SA.ZA$_x^{ki}$; **17** r. XVI 12: 1 ĝír mar-tu níĝ-ba $^{d}$*Ra-sa-ap* … 2 *bu*-DI níĝ-ba $^{d}$*A-da-ma gú-núm ma-lik-tum* ì-na-sum *in* ud **L.** é diĝir-diĝir-diĝir; **22** o. VI 4: *in* ud **L.** SA.ZA$_x^{ki}$; r. IV 2: (60 bracelets, 10 daggers) lú *in* **L.** SA.ZA$_x^{ki}$ *Ba-ga-ma* gaba-ru.

šu-mu-tak$_4$ «to hand over» **1** o IX 15; **3** o. II 16; r. IV 15; r. VI 10; r. X 8; r. XII 18; **4** o. X 22; r. VIII 4; r. IX 18; r. XI 16; r. XIII 1; r. XV 8; **5** r. XVI 2; **6** o. XV 13; o. XVI 4; r. VI 18; r. VII 15; r. XV 17; r. XVII 1; **7** o. X 15; r. V 6; r. VI 9; r. XIII 18; **8** o. II 4; o. IV 15; **9** o. IX 10; r. IX 4, 10; **10** o. VI 21; o. VIII 2; o. IX 7; r. I 14; r. V 12; **11** o. XII 22; **12** o. VI 23; o. XIV 17; o. XV 7; **13** o. II 5; o. IV 4; o. VII 6; o. IX 21; o. XII 7; r. II 19; r. XI 16; **14** o. II 17; o. III 20; o. V 6, 14; o. XX 6; r. I 15; r. V 19; r. VI 14; r. VII 7; r. VIII 9; r. X 1; r. XI 2; **15** o. III 8; o. IX 4; o. XVII 1; r. V 12; r. VI 6, 21; r. X 18; r. XIV 8; **16** o. XIV 15, 20; **17** o. II 14, 19; o. IX 9; o. XII 4; o. XVII 23; o. XX 13; r. VIII 27; r. X 22; r. XI 13; r. XXII 20; **19** o. II 11; o. III 12; o. VIII 2; o. X 14; o. XII 2; o. XVIII 17; r. VIII 19; r. XVI 10; r. XVIII 15; r. XIX 12; **20** o.

XVII 17; **21** o. III 6, 13; o. VII 17; o. VIII 2; o. XIV 23; o. XV 3; r. IX 14; **23** o. II 2; r. II 13; **24** o. II 10; r. III 2; **25** r. III 6.

(Krecher 1981, p. 137 nt. 9 has noted that the sign here read tak$_{4}$ should be the Eblaite form for KÍD "to leave, to abandon", a reading confirmed by the *Sign List* no. 131)

šu-níĝin «total sum» **6** l.ed. 10: **L.** 1 *mi-at* 98 ma-na kb an-na; **25** r. IX 1: **L.** 25 *g[u]-zi-tum*-TÚG 6 *mi-at* 61 túg-túg 60 lá-1 gada-TÚG 5 níĝ-lá-saĝ níĝ-lá-gaba 2 *mi-at* 23 íb-III-TÚG sa$_{6}$ gùn 6 *mi-at* 81 íb-III-TÚG gùn.

ŠÚ+ŠA «⅓ of a mina» (= 20 shekels) *passim.*

*šu-ti* (relative pronoun) see *ša*.

T

tak$_{4}$ «deposited; balance» **4** o. XV 21: 20 *gú-li-lum* gaba-ru é en **L.** IGI.IGI; **13** o. XVI 6: 2 *bu*-DI … 2 saĝ-*sù* níĝ-ba *Ti-šè-li-im ma-lik-tum Ì-mar*$^{ki}$ *in* ud DU.DU *si-in* SA.ZA$_{x}$$^{ki}$ **L.** AMA-*ra*; **19** o. XV 31: (104 daggers) lú **L.** igi-ḫi-du$_{8}$ *Za-ru*$_{12}$*-du*$^{<ki>}$; **20** o. XVII 4: 1 íb-lá 1 *si-ti-tum* 1 ĝír-kun sikil $^{d?}$*A*$_{5}$*-da-"bal"* lú *Lu-ba-an*$^{ki}$ *al*$_{6}$ tu-ra *Ib-rí-um* **L.**; **22** r. IX 2: AN.ŠÈ.GÚ 4 ma-na TAR 3 gín D. kg è lú mu-DU *I[b-rí-]um wa* **L.** kg É×PAP en-e[n].

TAR «half» **17** r. IX 15.

TAR «½ mina» (= 30 shekels) *passim.*

tar «to distribute»

tar-tar **16** r. VIII 19: (40 daggers) lú ĝuruš-ĝuruš **L.**

*ter*$_{6}$*-bí* «elevation» **20** r. III 22: 1 kù-sal níĝ-ba *Dar-ib-da-mu* dumu-munus en $^{d}$BAD-munus *si-in Lu-ba-an*$^{ki}$ *in* ud **L.** bur-KAK-*sù* $^{d?}$*A*$_{5}$*-da-"bal"*.

*ti-ba-ra-núm* (headdress) **15** o. XI 17: 1 ma-na 14 gín D. kg kin$_{5}$-ak … 2 **L.**; **24** r. I 11: 3 gín D. kg 1 *[m]a-ḫa-na-gúm* 1 *ša-mu* 1 *a-na-bù-bí-tum* 1 **L.**

*ti-gi-na* «torque» **7** o. II 15: 10 gín D. kb ⌜2⌝ **L.** 2 ĜIŠ-du; 13 r. X 18: TAR kb 2 **L.** 2 ĜIŠ-du; **15** o. X 18: 14 gín D. kg 2 **L.** 2 ĜIŠ-du 1 KA-*ḫu-a-tum*; o. XI 9: 1 ma-na 14 gín D. kg kin$_{5}$-ak … 2 **L.**; **18** o. II 7: 14 gín D. kg 2 *gú-li-lum wa* 2 **L.** *wa* 2 ĜIŠ-du, 16: 14 gín D. kg 2 *gú-li-lum wa* 2 **L.** *wa* 2 ĜIŠ-du; o. X 7: 15 gín D. kg *ni-zi-mu* 2 **L.**; o. XVI 16: 1 ma-na TAR kg kin$_{5}$-ak 2 **L.** …; o. XVIII 4: 8 gín D. kg *ni-zi-mu* 4 **L.** 4 ĜIŠ-du 4 ĝeštu$_{x}$-lá 2 kù-sal; **20** o. XV 8: 1 ma-na ŠÚ+ŠA gín D. kg kin$_{5}$-ak … 2 *ti-gi-na* ŠÚ+ŠA gín D; r. IV 15: ŠA.PI gín D. kg 2 **L.**; r. VI 6: ŠA.PI gín D. kg 2 **L.** *ma-l[ik-]tum*; **24** o. VII 10: TAR kg 2 **L.**

*ti-ki-na* **2** o. VI 4: ŠÚ+ŠA gín D. kg kin$_{5}$-ak 2 **L.** en.

til «to be defeated (said of a town)» **4** r. IX 22: (silver) Šubur *Na-gàr*$^{ki}$ šu-mu-tak$_{4}$ íb+III-TÚG babbar *Ma-rí*$^{ki}$ *wa* **L.**-*sù*; r. X 16: [ ] níĝ-"mul" àga-"kár"(ŠÈ) *Ma-rí*$^{ki}$ *wa* **L.** *Wa-ru*$_{12}$*-tum*; **7** r. VIII 24: (silver) níg-ba *Iš-dub-ì Ma-rí*$^{ki}$ níĝ-"mul" *Ar-ti-na-an*$^{ki}$ **L.**; r. XIII 6: (silver) [níĝ-ba] *Daš-na Ma-rí*$^{ki}$ níg-"mul" Kiš$^{ki}$ **L.**; **10** o. XVI 10: (silver) níĝ-ba *Ib-gi-tum Ma-rí*$^{ki}$ níĝ-"mul" *Na-gàr*$^{ki}$ **L.**; **11** o. VII 10: (silver) níĝ-ba *Ma-rí*$^{ki}$ níĝ-"mul" *Na-gàr*$^{ki}$ **L.**; **13** r. IX 19: [ ] *B[ù-]du-d[u]* ugula *Ar-ʾà-mu*$^{ki}$ *in* ud *Si-da-rí-in*$^{ki}$ **L.**

til-til **14** r. V 16: (silver) [níĝ-ba] *Wa-ru*$_{12}$*-tum Ma-rí*$^{ki}$ níĝ-"mul" Kiš$^{ki}$ **L.**; **15** r. X 25: (silver) níĝ-ba *Daš-na Ma-rí*$^{ki}$ níĝ-"mul" Kiš$^{ki}$ **L.**

til «to (be) complete» **15** o. III 27: [ ] *Ḫa-ra-il áš-du* 1 dib-*sù* **L.** *in Ša-nu-gú*$^{ki}$.

*ti-ša-nu* (decoration in shape of an animal of the caprine family) **7** r. XIV 2: 10 gín D. kb [ ] 4 **L.** 2 *bu*-DI; **14** r. VII 11: 10 gín D. kb [2 *b]u*-DI *wa* 4 **L.**; **20** r. X 6: 10 gín D. kb 2 *bu*-DI 4 **L.**

*ti-ša-na* **5** r. XIII 13: 10 gín D. kb 2 *bu*-DI 2 **L.**; **6** r. XIV 1: 10 gín D. kb 2 *bu*-DI 2 **L.**

(it is attested as the form of a toggle-pin, *bu*-DI, Conti – Bonechi 1992, p. 11).

ti-TÚG «ribbed clothing»

it qualifies aktum-TÚG **7** o. VIII 13; **11** o. IX 10; **18** r. XIII 7.

tu-da «to give birth (to)» **15** o. XVI 25: *Zi-mi-ni*-kù:babbar *ma-lik-tum Bur-ma-an*$^{ki}$ *in* ud dumu-munus **L.**; **16** r. XIII 28: [ ] s[ikil] *in* ud **L.**

túg «clothing» **12** r. II 17: 6 gín D. kb *Bù-sum Ma-rí*$^{ki}$ *a-dè* **L.**-*sù*.

túg-túg **6** o. XV 14: (silver) níĝ-ba *Puzur*$_{4}$*-ra-*$^{d}$Utu *Ma-rí*$^{ki}$ šu-mu-tak$_{4}$ **L.** *áš-da Na-zi*; **17** o. XVII 24: (silver) gur$_{8}$ ĜIŠ-gígir-sum šu-mu-tak$_{4}$ **L.**; **25** r. IX 3: šu-níĝin … 6 *mi-at* 61 **L.**

túg-NI.NI (a type of cloak for women) **2** r. V 8: 1 **L.** ḫul; r. XII 11: 7 **L.** ḫul; r. XIII 6: 14 **L.** ḫul; r. XVII 10: 1 **L.** ḫul; **5** o. I 4; 6 r. IX 9; r. XI 9; **7** o. VIII 14; o. XVII 5; r. VI 13; 9 o. XIV 10: 1 **L.** sa$_{6}$, 11; **11** r. II 15; **12** o. I 5; o. VIII 9; **13** o. XVII 2; r. V 9; **14** o. XVI 13; o. XXI 3; **15** o. VIII 6, 7: 1 **L.** sa$_{6}$; o. XII 12; o. XVII 12; r. III 11; **16** o. IV 10: 1 **L.** *Ma-rí*$^{ki}$; o. XIII 13; r. XI 14; **17** r. V 4; r. X 5; **18** o. IX 14; r. III 3; r. XIII 6; **19** o. VI 23; r. V 7; r. XVI 22; **20** o. XIII 24; r. VI 19; r. XIII 5; **25** o. I 4; o. II 2; o. III 3; o. IV 5; o. V 7.

túg-nu-tag «to weave; weaver» **6** o. II 11: 2 dam **L.** *Ma-rí*$^{ki}$.

tùn «axe»

tùn gal «big axe» **10** r. X 21: 20 **L.** zabar; r. XI 4: 1 ma-na an-na šub 30 **L.** urudu; **15** r. II 19: 10 gín D. an-na šub *si-in* 1 ma-na a-gar$_{5}$-gar$_{5}$ kin$_{5}$-ak 1 *ma-ḫa-ni-gúm wa* 1 **L.** en; **16** r. XV 8: TAR an-na šub *si-in* 4 ma-na ŠÚ+ŠA a-gar$_{5}$-gar$_{5}$ kin$_{5}$-ak 5 **L.** TAR.TAR.

tùn tur «small axe» **7** o. XIV 16: 8 gín D. an-na šub *si-in* 1 **L.** 1 dub-naĝar sal 1 *ma-za-ḫa-rúm* 1 UŠ×KÍD; **10** r. XI 1: 10 **L.** zabar; **12** r. XI 12: 1 ma-na ŠÚ+ŠA 3 gín D. an-na šub *si-in* 9 ma-na TAR gín D. a-gar$_{5}$-gar$_{5}$ kin$_{5}$-ak 6 **L.** lú TAR.TAR …; r. XII 12: 57 gín D. an-na šub *si-in* 6 ma-na ŠA.PI gín D. a-gar$_{5}$-gar$_{5}$ kin$_{5}$-ak 5 **L.** TAR.TAR…; **19** o. III 9: ŠÚ+ŠA 2 gín D. an-na šub *si-in* 1 m[a-]na TAR [4+]4 gín D. a-gar$_{5}$-gar$_{5}$ kin$_{5}$-ak 3 **L.** ŠA.PI-ŠA.PI lú šu-mu-tak$_{4}$ *si-in A-la-ga*$^{ki}$ *in* ud igi-ḫi-du$_{8}^{!}$(šu-du$_{8}$) *A-la-ga*$^{ki}$; **20** r. I 12–13: 17 gín D. an-na šub *si-in* 1 ma-na ŠA.PI gín D. a-gar$_{5}$[-gar$_{5}$] kin$_{5}$-ak 1 **L.** TAR 1 **L.** ŠÚ+ŠA gín D.

tur «small» **2** o. XI 13: 1 ĝír mar-tu *ra-ʾà-tum* **L.**; **4** o. XI 20: 12 zi-bar **L.**; **6** r. XIII 4: 1 útul **L.**; **12** r. XII 4: 6 dub-naĝar **L.** 5; **13** r. XI 1 *bu*-DI **L.**; **21** o. IX 7: 50 lá-2 DAM.KAK.UŠ **L.** sal
see dumu-munus tur en s.v. dumu-munus; tùn tur s.v. tùn.

tu-ra «illness» **15** r. VI 8: 1 ⌜íb⌝-lá 1 *si-ti-tum* 1 ĝír-kun sikil $^{d}$ʾ*A*$_{5}$*-da-“bal”* *Lu-ba-an*$^{ki}$ *Ib-rí-um* šu-mu-tak$_{4}$ *al*$_{6}$ **L.**-*sù*; r. X 5: 1 kù-sal [níĝ-b]a en $^{d}$*Ḫa-a-ba-du al*$_{6}$ **L.** ama-gal-*sù*; r. XII 9 and 18: 1 dib en *áš-du* dib-*sù* sikil $^{d}$ʾ*À-da al*$_{6}$ **L.** ama-gal-*sù wa* 2 *gú-li-lum-sù* sikil $^{d}$ʾ*A*$_{5}$*-da-“bal”* *Lu-ba-an*$^{ki}$ *al*$_{6}$ **L.**-*sù*, 30: 2 *gú-li-lum Ib-rí-um áš-du* 2 *gú-li-lum-sù* sikil $^{d}$ʾ*À-da al*$_{6}$ **L.** en; r. XIII 10: 1 dib *Ib-rí-um áš-du* 1 dib-*sù* sikil $^{d}$ʾ*À-da al*$_{6}$ **L.** en; r. XVI 11: [1 ĝír mar-t]u kg *Ib-rí-um áš-du* ĝír mar-tu-*sù* sikil $^{d}$*Áš-da-bíl al*$_{6}$ **L.** en; **19** o. I 18 and 22: 2 ĝír mar-tu kg *Ib-rí-um wa* sikil-*sù al*$_{6}$ **L.** *I-bí-zi-kir wa al*$_{6}$ **L.** en; o. II 13: 1 kù-sal níĝ-ba en $^{d}$*Ba-tum-ma-du áš-t*[*i*] ĝír mar-tu-*sù* šu-mu-tak$_{4}$ *al*$_{6}$ **L.** *Ib-rí-um*; o. IX 23: 2 kù-sal níĝ-ba $^{d}$*Ba-tum-ma-du wa* $^{d}$*Da-bi-na-du áš-ti* 2 ĝír mar-tu kg *al*$_{6}$ **L.** en; o. XII 4: 2 gí[r] mar-tu *wa* 2 kù-sal níg-ba $^{d}$ʾ*A*$_{5}$*-da-“bal”* *A-ru*$_{12}$*-ga-du*$^{ki}$ *wa* $^{d}$ʾ*A*$_{5}$*-da-“bal”* ʾ*À-ma-du*$^{ki}$ [ ]-⌜x⌝ [šu-m]u-tak$_{4}$ *al*$_{6}$ **L.**-*sù*; **20** o. XVII 2: 1 íb-lá 1 *si-ti-tum* 1 ĝír-kun sikil $^{d}$ʾ*A*$_{5}$*-da-“bal”* lú *Lu-ba-an*$^{ki}$ *al*$_{6}$ **L.** *Ib-rí-um* tak$_{4}$; **21** o. VIII 23: 1 *za-ḫa-da* … lul-gu-ak lú sikil é $^{d}$ʾ*À-da al*$_{6}$ **L.** *Ib-rí-um*; r. VIII 20: 1 íb-lá 1 *si-ti-tum* 1 ĝír-kun lú en sikil $^{d}$ʾ*À-da al*$_{6}$ **L.** *I-bí-zi-kir*.

tuš see al$_{6}$-tuš, ba-tuš.

tuš-LÚ×TIL «to reside, to occupy» **1** o. VII 16: *Du-bí-šum* lú *Ba-zi-da* **L.** *Kak-mi-um*$^{ki}$; **4** r. IX 2: *I-du-bù* **L.** *Ḫa-z*[*u-*]*wa-an*$^{ki}$; **5** r. IV 15: BÍL-*ma-lik* lú *Ba-ḫa-ga in* ud *Gú-rá-ma-an*$^{ki}$ **L.**; **6** r. VIII 12: *I-bí-šum* lú *Ti-ir in* ud **L.** *Zú-ti*$^{ki}$; **7** o. VIII 1: [ ] **L.** *Ma-rí*$^{ki}$ *áš-ti Du-du-lu*$^{ki}$, 9: *Ib-ḫur-ma-lik Kak-mi-um*$^{ki}$ **L.** *in Ar-ḫa-du*$^{ki}$; **9** r. II 15: *Du-bí* lú *Iš-da-má* **L.** *Ar-mi*$^{ki}$ *áš-ti Gul-da-ad*$^{ki}$; r. III 6: *En-àr-li-im* [dumu-ni]ta *Du-*[*bí*]*-šum A-ba-ad*$^{ki}$ **L.** *Ar-mi*$^{ki}$ *áš-ti Zú-mu-šar*$^{ki}$; r. IV 2: *Du-ur-il Bù-ra-tin*$^{ki}$ **L.** *Ar-mi*$^{[ki]}$ [*áš-ti*] [ $^{ki}$]; **11** o. VII 17: *Íl-gú-uš-ti* lú *I-gi* **L.** Kiš$^{ki}$ lú *A-bar-sal*$_{4}$$^{ki}$; **12** o. XII 19: *I-bí-zi-kir* lú *I-rí-gú-nu in* ud **L.** *in Ma-nu-wa-ad*$^{ki}$; **14** o. VIII 2: *Zú-za-bir*$_{5}$ lú *A-da-ad* **L.** *in Am*$_{6}$*-ʾà-rúm*$^{ki}$; r. VIII 14: *A-mur-da-mu* **L.** *Dur-zi-lum*$^{ki}$; r. IX 7: *I-bí-zi-kir* [**L.** *in*] *Ib-al*$_{6}$$^{ki}$; **15** o. IV 9: *Bar-za-ma-ù* ugula ʾ*À-šu*$^{ki}$ *in* ud **L.** *A-a-lu*$^{ki}$; o. XIII 26: *I-in-il* ugula *Ù-ša-li-ik*$^{ki}$ *in* ud **L.** *Kak-mi-um*$^{ki}$; **16** r. IV 9: *Ḫa-bù-zú* ʾ*À-bar-du*$^{ki}$ maškim *Za-ba-rúm* **L.** *Ḫal-sum*$^{ki}$; r. IX 6: *I-bí-zi-kir* dumu-nita *Ib-rí-um in* ud **L.** *Ḫal-sum*$^{ki}$; **17** o. I 14: *Íl-gú-uš-ti* lú *I-gi* **L.** *Kak-mi-um*$^{ki}$ ⌜*áš-ti*⌝ [GN]; o. XII 16: *Ḫa-zu-um* maškim *Ib-rí-um* **L.** *Ti-ma-tim*$^{ki}$ lú *Kak-mi-um*$^{ki}$, 25: *Du-bí-šum* lú *Gú-ma-ni-du* maškim *I-bí-zi-kir* **L.** *Kak-mi-um*$^{ki}$ *áš-ti Šu-ra-an*$^{ki}$; o. XVIII 5: ʾ*À:daš* **L.** *Ša-ra-bí-ig*$^{ki}$; **18** r. XVI 25: *Ga-nu-bù Sal-bu-um*$^{ki}$ **L.** *Ḫal-sum*$^{ki}$; **19** r. X 17: *Gi-ra-ma-lik* lú *I-bí-šum* **L.** *Ḫal-sum*$^{ki}$; r. XIV 12: *Bù-da-ì Maš-bar-rá*$^{ki}$ **L.** *Za-ḫi-ra-an*$^{ki}$ al$_{6}$-tuš *A-la-ga*$^{ki}$, 20: EN-*da-za A-rí-gú*$^{ki}$ **L.** *Nu-rí*$^{ki}$; **20** r. VIII 6: *Kùn-da-ba-an* [ ] *in* ud **L.** *in A-ru*$_{12}$*-ga-du*$^{ki}$; **21** o. XVI 24: [ ] **L.** *Ma-rí*$^{ki}$; **22** r. I 5: *Nu-ba-an*$^{ki}$ maškim *Sa-li-im* **L.** *in Ar-mi*$^{ki}$; **24** o. III 5: *Iš*$_{11}$*-ru-ud* lú *In-ma-lik* **L.** *in U*$_{9}$*-ru*$_{12}$$^{ki}$.

U

u$_{5}$ a) «to mount to ride» **1**(e) r. IV' 6: IGI.NITA **L.**; **2** r. X 5: IGI.NITA **L.**; **3** o. VII 1: IGI.NITA **L.**; **13** o. XVII 8: IGI.NITA **L.**; 16 r. IV 19: IGI.NITA **L.**; **17** o. IV 2: 2 IGI.NITA **L.**; **18** r. III 12: 3 IGI.NITA **L.**; **20** r. VII 2: 2 IGI.NITA **L.**
b) «merchant, courier» **4** r. III 18: 10 u$_{5}$ SA.ZA$_{x}$$^{ki}$; **21** r. XI 22: *Da-ti* … *Daš-na* … *A-rí-su* lú **L.** *Ma-rí*$^{ki}$.

UD.GÁNA **20** r. XI 21: [ ] l[u$_{x}$] **L.** ĜIŠ-sal ⌜dag⌝ é maḫ.

udu-nita «ram» **2** r. XII 20: 6 **L.** sa$_{6}$.

ugula «overseer» **3** r. II 9: *Ib-bí-um* **L.** é; **5** o. III 6: *Ba-ga-ma* **L.**; o. VII 10: *Ib-gi-da-mu* **L.** kad$_{4}$-kad$_{4}$; r. XVI 20: siki *I-bu*$_{16}$*-bù*$^{ki}$ **L.** é en šu-ba$_{4}$-ti; **6** r. XIV 15: *Ba-ga-ma* **L.** SA.ZA$_{x}$$^{ki}$; **9** o. XV 18: *A-šu-úr-il* **L.**; **12** o. V 8: *Zi-la-da-mu* **L.** kas$_{4}$; r. II 18: *Bù-su Ma-rí*$^{ki}$ *a-dè* túg-*sù* **L.** ki:lam$_{7}$ ga:eš$_{8}$ *in Maš-a*$^{ki}$.
ugula GN **2** o. V 17: *En-na-il* **L.** *Lum-na-an*$^{ki}$; o. XIV 3: *Rí-dam-ma-lik* **L.** *Šu-ti-gú*$^{ki}$; **3** o. I 4: *Rí-ì-ma-lik* **L.** *A-da-*⌜*áš*⌝$^{ki}$, 8: *Rí-ì-ma-lik* **L.** *Ig-du-ra*$^{ki}$; r. V 2: *Ḫáb-ra-ar* **L.** ʾ*A*$_{5}$*-da-tum*$^{ki}$; **4** r. VII 4: *Sa-ḫa-a* **L.** *Ù-si-gú*$^{ki}$; **5** r. VI 8: *I-ti-gi-ma-lik* **L.** *Mug-rí-ì*$^{ki}$; **6** r. II 13: *I-bí-gar-du* **L.** ʾ*À-ma-du*$^{ki}$; **7** o. II 2: *Du-bí* **L.** *A-ru*$_{12}$*-lu*$^{ki}$; **8** o. III 7: *I-nu-ud-da-mu* **L.** *Kak-mi-um*$^{⌜ki⌝}$; **9** r. VII 11: *En-na-il* **L.** *Lum-na-an*$^{ki}$; **11** r. VII 19: *Zi-ir-a-ḫu* **L.** *A-bar-sal*$_{4}$$^{ki}$; **13** o. II 17: *Mu-*NE*-a-du* **L.** *Ar-ḫa-du*$^{ki}$; o. IV 8: [*Rí-*]*dam-ma-lik* **L.** *Su-ti-gú*$^{ki}$; r. IX 16: *B*[*ù-*]*du-d*[*u*] **L.** *Ar-ʾà-mu*$^{ki}$; **14** o. V 3: *Mu-*NE*-a-du* **L.** *Ar-ḫa-du*$^{ki}$; o. XX 12: [ ] **L.** *Kul-ba-an*$^{ki}$; r. XIX 2': ⌜*Sa*⌝[*-ḫa-a*] **L.** *Ù-si-gú*$^{ki}$; **15** o. IV 7: *Bar-za-ma-ù* **L.** ʾ*À-šu*$^{ki}$; o. XIII 24: *I-in-il* **L** *Ù-ša-li-ik*$^{ki}$; **16** r. V 22: *Bar-za-ma-ù* **L.** *A-ru*$_{12}$*-ga-du*$^{ki}$; r. XV 12: *Wa-na* **L.** *A-la-ga*$^{ki}$; r. XVI 20: *Wa-na* **L.** *A-la-ga*$^{ki}$; **17** r. VIII 24: **L.** *Ib-al*$_{6}$$^{ki}$ DU.DU *Du-gú-ra-su*$^{ki}$; **18** o. XV 1: *Iš*$_{11}$*-gi-bar-zú wa Du-bí-ab* **L.** *Ti-*[*sum*]$^{ki}$; r. VI 18: *Iš*$_{11}$*-ru-ud* **L.** *Sal-ba-ù*$^{ki}$; **19** r. XIII 19: **L.** *Za-ḫi-ra-an*$^{ki}$; **21** o. VI 2: *Iš*$_{11}$*-ru-ud* **L.** *Sal-ba*$^{ki}$; **25** r. III 3: [ ] l[ú] *D*[*u-si*] **L.** *Ib-al*$_{6}$$^{ki}$.
see ugula BAR.AN and ugula BAR.AN-BAR.AN s.v. BAR.AN; ugula engar s.v. engar; ugula ĝiš s.v. ĝiš; ugula IGI.NITA s.v. IGI.NITA; ugula ir$_{11}$ s.v. ir$_{11}$; ugula sur$_{x}$-BAR.AN s.v. sur$_{x}$-BAR.AN.

ú-ḫáb «dull red» **2** r. IX 12; **5** o. XIV 11.

*ù*-NAM-*mi-lu* (a jewel) **16** r. XIII 17: ŠÚ+ŠA 6 gín D. kg kin$_{5}$-ak lul-gu-ak … 1 **L.** 8 gín D. sikil $^{d}$BAD-munus *Lu-ba-an*$^{ki}$.
(a jewel in general offered to gods, see TM.75.G.2382 o. III 5: $^{d}$*Ra-sa-ap* … 1 **L.** $^{d}$*A-da-ma-sù*; TM.75.G.10198 o. II 1: 1 **L.** $^{d}$*Ra-sa-ap wa* $^{d}$*A-dam-ma-sù*)

“ur$_{4}$” «collector (of goods); provider» **3** o. II 9: *En-na-*BAD ; **4** o. IV 3: *Ib-bí-um* **L.**; r. II 9: *Ib-bí-um* **L.**; r. V 4: *Ib-bí-um* **L.**; r. VII 14: *Ib-bí-um* **L.**; **5** o. II 3: *Wa-ba-rúm* **L.**; **6** r. VII 9: *Ba-lu-zú* **L.**; **8** o. XI

8: *Wa-ba-rúm* **L.**; r. IV 12': *Wa-ba-rúm* **L.**; **10** o. IX 16: **L.** *Mar-da-ma*-LUM[ki]; **11** r. V 10: *Uš-ga* **L.** *A-da-bí-ig*[ki]; **13** o. XII 3: *Ù-zu* **L.** *Ì-mar*[ki]; **18** o. IV 17: NI-*dim* **L.** *Na-gàr*[ki]; **19** o. X 13: *Ìr-ba$_x$-zé* **L.**; r. VI 22: *Ib-bi-um* **L.**; **20** o. VIII 1: *I-lu$_5$-za$_x$-ma-lik* **L.**; **23** r. V 8: *I-lu$_5$-za$_x$-ma-lik* **L.**

URI **8** o. XIII 7: ŠA.PI gín D. kb **L.** 1 íb-lá 1 kun; **9** r. XV 11: TAR kb **L.** 1 íb-lá 1 ĝír-kun; **14** o. VII 1: TAR kb **L.** 1 íb-lá 1 ĝír-kun kg; r. XIII 22: 1 ma-na 16 kb *ni-zi-mu* **L.** 10 lá-2 íb-lá 5 g[ír-kun] kb maš-maš; **16** o. VIII 3: 6 gín D. kb *ni-zi-mu* 7 íb-lá 5 ĝír-kun lú **L.** lú kg; **19** r. XIII 10: TAR kb **L.** 1 íb-lá 1 ĝír-kun.

uru[ki] «city»

uru[ki]-uru[ki] **15** o. VII 18: (silver) níĝ-ba *Wa-ru$_{12}$-tum Ma-rí*[ki] níĝ-"mul" *in* **L.** Kiš[ki] šu-ba$_4$-ti.

uru-bar «village; suburb» **9** o. XV 12: 2 ĝír mar-tu ti kg *Ib-rí-um* **L.** *in* níĝ-kas$_4$ lú sikil; r. I 4: 1 ĝír mar-tu kg *Ì-lum-a-ḫa* dumu-nita **L.** šu-ba$_4$-ti.

urudu «(not refined) copper» **4** o. XV 6: 1 útul **L.**; r. XV 18: 1 útul **L.**; **5** r. V 18: 1 ĜIŠ-banšur … 10 gín D. an-na šub *si-in* **L.**-*sù*; **6** r. II 20: 3 útul-útul **L.** maḫ; r. XIII 3: 2 ma-na TAR **L.**; **10** o. I 2: saĝ **L.** ${}^{d}$*Ku-ra*; r. IV 11: ⌜10⌝ útul **L.**, 16: 10 útul **L.**; r. XI 4: 30 tùn ⌜gal⌝ **L.**; **14** r. VI 5: 1 ĜIŠ-banšur maḫ … [x gín D. a-ga]r$_5$-gar$_5$ **L.**-*sù*; **15** r. XIV 20: 3 útul **L.** maḫ; **16** o. III 18: 1 útul **L.** maḫ; r. XIV 18: 1 útul **L.** maḫ, 21: 3 útul **L.** maḫ; r. XVI 6: 2 útul **L.** maḫ gibil; **18** o. I 15: 3 útul maḫ **L.**; o. XIII 17: 2 útul **L.**; r. XIX 4: [ ] ⌜x⌝ **L.**; **19** o. IX 5: 2 útul **L.** gibil maḫ; r. XVI 17: útul-útul maḫ **L.**; **20** r. XIV 10: ⌜útul⌝-útul maḫ **L.**

úš «death» **1**(e) r. II' 9': [ ] *Da-d*[*ub*] *Ìr-m*[*u*-]*da-mu* lú *Íl-zi Ìr-ga-bù* è *in* ud *Ìr-kab-da-mu si-mi* **L.**-*sù*; **3** r. XII 20: 2 íb-lá kg ì-ĝiš-saĝ 2 en *Ma-nu-wa-ad*[ki] *Ba-ga-ma* šu-mu-tak$_4$ *in* ud **L.** *ma-lik-tum*; **18** r. IV 25: 2 *bu*-DI ì-ĝiš-saĝ *Di-rín-da-mu* dam-diĝir *áš-du* **L.** *ma-lik-tum Lum-na-an*[ki]; **21** o. XI 24: AN.[Š]È.GÚ 1 *mi-at* 80 lá-1 ma-na kb lú è *in* ud [**L.** *Ib-rí-um*]; r. XVII 4: [AN.ŠÈ.GÚ x *mi-at* x ma-na x kb] ⌜è⌝ DIŠ m[u] **L.** *Ib-rí-um*.

see ḫi-úš.

UŠ×KÍD «blade» **7** o. XIV 18: 8 gín D. an-na šub *si-in* 1 tùn tur 1 dub-naĝar sal 1 *ma-za-ḫa-rúm* 1 **L.**; **12** r. XII 5: 1 ma-na ŠÚ+ŠA 3 gín D. an-na šub *si-in* 9 ma-na TAR gín D. a-gar$_5$-gar$_5$ kin$_5$-ak … 12 **L.**; **20** r. I 20: 17 gín D. an-na šub *si-in* 1 ma-na ŠA.PI gín D. a-gar$_5$[-gar$_5$] kin$_5$-ak … 1 **L.** 2 gín D.

útul «kettle» **4** o. XV 6: 3 gí[n] D. kb ZU.PIRIĜ 1 **L.** urudu; r. XV 18: [x kb] ZU.PIRIĜ 1 **L.** urudu; **6** r. XIII 4: 1 **L.** tur; **10** r. IV 11 and 16: [x gí]n [D.] kb ZU.PIRIĜ ⌜10⌝ **L.** urudu lú dam lú ĜIŠGAL-titab(MUNU$_4$.A) *wa* ZU.PIRIĜ 10 **L.** urudu lú *Du-si-gú*; **15** r. XIV 20: 10 gín D. kb ZU.PIRIĜ kin$_5$-ak 3 **L.** urudu maḫ; **16** o. III 18: 11 gín D. an-na šub *si-in zi-ba-ti* 1 **L.** urudu maḫ; r. XIV 18: 6 gín D. an-na šub *si-in zi-ba-du* 1 **L.** urudu maḫ, 21: 15 gín D. kb ZU.PIRIĜ 3 **L.** urudu maḫ; r. XVI 6: 13 ma-na ŠÚ+ŠA an-na šub *si-in* 4 *mi-at* ma-na a-gar$_5$-gar$_5$ kin$_5$-ak 2 **L.** urudu maḫ gibil; **18** o. I 15: ŠÚ+ŠA gín D. kb ZU.PIRIĜ 3 **L.** útul maḫ urudu *in* ud *ir-me*; o. IX 4: 11 ma-na an-na šub *si-in* 6 *mi-at* ma-na a-gar$_5$-gar$_5$ daḫ$_x$(MU.MU.MU) kin$_5$-ak 2 **L.** gibil; o. XIII 17: 10 na$_4$ PN kin$_5$-ak 2 **L.** urudu; o. XIV 10: 1 na$_4$ PN kin$_5$-ak 2 **L.**; **19** o. IX 5: 10 lá-1 ma-na 20 gín D. an-na šub *si-in* 2 *mi-at* 17 ma-na a-gar$_5$-g[ar$_5$] [k]in$_5$-ak sig$_4$-KI 2 **L.** urudu gibil maḫ.

útul-útul **6** r. I 20: ŠÚ+ŠA gín D. kb ZU.PIRIĜ 3 **L.** urudu maḫ; **19** r. XVI 17: ŠÚ+ŠA gín D. kb ZU.PIRIĜ **L.** maḫ urudu; **20** r. XIV 10: [x g]ín [D. an-n]a [šub *si-i*]*n* [x a-g]ar$_5$-gar$_5$ [*z*]*i*-⌜*ba*⌝-[*du*] **L.** maḫ urudu.

ùz-munus «female goat» **17** r. VII 8: 1 *gú-li-lum* **L.** a:tu$_{22}$ é *ma-tim* NE-*na-áš*[ki] *ma-lu-gi-iš* en.

ùz-nita (!) «male goat» **15** r. III 17: 2 kuš babbar **L.**

## W

*wa* «and» **1** o. X 14; o. XIII 4'; **2** o. VI 11; o. IX 11; o. XIV 17; o. XV 13; r. IV 7; r. VI 18; r. VIII 2; r. XIV 12; **3** o. II 20; o. VIII 23; o. XII 13; o. XIII 16; r. V 17; r. VI 14; r. VIII 6; r. IX 4; r. XIII 4, 14; r. XIV 3; **4** o. III 8; r. IV 21; r. VIII 12; r. IX 21; r. X 15; r. XII 22; **5** o. II 17; o. VII 11; o. X 5; r. IV 19; r. VI 18; r. XVI 13, 15; **6** o. III 19; o. VI 9, 11; o. VIII 5, 19, 22; o. XI 14; o. XIII 6; o. XV 3; o. XVI 8, 15; r. I 2, 8, 14; r. II 18; r. IV 4, 15; r. V 7, 24; r. VI 2; r. X 4, 6; r. XII 4; r. XIV 8; r. XV 15; r. XVI 22; r. XVII 31; **7** o. III 13; o. IX 10; r. VI 19; r. VIII 13; r. XII 12; r. XV 12, 22; **8** o. III 1; o. V 7; o. VIII 6; r. V 2', 14'; r. XI 10'; **9** o. III 18; o. V 4; o. XI 18; o. XII 9, 16; r. III 14; r. VI 18; r. VIII 10, 12, 14; r. X 2; r. XI 3, 5, 12; r. XIII 20; **10** o. VI 17; o. XIII 12; r. I 3; r. II 1; r. IV 3, 14; r. VI 2; r. IX 4; r. X 13; r. XVI 4; **12** o. II 8, 15, 17; o. III 13; o. V 19; o. VI 2; o. XI 18; o. XIV 14; r. VIII 17; r. IX 12, 14; **13** o. II 11; o. IV 12, 23; o. VI 3; o. VII 22; o. XII 18; o. XV 7, 9, 16; o. XVI 16; r. II 17; r. III 2, 15; r. IV 18; r. VI 6; r. VII 12, 17; r. VIII 5; r. X 12; r. XIV 19; **14** o. III 15; o. VI 20; o. XIII 4; o. XIV 13; o. XVIII 9, 11; o. XIX 2, 4; o. XXI 4, 8; r. V 17; r. VII 10; r. VIII 4; r. XI 12; r. XIII 13; **15** o. II 4; o. VI 4; o. VII 9, 24; o. XI 18; o. XIII 11, 14; r. II 1, 18; r. IV 5; r. VII 7, 17, 25; r. VIII 6, 17; r. X 14; r. XI 2; r. XII 12; r. XIII 23; **16** o. III 6; o. V 13, 15; r. VII 29; r. VIII 2, 11, 13, 15; r. X 19; r. XII 14; r. XIII 2, 16, 21; r. XV 28; **17** o. XVII 7; o. XIX 3, 10; r. I 29; r. II 6; r. VI 20, 22, 29; r. IX 19, 27; r. XI 7, 21; r. XIII 12; r. XIV 8, 13, 16, 22; r. XVII 4, 6, 18, 21; **18** o. I 22; o. II 6, 8, 15, 17; o. IV 8; o. VII 10, 15; o. VIII 4, 8; o. XIV 15, 27; o. XV 9, 22, 25; o. XVIII 9; r. I 9, 16; r. VII 10; r. VIII 8; r. X 6; r. XII 2; r. XIII 12, 14; r. XV 3; r. XVII 4, 29; **19** o. I 15, 20; o. III 20; o. VII 18; o. VIII 6, 10; o. IX 18; o. XI 24, 29; o. XIII 8; o. XV 20; o. XVII 8; o. XVIII 7, 12; r. II 17; r. III 21; r. V 20; r. VIII 3, 10, 14; r. IX 11; r. X 24; r. XI 19; r. XII 23; r. XV 4, 14; r. XVIII 9, 27; r. XIX 5; **20** o. II 19; r. XI 1; r. XV 3'; **21** o. II 5; o. VIII 1; o. XI 3; o. XII 16; o. XIII 13; r. I 22; r. II 10, 20, 23; r. III 18; r. IV 12, 16; r. V 8, 15, 20; r. XII 10; **22** o. I 11; r. II 2, 7; r. III 2; r. V 9; r. IX 1; **23** r. III 6; **24** o. I 9, 11; o. II 4; o. V 4, 9; r. I 4; r. III 13; r. IV 2, 8; **25** o. II 7; o. VIII 5.

# Z

ZA$_x$ «goods, property; treasure» **6** r. XVI 27: TAR an-na *ni-zi-mu* **L.** naĝar; **7** o. VII 11: ŠA.PI gín D. an-na šub *si-in ni-zi-mu* **L.** naĝar: o. XIV 20: 1 tùn tur 1 dub-naĝar sal 1 *ma-za-ḫa-rúm* 1 UŠ×KÍD *si-in* **L.** ⌜*Ib*⌝-[*r*]*í-um*; o. XV 18: 1 gud-I lú sig$_{17}$ lú **L.** *Ib-rí-um*; **11** o. V 21: 1 ma-na an-na šub *si-in ni-zi-mu* **L.** naĝar-naĝar; **12** o. X 8: ŠA.PI gín D. an-na šub *si-in* 6 ma-na 10 gín D. a-gar$_5$-gar$_5$ *ni-zi-mu* **L.** naĝar-naĝar; **14** r. XX 3': ⌜è⌝ *ni-zi-mu* **L.** ĝurus-ĝuruš; **15** o. XIV 25: 1 ma-na 10 gín D. an-na šub *si-in ni-zi-mu* **L.** naĝar-naĝar; **16** o. XII 17: 2 ĝír lú **L.** *Ib-rí-um*; r. XII 2: šum **L.** *Ib-rí-um*; **19** o. XIII 15: 3 gín D. kg kin$_5$-ak **L.** *a-si-ga-tim* ama-gal en; **20** o. XIII 3: [ ] 8 gín D. kb *zi-du-sù* **L.** en, 13: 4 ĝír 15 gín D. 2 ĝír 10 gín D. 4 gín D. kb *zi-du-sù* **L.** *Ib-rí-um*; o. XV 12: **L.** saĝ; **21** o. X 22: 1 kun **L.** *Ib-rí-um*.

ZA$_x$-ZA$_x$ **16** o. XII 4: 1 ma-na 50 gín D. <an-na> šub *si-in* 3[+x ma-n]a [T]AR gín D. ⌜a⌝-gar$_5$-gar$_5$ *ni-zi-mu* **L.** naĝar-naĝar; **18** r. II 9: 2 ma-na an-na šub *si-in* 12 ma-na a-gar$_5$-gar$_5$ *ni-zi-mu* **L.** naĝar-naĝar.

zabar «bronze» **4** r. XIV 2; **6** r. XIII 1; r. XV 8: 1 *li-im* ĜIŠ-gu-kak-gíd **L.**; **7** o. XVII 9: 2 ĝír **L.**; **10** r. X 21: 20 t[ùn] gal **L.**; r. XI 1: 10 tùn tur **L.**, 7: 1 *ma-ga-um* **L.**; **11** r. II 4: 21 á-MUŠEN **L.**; **12** o. IX 5: 1 *li-im* ĜIŠ-gu-kak-gíd **L.**; o. X 13: 2 *ma-ga-za-ʾà* **L.** gibil; **14** o. XV8: 1 balaĝ **L.**; **16** o. X 13: 13 á-MUŠEN **L.**, 16: 20 ĝír-kun **L.**, 17: 35 á-MUŠEN **L.**; **17** o. XVIII 9: 3 *mi-at* ĝír mar-tu **L.**; **19** o V 1: 1 *li-im* ĜIŠ-gu-kak-g[íd] **L.**; **20** o. I 14: 3 *li-im* ĜIŠ-gu-kak-gíd **L.**; **21** r. XII 12: 1 á-MUŠEN *wa* 2 ĝír-kun **L.**

zag «side» **3** o. III 3: 1 ½ gín D. kb nu$_{11}$-za 1 **L.** ĜIŠ-gígir-II; o. XIII 1: 1 gín D. kb [1 **L.**] ĜIŠ-gígir-II; r. IX 1: 3 gín D. kb nu$_{11}$-za 2 **L.** 2 ĜIŠ-gígir-II; **4** o. V 17: 1 ½ gín D. kb nu$_{11}$-za!(KUR) 1 **L.** ĜIŠ-gígir-II; o. XIII 8: 1 ½ gín D. kb nu$_{11}$-za!(KUR) 1 **L.** ĜIŠ-gígir-II; **5** r. VIII 8: 1 gín D. kb nu$_{11}$-za 1 **L.** ĜIŠ-gígir-II; **6** o. IX 12: 2 gín D. kb nu$_{11}$-za 1 **L.** ĜIŠ-gígir-II, 17: 1 ½ gín D. kb nu$_{11}$-za 1 **L.** ĜIŠ-gígir-II; r. V 18: 2 gín D. kb nu$_{11}$-za 1 **L.** ĜIŠ-gígir-{II-}II; **10** o. XII 4: 1 gín D. kb nu$_{11}$-za 1 **L.** 1 ĜIŠ-gígir-II; o. XIII 6: 1 ½ gín D. kb nu$_{11}$-za 1 **L.** 1 ĜIŠ-gígir-II; **13** o. III 8: [2 gín D. kg] nu$_{11}$-za 1 **L.**; o. VI 10: 1 gín D. kb nu$_{11}$-za 1 **L.** ĜIŠ-gígir-II; o. XV 12: 3 gín D. kb nu$_{11}$-za 2 **L.** 2 ĜIŠ-gígir-II; **14** o. VIII 21: ½ gín D. kg *ni-zi-mu* nu$_{11}$-za 2 **L.** 2 ĜIŠ-gígir-II; **15** o. VIII 12: 1 gín D. kb nu$_{11}$-za 1 **L.** ĜIŠ-gígir-II; **16** o. VI 13: 1 ½ gín D. kg nu$_{11}$-za 1 **L.**; r. XIV 5: 1 gín kg *zi-ba-du* 1 **L.**-*sù* kg en; **17** o. XV 1: 1 gín D. kb nu$_{11}$-za 1 **L.** ĜIŠ-gígir-II; r. I 13: 3 gín D. kb nu$_{11}$-za 2 **L.** 2 ĜIŠ-gígir-II; **18** r. XIV 13: 1 kg nu$_{11}$-za 1 **L.** ĜIŠ-gígir-II; **19** o. VII 11: 3 gín D. kb nu$_{11}$-za 2 **L.** ĜIŠ-gígir-II; o. X 16: 1 gín D. kb nu$_{11}$-za 1 **L.** ĜIŠ-gígir-II; **20** r. IV 4: 1 ½ gín D. kg nu$_{11}$-za 1 **L.** ĜIŠ-gígir-II.

za-gìn (za:gìn) «lapis lazuli» **8** r. III 9'.

gìn-gìn **2** o. VII 13; 13 o. XIV 14; **17** r. XX 20: 5 kb 15 *ḫa-za-nu* 2 **L.** 2 si$_4$ 1 šu-dub *Ib-rí-um*, **25**: 4 kb 15 *ḫa-za-nu* 2 **L.** 2 si$_4$ 1 šu-dub *I-bí-zi-kir*.

záḫ «fugitive» **8** r. IV x+1.

zàḫ «(to be) lost» **5** r. I 4: ⌜x⌝ g[ín] D. kb 1 *zú-zú-ba-tum* **L.** *Ib-rí-um*; **13** r. I 21: 1 BAR.AN *Na-zu-mu* **L.**; **14** o. XIV 3: [x] gí[n] D. a-gar$_5$-gar$_5$ lul-gu-ak 4 ĜIŠ-gu-kak-šub lú *Daš-na M*[*a*-]*rí*⌜ki⌝ *i*[*n*] *Bar-ga-u*$_9$ki **L.** *in* kaskal dAMA-*ra*; **15** o. VIII 21: 2 gín D. kb lul-gu-ak 1 *zú-zú-ba-tum* en **L.**; **17** r. III 4: *kam*$_4$-*ma-a-tum* **L.** *ša-ti* kù-sal ama-gal en; r. XIX 7: 10 kb lul-gu-ak 1 *zú-zú-ba-tum Ib-rí-um* **L.**

*za-ḫa-da* «battle-axe» **3** o. XIII 11: 1 gín D. kb *ni-zi-mu* nu$_{11}$-za 1 **L.** *I*[*b-rí-um*]; **7** o. VII 6: 1 gín D. kb *ni-zi-mu* nu$_{11}$-za 1 **L.** *Ib-rí-um*; o. XIII 20: 2 gín D. kg *ni-zi-mu* nu$_{11}$-za 2 **L.** en; o. XIV 12: 8 gín D. kg nu$_{11}$-za 1 **L.** *Ib-rí-um*; **10** o. IV 17: 2 gín D. kb *ni-zi-mu* nu$_{11}$-za 1 **L.** *Ib-rí-um*; **16** r. VI 13: 1 gín D. kg *ni-zi-mu* nu$_{11}$-za 1 **L.** *Ib-rí-um*; **17** r. I 28: 2 gín D. kb *ni-zi-mu* nu$_{11}$-⌜za⌝ 1 **L.** *wa* 1 ĜIŠ-MUNŠUB; r. II 8: 2 NI gín D. kg … nu$_{11}$-za 1 **L.** en; **18** o. XV 33: 3 kg *ni-zi-mu* nu$_{11}$-za 1 **L.** 1 [ĜI]Š?-PA-⌜x⌝-ga *Ib-rí-um*; r. I 27: 6 g[ín] D. kg *ni-zi-mu* nu$_{11}$-za 1 **L.** ⌜en⌝; **19** r. XI 3: 1 gín D. 6 NI kg *ni-zi-mu* nu$_{11}$-za 1 **L.** *Ib-rí-um*; r. XII 4: ŠÚ+ŠA gín D. an-na šub *si-in* <x a-gar$_5$-gar$_5$> 1 ĜIŠ-gu-kak-gíd 1 **L.** ĜIŠ-kak-ĜIŠ-kak 4 *zi-da-nu* ĜIŠ-sal lú ĜIŠ-gígir-II d*Á-la Gú-šè-bù*ki; **20** o. IX 12: 1 gín D. kg *ni-zi-mu* nu$_{11}$-za 1 **L.** [ ]; r. IV 10: 2 gín D. [k]g *ni-zi-mu* nu$_{11}$-za 1 **L.** *Ib-rí-um*; **21** o. VIII 13: 3 gín D. an-na šub *si-in* ŠÚ+ŠA a-gar$_5$-gar$_5$ 1 **L.**; **24** o. IV 4: 1 gín D. kg *ni-zi-mu* nu$_{11}$-za 1 **L.** en, 12: 1 gín D. kg *ni-zi-mu* nu$_{11}$-za 1 **L.** *Ib-rí-um*.

*za-ḫa-da ra-ʾà-tum* **6** o. VII 2: 1 **L.** kg

zarki «(provisions) wharehouse» (a place sometimes related to the gods Enki and Kamiš) **4** o. I 16: [ ] [x *g*]*ú*-[*l*]*i*-[*lum* x gí]n [D. ì]-na-sum SA.ZA$_x$ki *in* **L.** en.

zara$_6$-TÚG (a mantel for woman) **2** o. VIII 1; r. V 4; r. XIII 3; **6** r. VIII 16; **7** r. VI 12; r. XII 6; **11** o. II 16; o. XIII 2; **12** o. I 5; r. VI 16; **13** o. X 11; **14** o. VI 2; o. XVI 11; o. XXI 5; **15** o. VI 18; **16** o. IV 10; **17** o. VIII 17; o. IX 5; o. XVII 14; r. V 3; **18** r. III 4; **21** r. II 1; **25** o. III 2.

zé (an object) **2** r. II 13: 3 gín D. kb nu$_{11}$-za 2 **L.**-*sù*. (variant: gi-zé)

zi-bar «goblet» **2** o. III 7: 3 gín D. kb 1 **L.**; o. V 3: 3 gín D. kb 1 **L.**; **4** o. XI 20: 1 ma-na kb kin$_5$-ak 12 **L.** tur; **5** r. VI 10: 8 gín D. kg 2 **L.**; **10** r. VIII 10: 6 gín D. <kg> 1 **L.** en; **12** o. XIV 11: 6 gín D. kb 2 **L.**; **13** r. XI 5: [x] kb 1 **L.**; **15** o. VIII 24: 3 gín D. kg 1 **L.**; **18** o. III 14: 10 gín D. kg 1 **L.**; r. XI 15: 5 gín D. kb 1 **L.**, 26: 10 gín D. kb 3 **L.**; **21** r. X 20: 6 gín D. kg lul-gu-ak 1 **L.** en *ša-ti* sikil d?*A*$_5$-*da*-"*bal*" *Lu-ba-an*ki.

*zi-ba-tum* (a kind of handle, in general of small vessels) **2** o. I 12: 1 gín D. kg kin$_5$-ak 5 **L.**; **3** r. VII 14: 8 gín D. kb **L.** 4 ĜIŠ-šú 1 níĝ-bànda l[ú 2 šu]; **14** o. XV 7: [2 gín D. k]g **L.** 1 balaĝ zabar lú en; r. XIII

12: 3 kb **L.** *wa kam$_4$-ma-a-tum* 16 ĝír mar-tu kg ⸢10⸣ ĝír ⸢mar⸣-tu ti kg 15 g[ír] mar-tu zú AN.LAGAB×AN 2 ĝír mar-tu *ba-du-u$_4$* kg 6 ĝír mar-tu kb; **18** o. XII 14: TAR kg **L.** 2 KA-si en.

(*LLE*,I no. 674: ŠE.AN.U$_9$ = *zi-ba-tum*)

*zi-ba-du* **15** o. XVI 11: 2 gín kb **L.** 1 ĜIŠ-šú 1 níg-bànda kb; r. XV 12: 10 gín D. kb **L.** 1 *gú-bù* kg libir; **16** o. XI 7: TAR [(+x)] kg **L.** 14 ĝír mar-tu kg 7 ĝír mar-tu ti kg 17 ĝír mar-tu zú LAGAB×A kg; r. XIV 4: 1 gín kg **L.** 1 zag-*sù* kg, 17: 6 gín D. an-na šub *si-in* **L.** 1 útul dub maḫ; **18** o. XVII 19: 7 gín D. kb **L.** 1 ĜIŠ-šú 2 níg-bànda; **20** o. XI 8: [gín D. kg] **L.** [ ]⸢x⸣[ ]; r. X 1: [1] gín D. [kg] **L.** 1 pad an-zam$_x$; r. XIV 9: [x g]ín D. [an-n]a [šub *si-i*]*n* [x a-g]ar$_5$-gar$_5$ **L.** ⸢útul⸣-útul maḫ urudu; **21** r. III 15: 10 gín D. kb **L.** ĝír mar-tu; **24** o. IV 7: 1 gín D. kg **L.** 1 balaĝ maḫ.

*zi-ba-ti* **16** o. III 17: 11 gín D. an-na šub *si-in* **L.** 1 útul urudu maḫ.

*zi-ba-tum* (a topographic indication concerning the city of ʾAdani?) **2** o. IX 1: (62 garments, 21 kilts) ki:lam$_7$ **L.** *ʾÀ-da-ni*$^{ki}$; **9** r. XVI 15: (50 kilts) … ĜIŠ-gu-kak-gíd *Wa-ba-rúm* ⸢šu⸣-ba$_4$-ti ki:⸢lam$_7$⸣ **L.** *ʾÀ-da-ni*$^{ki}$.

*zi-da-nu* **19** r. XII 6: ŠÚ+ŠA gín D. an-na šub *si-in* <x a-gar$_5$-gar$_5$> 1 ĜIŠ-gu-kak-gíd 1 *za-ḫa-da* ĜIŠ-kak-ĜIŠ-kak 4 **L.** ĜIŠ-sal lú ĜIŠ-gígir-II $^{d}$*À-la Gú-šè-bù*$^{ki}$.

*zi-du* «alloy» **3** o. V 2: 2 ma-na kb **L.** 60 ĝír mar-tu SA.ZA$_x$$^{ki}$; **7** o. IV 8: TAR kg **L.** 10 ĝír mar-tu ti kg; r. II 18: 7 gín D. kg **L.** 1 ĝír mar-tu; **8** r. XI 14': 3 ma-na ŠÚ+ŠA gín D. kb **L.** 1 *mi-at* ĝír mar-tu *ba-du-u$_4$* kb; **9** o. X 10: 1 ma-na ŠÚ+ŠA gín D. kb **L.** [20$^{?}$+]10$^{?}$ g[ír] mar-tu; r. XII 12: 3 gín D. kb *ni-zi-mu* **L.** 4 ĝír mar-tu *ba-du-u$_4$* kb; **11** r. VII 23: 10 gín D. kg **L.** $^{d}$En-ki; **17** o. IX 13: 1 gín D. kg **L.** *ša-ga-tum* 1 ĝír mar-tu kg; o. XIII 21: 3 gín D. kg *ni-zi-mu* **L.** 3 *ša-ga-tum* 3 ĝír mar-tu; **18** r. VII 7: 40 ĝír mar-tu kg … 4 ma-na kg **L.**-*sù*, 15: 1 ĝír mar-tu 6 gín D. kg **L.**-*sù*; r. VIII 5: 20 ĝír mar-tu ti kù-gi *ʾà-lum* … 1 ma-na kg **L.**-*sù*, 13: 1 ĝír mar-tu 3 gín D. kg **L.**-*sù*; r. IX 5: 50 ĝír mar-tu ti kg … 2 ma-na TAR kg **L.**-*sù*, 12: 1 ĝír mar-tu 3 gín D. kg **L.**-*sù*; **19** o. XIV 3: 20 ĝír mar-tu kg … 2 ma-na kg lú mu-DU *Kab-lu$_5$-ul*$^{ki}$ **L.**-*sù*, 10: 1 ĝír mar-tu 6 kg **L.**-*sù*; o. XV 2: 40 ĝír mar-tu ti kg … 2 ma-na kg **L.**-*sù*, 10: 1 ĝír mar-tu 3 kg **L.**-*sù*; o. XVI 9: 40 ĝír mar-tu *ba-du-u$_9$* kg … 1 ma-na ŠA.PI gín D. kg **L.**-*sù*, 16: 1 ĝír mar-tu 2 ½ kg **L.**-*sù*; o. XVII 1: 60 ĝír mar-tu *ba-du-u$_9$* kbg … TAR kg **L.**-*sù*, 10: 1 ĝír mar-tu 3 kb *wa* ½ kg **L.**-*sù*; r. I 6: 80 ĝír mar-tu kg *ap* 10 lá-2 ma-na kg **L.**-*sù* lú mu-DU *Kab-lu$_5$-ul*$^{ki}$, 15: 1 ĝír mar-tu 6 gín D. kg **L.**-*sù*, 24: 20 ĝír mar-tu ti kg *ʾà-lum* … 1 [ma-na] ŠÚ+ŠA g[ín D.] kg **L.**-*sù*; r. II 5: 1 ĝír mar-tu 4 gín kg **L.**-*sù*, 14: 90 ĝír mar-tu ti kg … 4 ma-na TAR kg **L.**-*sù*, 22: 1 ĝír mar-tu 3 kg **L.**-*sù*; r. III 5: 50 ĝír mar-tu *ba-du-u$_9$* kg … 2 ma-na 5 gín D. kg **L.**-*sù*, 12: 1 ĝír mar-tu 2 ½ kg **L.**-*sù*, 23: 60 ĝír mar-tu *ba-du-u$_9$* kbg … [30 k]g [*w*]*a* 3 ma-na kb **L.**-*sù*; r. IV 2: 1 ĝír mar-tu 3 gín D. kb ½ kg **L.**-*sù*; **20** o. XIII 2: [ ] 8 gín D. kb **L.**-*sù*, 12: 4 ĝír 15 gín D. 2 ĝír 10 gín D. 4 gín D. kb **L.**-*sù*; **23** r. I 7: 1 gín D. kg **L.** *sa-ga-tum* 1 ĝír mar-tu.

*zi-tum* **4** o. VIII 2: 8 gín D. kb **L.** 4 ĝír-ĝír šu-du$_8$-máš; **6** o. VI 1: 1 ma-na kb **L.** 20 ĝír mar-tu *ba-du-u$_9$* kbg; **14** o. I 17: 7 gín D. kg **L.** 1 ĝír mar-tu; o. II 12: 7 gín D. kg **L.** 1 ⸢ĝír⸣ mar-tu.

zi-du$_8$ «entitlement» **6** o. X 3: 10 ma-na kb **L.** $^{d}$*ʾÀ-da.*

(see *ARET* XVI 21 §§ 4, 5: 1 ma-na kb **L.** *Mu-ru$_{12}$*$^{ki}$ PN$_1$ šu-ba$_4$-ti / 3 *mi-at* udu-udu **L.** *Mu-ru$_{12}$*$^{ki}$ PN$_2$ šu-ba$_4$-ti; *LLE*,I nos. 1028, 1029: ZI.GABA = *ʾà/a-ma-zu-um*; ZI.GABA.GABA = *da-da-me-zu-um*)

*zi-kir-ra-tum* «fastener» **8** o. XIV 10: 2 ma-na TAR 2 gín D. kg 4 s[aĝ ] 4 **L.** en.

*zi-ru$_{12}$* (a vessel) **5** r. XVI 12: 5 gín D. kg *ni-zi-mu* 1 **L.** *wa* 2 *gi-zu wa* níĝin-níĝin.

*zi-tum* see *zi-du.*

*zi-zi-ḫi-tum* (an object) **17** r. IV 11: 5 gín D. kb kin$_5$-ak 1 **L.**

zú «tooth; blade» **12** o. X 15: 7 gín D. an-na šub *si-in* 2 *ma-ga-za-ʾà* zabar gibil 2 **L.** bulug$_4$.

zú AN.LAGAB×AN/A.LAGAB×ḪAL «ivory (?)» **3** r. III 10: 17 gín D. kb níĝ-sa$_{10}$ 1 ĝír mar-tu **L.** A.LAGAB×ḪAL; **14** r. XI 24: [x gín D.] kb níĝ-sa$_{10}$ **L.** AN.LAGAB×AN; **19** o. XV 15: TAR an-na šub *si-in* 3 ma-na TAR 5 a-gar$_5$ kin$_5$-ak 12 ĝír mar-tu **L.** AN.LAGAB×A, 30: 10 lá-2 ĝír mar-tu **L.** AN.LAGAB×A kg.

zú-ak «tooth; nail; pointed» **7** o. XV 5: 6 *zú-zú-ba-tum* ĜIŠ-bar-ús **L.** 2 ĜIŠ-gígir-II; **19** o. VII 16: 2 ĜIŠ-zú ĜIŠ-gígir-II **L.**

ZU.PIRIĜ «hanger» **4** o. III 5: 10 ½ gín D. kb **L.** kin$_5$-ak *gú-li-lum wa* níĝ-anše-ak kù-sal; o. XV 1: 2 gín D. kb **L.** 2 *ḫu-bù*; o. XV 1: 2 gín D. kb **L.** 2 *ḫu-bù*, 5: 3 gí[n] D. kb **L.** 1 útul urudu; r. XII 24: 4 gín D. kb **L.** 2 dib; r. XV 17: [x kb] **L.** 1 útul urudu; **6** o. V 2: TAR kb **L.** kin$_5$-ak 23 dib a-gar$_5$-gar$_5$ kg; r. II 19: ŠÚ+ŠA gín D. kb **L.** 3 útul-útul! urudu maḫ; **7** r. IX 11: 2 gín D. kb **L.**-[*s*]*ù*; **9** r. V 2: 6 gín D. kb **L.** 2[+x] ⸢x⸣[- ] 3 [ ]; **10** o. XII 8: 3 gín D. kb **L.** ĜIŠ-šú níg-bànda šu-šu; r. II 14: ⸢4⸣ gín D. kb **L.** ⸢5⸣ *gú-li-lum*- II a-gar$_5$-gar$_5$ esi; r. IV 10: [x gí]n [D.] kb **L.** ⸢10⸣ útul! urudu!; **11** r. II 11: 5 gín D. kb **L.** *gú-li-lum-gú-li-lum* ĝuruš-ĝuruš; **14** o. XIX 7: 5 gín D. kb **L.** [ ]; **15** r. II 12: 1 gín D. kb **L.**-*sù*; r. XIV 18: 10 gín D. kb **L.** kin$_5$-ak 3 útul urudu maḫ; **16** o. III 20: 1 útul urudu maḫ 5 gín D. kb **L.**-*sù*; o. X 12: 15 gín D. kb **L.** 13 á-MUŠEN zabar; r. XIV 20: 15 gín D. kb **L.** 3 útul urudu maḫ; **17** o. XV 19: (30 bracelets) 2 gín D. kb **L.**-*sù*; **18** o. I 14: ŠÚ+ŠA gín D. kb **L.** 3 útul maḫ urudu; o. VIII 12: (126 bracelets) 4 gín D. kb **L.**-*sù*; o. IX 6: 2 útul gibil 5 m[a-]na [kb] **L.**-*sù*; **19** o. XVIII 15: (176 bracelets) 3 gín D. kb **L.**-*sù*; r. XVI 16: ŠÚ+ŠA gín D. kb **L.** útul-útul maḫ urudu; **20** o. IX 18: 1 gín D. kg **L.** *su-da-nu* kg BAR.AN en; **21** o. VI 16: [20+]30 gín D. kb **L.** [ ]; r. V 11: (51+[x] bracelets) 8 gín D. kb **L.**-*sù*.

*zú-zú-ba-tum* (part of the chariot) **4** o. III 23: [ ] [1+]1 **L.**; r. I 2: 7 gín D. kb kin$_5$-ak 3 **L.** ĝiš-gígir-II; r. X 3: 12 gín D. kb kin$_5$-ak 6 **L.** 2 ĝiš-gígir-II; **5** r. I 3: ⸢x⸣ g[ín] D. kb lul-gu-ak 1 **L.** zàḫ *Ib-rí-um*; r. II 1: [x gín D. kb kin$_5$-ak] 3 **L.**; **6** o. XV 24: 4 gín D. kb 3 **L.**; **7** o. XV 3: [x ma-na x] gín D. kb kin$_5$-ak 6 **L.** ĝiš-bar-ús zú-ak 2 ĝiš-gígir-II; r. X 21: 2 gín D. kb *ni-zi-mu* 2 **L.**; **10** r. I 7: 1 ½ gín D. kb 1 **L.**; **15** o. VIII 19: 2 gín D. kb lul-gu-ak 1 **L.** en zàḫ; **16** r. XV 1: 5 gín D. kb 3 **L.** ĝiš-gígir-II; **17** o. XV 4: 4 gín D. kb 2 **L.**; r. I 17: 5 gín D. kb kin$_5$-ak 3 **L.**; r. XIX 5: 10 kb lul-gu-ak 1 **L.** *Ib-rí-um* zàḫ; **18** r. V 13: 5 gín D. kb kin$_5$-ak 3 **L.** ĝiš-gígir-II *Ib-rí-um*; **21** o. VII 14: [ ] 3 **L.** ĝiš-gígir-II; o. XIII 21: 15 gín D. kb 3 **L.**; o. XVII 7: 5 gín D. kb 3 **L.**; r. VII 18: 5 gín D. kb kin$_5$-ak 3 **L.**

## X

⸢x⸣-UŠ **21** o. V 16: 10 gín D. an-na šub *si-in* 1 ma-na a-gar$_5$-gar$_5$ **L.** <gaba-ru>.

⸢x⸣-[x] **15** r. VI 26: 6 gín D. kg *ni-zi-mu* 10 **L.**

# List of the plates

# Archivi Reali di Ebla

Testi

XXI

On behalf of the Università degli Studi di Roma
„La Sapienza" edited by
Paolo Matthiae, Frances Pinnock,
and Alfonso Archi

MAIS



2023
Harrassowitz Verlag · Wiesbaden

Alfonso Archi, Gabriella Spada

# Annual Documents of the Metal Expenditures (è) from Minister Ibrium's Period

(Archive L. 2769)

Part 2

2023
Harrassowitz Verlag · Wiesbaden

Publication of this book was supported by a grant of the Fondazione OrMe.

The images of the plates can be downloaded at:
https://www.harrassowitz-verlag.de/isbn_9783447120937.ahtml


Inventory code: So for example 04o-10077.jpg refers to the text 4 obverse

Bibliografische Information der Deutschen Nationalbibliothek
Die Deutsche Nationalbibliothek verzeichnet diese Publikation in der Deutschen Nationalbibliografie; detaillierte bibliografische Daten sind im Internet über https://dnb.de abrufbar.

Bibliographic information published by the Deutsche Nationalbibliothek
The Deutsche Nationalbibliothek lists this publication in the Deutsche Nationalbibliografie; detailed bibliographic data are available in the Internet at https://dnb.de

For further information about our publishing program consult our website http://www.harrassowitz-verlag.de


Printed on permanent/durable paper.
Printing and binding: Memminger MedienCentrum AG
Printed in Germany

ISSN 1828-3039
ISBN 978-3-447-12093-7
eISBN 978-3-447-39475-8

PLATES

**Plate I**

1 obverse

**Plate II**

1 reverse

**Plate III**

2 obverse

**Plate IV**

2 reverse

**Plate V**

3 obverse

## Plate VI

3 reverse

**Plate VII**

4 obverse

**Plate VIII**

4 reverse

**Plate IX**

5 obverse

**Plate X**

5 reverse

**Plate XI**

6 obverse

**Plate XII**

6 reverse

**Plate XIII**

7 obverse

**Plate XIV**

7 reverse

**Plate XV**

8 obverse

**Plate XVI**

9 obverse

**Plate XVII**

9 reverse

**Plate XVIII**

10 obverse

**Plate XIX**

10 reverse

**Plate XX**

11 obverse

**Plate XXI**

11 reverse

**Plate XXII**

12 obverse

**Plate XXIII**

12 reverse

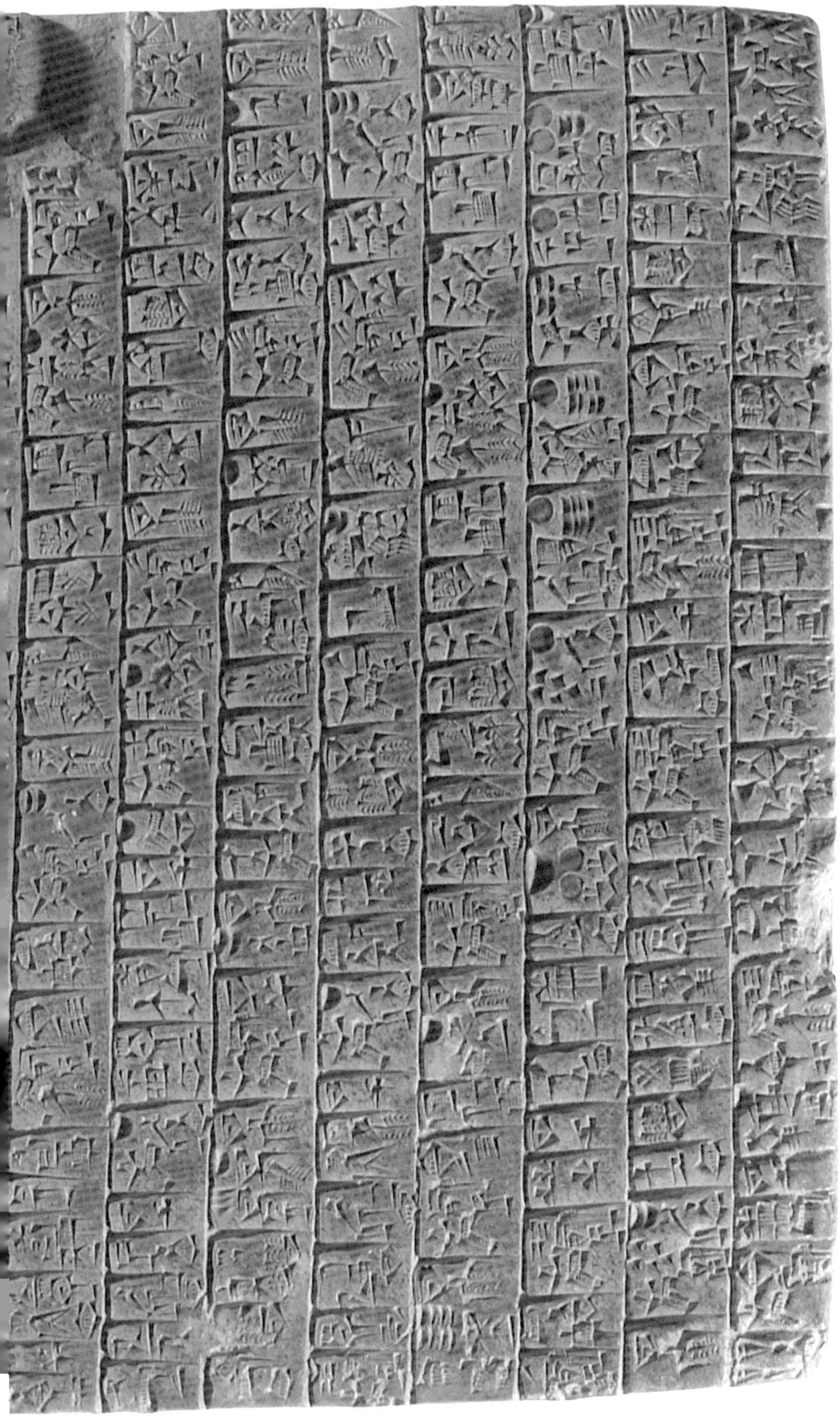

**Plate XXIV**

13 obverse

**Plate XXV**

13 reverse

**Plate XXVI**

14 obverse

**Plate XXVII**

14 reverse

**Plate XXVIII**

15 obverse

**Plate XXIX**

15 reverse

Plate XXX

16 obverse

**Plate XXXI**

16 reverse

**Plate XXXII**

17 obverse

**Plate XXXIII**

17 reverse

**Plate XXXIV**

18 obverse

**Plate XXXV**

18 reverse

**Plate XXXVI**

19 obverse

**Plate XXXVII**

19 reverse

Plate XXXVIII

20 obverse

**Plate XXXIX**

20 reverse

**Plate XL**

21 obverse

**Plate XLI**

21 reverse

**Plate XLII**

22 obverse

**Plate XLIII**

22 reverse

**Plate XLIV**

23 obverse

**Plate XLV**

23 reverse

**Plate XLVI**

24 obverse

**Plate XLVII**

24 reverse

**Plate XLVIII**

25 obverse

**Plate XLIX**

25 reverse